THE UNIDROIT PRINCIPLES IN PRACTICE

Caselaw and Bibliography on the
UNIDROIT Principles of
International Commercial Contracts

2nd Edition

Incorporating the UNIDROIT Principles 2004

Edited by
Michael Joachim Bonell

Published and distributed by *Transnational Publishers, Inc.*
Ardsley Park Science and Technology Center
410 Saw Mill River Road
Ardsley, NY 10502

Phone: 914–693–5100
Fax: 914–693–4430
E-mail: info@transnationalpubs.com
Web: www.transnationalpubs.com

Library of Congress Cataloging-in-Publication Data

(On file with publisher.)

ISBN 1-57105-346-8

Manufactured in the United States of America

TABLE OF CONTENTS

Preface to the Second Edition xi
Introduction to the First Edition xv
Acknowledgments to the First Edition xxi

PART I

LIST OF CASES BY DATE
LIST OF CASES BY ADJUDICATING COURT
GENERAL BIBLIOGRAPHY

LIST OF CASES BY DATE 3
LIST OF CASES BY ADJUDICATING COURT 11
GENERAL BIBLIOGRAPHY 17
UNIDROIT Principles in General 17
UNIDROIT Principles and Similar Projects 27
UNIDROIT Principles and International Commercial Arbitration 35

PART II

TEXT OF THE UNIDROIT PRINCIPLES & OFFICIAL COMMENTS
ISSUES & CASES AND BIBLIOGRAPHY

Preamble *(Purpose of the Principles)* 43

CHAPTER 1: GENERAL PROVISIONS 67

Article 1.1 *(Freedom of contract)* 69
Article 1.2 (*No form required)* 71
Article 1.3 (*Binding character of contract)* 73
Article 1.4 *(Mandatory rules)* 75
Article 1.5 *(Exclusion or modification by the parties)* 77
Article 1.6 *(Interpretation and supplementation of the Principles)* 79
Article 1.7 *(Good faith and fair dealing)* 83
Article 1.8 (*Inconsistent behaviour*) 88
Article 1.9 *(Usages and practices)* 92
Article 1.10 *(Notice)* 96
Article 1.11 *(Definitions)* 99

Article 1.12 (*Computation of time set by parties*) 101

CHAPTER 2: FORMATION AND AUTHORITY OF AGENTS

Section 1: Formation 103

Article 2.1.1 *(Manner of formation)* 107
Article 2.1.2 *(Definition of offer)* 109
Article 2.1.3 *(Withdrawal of offer)* 112
Article 2.1.4 *(Revocation of offer)* 113
Article 2.1.5 *(Rejection of offer)* 116
Article 2.1.6 *(Mode of acceptance)* 117
Article 2.1.7 *(Time of acceptance)* 120
Article 2.1.8 *(Acceptance within a fixed period of time)* 122
Article 2.1.9 *(Late acceptance. Delay in transmission)* 123
Article 2.1.10 *(Withdrawal of acceptance)* 125
Article 2.1.11 *(Modified acceptance)* 126
Article 2.1.12 *(Writings in confirmation)* 129
Article 2.1.13 *(Conclusion of contract dependent on agreement on specific matters or in a particular form)* 132
Article 2.1.14 *(Contract with terms deliberately left open)* 135
Article 2.1.15 *(Negotiations in bad faith)* 138
Article 2.1.16 *(Duty of confidentiality)* 141
Article 2.1.17 *(Merger clauses)* 144
Article 2.1.18 *(Modification in a particular form)* 146
Article 2.1.19 *(Contracting under standard terms)* 148
Article 2.1.20 *(Surprising terms)* 151
Article 2.1.21 *(Conflict between standard terms and non-standard terms)* 154
Article 2.1.22 *(Battle of forms)* 156

Section 2: Authority of agents 159

Article 2.2.1 *(Scope of the Section)* 160
Article 2.2.2 (*Establishment and scope of the authority of the agent*) 163
Article 2.2.3 (*Agency disclosed*) 135
Article 2.2.4 (*Agency undisclosed*) 138
Article 2.2.5 (*Agent acting without or exceeding its authority*) 170
Article 2.2.6 (*Liability of agent acting without or exceeding its authority*) 172
Article 2.2.7 (*Conflict of interests*) 174
Article 2.2.8 (*Sub-agency*) 177
Article 2.2.9 (*Ratification*) 179
Article 2.2.10 (*Termination of authority*) 182

CHAPTER 3: VALIDITY 185

Article 3.1 *(Matters not covered)* 188
Article 3.2 *(Validity of mere agreement)* 189
Article 3.3 *(Initial impossibility)* 191
Article 3.4 *(Definition of mistake)* 193
Article 3.5 *(Relevant mistake)* 195
Article 3.6 *(Error in expression or transmission)* 199
Article 3.7 *(Remedies for non-performance)* 201
Article 3.8 *(Fraud)* 203
Article 3.9 *(Threat)* 205
Article 3.10 *(Gross disparity)* 207
Article 3.11 *(Third persons)* 211
Article 3.12 *(Confirmation)* 213
Article 3.13 *(Loss of right to avoid)* 214
Article 3.14 *(Notice of avoidance)* 216
Article 3.15 *(Time limits)* 218
Article 3.16 *(Partial avoidance)* 220
Article 3.17 *(Retroactive effect of avoidance)* 221
Article 3.18 *(Damages)* 223
Article 3.19 *(Mandatory character of the provisions)* 224
Article 3.20 *(Unilateral declarations)* 225

CHAPTER 4: INTERPRETATION 227

Article 4.1 *(Intention of the parties)* 229
Article 4.2 *(Interpretation of statements and other conduct)* 232
Article 4.3 *(Relevant circumstances)* 234
Article 4.4 *(Reference to contract or statement as a whole)* 238
Article 4.5 *(All terms to be given effect)* 240
Article 4.6 *(Contra proferentem rule)* 242
Article 4.7 *(Linguistic discrepancies)* 244
Article 4.8 *(Supplying an omitted term)* 246

CHAPTER 5: CONTENT AND THIRD PARTY RIGHTS

Section 1: Content 249

Article 5.1.1 *(Express and implied obligations)* 250
Article 5.1.2 *(Implied obligations)* 251
Article 5.1.3 *(Co-operation between the parties)* 253
Article 5.1.4 *(Duty to achieve a specific result. Duty of best efforts)* 255
Article 5.1.5 *(Determination of kind of duty involved)* 258

Article 5.1.6 *(Determination of quality of performance)* 261
Article 5.1.7 *(Price determination)* 263
Article 5.1.8 *(Contract for an indefinite period)* 266
Article 5.1.9 *(Release by agreement)* 268

Section 2: Third party rights 270

Article 5.2.1 (*Contracts in favour of third parties*) 271
Article 5.2.2 (*Third party identifiable*) 274
Article 5.2.3 (*Exclusion and limitation clauses*) 275
Article 5.2.4 (*Defences)* 276
Article 5.2.5 (*Revocation*) 277
Article 5.2.6 (*Renunciation*) 279

CHAPTER 6: PERFORMANCE

Section 1: Performance in General 281

Article 6.1.1 *(Time of performance)* 282
Article 6.1.2 *(Performance at one time or in instalments)* 284
Article 6.1.3 *(Partial performance)* 285
Article 6.1.4 *(Order of performance)* 288
Article 6.1.5 *(Earlier performance)* 290
Article 6.1.6 *(Place of performance)* 293
Article 6.1.7 *(Payment by cheque or other instrument)* 296
Article 6.1.8 *(Payment by funds transfer)* 298
Article 6.1.9 *(Currency of payment)* 300
Article 6.1.10 *(Currency not expressed)* 304
Article 6.1.11 *(Costs of performance)* 305
Article 6.1.12 *(Imputation of payments)* 306
Article 6.1.13 *(Imputation of non-monetary obligations)* 308
Article 6.1.14 *(Application for public permission)* 309
Article 6.1.15 *(Procedure in applying for permission)* 314
Article 6.1.16 *(Permission neither granted nor refused)* 317
Article 6.1.17 *(Permission refused)* 319

Section 2: Hardship 322

Article 6.2.1 *(Contract to be observed)* 325
Article 6.2.2 *(Definition of hardship)* 327
Article 6.2.3 *(Effects of hardship)* 333

CHAPTER 7: NON-PERFORMANCE

Section 1: Non-performance in general 339

Article 7.1.1 *(Non-performance defined)* 342
Article 7.1.2 *(Interference by the other party)* 343
Article 7.1.3 *(Withholding performance)* 344
Article 7.1.4 *(Cure by non-performing party)* 347
Article 7.1.5 *(Additional period for performance)* 352
Article 7.1.6 *(Exemption clauses)* 355
Article 7.1.7 *(Force majeure)* 359

Section 2: Right to performance 362

Article 7.2.1 *(Performance of monetary obligation)* 363
Article 7.2.2 *(Performance of non-monetary obligation)* 364
Article 7.2.3 *(Repair and replacement of defective performance)* 368
Article 7.2.4 *(Judicial penalty)* 370
Article 7.2.5 *(Change of remedy)* 373

Section 3: Termination 375

Article 7.3.1 *(Right to terminate the contract)* 377
Article 7.3.2 *(Notice of termination)* 382
Article 7.3.3 *(Anticipatory non-performance)* 384
Article 7.3.4 *(Adequate assurance of due performance)* 385
Article 7.3.5 *(Effects of termination in general)* 387
Article 7.3.6 *(Restitution)* 389

Section 4: Damages 393

Article 7.4.1 *(Right to damages)* 395
Article 7.4.2 *(Full compensation)* 397
Article 7.4.3 *(Certainty of harm)* 401
Article 7.4.4 *(Foreseeability of harm)* 404
Article 7.4.5 *(Proof of harm in case of replacement transaction)* 406
Article 7.4.6 *(Proof of harm by current price)* 408
Article 7.4.7 *(Harm due in part to aggrieved party)* 410
Article 7.4.8 *(Mitigation of harm)* 413
Article 7.4.9 *(Interest for failure to pay money)* 416
Article 7.4.10 *(Interest on damages)* 421
Article 7.4.11 *(Manner of monetary redress)* 423
Article 7.4.12 *(Currency in which to assess damages)* 425

Article 7.4.13 *(Agreed payment for non-performance)* 426

CHAPTER 8: SET-OFF

Article 8.1 (*Conditions of set-off*) 432
Article 8.2 (*Foreign currency set-off*) 439
Article 8.3 (*Set-off by notice*) 441
Article 8.4 (*Content of notice*) 442
Article 8.5 (*Effect of set-off*) 444

CHAPTER 9: ASSIGNMENT OF RIGHTS, TRANSFER OF OBLIGATIONS, ASSIGNMENT OF CONTRACTS

Section 1: Assignment of rights 447

Article 9.1.1 (*Definitions*) 448
Article 9.1.2 (*Exclusions*) 450
Article 9.1.3 (*Assignability of non-monetary rights*) 452
Article 9.1.4 (*Partial assignment*) 453
Article 9.1.5 (*Future rights*) 455
Article 9.1.6 (*Rights assigned without individual specification*) 457
Article 9.1.7 (*Agreement between assignor and assignee sufficient*) 458
Article 9.1.8 (*Obligor's additional costs*) 460
Article 9.1.9 (*Non-assignment clauses*) 462
Article 9.1.10 (*Notice to the obligor*) 465
Article 9.1.11 (*Successive assignments*) 468
Article 9.1.12 (*Adequate proof of assignment*) 470
Article 9.1.13 (*Defences and rights of set-off*) 472
Article 9.1.14 (*Rights related to the right assigned*) 474
Article 9.1.15 (*Undertakings of the assignor*) 476

Section 2: Transfer of obligations 480

Article 9.2.1 (*Modes of transfer*) 480
Article 9.2.2 (*Exclusion*) 483
Article 9.2.3 (*Requirement of obligee's consent to transfer*) 484
Article 9.2.4 (*Advance consent of obligee*) 486
Article 9.2.5 (*Discharge of old obligor*) 488
Article 9.2.6 (*Third party performance*) 491
Article 9.2.7 (*Defences and rights of set-off*) 493
Article 9.2.8 (*Rights related to the obligation transferred*) 495

Section 3: Assignment of contracts 498

Article 9.3.1 (*Definitions*) 498
Article 9.3.2 (*Exclusion*) 499
Article 9.3.3 (*Requirement of consent of the other party*) 500
Article 9.3.4 (*Advance sonsent of the other party*) 501
Article 9.3.5 (*Discharge of the assignor*) 503
Article 9.3.6 (*Defences and rights of set-off*) 506
Article 9.3.7 (*Rights transferred with the contract*) 508

CHAPTER 10: LIMITATION PERIODS 511

Article 10.1 (*Scope of the Chapter*) 512
Article 10.2 (*Limitation periods*) 515
Article 10.3 (*Modification of limitation periods by the parties*) 520
Article 10.4 (*New limitation period by acknowledgement*) 522
Article 10.5 (*Suspension by judicial proceedings*) 526
Article 10.6 (*Suspension by arbitral proceedings*) 529
Article 10.7 (*Alternative dispute resolution*) 531
Article 10.8 (*Suspension in case of force majeure, death or incapacity*) 533
Article 10.9 (*Effects of expiration of limitation period*) 536
Article 10.10 (*Right of set-off*) 538
Article 10.11 (*Restitution*) 539

PART III

DECISIONS REPORTED: ABSTRACT AND FULL TEXT

DECISIONS REPORTED: ABSTRACTS AND FULL TEXT 543

PREFACE TO THE SECOND EDITION

There are several reasons that justify a new edition of this book, first published in 2002.

One reason is the appearence in 2004 of a second, enlarged edition of the UNIDROIT Principles containing, in addition to two new paragraphs in the Preamble and a new provison on inconsistent behaviour in Chapter 1, five new chapters or sections on authority of agents, third party rights, set-off, assignment of rights, transfer of obligations and assignment of contracts, and limitation periods, respectively.[1] The present volume reproduces the text of both the black letter rules and the comments of the 2004 edition of the UNIDROIT Principles, together with a list of "issues", i.e. questions that have arisen or are likely to arise in connection with their application, which have been prepared also with respect to the new provisions.

Another, and even more important, reason is the continuously growing body of case law concerning the UNIDROIT Principles. While the total number of decisions reported in the first edition of this book was 68, the new edition contains 130 decisions, 101 of which are arbitral awards and 27 court decisions,[2] thereby contradicting the widespread belief that in view of their non-binding nature the UNIDROIT Principles can only be relevant in the context of arbitration. To be sure, of all the arbitral awards, let alone court decisions, rendered world-wide those referring in one way or another to the UNIDROIT Principles still represent only a small percentage. Yet, as compared to the reception in practice of other uniform law instruments, the performance of the UNIDROIT Principles is more than satisfactory: suffice it to mention that it took the U.N. Convention on Contracts for the International Sale of Goods (CISG), adopted in 1980 by more than 60 States, eight years to come into force and another four years before the first 100 decisions applying it had been rendered. Moreover, the number of arbitral awards concerning the UNIDROIT Principles is in fact much greater than those reported in this book, but given their confidential nature they remain unknown and/or cannot be listed here. Thus, the International Court of Arbitration of the International Chamber of Commerce which administers the majority of international arbitration proceedings, after having

---

[1] For further details see M. J. BONELL, An International Restatement of Contract Law, 3rd ed., Transnational Publ. 2005.

[2] The remaining two are decisions by other adjudicating bodies.

published two fairly comprehensive surveys of arbitral awards of this kind in 1999 and in 2001, has since provided only one further survey in 2005 covering 10 awards from the period 2001 - 2002, while according to the same source of information the total number of ICC awards referring in one way or another to the UNIDROIT Principles amounts to an average of 15 per year.

Last but not least, the new edition of this book was also prompted by the favourable reception the first edition received not only among academics but also and above all by practicioners who appear to be particularly interested in an easily accessible and updated reporting service of all the decisions rendered by domestic courts and arbitral tribunals world-wide and referring to the UNIDROIT Principles. For this reason the structure of the first edition has remained basically unchanged, i.e. the decisions are listed not only in chronological order and by adjudicating body but also by the specific issues they address, and each single decision is published in the form of an abstract followed by (excerpts of) the original full text version where available. Moreover, also the bibliography on the UNIDROIT Principles in general, their relationships with similar projects and their role in international commercial arbitration, as well as the specific bibliographies on each chapter or section of the UNIDROIT Principles, have been updated so as to include at least the most important and/or linguistically accessible contributions published wordwide over the last years.

***

My special thanks go to the International Institute for the Unification of Private Law (UNIDROIT) for allowing me to reproduce the text of the 2004 edition of the UNIDROIT Principles.

I would also like to thank the International Court of Arbitration of the International Chamber of Commerce for granting permission to reproduce excerpts from ICC awards published in the ICC International Court of Arbitration Bulletin and referring to the UNIDROIT Principles. I am equally very grateful to all the other Arbitration Centres, as well as to Colleagues involved in *ad hoc* arbitrations, for having provided information on awards renderd under their auspices or with their partecipation. I can only hope that also in the future those who come to know of award in which the UNIDROIT Principles have been referred to will share their information by providing excerpts or abstracts of those awards, thereby enabling legal scholars and practitioners alike to have a better knowledge of how the UNIDROIT Principles are being applied in practice.

Last but not least, I would like to express my sincerest appreciation to Silvia Sabbatini for her most valuable assistance in editing and preparing the texts for publication.

Rome, July 2006 Michael Joachim Bonell

INTRODUCTION TO THE FIRST EDITION

I.

If – as is nowadays generally admitted – uniform law is not an end in itself but has to serve a specific purpose in practice, the preparation of a single uniform law instrument represents only a first, albeit important, step. What in the final analysis really matters is that the instrument in question does not remain a dead letter but is actually applied in practice. Hence the importance of not just limiting oneself to celebrate – as is often the case – the proliferation on paper of uniform law instruments dealing with the disparate subjects, but also to monitor the acceptance of those instruments by their potential beneficiaries within the legal and business communities concerned.

These remarks, if already pertinent with respect to legally binding instruments such as international conventions or uniform laws, apply even more so with respect to so-called "soft law" products. Indeed while the former, once adopted by an international treaty and implemented by the individual States, become integral parts of the respective domestic law, the latter are as such not binding and can only expect to be applied in practice thanks to their persuasive value.

The UNIDROIT Principles of International Commercial Contracts, published in 1994 following years of intensive preparatory work and deliberations by a group of experts representing the world's most important legal systems, are a typical example of soft law. As the Governing Council of UNIDROIT stated in its Introduction to the Principles "[they] are not a binding instrument and [ ] in consequence their acceptance will depend upon their persuasive authority [ ] The Council is confident that those to whom the UNIDROIT Principles are addressed will appreciate their intrinsic merits and derive full advantage from their use".

Eight years after the appearance of the UNIDROIT Principles it is fair to say that they have been extremely well received both in academic circles and in practice.

Right from the start the UNIDROIT Principles – available in some 20 different language versions including all the major international languages – were the subject of numerous seminars and colloquia all over the world. In addition the volume of scholarly writings dealing with them is constantly increasing and – what is even more important – their reception is generally very positive.

As to the different ways in which the UNIDROIT Principles are being used in practice it may be mentioned first of all that numerous countries all over the world have taken them as a source of inspiration for their law reform projects. The UNIDROIT Principles are likewise increasingly being relied on by lawyers and business persons as a guide in the negotiating and drafting of international commercial contracts. Most importantly, arbitrators and judges are more and more frequently resorting to the UNIDROIT Principles in resolving transnational commercial disputes.

II.

Over the last years there have been a number of initiatives to monitor and report on how the UNIDROIT Principles are being received in practice.

As early as 1996 UNIDROIT itself launched a formal inquiry with a view to gathering more detailed information as to the different ways in which the Principles were being used in actual practice. The results of the inquiry were encouraging enough to induce the Institute to continue to collect information on the UNIDROIT Principles and to publish in its *Uniform Law Review* select bibliographies and summaries of the first decisions relating to them. Moreover, the International Academy of Comparative Law at its 1998 Bristol Congress devoted a special section to the UNIDROIT Principles prompting national reporters from all five continents to assess the compatibility of the Principles with their domestic law. On its part the International Court of Arbitration of the International Chamber of Commerce in 1999 and 2001 published in its Bulletin an ample survey of ICC awards applying the UNIDROIT Principles.

The present volume is the first attempt to provide a comprehensive collection of all reported decisions that have been rendered by domestic courts and arbitral tribunals world-wide and have referred in one way or another to the UNIDROIT Principles.

The decisions, some of which have not yet been published, are listed not only in chronological order and by adjudicating body (*cf.* Part I) but also by the specific issues they address. For this purpose each individual provision of the UNIDROIT Principles (and the Official Comments thereto) is followed by a list of questions which have arisen or are likely to arise in connection with the respective provision, and to which the relevant decisions, if any, are linked (*cf.* Part II). Of each of these decisions an abstract has been prepared which is published together with (excerpts of) the original full text version where available (*cf.* Part III).

Moreover the volume contains an exhaustive bibliography which is divided into a general bibliography on (i) the UNIDROIT Principles in general; (ii) the UNIDROIT Principles and similar projects; and (iii) the UNIDROIT Principles and international commercial arbitration; and specific bibliographies on each Chapter or Section of the Principles.

III.

While this is clearly not the place to make an in-depth analysis of the content of the international case-law on the UNIDROIT Principles reported in this volume, some conclusions of a more general nature may be drawn.

To begin with, the UNIDROIT Principles are playing a much greater role in the context of arbitration than in litigation before domestic courts. This is not surprising. While domestic courts are traditionally bound to apply a particular national law, be it their own law or that of a foreign country applicable by virtue of the conflict of laws rules of the forum, international arbitrators generally have discretionary power to base their decisions on principles and rules of an a-national or supra-national nature. This means however that, given the confidential nature of most of the arbitral awards, a large number of decisions remain unknown and cannot be reported here.

Threee categories of decisions may be identified on the basis of the way in which the UNIDROIT Principles have been used.

First of all there are those in which the UNIDROIT Principles have been applied as the law governing the substance of the dispute. Sometimes this has been expressly requested by the parties either in the contract itself or at the beginning of the arbitration proceedings. More often however the contracts merely referred to "general principles of law", "principles of international law", "*lex mercatoria*" or the like, and the arbitrators applied the UNIDROIT Principles on the assumption that they represented a particularly authoritative expression of similar supra-national or transnational principles and rules of law. While such an approach has received express confirmation by domestic courts, there has recently been a tendency to go even further and apply the UNIDROIT Principles – either alone or in conjunction with the otherwise applicable law – even in the absence of any choice of law clause in the contract. In so doing the arbitrators relied on statutory provisions or arbitration rules according to which they may "apply the rules of law which [they] determine to be appropriate" and "in all cases [...] shall tale account of [...] the relevant trade usages" (*cf. e.g.* Article 17 of the ICC Rules of Arbitration).

It is worth mentioning that in this context sometimes reference has been made not only to the UNIDROIT Principles but also to the Principles of European Contract Law. Significantly enough however such joint reference, where made, has been done so only in general terms or with respect to issues for which the two instruments provide substantially the same solutions, thereby dissipating the fear that the co-existence of the UNIDROIT Principles and the European Principles would cause uncertainty and conflicts in practice.

Secondly there are decisions in which the UNIDROIT Principles were referred to as a means of interpreting and supplementing international uniform law. For obvious reasons most of them concerned the United Nations Convention on Contracts for the International Sale of Goods (CISG), Article 7 of which expressly states that the Convention should be interpreted taking into account its international character and the need to promote uniformity and that gaps should be filled whenever possible by the general principles underlying it.

In a third category of cases – which by the way represents almost half of the reported cases – the UNIDROIT Principles have been used as a means of interpreting and supplementing the otherwise applicable domestic law. This may come as a surprise since the possibility of using the UNIDROIT Principles for this purpose has not been expressly stated in the Preamble. More important, the domestic laws governing the individual contracts in the cases in question were far from being only those of less developed countries or countries in transition to a market economy. Indeed, they include *inter alia* the laws of Australia, France, Italy, Switzerland and the State of New York, thus confirming that even higly sophisticated legal systems do not always provide clear and/or satisfactory solutions to the special needs of current international commercial transactions, while the UNIDROIT Principles may actually offer such a solution.

IV.

Obviously not all the parts of the UNIDROIT Principles have proved to be of equal importance in the context of international dispute resolution. Among those most frequently applied were Article 1.7 on the duty of the parties to act in accordance with good faith and fair dealing in international trade, Chapter 4 on contract interpretation, Chapter 7, Section 3 on contract termination in case of breach, and Chapter 7, Section 4 on damages.

It is worth noting that none of the provisions contained in the UNIDROIT Principles, which occasionally had been criticised as a possibile source of abuse, have so far actually had this effect. This is true in particular of Article 3.10 on gross disparity and Articles 6.2.1 to 6.2.3 on hardship: not only did they not induce frivolous litigation but in the relatively rare cases where they were invoked by a party to avoid the contract for original gross disparity or to have it terminated or revised for supervening hardship, they, more often than not, served to confirm the validity of the contract or to impose performance according to the originally agreed terms.

Finally, it is fair to say that there were cases where the incompleteness of the UNIDROIT Principles became an issue in the sense that, although applicable, the Principles could not provide a solution to the matter at stake. In particular it occurred in disputes involving the authority of an agent and limitation periods. As if it were necessary, this confirms the need for a new, enlarged edition of the UNIDROIT Principles covering matters not dealt with in the first edition. Fortunately, work to this end is already underway and the new edition of the UNIDROIT Principles containing additional chapters on the authority of agents, limitations periods, assignment of rights, transfer of obligations and assignment of contracts, set-off and third party rights is expected to be published within the next two years or so.

MICHAEL JOACHIM BONELL

ACKNOWLEDGMENTS TO THE FIRST EDITION

Special thanks go first of all to the International Court of Arbitration of the International Chamber of Commerce for granting permission to reproduce excerpts from ICC awards published in the ICC International Court of Arbitration Bulletin and referring to the UNIDROIT Principles.

I am equally grateful to the Arbitral Tribunal of the City of Panama, the Court of Arbitration of the Zürich Chamber of Commerce, the International Arbitration Court of the Chamber of Commerce and Industry of the Russian Federation, the International Court of Arbitration of the Economic Chamber of the Czech Republic (Prague), the National and International Arbitration Chamber of Milan, the United Nations Compensation Commission (Geneva), the Vienna International Court of Arbitration, as well as to Colleagues involved in *ad hoc* arbitrations, for having provided information on award renderd under their auspices or by them.

It is strongly hoped that also in the future those who come to know of award in which the UNIDROIT Principles have been applied will share their information by providing excerpts or abstracts of those awards, thereby enabling legal scholars and practitioners alike to have a better knowledge of how the UNIDROIT Principles are being applied in practice.

Lastly I would like to thank Ms. Yahaira Alonzo and Ms. Paula Howarth for their invaluable assistance in editing and preparing the texts for publication.

Rome, December 2001

The Editor

PART I

LIST OF CASES BY DATE (*)

LIST OF CASES BY ADJUDICATING COURT (*)

GENERAL BIBLIOGRAPHY

(*) The numbers between square brackets indicate the page number of the abstracts and the full text (where available) of the corresponding decision.

Cases Listed by Date

AD HOC ARBITRATION
- Arbitral Award (place and date unknown) [544]
- Arbitral Award, New York (date unknown) [545]
- Arbitral Award, New York (date unknown) [546]

INTERNATIONAL CHAMBER OF COMMERCE INTERNATIONAL COURT OF ARBITRATION
- Arbitral Award (date unknown) [543]

1990

SCHIEDSGERICHT BERLIN
- Arbitral Award No. SG 126/90 (date unknown) [547]

1994

INTERNATIONALES SCHIEDSGERICHT DER BUNDESKAMMER DER GEWERBLICHEN WIRTSCHAFT – WIEN:
- Arbitral Award No. SCH-4318 of June 15, 1994 [548]
- Arbitral Award No. SCH-4366 of June 15, 1994 [554]

SCHIEDSGERICHT DER ZÜRICHER HANDELSKAMMER
- Arbitral Award of November 25, 1994 [559]

1995

AD HOC ARBITRATION
- Arbitral Award, Auckland (date unknown) [564]

INTERNATIONAL CHAMBER OF COMMERCE INTERNATIONAL COURT OF ARBITRATION
- Arbitral Award No. 8128 (date unknown) [565]
- Arbitral Award (First Partial) No. 7110 of June 1995 [572]
- Arbitral Award No. 8240 of July 1995 [591]

LONDON COURT OF ARBITRATION
- Arbitral Award (date unknown) [571]

SUPREME COURT OF THE NETHERLANDS, NETHERLANDS
- Decision No. 15754 of September 22, 1995 [593]

1996

AD HOC ARBITRATION
- Arbitral Award of December 4, 1996, Rome [664]

ARBITRAL COURT OF THE ECONOMIC CHAMBER AND THE AGRARIAN CHAMBER OF CZECH REPUBLIC – PRAGUE
- Arbitral Award No. Rsp 88/94 of December 17, 1996 [669]

ARBITRATION COURT OF THE HUNGARIAN CHAMBER OF COMMERCE AND INDUSTRY
- Arbitral Award of November 17, 1996 [655]

CAMERA ARBITRALE NAZIONALE ED INTERNAZIONALE DI MILANO
- Arbitral Award No. A-1795/51 of December 1, 1996 [662]

COUR D'APPEL DE GRENOBLE, FRANCIA
- Decision of January 24, 1996 [611]
- Decision of October 23, 1996 [643]

INTERNATIONAL CHAMBER OF COMMERCE INTERNATIONAL COURT OF ARBITRATION
- Arbitral Award of April 25, 1996 [617]
- Arbitral Award No. 5835 of June 1996 [618]
- Arbitral Award No. 7375 of June 5, 1996 [622]
- Arbitral Award No. 8486 of September 1996 [633]
- Arbitral Award No. 8540 of September 4, 1996 [636]
- Arbitral Award No. 8261 of September 27, 1996 [642]
- Arbitral Award No. 8502 of November 1996 [651]
- Arbitral Award No. 8331 of December 1996 [656]
- Arbitral Award No. 8769 of December 1996 [659]
- Arbitral Award No. 8874 of December 1996 [660]

1997

AD HOC ARBITRATION
- Arbitral Award of April 21, 1997, Paris [679]
- Arbitral Award of December 1997, New York [710]
- Arbitral Award of December 10, 1997, Buenos Aires [715]

FEDERAL COURT, AUSTRALIA
- Decision No. 558 of June 30, 1997 [685]

INTERNATIONAL ARBITRATION COURT OF THE CHAMBER OF COMMERCE AND INDUSTRY OF THE RUSSIAN FEDERATION
- Arbitral Award No. 116 of January 20, 1997 [670]
- Arbitral Award No. 229 of June 5, 1997 [683]
- Arbitral Award No. 225 of September 2, 1997 [702]

INTERNATIONAL CHAMBER OF COMMERCE INTERNATIONAL COURT OF ARBITRATION
- Arbitral Award No. 8264 of April 1997 [675]
- Arbitral Award No. 7365/FMS of May 5, 1997 [680]

- Arbitral Award No. 8873 of July 1997 [699]
- Arbitral Award No. 8817 of December 1997 [712]

RB ZWOLLE, NETHERLANDS
- Decision No. HA ZA 95-640 of March 5, 1997 [671]

SUPREME COURT, VENEZUELA
- Decision of October 9, 1997 [708]

UNITED NATION COMPENSATION COMMISSION, PANEL F1
- Recommendation No. S/AC.26 of September 23, 1997 [703]

1998

AD HOC ARBITRATION
- Arbitral Award of January 28, 1998, Helsinki [717]

COUR D'APPEL DE PARIS, FRANCE
- Decision (1er Ch. C.) of March 5, 1998 [732]

INTERNATIONAL CHAMBER OF COMMERCE INTERNATIONAL COURT OF ARBITRATION
- Arbitral Award No. 9029 of March 1998 [718]
- Arbitral Award No. 9117 of March 1998 [727]
- Arbitral Award (Second Partial) No. 7110 of April 1998 [734]
- Arbitral Award No. 8223 of April 1998 [739]
- Arbitral Award No. 8908 of September 1998 [750]
- Arbitral Award No. 9419 of September 1998 [755]
- Arbitral Award No. 9333 of October 1998 [759]
- Arbitral Award No. 9593 of December 1998 [762]

SUPREME COURT OF NEW SOUTH WALES, AUSTRALIA
- Decision No. NSWSC 483 of July 16, 1998 [742]

UNITED STATES DISTRICT COURT, S.D. CALIFORNIA
- Decision No. 98-1165-B of December 7, 1998 [764]

1999

INTERNATIONAL ARBITRATION COURT OF THE CHAMBER OF COMMERCE AND INDUSTRY OF THE RUSSIAN FEDERATION
- Arbitral Award No. 152/1998 of April 16, 1999 [798]
- Arbitral Award No. 302/1997 of July 27, 1999 [802]

INTERNATIONAL CHAMBER OF COMMERCE INTERNATIONAL COURT OF ARBITRATION
- Arbitral Award No. 8547 of January 1999 [770]
- Arbitral Award (Partial) No. 9875 of January 1999 [774]
- Arbitral Award (Partial) No. 9474 of February 1999 [777]
- Arbitral Award No. 9479 of February 1999 [786]
- Arbitral Award No. 9594 of March 1999 [794]
- Arbitral Award No. 9753 of May 1999 [799]
- Arbitral Award (Partial) No. 9759 of August 1999 [803]

- Arbitral Award No. 7819 of September 1999 [809]

SUPREME COURT OF NEW SOUTH WALES, AUSTRALIA

- Decision No. 996 of October 1, 1999 [811]

2000

COURT OF APPEAL OF NEW ZEALAND, NEW ZEALAND

- Decision No. (2000) NZCA 350 of November 27, 2000 [869]

INTERNATIONAL CENTRE FOR SETTLEMENT OF INVESTMENT DISPUTES (ICSID)

- Arbitral Award No. ARB(AF)/98/1 of March 20, 2000 [826]

INTERNATIONAL CHAMBER OF COMMERCE INTERNATIONAL COURT OF ARBITRATION

- Arbitral Award No. 10021 (date unknown) [817]
- Arbitral Award No. 9875 of March 2000 [820]
- Arbitral Award No. 10114 of March 2000 [824]
- Arbitral Award No. 9797/CK/AER/ACS of July 28, 2000 [834]
- Arbitral Award No. 9651 of August 2000 [854]
- Arbitral Award (Partial) No. 10022 of October 2000 [862]
- Arbitral Award No. 10335 of October 2000 [864]
- Arbitral Award No. 10346 of December 2000 [883]

2001

AD HOC ARBITRATION

- Arbitral Award of April 30, 2001, San José (Costa Rica) [945]

ARBITRAL TRIBUNAL OF THE CITY OF PANAMA

- Arbitral Award of February 24, 2001 [931]

ARBITRATION INSTITUTE OF THE STOCKHOLM CHAMBER OF COMMERCE

- Arbitral Award (Partial) No. 117/1999 (date unknown) [895]

COURT OF APPEAL OF NEW ZEALAND, NEW ZEALAND

- Decision No. NZCA 348 of October 3, 2001 [974]

INTERNATIONAL ARBITRATION COURT OF THE CHAMBER OF COMMERCE AND INDUSTRY OF THE RUSSIAN FEDERATION

- Arbitral Award No. 88/2000 of January 25, 2001 [921]

INTERNATIONAL CHAMBER OF COMMERCE INTERNATIONAL COURT OF ARBITRATION

- Arbitral Award No. 10422 (date unknown) [902]
- Arbitral Award No. 9771 of January 2001 [918]
- Arbitral Award No. 10578 of April 2001 [942]
- Arbitral Award No. 9950 of June 2001 [948]
- Arbitral Award No. 11227 of June 2001 [951]
- Arbitral Award No. 11051 of July 2001 [953]
- Arbitral Award No. 9078 of October 2001 [970]
- Arbitral Award No. 9994 of December 2001 [985]
- Arbitral Award No. 11295 of December 2001 [988]

SUPREME COURT OF THE NETHERLANDS, NETHERLANDS
- Decision No. R99/120HR of February 2, 2001 [922]
- Decision No. C99/315HR of July 13, 2001 [956]

2002

ARBITRATION CENTRE OF THE COSTA RICAN CHAMBER OF COMMERCE
- Arbitral Award of July 29, 2002 [1003]
ARBITRATION COURT OF THE LAUSANNE CHAMBER OF COMMERCE AND INDUSTRY
- Arbitral Award of January 25, 2002 [991]
- Arbitral Award (Partial) of May 17, 2002 [1001]
CAMERA ARBITRALE NAZIONALE ED INTERNAZIONALE DI MILANO
- Arbitral Award of November 28, 2002 [1034]
CORTE ARBITRALE DELLA ASSOCIAZIONE ITALIANA ARBITRATO
- Arbitral Award No. 91/2001 of September 2002 [1005]
COURT OF JUSTICE OF THE EUROPEAN COMMUNITIES
- Decision No. C-334/00 of September 17, 2002 [1010]
HOF'S-HERTOGENBOSCH, NETHERLANDS
- Decision of October 16, 2002 [1027]
INTERNATIONAL ARBITRATION COURT OF THE CHAMBER OF COMMERCE AND INDUSTRY OF THE RUSSIAN FEDERATION
- Arbitral Award No. 11/2002 of November 5, 2002 [1030]
- Arbitral Award No. 217/2001 of November 6, 2002 [1032]
INTERNATIONAL CHAMBER OF COMMERCE INTERNATIONAL COURT OF ARBITRATION
- Arbitral Award No. 10385 of March 2002 [994]
- Arbitral Award (Partial) No. 11375, of March 2002 [999]
SUPREME COURT OF THE NETHERLANDS
- Decision No. C01/157HR of December 20, 2002 [1036]

2003

ARBITRATION CENTRE OF THE COSTA RICAN CHAMBER OF COMMERCE
- Arbitral Award of June 1, 2003 [1065]
ARBITRATION COURT OF THE LAUSANNE CHAMBER OF COMMERCE AND INDUSTRY
- Arbitral Award of January 31, 2003 [1056]
FEDERAL COURT OF AUSTRALIA
- Decision No. NG733/1997 of February 12, 2003 [1058]
INTERNATIONAL ARBITRATION COURT OF THE CHAMBER OF COMMERCE AND INDUSTRY OF THE RUSSIAN FEDERATION
- Arbitral Award No. 134/2002 of April 4, 2003 [1061]
- Arbitral Award No. 97/2002 of June 6, 2003 [1067]

INTERNATIONAL CHAMBER OF COMMERCE INTERNATIONAL COURT OF ARBITRATION
- Arbitral Award (Partial) No. 12111 of January 6, 2003 [1054]
- Arbitral Award No. 12111 of October 3, 2003 [1074]

SUPREME COURT, POLAND
- Decision No. III CZP 61/03 of November 6, 2003 [1076]

SUPREME ECONOMIC COURT OF THE REPUBLIC OF BELARUS, BELARUS
- Decision No. 7-5/2003 of May 20, 2003 [1063]
- Decision No. 8-5/2003 of May 20, 2003 [1064]

2004

AD HOC ARBITRATION
- Arbitral Award of March 4, 2004 (place unknown) [1077]

HANDELSGERICHT ST. GALLEN, SWITZERLAND
- Decision of November 12, 2004 [1084]

INTERNATIONAL ARBITRATION COURT OF THE CHAMBER OF COMMERCE AND INDUSTRY OF THE RUSSIAN FEDERATION
- Arbitral Award No. 100/2002 of May 19, 2004 [1082]
- Arbitral Award No. 174/2003 of November 12, 2004 [1088]

TRIBUNAL OF INTERNATIONAL COMMERCIAL ARBITRATION AT THE UKRAINIAN CHAMBER OF COMMERCE AND TRADE
- Arbitral Award of December 22, 2004 [1089]

2005

AD HOC ARBITRATION
- Arbitral Award of August 19, 2005, Brussels [1108]

ARBITRATION INSTITUTE OF THE STOC KHOLM CHAMBER OF COMMERCE
- Arbitral Award of March 29, 2005 [1104]

BUNDESGERICHT, SWITZERLAND
- Decision of December 20, 2005 [1126]

GUANGDONG INTERMEDIATE PEOPLE'S COURT, PEOPLE'S REPUBLIC OF CHINA
- Decision of April 28, 2005 [1105]

HIGH COURT OF JUSTICE (QUEEN'S BENCH DIVISION), UNITED KINGDOM
- Decision 2004 Folio 272 of December 4, 2005 [1110]

OVERSEAS PRIVATE INVESTMENT CORP., USA
- Administrative Determination of August 2, 2005 [1106]

TRIBUNALE PADOVA – SEZ. ESTE, ITALY
- Decision of January 11, 2005 [1090]

2006

COURT OF APPEAL (CIVIL DIVISION), UNITED KINGDOM

- Decision No. 2006 EWCA civ. 69 of February 17, 2006 [1142]

TRIBUNALE PADOVA – SEZ. ESTE, ITALY

- Decision of January 10, 2006 [1132]

XIAMEN INTERMEDIATE PEOPLE'S COURT, PEOPLE'S REPUBLIC OF CHINA

- Decision (date unknown) [1131]

Cases Listed by Court

A. SUPRANATIONAL COURTS

COURT OF JUSTICE OF THE EUROPEAN COMMUNITIES
- Decision No. C-334/00 of September 17, 2002 [1010]

B. DOMESTIC COURTS

BUNDESGERICHT, SWITZERLAND
- Decision of December 20, 2005 [1126]

COUR D'APPEL DE GRENOBLE, FRANCIA
- Decision of January 24, 1996 [611]
- Decision of October 23, 1996 [643]

COUR D'APPEL DE PARIS, FRANCE
- Decision (1er Ch. C.) of March 5, 1998 [732]

COURT OF APPEAL (CIVIL DIVISION), UNITED KINGDOM
- Decision No. 2006 EWCA civ. 69 of February 17, 2006 [1142]

COURT OF APPEAL OF NEW ZEALAND, NEW ZEALAND
- Decision No. (2000) NZCA 350 of November 27, 2000 [869]
- Decision No.NZCA 348 of October 3, 2001 [974]

FEDERAL COURT, AUSTRALIA
- Decision No. 558 of June 30, 1997 [685]
- Decision No. NG733/1997 of February 12, 2003 [1058]

GUANGDONG INTERMEDIATE PEOPLE'S COURT, PEOPLE'S REPUBLIC OF CHINA
- Decision of April 28, 2005 [1105]

HANDELSGERICHT ST. GALLEN, SWITZERLAND
- Decision of November 12, 2004 [1084]

HIGH COURT OF JUSTICE (QUEEN'S BENCH DIVISION), UNITED KINGDOM
- Decision 2004 Folio 272 of December 4, 2005 [1110]

HOF'S-HERTOGENBOSCH, NETHERLANDS
- Decision of October 16, 2002 [1027]

RB ZWOLLE, NETHERLANDS
- Decision No. HA ZA 95-640 of March 5, 1997 [671]

SUPREME COURT OF THE NETHERLANDS, NETHERLANDS
- Decision No. 15754 of September 22, 1995 [593]
- Decision No. R99/120HR of February 2, 2001 [922]
- Decision No. C99/315HR of July 13, 2001 [956]
- Decision No. C01/157HR of December 20, 2002 [1036]

SUPREME COURT OF NEW SOUTH WALES, AUSTRALIA
- Decision No. NSWSC 483 of July 16, 1998 [742]
- Decision No. 996 of October 1, 1999 [811]
SUPREME COURT, POLAND
- Decision No. III CZP 61/03 of November 6, 2003 [1076]
SUPREME COURT, VENEZUELA
- Decision of October 9, 1997 [708]
SUPREME ECONOMIC COURT OF THE REPUBLIC OF BELARUS, BELARUS
- Decision No. 7-5/2003 of May 20, 2003 [1063]
- Decision No. 8-5/2003 of May 20, 2003 [1064]
TRIBUNALE PADOVA – SEZ. ESTE, ITALY
- Decision of January 11, 2005 [1090]
- Decision of January 10, 2006 [1132]
UNITED STATES DISTRICT COURT, S.D. CALIFORNIA
- Decision No. 98-1165-B of December 7, 1998 [764]
XIAMEN INTERMEDIATE PEOPLE'S COURT, PEOPLE'S REPUBLIC OF CHINA
- Decision of 2006 (date unknown) [1131]

C. ARBITRAL AWARDS

AD HOC ARBITRATION
- Arbitral Award (place and date unknown) [544]
- Arbitral Award, New York (date unknown) [545]
- Arbitral Award, New York (date unknown) [546]
- Arbitral Award 1995, Auckland (date unknown) [564]
- Arbitral Award of December 4, 1996, Rome [664]
- Arbitral Award of April 21, 1997, Paris [679]
- Arbitral Award of December 1997, New York [710]
- Arbitral Award of December 10, 1997, Buenos Aires [715]
- Arbitral Award of January 28, 1998, Helsinki [717]
- Arbitral Award of April 30, 2001, San José (Costa Rica) [945]
- Arbitral Award of March 4, 2004 (place unknown) [1077]
- Arbitral Award of August 19, 2005, Brussels [1108]
ARBITRAL COURT OF THE ECONOMIC CHAMBER AND THE AGRARIAN CHAMBER OF CZECH REPUBLIC – PRAGUE
- Arbitral Award Rsp 88/94 of December 17, 1996 [669]
ARBITRAL TRIBUNAL OF THE CITY OF PANAMA
- Arbitral Award of February 24, 2001 [931]
ARBITRATION CENTRE OF THE COSTA RICAN CHAMBER OF COMMERCE
- Arbitral Award of July 29, 2002 [1003]
- Arbitral Award of June 1, 2003 [1065]
ARBITRATION COURT OF THE HUNGARIAN CHAMBER OF COMMERCE AND INDUSTRY
- Arbitral Award of November 17, 1996 [655]

ARBITRATION COURT OF THE LAUSANNE CHAMBER OF COMMERCE AND INDUSTRY
- Arbitral Award of January 25, 2002 [991]
- Arbitral Award (Partial) of May 17, 2002 [1001]
- Arbitral Award of January 31, 2003 [1056]

ARBITRATION INSTITUTE OF THE STOCKHOLM CHAMBER OF COMMERCE
- Arbitral Award (Partial) 117/1999 of 2001 (date unknown) [895]
- Arbitral Award of March 29, 2005 [1104]

CAMERA ARBITRALE NAZIONALE ED INTERNAZIONALE DI MILANO
- Arbitral Award No. A-1795/51 of December 1, 1996 [662]
- Arbitral Award of November 28, 2002 [1034]

CORTE ARBITRALE DELLA ASSOCIAZIONE ITALIANA ARBITRATO
- Arbitral Award No. 91/2001 of September 2002 [1005]

INTERNATIONAL ARBITRATION COURT OF THE CHAMBER OF COMMERCE AND INDUSTRY OF THE RUSSIAN FEDERATION
- Arbitral Award No. 116 of January 20, 1997 [670]
- Arbitral Award No. 229 of June 5, 1997 [683]
- Arbitral Award No. 225 of September 2, 1997 [702]
- Arbitral Award No. 152/1998 of April 16, 1999 [798]
- Arbitral Award No. 302/1997 of July 27, 1999 [802]
- Arbitral Award No. 88/2000 of January 25, 2001 [921]
- Arbitral Award No. 11/2002 of November 5, 2002 [1030]
- Arbitral Award No. 217/2001 of November 6, 2002 [1032]
- Arbitral Award No. 134/2002 of April 4, 2003 [1061]
- Arbitral Award No. 97/2002 of June 6, 2003 [1067]
- Arbitral Award No. 100/2002 of May 19, 2004 [1082]
- Arbitral Award No. 174/2003 of November 12, 2004 [1088]

INTERNATIONAL CENTRE FOR SETTLEMENT OF INVESTMENT DISPUTES (ICSID)
- Arbitral Award No. ARB(AF)/98/1 of March 20, 2000 [826]

INTERNATIONAL CHAMBER OF COMMERCE INTERNATIONAL COURT OF ARBITRATION
- Arbitral Award (date unknown) [543]
- Arbitral Award No. 8128 of 1995 (date unknown) [565]
- Arbitral Award (First Partial) No. 7110 of June 1995 [572]
- Arbitral Award No. 8240 of July 1995 [591]
- Arbitral Award of April 25, 1996 [617]
- Arbitral Award No. 5835 of June 1996 [618]
- Arbitral Award No. 7375 of June 5, 1996 [622]
- Arbitral Award No. 8486 of September 1996 [633]
- Arbitral Award No. 8540 of September 4, 1996 [636]
- Arbitral Award No. 8261 of September 27, 1996 [642]
- Arbitral Award No. 8502 of November 1996 [651]
- Arbitral Award No. 8331 of December 1996 [656]
- Arbitral Award No. 8769 of December 1996 [659]
- Arbitral Award No. 8874 of December 1996 [660]

- Arbitral Award No. 8264 of April 1997 [675]
- Arbitral Award No. 7365/FMS of May 5, 1997 [680]
- Arbitral Award No. 8873 of July 1997 [699]
- Arbitral Award No. 8817 of December 1997 [712]
- Arbitral Award No. 9029 of March 1998 [718]
- Arbitral Award No. 9117 of March 1998 [727]
- Arbitral Award (Second Partial) No. 7110 of April 1998 [734]
- Arbitral Award No. 8223 of April 1998 [739]
- Arbitral Award No. 8908 of September 1998 [750]
- Arbitral Award No. 9419 of September 1998 [755]
- Arbitral Award No. 9333 of October 1998 [759]
- Arbitral Award No. 9593 of December 1998 [762]
- Arbitral Award No. 8547 of January 1999 [770]
- Arbitral Award (Partial) No. 9875 of January 20, 1999 [774]
- Arbitral Award (Partial) No. 9474 of February 1999 [777]
- Arbitral Award No. 9479 of February 1999 [786]
- Arbitral Award No. 9594 of March 1999 [794]
- Arbitral Award No. 9753 of May 1999 [799]
- Arbitral Award (Partial) 9759 of August 1999 [803]
- Arbitral Award No. 7819 of September 1999 [809]
- Arbitral Award No. 10021 of 2000 (date unknown) [817]
- Arbitral Award No. 9875 of March 2000 [820]
- Arbitral Award No. 10114 of March 2000 [824]
- Arbitral Award No. 9797/CK/AER/ACS of July 28, 2000 [834]
- Arbitral Award No. 9651 of August 2000 [854]
- Arbitral Award (Partial) No. 10022 of October 2000 [862]
- Arbitral Award No. 10335 of October 2000 [864]
- Arbitral Award No. 10346 of December 2000 [883]
- Arbitral Award No. 10422 of 2001 (date unknown) [902]
- Arbitral Award No. 9771 of January 2001 [918]
- Arbitral Award No. 10578 of April 2001 [942]
- Arbitral Award No. 9950 of June 2001 [948]
- Arbitral Award No. 11227 of June 2001 [951]
- Arbitral Award No. 11051 of July 2001 [953]
- Arbitral Award No. 9078 of October 2001 [970]
- Arbitral Award No. 9994 of December 2001 [985]
- Arbitral Award No. 11295 of December 2001 [988]
- Arbitral Award No. 10385 of March 2002 [994]
- Arbitral Award (Partial) No. 11375 of March 2002 [999]
- Arbitral Award (Partial) No. 12111 of January 6, 2003 [1054]
- Arbitral Award No. 12111 of October 3, 2003 [1074]

INTERNATIONALES SCHIEDSGERICHT DER BUNDESKAMMER DER GEWERBLICHEN WIRTSCHAFT – WIEN:
- Arbitral Award No. SCH-4318 of June 15, 1994 [548]
- Arbitral Award No. SCH-4366 of June 15, 1994 [554]

LONDON COURT OF ARBITRATION
- Arbitral Award 1995 (date unknown) [571]
SCHIEDSGERICHT BERLIN
- Arbitral Award No. 126/90 (date unknown) [547]
SCHIEDSGERICHT DER ZÜRICHER HANDELSKAMMER
- Arbitral Award of November 25, 1994 [559]
TRIBUNAL OF INTERNATIONAL COMMERCIAL ARBITRATION AT THE UKRAINIAN CHAMBER OF COMMERCE AND TRADE
- Arbitral Award of December 22, 2004 [1089]

D. – OTHER ADJUDICATING BODIES

OVERSEAS PRIVATE INVESTMENT CORP. USA
- Administrative Determination of August 2, 2005 [1106]
UNITED NATION COMPENSATION COMMISSION, PANEL F1
- Recommendation No. S/AC.26 of September 23, 1997 [703]

GENERAL BIBLIOGRAPHY

1. The UNIDROIT Principles in general

ADDIS F., Note introduttive ai Principi UNIDROIT, in VETTORI G. (ed.), Materiali e Commenti sul Nuovo Diritto dei Contratti, Cedam, Padova 1999, 926-934.

ALPA G., Italy, in BONELL M.J. (ed.), A New Approach to International Commercial Contracts. The UNIDROIT Principles of International Commercial Contracts, Kluwer Law International, 1999, 175-190.

ALPA G., (Principi UNIDROIT) Quadro di sintesi, in ALPA G. / BESSONE M. (eds.), Giurisprudenza sistematica di diritto civile e commerciale, I, Utet, Torino 1999, 195-216.

ALPA G., Prime note di raffronto tra i Principi dell'UNIDROIT e il sistema contrattuale italiano, in Contratto e impresa / Europa, 1996, 316-336.

ALTERINI A.A., Los Principios de UNIDROIT y las soluciones del derecho común, in UNIDROIT (ed.), The UNIDROIT Principles: a Common Law of Contracts for the Americas?, 1998, 259-274.

BANNES F.-M., L'impact de l'adoption des Principes UNIDROIT 1994 sur l'unification du droit commercial international: réalité ou utopie?, in Revue de la recherche juridique - droit prospectif, 1996, 933-970.

BANREVY G., Az UNIDROIT "Alapelvek" és a "*lex mercatoria*", in Iustum, Aequum, Salutare (Festschrift in Honour of Professor J. Zlinszky), Budapest 1998, 41-50.

BASEDOW J., Uniform law Conventions and the UNIDROIT Principles of International Commercial Contracts, in International Uniform Law Conventions, *Lex Mercatoria* and UNIDROIT Principles. Symposium held at Verona University (Italy), Faculty of Law, 4-6 November 1999, in Uniform Law Review 2000, 129-139.

BASEDOW J. (ed.), Europäische Vertragsrechtsvereinheitlichung und deutsches Recht, J. C. B. Mohr (Siebeck), Tübingen 2000.

BASEDOW J., Germany, in BONELL M.J. (ed.), A New Approach to International Commercial Contracts. The UNIDROIT Principles of International Commercial Contracts, Kluwer Law International, 1999, 125-150.

BEALE H., Finding the remaining traps instead of unifying contract law, in GRUNDMANN, S. - STUYCK, J. (eds.) - An Academic Green Paper on European Contract Law, Kluwer Law International, The Hague 2002, 67-72.

BEN-OLIEL R., The UNIDROIT Principles of International Commercial Contracts: A comment, in RABELLO A.M. (ed.), The Principles of UNIDROIT and Modern National Codifications, Jerusalem, Harry and Michael Sacher Institute for Legislative Research and Comparative Law, Faculty of Law, The Hebrew University of Jerusalem, 2001,139-148.

BERAUDO J.P., The Interamerican Congress on UNIDROIT Principles, in ICC International Court of Arbitration Bulletin, n. 8, 1997, 48 *et seq*.

BERAUDO J.P., Les Principes d'UNIDROIT relatifs au droit du commerce international, in La Semaine Juridique, 1995, 189-194.

BERGER K.P., The *Lex Mercatoria* Doctrine and the UNIDROIT Principles of International Commercial Contracts, in 28 Law and Policy in International Business, n. 4, 1997, 943-990.

BERGER K.P., Die UNIDROIT-Prinzipien für Internationale Handelsverträge, in Zeitschrift für Vergleichende Rechtswissenschaft, 1995, 217-236.

BOELE-WOELKI K., Terms of Co-Existence: the CISG and the UNIDROIT Principles, in SARCEVIC P. / VOLKEN P. (eds), The International Sale of Goods, Kluwer Law International, The Hague/London/New York 2001, 203-240.

BONASSIES P., Le droit positif francais en 1995. I. Legislation. 1. Droit maritime. Sources. "Principes relatifs aux contrats du commerce international" (UNIDROIT), in Le droit maritime français, 1996, 3-273.

BONELL M.J., An International Restatement of Contract Law. The UNIDROIT Principles of International Commercial Contracts, 3rd ed., Transnational Publications Inc., Ardsley, New York 2005.

BONELL M.J., UNIDROIT Principles 2004 - A Further Step Towards a Global Contract Law, in Uniform Commercial Code Law Journal 2004, 49-90.

BONELL M.J., The UNIDROIT Principles of International Commercial Contracts prepared by the International Institute for the Unification of Private Law (UNIDROIT), in Transnational Law in Commercial Legal Practice, Quadis Publishing, Münster 1999, 7-44.

BONELL M.J., General Report, in BONELL M.J. (ed.), A New Approach to International Commercial Contracts. The UNIDROIT Principles of International Commercial Contracts, Kluwer Law International, 1999, 1-17.

BONELL M.J. (ed.), A New Approach to International Commercial Contracts. The UNIDROIT Principles of International Commercial Contracts, Kluwer Law International, 1999.

BONELL M.J., I Principi UNIDROIT. Un approccio moderno al diritto dei contratti, in VETTORI G. (ed.), Materiali e Commenti sul Nuovo Diritto dei Contratti, Cedam, Padova 1999, 935-955.

BONELL M.J., The UNIDROIT Principles: What Next?, in Uniform Law Review / Revue de droit uniforme, 1998, 275-286.

BONELL M.J., The UNIDROIT Principles of International Commercial Contracts: General Presentation, in UNIDROIT (ed.), The UNIDROIT Principles: a Common Law of Contracts for the Americas?, 1998, 21-28.

BONELL M.J., The UNIDROIT Principles: First Practical Experiences, in 1 European Journal of Law Reform, n. 3, 1998-1999, 193-202.

BONELL M.J., The UNIDROIT Principles - A Modern Approach to Contract Law, in WEYERS H.-L. (ed.), Europäisches Vertragsrecht, Nomos, Baden-Baden 1997, 9-21.

BONELL M.J., The UNIDROIT Principles of International Commercial Contracts: Towards a New *Lex Mercatoria*?, in Revue de droit des affaires internationales / International Business Law, 1997, 145-163.

BONELL M.J., The UNIDROIT Principles in Practice: The Experience of the First Two Years, in 2 Uniform Law Review / Revue de droit uniforme, n. 1, 1997, 34-45.

BONELL M.J., Erste Entscheidungen zu den UNIDROIT Principles, in ASA (Association suisse de l'arbitrage) Bulletin, n. 4, 1997, 600-607.

BONELL M.J., I Principi UNIDROIT dei contratti commerciali internazionali: un approccio nuovo alla disciplina dei contratti internazionali, in BONELL M.J. /

BONELLI F. (eds.), Contratti commerciali internazionali e Principi UNIDROIT, Giuffré, Milano 1997, 7-19.

BONELL M.J. / BONELLI F. (eds.), Contratti commerciali internazionali e Principi UNIDROIT, Giuffré, Milano 1997.

BONELL M.J., Die UNIDROIT Prinzipien der internationalen Handelsverträge - eine neue *Lex Mercatoria*?, in Zeitschrift für Rechtsvergleichung, 1996, 152-157.

BONELL M.J., Il progetto dell'UNIDROIT per la elaborazione di Principi per i contratti commerciali internazionali, in BONELL M.J. / SCHIPANI S. (eds.), "Principi per i contratti commerciali internazionali" e il sistema giuridico latinoamericano, Cedam, Padova 1996, 9-19.

BONELL M.J., I Principi UNIDROIT dei contratti commerciali internazionali: origini, natura e finalità, in Diritto del commercio internazionale, 1995, 3-22.

BONELL M.J., Unification of Law by Non-Legislative Means: The UNIDROIT Draft Principles for International Commercial Contracts, in 40 American Journal of Comparative Law, n. 3, 1992, 617-633.

BONELL M.J., A "Restatement" of Principles for International Commercial Contracts: An Academic Exercise or A Practical Need?, in Revue de Droit des Affaires Internationales, 1988, 873-888.

BONELL M.J., The UNIDROIT Initiative for the Progressive Codification of International Trade Law, in 27 International and Comparative Law Quarterly, 1978, 413-441.

BONELL M.J. / PELEGGI R. (eds.), Rassegna giurisprudenziale sui Principi UNIDROIT dei contratti commerciali internazionali, in Diritto del commercio internazionale, 16, 2002, 443-461.

BONELL M.J. / PELEGGI R. (eds.), Rassegna giurisprudenziale sui Principi UNIDROIT dei contratti commerciali internazionali, in Diritto del Commercio Internazionale, 18, 2004, 161-186.

BONELL M.J. / SCHIPANI S. (eds.), "Principi per i contratti commerciali internazionali" e il sistema giuridico latinoamericano, Cedam, Padova 1996.

BORTOLOTTI F., Il Codice UNIDROIT alla prova dei fatti, in Focus Commercio Internazionale, 1995, 604-605.

BRIDGE M., The UK Sale of Goods Act, the CISG and the UNIDROIT Principles, in SARCEVIC P. - VOLKEN P. (eds), The International Sale of Goods, Kluwer Law International, The Hague/London/New York 2001, 115-255.

BRÖDERMANN E., Die erweiterten UNIDROIT Principles 2004, in Recht der Internationalen Wirtschaft 2004, 721-735.

BUREAU D., Les nouveaux Principes UNIDROIT: Colloque de l'Institut de la CCI (Paris, 20-21 octobre 1994), in Revue de l'arbitrage, 1994, 787-791.

BURKART F. / KOCH D., "UNIDROIT Principles" - eine neue Rechtsgrundlage für internationale Verträge, in Schweizerische Zeitschrift für Wirtschaftsrechts, 1998, 68-71.

CARBONE S.M., Principi dei contratti internazionali e norme di origine internazionale (con particolare riguardo al diritto uniforme), in BONELL M. J. / BONELLI F. (eds.), Contratti commerciali internazionali e Principi UNIDROIT, Giuffré, Milano 1997, 23-38.

CERUTTI R., Das U.S. amerikanische Warenkaufrecht mit rechtsvergleichenden Hinweisen auf das schweizerische und das deutsche Recht, das CISG sowie die UNIDROIT Principles, Schulthess Polygraphischer Verlag, Zürich 1998.

COSMIVICI P. M. / MUNTEANU R., Romania, in BONELL M.J. (ed.), A New Approach to International Commercial Contracts. The UNIDROIT Principles of International Commercial Contracts, Kluwer Law International, 1999, 281-300.

CONTRATACIÓN INTERNACIONAL, Romania in M.J. BONELL (ed.), A New Approach to International Commercial Contracts. The UNIDROIT Principles of International Commercial Contracts, Kluwer Law International, 1999, 281 – 300.

CRÉPEAU P.A., The UNIDROIT Principles of International Commercial Contracts, in RABELLO A.M. (ed.), The Principles of UNIDROIT and Modern National Codifications, Jerusalem, Harry and Michael Sacher Institute for Legislative Research and Comparative Law, Faculty of Law, The Hebrew University of Jerusalem, 2000, 21-61

CREPEAU P.A. / CHARPENTIER E.M., Les Principes d'UNIDROIT et le Code civil du Québec: valeurs partagées?, Carswell, Toronto 1998.

CRÉPEAU P.A., Présentation générale du projet d'UNIDROIT relatif aux contrats de commerce international, (paper presented at the 12th seminar on international commercial law organised by the Ministry of Justice of Ottawa on 20th October 1994).

DANHAN H., China, in BONELL M.J. (ed.), A New Approach to International Commercial Contracts. The UNIDROIT Principles of International Commercial Contracts, Kluwer Law International, 1999, 65-70.

DANNES F.-M., L'impact de l'adoption des Principes UNIDROIT sur l'unification du droit commercial international: réalité ou utopie?, in Revue de la recherche juridique 1996, 933.

DASSER F., Vertragstypenrecht im Wandel, Schulthess, Zürich; Nomos, Baden-Baden 2000.

DATE-BAH S.K., The UNIDROIT Principles of International Commercial Contracts and the Harmonisation of the Principles of Commercial Contracts in West and Central Africa [résumé in French], in Uniform Law Review / Revue de droit uniforme, 9, 2004, 269-273.

DE LY F., Netherlands, in BONELL M.J. (ed.), A New Approach to International Commercial Contracts. The UNIDROIT Principles of International Commercial Contracts, Kluwer Law International, 1999, 203-235.

DE MIGUEL ASENSIO P.A., Armonización normativa y régimen jurídico de los contratos mercantiles internacionales, in 12 Diritto del Commercio Internazionale 1998, 859-883.

DI MAJO A., I principi dei contratti commerciali internazionali dell'UNIDROIT, in Contratto e impresa / Europa, 1996, 287-296.

DI MAJO A., I "*Principles*" dei contratti commerciali internazionali tra *Civil Law* e *Common Law*, in Rivista di diritto civile, n. 1, 1995, 609-627.

DROBNIG U., Vereinheitlichung von Zivilrecht durch *soft law*: neuere Erfahrungen und Einsichten, in BASEDOW J. / DROBNIG U./ ELLGER R. [*et al.*] (eds.), Aufbruch nach Europa. 75 Jahre Max-Planck-Institut für Privatrecht, Mohr, Tübingen 2001, 745-756.

DROBIG U., Der Stand der internationalen Überlegungen: Die UNIDROIT Principles of International Commercial Contracts, in GRUNDMANN S. / MEDICUS D. / ROLLAND W. (eds.), Europäisches Kaufgewährleistungsrecht. Reform and Internationalisierung des deutschen Schuldrechts, Carl Heymanns Verlag, Köln/Berlin/Bonn 2000, 49-60.

FAHRI DE MONTALBAN D., Los Principios UNIDROIT para los contratos comerciales internacionales, in Derecho Economico, 26, 39 *et seq.*

FARNSWORTH E.A., An International Restatement: The UNIDROIT Principles of

International Commercial Contracts, in University of Baltimore Law Review, n. 26, 1997, 1-7.

FARNSWORTH E.A., The American Provenance of the UNIDROIT Principles, in 72 Tulane Law Review, n. 6, 1998, 1985-1994.

FAUVARQUE-COSSON B., Les contrats du commerce international, une approche nouvelle: les Principes d'UNIDROIT relatifs aux contrats du commerce international, in Revue internationale de droit comparé, 1998, 463-489.

FAUVARQUE-COSSON B., France, in BONELL M.J. (ed.), A New Approach to International Commercial Contracts. The UNIDROIT Principles of International Commercial Contracts, Kluwer Law Int., 1999, 95-123.

FONTAINE M., The UNIDROIT Principles 2004, in Nederlands Tijdschrift voor Handelsrecht 2006, 7 – 12.

FONTAINE M., *Ius commune* et harmonization du droit des contrats, in WIJFFELS A. (ed.), Le Code civil entre *ius commune* et droit privé européen, Bruylant 2005, 75 – 91.

FONTAINE M., The UNIDROIT Principles: An Expression of Current Contract Practice?, in ICC International Court of Arbitration Bulletin, 2002, Special Supplement, 95-104.

FONTAINE M., Belgium, in BONELL M.J. (ed.), A New Approach to International Commercial Contracts. The UNIDROIT Principles of International Commercial Contracts, Kluwer Law Int., 1999, 55-64.

FONTAINE M., Les Principes pour les contrats commerciaux internationaux élaborés par UNIDROIT, in Revue de droit international et de droit comparé, 1991, 23-40.

FORTIER V., Le contrat du commerce international à l'aune du raisonnable, in Journal de droit international, n. 2, 1996, 315-379.

FRICK J.G., Die UNIDROIT-Prinzipien für internationale Handelsverträge, in 47 Recht der Internationalen Wirtschaft 2001, 416-422.

FURMSTON M.P., United Kingdom, in BONELL M.J. (ed.), A New Approach to International Commercial Contracts. The UNIDROIT Principles of International Commercial Contracts, Kluwer Law International, 1999, 379-385.

FURMSTON M.P., An English View of the UNIDROIT Principles of International Commercial Contracts, in Uniform Law Review / Revue de droit uniforme 1998, 419-424.

FURMSTON M.P., UNIDROIT General Principles for International Commercial Contracts, 10 Journal of Contract Law, 1996, 11-20.

GAMA JR. L., Contratos Internacionais à luz dos Principios do UNIDROIT 2004: *Soft Law*, Arbitragem e Jurisdicao, Renovar (Brasil), 2006, i – 575.

GIARDINA A., Les Principes UNIDROIT sur les contrats internationaux, in Journal du droit international, 1995, 547-558.

GLENN H.P., An international private law of contract, in BORCHERS P.J. - ZEKOLL J. (ed.), International Conflict of Laws for the Third Millennium. Essays in Honor of Friedrich K. Juenger, Transnational Publishers Inc., Ardsley, N.Y. 2000, 53-64.

GORDLEY J., An American Perspective on the UNIDROIT Principles, in CENTRO DI STUDI E RICERCHE DI DIRITTO COMPARATO E STRANIERO (ed.), Saggi, conferenze e seminari, n. 22, Roma 1996.

HARTKAMP A.S., The UNIDROIT Principles for International Commercial Contracts and the New Dutch Civil Code, CJHB, Kluwer 1994, 127-137.

HERBER R., "*Lex mercatoria*" und "Principles" - gefährliche Irrlichter im internationalen Kaufrecht, in Internationales Handelsrecht, 3, 2003, 1-10.

HEUTGER V., UNIDROIT Principles of International Commercial Contracts 2004, in European Review of Private Law 2005, 83 – 90.

HEUTGER V., Die Aktualität der "UNIDROIT Prinzipien" - zur Neuauflage 2004. Die "UNIDROIT Principles" 2004 und ihre Anwendung in der Schweiz, Jusletter 29. November 2004, 1-5.

HILL R., A Businessman's View of the UNIDROIT Principles, in 13 Journal of International Arbitration, 1996, 163-170.

HINESTROSA F., De los principios generales del derecho a los principios generales del contrato, in Revista de Derecho Privado [Universidad Externado de Colombia] 2000, n. 5, 3- 22.

HINESTROSA F., Des principes généraux du droit aux principes généraux des contrats, in Uniform Law Review / Revue de droit uniforme 1998, 501-517.

HIROSE H., The Place of the UNIDROIT Principles in Non-Western Legal Traditions, (paper presented at the Bi-annual 25th Conference of the International Bar Association held in Melbourne on 9-14 October 1994).

HORN N., The Use of Transnational Law in the Contract Law of International Trade and Finance, in BERGER K.P., The Practice of Transnational Law, Kluwer Law International, The Hague 2001, 67-80.

HUET J., Conclusions, in UNIDROIT Principles for International Commercial Contracts: A New *Lex Mercatoria*?, ICC Publication n. 490/1, 1995, 263-282.

HULTMARK CH., Sweden, in BONELL M.J. (ed.), A New Approach to International Commercial Contracts. The UNIDROIT Principles of International Commercial Contracts, Kluwer Law International, 1999, 301-330.

HULTMARK CH., Internationaliseringen av svenk avtalsratt - UNIDROIT Principles of International Commercial Contracts, in 7 Juridisk Tidskrift, 1995-1996, 655-669.

HYLAND R., On Setting Forth the Law of Contract: A Forward, in 40 American Journal of Comparative Law, n. 3, 1992, 541-550.

ILLESCAS ORTÍZ R. / PERALES VISCASILLAS P., Derecho mercantil internacional. El derecho uniforme, Editorial Centro de Estudios Ramón Areces, Universidad Carlos III de Madrid, Madrid 2003.

INSTITUTE OF INTERNATIONAL BUSINESS LAW AND PRACTICE (ed.), UNIDROIT Principles for International Commercial Contracts: A New *Lex Mercatoria*?, ICC Publication n. 490/1, 1995.

IZADI B., Iran, in BONELL M.J. (ed.), A New Approach to International Commercial Contracts. The UNIDROIT Principles of International Commercial Contracts, Kluwer Law International, 1999, 151-165.

JANSSEN A., Die Einbeziehung von allgemeinen Geschäftsbedingungen in internationale Kaufverträge und die Bedeutung der UNIDROIT- und der Lando-Principles, in IHR- Internationales Handelsrecht, 4 (2004), 194 – 200.

KAHN PH., Les contrats internationaux de coopération scientifique et technique inter-entreprises face aux Principes d'UNIDROIT, in Uniform Law Review / Revue de droit uniforme, 1998, 519 – 524.

KAROLLUS M., Principles of International Commercial Contracts, in 61 Rabels-Zeitschrift, 1997, 582-592.

KAVASS I., UNIDROIT Principles of International Commercial Contracts, in 23 International Journal of Legal Information 1995, 201-203.

KESSEDJIAN C., Un exercice de rénovation des sources du droit des contrats du commerce international: Les Principes proposés par l'UNIDROIT, in Revue critique de droit international privé, 1995, 641-670.

KING D.B., Convergence of Contract Law Systems and the UNIDROIT Principles of International Commercial Contracts: A Search for the Nature of Contract, Ch. 4, Hart Publishing, 1998, 97-104.

KOMAROV A.S., The UNIDROIT Principles of International Commercial Contracts: A Russian View, in 1 Uniform Law Review / Revue de droit uniforme, n. 2, 1996, 247-254.

KRONKE H., From International Uniform Conventions to Model Laws - From Guides to Principles, in PERRET L. - BISSON A.-F. - MARIANI N. (eds.), Evolution des systèmes juridiques, bijuridisme et commerce international. The evolution of legal systems, bijuralism and international trade. Textes présentés lors d'un colloque organisée par la Faculté de droit de l'Université d'Ottawa, le Ministère de la Justice du Canada et le Patrimoine canadien, tenu à Ottawa, Ont., du 20 au 21 oct. 2000, Wilson & Lafleur, Ottawa 2002, 283-304.

KRONKE H., Les Principes d'UNIDROIT et les contrats internationaux: aspects pratiques - Profil de la problématique. Journées Maximilien-Caron 2001 (Faculté de droit, Université de Montréal) - Les Principes d'UNIDROIT et les contrats internationaux: aspects pratiques, in Revue Juridique Thémis, 36, 2002, 331-334.

KRÜGER H., Rechtseinheit von unten? Restatements of the law als Alternativen internationaler und europäischer Rechtsvereinheitlichung, Nomos, Baden-Baden 2005, 183.

LALIVE P., Préface, in UNIDROIT Principles for International Commercial Contracts: A New *Lex Mercatoria*?, ICC Publication n. 490/1, 1995, 7-8.

LANDO O., The CISG and the UNIDROIT Principles in a Global Commercial Code, in Mélanges offerts à Marcel Fontaine, Larcier, Paris 2003, 451-472.

LARROUMET CH., La valeur des Principes d'UNIDROIT applicables aux contrats du commerce international, in La Semaine Juridique, ed. G., Doctrine, 1997, 147-152.

LEDUC A., L'emergence d'une nouvelle *lex mercatoria* à l'enseigne des principes d'UNIDROIT relativs aux contrats du commerce international: thèse et antithèse, in Revue Juridique Thèmis 2001, 429-451.

LEIBLE S., El significado de los principios de UNIDROIT para la seguridad jurídica en el comercio internacional, in Derechos de los Negocios (Septiembre 1999), 11-20.

LETE ACHIRICA J., Los Principios de UNIDROIT sobre los contratos comerciales internacionales, in Actualidad Civil, 1996, 127-136.

LETTERMAN G.G., UNIDROIT's rules in practice. Standard international contracts and applicable rules, Kluwer Law International, The Hague 2001.

LEYVA SAAVEDRA J., Los principios sobre los contratos comerciales internacionales del UNIDROIT, in LEYVA SAAVEDRA J., Contratos de empresa, Tomo I (Tratado de derecho privado, vol. II), Editorial San Marco, Lima 1997, 145-183.

LINZER P., Non-["Un-"?] American Law and the Core Curriculum, in 72 Tulane Law Review n. 6, 1998, 2031-2042.

LINZER P., The UNIDROIT Principles of International Commercial Contracts: Should American Lawyers Pull Their Hair Out Over Them?, in 13 Texas Transnational Law Quarterly, 1997.

LOOKOFSKY J., Denmark, in BONELL M.J. (ed.), A New Approach to International Commercial Contracts. The UNIDROIT Principles of International Commercial Contracts, Kluwer Law International, 1999, 71-93.

LOUSIN A., The UNIDROIT Principles, in 30 John Marshall Law Review 1997,

761-765.
MÁRQUES GONZÁLES J. A., La teoría de las obligaciones en los Principios sobre los contratos comerciales internacionales, in Revista Mexicana de Derecho, Colegio de Notarios del Distrito Federal, no. 1, 1999, 239-255.
MARRELLA F., La nuova *lex mercatoria*. Principi UNIDROIT ed usi dei contratti del commercio internazionale, in Trattato di diritto commerciale e di diritto pubblico dell'economia, 30, Cedam, Padova 2003.
MARRELLA F., *Lex mercatoria* e Principi UNIDROIT. Per una ricostruzione sistematica del diritto del commercio internazionale, in Contratto e Impresa / Europa, 2000, 29-79.
MARTY R., Conflits d'application entre les Principes d'UNIDROIT et la loi francaise applicable au contrat. A propos d'un dualisme juridique, in Dalloz Affaires 1997, 100-106.
MATHER H., Choice of law for international sales issues not reseolved by the CISG, in Journal of Law and Commerce, 20, 2001, 155-208.
MAYER U., Die UNIDROIT-Prinzipien für internationale Handelsverträge. Zielstzung, Anwendungsbereich und ihre Bedeutung für die schweizerische Rechtspraxis, in Aktuelle Juristische Praxis, 4, 1998, 499-514.
MICHAELS R., Privatautonomie und Privatkodification. Zu Anwendbarkeit und Geltung allgemeiner Vertragsrechtsprinzipien, in 62 Rabels-Zeitschrift, 1998, 580-626.
MOENS A. / COHN L. / PEACOCK D., Australia, in BONELL M.J. (ed.), A New Approach to International Commercial Contracts. The UNIDROIT Principles of International Commercial Contracts, Kluwer Law International, 1999, 19-54.
MORAN BOVIO D. (ed.), Comentario a los Principios de UNIDROIT para los Contratos del Comercio Internacional, Editorial Aranzadi, 1999.
MOURRE A. – JOLIVET E., La réception des Principes d'UNIDROIT dans les contrats modèles de la Chambre de commerce international [abstract in English], in Uniform Law Review, 2005, 275 – 293.
NAFZIGER J.A.R. / SYMEONIDES S.C. (eds.), Law and justice in a multistate world. Essays in honor of Arthur T. von Mehren, Law and justice in a Transnational Publishers, Ardsley, N.Y. 2002.
NET L., Vietnam, in BONELL M.J. (ed.), A New Approach to International Commercial Contracts. The UNIDROIT Principles of International Commercial Contracts, Kluwer Law International, 1999, 421-431.
NET L., UNIDROIT Principles of International Commercial Contracts and Vietnamese contract law, in Revue de droit Vietnamien / Vietnamese Law Journal 1998, No. 19, 29-33.
NEWMAN L.W. / BURROWS M., General Principles of International Commercial Law, The Practice of International Litigation, Part. VI, Juris Publishing Inc. 1998, 49-56.
OVIEDO ALBÁN J., UNIDROIT y la unificación del derecho privado: referencia a los principios para los contratos comerciales internacionales, in LUIS CALVO CARAVACA A. / PILAR BLANCO-MORALES L. (eds.), Globalización y derecho, Editorial Colex, Madrid 2003.
PARRA RODRIGUEZ C., El nuevo Derecho Internacional de los contratos, Barcelona 2001.
PATOCCHI P.M. / FAVRE-BULLE X., Les Principes UNIDROIT relatifs aux contrats du commerce international. Une solution, in Semaine Judiciaire, 1998, 569-616.
PERILLO J.M., UNIDROIT Principles of International Commercial Contracts: The

Black Letter Text and a Review, in 43 Fordham Law Review, 1994, 281-317.

PERNAZZA F., I Principi UNIDROIT dei contratti commerciali internazionali: codificazione ed innovazione in un nuovo modello di uniformazione del diritto, in Rivista del diritto commerciale, n. 2, 1996, 297-306.

PERNAZZA F., Il progetto UNIDROIT sui *Principles for International Commercial Contracts* e l'unità e specificità del sistema giuridico latino-americano, in Diritto del commercio internazionale 1994, 491-520.

PETERS L., The UNIDROIT Principles 2004, in IBA (ed.), Newsletter: International Sales and Related Commercial Transactions, August 2005, 22-25.

PETZ T., Die UNIDROIT Prinzipien für internationale Handelsverträge, Verlag Österreich, Juristische Schriftenreih, Band 177, 2001.

RABELLO A.M., Israel, in BONELL M.J. (ed.), A New Approach to International Commercial Contracts. The UNIDROIT Principles of International Commercial Contracts, Kluwer Law International, 1999, 167-173.

RABELLO A.M. (ed.) The Principles of UNIDROIT and Modern National Codifications, Jerusalem, Harry and Michael Sacher Institute for Legislative Research and Comparative Law, Faculty of Law, The Hebrew University of Jerusalem, 2001.

RABELLO A.M. / LERNER P., The UNIDROIT Principles of International Contracts and Israeli Law, in RABELLO A.M. (ed.), The Principles of UNIDROIT and Modern National Codifications, Jerusalem, Harry and Michael Sacher Institute for Legislative Research and Comparative Law, Faculty of Law, The Hebrew University of Jerusalem, 2001, 7-32.

RAZUMOV K., Les contrats commerciaux internationaux et les nouveaux Principes UNIDROIT: la pratique contractuelle commerciale russe, in UNIDROIT Principles for International Commercial Contracts: A New *Lex Mercatoria*?, ICC Publication n. 490/1, 1995, 95-113.

ROSE A.D., A Fresh Approach, in Law Institute Journal, 19, 1995, 928 *et seq*.

ROSETT A., The UNIDROIT Principles of International Commercial Contracts: a New Approach to International Commercial Contracts, in 46 American Journal of Comparative Law 1998, 347-360.

ROSETT A. / GORDON M.W., United States, in BONELL M.J. (ed.), A New Approach to International Commercial Contracts. The UNIDROIT Principles of International Commercial Contracts, Kluwer Law International, 1999, 387-419.

ROUTANO E., UNIDROIT ja kansainväliset kaupalliset sopimukset, in Defensor Legis, 1996, 375-380.

SABOURIN F., Québec, in BONELL M.J. (ed.), A New Approach to International Commercial Contracts. The UNIDROIT Principles of International Commercial Contracts, Kluwer Law International, 1999, 237-280.

SAIDOV D., UNIDROIT Principles of International Commercial Contracts 2004, in Lloyd's Maritime and Commercial Law Quarterly 2005, 405 – 406.

SANTOS BELANDRO R.B., Los principios aplicables a los contratos mercatiles internacionales: una nueva labor de UNIDROIT, Revista de derecho comercial y de la impresa 1996, 13-53.

SATTAR I.M., The UNIDROIT Principles of International Commercial Contracts and WTO: Between an "International Restatement and a "Globalization" of Contract Law?, in 5 Indiana Journal of Global Legal Studies 1997, 375-388.

SCHILF S., Allgemeine Vertragsgrundregeln als Vertragsstatut, Mohr Siebeck

2005, vii – 451.
SCHILF S., UNIDROIT Principles 2004 - Auf dem Weg zu einem Allgemeinen Teil des internationalen Einheitsprivatrechts, in Internationales Handelsrecht 4, 2004, 236-246.
SCHLECHTRIEM P., Die UNIDROIT Grundregeln der internationaler Handelsverträge 2004, in BLAHO P. – SVIDRON J. (eds.), Kodifikation, Europäisierung und Harmonisierung des Privatrechts, Bratislava 2005, 31 – 42.
SCHLECHTRIEM P., Symposium: UNIDROIT Principles of International Commercial Contracts, in Juristenzeitung 1996, 191-192.
SETO HARDJOWAHONO B., The UNIDROIT Principles and the law governing commercial contracts in Southeast Asia, in Uniform Law Review / Revue de droit uniforme, 7, 2002, 1005-1015.
SIQUEIROS J.L., Los Nuevos Principios de UNIDROIT 2004 sobre Contratos Comerciales Internacionales, Revista de Derecho Privado 2005, 129 – 145.
TRAHAN A.-M., Les Principes d'UNIDROIT relatifs aux contrats du commerce international, Les Principes d'UNIDROIT et les contrats internationaux: aspects pratiques, in Revue Juridique Thémis, vol. 36, no. 2, 2002, 623-635.
TRATAR B., Nacela UNIDROIT za mednarodne gospodarske pogodbe v luci spremembe paradigme v mednarodnem gospodarskem pravu, in Pravnik 1999, 428-455.
UNIVERSIDAD NACIONAL AUTÓNOMA DE MÉXICO - UNIVERSIDAD PANAMERICANA, Contratación internacional. Comentarios a los Principios sobre los Contratos Comerciales Internacionales del UNIDROIT, Universidad Nacional Autónoma de México - Universidad Panamericana, 1998.
VALINO DEL RIO E., Historia de los modernos intentos de unificación en el ámbito del derecho privado patrimonial. Los principios sobre los contratos comerciales internacionales y su inspiración romanistica, Palao Moreno G., (ed.), Derecho patrimonial europeo, Cizur Menor, Aranzadi, 2003, 403 – 418.
VAN HOUTTE H., De "UNIDROIT Principles of International Commercial Contracts" en de Belgische rechtspraktijk, Tijdschrift voor Belgisch Handelsrecht, 1995, 348 *et seq.*
VAN HOUTTE H., The UNIDROIT Principles of International Commercial Contracts, in 11 Arbitration International, 1995, 373-390.
VANDOMME L., La négociation des contrats internationaux, Revue de droit des affaires internationals / International Business Law Review [in English and French], 2003, 487 – 501.
VATIER FUENZALIDA C., [Book review of] UNIDROIT: Principios sobre los Contratos Comerciales Internacionales, version española de A.M. Garro (Roma, 1995), in Revista Critica de Derecho Immobiliario 1999, Núm. 650, 327-333.
VEYTIA H., Mexico, in BONELL M.J. (ed.), A New Approach to International Commercial Contracts. The UNIDROIT Principles of International Commercial Contracts, Kluwer Law International, 1999, 193-201.
VEYTIA H., The Requirement of Justice and Equity in Contracts, in 69 Tulane Law Review 1995, 1191-1207.
WEINTRAUB R.J., *Lex mercatoria* and the UNIDROIT Principles of International Commercial Contracts, in BORCHERS P.J. / ZEKOLL J. (eds.), International Conflict of Laws for the Third Millennium. Essays in Honor of Friedrich K. Juenger, Transnational Publishers Inc., Ardsley, N.Y. 2001, 141-154.

WERRO F. / BELSER E.M., Switzerland, in BONELL M.J. (ed.), A New Approach to International Commercial Contracts. The UNIDROIT Principles of International Commercial Contracts, Kluwer Law International, 1999, 331-378.

WIDMER P., Les Principes UNIDROIT: Une nouvelle forme de "codification" au niveau transnational, in DUNAND - WINIGER (eds.), Le code civil francais dans le droit européen, Brylant, 2005, 235 – 256.

WIDMER P., Principes relatifs aux contrats du commerce international, in Schweizerische Zeitschrift für internationales und europäisches Recht 1995, 83-84.

WILHELMSSON T., Standard form conditions, HARTKAMP A., *et al.*, (eds.), Towards a European Civil Code, 3rd fully revised and expanded edition, Nijmegen, Ars Aequi Libri, 2004, 431 – 444.

WITZ C., Principes relatifs aux contrats du commerce international, in Revue internationale de droit comparé 1995, 799-800.

YAMASHITA R., Japan, in BONELL M.J. (ed.), A New Approach to International Commercial Contracts. The UNIDROIT Principles of International Commercial Contracts, Kluwer Law International, 1999, 191-192.

ZIMMERMANN R., Die UNIDROIT-Grundregeln der internationalen Handelsverträge 2004 in vergleichender Perspective, Zeitschrift für Europäisches Privatrecht 2/2005, 264 – 290.

2. UNIDROIT Principles and Similar Projects

ACADEMIE DES PRIVATISTES EUROPEENS, Code européen des contrats. Projecto preliminar coordinado por G. Gandolfi, Giuffrè, Milano 2000.

AKADEMIE EUROPÄISCHER PRIVATRECHTSWISSENSCHAFTLER, Europäisches Vertragsgesetzbuch. Vorentwurf, in Zeitschrift für Europäisches Privatrecht, 10, 2002, 139-172.

AKADEMIE EUROPÄISCHER PRIVATRECHTSWISSENSCHAFTLER, Europäisches Vertragsgesetzbuch. Vorentwurf. Art. 118 - Art. 173, in Zeitschrift für Europäisches Privatrecht, 10, 2002, 365-394.

ALESSI R., Luci ed ombre del nascente diritto europeo dei contratti, in ALESSI R. (ed.), Diritto europeo e autonomia contrattuale, Flaccovio, Palermo 1999, 7-46.

ALPA G., Il "Quadro comune di riferimento" e le nuove prospettive di diritto contrattuale europeo, in I Contratti, 2005, 308-310.

ALPA G., Diritto privato europeo: fonti normative e programmi di armonizzazione, in La nuova giurisprudenza civile commentata, 2003, II, 16-34.

AMOUSSOU-GUENOU R., Perspectives des Principes Asean (ou Asiatiques) du droit des contrats, in Revue de droit des affaires international 2005, 573 *et seq*.

BAR C. VON / LANDO O. / SWANN S., Communication on European contract law : joint response of the Commission on European Contract Law and the Study Group on a European Civil Code, in European Review of Private Law, 10, 2002, 183-248.

BAR C. VON / LANDO O. (eds.), Communication on European Contract Law: Joint Response of the Commission on European Contract Law and the Study group on a European Civil Code, in Europa e diritto privato, 2002, 133-200.

BAR C. VON, Paving the way forward with Principles of European Private Law, in GRUNDMANN S. - STUYCK J. (eds.), An Academic Green Paper on European Contract Law, Kluwer Law International, The Hague/London/New York 2002, 137-157.

BARRETT G. / BERNADEAU L. (eds.), Towards a European Civil Code. Reflections on the codification of civil law in Europe, in ERA-Forum, Special Issue, ERA, Trier 2002, 3-120.

BASEDOW J., The case for a European Contract Act, in GRUNDMANN S. - STUYCK J. (eds.), An Academic Green Paper on European Contract Law, Kluwer Law International, The Hague 2002, 147-157.

BASEDOW J., The renascence of uniform law: European contract law and its components, in 18 Legal Studies, n. 2, 1998, 121-145.

BEALE H., Finding the remaining traps instead of unifying contract law, in GRUNDMANN S. - STUYCK J. (eds.), An Academic Green Paper on European Contract Law, Kluwer Law International, The Hague 2002, 67-72.

BERGER K.P., The New Law Merchant and the Global Market Place; A 21st Century View of Transnational Commercial Law, in BERGER K.P. (ed.), The Practice of Transnational Law, Kluwer Law International, The Hague 2001, 1-22.

BERGER K.P., Harmonisation of European contract law: The influence of comparative law, in 50 International and Comparative Law Quarterly 2001, 877-900.

BERGER K.P., Einheitliche Rechtsstrukturen durch außergesetzilche Rechtsvereinheitlichung, in Juristenzeitung, n. 8, 1999, 369-377.

BERGER K.P., Formalisierte oder "schleichende" Kodifizierung des transnationalen Wirtschaftsrechts, de Gruyter, Berlin/New York 1996.

BLASE F., Die Grundregeln des Europäischen Vertragsrechts als Recht grenzüberschreitender Verträge, Quadis Publishing, Münster 2001.

BOELE-WOELKI K., European and UNIDROIT Principles of Contract Law, in VON HOFFMAN B. (ed.), European Private International Law, Ars Aequi Libri, Nijmegen 1998, 67-85.

BONELL, An international Restatement of Contract Law. The UNIDROIT Principles of International Commercial Contracts, 3rd ed., Transnational Publications Inc., Ardsley, New York, 2005, at 335 – 359.

BONELL M.J., Verso un codice europeo dei contratti?, in 1 Europa e diritto privato, 1998, 171-191.

BONELL M.J., The UNIDROIT Principles of International Commercial Contracts and the Principles of European Contract Law: A Comparison, in CRANSTON R. (ed.), Making Commercial Law. Essays in Honour of Roy Goode, Clarendon Press, Oxford 1997, 91-101.

BONELL M.J., Zásady UNIDROIT a Zásady európskeho zmluvného práva - podobné pravidlá pre zhodné ciele?, in 80 Právny Obzor, 1997, 109-129.

BONELL M.J., The UNIDROIT Principles of International Commercial Contracts and the Principles of European Contract Law: Similar Rules for the Same Purposes?, in 1 Uniform Law Review / Revue de droit uniforme, n. 2, 1996, 229-246.

BONELL M.J., Unificazione internazionale del diritto, in Enciclopedia del diritto, vol. XLV, Giuffré, Milano 1992, 720-734.

BONELL M.J. / PELEGGI R., UNIDROIT Principles of International Commercial Contracts and Principles of European Contract Law: A Synoptical Table, in Uniform Law Review 2004, 315-396.

BROGGINI G., Le droit des contrats entre fragmentation et globalisation, in VACCA L. (ed.), Il contratto inadempiuto. Realtà e tradizione del diritto contrattuale europeo, Giappichelli, Torino 1999, 411-426.

BROGGINI G., Was bedeutet heute gemeineuropäisches Vertragsrecht?, in Zeitschrift für Rechtsvergleichung, Internationales Privatrecht und Europarecht, n. 6, 1997, 221-229.

BROGGINI G., Conflitto di leggi, armonizzazione e unificazione nel diritto europeo delle obbligazioni e delle imprese, in Rivista di diritto internazionale privato e processuale, 1995, 241-264.

BUSCH D. / HONDIUS E. / KOOTEN H. VAN / SCHELHAAS H. / SCHRAMA W. (eds.), The Principles of European Contract Law and Dutch Law. A Commentary, Ars Aequi Libri, Nijmegen; Kluwer Law International, The Hague/London/Boston 2002.

BUSSANI M., The contract law codification process in Europe: Policies, targets and time dimensions, in GRUNDMANN S. - STUYCK J. (eds.), An Academic Green Paper on European Contract Law, Kluwer Law International, The Hague 2002, 159-179.

CAMARA LAPUENTE S., The hypothetical "European Civil Code": why, how, when?, in ERA-Forum. Special Issue European Contract Law, 2002, no. 2, 89-98.

CANARIS C.W., Die Stellung der "UNIDROIT Principles" und der "Principles of European Contract Law" im System der Rechtsquellen, in BASEDOW J. (ed.), Europäische Vertragsrechtsvereinheitlichung und deutsches Recht, J.C.B. Mohr (Siebeck), Tübingen 2000, 5-31.

CASTRONOVO C., Natura e modi di un codice europeo nell'esperienza della Commissione Lando, in ALPA G. - BUCCICO E.N. (eds.), La riforma dei codici civili e il progetto di un codice civile europeo. Materiali dei seminari 2001, Giuffrè, Milano 2002, 145-155.

CASTRONOVO C., Principi di diritto europeo dei contratti, Parte III. Introduzione, in Europa e diritto privato, 2002, 949-954.

CASTRONOVO C., Il contratto nei Principi di diritto europeo, in MAZZAMUTO S. (ed.), Il contratto e le tutele. Prospettive di diritto europeo, Giappichelli Editore, Torino 2002, 30-59.

CASTRONOVO C., Savigny, i moderni e la Codificazione Europea, in Europa e diritto privato, 2001, 219-256.

CASTRONOVO C. (ed.), Principi di diritto europeo dei contratti. Parte I e II, Giuffrè, Milano 2001.

CASTRONOVO C., Il diritto europeo delle obbligazioni e dei contratti: codice o *restatement*?, in ALESSI R. (ed.), Diritto europeo e autonomia contrattuale, Flaccovio, Palermo 1999, 157-168.

CASTRONOVO C., I "Principi di diritto europeo dei contratti" e l'idea di codice, in Rivista di diritto commerciale, n. 1, 1995, 21-38.

CAUFFMAN C., De principles of European contract law, in Tijdschrift voor privaatrecht, 38, 2001, 1231-1309.

CHARBIT N., L'esperanto du droit? La recontre du droit communautaire et du droit des contrats. A propos de la Communication de la Commission européenne relative au droit européen des contrats, in La Semaine juridique. Edition générale, 2 Janvier 2002, 9-16.

COEN C., Vertragsscheitern und Rückabwicklung. Eine rechtsvergleichende Untersuchung zum englischen und deutschen Recht, zum UN-Kaufrecht sowie zu den UNIDROIT Principles und den Principles of European contract law, Duncker & Humblot, Berlin 2003 (Beiträge zum europäischen Wirtschaftsrecht, 22).

CORTES E., El sistema europeo de la responsabilidad contractual y las normas de derecho uniforme, in La culpa contractual en el sistema jurídico latinoamericano, Universidad Externado de Colombia, Bogotá 2001, 89-113.

DE MOT J. / DE GEEST G., De toekomst van het Europees Privaatrecht na het Groenboek, in Nederlands Juristenblad 2002, No. 18, 881-890.

DI MAJO A., Il contratto e l'obbligazione nei principi, in Europa e diritto privato, 2002, 883-896.

DIEZ-PICAZO L. / ROCA TRIAS E. / MORALES A.M., Los Principios del derecho europeo de contratos, Civitas Ediciones, 2002.

DOTEVALL R., Ekvivalensprincipen och jämkning av långvariga avtål, Svensk Jurist Tidning, 87, 2002, 441-457.

DRAETTA U., Principi UNIDROIT per i contratti commerciali internazionali e progetto di codice europeo dei contratti: due proposte a confronto, in Diritto del commercio internazionale, 1994, 681-729.

DREXL J., Community legislation continued: complete harmonisation, framework legislation or non-binding measures - Alternative approaches to European contract law, in European Business Law Review, 13, 2002, 557-582.

FAGES B., Einige neuere Entwicklungen des französischen Vertragsrechts im Lichte der Lando-Kommission, in Zeitschrift für Europäisches Privatrecht, 2003, 514-524.

FAUVARQUE-COSSON B., Droit européen des contrats: première réaction au plan d'action de la Commission, in Recueil Dalloz, 179, 2003, 1171-1173.

FAUVARQUE-COSSON B., Faut-il un Code civil européen?, in Revue trimestrelle de droit civil, 2002, No. 3, 463-480.

FERRI G.B., Il Code européen des contrats, in Contratto e impresa / Europa, 7, 2002, No. 1, 27-39.

FERRI G.B., L'"invisibile" presenza della causa del contratto, in Europa e diritto privato, 2002, 897-914.

FLETCHNER H.M., The CISG's impact on international unification efforts: the UNIDROIT Principles of International Commercial Contracts and the Principles of European Contract Law , in FERRARI F. (ed.), The 1980 Uniform Sales Law. Old issues revisited in the light of recent experiences. Verona Conference 2003, Giuffrè, Milano; Sellier European Publishers, München 2003, 169-197.

FONTAINE M., *Ius commune* et harmonisation du droit des contrats, in WIJFFELS A. (ed.), Le Code civil entre *ius commune* et droit privé européen, Bruylant 2005, 75 – 91.

FONTAINE M., Le projet d'Acte uniforme OHADA sur les contrats et les Principes d'UNIDROIT relatifs aux contrats du commerce international, in Uniform Law Review / Revue de droit uniforme, 9, 2004, 253-266.

FUENZALIDA C.V., Para la unificación internacional del derecho de obligaciones en la Comunidad Europea, in Revista de derecho privado 1996, 223-230.

GANDOLFI G., Der Vorentwurf eines Europäischen Vertragsgesetzbuchs, in Zeitschrift für Europäisches Privatrecht, 10, 2002, 1-4.

GANDOLFI G., Sul progetto di un "codice europeo dei contratti", in Rassegna di diritto civile 1996, 105-116.

GRASSO G., La disciplina dell'invalidità nei principi di diritto europeo dei contratti, Jovene editore, Napoli 2005.

GENTILI A., L'equilibrio del contratto nei principi del diritto contracttuale europeo, in ALPA G. - BUCCICO E.N. (eds.), La riforma dei codici civili e il progetto di un codice civile europeo. Materiali dei seminari 2001, Giuffrè, Milano 2002, 3-6 (Rassegna forense. Quaderni, 10).

GERVEN W. VAN, A common law for Europe: The future meeting the past?, European Review of Private Law, 9, 2001, 485-50.

GHESTIN J., Faut-il conserver la cause en droit européen des contrats?, in European Review of Private Law 9, (2001), 485 *et seq.*

GOODE R., The harmonization of dispositive contract and commercial law – should the European Community be involved?, in Senationalisierung des Privatrechts? Symposium anlässlich des 70. Geburstages von Karl Kreuzer, Mohr Siebeck 2005, 19 – 32.

GOODE R., International Restatement and National Law, in SWANDLING W. - JONES G. (eds.), The Search for Principles. Essays in Honour of Lord Goff of Chieveley, Oxford University Press, 2000, 45-58.

GOODE R., International Restatements of Contract and English Contract Law, in 2 Uniform Law Review / Revue de droit uniforme, n. 2, 1997, 231-248.

GRIDEL J.-P., Sur l'hypothèse d'un Code européen des contrats: les propositions de l'Académie des privatistes européens (Pavie), in Gazette du Palais, 123, 2003, 240-278.

GRIGOLEIT H.C., Irrtum, Täuschung und Informationspflichten in den European Principles und in den UNIDROIT-Principles, in SCHULZE R. / EBERS M. / GRIGOLEIT H.C. (eds.), Informationspflichten und Vertragsabschluss im *Acquis communautaire*. Information requirements and formation of contract in the *acquis communautaire*, Mohr Siebeck, Tübingen 2003, 201-230.

GRUNDMANN S., Harmonisierung, Europäischer Kodex, Europäisches System der Vertragsrechte. Die Perspektiven der Kommissionsmitteilung zum Europäischen Vertragsrecht, in Neue Juristische Wochenschrift, 6, 2002, 393-400.

GRUNDMANN S., The structure of European contract law, in European Review of Private Law, 9, 2001, 505-528.

GRUNDMANN S. / STUYCK J. (eds.), An Academic Greenpaper on European Contract Law, Kluwer Law International, The Hague/Boston/London 2002 (Private Law in European Context Series, 2).

GRUNDMANN S. / STUYCK J., An Academic Green Paper on European Contract Law - Scope, common ground and debated issues, in: GRUNDMANN S. - STUYCK J. (eds.), An Academic Green Paper on European Contract Law, Kluwer Law International, The Hague 2002, 3-35.

GUILLEMARD S., A comparative study of the UNIDROIT Principles, the Principles of the European Law of Contracts, and some dispositions of the CISG applicable to the formation of international contracts, in Review of the Convention on Contracts for the International Sale of Goods (CISG), 2000-2001, 83-113.

HAAZEN O.E., Comparative law and economics en het Europees privaatrecht als ongemengd rechtsstelsel, in 73 Nederlands Juristenblad, 1998, 1227-1233

HARTKAMP A.S., Principles of Contract Law, in HARTKAMP A.S. / HESSELINK M.W. / HONDIUS E.H. / JOUSTRA C. / DU PERRON E. / VELDMAN M. (eds.), Towards a European Civil Code, 3rd ed., Kluwer Law International, 2004, 125-143.

HARTKAMP A.S., The UNIDROIT Principles for International Commercial Contracts and the Principles of European Contract Law, in European Review of Private Law, 1994, 341-357.

HEGGBERGET L.M. / NYLAND E., Formuleringen av internasjonale kontraktsrettslige grunnprinsipper ogbetydningen for norsk rett, in Tidsskrift for Rettsvitenskap 2000, 251-323.

HESSELINK M.W., The politics of European contract law: Who has an interest in what kind of contract law for Europe?, in GRUNDMANN S. / STUYCK J. (eds.) - An Academic Green Paper on European Contract Law, Kluwer Law International, The Hague 2002, 181-191.

HEUTGER V., UNIDROIT Principles of International Commercial Contracts 2004, in European Review of Private Law 2005, 83-90.

HOEKSTRA M.J., De UNIDROIT Principles of International Commercial Contracts en de Principles of European Contract Law: Een Vergelijking, in GROSHEIDE F.W. / BOELE-WOELKI K. (eds.), Europees Privaatrecht, Molengrafica, Lelystad 1996, 3-44.

HONDIUS E., European Private Law - Survey 2000-2002, in European Review of Private Law, Vol. 10, no. 6, 2002, 865-900.

HONKA H., Contract Law and International Trade, in MAHONEN J. (ed.), International Market Change and the Law, Publications of Turku Law School, 1996, 7 -97.

JAGUSH S., Recent Codification Efforts: An Assessment, in E. Gaillard (ed.), Toward a Uniform International Arbitration Law? Juris Publishing Inc., N.Y. 2005, 63 – 90.

JANSSEN A., Die Einbeziehung von allgemeinen Geschäftsbedingungen in internationale Kaufverträge und die Bedeutung der UNIDROIT- und der Lando-Principles, in IHR, Internationales Handelsrecht, 4 (2004), 194 - 200

KIENINGER E.-M., Europäisches Vertragsrecht in der Lehre - Bericht über die Podiumsdiskussion, in BASEDOW J. (ed.), Europäische Vertragsrechtsvereinheitlichung und deutsches Recht, Mohr Siebeck, Tübingen 2000, 215-218.

KIRCHNER CH., Europäisches Vertragsrecht, in WEYERS H.L. (ed.), Europäisches Vertragsrecht, Nomos, Baden-Baden 1997, 103-137.

KOMMISSION FÜR EUROPÄISCHES VERTRAGSRECHT, Grundregeln des Europäischen Vertragsrechts. Teile I und II. Deutsche Ausgabe von Christian von Bar und Reinhard Zimmermann, Sellier, München 2002.

KRONKE H., Brauchen wir ein europäisches Zivilgesetzbuch?, Institut für Rechtspolitik an der Universität Trier, Heft 11, 2002.

KRONKE H., Les Principes d'UNIDROIT et les contrats internationaux: aspects pratiques - Profil de la problématique. Journées Maximilien-Caron 2001 (Faculté de droit, Université de Montréal) - Les Principes d'UNIDROIT et les contrats internationaux: aspects pratiques, in Revue Juridique Thémis, 36, 2002, 331-334.

KRONKE H., From International Uniform Conventions to Model Laws - From Guides to Principles, in PERRET L. - BISSON A.-F. - MARIANI N. (eds.), Evolution des systèmes juridiques, bijuridisme et commerce international. The evolution of legal systems, bijuralism and international trade. Textes présentés lors d'un colloque organisée par la Faculté de droit de l'Université d'Ottawa, le Ministèere de la Justice du Canada et le Patrimoine canadien, tenu à Ottawa, Ont., du 20 au 21 oct. 2000, Wilson & Lafleur, Ottawa 2002, 283-304.

KRÜGER H., Rechtseinheit von unten? Restatements of the law als Alternativen internationaler und europäischer Rechtsvereinheitlichung, Nomos, Baden-Baden 2005, 183.

LANDO O., Der Aktionplan der EG-Kommission zum europäischen Vertragsrecht, in Recht der Internationalen Wirtschaft 2005, 1-6.

LANDO O., The European Principles in an Integrated World, in European Review of Contract Law, n. 1/2005, 3 – 18.

LANDO O., Principles of European Contract Law and UNIDROIT Pirnciples: moving from harmonization to unification?, in Uniform Law Review / Revue de droit uniforme, 8 (2003), 123 – 134.

LANDO O., Does the European Union need a Civil Code?, in Recht der Internationalen Wirtschaft, 49, 2003, 1-15.

LANDO O., Why does Europe need a civil code?, in GRUNDAMANN S. - STUYCK J. (eds.), An Academic Green Paper on European Contract Law, Kluwer Law International, The Hague 2002, 207-213.

LANDO O., The future development of the Principles of European Contract Law and a European Civil Code, in BARRETT G. - BERNADEAU L. (eds.), Towards a European Civil Code. Reflexions on the codification of civil law in Europe, in ERA-Forum. Special Issue, ERA, Trier 2002, 40-46.

LANDO O., A short introduction to the Principles of European Contract Law, in BARRETT G. - BERNADEAU L. (eds.), Towards a European Civil Code. Reflexions on the codification of civil law in Europe, in ERA-Forum. Special Issue, ERA, Trier 2002, 57-66.

LANDO O., The Harmonization of European Contract Law Through a Restatement of Principles, Centre for the Advanced Study of European and Comparative Law, University of Oxford 1997.

LANDO O. / CLIVE E. / PRÜM A. / ZIMMERMANN R. (eds.), Principles of European Contract Law. Part III, Kluwer Law International, The Hague [*et al.*] 2003.

LANDO O. – BEALE H. (eds.), Principles of European Contract Law, Parts I and II (combined and revised), Kluwer Law International 2000.

LEFEBVRE G. / SIBIDI DARANKOUM E., Phénomèn transnational et droit des contrats: les Principes Européens, in Revue de Droit des Affairs Internationales / International Business Law, n. 1, 1999, 47-78.

LÓPEZ RODRÍGEZ A.M., *Lex mercatoria* and Harmonization of Contract Law in the EU, DJOF Publishing, Copenhagen 2003.

LURGER B., Grundfragen der Vereinheitlichung des Vertragsrechts in der Europäischen Union, Springer, Wien 2002, 7-55.

MALAURIE P., Droit européen des contrats. Le Code civil européen des obligations et des contrats. Une question toujours ouverte. Colloque de Leuven (30 nov. - 1er déc. 2001), in La Semaine Juridique. Edition générale, 6 Février 2002, 281-285.

MALINVAUD P., Réponse - hors délai - à la Commission européenne: à propos d'un code européen des contrats (1), in Recueil Dalloz, 178, 2002, 2542-2551.

MATTEI U., Hard Minimal Code Now - A Critique of Softness and a Plea for Responsibility in the European Debate over Codification, in GRUNDMANN S. - STUYCK J. (eds.), An Academic Green Paper on European Contract Law, Kluwer Law International, The Hague 2002, 215-233.

MATTEI U., Il problema della codificazione civile europea e la cultura giuridica. Pregiudizi, strategie e sviluppi, in Contratto e impresa / Europa, n. 1, 1998, 207-227.

MAZEAUD D., A propos du droit virtuel des contracts - Réflexions sur les principes d'UNIDROIT et de la Commission Lando, in Mélanges Cabrillac, Paris 1999, 205-236.

MAZZAMUTO S., Equivoci e concettualismi nel diritto europeo dei contratti: il dibattito sulla vendita dei beni al consumo, in Europa e diritto privato, 4, 2004, 1029-1125.

MAZZAMUTO S., I principi di diritto europeo dei contratti nel canone di Carlo Castronovo, in Europa e diritto privato, 2002, 847-870.

MAZZAMUTO S. (ed.), Il contratto e le tutele. Prospettive di diritto europeo, Giappichelli Editore, Torino 2002.

MENGONI L., L'Europa dei codici o un codice per l'Europa?, in CENTRO DI STUDI E RICERCHE DI DIRITTO COMPARATO E STRANIERO (ed.), Saggi, conferenze e seminari, n. 7, Roma 1992.

MÖLLERS T.M.J., European Directives on Civil Law - The German Approach: Towards the Recodification and New Foundation of Civil Law Principles, in European Review of Private Law, Vol. 10, no. 6, 2002, 777-798.

MOURRE A., - JOLIVET E., La reception des Principes d'UNIDROIT dans les contrats modèles de la Chambre de commerce international (abstract in English), Uniform Law Review, 2004, 275 – 293.

MÜLLER-GRAF P.C., Private Law Unification by Means Other Than of Codification, in HARTKAMP A.S. / HESSELINK M.W. / HONDIUS E.H. / DU PERRON C.E. / VRANKEN J.M.B. (eds.), Towards a European Civil Code, Martinus Nijhoff Pub., Dordrecht 1994, 19-36.

NIGLIA L., The Transformation of Contract in Europe, Kluwer Law International, The Hague/London/New York 2003.

PELEGGI. R., La compensazione nei Principi UNIDROIT dei contratti commerciali internazionali e nei Principi di Diritto Europeo dei Contratti: un primo confronto, in Diritto del commercio internazionale, 16, 2002, 927-950.

REICH N., Critical Comments on the Commission Communication On European Contract Law, in GRUNDMANN S. - STUYCK J. (eds.), An Academic Green Paper on European Contract Law, Kluwer Law International, The Hague 2002, 283-291.

ROSETT A., Unification, Harmonization, Restatement, Codification, and Reform in International Commercial Law, in 40 American Journal of Comparative Law, 1992, 683-697.

ROUHETTE G., Les codifications du droit des contrats, in Droits - Revue française de théorie, de philosophie et de culture juridiques, n. 24, 1996, 113-124.

SÁNCHEZ LORENZO S.A., Derecho Privado Europeo, Editorial Comares, Granada 2002 (Estudios de Derecho Privado Europeo, 2).

SANDROCK O., Neue Herausforderungen an das Internationale Wirtschaft, in Zeitschrift für Vergleichende Rechtswissenschaft, n. 3, 1999, 227-259.

SANDROCK O., Das Privatrecht am Ausgang des 20. Jahrhunders: Deutschland - Europa - und die Welt, in Juristenzeitung, 1996, 1-9.

SCHILF S., Allegemeine Vertragsgrundregeln als Vertragsstatut, Mohr Siebeck 2005, vii – 451.

SCHLECHTRIEM P., Rechtsvereinheitlichung in Europa und Schuldrechtsreform in Deutschland, in Zeitschrift für Europäisches Privatrecht, 1993, 217-246.

SCHWINTOWSKI H.-P., Auf dem Wege zu einem Europäischen Zivilgesetzbuch, in Juristen-Zeitung, 57, 2002, 205-211.

SCOGNAMIGLIO C., Il danno non patrimoniale contrattuale, in MAZZAMUTO S. (ed.), Il contratto e le tutele. Prospettive di diritto europeo, Giappichelli, Torino 2002, 467-478.

SOMMA A., Giustizia sociale nel diritto europeo dei contratti!, in Rivista critica

del diritto privato, 1, 2005, 75-97.
STAUDENMAYER D., The Commission Communication on European Contract Law: What future for European Contract Law, in European Review of Private Law, 10, 2002, 249-260.
STORME M.E., Functions and Character of Uniform Principles of Contract Law, in RABELLO A.M. (ed.), Essays on European Law and Israel, The Harry and Michael Sacher Institute, Jerusalem 1996, 419-432.
STORME M.E., Applications possibles et caractères généraux des principes de droit uniforme des contrats, in Revue de droit international et de droit comparé, 1995, 309-325.
SWANN S., A European civil code. Legal and political foundations, in: ALPA G. - BUCCICO E.N. (eds.), La riforma dei codici civili e il progetto di un codice civile europeo. Materiali dei seminari 2001, Giuffrè, Milano 2002, 7-57 (Rassegna forense. Quaderni, 10).
TIMOTEO M., The harmonization of contract law and the role of comparative law, in Revue de droit comparé (Institut japonais de droit comparé), 35, 2002, no. 4, 27-47.
TRAMHEL J., UNIDROIT & OAS: Supplementary Initiatives for the Furtherance of International Contract Law, in UNIDROIT (ed.), The UNIDROIT Principles: a Common Law of Contracts for the Americas?, 1998, 311-316.
VETTORI G., Buona fede e diritto europeo dei contratti, in Europa e diritto privato, 2002, 915-936.
VITUCCI P., L'atto unilaterale nei *Principles* e in altre compilazioni sul diritto europeo dei contratti, in Europa e diritto privato, 2002, 937-954.
WILHELMSSON T., International *lex mercatoria* and local consumer law: an impossible combination?, in Uniform Law Review / Revue de droit uniforme, 8, 2003, 141-154.
WILHELMSSON T., The Design of an Optional (re)Statement of European Contract Law - Real Life Instead of Dead Concepts, in GRUNDMANN S. - STUYCK J. (eds.), An Academic Green Paper on European Contract Law, Kluwer Law International, The Hague 2002, 353-372.
WILHELMSSON T., The Legal, the Cultural and the Political - Conclusions from Different Perspectives on Harmonisation of European Contract Law, in European Business Law Review, 13, 2002, 541-555.
ZIMMERMANN R., Die UNIDROIT-Grundregeln der internationalen Handelsverträge 2004 in vergleichender Perspektive, Zeitschrift für Europäisches Privatrecht 2/2005, 264 – 190.
ZIMMERMANN R., Konturen eines Europäischen Vertragsrecht, in Juristenzeitung, 1995, 477-491.

3. UNIDROIT Principles and International Commercial Arbitration

BERGER K.P., Internationale Investitionsverträge und Schiedsgerichtsbarkeit, in Zeitschrift für vergleichende Rechtswissenschaft, 102, 2003, 1-32.
BERGER K.P., Renegotiations and Adaptation of International Investment Contracts: the Role of Contract Drafters and Arbitrators in International Commercial Arbitration. A Symposium sponsored by Vanderbilt University Law and Business Program and Vanderbilt Journal of Transnational Law, March 2003, in 36 Vanderbilt Journal of Transnational Law 2003, 1347-

1380.

BERGER K.P., International Arbitral Practice and the UNIDROIT Principles of International Commercial Contracts, in 46 American Journal of Comparative Law, 1998, 129-150.

BERGER K.P. / DUBBERSTEIN H. / LEHMANN S. / PETZOLD V., The Central Enquiry on the Use of Transnational Law in International Contract Law and Arbitration - Background, Procedure and Selected Results, in BERGER K.P. (ed.), The Practice of Transnational Law, Kluwer Law International, The Hague 2001, 91-113.

BERGER K.P. / DUBBERSTEIN H. / LEHMANN S. / PETZOLD V., Anwendung Transnationalen Rechts in der Internationalen Vertrags- und Schiedspraxis, in Zeitschrift für vergleichende Rechtswissenschaft, 101, 2002, 12-37.

BERNARDINI P., International Arbitration and A-National Rules of Law, in ICC International Court of Arbitration Bulletin Vol. 15/No. 2, 2004, 58-69.

BLASE F., Proposing a New Road Map for an Old Minefield. The Determination of the Rules Governing the Substance of the Dispute in International Commercial Arbitration, in 20 Journal of International Arbitration 2003, 267 *et seq.*

BLASE F., Die Grundregeln des Europäischen Vertragsrechts als Recht grenzüberschreitender Verträge, Quadis Publishing, Münster 2001.

BLESSING M., Choice of Substantive Law in International Arbitration, in 14 Journal of International Arbitration, 1997, 39-65.

BÖCKSTIEGEL K.-H., The Applcation of the UNIDROIT Principles to Contracts Involving States or Intergovernmental Organizations, in ICC International Court of Arbitration Bulletin, 2002, Special Supplement, 51-55.

BONELL M.J., An International Restatement of Contract Law. The UNIDROIT Principles of International Commercial Contracts 3rd ed., Transnational Publications Inc., Ardsley, New York, 2005, 192 – 228, 277 – 300.

BONELL M.J., The UNIDROIT Principles as a Means of Interpreting and Supplementing International Uniform Law, in ICC International Court of Arbitration Bulletin, 2002, Special Supplement, 29-38.

BONELL M.J., I Principi UNIDROIT e il diritto transnazionale, in MAZZAMUTO S. (ed.), Il contratto e le tutele. Prospettive di diritto europeo, Giappichelli Editore, Torino 2002, 60-82.

BONELL M.J., The UNIDROIT Principles and Transnational Law, in BERGER K.P. (ed.), The Practice of Transnational Law, Kluwer Law International, The Hague/London/Boston 2001, 23-41.

BONELL M.J., Un arbitrato "globale" deciso sulla base dei Principi UNIDROIT, in Diritto del Commercio Internazionale 2001, 15, 211-236.

BONELL M.J., A "Global" Arbitration decided on the Basis of the UNIDROIT Principles: In re Andersen Consulting Business Unit Member Firms v. Arthur Andersen Business Unit Member Firms and Andersen Worldwide Société Coopérative, in 17 Arbitration International 2001, 249-261.

BONELL M.J., The UNIDROIT Principles and Transnational Law, in Uniform Law Review / Revue de Droit Uniforme 2000, 199-218.

BONELL M.J., The UNIDROIT Principles of International Commercial Contracts: the first 50 or so decisions, New Trends in International Trade Law. Contributions on the occasion of the 10th Anniversary of the International Trade Law Course, Giappichelli Editore, Torino 2000, 65-80.

BONELL M.J., UNIDROIT Principles: a significant recognition by a United States District Court, in Uniform Law Review / Revue de Droit Uniforme 1999,

651-663.
BONELL M.J. / MONFELI T., Rassegna giurisprudenziale sui Principi UNIDROIT dei Contratti Commerciali Internazionali, in Diritto del Commercio Internazionale 2001, 15, 169-210.
BORTOLOTTI F., The UNIDROIT Principles and the Arbitral Tribunals, in Uniform Law Review / Revue de Droit Uniforme, 2000, 141-152.
BRAZIL P., Principles of International Commercial Contracts in the Context of International Commercial Arbitration, in Mealey's International Arbitration Review 1996, 75-83.
BRÖDERMANN E., Die erweiterten UNIDROIT Principles 2004, in Recht Der Internationalen Wirtschaft 2004, 721-735.
BROWER C.N., The Privatization of Rules of Decision in International Commercial Arbitration, in BRINER R. / FORTIER L.Y. / BERGER K.P. / BREDOW J. (eds.), Law of International Business and Dispute Settlement in the 21st Century / Recht der Internationalen Wirtschaft und Streitbeilegung im 21. Jahrhundert - Liber Amicorum Karl-Heinz Böckstiegel, Carl Heymanns Verlag, Köln 2001, 111-123.
BROWER C.N. / SHARPE J.K., The Creeping Codification of Transnational Commercial Law: An Arbitrator's Perspective, in 45 Virginia Journal of International Law 2004, 199-220.
CRAWFORD J. / SINCLAIR A., The UNIDROIT Principles and Their Application to State Contracts, in ICC International Court of Arbitration Bulletin, 2002, Special Supplement, 57-75.
CRUZ MIRAMONTES R., El arbitraje y su función en la aplicación de los Principios sobre los Contratos Comerciales Internacionales, in UNIVERSIDAD NACIONAL AUTÓNOMA DE MÉXICO - UNIVERSIDAD PANAMERICANA (ed.), Contratación Internacional, Comentarios a los Principios sobre los Contratos Comerciales Internacionales del UNIDROIT, 1998, 253-264.
DA GAMA E SOUZA Jr. L., The UNIDROIT Principles of International Commercial Contracts and Their Applicability in the MERCOSUR Countries. Les Principes d'UNIDROIT et les contrats internationaux: aspects pratiques, in Revue Juridique Thémis, Vol. 36, No. 2, 2002, 375-419.
DERAINS Y., The Role of the UNIDROIT Principles in International Commercial Arbitration (1): a European Perspective, in ICC International Court of Arbitration Bulletin, 2002, Special Supplement, 9-20.
DESSEMONTET F., Use of the UNIDROIT Principles to Interpret and Supplement Domestic Law, in ICC International Court of Arbitration Bulletin, 2002, Special Supplement, 39-50.
DROBNIG U., Vereinheitlichung von Zivilrecht durch *Soft Law*: neuere Erfahrungen und Einsichten, in BASEDOW J. / DROBNIG U. / ELLGER R. [*et al.*] (eds.), Aufbruch nach Europa. 75 Jahre Max-Planck-Institut für Privatrecht, Mohr, Tübingen 2001, 745-756.
FARNSWORTH E.A., The Role of the UNIDROIT Principles in International Commercial Arbitration (2): a Us Perspective on Their Aims and Application, in ICC International Court of Arbitration Bulletin, 2002, Special Supplement, 21-28.
FONTAINE M., *Ius commune* et harmonisation du droit des contrats, in WIJFFELS A. (ed.), Le Code civil entre *ius commune* et le droit privé européen, Bruylant 2005, 75 – 91.
FORTIER Y.L., The New *Lex Mercatoria*, or Back to the Future, in Arbitration International 17, 2001, 121-128.

FURMSTON M.P., The UNIDROIT Principles and International Commercial Arbitration, Institute of International Business Law and Practice, in UNIDROIT Principles for International Commercial Contracts: A New *Lex Mercatoria*?, ICC Publication N. 490/1, 1995.

GALGANO F., Die Globalisierung im Spiegel des Rechts, in Zeitschrift für Europäisches Privatrecht, 2003, 237-242.

GALGANO F. / MARRELLA F., Interpretación del contrato y "*Lex Mercatoria*", in Revista de Derecho Comparado: Interpretación de los contratos, 3, 2000, 7-57.

GARRO A.M., The Contribution of the UNIDROIT Principles to the Advancement of International Commercial Arbitration, in Tulane Journal of International and Comparative Law, N. 1/2, 1994, 93-128.

HOLTZMANN H.M., Application of the UNIDROIT Principles of International Commercial Contracts in Arbitrations Governed by the UNCITRAL Model Law on International Commercial Arbitration, in UNIDROIT (ed.), The UNIDROIT Principles: A Common Law of Contracts for the Americas?, 1998, 161-166.

JAGUSH S., Recent Codification Efforts: An Assessment, in E. GAILLARD (ed.), Towards a Uniform International Arbitration Law?, Juris Publishing Inc., N.Y. 2005, 63 – 90.

JOLIVET E., The UNIDROIT Principles in ICC Arbitration, in ICC International Court of Arbitration Bulletin, 2005 Special Supplement, 65 – 72.

KRONKE H., From International Uniform Conventions to Model Laws - From Guides to Principles, in PERRET L. / BISSON A.-F. / MARIANI N. (eds.), Evolution des systèmes juridiques, bijuridisme et commerce international. The Evolution of Legal Systems, Bijuralism and International Trade. Textes présentés lors d'un colloque organisée par la Faculté de Droit de l'Université d'Ottawa, le Ministère de la Justice du Canada et le Patrimoine Canadien, tenu à Ottawa, Ont., du 20 au 21 Oct. 2000, Wilson & Lafleur, Ottawa 2002, 283-304.

LALIVE P., The UNIDROIT Principles as *Lex Contractus*, with or without an Explicit or Tacit Choice of Law: an Arbitrator's Perspective, in ICC International Court of Arbitration Bulletin, 2002, Special Supplement, 77-94.

LALIVE P., L'arbitrage international et les Principes UNIDROIT, in BONELL M.J. / BONELLI F. (eds.), Contratti commerciali internazionali e Principi UNIDROIT, Giuffrè, Milano 1997, 71-89.

LANDO O., Assessing the Role of the UNIDROIT Principles in the Harmonization of Arbitration Law, 3 Tulane Journal of International and Comparative Law n. 1/2, 1994, 129-143.

LEW J.D.M., The UNIDROIT Principles as *Lex Contractus* Chosen by the Parties and Without an Explicit Choice-of-Law Clause: The Perspective of Councel, in ICC International Court of Arbitration Bulletin, 2002, Special Supplement, 85-94.

LÓPEZ RODRÍGEZ A.M., Lex Mercatoria and Harmonization of Contract Law in the Eu, Djof Publishing, Copenhagen 2003.

LUZZATTO R., I Principi UNIDROIT e l'arbitrato commerciale internazionale, in BONELL M.J. / BONELLI F. (eds.), Contratti commerciali internazionali e Principi UNIDROIT, Giuffrè, Milano 1997, 91-104.

MARRELLA F., Choice of Law in Third-Millenium Arbitrations: the Relevance of the UNIDROIT Principles of International Commercial Contracts, in International Commercial Arbitration. A Symposium sponsored by

Vanderbilt University Law and Business Program and Vanderbilt Journal of Transnational Law, March 2003, in 36 Vanderbilt Journal of Transnational Law 2003, 1137-1188.

MARRELLA F., Nuovi sviluppi dei Principi UNIDROIT sui contratti commerciali internazionali nell'arbitrato CCI, in Contratto e Impresa / Europa, 7, 2002, No. 1, 40-53.

MARRELLA F., UNIDROIT Principles of International Commercial Contracts in ICC Arbitration, 1999-2001, in ICC International Court of Arbitration Bulletin, Vol. 12, Issue 2, 49-55.

MARRELLA F., Extracts from ICC Awards referring to the UNIDROIT Principles of International Commercial Contracts, in ICC International Court of Arbitration Bulletin, Vol. 12, Issue 2, 49-115.

MARRELLA F. / GÉLINAS F., The UNIDROIT Principles of International Commercial Contracts in ICC Arbitration: A Preliminary Assessment [including extracts from ICC awards referring to the UNIDROIT Principles of International Commercial Contracts and a bibliography], in ICC International Court of Arbitration Bulletin 1999, No. 2, 26-119.

MARRELLA F. / GELINAS F., Les Principes d'UNIDROIT relatifs aux contrats du commerce international dans l'arbitrage de la CCI [avec extraits de sentences faisant référence aux Principes d'UNIDROIT et une bibliographie], in ICC Bulletin de la Cour Internationale d'Arbitrage de la CCI 1999, No. 2, 21-122.

MAYER P., Reflections on the International Arbitrors Duty to apply the Law, in 17 Arbitration International 2001, 235-247.

MISTELIS L., The UNIDROIT Principles applied as "Most Appropriate Rule of Law" in a Swedish Arbitral Award, in Uniform Law Review / Revue de Droit Uniforme, 7, 2003, 631-640.

NAFZIGER J.A.R. / SYMEONIDES S.C. (eds.), Law and Justice in a Multistate World. Essays in Honor of Arthur T. Von Mehren, Transnational Publishers, Ardsley, N.Y. 2002.

NOTTAGE L., The Vicissitudes of Transnational Commercial Arbitration and the *Lex Mercatoria*: a View from the Periphery, in Arbitration International, 16, 2000, 53-78.

OGUZ A., Hukuk Tahiri ve Karþýlaþtýrmaltý Hukuk Açýsýdan Uluslararasý icaret Hukuku (*Lex Mercatoria*) - UNIDROIT Ýlkelerinin *Lex Mercatoria* Niteliði, Ankara Üniversiteti Hukuk Fakültesi Dergisi, 50, 2001, 11-54.

PELEGGI R., L'applicazione dei Principi UNIDROIT *en voie directe* alla luce di un recente lodo della Corte Arbitrale della Camera di Commercio Internazionale, in Diritto del commercio internazionale, 2004, 483 – 507.

RAESCHKE-KESSLER H., Should an Arbitrator in an International Arbitration Procedure apply the UNIDROIT Principles?, in The UNIDROIT Principles for International Commercial Contracts: A New *Lex Mercatoria*?, ICC Publication N. 490/1, 1995, 167-180.

RAMBERG J., The Creativity of Arbitrators in the Context of the UNIDROIT Principles of International Commercial Contracts, in Uniform Law Review / Revue de Droit Uniforme, 1998, 651-656.

RICCOMAGNO M., The UNIDROIT Principles in the Context of International Commercial Arbitration, Arbitration (Paper presented at the Bi-Annual 25th Conference of the International Bar Association held in Melbourne on 9-14 October 1994).

SANDROCK O., Die objektive Anknüpfung von Verträgen nach § 1051 Abs. 2 ZPO, in Recht der internationalen Wirtschaft 2000, 321-328.

SILVA ROMERO E., Las normas jurídicas aplicables en el arbitraje comercial internacional. Breve contribución al derecho internacional privado colombiano, Revista de Derecho Privado. Universidad de los Andes, 28, 2002, 3-43.

SIQUEIROS J.L., Los Principios de UNIDROIT como normativa aplicable por los árbitros en controversias comerciales internacionales, in UNIDROIT (ed.), The UNIDROIT Principles: A Common Law of Contracts for the Americas?, 1998, 151-159.

SMITH J.F., Mediation and the Principles of UNIDROIT, in Comentarios a los Principios sobre los Contratos Comerciales Internacionales del UNIDROIT, Universidad Nacional Autónoma de México, 1998, 237-251.

TRAISCI F.P., Principi UNIDROIT, *lex mercatoria* e diritto del commercio internazionale: note a margine di un lodo arbitrale, in Diritto del Commercio Internazionale, N. 2, 1999, 474-494.

VAGTS D.F., Arbitration and the UNIDROIT Principles, in Comentarios a los Principios sobre los Contratos Comerciales Internacionales del UNIDROIT, Universidad Nacional Autónoma de México, 1998, 265-277.

VAN HOUTTE H., UNIDROIT Principles of International Commercial Contracts and International Commercial Arbitration: Their Reciprocal Relevance, in UNIDROIT Principles for International Commercial Contracts: A New *Lex Mercatoria*?, ICC Publication N. 490/1, 1995, 181-197.

VILLA A.V., La "ley aplicable" por los árbitros al fondo de la cuestión sometida A arbitraje en el reglamento de procedimientos de CIAC, in Revista de Derecho del Mercosur, 4, 1999, 109-117.

VISCHER F., Die kollisionsrechtliche Bedeutung der Wahl einer nichtstaatlichen Ordnung für den staatlichen Richter am Beispiel der UNIDROIT Principles of International Commercial Contracts, in SCHWENZER I. / HAGER G. (eds.), Festschrift für Peter Schlechtriem zum 70. Geburtstag, J.B.C. Mohr (Paul Siebeck), Tübingen 2003, 445-454.

WILLIAMS D.A.R., The Further Development of International Commercial Arbitration through the UNIDROIT Principles of International Commercial Contracts, in 2 New Zealand Business Law Quarterly, 1996, 7-21.

WORTMANN B., Choice of Law by Arbitrators: the Applicable Conflict of Laws System, in Arbitration International 1998, 97-113.

PART II

TEXT OF THE UNIDROIT PRINCIPLES & OFFICIAL COMMENTS

ISSUES & CASES (*)

BIBLIOGRAPHY

(*) The numbers between square brackets indicate the page number of the abstracts and the full text (where available) of the corresponding decision.

PREAMBLE

(Purpose of the Principles)

These Principles set forth general rules for international commercial contracts.

They shall be applied when the parties have agreed that their contract be governed by them.(*)

They may be applied when the parties have agreed that their contract be governed by general principles of law, the lex mercatoria or the like.

They may be applied when the parties have not chosen any law to govern their contract.

They may be used to interpret or supplement international uniform law instruments.

They may be used to interpret or supplement domestic law.

They may serve as a model for national and international legislators.

COMMENT

The Principles set forth general rules which are basically conceived for "international commercial contracts".

1. "International" contracts

The international character of a contract may be defined in a great variety of ways. The solutions adopted in both national and international legislation range from a reference to the place of business or habitual residence of the parties in different countries to the adoption of more general criteria such as the

---

(*) Parties wishing to provide that their agreement be governed by the Principles might use the following words, adding any desired exceptions or modifications:

"This contract shall be governed by the UNIDROIT Principles (2004) [except as to Articles ...]".

Parties wishing to provide in addition for the application of the law of a particular jurisdiction might use the following words:

"This contract shall be governed by the UNIDROIT Principles (2004) [except as to Articles...], supplemented when necessary by the law of [jurisdiction X]".

contract having "significant connections with more than one State", "involving a choice between the laws of different States", or "affecting the interests of international trade".

The Principles do not expressly lay down any of these criteria. The assumption, however, is that the concept of "international" contracts should be given the broadest possible interpretation, so as ultimately to exclude only those situations where no international element at all is involved, *i.e.* where all the relevant elements of the contract in question are connected with one country only.

2. "Commercial" contracts

The restriction to "commercial" contracts is in no way intended to take over the distinction traditionally made in some legal systems between "civil" and "commercial" parties and/or transactions, *i.e.* to make the application of the Principles dependent on whether the parties have the formal status of "merchants" (*commerçants*, *Kaufleute*) and/or the transaction is commercial in nature. The idea is rather that of excluding from the scope of the Principles so-called "consumer transactions" which are within the various legal systems being increasingly subjected to special rules, mostly of a mandatory character, aimed at protecting the consumer, *i.e.* a party who enters into the contract otherwise than in the course of its trade or profession.

The criteria adopted at both national and international level also vary with respect to the distinction between consumer and non-consumer contracts. The Principles do not provide any express definition, but the assumption is that the concept of "commercial" contracts should be understood in the broadest possible sense, so as to include not only trade transactions for the supply or exchange of goods or services, but also other types of economic transactions, such as investment and/or concession agreements, contracts for professional services, etc.

3. The Principles and domestic contracts between private persons

Notwithstanding the fact that the Principles are conceived for international commercial contracts, there is nothing to prevent private persons from agreeing to apply the Principles to a purely domestic contract. Any such agreement would however be subject to the mandatory rules of the domestic law governing the contract.

4. The Principles as rules of law governing the contract

a. *Express choice by the parties*

As the Principles represent a system of principles and rules of contract law which are common to existing national legal systems or best adapted to the special requirements of international commercial transactions, there might be good reasons for the parties to choose them expressly as the rules of law governing their contract. In so doing the parties may refer to the Principles exclusively or in conjunction with a particular domestic law which should apply to issues not covered by the Principles.

Parties who wish to choose the Principles as the rules of law governing their contract are well advised to combine such a choice of law clause with an arbitration agreement.

The reason for this is that the freedom of choice of the parties in designating the law governing their contract is traditionally limited to national laws. Therefore, a reference by the parties to the Principles will normally be considered to be a mere agreement to incorporate them in the contract, while the law governing the contract will still have to be determined on the basis of the private international law rules of the forum. As a result, the Principles will bind the parties only to the extent that they do not affect the rules of the applicable law from which the parties may not derogate. See comment 2 to Art.1.4.

The situation is different if the parties agree to submit disputes arising from their contract to arbitration. Arbitrators are not necessarily bound by a particular domestic law. This is self-evident if they are authorised by the parties to act as *amiable compositeurs* or *ex aequo et bono.* But even in the absence of such an authorisation parties are generally permitted to choose "rules of law" other than national laws on which the arbitrators are to base their decisions. See in particular Art. 28(1) of the *1985 UNCITRAL Model Law on International Commercial Arbitration*; see also Art. 42(1) of the *1965 Convention on the Settlement of Investment Disputes between States and Nationals of other States (ICSID Convention).*

In line with this approach, the parties would be free to choose the Principles as the "rules of law" according to which the arbitrators would decide the dispute, with the result that the Principles would apply to the exclusion of any particular national law, subject only to the application of those rules of domestic law which are mandatory irrespective of which law governs the contract. See comment 3 to Art.1.4.

In disputes falling under the ICSID Convention, the Principles might even be applicable to the exclusion of any domestic rule of law.

b. *The Principles applied as a manifestation of "general principles of law", the lex mercatoria" or the like referred to in the contract*

Parties to international commercial contracts who cannot agree on the choice of a particular domestic law as the law applicable to their contract sometimes provide that it shall be governed by the "general principles of law", by the "usages and customs of international trade", by the *lex mercatoria*, etc.

Hitherto, such reference by the parties to not better identified principles and rules of a supranational or transnational character has been criticised, among other grounds, because of the extreme vagueness of such concepts. In order to avoid, or at least to reduce considerably, the uncertainty accompanying the use of such rather vague concepts, it might be advisable, in order to determine their content, to have recourse to a systematic and well-defined set of rules such as the Principles.

c. *The Principles applied in the absence of any choice of law by the parties*

The Principles may however be applied even if the contract is silent as to the applicable law. If the parties have not chosen the law governing their contract, it has to be determined on the basis of the relevant rules of private international law. In the context of international commercial arbitration such rules are very flexible, permitting arbitral tribunals to apply "the rules of law which it determines to be appropriate" (see *e.g.* Art. 17(1) of the *1998 Rules of Arbitration of the International Chamber of Commerce*; Art. 24(1) of the *Rules of the Arbitration of the Institute of the Stockholm Chamber of Commerce*). Normally arbitral tribunals will apply a particular domestic law as the proper law of the contract, yet exceptionally they may resort to a-national or supra-national rules such as the Principles. This may occur when it can be inferred from the circumstances that the parties intended to exclude the application of any domestic law (*e.g.* where one of the parties is a State or a government agency and both parties have made it clear that neither would accept the application of the other's domestic law or that of a third country), or when the contract presents connecting factors with many countries none of which is predominant enough to justify the application of one domestic law to the exclusion of all the others.

5. The Principles as a means of interpreting and supplementing international uniform law instruments

International uniform law instruments may give rise to questions concerning the precise meaning of their individual provisions and may present gaps.

Traditionally international uniform law has been interpreted on the basis of, and supplemented by, principles and criteria of domestic law, be it the law of the forum or that which would, according to the relevant rules of private international law, be applicable in the absence of an international uniform law.

Recently, both courts and arbitral tribunals have increasingly abandoned such a "conflictual" approach, seeking instead to interpret and supplement international uniform law by reference to autonomous and internationally uniform principles and criteria. This approach, expressly sanctioned in the most recent conventions (see, *e.g.*, Art. 7 of the *1980 UN Convention on Contracts for the International Sale of Goods (CISG)*), is based on the assumption that international uniform law, even after its incorporation into the various national legal systems, only formally becomes an integrated part of the latter, whereas from a substantive point of view it does not lose its original character of a special body of law autonomously developed at international level and intended to be applied in a uniform manner throughout the world.

Until now, such autonomous principles and criteria for the interpretation and supplementing of international uniform law instruments have had to be found in each single case by the judges and arbitrators themselves on the basis of a comparative survey of the solutions adopted in the different national legal systems. The Principles could considerably facilitate their task in this respect.

6. The Principles as a means of interpreting and supplementing domestic law

The Principles may also be used to interpret and supplement domestic law. In applying a particular domestic law, courts and arbitral tribunals may be faced with doubts as to the proper solution to be adopted under that law, either because different alternatives are available or because there seem to be no specific solutions at all. Especially where the dispute relates to an international commercial contract, it may be advisable to resort to the Principles as a source of inspiration. By so doing the domestic law in question would be interpreted and supplemented in accordance with internationally accepted standards and/or the special needs of cross-border trade relationships.

7. The Principles as a model for national and international legislators

In view of their intrinsic merits the Principles may in addition serve as a model to national and international law-makers for the drafting of legislation in the field of general contract law or with respect to special types of transactions. At a national level, the Principles may be particularly useful to those countries which lack a developed body of legal rules relating to contracts and which intend to update their law, at least with respect to foreign economic relationships, to current international standards. Not too different is the situation of those countries with a well-defined legal system, but which after the recent dramatic changes in their socio-political structure have an urgent need to rewrite their laws, in particular those relating to economic and business activities.

At an international level the Principles could become an important term of reference for the drafting of conventions and model laws.

So far the terminology used to express the same concept differs considerably from one instrument to another, with the obvious risk of misunderstandings and misinterpretations. Such inconsistencies could be avoided if the terminology of the Principles were to be adopted as an international uniform glossary.

8. Other possible uses of the Principles

The list set out in the Preamble of the different ways in which the Principles may be used is not exhaustive.

Thus, the Principles may also serve as a guide for drafting contracts. In particular the Principles facilitate the identification of the issues to be addressed in the contract and provide a neutral legal terminology equally understandable by all the parties involved. Such a use of the Principles is enhanced by the fact that they are available in a large number of languages.

The Principles may also be used as a substitute for the domestic law otherwise applicable. This is the case whenever it proves impossible or extremely difficult to establish the relevant rule of that particular domestic law with respect to a specific issue, *i.e.* it would entail disproportionate efforts and/or costs. The reasons for this generally lie in the special character of the legal sources of the domestic law in question and/or the cost of accessing them.

Furthermore, the Principles may be used as course material in universities and law schools, thereby promoting the teaching of contract law on a truly comparative basis.

Issues & Cases

1 MATERIAL SCOPE OF APPLICATION OF PRINCIPLES

1.1 INTERNATIONAL COMMERCIAL CONTRACTS

- OCTOBER 9, 1997 VENEZUELA SUPREME COURT OF VENEZUELA [708]

1.1.1 CONTRACTS V. UNILATERAL ACTS

1.1.2 INTERNATIONAL V. DOMESTIC CONTRACTS

- OCTOBER 9, 1997 VENEZUELA SUPREME COURT OF VENEZUELA [708]

1.1.3 COMMERCIAL V. CONSUMER TRANSACTIONS

2. APPLICABILITY OF PRINCIPLES

2.1 AS RULES OF LAW GOVERNING THE CONTRACT

2.1.1 PRINCIPLES EXPRESSLY CHOSEN BY THE PARTIES

- NOVEMBER 12, 2004 SWITZERLAND, HANDELSGERICHT ST. GALLEN [1084]
- DECEMBER 20, 2005 SWITZERLAND, BUNDESGERICHT [1126]

2.1.1.1 IN DISPUTES BEFORE STATE COURT

- NOVEMBER 12, 2004 SWITZERLAND, HANDELSGERICHT ST. GALLEN [1084]
- JANUARY 11, 2005 ITALY TRIBUNALE PADOVA – SEZ. ESTE [1090]
- DECEMBER 20, 2005 SWITZERLAND, BUNDESGERICHT [1126]

2.1.1.2 IN DISPUTES BEFORE ARBITRAL TRIBUNAL

- -- ARBITRAL AWARD AD HOC ARBITRATION, NEW YORK [546]

- December 1996 Arbitral Award ICC International Court of Arbitration (No. 8331) [656]
- December 1, 1996 Arbitral Award, Camera Arbitrale Nazionale ed Internazionale di Milano (No. A-1795/51) [662]
- January 20, 1997 Arbitral Award International Arbitration Court of the Chamber of Commerce and Industry of the Russian Federation (No. 116) [670]
- April 21, 1997 Arbitral Award Ad hoc Arbitration Paris [679]
- March 2000 Arbitral Award ICC International Court of Arbitration (No. 10114) [824]
- January 25, 2002 Arbitral Award Arbitration Court of the Lausanne Chamber of Commerce and Industry [991]
- May 17, 2002 Arbitral Award (Partial) Arbitration Court of the Lausanne Chamber of Commerce and Industry [1001]
- January 31, 2003 Arbitral Award Arbitration Court of the Lausanne Chamber of Commerce and Industry [1056]
- December 22, 2004 Arbitral Award Tribunal of International Commercial Arbitration at the Ukrainian Chamber of Commerce and Trade [1089]

2.1.2 Principles as expression of the "lex mercatoria" referred to in the contract

- April 30, 2001 Arbitral Award Ad hoc arbitration San José (Costa Rica) [945]
- November 5, 2002 Arbitral Award International Arbitration Court at the Chamber of Commerce and Industry of the Russian Federation (No. 11/2002) [1030]
- January 6, 2003 Arbitral Award (Partial) ICC International Court of Arbitration (No. 12111) [1054]

2.1.3 Principles as expressione of "general principles of law" referred to in the contract

- -- Arbitral Award Ad hoc Arbitration, New York [545]

- JUNE 1995 ARBITRAL AWARD ICC (FIRST PARTIAL) INTERNATIONAL COURT OF ARBITRATION (NO. 7110) [572]
- APRIL 1997 ARBITRAL AWARD ICC INTERNATIONAL COURT OF ARBITRATION (NO. 8264) [675]
- MAY 5, 1997 ARBITRAL AWARD ICC INTERNATIONAL COURT OF ARBITRATION (NO. 7365/FMS) [680]
- SEPTEMBER 23, 1997 UNITED NATIONS COMPENSATION COMMISSION, PANEL F1 (NO. S/AC.26) [703]
- DECEMBER 1997 ARBITRAL AWARD AD HOC ARBITRATION, NEW YORK [710]
- DECEMBER 7, 1998 USA UNITED STATES DISTRICT COURT, S.D. CALIFORNIA (NO. 98-1165-B) [764]
- FEBRUARY 1999 ARBITRAL AWARD (PARTIAL) ICC INTERNATIONAL COURT OF ARBITRATION (NO. 9474) [777]
- SEPTEMBER 1999 ARBITRAL AWARD ICC INTERNATIONAL COURT OF ARBITRATION (NO. 7819) [809]
- JULY 28, 2000 ARBITRAL AWARD ICC INTERNATIONAL COURT OF ARBITRATION (NO. 9797/CK/AER/ACS) [834]
- JANUARY 6, 2003 ARBITRAL AWARD (PARTIAL) ICC INTERNATIONAL COURT OF ARBITRATION (NO. 12111) [1054]
- AUGUST 19, 2005 ARBITRAL AWARD AD HOC ARBITRATION, BRUSSELS [1108]

2.1.4 PRINCIPLES APPLIED IN THE ABSENCE OF ANY CHOICE-OF-LAW CLAUSE

- JANUARY 2001 ARBITRAL AWARD ICC INTERNATIONAL COURT OF ARBITRATION (NO. 9771) [918]

2.1.4.1 PRINCIPLES AS "THE RULES OF LAW [ARBITRATORS] DETERMINE TO BE APPROPRIATE"

- 1995 ARBITRAL AWARD LONDON COURT OF ARBITRATION [571]
- JUNE 5, 1996 ARBITRAL AWARD ICC INTERNATIONAL COURT OF ARBITRATION (NO. 7375) [622]

- SEMPTEMBER 27, 1996 ARBITRAL AWARD ICC INTERNATIONAL COURT OF ARBITRATION (NO. 8261) [645]
- SEPTEMBER 1998 ARBITRAL AWARD ICC INTERNATIONAL COURT OF ARBITRATION (NO. 9419) [755]
- JANUARY 1999 ARBITRAL AWARD (PARTIAL) ICC INTERNATIONAL COURT OF ARBITRATION (NO. 9875) [774]
- APRIL 16, 1999 ARBITRAL AWARD INTERNATIONAL ARBITRATION COURT OF THE CHAMBER OF COMMERCE AND INDUSTRY OF THE RUSSIAN FEDERATION (NO. 152/1998) [798]
- 2001 ARBITRAL AWARD (PARTIAL) ARBITRATION INSTITUTE OF THE STOCKHOLM CHAMBER OF COMMERCE (NO. 117/1999) [895]
- 2001 ARBITRAL AWARD ICC INTERNATIONAL COURT OF ARBITRATION (NO. 10422) [902]
- JANUARY 25, 2001 ARBITRAL AWARD INTERNATIONAL ARBITRATION COURT OF THE CHAMBER OF COMMERCE AND INDUSTRY OF THE RUSSIAN FEDERATION (NO. 88/2000) [921]
- MARCH 2002 ARBITRAL AWARD ICC INTERNATIONAL COURT OF ARBITRATION (NO. 10385) [994]
- MARCH 29, 2005 ARBITRAL AWARD ARBITRATION INSTITUTE OF THE STOCKHOLM CHAMBER OF COMMERCE [1104]

2.1.4.2 PRINCIPLES AS "RELEVANT TRADE USAGES" TO BE TAKEN INTO ACCOUNT IN ALL CASES BY ARBITRATORS

- NOVEMBER 1996 ARBITRAL AWARD ICC INTERNATIONAL COURT OF ARBITRATION (NO. 8502) [651]
- JUNE 5, 1997 ARBITRAL AWARD INTERNATIONAL ARBITRATION COURT OF THE CHAMBER OF COMMERCE AND INDUSTRY OF THE RUSSIAN FEDERATION (NO. 229/1996) [683]
- DECEMBER 10, 1997 ARBITRAL AWARD AD HOC ARBITRATION, BUENOS AIRES [715]
- MARCH 1998 ARBITRAL AWARD ICC INTERNATIONAL COURT OF ARBITRATION (NO. 9029) [718]

- FEBRUARY 1999 ARBITRAL AWARD ICC INTERNATIONAL COURT OF ARBITRATION (NO. 9479) [786]
- JULY 27, 1999 ARBITRAL AWARD INTERNATIONAL ARBITRATION COURT OF THE CHAMBER OF COMMERCE AND INDUSTRY OF THE RUSSIAN FEDERATION (NO. 302/1997) [802]
- 2000 ARBITRAL AWARD ICC INTERNATIONAL COURT OF ARBITRATION (NO. 10021) [817]
- OCTOBER 2000 ARBITRAL AWARD (PARTIAL) ICC INTERNATIONAL COURT OF ARBITRATION (NO. 10022) [862]
- NOVEMBER 6, 2002 ARBITRAL AWARD INTERNATIONAL ARBITRATION COURT OF THE CHAMBER OF COMMERCE AND INDUSTRY OF THE RUSSIAN FEDERATION (NO. 217/2001) [1032]
- NOVEMBER 12, 2004 ARBITRAL AWARD INTERNATIONAL ARBITRATION COURT AT THE CHAMBER OF COMMERCE AND INDUSTRY OF THE RUSSIAN FEDERATION (NO. 174/2003) [1088]

2.1.5 PRINCIPLES AND ARBITRATION EX AEQUO ET BONO

- DECEMBER 1996 ARBITRAL AWARD ICC INTERNATIONAL COURT OF ARBITRATION (NO. 8874) [660]
- DECEMBER 10, 1997 ARBITRAL AWARD AD HOC ARBITRATION, BUENOS AIRES [715]
- FEBRUARY 24, 2001 ARBITRAL AWARD ARBITRAL TRIBUNAL OF THE CITY OF PANAMA [931]

2.2 AS SUBSTITUTE FOR DOMESTIC LAW OTHERWISE APPLICABLE

2.3 AS MEANS FOR INTERPRETING AND SUPPLEMENTING DOMESTIC LAW OTHERWISE APPLICABLE

- -- ARBITRAL AWARD AD HOC ARBITRATION (PLACE UNKNOWN) [544]
- 1990 ARBITRAL AWARD SCHIEDSGERICHT BERLIN (NO. SG 126/90) [547]
- NOVEMBER 25, 1994 ARBITRAL AWARD ZÜRICH CHAMBER OF COMMERCE [559]
- 1995 ARBITRAL AWARD AD HOC ARBITRATION, AUCKLAND [564]
- JULY 1995 ARBITRAL AWARD ICC INTERNATIONAL COURT OF ARBITRATION (NO. 8240) [591]
- SEPTEMBER 22, 1995 NETHERLANDS, SUPREME COURT OF THE NETHERLANDS (NO. 15754) [593]

- JANUARY 24, 1996 FRANCE COUR D'APPEL DE GRENOBLE [611]
- APRIL 25, 1996 ARBITRAL AWARD ICC INTERNATIONAL COURT OF ARBITRATION [617]
- JUNE 1996 ARBITRAL AWARD ICC INTERNATIONAL COURT OF ARBITRATION (NO. 5835) [618]
- SEPTEMBER 1996 ARBITRAL AWARD ICC INTERNATIONAL COURT OF ARBITRATION (NO. 8486) [633]
- SEPTEMBER 4, 1996 ARBITRAL AWARD ICC INTERNATIONAL COURT OF ARBITRATION (NO. 8540) [636]
- DECEMBER 4, 1996 ARBITRAL AWARD AD HOC ARBITRATION, ROME [664]
- DECEMBER 17, 1996 ARBITRAL AWARD ARBITRAL COURT OF THE ECONOMIC CHAMBER AND THE AGRARIAN CHAMBER OF THE CZECH REPUBLIC (NO. RSP 88/94) [669]
- MARCH 5,1997 NETHERLANDS RB ZWOLLE (NO. HA ZA 95-640) [671]
- APRIL 21, 1997 ARBITRAL AWARD AD HOC ARBITRATION, PARIS [679]
- JUNE 30, 1997 AUSTRALIA FEDERAL COURT OF AUSTRALIA (NO. 558) [685]
- SEPTEMBER 2, 1997 ARBITRAL AWARD INTERNATIONAL ARBITRATION COURT OF THE CHAMBER OF COMMERCE AND INDUSTRY OF THE RUSSIAN FEDERATION (NO. 225/1996) [702]
- JANUARY 28, 1998 ARBITRAL AWARD AD HOC ARBITRATION, HELSINKI [717]
- MARCH 5, 1998 FRANCE COUR D'APPEL DE PARIS (1ER CH. C.) [732]
- APRIL 1998 ARBITRAL AWARD ICC INTERNATIONAL COURT OF ARBITRATION (NO. 8223) [739]
- JULY 16, 1998 AUSTRALIA SUPREME COURT OF NEW SOUTH WALES (NO. NSWSC 483) [742]
- SEPTEMBER 1998 ARBITRAL AWARD ICC INTERNATIONAL COURT OF ARBITRATION (NO. 8908) [750]
- OCTOBER 1998 ARBITRAL AWARD ICC INTERNATIONAL COURT OF ARBITRATION (NO. 9333) [759]

- December 1998 Arbitral Award ICC International Court of Arbitration (No. 9593) [762]
- March 1999 Arbitral Award ICC International Court of Arbitration (No. 9594) [794]
- May 1999 Arbitral Award ICC International Court of Arbitration (No. 9753) [799]
- September 1999 Arbitral Award ICC International Court of Arbitration (No. 7819) [809]
- October 1, 1999 Australia Supreme Court of New South Wales (No. 996) [811]
- 2000 Arbitral Award ICC International Court of Arbitration (No. 10021) [817]
- August 2000 Arbitral Award ICC International Court of Arbitration (No. 9651) [854]
- October 2000 Arbitral Award ICC International Court of Arbitration (No. 10335) [864]
- November 27, 2000 New Zealand Court of Appeal of New Zealand (No. (2000) NZCA 350) [869]
- December 2000 Arbitral Award ICC International Court of Arbitration (No. 10346) [883]
- February 2, 2001 Netherlands Supreme Court of the Netherlands (No. R99/120 HR) [922]
- April 2001 Arbitral Award ICC International Court of Arbitration (No. 10578) [942]
- June 2001 Arbitral Award ICC International Court of Arbitration (No. 11227) [951]
- June 2001 Arbitral Award ICC International Court of Arbitration (No. 9950) [948]
- July 2001 Arbitral Award ICC International Court of Arbitration (No. 11051) [953]
- July 13, 2001 Netherlands Supreme Court of the Netherlands (No. C99/315 HR) [956]
- October 2001 Arbitral Award ICC International Court of Arbitration (No. 9078) [970]

- October 3, 2001 New Zealand Court of Appeal of New Zealand (No. NZCA 348) [974]
- December 2001 Arbitral Award ICC International Court of Arbitration (No. 11295) [988]
- December 2001 Arbitral Award ICC International Court of Arbitration (No. 9994) [985]
- March 2002 Arbitral Award (Partial) ICC International Court of Arbitration (No. 11375) [999]
- July 29, 2002 Arbitral Award Arbitration Centre of the Costa Rican Chamber of Commerce [1003]
- September 2002 Arbitral Award Corte Arbitrale della Associazione Italiana Arbitrato (No. 91/2001) [1005]
- November 6, 2002 Arbitral Award International Arbitration Court of the Chamber of Commerce and Industry of the Russian Federation (No. 217/2001) [1032]
- November 28, 2002 Arbitral Award Camera Arbitrale Nazionale e Internazionale di Milano [1034]
- December 20, 2002 Netherlands Supreme Court of the Netherlands (No. C01/157 HR) [1036]
- February 12, 2003 Australia Federal Court of Australia (No. NG733 of 1997) [1058]
- April 4, 2003 Arbitral Award International Arbitration Court of the Chamber of Commerce and Industry of the Russian Federation (No. 134/2002) [1061]
- June 1, 2003 Arbitral Award Arbitration Centre of the Costa Rican Chamber of Commerce [1065]
- November 6, 2003 Poland Supreme Court (No. III CZP 61/03) [1076]
- March 4, 2004 Arbitral Award Ad hoc Arbitration (Place unknown) [1077]
- December 4, 2005 United Kingdom High Court of Justice (Queen's Bench Division) (2004 Folio 272) [1110]

- AUGUST 2, 2005 OVERSEAS PRIVATE INVESTMENT CORP. USA ADIMINISTRATIVE DETERMINATION [1106]
- FEBRUARY 17, 2006 UNITED KINGDOM COURT OF APPEAL (CIVIL DIVISION) (NO. 2006 EWCA CIV. 69) [1142]

2.4 AS MEANS FOR INTERPRETING AND SUPPLEMENTING INTERNATIONAL UNIFORM LAW INSTRUMENTS

2.4.1 PRINCIPLES AND CISG

- JUNE 15, 1994 ARBITRAL AWARD INTERNATIONALES SCHIEDSGERICHT DER BUNDESKAMMER DER GEWERBLICHEN WIRTSCHAFT – WIEN (NO. SCH-4318) [548]
- JUNE 15, 1994 ARBITRAL AWARD INTERNATIONALES SCHIEDSGERICHT DER BUNDESKAMMER DER GEWERBLICHEN WIRTSCHAFT – WIEN (NO. SCH-4366) [554]
- 1995 ARBITRAL AWARD ICC INTERNATIONAL COURT OF ARBITRATION (NO. 8128) [565]
- OCTOBER 23, 1996 FRANCE COUR D'APPEL DE GRENOBLE [643]
- DECEMBER 1996 ARBITRAL AWARD ICC INTERNATIONAL COURT OF ARBITRATION (NO. 8769) [659]
- JUNE 5, 1997 ARBITRAL AWARD INTERNATIONAL ARBITRATION COURT OF THE CHAMBER OF COMMERCE AND INDUSTRY OF THE RUSSIAN FEDERATION (NO. 229/1996) [683]
- DECEMBER 1997 ARBITRAL AWARD ICC INTERNATIONAL COURT OF ARBITRATION (NO. 8817) [712]
- MARCH 1998 ARBITRAL AWARD ICC INTERNATIONAL COURT OF ARBITRATION (NO. 9117) [727]
- NOVEMBER 27, 2000 NEW ZEALAND COURT OF APPEAL OF NEW ZEALAND (NO. (2000) NZCA 350) [869]
- OCTOBER 16, 2002 NETHERLANDS HOF'S-HERTOGENBOSCH [1027]
- MAY 20, 2003 BELARUS SUPREME ECONOMIC COURT OF THE REPUBLIC OF BELARUS (NO. 7-5/2003) [1063]

- MAY 20, 2003 BELARUS SUPREME ECONOMIC COURT OF THE REPUBLIC OF BELARUS (NO. 8-5/2003) [1064]
- JUNE 6, 2003 ARBITRAL AWARD INTERNATIONAL ARBITRATION COURT OF THE CHAMBER OF COMMERCE AND INDUSTRY OF THE RUSSIAN FEDERATION (NO. 97/2002) [1067]
- MAY 19, 2004 ARBITRAL AWARD INTERNATIONAL ARBITRATION COURT AT THE CHAMBER OF COMMERCE AND INDUSTRY OF THE RUSSIAN FEDERATION (NO. 100/2002) [1082]
- 2006 PEOPLE'S REPUBLIC OF CHINA XIAMEN INTERMEDIATE PEOPLE'S COURT [1131]
- FEBRUARY 17, 2006 UNITED KINGDOM COURT OF APPEAL (CIVIL DIVISION) (NO. 2006 EWCA CIV. 69) [1142]

2.4.2 PRINCIPLES AND OTHER INTERNATIONAL INSTRUMENTS

- OCTOBER 9, 1997 VENEZUELA SUPREME COURT OF VENEZUELA [708]
- JANUARY 1999 ARBITRAL AWARD ICC INTERNATIONAL COURT OF ARBITRATION (NO. 8547) [770]
- SEPTEMBER 17, 2002 COURT OF JUSTICE OF THE EUROPEAN COMMUNITIES (NO. C-334/00) [1010]
- JANUARY 10, 2006 ITALY TRIBUNALE PADOVA – SEZ. ESTE [1132]

2.5 AS GUIDE FOR DRAFTING CONTRACTS

- MARCH 20, 2000 ARBITRAL AWARD INTERNATIONAL CENTRE FOR SETTLEMENT OF INVESTMENT DISPUTES (ICSID) (NO. ARB(AF)/98/1) [826]

2.5.1 PRINCIPLES AS MODEL CONTRACT CLAUSES

- MARCH 20, 2000 ARBITRAL AWARD INTERNATIONAL CENTRE FOR SETTLEMENT OF INVESTMENT DISPUTES (ICSID) (NO. ARB(AF)/98/1) [826]

2.5.2 PRINCIPLES AS CHECK-LIST

2.5.3 PRINCIPLES AS LINGUA FRANCA

2.6 AS MODEL FOR NATIONAL AND INTERNATIONAL LEGISLATORS

2.7 AS TEACHING MATERIALS

3. PRINCIPLES AND SIMILAR INSTRUMENTS (E.G. PRINCIPLES OF EUROPEAN CONTRACT LAW)

- 1995 ARBITRAL AWARD ICC INTERNATIONAL COURT OF ARBITRATION (NO. 8128) [565]

- FEBRUARY 1999 ARBITRAL AWARD (PARTIAL) ICC INTERNATIONAL COURT OF ARBITRATION (NO. 9474) [777]
- OCTOBER 1, 1999 AUSTRALIA SUPREME COURT OF NEW SOUTH WALES (NO. 996) [811]
- JULY 28, 2000 ARBITRAL AWARD ICC INTERNATIONAL COURT OF ARBITRATION (NO. 9797/CK/AER/ACS) [834]
- OCTOBER 2000 ARBITRAL AWARD (PARTIAL) ICC INTERNATIONAL COURT OF ARBITRATION (NO. 10022) [862]
- OCTOBER 16, 2002 NETHERLANDS HOF'S-HERTOGENBOSCH [1027]
- JANUARY 6, 2003 ARBITRAL AWARD (PARTIAL) ICC INTERNATIONAL COURT OF ARBITRATION (NO. 12111) [1054]
- FEBRUARY 12, 2003 AUSTRALIA FEDERAL COURT OF AUSTRALIA (NO. NG733 OF 1997) [1058]

BIBLIOGRAPHY

ADAME GODDARD J., Hacia un concepto international de contrato (o la interpretación de la palabra "contrato" en los Principios de UNIDROIT), in Contratación internacional, Comentarios a los principios sobre los Contratos Comerciales Internacionales del UNIDROIT, Universidad Nacional Autónoma de México – Universidad Panamericana (ed.), 1998, 15-32.

ABASCAL J.M., Los Principios de UNIDROIT como instrumento para interpretar o suplementar textos internacionales de derecho uniforme o textos de derecho interno, in UNIDROIT (ed.), The UNIDROIT Principles: a Common Law of Contracts for the Americas?, 1998, 211-220.

AMOUSSOU–GUENOU R., Perspectives del Principes Asean (ou Asiatiques) du droit des contrats, in Revue de droit des affaires international, 2005, 573 *et seq.*

ASENSIO P.A., Armonización normativa y régimen juridico de los contratos mercantiles internacionales, in Diritto del commercio internazionale, 4, 1998, 859-883.

BARON, G., Do the UNIDROIT Principles of International Commercial Contracts form a New *Lex Mercatoria*?, in Arbitration International, 1999, 115-130.

BASEDOW J., Uniform Law Conventions and the UNIDROIT Principles of International Commercial Contracts, in Uniform Law Review / Revue de droit uniforme, 2000, 129-139.

BASEDOW J., Die UNIDROIT -Prinzipien der Internationalen Handelsverträge und die Übereinkommen des einheitlichen Privatrechts – Eine theoretische Studie zur praktischen Anwendung des internationalen Transportrechts, besonders der CMR, in Festschrift für Ulrich Drobnig zum siebzigsten Geburtstag, Mohr Siebeck, Tübingen 1998, 19-38.

BERAUDO J.P., Los Principios de UNIDROIT como instrumento para interpretar o suplementar textos internacionales de derecho uniforme o textos de derecho interno,

UNIDROIT (ed.), The UNIDROIT Principles: a Common Law of Contracts for the Americas?, 1998, 235-238.

BERGER, K.P., The Creeping Codification of the *Lex Mercatoria*, Kluwer Law International, The Hague – London – Boston, 1999.

BERGER, K.P., The relationship between the UNIDROIT Principles of International Commercial Contracts and the new lex mercatoria, in Uniform Law Review / Revue de droit uniforme, 2000, 153-170.

BLASE F., Die Grundregeln des Europäischen Vertragsrechts als Recht grenzüberschreitender Verträge, in Quadis Publishing, Münster 2001.

BLASE F., Proposing a New Road Map for an Old Minefield. The Determination of the Rules Governing the Substance of the Dispute in International Commercial Arbitration, in 20 Journal of International Arbitration 2003, 267 *et seq.*

BÖCKSTIEGEL K.-H., The Application of the UNIDROIT Principles to Contracts Involving States or Intergovernmental Organizations, in ICC International Court of Arbitration Bulletin, 2002, Special Supplement, 51 – 55.

BOELE-WOELKI K., Terms of Coexistence: the CISG and the UNIDROIT Principles, in: SARCEVIC, P. - VOLKEN, P. (eds.), The International Sale of Goods Revisited, Kluwer Law International, The Hague 2001, 203-240.

BOELE-WOELKI K., Die Anwendung der UNIDROIT-Principles auf internationale Handelsverträge, in Praxis des Internationalen Privat- und Verfahrensrecht, 1997, 161-171.

BOELE-WOELKI K., Principles and Private International Law: The UNIDROIT Principles of International Commercial Contracts and the Principles of European Contract Law: How to apply them to international contracts, in 1 Uniform Law Review n. 4, 1996, 652-678.

BOELE-WOELKI K., Principles en IPR. Enkele beschouwingen over de toepassing van de UNIDROIT Principles of International Commercial Contracts en de Principles of European Contract Law op internationale overeenkomsten, Koninklijke Vermande, Lelystad 1995.

BOGGIANO A., La Convention interaméricaine sur la loi applicable aux contrats internationaux et les Principes d' UNIDROIT, in 1 Uniform Law Review / Revue de droit uniforme, n. 2, 1996, 219-228.

BONELL M.J., An International Restatement of Contract Law. The UNIDROIT Principles of International Commercial Contracts, 3rd ed., Transnational Publications Inc., Ardsley (New York), 2005, at 68 – 82, 173 – 261.

BONELL M.J., UNIDROIT Principles 2004 – A Further Step Towards a Global Contract Law, in Uniform Commercial Code Law Journal, 2004, 49 – 90.

BONELL M.J., Responsabilità precontrattuale, Convenzione di Bruxelles sulla competenza giurisdizionale e l'esecuzione delle sentenze e ... Principi UNIDROIT (Corte di Giustizia, 17 settembre 2002), in Diritto del commercio internazionale, 17 (2003), 169 – 191.

BONELL M.J., The UNIDROIT Principles as a Means of Intepreting and Supplementing International Uniform Law, in ICC International Court of Arbitration Bulletin, 2002, Special Supplement, 29 – 38.

BONELL M.J., The UNIDROIT Principles and Transnational Law, in: BERGER, K.P., The Practice of Transnational Law, Kluwer Law International, The Hague 2001, 23-41.

BONELL M.J., A 'Global' arbitration decided on the basis of the UNIDROIT Principles: in re Andersen Consulting Business Unit Member Firms v. Arthur Andersen Business Unit Member Firms and Andersen Worldwide Société Coopérative, in 17 Arbitration International 2001, 249 – 261.

BONELL M.J., The UNIDROIT Principles of International Commercial Contracts and the harmonisation of international sales law, in FLETCHER I. / MISTELIS, L. /CREMONA, M. (Eds.), Foundations and Perspectives of International Trade Law, London, Sweet and Maxwell, 2001, 298 – 309.

BONELL M.J., UNIDROIT Principles of International Commercial Contracts and CISG: Alternatives or Complementary Instruments?, in 24 International Sales 1999, 9-14; Business Law International, n. 2, 2000, 89-98.

BONELL M.J., UNIDROIT Principles: a significant recognition by a United States District Court, in Uniform Law Review / Revue de droit uniforme 1999, 651 – 663.

BONELL M.J., UNIDROIT Principles and the *Lex Mercatoria*, in Carbonneau T.E. (ed.), *Lex Mercatoria* and Arbitration, Juris Publ., Kluwer Law International, 1998, 249-255.

BONELL M.J., The UNIDROIT Principles of International Commercial Contracts and the Vienna Sales Convention (CISG): Alternative or Complementary Instruments?, in 1 Uniform Law Review / Revue de droit uniforme, n. 1, 1996, 26-39.

BORJAS HERNANDEZ L., Los Principios de UNIDROIT: ¿Un modelo posible con miras a la armonización del derecho de los contratos comerciales internacionales en el contexto de la integración regional en las Américas?, in UNIDROIT (ed.), The UNIDROIT Principles: a Common Law of Contracts for the Americas?, 1998, 137-145.

BORTOLOTTI F., Reference to the UNIDROIT Principles in Contract Practice and Model Contracts, in ICC International Court of Arbitration Bulletin, 2005 Special Supplement, 57 – 64.

BORTOLOTTI F., Manuale di diritto commerciale internazionale, I, Diritto dei contratti internazionali, 2 ed., CEDAM 2001, 73 – 98.

BRIDGE, M., The UK Sale of Goods Act, the CISG and the UNIDROIT Principles, in: SARCEVIC, P. - VOLKEN, P. (eds.), The International Sale of Goods Revisited, Kluwer Law International, The Hague 2001, 115-155.

BRÖDERMANN E., Dier erweiterten UNIDROIT Principles 2004, in Recht der Internationalen Wirtshaft 2004, 721 – 735.

BURKART F., Interpretatives Zusammenwirken von CISG und UNIDROIT Principles, Baden-Baden, Nomos Verlagsgesellschaft, 2000, xxvii – 314.

CANARIS, C. W., Die Stellung der "UNIDROIT Principles" und der "Principles of European Contract Law" im System der Rechtsquellen, in BASEDOW, J. (ed.), Europäische Vertragsrechtsvereinheitlichung und deutsches Recht, J. C. B. Mohr (Siebeck), Tübingen 2000, 5 – 31.

DA GAMA E SOUZA JR., The UNIDROIT Principles of International Commercial Contracts and Their Applicability in the MERCOSUR Countries, in Les Principes d'UNIDROIT et les contrats internationaux: aspect pratiques, in Revue Juridique Thémis, vol. 36, no. 2 (2002), 375 – 419.

DARANKOUM E.S., L'application des Principes d'UNIDROIT par les arbitres internationaux et par les juges étatiques, in Les Principes d'UNIDROIT et les contrats internationaux: aspect pratiques, in Revue Juridique Thémis, vol. 36, no. 2 (2002), 421 – 480.

DE LY F., Choice of law clauses, UNIDROIT Principles of International Commercial Contracts and Article 3 Rome Convention: The *lex mercatoria* before domestic courts or arbitration privilege?, in Etudes offertes à Barthélemy Mercadal, Paris 2002, 133 – 145.

DESSEMONTET F., Use of the UNIDROIT Principles to Interpret and Supplement Domestic Law, in ICC International Court of Arbitration Bulletin, 2002, Special Supplement, 39 – 50.

DROBNIG U., The UNIDROIT Principles in the Conflict of Laws, in Uniform Law Review / Revue de droit uniforme, 1998, 385-395.

DROBNIG U., The Use of the UNIDROIT Principles by National and Supranational Courts, in Institute of International Business Law and Practice (ed.), UNIDROIT Principles for International Commercial Contracts: A New Lex Mercatoria?, ICC Publication n. 490/1, 1995, 223-232.

ENDERLEIN F., The UNIDROIT Principles as a Means for the Interpretation of International Uniform Laws (paper presented at the Bi-annual 25th Conference of the International Bar Association held in Melbourne on 9-14 October 1994).

FARNSWORTH E.A., The Role of the UNIDROIT Principles in International Commercial Arbitration (2): A US Perspective on Their Aims and Application, in ICC International Court of Arbitration Bulletin, 2002, Special Supplement, 21 – 28.

FERNANDEZ-ARMESTO J., NOTE on Separate Arbitral Award rendered in 2001 in SCC case 117/1999, in Stockholm Arbitration Report, 2001:1, 71 – 82.

FERRARI F., General Principles and International Uniform Commercial Law Conventions: A Study of the 1980 Vienna Sales Convention and the 1988 UNIDROIT Conventions on International Factoring and Leasing and the UNIDROIT Principles in 1 European Journal of Law Reform, n. 3, 1998-1999, 217-241.

FERRARI F., Das Verhältnis zwischen den UNIDROIT-Grundsätzen und den allgemeinen Grundsätzen internationaler Einheitsprivatrecht-konvention, in Juristenzeitung, n. 1, 1998, 9-17.

FERRARI F., Le champ d'application des principes pour les contrats commerciaux internationaux élaborés par UNIDROIT, in Revue internationale de droit comparé, n. 4, 1996, 986 *et seq.*

FERRARI F., I "Principi per i contratti commerciali internazionali" dell' UNIDROIT ed il loro ambito di applicazione, in Contratto e impresa / Europa, 1996, 297 *et seq.*

FERRARI F., Defining the Sphere of Application of the 1994 "UNIDROIT Principles of International Commercial Contracts", in 69 Tulane Law Review 1995, 1225-1237.

FONTAINE M., *Ius commune* et harmonization du droit des contrats, in WIJFFELS A. (ed.), Le Code civil entre *ius commune* et droit privé européen, Bruylant 2005, 75 – 91.

FONTAINE M., The Draft OHADA Uniform Act on Contracts and the UNIDROIT Principles of International Commercial Contracts, in Uniform Law Review /Revue de droit uniforme, 9 (2004), 573 – 584.

FONTAINE M., The UNDROIT Principles: An Expression of Current Contract Practice?, in ICC International Court of Arbitration Bulletin, 2002, Special Supplement, 95 – 104

GAILLARD E., Use of General Principles of International Law in International Long-Term Contracts, in International Business Lawyers, n. 5, 1999, 214-224.

GAMA JR. L., Contratos Internacionais à luz dos Princìpios do UNIDROIT 2004: *Soft Law*, Arbitragem e Jurisdicao, Renovar (Brasil) 2006, 1- 575.

GARRO A.M., The Gap-Filling Role of the UNIDROIT Principles in International Sales Law: Some Comments on the Interplay between the Principles and CISG, in 69 Tulane Law Review 1995, 1149-1257.

GARRO A.M., Unification and Harmonization of Private Law in Latin America, in 40 American Journal of Comparative Law 1992, 587-616.

GIARDINA A., I Principi UNIDROIT quale legge regolatrice dei contratti internazionali (i Principi ed il diritto internazionale privato), in BONELL M.J. / BONELLI F. (eds.), Contratti commerciali internazionali e Principi UNIDROIT, Giuffré, Milano 1997, 55-70.

HARTKAMP A.S., The Use of the UNIDROIT Principles of International Commercial Contracts by National and Supranational Courts, in Institute of International Business Law and Practice (ed.), UNIDROIT Principles for International Commercial Contracts: A New *Lex Mercatoria*?, ICC Publication n. 490/1, 1995, 253-261.

HARTKAMP A.S., The UNIDROIT Principles for International Commercial Contracts and the United Nations Convention on Contracts for the International Sale of Goods, in Asser Institute (ed.), Comparability and Evaluation. Essays on Comparative Law, Private International Law and International Commercial Arbitration, Nijhoff Publishers 1994, 95-98.

HERBER R., "*Lex mercatoria*" und "*Principles*" – gefährliche Irrlichter im internationalen Kaufrecht, in Internationales Handelsrecht, 3 (2003), 1 – 10.

HERRE J., Utfyllnad av CISG med UNIDROIT och European Principles, in V. Hagstrøm / P. Lødrup / M. Aarbakke (eds.), Ånd og rett, Festskrift til Birger Stuevold Lassen, Universitetsforlaget, Oslo 1997.

JENKINS, S.H., Teaching Sales Law in a Global Context: the Reciprocal Influence of Domestic Sales Law (Article 2) on Private International Law (CISG & UNIDROIT) and Private International Law on Revised Article 2, in 72 Tulane Law Review, n. 6, 1998, 1925-1929.

JUENGER F.K., The *lex mercatoria* and private international law, in Uniform Law Review / Revue de droit uniforme, 2000, 171-187.

JUENGER F.K., The UNIDROIT Principles of Commercial Contracts and Inter-american Contract Choice of Law, in Contratación Internacional, Comentarios a los Principios sobre los Contratos Comerciales Internacionales del UNIDROIT, Universidad Nacional Autónoma de México, Universidad Panamericana, México 1998, 229-236.

JUENGER F.K., Contract Choice of Law in the Americas, in UNIDROIT (ed.), The UNIDROIT Principles: a Common Law of Contracts for the Americas?, 1998, 77-88.

KAHN PH., Les Principes UNIDROIT comme droit applicable aux contrats internationaux, in BONELL M.J. / BONELLI F. (eds.), Contratti commerciali internazionali e Principi UNIDROIT, Giuffré, Milano 1997, 39-53.

KEMELMAJER DE CARLUCCI, A., Adecuación de los Principios de los contratos de UNIDROIT para la armonización del régimen interno de los contratos en un Código Latinoamericano tipo, in Roma e America. Diritto Romano Comune. Rivista di diritto dell'integrazione e unificazione del diritto in Europa e in America Latina. Unificazione del diritto dei contratti in America Latina, n. 7, 1999, 231-247.

KÖHLER M., Die Haftung nach UN-Kaufrecht im Spannungsverhältnis zwischen Vertrag und Delikt, Tübingen, J.B.C. Mohr (Paul Siebeck), 2003, xv – 290.

KOZOLCHYK B. The UNIDROIT Principles as a model for the unification of the best contractual practices in the Americas, in UNIDROIT (ed.), The UNIDROIT Principles: a Common Law of Contracts for the Americas?, 1998, 93-117.

LEON STEFFENS A., Principios para contratos comerciales internacionales : Algunas consideraciones de derecho internacional privado en torno al proyecto de UNIDROIT, in BONELL M.J. / SCHIPANI S. (eds.), "Principi per i contratti commerciali internazionali" e il sistema giuridico latinoamericano, Padova 1996, 45-50.

LEW J.D.M., The UNIDROIT Principles as *Lex Contractus* Chosen by the Parties and Withourt and Explicit Choce-of-Law Clause: The Perspective of Counsel, in ICC International Court of Arbitration Bulletin, 2002, Special Supplement, 85 – 94.

LOOKOFSKY, J., The Limits of Commercial Contract Freedom: Under the UNIDROIT Restatement and Danish Law, in The American Journal of Comparative Law, 1998, 485 – 508.

MANKOWSKI P., Überlegungen zur sach- und interessengerechten Rechtswahl für Verträge des internationalen Wirtschaftsverkehrs, in Recht der Internationalen Wirtschaft, 49 (2003), 2 – 15.

MARQUIS L., Les Principes d'UNIDROIT: synthèse et perspective, in Les Principes d'UNIDROIT et les contrats internationaux: aspects pratiques, in Revue Juridique Thémis, vol. 36, no. 2 (2002), 539 – 559.

MARRELLA F., Autonomia privata e contratti internazionali, in Contratto e impresa / Europa 2003, 823 – 868.

MARTINEZ CAZON S.N., A Practitioner's View of the Applicability of the UNIDROIT Principles of International Commercial Contracts in Interpreting International Uniform Laws (paper presented at the Bi-annual 25th Conference of the International Bar Association held in Melbourne on 9-14 October 1994).

MATHER H., Choice of law for international sales issues not resolved by the CISG, in Journal of Law and Commerce, 20 (2001) spring, 155 – 208.

MAYER P., Principes UNIDROIT et *Lex Mercatoria*, in F. FOUCHARD – L. VOGEL (eds.), L'actualité de la pensée de Berthold Goldmann, L.G.D.J., 2003, 31 – 36.

MELÉNDEZ M.A.P., Preámbulo, in Comentario a los Principios de UNIDROIT para los Contratos del Comercio International, Aranzadi, Pamplona 1999, 21-48.

MEYER O., The UNIDROIT Principles and their impact on European private law – some comments on the opinion (31 january 2002) of Advocat General L.A. Geelhoed, Court of Justice of the European Communities in case C-334/00 – Tacconi, in Uniform Law Review / Revue de droit uniforme, 7 (2002), 1222 . 1227.

MICHAELS, R., Privatautonomie und Privatkodification. Zu Anwendbarkeit und Geltung allgemeiner Vertragsrechtsprinzipien, in 62 RabelsZeitschrift, 1998, 580-626.

MOURRE A. – JOLIVET E., La réception del Principes d'UNIDROIT dans les contrats modèles de la Chambre de commerce international, in Uniform Law Review, 2004, 275 – 293 (abstract in English).

MUSTILL M.J., The Use of the UNIDROIT Principles by National and Supranational Courts (paper presented at the international colloquium on "UNIDROIT Principles of International Commercial Contracts: A New *Lex Mercatoria*?", organized by the Institute of International Business Law and Practice of the ICC in Paris, on 20-21 October 1994).

NGUYEN M.H., Les Principes UNIDROIT: Jurisprudence et expériences pour le Vietnam, in Revue de droit des affaires internationales / International Business Law, no. 5/2005, 619 *et seq*.

NGUYEN M.H., The Use of the UNIDROIT Principles by National and Supranational Courts, (paper presented at the international colloquium on "UNIDROIT Principles of International Commercial Contracts: A New *Lex Mercatoria*?", organized by the Institute of International Business Law and Practice of the ICC in Paris, on 20 – 21 October 1994).

OLAVO BAPTISTA L., The UNIDROIT Principles – a possible model for the harmonisation of international contract law in the context of the regional integration of the Americas, with special reference to MERCOSUR, in UNIDROIT (ed.), The UNIDROIT Principles: a Common Law of Contracts for the Americas?, 1998, 119-135.

OLAVO BAPTISTA L., Os "Projeto de Princìpios para Contractos comerciais internacionais" da UNIDROIT, Aspectos de direito internacional privado, in BONELL M.J. / SCHIPANI S. (eds.), "Principi per i contratti commerciali internazionali" e il sistema giuridico latinoamericano, Padova 1996, 23-33.

OLAVO BAPTISTA L., The UNIDROIT Principles for International Commercial Law Project: Aspects of International Private Law, in 69 Tulane Law Review 1995, 1209-1224.

ONNANA ETOUNDI F., Les Principes d'UNIDROIT et la sécurité juridique des transactions commerciales dans l'avant-projet d'Acte uniforme OHADA sur le droit des contrats, in Uniform Law Review, 2005, 683 – 716.

OPERTTI BADÁN D., El estado actual del tratamiento jurídico de los contratos internacionales en el continente americano, in UNIDROIT (ed.), The UNIDROIT Principles: a Common Law of Contracts for the Americas?, 1998, 29-75.

PARRA-ARANGUREN G., El proyeto de "Principios" de UNIDROIT: Aspectos de derecho internacional privado, in BONELL M.J. / SCHIPANI S. (eds.), "Principi per i contratti commerciali internazionali" e il sistema giuridico latinoamericano, Padova 1996, 35-43.

PARRA-ARANGUREN G., Conflict of Law Aspects of the UNIDROIT Principles of International Commercial Contracts, in 69 Tulane Law Review, n. 5, 1995, 1239-1252.

PARRA-ARANGUREN G., Aspectos de Derecho Internacional Privado de los Principios para los contratos mercantiles internacionales elaborados por el UNIDROIT, in Revista de la Facultad de Ciencias Jurìdicas y Polìticas de la Universidad Central de Venezuela 1994, 167-180.

PELEGGI R., L'applicazione dei Principi UNIDROIT *en voie directe* alla luce di un recente lodo della Corte Arbitrale della Camera di Commercio Internazionale, in Diritto del commercio internazionale, 2004, 483 – 507.

PERALES VISCASILLAS M., Los Principios de UNIDROIT como objeto y como instrumento de interpretación, in UNIDROIT (ed.), The UNIDROIT Principles: a Common Law of Contracts for the Americas?, 1998, 303-309.

PERALES VISCASILLAS M., Los Principios de UNIDROIT y CISG: su mutua interacción, in Contratación internacional, Comentarios a los principios sobre los Contratos Comerciales Internacionales del UNIDROIT, Universidad Nacional Autónoma de México – Universidad Panamericana (ed.) 1998, 187-208.

PERALES VISCASILLAS P., El derecho uniforme del Comercio Internacional: los Principios de UNIDROIT (Ámbito de aplicación y Disposiciones Generales), in Revista de derecho mercantil 1997, 221-297.

PERALES VISCASILLAS P., UNIDROIT Principles of International Commercial Contracts: Sphere of Application and General Provisions, in 13 Arizona Journal of International and Comparative Law 1996, 383-441.

PEREZNIETO CASTRO L., Los Principios de UNIDROIT y la Convención Interamericana sobre el Derecho Aplicable a los Contratos, in Contratación internacional, Comentarios a los principios sobre los Contratos Comerciales Internacionales del UNIDROIT, Universidad Nacional Autónoma de México – Universidad Panamericana (ed.) 1998, 209-216.

PRUJINER A., Comme utiliser les Principes d'UNIDROIT dans la pratique contractuelle, in Les Principes d'UNIDROIT et les contrats internationaux: aspects pratiques, in Revue Juridique Thémis, vol. 36, no. 2 (2002), 561 – 582.

RIPPE S., Problemas de Derecho Internacional Privado en materia de contratos comerciales internacionales, con especial referencia a la aplicabilidad imperativa de los Principios del Proyecto UNIDROIT en los Estados partes del MERCOSUR, in BONELL M.J. / SCHIPANI S. (eds.), "Principi per i contratti commerciali internazionali" e il sistema giuridico latinoamericano, Padova 1996, 51-57.

SAMTLEBEN, J., Versuch über die Konvention von Mexico über das auf internationale Schuldverträge anwendbare Recht, in IPRax, n. 5, 1998.

SCHILF S., Allgemeine Vertragsgrundregeln als Vertragsstatut, Mohr Siebeck 2005, vii–451.

SCHIPANI S., Los Principios de UNIDROIT en America, el derecho común y la asimetría estructural entre las partes en la contratación internacional entre Norte y Sur, in

UNIDROIT (ed.), The UNIDROIT Principles: a Common Law of Contracts for the Americas?, 1998, 251-259.

SETO HARDJOWAHONO B., The UNIDROIT Principles and the law governing commercial contracts in Southeast Asia, in Uniform Law Review / Revue de droit uniforme, 7 (2002), 1005 – 1015.

SINCLAIR A., Using the UNIDROIT Principles of International Commercial Contracts in International Commercial Arbitration, in International Arbitration Law Review, no. 6/2003, 65 – 74.

SIQUEIROS J.L., Los Principios de UNIDROIT y la Convención Interamericana Sobre el Derecho Aplicable a los Contratos Internacionales, in Contratación internacional, Comentarios a los principios sobre los Contratos Comerciales Internacionales del UNIDROIT, Universidad Nacional Autónoma de México – Universidad Panamericana (ed.) 1998, 217-228.

TALLON D., L'application des Principies UNIDROIT par les tribunaux étatiques, in Institute of International Business Law and Practice (ed.), UNIDROIT Principles for International Commercial Contracts: A New *Lex Mercatoria*?, ICC Publication n. 490/1, 1995, 243-249.

TALPIS J.A., Retour vers le futur: application en droit québécois des Principes d'UNIDROIT au lieu d'une loi nationale, in Les Principes d'UNIDROIT et les contrats internationaux: aspects pratiques, in Revue Juridique Thémis, vol. 36, no. 2 (2002), 609 – 622.

TRAISCI F.P., Principi UNIDROIT, *lex mercatoria* e diritto del commercio internazionale: note a margine di un lodo arbitrale, in Diritto del commercio internazionale, n. 2, 1999, 474 – 494.

VENEZIANO, A., L'application des Principes d' UNIDROIT dans la vente internationale (en francais et en anglais), in: Revue de droit des affaires internationales 2001, 477-488.

VEYTIA H., Los Principios ante la problemática de la ley aplicable a los contratos mercantiles en materia internacional, in BONELL M.J. / SCHIPANI S. (eds.), "Principi per i contratti commerciali internazionali" e il sistema giuridico latinoamericano, Padova 1996, 59-67.

VISHER F., Die kollisionrechtliche Bedeutung der Wahl einer nichtstaatlichen Ordnung für den staatlichen Richter am Beispiel der UNIDROIT Principles of International Commercial Contracts, in SCHWENZER I. – HAGER G. (eds.) – Festschrift für Peter Schlechtriem zum 70. Geburtstag, Tübingen, J.B.C. Mohr (Paul Siebeck), 2003, 445 – 454.

VISCHER F., The Relevance of the UNIDROIT Principles for Judges and Arbitrators in Disputes Arising out of International Contracts, in 1, European Journal of Law Reform, n. 3, 1998-1999, 203-216.

VULLIETY J.-P., Le contrat-type pour les joint ventures contractuelles du Centre du commerce international au regard des Principes d'UNIDROIT et d'autres nromes d'unification du droit des contrats (abstract in English), in Uniform Law Review, 2004, 295 – 314.

WICHARD J., Die Anwendung der UNIDROIT-Prinzipien für internationale Handelsverträge durch Schiedsgerichte und staatliche Gerichte, in 60 RabelsZeitschrift, 1996, 269-302

ZIEGEL J.S., The UNIDROIT Contract Principles, CISG and National Law, in UNIDROIT (ed.), The UNIDROIT Principles: a Common Law of Contracts for the Americas?, 1998, 221-233.

CHAPTER 1
GENERAL PROVISIONS

BIBLIOGRAPHY

BARCELLONA M., La buona fede e il controllo giudiziale del contratto, in MAZZAMUTO S. (ed.), Il contratto e le tutele. Prospettive di diritto europeo, Torino, G. Giappichelli Editore, 2002, 305 – 331.

BONELL M.J., Soft Law and Party Autonomy: The Case of the UNIDROIT Principles, in 51 Loyola Law Review (2005), 229 – 252.

BONELL M.J., An International Restatement of Contract Law. The UNIDROIT Principles of International Commercial Contracts, 3rd ed., Transnational Publications Inc., Ardsley, New York, 2005, at 88 – 96, 97 – 102, 127 – 151.

BRASSEUR P., in FONTAINE, M. (ed.), Le processus de formation du contrat. Bruylant, Bruxelles, 2002, 619-622.

CHARPENTIER E., L'émergence d'un ordre public ... privé: une présentation des Principes d'UNIDROIT, in Les Principes d'UNIDROIT et les contrats internationaux: aspects pratiques, in Revue Juridique Thémis, vol. 36, no. 2 (2002), 355 – 419.

DI MAJO A., L'osservanza della buona fede nei Principi UNIDROIT sui contratti commerciali internazionali, in BONELL M.J./BONELLI F. (eds.), Contratti commerciali internazionali e Principi UNIDROIT, Giuffrè, Milano 1997, 143-160.

FARNSWORTH E.A., Duties of Good Faith and Liability for Bad Faith Under the UNIDROIT Principles, Relevant International Conventions and National Laws, in 3 Tulane Journal of International and Comparative Law, n. 1/2, 1994, 47-63.

FERRI G.B., Il ruolo dell'autonomia delle parti e la rilevanza degli usi nei Principi UNIDROIT, in BONELL M.J. / BONELLI F. (eds.), Contratti commerciali internazionali e Principi UNIDROIT, Giuffrè, Milano 1997, 123-141.

FONTAINE M., Du droit "mou" ... impératif?, Etudes offertes à Barthélemy Mercadal, Paris, 2002, 159 – 167.

GAUTRAIS V., Les Principes d'UNIDROIT face au contrat électronique, in Les Principes d'UNIDROIT et les contrats internationaux: aspects pratiques, in Revue Juridique Thémis, Vol. 36, no. 2 (2002), 481 – 517.

GUTIERREZ FALLA L.F., Good Faith in Commercial Law and the UNIDROIT Principles of International Commercial Contracts, in PennState International Law Review, vol 23 (2005), 507 – 520.

HARTKAMP A.S., The Concept of Good Faith in the UNIDROIT Principles for International Commercial Contracts, in 3 Tulane Journal of International and Comparative Law, n.1/2, 1994, 65-71.

HESSELINK M.W., De goede trouw bij de uitvoering van de overeenkomst in het Franse recht, de UNIDROIT Principles en de Principles of European Contract Law, in F.W. GROSHEIDE / K. BOELE-WOELKI (eds.), Europees Privaatrecht, Molengrafica, Koninklijke Vermande BV, Lelystad 1995, 47-95.

JUENGER F.K., Listening to Law Professors Talk About Good Faith, in 69 Tulane Law Review, n. 5, 1995, 1253-1257.

LANDO O., The Role of Party Autonomy and the Relevance of Usages, in BONELL M.J. / BONELLI F. (eds.), Contratti commerciali internazionali e Principi UNIDROIT, Giuffré, Milano 1997, 107-122.

LANDO O., The CISG and the UNIDROIT Principles in a Global Commercial Code, in Mélanges offerts à Marcel Fontaine, Paris, Larcier, 2003, 451 – 472.

LOOKOFSKY J., The Limits of Commercial Contract Freedom: Under the UNIDROIT Restatement and Danish Law, in The American Journal of Comparative Law, 1998, 485 – 508.

MARRELLA F., Autonomia privata e contratti internazionali, in Contratto e impresa / Europa 2003, 823 – 867.

MELÉNDEZ M.A.P., Disposiciones generales, in Comentario a los Principios de UNIDROIT para los Contratos del Comercio Internacional, Aranzadi, Pamplona, 1999, 49 – 96.

MOREIRA ALVES J.C., Comentário sobre o artigo 1.6 do Projeto UNIDROIT sobre Princípios aplicáveis aos contratos internacionais, in BONELL M.J. / SCHIPANI S. (eds.), "Principi per i contratti commerciali internazionali" e il sistema giuridico latinoamericano, Padova 1996, 75-78.

PAES BARROS DE LEAES L.G., Notas sobre Boa-Fè e Lealdade negocial, in BONELL M.J. / SCHIPANI S. (eds.), "Principi per i contratti commerciali internazionali" e il sistema giuridico latinoamericano, Padova 1996, 71-73.

PERALES VISCASILLAS P., El derecho uniforme del Comercio Internacional: los Principios de UNIDROIT (Ámbito de aplicación y Disposiciones Generales), in Revista de derecho mercantil 1997, 221-297.

PERALES VISCASILLAS P., UNIDROIT Principles of International Commercial Contracts: Sphere of Application and General Provisions, in 13 Arizona Journal of International and Comparative Law, 1996, 383-441.

ROBIN G., Le principe de la bonne foi dans les contrats internationaux, in Revue de droit des affaires internationales / International Business Law, no. 6/2005, 659 – 727.

ROBIN G., Le principe de la bonne foi dans les contrats internationaux, in Centro di studi e ricerche di diritto comparato e straniero (ed.), Saggi, conferenze e seminari, n. 24, Roma 1997.

SCHLECHTRIEM P., Good faith in German Law and in International Uniform Laws, in Centro di studi e ricerche di diritto comparato e straniero (ed.), Saggi, conferenze e seminari, n. 24, Roma 1997.

VEYTIA H., El capítulo uno de los Principios del UNIDROIT: "Disposiciones generales", in Contratación internacional, Comentarios a los principios sobre los Contratos Comerciales Internacionales del UNIDROIT, Universidad Nacional Autónoma de México – Universidad Panamericana (ed.) 1998, 33-52.

WEIDEMANN C., Lückenergänzung und richterliche Fortbildung nach Art. 1.6. II der UNIDROIT-Principles for International Commercial Contracts. Methode und Beispiele: Rückgewährschuldverhältnisse, postvertragliche Pflichten, objektive Beweislast. Europäische Hochschulschriften, Reihe II, Rechtswissenschaft, 3213, Frankfurt a. M. 2001.

ARTICLE 1.1
(Freedom of contract)

The parties are free to enter into a contract and to determine its content.

COMMENT

1. Freedom of contract as a basic principle in the context of international trade

The principle of freedom of contract is of paramount importance in the context of international trade. The right of business people to decide freely to whom they will offer their goods or services and by whom they wish to be supplied, as well as the possibility for them freely to agree on the terms of individual transactions, are the cornerstones of an open, market-oriented and competitive international economic order.

2. Economic sectors where there is no competition

There are of course a number of possible exceptions to the principle laid down in the present article.

As concerns the freedom to conclude contracts with any other person, there are economic sectors which States may decide in the public interest to exclude from open competition. In such cases the goods or services in question can only be requested from the one available supplier, which will usually be a public body, and which may or may not be under a duty to conclude a contract with whoever makes a request, within the limits of the availability of the goods or services.

3. Limitation of party autonomy by mandatory rules

With respect to the freedom to determine the content of the contract, in the first instance the Principles themselves contain provisions from which the parties may not derogate. See Art. 1.5.

Moreover, there are both public and private law rules of mandatory character enacted by States (*e.g.* anti-trust, exchange control or price laws; laws imposing special liability regimes or prohibiting grossly unfair contract terms, etc.), which may prevail over the rules contained in the Principles. See Art. 1.4.

Issues & Cases

1. FREEDOM OF CONTRACT AS A BASIC PRINCIPLE IN INTERNATIONAL TRADE

1.1 FREEDOM TO CONCLUDE CONTRACT WITH ANY OTHER PERSON
- 1.1.1 ECONOMIC SECTORS EXCLUDED FROM OPEN COMPETITION
  - 1.1.1.1 DUTY TO CONCLUDE A CONTRACT WITH WHOEVER MAKES A REQUEST

1.2 FREEDOM TO DETERMINE THE CONTENT OF THE CONTRACT
- SEPTEMBER 4, 1996 ARBITRAL AWARD ICC INTERNATIONAL COURT OF ARBITRATION (NO. 8540) [636]
- 1.2.1 LIMITATION BY MANDATORY RULES
  - 1.2.1.1 MANDATORY RULES PROVIDED BY PRINCIPLES (SEE ART. 1.5)
  - 1.2.1.2 MANDATORY RULES PROVIDED BY THE LAW APPLICABLE TO THE CONTRACT (SEE ART. 1.4)

ARTICLE 1.2
(No form required)

Nothing in these Principles requires a contract, statement or any other act to be made in or evidenced by a particular form. It may be proved by any means, including witnesses.

COMMENT

1. Contracts as a rule not subject to formal requirements

This article states the principle that the conclusion of a contract is not subject to any requirement as to form. The same principle also applies to the subsequent modification or termination of a contract by agreement of the parties.

The principle, which is to be found in many, although not in all, legal systems, seems particularly appropriate in the context of international trade relationships where, thanks to modern means of communication, many transactions are concluded at great speed and by a mixture of conversations, telefaxes, paper contracts, e-mail and web communication.

The first sentence of the article takes into account the fact that some legal systems regard formal requirements as matters relating to substance, while others impose them for evidentiary purposes only. The second sentence is intended to make it clear that to the extent that the principle of freedom of form applies, it implies the admissibility of oral evidence in judicial proceedings.

2. Statements and other unilateral acts

The principle of no requirement as to form applies also to statements and other unilateral acts. The most important such acts are statements of intent made by parties either in the course of the formation or performance of a contract (*e.g.* an offer, acceptance of an offer, confirmation of the contract by the party entitled to avoid it, determination of the price by one of the parties, etc.), or in other contexts (*e.g.* the grant of authority by a principal to an agent, the ratification by a principal of an act performed by an agent without authority, the obligor's acknowledgement of the obligee's right before the expiration of the general limitation period, etc.).

3. Possible exceptions under the applicable law

The principle of no requirement as to form may of course be overridden by the applicable law. See Art. 1.4. National laws as well as international instruments may impose special requirements as to form with respect either to the contract as a whole or to individual terms (*e.g.* arbitration agreements; jurisdiction clauses).

4. Form requirements agreed by the parties

Moreover, the parties may themselves agree on a specific form for the conclusion, modification or termination of their contract or for any other statement they may make or unilateral act they may perform in the course of the formation or performance of their contract or in any other context. In this connection see, in particular, Arts. 2.1.13, 2.1.17 and 2.1.18.

Issues & Cases

1. IN GENERAL NO PARTICULAR FORM REQUIRED
   - DECEMBER 4, 1996 ARBITRAL AWARD AD HOC ARBITRATION, ROME [664]

   1.1 FOR SUBSTANTIVE PURPOSES

   1.2 FOR EVIDENTIARY PURPOSES

      1.2.1 ADMISSIBILITY OF ALL EVIDENCE, INCLUDING TESTIMONY BY WITNESSES

2. PARTICULAR FORM REQUIRED EXCEPTIONALLY

   2.1 BY DOMESTIC LAW

   2.2 BY INTERNATIONAL INSTRUMENTS

   2.3 BY CONTRACTUAL AGREEMENT (SEE ARTS. 2.1.13, 2.1.17, 2.1.18)

ARTICLE 1.3
(Binding character of contract)

A contract validly entered into is binding upon the parties. It can only be modified or terminated in accordance with its terms or by agreement or as otherwise provided in these Principles.

COMMENT

1. The principle *pacta sunt servanda*

This article lays down another basic principle of contract law, that of *pacta sunt servanda.*

The binding character of a contractual agreement obviously presupposes that an agreement has actually been concluded by the parties and that the agreement reached is not affected by any ground of invalidity. The rules governing the conclusion of contractual agreements are laid down in Chapter 2 Section 1 of the Principles, while the grounds of invalidity are dealt with in Chapter 3, as well as in individual provisions in other chapters (see, *e.g.*, Arts. 7.1.6 and 7.4.13(2)). Additional requirements for the valid conclusion of contracts may be found in the applicable national or international mandatory rules.

2. Exceptions

A corollary of the principle of *pacta sunt servanda* is that a contract may be modified or terminated whenever the parties so agree. Modification or termination without agreement are on the contrary the exception and can therefore be admitted only when in conformity with the terms of the contract or when expressly provided for in the Principles. See Arts. 3.10(2), 3.10(3), 3.13, 5.1.8, 6.1.16, 6.2.3, 7.1.7, 7.3.1 and 7.3.3.

3. Effects on third persons

By stating the principle of the binding force of the contract between the parties, this article does not intend to prejudice any effect which that contract may have vis-à-vis third persons under the applicable law. Thus, a seller may in some jurisdictions be under a contractual duty to protect the physical integrity and property not only of the buyer, but also of accompanying persons during their presence on the seller's premises.

Similarly the Principles do not deal with the effects of avoidance and termination of a contract on the rights of third persons.

With respect to cases where the agreement between the parties by its very nature is intended to affect the legal relations of another person, see Section 2 of Chapter 2 on "Authority of Agents", Section 2 of Chapter 5 on "Third Party Rights" and Chapter 9 on "Assignment of Rights, Transfer of Obligations, Assignment of Contracts".

Issues & Cases

1. **BINDING CHARACTER OF CONTRACT**
   1.1 **IN GENERAL**
   - SEPTEMBER 4, 1996 ARBITRAL AWARD ICC INTERNATIONAL COURT OF ARBITRATION (NO. 8540) [636]
   - DECEMBER 1, 1996 ARBITRAL AWARD CAMERA ARBITRALE NAZIONALE ED INTERNAZIONALE DI MILANO (NO. A-1795/51) [662]
   - MAY, 1999 ARBITRAL AWARD ICC INTERNATIONAL COURT OF ARBITRATION (NO. 9753) [809]

   1.2 **MODIFICATION OR TERMINATION ONLY BY AGREEMENT OF THE PARTIES**
   1.2.1 **MODIFICATION**
   1.2.2 **TERMINATION**
   - JANUARY 25, 2002 ARBITRAL AWARD ARBITRATION COURT OF THE LAUSANNE CHAMBER OF COMMERCE AND INDUSTRY [991]

2. **EXCEPTIONS**
   2.1 **MODIFICATION OR TERMINATION WITHOUT AGREEMENT OF THE PARTIES**
   2.1.1 **ACCORDING TO THE TERMS OF THE CONTRACT**
   2.1.1.1 **MODIFICATION**
   2.1.1.2 **TERMINATION**
   2.1.2 **ACCORDING TO OTHER PROVISIONS OF PRINCIPLES**
   - JANUARY 25, 2002 ARBITRAL AWARD ARBITRATION COURT OF THE LAUSANNE CHAMBER OF COMMERCE AND INDUSTRY [991]

   2.1.2.1 **MODIFICATION (SEE ARTS. 3.10(2), 3.10(3), 3.13 AND 6.2.3)**
   2.1.2.2 **TERMINATION (SEE ARTS. 5.1.8, 6.1.16, 6.2.3, 7.1.7, 7.3.1 AND 7.3.3)**

3. **EFFECTS OF CONTRACT ON THIRD PERSONS OUTSIDE SCOPE OF PRINCIPLES**

ARTICLE 1.4
(Mandatory rules)

Nothing in these Principles shall restrict the application of mandatory rules, whether of national, international or supranational origin, which are applicable in accordance with the relevant rules of private international law.

COMMENT

1. Mandatory rules prevail

Given the particular nature of the Principles, they cannot be expected to prevail over applicable mandatory rules, whether of national, international or supranational origin. In other words, mandatory provisions, whether enacted by States autonomously or to implement international conventions, or adopted by supranational entities, cannot be overruled by the Principles.

2. Mandatory rules applicable in the event of mere incorporation of the Principles in the contract

In cases where the parties' reference to the Principles is considered to be only an agreement to incorporate them in the contract, the Principles will first of all encounter the limit of the mandatory rules of the law governing the contract, *i.e.* they will bind the parties only to the extent that they do not affect the rules of the applicable law from which parties may not contractually derogate. In addition, the mandatory rules of the forum, and possibly also those of third States, will likewise prevail, provided that they claim application whatever the law governing the contract and, in the case of the rules of third States, there is a close connection between those States and the contract in question.

3. Mandatory rules applicable if the Principles are the law governing the contract

Yet, even where, as may be the case if the dispute is brought before an arbitral tribunal, the Principles are applied as the law governing the contract, they cannot prejudice the application of those mandatory rules which claim application irrespective of which law is applicable to the contract (*lois d'application nécessaire*). Examples of such internationally mandatory rules, the application of which cannot be excluded simply by choosing another law, are to be found in the field of foreign exchange regulations (see Article VIII(2)(b) of the *Agreement of the International Monetary Fund, (Bretton Woods*

Agreement)), import-export licences (see Arts. 6.1.14 - 6.1.17 on public permission requirements), regulations pertaining to restrictive trade practices, etc.

4. Recourse to the rules of private international law relevant in each individual case

Both courts and arbitral tribunals differ considerably in the way in which they determine the mandatory rules applicable to international commercial contracts. For this reason the present article deliberately refrains from entering into the merit of the various questions involved, in particular whether in addition to the mandatory rules of the forum and of the *lex contractus* those of third States are also to be taken into account and if so, to what extent and on the basis of which criteria. These questions are to be settled in accordance with the rules of private international law which are relevant in each particular case (see, for instance, Art. 7 of the *1980 Rome Convention on the Law applicable to Contractual Obligations*; Art. 11 of the *1994 Inter-American Convention on the Law Applicable to International Contracts*).

Issues & Cases

1. MANDATORY RULES PREVAILING OVER PRINCIPLES
   - 1.1 NATIONAL MANDATORY RULES
   - 1.2 INTERNATIONAL MANDATORY RULES
   - 1.3 SUPRANATIONAL MANDATORY RULES
2. MANDATORY RULES APPLICABLE IF PRINCIPLES ARE INCORPORATED IN THE CONTRACT
   - 2.1 MANDATORY RULES OF THE LAW GOVERNING THE CONTRACT
     - -- ARBITRAL AWARD AD HOC ARBITRATION (PLACE UNKNOWN) [544]
3. MANDATORY RULES APPLICABLE IF PRINCIPLES ARE APPLIED AS RULES OF LAW GOVERNING THE CONTRACT
   - 3.1 MANDATORY RULES TO BE APPLIED IRRESPECTIVE OF THE LAW GOVERNING THE CONTRACT (LOIS D'APPLICATION NÉCESSAIRE) (SEE ALSO ARTS. 6.1.14 – 6.1.17)
     - 3.1.1 ORDER PUBLIC OF THE FORUM STATE
     - 3.1.2 MANDATORY RULES OF THIRD STATES
       - 3.1.2.1 FOREIGN EXCHANGE REGULATIONS
       - 3.1.2.2 IMPORT-EXPORT LICENSES REGULATIONS
       - 3.1.2.3 RESTRICTIVE TRADE PRACTICES REGULATIONS

ARTICLE 1.5
(Exclusion or modification by the parties)

The parties may exclude the application of these Principles or derogate from or vary the effect of any of their provisions, except as otherwise provided in the Principles.

COMMENT

1. The non-mandatory character of the Principles

The rules laid down in the Principles are in general of a non-mandatory character, *i.e.* the parties may in each individual case either simply exclude their application in whole or in part or modify their content so as to adapt them to the specific needs of the kind of transaction involved. See the Model Clause in the footnote to the second paragraph of the Preamble.

2. Exclusion or modification may be express or implied

The exclusion or modification of the Principles by the parties may be either express or implied. There is an implied exclusion or modification when the parties expressly agree on contract terms which are inconsistent with provisions of the Principles and it is in this context irrelevant whether the terms in question have been negotiated individually or form part of standard terms incorporated by the parties in their contract.

If the parties expressly agree to the application of some only of the chapters of the Principles (*e.g.* "As far as the performance and non-performance of this contract is concerned, the UNIDROIT Principles shall apply"), it is presumed that the chapters concerned will be applied together with the general provisions of Chapter 1.

3. Mandatory provisions to be found in the Principles

A few provisions of the Principles are of a mandatory character, *i.e.* their importance in the system of the Principles is such that parties should not be permitted to exclude or to derogate from them as they wish. It is true that given the particular nature of the Principles the non-observance of this precept may have no consequences. On the other hand, it should be noted that the provisions in question reflect principles and standards of behaviour which are of a mandatory character under most domestic laws also.

Those provisions of the Principles which are mandatory are normally expressly indicated as such. This is the case with Art. 1.7 on good faith and fair dealing, with the provisions of Chapter 3 on substantive validity, except in so far as they relate or apply to mistake and to initial impossibility (see Art. 3.19), with Art. 5.1.7(2) on price determination, with Art. 7.4.13(2) on agreed payment for non-performance and Art. 10.3(2) on limitation periods. Exceptionally, the mandatory character of a provision is only implicit and follows from the content and purpose of the provision itself (see, *e.g.*, Arts. 1.8 and 7.1.6).

Issues & Cases

1. NON-MANDATORY CHARACTER OF PRINCIPLES
2. TOTAL EXCLUSION OF PRINCIPLES
   - 2.1 EXPRESS EXCLUSION
     - 2.1.1 REQUIREMENTS FOR EXCLUSION AGREEMENT
   - 2.2 IMPLIED EXCLUSION
     - 2.2.1 PARTIES' AGREEMENT ON CONTRACT TERMS INCONSISTENT WITH PRINCIPLES' PROVISIONS
       - 2.2.1.1 CONTRACT TERMS INDIVIDUALLY NEGOTIATED
       - 2.2.1.2 STANDARD TERMS
3. PARTIAL EXCLUSION OF PRINCIPLES
   - 3.1 EXPRESS DEROGATION
   - 3.2 IMPLIED DEROGATION
   - 3.3 MANDATORY PROVISION OF PRINCIPLES

ARTICLE 1.6

(Interpretation and supplementation of the Principles)

(1) In the interpretation of these Principles, regard is to be had to their international character and to their purposes including the need to promote uniformity in their application.

(2) Issues within the scope of these Principles but not expressly settled by them are as far as possible to be settled in accordance with their underlying general principles.

COMMENT

1. Interpretation of the Principles as opposed to interpretation of the contract

The Principles, like any other legal text, be it of a legislative or of a contractual nature, may give rise to doubts as to the precise meaning of their content. The interpretation of the Principles is however different from that of the individual contracts to which they apply. Even if the Principles are considered to bind the parties only at contractual level, *i.e.* their application is made dependent on their incorporation in individual contracts, they remain an autonomous set of rules worked out with a view to their application in a uniform manner to an indefinite number of contracts of different types entered into in various parts of the world. As a consequence they must be interpreted in a different manner from the terms of each individual contract. The rules for the interpretation of contracts (as well as of statements by or other conduct of the parties) are laid down in Chapter 4. The present article deals with the manner in which the Principles as such are to be interpreted.

2. Regard to the international character of the Principles

The first criterion laid down by this article for the interpretation of the Principles is that regard is to be had to their "international character". This means that their terms and concepts are to be interpreted autonomously, *i.e.* in the context of the Principles themselves and not by reference to the meaning which might traditionally be attached to them by a particular domestic law.

Such an approach becomes necessary if it is recalled that the Principles are the result of thorough comparative studies carried out by lawyers coming from totally different cultural and legal backgrounds. When drafting the individual provisions, these experts had to find sufficiently neutral legal language on which they could reach a common understanding. Even in the exceptional cases where terms or concepts peculiar to one or more national laws are employed, the intention was never to use them in their traditional meaning.

3. Purposes of the Principles

By stating that in the interpretation of the Principles regard is to be had to their purposes, this article makes it clear that they are not to be construed in a strict and literal sense but in the light of the purposes and the rationale underlying the individual provisions as well as the Principles as a whole. The purpose of the individual provisions can be ascertained both from the text itself and from the comments thereon. As to the purposes of the Principles as a whole, this article, in view of the fact that the Principles' main objective is to provide a uniform framework for international commercial contracts, expressly refers to the need to promote uniformity in their application, *i.e.* to ensure that in practice they are to the greatest possible extent interpreted and applied in the same way in different countries. As to other purposes, see the remarks contained in the Introduction. See further Art. 1.7 which, although addressed to the parties, may also be seen as an expression of the underlying purpose of the Principles as such to promote the observance of good faith and fair dealing in contractual relations.

4. Supplementation of the Principles

A number of issues which would fall within the scope of the Principles are not settled expressly by them. In order to determine whether an issue is one that falls within the scope of the Principles even though it is not expressly settled by them, or whether it actually falls outside their scope, regard is to be had first to what is expressly stated either in the text or in the comments (see, *e.g.*, comment 3 on Art. 1.3; comment 4 on Art. 1.4; Art. 2.2.1(2) and (3) and comment 5 on Art. 2.2.1; comment 5 on Art. 2.2.7; comment 5 on Art. 2.2.9; comment 1 on Art. 2.2.10; Art. 3.1; comment 1 on Art. 6.1.14; Art. 9.1.2; Art. 9.2.2; Art. 9.3.2). A useful additional guide in this respect is the subject-matter index of the Principles.

The need to promote uniformity in the application of the Principles implies that when such gaps arise a solution should be found, whenever possible, within the system of the Principles itself before resorting to domestic laws.

The first step is to attempt to settle the unsolved question through an application by analogy of specific provisions. Thus, Art. 6.1.6 on place of performance should also govern restitution. Similarly, the rules laid down in Art. 6.1.9 with respect to the case where a monetary obligation is expressed in a currency other than that of the place for payment may also be applied when the monetary obligation is expressed by reference to units of account such as the Special Drawing Right (SDR). If the issue cannot be solved by a mere extension of specific provisions dealing with analogous cases, recourse must be made to their underlying general principles, *i.e.* to the principles and rules which may be applied on a much wider scale because of their general character. Some of these fundamental principles are expressly stated in the Principles (see, *e.g.*, Arts. 1.1, 1.3, 1.5, 1.7 and 1.8). Others have to be extracted from specific provisions, *i.e.* the particular rules contained therein must be analysed in order to see whether they can be considered an expression of a more general principle, and as such capable of being applied also to cases different from those specifically regulated.

Parties are of course always free to agree on a particular national law to which reference should be made for the supplementing of the Principles. A provision of this kind could read "This contract is governed by the UNIDROIT Principles supplemented by the law of country X", or "This contract shall be interpreted and executed in accordance with the UNIDROIT Principles. Questions not expressly settled therein shall be settled in accordance with the law of country X". See the Model Clause in the footnote to the second paragraph of the Preamble.

Issues & Cases

1. **INTERPRETATION OF PRINCIPLES**
   - 1.1 **INTERPRETATION OF PRINCIPLES DISTINGUISHED FROM INTERPRETATION OF CONTRACT**
   - 1.2 **CONSIDERATION OF INTERNATIONAL CHARACTER OF PRINCIPLES**
   - 1.3 **NEED FOR UNIFORM APPLICATION OF PRINCIPLES**
   - 1.4 **PURPOSES OF PRINCIPLES**
2. **GAPS IN PRINCIPLES**
   - 2.1 **MATTERS GOVERNED BUT NOT EXPRESSLY SETTLED BY PRINCIPLES**
   - 2.2 **MATTERS EXCLUDED FROM SCOPE OF PRINCIPLES**
     - APRIL 1998 ARBITRAL AWARD (SECOND PARTIAL) ICC INTERNATIONAL COURT OF ARBITRATION (NO. 7110) [734]
     - JULY 27, 1999 ARBITRAL AWARD INTERNATIONAL ARBITRATION COURT OF THE CHAMBER OF COMMERCE AND INDUSTRY OF THE RUSSIAN FEDERATION (NO. 302/1997) [802]
   - 2.3 **METHODS FOR FILLING IN GAPS**
     - JULY 27, 1999 ARBITRAL AWARD INTERNATIONAL ARBITRATION COURT OF THE CHAMBER OF COMMERCE AND INDUSTRY OF THE RUSSIAN FEDERATION (NO. 302/1997) [802]

- AUGUST 1999 ARBITRAL AWARD (PARTIAL) ICC INTERNATIONAL COURT OF ARBITRATION (NO. 9759) [803]

2.3.1 RECOURSE TO BASIC IDEAS UNDERLYING PRINCIPLES

- JULY 27, 1999 ARBITRAL AWARD INTERNATIONAL ARBITRATION COURT OF THE CHAMBER OF COMMERCE AND INDUSTRY OF THE RUSSIAN FEDERATION (NO. 302/1997) [802]

2.3.1.1 EXAMPLES OF SUCH BASIC IDEAS

2.3.2 RECOURSE TO OTHER GENERAL PRINCIPLES OF LAW

- APRIL 1998 ARBITRAL AWARD (SECOND PARTIAL) ICC INTERNATIONAL COURT OF ARBITRATION (NO. 7110) [734]

2.3.3 RECOURSE TO DOMESTIC LAW

ARTICLE 1.7
(Good faith and fair dealing)

(1) Each party must act in accordance with good faith and fair dealing in international trade.

(2) The parties may not exclude or limit this duty.

COMMENT

1. "Good faith and fair dealing" as a fundamental idea underlying the Principles

There are a number of provisions throughout the different chapters of the Principles which constitute a direct or indirect application of the principle of good faith and fair dealing. See above all Art. 1.8, but see also for instance, Arts 1.9(2); 2.1.4(2)(b), 2.1.15, 2.1.16, 2.1.18 and 2.1.20; 2.2.4(2), 2.2.5(2), 2.2.7 and 2.2.10; 3.5, 3.8 and 3.10; 4.1(2), 4.2(2), 4.6 and 4.8; 5.1.2 and 5.1.3; 5.2.5; 6.1.3, 6.1.5, 6.1.16(2) and 6.1.17(1); 6.2.3(3)(4); 7.1.2, 7.1.6 and 7.1.7; 7.2.2(b)(c); 7.4.8 and 7.4.13; 9.1.3, 9.1.4 and 9.1.10(1). This means that good faith and fair dealing may be considered to be one of the fundamental ideas underlying the Principles. By stating in general terms that each party must act in accordance with good faith and fair dealing, para. (1) of this article makes it clear that even in the absence of special provisions in the Principles the parties' behaviour throughout the life of the contract, including the negotiation process, must conform to good faith and fair dealing.

Illustrations

1. A grants B forty-eight hours as the time within which B may accept its offer. When B, shortly before the expiry of the deadline, decides to accept, it is unable to do so: it is the weekend, the fax at A's office is disconnected and there is no telephone answering machine which can take the message. When on the following Monday A refuses B's acceptance A acts contrary to good faith since when it fixed the time-limit for acceptance it was for A to ensure that messages could be received at its office throughout the forty-eight hour period.

2. A contract for the supply and installation of a special production line contains a provision according to which A, the seller, is obliged to communicate to B, the purchaser, any improvements made by A to the technology of that line. After a year B learns of an important improvement of which it had not been informed. A is not excused by the fact that the production of that particular type of production line is no longer its responsibility

but that of C, a wholly-owned affiliated company of A. It would be against good faith for A to invoke the separate entity of C, which was specifically set up to take over this production in order to avoid A's contractual obligations vis-à-vis B.

3. A, an agent, undertakes on behalf of B, the principal, to promote the sale of B's goods in a given area. Under the contract A's right to compensation arises only after B's approval of the contracts procured by A. While B is free to decide whether or not to approve the contracts procured by A, a systematic and unjustified refusal to approve any contract procured by A would be against good faith.

4. Under a line of credit agreement between A, a bank, and B, a customer, A suddenly and inexplicably refuses to make further advances to B whose business suffers heavy losses as a consequence. Notwithstanding the fact that the agreement contains a term permitting A to accelerate payment "at will", A's demand for payment in full without prior warning and with no justification would be against good faith.

2. Abuse of rights

A typical example of behaviour contrary to the principle of good faith and fair dealing is what in some legal systems is known as "abuse of rights". It is characterised by a party's malicious behaviour which occurs for instance when a party exercises a right merely to damage the other party or for a purpose other than the one for which it had been granted, or when the exercise of a right is disproportionate to the originally intended result.

Illustrations

5. A rents premises from B for the purpose of setting up a retail business. The rental contract is for five years, but when three years later A realises that business in the area is very poor, it decides to close the business and informs B that it is no longer interested in renting the premises. A's breach of contract would normally lead to B's having the choice of either terminating the contract and claiming damages or requesting specific performance. However, under the circumstances B would be abusing its rights if it required B to pay the rent for the remaining two years of the contract instead of terminating the contract and claiming damages from B for the rent it has lost for the length of time necessary to find a new tenant.

6. A rents premises from B for the purpose of opening a restaurant. During the summer months A sets up a few tables out

of doors, but still on the owner's property. On account of the noise caused by the restaurant's customers late at night, B has increasing difficulties finding tenants for apartments in the same building. B would be abusing its rights if, instead of requesting A to desist from serving out of doors late at night, it required A not to serve out of doors at all.

3. "Good faith and fair dealing in international trade"

The reference to "good faith and fair dealing in international trade" first makes it clear that in the context of the Principles the two concepts are not to be applied according to the standards ordinarily adopted within the different national legal systems. In other words, such domestic standards may be taken into account only to the extent that they are shown to be generally accepted among the various legal systems. A further implication of the formula used is that good faith and fair dealing must be construed in the light of the special conditions of international trade. Standards of business practice may indeed vary considerably from one trade sector to another, and even within a given trade sector they may be more or less stringent depending on the socio-economic environment in which the enterprises operate, their size and technical skill, etc.

It should be noted that the provisions of the Principles and/or the comments thereto at times refer only to "good faith" or to "good faith and fair dealing". Such references should always be understood as a reference to "good faith and fair dealing in international trade" as specified in this article.

Illustrations

7. Under a contract for the sale of high-technology equipment the purchaser loses the right to rely on any defect in the goods if it does not give notice to the seller specifying the nature of the defect without undue delay after it has discovered or ought to have discovered the defect. A, a buyer operating in a country where such equipment is commonly used, discovers a defect in the equipment after having put it into operation, but in its notice to B, the seller of the equipment, A gives misleading indications as to the nature of the defect. A loses its right to rely on the defect since a more careful examination of the defect would have permitted it to give B the necessary specifications.

8. The facts are the same as in Illustration 5, the difference being that A operates in a country where this type of equipment is so far almost unknown. A does not lose its right to rely on the defect because B, being aware of A's lack of technical knowledge, could not reasonably have expected A properly to identify the nature of the defect.

4. The mandatory nature of the principle of good faith and fair dealing

The parties' duty to act in accordance with good faith and fair dealing is of such a fundamental nature that the parties may not contractually exclude or limit it (para. (2)). As to specific applications of the general prohibition to exclude or limit the principle of good faith and fair dealing between the parties, see Arts. 3.19, 7.1.6 and 7.4.13.

On the other hand, nothing prevents parties from providing in their contract for a duty to observe more stringent standards of behaviour.

Issues & Cases

1. GOOD FAITH AND FAIR DEALING IN INTERNATIONAL TRADE

- SEPTEMBER 4, 1996 ARBITRAL AWARD ICC INTERNATIONAL COURT OF ARBITRATION (NO. 8540) [636]
- DECEMBER 4, 1996 ARBITRAL AWARD AD HOC ARBITRATION, ROME [664]
- MARCH 5, 1997 NETHERLANDS RB ZWOLLE (NO. HA ZA 95-640) [671]
- JUNE 30, 1997 AUSTRALIA FEDERAL COURT OF AUSTRALIA (NO. 558) [685]
- SEPTEMBER 1998 ARBITRAL AWARD ICC INTERNATIONAL COURT OF ARBITRATION (NO. 8908) [750]
- OCTOBER 1, 1999 AUSTRALIA SUPREME COURT OF NEW SOUTH WALES (NO. 996) [811]
- MARCH 2000 ARBITRAL AWARD ICC INTERNATIONAL COURT OF ARBITRATION (NO. 9875) [820]
- MARCH 20, 2000 ARBITRAL AWARD INTERNATIONAL CENTRE FOR SETTLEMENT OF INVESTMENT DISPUTES (ICSID) (NO. ARB(AF)/98/1) [826]
- JULY 28, 2000 ARBITRAL AWARD ICC INTERNATIONAL COURT OF ARBITRATION (NO. 9797/CK/AER/ACS) [834]
- APRIL 30, 2001 ARBITRAL AWARD AD HOC ARBITRATION SAN JOSÉ (COSTA RICA) [945]
- OCTOBER 3, 2001 NEW ZEALAND COURT OF APPEAL OF NEW ZEALAND (NO. NZCA 348) [974]
- FEBRUARY 12, 2003 AUSTRALIA FEDERAL COURT OF AUSTRALIA (NO. NG 733 OF 1997) [ ]

- MARCH 4, 2004 ARBITRAL AWARD AD HOC ARBITRATION (PLACE UNKNOWN) [1077]

1.1 AS A DIFFERENT ONE FROM CORRESPONDING STANDARDS IN DOMESTIC LAW

- MARCH 5, 1997 NETHERLANDS RB ZWOLLE (HA ZA 95-640) [671]

2. GOOD FAITH AND FAIR DEALING AS BASIC IDEA UNDERLYING PRINCIPLES (SEE ARTS. 2.1.4(2)(B), 2.1.15, 2.1.16, 2.1.18, 2.1.10, 3.5, 3.8, 3.10, 4.1(2), 4.2(2), 4.6, 4.8, 5.1.2, 5.1.3, 6.1.3)

- APRIL 1998 ARBITRAL AWARD (SECOND PARTIAL) ICC INTERNATIONAL COURT OF ARBITRATION (NO. 7110) [734]
- MAY 1999 ARBITRAL AWARD ICC INTERNATIONAL COURT OF ARBITRATION (NO. 9753) [799]
- JULY 28, 2000 ARBITRAL AWARD ICC INTERNATIONAL COURT OF ARBITRATION (NO. 9797/CK/AER/ACS) [834]
- OCTOBER 2000 ARBITRAL AWARD ICC INTERNATIONAL COURT OF ARBITRATION (NO. 10335) [864]
- DECEMBER 2000 ARBITRAL AWARD ICC INTERNATIONAL COURT OF ARBITRATION (NO. 10346) [883]
- JANUARY 25, 2002 ARBITRAL AWARD ARBITRATION COURT OF THE LAUSANNE CHAMBER OF COMMERCE AND INDUSTRY [991]
- MAY 17, 2002 ARBITRAL AWARD (PARTIAL) ARBITRATION COURT OF THE LAUSANNE CHAMBER OF COMMERCE AND INDUSTRY [1001]
- JUNE 1, 2003 ARBITRAL AWARD ARBITRATION CENTRE OF THE COSTA RICAN CHAMBER OF COMMERCE [1065]

3. MANDATORY NATURE OF PRINCIPLE OF GOOD FAITH AND FAIR DEALING

- MARCH 20, 2000 ARBITRAL AWARD INTERNATIONAL CENTRE FOR SETTLEMENT OF INVESTMENT DISPUTES (ICSID) (ARB(AF)/98/1) [826]
- FEBRUARY 12, 2003 AUSTRALIA FEDERAL COURT OF AUSTRALIA (NO. NG733 OF 1997) [1058]

ARTICLE 1.8
(Inconsistent Behaviour)

A party cannot act inconsistently with an understanding it has caused the other party to have and upon which that other party reasonably has acted in reliance to its detriment.

COMMENT

1. Inconsistent behaviour and "good faith and fair dealing"

This provision is a general application of the principle of good faith and fair dealing (Art. 1.7). It is reflected in other more specific provisions of the Principles. See, for example, Arts. 2.1.4(2)(b), 2.1.18, 2.1.20, 2.2.5(2) and comment 3 on Art. 10.4. It imposes a responsibility on a party not to occasion detriment to another party by acting inconsistently with an understanding concerning their contractual relationship which it has caused that other party to have and upon which that other party has reasonably acted in reliance.

The prohibition contained in this article can result in the creation of rights and in the loss, suspension or modification of rights otherwise than by agreement of the parties. This is because the understanding relied upon may itself be inconsistent with the agreed or actual rights of the parties. The article does not provide the only means by which a right might be lost or suspended because of one party's conduct. See, for example, Arts. 3.12 and 7.1.4(3).

2. An understanding reasonably relied upon

There is a variety of ways in which one party may cause the other party to have an understanding concerning their contract, its performance, or enforcement. The understanding may result, for example, from a representation made, from conduct, or from silence when a party would reasonably expect the other to speak to correct a known error or misunderstanding that was being relied upon.

So long as it relates in some way to the contractual relationship of the parties, the understanding for the purposes of this article is not limited to any particular subject-matter. It may relate to a matter of fact or of law, to a matter of intention, or to how one or other of the parties can or must act.

The important limitation is that the understanding must be one on which, in the circumstances, the other party can and does reasonably rely. Whether the reliance is reasonable is a matter of fact in the circumstances having regard, in particular, to the communications and conduct of the parties, to the nature and setting of the parties' dealings and to the expectations they could reasonably entertain of each other.

Illustrations

1. A has negotiated with B over a lengthy period for a contract of lease of B's land under which B is to demolish a building and construct a new one to A's specification. A communicates with B in terms that induce B reasonably to understand that their contract negotiations have been completed, and that B can begin performance. B then demolishes the building and engages contractors to build the new building. A is aware of this and does nothing to stop it. A later indicates to B that there are additional terms still to be negotiated. A will be precluded from departing from B's understanding.

2. B mistakenly understands that its contract with A can be performed in a particular way. A is aware of this and stands by while B's performance proceeds. B and A meet regularly. B's performance is discussed but no reference is made by A to B's mistake. A will be precluded from insisting that the performance was not that which was required under the contract.

3. A regularly uses B to do sub-contract work on building sites. That part of A's business and the employees involved in it are taken over by A1, a related business. There is no change in the general course of business by which B obtains its instruction to do work. B continues to provide sub-contract services and continues to bill A for work done believing the work is being done for A. A does not inform B of its mistake. A is precluded from denying that B's contract for work done is with it and must pay for the work done.

4. Because of difficulties it is experiencing with its own suppliers, A is unable to make deliveries on time to B under their contract. The contract imposes penalties for late delivery. After being made aware of A's difficulties, B indicates it will not insist on strict compliance with the delivery schedule. A year later B's business begins to suffer from A's late deliveries. B seeks to recover penalties for the late deliveries to date and to require compliance with the delivery schedule for the future. It will be precluded from recovering the penalties but will be able to insist on compliance with the schedule if reasonable notice is given that compliance is required for the future.

5. B is indebted to A in the sum of AUS $10,000. Though the debt is due A takes no steps to enforce it. B assumes in consequence that A has pardoned the debt. A has done nothing to indicate that such actually is the case. It later demands payment. B cannot rely on A's inaction to resist that demand.

3. Detriment and preclusion

The responsibility imposed by the article is to avoid detriment being occasioned in consequence of reasonable reliance. This does not necessarily require that the party seeking to act inconsistently must be precluded from so doing. Preclusion is only one way of avoiding detriment. There may, in the circumstances, be other reasonable means available that can avert the detriment the relying party would otherwise experience if the inconsistent action were allowed as, for example, by giving reasonable notice before acting inconsistently (see Illustration 4), or by paying for costs or losses incurred by reason of reliance.

Illustrations

6. A and B are parties to a construction contract which requires that additional works be documented in writing and be certified by the site architect. A's contract manager orally requests B to do specified additional work on a time and materials basis and assures B it will be documented appropriately in due course. B commissions design works for the additional work at which stage A indicates that the work is not required. The cost incurred in commissioning the design work is far less than the cost that would be incurred if the additional work were to be done. If A pays B the costs incurred by B for the design work, B cannot then complain of A's inconsistent behaviour.

7. A fails to meet on time a prescribed milestone in a software development contract with B. B is entitled under the contract to terminate the contract because of that failure. B continues to require and pay for changes to the software and acts co-operatively with A in continuing the software development program. A's continued performance is based on B's conduct subsequent to the breach. B will in such circumstances be precluded from exercising its right to terminate for the failure to meet the milestone. However, under the Principles B will be able to allow A an additional period of time for performance (Art. 7.1.5) and to exercise its right to terminate if the milestone is not met in that period.

Issues & Cases

1. Inconsistent Behaviour

- March 4, 2004 Arbitral Award Ad hoc Arbitration (Place unknown) [1077]

1.1 A Party's acting inconsistently with understanding which other party has

1.2 OTHER PARTY'S REASONABLE RELIANCE UPON SUCH UNDERSTANDING

1.3 OTHER PARTY'S DETRIMENT

2. RESPONSIBILITY FOR INCONSISTENT BEHAVIOUR

2.1 PARTY PRECLUDED FROM ACTING INCONSISTENTLY

- APRIL 30, 2001 ARBITRAL AWARD AD HOC ARBITRATION SAN JOSÉ (COSTA RICA) [ ]
- MARCH 4, 2004 ARBITRAL AWARD AD HOC ARBITRATION (PLACE UNKNOWN) [1077]

2.2 OTHER WAYS OF AVOIDING OTHER PARTY'S DETRIMENT

ARTICLE 1.9
(Usages and practices)

(1) The parties are bound by any usage to which they have agreed and by any practices which they have established between themselves.

(2) The parties are bound by a usage that is widely known to and regularly observed in international trade by parties in the particular trade concerned except where the application of such a usage would be unreasonable.

COMMENT

1. Practices and usages in the context of the Principles

This article lays down the principle according to which the parties are in general bound by practices and usages which meet the requirements set forth in the article. Furthermore, these same requirements must be met by practices and usages for them to be applicable in the cases and for the purposes expressly indicated in the Principles. See, for instance, Arts. 2.1.6(3), 4.3, and 5.1.2.

2. Practices established between the parties

A practice established between the parties to a particular contract is automatically binding, except where the parties have expressly excluded its application. Whether a particular practice can be deemed to be "established" between the parties will naturally depend on the circumstances of the case, but behaviour on the occasion of only one previous transaction between the parties will not normally suffice.

Illustration

1. A, a supplier, has repeatedly accepted claims from B, a customer, for quantitative or qualitative defects in the goods as much as two weeks after their delivery. When B gives another notice of defects only after a fortnight, A cannot object that it is too late since the two-weeks' notice amounts to a practice established between A and B which will as such be binding on A.

3. Agreed usages

By stating that the parties are bound by usages to which they have agreed, para. (1) of this article merely applies the general principle of freedom of contract laid down in Art. 1.1. Indeed, the parties may either negotiate all the terms of their contract, or for certain questions simply refer to other sources including usages. The parties may stipulate the application of any usage, including a usage developed within a trade sector to which neither party belongs, or a usage relating to a different type of contract. It is even conceivable that the parties will agree on the application of what are sometimes misleadingly called usages, *i.e.* a set of rules issued by a particular trade association under the title of "Usages", but which only in part reflects established general lines of conduct.

4. Other applicable usages

Para. (2) lays down the criteria for the identification of usages applicable in the absence of a specific agreement by the parties. The fact that the usage must be "widely known to and regularly observed [...] by parties in the particular trade concerned" is a condition for the application of any usage, be it at international or merely at national or local level. The additional qualification "in international trade" is intended to avoid usages developed for, and confined to, domestic transactions also being invoked in transactions with foreigners.

Illustration

2. A, a real estate agent, invokes a particular usage of the profession in its country vis-à-vis B, a foreign customer. B is not bound by such a usage if that usage is of a local nature and relates to a trade which is predominantly domestic in character.

Only exceptionally may usages of a purely local or national origin be applied without any reference thereto by the parties. Thus, usages existing on certain commodity exchanges or at trade exhibitions or ports should be applicable provided that they are regularly followed with respect to foreigners as well. Another exception concerns the case of a businessperson who has already entered into a number of similar contracts in a foreign country and who should therefore be bound by the usages established within that country for such contracts.

Illustrations

3. A, a terminal operator, invokes a particular usage of the port where it is located vis-à-vis B, a foreign carrier. B is bound by this local usage if the port is normally used by foreigners and the usage in question has been regularly observed with respect to all customers, irrespective of their place of business and of their nationality.

4. A, a sales agent from country X, receives a request from B, one of its customers in country Y, for the customary 10% discount

upon payment of the price in cash. A may not object to the application of such a usage on account of its being restricted to country Y if A has been doing business in that country for a certain period of time.

5. Application of usage unreasonable

A usage may be regularly observed by the generality of business people in a particular trade sector but its application in a given case may nevertheless be unreasonable. Reasons for this may be found in the particular conditions in which one or both parties operate and/or the atypical nature of the transaction. In such cases the usage will not be applied.

Illustration

5. A usage exists in a commodity trade sector according to which the purchaser may not rely on defects in the goods if they are not duly certified by an internationally recognised inspection agency. When A, a buyer, takes over the goods at the port of destination, the only internationally recognised inspection agency operating in that port is on strike and to call another from the nearest port would be excessively costly. The application of the usage in this case would be unreasonable and A may rely on the defects it has discovered even though they have not been certified by an internationally recognised inspection agency.

6. Usages prevail over the Principles

Both courses of dealing and usages, once they are applicable in a given case, prevail over conflicting provisions contained in the Principles. The reason for this is that they bind the parties as implied terms of the contract as a whole or of single statements or other conduct on the part of one of the parties. As such, they are superseded by any express term stipulated by the parties but, in the same way as the latter, they prevail over the Principles, the only exception being those provisions which are specifically declared to be of a mandatory character. See comment 3 on Art. 1.5.

Issues & Cases

1. BINDING CHARACTER OF USAGES AND PRACTICES

- DECEMBER 1997 ARBITRAL AWARD ICC INTERNATIONAL COURT OF ARBITRATION (NO. 8817) [712]

1.1 PRACTICES ESTABLISHED BETWWEN PARTIES

- December 1997 Arbitral Award ICC International Court of Arbitration (No. 8817) [712]
- January 25, 2002 Arbitral Award Arbitration Court of the Lausanne Chamber of Commerce and Industry [991]

1.2 **Usages expressly agreed between parties**

1.3 **Applicability of usages not expressly agreed to by parties**

- October 2000 Arbitral Award ICC International Court of Arbitration (No. 10335) [864]

1.3.1 **Usages widely known to regularly observed in international trade by parties in the trade concerned**

- April 30, 2001 Arbitral Award Ad hoc Arbitration San José (Costa Rica) [945]

1.3.2 **Local usages**

2. **Unreasonable usages**

3. **Usages to prevail over provisions of Principles (see Arts. 1.1 and 1.5)**

ARTICLE 1.10
(Notice)

(1) Where notice is required it may be given by any means appropriate to the circumstances.

(2) A notice is effective when it reaches the person to whom it is given.

(3) For the purpose of paragraph (2) a notice "reaches" a person when given to that person orally or delivered at that person's place of business or mailing address.

(4) For the purpose of this article "notice" includes a declaration, demand, request or any other communication of intention.

COMMENT

1. Form of notice

This article first lays down the principle that notice or any other kind of communication of intention (declarations, demands, requests, etc.) required by individual provisions of the Principles are not subject to any particular requirement as to form, but may be given by any means appropriate in the circumstances. Which means are appropriate will depend on the actual circumstances of the case, in particular on the availability and the reliability of the various modes of communication, and the importance and/or urgency of the message to be delivered. For an electronic notice to be "appropriate to the circumstances" the addressee must expressly or impliedly have consented to receive electronic communications in the way in which the notice was sent by the sender, *i.e.* of that type, in that format and to that address. The addressee's consent may be inferred from the addressee's statements or conduct, from practices established between the parties, or from applicable usages.

Illustration

1. Seller A and buyer B have a longstanding business relationship in the course of which they have always negotiated and concluded their contracts by telephone. On discovering a defect in the goods supplied on one occasion, B immediately sends A notice thereof by e-mail. A, who does not regularly read its e-mail and had no reason to expect an e-mail from B, on discovering B's notice three weeks after it had been sent rejects it as being too late. B may not

object that it had given prompt notice of the defects since the notice was not given by a means appropriate to the circumstances.

2. Seller A and buyer B have a longstanding business relationship in the course of which they have regularly communicated by electronic means. On discovering a defect in the goods supplied on one occasion, B immediately sends A notice thereof by e-mail to an e-mail address different from the one normally used. A, who had no reason to expect an e-mail from B at that address, on discovering B's notice three weeks after it had been sent rejects it as being too late. B may not object that it had given prompt notice of the defects since the notice was not given by a means appropriate to the circumstances.

2. Receipt principle

With respect to all kinds of notices the Principles adopt the so-called "receipt" principle, *i.e.* they are not effective unless and until they reach the person to whom they are given. For some communications this is expressly stated in the provisions dealing with them: see Arts. 2.1.3(1), 2.1.3(2), 2.1.5, 2.1.6(2), 2.1.8(1) and 2.1.10; 9.1.10 and 9.1.11. The purpose of para. (2) of the present article is to indicate that the same will also be true in the absence of an express statement to this effect: see Arts. 2.1.9, 2.1.11; 2.2.9; 3.13, 3.14; 6.1.16, 6.2.3; 7.1.5, 7.1.7; 7.2.1, 7.2.2; 7.3.2, 7.3.4; and 8.3.

3. Dispatch principle to be expressly stipulated

The parties are of course always free expressly to stipulate the application of the dispatch principle. This may be appropriate in particular with respect to the notice a party has to give in order to preserve its rights in cases of the other party's actual or anticipated non-performance when it would not be fair to place the risk of loss, mistake or delay in the transmission of the message on the former. This is all the more true if the difficulties which may arise at international level in proving effective receipt of a notice are borne in mind.

4. "Reaches"

It is important in relation to the receipt principle to determine precisely when the communications in question "reach" the addressee. In an attempt to define the concept, para. (3) of this article draws a distinction between oral and other communications. The former "reach" the addressee if they are made personally to it or to another person authorised by it to receive them. The latter "reach" the addressee as soon as they are delivered either to the addressee personally or to its place of business or (electronic) mailing address. The particular communication in question need not come into the hands of the addressee or actually be read by the addressee. It is sufficient that it be handed over to an employee of the addressee authorised to accept it, or that it be placed in the addressee's mailbox, or received by the addressee's fax or telex machine, or, in the case of electronic communications, that it has entered the addressee's server (see *e.g.* Art. 15(2) of the *1996 UNCITRAL Model Law on Electronic Commerce*).

Issues & Cases

1. **MEANING OF NOTICE**
2. **FORM AND CONTENT OF NOTICE**
   - 2.1 **FREEDOM OF FORM**
   - 2.2 **MEANS APPROPRIATE TO CIRCUMSTANCES**
3. **RECEIPT PRINCIPLE AS THE RULE**
   - 25.04.1996 ARBITRAL AWARD ICC INTERNATIONAL COURT OF ARBITRATION [ ]
   - 3.1 **MEANING OF "REACHES"**
4. **DISPATCH PRINCIPLE TO BE EXPRESSLY STIPULATED**

ARTICLE 1.11
(Definitions)

In these Principles

– "court" includes an arbitral tribunal;

– where a party has more than one place of business the relevant "place of business" is that which has the closest relationship to the contract and its performance, having regard to the circumstances known to or contemplated by the parties at any time before or at the conclusion of the contract;

– "obligor" refers to the party who is to perform an obligation and "obligee" refers to the party who is entitled to performance of that obligation.

– "writing" means any mode of communication that preserves a record of the information contained therein and is capable of being reproduced in tangible form.

COMMENT

1. Courts and arbitral tribunals

The importance of the Principles for the purpose of the settlement of disputes by means of arbitration has already been stressed (see above the comments on the Preamble). In order however to avoid undue heaviness of language, only the term "court" is used in the text of the Principles, on the understanding that it covers arbitral tribunals as well as courts.

2. Party with more than one place of business

For the purpose of the application of the Principles a party's place of business is of relevance in a number of contexts such as the place for the delivery of notices (Art. 1.10(3)); a possible extension of the time of acceptance because of a holiday falling on the last day (Art. 1.12); the place of performance (Art. 6.1.6) and the determination of the party who should apply for a public permission (Art. 6.1.14(a)).

With reference to a party with multiple places of business (normally a central office and various branch offices) the present article lays down the rule that the relevant place of business should be considered to be that which has the closest relationship to the contract and to its performance. Nothing is said with respect to the case where the place of the conclusion of the contract and that of performance differ, but in such a case the latter would seem to be the more relevant one. In the determination of the place of business which has the closest relationship to a given contract and to its performance, regard is to be had to the circumstances known to or contemplated by both parties at any time before or at the conclusion of the contract. Facts known only to one of the parties or of which the parties became aware only after the conclusion of the contract cannot be taken into consideration.

3. "Obligor" - "obligee"

Where necessary, to better identify the party performing and the party receiving performance of obligations the terms "obligor" and "obligee" are used, irrespective of whether the obligation is non-monetary or monetary.

4. "Writing"

In some cases the Principles refer to a "writing" or a "contract in writing". See Arts. 2.1.12, 2.1.17 and 2.1.18. The Principles define this formal requirement in functional terms. Thus, a writing includes not only a telegram and a telex, but also any other mode of communication, including electronic communications, that preserves a record and can be reproduced in tangible form. This formal requirement should be compared with the more flexible form of a "notice". See Art. 1.10(1).

Issues & Cases

1. MEANING OF "COURT"
2. CONCEPT OF "PLACE OF BUSINESS"
3. "OBLIGOR" AND "OBLIGEE" DEFINED
4. MEANING OF "WRITING"
   - 4.1 COMMUNICATIONS BY TELEGRAPH OR TELEX
   - 4.2 COMMUNICATIONS BY OTHER MEANS (FACSIMILE, ELECTRONIC DATA EXCHANGE, ETC.)

ARTICLE 1.12
(Computation of time set by parties)

(1) Official holidays or non-business days occurring during a period set by parties for an act to be performed are included in calculating the period.

(2) However, if the last day of the period is an official holiday or a non-business day at the place of business of the party to perform the act, the period is extended until the first business day which follows, unless the circumstances indicate otherwise.

(3) The relevant time zone is that of the place of business of the party setting the time, unless the circumstances indicate otherwise.

COMMENT

The parties may, either unilaterally or by agreement, fix a period of time within which certain acts must be done. See, *e.g.*, Arts. 2.1.7, 2.2.9(2), and 10.3.

In fixing the time limit the parties may either indicate merely a period of time (*e.g.* "Notice of defects in the goods must be given within ten days after delivery") or a precise date (*e.g.* "Offer firm until 1 March").

In the first case the question arises of whether or not holidays or non-business days occurring during the period of time are included in calculating the period of time, and according to para. (1) of this article the answer is in the affirmative.

In both of the above-mentioned cases, the question may arise of what the effect would be of a holiday or non-business day falling at the expiry of the fixed period of time at the place of business of the party to perform the act. Para. (2) provides that in such an eventuality the period is extended until the first business day that follows, unless the circumstances indicate otherwise.

Finally, whenever the parties are situated in different time zones, the question arises as to what time zone is relevant, and according to para. (3) it is the time zone of the place of business of the party setting the time limit, unless the circumstances indicate otherwise.

Illustration

1. A sales contract provides that buyer A must give notice of defects of the goods within 10 days after delivery. The goods are delivered on Friday 16 December. A gives notice of defects on Monday 2 January and seller B rejects it as being untimely. A may

not object that the holidays and non-business days which occurred between 16 December and 2 January should not be counted when calculating the ten days of the time limit.

2. Offeror A indicates that its offer is firm until 1 March. Offeree B accepts the offer on 2 March because 1 March was a holiday at its place of business. A may not object that the fixed time limit for acceptance had expired on 1 March.

3. Offeror A sends an offer to offeree B by e-mail on a Saturday indicating that the offer is firm for 24 hours. If B intends to accept, it must do so within 24 hours, even though the time limit elapses on a Sunday, since under the circumstances the time limit fixed by A was to be understood as absolute.

4. The facts are the same as in Illustration 2, the difference being that A is situated in Frankfurt and B in New York, and the time limit fixed for acceptance is "by 5 p.m. tomorrow at the latest". A must accept by 5 p.m. Frankfurt time.

5. A charterparty concluded between owner A, situated in Tokyo, and charterer B, situated in Kuwait City, provides for payment of the freight by B at A's bank in Zurich, Switzerland, on a specific date by 5 p.m. at latest. The relevant time zone is neither that of A nor that of B, but that of Zurich where payment is due.

Issues & Cases

1. **TIME PERIOD SET BY PARTIES AND HOLIDAYS**
   1.1 **HOLIDAYS OCCOURRING DURING PERIOD INCLUDED IN CALCULATING PERIOD**
   1.2 **HOLIDAY FALLING AT EXPIRY OF PERIOD**
2. **TIME PERIOD SET BY PARTIES AND RELEVANT TIME ZONE**

CHAPTER 2

FORMATION AND AUTHORITY OF AGENTS

SECTION 1: FORMATION

BIBLIOGRAPHY

BONELL M.J., An International Restatement of Contract Law. The UNIDROIT Principles of International Commercial Contracts, 3rd ed., Transnational Publications Inc., Ardsley, New York, 2005, at 105 – 113, 153 - 158.

BONELL M.J., *Soft Law* and Party Autonomy: The Case of the UNIDROIT Principles, in 51 Loyola Law Review (2005).

BONELL M.J., Responsabilità precontrattuale, Convenzione di Bruxelles sulla competenza giurisdizionale e l'esecuzione delle sentenze e ... Principi UNIDROIT (Corte di Giustizia, 17 settembre 2002), in Diritto del commercio internazionale, 17 (2003), 169 – 191.

BONELL M.J., Pre-contractual liability, the Brussels Jurisdiction Convention and ... the UNIDROIT Principles (Case 334/00 Tacconi v. HWS), in Mélanges offerts à Marcel Fontaine, Paris, Larcier, 2003, 359 – 370.

BRASSEUR P., in: FONTAINE, M., Le processus de formation du contrat. Bruylant, Bruxelles, 2002, 619-622.

CRIVELLARO A., La rilevanza dei preamboli nell'interpretazione dei contratti internazionali, in Diritto del commercio internazionale, 2001, 777 – 792.

DARANKOUM E.S., L'application des Principes d'UNIDROIT par les arbitres internationaux et par les juges étatiques, in Les Principes d'UNIDROIT et les contrats internationaux: aspects pratiques, in Revue Juridique Thémis, vol. 36, no. 2 (2002), 421 – 480.

DE CONINCK B., in FONTAINE, M. (ed.) Le processus de formation du contrat. Bruylant, Bruxelles, 2002, 95-105.

DELFORGE C., in FONTAINE, M. (ed.) Le processus de formation du contrat. Bruylant, Bruxelles, 2002, 330-352.

DE NOVA G., The UNIDROIT Principles as a Guide for Drafting International Contracts, in Institute of International Business Law and Practice (ed.), UNIDROIT Principles for International Commercial Contracts: A New *Lex Mercatoria*?, ICC Publication n. 490/1, 1995, 115-128.

DI MAJO A., L'osservanza della buona fede nei Principi UNIDROIT sui contratti commerciali internazionali, in BONELL M.J. / BONELLI F. (eds.), Contratti commerciali internazionali e Principi UNIDROIT, Giuffrè, Milano 1997, 143-160.

FARNSWORTH E.A., The UNIDROIT Principles: A new *lingua franca* for the drafting of international commercial contracts?, in UNIDROIT (ed.), The UNIDROIT Principles: a Common Law of Contracts for the Americas?, 1998, 193-199.

FARNSWORTH E.A., Contract Formation: Two Models Compared, in BONELL M.J. / BONELLI F. (eds.), Contratti commerciali internazionali e Principi UNIDROIT, Giuffrè, Milano 1997, 171-181.

FARNSWORTH E.A., An American View of the Principles as a Guide to Drafting Contracts, in Institute of International Business Law and Practice (ed.), UNIDROIT Principles for International Commercial Contracts: A New *Lex Mercatoria*?, ICC Publication n. 490/1, 1995, 85-93.

FARNSWORTH E.A., Duties of Good Faith and Liability for Bad Faith Under the UNIDROIT Principles, Relevant International Conventions and National Laws, in 3 Tulane Journal of International and Comparative Law, n. 1/2, 1994, 47-63.

FONTAINE M., in: FONTAINE, M. (ed.), Le processus de formation du contrat. Bruylant, Bruxelles, 2002, 849-897.

FONTAINE M., Les Principes UNIDROIT, guide de la rédaction des contrats internationaux, in Institute of International Business Law and Practice (ed.), UNIDROIT Principles for International Commercial Contracts: A New *Lex Mercatoria*?, ICC Publication n. 490/1, 1995, 73-84.

GAYMER V., The UNIDROIT Principles as a Guide for Drafting Contracts, A View from an International Commercial Lawyer, in Institute of International Business Law and Practice (ed.), UNIDROIT Principles for International Commercial Contracts: A New *Lex Mercatoria*?, ICC Publication n. 490/1, 1995, 95-102.

GAUTRAIS V., Les Principes d'UNIDROIT face au contrat électronique, in Les Principes d'UNIDROIT et les contrats internationaux: aspects pratiques, in Revue Juridique Thémis, vol. 36, no. 2 (2002), 481 – 517.

GUILLEMARD S., A comparative study of the UNIDROIT Principles, the Principles of the European Law of Contracts, and some dispositions of the CISG applicable to the formation of international contracts, in Review of the Convention on Contracts for the International Sale of Goods (CISG), (2000 – 2001), 83 – 113.

HAGER J., Die *culpa in contrahendo* in den UNIDROIT-Prinzipien und den Prinzipien des Europäisches Vertragsrechts aus der Sicht des deutschen Bürgerlichen Rechts, in BASEDOW J., (ed.), Europäische Vertragsrechtsvereinheitlichung und deutsches Recht, J.C.B. Mohr (Siebeck), Tübingen 2000, 67 – 84.

HINESTROSA F., Los Principios de UNIDROIT: Una nueva *lingua franca*, in UNIDROIT (ed.), The UNIDROIT Principles: a Common Law of Contracts for the Americas?, 1998, 185-191.

VAN HOUTTE H., The UNIDROIT Principles as a Guide for Drafting Contracts, in Institute of International Business Law and Practice (ed.), UNIDROIT Principles for International Commercial Contracts: A New *Lex Mercatoria*?, ICC Publication n. 490/1, 1995, 129-135.

ILLESCAS ORTIZ R., Los Principios de UNIDROIT: ¿una nueva *lingua franca* para la redacción de los contratos comerciales internacionales?, in Comentario a los Principios de UNIDROIT para los Contratos del Comercio International, Aranzadi, Pamplona, 1999, 389-397.

ILLESCAS ORTIZ J., Los Principios de UNIDROIT: ¿Una nueva *lingua franca* para la redacción de los contratos comerciales internacionales?, in UNIDROIT (ed.), The UNIDROIT Principles: a Common Law of Contracts for the Americas?, 1998, 201-209.

JANSSEN A., Die Einbeziehung von allgemeinen Geschäftsbedingungen in internationale Kaufverträge und die Bedeutung der UNIDROIT – und der Lando-Principles, in IHR – Internationales Handelsrecht, 4 (2004), 194 – 200.

KAUFMANN S., Parol Evidence Rule und Merger Clause im Internationalen Einheitsrecht, Lang 2004.

KÖHLER H., Das Verfahren des Vertragsschlusses, in BASEDOW, J. (ed.), Europäische Vertragsrechtsvereinheitlichung und deutsches Recht, J.C.B. Mohr (Siebeck), Tübingen 2000, 33 – 65.

KRAMER E.A., "Battle of the Forms", in Festschrift für Peter Gauch zum 65. Geburtstag, Schulthess 2004, 493 – 506.

LANDO O., The CISG and the UNIDROIT Principles in a Global Commercial Code, in Mélanges offerts à Marcel Fontaine, Paris, Larcier, 2003, 451 – 472.

LEVY D.A., Contract formation under the UNIDROIT Principles of International Commercial Contracts, UCC, Restatement, and CISG, in 30 Uniform Commercial Code Law Journal 1998, 249-300.

LUIG E., Der internationale Vertragsschluβ. Der Vergleich von UN-Kuafrecht, UNIDROIT-Principles und Principles of European Contract Law, Bern, Berlin, Peter Lang Verlag, 2003, XLVI – 301 (Europäische Hochschulschriften, Reihe 2. Rechtswissenschaften, 3076).

MEYER O., The UNIDROIT Principles and their impact on European private law – some comments on the opinion (31 January 2002) of Advocat General L.A. Geelhoed, Court of Justice of the European Communities in case C-334/00 – Tacconi .

MOREIRA ALVES J.C., Comentàrio ao capìtulo 2 do Projeto UNIDROIT sobre Princípios para os contratos comerciaes internacionais em confronto com os sistemas jurìdicos dos paises latino-americanos que integram o MERCOSUR, in BONELL M.J. / SCHIPANI S. (eds.), "Principi per i contratti commerciali internazionali" e il sistema giuridico latinoamericano, Padova 1996, 81-107.

MURRAY J.E., The definitive "battle of forms": chaos revisited, in Journal of Law and Commerce, 20 (2000), 1 – 48.

OVIEDO ALBÁN J. – URBINA GALIANO L. – POSADA NUÑEZ L., La formación del contrato en los Principios de UNIDROIT para los contratos comerciales internacionales (comparación con las normas colombianas), Universitas Juridica, No. 96 Publicación de la Pontificia Universidad Javeriana Facultad de Ciencias Jurídicas.

PERALES VISCASILLAS P., Formación, in Comentario a los Principios de UNIDROIT para los Contratos del Comercio Internacional, Aranzadi, Pamplona, 1999, pp. 97-160.

PERALES VISCASILLAS P., Contract conclusion under CISG, in 16 Journal of Law and Commerce (1997), no. 2, 315 – 344.

PERALES VISCASILLAS P., La batalla de los formularios en la Convención de Viena de 1980 sobre compravendita internacional de mercaderías: una comparación con la sección 2-207 UCC y los Principios de UNIDROIT, in La Ley 1996, 1-12.

SCHILF S., Writing in Confirmation: Valid Evidence of a Sales Contract? Reflections on a Danish Case Regarding Usages, CISG and the UNIDROIT Principles, in: Uniform Law Review / Revue de droit uniforme 1999, 1004-1009.

SCHLECHTRIEM P., Battle of the Forms in International Contract Law: Evaluation of Approaches in German Law, UNIDROIT Principles, PECL, CISG; UCC Approaches Under Consideration, in Review of the Convention on Contracts for the International Sale of Goods (2002 – 2003), 2004, 195 – 216.

SCHLOSSER, P., Rechtszersplitterung durch internationales Einheitsrecht? Eine Studie zu kaufmännischen Bestätigungsschreiben und Rechnungsaufdrucken nach deutschem materiellen Recht, nach § 1031 ZPO, nach Art. 17 EuGVÜ, nach Art. 9 Abs. 2 CISG und Nr. 2.12 UNIDROIT -Grundsätzen, in BEUTHIEN V. / FUCHS M: / ROTH H: / SCHIEMANN G. / WACKE A. (eds.), Festschrift für Dieter Medicus zum 70. Geburtstag, Carl Heymanns Verlag, Köln 1999.

SCHNYDER K. / STRAUB R.M., The Conclusion of a Contract in Accordance with UNIDROIT Principles, in 1 European Journal of Law Reform, n. 3, 1998-1999, 243-268.

SUCHANKOVA M., Les Principes d'UNIDROIT et la responsabilité précontractuelle en cas d'échec des négociations, in 6, Revue de droit des affaires internationales / International Business Law Journal, 1997, 691-702.

TREVIÑO AZCUÉ J.C., La formación del contrato en los Principios sobre los Contratos Internacionales de UNIDROIT, in Contratación internacional, Comentarios a los principios sobre los Contratos Comerciales Internacionales del UNIDROIT, Universidad Nacional Autónoma de México – Universidad Panamericana (ed.) 1998, 53-80.

VANDOMME L., La négociation des contrats internationaux, in Revue de droit des affaires internationales / International Business Law Review (in English and French), 2003, 487 – 501.

WILHELMSSON T., Standard form conditions, in HARTKAMP A., *et al.* (eds.) Towards a European Civil Code, 3rd fully revised and expanded edition, Nijmegen, Ars Aequi Libri, 2004, 431 – 444.

ARTICLE 2.1.1
(Manner of formation)

A contract may be concluded either by the acceptance of an offer or by conduct of the parties that is sufficient to show agreement.

COMMENT

1. Offer and acceptance

Basic to the Principles is the idea that the agreement of the parties is, in itself, sufficient to conclude a contract (see Art. 3.2). The concepts of offer and acceptance have traditionally been used to determine whether, and if so when, the parties have reached agreement. As this article and this chapter make clear, the Principles retain these concepts as essential tools of analysis.

2. Conduct sufficient to show agreement

In commercial practice contracts, particularly when related to complex transactions, are often concluded after prolonged negotiations without an identifiable sequence of offer and acceptance. In such cases it may be difficult to determine if and when a contractual agreement has been reached. According to this article a contract may be held to be concluded even though the moment of its formation cannot be determined, provided that the conduct of the parties is sufficient to show agreement. In order to determine whether there is sufficient evidence of the parties' intention to be bound by a contract, their conduct has to be interpreted in accordance with the criteria set forth in Art. 4.1 *et seq.*

Illustration

1. A and B enter into negotiations with a view to setting up a joint venture for the development of a new product. After prolonged negotiations without any formal offer or acceptance and with some minor points still to be settled, both parties begin to perform. When subsequently the parties fail to reach an agreement on these minor points, a court or arbitral tribunal may decide that a contract was nevertheless concluded since the parties had begun to perform, thereby showing their intention to be bound by a contract.

3. Automated contracting

The language of this article is sufficiently broad to cover also cases of so-called automated contracting, *i.e.* where the parties agree to use a system capable of setting in motion self-executing electronic actions leading to the conclusion of a contract without the intervention of a natural person.

Illustration

2. Automobile manufacturer A and components supplier B set up an electronic data interchange system which, as soon as A's stocks of components fall below a certain level, automatically generates orders for the components and executes such orders. The fact that A and B have agreed on the operation of such a system makes the orders and performances binding on A and B, even though they have been generated without the personal intervention of A and B.

Issues & Cases

1. **CONTRACT CONCLUDED BY SEQUENCE OF OFFER AND ACCEPTANCE**
   - AUGUST 2, 2005 OVERSEAS PRIVATE INVESTMENT CORP. USA ADMINISTRATIVE DETERMINATION [1106]
2. **OTHER CONDUCT OF PARTIES SUFFICIENT TO SHOW AGREEMENT**
   - DECEMBER 4, 1996 ARBITRAL AWARD AD HOC ARBITRATION, ROME [664]
   - AUGUST 2, 2005 OVERSEAS PRIVATE INVESTMENT CORP. USA ADMINISTRATIVE DETERMINATION [1106]

1.2 LETTERS OF INTENT, MEMORANDA OF UNDERSTANDING, ETC.

ARTICLE 2.1.2
(Definition of offer)

A proposal for concluding a contract constitutes an offer if it is sufficiently definite and indicates the intention of the offeror to be bound in case of acceptance.

COMMENT

In defining an offer as distinguished from other communications which a party may make in the course of negotiations initiated with a view to concluding a contract, this article lays down two requirements: the proposal must (i) be sufficiently definite to permit the conclusion of the contract by mere acceptance and (ii) indicate the intention of the offeror to be bound in case of acceptance.

1. Definiteness of an offer

Since a contract is concluded by the mere acceptance of an offer, the terms of the future agreement must already be indicated with sufficient definiteness in the offer itself. Whether a given offer meets this requirement cannot be established in general terms. Even essential terms, such as the precise description of the goods or the services to be delivered or rendered, the price to be paid for them, the time or place of performance, etc., may be left undetermined in the offer without necessarily rendering it insufficiently definite: all depends on whether or not the offeror by making the offer, and the offeree by accepting it, intends to enter into a binding agreement, and whether or not the missing terms can be determined by interpreting the language of the agreement in accordance with Arts. 4.1 *et seq.*, or supplied in accordance with Arts. 4.8 or 5.1.2. Indefiniteness may moreover be overcome by reference to practices established between the parties or to usages (see Art. 1.9), as well as by reference to specific provisions to be found elsewhere in the Principles (*e.g.* Arts. 5.1.6 (Determination of quality of performance), 5.1.7 (Price determination), 6.1.1 (Time of performance), 6.1.6 (Place of performance), and 6.1.10 (Currency not expressed)).

Illustration

1. A has for a number of years annually renewed a contract with B for technical assistance for A's computers. A opens a second office with the same type of computers and asks B to provide assistance also for the new computers. B accepts and, despite the fact that A's offer does not specify all the terms of the agreement, a contract has been concluded since the missing terms

can be taken from the previous contracts as constituting a practice established between the parties.

2. Intention to be bound

The second criterion for determining whether a party makes an offer for the conclusion of a contract, or merely opens negotiations, is that party's intention to be bound in the event of acceptance. Since such an intention will rarely be declared expressly, it often has to be inferred from the circumstances of each individual case. The way in which the proponent presents the proposal (*e.g.* by expressly defining it as an "offer" or as a mere "declaration of intent") provides a first, although not a decisive, indication of possible intention. Of even greater importance are the content and the addressees of the proposal. Generally speaking, the more detailed and definite the proposal, the more likely it is to be construed as an offer. A proposal addressed to one or more specific persons is more likely to be intended as an offer than is one made to the public at large.

Illustrations

2. After lengthy negotiations the Executive Directors of two companies, A and B, lay down the conditions on which B will acquire 51% of the shares in company C which is totally owned by A. The "Memorandum of Agreement" signed by the negotiators contains a final clause stating that the agreement is not binding until approved by A's Board of Directors. There is no contract before such approval is given by them.

3. A, a government agency, advertises for bids for the setting up of a new telephone network. Such an advertisement is merely an invitation to submit offers, which may or may not be accepted by A. If, however, the advertisement indicates in detail the technical specifications of the project and states that the contract will be awarded to the lowest bid conforming to the specifications, it may amount to an offer with the consequence that the contract will be concluded once the lowest bid has been identified.

A proposal may contain all the essential terms of the contract but nevertheless not bind the proponent in case of acceptance if it makes the conclusion of the contract dependent on the reaching of agreement on some minor points left open in the proposal. See Art. 2.1.13.

Issues & Cases

1. REQUIREMENTS FOR OFFER

1.1 DEFINITENESS OF TERMS

1.1.1 DETERMINATION OF PRICE NOT NECESSARY (SEE ART. 5.1.7)
1.2 INDICATION OF OFFEROR'S INTENTION TO BE BOUND
2. PUBLIC OFFERS

ARTICLE 2.1.3
(Withdrawal of offer)

(1) An offer becomes effective when it reaches the offeree.

(2) An offer, even if it is irrevocable, may be withdrawn if the withdrawal reaches the offeree before or at the same time as the offer.

COMMENT

1. When an offer becomes effective

Para. (1) of this article, which is taken literally from Art. 15 CISG, provides that an offer becomes effective when it reaches the offeree (see Art. 1.10(2)). For the definition of "reaches" see Art. 1.10(3). The time at which the offer becomes effective is of importance as it indicates the precise moment as from which the offeree can accept it, thus definitely binding the offeror to the proposed contract.

2. Withdrawal of an offer

There is, however, a further reason why it may in practice be important to determine the moment at which the offer becomes effective. Indeed, up to that time the offeror is free to change its mind and to decide not to enter into the agreement at all, or to replace the original offer by a new one, irrespective of whether or not the original offer was intended to be irrevocable. The only condition is that the offeree is informed of the offeror's altered intentions before or at the same time as the offeree is informed of the original offer. By expressly stating this, para. (2) of the present article makes it clear that a distinction is to be drawn between "withdrawal" and "revocation" of an offer: before an offer becomes effective it can always be withdrawn whereas the question of whether or not it may be revoked (see Art. 2.1.4) arises only after that moment.

Issues & Cases

1. WHEN OFFER BECOMES EFFECTIVE
   - 1.1 UPON RECEIPT BY OFFEREE
2. WITHDRAWAL OF OFFER
   - 2.1 MUST REACH OFFEREE BEFORE OR AT THE SAME TIME AS OFFER
   - 2.2 WITHDRAWAL DESPITE IRREVOCABILITY OF OFFER

ARTICLE 2.1.4
(Revocation of offer)

(1) Until a contract is concluded an offer may be revoked if the revocation reaches the offeree before it has dispatched an acceptance.

(2) However, an offer cannot be revoked

(a) if it indicates, whether by stating a fixed time for acceptance or otherwise, that it is irrevocable; or

(b) if it was reasonable for the offeree to rely on the offer as being irrevocable and the offeree has acted in reliance on the offer.

COMMENT

The problem of whether an offer is or is not revocable is traditionally one of the most controversial issues in the context of the formation of contracts. Since there is no prospect of reconciling the two basic approaches followed in this respect by the different legal systems, *i.e.* the common law approach according to which an offer is as a rule revocable, and the opposite approach followed by the majority of civil law systems, the only remaining possibility is that of selecting one approach as the main rule, and the other as the exception.

1. Offers as a rule revocable

Para. (1) of this article, which is taken literally from Art. 16 CISG, states that until the contract is concluded offers are as a rule revocable. The same paragraph, however, subjects the revocation of an offer to the condition that it reach the offeree before the offeree has dispatched an acceptance. It is thus only when the offeree orally accepts the offer, or when the offeree may indicate assent by performing an act without giving notice to the offeror (see Art. 2.1.6(3)), that the offeror's right to revoke the offer continues to exist until such time as the contract is concluded. Where, however, the offer is accepted by a written indication of assent, so that the contract is concluded when the acceptance reaches the offeror (see Art. 2.1.6(2)), the offeror's right to revoke the offer terminates earlier, *i.e.* when the offeree dispatches the acceptance. Such a solution may cause some inconvenience to the offeror who will not always know whether or not it is still possible to revoke the offer. It is, however, justified in view of the legitimate interest of the offeree in the time available for revocation being shortened.

As to the determination of the time of dispatch, see Art. 2.1.8 and the comment thereto.

2. Irrevocable offers

Para. (2) provides for two important exceptions to the general rule as to the revocability of offers: (i) where the offer contains an indication that it is irrevocable and (ii) where the offeree, having other good reasons to treat the offer as being irrevocable, has acted in reliance on that offer.

a. *Indication of irrevocability contained in the offer*

The indication that the offer is irrevocable may be made in different ways, the most direct and clear of which is an express statement to that effect by the offeror (*e.g.* "This is a firm offer"; "We shall stand by our offer until we receive your answer"). It may, however, simply be inferred from other statements by, or conduct of, the offeror. The indication of a fixed time for acceptance may, but need not necessarily, amount by itself to an implicit indication of an irrevocable offer. The answer must be found in each case through a proper interpretation of the terms of the offer in accordance with the various criteria laid down in the general rules on interpretation in Chapter 4. In general, if the offeror operates within a legal system where the fixing of a time for acceptance is considered to indicate irrevocability, it may be assumed that by specifying such a fixed time the offeror intends to make an irrevocable offer. If, on the other hand, the offeror operates in a legal system where the fixing of a time for acceptance is not sufficient to indicate irrevocability, the offeror will not normally have had such an intention.

Illustrations

1. A, a travel agency, informs a client of a cruise in its brochure for the coming New Year holidays. It urges the client to book within the next three days, adding that after that date there will probably be no more places left. This statement by itself will not be considered to indicate that the offer is irrevocable during the first three days.

2. A invites B to submit a written offer of the terms on which B is prepared to construct a building. B presents a detailed offer containing the statement "Price and other conditions are not good after 1 September". If A and B operate within a legal system where such a statement is considered to be an indication that the offer is irrevocable until the specified date, B can expect the offer to be understood as being irrevocable. The same may not necessarily be the case if the offeree operates in a legal system where such a statement is not considered as being sufficient to indicate that the offer is irrevocable.

b. *Reliance by offeree on irrevocability of offer*

The second exception to the general rule regarding the revocability of offers, *i.e.* where "it was reasonable for the offeree to rely on the offer as being irrevocable", and "the offeree has acted in reliance on the offer", is an application of the general principle prohibiting inconsistent behaviour laid down in Art. 1.8. The reasonable reliance of the offeree may have been induced either by the conduct of the offeror, or by the nature of the offer itself (*e.g.* an offer whose acceptance requires extensive and costly investigation on the part of the offeree or an offer made with a view to permitting the offeree in turn to make an offer to a third party). The acts which the offeree must have performed in reliance on the offer may consist in making preparations for production, buying or hiring of materials or equipment, incurring expenses etc., provided that such acts could have been regarded as normal in the trade concerned, or should otherwise have been foreseen by, or known to, the offeror.

Illustrations

3. A, an antique dealer, asks B to restore ten paintings on condition that the work is completed within three months and that the price does not exceed a specific amount. B informs A that, so as to know whether or not to accept the offer, B finds it necessary to begin work on one painting and will then give a definite answer within five days. A agrees, and B, relying on A's offer, begins work immediately. A may not revoke the offer during those five days.

4. A seeks an offer from B for incorporation in a bid on a project to be assigned within a stated time. B submits an offer on which A relies when calculating the price of the bid. Before the expiry of the date, but after A has made the bid, B informs A that it is no longer willing to stand by its offer. B's offer is irrevocable until the stated date since in making its bid A relied on B's offer.

Issues & Cases

1. **REVOCATION OF OFFER**
   - 1.1 **MUST REACH OFFEREE BEFORE DISPATCH OF ACCEPTANCE**
   - 1.2 **FORM OF REVOCATION**
   - 1.3 **PUBLIC OFFERS**
2. **IRREVOCABLE OFFERS**
   - 2.1 **INDICATION OF IRREVOCABILITY BY OFFEROR**
     - 1.1.1 **EXPLICIT DECLARATION OF IRREVOCABILITY**
     - 1.1.2 **FIXING DEFINITE TIME FOR ACCEPTANCE**
     - 1.1.3 **OTHER STATEMENTS OF CONDUCT BY OFFEROR**
   - 2.2. **OFFEREE'S RELIANCE ON IRREVOCABILITY OF OFFER**

ARTICLE 2.1.5
(Rejection of offer)

An offer is terminated when a rejection reaches the offeror.

COMMENT

1. Rejection may be express or implied

An offer may be rejected either expressly or impliedly. A frequent case of implied rejection is a reply to an offer which purports to be an acceptance but which contains additions, limitations or other modifications (see Art. 2.1.11(1)).

In the absence of an express rejection the statements by, or the conduct of, the offeree must in any event be such as to justify the belief of the offeror that the offeree has no intention of accepting the offer. A reply on the part of the offeree which merely asks whether there would be a possible alternative (*e.g.* "Is there any chance of the price being reduced?", or "Could you deliver a couple of days earlier?") would not normally be sufficient to justify such a conclusion.

It should be recalled that a rejection will bring about the termination of any offer, irrespective of whether it was revocable or irrevocable according to Art. 2.1.4.

Illustration

A receives an offer from B stating that the offer will be firm for two weeks. A replies by return of post asking for partially different conditions which B does not accept. A may no longer accept the original offer even though there are still several days left before the expiry of the two week period since by making a counter-offer A implicitly rejected the original offer.

2. Rejection only one cause of termination of an offer

Rejection by the offeree is only one of the causes of termination of an offer. Other causes are dealt with in Arts. 2.1.4(1) and 2.1.7.

Issues & Cases

1. TERMINATION OF OFFER BY REJECTION
   1.1 EXPLICIT REJECTION
   1.2 IMPLICIT REJECTION
2. TERMINATION DESPITE IRREVOCABILITY OF OFFER

ARTICLE 2.1.6
(Mode of acceptance)

(1) A statement made by or other conduct of the offeree indicating assent to an offer is an acceptance. Silence or inactivity does not in itself amount to acceptance.

(2) An acceptance of an offer becomes effective when the indication of assent reaches the offeror.

(3) However, if, by virtue of the offer or as a result of practices which the parties have established between themselves or of usage, the offeree may indicate assent by performing an act without notice to the offeror, the acceptance is effective when the act is performed.

COMMENT

1. Indication of assent to an offer

For there to be an acceptance the offeree must in one way or another indicate "assent" to the offer. The mere acknowledgement of receipt of the offer, or an expression of interest in it, is not sufficient. Furthermore, the assent must be unconditional, *i.e.* it cannot be made dependent on some further step to be taken by either the offeror (*e.g.* "Our acceptance is subject to your final approval") or the offeree (*e.g.* "We hereby accept the terms of the contract as set forth in your Memorandum and undertake to submit the contract to our Board for approval within the next two weeks"). Finally, the purported acceptance must contain no variation of the terms of the offer or at least none which materially alters them (see Art. 2.1.11).

2. Acceptance by conduct

Provided that the offer does not impose any particular mode of acceptance, the indication of assent may either be made by an express statement or be inferred from the conduct of the offeree. Para. (1) of this article does not specify the form such conduct should assume: most often it will consist in acts of performance, such as the payment of an advance on the price, the shipment of goods or the beginning of work at the site, etc.

3. Silence or inactivity

By stating that "[s]ilence or inactivity does not in itself amount to acceptance", para. (1) makes it clear that as a rule mere silence or inactivity on the part of the offeree does not allow the inference that the offeree assents to the offer. The situation is different if the parties themselves agree that silence shall amount to acceptance, or if there exists a course of dealing or usage to that effect. In no event, however, is it sufficient for the offeror to state unilaterally in its offer that the offer will be deemed to have been accepted in the absence of any reply from the offeree. Since it is the offeror who takes the initiative by proposing the conclusion of the contract, the offeree is free not only to accept or not to accept the offer, but also simply to ignore it.

Illustrations

1. A requests B to set out the conditions for the renewal of a contract for the supply of wine, due to expire on 31 December. In its offer B includes a provision stating that "if we have not heard from you at the latest by the end of November, we will assume that you have agreed to renew the contract on the conditions as indicated above". A finds the proposed conditions totally unacceptable and does not even reply. The former contract expires on the fixed date without a new contract having been agreed between the parties.

2. Under a long-term agreement for the supply of wine B regularly met A's orders without expressly confirming its acceptance. On 15 November A orders a large stock for New Year. B does not reply, nor does it deliver at the requested time. B is in breach since, in accordance with the practice established between the parties, B's silence in regard to A's order amounts to an acceptance.

4. When acceptance becomes effective

According to para. (2) an acceptance becomes effective at the moment the indication of assent reaches the offeror (see Art. 1.10(2)). For the definition of "reaches" see Art. 1.10(3). The reason for the adoption of the "receipt" principle in preference to the "dispatch" principle is that the risk of transmission is better placed on the offeree than on the offeror, since it is the former who chooses the means of communication, who knows whether the chosen means of communication is subject to special risks or delay, and who is consequently best able to take measures to ensure that the acceptance reaches its destination.

As a rule, an acceptance by means of mere conduct likewise becomes effective only when notice thereof reaches the offeror. It should be noted, however, that special notice to this effect by the offeree will be necessary only in cases where the conduct will not of itself give notice of acceptance to the offeror within a reasonable period of time. In all other cases, *e.g.* where the conduct consists in the payment of the price, or the shipment of the goods by air or by some other rapid mode of transportation, the same effect may well be achieved simply by the bank or the carrier informing the offeror of the funds transfer or of the consignment of the goods.

An exception to the general rule of para. (2) is to be found in the cases envisaged in para. (3), *i.e.* where "by virtue of the offer or as a result of practices which the parties have established between themselves or of usage, the offeree may indicate assent by performing an act without notice to the offeror". In such cases the acceptance is effective at the moment the act is performed, irrespective of whether or not the offeror is promptly informed thereof.

Illustrations

3. A asks B to write a special program for the setting up of a data bank. Without giving A notice of acceptance, B begins to write the program and, after its completion, insists on payment in accordance with the terms set out in A's offer. B is not entitled to payment since B's purported acceptance of A's offer never became effective as B never notified A of it.

4. The facts are the same as in Illustration 3, the difference being that in the offer B is informed of A's absence for the following two weeks, and that if B intends to accept the offer B should begin writing the program immediately so as to save time. The contract is concluded once B begins to perform, even if B fails to inform A thereof either immediately or at a later stage.

This article corresponds to paras. (1), (2) first part and (3) of Art. 18 CISG.

Issues & Cases

1. **MODE OF ACCEPTANCE**
   - DECEMBER 4, 1996 ARBITRAL AWARD AD HOC ARBITRATION, ROME [664]

   1.1 **BY STATEMENTS**

   1.2 **BY OTHER CONDUCT INDICATING ASSENT**
   - DECEMBER 4, 1996 ARBITRAL AWARD AD HOC ARBITRATION, ROME [664]

   1.2.1 **PERFORMANCE OF PREPARATORY ACTS**

   1.2.2 **SILENCE OR INACTIVITY**

2. **WHEN ACCEPTANCE BECOMES EFFECTIVE**

   2.1 **UPON RECEIPT OF INDICATION OF ASSENT BY OFFEROR**

   2.2 **UPON PERFORMANCE OF ACT EFFECTIVE AS ACCEPTANCE**

ARTICLE 2.1.7
(Time of acceptance)

An offer must be accepted within the time the offeror has fixed or, if no time is fixed, within a reasonable time having regard to the circumstances, including the rapidity of the means of communication employed by the offeror. An oral offer must be accepted immediately unless the circumstances indicate otherwise.

COMMENT

With respect to the time within which an offer must be accepted, this article, which corresponds to the second part of para. (2) of Art. 18 CISG, distinguishes between written and oral offers.

As concerns written offers, all depends upon whether or not the offer indicated a specific time for acceptance: if it did, the offer must be accepted within that time, while in all other cases the indication of assent must reach the offeror "within a reasonable time having regard to the circumstances, including the rapidity of the means of communication employed by the offeror".

Illustrations

1. A sends B an offer on Monday indicating that if B intends to accept, it must do so by Friday at the latest. B's acceptance reaches A on the Monday of the following week. A may reject B's acceptance as being too late.

2. A sends B an offer on Monday morning by e-mail, urging B to reply "as soon as possible". Although on previous occasions A and B had already communicated by e-mail, B accepts A's offer by letter which reaches A on Thursday. B's acceptance is too late since under the circumstances an acceptance by a letter which reaches A three days after its e-mail was not made "as soon as possible".

Oral offers must be accepted immediately unless the circumstances indicate otherwise. An offer is to be considered oral not only when made in the presence of the offeree, but whenever the offeree can respond immediately. This is the case of an offer made over the phone or communicated electronically in real time (*e.g.* in "chat rooms").

It is important to note that the rules laid down in this article also apply to situations where, in accordance with Art. 2.1.6(3), the offeree may indicate assent by performing an act without notice to the offeror: in these cases it is the act of performance which has to be accomplished within the respective periods of time.

For the determination of the precise starting point of the period of time fixed by the offeror, see Art. 2.1.8; as to the calculation of holidays falling within that period of time, see Art. 1.12; as to cases of late acceptance and of delay in transmission, see Art. 2.1.9.

Issues & Cases

1. **WHEN ACCEPTANCE MUST BE MADE**
   - 1.1 **IMMEDIATELY IN CASE OF ORAL OFFERS**
   - 1.2 **WITHIN TIME FIXED BY OFFEROR**
   - 1.3 **IN OTHER CASES, WITHIN REASONABLE TIME**

ARTICLE 2.1.8
(Acceptance within a fixed period of time)

A period of acceptance fixed by the offeror begins to run from the time that the offer is dispatched. A time indicated in the offer is deemed to be the time of dispatch unless the circumstances indicate otherwise.

COMMENT

Whenever an offeror fixes a period of time for acceptance the question arises of when the period begins to run. According to this article it begins to run from the moment the offer is dispatched, *i.e.* has left the sphere of control of the offeror. As to when this occurs there is a presumption that the time of dispatch is the time indicated in the offer. For instance, in the case of a letter, the date of despatch will be the date shown on the letter; in the case of an e-mail, it will be the time indicated as the sending time by the offeror's server; etc. However, the presumption may be rebutted if in a given case the circumstances indicate otherwise. Thus, if the date shown on a fax letter is prior to the sending date printed by the fax machine, the latter date should prevail. Likewise, if the date shown on a letter is later than the delivery date of the letter, it is clear that the latter was written in by mistake and should therefore be disregarded.

Issues & Cases

1. BEGINNING OF PERIOD FOR ACCEPTANCE
   1.1 TIME OF DISPATCH OF OFFER
      1.1.1 TIME INDICATED IN OFFER DEEMED TO BE TIME OF DISPATCH
      1.1.2 OTHER CASES

ARTICLE 2.1.9
(Late acceptance. Delay in transmission)

(1) A late acceptance is nevertheless effective as an acceptance if without undue delay the offeror so informs the offeree or gives notice to that effect.

(2) If a communication containing a late acceptance shows that it has been sent in such circumstances that if its transmission had been normal it would have reached the offeror in due time, the late acceptance is effective as an acceptance unless, without undue delay, the offeror informs the offeree that it considers the offer as having lapsed.

COMMENT

1. Late acceptance normally ineffective

According to the principle laid down in Art. 2.1.7 for an acceptance to be effective it must reach the offeror within the time fixed by the latter or, if no time is fixed, within a reasonable time. This means that as a rule an acceptance which reaches the offeror thereafter is without effect and may be disregarded by the offeror.

2. Offeror may nevertheless "accept" late acceptance

Para. (1) of this article, which corresponds to Art. 21 CISG, states that the offeror may nevertheless consider a late acceptance as having arrived in time and thus render it effective, provided that the offeror "without undue delay [...] so informs the offeree or gives notice to that effect". If the offeror takes advantage of this possibility, the contract is to be considered as having been concluded as soon as the late acceptance reaches the offeror and not when the offeror informs the offeree of its intention to consider the late acceptance effective.

Illustration

1. A indicates 31 March as the deadline for acceptance of its offer. B's acceptance reaches A on 3 April. A, who is still interested in the contract, intends to "accept" B's late acceptance, and immediately informs B of its intention. Notwithstanding the

fact that this notice only reaches B on 5 April the contract is concluded on 3 April.

3. Acceptance late because of delay in transmission

As long as the acceptance is late because the offeree did not send it in time, it is natural to consider it as having no effect unless the offeror expressly indicates otherwise. The situation is different when the offeree has replied in time, but the acceptance reaches the offeror late because of an unexpected delay in transmission. In such a case the reliance of the offeree on the acceptance having arrived in time deserves protection, with the consequence that the late acceptance is considered to be effective unless the offeror objects without undue delay. The only condition required by para. (2) is that the communication containing the late acceptance shows that it has been sent in such circumstances that, had its transmission been normal, it would have reached the offeror in due time.

Illustration

2. The facts are the same as in Illustration 1, the difference being that B, knowing that the normal time for transmission of letters by mail to A is three days, sends its letter of acceptance on 25 March. Owing to a strike of the postal service in A's country the letter, which shows the date of its mailing on the envelope, only arrives on 3 April. B's acceptance, though late, is nevertheless effective unless A objects without undue delay.

3. The facts are the same as in Illustration 1, the difference being that B, after receiving A's offer, accepts it on 30 March by e-mail. Due to technical problems at A's server, the e-mail reaches A only on 1 April. B's acceptance, though late, is nevertheless effective unless A objects without undue delay.

Issues & Cases

1. LATE ACCEPTANCE
   - 1.1 LATE DISPATCH OF ACCEPTANCE
   - 1.2 ACCEPTANCE DISPATCHED ON TIME BUT DELAYED EN ROUTE

ARTICLE 2.1.10
(Withdrawal of acceptance)

An acceptance may be withdrawn if the withdrawal reaches the offeror before or at the same time as the acceptance would have become effective.

COMMENT

With respect to the withdrawal of an acceptance the present article lays down the same principle as that contained in Art. 2.1.3 concerning the withdrawal of an offer, *i.e.* that the offeree may change its mind and withdraw the acceptance provided that the withdrawal reaches the offeror before or at the same time as the acceptance.

It should be noted that while the offeror is bound by the offer and may no longer change its mind once the offeree has dispatched the acceptance (see Art. 2.1.4(1)), the offeree looses its freedom of choice only at a later stage, *i.e.* when the notice of acceptance reaches the offeror.

This article corresponds to Art. 22 CISG.

Issues & Cases

1. WITHDRAWAL OF ACCEPTANCE
   1.1 MUST REACH OFFEROR BEFORE OR AT THE SAME TIME AS ACCEPTANCE
   1.2 FORM OF WITHDRAWAL OF ACCEPTANCE

ARTICLE 2.1.11
(Modified acceptance)

(1) A reply to an offer which purports to be an acceptance but contains additions, limitations or other modifications is a rejection of the offer and constitutes a counter-offer.

(2) However, a reply to an offer which purports to be an acceptance but contains additional or different terms which do not materially alter the terms of the offer constitutes an acceptance, unless the offeror, without undue delay, objects to the discrepancy. If the offeror does not object, the terms of the contract are the terms of the offer with the modifications contained in the acceptance.

COMMENT

1. Acceptance with modifications normally to be considered a counter-offer

In commercial dealings it often happens that the offeree, while signifying to the offeror its intention to accept the offer ("acknowledgement of order"), nevertheless includes in its declaration terms additional to or different from those of the offer. Para. (1) of this article provides that such a purported acceptance is as a rule to be considered a rejection of the offer and that it amounts to a counter-offer by the offeree, which the offeror may or may not accept either expressly or impliedly, *e.g.* by an act of performance.

2. Modifications which do not alter the nature of the acceptance

The principle according to which the acceptance must be the mirror image of the offer implies that even unimportant differences between the offer and the acceptance permit either party at a later stage to question the existence of the contract. In order to avoid such a result, which a party may well seek merely because market conditions have changed unfavourably, para. (2) provides for an exception to the general rule laid down in para. (1) by stating that if the additional or modified terms contained in the acceptance do not "materially" alter the terms of the offer, the contract is concluded with those modifications unless the offeror objects without undue delay.

What amounts to a "material" modification cannot be determined in the abstract but will depend on the circumstances of each case. Additional or different terms relating to the price or mode of payment, place and time of performance of a non-monetary obligation, the extent of one party's liability to the other or the settlement of disputes, will normally, but need not necessarily, constitute a material modification of the offer. An important factor to be taken into account in this respect is whether the additional or different terms are commonly used in the trade sector concerned and therefore do not come as a surprise to the offeror.

Illustrations

1. A orders a machine from B to be tested on A's premises. In its acknowledgement of order B declares that it accepts the terms of the offer, but adds that it wishes to be present at the testing of the machine. The additional term is not a "material" modification of the offer and will therefore become part of the contract unless A objects without undue delay.

2. The facts are the same as in Illustration 1, the difference being that in its acknowledgement of order B adds an arbitration clause. Unless the circumstances indicate otherwise, such a clause amounts to a "material" modification of the terms of the offer, with the result that B's purported acceptance would constitute a counter-offer.

3. A orders a stated quantity of wheat from B. In its acknowledgement of order B adds an arbitration clause which is standard practice in the commodity sector concerned. Since A cannot be surprised by such a clause, it is not a "material" modification of the terms of the offer and, unless A objects without undue delay, the arbitration clause becomes part of the contract.

Issues & Cases

1. MODIFIED ACCEPTANCE

- SEPTEMBER 1998 ARBITRAL AWARD ICC INTERNATIONAL COURT OF ARBITRATION (NO. 8908) [750]

1.1 CONSTITUING COUNTER-OFFER

1.2 CONSTITUING ACCEPTANCE WHERE MODIFICATIONS NOT MATERIAL AND NOT OBJECTED TO BY OFFEROR

- SEPTEMBER 1998 ARBITRAL AWARD ICC INTERNATIONAL COURT OF ARBITRATION (NO. 8908) [750]
- 2001 ARBITRAL AWARD ICC INTERNATIONAL COURT OF ARBITRATION (NO. 10422) [902]
- JUNE 2001 ARBITRAL AWARD ICC INTERNATIONAL COURT OF ARBITRATION (NO. 11227) [951]

1.2.1 EXAMPLES OF NON-MATERIAL MODIFICATIONS

- 2001 ARBITRAL AWARD ICC INTERNATIONAL COURT OF ARBITRATION (NO. 10422) [902]

1.2.2 EXAMPLE OF MATERIAL MODIFICATIONS

2. DIFFERENCE WITH WRITINGS IN CONFIRMATION (SEE ART. 2.1.12)

3. DIFFERENCE WITH BATTLE OF FORMS (SEE ART. 2.1.22)

ARTICLE 2.1.12
(Writings in confirmation)

If a writing which is sent within a reasonable time after the conclusion of the contract and which purports to be a confirmation of the contract contains additional or different terms, such terms become part of the contract, unless they materially alter the contract or the recipient, without undue delay, objects to the discrepancy.

COMMENT

1. "Writings in confirmation"

This article deals with the situation where a contract has already been concluded either orally or by the exchange of written communications limited to the essential terms of the agreement, and one party subsequently sends the other a document intended simply to confirm what has already been agreed upon, but which in fact contains terms which are additional to or different from those previously agreed by the parties. In theory, this situation clearly differs from that envisaged in Art. 2.1.11, where a contract has not yet been concluded and the modifying terms are contained in the offeree's purported acceptance. Yet, since in practice it may be very difficult if not impossible to distinguish between the two situations, the present article adopts with respect to modifying terms contained in a writing in confirmation the same solution as that envisaged in Art. 2.1.11. In other words, just as for the modifications contained in an acknowledgement of order, it is provided that terms additional to or different from those previously agreed by the parties contained in a writing in confirmation become part of the contract, provided that they do not "materially" alter the agreement and that the recipient of the document does not object to them without undue delay.

It goes without saying that also in the context of writings in confirmation the question of which of the new terms "materially" alter the terms of the previous agreement can be answered definitely only in the light of the circumstances of each individual case. On the other hand, the present article clearly does not apply to cases where the party sending the writing in confirmation expressly invites the other party to return it duly counter-signed for acceptance. In such circumstances it is irrelevant whether the writing contains modifications, and if so whether or not these modifications are "material" since the writing must in any case be expressly accepted by the addressee if there is to be a contract.

Illustrations

1. A orders by telephone a machine from B, who accepts the order. The following day A receives a letter from B confirming the terms of their oral agreement but adding that B wishes to be present at the testing of the machine on A's premises. The additional term is not a "material" modification of the terms previously agreed between the parties and will therefore become part of the contract unless A objects without undue delay.

2. The facts are the same as in Illustration 1, the difference being that the modification contained in B's writing in confirmation consists in the addition of an arbitration clause. Unless the circumstances indicate otherwise such a clause amounts to a "material" modification of the terms previously agreed between the parties with the result that it will not become part of the contract.

3. A orders by e-mail a stated quantity of wheat and B accepts immediately by e-mail. Later on the same day B sends a letter to A confirming the terms of their agreement but adding an arbitration clause which is standard practice in the commodity sector concerned. Since A cannot be surprised by such a clause, it is not a "material" modification of the terms previously agreed and, unless A objects without undue delay, the arbitration clause becomes part of the contract.

2. Writing in confirmation to be sent within a reasonable time after conclusion of the contract

The rule according to which silence on the part of the recipient amounts to acceptance of the content of the writing in confirmation, including any non-material modifications of the terms previously agreed, presupposes that the writing is sent "within a reasonable time after the conclusion of the contract". Any writing of this kind sent after a period of time which, in the circumstances, appears to be unreasonably long, loses any significance, and silence on the part of the recipient may therefore no longer be interpreted as acceptance of its content.

3. Invoices

For the purposes of this article, the term "writing in confirmation" is to be understood in a broad sense, *i.e.* as covering also those cases where a party uses the invoice or another similar document relating to performance to specify the conditions of the contract concluded either orally or by informal correspondence, provided that such use is customary in the trade sector and/or country concerned.

Issues & Cases

1. NOTION OF "WRITINGS IN CONFIRMATION"
   1.1 LETTERS OF CONFIRMATION
   1.2 INVOICES
2. CONDITIONS FOR MODIFYING TERMS TO BECOME PART OF THE CONTRACT
   - DECEMBER 4, 1996 ARBITRAL AWARD AD HOC ARBITRATION, ROME [664]

   2.1 WRITING TO BE SENT WITHIN REASONABLE TIME AFTER CONCLUSION OF CONTRACT
   2.2 MODIFYING TERMS NON MATERIAL
   2.3 SILENCE OF RECIPIENT
3. DIFFERENCE WITH MODIFIED ACCEPTANCE (ART. 2.1.12)
4. DIFFERENCE WITH BATTLE OF FORMS (SEE ART. 2.1.22)

ARTICLE 2.1.13
(Conclusion of contract dependent on agreement on specific matters or in a particular form)

Where in the course of negotiations one of the parties insists that the contract is not concluded until there is agreement on specific matters or in a particular form, no contract is concluded before agreement is reached on those matters or in that form.

COMMENT

1. Conclusion of contract dependent on agreement on specific matters

As a rule, a contract is concluded if the parties reach agreement on the terms which are essential to the type of transaction involved, while minor terms which the parties have not settled may subsequently be implied either in fact or by law. See comment 1 on Art. 2.1.2 and also Arts. 4.8 and 5.1.2.

Illustration

1. A agrees with B on all the terms which are essential to their intended contract for the distribution of A's goods. When the question subsequently arises of who should bear the costs of the publicity campaign, neither party may claim that no contract has come into existence by reason of the silence of the contract on this point, as the missing term is not essential to the type of transaction in question and will be implied in fact or by law.

Parties may, however, in a given case consider specific matters to be of such importance that they do not intend to enter into a binding agreement unless these matters are settled in a satisfactory manner. If the parties, or one only of them, make such an intention explicit, the contract as such does not come into existence without agreement on those matters. By using the word "insists", the present article makes it clear that it is not sufficient for the parties to manifest their intention to this effect simply in passing, but that it must be done unequivocally.

Illustration

2. The facts are the same as in Illustration 1, the difference being that during the negotiations B repeatedly declares that the question of who should bear the cost of the publicity campaign must be settled expressly. Notwithstanding their agreement on all the essential terms of the contract, no contract has come into

existence between A and B since B had insisted that the conclusion of the contract was dependent on agreement regarding that specific term.

2. Conclusion of contract dependent on agreement in a particular form

In commercial practice, particularly when transactions of considerable complexity are involved, it is quite frequent that after prolonged negotiations the parties sign an informal document called "Preliminary Agreement", "Memorandum of Understanding", "Letter of Intent" or the like, containing the terms of the agreement so far reached, but at the same time state their intention to provide for the execution of a formal document at a later stage ("Subject to Contract", "Formal Agreement to follow"). In some cases the parties consider their contract as already being concluded and the execution of the formal document only as confirmation of the already complete agreement. If, however, both parties, or only one of them, make it clear that they do not intend to be bound unless the formal document has been drawn up, there will be no contract until that time even if the parties have agreed on all the relevant aspects of their transaction.

Illustrations

3. After prolonged negotiations A and B sign a "Memorandum of Understanding" containing the terms of an agreement for a joint venture for the exploration and exploitation of the continental shelf of country X. The parties agree that they will at a later stage draw up the agreement in formal documents to be signed and exchanged at a public ceremony. If the "Memorandum" already contains all the relevant terms of the agreement and the subsequent documents are intended merely to permit the agreement to be properly presented to the public, it may be taken that the contract was already concluded when the first written document was signed.

4. The facts are the same as in Illustration 3, the difference being that the "Memorandum of Understanding" contains a clause such as "Not binding until final agreement is executed" or the like. Until the signing and the exchange of the formal documents there is no binding contract.

Issues & Cases

1. CONCLUSION OF CONTRACT DEPENDENT ON AGREEMENT ON SPECIFIC MATTERS

- 2001 ARBITRAL AWARD ICC INTERNATIONAL COURT OF ARBITRATION (NO. 10422) [902]

1.1 INTENTION MUST BE EXPRESSED UNEQUIVOCALLY

2. CONCLUSION OF CONTRACT DEPENDENT ON AGREEMENT IN A SPECIFIC FORM

- FEBRUARY 2, 2001 NETHERLANDS SUPREME COURT OF THE NETHERLANDS (NO. R99/120 HR) [922]

2.1 INTENTION MUST BE EXPRESSED UNEQUIVOCALLY

2.1.1 CLAUSES SUCH AS "SUBJECT TO CONTRACT", "FORMAL AGREEMENT TO FOLLOW", ETC.

ARTICLE 2.1.14
(Contract with terms deliberately left open)

(1) If the parties intend to conclude a contract, the fact that they intentionally leave a term to be agreed upon in further negotiations or to be determined by a third person does not prevent a contract from coming into existence.

(2) The existence of the contract is not affected by the fact that subsequently

(a) the parties reach no agreement on the term; or

(b) the third person does not determine the term,

provided that there is an alternative means of rendering the term definite that is reasonable in the circumstances, having regard to the intention of the parties.

COMMENT

1. Contract with terms deliberately left open

A contract may be silent on one or more issues because the parties simply did not think of them during the negotiations. Provided that the parties have agreed on the terms essential to the type of transaction concerned, a contract will nonetheless have been concluded and the missing terms will be supplied on the basis of Arts. 4.8 or 5.1.2. See comment 1 on Art. 2.1.2. Quite different is the case dealt with in the present article: here the parties intentionally leave open one or more terms because they are unable or unwilling to determine them at the time of the conclusion of the contract, and refer for their determination to an agreement to be made by them at a later stage, or to a third person.

This latter situation, which is especially frequent in, although not confined to, long-term transactions, gives rise in essence to two problems: first, whether the fact that the parties have intentionally left terms open prevents a contract from coming into existence and second, if this is not the case, what will happen to the contract if the parties subsequently fail to reach agreement or the third person fails to make the determination.

2. Open terms not in themselves an impediment to valid conclusion of contract

Para. (1) states that if the parties intended to conclude a contract, the fact that they have intentionally left a term to be agreed upon in further negotiations or to be determined by a third person does not prevent a contract from coming into existence.

In cases where it is not expressly stated, the parties' intention to conclude a contract notwithstanding the terms left open may be inferred from other circumstances, such as the non-essential character of the terms in question, the degree of definiteness of the agreement as a whole, the fact that the open terms relate to items which by their very nature can be determined only at a later stage, the fact that the agreement has already been partially executed, etc.

Illustration

1. A, a shipping line, enters into a detailed agreement with B, a terminal operator, for the use of B's container terminal. The agreement fixes the minimum volume of containers to be discharged or loaded annually and the fees payable, while the fees for additional containers are left to be determined if and when the minimum volume is reached. Two months later A learns that B's competitor would offer better conditions and refuses to perform, claiming that the agreement with B never resulted in a binding contract because the question of the fees had not been settled. A is liable for non-performance because the detailed character of the agreement as well as the fact that both A and B began performance immediately indicate clearly that their intention was to enter into a binding agreement.

3. Failure of mechanism provided for by parties for determination of open terms

If the parties are unable to reach agreement on the open terms or the third person does not determine them, the question arises as to whether or not the contract comes to an end. According to para. (2) of this article the existence of the contract is not affected "provided that there is an alternative means of rendering the term definite that is reasonable in the circumstances, having regard to the intention of the parties". A first alternative exists whenever the missing term may be supplied on the basis of Art. 5.1.2; if the parties have deferred the determination of the missing term to a third person to be nominated by an instance such as the President of the Tribunal, or of the Chamber of Commerce, etc., it may also consist in the appointment of a new third person. The cases in which a given contract may be upheld by resorting to such alternative means will, however, be quite rare in practice. Few problems should arise as long as the term to be implemented is of minor importance. If, on the other hand, the term in question is essential to the type of transaction concerned, there must be clear evidence of the intention of the parties to uphold the contract: among the factors to be taken into account in this connection are whether the term in question relates to items which by their very nature can be determined only at a later stage, whether the agreement has already been partially executed, etc.

Illustration

2. The facts are the same as in Illustration 1, the difference being that when the minimum volume of containers to be loaded or unloaded is reached the parties fail to agree on the fees payable in respect of the additional containers. A stops performing, claiming that the contract has come to an end. A is liable for non-performance, since the fact that the parties have started performing without making future agreement on the missing term a condition for the continuation of their business relationship is sufficient evidence of their intention to uphold the contract even in the absence of such agreement. The fees for the additional containers will be determined according to the criteria laid down in Art. 5.1.7.

Issues & Cases

1. **CONTRACT WITH TERMS DELIBERATELY LEFT OPEN V. CONTRACT WITH MISSING TERMS (SEE E.G. ARTS. 4.8, 5.1.2, 5.1.6, 5.1.7, 6.1.1(C), 6.1.6, 6.1.7, 6.1.10, 6.1.11 AND 7.4.9)**
2. **VALID CONCLUSION OF CONTRACT NOTWITHSTANDING OPEN TERMS**
   - **2.1 EXPRESS STATEMENT BY PARTIES**
   - **2.2 INFERENCE FROM OTHER CIRCUMSTANCES**
     - APRIL 1998 ARBITRAL AWARD (SECOND PARTIAL) ICC INTERNATIONAL COURT OF ARBITRATION (NO. 7110) [734]
     - JUNE 2001 ARBITRAL AWARD ICC INTERNATIONAL COURT OF ARBITRATION (NO. 11227) [951]
3. **MECHANISM PROVIDED FOR BY PARTIES FOR DETERMINATION OF OPEN TERMS**
   - **3.1 FURTHER NEGOTIATION BETWEEN PARTIES**
     - APRIL 1998 ARBITRAL AWARD (SECOND PARTIAL) ICC INTERNATIONAL COURT OF ARBITRATION (NO. 7110) [734]
   - **3.2 DETERMINATION BY THIRD PERSON**
4. **FAILURE OF MECHANISM PROVIDED FOR BY PARTIES FOR DETERMINATION OF OPEN TERMS**

ARTICLE 2.1.15
(Negotiations in bad faith)

(1) A party is free to negotiate and is not liable for failure to reach an agreement.

(2) However, a party who negotiates or breaks off negotiations in bad faith is liable for the losses caused to the other party.

(3) It is bad faith, in particular, for a party to enter into or continue negotiations when intending not to reach an agreement with the other party.

COMMENT

1. Freedom of negotiation

As a rule, parties are not only free to decide when and with whom to enter into negotiations with a view to concluding a contract, but also if, how and for how long to proceed with their efforts to reach an agreement. This follows from the basic principle of freedom of contract enunciated in Art. 1.1, and is essential in order to guarantee healthy competition among business people engaged in international trade.

2. Liability for negotiating in bad faith

A party's right freely to enter into negotiations and to decide on the terms to be negotiated is, however, not unlimited, and must not conflict with the principle of good faith and fair dealing laid down in Art. 1.7. One particular instance of negotiating in bad faith which is expressly indicated in para. (3) of this article is that where a party enters into negotiations or continues to negotiate without any intention of concluding an agreement with the other party. Other instances are where one party has deliberately or by negligence misled the other party as to the nature or terms of the proposed contract, either by actually misrepresenting facts, or by not disclosing facts which, given the nature of the parties and/or the contract, should have been disclosed. As to the duty of confidentiality, see Art. 2.1.16.

A party's liability for negotiating in bad faith is limited to the losses caused to the other party (para. (2)). In other words, the aggrieved party may recover the expenses incurred in the negotiations and may also be compensated for the lost opportunity to conclude another contract with a third person (so-called reliance or negative interest), but may generally not recover the profit which would have resulted had the original contract been concluded (so-called expectation or positive interest).

Only if the parties have expressly agreed on a duty to negotiate in good faith, will all the remedies for breach of contract be available to them, including the remedy of the right to performance.

Illustrations

1. A learns of B's intention to sell its restaurant. A, who has no intention whatsoever of buying the restaurant, nevertheless enters into lengthy negotiations with B for the sole purpose of preventing B from selling the restaurant to C, a competitor of A's. A, who breaks off negotiations when C has bought another restaurant, is liable to B, who ultimately succeeds in selling the restaurant at a lower price than that offered by C, for the difference in price.

2. A, who is negotiating with B for the promotion of the purchase of military equipment by the armed forces of B's country, learns that B will not receive the necessary export licence from its own governmental authorities, a pre-requisite for permission to pay B's fees. A does not reveal this fact to B and finally concludes the contract, which, however, cannot be enforced by reason of the missing licences. A is liable to B for the costs incurred after A had learned of the impossibility of obtaining the required licences.

3. A enters into lengthy negotiations for a bank loan from B's branch office. At the last minute the branch office discloses that it had no authority to sign and that its head office has decided not to approve the draft agreement. A, who could in the meantime have obtained the loan from another bank, is entitled to recover the expenses entailed by the negotiations and the profits it would have made during the delay before obtaining the loan from the other bank.

4. Contractor A and supplier B enter into a pre-bid agreement whereby they undertake to negotiate in good faith for the supply of equipment in the event that A succeeds in becoming prime contractor for a major construction project. A is awarded the construction contract, but after preliminary contacts with B refuses to continue the negotiations. B may request enforcement of the duty to negotiate in good faith.

3. Liability for breaking off negotiations in bad faith

The right to break off negotiations also is subject to the principle of good faith and fair dealing. Once an offer has been made, it may be revoked only within the limits provided for in Art. 2.1.4. Yet even before this stage is reached, or in a negotiation process with no ascertainable sequence of offer and acceptance, a party may no longer be free to break off negotiations abruptly and without justification. When such a point of no return is reached depends of course on the circumstances of the case, in particular the extent to which the other party, as a result of the conduct of the first party, had reason to rely on the positive outcome of the negotiations, and on the number of issues relating to the future contract on which the parties have already reached agreement.

Illustration

4. A assures B of the grant of a franchise if B takes steps to gain experience and is prepared to invest US$ 150,000. During the next two years B makes extensive preparations with a view to concluding the contract, always with A's assurance that B will be granted the franchise. When all is ready for the signing of the agreement, A informs B that the latter must invest a substantially higher sum. B, who refuses, is entitled to recover from A the expenses incurred with a view to the conclusion of the contract.

Issues & Cases

1. FREEDOM OF NEGOTIATION (SEE ART. 1.1)
2. NEGOTIATING IN BAD FAITH
   - SEPTEMBER 4, 1996 ARBITRAL AWARD ICC INTERNATIONAL COURT OF ARBITRATION (NO. 8540) [636]

   2.1 ENTERING INTO OR CONTINUING NEGOTIATIONS WITHOUT ANY INTENTION TO REACH AGREEMENT
   - SEPTEMBER 4, 1996 ARBITRAL AWARD ICC INTERNATIONAL COURT OF ARBITRATION (NO. 8540) [636]

   2.2 FRAUDOLENT OR NEGLIGENT MISREPRESENTATION
   - AUGUST 2000 ARBITRAL AWARD ICC INTERNATIONAL COURT OF ARBITRATION (NO. 9651) [854]

   2.3 NON DISCLOSURE OF RELEVANT FACTS

   2.4 BREACH OF CONFIDENTIALITY (SEE ART. 2.1.16)

   2.5 BREAKING OFF NEGOTIATIONS ABRUPTLY AND WITHOUT JUSTIFICATION
   - SEPTEMBER 17, 2002 COURT OF JUSTICE OF THE EUROPEAN COMMUNITIES (NO. C-334/00) [1010]
3. LIABILITY FOR NEGOTIATING IN BAD FAITH

   3.1 LIABILITY LIMITED TO LOSSES CAUSED TO THE OTHER PARTY (SO-CALLED RELIANCE OR NEGATIVE INTEREST)

ARTICLE 2.1.16
(Duty of confidentiality)

Where information is given as confidential by one party in the course of negotiations, the other party is under a duty not to disclose that information or to use it improperly for its own purposes, whether or not a contract is subsequently concluded. Where appropriate, the remedy for breach of that duty may include compensation based on the benefit received by the other party.

COMMENT

1. Parties in general not under a duty of confidentiality

Just as there exists no general duty of disclosure, so parties, when entering into negotiations for the conclusion of a contract, are normally under no obligation to treat the information they have exchanged as confidential. In other words, since a party is normally free to decide which facts relevant to the transaction under negotiation to disclose, such information is as a rule to be considered non-confidential, *i.e.* information which the other party may either disclose to third persons or use for purposes of its own should no contract be concluded.

Illustration

1. A invites B and C, producers of air-conditioning systems, to submit offers for the installation of such a system. In their offers B and C also provide some technical details regarding the functioning of their respective systems, with a view to enhancing the merits of their products. A decides to reject B's offer and to continue negotiations only with C. A is free to use the information contained in B's offer in order to induce C to propose more favourable conditions.

2. Confidential information

A party may have an interest in certain information given to the other party not being divulged or used for purposes other than those for which it was given. As long as that party expressly declares that such information is to be considered confidential, the situation is clear, for by receiving the information the other party implicitly agrees to treat it as confidential. The only problem which may arise is that if the period during which the other party is not to disclose the information is too long, this might contravene the applicable laws prohibiting restrictive trade practices. Yet even in the absence of such an express declaration the receiving party may be under a duty of confidentiality. This is the case where, in view of the particular nature of the information or the professional qualifications of the parties, it would be contrary to the general principle of good faith and fair dealing for the receiving party to disclose it, or to use it for its own purposes after the breaking off of negotiations.

Illustrations

2. The facts are the same as in Illustration 1, the difference being that in its offer B expressly requests A not to divulge certain technical specifications contained therein. A may not use this information in its negotiations with C.

3. A is interested in entering into a joint venture agreement with B or C, the two leading car manufacturers in country X. Negotiations progress with B in particular, and A receives fairly detailed information relating to B's plans for a new car design. Although B does not expressly request A to treat this information as confidential, because it is for a new car design A may be under a duty not to disclose it to C, nor is A allowed to use those plans for its own production process should the negotiations not result in the conclusion of a contract.

3. Damages recoverable

The breach of confidentiality implies first liability in damages. The amount of damages recoverable may vary, depending on whether or not the parties entered into a special agreement for the non-disclosure of the information. Even if the injured party has not suffered any loss, it may be entitled to recover from the non-performing party the benefit the latter received by disclosing the information to third persons or by using it for its own purposes. If necessary, for example when the information has not yet been disclosed or has been disclosed only partially, the injured party may also seek an injunction in accordance with the applicable law.

Issues & Cases

1. PARTIES IN GENERAL NOT UNDER A DUTY OF CONFIDENTIALITY
2. CONFIDENTIAL INFORMATION
   - JANUARY 31, 2003 ARBITRAL AWARD ARBITRATION COURT OF THE LAUSANNE CHAMBER OF COMMERCE AND INDUSTRY [1056]

2.1 EXPRESSED DECLARED SO BY PARTY
2.2 DEPENDING ON OTHER CIRCUMSTANCES
3. BREACH OF DUTY OF CONFIDENTIALITY
- MAY 17, 2002 ARBITRAL AWARD (PARTIAL) ARBITRATION COURT OF THE LAUSANNE CHAMBER OF COMMERCE AND INDUSTRY [1001]

3.1 DISCLOSURE OF INFORMATION
3.2 IMPROPER USE OF INFORMATION FOR PERSONAL PURPOSES
4. REMEDIES FOR BREACH OF CONFIDENTIALITY
4.1 DAMAGES
4.2 INJUNCTION

ARTICLE 2.1.17
(Merger clauses)

A contract in writing which contains a clause indicating that the writing completely embodies the terms on which the parties have agreed cannot be contradicted or supplemented by evidence of prior statements or agreements. However, such statements or agreements may be used to interpret the writing.

COMMENT

If the conclusion of a contract is preceded by more or less extended negotiations, the parties may wish to put their agreement in writing and declare that document to constitute their final agreement. This can be achieved by an appropriately drafted "merger" or "integration" clause (*e.g.* "This contract contains the entire agreement between the parties"). However, the effect of such a clause is not to deprive prior statements or agreements of any relevance: they may still be used as a means of interpreting the written document. See also Art. 4.3(a).

A merger clause of course covers only prior statements or agreements between the parties and does not preclude subsequent informal agreements between them. The parties are, however, free to extend an agreed form even to future amendments. See Art. 2.1.18.

This article indirectly confirms the principle set out in Art. 1.2 in the sense that, in the absence of a merger clause, extrinsic evidence supplementing or contradicting a written contract is admissible.

Issues & Cases

1. **MERGER CLAUSES DEFINED**
   - MARCH 1998 ARBITRAL AWARD ICC INTERNATIONAL COURT OF ARBITRATION (NO. 9117) [727]

   1.1 **CONTRACT TERMS CANNOT BE CONTRADICTED OR SUPPLEMENTED BY PRIOR STATEMENTS OR AGREEMENTS**
   - MARCH 1998 ARBITRAL AWARD ICC INTERNATIONAL COURT OF ARBITRATION (NO. 9117) [727]

   1.2 **PRIOR STATEMENTS OR AGREEMENTS CAN ONLY BE USED AS A MEANS OF INTERPRETING CONTRACT TERMS**

- NOVEMBER 28, 2002 ARBITRAL AWARD CAMERA ARBITRALE NAZIONALE E INTERNAZIONALE DI MILANO [1034]
- FEBRUARY 17, 2006 UNITED KINGDOM COURT OF APPEAL (CIVIL DIVISION) (NO. 2006 EWCA CIV. 69) [1142]

2. EFFECTS OF MERGER CLAUSE

ARTICLE 2.1.18
(Modification in a particular form)

A contract in writing which contains a clause requiring any modification or termination by agreement to be in a particular form may not be otherwise modified or terminated. However, a party may be precluded by its conduct from asserting such a clause to the extent that the other party has acted in reliance on that conduct.

COMMENT

Parties concluding a written contract may wish to ensure that any modification or termination by agreement will also be in writing or otherwise in a particular form and to this end include a special clause in the contract (*e.g.* "Any modification of this Contract may be made only by a writing signed by both Parties"; "Alterations to the above-indicated Time-schedule must be confirmed in writing by the Engineer's representative on site").

This article states that as a rule such a clause renders any oral modification or termination ineffective, thus rejecting the idea that an oral modification or termination of the contract may be seen as an implied abrogation of the "no oral modification" clause.

Yet there is an exception to the general rule. In application of the general principle prohibiting inconsistent behaviour (see Art. 1.8), this article specifies that a party may be precluded by its conduct from invoking the written modification clause to the extent that the other party has acted in reliance on that conduct.

Illustration

A, a contractor, contracts with B, a school board, for the construction of a new school building. The contract provides that the second floor of the building is to have sufficient bearing capacity to support the school library. Notwithstanding a "no oral modification" clause in the same contract, the parties orally agree that the second floor of the building should be of non-bearing construction. A completes construction according to the modification, and B, who has observed the progress of the construction without making any objections, only at this point objects to how the second floor has been constructed. A court may decide that B is not entitled to invoke the "no oral modification" clause as A reasonably relied on the oral modification, and is therefore not liable for non-performance.

Issues & Cases

1. NO-ORAL MODIFICATION CLAUSES
   - MARCH 1998 ARBITRAL AWARD ICC INTERNATIONAL COURT OF ARBITRATION (NO. 9117) [727]

1.1 NON APPLICABLE IN CASE OF DETRIMENTAL RELIANCE
   - FEBRUARY 12, 2003 AUSTRALIA FEDERAL COURT OF AUSTRALIA (NO. NG733 OF 1997) [1058]

ARTICLE 2.1.19
(Contracting under standard terms)

(1) Where one party or both parties use standard terms in concluding a contract, the general rules on formation apply, subject to Articles 2.1.20 - 2.1.22.

(2) Standard terms are provisions which are prepared in advance for general and repeated use by one party and which are actually used without negotiation with the other party.

COMMENT

1. Contracting under standard terms

This article is the first of four articles (Arts. 2.1.19 - 2.1.22) which deal with the special situation where one or both parties use standard terms in concluding a contract.

2. Notion of "standard terms"

"Standard terms" are to be understood as those contract provisions which are prepared in advance for general and repeated use by one party and which are actually used without negotiation with the other party (para. (2)). What is decisive is not their formal presentation (*e.g.* whether they are contained in a separate document or in the contract document itself; whether they have been issued on pre-printed forms or are only contained in an electronic file, etc.), nor who prepared them (the party itself, a trade or professional association, etc.), nor their volume (whether they consist of a comprehensive set of provisions covering almost all the relevant aspects of the contract, or of only one or two provisions regarding, for instance, exclusion of liability and arbitration). What is decisive is the fact that they are drafted in advance for general and repeated use and that they are actually used in a given case by one of the parties without negotiation with the other party. This latter requirement obviously relates only to the standard terms as such, which the other party must accept as a whole, while the other terms of the same contract may well be the subject of negotiation between the parties.

3. General rules on formation apply

Usually, the general rules on formation apply irrespective of whether or not one or both parties use standard terms (para. (1)). It follows that standard terms proposed by one party bind the other party only on acceptance, and that it depends upon the circumstances of the case whether the two parties must refer to the standard terms expressly or whether the incorporation of such terms may be implied. Thus, standard terms contained in the contract document itself will normally be binding upon the mere signature of the contract document as a whole, at least as long as they are reproduced above that signature and not, for instance, on the reverse side of the document. On the other hand, standard terms contained in a separate document or electronic file will normally have to be referred to expressly by the party intending to use them. Implied incorporation may be admitted only if there exists a practice established between the parties or usage to that effect. See Art. 1.9.

Illustrations

1. A intends to conclude an insurance contract with B covering the risk of liability for accidents of A's employees at work. The parties sign a model contract form presented by B after filling in the blank spaces relating, among other matters, to the premium and to the maximum amount insured. By virtue of its signature, A is bound not only by the terms which it has individually negotiated with B, but also by the General Conditions of the National Insurers' Association, which are printed on the form.

2. A normally concludes contracts with its customers on the basis of its own standard terms which are printed as a separate document. When making an offer to B, a new customer, A fails to make an express reference to the standard terms. B accepts the offer. The standard terms are not incorporated in the contract unless A can prove that B knew or ought to have known of A's intention to conclude the contract only on the basis of its own standard terms, *e.g.* because the same standard terms had regularly been adopted in previous transactions.

3. A intends to buy grain on the commodity exchange in London. In the contract concluded between A and B, a broker on that exchange, no express reference is made to the standard terms which normally govern brokerage contracts concluded at the exchange in question. The standard terms are nevertheless incorporated in the contract because their application to the kind of contract in question amounts to a usage.

Issues & Cases

1. **'STANDARD TERMS' DEFINED**

- APRIL 1998 ARBITRAL AWARD ICC INTERNATIONAL COURT OF ARBITRATION (NO. 8223) [739]

1.1 TERMS PREPARED IN ADVANCE FOR GENERAL AND REPEATED USE BY ONE PARTY

- APRIL 1998 ARBITRAL AWARD ICC INTERNATIONAL COURT OF ARBITRATION (NO. 8223) [739]

1.2 TERMS USED WITHOUT NEGOTIATION WITH THE OTHER PARTY (SEE ART. 2.1.21)

2. GENERAL RULES ON FORMATION APPLY

2.1 STANDARD TERMS CONTAINED IN THE CONTRACT DOCUMENT ITSELF

- OCTOBER 16, 2002 NETHERLANDS HOF'S-HERTOGENBOSCH [1027]

2.2 STANDARD TERMS CONTAINED IN A SEPARATE DOCUMENT

ARTICLE 2.1.20
(Surprising terms)

(1) No term contained in standard terms which is of such a character that the other party could not reasonably have expected it, is effective unless it has been expressly accepted by that party.

(2) In determining whether a term is of such a character regard shall be had to its content, language and presentation.

COMMENT

1. Surprising terms in standard terms not effective

A party which accepts the other party's standard terms is in principle bound by them irrespective of whether or not it actually knows their content in detail or fully understands their implications. An important exception to this rule is, however, laid down in this article which states that, notwithstanding its acceptance of the standard terms as a whole, the adhering party is not bound by those terms which by virtue of their content, language or presentation are of such a character that it could not reasonably have expected them. The reason for this exception is the desire to avoid a party which uses standard terms taking undue advantage of its position by surreptitiously attempting to impose terms on the other party which that party would scarcely have accepted had it been aware of them. For other articles intended to protect the economically weaker or less experienced party, see Arts. 3.10 and 4.6.

2. Terms "surprising" by virtue of their content

A particular term contained in standard terms may come as a surprise to the adhering party first by reason of its content. This is the case whenever the content of the term in question is such that a reasonable person of the same kind as the adhering party would not have expected it in the type of standard terms involved. In determining whether or not a term is unusual, regard must be had on the one hand to the terms which are commonly to be found in standard terms generally used in the trade sector concerned, and on the other to the individual negotiations between the parties. Thus, for example, a term excluding or limiting the contractual liability of the proponent may or may not be considered to be "surprising", and in consequence ineffective in a particular case, its effectiveness depending on whether or not terms of that kind are common in the trade sector concerned, and are consistent with the way in which the parties conducted their negotiations.

Illustration

1. A, a travel agency, offers package tours for business trips. The terms of the advertisement give the impression that A is acting as a tour operator who undertakes full responsibility for the various services comprising the package. B books a tour on the basis of A's standard terms. Notwithstanding B's acceptance of the terms as a whole, A may not rely on a term stating that, with respect to the hotel accommodation, it is acting merely as an agent for the hotelkeeper, and therefore declines any liability.

3. Terms "surprising" by virtue of their language or presentation

Other reasons for a particular term contained in standard terms being surprising to the adhering party may be the language in which it is couched, which may be obscure, or the way in which it is presented typographically, for instance in minute print. In order to determine whether or not this is the case, regard is to be had not so much to the formulation and presentation commonly used in the type of standard terms involved, but more to the professional skill and experience of persons of the same kind as the adhering party. Thus, a particular wording may be both obscure and clear at the same time, depending on whether or not the adhering party belongs to the same professional category as the party using the standard terms.

The language factor may also play an important role in the context of international transactions. If the standard terms are drafted in a foreign language it cannot be excluded that some of its terms, although fairly clear in themselves, will turn out to be surprising for the adhering party who could not reasonably have been expected fully to appreciate all their implications.

Illustrations

2. A, an insurance company operating in country X, is an affiliate of B, a company incorporated in country Y. A's standard terms comprise some 50 terms printed in small type. One of the terms designates the law of country Y as the applicable law. Unless this term is presented in bold letters or in any other way apt to attract the attention of the adhering party, it will be without effect since customers in country X would not reasonably expect to find a choice-of-law clause designating a foreign law as the law governing their contracts in the standard terms of a company operating in their own country.

3. A, a commodity dealer operating in Hamburg, uses in its contracts with its customers standard terms containing, among

others, a provision stating "Hamburg - Freundschaftliche Arbitrage". In local business circles this clause is normally understood as meaning that possible disputes are to be submitted to a special arbitration governed by particular rules of procedure of local origin. In contracts with foreign customers this clause may be held to be ineffective, notwithstanding the acceptance of the standard terms as a whole, since a foreign customer cannot reasonably be expected to understand its exact implications, and this irrespective of whether or not the clause has been translated into its own language.

4. Express acceptance of "surprising" terms

The risk of the adhering party being taken by surprise by the kind of terms so far discussed clearly no longer exists if in a given case the other party draws the adhering party's attention to them and the adhering party accepts them. The present article therefore provides that a party may no longer rely on the "surprising" nature of a term in order to challenge its effectiveness, once it has expressly accepted the term.

Issues & Cases

1. "SURPRISING TERMS" DEFINED
   - 1.1 TERMS "SURPRISING" BY VIRTUE OF THEIR CONTENT
     - OCTOBER 16, 2002 NETHERLANDS HOF'S-HERTOGENBOSCH [1027]
   - 1.2 TERMS "SURPRISING" BY VIRTUE OF THEIR LANGUAGE OR PRESENTATION
2. "SURPRISING TERMS" INEFFECTIVE UNLESS EXPRESSLY ACCEPTED BY THE ADHERING PARTY

ARTICLE 2.1.21

(Conflict between standard terms and non-standard terms)

In case of conflict between a standard term and a term which is not a standard term the latter prevails.

COMMENT

Standard terms are by definition prepared in advance by one party or a third person and incorporated in an individual contract without their content being discussed by the parties (see Art. 2.1.19(2)). It is therefore logical that whenever the parties specifically negotiate and agree on particular provisions of their contract, such provisions will prevail over conflicting provisions contained in the standard terms since they are more likely to reflect the intention of the parties in the given case.

The individually agreed provisions may appear in the same document as the standard terms, but may also be contained in a separate document. In the first case they may easily be recognised on account of their being written in characters different from those of the standard terms. In the second case it may be more difficult to distinguish between the provisions which are standard terms and those which are not, and to determine their exact position in the hierarchy of the different documents. To this effect the parties often include a contract provision expressly indicating the documents which form part of their contract and their respective weight.

Special problems may however arise when the modifications to the standard terms have only been agreed upon orally, without the conflicting provisions contained in the standard terms being struck out, and those standard terms contain a provision stating the exclusive character of the writing signed by the parties, or that any addition to or modification of their content must be in writing. For these cases see Arts. 2.1.17 and 2.1.18.

Issues & Cases

1. **PREVALENCE OF INDIVIDUALLY AGREED TERMS OVER STANDARD TERMS**

- JANUARY 24, 1996 FRANCE COUR D'APPEL DE GRENOBLE [611]

1.1 **INDIVIDUALLY AGREED TERMS AND STANDARD TERMS CONTAINED IN THE SAME CONTRACT DOCUMENT**

- JANUARY 24, 1996 FRANCE COUR D'APPEL DE GRENOBLE [611]

1.2 **INDIVIDUALLY TERMS AGREED ORALLY**

1.2.1 CONFLICT WITH "MERGER CLAUSES" CONTAINED IN STANDARD TERMS (SEE ART. 2.1.17)
1.2.2 CONFLICT WITH "NO ORAL MODIFICATION CLAUSES" CONTAINED IN STANDARD TERMS (SEE ART. 2.1.18)

ARTICLE 2.1.22
(Battle of forms)

Where both parties use standard terms and reach agreement except on those terms, a contract is concluded on the basis of the agreed terms and of any standard terms which are common in substance unless one party clearly indicates in advance, or later and without undue delay informs the other party, that it does not intend to be bound by such a contract.

COMMENT

1. Parties using different standard terms

It is quite frequent in commercial transactions for both the offeror when making the offer, and the offeree when accepting it, each to refer to its own standard terms. In the absence of express acceptance by the offeror of the offeree's standard terms, the problem arises as to whether a contract is concluded at all and if so, which, if either, of the two conflicting sets of standard terms should prevail.

2. "Battle of forms" and general rules on offer and acceptance

If the general rules on offer and acceptance were to be applied, there would either be no contract at all since the purported acceptance by the offeree would, subject to the exception provided for in Art. 2.1.11(2), amount to a counter-offer, or if the two parties have started to perform without objecting to each other's standard terms, a contract would be considered to have been concluded on the basis of those terms which were the last to be sent or to be referred to (the "last shot").

3. The "knock-out" doctrine

The "last shot" doctrine may be appropriate if the parties clearly indicate that the adoption of their standard terms is an essential condition for the conclusion of the contract. Where, on the other hand, the parties, as is very often the case in practice, refer to their standard terms more or less automatically, for example by exchanging printed order and acknowledgement of order forms with the respective terms on the reverse side, they will normally not even be aware of the conflict between their respective standard terms. There is in such cases no reason to allow the parties subsequently to question the very existence of the contract or, if performance has commenced, to insist on the application of the terms last sent or referred to.

It is for this reason that the present article provides, notwithstanding the general rules on offer and acceptance, that if the parties reach an agreement except on their standard terms, a contract is concluded on the basis of the agreed terms and of any standard terms which are common in substance ("knock-out" doctrine).

Illustration

1. A orders a machine from B indicating the type of machine, the price and terms of payment, and the date and place of delivery. A uses an order form with its "General Conditions for Purchase" printed on the reverse side. B accepts by sending an acknowledgement of order form on the reverse side of which appear its own "General Conditions for Sale". When A subsequently seeks to withdraw from the deal it claims that no contract was ever concluded as there was no agreement as to which set of standard terms should apply. Since, however, the parties have agreed on the essential terms of the contract, a contract has been concluded on those terms and on any standard terms which are common in substance.

A party may, however, always exclude the operation of the "knock-out" doctrine by clearly indicating in advance, or by later and without undue delay informing the other, that it does not intend to be bound by a contract which is not based on its own standard terms. What will in practice amount to such a "clear" indication cannot be stated in absolute terms but the inclusion of a clause of this kind in the standard terms themselves will not normally be sufficient since what is necessary is a specific declaration by the party concerned in its offer or acceptance.

Illustrations

2. The facts are the same as in Illustration 1, the difference being that A claims that the contract was concluded on the basis of its standard terms since they contain a clause which states that "Deviating standard terms of the party accepting the order are not valid if they have not been confirmed in writing by us". The result will be the same as in Illustration 1, since merely by including such a clause in its standard terms A does not indicate with sufficient clarity its determination to conclude the contract only on its own terms.

3. The facts are the same as in Illustration 1, the difference being that the non-standard terms of A's offer contain a statement to the effect that A intends to contract only on its own standard terms. The mere fact that B attaches its own standard terms to its

acceptance does not prevent the contract from being concluded on the basis of A's standard terms.

Issues & Cases

1. **BATTLE OF FORMS DEFINED**
   - JULY 13, 2001 NETHERLANDS SUPREME COURT OF THE NETHERLANDS (NO. C99/315 HR) [956]

   1.1 **DIFFERENCE WITH MODIFIED ACCEPTANCE (SEE ART. 2.1.11)**

   1.2 **DIFFERENCE WITH WRITINGS IN CONFIRMATION (SEE ART. 2.1.12)**
2. **"LAST-SHOT" DOCTRINE**
3. **"KNOCK-OUT" DOCTRINE**
   - JULY 13, 2001 NETHERLANDS SUPREME COURT OF THE NETHERLANDS (NO. C99/315 HR) [956]

   3.1 **EXCLUSION BY PARTIES**

SECTION 2: AUTHORITY OF AGENTS

BIBLIOGRAPHY

BONELL M.J., Agency, in HARTKAMP A.S. / HESSELINK M.W. / HONDIUS E.H. / JOUSTRA C. / DU PERRON E. / VELDMAN M. (eds.), Towards a European Civil Code, 3rd ed., Kluwer Law International 2004, 381 – 397.

REYNOLDS F., Authority of Agents, in ICC International Court of Arbitration Bulletin, 2005 Special Supplement, 9 – 16.

ARTICLE 2.2.1
(Scope of the Section)

(1) This Section governs the authority of a person, the agent, to affect the legal relations of another person, the principal, by or with respect to a contract with a third party, whether the agent acts in its own name or in that of the principal.

(2) It governs only the relations between the principal or the agent on the one hand, and the third party on the other.

(3) It does not govern an agent's authority conferred by law or the authority of an agent appointed by a public or judicial authority.

COMMENT

1. Scope of the Section

This Section governs the authority of an agent to affect the legal relations between its principal and a third party. In other words, it focuses on the external relations between the principal or the agent on the one hand and the third party on the other, and is not concerned with the internal relations between the principal and the agent. Even those provisions which deal with issues affecting both the internal and the external relations (see, *e.g.*, Arts. 2.2.2 and 2.2.10 on the establishment and termination of the agent's authority, Art. 2.2.7 on conflict of interests and Art. 2.2.8 on sub-agency), consider those issues only with respect to their effects on the third party.

The rights and duties as between principal and agent are governed by their agreement and the applicable law which, with respect to specific types of agency relationships such as those concerning so-called "commercial agents", may provide mandatory rules for the protection of the agent.

2. Authority to contract

The Section deals only with agents who have authority to conclude contracts on behalf of their principals. Intermediaries whose task it is merely to introduce two parties to one another with a view to their concluding a contract (*e.g.* real estate agents), or to negotiate contracts on behalf of a principal but who have no authority to bind the principal (as may be the case of commercial agents) are outside the scope of the Section.

On the other hand, the wording "the authority [...] to affect the legal relations of [...] the principal by or with respect to a contract with a third party" used in para. (1) is to be understood in a broad sense, so as to comprise any act by the agent aimed at concluding a contract or which relates to its performance, including giving a notice to, or receiving it from, the third party.

3. Irrelevant whether agent acts in its own name or in that of its principal

Contrary to a number of legal systems that distinguish between "direct representation" and "indirect representation" depending on whether the agent acts in the principal's name or in its own name, no such distinction is made in this Section. As to the distinction between "disclosed" and "undisclosed" agency, see Arts. 2.2.3 and 2.2.4.

4. Voluntary nature of the relationship between principal and agent

A further condition for the application of this Section is the voluntary nature of the relationship between principal and agent. Cases where the agent's authority is conferred by law (*e.g.* in the field of family law, matrimonial property and succession), or is derived from judicial authorisation (*e.g.* acting for a person without capacity to act), are outside the scope of this Section.

5. Agents of companies

The authority of organs, officers or partners of a corporation, partnership or other entity, with or without legal personality, is traditionally governed by special rules, sometimes even of a mandatory character, which by virtue of their specific scope necessarily prevail over the general rules on the authority of agents laid down in this Section. Thus, for instance, if under the special rules governing the authority of its organs or officers a corporation is prevented from invoking any limitation to their authority against third parties, that corporation may not rely on Art. 2.2.5(1) to claim that it is not bound by an act of its organs or officers that falls outside the scope of their authority.

On the other hand, as long as the general rules laid down in this Section do not conflict with the above-mentioned special rules on the authority of organs, officers or partners, they may well be applied in lieu of the latter. Thus, for instance, a third party seeking to demonstrate that the contract it has concluded with an officer of a corporation binds that corporation, may invoke either the special rules governing the authority of that corporation's organs or officers or, as the case may be, the general rules on apparent authority laid down in Art. 2.2.5(2).

Illustrations

1. A, a Chief Executive Officer of Ruritanian company B, has under the company's articles authority to carry out all transactions

falling within the company's ordinary course of business. A enters into a contract with third party C that clearly falls outside the scope of B's ordinary business. According to Section 35A of the Ruritanian Companies Act, "[i]n favour of a person dealing with a company in good faith, the power of the board of directors to bind the company, or authorise others to do so, shall be deemed to be free of any limitation under the company's constitution" and "[...] a person shall not be regarded as acting in bad faith by reason only of his knowing that an act is beyond the powers of the directors under the company's constitution [...]". B is bound by the contract between A and C even if C knew or ought to have known of the limitations to A's authority, and B may not rely on Art. 2.2.5(1) to claim the contrary.

2. A, Managing Director of Ruritanian company B, has been given by the Board of Directors of the company the authority to carry out all transactions falling within the company's ordinary course of business except the hiring and dismissal of employees. A hires C as the new accountant of B's branch in foreign country X. B refuses to be bound by this appointment on account of A's lack of authority to hire employees. C may overcome B's objection by invoking Section 35A of the Ruritanian Companies Act. Yet C, who as a national of foreign country X may not be familiar with that special provision of the Ruritanian Companies Act, may equally rely on the general rule on apparent authority laid down in Art. 2.2.5(2) and claim that, in view of A's position as Managing Director of B, it was reasonable for C to believe that A had the authority to hire employees.

Issues & Cases

1. AUTHORITY OF AGENTS
   1.1 ONLY EXTERNAL RELATIONSHIP BETWEEN PARINCIPAL/AGENT AND THIRD PARTY AFFECTED
2. AUTHORITY OF OFFICERS OF COMPANIES
   2.1 GOVERNED BY SPECIAL RULES OF COMPANY LAW
   2.2 GOVERNED BY GENERAL RULES ON AGENCY

ARTICLE 2.2.2
(Establishment and scope of the authority of the agent)

(1) The principal's grant of authority to an agent may be express or implied.

(2) The agent has authority to perform all acts necessary in the circumstances to achieve the purposes for which the authority was granted.

COMMENT

1. Express or implied grant of authority

Para. (1) makes it clear that the granting of authority to the agent by the principal is not subject to any particular requirement of form and that it may be either express or implied.

The most common case of express authority is a power of attorney, but the principal may also confer authority on the agent in an oral statement or written communication or, in the case of a corporate entity, in a resolution by its board of directors. The granting of express authority in writing has the obvious advantage of providing clear evidence of the existence and precise scope of the agent's authority to all parties concerned (principal, agent and third parties).

An implied authority exists whenever the principal's intention to confer authority on an agent can be inferred from the principal's conduct (*e.g.* the assigning of a particular task to the agent) or other circumstances of the case (*e.g.* the terms of the express authorisation, a particular course of dealing between the two parties or a general trade usage).

Illustration

1. B appoints A as Manager of B's apartment building. A has implied authority to conclude short term lease contracts relating to the individual apartments.

2. Scope of the authority

The broader the mandate conferred on the agent, the broader the scope of its authority. Accordingly, para. (2) makes it clear that the agent's authority, unless otherwise provided by the principal in its authorisation, is not limited to its express terms, but extends to all acts necessary in the circumstances to achieve the purposes for which the authority was granted.

Illustration

2. Owner B consigns to shipmaster A a cargo to be carried to country X within 10 days. With only three days of navigation left,

the ship is damaged and must stop in the nearest port for repairs. A has implied authority to unload the cargo and consign it to another shipmaster to be carried to destination on another ship.

Issues & Cases

1. **EXPRESS GRANT OF AUTHORITY**
2. **IMPLIED GRANT OF AUTHORITY**
   - **2.1 INFERRED FROM THE PRINCIPAL'S CONDUCT**
   - **2.2 INFERRED FROM OTHER CIRCUMSTANCES**
3. **SCOPE OF AUTHORITY**
   - **3.1 EXPRESSLY FIXED BY PRINCIPAL**
   - **3.2 INFERRED FROM CIRCUMSTANCES**

ARTICLE 2.2.3
(Agency disclosed)

(1) Where an agent acts within the scope of its authority and the third party knew or ought to have known that the agent was acting as an agent, the acts of the agent shall directly affect the legal relations between the principal and the third party and no legal relation is created between the agent and the third party.

(2) However, the acts of the agent shall affect only the relations between the agent and the third party, where the agent with the consent of the principal undertakes to become the party to the contract.

COMMENT

1. "Disclosed" agency

With respect to the effects of the acts of the agent, this Section distinguishes between two basic situations: one in which the agent acts on behalf of a principal and within the scope of its authority and the third party knows or ought to know that the agent is acting as an agent, and the other in which the agent acts on behalf of a principal within the scope of its authority but the third party neither knows nor ought to know that the agent is acting as an agent. The first situation, which is the normal one, may be referred to as "disclosed" agency and is dealt with in the present article.

2. Agent's acts directly affect legal relations between principal and third party

In the case of a "disclosed" agency, the rule is that the agent's acts directly affect the principal's legal position vis-à-vis the third party (para. (1)). Thus, a contract made by the agent directly binds the principal and the third party to each other. Likewise, any communication of intention that the agent makes to, or receives from, the third party affects the principal's legal position as if the principal itself had made or received it.

Illustrations

1. A, a sales representative for computer manufacturer B, accepts the order placed by university C for the purchase of a certain number of computers. The sales contract directly binds B

vis-à-vis C with the result that it is B, and not A, who is under an obligation to deliver the goods to C and who is entitled to payment by C.

2. The facts are the same as in Illustration 1, the difference being that one of the computers delivered is defective. The notice of such defects given by C to A directly affects B.

3. Acting in the principal's name not necessary

For the establishment of a direct relationship between the principal and the third party it is sufficient that the agent acts within the scope of its authority and that the third party knows or ought to know that the latter acts on behalf of another person. By contrast, it is as a rule not necessary for the agent to act in the principal's name (see also Art. 2.2.1(1)).

In practice, however, there might be cases where it is in the agent's own interest to indicate expressly the identity of the person on whose behalf it is acting. Thus, whenever the contract requires the signature of the parties, the agent is well advised not simply to sign in its own name, but to add language such as "for and on behalf of" followed by the principal's name, so as to avoid any risk of being held personally liable under the contract.

Illustrations

3. The facts are the same as in Illustration 1. For the sales contract to directly bind B vis-à-vis C it is irrelevant whether A, when accepting C's order over the telephone, acts in its own name or expressly states that it is accepting in the name of B.

4. Computer specialist A is contacted by research centre C with a view to creating a computer programme for a special database on international case law. A, when signing the contract in its capacity as employee of software company B, should expressly state that it is acting on behalf of B. If A merely signs the contract without indicating B, C may hold A personally liable under the contract

4. Agent undertakes to become party to the contract

An agent, though openly acting on behalf of a principal, may exceptionally itself become party to the contract with the third party (para. (2)). This is the case, in particular, where a principal, who wants to remain anonymous, instructs the agent to act as a so-called "commission agent", *i.e.* to deal with the third party in its own name without establishing any direct relation between the principal and the third party. This is also the case where the third party makes it clear that it does not intend to contract with anyone other than the agent and the agent, with the consent of the principal, agrees that it alone and not the principal will be bound by the contract. In both cases it will follow from the terms of the agreement between the principal and the agent that, once the agent has acquired its rights under the contract with the third party, it will transfer them to the principal.

Entirely different is the case where the agent steps in and, in violation of its agreement with the principal, decides to become party to the contract with the third party. In so doing the agent no longer acts as an agent, and this case therefore falls outside the scope of this Section.

Illustrations

5. Dealer B, expecting a substantial increase in the price of wheat, decides to purchase a large quantity of wheat. B, wishing to remain anonymous, entrusts commission agent A with this task. Even though supplier C knows that A is purchasing on behalf of a principal, the purchase contract is binding on A and C and does not directly affect B's legal position.

6. Confirming house A, acting on behalf of overseas buyer B, places an order with supplier C for the purchase of certain goods. Since C, who does not know B, insists on A's confirmation of B's order, A accepts to be held liable itself vis-à-vis C. Even though C knows that A is purchasing on behalf of B, the purchase contract is binding on A and C and does not directly affect B's legal position.

7. Dealer B instructs agent A to purchase a certain quantity of oil on its behalf. When A is about to conclude the contract with supplier C, the news arrives that the oil producing countries intend to reduce production substantially. A, expecting a rise in oil prices, decides to purchase the oil on its own behalf and enters into the contract with C as the only other party. In so doing A has ceased to act as agent for the principal and the consequences of its acts are no longer governed by this Section.

Issues & Cases

1. **DISCLOSED AGENCY**
   - 1.1 **THIRD PARTY'S ACTUAL OR CONSTRUCTIVE KNOWLEDGE OF AGENT'S ACTING AS AGENT**
   - 1.2 **AGENT'S ACTING IN THE NAME OF PRINCIPAL IRRELEVANT**
2. **AGENT'S ACTS DIRECTLY BINDING PRINCIPAL VIS-À-VIS THIRD PARTY**
   - 2.1 **EXCEPTIONS**
     - 2.1.1 **"COMMISSION AGENT"**

ARTICLE 2.2.4
(Agency undisclosed)

(1) Where an agent acts within the scope of its authority and the third party neither knew nor ought to have known that the agent was acting as an agent, the acts of the agent shall affect only the relations between the agent and the third party.

(2) However, where such an agent, when contracting with the third party on behalf of a business, represents itself to be the owner of that business, the third party, upon discovery of the real owner of the business, may exercise also against the latter the rights it has against the agent.

COMMENT

1. "Undisclosed" agency

This article deals with what may be referred to as "undisclosed" agency, *i.e.* the situation where an agent acts within the scope of its authority on behalf of a principal but the third party neither knows nor ought to know that the agent is acting as an agent.

2. Agent's acts directly affect only the relations between agent and third party

Para. (1) provides that in the case of an "undisclosed" agency the agent's acts affect only the relations between the agent and the third party and do not directly bind the principal vis-à-vis the third party.

Illustration

1. Art dealer A purchases a painting from artist C. When entering into the contract A does not disclose the fact that it is acting on behalf of client B, nor has C any reason to believe that A is not acting on its own behalf. The contract is binding on A and C only, and does not give rise to a direct relationship between client B and artist C.

3. Third party's right of action against principal

Notwithstanding the rule laid down in para. (1), the third party may exceptionally have a right of direct action also against the principal. More precisely, according to para. (2), if the third party believes that it is dealing with the owner of a business while in fact it is dealing with the owner's agent, it may, upon discovery of the real owner, exercise also against the owner the rights it has against the agent.

Illustration

2. Manufacturer A, after having transferred its assets to a newly formed company X, continues to contract in its own name without disclosing to supplier B that it is in fact acting only as the Managing Director of X. Upon discovery of the existence of X, B has a right of action also against that company.

Issues & Cases

1. "UNDISCLOSED" AGENCY
   1.1 THIRD PARTY'S LACK OF KNOWLEDGE OF AGENT'S ACTING AS AGENT
2. AGENT'S ACTS BINDING AGENT VIS-À-VIS THIRD PARTY
   2.1 EXCEPTION
      2.2.1 AGENT REPRESENTING ITSELF AS OWNER OF BUSINESS
         2.2.1.1 THIRD PARTY'S RIGHT OF ACTION AGAINST PRINCIPAL

ARTICLE 2.2.5
(Agent acting without or exceeding its authority)

(1) Where an agent acts without authority or exceeds its authority, its acts do not affect the legal relations between the principal and the third party.

(2) However, where the principal causes the third party reasonably to believe that the agent has authority to act on behalf of the principal and that the agent is acting within the scope of that authority, the principal may not invoke against the third party the lack of authority of the agent.

COMMENTS

1. Lack of authority

Para. (1) expressly states that where an agent acts without authority, its acts do not bind the principal and the third party to each other. The same applies to the case where the agent has been granted authority of limited scope and acts exceeding its authority.

As to the liability of the false agent *vis-à-vis* the third party, see Art. 2.2.6.

Illustration

1. Principal B authorises agent A to buy on its behalf a specific quantity of grain but without exceeding a certain price. A enters into a contract with seller C for the purchase of a greater quantity of grain and at a higher price than that authorised by B. On account of A's lack of authority, the contract between A and C does not bind B, nor does it become effective between A and C.

2. Apparent authority

There are two cases in which an agent, though acting without authority or exceeding its authority, may bind the principal and the third party to each other.

The first case occurs whenever the principal ratifies the agent's act and is dealt with in Art. 2.2.9.

The second case is that of so-called "apparent authority" and is dealt with in para. (2) of the present article. According to this provision a principal, whose conduct leads a third party reasonably to believe that the agent has authority to act on its behalf, is prevented from invoking against the third party the lack of authority of the agent and is therefore bound by the latter's act.

Apparent authority, which is an application of the general principle of good faith (see Art. 1.7) and of the prohibition of inconsistent behaviour (see Art. 1.8), is especially important if the principal is not an individual but an organisation. In dealing with a corporation, partnership or other business association a third party may find it difficult to determine whether the persons acting for the organisation have actual authority to do so and may therefore prefer, whenever possible, to rely on their apparent authority. For this purpose the third party only has to demonstrate that it was reasonable for it to believe that the person purporting to represent the organisation was authorised to do so, and that this belief was caused by the conduct of those actually authorised to represent the organisation (Board of Directors, executive officers, partners, etc.). Whether or not the third party's belief was reasonable will depend on the circumstances of the case (position occupied by the apparent agent in the organisation's hierarchy, type of transaction involved, acquiescence of the organisation's representatives in the past, etc.).

Illustrations

2. A, a manager of one of company B's branch offices, though lacking actual authority to do so, engages construction company C to redecorate the branch's premises. In view of the fact that a branch manager normally would have authority to enter into such a contract, B is bound by the contract with C since it was reasonable for C to believe that A had actual authority to enter into the contract.

3. A, Chief Financial Officer of company B, though lacking authority to do so, has, with the acquiescence of the Board of Directors, repeatedly entered into financial transactions with bank C on behalf of B. On the occasion of a new transaction which proves to be disadvantageous to B, B's Board of Directors raises against C the objection of A's lack of authority. C may defeat this objection by claiming that B is bound by A's apparent authority to enter into the financial transaction on B's behalf.

Issues & Cases

1. AGENT ACTING WITHOUT OR EXCEEDING AUTHORITY
   - 1.1 AGENT'S ACTS NOT BINDING THE PRINCIPAL
2. APPARENT AUTHORITY
   - 2.1 PRINCIPAL MAY NOT INVOKE VIS-À-VIS THIRD PARTY AGENT'S LACK OF AUTHORITY
   - 2.2 APPARENT AUTHORITY OF OFFICERS OF COMPANY

ARTICLE 2.2.6
(Liability of agent acting without or exceeding its authority)

(1) An agent that acts without authority or exceeds its authority is, failing ratification by the principal, liable for damages that will place the third party in the same position as if the agent had acted with authority and not exceeded its authority.

(2) However, the agent is not liable if the third party knew or ought to have known that the agent had no authority or was exceeding its authority.

COMMENT

1. Liability of false agent

It is generally recognised that an agent acting without authority or exceeding its authority shall, failing ratification by the principal, be liable for damages to the third party. Para. (1), in stating that the false agent shall be liable to pay the third party such compensation as will place the third party in the same position as it would have been in if the agent had acted with authority, makes it clear that the liability of the false agent is not limited to the so-called reliance or negative interest, but extends to the so-called expectation or positive interest. In other words, the third party may recover the profit that would have resulted if the contract concluded with the false agent had been a valid one.

Illustration

1. Agent A, without being authorised by principal B, enters into a contract with third party C for the sale of a cargo of oil belonging to B. Failing B's ratification of the contract, C may recover from A the difference between the contract price and the current market price.

2. Third party's knowledge of agent's lack of authority

The false agent is liable to the third party only to the extent that the third party, when entering into the contract with the false agent, neither knew nor ought to have known that the latter was acting without authority or exceeding its authority.

Illustration

2. A, a junior employee of company B, without having authority to do so engages construction company C to redecorate

B's premises. B refuses to ratify the contract. Nevertheless C may not request damages from A since it should have known that an employee of A's rank normally has no authority to enter into such a contract.

Issues & Cases

1. LIABILITY OF FALSE AGENT VIS-À-VIS THIRD PARTY
1.1 COVERING THIRD PARTY'S EXPECTATION OR POSITIVE INTEREST
2. LIABILITY OF FALSE AGENT EXCLUDED
2.1 THIRD PARTY'S ACTUAL OR CONSTRUCTIVE KNOWLEDGE OF AGENT'S LACK OF AUTHORITY

ARTICLE 2.2.7
(Conflict of interests)

(1) If a contract concluded by an agent involves the agent in a conflict of interests with the principal of which the third party knew or ought to have known, the principal may avoid the contract. The right to avoid is subject to Articles 3.12 and 3.14 to 3.17.

(2) However, the principal may not avoid the contract

(a) if the principal had consented to, or knew or ought to have known of, the agent's involvement in the conflict of interests; or

(b) if the agent had disclosed the conflict of interests to the principal and the latter had not objected within a reasonable time.

COMMENT

1. Conflict of interests between agent and principal

It is inherent in any agency relationship that the agent, in fulfilling its mandate, will act in the interest of the principal and not in its own interest or in that of anyone else if there is a conflict between such an interest and that of the principal.

The most frequent cases of potential conflict of interests are those where the agent acts for two principals and those where the agent concludes the contract with itself or with a firm in which it has an interest. However, in practice even in such cases a real conflict of interests may not exist. Thus, for instance, the agent's acting for two principals may be in conformity with the usages of the trade sector concerned, or the principal may have conferred on the agent a mandate which is so stringent as to leave it no margin for manoeuvre.

2. Conflict of interests as grounds for avoidance of the contract

Para. (1) of this article lays down the rule that a contract concluded by an agent acting in a situation of real conflict of interests may be avoided by the principal, provided that the third party knew or ought to have known of the conflict of interests.

The requirement of the actual or constructive knowledge of the third party is intended to protect the innocent third party's interest in preserving the contract. This requirement is obviously no longer relevant where the agent concludes the contract with itself and is therefore at one and the same time agent and third party.

Illustrations

1. Solicitor A is requested by foreign client B to purchase on its behalf an apartment in A's city. A buys the apartment client C has requested A to sell on its behalf. B may avoid the contract if it can prove that C knew or ought to have known of A's conflict of interests. Likewise, C may avoid the contract if it can prove that B knew or ought to have known of A's conflict of interests

2. Sales agent A, requested by retailer B to purchase certain goods on its behalf, purchases the goods from company C in which A is a majority shareholder. B may avoid the contract if it can prove that C knew or ought to have known of A's conflict of interests.

3. Client B instructs bank A to buy on its behalf one thousand shares of company X at the closing price of day M on the stock exchange of city Y. Even if A sells B the requested shares from out of those it has in its own portfolio, there can be no conflict of interests because B's mandate leaves A no margin for manoeuvre.

4. A, Chief Executive Officer of company B, has authority to appoint the company's counsel in the event of a law suit being brought by or against B. A appoints itself as B's counsel. B may avoid the contract.

3. Procedure for avoidance

As to the procedure for avoidance, the provisions laid down in Arts. 3.12 (*Confirmation*), 3.14 (*Notice of avoidance*), 3.15 (*Time limits*), 3.16 (*Partial avoidance*) and 3.17 (*Retroactive effect of avoidance*) apply.

4. Avoidance excluded

According to para. (2), the principal loses its right to avoid the contract if it has given its prior consent to the agent's acting in a situation of conflict of interests, or at any rate knew or ought to have known that the agent would do so. The right of avoidance is likewise excluded if the principal, having been informed by the agent of the contract it has concluded in a situation of conflict of interests, raises no objection.

Illustration

5. The facts are the same as in Illustration 1, the difference being that before concluding the contract A duly informs B that it

is acting as agent also for C. If B does not object B loses its right to avoid the contract. Likewise, if A duly informs C that it is acting as agent also for B and C does not object, C loses its right to avoid the contract.

5. Issues not covered by the present article

In conformity with the scope of this Section set out in Art. 2.2.1, the present article addresses only the impact that the agent's involvement in a conflict of interests situation may have on the external relationship. Issues such as the agent's duty of full disclosure vis-à-vis the principal and the principal's right to damages from the agent may be settled on the basis of other provisions of the Principles (see Arts. 1.7, 3.18, 7.4.1 *et seq.*) or are otherwise governed by the law applicable to the internal relationship between principal and agent.

Issues & Cases

1. AGENT ACTING IN CONFLICT OF INTEREST WITH PRINCIPAL
   - 1.1 AGENT ACTING FOR TWO PRINCIPALS
   - 1.2 AGENT CONTRACTING WITH ITSELF
2. PRINCIPAL ENTITLED TO AVOID CONTRACT WITH THIRD PARTY
   - 2.1 THIRD PARTY'S KNOWLEDGE OF CONFLICT OF INTEREST REQUIRED
3. PRINCIPAL'S RIGHT TO AVOID THE CONTRACT WITH THIRD PARTY EXCLUDED
   - 3.1 PRINCIPAL CONSENTED OR KNEW OF AGENT'S CONFLICT OF INTEREST
   - 3.2 AGENT DISCLOSED CONFLICT OF INTEREST

ARTICLE 2.2.8
(Sub-agency)

An agent has implied authority to appoint a sub-agent to perform acts which it is not reasonable to expect the agent to perform itself. The rules of this Section apply to the sub-agency.

COMMENTS

1. Role of sub-agents

In carrying out the mandate conferred on it by the principal, an agent may find it convenient or even necessary to avail itself of the services of other persons. This is the case, for instance, where certain tasks are to be performed in a place distant from the agent's place of business, or if a more efficient performance of the agent's mandate requires distribution of work.

2. Implied authority to appoint sub-agents

Whether or not the agent is authorised to appoint one or more sub-agents depends on the terms of the authority granted by the principal. Thus, the principal may expressly exclude the appointment of sub-agents or make it conditional upon its prior approval. If nothing is said in the authorisation as to the possibility of appointing sub-agents and the terms of the authority granted are not otherwise inconsistent with such a possibility, the agent has the right under this article to appoint sub-agents. The only limitation is that the agent may not entrust the sub-agent(s) with tasks that it is reasonable to expect the agent itself to perform. This is the case in particular of acts requiring the agent's personal expertise.

Illustrations

1. Chinese museum B instructs a London-based art dealer A to buy a particular piece of Greek pottery on sale at a private auction in Germany. A has implied authority to appoint German sub-agent S to purchase that piece of pottery at the auction in Germany and to send it to B.

2. The facts are the same as in Illustration 1, the difference being that B does not specify the particular piece of Greek pottery to be acquired at the auction in Germany as it relies on A's expertise to choose the most suitable item offered for sale. A is expected to make the purchase at the auction itself, but once it has

purchased the piece of pottery, it may appoint sub-agent S to send it to B.

3. Effects of a sub-agent's acts

The present article expressly states that the rules of this Section apply to the sub-agency. In other words, the acts of a sub-agent legitimately appointed by the agent bind the principal and the third party to each other, provided that those acts are within both the agent's authority and the authority conferred on the sub-agent by the agent, which may be more limited.

Illustration

3. The facts are the same as in Illustration 1. The purchase of the piece of Greek pottery by S directly binds B provided that it is within both the authority that B has granted to A and the authority that A has granted to S.

Issues & Cases

1. AGENT'S IMPLIED AUTHORITY TO APPOINT SUB-AGENTS
   1.1 ONLY FOR ACTS NOT REASONABLY EXPECTED TO BE PERFORMED BY AGENT ITSELF
2. SUB-AGENT'S ACTS DIRECTLY BIND PRINCIPAL

ARTICLE 2.2.9
(Ratification)

(1) An act by an agent that acts without authority or exceeds its authority may be ratified by the principal. On ratification the act produces the same effects as if it had initially been carried out with authority.

(2) The third party may by notice to the principal specify a reasonable period of time for ratification. If the principal does not ratify within that period of time it can no longer do so.

(3) If, at the time of the agent's act, the third party neither knew nor ought to have known of the lack of authority, it may, at any time before ratification, by notice to the principal indicate its refusal to become bound by a ratification.

COMMENT

1. Notion of ratification

This article lays down the generally accepted principle whereby acts which have no effect on the principal because they have been carried out by an agent holding itself out to have authority but actually without authority or exceeding its authority, may be authorised by the principal at a later stage. Such subsequent authorisation is known as "ratification".

Like the original authorisation, ratification is not subject to any requirement as to form. As it is a unilateral manifestation of intent, it may be either express or implied from words or conduct and, though normally communicated to the agent, to the third party, or to both, it need not be communicated to anyone, provided that it is manifested in some way and can therefore be ascertained by probative material.

Illustration

Agent A purchases on behalf of principal B goods from third party C at a price higher than that which A is authorised to pay. Upon receipt of C's bill, B makes no objection and pays it by bank transfer. The payment amounts to ratification of A's act even if B does not expressly declare its intention to ratify, fails to inform both A and C of the payment and C is only subsequently informed of the payment by its bank.

2. Effects of ratification

On ratification the agent's acts produce the same effects as if they had been carried out with authority from the outset (para. (1)). It follows that the third party may refuse partial ratification of the agent's acts by the principal as it would amount to a proposal by the principal to modify the contract that the third party has concluded with the agent. In turn, the principal may not revoke ratification after it has been brought to the attention of the third party. Otherwise the principal would be in a position to withdraw unilaterally from the contract with the third party.

3. Time of ratification

The principal may in principle ratify at any time. The reason for this is that normally the third party does not even know that it has contracted with an agent who did not have authority or who exceeded its authority. However, even if the third party knows from the outset, or subsequently becomes aware, that the agent was a false agent, it will have a legitimate interest not to be left in doubt indefinitely as to the ultimate fate of the contract concluded with the false agent. Accordingly, para. (2) grants the third party the right to set a reasonable time limit within which the principal must ratify if it intends to do so. It goes without saying that in such a case ratification must be notified to the third party.

4. Ratification excluded by third party

A third party, who when dealing with the agent neither knew nor ought to have known of that agent's lack of authority, may exclude ratification by giving the principal notice to this effect any time before ratification by the latter. The reason for granting the innocent third party such a right is to avoid that the principal is the only one in a position to speculate and to decide whether or not to ratify depending on market developments.

5. Third persons' rights not affected

This article deals only with the effects of ratification on the three parties directly involved in the agency relationship, *i.e.* the principal, the agent and the third party. In accordance with the scope of this Section as defined in Art. 2.2.1, the rights of other third persons are not affected. For instance, if the same goods have been sold first by the false agent to C, and subsequently by the principal to another person D, the conflict between C and D as a result of the principal's subsequent ratification of the first sale will have to be solved by the applicable law.

Issues & Cases

1. RATIFICATION OF FALSE AGENT'S ACTS BY PRINCIPAL
    - 1.1 NO REQUIREMENTS AS TO FORM
        - 1.1.1 RATIFICATION BY PRINCIPAL'S CONDUCT
2. TIME OF RATIFICATION
    - 2.1 THIRD PARTY'S RIGHT TO SET REASONABLE PERIOD OF TIME FOR RATIFICATION
3. PARTIAL RATIFICATION
4. REVOCATION OF RATIFICATION
5. REVOCATION EXCLUDED BY THIRD PARTY
    - 5.1 CONDITIONS

ARTICLE 2.2.10
(Termination of authority)

(1) Termination of authority is not effective in relation to the third party unless the third party knew or ought to have known of it.

(2) Notwithstanding the termination of its authority, an agent remains authorised to perform the acts that are necessary to prevent harm to the principal's interests.

COMMENT

1. Grounds for termination not covered by the present article

There are several grounds on which the agent's authority may be terminated: revocation by the principal, renunciation by the agent, completion of the act(s) for which authority had been granted, loss of capacity, bankruptcy, death or cessation of the existence of the principal or the agent, etc. What exactly constitutes a ground for termination and the way it operates as between the principal and the agent falls outside the scope of the present article and is to be determined in accordance with the applicable laws (*e.g.* the law governing the internal relations between principal and agent, the law governing their legal status or personality, the law governing bankruptcy, etc.) which may vary considerably from one country to another.

2. Termination effective vis-à-vis third party

Whatever the grounds for termination of the agent's authority, in relation to the third party termination is not effective unless the third party knew or ought to have known of it (para. (1)). In other words, even if the agent's authority has been terminated for one reason or another, the agent's acts continue to affect the legal relationship between the principal and the third party as long as the third party is neither aware of nor ought to know that the agent no longer has authority.

Obviously the situation is clear whenever either the principal or the agent gives the third party notice of the termination. In the absence of such notice it will depend on the circumstances of the case whether the third party ought to have known of the termination.

Illustrations

1. Principal B opens a branch office in city X. An advertisement published in the local newspaper indicates Managing Director A as

having full authority to act on behalf of B. When B subsequently revokes A's authority, a similar notice thereof in the same newspaper is sufficient to make the termination effective vis-à-vis B's customers in city X.

2. Retailer C has repeatedly placed orders with sales representative A for the purchase of goods sold by principal B. A continues to accept orders from C even after its authority has been terminated on account of B's bankruptcy. The mere fact that the bankruptcy proceedings were given the publicity required by the applicable law is not sufficient to make the termination effective vis-à-vis C.

3. Authority of necessity

Even after termination of the agent's authority the circumstances of the case may make it necessary for the agent to perform additional acts in order to prevent the principal's interests from being harmed.

Illustration

3. Agent A has authority to purchase a certain quantity of perishable goods on behalf of principal B. After the purchase of the goods A is informed of B's death. Notwithstanding the termination of its authority, A continues to be authorised either to resell the goods or to store them in a suitable warehouse.

4. Restriction of authority also covered

The rules of this article apply not only to termination but, with appropriate modifications, also to subsequent restrictions of an agent's authority.

Issues & Cases

1. **TERMINATION OR SUBSEQUENT RESTRICTION OF AUTHORITY**
   1.1 **EFFECTIVE VIS-À-VIS THIRD PARTY ONLY UPON ACTUAL OR CONSTRUCTIVE KNOWLEDGE THEREOF BY THIRD PARTY**
2. **AUTHORITY OF NECESSITY**

CHAPTER 3

VALIDITY

BIBLIOGRAPHY

ADRIAN HERNANDEZ T.M., Las "ventajas desproporcionadas" en los Principios de UNIDROIT sobre los contratos comerciales internacionales, in UNIDROIT (ed.), The UNIDROIT Principles: a Common Law of Contracts for the Americas?, 1998, 293-298.

ALPA G., La protezione della parte debole nei Principi dell'UNIDROIT, in ALPA G. / BESSONE M. (eds.), Giurisprudenza sistematica di diritto civile e commerciale, I, Utet, Torino, 1999, 217-232.

ALPA G., La protezione della parte debole di origine internazionale (con particolare riguardo al diritto uniforme), in BONELL M.J. / BONELLI F. (eds.), Contratti commerciali internazionali e Principi UNIDROIT, Giuffré, Milano 1997, 225-246.

BARALDI M., Il governo giudiziario della discrezionalità contrattuale, in Contratto e Impresa 2005, 501 – 538.

BONELL M.J., An International Restatement of Contract Law. The UNIDROIT Principles of International Commercial Contracts, 3rd ed., Transnational Publications Inc., Ardsley, New York, 2005 at 165 - 172.

BONELL M.J., Policing the International Commercial Contract against Unfairness under the UNIDROIT Principles, in 3 Tulane Journal of International and Comparative Law, n. 1/2, 1994, 73-91; also in Diritto del Commercio Internazionale, 1994, 251-267.

BORTOLOTTI F., Manuale di diritto commerciale internazionale, I, Diritto dei contratti internazionali, 2 ed., CEDAM 2001, 73 – 75.

BRECCIA U., Morte e resurrezione della causa: la tutela, in MAZZAMUTO S. (ed.), Il contratto e le tutele (2002), 241 – 266.

CHAPPUIS CH., L'intervention du tribunal dans le contrat. Convergence entre les Principes UNIDROIT et le droit suisse, in Liber Amicorum Claude Reymond, Litec, Paris 2004, 53 – 72.

COEN C., Vertragsscheitern und Rückabwiklung. Eine rechtsvergleichende Untersuchung zum englishen und deutschen Recht, zum UN-Kaufrecht sowie zu den UNIDROIT Principles und den Principles of European Contract Law, Berlin, Dunker & Humblot, 2003, 455 (Beiträge zum europäischen Wirtshaftsrecht, 22).

CORAPI D., L'equilibrio delle posizioni contrattuali nei Principi UNIDROIT, in Europa e Diritto Privato, 2002, n. 1, 23 – 40.

D'ANGELO A., Principi UNIDROIT e regole causalistiche, in ALPA G. – BESSONE M., (eds.), Giurisprudenza sistematica di diritto civile e commerciale, I, Utet, Torino, 1999, 235-238.

DOTEVALL R., Ekvivalensprincipen och jämkning av långvariga avtål, in Svensk Jurist Tidning, 87 (2002), 441 – 457.

DROBNIG U., Protection of the Weaker Party, in Bonell M.J. / Bonelli F. (eds.), Contratti commerciali internazionali e Principi UNIDROIT, Giuffré, Milano 1997, 215-224.

DROBNIG U., Substantive Validity, in 40 American Journal of Comparative Law, n. 3, 1992, 635-644.

FERRI G.B., L' "invisibile" presenza della causa del contratto, in Europa e diritto privato, 2002, 897 – 914.

GHESTIN J., Faut-il conserver la cause en droit européen des contrats?, in European Review of Contract Law, n. 4/2005, 396 – 416.

GORDLEY, J., An American Perspective on the UNIDROIT Principles, in Centro di studi e ricerche di diritto comparato e straniero (ed.), Saggi, conferenze e seminari, n. 22, Roma 1996, 1-6.

GRIGOLEIT H.C., Irrtum, Täuschung und Informationspflichten in den European Principles und in den UNIDROIT-Principles, in SCHULZE R. – EBERS M. – GRIGOLEIT H.G. (Hrsg.) – Informationsplifchten und Vertragsabschluss im *Acquis communautaire*. Information requirements and formation of contract in the *acquis communautaire*, Tubingen, Mohr Siebeck, 2003, 201 – 230.

HERRERA A.L., Validez, in Comentario a los Principios de UNIDROIT para los Contratos del Comercio Internacional, Aranzadi, Pamplona, 1999, 161-223.

HINESTROSA F., Capitolo 3. Validez., in BONELL M.J. / SCHIPANI S. (eds.), "Principi per i contratti commerciali internazionali" e il sistema giuridico latinoamericano, Padova 1996, 111-137.

KRAMER E., Die Gültigkeit der Verträge nach den UNIDROIT Principles of International Commercial Contracts, in Zeitschrift für Europäisches Privatrecht, 2, 1999, 209-228.

KRAMER E., Contractual Validity According to the UNIDROIT Principles, in 1 European Journal of Law Reform, n. 3, 1998-1999, 269-288.

KRAMER E., "Fair Dealing in International Trade" et vices du consentement, in BONELL M.J. / BONELLI F. (eds.), Contratti commerciali internazionali e Principi UNIDROIT, Giuffré, Milano 1997, 161-169.

KRAMER E.A. – PROBST T., Defects in the Contracting Process, Chapter II, International Encyclopedia of Comparative Law, Vol. II, Contracts in general (A. Von MEHREN ed.), Tübingen, Mohr Siebeck, 2001.

LINZER P., Validity under Chapter 3 of the UNIDROIT Principles of International Commercial Contracts, in Contratación internacional, Comentarios a los principios sobre los Contratos Comerciales Internacionales del UNIDROIT, Universidad Nacional Autónoma de México – Universidad Panamericana (ed.) 1998, 81-93.

PIERAZZI E.M., La giustizia del contratto, Contratto e impresa 2005, 646 – 657.

PONTIROLI L., La protezione del 'contraente debole' nei Principles of International Commercial Contracts di UNIDROIT: much ado about nothing?, in Giurisprudenza commerciale, Luglio – Agosto 1997, 566-606.

SICCHIERO G.-L. Tramonto della causa del contratto?, in Contratto e Impresa 2003, 100 – 130.

TIMOTEO M., Nuove regole in materia di squilibrio contrattuale: l'articolo 3.10 dei Principi UNIDROIT, in Contratto e Impresa/ Europa, 1997, gennaio-giugno, 140-175.

VITUCCI P., L'atto unilaterale nei *Principles* e in altre compilazioni sul diritto europeo dei contratti, in Europa e diritto privato, 2002, 937 – 954.

VOLPE F., I Principi UNIDROIT e l'eccesivo squilibrio del contenuto contrattuale (*gross disparity*), in Revista Dotrinària, Rio de Janeiro, 2000, 115 – 143.

WOLF, M., Willensmängel und sonstige Beeinträchtigungen der Entscheidungsfreiheit in einem europäischen Vertragsrecht, in BASEDOW, J. (ed.), Europäische Vertragsrechts-vereinheitlichung und deutsches Recht, J. C. B. Mohr (Siebeck), Tübingen 2000, 85 – 128.

ZIMMERMANN R., Die Rückabwicklung fehlgeschlagener Verträge nach den Principles of European Contract Law, den UNIDROIT-Principles und dem *Avant-projet* eines *Code Européen des Contrats*, in HONSELL H., *et al.*, (eds.), Privatrecht und Methode. Festschrift für Ernst A. Kramer, Basel, Helbing & Lichtenhahn, 2004, 735 – 754.

ZIMMERMANN R., *Restitutio in Integrum*: The Unwinding of Failed Contracts under the Principles of European Contract Law, the UNIDROIT Principles and the *Avant-projet* d'un *Code Européen des Contrats*, in Uniform Law Review 2005, 719 – 734.

ARTICLE 3.1
(Matters not covered)

These Principles do not deal with invalidity arising from

(a) lack of capacity;

(b) immorality or illegality.

COMMENT

This article makes it clear that not all the grounds of invalidity of a contract to be found in the various national legal systems fall within the scope of the Principles. This is in particular the case of lack of capacity and immorality or illegality. The reason for their exclusion lies both in the inherent complexity of questions of status and of public policy and the extremely diverse manner in which they are treated in domestic law. In consequence, matters such as *ultra vires* or the illegal or immoral content of contracts will continue to be governed by the applicable law.

As to the authority of organs, officers or partners of a corporation, partnership or other entities to bind their respective entities, see comment 5 on Art. 2.2.1.

Issues & Cases

1. OUTSIDE SCOPE OF PRINCIPLES
   - 1.1 LACK OF CAPACITY
   - 1.2 LACK OF AUTHORITY
   - 1.3 IMMORALITY OR ILLEGALITY

ARTICLE 3.2
(Validity of mere agreement)

A contract is concluded, modified or terminated by the mere agreement of the parties, without any further requirement.

COMMENT

The purpose of this article is to make it clear that the mere agreement of the parties is sufficient for the valid conclusion, modification or termination by agreement of a contract, without any of the further requirements which are to be found in some domestic laws.

1. No need for consideration

In common law systems, consideration is traditionally seen as a prerequisite for the validity or enforceability of a contract as well as for its modification or termination by the parties.

However, in commercial dealings this requirement is of minimal practical importance since in that context obligations are almost always undertaken by both parties. It is for this reason that Art. 29(1) CISG dispenses with the requirement of consideration in relation to the modification and termination by the parties of contracts for the international sale of goods. The fact that the present article extends this approach to the conclusion, modification and termination by the parties of international commercial contracts in general can only bring about greater certainty and reduce litigation.

2. No need for *cause*

This article also excludes the requirement of *cause* which exists in some civil law systems and is in certain respects functionally similar to the common law "consideration".

Illustration

1. At the request of its French customer A, bank B in Paris issues a guarantee on first demand in favour of C, a business partner of A in England. Neither B nor A can invoke the possible absence of consideration or *cause* for the guarantee.

It should be noted however that this article is not concerned with the effects which may derive from other aspects of *cause*, such as its illegality. See comment 2 on Art. 3.3.

3. All contracts consensual

Some civil law systems have retained certain types of "real" contract, *i.e.* contracts concluded only upon the actual handing over of the goods concerned. Such rules are not easily compatible with modern business perceptions and practice and are therefore also excluded by the present article.

Illustration

2. Two French businessmen, A and B, agree with C, a real estate developer, to lend C 300,000 euros on 2 July. On 25 June, A and B inform C that, unexpectedly, they need the money for their own business. C is entitled to receive the loan, although the loan is generally considered a "real" contract in France.

Issues & Cases

1. AGREEMENT SUFFICIENT FOR VALID CONCLUSION, MODIFICATION OR TERMINATION OF CONTRACT
   - 1.1 NO NEED FOR CONSIDERATION
   - 1.2 NO NEED FOR CAUSE
   - 1.3 NO NEED FOR OTHER REQUIREMENTS

ARTICLE 3.3
(Initial impossibility)

(1) The mere fact that at the time of the conclusion of the contract the performance of the obligation assumed was impossible does not affect the validity of the contract.

(2) The mere fact that at the time of the conclusion of the contract a party was not entitled to dispose of the assets to which the contract relates does not affect the validity of the contract.

COMMENT

1. Performance impossible from the outset

Contrary to a number of legal systems which consider a contract of sale void if the specific goods sold have already perished at the time of conclusion of the contract, para. (1) of this article, in conformity with the most modern trends, states in general terms that the mere fact that at the time of the conclusion of the contract the performance of the obligation assumed was impossible does not affect the validity of the contract.

A contract is valid even if the assets to which it relates have already perished at the time of contracting, with the consequence that initial impossibility of performance is equated with impossibility occurring after the conclusion of the contract. The rights and duties of the parties arising from one party's (or possibly even both parties') inability to perform are to be determined according to the rules on non-performance. Under these rules appropriate weight may be attached, for example, to the fact that the obligor (or the obligee) already knew of the impossibility of performance at the time of contracting.

The rule laid down in para. (1) also removes possible doubts as to the validity of contracts for the delivery of future goods.

If an initial impossibility of performance is due to a legal prohibition (*e.g.* an export or import embargo), the validity of the contract depends upon whether under the law enacting the prohibition the latter is intended to invalidate the contract or merely to prohibit its performance.

Para. (1) moreover departs from the rule to be found in some civil law systems according to which the object (*objet*) of a contract must be possible.

The paragraph also deviates from the rule of the same systems which requires the existence of a *cause*, since, in a case of initial impossibility, the *cause* for a counter-performance is lacking. See Art. 3.2.

2. Lack of legal title or power

Para. (2) of this article deals with cases where the party promising to transfer or deliver assets was not entitled to dispose of the assets because it lacked legal title or the right of disposition at the time of the conclusion of the contract.

Some legal systems declare a contract of sale concluded in such circumstances to be void. Yet, as in the case with initial impossibility, and for even more cogent reasons, para. (2) of this article considers such a contract to be valid. Indeed, a contracting party may, and often does, acquire legal title to, or the power of disposition over, the assets in question after the conclusion of the contract. Should this not occur, the rules on non-performance will apply.

Cases where the power of disposition is lacking must be distinguished from those of lack of capacity. The latter relate to certain disabilities of a person which may affect all or at least some types of contract concluded by it, and falls outside the scope of the Principles. See Art. 3.1(a).

Issues & Cases

1. INITIAL IMPOSSIBILITY OF PERFORMANCE
   1.1 VALIDITY OF CONTRACT NOT AFFECTED AND TO BE CONSIDERED AS A CASE OF NON-PERFORMANCE
      - MARCH 20, 2000 ARBITRAL AWARD INTERNATIONAL CENTRE FOR SETTLEMENT OF INVESTMENT DISPUTES (ICSID) (ARB(AF)/98/1) [826]

      1.1.1 PARTY'S KNOWLEDGE OF INITIAL IMPOSSIBILITY
2. LACK OF LEGAL TITLE OR OF RIGHT OF DISPOSITION AT TIME OF CONCLUSION OF CONTRACT
   2.1 VALIDITY OF CONTRACT NOT AFFECTED
      2.1.1 SUBSEQUENT ACQUISITION OF TITLE OR RIGHT OF DISPOSITION
      2.1.2 NO SUBSEQUENT ACQUISITION OF TITLE OR RIGHT OF DISPOSITION

ARTICLE 3.4
(Definition of mistake)

Mistake is an erroneous assumption relating to facts or to law existing when the contract was concluded.

COMMENT

1. Mistake of fact and mistake of law

This article equates a mistake relating to facts with a mistake relating to law. Identical legal treatment of the two types of mistake seems justified in view of the increasing complexity of modern legal systems. For cross-border trade the difficulties caused by this complexity are exacerbated by the fact that an individual transaction may be affected by foreign and therefore unfamiliar legal systems.

2. Decisive time

The article indicates that the mistake involves an erroneous assumption relating to the factual or legal circumstances that exist at the time of the conclusion of the contract.

The purpose of fixing this time element is to distinguish cases where the rules on mistake with their particular remedies apply from those relating to non-performance. Indeed, a typical case of mistake may, depending on the point of view taken, often just as well be seen as one involving an obstacle which prevents or impedes the performance of the contract. If a party has entered into a contract under a misconception as to the factual or legal context and therefore misjudged its prospects under that contract, the rules on mistake will apply. If, on the other hand, a party has a correct understanding of the surrounding circumstances but makes an error of judgment as to its prospects under the contract, and later refuses to perform, then the case is one of non-performance rather than mistake.

Issues & Cases

1. MISTAKE DEFINED

- DECEMBER 4, 1996 ARBITRAL AWARD AD HOC ARBITRATION, ROME [664]

1.1 MISTAKE OF FACTS

- DECEMBER 4, 1996 ARBITRAL AWARD AD HOC ARBITRATION, ROME [664]

1.2 MISTAKE OF LAW

- DECEMBER 20, 2002 NETHERLANDS SUPREME COURT OF THE NETHERLANDS (NO. C01/157 HR) [1036]

1.3 DELIMITATION TO ERRORS OF JUDGEMENT

2. DECISIVE TIME

ARTICLE 3.5
(Relevant mistake)

(1) A party may only avoid the contract for mistake if, when the contract was concluded, the mistake was of such importance that a reasonable person in the same situation as the party in error would only have concluded the contract on materially different terms or would not have concluded it at all if the true state of affairs had been known, and

(a) the other party made the same mistake, or caused the mistake, or knew or ought to have known of the mistake and it was contrary to reasonable commercial standards of fair dealing to leave the mistaken party in error; or

(b) the other party had not at the time of avoidance acted in reliance on the contract.

(2) However, a party may not avoid the contract if

(a) it was grossly negligent in committing the mistake; or

(b) the mistake relates to a matter in regard to which the risk of mistake was assumed or, having regard to the circumstances, should be borne by the mistaken party.

COMMENT

This article states the conditions necessary for a mistake to be relevant with a view to avoidance of the contract. The introductory part of para. (1) determines the conditions under which a mistake is sufficiently serious to be taken into account; sub-paras. (a) and (b) of para. (1) add the conditions regarding the party other than the mistaken party; para. (2) deals with the conditions regarding the mistaken party.

1. Serious mistake

To be relevant, a mistake must be serious. Its weight and importance are to be assessed by reference to a combined objective/subjective standard, namely what "a reasonable person in the same situation as the party in error" would have done if it had known the true circumstances at the time of the conclusion of the contract. If it would not have contracted at all, or would have done so only on materially different terms, then, and only then, is the mistake considered to be serious.

In this context the introductory part of para. (1) relies on an open-ended formula, rather than indicating specific essential elements of the contract to which the mistake must relate. This flexible approach allows full account to be taken of the intentions of the parties and the circumstances of the case. In ascertaining the parties' intentions, the rules of interpretation laid down in Chapter 4 must be applied. General commercial standards and relevant usages will be particularly important.

Normally in commercial transactions certain mistakes, such as those concerning the value of goods or services or mere expectations or motivations of the mistaken party, are not considered to be relevant. The same is true of mistakes as to the identity of the other party or its personal qualities, although special circumstances may sometimes render such mistakes relevant (*e.g.* when services to be rendered require certain personal qualifications or when a loan is based upon the credit-worthiness of the borrower).

The fact that a reasonable person would consider the circumstances erroneously assumed to be essential is however not sufficient, since additional requirements concerning both the mistaken and the other party must be met if a mistake is to become relevant.

2. Conditions concerning the party other than the mistaken party

A mistaken party may avoid the contract only if the other party satisfies one of four conditions laid down in para. (1).

The first three conditions indicated in sub-para. (a) have in common the fact that the other party does not deserve protection because of its involvement in one way or another with the mistaken party's error.

The first condition is that both parties laboured under the same mistake.

Illustration

1. A and B, when concluding a contract for the sale of a sports car, were not and could not have been aware of the fact that the car had in the meantime been stolen. Avoidance of the contract is admissible.

However, if the parties erroneously believe the object of the contract to be in existence at the time of the conclusion of the contract, while in reality it had already been destroyed, Art. 3.3 has to be taken into account.

The second condition is that the error of the mistaken party is caused by the other party. This is the case whenever the error can be traced to specific representations made by the latter party, be they express or implied, negligent or innocent, or to conduct which in the circumstances amounts to a representation.

Even silence may cause an error. A mere "puff" in advertising or in negotiations will normally be tolerated.

If the error was caused intentionally, Art. 3.8 applies.

The third condition is that the other party knew or ought to have known of the error of the mistaken party and that it was contrary to reasonable commercial standards of fair dealing to leave the mistaken party in error. What the other party ought to have known is what should have been known to a reasonable person in the same situation as that party. In order to avoid the contract the mistaken party must also show that the other party was under a duty to inform it of its error.

The fourth condition is laid down in sub-para. (b) and is that the party other than the mistaken party had not, up to the time of avoidance, acted in reliance on the contract. For the time of avoidance, see Arts. 3.15 and 1.10.

3. Conditions concerning the mistaken party

Para. (2) of the present article mentions two cases in which the mistaken party may not avoid the contract.

The first of these, dealt with in sub-para. (a), is that the error is due to the gross negligence of the mistaken party. In such a situation it would be unfair to the other party to allow the mistaken party to avoid the contract.

Sub-para. (b) contemplates the situation where the mistaken party either has assumed the risk of mistake or where this risk should in the circumstances be borne by it. An assumption of the risk of mistake is a frequent feature of speculative contracts. A party may conclude a contract in the hope that its assumption of the existence of certain facts will prove to be correct, but may nevertheless undertake to assume the risk of this not being so. In such circumstances it will not be entitled to avoid the contract for its mistake.

Illustration

2. A sells to B a picture "attributed" to the relatively unknown painter C at a fair price for such paintings. It is subsequently discovered that the work was painted by the famous artist D. A cannot avoid its contract with B on the ground of its mistake, since the fact that the picture was only "attributed" to C implied the risk that it might have been painted by a more famous artist.

Sometimes both parties assume a risk. However, speculative contracts involving conflicting expectations of future developments, *e.g.* those concerning prices and exchange rates, may not be avoided on the ground of mistake, since the mistake would not be one as to facts existing at the time of the conclusion of the contract.

Issues & Cases

1. AVOIDANCE OF CONTRACT FOR MISTAKE
   - NOVEMBER 25, 1994 ARBITRAL AWARD ZÜRICH CHAMBER OF COMMERCE [559]
   - DECEMBER 4, 1996 ARBITRAL AWARD AD HOC ARBITRATION, ROME [664]

1.1 SERIOUS MISTAKE
   - NOVEMBER 25, 1994 ARBITRAL AWARD ZÜRICH CHAMBER OF COMMERCE [559]

1.1.1 CRITERIA FOR ASSESSMENT OF IMPORTANCE OF MISTAKE
   - DECEMBER 4, 1996 ARBITRAL AWARD, AD HOC ARBITRATION, ROME [664]

1.1.1.1 INTENTION OF PARTIES

1.1.1.2 CIRCUMSTANCES OF THE CASE

1.1.1.3 GENERAL COMMERCIAL STANDARDS AND USAGES
   - DECEMBER 4, 1996 ARBITRAL AWARD AD HOC ARBITRATION, ROME [664]

1.2 CONDITIONS CONCERNING PARTY OTHER THAN THE MISTAKEN PARTY

1.2.1 LABOURING UNDER THE SAME MISTAKE (SEE ALSO ART. 3.3)

1.2.2 CAUSING ERROR OF MISTAKEN PARTY

1.2.2.1 BY MAKING SPECIFIC REPRESENTATION

1.2.2.2 BY SILENCE
   - FEBRUARY 1999 ARBITRAL AWARD (PARTIAL) ICC INTERNATIONAL COURT OF ARBITRATION (NO. 9474) [777]

1.2.3 LEAVING MISTAKEN PARTY IN ERROR

1.2.3.1 DUTY TO INFORM MISTAKEN PARTY ABOUT ERROR

1.2.4 NOT HAVING ACTED IN RELIANCE ON CONTRACT

2. MISTAKEN PARTY PREVENTED FROM AVOIDING CONTRACT

2.1 ERROR DUE TO ITS OWN GROSS NEGLIGENCE

2.2 RISK OF MISTAKE TO BE BORNE BY IT

ARTICLE 3.6
(Error in expression or transmission)

An error occurring in the expression or transmission of a declaration is considered to be a mistake of the person from whom the declaration emanated.

COMMENT

This article equates an error in the expression or transmission of a declaration with an ordinary mistake of the person making the declaration or sending it and thus the rules of Art. 3.5 and of Arts. 3.12 to 3.19 apply also to these kinds of error.

1. Relevant mistake

If an error in expression or transmission is of sufficient magnitude (especially if it has resulted in the misstatement of figures), the receiver will be, or ought to be, aware of the error. Since nothing in the Principles prevents the receiver/offeree from accepting the erroneously expressed or transmitted offer, it is for the sender/offeror to invoke the error and to avoid the contract provided that the conditions of Art. 3.5 are met, in particular that it was contrary to reasonable commercial standards of fair dealing for the receiver/offeree not to inform the sender/offeror of the error.

In some cases the risk of the error may have been assumed by, or may have to be imposed upon, the sender if it uses a method of transmission which it knows or ought to know to be unsafe either in general or in the special circumstances of the case.

Illustration

A, a potential Italian client, asks B, an English law firm, for legal advice and by way of reply receives a telegram indicating that B's hourly rate is "£150", whereas the form handed by B to the English post office had read "£250". Since it is well known that numbers in telegrams are often wrongly transmitted, B is considered to have assumed that risk and is not entitled to invoke the error in the transmission, even if the other conditions of Art. 3.5 are met.

2. Mistakes on the part of the receiver

Transmission ends as soon as the message reaches the receiver. See Art. 1.10.

If the message is correctly transmitted, but the receiver misunderstands its content, the case falls outside the scope of the present article.

If the message is correctly transmitted to the receiver's machine which, however, due to a technical fault, prints out a mutilated text, the case is again outside the scope of this article. The same is true if, at the receiver's request, a message is given orally to the receiver's messenger who misunderstands it or transmits it wrongly.

In the two above-mentioned situations the receiver may however be entitled to invoke its own mistake in accordance with Art. 3.5, if it replies to the sender and bases its reply upon its own misunderstanding of the sender's message and if all the conditions of Art. 3.5 are met.

Issues & Cases

1. ERROR IN EXPRESSION OR TRANSMISSION CONSIDERED TO BE MISTAKE BY SENDER HARDWARE
   1.1 REQUIREMENTS FOR AVOIDANCE OF CONTRACT THE SAME AS THOSE LAID DOWN IN ART. 3.5
      1.1.1 RECIPIENT'S DUTY TO INFORM SENDER OF ERROR
      1.1.2 SENDER'S RISK FOR UNSAFE METHODS OF TRANSMISSION
2. ERROR IN EXPRESSION OR TRANSMISSION TO BE DISTINGUISHED FROM MESSAGE CORRECTLY TRANSMITTED BUT MISUNDERSTOOD BY RECEIVER (SEE ART. 3.5)
3. ERROR IN EXPRESSION OR TRANSMISSION TO BE DISTINGUISHED FROM MESSAGE CORRECTLY TRANSMITTED BUT WRONGLY RECORDED AND/OR PRINTED OUT BY RECEIVER'S

ARTICLE 3.7
(Remedies for non-performance)

A party is not entitled to avoid the contract on the ground of mistake if the circumstances on which that party relies afford, or could have afforded, a remedy for non-performance.

COMMENT

1. Remedies for non-performance preferred

This article is intended to resolve the conflict which may arise between the remedy of avoidance for mistake and the remedies for non-performance. In the event of such a conflict, preference is given to the remedies for non-performance since they seem to be better suited and are more flexible than the radical solution of avoidance.

2. Actual and potential conflicts

An actual conflict between the remedies for mistake and those for non-performance arises whenever the two sets of remedies are invoked in relation to what are essentially the same facts.

Illustration

A, a farmer, who finds a rusty cup on the land sells it to B, an art dealer, for 10,000 euros. The high price is based upon the assumption of both parties that the cup is made of silver (other silver objects had previously been found on the land). It subsequently turns out that the object in question is an ordinary iron cup worth only 1,000 euros. B refuses to accept the cup and to pay for it on the ground that it lacks the assumed quality. B also avoids the contract on the ground of mistake as to the quality of the cup. B is entitled only to the remedies for non-performance.

It may be that the conflict between the two sets of remedies is only potential, since the mistaken party could have relied upon a remedy for non-performance, but is actually precluded from doing so by special circumstances, for example because a statutory limitation period has lapsed. Even in such a case the present article applies with the consequence that the remedy of avoidance for mistake is excluded.

Issues & Cases

1. **REMEDIES FOR NON-PERFORMANCE PREFERRED**
   1.1 **ACTUAL CONFLICTS BETWEEN TWO SETS OF REMEDIES**
   1.2 **POTENTIAL CONFLICTS BETWEEN TWO SETS OF REMEDIES**

ARTICLE 3.8
(Fraud)

A party may avoid the contract when it has been led to conclude the contract by the other party's fraudulent representation, including language or practices, or fraudulent non-disclosure of circumstances which, according to reasonable commercial standards of fair dealing, the latter party should have disclosed.

COMMENT

1. Fraud and mistake

Avoidance of a contract by a party on the ground of fraud bears some resemblance to avoidance for a certain type of mistake. Fraud may be regarded as a special case of mistake caused by the other party. Fraud, like mistake, may involve either representations, whether express or implied, of false facts or non-disclosure of true facts.

2. Notion of fraud

The decisive distinction between fraud and mistake lies in the nature and purpose of the defrauding party's representations or non-disclosure. What entitles the defrauded party to avoid the contract is the "fraudulent" representation or non-disclosure of relevant facts. Such conduct is fraudulent if it is intended to lead the other party into error and thereby to gain an advantage to the detriment of the other party. The reprehensible nature of fraud is such that it is a sufficient ground for avoidance without the need for the presence of the additional conditions laid down in Art. 3.5 for the mistake to become relevant.

A mere "puff" in advertising or negotiations does not suffice.

Issues & Cases

1. AVOIDANCE OF CONTRACT FOR FRAUD
   - DECEMBER 4, 1996 ARBITRAL AWARD AD HOC ARBITRATION, ROME [664]

   1.1 FRAUDOLENT REPRESENTATION OF FALSE FACTS
   - DECEMBER 4, 1996 ARBITRAL AWARD AD HOC ARBITRATION, ROME [664]

- AUGUST 2000 ARBITRAL AWARD ICC INTERNATIONAL COURT OF ARBITRATION (NO. 9651) [854]

1.2 FRAUDOLENT NON-DISCLOSURE OF TRUE FACTS

- FEBRUARY 1999 ARBITRAL AWARD (PARTIAL) ICC INTERNATIONAL COURT OF ARBITRATION (NO. 9474) [777]

1.3 MERE "PUFF" IN ADVERTISING OR NEGOTIATIONS

ARTICLE 3.9
(Threat)

A party may avoid the contract when it has been led to conclude the contract by the other party's unjustified threat which, having regard to the circumstances, is so imminent and serious as to leave the first party no reasonable alternative. In particular, a threat is unjustified if the act or omission with which a party has been threatened is wrongful in itself, or it is wrongful to use it as a means to obtain the conclusion of the contract.

COMMENT

This article permits the avoidance of a contract on the ground of threat.

1. Threat must be imminent and serious

Threat of itself is not sufficient. It must be of so imminent and serious a character that the threatened person has no reasonable alternative but to conclude the contract on the terms proposed by the other party. The imminence and seriousness of the threat must be evaluated by an objective standard, taking into account the circumstances of the individual case.

2. Unjustified threat

The threat must in addition be unjustified. The second sentence of the present article sets out, by way of illustration, two examples of an unjustified threat. The first envisages a case where the act or omission with which the contracting party has been threatened is wrongful in itself (*e.g.* a physical attack). The second refers to a situation where the threatened act or omission is in itself lawful, but the purpose to be achieved is wrongful (*e.g.* the bringing of a court action for the sole purpose of inducing the other party to conclude the contract on the terms proposed).

Illustration

1. A, who is in default with the repayment of a loan, is threatened by B, the lender, with proceedings for the recovery of the money. The only purpose of this threat is to obtain on particularly advantageous terms a lease of A's warehouse. A signs the lease, but is entitled to avoid the contract.

3. Threat affecting reputation or economic interests

For the purpose of the application of the present article, threat need not necessarily be made against a person or property, but may also affect reputation or purely economic interests.

Illustration

2. Faced with a threat by the players of a basketball team to go on strike unless they receive a much higher bonus than had already been agreed for winning the four remaining matches of the season, the owner of the team agrees to pay the requested bonus. The owner is entitled to avoid the new contract with the players, since the strike would have led automatically to the team being relegated to a minor league and therefore represented a serious and imminent threat to both the reputation and the financial position of the club.

Issues & Cases

1. **AVOIDANCE OF CONTRACT FOR THREAT**
   - 1.1 **IMMINENT AND SERIOUS THREAT**
   - 1.2 **UNJUSTIFIED THREAT**
     - AUGUST 2000 ARBITRAL AWARD ICC INTERNATIONAL COURT OF ARBITRATION (NO. 9651) [854]
     - 1.2.1 **WRONGFUL ACT OR OMISSION**
     - 1.2.2 **WRONGFUL PURPOSE TO BE ACHIEVED**
   - 1.3 **THREAT AFFECTING REPUTATION OR ECONOMIC INTERESTS**

ARTICLE 3.10
(Gross disparity)

(1) A party may avoid the contract or an individual term of it if, at the time of the conclusion of the contract, the contract or term unjustifiably gave the other party an excessive advantage. Regard is to be had, among other factors, to

(a) the fact that the other party has taken unfair advantage of the first party's dependence, economic distress or urgent needs, or of its improvidence, ignorance, inexperience or lack of bargaining skill, and

(b) the nature and purpose of the contract.

(2) Upon the request of the party entitled to avoidance, a court may adapt the contract or term in order to make it accord with reasonable commercial standards of fair dealing.

(3) A court may also adapt the contract or term upon the request of the party receiving notice of avoidance, provided that that party informs the other party of its request promptly after receiving such notice and before the other party has acted in reliance on it. The provisions of Article 3.13(2) apply accordingly.

COMMENT

1. Excessive advantage

This provision permits a party to avoid a contract in cases where there is a gross disparity between the obligations of the parties, which gives one party an unjustifiably excessive advantage.

The excessive advantage must exist at the time of the conclusion of the contract. A contract which, although not grossly unfair when entered into, becomes so later may be adapted or terminated under the rules on hardship contained in Chapter 6, Section 2.

As the term "excessive" advantage denotes, even a considerable disparity in the value and the price or some other element which upsets the equilibrium of performance and counter-performance is not sufficient to permit the avoidance or the adaptation of the contract under this article. What is required is that the disequilibrium is in the circumstances so great as to shock the conscience of a reasonable person.

2. Unjustifiable advantage

Not only must the advantage be excessive, it must also be unjustifiable. Whether this requirement is met will depend upon an evaluation of all the relevant circumstances of the case. Para. (1) of the present article refers in particular to two factors which deserve special attention in this connection.

a. *Unequal bargaining position*

The first factor is that one party has taken unfair advantage of the other party's dependence, economic distress or urgent needs, or its improvidence, ignorance, inexperience, or lack of bargaining skill (sub-para. (a)). As to the dependence of one party vis-à-vis the other, superior bargaining power due to market conditions alone is not sufficient.

Illustration

A, the owner of an automobile factory, sells an outdated assembly line to B, a governmental agency from a country eager to set up its own automobile industry. Although A makes no representations as to the efficiency of the assembly line, it succeeds in fixing a price which is manifestly excessive. B, after discovering that it has paid an amount which corresponds to that of a much more modern assembly line, may be entitled to avoid the contract.

b. *Nature and purpose of the contract*

The second factor to which special regard must be had is the nature and purpose of the contract (sub-para. (b)). There are situations where an excessive advantage is unjustifiable even if the party who will benefit from it has not abused the other party's weak bargaining position.

Whether this is the case will often depend upon the nature and purpose of the contract. Thus, a contract term providing for an extremely short period for giving notice of defects in goods or services to be supplied may or may not be excessively advantageous to the seller or supplier, depending on the character of the goods or services in question. Equally, an agent's fee expressed in terms of a fixed percentage of the price of the goods or services to be sold or rendered, although justified in the event of the agent's contribution to the conclusion of the transaction being substantial and/or the value of the goods or services concerned not being very high, may well turn out to confer an excessive advantage on the agent if the latter's contribution is almost negligible and/or the value of the goods or services are extraordinarily high.

c. *Other factors*

Other factors may need to be taken into consideration, for example the ethics prevailing in the business or trade.

3. Avoidance or adaptation

The avoidance of the contract or of any of its individual terms under this article is subject to the general rules laid down in Arts. 3.14 - 3.18.

However, according to para. (2) of the present article, at the request of the party who is entitled to avoidance, the court may adapt the contract in order to bring it into accord with reasonable commercial standards of fair dealing. Similarly, according to para. (3) the party receiving notice of avoidance may also request such adaptation provided it informs the avoiding party of its request promptly after receiving the notice of avoidance, and before the avoiding party has acted in reliance on that notice.

If the parties are in disagreement as to the procedure to be adopted, it will be for the court to decide whether the contract is to be avoided or adapted and, if adapted, on which terms.

If, in its notice or subsequently, a party entitled to avoidance requests adaptation only, its right to avoidance will be lost. See Art. 3.13(2).

Issues & Cases

1. NOTION OF GROSS DISPARITY

- MARCH 1998 ARBITRAL AWARD ICC INTERNATIONAL COURT OF ARBITRATION (NO. 9029) [718]

1.1 GROSS DISPARITY BETWEEN OBLIGATIONS OF PARTIES

1.2 MUST EXIST AT TIME OF CONCLUSION OF CONTRACT

- MARCH 1998 ARBITRAL AWARD ICC INTERNATIONAL COURT OF ARBITRATION (NO. 9029) [718]

1.3 MUST BE UNJUSTIFIABLE

1.3.1 ABUSE OF OTHER PARTY'S WEAK BARGAINING POWER

1.3.1.1 STATUS OF DEPENDENCE

1.3.1.2 ECONOMIC DISTRESS OR URGENT NEEDS

1.3.1.3 PERSONAL WEAKNESS

- MARCH 1998 ARBITRAL AWARD ICC INTERNATIONAL COURT OF ARBITRATION (NO. 9029) [718]

1.3.2 UNFAIRNESS WITH REGARD TO NATURE AND PURPOSE OF CONTRACT

1.3.2.1 GENERAL ETHICS AND PRACTICES IN TRADE SECTOR CONCERNED

2. AVOIDANCE OF CONTRACT OR OF INDIVIDUAL TERM

3. ADAPTATION OF CONTRACT OR OF INDIVIDUAL TERM BY COURT

3.1 UPON REQUEST OF PARTY ENTITLED TO AVOIDANCE

3.2 UPON REQUEST OF PARTY RECEIVING NOTICE OF AVOIDANCE

ARTICLE 3.11
(Third persons)

(1) Where fraud, threat, gross disparity or a party's mistake is imputable to, or is known or ought to be known by, a third person for whose acts the other party is responsible, the contract may be avoided under the same conditions as if the behaviour or knowledge had been that of the party itself.

(2) Where fraud, threat or gross disparity is imputable to a third person for whose acts the other party is not responsible, the contract may be avoided if that party knew or ought to have known of the fraud, threat or disparity, or has not at the time of avoidance acted in reliance on the contract.

COMMENT

This article deals with situations, frequent in practice, in which a third person has been involved or has interfered in the negotiation process, and the ground for avoidance is in one way or another imputable to that person.

1. Third person for whom a party is responsible

Para. (1) is concerned with cases in which fraud, threat, gross disparity or a party's mistake is caused by a third person for whose acts the other party is responsible, or cases in which, without causing the mistake, the third person knew or ought to have known of it. A party is responsible for the acts of a third person in a variety of situations ranging from those in which that person is an agent of the party in question to those where the third person acts for the benefit of that party on its own initiative. In all such cases it seems justified to impute to that party the third person's acts or its knowledge, whether actual or constructive, of certain circumstances, and this irrespective of whether the party in question knew of the third person's acts.

2. Third person for whom a party is not responsible

Para. (2) deals with cases where a party is defrauded, threatened or otherwise unduly influenced by a third person for whom the other party is not responsible. Such acts may be imputed to the latter party only if it knew or ought to have known of them.

There is however one exception to this rule: the defrauded, threatened or otherwise unduly influenced party is entitled to avoid the contract, even if the other party did not know of the third person's acts, whenever the latter party has not acted in reliance on the contract before the time of avoidance. This exception is justified because in this situation the other party is not in need of protection.

Issues & Cases

1. **GROUND OF AVOIDANCE IMPUTABLE TO THIRD PERSON**
   - 1.1 **THIRD PERSON FOR WHOM A PARTY IS RESPONSIBLE**
     - 1.1.1 **THIRD PERSON'S ACTS OR KNOWLEDGE IMPUTED TO PARTY IRRESPECTIVE OF THAT PARTY'S KNOWLEDGE**
   - 1.2 **THIRD PERSON FOR WHOM A PARTY IS NOT RESPONSIBLE**
     - 1.2.1 **THIRD PERSON'S ACTS OR KNOWLEDGE IMPUTED TO PARTY ONLY IF THAT PARTY KNEW OR OUGHT TO HAVE KNOWN OF THEM**
     - 1.2.2 **EXCEPTIONS**

ARTICLE 3.12
(Confirmation)

If the party entitled to avoid the contract expressly or impliedly confirms the contract after the period of time for giving notice of avoidance has begun to run, avoidance of the contract is excluded.

COMMENT

This article lays down the rule according to which the party entitled to avoid the contract may either expressly or impliedly confirm the contract.

For there to be an implied confirmation it is not sufficient, for example, for the party entitled to avoid the contract to bring a claim against the other party based on the latter's non-performance. A confirmation can only be assumed if the other party acknowledges the claim or if a court action has been successful.

There is also confirmation if the party entitled to avoidance continues to perform the contract without reserving its right to avoid the contract.

Issues & Cases

1. CONFIRMATION OF CONTRACT BY PARTY ENTITLED TO AVOIDANCE
    - APRIL 21, 1997 ARBITRAL AWARD AD HOC ARBITRATION, PARIS [679]
    - DECEMBER 10, 1997 ARBITRAL AWARD AD HOC ARBITRATION, BUENOS AIRES [715]

1.1 EXPLICIT CONFIRMATION

1.2 IMPLICIT CONFIRMATION

1.2.1 UNCONDITIONAL PERFORMANCE OF THE CONTRACT

1.2.2 CLAIM BASED ON NON-PERFORMANCE

1.2.3 OTHER CASES

- APRIL 21, 1997 ARBITRAL AWARD AD HOC ARBITRATION, PARIS [679]
- DECEMBER 10, 1997 ARBITRAL AWARD AD HOC ARBITRATION, BUENOS AIRES [715]

ARTICLE 3.13
(Loss of right to avoid)

(1) If a party is entitled to avoid the contract for mistake but the other party declares itself willing to perform or performs the contract as it was understood by the party entitled to avoidance, the contract is considered to have been concluded as the latter party understood it. The other party must make such a declaration or render such performance promptly after having been informed of the manner in which the party entitled to avoidance had understood the contract and before that party has acted in reliance on a notice of avoidance.

(2) After such a declaration or performance the right to avoidance is lost and any earlier notice of avoidance is ineffective.

COMMENT

1. Performance of the contract as understood by the mistaken party

According to this article a mistaken party may be prevented from avoiding the contract if the other party declares itself willing to perform or actually performs the contract as it was understood by the mistaken party. The interest of the other party in so doing may lie in the benefit to be derived from the contract, even in its adapted form.

Such regard for the interests of the other party is only justified in the case of mistake and not in other cases of defective consent (threat and fraud) where it would be extremely difficult to expect the parties to keep the contract alive.

2. Decision to be made promptly

The other party has to declare its decision to perform or actually to perform the contract in its adapted form promptly after having been informed of the manner in which the mistaken party had understood the contract. How the other party is to receive the information about the erroneous understanding of the terms of the contract will depend on the circumstances of the case.

3. Loss of right to avoid

Para. (2) expressly states that after the other party's declaration or performance the right of the mistaken party to avoid the contract is lost and that any earlier notice of avoidance becomes ineffective.

Conversely, the other party is no longer entitled to adapt the contract if the mistaken party has not only given notice of avoidance but has also acted in reliance on that notice.

4. Damages

The adaptation of the contract by the other party does not preclude the mistaken party from claiming damages in accordance with Art. 3.18 if it has suffered loss which is not compensated by the adaptation of the contract.

Issues & Cases

1. CONFIRMATION OF CONTRACT AVOIDABLE FOR MISTAKE
   - 1.1 PERFORMANCE AS UNDERSTOOD BY MISTAKEN PARTY
   - 1.2 TIME LIMITS
     - 1.2.1 REAL PERFORMANCE
     - 1.2.2 WILLINGNESS TO RENDER SUCH PERFORMANCE
2. EFFECTS OF CONFIRMATION
   - 2.1 LOSS OF RIGHT TO AVOIDANCE OF MISTAKEN PARTY
   - 2.2 INEFFECTIVENESS OF EARLIER NOTICE OF AVOIDANCE
   - 2.3 DAMAGES

ARTICLE 3.14
(Notice of avoidance)

The right of a party to avoid the contract is exercised by notice to the other party.

COMMENT

1. The requirement of notice

This article states the principle that the right of a party to avoid the contract is exercised by notice to the other party without the need for any intervention by a court.

2. Form and content of notice

No provision is made in this article for any specific requirement as to the form or content of the notice of avoidance. It follows that in accordance with the general rule laid down in Art. 1.10(1), the notice may be given by any means appropriate to the circumstances. As to the content of the notice, it is not necessary that the term "avoidance" actually be used, or that the reasons for avoiding the contract be stated expressly. However, for the sake of clarity a party would be well advised to give some reasons for the avoidance in its notice, although in cases of fraud or gross disparity the avoiding party may assume that those reasons are already known to the other party.

Illustration

A, B's employer, threatens B with dismissal if B does not sell A a Louis XVI chest of drawers. B ultimately agrees to the sale. Two days later A receives a letter from B announcing B's resignation and stating that B has sold the chest of drawers to C. B's letter is sufficient notice of avoidance of the contract of sale with A.

3. Notice must be received

The notice of avoidance becomes effective when it reaches the other party. See Art. 1.10(2).

Issues & Cases

1. AVOIDANCE BY MERE NOTICE
   1.1 NO NEED FOR COURT INTERVENTION
2. FORM AND CONTENT OF NOTICE

- DECEMBER 10, 1997 ARBITRAL AWARD AD HOC ARBITRATION, BUENOS AIRES [715]

3. **NOTICE MUST REACH OTHER PARTY (SEE ART. 1.9(2))**
4. **TIME LIMITS (SEE ART. 3.15)**

ARTICLE 3.15
(Time limits)

(1) Notice of avoidance shall be given within a reasonable time, having regard to the circumstances, after the avoiding party knew or could not have been unaware of the relevant facts or became capable of acting freely.

(2) Where an individual term of the contract may be avoided by a party under Article 3.10, the period of time for giving notice of avoidance begins to run when that term is asserted by the other party.

COMMENT

According to para. (1) of this article notice of avoidance must be given within a reasonable time after the avoiding party became aware or could not have been unaware of the relevant facts or became capable of acting freely. More precisely, the mistaken or defrauded party must give notice of avoidance within a reasonable time after it became aware or could no longer be unaware of the mistake or fraud. The same applies in cases of gross disparity which result from an abuse of the innocent party's ignorance, improvidence or inexperience. In cases of threat or abuse of the innocent party's dependence, economic distress or urgent needs the period runs from the time the threatened or abused party becomes capable of acting freely.

In case of avoidance of an individual term of the contract in accordance with Art. 3.10, para. (2) of this article states that the period of time for giving notice begins to run when that term is asserted by the party.

Issues & Cases

1. NOTICE OF AVOIDANCE TO BE GIVEN WITHIN REASONABLE TIME
   1.1 REASONABLE TIME
      - JULY 27, 1999 ARBITRAL AWARD INTERNATIONAL ARBITRATION COURT OF THE CHAMBER OF COMMERCE AND INDUSTRY OF THE RUSSIAN FEDERATION (NO. 302/1997) [802]
   1.2 BEGINNING OF PERIOD

1.2.1 IN CASE OF MISTAKE AND FRAUD, WHEN MISTAKEN OR DEFRAUDED PARTY BECOMES AWARE OF MISTAKE OR FRAUD

1.2.2 IN CASE OF THREAT AND GROSS DISPARITY, WHEN TREATENED OR EXPLOITED PARTY BECOMES CAPABLE OF ACTING FREELY

ARTICLE 3.16
(Partial avoidance)

Where a ground of avoidance affects only individual terms of the contract, the effect of avoidance is limited to those terms unless, having regard to the circumstances, it is unreasonable to uphold the remaining contract.

COMMENT

This article deals with situations where the grounds of avoidance affect only individual terms of the contract. In such cases the effects of avoidance will be limited to the terms affected unless it would in the circumstances be unreasonable to uphold the remaining contract. This will generally depend upon whether or not a party would have entered into the contract had it envisaged that the terms in question would have been affected by grounds of avoidance.

Illustrations

1. A, a contractor, agrees to build two houses on plots of land X and Y for B, one of which B intends to live in and the other to rent. B was mistaken in assuming that it had a licence to build on both plots, since in fact the licence covered only plot X. Unless the circumstances indicate otherwise, notwithstanding the avoidance of the contract concerning the building of the house on plot Y, it would be reasonable to uphold the remaining contract concerning the building of the house on plot X.

2. The situation is the same as in Illustration 1, the difference being that a school was to be built on plot X and living quarters for the students on plot Y. Unless the circumstances indicate otherwise, after the avoidance of the contract concerning the building of the living quarters on plot Y it would not be reasonable to uphold the remaining contract for the building of the school on plot X.

Issues & Cases

1. AVOIDANCE OF INDIVIDUAL TERMS OF CONTRACT

1.1 EFFECTS OF AVOIDANCE LIMITED TO THE AFFECTED TERMS

1.1.1 EXCEPTIONS

ARTICLE 3.17
(Retroactive effect of avoidance)

(1) Avoidance takes effect retroactively.

(2) On avoidance either party may claim restitution of whatever it has supplied under the contract or the part of it avoided, provided that it concurrently makes restitution of whatever it has received under the contract or the part of it avoided or, if it cannot make restitution in kind, it makes an allowance for what it has received.

COMMENT

1. Avoidance generally of retroactive effect

Para. (1) of this article states the rule that avoidance takes effect retroactively. In other words, the contract is considered never to have existed. In the case of a partial avoidance under Art. 3.16 the rule applies only to the avoided part of the contract.

There are however individual terms of the contract which may survive even in cases of total avoidance. Arbitration, jurisdiction and choice-of-law clauses are considered to be different from the other terms of the contract which may be upheld notwithstanding the avoidance of the contract in whole or in part. Whether in fact such clauses remain operative is to be determined by the applicable domestic law.

2. Restitution

According to para. (2) of the present article either party may claim restitution of what it has supplied under the contract or the part of it avoided. The only condition for such restitution is that each party makes restitution of whatever it has received under the contract or the part of it avoided. If restitution in kind is not possible, as is typically the case with services, a party must make an allowance for what it has received, except where the performance received is of no value to it.

Illustration

A commissions B to decorate a restaurant. B begins the work. When A later discovers that B is not the famous decorator who had made similar decorations in a number of another restaurants, A avoids the contract. Since the decorations so far made cannot be returned and they have no value for A, B is not entitled to any allowance from A for the work done.

Issues & Cases

1. **RETROACTIVE EFFECT OF AVOIDANCE**
   - 1.1 **UPHOLDING OF INDIVIDUAL TERMS**
2. **RESTITUTION**
   - 2.1 **RESTITUTION IN KIND**
   - 2.2 **ALLOWANCE IF RESTITUTION IN KIND IS NOT POSSIBLE**

ARTICLE 3.18
(Damages)

Irrespective of whether or not the contract has been avoided, the party who knew or ought to have known of the ground for avoidance is liable for damages so as to put the other party in the same position in which it would have been if it had not concluded the contract.

COMMENT

1. Damages if ground for avoidance known to the other party

This article provides that a party which knew or ought to have known of a ground for avoidance is liable for damages to the other party. The right to damages arises irrespective of whether or not the contract has been avoided.

2. The measure of damages

Unlike the damages in case of non-performance under Chapter 7, Section 4, the damages contemplated by the present article are intended simply to put the other party in the same position in which it would have been if it had not concluded the contract.

Illustration

A sells software to B, and could not have been unaware of B's mistake as to its appropriateness for the use intended by B. Irrespective of whether or not B avoids the contract, A is liable to B for all the expenses incurred by B in training its personnel in the use of the software, but not for the loss suffered by B as a consequence of the impossibility to use the software for the intended purpose.

Issues & Cases

1. RIGHT TO DAMAGES
    - 1.1 PARTY'S KNOWLEDGE OF GROUND FOR AVOIDANCE (SEE ART. 2.1.15)
    - 1.2 AVOIDANCE OF CONTRACT IRRELEVANT
2. MEASURE OF DAMAGES
    - 2.1 RELIANCE (OR NEGATIVE) INTERESTS

ARTICLE 3.19
(Mandatory character of the provisions)

The provisions of this Chapter are mandatory, except insofar as they relate to the binding force of mere agreement, initial impossibility or mistake.

COMMENT

This article declares the provisions of this Chapter relating to fraud, threat and gross disparity to be of a mandatory character. It would be contrary to good faith for the parties to exclude or modify these provisions when concluding their contract. However, nothing prevents the party entitled to avoidance to waive that right once it learns of the true facts or is able to act freely.

On the other hand, the provisions of this Chapter relating to the binding force of mere agreement, to initial impossibility or to mistake are not mandatory. Thus the parties may well reintroduce special requirements of domestic law, such as consideration or *cause*; they may likewise agree that their contract shall be invalid in case of initial impossibility, or that mistake by one of them is not a ground for avoidance.

Issues & Cases

1. MANDATORY CHARACTER OF THE PROVISIONS OF CHAPTER 3
2. EXCEPTIONS
   - 2.1 ART. 3.2
   - 2.2 ART. 3.3
   - 2.3 ARTS. 3.5, 3.6 AND 3.13

ARTICLE 3.20
(Unilateral declarations)

The provisions of this Chapter apply with appropriate adaptations to any communication of intention addressed by one party to the other.

COMMENT

This article takes account of the fact that apart from the contract itself the parties, either before or after the conclusion of the contract, often exchange a number of communications of intention which may likewise be affected by invalidity.

In a commercial setting, the most important example of unilateral communications of intention which are external, but preparatory, to a contract are bids for investment, works, delivery of goods or provision of services. Communications of intention made after the conclusion of a contract take a variety of forms, such as notices, declarations, demands and requests. In particular, waivers and declarations by which a party assumes an obligation may be affected by a defect of consent.

Issues & Cases

1. APPLICATION BY ANALOGY OF THE PROVISIONS OF CHAPTER 3 ON OTHER COMMUNICATIONS OF INTENTION
   1.1 COMMUNICATIONS MADE BEFORE CONCLUSION OF CONTRACT
   1.2 COMMUNICATIONS MADE AFTER CONCLUSION OF CONTRACT

CHAPTER 4

INTERPRETATION

BIBLIOGRAPHY

ADAME GODDARD J., Las Reglas de interpretación de los contratos internacionales desde la perspectiva del derecho mexicano, in BONELL M.J. / SCHIPANI S. (eds.), "Principi per i contratti commerciali internazionali" e il sistema giuridico latinoamericano, Padova 1996, 155-167.

AIMONE GIBSON E., Interpretación de los contratos. Comentario al Capítulo IV de los "*Principles*", in BONELL M.J. / SCHIPANI S. (eds.), "Principi per i contratti commerciali internazionali" e il sistema giuridico latinoamericano, Padova 1996, 141-153.

BAUMANN A., Regeln der Auslegung internationaler Handelsgeschäfte. Eine vergleichende Untersuchung der UNIDROIT Principles, der Principles of European Contract Law, des Uniform Commercial Code und des deutschen Rechts, in V&R Unipress, 2004.

BELSER, E.M., Die Auslegung des Vertrages – Richterliche Inhaltsgestaltung zwischen Freiheit und Gerechtigkeit, in L'européanisation du droit privé. Vers un code civil européen?, in ed. Univ. Fribourg, 1998, 237-267.

BONELL M.J., A 'Global' arbitration decided on the basis of the UNIDROIT Principles: In re Andersen Consulting Business Unit Member Firms v. Arthur Andersen Business Unit Member Firms and Andersen Worldwide Société Coopérative, in 17 Arbitration International 2001, 249 – 261.

CARBONE S.M., Interpretazione dei contratti internazionali e Principi UNIDROIT, in ALPA G. / BESSONE M., (eds.), Giurisprudenza sistematica di diritto civile e commerciale, I, Utet, Torino, 1999, 239-252.

CHAPPUIS Ch., L'intervention du tribunal dans le contrat. Convergence entre les Principes UNIDROIT et le droit suisse, in Liber Amicorum Claude Reymond, Litec, Paris 2004, 53 – 72.

FERRI G.B., L'"invisibile" presenza della causa del contratto, in Europa e diritto privato, 2002, 897 – 914.

GORRIZ LOPEZ, C., L'interpretazione del contratto nei Principi UNIDROIT dei contratti commerciali internazionali, in Contratto e impresa / Europa, 1998, 467-488.

KAUFMANN S., Parol Evidence Rule und Merger Clause im Internationalen Einheitsrecht, Lang 2004.

MENYHÁRD A., A szerződés akarathibák miatti érvénytelensége, Budapest, in Az Elte Állam-és Jogtudományi, 2000 (A Szladitis Szeminárium Kiadványai, 1).

NET L., Rules of interpretation of contracts under the UNIDROIT Principles and their possible adoption in Vietnamese law, in Uniform Law Review / Revue de droit uniforme, 7 (2002), 1017 – 1030.

TERNERO M.C., Interpretación, in Comentario a los Principios de UNIDROIT para los Contratos del Comercio Internacional, Aranzadi, Pamplona, 1999, 225-244.

WEIDEMANN C., Lückenergänzung and richterliche Fortbildung nach Art. 1.6 II der UNIDROIT-Principles for International Commercial Contracts. Methode and Beispiele: Rückgewärschuldverhältnisse, postvertragliche Pflichten, objecktive Beweislast, Frankfurt a.M., Berlin, Bern, Peter Lang, 2001, 277. (Europäische Hochschuldschriften. Reihe II. Rechtswissenschaft, 3213).

ARTICLE 4.1
(Intention of the parties)

(1) A contract shall be interpreted according to the common intention of the parties.

(2) If such an intention cannot be established, the contract shall be interpreted according to the meaning that reasonable persons of the same kind as the parties would give to it in the same circumstances.

COMMENT

1. Common intention of the parties to prevail

Para. (1) of this article lays down the principle that in determining the meaning to be attached to the terms of a contract, preference is to be given to the intention common to the parties. In consequence, a contract term may be given a meaning which differs both from the literal sense of the language used and from the meaning which a reasonable person would attach to it, provided that such a different understanding was common to the parties at the time of the conclusion of the contract.

The practical importance of the principle should not be over-estimated, first because parties to commercial transactions are unlikely to use language in a sense entirely different from that usually attached to it, and secondly because even if this were to be the case it would be extremely difficult, once a dispute arises, to prove that a particular meaning which one of the parties claims to have been their common intention was in fact shared by the other party at the time of the conclusion of the contract.

2. Recourse to the understanding of reasonable persons

For those cases where the common intention of the parties cannot be established, para. (2) provides that the contract shall be interpreted in accordance with the meaning which reasonable persons of the same kind as the parties would give to it in the same circumstances. The test is not a general and abstract criterion of reasonableness, but rather the understanding which could reasonably be expected of persons with, for example, the same linguistic knowledge, technical skill, or business experience as the parties.

3. How to establish the common intention of the parties or to determine the understanding of reasonable persons

In order to establish whether the parties had a common intention and, if so, what that common intention was, regard is to be had to all the relevant circumstances of the case, the most important of which are listed in Art. 4.3. The same applies to the determination of the understanding of reasonable persons when no common intention of the parties can be established.

4. Interpretation of standard terms

Both the "subjective" test laid down in para. (1) and the "reasonableness" test in para. (2) may not always be appropriate in the context of standard terms. Indeed, given their special nature and purpose, standard terms should be interpreted primarily in accordance with the reasonable expectations of their average users irrespective of the actual understanding which either of the parties to the contract concerned, or reasonable persons of the same kind as the parties, might have had. For the definition of "standard terms", see Art. 2.1.19(2).

Issues & Cases

1. INTERPRETATION OF CONTRACT

- NOVEMBER 25, 1994 ARBITRAL AWARD ZÜRICH CHAMBER OF COMMERCE [559]
- 1995 ARBITRAL AWARD AD HOC ARBITRATION, AUCKLAND [564]
- SEPTEMBER 1998 ARBITRAL AWARD ICC INTERNATIONAL COURT OF ARBITRATION (NO. 8908) [750]
- MARCH 20, 2000 ARBITRAL AWARD INTERNATIONAL CENTRE FOR SETTLEMENT OF INVESTMENT DISPUTES (ICSID) (NO. ARB(AF)/98/1) [826]

1.1 ACCORDING TO COMMON INTENTION OF PARTIES

- 1995 ARBITRAL AWARD LONDON COURT OF ARBITRATION [571]
- SEPTEMBER 1998 ARBITRAL AWARD ICC INTERNATIONAL COURT OF ARBITRATION (NO. 8908) [750]
- OCTOBER 2000 ARBITRAL AWARD ICC INTERNATIONAL COURT OF ARBITRATION (NO. 10335) [864]
- NOVEMBER 27, 2000 NEW ZEALAND COURT OF APPEAL OF NEW ZEALAND (NO. (2000)NZCA 350) [869]
- DECEMBER 2001 ARBITRAL AWARD ICC INTERNATIONAL COURT OF ARBITRATION (NO. 11295) [988]
- NOVEMBER 5, 2002 ARBITRAL AWARD INTERNATIONAL ARBITRATION COURT AT THE

CHAMBER OF COMMERCE AND INDUSTRY OF THE RUSSIAN FEDERATION (NO. 11/2002) [1030]

- DECEMBER 4, 2005 UNITED KINGDOM HIGH COURT OF JUSTICE (QUEEN'S BENCH DIVISION) (NO. 2004 FOLIO 272) [1110]
- FEBRUARY 17, 2006 UNITED KINGDOM COURT OF APPEAL (CIVIL DIVISION) (NO. 2006 EWCA CIV. 69) [1142]

1.2 ACCORDING TO UNDERSTANDING OF REASONABLE PERSONS

- NOVEMBER 25, 1994 ARBITRAL AWARD ZÜRICH CHAMBER OF COMMERCE [559]
- 1995 ARBITRAL AWARD AD HOC ARBITRATION, AUCKLAND [564]
- MARCH 2000 ARBITRAL AWARD ICC INTERNATIONAL COURT OF ARBITRATION (NO. 9875) [820]
- JULY 28, 2000 ARBITRAL AWARD ICC INTERNATIONAL COURT OF ARBITRATION (NO. 9797/CK/AER/ACS) [834]
- AUGUST 2000 ARBITRAL AWARD ICC INTERNATIONAL COURT OF ARBITRATION (NO. 9651) [854]
- OCTOBER 2000 ARBITRAL AWARD ICC INTERNATIONAL COURT OF ARBITRATION (NO. 10335) [864]
- APRIL 30, 2001 ARBITRAL AWARD AD HOC ARBITRATION SAN JOSÉ (COSTA RICA) [945]
- DECEMBER 2001 ARBITRAL AWARD ICC INTERNATIONAL COURT OF ARBITRATION (NO. 11295) [988]
- JANUARY 25, 2002 ARBITRAL AWARD ARBITRATION COURT OF THE LAUSANNE CHAMBER OF COMMERCE AND INDUSTRY [991]
- JANUARY 31, 2003 ARBITRAL AWARD ARBITRATION COURT OF THE LAUSANNE CHAMBER OF COMMERCE AND INDUSTRY [1056]

1.3 SPECIAL CRITERIA FOR STANDARD TERMS

2. RELEVANT CIRCUMSTANCES (SEE ART. 4.3)

ARTICLE 4.2

(Interpretation of statements and other conduct)

(1) The statements and other conduct of a party shall be interpreted according to that party's intention if the other party knew or could not have been unaware of that intention.

(2) If the preceding paragraph is not applicable, such statements and other conduct shall be interpreted according to the meaning that a reasonable person of the same kind as the other party would give to it in the same circumstances.

COMMENT

1. Interpretation of unilateral acts

By analogy to the criteria laid down in Art. 4.1 with respect to the contract as a whole, this article states that in the interpretation of unilateral statements or conduct preference is to be given to the intention of the party concerned, provided that the other party knew (or could not have been unaware) of that intention, and that in all other cases such statements or conduct are to be interpreted according to the understanding that a reasonable person of the same kind as the other party would have had in the same circumstances.

In practice the principal field of application of this article, which corresponds almost literally to Art. 8(1) and (2) CISG, will be in the process of the formation of contracts where parties make statements and engage in conduct whose precise legal significance may have to be established in order to determine whether or not a contract is ultimately concluded. There are however also unilateral acts performed after the conclusion of the contract which may give rise to problems of interpretation: for example, a notification of defects in goods, notice of avoidance or of termination of the contract, etc.

2. How to establish the intention of the party performing the act or to determine the understanding of a reasonable person

In applying both the "subjective" test laid down in para. (1) and the "reasonableness" test in para. (2), regard is to be had to all the relevant circumstances, the most important of which are listed in Art. 4.3.

Issues & Cases

1. INTERPRETATION OF UNILATERAL ACTS

- NOVEMBER 25, 1994 ARBITRAL AWARD ZÜRICH CHAMBER OF COMMERCE [559]
- 1995 ARBITRAL AWARD AD HOC ARBITRATION, AUCKLAND [564]
- DECEMBER 1, 1996 ARBITRAL AWARD CAMERA ARBITRALE NAZIONALE ED INTERNAZIONALE DI MILANO (NO. A-1795/51) [662]
- MARCH 20, 2000 ARBITRAL AWARD INTERNATIONAL CENTRE FOR SETTLEMENT OF INVESTMENT DISPUTES (ICSID) (NO. ARB(AF)/98/1) [826]

1.1 ACCORDING TO INTENTION OF PARTY CONCERNED

- OCTOBER 2000 ARBITRAL AWARD ICC INTERNATIONAL COURT OF ARBITRATION (NO. 10335) [864]

1.2 ACCORDING TO UNDERSTANDING OF REASONABLE PERSON

- NOVEMBER 25, 1994 ARBITRAL AWARD ZÜRICH CHAMBER OF COMMERCE [559]
- 1995 ARBITRAL AWARD LONDON COURT OF ARBITRATION [571]
- 1995 ARBITRAL AWARD AD HOC ARBITRATION, AUCKLAND [564]
- DECEMBER 1, 1996 ARBITRAL AWARD CAMERA ARBITRALE NAZIONALE ED INTERNAZIONALE DI MILANO (NO. A-1795/51) [666]
- APRIL 16, 1999 ARBITRAL AWARD INTERNATIONAL ARBITRATION COURT OF THE CHAMBER OF COMMERCE AND INDUSTRY OF THE RUSSIAN FEDERATION (NO. 152/1998) [798]
- MARCH 2000 ARBITRAL AWARD ICC INTERNATIONAL COURT OF ARBITRATION (NO. 9875) [820]
- AUGUST 2000 ARBITRAL AWARD ICC INTERNATIONAL COURT OF ARBITRATION (NO. 9651) [854]
- OCTOBER 2000 ARBITRAL AWARD ICC INTERNATIONAL COURT OF ARBITRATION (NO. 10335) [864]
- JANUARY 25, .2002 ARBITRAL AWARD ARBITRATION COURT OF THE LAUSANNE CHAMBER OF COMMERCE AND INDUSTRY [ ]

2. RELEVANT CIRCUMSTANCES (SEE ART. 4.3)

ARTICLE 4.3
(Relevant circumstances)

In applying Articles 4.1 and 4.2, regard shall be had to all the circumstances, including

(a) preliminary negotiations between the parties;

(b) practices which the parties have established between themselves;

(c) the conduct of the parties subsequent to the conclusion of the contract;

(d) the nature and purpose of the contract;

(e) the meaning commonly given to terms and expressions in the trade concerned;

(f) usages.

COMMENT

1. Circumstances relevant in the interpretation process

This article indicates circumstances which have to be taken into consideration when applying both the "subjective" test and the "reasonableness" test in Arts. 4.1 and 4.2. The list mentions only those circumstances which are the most important and is in no way intended to be exhaustive.

2. "Particular" and "general" circumstances compared

Of the circumstances listed in the present article some relate to the particular relationship which exists between the parties concerned, while others are of a more general character. Although in principle all the circumstances listed may be relevant in a given case, the first three are likely to have greater weight in the application of the "subjective" test.

Illustrations

1. A contract for the writing of a book between A and B, a publisher, indicates that the book should consist of "about 300 pages". During their negotiations B had assured A that an approximate indication of the number of pages was necessary for administrative reasons and that A was not bound to stick precisely to that number of pages, but could exceed it, substantially if need be. A submits a manuscript of 500 pages. In interpreting the

meaning of "about 300 pages" due consideration should be given to these preliminary negotiations. See Art. 4.3(a).

2. A, a Canadian manufacturer, and B, a United States retailer, conclude a number of contracts for the delivery of optical lenses in which the price is always expressed in Canadian dollars. A makes B a new offer indicating the price in "dollars" without further specification, but intending to refer again to Canadian dollars. In the absence of any indication to the contrary, A's intention will prevail. See Art. 4.3(b).

The remaining circumstances listed in this article, *i.e.* the nature and purpose of the contract, the meaning commonly given to terms and expressions in a trade concerned and usages, are important primarily, although not exclusively, in the application of the "reasonableness" test.

The criteria in sub-paras. (e) and (f) may at first sight appear to overlap. There is however a difference between them: while the "usages" apply only if they meet the requirements laid down in Art. 1.9, the "meaning commonly given [...] in the trade concerned" can be relevant even if it is peculiar to a trade sector to which only one, or even neither, party belongs, provided that the expression or term concerned is one which is typical in that trade sector.

Illustrations

3. A and B conclude a contract for the sale of a cargo of oil at US$ 20.5 per barrel. The parties subsequently disagree on the size of the barrel to which they had referred, A having intended a barrel of 42 standard gallons and B one of 36 Imperial gallons. In the absence of any indications to the contrary, A's understanding prevails, since in the international oil trade it is a usage to measure barrels in standard gallons. See Art. 4.3(f)

4. A, a shipowner, concludes a charterparty agreement with B for the carriage of grain containing the standard term "whether in berth or not" with respect to the commencement of the lay-time of the ship after its reaching the port of destination. When it subsequently emerges that the parties attached different meanings to the term, preference should, in the absence of any indication to the contrary, be given to the meaning commonly attached to it in the shipping trade since the term is typical in the shipping trade. See Art. 4.3(e).

3. "Merger" clauses

Parties to international commercial transactions frequently include a provision indicating that the contract document completely embodies the terms on which they have agreed. For the effect of these so-called "merger" or "integration" clauses, in particular whether and to what extent they exclude the relevance of preliminary negotiations between the parties, albeit only for the purpose of the interpretation of the contract, see Art. 2.1.17.

Issues & Cases

1. CIRCUMSTANCES RELEVANT IN INTERPRETATION PROCESS
    - 1995 ARBITRAL AWARD AD HOC ARBITRATION, AUCKLAND [564]
    - APRIL 21, 1997 ARBITRAL AWARD AD HOC ARBITRATION, PARIS [679]
    - MARCH 1998 ARBITRAL AWARD ICC INTERNATIONAL COURT OF ARBITRATION (NO. 9117) [727]
    - SEPTEMBER 1998 ARBITRAL AWARD ICC INTERNATIONAL COURT OF ARBITRATION (NO. 8908) [750]

1.1 PRELIMINARY NEGOTIATIONS
    - NOVEMBER 27, 2000 NEW ZEALAND COURT OF APPEAL OF NEW ZEALAND (NO. (2000) NZCA 350) [869]
    - DECEMBER 4, 2005 UNITED KINGDOM HIGH COURT OF JUSTICE (QUEEN'S BENCH DIVISION) (NO. 2004 FOLIO 272) [1110]
    - FEBRUARY 17, 2006 UNITED KINGDOM COURT OF APPEAL (CIVIL DIVISION) (NO. 2006 EWCA CIV. 69) [1142]

1.2 PRACTICES ESTABLISHED BETWEEN PARTIES
    - MARCH 3, 1998 ARBITRAL AWARD ICC INTERNATIONAL COURT OF ARBITRATION (NO. 9117) [727]

1.3 PARTIES' CONDUCT SUBSEQUENT TO CONCLUSION OF CONTRACT
    - 1995 ARBITRAL AWARD AD HOC ARBITRATION, AUCKLAND [564]
    - APRIL 21, 1997 ARBITRAL AWARD AD HOC ARBITRATION, PARIS [679]
    - SEPTEMBER 1998 ARBITRAL AWARD ICC INTERNATIONAL COURT OF ARBITRATION (NO. 8908) [750]
    - JANUARY 25, 2002 ARBITRATION AWARD ARBITRATION COURT OF THE LAUSANNE CHAMBER OF COMMERCE AND INDUSTRY [991]

1.4 NATURE AND PURPOSE OF CONTRACT

- 1995 ARBITRAL AWARD LONDON COURT OF ARBITRATION [571]
- SEPTEMBER 1998 ARBITRAL AWARD ICC INTERNATIONAL COURT OF ARBITRATION (NO. 8908) [750]
- OCTOBER 2000 ARBITRAL AWARD ICC INTERNATIONAL COURT OF ARBITRATION (NO. 10335) [864]
- NOVEMBER 27, 2000 NEW ZEALAND COURT OF APPEAL OF NEW ZEALAND (NO. (2000) NZCA 350) [869]
- NOVEMBER 5, 2002 ARBITRAL AWARD INTERNATIONAL ARBITRATION COURT AT THE CHAMBER OF COMMERCE AND INDUSTRY OF THE RUSSIAN FEDERATION (NO. 11/2002) [1030]

1.4 MEANING COMMONLY GIVEN TO TERMS AND EXPRESSION IN THE TRADE CONCERNED

- OCTOBER 2000 ARBITRAL AWARD ICC INTERNATIONAL COURT OF ARBITRATION (NO. 10335) [864]

1.6 USAGES

- OCTOBER 2000 ARBITRAL AWARD ICC INTERNATIONAL COURT OF ARBITRATION (NO. 10335) [864]

1.7 OTHER RELEVANT CIRCUMSTANCES

- NOVEMBER 27, 2000 NEW ZEALAND COURT OF APPEAL OF NEW ZEALAND (NO. (2000) NZCA 350) [869]
- DECEMBER 4, 2005 UNITED KINGDOM HIGH COURT OF JUSTICE (QUEEN'S BENCH DIVISION) (NO. 2004 FOLIO 272) [1110]

2. MERGER CLAUSES (SEE ART. 2.1.17)

3. PAROL EVIDENCE RULE

ARTICLE 4.4
(Reference to contract or statement as a whole)

Terms and expressions shall be interpreted in the light of the whole contract or statement in which they appear.

COMMENT

1. Interpretation in the light of the whole contract or statement

Terms and expressions used by one or both parties are clearly not intended to operate in isolation but have to be seen as an integral part of their general context. In consequence they should be interpreted in the light of the whole contract or statement in which they appear.

Illustration

A, a licensee, hears that, despite a provision in their contract granting A an exclusive licence, B, the licensor, has concluded a similar contract with C, one of A's competitors. A sends B a letter complaining of B's breach and ending with the words "your behaviour has clearly demonstrated that it was a mistake on our part to rely on your professional correctness. We hereby avoid the contract we have with you". Despite the use of the term "avoid", A's words interpreted in the light of the letter as a whole, must be understood as a notice of termination.

2. In principle no hierarchy among contract terms

In principle there is no hierarchy among contract terms, in the sense that their respective importance for the interpretation of the remaining part of the contract is the same regardless of the order in which they appear. There are, however, exceptions to this rule. First, declarations of intent made in the preamble may or may not be of relevance for the interpretation of the operative provisions of the contract. Secondly, it goes without saying that, in cases of conflict, provisions of a specific character prevail over provisions laying down more general rules. Finally, the parties may themselves expressly establish a hierarchy among the different provisions or parts of their contract. This is frequently the case with complex agreements consisting of different documents relating to the legal, economic and technical aspects of the transaction.

Issues & Cases

1. **INTERPRETATION IN THE LIGHT OF THE WHOLE CONTRACT OR STATEMENT**
   - **1.1 RELEVANCE OF PREAMBLE**
     - JANUARY 25, 2002 ARBITRAL AWARD ARBITRATION COURT OF THE LAUSANNE CHAMBER OF COMMERCE AND INDUSTRY [991]
   - **1.2 GENERAL TERMS V. SPECIFIC TERMS**
   - **1.3 STANDARD TERMS V. INDIVIDUALLY NEGOTIATED TERMS (SEE ART. 2.1.21)**
   - **1.4 AGREED HIERARCHY OF CONTRACT DOCUMENTS**

ARTICLE 4.5
(All terms to be given effect)

Contract terms shall be interpreted so as to give effect to all the terms rather than to deprive some of them of effect.

COMMENT

It is to be expected that when drafting their contract parties do not use words to no purpose. It is for this reason that this article lays down the rule that unclear contract terms should be interpreted so as to give effect to all the terms rather than to deprive some of them of effect. The rule however comes into play only if the terms in question remain unclear notwithstanding the application of the basic rules of interpretation laid down in Arts. 4.1 - 4.3.

Illustration

A, a commercial television network, enters into an agreement with B, a film distributor, for the periodic supply of a certain number of films to be transmitted on A's network in the afternoon, when only those films that are admissible for all viewers may be transmitted. According to the contract the films submitted must "have passed the admission test" of the competent censorship commission. A dispute arises between A and B as to the meaning of this term. B maintains that it implies only that the films must have been released for circulation, even if they are X-rated, while A insists that they must have been classified as admissible for everybody. If it is not possible otherwise to establish the meaning to be attached to the term in question, A's understanding prevails since B's interpretation would deprive the provision of any effect.

Issues & Cases

1. INTERPRETATION OF CONTRACT TERMS SO AS TO GIVE EFFECT TO ALL OF THEM

- DECEMBER 1996 ARBITRAL AWARD ICC INTERNATIONAL COURT OF ARBITRATION (NO. 8331) [656]
- JANUARY 1999 ARBITRAL AWARD ICC INTERNATIONAL COURT OF ARBITRATION (NO. 8547) [770]

- AUGUST 1999 ARBITRAL AWARD (PARTIAL) ICC INTERNATIONAL COURT OF ARBITRATION (NO. 9759) [803]
- MARCH 2000 ARBITRAL AWARD ICC INTERNATIONAL COURT OF ARBITRATION (NO. 9875) [820]
- 2001 ARBITRAL AWARD ICC INTERNATIONAL COURT OF ARBITRATION (NO. 10422) [902]
- JANUARY 25, 2002 ARBITRAL AWARD ARBITRATION COURT OF THE LAUSANNE CHAMBER OF COMMERCE AND INDUSTRY [991]

2. RELATION WITH OTHER CANONS OF INTERPRETATION

ARTICLE 4.6
(Contra proferentem rule)

If contract terms supplied by one party are unclear, an interpretation against that party is preferred.

COMMENT

A party may be responsible for the formulation of a particular contract term, either because that party has drafted it or otherwise supplied it, for example, by using standard terms prepared by others. Such a party should bear the risk of possible lack of clarity of the formulation chosen. It is for this reason that the present article states that if contract terms supplied by one party are unclear, there is a preference for their interpretation against that party. The extent to which this rule applies will depend on the circumstances of the case; the less the contract term in question was the subject of further negotiations between the parties, the greater the justification for interpreting it against the party who included it in the contract.

Illustration

A contract between A, a contractor, and B for the construction of an industrial plant contains a provision drafted by A and not discussed further stating that "[t]he Contractor shall be liable for and shall indemnify the Purchaser for all losses, expenses and claims in respect of any loss of or damage to physical property (other than the works), death or personal injury caused by negligence of the Contractor, its employees and agents". One of A's employees plays around with some of B's equipment after working hours and damages it. A denies liability, contending that the provision in question covers only cases where A's employees act within the scope of their employment. In the absence of any indication to the contrary, the provision will be interpreted in the manner which is less favourable to A, *i.e.* as also covering cases where his employees are not acting within the scope of their employment.

Issues & Cases

1. INTERPRETATION OF UNCLEAR CONTRACT TERMS SUPPLIED BY ONE PARTY

- JANUARY 24, 1996 FRANCE COUR D'APPEL DE GRENOBLE [611]
- SEPTEMBER 27, 1996 ARBITRAL AWARD ICC INTERNATIONAL COURT OF ARBITRATION (NO. 8261) [642]
- DECEMBER 10, 1997 ARBITRAL AWARD AD HOC ARBITRATION, BUENOS AIRES [715]

1.1 SUPPLYING CONTRACT TERMS DEFINED

1.2 INTERPRETATION AGAINST SUPPLYING PARTY PREFERRED

- JANUARY 24, 1996 FRANCE COUR D'APPEL DE GRENOBLE [611]
- SEPTEMBER 27, 1996 ARBITRAL AWARD ICC INTERNATIONAL COURT OF ARBITRATION (NO. 8261) [642]
- DECEMBER 10, 1997 ARBITRAL AWARD AD HOC ARBITRATION, BUENOS AIRES [715]

1.2.1 CIRCUMSTANCES DETERMINING EXTENT OF PREFERENCE

- MAY 17, 2002 ARBITRAL AWARD (PARTIAL) ARBITRATION COURT OF THE LAUSANNE CHAMBER OF COMMERCE AND INDUSTRY [1001]

2. RELATION WITH OTHER CANONS OF INTERPRETATION

- DECEMBER 4, 2005 UNITED KINGDOM HIGH COURT OF JUSTICE (QUEEN'S BENCH DIVISION) (NO. 2004 FOLIO 272) [1110]

ARTICLE 4.7
(Linguistic discrepancies)

Where a contract is drawn up in two or more language versions which are equally authoritative there is, in case of discrepancy between the versions, a preference for the interpretation according to a version in which the contract was originally drawn up.

COMMENT

International commercial contracts are often drawn up in two or more language versions which may diverge on specific points. Sometimes the parties expressly indicate which version shall prevail. If all versions are equally authoritative the question arises of how possible discrepancies should be dealt with. The present article does not lay down a hard and fast rule, but merely indicates that preference should be given to the version in which the contract was originally drawn up or, should it have been drawn up in more than one original language version, to one of those versions.

Illustration

1. A and B, neither of them native English speakers, negotiate and draw up a contract in English before translating it into their respective languages. The parties agree that all three versions are equally authoritative. In case of divergencies between the texts, the English version will prevail unless circumstances indicate the contrary.

A situation where a different solution may be preferable could arise where the parties have contracted on the basis of internationally and widely known instruments such as INCOTERMS or the *Uniform Customs and Practices on Documentary Credits*. In case of divergencies between the different versions used by the parties it may be preferable to refer to yet another version if that version is much clearer than the ones used.

Illustration

2. A contract between a Mexican and a Swedish company drawn up in three equally authoritative versions, Spanish, Swedish and English, contains a reference to INCOTERMS 2000. If the French version of INCOTERMS is much clearer than the other three on a point in dispute, that version might be referred to.

Issues & Cases

1. **DISCREPANCY BETWEEN DIFFERENT LANGUAGE VERSIONS**
   1.1 **EQUALLY AUTHORITATIVE VERSIONS**
      - NOVEMBER 6, 2002 ARBITRAL AWARD INTERNATIONAL ARBITRATION COURT OF THE CHAMBER OF COMMERCE AND INDUSTRY OF THE RUSSIAN FEDERATION (NO. 217/2001) [1032]

   1.2 **PREFERENCE FOR INTERPRETATION ACCORDING TO ORIGINAL VERSIONE OF CONTRACT**
      - NOVEMBER 6, 2002 ARBITRAL AWARD INTERNATIONAL ARBITRATION COURT OF THE CHAMBER OF COMMERCE AND INDUSTRY OF THE RUSSIAN FEDERATION (NO. 217/2001) [1032]

2. **DISCREPANCIES BETWEEN DIFFERENT LANGUAGE VERSIONS OF INTERNATIONAL INSTRUMENTS REFERRED TO BY PARTIES**

ARTICLE 4.8
(Supplying an omitted term)

(1) Where the parties to a contract have not agreed with respect to a term which is important for a determination of their rights and duties, a term which is appropriate in the circumstances shall be supplied.

(2) In determining what is an appropriate term regard shall be had, among other factors, to

(a) the intention of the parties;

(b) the nature and purpose of the contract;

(c) good faith and fair dealing;

(d) reasonableness.

COMMENT

1. Supplying of omitted terms and interpretation

Articles 4.1 - 4.7 deal with the interpretation of contracts in the strict sense, *i.e.* with the determination of the meaning which should be given to contract terms which are unclear. This article addresses a different though related issue, namely that of the supplying of omitted terms. Omitted terms or gaps occur when, after the conclusion of the contract, a question arises which the parties have not regulated in their contract at all, either because they preferred not to deal with it or simply because they did not foresee it.

2. When omitted terms are to be supplied

In many cases of omitted terms or gaps in the contract the Principles will themselves provide a solution to the issue. See, for example, Arts. 5.1.6, (Determination of quality of performance), 5.1.7 (Price determination), 6.1.1 (Time of performance), 6.1.4 (Order of performance), 6.1.6 (Place of performance) and 6.1.10 (Currency not expressed). See also, in general, Art. 5.1.2 on implied obligations. However, even when there are such suppletive, or "stop-gap", rules of a general character they may not be applicable in a given case because they would not provide a solution appropriate in the circumstances in view of the expectations of the parties or the special nature of the contract. This article then applies.

3. Criteria for the supplying of omitted terms

The terms supplied under the present article must be appropriate to the circumstances of the case. In order to determine what is appropriate, regard is first of all to be had to the intention of the parties as inferred from, among other factors, the terms expressly stated in the contract, prior negotiations or any conduct subsequent to the conclusion of the contract.

Illustration

1. The parties to a construction contract agree on a special interest rate to be paid by the purchaser in the event of delay in payment of the price. Before the beginning of the work, the parties decide to terminate the contract. When the constructor delays restitution of the advance payment the question arises of the applicable interest rate. In the absence of an express term in the contract dealing with this question, the circumstances may make it appropriate to apply the special interest rate agreed for delay in payment of the price by the purchaser also to delay in restitution by the constructor.

If the intention of the parties cannot be ascertained, the term to be supplied may be determined in accordance with the nature and purpose of the contract, and the principles of good faith and fair dealing and reasonableness.

Illustration

2. A distribution franchise agreement provides that the franchisee may not engage in any similar business for a year after the termination of the agreement. Although the agreement is silent on the territorial scope of this prohibition, it is, in view of the particular nature and purpose of a franchise agreement, appropriate that the prohibition be restricted to the territory where the franchisee had exploited the franchise.

Issues & Cases

1. **NOTION OF OMITTED TERMS**
   - 1.1 **TERMS NOT DELIBERATELY LEFT OPEN BY PARTIES (SEE ART. 2.1.14)**
   - 1.2 **TERMS IMPORTANT FOR DETERMINATION OF PARTIES' RIGHTS AND DUTIES**
   - 1.3 **ISSUES NOT SETTLED BY GAP-FILLING RULES OF PRINCIPLES**
2. **CRITERIA FOR SUPPLYING OMITTED TERMS**
   - SEPTEMBER 27, 1996 ARBITRAL AWARD ICC INTERNATIONAL COURT OF ARBITRATION (NO. 8261) [642]
   - SEPTEMBER 1998 ARBITRAL AWARD ICC INTERNATIONAL COURT OF ARBITRATION (NO. 8908) [750]

2.1 INTENTION OF PARTIES

- DECEMBER 2001 ARBITRAL AWARD ICC INTERNATIONAL COURT OF ARBITRATION (NO. 11295) [988]

2.2 NATURE OF PURPOSE OF CONTRACT

- DECEMBER 2001 ARBITRAL AWARD ICC INTERNATIONAL COURT OF ARBITRATION (NO. 11295) [988]

2.3 GOOD FAITH AND FAIR DEALING

- SEPTEMBER 1998 ARBITRAL AWARD ICC INTERNATIONAL COURT OF ARBITRATION (NO. 8908) [750]
- JULY 28, 2000 ARBITRAL AWARD ICC INTERNATIONAL COURT OF ARBITRATION (NO. 9797/CK/AER/ACS) [834]

2.4 REASONABLENESS

- SEPTEMBER 27, 1996 ARBITRAL AWARD ICC INTERNATIONAL COURT OF ARBITRATION (NO. 8261) [642]

3. SUPPLYING OMITTED TERMS V. IMPLIED OBLIGATIONS (SEE ART. 5.1.2)

CHAPTER 5

CONTENT AND THIRD PARTY RIGHTS

SECTION 1: CONTENT

BIBLIOGRAPHY

BEGINES J.L.P., Contenido, in Comentario a los Principios de UNIDROIT para los Contratos del Comercio Internacional, Aranzadi, Pamplona, 1999, 245-273.

BONELL M.J., A 'Global' arbitration decided on the basis of the UNIDROIT Principles: In re Andersen Consulting Business Unit Member Firms v. Arthur Andersen Business Unit Member Firms and Andersen Worldwide Société Coopérative, in 17 Arbitration International 2001, 249 – 261.

CHAPPUIS Ch., L'intervention du tribunal dans le contrat. Convergence entre les Principes UNIDROIT et le droit suisse, in Liber Amicorum Claude Reymond, Litec, Paris 2004, 53 – 72.

DI MAJO A., L'osservanza della buona fede nei Principi UNIDROIT sui contratti commerciali internazionali, in BONELL M.J. / BONELLI F. (eds.), Contratti commerciali internazionali e Principi UNIDROIT, Giuffré, Milano 1997, 143-160.

FERRI G.B., L' "invisibile" presenza della causa del contratto, in Europa e diritto privato, 2002, 897 – 914.

FONTAINE M., Content and Performance, in 40 American Journal of Comparative Law, n. 3, 1992, 645-656.

GARRO A., El contenido del contrato bajo los Principios de UNIDROIT aplicables a los contratos comerciales internacionales, in BONELL M.J. – SCHIPANI S. (eds.), "Principi per i contratti commercial internazionali" e il sistema giuridico latinoamericano, Padova, 1996, 171-206.

GORDLEY, J., An American Perspective on the UNIDROIT Principles, in Centro di studi e ricerche di diritto comparato e straniero (ed.), Saggi, conferenze e seminari, n. 22, Roma 1996, 24-28

MARRELLA F., Contratti di vendita internazionale privi di prezzo, questione preliminare e Principi UNIDROIT, in Rivista dell'arbitrato 2002, 129 - 138

SCHLECHTRIEM P., Good faith in German Law and in International Uniform Laws, in Centro di studi e ricerche di diritto comparato e straniero: saggi, conferenze e seminari, n. 24, Roma 1997.

ARTICLE 5.1.1
(Express and implied obligations)

The contractual obligations of the parties may be express or implied.

COMMENT

This provision restates the widely accepted principle according to which the obligations of the parties are not necessarily limited to that which has been expressly stipulated in the contract. Other obligations may be implicit (see Art. 5.1.2, comments and illustrations).

Close links exist between this rule and some of the other provisions of the Principles. Thus Art. 5.1.1 is a direct corollary of the rule according to which "[e]ach party must act in accordance with good faith and fair dealing in international trade" (Art. 1.7). Insofar as the rules on interpretation (Chapter 4) provide criteria for filling lacunae (besides criteria for solving ambiguities), those rules may assist in determining the precise content of the contract and therefore in establishing the terms which must be considered as implied.

Issues & Cases

1. **OBLIGATIONS EXPRESSLY STIPULATED**
2. **IMPLIED OBLIGATIONS (SEE ARTS. 1.7 AND 5.1.2)**
    - MAY 5, 1997 ARBITRAL AWARD ICC INTERNATIONAL COURT OF ARBITRATION (NO. 7365/FMS) [680]

ARTICLE 5.1.2
(Implied obligations)

Implied obligations stem from

(a) the nature and purpose of the contract;

(b) practices established between the parties and usages;

(c) good faith and fair dealing;

(d) reasonableness.

COMMENT

This article describes the sources of implied obligations. Different reasons may account for the fact that they have not been expressly stated. The implied obligations may for example have been so obvious, given the nature or the purpose of the obligation, that the parties felt that the obligations "went without saying". Alternatively, they may already have been included in the practices established between the parties or prescribed by trade usages according to Art. 1.9. Yet again, they may be a consequence of the principles of good faith and fair dealing and reasonableness in contractual relations.

Illustrations

1. A rents a full computer network to B and installs it. The contract says nothing as to A's possible obligation to give B at least some basic information concerning the operation of the system. This may however be considered to be an implied obligation since it is obvious, and necessary for the accomplishment of the purpose of such a contract, that the provider of sophisticated goods should supply the other party with a minimum of information. See Art. 5.1.2(a).

2. A broker who has negotiated a charterparty claims the commission due. Although the brokerage contract is silent as to the time when the commission is due, the usages of the sector can provide an implied term according to which the commission is due, for example only when the hire is earned, or alternatively when the charterparty was signed, regardless of whether or not the hire will effectively be paid. See Art. 5.1.2(b).

3. A and B, who have entered into the negotiation of a co-operation agreement, conclude an agreement concerning a complex feasibility study, which will be most time-consuming for A. Long before the study is completed, B decides that it will not pursue the negotiation of the co-operation agreement. Even though

nothing has been stipulated regarding such a situation, good faith requires B to notify A of its decision without delay. See Art. 5.1.2(c).

Issues & Cases

1. SOURCES OF IMPLIED OBLIGATIONS
    - MAY 5, 1997 ARBITRAL AWARD ICC INTERNATIONAL COURT OF ARBITRATION (NO. 7365/FMS) [680]

    1.1 NATURE AND PURPOSE OF THE CONTRACT

    1.2 PRACTICES ESTABLISHED BETWEEN THE PARTIES

    1.3 USAGES

    1.4 GOOD FAITH AND FAIR DEALING
    - MAY 5, 1997 ARBITRAL AWARD ICC INTERNATIONAL COURT OF ARBITRATION (NO. 7365/FMS) [680]
    - JULY 28, 2000 ARBITRAL AWARD ICC INTERNATIONAL COURT OF ARBITRATION (NO. 9797/CK/AER/ACS) [834]
    - MARCH 2002 ARBITRAL AWARD (PARTIAL) ICC INTERNATIONAL COURT OF ARBITRATION (NO. 11375) [999]

    1.5 REASONABLENESS

2. IMPLIED OBLIGATIONS V. SUPPLYING OMITTED TERMS

ARTICLE 5.1.3
(Co-operation between the parties)

Each party shall cooperate with the other party when such co-operation may reasonably be expected for the performance of that party's obligations.

COMMENT

A contract is not merely a meeting point for conflicting interests but must also, to a certain extent, be viewed as a common project in which each party must cooperate. This view is clearly related to the principle of good faith and fair dealing (Art. 1.7) which permeates the law of contract, as well as to the obligation to mitigate harm in the event of non-performance (Art. 7.4.8).

The duty of co-operation must of course be confined within certain limits (the provision refers to reasonable expectations), so as not to upset the allocation of duties in the performance of the contract. Although the principal concern of the provision is the duty not to hinder the other party's performance, there may also be circumstances which call for more active co-operation.

Illustrations

1. A, after contracting with B for the immediate delivery of a certain quantity of oil, buys all the available oil on the spot market from another source. Such conduct, which will hinder B in performing its obligation, is contrary to the duty of co-operation.

2. A, an art gallery in country X, buys a sixteenth century painting from B, a private collector in country Y. The painting may not be exported without a special authorisation and the contract requires B to apply for that permission. B, who has no experience of such formalities, encounters serious difficulties with the application whereas A is familiar with such procedures. In these circumstances, and notwithstanding the contractual provision, A can be expected to give at least some assistance to B.

Issues & Cases

1. DUTY TO CO-OPERATE

- DECEMBER 1998 ARBITRAL AWARD ICC INTERNATIONAL COURT OF ARBITRATION (NO. 9593) [762]

- MARCH 20, 2000 ARBITRAL AWARD INTERNATIONAL CENTRE FOR SETTLEMENT OF INVESTMENT DISPUTES (ICSID) (NO. ARB(AF)/98/1) [826]
- JULY 28, 2000 ARBITRAL AWARD ICC INTERNATIONAL COURT OF ARBITRATION (NO. 9797/CK/AER/ACS) [834]
- DECEMBER 2000 ARBITRAL AWARD ICC INTERNATIONAL COURT OF ARBITRATION (NO. 10346) [883]
- APRIL 30, 2001 ARBITRAL AWARD AD HOC ARBITRATION SAN JOSÉ (COSTA RICA) [945]
- MARCH 2002 ARBITRAL AWARD (PARTIAL) ICC INTERNATIONAL COURT OF ARBITRATION (NO. 11375) [999]

2. LIMITS OF DUTY TO CO-OPERATE

2.1 REASONABLE EXPECTATIONS OF THE OTHER PARTY

ARTICLE 5.1.4

(Duty to achieve a specific result

Duty of best efforts)

(1) To the extent that an obligation of a party involves a duty to achieve a specific result, that party is bound to achieve that result.

(2) To the extent that an obligation of a party involves a duty of best efforts in the performance of an activity, that party is bound to make such efforts as would be made by a reasonable person of the same kind in the same circumstances.

COMMENT

1. Distinction between the duty to achieve a specific result and the duty of best efforts

The degree of diligence required of a party in the performance of an obligation varies considerably depending upon the nature of the obligation incurred. Sometimes a party is bound only by a duty of best efforts. That party must then exert the efforts that a reasonable person of the same kind would exert in the same circumstances, but does not guarantee the achievement of a specific result. In other cases, however, the obligation is more onerous and such a specific result is promised.

The distinction between a "duty to achieve a specific result" and a "duty of best efforts" corresponds to two frequent and typical degrees of severity in the assumption of a contractual obligation, although it does not encompass all possible situations.

Obligations of both types may coexist in the same contract. For instance, a firm that repairs a defective machine may be considered to be under a duty of best efforts concerning the quality of the repair work in general, and under a duty to achieve a specific result as regards the replacement of certain spare parts.

2. Distinction provides criteria for determining whether a party has performed its obligations

Taken together, the two paragraphs of this article provide judges and arbitrators with criteria by which correct performance can be evaluated. In the case of an obligation to achieve a specific result, a party is bound simply to achieve the promised result, failure to achieve which amounts in itself to non-performance, subject to the application of the force majeure provision (Art. 7.1.7). On the other hand, the assessment of non-performance of an obligation of best efforts calls for a less severe judgment, based on a comparison with the efforts a reasonable person of the same kind would have made in similar circumstances. This distinction signifies that more will be expected from a highly specialised firm selected for its expertise than from a less sophisticated partner.

Illustrations

1. A, a distributor, promises that it will reach a quota of 15,000 sales within a year in the contract zone. If at the end of the period A has sold only 13,000 items, it has clearly failed to perform its obligation. See Art. 5.1.4(1).

2. B, another distributor, promises "to use our best efforts to expand the sales of the product" in the contract zone, without any stipulation that it must reach a minimum quantity. This provision creates an obligation of best efforts; it obliges B to take all the steps that a reasonable person, placed in similar circumstances (nature of the product, characteristics of the market, importance and experience of the firm, presence of competitors, etc.) would take to promote the sales (advertising, visits to customers, proper service, etc.). B does not promise the specific result of selling a certain number of items per year, but does undertake to do all that can be expected of it when acting as a reasonable person. See Art. 5.1.4(2).

Issues & Cases

1. **DUTY TO ACHIEVE SPECIFIC RESULT**
   - MARCH 20, 2000 ARBITRAL AWARD INTERNATIONAL CENTRE FOR SETTLEMENT OF INVESTMENT DISPUTES (ICSID) (NO. ARB(AF)/98/1) [826]

   1.1 **FAILURE TO ACHIEVE RESULT AMOUNTS TO NON-PERFORMANCE**

2. **DUTY OF BEST EFFORTS**
   - DECEMBER 1996 ARBITRAL AWARD ICC INTERNATIONAL COURT OF ARBITRATION (NO. 8331) [656]
   - JULY 28, 2000 ARBITRAL AWARD ICC INTERNATIONAL COURT OF ARBITRATION (NO. 9797/CK/AER/ACS) [834]

   2.1 **EFFORTS OF REASONABLE PERSON**

- JANUARY 25, 2002 ARBITRAL AWARD
  ARBITRATION COURT OF THE LAUSANNE CHAMBER OF COMMERCE AND INDUSTRY [991]

2.2 PARTICULAR EFFORT REQUESTED

2.2.1 WITH REGARD TO EXPERTISE OF PERFORMING PARTY

2.2.2 WITH REGARD TO NATURE OF OBLIGATION

3. COEXISTANCE OF BOTH KINDS OF DUTIES IN SAME CONTRACT

ARTICLE 5.1.5
(Determination of kind of duty involved)

In determining the extent to which an obligation of a party involves a duty of best efforts in the performance of an activity or a duty to achieve a specific result, regard shall be had, among other factors, to

(a) the way in which the obligation is expressed in the contract;

(b) the contractual price and other terms of the contract;

(c) the degree of risk normally involved in achieving the expected result;

(d) the ability of the other party to influence the performance of the obligation.

COMMENT

1. Criteria for determining the nature of the obligation

It is important to determine whether an obligation involves a duty to achieve a specific result or simply a duty of best efforts, as the obligation is more onerous in the former case. Such a determination may sometimes be difficult. This article therefore establishes criteria which may offer guidance to parties, judges and arbitrators, although the list is not exhaustive. The problems involved are frequently matters of interpretation.

2. Nature of the obligation as expressed by the contract

The way in which an obligation is expressed in the contract may often be of assistance in determining whether the parties intended to create a duty to achieve a specific result or a duty of best efforts.

Illustration

1. A, a contractor, agrees to build storage facilities for B, who is most keen that the work be finished in an unusually short time. If A undertakes that "the work will be completed before 31 December", it assumes an obligation to achieve the specific result of meeting that deadline. If it merely undertakes "to try to complete the work before 31 December", its obligation involves a

duty of best efforts to attempt to meet the deadline, but no guarantee that it will definitely be met. See Art. 5.1.5(a).

3. Price or other terms of the contract

The contractual price or other terms of the contract may also offer clues as to the nature of an obligation. An unusually high price or another particular non-monetary reciprocal obligation may indicate a duty to achieve a specific result in cases where a mere duty of best efforts would normally be assumed. Clauses linking payment of the price to the successful outcome of the operation, penalty clauses applicable if the result is not achieved and hardship clauses enabling a party to adapt the contract if circumstances make it too harsh to perform as initially agreed are other examples of contractual terms which may - in one way or another - assist in determining the nature of the obligation in question. See Art. 5.1.5(b).

4. Degree of risk in performance of an obligation

When a party's performance of an obligation normally involves a high degree of risk it is generally to be expected that that party does not intend to guarantee a result, and that the other party does not expect such a guarantee. The opposite conclusion will be drawn when the desired result can as a rule be achieved without any special difficulty. See Art. 5.1.5(c).

Illustrations

2. A space agency undertakes to put a telecommunication satellite into orbit, the rate of failure of past launchings having been 22%. The space agency cannot be expected to guarantee that the orbiting will be successful. The obligation is merely to observe the degree of diligence required for such launchings in view of the present state of technology.

3. A promises to deliver 20 tons of steel to B on 30 June. Such a relatively simple operation is subject to no special risk. A is committed to the specific result of delivering the required quantity of steel on the date specified and not merely to attempting to do so.

5. Influence of obligee over performance of an obligation

In some situations one party may have a degree of influence over the performance of the other party's obligations. This fact may transform into duties of best efforts obligations which might otherwise be characterised as duties to achieve specific results.

Illustration

4. A is prepared to provide B with the technical assistance necessary to apply a newly discovered chemical process, and it is agreed that B will send some of its engineers to attend training sessions organised by A. A cannot promise that the new process will be mastered by the other party, since that result depends in part on B's effectively sending its engineers to the training sessions, on those engineers' competence and on their attentiveness at the sessions. See Art. 5.1.5(d).

Issues & Cases

1. CRITERIA FOR DETERMINING NATURE OF OBLIGATION
   - 1.1 EXPRESSIONS USED BY PARTIES IN DEFINING OBLIGATIONS
   - 1.2 OTHER TERMS OF CONTRACT
     - 1.2.1 PRICE
     - 1.2.2 PAYMENT DEPENDING ON PERFORMANCE OF OBLIGATION V. PAYMENT DEPENDING ON OBTAINING RESULT
     - 1.2.3 PENALTY CLAUSES
     - 1.2.4 HARDSHIP CLAUSES
     - 1.2.5 OTHER TERMS
   - 1.3 DEGREE OF RISK NORMALLY INVOLVED IN PERFORMING OBLIGATION
     - 1.3.1 PERFORMANCE REQUIRING HIGH DILIGENCE
     - 1.3.2 PERFORMANCE NOT SUBJECT TO SPECIAL RISK
   - 1.4 INFLUENCE OF ONE PARTY IN PERFORMANCE OF OTHER PARTY'S OBLIGATIONS

ARTICLE 5.1.6
(Determination of quality of performance)

Where the quality of performance is neither fixed by, nor determinable from, the contract a party is bound to render a performance of a quality that is reasonable and not less than average in the circumstances.

COMMENT

Standards have been set in Art. 5.1.4 concerning the exercise of "best efforts", but quality of performance is a wider problem addressed by Art. 5.1.6. If goods are to be supplied, or services rendered, it is not sufficient to supply those goods or to render those services; they must also be of a certain quality.

The contract will often be explicit as regards the quality due ("grade 1 oil"), or it will provide elements making that quality determinable. In other cases, the rule established by Art. 5.1.6 is that the quality must be "reasonable and not less than average in the circumstances". Two criteria are thus combined.

Illustration

1. A undertakes to build a hotel next to a busy railway station. The contract provides for "adequate sound isolation", the quality of which is not more precisely determined. It is, however, determinable from the contract that the sound isolation must meet the high standards needed in view of the hotel's proximity to a railway station.

1. Performance must be of average quality

The minimum requirement is that of providing goods of average quality. The supplier is not bound to provide goods or services of superior quality if that is not required by the contract, but neither may it deliver goods or services of inferior quality. This average quality is determined according to the circumstances, which normally means that which is available on the relevant market at the time of performance (there may for example have been a recent technological advance). Other factors may also be of relevance, such as the specific qualifications for which the performing party was chosen.

Illustration

2. A buys 500 kgs. of oranges from B. If the contract says nothing more precise, and no other circumstances call for a different solution, those oranges may not be of less than average

quality. Average quality will however suffice unless it is unreasonably defective.

2. Performance must be reasonable

The additional reference to reasonableness is intended to prevent a party from claiming that it has performed adequately if it has rendered an "average" performance in a market where the average quality is most unsatisfactory and is intended to give the judge or arbitrator an opportunity to raise those insufficient standards.

Illustration

3. A company based in country X organises a banquet to celebrate its 50th anniversary. Since the cuisine in country X is mediocre, the company orders the meal from a renowned restaurant in Paris. In these circumstances the quality of the food provided must not be less than the average standards of the Parisian restaurant; it would clearly not be sufficient simply to meet the average standards of country X.

Issues & Cases

1. QUALITY OF PERFORMANCE NEITHER DETERMINED NOR DETERMINABLE FROM CONTRACT
   1.1 PERFORMANCE OF AVERAGE QUALITY AS MINIMUM REQUIREMENT
      1.1.1 QUALITY AVAILABLE ON RELEVANT MARKET AT TIME OF PERFORMANCE
      1.1.2 SPECIFIC QUALIFICATIONS OF PERFORMING PARTY
   1.2 PERFORMANCE OF REASONABLE QUALITY

ARTICLE 5.1.7
(Price determination)

(1) Where a contract does not fix or make provision for determining the price, the parties are considered, in the absence of any indication to the contrary, to have made reference to the price generally charged at the time of the conclusion of the contract for such performance in comparable circumstances in the trade concerned or, if no such price is available, to a reasonable price.

(2) Where the price is to be determined by one party and that determination is manifestly unreasonable, a reasonable price shall be substituted notwithstanding any contract term to the contrary.

(3) Where the price is to be fixed by a third person, and that person cannot or will not do so, the price shall be a reasonable price.

(4) Where the price is to be fixed by reference to factors which do not exist or have ceased to exist or to be accessible, the nearest equivalent factor shall be treated as a substitute.

COMMENT

1. General rule governing price determination

A contract usually fixes the price to be paid, or makes provision for its determination. If however this is not the case, para. (1) of this article presumes that the parties have made reference to the price generally charged at the time of the conclusion of the contract for such performance in comparable circumstances in the trade concerned. All these qualifications are of course significant. The provision also permits the rebuttal of the presumption if there is any indication to the contrary.

This article is inspired by Art. 55 CISG. The rule has the necessary flexibility to meet the needs of international trade.

It is true that in some cases the price usually charged on the market may not satisfy the reasonableness test which prevails elsewhere in this article. Recourse would then have to be made to the general provision on good faith and fair dealing (Art. 1.7), or possibly to some of the provisions on mistake, fraud and gross disparity (Chapter 3).

Some international contracts relate to operations which are unique or at least very specific, in respect of which it is not possible to refer to the price charged for similar performance in comparable circumstances. According to para. (1) the parties are then deemed to have made reference to a reasonable price and the party in question will fix the price at a reasonable level, subject to the possible review by courts or arbitral tribunals.

Illustrations

1. A, a firm specialised in express mailing throughout the world, receives from B a parcel to be delivered as soon as possible from France to the United States. Nothing is said as to the price. A should bill B with the price usually charged in the sector for such a service.

2. The next order which A receives from B is one to deliver another parcel as soon as possible to Antarctica where a team of explorers is in need of urgent supplies. Again, nothing is said as to price, but since no possible market comparison can be made A must act reasonably when fixing the price.

2. Determination of price by one party

In some cases the contract expressly provides that the price will be determined by one of the parties. This happens frequently in several sectors, for example the supply of services. The price cannot easily be determined in advance, and the performing party is in the best position to place a value on what it has done.

In those cases where the parties have made such a provision for determining the price, it will be enforced. To avoid possible abuses however, para. (2) enables judges or arbitrators to replace a manifestly unreasonable price by a reasonable one. This provision is mandatory.

3. Determination of price by third person

A provision that the price will be determined by a third person can give rise to serious difficulty if that third person is unable to accomplish the mission (not being the expert he or she was thought to be) or refuses to do so. Para. (3) provides that the price, possibly determined by judges or arbitrators, shall be reasonable. If the third person determines the price in circumstances that may involve fraud, gross disparity or threat, Art. 3.11(2) may apply.

4. Determination of price by reference to external factors

In some situations the price is to be fixed by reference to external factors, typically a published index, or quotations on a commodity exchange. In cases where the reference factor ceases to exist or to be accessible, para. (4) provides that the nearest equivalent factor shall be treated as a substitute.

Illustration

3. The price of a construction contract is linked to several indexes, including the "official index of charges in the construction sector", regularly published by the local Government. Several instalments of the price still have to be calculated when that index ceases to be published. The Construction Federation, a private trade association, decides however to start publishing a similar index to replace the former one and in these circumstances the new index will serve as a substitute.

Issues & Cases

1. **PRICE NOT DETERMINED NOR DETERMINABLE FROM CONTRACT**
    - 1.1 **PRICE GENERALLY CHARGED AT TIME OF CONCLUSION OF CONTRACT FOR PERFORMANCE OF SAME TYPE**
        - SEPTEMBER 1999 ARBITRAL AWARD ICC INTERNATIONAL COURT OF ARBITRATION (NO. 7819) [809]
    - 1.2 **REASONABLE PRICE**
2. **DETERMINATION OF PRICE BY ONE PARTY**
    - 2.1 **DETERMINATION MANIFESTLY UNREASONABLE**
        - 2.1.1 **REPLACEMENT BY REASONABLE PRICE**
3. **DETERMINATION OF PRICE BY THIRD PERSON**
    - 3.1 **THIRD PERSON DOES NOT ACCOMPLISH ITS MISSION**
        - 3.1.1 **RECOURSE TO REASONABLE PRICE**
4. **DETERMINATION OF PRICE BY REFERENCE TO EXTERNAL FACTORS**
    - 4.1 **EXTERNAL FACTORS INEXISTENT**
        - 4.1.1 **RECOURSE TO NEAREST EQUIVALENT FACTORS**

ARTICLE 5.1.8
(Contract for an indefinite period)

A contract for an indefinite period may be ended by either party by giving notice a reasonable time in advance.

COMMENT

The duration of a contract is often specified by an express provision, or it may be determined from the nature and purpose of the contract (*e.g.* technical expertise provided in order to assist in performing specialised work). However, there are cases when the duration is neither determined nor determinable. Parties can also stipulate that their contract is concluded for an indefinite period.

This article provides that in such cases either party may end the contractual relationship by giving notice a reasonable time in advance. What a reasonable time in advance will be will depend on circumstances such as the period of time the parties have been cooperating, the importance of their relative investments in the relationship, the time needed to find new partners, etc.

The rule can be understood as a gap-filling provision in cases where parties have failed to specify the duration of their contract. More generally, it also relates to the widely recognised principle that contracts may not bind the parties eternally and that they may always opt out of such contracts provided they give notice a reasonable time in advance.

This situation is to be distinguished from the case of hardship which is covered by Arts. 6.2.1 - 6.2.3. Hardship requires a fundamental change of the equilibrium of the contract, and gives rise, at least in the first instance, to renegotiations. The rule in this article requires no special condition to be met, except that the duration of the contract be indefinite and that it permit unilateral cancellation.

Illustration

A agrees to distribute B's products in country X. The contract is concluded for an indefinite period. Either party may cancel this arrangement unilaterally, provided that it gives the other party notice a reasonable time in advance.

Issues & Cases

1. INDEFINITE DURATION OF CONTRACT

   1.1 EITHER PARTY'S RIGHT TO END CONTRACT UNILATERALLY

- FEBRUARY 1999 ARBITRAL AWARD ICC INTERNATIONAL COURT OF ARBITRATION (NO. 9479) [786]

1.1.1 **NOTICE REASONABLE TIME IN ADVANCE**

- 2000 ARBITRAL AWARD ICC INTERNATIONAL COURT OF ARBITRATION (NO. 10021) [817]

ARTICLE 5.1.9
(Release by agreement)

(1) An obligee may release its right by agreement with the obligor.

(2) An offer to release a right gratuitously shall be deemed accepted if the obligor does not reject the offer without delay after having become aware of it.

COMMENT

An obligee may wish to release the obligor from its obligation (or, in case the obligor owes more than one obligation, from more than one or from all its obligations). The release may either be a separate act, or constitute a part of a more complex transaction between the parties, *e.g.* a compromise which settles a dispute between them.

This article provides that such renunciation of the obligee's right(s) requires an agreement between the parties, irrespective or whether the obligee renounces its right(s) for value or gratuitously.

In the latter case, while the obligor should not be compelled to accept a benefit against its will, it will normally consent to accepting the benefit. For this reason para. (2) provides that a gratuitous offer shall be deemed accepted if the obligor does not reject the offer without delay after having become aware of it.

Illustrations

1. Company A is in financial difficulties and needs the co-operation of its creditors in order to survive. Bank B is prepared to renounce 50% of its claim against A and the interest that has fallen due on condition that A pay an interest of 9% (instead of the 5% paid previously) on the remaining debt. B sends a notice to this effect on 15 January. By 22 January A has not reacted to the notice. B's renunciation will only be effective after A has accepted B's offer in accordance with Art. 2.1.6 *et seq*.

2. Company A is in financial difficulties and needs the co-operation of its creditors in order to survive. Bank B is prepared to renounce 50% of its claim against A and the interest that has fallen due and sends A a notice to this effect on 15 January. By 22 January A has not reacted to the notice. B's offer is deemed to be accepted by A.

Issues & Cases

1. RENOUNCIATION OF A RIGHT
   1.1 FOR VALUE
   1.2 GRATUITOUSLY

SECTION 2: THIRD PARTY RIGHTS

BIBLIOGRAPHY

MÜLLER H.-F., Die Einfürung des Vertrages zugunsten Dritter in das englishe Recht. Eine vergleichende Betrachtung aus deutscher und gemeineuropäischer Perspecktive, in RabelsZeitschrift für ausländisches und internationales Privatrecht 67 (2003), 140 – 165.

ARTICLE 5.2.1
(Contracts in favour of third parties)

(1) The parties (the "promisor" and the "promisee") may confer by express or implied agreement a right on a third party (the "beneficiary").

(2) The existence and content of the beneficiary's right against the promisor are determined by the agreement of the parties and are subject to any conditions or other limitations under the agreement.

COMMENT

Usually contracts are intended by the parties to create rights and obligations between themselves. In such cases only the parties will acquire rights and duties under the contract. The mere fact that a third party will benefit from the performance of the contract does not in itself give that third party any rights under the contract.

Illustration

1. Professor A makes a contract with the University of Utopia under which he agrees to give forty one-hour lectures comparing the Utopian and Ruritanian laws of contract. A only appears for twenty lectures and does not mention Ruritanian law in the lectures. T, a student, does not acquire rights under the contract between A and the University.

However, third parties are not always left without rights. The underlying principle is that of the autonomy of the parties, who, if they wish to create rights in a third party, should be free to do so. The parties may state expressly that this is their intention, but this is not essential since the intention to benefit the third party may be implicit in the contract. In cases where implied intention is alleged, the decision will turn on all the terms of the contract and the circumstances of the case.

The following are illustrations of implicit intention.

Illustrations

2. A takes out a policy of insurance on its fleet of lorries which are regularly driven by its employees. The contract provides that the insurance company will cover anyone driving a lorry with A's consent. An employee, T, has an accident while driving the lorry. T is covered in respect of his liability for the accident.

3. A sells his business to B on the terms that B will pay A £1,000 a month for the rest of his life and will pay A's wife, T, £500 a month if A predeceases her. A dies. B refuses to pay T anything. T is entitled to the £500 a month.

4. T, the International World University, wishes to build a new law library on land owned by the University. For legitimate tax reasons the contract for the erection of the library is made by Denning Ltd, a company wholly owned by the University, although the contractor well knows that when completed the library will be occupied and used by T. The building has been badly done and it will cost US $5,000,000 to complete it satisfactorily. T can recover the cost of the remedial work.

5. A, the developer of a shopping mall, concludes a contract with B, a security firm, to provide security at the mall. Both A and B know that the shops will be operated by tenants of A. These tenants are told that one of the major attractions of the mall will be the high level of security provided by B. It is a term of the contract between A and B that all employees of B working at the mall will be ex-policemen personally selected by the chief executive of B. In fact, selection is delegated to a consultancy firm which recruits many unsuitable people. There are many thefts at the shops. Tenants who suffer losses will have contractual claims against B.

The following are illustrations where there is no such implicit intention unless the circumstances clearly indicate otherwise.

Illustrations

6. A goes to an expensive furrier and selects and buys a coat. He tells the assistant (truthfully) that he is buying it for T, the wife of a visiting head of State. By the side of the coat is a prominent card saying "It looks like mink, it feels like mink but is guaranteed man made." A gives the coat to T. In fact, owing to a mistake by the furrier, the coat is a real mink coat and T is subjected to violent and hostile criticism by animal lovers in her country. T has no enforceable contract right.

7. A, a company with a large factory, concludes a contract with a company operating the local sewage system. Under the contract, A is entitled to discharge its waste into the sewer but undertakes not to discharge certain types of waste. In breach of this undertaking, A discharges waste which blocks the sewer and causes damage to T, another user of the sewer. T has no enforceable contract right.

8. A, a Japanese company, sells materials to B, a Swiss company. A knows that B plans to resell the materials to T, a German pharmaceutical company, which will use the materials for the manufacture of a new drug under a contract which will effectively limit B's liability to T to US $1,000,000. The materials are defective and T's losses greatly exceed US $1,000,000. T has no enforceable contract right against A.

The application of this article will often come up in the context of an associated claim in tort. This possibility is outside the scope of the Principles.

It follows from the scheme of this article that an express statement that the parties do not intend to create rights in a third party will be effective. It also follows that the promisor and promisee enjoy broad powers to shape the rights created in favour of the beneficiary. In this context the word "rights" should be interpreted liberally. In principle, a third party beneficiary will have the full range of contractual remedies including the right to performance and damages.

Issues & Cases

1. PARTIES CONFERRING RIGHTS ON THIRD PARTY
    1.1 BY EXPRESS AGREEMENT
    1.2 BY IMPLIED AGREEMENT
2. BENEFICIARY'S RIGHTS AGAINST PROMISSOR DETERMINED BY PARTIES' AGREEMENT
    2.1 CONDITIONS OR LIMITATIONS TO BENEFICIARY'S RIGHTS

ARTICLE 5.2.2
(Third party identifiable)

The beneficiary must be identifiable with adequate certainty by the contract but need not be in existence at the time the contract is made.

COMMENT

The parties may well wish to make a contract in which the identity of the third party is not known at the time the contract is made, but a mechanism is provided by which it will become known by the time performance is due. This might be by providing that the parties, or one of them, can identify the beneficiary at a later date, or by choosing a definition of the beneficiary which later circumstances will serve to make the identity clear.

Illustrations

1. A married man with children but no grandchildren makes a contract with the XYZ insurance company under which A pays £10 a month to the insurance company and they promise to pay £10,000 to each of his grandchildren on his death. Grandchildren born after the date of the contract but before A's death are entitled to £10,000.

2. Company A launches a takeover bid for company B, a public company whose shares are traded on leading stock exchanges. Company B engages C, a leading firm of accountants, to prepare a report on B for distribution to shareholders. The contract between B and C requires C to produce an honest, thorough and competent report. Owing to incompetence C produces a report that is much too favourable to B. As a result the majority of shareholders (T1) vote to reject A's offer. Some shareholders show copies of the report to friends (T2) who buy shares in B. T1 can acquire rights under the contract between B and C but T2 cannot.

Issues & Cases

1. BENEFIARY'S IDENTITY
   1.1 MUST BE IDENTIFIABLE WITH ADEQUATE CERTAINTY
2. BENEFICIARY NEED NOT BE IN EXISTENCE AT TIME OF CONCLUSION OF CONTRACT

ARTICLE 5.2.3
(Exclusion and limitation clauses)

The conferment of rights in the beneficiary includes the right to invoke a clause in the contract which excludes or limits the liability of the beneficiary.

COMMENT

Contractual provisions limiting or excluding liability of those who are not parties to the contract are very common particularly in contracts of carriage, where they often form part of a settled pattern of insurance. Perhaps the best known example is the so-called Himalaya clause, which in some form is frequently to be found in bills of lading. In general the autonomy of the parties should be respected in this area too.

Illustration

A, the owner of goods, makes a contract with a sea carrier to carry them from Zenda to Xanadu. The bill of lading is subject to the Hague Rules and purports to exclude the liability of (a) the master and crew; (b) stevedores employed in loading and unloading the cargo; and (c) the owners of ships onto which the goods may be transhipped. These exclusions will be effective.

Another situation which would be covered by this article arises where the promisor and promisee agree that the beneficiary shall be released from an obligation which it owed to the promisor.

Issues & Cases

1. BENEFICIARY ENTITLED TO INVOKE CLAUSES EXCLUDING OR LIMITING LIABILITY
   1.1 HIMALAYA CLAUSES
   1.2 PARTIES' AGREEMENT TO RELEASE BENEFICIARY FROM OBLIGATION

ARTICLE 5.2.4
(Defences)

The promisor may assert against the beneficiary all defences which the promisor could assert against the promisee.

COMMENT

Under Art. 5.2.1 the content of the beneficiary's right may be made subject to any conditions or limitations devised by the parties. The promisor and promisee may devise a contract in which the position of the beneficiary is significantly different from that of the promisee. The parties' autonomy is in principle unlimited but they may well not provide expressly for all possibilities. The normal default rule will therefore be as stated in the present article.

Illustrations

1. A takes out a policy of life insurance with insurance company B in favour of T. The contract provides for the payment of premiums for 25 years but after 5 years A stops paying premiums. The position of T will be modelled on that of A if the policy had been in his favour. Such policies do not usually deny all return on the premiums paid. If, however, the policy had been liable to be set aside by the insurance company, for instance because A had not made material disclosure, then B would normally be entitled to raise this defence against T.

2. Company C takes out a policy of fidelity insurance with insurance company D to cover dishonest employees. The insurance policy provides that D will indemnify in full customers (T) who are defrauded by employees of C and that it will indemnify C only if C has not been negligent in the selection or supervision of the employees. Clearly in such a contract D will have defences against C which it cannot raise against T.

Issues & Cases

1. PROMISOR ENTITLED TO ASSERT AGAINST BENEFICIARY ALL DEFENCES IT HAS AGAINST PROMISEE
2. EXCEPTIONS (SEE ART. 5.2.1(2))

ARTICLE 5.2.5
(Revocation)

The parties may modify or revoke the rights conferred by the contract on the beneficiary until the beneficiary has accepted them or reasonably acted in reliance on them.

COMMENT

It might be the rule that the promisor and promisee are free to revoke the third party's rights at any time or, contrariwise, that the third party's rights are immutable once the contract is concluded. It appears that few systems adopt either of these extreme positions. The solution adopted is that the third party's rights become irrevocable once the third party has either accepted the rights or has reasonably acted in reliance on them. It will, of course, be open to the parties to provide for a different regime in the contract either by making the beneficiary's rights irrevocable sooner, or by preserving a right of revocation even after the beneficiary has acted in reliance on the rights. There may well be situations where a right of revocation is given only to one party. For example, in a contract of life insurance it might be provided that the insured can change the beneficiary. There might be relevant usages which limit the possibility of revocation.

Illustration

A, the main contractor on a major construction contract, takes out a policy of insurance with the insurance company B to cover damage to the work in progress. The policy is expressed to cover the interests of all sub-contractors involved in the contract and the sub-contractors are all told of the policy. T, a sub-contractor, does not take out any insurance himself, but does not tell A or B. Absent clear words to the contrary, T's reliance makes the contract between A and B irrevocable.

Issues & Cases

1. REVOCATION OF RIGHTS CONFERRED ON BENEFICIARY
   1.1 UNTIL ACCEPTANCE BY BENEFICIARY
   1.2 UNTIL BENEFICIARY HAS REASONBLY ACTED IN RELIANCE THEREON
2. EXCEPTIONS (SEE ART. 5.2.1(1))
   2.1 IRREVOCABILITY

2.2 **REVOCATION ALSO AFTER ACCEPTANCE BY BENEFICIARY**

2.3 **REVOCATION ALSO AFTER BENEFICIARY HAS ACTED IN RELIANCE THEREON**

2.4 **REVOCATION ONLY BY ONE PARTY**

2.5 **ACCORDING TO USAGES**

ARTICLE 5.2.6
(Renunciation)

The beneficiary may renounce a right conferred on it.

COMMENT

The scheme of this Section assumes that, absent contrary provision, the contract between promisor and promisee creates rights in the beneficiary at once, without any need for acceptance by the beneficiary.

Although the third party will usually welcome the benefit which the parties have conferred upon it, it cannot be forced to accept it. It follows that the third party may expressly or impliedly renounce the benefit.

However, once the beneficiary has done something that amounts to acceptance, it should not normally be entitled to renounce.

Illustration

On the facts given in the illustration to Art. 5.2.5, T, a sub-contractor, may not wish to take advantage of the insurance taken out by the main contractor because it already has relevant insurance in place (and he knows that there will be difficulties if there are two insurances covering the same risk). T is entitled to renounce.

Issues & Cases

1. RENUNCIATION OF RIGHTS BY BENEFICIARY
   - 1.1 EXPLICIT RENUNCIATION
   - 1.2 IMPLICIT RENUNCIATION
2. BENEFICIARY NOT ENTITLED TO RENOUNCE

CHAPTER 6

PERFORMANCE

SECTION 1: PERFORMANCE IN GENERAL

BIBLIOGRAPHY

BEN-OLIEL, R., The UNIDROIT Principles of International Commercial Contracts: A Comment, in: RABELLO, A.M. (ed.), The Principles of UNIDROIT and Modern National Codifications, Jerusalem, Harry and Michael Sacher Institute for Legislative Research and Comparative Law, Faculty of Law, The Hebrew University of Jerusalem 2001, 139-148.

CUSMAI, S., L'esecuzione del contratto nei principi di diritto europeo e nei principi dei contratti commerciali internazionali. Appunti sull'influenza di *common law* e di *civil law*, in Vita notarile, n. 3, 1998, 1847-1885.

ERNST, W., Die Verpflichtung zur Leistung in den Principles of European Contract Law und in den *Principles of International Commercial Contracts*, in BASEDOW, J. (ed.), Europäische Vertragsrechtsvereinheitlichung und deutsches Recht, J. C. B. Mohr (Siebeck), Tübingen 2000, 129 – 157.

FONTAINE M., "*Paiement*" et "*Performance*". Réflexions sur les difficultés du dialogue comparatif à propos des Principes d'UNIDROIT, in Mélanges en l'honneur de Denis Tallon. D'ici, d'ailleurs: harmonisation et dynamique du droit. Paris, Société de législation comparée, 1999, 57-67.

FONTAINE M., Content and Performance, in 40 American Journal of Comparative Law, n. 3, 1992, 645-656.

PARRA A.M., Cumplimiento, in Comentario a los Principios de UNIDROIT para los Contratos del Comercio Internacional, Aranzadi, Pamplona, 1999, 275-316.

RIVERA J.C., Reglas sobre cumplimiento de los contratos. Disposiciones sobre el pago, in BONELL M.J. / SCHIPANI S. (eds.), "Principi per i contratti commerciali internazionali" e il sistema giuridico latinoamericano, Padova 1996, 239-249.

TRAKMAN L.E., Performance and the UNIDROIT: An Evaluation of Article 6.1, in Contratación internacional, Comentarios a los principios sobre los Contratos Comerciales Internacionales del UNIDROIT, Universidad Nacional Autónoma de México – Universidad Panamericana (ed.) 1998, 95-110.

ARTICLE 6.1.1
(Time of performance)

A party must perform its obligations:

(a) if a time is fixed by or determinable from the contract, at that time;

(b) if a period of time is fixed by or determinable from the contract, at any time within that period unless circumstances indicate that the other party is to choose a time;

(c) in any other case, within a reasonable time after the conclusion of the contract.

COMMENT

With a view to determining when a contractual obligation is to be performed, this article, which is inspired by Art. 33 CISG, distinguishes three situations. The first is where the contract stipulates the precise time for performance or makes it determinable. If the contract does not specify a precise moment but a period of time for performing, any time during that period chosen by the performing party will be acceptable unless circumstances indicate that the other party is to choose the time. Finally, in all other cases, performance is due within a reasonable time.

Illustrations

1. A offers to advise B in the latter's plans to buy computer equipment and software, and it is agreed that A's experts will visit B "in May" It is in principle for A to announce when precisely in May that visit will take place. The circumstances may however leave the option to B, as would be the case if the contract expressly left to B the choice of the precise dates, or where, for example, it was understood that some of B's staff who are often absent on business trips must be present when A's experts arrive. See Art. 6.1.1(b).

2. A, a building contractor, encounters unusual difficulties when excavating a site, and needs special equipment to continue the work which it does not have. A immediately telephones B, another contractor, who has the necessary equipment and agrees to lend it to A. Nothing however is said as to when the equipment should be delivered to A. Performance is then to take place "within

a reasonable time" in the circumstances. Since the work has been interrupted because of the above-mentioned difficulties, A urgently needs to receive the equipment and in such a case "within a reasonable time" probably means that performance is due almost immediately. See Art. 6.1.1(c).

Issues & Cases

1. PRECISE TIME FOR PERFORMANCE
   1.1 OBLIGATION TO BE PERFORMED AT THAT TIME
2. PERIOD OF TIME FOR PERFORMANCE
   2.1 OBLIGATION TO BE PERFORMED AT ANY TIME WITHIN THAT PERIOD
      2.1.1 AT PRECISE TIME TO BE CHOSEN BY OTHER PARTY
3. PERFORMANCE WITHIN REASONABLE TIME

ARTICLE 6.1.2
(Performance at one time or in instalments)

In cases under Article 6.1.1(b) or (c), a party must perform its obligations at one time if that performance can be rendered at one time and the circumstances do not indicate otherwise.

COMMENT

A party's performance is of necessity sometimes rendered at one time (*e.g.* delivery of a single object), or, alternatively, must take place over a period of time (*e.g.* construction). There are however also cases where it can be rendered either at one time or in instalments (*e.g.* delivery of quantities of goods). This article addresses the latter situation, in circumstances where there is no contractual provision as to how such performance should be rendered, or where it is not determinable from the contract. The principle stated is that performance is due at one time, unless the circumstances indicate otherwise.

Illustrations

1. A promises to deliver 100 tons of coal to B "in March". It would be materially possible and perhaps convenient for A to deliver the 100 tons in instalments, for instance 25 tons each week of the month. In principle however, according to Art. 6.1.2, A must deliver the 100 tons at one time.

2. The facts are the same as in Illustration 1, the difference being that B needs the coal gradually, to meet the needs of its operations. B also has limited storage facilities and could not cope adequately with a consignment of 100 tons at any one time. A knows of B's specific needs. Here the circumstances suggest that A should instead deliver in instalments during the month of March.

Issues & Cases

1. PERFORMANCE CAPABLE OF BEING RENDERED AT ONE TIME
   1.1 AS A RULE TO BE RENDERED AT ONE TIME
   1.2 EXCEPTIONALLY PERFORMANCE IN INSTALMENTS (SEE ART. 6.1.3)

ARTICLE 6.1.3
(Partial performance)

(1) The obligee may reject an offer to perform in part at the time performance is due, whether or not such offer is coupled with an assurance as to the balance of the performance, unless the obligee has no legitimate interest in so doing.

(2) Additional expenses caused to the obligee by partial performance are to be borne by the obligor without prejudice to any other remedy.

COMMENT

1. Partial performance distinguished from performance at one time or in instalments

The situation covered by this article should be distinguished from that of Art. 6.1.2.

The provision on "[p]erformance at one time or in instalments" attempts to solve a preliminary question which concerns only certain special cases. If a party's performance can be rendered at one time or in instalments and if the contract does not make it clear or determinable how that party is to perform, it must in principle perform at one time.

The present article has a more general scope. It provides that at the time performance is due the obligee may in principle reject an offer of partial performance. This applies at maturity, irrespective of whether what is due then is a global performance or an instalment of a wider obligation (which, in some cases, has been previously determined on the basis of Art. 6.1.2).

Illustration

1. A owes US $1,000,000 to a bank and it has been agreed that A will pay back US $100,000 on the first day of each month, starting in January. On 1 April A offers to reimburse only US $50,000, and the balance two weeks later. In principle, the bank is entitled to refuse A's proposal.

2. Obligee entitled in principle to reject partial performance

When performance is due at maturity (be it the whole performance or an instalment), that which is due must be performed completely. In principle, the obligee may reject an offer of partial performance, whether or not it is coupled with an assurance as to the balance of the performance, since it is entitled to receive the whole of what was stipulated. Subject to what will be said below, partial performance normally constitutes a breach of contract. A party who does not obtain full performance at maturity may resort to the available remedies. As a rule, the obligee has a legitimate interest in requiring full performance of what was promised at the time that performance is due.

The obligee may of course also refrain from rejecting the offer to perform in part, while reserving its rights as to the breach, or may accept it without any reservation, in which case partial performance can no longer be treated as a non-performance.

Illustration

2. A wishes to open a branch office in Brussels and rents the necessary office space in a building under construction, due to be finished in time for the move on 1 September. On that date, only four of the ten offices are made available for A, with an assurance that the remaining six will be ready in one month. In principle, A may refuse to move into those four offices.

3. Obligee's right to reject partial performance conditional on its legitimate interest in so doing

There may be situations where the obligee's legitimate interest in receiving full performance is not apparent and where temporary acceptance of partial performance will not cause any significant harm to the obligee. If the party tendering partial performance proves this to be the case, the obligee cannot then refuse such partial performance (subject to para. (2)), and there is no non-performance in such cases. This may be seen as a consequence of the general principle of good faith and fair dealing enunciated in Art. 1.7.

Illustration

3. An airline promises to transport 10 automobiles from Italy to Brazil in one single consignment due to be delivered on a definite date. When performance is due, some circumstances make it difficult, although not impossible, for the airline to find sufficient space in a single aircraft. The airline suggests making two successive deliveries within a week. It is established that this will cause no inconvenience to the purchaser of the cars, which will not actually be used before the following month. In such a case the obligee has no legitimate interest in refusing partial performance.

4. Additional expenses entailed by partial performance to be borne by obligor

If partial performance is accepted, it may entail additional expenses for the obligee. In all cases, such expenses are to be borne by the other party. If partial performance amounts to a non-performance (as it usually does), these expenses will be part of the damages, without prejudice to any other available remedy. If partial performance does not amount to a non-performance (the obligee has been shown not to have any legitimate interest in rejecting the offer of partial performance, or has found the offer to be acceptable without reservation), it will only be entitled to those expenses.

Illustration

4. The facts are the same as in Illustration 3. If the purchaser has to meet additional expenses on account of having to make double arrangements for picking up the cars at the airport, those extra costs will be borne by the airline.

Issues & Cases

1. **PARTIAL PERFORMANCE DEFINED**
    1.1 **OFFER TO PERFORM IN PART V. PERFORMANCE IN INSTALMENTS**
2. **OBLIGEE'S RIGHT TO REJECT PARTIAL PERFORMANCE**
    2.1 **OBLIGEE'S LEGITIMATE INTEREST IN SO DOING**
3. **OBLIGOR TO BEAR ADDITIONAL EXPENSES**

ARTICLE 6.1.4
(Order of performance)

(1) To the extent that the performances of the parties can be rendered simultaneously, the parties are bound to render them simultaneously unless the circumstances indicate otherwise.

(2) To the extent that the performance of only one party requires a period of time, that party is bound to render its performance first, unless the circumstances indicate otherwise.

COMMENT

In bilateral contracts, where both parties have obligations towards the other, the basic but complex question arises of which party is to perform first. If the parties have not made any specific arrangements, then in practice much will depend on usages and it must also be recalled that there are often several obligations on each side which may have to be performed at different times.

This article states two broad principles, while recognising that in both cases the circumstances may indicate otherwise. In effect, the main purpose of this article is to draw the parties' attention to the problem of order of performance, and to encourage them, where necessary, to draft appropriate contractual provisions.

A distinction is drawn between cases where the parties' performances can be rendered simultaneously and those where the performance of only one party requires a period of time.

1. Simultaneous performance to be made when possible

In the first situation, the rule is that the parties are bound to perform simultaneously (para. (1)). A seller is entitled to payment on delivery but circumstances may indicate otherwise, for example any exception originating from the terms of the contract or from usages which may allow a party to perform some time after the other.

Illustration

1. A and B agree to barter a certain quantity of oil against a certain quantity of cotton. Unless circumstances indicate otherwise, the commodities should be exchanged simultaneously.

2. Exception where performance requires a period of time

If the performance of only one party's obligation by its very nature requires a period of time, for example in construction and most service contracts, the rule established in para. (2) is that that party is bound to render its performance first. Circumstances may frequently however indicate the contrary. Thus, insurance premiums are normally paid in advance, as also are rent and freight charges. In construction contracts, payments are usually made in agreed instalments throughout the duration of the work.

Illustration

2. A promises to write a legal opinion to assist B in an arbitration. If no arrangement is made as to when A should be paid for the services, A must prepare the opinion before asking to be paid.

3. Relation of order of performance to withholding of performance

This article sets out the rules which will condition the application of Art. 7.1.3 concerning the withholding of performance.

Issues & Cases

1. PARTIES' PERFORMANCE CAPABLE OF BEING RENDERED SIMULTANEOUSLY
   1.1 SIMULTANEOUS PERFORMANCE THE RULE (SEE ALSO ART. 7.1.3)
   1.2 EXCEPTIONS
2. ONE PARTY'S OBLIGATION REQUIRING A PERIOD OF TIME
   2.1 AS A RULE THAT PARTY BOUND TO RENDER ITS PERFORMANCE FIRST (SEE ALSO ART. 7.1.3)
   2.2 EXCEPTIONS
       - FEBRUARY 12, 2003 AUSTRALIA FEDERAL COURT OF AUSTRALIA (NO. NG733 OF 1997) [1058]

ARTICLE 6.1.5
(Earlier performance)

(1) The obligee may reject an earlier performance unless it has no legitimate interest in so doing.

(2) Acceptance by a party of an earlier performance does not affect the time for the performance of its own obligations if that time has been fixed irrespective of the performance of the other party's obligations.

(3) Additional expenses caused to the obligee by earlier performance are to be borne by the obligor, without prejudice to any other remedy.

COMMENT

1. Obligee in principle entitled to reject earlier performance

When performance is due at a certain moment (to be determined in accordance with Art. 6.1.1), it must take place at that time and in principle the obligee may reject an earlier performance. Usually, the time set for performance is geared to the obligee's activities, and earlier performance may cause it inconvenience. The obligee has therefore a legitimate interest in refusing it. Earlier performance, in principle, constitutes non-performance of the contract.

The obligee may of course also abstain from rejecting an earlier performance while reserving its rights as to the non-performance. It may also accept such performance without reservation, in which case earlier performance can no longer be treated as non-performance.

Illustration

1. A agrees to carry out the annual maintenance of all lifts in B's office building on 15 October. A's employees arrive on 14 October, a day on which important meetings, with many visitors, are taking place in the building. B is entitled to refuse such earlier performance which would cause it obvious inconvenience.

2. Obligee's right to reject earlier performance conditional on its legitimate interest in so doing

Situations may arise in which the obligee's legitimate interest in timely performance is not apparent and when its accepting earlier performance will not cause it any significant harm. If the party offering earlier performance proves this to be the case, the other party cannot reject earlier performance.

Illustration

2. The facts are the same as in Illustration 1, the difference being that neither 14 nor 15 October has any special significance. A can probably prove that B has no legitimate interest in refusing the earlier performance.

3. Effect of acceptance by obligee on its own performance of earlier performance of the other party's obligations

If one party accepts earlier performance by the other, the question arises of whether this affects the time for performance of its own obligations. Para. (2) deals with cases where obligations are due at a certain time which is not linked to the performance of the other party's obligations; that time for performance remains unchanged.

This provision does not however deal with the converse case where the performances are linked in time. Several situations may then arise. This circumstance may in itself establish the obligee's legitimate interest in rejecting earlier performance. If earlier performance is thus rejected, the obligee's time of performance is unaffected. If earlier performance is accepted with all due reservations as to the non-performance involved, the obligee may also reserve its rights as to its time for performance. If earlier performance is acceptable to the obligee it may at the same time decide whether or not to accept the consequences as regards its own obligations.

Illustrations

3. B undertakes to deliver goods to A on 15 May and A to pay the price on 30 June. B wishes to deliver the goods on 10 May and A has no legitimate interest in refusing such earlier performance. This will however have no effect on the time agreed for payment of the price, which was determined irrespective of the date of delivery.

4. B undertakes to deliver goods to A on 15 May and A to pay the price "on delivery". If B tenders the goods on 10 May, A, depending on the circumstances, may reject such earlier performance, claiming that it is not in a position to pay at that date, take delivery of the goods subject to observing the original deadline for payment of the price, or decide to accept the goods and pay for them immediately.

4. Additional expenses entailed by earlier performance to be borne by the performing party

If earlier performance is accepted, it may entail additional expenses for the obligee. In all cases, such expenses are to be borne by the other party. If earlier performance amounts to non-performance (the normal case), those expenses will be part of the damages, without prejudice to any other remedy available. If earlier performance does not amount to non-performance (the obligee has been shown not to have any legitimate interest in rejecting the offer of earlier performance, or has found that offer to be acceptable without reservation), the obligee will only be entitled to those expenses.

Illustration

5. A has no legitimate interest in refusing delivery of goods on 10 May instead of 15 May, but some additional storage fees are payable for those five extra days. Those costs will be borne by B.

Issues & Cases

1. EARLIER PERFORMANCE DEFINED
2. OBLIGEE'S RIGHT TO REJECT EARLIER PERFORMANCE
   2.1 OBLIGEE'S LEGITIMATE INTEREST IN SO DOING
3. OBLIGOR TO BEAR ADDITIONAL EXPENSES

ARTICLE 6.1.6
(Place of performance)

(1) If the place of performance is neither fixed by, nor determinable from, the contract, a party is to perform:

(a) a monetary obligation, at the obligee's place of business;

(b) any other obligation, at its own place of business.

(2) A party must bear any increase in the expenses incidental to performance which is caused by a change in its place of business subsequent to the conclusion of the contract.

COMMENT

1. Place of performance fixed by, or determined from, the contract when possible

The place where an obligation is to be performed is often determined by an express term of the contract or is determinable from it. It is obvious, for instance, that an obligation to build must be performed on the construction site, and that an obligation to transport goods must be performed in accordance with the agreed route.

2. Need for suppletive rules

Rules are however needed to cover cases where the contract is silent on the matter and circumstances do not indicate where performance should take place. Para. (1) provides two solutions.

The general rule is that a party is to perform its obligations at its own place of business. The second rule is specific to monetary obligations where the converse solution applies, namely that the obligor is to perform its obligations at the obligee's place of business (subject to the application of Art. 6.1.8 concerning payments by funds transfers).

These solutions may not be the most satisfactory in all cases, but they do reflect the need for rules where the parties have not made any other arrangement or where the circumstances do not indicate otherwise.

Illustrations

1. A wishes some of its engineers to learn the language of country X, where they will be employed for some time. It agrees

with B, a language school, for a series of intensive lessons. If nothing else is stipulated, the lessons are to take place at B's place of business. See Art. 6.1.6(1)(b)

2. The facts are the same as in Illustration 1. The language school sends its bill to A. The cost of the lessons must, in principle, be paid at B's place of business. See Art. 6.1.6(1)(a).

3. Consequences of change in a party's place of business subsequent to conclusion of contract

In view of the importance of the parties' respective places of business for the application of para. (1), it is necessary to cater for the situation where a party changes its location after the conclusion of the contract, a move which may involve additional expense for the performing party. The rule established in para. (2) is that each party must bear any such increase of expenses occasioned by a change in its place of business.

It is moreover possible that a party's move may entail other inconvenience for the other party. The obligation to act in good faith (Art. 1.7) and the duty to cooperate (Art. 5.1.3) will often impose on the moving party an obligation to inform the other party in due time so as to enable the latter to make such arrangements as may be necessary.

Illustrations

3. A enters into a technical assistance agreement with B, under the terms of which A undertakes to train ten of B's engineers for a period of two months on A's premises. The engineers are to be accommodated at a local hotel which offers very reasonable rates on account of A's location in a rural area. After the agreement has been concluded, but before B's engineers arrive, A notifies B that it has moved to the capital city where hotel rates are much higher. Irrespective of whether the initial costs of accommodation were to be paid by A or by B, the additional costs will be borne by A.

4. Each year on 3 May, A must pay royalties to B at B's place of business. B moves to another country, to which it takes some time (*e.g.* two months) for a payment to arrive. A formerly gave its bank the transfer order on or about 15 April, but from now on the order must be given towards the end of March at the latest if A wishes to avoid late payment. B is under a duty to inform A of its new place of business in sufficient time to permit A to make the necessary arrangements for payment and B will bear the additional costs.

Issues & Cases

1. **PLACE OF PERFORMANCE NOT DETERMINED NOR DETERMINABLE FROM CONTRACT**
   - OCTOBER 23, 1996 FRANCE COUR D'APPEL DE GRENOBLE [643]

   1.1 **MONETARY OBLIGATIONS TO BE PERFORMED AT OBLIGEE'S PLACE OF BUSINESS**
   - OCTOBER 23, 1996 FRANCE COUR D'APPEL DE GRENOBLE [643]

   1.2 **OTHER OBLIGATIONS TO BE PERFORMED AT OBLIGOR'S PLACE OF BUSINESS**
   - JANUARY 10, 2006 ITALY TRIBUNALE PADOVA – SEZ. ESTE [1132]

2. **CHANGE OF PLACE OF BUSINESS SUBSEQUENT TO CONCLUSION OF CONTRACT**

   2.1 **ADDITIONAL EXPENSES TO BE BORN BY PARTY CONCERNED**

ARTICLE 6.1.7
(Payment by cheque or other instrument)

(1) Payment may be made in any form used in the ordinary course of business at the place for payment.

(2) However, an obligee who accepts, either by virtue of paragraph (1) or voluntarily, a cheque, any other order to pay or a promise to pay, is presumed to do so only on condition that it will be honoured.

COMMENT

Discharge of monetary obligations is frequently made by cheques or similar instruments, or by transfers between financial institutions. The problems involved have however very seldom been the subject of codification, one notable exception being the *UNCITRAL Model Law on International Credit Transfers.* Without attempting to provide a detailed regulation, which would not be compatible with the very rapid evolution of techniques in this field, Arts. 6.1.7 and 6.1.8 establish some basic principles which should be of assistance in regard to international payments.

1. General rule regarding form of payment

Para. (1) allows for payment to be made in any form that is usual at the place for payment. Subject to the reservation contained in para. (2), the obligor may for instance pay in cash, by cheque, banker's draft, a bill of exchange, credit card, or in any other form such as the newly developing electronic means of payment, provided it chooses a mode that is usual at the place for payment, *i.e.* normally at the obligee's place of business. In principle, the obligee should be satisfied to receive payment in a form that is customary at its place of business.

Illustration

1. A, an importer in Luxembourg, receives a bill for goods bought from B, a firm in Central America, and sends a eurocheque in payment. B may reject this mode of payment if the banks in its country are not familiar with eurocheques.

2. Presumption that payment will be honoured a condition for acceptance

Para. (2) states the generally recognised principle according to which the obligee's acceptance of an instrument that has to be honoured by a financial institution or another person (a third person or the obligor itself) is given only on condition that the instrument will actually be honoured.

The presumption can sometimes be overturned by usages. There are for instance countries where delivery of instruments such as certified cheques, banker's drafts and cashier's cheques is considered as being equivalent to payment by the obligor, with the consequence that the risk of the bank's insolvency is transferred to the obligee. In such countries, the rule in Art. 6.1.7(2) would apply only to so-called personal cheques.

Illustration

2. A, a contractor, must pay B, a sub-contractor, for work completed by the latter on a building site. A is experiencing a cash-flow crisis as its client C is late in paying the first instalment due. C has however given A a set of promissory notes up to the amount of its debt. A offers to pay B by assigning a sufficient number of promissory notes. If B accepts them (in this case it probably does not have to do so as this is not a usual form of payment), the effectiveness of the payment by A to B is conditional on C's honouring the promissory notes at maturity.

Issues & Cases

1. **PAYMENT TO BE MADE IN ANY FORM USUAL AT PLACE OF PAYMENT**
2. **PAYMENT BY AN INSTRUMENT TO BE HONOURED BY ANOTHER PERSON**
   - DECEMBER 17, 1996 ARBITRAL AWARD ARBITRAL COURT OF THE ECONOMIC CHAMBER AND THE AGRARIAN CHAMBER OF THE CZECH REPUBLIC (NO. RSP 88/94) [669]

   2.1 **IMPLIED CONDITION THAT INSTRUMENT WILL BE HONOURED**
   - DECEMBER 17, 1996 ARBITRAL AWARD ARBITRAL COURT OF THE ECONOMIC CHAMBER AND THE AGRARIAN CHAMBER OF THE CZECH REPUBLIC (NO. RSP 88/94) [669]

   2.2 **EXCEPTIONS**

ARTICLE 6.1.8
(Payment by funds transfer)

(1) Unless the obligee has indicated a particular account, payment may be made by a transfer to any of the financial institutions in which the obligee has made it known that it has an account.

(2) In case of payment by a transfer the obligation of the obligor is discharged when the transfer to the obligee's financial institution becomes effective.

COMMENT

1. Admissibility of funds transfers

Although the principle enunciated in Art. 6.1.6 that payment of a monetary obligation should be made at the obligee's place of business still stands, para. (1) of this article provides that it can also be made to one of the financial institutions in which the obligee has made it known that it keeps an account. If however the obligee has indicated a particular account, payment should then be made to that account. Naturally, the obligee can also make it known that it does not wish payment to be made by transfer.

Illustration

1. A, a shipyard established in Helsinki, repairs a ship belonging to B, a Swedish company, and the bill is sent on a letter-head that mentions a bank account in Finland and another in Sweden. Unless A states that payment has to be made to the Finnish account, or by a means other than a bank transfer, B is entitled to make payment to the Swedish account.

2. Time at which the obligor's obligation is discharged by a funds transfer

Para. (2) of this article deals with the difficult question of determining when a payment by funds transfer is to be considered as completed, *i.e.* when the obligor's obligation is discharged. This matter is of importance, for example when deciding whether a payment was made in time, or in the event of one of the banks not forwarding the funds it has received. The choice of a satisfactory solution has been the centre of considerable controversy in many countries and international fora. Various possible times have been suggested such as that of the debiting of the account of the transferor, the crediting to the account of the transferee bank, the notice of credit to that account, the decision of the transferee bank to accept a credit transfer, the entry of credit to the transferee's account, the notice of credit to the transferee, etc. The matter is further complicated by the changes in the procedures for the transfer of funds entailed by new electronic transfer mechanisms, while bank practices may also differ from one case to another.

This uncertainty makes it extremely difficult to establish a definite rule providing when payment by a transfer is completed. Para. (2) of this article nevertheless serves a useful purpose in that it states the basic principle which will permit the finding of a more precise rule in each case. Such a payment will be effective when the transfer to the obligee's financial institution becomes effective, a solution founded on the notion that the institution acts as the obligee's agent. This means that the payment will not be effective simply because an order has been given to the transferor's financial institution, and the transferor's account has been debited. However, payment is effective before the transferee is notified or credited with it by its financial institution although the precise moment at which payment to the obligee's financial institution can be considered as being effective will depend on banking practices in the case concerned.

Illustration

2. A, a licensee, gives its bank, C, a transfer order for US $5,000, royalties due to B, a licensor, who has an account with Bank D. C debits A's account, but fails to forward the funds to D and becomes bankrupt. A has not effectively paid B.

Issues & Cases

1. **PAYMENT BY FUNDS TRANSFERS**
   1.1 **ADMISSABLE TO ANY FINANCIAL INSTITUTION IN WHICH OBLIGEE INFORMS TO HAVE ACCOUNT**
2. **TIME WHEN OBLIGOR'S OBLIGATION IS DISCHARGED**

ARTICLE 6.1.9
(Currency of payment)

(1) If a monetary obligation is expressed in a currency other than that of the place for payment, it may be paid by the obligor in the currency of the place for payment unless

(a) that currency is not freely convertible; or

(b) the parties have agreed that payment should be made only in the currency in which the monetary obligation is expressed.

(2) If it is impossible for the obligor to make payment in the currency in which the monetary obligation is expressed, the obligee may require payment in the currency of the place for payment, even in the case referred to in paragraph (1)(b).

(3) Payment in the currency of the place for payment is to be made according to the applicable rate of exchange prevailing there when payment is due.

(4) However, if the obligor has not paid at the time when payment is due, the obligee may require payment according to the applicable rate of exchange prevailing either when payment is due or at the time of actual payment.

COMMENT

Monetary obligations are usually expressed in a certain currency (currency of account), and payment must normally be made in the same currency. However, when the currency of the place for payment is different from the currency of account, paras. (1) and (2) of this article provide for those cases where the obligor may or must make payment in the former currency.

1. Monetary obligation expressed in currency different from that of place for payment

As a general rule, the obligor is given the alternative of paying in the currency of the place for payment, which may have definite practical advantages and, if that currency is freely convertible, this should cause no difficulty to the obligee.

If, however, the currency of the place for payment is not freely convertible, the rule does not apply. Parties may also exclude the application of the rule by agreeing that payment is to be made only in the currency in which the monetary obligation is expressed (*effectivo* clause): If it has an interest in the payment actually being made in the currency of account, the obligee should specify this in the contract.

Illustrations

1. A French firm receives an order for machinery from a Brazilian buyer, the price being expressed in United States dollars. According to Art. 6.1.6, payment of that monetary obligation must in principle be made at the obligee's place of business, *i.e.* France. If the Brazilian firm finds it more convenient, it may pay the price in euros. See Art. 6.1.9(1).

2. The same French firm frequently needs to buy from United States sources certain parts to be included in the machines, and has stipulated that the Brazilian buyer should pay only in dollars. In this case, payment may only be made in dollars. See Art. 6.1.9(1)(b).

3. The same French firm has a plant in country X, where the machines will be assembled. The contract provides that the Brazilian buyer has to pay the price to the firm's subsidiary in country X. Since the currency of country X is not convertible, payment may only be made in dollars. See Art. 6.1.9(1)(a).

2. Impossibility for obligor to make payment in currency in which obligation is expressed

In some instances, the obligor may find it impossible to make payment in the currency in which the obligation was expressed. This may be the result of the application of exchange regulations or other mandatory rules, or due to any other cause preventing the obligor from obtaining that currency in sufficient quantity. Para. (2) gives the obligee the option of requiring payment in the currency of the place for payment, even if the contract contains an *effectivo* clause. This is an additional option open to the obligee who may find it acceptable or even advantageous in the circumstances. It does not preclude the exercise of any available remedy in the event of the obligor's inability to pay in the currency of account amounting to a non-performance of the contract (*e.g.* damages).

Illustration

4. A, a Swiss bank, lends US $1,000,000 to B, to be reimbursed in Lugano. At maturity, B is unable to find the necessary dollars. A, which knows that B has deposits in Swiss

francs with another local bank, may require payment in Swiss francs, even though the loan agreement stipulated that reimbursement was to be made only in United States dollars. See Art. 6.1.9(2).

3. Determination of applicable rate of exchange

Paras. (3) and (4) deal with the problem of the determination of the rate of exchange to be chosen when payment is made in the currency of the place for payment rather than in a different currency stipulated in the contract. This may occur when the obligor avails itself of para. (1), or the obligee the provisions of para. (2).

Two widely accepted solutions are offered. In normal cases, the rate of exchange is that prevailing when payment is due. If, however, the obligor is in default, the obligee is given an option between the rate of exchange prevailing when payment was due or the rate at the time of actual payment.

The double reference to the "applicable" rate is justified by the fact that there may be different rates of exchange depending on the nature of the operation.

Illustration

5. The facts are the same as in Illustration 4. A chooses to be reimbursed in Swiss francs and payment, which was due on 10 April, actually takes place on 15 September. The rate of exchange on 10 April was Sfrs. 2 to US $1. By 15 September it has become Sfrs. 2,15 to US $1. A is entitled to apply the latter rate. If the dollar had depreciated rather than increased in value, A would have chosen the rate applicable on 10 April.

Issues & Cases

1. MONETARY OBLIGATION EXPRESSED IN CURRENCY DIFFERENT FROM THAT OF PLACE FOR PAYMENT
   - 1.1 MAY BE PAID IN CURRENCY OF PLACE FOR PAYMENT
   - 1.2 EXCEPTIONS
     - 1.2.1 CURRENCY OF PLACE OF PAYMENT NOT FREELY CONVERTIBLE
     - 1.2.2 "EFFECTIVO-CLAUSE"
       - 1.2.2.1 EXCEPTION FROM "EFFECTIVO-CLAUSE"
2. RATE OF EXCHANGE BETWEEN CURRENCY OF ACCOUNT AND CURRENCY OF PAYMENT
   - JULY 1995 ARBITRAL AWARD ICC INTERNATIONAL COURT OF ARBITRATION (NO. 8240) [591]

2.1 RATE PREVAILING WHEN PAYMENT IS DUE

- JULY 1995 ARBITRAL AWARD ICC INTERNATIONAL COURT OF ARBITRATION (NO. 8240) [591]

2.1 IN CASE OF DEFAULT BY OBLIGOR, OBLIGEE'S OPTION BETWEEN RATE PREVAILING WHEN PAYMENT IS DUE AND RATE AT TIME OF ACTUAL PAYMENT

ARTICLE 6.1.10
(Currency not expressed)

Where a monetary obligation is not expressed in a particular currency, payment must be made in the currency of the place where payment is to be made.

COMMENT

Determining the currency of payment gives rise to a special problem if the contract does not state the currency in which a monetary obligation is due. Although such cases may be infrequent, they do exist; a contract may for example state that the price will be the "current price", or that it will be determined by a third person, or that some expenses or costs will be reimbursed by one party to the other, without specifying in which currency those sums are due. The rule laid down in Art. 6.1.10 is that in such situations payment must be made in the currency of the place where payment is to be made.

Article 6.1.10 is not concerned with the currency in which damages are to be assessed, a matter dealt with in Art. 7.4.12 in the context of non-performance.

Illustration

A US client, A, instructs its broker, B, to buy shares on the Frankfurt stock exchange. If B pays for them in euros, should A be billed in euros or in dollars? If A is to pay B in Boston, it will pay in dollars.

Issues & Cases

1. CURRENCY OF PAYMENT NOT EXPRESSED
   1.2 CURRENCY OF PLACE OF PAYMENT

ARTICLE 6.1.11
(Costs of performance)

Each party shall bear the costs of performance of its obligations.

COMMENT

The performance of obligations often entails costs, which may be of different kinds: transportation costs in delivering goods, bank commission in making a monetary transfer, fees to be paid when applying for a permission, etc. In principle, such costs are to be borne by the performing party.

Other arrangements may of course be made by the parties and there is nothing to prevent the performing party from including those costs in advance in the price it quotes. The rule set out in Art. 6.1.11 applies in the absence of such arrangements.

The provision states who shall bear the costs, not who shall pay them. Usually, it will be the same party, but there may be different situations, for example where tax regulations place the burden of payment on a specific party; in such cases, if the person who has to pay is different from the person who must bear the costs under Art. 6.1.11, the latter must reimburse the former.

Illustration

A, a consultant, agrees to send five experts to perform an audit of B's firm. Nothing is said concerning the experts' travel expenses, and A does not take those costs into account when determining its fees. A may not add the travel expenses to the bill.

Issues & Cases

1. COSTS OF PERFORMANCE TO BE BORNE BY PERFORMING PARTY
   1.1 EXCEPTIONS

ARTICLE 6.1.12
(Imputation of payments)

(1) An obligor owing several monetary obligations to the same obligee may specify at the time of payment the debt to which it intends the payment to be applied. However, the payment discharges first any expenses, then interest due and finally the principal.

(2) If the obligor makes no such specification, the obligee may, within a reasonable time after payment, declare to the obligor the obligation to which it imputes the payment, provided that the obligation is due and undisputed.

(3) In the absence of imputation under paragraphs (1) or (2), payment is imputed to that obligation which satisfies one of the following criteria in the order indicated:

(a) an obligation which is due or which is the first to fall due;

(b) the obligation for which the obligee has least security;

(c) the obligation which is the most burdensome for the obligor;

(d) the obligation which has arisen first.

If none of the preceding criteria applies, payment is imputed to all the obligations proportionally.

COMMENT

Arts. 6.1.12 and 6.1.13 deal with the classic problem of imputation of payments. If an obligor owes several monetary obligations at the same time to the same obligee and makes a payment the amount of which is not sufficient to discharge all those debts, the question arises of the debts to which that payment applies.

Art. 6.1.12, which is inspired by widely recognised principles, offers the obligor the possibility of imputing its payment to a particular debt, provided that any expenses and interest due are discharged before the principal. In the absence of any imputation by the obligor, this provision enables the obligee to impute the payment received, although not to a disputed debt. Para. (3) lays down criteria which will govern in the absence of any imputation by either party.

Illustration

A receives under separate contracts three loans, each of US $100,000, from bank B payment of which is due on 31 December. B receives US $100,000 from A on 2 January with the imprecise message: "Reimbursement of the loan". B pays little attention to the matter and at first does not react, but three months later sues A for payment of the remaining US $200,000 and the parties disagree as to which of the loans had been reimbursed by the January payment. B had similar security in each case, but the interest rates were not the same: 8% on the first loan, 8,50% on the second and 9% on the third. The January payment will be imputed to the third loan.

Issues & Cases

1. **IMPUTATION OF PAYMENTS**
   - 1.1 **OBLIGOR'S RIGHT TO IMPUTE PAYMENT TO SPECIFIC DEBT**
   - 1.2 **OTHERWISE OBLIGEE'S RIGHT TO IMPUTE PAYMENT RECEIVED**
   - 1.3 **ORDER OF IMPUTATION IN ABSENCE OF EITHER PARTY'S SPECIFICATION**

ARTICLE 6.1.13
(Imputation of non-monetary obligations)

Article 6.1.12 applies with appropriate adaptations to the imputation of performance of non-monetary obligations.

COMMENT

The problem of imputation of payments normally concerns monetary obligations, but similar difficulties may sometimes occur in relation to obligations of a different nature. Art. 6.1.13 provides that the rules governing monetary obligations will apply, with appropriate adaptations to these cases also.

Illustration

A is performing construction work on several sites in an African country and, through five separate and successive contracts with B, purchases different quantities of cement, all to be delivered in Antwerp on the same date and to be loaded on the same ship. The contracts are similar, except that the third and fifth contracts stipulate very high liquidated damages in the event of late delivery. On account of certain difficulties, B can only deliver part of what it was supposed to. Upon delivery B is entitled to specify that the quantities delivered are to be imputed to the third and fifth contracts.

Issues & Cases

1. IMPUTATION OF NON-MONETARY OBLIGATIONS (SEE ART. 6.1.13)

ARTICLE 6.1.14
(Application for public permission)

Where the law of a State requires a public permission affecting the validity of the contract or its performance and neither that law nor the circumstances indicate otherwise

(a) if only one party has its place of business in that State, that party shall take the measures necessary to obtain the permission;

(b) in any other case the party whose performance requires permission shall take the necessary measures.

COMMENT

If the validity or the performance of a contract is subject to compliance with public permission requirements, several issues arise as to who has the burden of filing the application (Art. 6.1.14), the time for filing (Art. 6.1.15), the legal consequences of failure to obtain an administrative decision in due time (Art. 6.1.16) and the rejection of the application (Art. 6.1.17)

1. Scope of the permission requirement

The Principles do not deal with the relevance of public permission requirements. What kind of public permission is required, if any, is to be determined under the applicable law, including the rules of private international law.

Courts tend to give effect only to the public permission requirements of the *lex fori*, and sometimes to those prescribed by the *lex contractus*. Arbitral tribunals may enjoy wider discretion than courts in deciding which public permissions are relevant to the contract.

Under the relevant conflict of laws rules public permission requirements of the law of other jurisdictions connected with the contract may also come into play (see Art. 7(2) of the *1980 Rome Convention on the Law Applicable to Contractual Obligations*; Art. 11(2) of the *1994 Inter-American Convention on the Law Applicable to International Contracts*). Long-arm statutes in some jurisdictions too may impose public permission requirements on licensees or subsidiaries of companies located abroad. This article assumes that the requirements prescribed by the applicable law are to be observed.

a. *Broad notion of "public permission"*

The term "public permission" is to be given a broad interpretation. It includes all permission requirements established pursuant to a concern of a public nature, such as health, safety, or particular trade policies. It is irrelevant whether a required licence or permit is to be granted by a governmental or by a non-governmental institution to which Governments have delegated public authority for a specific purpose. Thus, the authorisation of payments by a private bank pursuant to foreign exchange regulations is in the nature of a "public permission" for the purposes of this article.

b. *Timing of public permission*

The provisions on public permissions refer primarily to those required by the applicable law or by a regulation in force at the time of the conclusion of the contract. However, these provisions may also apply to public permissions that may be introduced after the conclusion of the contract.

c. *Public permission may affect the contract in whole or in part*

The provisions on public permissions apply both to those requirements affecting the contract as a whole and to those merely affecting individual terms of the contract. However, where the legal consequences of failing to obtain a public permission differ according to whether such permission affects the contract in whole or in part, different rules are established. See Arts. 6.1.16 (2) and 6.1.17.

d. *Public permission may affect the validity or performance of a contract*

The absence of the required permission may affect the validity of a contract or render its performance impossible. Notwithstanding differences in the legal consequences of failing to obtain a required public permission, the problems raised in connection with the application for, or the obtaining of, a public permission are the same. As to the further consequences, Art. 6.1.17(2) provides that the rules on non-performance apply to a situation where the refusal of a permission makes the performance of a contract impossible in whole or in part.

2. Duty to inform of the existence of a public permission requirement

There is as a rule no duty to provide information concerning the requirement to obtain a public permission. However, the existence of such a requirement must be disclosed by the party upon whom rests the burden of obtaining a public permission when such permission is required under rules which are not generally accessible. Thus, the overriding principle of good faith (Art. 1.7) may require the party whose place of business is located in the State requiring a public permission to inform the other party of the existence of that requirement. Failure to do so may lead a court to disregard the permission requirement altogether or to conclude that the party who failed to communicate the existence of the requirement implicitly guaranteed that it would be obtained.

3. Which party is bound to take measures to obtain a public permission

a. *Party with place of business in State requiring public permission*

The rule set out in sub-para. (a) of this article which places the burden to apply on the party who has its place of business in the State which requires the relevant public permission reflects current international trade practices. It is that party who is in the best position to apply promptly for a public permission, since it is probably more familiar with the application requirements and procedures.

If a party needs further information from the other to file an application (*e.g.* information relating to the final destination of the goods, or information as to the purpose or subject matter of the contract), the other party must furnish such information pursuant to the duty of co-operation (Art. 5.1.3). Should that party not furnish such information it may not rely on the obligation of the first party. This duty to cooperate with the other party applies even if the contract stipulates that one of the parties bears the burden of applying for a public permission. Thus, if the parties have incorporated in their contract the term "ex works", which imposes far-reaching obligations on the buyer, the seller is nevertheless bound "to render the buyer, at the latter's request, risk and expense, every assistance in obtaining [...] any export licence or other official authorisation necessary for the export of the goods" (INCOTERMS 2000, A 2, see also B 2).

b. *Party whose performance requires public permission*

Sub-para. (b) of this article contemplates those cases where none of the parties has a place of business in the State requiring the permission. It also envisions a contract which is truly international notwithstanding the fact that both parties have their places of business in that State. In either case, the party whose performance requires the public permission is bound to take the necessary measures to obtain such a permission.

Illustration

1. A, a contractor whose place of business is located in country X, sells a plant on a turn-key basis to B, whose place of business is located in country Y. Acceptance is to take place after performance tests in country Y. On the one hand, A has to apply for all public permissions required in country X, as well as for permissions in third countries (transit, sub-deliveries). On the other, B has to apply for import licences, as well as for all other permissions relating to the site, the use of local services, and the technology imported into country Y. A is also bound to furnish the

information and documentation needed by B to obtain import licences and other permissions related to B's performance. A is not responsible for applying for public permissions in country Y, unless this is agreed in the contract or is required, explicitly or implicitly, by the applicable law or the circumstances of the case (*e.g.* the applicable law may require certain technical permits in country Y to be applied for by the licensor).

c. *Suppletory nature of provisions on public permissions*

The purpose of this article is to determine the party who must apply for a public permission in those cases where it is not clear who is to bear that burden. It is a suppletory rule to be applied when neither the contract, nor the law requiring the permission or the circumstances specify which party is under an obligation to apply for the required public permission.

Illustration

2. The law of country X subordinates the granting of an export licence for computers to a sworn declaration indicating the country where the computers will ultimately be sent. However, neither the contract nor the law of country X indicates which party bears the burden of applying for a licence. Since it is reasonable to suppose that only the buyer knows what it plans to do with the computers, the policy behind the rule imposing the permission requirement leads to the conclusion that it is the buyer who has to file the application.

4. Nature of obligation to take the "necessary measures"

The party who has to apply for the permission must take the "necessary measures" to obtain such permission, but is not responsible for the outcome of the application. That party is bound to exhaust available local remedies to obtain the permission, provided that they have a good chance of success and that resorting to local remedies appears reasonable in view of the circumstances of the case (*e.g.* the value of the transaction, time constraints).

Which measures have to be taken depends on the relevant regulations and the procedural mechanisms available in the State where the permission is to be granted. The obligation is in the nature of an obligation of best efforts (see Art. 5.1.4(2)).

Illustration

3. A, a principal whose place of business is in country X, enters into a contract with B, a self-employed agent, whose place of business is in country Y. B, who has no authority to conclude contracts, is to represent A in countries Y and Z. Among other

duties, B must exhibit A's goods at a fair which is to take place in country Z. B must apply for all permissions which are required to undertake these professional activities in countries Y and Z. B's duty to take "necessary measures" includes that of applying for public permissions required to import A's goods temporarily into countries Y and Z, as well as any other public permission that would enable B to participate in the fair. However, unless otherwise agreed, B is not required to apply for public permissions required for goods imported through B by customers located in countries Y and Z.

Issues & Cases

1. **RELEVANCE OF PUBLIC PERMISSION REQUIREMENTS (SEE ART. 1.4)**
   1.1 **PUBLIC PERMISSION REQUIREMENTS OF LEX FORI**
   1.2 **PUBLIC PERMISSION OF LAW GOVERNING CONTRACT**
   1.3 **PUBLIC PERMISSION REQUIREMENTS OF THIRD STATES**
2. **PARTY BOUND TO APPLY FOR PERMISSION**
   2.1 **PARTY WITH PLACE OF BUSINESS IN STATE REQUIRING PERMISSION**
   2.2 **PARTY WHOSE PERFORMANCE REQUIRES PERMISSION**

ARTICLE 6.1.15
(Procedure in applying for permission)

(1) The party required to take the measures necessary to obtain the permission shall do so without undue delay and shall bear any expenses incurred.

(2) That party shall whenever appropriate give the other party notice of the grant or refusal of such permission without undue delay.

COMMENT

1. Time for filing an application

The party under an obligation to obtain a public permission must take action immediately after the conclusion of the contract and pursue this action as necessary under the circumstances.

2. Expenses

According to Art. 6.1.11, each party shall bear the costs of performance of its obligations. This rule has been restated in para. (1) of the present article for the sake of clarity.

3. Duty to give prompt notice of the grant or refusal of the permission

The parties to the contract need to know as soon as possible whether the permission can be obtained. Accordingly, para. (2) of this article provides that the party required to take the necessary measures must inform the other of the outcome of the application. This duty of information extends to other relevant facts, such as for example the timing and outcome of the application, whether a refusal is subject to appeal and whether an appeal is to be lodged.

4. Duty to give notice "whenever appropriate"

The "appropriateness" of giving notice of the grant or refusal refers to the need to give notice and the manner of providing it. The necessity of giving notice obviously exists where such notice is required by law, but may also be inferred from the mere fact that a permission requirement is referred to in the contract.

The "appropriateness" of the duty to give notice is also related to the relevance of the information to be provided. Accordingly, the applying party is not bound to inform the other party of the outcome of that application in cases where the latter party obtains the information from the granting authority, or where applications for permissions are regularly granted. The fact that the permission is, contrary to normal practice, refused in a given case makes the obligation to inform more compelling.

This article does not establish particular requirements concerning the formalities relating to the communication. See Art. 1.10.

5. Consequences of the failure to inform

Failure to provide information regarding the grant or refusal of the permission amounts to non-performance. Accordingly, the general consequences of non-performance, as set forth in Chapter 7, apply. The duty to give notice of the grant of the public permission is a contractual obligation arising at the time the contract comes into existence. The duty to give notice of the refusal of the permission is part of the duty to take the "necessary measures" to obtain the permission under Art. 6.1.14 (see comment 4).

Illustrations

1. A, whose place of business is in country X, and B, a contractor, enter into a contract for the construction of a plant in country X. The parties agree that B is not bound to begin the construction and A's advance payments are not due until the grant of a permission by the authorities of country X.

A applies for and obtains the permission but fails to inform B that the permission has been granted. Two months later, B learns through inquiries with the authorities of country X that the permission has been granted and begins work on the construction of the plant.

Although the parties had agreed that their performances were due as of the time of the granting of the permission, A's failure to inform B that the permission has been granted precludes A from relying on B's failure to perform as of that date (see Art. 7.1.2). Thus, the contractual period begins to run for B as from when it learns of the granting of the permission.

Moreover, B may also claim damages if it is able to establish, for example, damage resulting from failure to use its production capacity, additional costs arising from storing raw materials during that two-month period, etc. (see Art. 7.4.1 *et seq.*). A, who from the very beginning had notice of the grant of the permission, must observe the original date of its performance, as provided for in the contract. If A fails to make an advance payment due four weeks after the granting of the permission, A must pay interest as from that date.

2. The facts are the same as in Illustration 1, the difference being that the proper authority simultaneously informs A and B that the permission has been granted. B may not avail itself of A's failure to inform in order to postpone its performance, nor is it entitled to damages for A's failure to inform.

Issues & Cases

1. **PROCEDURE IN APPLYING FOR PERMISSION**

 1.1 **TIME FOR FILLING AN APPLICATION**

 - JANUARY 25, 2002 ARBITRAL COURT OF THE LAUSANNE CHAMBER OF COMMERCE AND INDUSTRY [991]

 1.2 **EXPENSES**

 1.3 **DUTY TO GIVE PROMPT NOTICE OF GRANT OR REFUSAL OF PERMISSION**

 - JANUARY 25, 2002 ARBITRAL COURT OF THE LAUSANNE CHAMBER OF COMMERCE AND INDUSTRY [991]

 1.3 **CONSEQUENCES OF FAILURE TO GIVE NOTICE (SEE CHAPTER 7)**

 - JANUARY 25, 2002 ARBITRAL COURT OF THE LAUSANNE CHAMBER OF COMMERCE AND INDUSTRY [991]

ARTICLE 6.1.16
(Permission neither granted nor refused)

(1) If, notwithstanding the fact that the party responsible has taken all measures required, permission is neither granted nor refused within an agreed period or, where no period has been agreed, within a reasonable time from the conclusion of the contract, either party is entitled to terminate the contract.

(2) Where the permission affects some terms only, paragraph (1) does not apply if, having regard to the circumstances, it is reasonable to uphold the remaining contract even if the permission is refused.

COMMENT

Whereas Arts. 6.1.14 and 6.1.15 are concerned with the duties of the contracting parties, Arts. 6.1.16 and 6.1.17 deal with the legal consequences in cases respectively where there has been no decision on the application within a given period or where the public permission has been refused.

1. No decision taken as regards the permission

Para. (1) of the present article deals with the "nothing happens" situation, that is to say a situation where permission has neither been granted nor refused within the agreed period or, where no period has been agreed, within a reasonable time from the conclusion of the contract. The reasons for the absence of a pronouncement may vary, for example the slow pace of processing the application, a pending appeal, etc. In any event there is no longer any reason to keep the parties waiting and either party is entitled to terminate the contract.

2. Termination of the contract

Remedies other than termination may be appropriate depending on the legal role played by the permission in the creation of the contractual obligations. This is in particular the case where the granting of the public permission is a condition for the validity of the contract, since in the absence of the permission either party may simply disregard the contract. The reason why this article provides also in these cases for the termination of the contract is that the parties are, with a view to obtaining the permission, under a number of obligations which cannot be allowed to exist indefinitely.

The entitlement of the party responsible for obtaining the permission to terminate the contract under this article is conditional on that party's having taken "the necessary measures" to that effect.

Illustration

1. A, situated in country X, sells rifles to B for resale by B in the hunting season starting in four months. The validity of the sale is subject to a public permission to be granted by the authorities of country X. No period is agreed for obtaining that permission. Notwithstanding the fact that A takes all the necessary measures to obtain the permission, after three months no decision has yet been taken on A's application. Either party may terminate the contract.

The termination envisaged under this article has no consequences for the expenses so far incurred by the parties for the purpose of obtaining the permission. The expenses will be borne by the party who has assumed the risk of not obtaining the permission.

3. Permission affecting individual terms only

Where the permission affects some terms only of the contract, para. (2) of this article excludes the right of termination in cases where, even if the permission had been refused, it would according to Art. 6.1.17(1) nevertheless be reasonable to uphold the contract.

Illustration

2. A, situated in country X, enters into a contract with B, containing a penalty clause for delay, the validity of which is subject to a public permission to be granted by the authorities of country X. Notwithstanding the fact that A takes all the necessary measures to obtain the permission, time continues to pass without any decision being taken. It would be reasonable in the circumstances to uphold the contract. Even if the permission were to have been refused, neither party may terminate the contract.

Issues & Cases

1. **PERMISSION NEITHER GRANTED NOR REFUSED**
   - 1.1 **EITHER PARTY'S RIGHT TO TERMINATE CONTRACT**
   - 1.2 **PERMISSION AFFECTING INDIVIDUAL TERMS ONLY**

ARTICLE 6.1.17
(Permission refused)

(1) The refusal of a permission affecting the validity of the contract renders the contract void. If the refusal affects the validity of some terms only, only such terms are void if, having regard to the circumstances, it is reasonable to uphold the remaining contract.

(2) Where the refusal of a permission renders the performance of the contract impossible in whole or in part, the rules on non-performance apply.

COMMENT

1. Application for permission rejected

This article contemplates the situation where the application for a permission is expressly refused. The nature of the obligation imposed on the responsible party with respect to the application for the permission is such that a refusal under this article is one which is not subject to an appeal which has a reasonable prospect of success. See comment 4 on Art. 6.1.14. Moreover, means of recourse against the refusal need not be exhausted whenever a final decision on the permission would be taken only after the time at which the contract could meaningfully be performed.

2. Legal consequences of a refusal of permission

The consequences of a refusal to grant the permission vary depending on whether the permission affects the validity of the contract or its performance.

a. *Refusal of permission affecting validity of the contract*

Where the permission affects the validity of the whole contract, a refusal renders the whole contract void, *i.e.* the contract is considered as never having come into being.

Illustration

1. A, situated in country X, enters into a contract with B, the validity of which is subject to a public permission to be granted by the authorities of country X. Notwithstanding the fact that A takes all the necessary measures to obtain the permission, A's

application is refused. The contract is considered never to have come into existence.

Where, on the other hand, a refusal affects the validity of some terms only of the contract, only such terms are void, while the remaining part of the contract may be upheld provided that such a result is reasonable in the circumstances.

Illustration

2. A, situated in country X, enters into a contract with B, containing a penalty clause for delay, the validity of which is subject to a public permission to be granted by the authorities of country X. Notwithstanding the fact that A takes all the necessary measures to obtain the permission, A's application is refused. If it is reasonable in the circumstances, the contract will be upheld without the penalty clause.

b. *Refusal rendering performance of the contract impossible*

If the refusal of the permission renders the performance impossible in whole or in part, para. (2) of this article refers to the rules on non-performance embodied in Chapter 7.

Illustration

3. Under a contract entered into with B, A owes B US $100,000. The transfer of the sum from country X, where A is situated, to B's bank account in country Y is subject to a permission by the Central Bank of country X. Notwithstanding the fact that A takes all the necessary measures to obtain the permission, A's application is refused. The refusal of the permission renders it impossible for A to pay B. The consequences of A's non-performance are determined in accordance with the provisions of Chapter 7.

The refusal of the permission may render impossible the performance of a party only in the State imposing the permission requirement, while it may be possible for that party to perform the same obligation elsewhere. In such cases the general principle of good faith (see Art. 1.7) will prevent that party from relying on the refusal of the permission as an excuse for non-performance.

Illustration

4. The facts are the same as in Illustration 3, the difference being that A has in country Z, where no such permission requirement exists, sufficient funds to pay B. A may not rely on the refusal of the permission by the authorities of country X as an excuse for not paying B.

Issues & Cases

1. **REFUSAL OF PERMISSION AFFECTING VALIDITY OF CONTRACT OR SINGLE TERMS THEREOF**
   1.1 **CONTRACT OR SINGLE TERMS VOID**
2. **REFUSAL OF PERMISSION RENDERING PERFORMANCE OF CONTRACT IMPOSSIBLE**
   2.1 **RULES ON NON-PERFORMANCE APPLY (SEE CHAPTER 7)**

SECTION 2: HARDSHIP

BIBLIOGRAPHY

BARALDI M., Il governo giudiziario della discrezionalità contrattuale, in Contratto e impresa 2005, 501 – 538.

BERGER K.P., Internazionale Investitionsverträge und Schiedsgerichtsbarkeit, in Zeitschrift für Vergleichende Rechtswissenschaft 2003, 1 – 32.

BERNARDINI P., Hardship e Force majeure, in BONELL M.J. / BONELLI F. (eds.), Contratti commerciali internazionali e Principi UNIDROIT, Giuffrè, Milano 1997. 193 – 214.

BONELL M.J., An International Restatement of Contract Law. The UNIDROIT Principles of International Commercial Contracts, 3rd ed., Transnational Publications Inc., Ardsley, New York, 2005, at 117 – 124.

BONELL M.J., A 'Global' arbitration decided on the basis of the UNIDROIT Principles: In re Andersen Consulting Business Unit Member Firms v. Arthur Andersen Business Unit Member Firms and Andersen Worldwide Société Coopérative, in 17 Arbitration International 2001, 249 – 261.

BORTOLOTTI F., Manuale di diritto commerciale internazionale, I, Diritto dei contratti internazionali, 2 ed., CEDAM, 2001, 141 – 143.

CHAPPUIS Ch., L'intervention du tribunal dans le contrat. Convergence entre les Principes UNIDROIT et le droit suisse, in Liber Amicorum Claude Reymond, Litec, Paris 2004, 53 – 72.

CIRIELLI S.E., Clausola di *hardship* e adattamento nel contratto commerciale internazionale, Contratto e impresa / Europa, 1998, 733 – 789.

CORAPI D., L'equilibrio delle posizioni contrattuali nei Principi UNIDROIT, Europa e Diritto Privato, 2002, n. 1, 23 – 40.

DARANKOUM E.S., L'application des Principes d'UNIDROIT par les arbitres internationaux et par les juges étatiques, Les Principes d'UNIDROIT et les contrats internationaux: aspects pratiques, in Revue Juridique Thémis, vol 36, no. 2 (2002), 421 – 480.

DOUDKO A.G., Hardship in contract: The approach of the UNIDROIT Principles and legal developments in Russia, Uniform Law Review / Revue de droit uniforme, 2000, 483 – 509.

DRAETTA U., Les clauses de force majeure et de hardship dans les contrats internationaux, in 15 Diritto del Commercio Internazionale, 2001, 297 – 308.

ERNST W., Die Verpflichtung zur Leistung in den Principles of European Contract Law und in den Principles of International Commercial Contracts, in BASEDOW J. (ed.), Europäische Vertragsrechtsvereinheitlichung und deutsches Recht, J.C.B. Mohr (Siebeck), Tübingen 2000, 129 – 157.

FAUVARQUE-COSSON B., Le changement de circonstances, in Revue des contrats, 2004, 67 – 92.

FONTAINE M., Les dispositions relatives au *hardship* et à la force majeure, in BONELL M.J. / BONELLI F. (eds.), Contratti commerciali internazionali e Principi UNIDROIT, Giuffrè, Milano 1997, 183 – 191.

GROSHEIDE F.W., Evenwicht in Internationale Commerciële Contracts-vehou-dingen. Opmerkingen geïnspireerd door de regeling van *hardship* in de Principles of International Commercial Contracts, F.W. GROSHEIDE / K. BOELE-WOELKI (eds.), Europees Privaatrecht, Molengrafica, Koninklijke Vermande B.V., Lelystad 1996.

JENKINS S.H., Exemption for Non-Performance: UCC, CISG, UNIDROIT Principles – A Comparative Assessment, in 72 Tulane Law Review, n. 6, 1998, 2015 – 2030.

KRÖLL S., Ergänzung und Anpassung von Verträgen durch Schiedsgerichte, C. Heymanns Verlag KG, Köln-Berlin-Bonn-München, 1998.

KUIJER M., Een vergelijking van 'hardship' uit de UNIDROIT-regeling met de onvoorziene omstandigheden uit artikel 6:258 van het BW, Ars Aequi 1996, 16 *et seq.*

LANDO O., The CISG and the UNIDROIT Principles in a Global Commercial Code, in Mélanges offerts à Marcel Fontaine, Paris, Larcier, 2003, 451 – 472.

LEHRBERG B., Renegotiation clauses, the doctrine of assumptions and unfair contract terms, in European Review of Private Law, n. 3, 1998, 265 – 283.

LURGER B., Grundfragen der Vereinheitlichung des Vertragsrechts in der Europäischen Union, Springer, Wien, 2002, 486 – 522.

MARASCO P.G., La rinegoziazione e l'intervento del giudice nella gestione del contratto, in Contratto e impresa 2005, 539 – 578.

MASKOW D, Hardship and *Force Majeure*, in 40 American Journal of Comparative Law, n. 3, 1992, 657 – 669.

NGUYEN M.H., Les Principes UNIDROIT: Jurisprudence et expériences pour le Vietnam, in Revue de droit des affaires internationales / International Business Law, no. 5/2005, 619 – 636.

PERILLO J.M., *Force Majeure* and Hardship Under the UNIDROIT PRINCIPLES of International Commercial Contracts, in 5 Tulane Journal of International & Comparative Law, 1997, 5 – 28; also in Comentarios a los Principios sobre los Contratos Comerciales Internacionales del UNIDROIT, Universidad Nacional Autónoma de México, 1998, 111 – 133.

PERILLO J.M., Hardship and its Impact on Contractual Obligations: A Comparative Analysis, in Centro di studi e ricerche di diritto comparato e straniero: Saggi, Conferenze e Seminari, n. 20, Roma 1996.

PIERAZZI E.M., La giustizia del contratto, in Contratto e impresa 2005, 646 – 657.

PRADO M.C.A., La théorie du *hardship* dans les Principes de l'UNIDROIT relatifs aux contrats du commerce international. Une approche comparative des Principes et les solutions adoptées par le droit francais, in Diritto del commercio internazionale 1997, 323 – 373.

RIMKE J., *Force majeure* and hardship: Application in International Trade Practice with Specific Regard to the CISG and the UNIDROIT Principles of International Contracts, in Revue of the Convention on Contracts for the International Sale of Goods (CISG), 1999 – 2000, 193 – 244.

RIPPEN E.E., Verandering van omstandigheden in het Engelse contractenrecht. Een vergelijking met de UNIDROIT-Principles en de Principles of European Contract Law, in F.W. GROSHEIDE / K. BOELE-WOELKI (eds.), Europees Privaat-recht, Molengrafica, Koninklijke Vermande B.V., Lelystad 1996.

RIVEIRA J.O., Hardship under the UNIDROIT Principles of International Commercial Contracts, in AKSEN G. – BÖCKSTIEGEL K.-M. – MUSTILL M.J. – PATOCCHI P.M. – WHITESELL A.M. (eds.), Global Reflections on International Law, Commerce and Dispute Resolution. Liber Amicorum in Honour of Robert Briner, Paris 2005, 677 – 691.

TALLON D., Hardship in HARTKAMP A., *et al.*, (eds.), Towards a European Civil Code, 3rd fully revised and expanded edition, Nijmegen, Ars Aequi Libri, 2004, 499 – 504.

TRAISCI F.P., Sopravvenienze contrattuali e rinegoziazione nei sistemi di *civil* e di *common law*, Edizioni Scientifiche Italiane, Napoli 2003.

ZACCARIA E.CH., L'adattamento dei contratti a lungo termine nell'esperienza giuridica statunitense: aspirazioni teoriche e prassi giurisprudenziale, in Contratto e impresa 2006, 478 – 516.

ARTICLE 6.2.1
(Contract to be observed)

Where the performance of a contract becomes more onerous for one of the parties, that party is nevertheless bound to perform its obligations subject to the following provisions on hardship.

COMMENT

1. Binding character of the contract the general rule

The purpose of this article is to make it clear that as a consequence of the general principle of the binding character of the contract (see Art. 1.3) performance must be rendered as long as it is possible and regardless of the burden it may impose on the performing party. In other words, even if a party experiences heavy losses instead of the expected profits or the performance has become meaningless for that party the terms of the contract must nevertheless be respected.

Illustration

In January 1990 A, a forwarding agent, enters into a two-year shipping contract with B, a carrier. Under the contract B is bound to ship certain goods from Hamburg to New York at a fixed price, on a monthly basis throughout the two-year period. Alleging a substantial increase in the price of fuel in the aftermath of the 1990 Gulf crisis, B requests a five per cent increase in the rate for August 1990. B is not entitled to such an increase because B bears the risk of its performance becoming more onerous.

2. Change in circumstances relevant only in exceptional cases

The principle of the binding character of the contract is not however an absolute one. When supervening circumstances are such that they lead to a fundamental alteration of the equilibrium of the contract, they create an exceptional situation referred to in these Principles as "hardship" and dealt with in the following articles of this section.

The phenomenon of hardship has been acknowledged by various legal systems under the guise of other concepts such as frustration of purpose, *Wegfall der Geschäftsgrundlage*, *imprévision*, *eccessiva onerosità sopravvenuta*, etc. The term "hardship" was chosen because it is widely known in international trade practice as confirmed by the inclusion in many international contracts of so-called "hardship clauses".

Issues & Cases

1. **CHANGE IN CIRCUMSTANCES RELEVANT ONLY IN EXCEPTIONAL CASE (SEE ART. 1.3)**
    - SEPTEMBER 1996 ARBITRAL AWARD ICC INTERNATIONAL COURT OF ARBITRATION (NO. 8486) [633]
    - FEBRUARY 1999 ARBITRAL AWARD ICC INTERNATIONAL COURT OF ARBITRATION (NO. 9479) [786]
    - MARCH 20, 2000 ARBITRAL AWARD INTERNATIONAL CENTRE FOR SETTLEMENT OF INVESTMENT DISPUTES (ICSID) (ARB(AF)/98/1) [826]

ARTICLE 6.2.2
(Definition of hardship)

There is hardship where the occurrence of events fundamentally alters the equilibrium of the contract either because the cost of a party's performance has increased or because the value of the performance a party receives has diminished, and

(a) the events occur or become known to the disadvantaged party after the conclusion of the contract;

(b) the events could not reasonably have been taken into account by the disadvantaged party at the time of the conclusion of the contract;

(c) the events are beyond the control of the disadvantaged party; and

(d) the risk of the events was not assumed by the disadvantaged party.

COMMENT

1. Hardship defined

This article defines hardship as a situation where the occurrence of events fundamentally alters the equilibrium of the contract, provided that those events meet the requirements which are laid down in sub-paras. (a) to (d).

2. Fundamental alteration of equilibrium of the contract

Since the general principle is that a change in circumstances does not affect the obligation to perform (see Art. 6.2.1), it follows that hardship may not be invoked unless the alteration of the equilibrium of the contract is fundamental. Whether an alteration is "fundamental" in a given case will of course depend upon the circumstances.

Illustration

1. In September 1989 A, a dealer in electronic goods situated in the former German Democratic Republic, purchases stocks from B, situated in country X, also a former socialist country. The goods are to be delivered by B in December 1990. In November 1990, A

informs B that the goods are no longer of any use to it, claiming that after the unification of the German Democratic Republic and the Federal Republic of Germany there is no longer any market for such goods imported from country X. Unless the circumstances indicate otherwise, A is entitled to invoke hardship.

a. *Increase in cost of performance*

In practice a fundamental alteration in the equilibrium of the contract may manifest itself in two different but related ways. The first is characterised by a substantial increase in the cost for one party of performing its obligation. This party will normally be the one who is to perform the non-monetary obligation. The substantial increase in the cost may, for instance, be due to a dramatic rise in the price of the raw materials necessary for the production of the goods or the rendering of the services, or to the introduction of new safety regulations requiring far more expensive production procedures.

b. *Decrease in value of the performance received by one party*

The second manifestation of hardship is characterised by a substantial decrease in the value of the performance received by one party, including cases where the performance no longer has any value at all for the receiving party. The performance may be that either of a monetary or of a non-monetary obligation. The substantial decrease in the value or the total loss of any value of the performance may be due either to drastic changes in market conditions (*e.g.* the effect of a dramatic increase in inflation on a contractually agreed price) or the frustration of the purpose for which the performance was required (*e.g.* the effect of a prohibition to build on a plot of land acquired for building purposes or the effect of an export embargo on goods acquired with a view to their subsequent export).

Naturally the decrease in value of the performance must be capable of objective measurement: a mere change in the personal opinion of the receiving party as to the value of the performance is of no relevance. As to the frustration of the purpose of the performance, this can only be taken into account when the purpose in question was known or at least ought to have been known to both parties.

3. Additional requirements for hardship to arise

a. *Events occur or become known after conclusion of the contract*

According to sub-para. (a) of this article, the events causing hardship must take place or become known to the disadvantaged party after the conclusion of the contract. If that party had known of those events when entering into the contract, it would have been able to take them into account at that time and may not subsequently rely on hardship.

b. *Events could not reasonably have been taken into account by disadvantaged party*

Even if the change in circumstances occurs after the conclusion of the contract, sub-para. (b) of this article makes it clear that such circumstances cannot cause hardship if they could reasonably have been taken into account by the disadvantaged party at the time the contract was concluded.

Illustration

2. A agrees to supply B with crude oil from country X at a fixed price for the next five years, notwithstanding the acute political tensions in the region. Two years after the conclusion of the contract, a war erupts between contending factions in neighbouring countries. The war results in a world energy crisis and oil prices increase drastically. A is not entitled to invoke hardship because such a rise in the price of crude oil was not unforeseeable.

Sometimes the change in circumstances is gradual, but the final result of those gradual changes may constitute a case of hardship. If the change began before the contract was concluded, hardship will not arise unless the pace of change increases dramatically during the life of the contract.

Illustration

3. In a sales contract between A and B the price is expressed in the currency of country X, a currency whose value was already depreciating slowly against other major currencies before the conclusion of the contract. One month afterwards a political crisis in country X leads to a massive devaluation of the order of 80% of its currency. Unless the circumstances indicate otherwise, this constitutes a case of hardship, since such a dramatic acceleration of the loss of value of the currency of country X was not foreseeable.

c. *Events beyond the control of disadvantaged party*

Under sub-para. (c) of this article a case of hardship can only arise if the events causing the hardship are beyond the control of the disadvantaged party.

d. *Risks must not have been assumed by disadvantaged party*

Under sub-para. (d) there can be no hardship if the disadvantaged party had assumed the risk of the change in circumstances. The word "assumption" makes it clear that the risks need not have been taken over expressly, but that this may follow from the very nature of the contract. A party who enters into a speculative transaction is deemed to accept a certain degree of risk, even though it may not have been fully aware of that risk at the time it entered into the contract.

Illustration

4. A, an insurance company specialised in the insurance of shipping risks, requests an additional premium from those of its customers who have contracts which include the risks of war and civil insurrection, so as to meet the substantially greater risk to which it is exposed following upon the simultaneous outbreak of war and civil insurrection in three countries in the same region. A is not entitled to such an adaptation of the contract, since by the war and civil insurrection clause insurance companies assume these risks even if three countries are affected at the same time.

4. Hardship relevant only to performance not yet rendered

By its very nature hardship can only become of relevance with respect to performances still to be rendered: once a party has performed, it is no longer entitled to invoke a substantial increase in the costs of its performance or a substantial decrease in the value of the performance it receives as a consequence of a change in circumstances which occurs after such performance.

If the fundamental alteration in the equilibrium of the contract occurs at a time when performance has been only partially rendered, hardship can be of relevance only to the parts of the performance still to be rendered.

Illustration

5. A enters into a contract with B, a waste disposal company in country X, for the purpose of arranging the storage of its waste. The contract provides for a four-year term and a fixed price per ton of waste. Two years after the conclusion of the contract, the environmental movement in country X gains ground and the Government of country X prescribes prices for storing waste which are ten times higher than before. B may successfully invoke hardship only with respect to the two remaining years of the life of the contract.

5. Hardship normally relevant to long-term contracts

Although this article does not expressly exclude the possibility of hardship being invoked in respect of other kinds of contracts, hardship will normally be of relevance to long-term contracts, *i.e.* those where the performance of at least one party extends over a certain period of time.

6. Hardship and force majeure

In view of the respective definitions of hardship and force majeure (see Art. 7.1.7) under these Principles there may be factual situations which can at the same time be considered as cases of hardship and of force majeure. If this is the case, it is for the party affected by these events to decide which remedy to pursue. If it invokes force majeure, it is with a view to its non-performance being excused. If, on the other hand, a party invokes hardship, this is in the first instance for the purpose of renegotiating the terms of the contract so as to allow the contract to be kept alive although on revised terms.

7. Hardship and contract practice

The definition of hardship in this article is necessarily of a rather general character. International commercial contracts often contain much more precise and elaborate provisions in this regard. The parties may therefore find it appropriate to adapt the content of this article so as to take account of the particular features of the specific transaction.

Issues & Cases

1. NOTION OF HARDSHIP
    - 1990 ARBITRAL AWARD SCHIEDSGERICHT BERLIN (NO. SG 126/90) [547]
    - MAY 5, 1997 ARBITRAL AWARD ICC INTERNATIONAL COURT OF ARBITRATION (NO. 7365/FMS) [680]
    - JULY 1997 ARBITRAL AWARD ICC INTERNATIONAL COURT OF ARBITRATION (NO. 8873) [699]
    - MARCH 1998 ARBITRAL AWARD ICC INTERNATIONAL COURT OF ARBITASTION (NO. 9029) [718]
    - MARCH20,2000 ARBITRAL AWARD INTERNATIONAL CENTRE FOR THE SETTLEMENT OF INVESTMENT DISPUTES (ICSID) (NO. ARB(AF)/98/1) [826]

1.1 FUNDAMENTAL ALTERATION OF CONTRACTUAL EQUILIBRIUM
    - 1990 ARBITRAL AWARD SCHIEDSGERICHT BERLIN (NO. SG 126/90) [547]
    - FEBRUARY 1999 ARBITRAL AWARD ICC INTERNATIONAL COURT OF ARBITRATION (NO. 9479) [786]

- December 2001 Arbitral Award ICC International Court of Arbitration (No. 9994) [985]

1.1.1 **Increase in cost of performance**

- July 1997 Arbitral Award ICC International Court of Arbitration (No. 8873) [699]
- December 2001 Arbitral Award ICC International Court of Arbitration (No. 9994) [985]

1.1.2 **Decrease in value of counter-performance**

- -- Arbitral Award Ad hoc Arbitration, (Place unknown) [544]
- 1990 Arbitral Award Schiedsgericht Berlin (No. SG 126/90) [547]
- May 5, 1997 Arbitral Award ICC International Court of Arbitration (No. 7365/FMS) [680]

1.2 **Events occurring after conclusion of contract**

1.3 **Events unforeseeable by disadvantaged party**

1.4 **Events beyond control of disadvantaged party**

- 2000 Arbitral Award ICC International Court of Arbitration (No. 10021) [817]

1.5 **Risks not assumed by disadvantaged party**

- March 1998 Arbitral Award ICC International Court of Arbitration (No. 9029) [718]

2. **Fundamental alteration when performance has been partially rendered**
3. **Hardship v. Force majeure (Art. 7.1.7)**
4. **Hardship clauses**

ARTICLE 6.2.3
(Effects of hardship)

(1) In case of hardship the disadvantaged party is entitled to request renegotiations. The request shall be made without undue delay and shall indicate the grounds on which it is based.

(2) The request for renegotiation does not in itself entitle the disadvantaged party to withhold performance.

(3) Upon failure to reach agreement within a reasonable time either party may resort to the court.

(4) If the court finds hardship it may, if reasonable,

(a) terminate the contract at a date and on terms to be fixed, or

(b) adapt the contract with a view to restoring its equilibrium.

COMMENT

1. Disadvantaged party entitled to request renegotiations

Since hardship consists in a fundamental alteration of the equilibrium of the contract, para. (1) of this article in the first instance entitles the disadvantaged party to request the other party to enter into renegotiation of the original terms of the contract with a view to adapting them to the changed circumstances.

Illustration

1. A, a construction company situated in country X, enters into a lump sum contract with B, a governmental agency, for the erection of a plant in country Y. Most of the sophisticated machinery has to be imported from abroad. Due to an unexpected devaluation of the currency of country Y, which is the currency of payment, the cost of the machinery increases dramatically. A is entitled to request B to renegotiate the original contract price so as to adapt it to the changed circumstances.

A request for renegotiations is not admissible where the contract itself already incorporates a clause providing for the automatic adaptation of the contract (*e.g.* a clause providing for automatic indexation of the price if certain events occur).

Illustration

2. The facts are the same as in Illustration 1, the difference being that the contract contains a price indexation clause relating to variations in the cost of materials and labour. A is not entitled to request a renegotiation of the price.

However, even in such a case renegotiation on account of hardship would not be precluded if the adaptation clause incorporated in the contract did not contemplate the events giving rise to hardship.

Illustration

3. The facts are the same as in Illustration 2, the difference being that the substantial increase in A's costs is due to the adoption of new safety regulations in country Y. A is entitled to request B to renegotiate the original contract price so as to adapt it to the changed circumstances.

2. Request for renegotiations without undue delay

The request for renegotiations must be made as quickly as possible after the time at which hardship is alleged to have occurred (para. (1)). The precise time for requesting renegotiations will depend upon the circumstances of the case: it may, for instance, be longer when the change in circumstances takes place gradually (see comment 3(b) on Art. 6.2.2).

The disadvantaged party does not lose its right to request renegotiations simply because it fails to act without undue delay. The delay in making the request may however affect the finding as to whether hardship actually existed and, if so, its consequences for the contract.

3. Grounds for request for renegotiations

Para. (1) of this article also imposes on the disadvantaged party a duty to indicate the grounds on which the request for renegotiations is based so as to permit the other party better to assess whether or not the request for renegotiations is justified. An incomplete request is to be considered as not being raised in time, unless the grounds of the alleged hardship are so obvious that they need not be spelt out in the request.

Failure to set forth the grounds on which the request for renegotiations is based may have similar effects to those resulting from undue delay in making the request (see comment 2 on this article).

4. Request for renegotiations and withholding of performance

Para. (2) of this article provides that the request for renegotiations does not of itself entitle the disadvantaged party to withhold performance. The reason for this lies in the exceptional character of hardship and in the risk of possible abuses of the remedy. Withholding performance may be justified only in extraordinary circumstances.

Illustration

4. A enters into a contract with B for the construction of a plant. The plant is to be built in country X, which adopts new safety regulations after the conclusion of the contract. The new regulations require additional apparatus and thereby fundamentally alter the equilibrium of the contract making A's performance substantially more onerous. A is entitled to request renegotiations and may withhold performance in view of the time it needs to implement the new safety regulations, but it may also withhold the delivery of the additional apparatus, for as long as the corresponding price adaptation is not agreed.

5. Renegotiations in good faith

Although nothing is said in this article to that effect, both the request for renegotiations by the disadvantaged party and the conduct of both parties during the renegotiation process are subject to the general principle of good faith (Art. 1.7) and to the duty of co-operation (Art. 5.1.3). Thus the disadvantaged party must honestly believe that a case of hardship actually exists and not request renegotiations as a purely tactical manoeuvre. Similarly, once the request has been made, both parties must conduct the renegotiations in a constructive manner, in particular by refraining from any form of obstruction and by providing all the necessary information.

6. Resort to the court upon failure to reach an agreement

If the parties fail to reach agreement on the adaptation of the contract to the changed circumstances within a reasonable time, para. (3) of the present article authorises either party to resort to the court. Such a situation may arise either because the non-disadvantaged party completely ignored the request for renegotiations or because the renegotiations, although conducted by both parties in good faith, did not achieve a positive outcome.

How long a party must wait before resorting to the court will depend on the complexity of the issues to be settled and the particular circumstances of the case.

7. Court measures in case of hardship

According to para. (4) of this article a court which finds that a hardship situation exists may react in a number of different ways.

A first possibility is for it to terminate the contract. However, since termination in this case does not depend on a non-performance by one of the parties, its effects on the performances already rendered might be different from those provided for by the rules governing termination in general (Arts. 7.3.1. *et seq.*). Accordingly, para. (4)(a) provides that termination shall take place "at a date and on terms to be fixed" by the court.

Another possibility would be for a court to adapt the contract with a view to restoring its equilibrium (para. (4)(b)). In so doing the court will seek to make a fair distribution of the losses between the parties. This may or may not, depending on the nature of the hardship, involve a price adaptation. However, if it does, the adaptation will not necessarily reflect in full the loss entailed by the change in circumstances, since the court will, for instance, have to consider the extent to which one of the parties has taken a risk and the extent to which the party entitled to receive a performance may still benefit from that performance.

Para. (4) of this article expressly states that the court may terminate or adapt the contract only when this is reasonable. The circumstances may even be such that neither termination nor adaptation is appropriate and in consequence the only reasonable solution will be for the court either to direct the parties to resume negotiations with a view to reaching agreement on the adaptation of the contract, or to confirm the terms of the contract as they stand.

Illustration

5. A, an exporter, undertakes to supply B, an importer in country X, with beer for three years. Two years after the conclusion of the contract new legislation is introduced in country X prohibiting the sale and consumption of alcoholic drinks. B immediately invokes hardship and requests A to renegotiate the contract. A recognises that hardship has occurred, but refuses to accept the modifications of the contract proposed by B. After one month of fruitless discussions B resorts to the court.

If B has the possibility to sell the beer in a neighbouring country, although at a substantially lower price, the court may decide to uphold the contract but to reduce the agreed price.

If on the contrary B has no such possibility, it may be reasonable for the court to terminate the contract, at the same time however requiring B to pay A for the last consignment still en route.

Issues & Cases

1. **EFFECTS OF HARDSHIP**
   - 1990 ARBITRAL AWARD SCHIEDSGERICHT BERLIN (NO. SG 126/90) [547]
   - MAY 5, 1997 ARBITRAL AWARD ICC INTERNATIONAL COURT OF ARBITRATION (NO. 7365/FMS) [680]
   - JULY 1997 ARBITRAL AWARD ICC INTERNATIONAL COURT OF ARBITRATION (NO. 8873) [699]
   - MARCH 20, 2000 ARBITRAL AWARD INTERNATIONAL CENTRE FOR SETTLEMENT OF INVESTMENT DISPUTES (ICSID) (NO. ARB(AF)/98/1) [826]
   - DECEMBER 2001 ARBITRAL AWARD ICC INTERNATIONAL COURT OF ARBITRATION (NO. 9994) [985]

1.1 **RIGHT OF DISADVANTAGED PARTY TO REQUEST RENEGOTIATIONS**
   - -- ARBITRAL AWARD AD HOC ARBITRATION (PLACE UNKNOWN) [544]
   - JULY 1997 ARBITRAL AWARD ICC INTERNATIONAL COURT OF ARBITRATION (NO. 8873) [699]
   - 2000 ARBITRAL AWARD ICC INTERNATIONAL COURT OF ARBITRATION (NO. 10021) [817]
   - DECEMBER 2001 ARBITRAL AWARD ICC INTERNATIONAL COURT OF ARBITRATION (NO. 9994) [985]

1.1.1 **REQUEST TO BE MADE WITHOUT UNDUE DELAY**

1.1.2 **INDICATION OF GROUNDS FOR REQUEST**

1.1.3 **RENEGOTIATIONS IN GOOD FAITH (SEE ART. 1.7)**

1.2 **NO AUTOMATIC RIGHT TO WITHHOLD PERFORMANCE**

1.3 **RIGHT TO RESORT TO COURT**
   - -- ARBITRAL AWARD AD HOC ARBITRATION (PLACE UNKNOWN) [544]

1.3.1 **TERMINATION OF CONTRACT BY COURT**
   - 1990 ARBITRAL AWARD SCHIEDSGERICHT BERLIN (NO. SG 126/90) [547]
   - MAY 5, 1997 ARBITRAL AWARD ICC INTERNATIONAL COURT OF ARBITRATION (NO. 7365/FMS) [680]
   - FEBRUARY 1999 ARBITRAL AWARD ICC INTERNATIONAL COURT OF ARBITRATION (NO. 9479) [786]

- 2000 ARBITRAL AWARD ICC INTERNATIONAL COURT OF ARBITRATION (NO. 10021) [817]
- JULY 28, 2000 ARBITRAL AWARD ICC INTERNATIONAL COURT OF ARBITRATION (NO. 9797/CK/AER/ACS) [834]
- APRIL 28, 2005 PEOPLE'S REPUBLIC OF CHINA GUANGDONG INTERMEDIATE PEOPLE'S COURT [1105]

1.3.1.1 TERMINATION ON TERMS TO BE FIXED BY COURT

- JULY 28, 2000 ARBITRAL AWARD ICC INTERNATIONAL COURT OF ARBITRATION (NO. 9797/CK/AER/ACS) [834]

1.3.2 ADAPTATION OF CONTRACT BY COURT

- MAY 5, 1997 ARBITRAL AWARD ICC INTERNATIONAL COURT OF ARBITRATION (NO. 7365/FMS) [680]
- FEBRUARY 1999 ARBITRAL AWARD ICC INTERNATIONAL COURT OF ARBITRATION (NO. 9479) [786]

CHAPTER 7

NON-PERFORMANCE

SECTION 1: NON-PERFORMANCE IN GENERAL

Bibliography

Banchio E. C., Principios aplicables en materia de Caso Fortuìto o Fuerza Mayor, in Bonell M.J. / Schipani S. (eds.), "Principi per i contratti commerciali internazionali" e il sistema giuridico latinoamericano, Padova 1996, 291-306.

Bernardini P., Hardship e Force majeure, in Bonell M.J. / Bonelli F. (eds.), Contratti commerciali internazionali e Principi Unidroit, Giuffré, Milano 1997, 193-214.

Bonell, M.J., An International Restatement of Contract Law. The Unidroit Principles of International Commercial Contracts, 3rd ed., Transnational Publications Inc., Ardsley, New York, 2005, at 159 – 162.

Castronovo C., Inadempimento ed esatto adempimento nei Principi Unidroit, in Bonell M.J. / Bonelli F. (eds.), Contratti commerciali internazionali e Principi Unidroit, Giuffré, Milano 1997, 271-294.

Contreras Vaca F.J., Resolución del contrato por incumplimiento, in Contratación internacional, Comentarios a los principios sobre los Contratos Comerciales Internacionales del Unidroit, Universidad Nacional Autónoma de México – Universidad Panamericana (ed.) 1998, 135-174.

Cortes E., El sistema europeo de la responsabilidad contractual y las normas de derecho uniforme, in La culpa contractual en el sistema juridico latinoamericano, Bogotá, Universidad Externado de Colombia, 2001, 89 – 113.

Darankoum E.S., L'application des Principes d'Unidroit par les arbitres internationaux et par les juges étatiques, in Les Principes d'Unidroit et les contrats internationaux: aspects pratiques, in Revue Juridique Thémis, vol. 36, no. 2 (2002), 421 – 480.

Dawwas, A., Non-performance and damages under CISG and the Unidroit Principles, in Comparative Law Review, 1997, 225-277.

Draetta, U., Les clauses de force majeure et de *hardship* dans les contrats internationaux, in: Diritto del Commercio Internazionale 2001, 297-308.

Eberhard S., Les sanctions de l'inexécution du contrat et les Principes Unidroit, Lausanne 2005, 323.

Ferri G.B., L'"invisibile" presenza della causa del contratto, in Europa e diritto privato 2002, 897 – 914.

Fontaine, M., Les clauses exonératoires et les indemnités contractuelles dans les Principes d'Unidroit: Observations critiques, in Uniform Law Review / Revue de droit uniforme, 1998, 405 – 417.

Fontaine M., Les dispositions relatives au *hardship* et à la force majeure, in Bonell M.J. / Bonelli F. (eds.), Contratti commerciali internazionali e Principi Unidroit, Giuffré, Milano 1997, 183-191.

Furmston, M.P., Breach of Contract, in 40 American Journal of Comparative Law, n. 3, 1992, 671-674.

HUBER U., Die Haftung des Schuldners und das Recht des Gläubigers zur Vertragsaufhebung nach den UNIDROIT Principles und den Principles of European Contract Law, in L. VACCA (ed.), Il contratto inadempiuto. Realtà e tradizione del diritto contrattuale europeo, Giappichelli, Torino 1999, 393-410.

JENKINS S.H., Exemption for Non-Performance: UCC, CISG, UNIDROIT Principles – A Comparative Assessment, in 72 Tulane Law Review, n. 6, 1998, 2015-2030.

LURGER B., Grundfragen der Vereinheitlichung des Vertragsrechts in der Europäischen Union, Springer, Wien, 2002, 486 – 522.

MASKOW D., Hardship and *Force Majeure*, in 40 American Journal of Comparative Law, n. 3, 1992, 657-669.

MEDICUS D., Voraussetzungen einer Haftung für Vertragsveletzung, in Basedow J. (ed.), Europäische Vertragsvereinheitlichung und deutsches Recht, 179 – 193.

MONFELI, T., Il diritto alla correzione dell'inadempimento dal diritto nordamericano ai Principi UNIDROIT, in Diritto del commercio internazionale, 2, 1999, 273-317.

MORAN BOVIO D., Incumplimiento, in MORAN BOVIO D. (ed.), Comentario a los Principios de UNIDROIT para los Contratos del Comercio Internacional, Aranzadi, Pamplona 1999, 317-388.

OLMO GUARIDO N. DEL, El caso fortuito: su incidencia en la ejecución de las obligaciones, Cizur Menor, Aranzadi, 2004, 308.

PAES DE BARROS LEAES L.G., Notas sobre o Capìtulo 7: Inexecuçao, in BONELL M.J. / SCHIPANI S. (eds.), "Principi per i contratti commerciali internazionali" e il sistema giuridico latinoamericano, Padova 1996, 279-289.

PERILLO J.M., *Force Majeure* and Hardship Under the UNIDROIT Principles of International Commercial Contracts, in Contratación internacional, Comentarios a los principios sobre los Contratos Comerciales Internacionales del UNIDROIT, Universidad Nacional Autónoma de México – Universidad Panamericana (ed.) 1998, 111-133.

PERILLO J.M., *Force Majeure* and Hardship Under the UNIDROIT Principles of International Commercial Contracts, in 5 Tulane Journal of International & Comparative Law (1997), 5-28.

RIMKE, J., *Force majeure* and Hardship: Application in International Trade Practice with Specific Regard to the CISG and the UNIDROIT Principles of International Commercial Contracts, in: Review of the Convention on Contracts for the International Sale of Goods (CISG) 1999-2000 (2000), 193-243.

ROSETT A., UNIDROIT Principles and Harmonization of International Commercial Law: Focus on Chapter Seven, in Uniform Law Review / Revue de droit uniforme 1997, 441-450.

ROSETT A., The UNIDROIT Principles of International Commercial Contracts. An Introduction to Chapter Seven: Non-Performance, in Contratación internacional, Comentarios a los principios sobre los Contratos Comerciales Internacionales del UNIDROIT , Universidad Nacional Autónoma de México – Universidad Panamericana (ed.) 1998, 175-186.

SCHIPANI S., I Principi di UNIDROIT e il diritto romano (Alcune annotazioni su *favor debitoris* e asimmetrie del commercio internazionale), in Studi in onore di Pietro Rescigno, I, Teoria generale e storia del diritto, Milano, Giuffrè Editore, 1998, 753 – 782.

SCHLECHTRIEM P., UNIDROIT -Principles (Einheitliche Prinzipien für Verträge) und Werkvertragsrecht, in K. VYGEN / BÖGGERING P. (eds.), Dem Baurecht ein Forum, Festschrift für Götz von Craushaar, Werner Verlag 1997, 157-167.

TAILLON D., Le droit français de l'inexécution confronté aux instruments d'unification, in L. VACCA (ed.), Il contratto inadempiuto. Realtà e tradizione del diritto contrattuale europeo, Giappichelli, Torino 1999, 379-392.

VAN DER MERSCH M. – PHILIPPE D., L'inéxecution dans les contrats du commerce international, in FONTAINE M. – VINEY G. (eds.), Les sanctions de l'inéxecution des obligations contractuelles, Bruxelles – Paris 2001, 701 - 785

ARTICLE 7.1.1
(Non-performance defined)

Non-performance is failure by a party to perform any of its obligations under the contract, including defective performance or late performance.

COMMENT

This article defines "non-performance" for the purpose of the Principles. Particular attention should be drawn to two features of the definition.

The first is that "non-performance" is defined so as to include all forms of defective performance as well as complete failure to perform. So it is non-performance for a builder to erect a building which is partly in accordance with the contract and partly defective or to complete the building late.

The second feature is that for the purposes of the Principles the concept of "non-performance" includes both non-excused and excused non-performance.

Non-performance may be excused by reason of the conduct of the other party to the contract (see Arts. 7.1.2 (Interference by the other party) and 7.1.3 (Withholding performance) and comments) or because of unexpected external events (Art. 7.1.7 (Force majeure) and comment). A party is not entitled to claim damages or specific performance for an excused non-performance of the other party but a party who has not received performance will as a rule be entitled to terminate the contract whether or not the non-performance is excused. See Art. 7.3.1 *et seq.* and comment.

There is no general provision dealing with cumulation of remedies. The assumption underlying the Principles is that all remedies which are not logically inconsistent may be cumulated. So, in general, a party who successfully insists on performance will not be entitled to damages but there is no reason why a party may not terminate a contract for non-excused non-performance and simultaneously claim damages. See Arts. 7.2.5 (Change of remedy), 7.3.5 (Effects of termination in general) and 7.4.1 (Right to damages).

Issues & Cases

1. NON-PERFORMANCE DEFINED

- MARCH 20, 2000 ARBITRAL AWARD INTERNATIONAL CENTRE FOR SETTLEMENT OF INVESTMENT DISPUTES (ICSID) (ARB(AF)/98/1) [826]

1.1 BROAD NOTION OF NON-PERFORMANCE

ARTICLE 7.1.2
(Interference by the other party)

A party may not rely on the non-performance of the other party to the extent that such non-performance was caused by the first party's act or omission or by another event as to which the first party bears the risk.

COMMENT

1. Non-performance caused by act or omission of the party alleging non-performance

This article can be regarded as providing two excuses for non-performance. However conceptually, it goes further than this. When the article applies, the relevant conduct does not become excused non-performance but loses the quality of non-performance altogether. It follows, for instance, that the other party will not be able to terminate for non-performance.

Two distinct situations are contemplated. In the first, one party is unable to perform either wholly or in part because the other party has done something which makes performance in whole or in part impossible.

Illustration

1. A agrees to perform building work on B's land beginning on 1 February. If B locks the gate to the land and does not allow A entry, B cannot complain that A has failed to begin work. B's conduct will often amount to non-excused non-performance either because of an express provision entitling A to access to the land or because B's conduct infringes the obligations of good faith and co-operation. This result does not however depend on B's non-performance being non-excused. The result will be the same where B's non-performance is excused, for instance because access to the land is barred by strikers.

The Principles contemplate the possibility of one party's interference acting only as a partial impediment to performance by the other party and in such cases it will be necessary to decide the extent to which non-performance was caused by the first party's interference and that to which it was caused by other factors.

2. Non-performance caused by event for which party alleging non-performance bears the risk

Another possibility is that non-performance may result from an event the risk of which is expressly or impliedly allocated by the contract to the party alleging non-performance.

Illustration

2. A, a builder, concludes a construction contract to be performed on the premises of B who already has many buildings on those premises which are the subject of an insurance policy covering any damage to the buildings. If the parties agree that the risk of accidental damage is to fall on B as the person insured, there would normally be no reason to reject the parties' allocation of risk since risks of this kind are normally covered by insurance. Even therefore if a fire were to be caused by A's negligence, the risk may be allocated to B although it would clearly need more explicit language to carry this result than would be the case if the fire which destroyed the building were the fault of neither party.

Issues & Cases

1. **NON-PERFORMANCE CAUSED BY OTHER PARTY'S INTERFERENCE**
   - 1.1 **ACT OR OMISSION BY OTHER PARTY**
     - 1.1.1 **FAULT NOT RELEVANT**
   - 1.2 **EVENT FOR WHICH OTHER PARTY BEARS THE RISK**
2. **LOSS OF RIGHT TO REMEDIES BY OTHER PARTY**

ARTICLE 7.1.3
(Withholding performance)

(1) Where the parties are to perform simultaneously, either party may withhold performance until the other party tenders its performance.

(2) Where the parties are to perform consecutively, the party that is to perform later may withhold its performance until the first party has performed.

COMMENT

This article must be read together with Art. 6.1.4 (Order of performance). The present article is concerned with remedies and corresponds in effect to the civil law concept of *exceptio non adimpleti contractus.*

Illustration

A agrees to sell to B a thousand tons of white wheat, cif Rotterdam, payment to be made by confirmed letter of credit opened in euros on a German bank. A is not obliged to ship the goods unless and until B opens the letter of credit in conformity with its contractual obligations.

The text does not explicitly address the question which arises where one party performs in part but does not perform completely. In such a case the party entitled to receive performance may be entitled to withhold performance but only where in normal circumstances this is consonant with good faith (Art. 1.7).

Issues & Cases

1. **RIGHT TO WITHHOLD PERFORMANCE IN CASE OF OTHER PARTY'S NON-PERFORMANCE (SEE ALSO ARTS. 6.1.4, 7.3.4 AND 1.7)**

   1.1 **SIMULTANEOUS PERFORMANCE**

   - APRIL 1998 ARBITRAL AWARD (SECOND PARTIAL) ICC INTERNATIONAL COURT OF ARBITRATION (NO. 7110) [734]
   - AUGUST 19, 2005 ARBITRAL AWARD AD HOC ARBITRATION, BRUSSELS [1108]

   1.2 **CONSECUTIVE PERFORMANCE**

2. RIGHT TO WITHHOLD PERFORMANCE IN CASE OF OTHER PARTY'S PARTIAL NON-PERFORMANCE

- JANUARY 1999 ARBITRAL AWARD ICC INTERNATIONAL COURT OF ARBITRATION (NO. 8547) [770]

ARTICLE 7.1.4
(Cure by non-performing party)

(1) The non-performing party may, at its own expense, cure any non-performance, provided that

(a) without undue delay, it gives notice indicating the proposed manner and timing of the cure;

(b) cure is appropriate in the circumstances;

(c) the aggrieved party has no legitimate interest in refusing cure; and

(d) cure is effected promptly.

(2) The right to cure is not precluded by notice of termination.

(3) Upon effective notice of cure, rights of the aggrieved party that are inconsistent with the non-performing party's performance are suspended until the time for cure has expired.

(4) The aggrieved party may withhold performance pending cure.

(5) Notwithstanding cure, the aggrieved party retains the right to claim damages for delay as well as for any harm caused or not prevented by the cure.

COMMENT

1. General principle

Para. (1) of this article provides that, if certain conditions are met, the non-performing party may cure by correcting the non-performance. In effect, by meeting these conditions, the non-performing party is able to extend the time for performance for a brief period beyond that stipulated in the contract, unless timely performance is required by the agreement or the circumstances. This article thus favours the preservation of the contract. It also reflects the policy of minimising economic waste, as incorporated in Art. 7.4.8 (Mitigation of harm), and the basic principle of good faith stated in Art. 1.7. This article is related to the cure provisions contained in Arts. 37 and 48 CISG and in some domestic laws governing contracts and sales. Even many of those legal systems that do not have a rule permitting cure would normally take a reasonable offer of cure into account in assessing damages.

2. Notice of cure

Cure may be effected only after the non-performing party gives notice of cure. The notice must be reasonable with regard to its timing and content as well as to the manner in which it is communicated. Notice of cure must be given without undue delay after the non-performing party learns of the non-performance. To the extent information is then available, the notice must indicate how cure is to be effected and when. Notice must also be communicated to the aggrieved party in a manner that is reasonable in the circumstances.

Notice of cure is considered to be "effective" when the requirements of para. (1)(a) - (c) have been met.

3. Appropriateness of cure

Whether cure is appropriate in the circumstances depends on whether it is reasonable, given the nature of the contract, to permit the non-performing party to make another attempt at performance. As indicated in para. (2), cure is not precluded merely because the failure to perform amounts to a fundamental non-performance. The factors to be considered in determining the appropriateness of cure include whether the proposed cure promises to be successful in resolving the problem and whether the necessary or probable delay in effecting cure would be unreasonable or would itself constitute a fundamental non-performance. However, the right to cure is not defeated by the fact that the aggrieved party subsequently changes its position. If the non-performing party gives effective notice of cure, the aggrieved party's right to change position is suspended. Nonetheless, the situation may be different if the aggrieved party has changed position before receiving notice of cure.

4. The aggrieved party's interest

The non-performing party may not cure if the aggrieved party can demonstrate a legitimate interest in refusing cure. However, if notice of cure is properly given and if cure is appropriate in the circumstances, it is presumed that the non-performing party should be permitted to cure. A legitimate interest may arise, for example, if it is likely that, when attempting cure, the non-performing party will cause damage to person or property. On the other hand, a legitimate interest is not present if, on the basis of the non-performance, the aggrieved party has simply decided that it does not wish to continue contractual relations.

Illustration

1. A agrees to construct a road on B's property. When the road is complete, B discovers that the road grade is steeper than the contract permits. B also discovers that, during construction, A's trucks caused damage to B's timber. A gives notice of cure to regrade the road. Even if cure would otherwise be appropriate in

the circumstances, B's desire to prevent further damage to the timber may provide a legitimate interest for refusing cure.

5. Timing of cure

Cure must be effected promptly after notice of cure is given. Time is of the essence in the exercise of the right to cure. The non-performing party is not permitted to lock the aggrieved party into an extended waiting period. The lack of inconvenience on the part of the aggrieved party does not justify the non-performing party in delaying cure.

6. Proper forms of cure

Cure may include repair and replacement as well as any other activities that remedy the non-performance and give to the aggrieved party all that it is entitled to expect under the contract. Repairs constitute cure only when they leave no evidence of the prior non-performance and do not threaten the value or the quality of the product as a whole. It is left to the courts to determine the number of times the non-performing party may attempt a cure.

Illustration

2. A agrees to install an assembly line for high temperature enamel painting in B's factory. The motors are installed with insufficient lubricant and as a result "lock up" after a few hours of operation. A replaces the motors in a timely fashion, but refuses to examine and test the rest of the equipment to ensure that other parts of the line have not been damaged. A has not effectively cured.

7. Suspension of other remedies

When the non-performing party has given effective notice of cure, the aggrieved party may, in accordance with para. (4), withhold its own performance but, pursuant to para. (3), may not exercise any remedies inconsistent with the non-performing party's right to cure until it becomes clear that a timely and proper cure has not been or will not be effected. Inconsistent remedies include giving notice of termination, entering into replacement transactions and seeking damages or restitution.

8. Effect of a notice of termination

If the aggrieved party has rightfully terminated the contract pursuant to Arts. 7.3.1(1) and 7.3.2(1), the effects of termination (Art. 7.3.5) are also suspended by an effective notice of cure. If the non-performance is cured, the notice of termination is inoperative. On the other hand, termination takes effect if the time for cure has expired and any fundamental non-performance has not been cured.

9. Right of aggrieved party to damages

Under para. (5) of this article, even a non-performing party who successfully cures is liable for any harm that, before cure, was occasioned by the non-performance, as well as for any additional harm caused by the cure itself or by the delay or for any harm which the cure does not prevent. The principle of full compensation for damage suffered, as provided in Art. 7.4.2, is fundamental to these Principles.

10. The aggrieved party's obligations

The decision to invoke this article rests on the non-performing party. Once the aggrieved party receives effective notice of cure, it must permit cure and, as provided in Art. 5.1.3, cooperate with the non-performing party. For example, the aggrieved party must permit any inspection that is reasonably necessary for the non-performing party to effect cure. If the aggrieved party refuses to permit cure when required to do so, any notice of termination is ineffective. Moreover, the aggrieved party may not seek remedies for any non-performance that could have been cured.

Illustration

3. A agrees to construct a shed on B's property in order to protect B's machinery from the weather. The roof is constructed in a defective manner. During a storm, water leaks into the shed and B's machinery is damaged. B gives notice of termination. A gives timely notice of cure. B does not wish to deal further with A and refuses the cure. If cure is appropriate in the circumstances and the other conditions for cure are met, B cannot invoke remedies for the faulty construction but can recover for damage caused to the machinery before the cure was to be effected. If cure is inappropriate in the circumstances, or if the proposed cure could not have solved the problem, the contract is terminated by B's notice.

Issues & Cases

1. RIGHT TO CURE NON-PERFORMANCE (SEE ALSO ART. 5.1.3)

- MARCH 20, 2000 ARBITRAL AWARD INTERNATIONAL CENTRE FOR SETTLEMENT OF INVESTMENT DISPUTES (ICSID) (ARB(AF)/98/1) [826]

1.1 NOTICE OF CURE
1.2 APPROPRIATENESS OF CURE
1.3 PROMPTNESS OF CURE
1.4 PROPER FORMS OF CURE
1.5 AGGRIEVED PARTY'S INTEREST TO REFUSE CURE
2. RIGHT TO CURE NOT IMPAIRED BY NOTICE OF TERMINATION
3. SUSPENSION OF REMEDIES INCONSISTENT WITH CURE DURING TIME OF CURE
4. RIGHT TO DAMAGES NOT IMPAIRED

ARTICLE 7.1.5
(Additional period for performance)

(1) In a case of non-performance the aggrieved party may by notice to the other party allow an additional period of time for performance.

(2) During the additional period the aggrieved party may withhold performance of its own reciprocal obligations and may claim damages but may not resort to any other remedy. If it receives notice from the other party that the latter will not perform within that period, or if upon expiry of that period due performance has not been made, the aggrieved party may resort to any of the remedies that may be available under this Chapter.

(3) Where in a case of delay in performance which is not fundamental the aggrieved party has given notice allowing an additional period of time of reasonable length, it may terminate the contract at the end of that period. If the additional period allowed is not of reasonable length it shall be extended to a reasonable length. The aggrieved party may in its notice provide that if the other party fails to perform within the period allowed by the notice the contract shall automatically terminate.

(4) Paragraph (3) does not apply where the obligation which has not been performed is only a minor part of the contractual obligation of the non-performing party.

COMMENT

This article deals with the situation where one party performs late and the other party is willing to give extra time for performance. It is inspired by the German concept of *Nachfrist* although similar results are obtained by different conceptual means in other legal systems.

1. Special characteristics of late performance

The article recognises that late performance is significantly different from other forms of defective performance. Late performance can never be remedied since once the date for performance has passed it will not occur again, but nevertheless in many cases the party who is entitled to performance will much prefer even a late performance to no performance at all. Secondly, at the moment when a party fails to perform on time it is often unclear how late performance will in fact be. The commercial interest of the party receiving performance may often therefore be that a reasonably speedy completion, although late, will be perfectly acceptable but that a long delayed completion will not. The procedure enables that party to give the performing party a second chance without prejudicing its other remedies.

2. Effects of granting extension of time for performance

The party who grants the extension of time cannot terminate or seek specific performance during the extension time. The right to recover damages arising from late performance is not affected.

The position at the end of the period of extension depends on whether the late performance was already fundamental at the time when the extension was granted. In this situation, if the contract is not completely performed during the extension, the right to terminate for fundamental non-performance simply springs into life again as soon as the extension period expires. On the other hand, if the late performance was not yet fundamental, termination would only be possible at the end of the period of extension if the extension was reasonable in length.

Illustrations

1. A agrees to construct a special bullet-proof body for B's Rolls Royce. The contract provides that the body is to be finished by 1 February so that the car can be shipped to B's country of residence. On 31 January the car is needed but not yet quite finished. A assures B that it will be able to complete the work if given another week and B agrees to a week's extension of time. If the car is finished within the week B must accept it but may recover any damages, for example extra shipping charges. If the work is not finished within the week, B may refuse to accept delivery and terminate the contract.

2. A, a company in country X, concludes a contract with B, a company in country Y, to build 100 km. of motorway in the latter country. The contract provides that the motorway will be finished within two years from the start of the work. After two years, A has in fact built 85 km. and it is clear that it will take at least three more months to finish the motorway. B gives A notice to complete within a further month. B is not entitled to terminate at the end of the month because the additional period of time is not reasonable; it shall be extended to the reasonable period of three months.

Issues & Cases

1. AGGRIEVED PARTY FIXING ADDITIONAL TIME FOR PERFORMANCE
    - MARCH 20, 2000 ARBITRAL AWARD INTERNATIONAL CENTRE FOR SETTLEMENT OF INVESTMENT DISPUTES (ICSID) (NO. ARB(AF)/98/1) [826]

    1.1 CONSEQUENCE OF FIXING ADDITIONAL TIME
        1.1.1 DURING ADDITIONAL TIME AGGRIEVED PARTY ENTITLED TO WITHHOLD PERFORMANCE AND TO CLAIM DAMAGES BUT NOT TO RESORT TO OTHER REMEDIES
        1.1.2 UPON EXPIRATION OF ADDITIONAL TIME AGGRIEVED PARTY ENTITLED TO RESORT TO ANY REMEDY
2. EXTENSION OF TIME FOR PERFORMANCE IN CASE OF DELAY NOT AMOUNTING TO FUNDAMENTAL NON-PERFORMANCE
    2.1 UPON EXPIRATION OF ADDITIONAL TIME AGGRIEVED PARTY'S RIGHT TO TERMINATE CONTRACT
        2.1.1 CONDITIONS

ARTICLE 7.1.6
(Exemption clauses)

A clause which limits or excludes one party's liability for non-performance or which permits one party to render performance substantially different from what the other party reasonably expected may not be invoked if it would be grossly unfair to do so, having regard to the purpose of the contract.

COMMENT

1. The need for a special rule on exemption clauses

The Principles contain no general rule permitting a court to strike down abusive or unconscionable contract terms. Apart from the principle of good faith and fair dealing (Art. 1.7) which may exceptionally be invoked in this respect, there is only one provision permitting the avoidance at any time of the contract as a whole as well as of any of its individual terms when they unjustifiably give one party an excessive advantage (Art. 3.10).

The reason for the inclusion of a specific provision on exemption clauses is that they are particularly common in international contract practice and tend to give rise to much controversy between the parties.

Ultimately, the present article has opted in favour of a rule which gives the court a broad discretionary power based on the principle of fairness. Terms regulating the consequences of non-performance are in principle valid but the court may ignore clauses which are grossly unfair.

2. "Exemption clauses" defined

For the purpose of this article exemption clauses are in the first instance those terms which directly limit or exclude the non-performing party's liability in the event of non-performance. Such clauses may be expressed in different ways (*e.g.* fixed sum, ceiling, percentage of the performance in question, deposit retained).

Exemption clauses are further considered to be those which permit a party to render a performance substantially different from what the other party reasonably expected. In practice clauses of this kind are in particular those whose purpose or effect is to allow the performing party unilaterally to alter the character of the performance promised in such a way as to transform the contract. Such clauses are to be distinguished from those which are limited to defining the performance undertaken by the party in question.

Illustration

1. A tour operator offers at a high price a tour providing for accommodation in specifically designated luxury hotels. A term of the contract provides that the operator may alter the accommodation if the circumstances so require. If the operator puts up its clients in second class hotels, it will be liable to them notwithstanding the contractual term since the clients expected to be accommodated in hotels of a category similar to that which had been promised.

2. A hotelkeeper exhibits a notice to the effect that the hotel is responsible for cars left in the garage but not for objects contained in the cars. This term is not an exemption clause for the purpose of this article since its purpose is merely that of defining the scope of the hotelkeeper's obligation.

3. Exemption clauses to be distinguished from forfeiture clauses

Exemption clauses are to be distinguished from forfeiture clauses which permit a party to withdraw from a contract on payment of an indemnity. In practice, however, there may be forfeiture clauses which are in reality intended by the parties to operate as disguised exemption clauses.

4. Exemption clauses and agreed payment for non-performance

A contract term providing that a party who does not perform is to pay a specified sum to the aggrieved party for such non-performance (see Art. 7.4.13) may also have the effect of limiting the compensation due to the aggrieved party. In such cases the non-performing party may not be entitled to rely on the term in question if the conditions laid down in the present article are satisfied.

Illustration

3. A enters into a contract with B for the building of a factory. The contract contains a penalty clause providing for payment of 10,000 Australian dollars for each week of delay. The work is not completed within the agreed period because A deliberately suspends the work for another project which was more lucrative for it and in respect of which the penalty for delay was higher. The actual harm suffered by B as a result of the delay amounts to 20,000 Australian dollars per week. A is not entitled to rely on the penalty clause and B may recover full compensation of the actual harm sustained, as the enforcement of that clause would in the circumstances be grossly unfair in view of A's deliberate non-performance.

5. Cases where exemption clauses may not be relied upon

Following the approach adopted in most national legal systems this article starts out from the assumption that in application of the doctrine of freedom of contract (Art. 1.1) exemption clauses are in principle valid. A party may not however invoke such a clause if it would be grossly unfair to do so.

This will above all be the case where the term is inherently unfair and its application would lead to an evident imbalance between the performances of the parties. Moreover, there may be circumstances in which even a term that is not in itself manifestly unfair may not be relied upon: for instance, where the non-performance is the result of grossly negligent conduct or where the aggrieved party could not have obviated the consequences of the limitation or exclusion of liability by taking out appropriate insurance.

In all cases regard must be had to the purpose of the contract and in particular to what a party could legitimately have expected from the performance of the contract.

Illustrations

4. A, an accountant, undertakes to prepare B's accounts. The contract contains a term excluding any liability of A for the consequences arising from any inaccuracy whatsoever in A's performance of the contract. As a result of a serious mistake by A, B pays 100% more taxes than were due. A may not rely on the exemption clause which is inherently unfair.

5. A, a warehouse operator, enters into a contract with B for the surveillance of its premises. The contract contains a term limiting B's liability. Thefts occur in the terminal resulting in loss exceeding the amount of the limitation. Although the term, agreed upon by two professional parties, is not inherently unfair, it may not be relied upon by B if the thefts are committed by B's servants in the course of their employment.

6. Consequence of inability to rely on exemption clauses

If a party is not entitled to rely on an exemption clause, its liability is unaffected and the aggrieved party may obtain full compensation for the non-performance. Contrary to the rule laid down with respect to agreed payment for non-performance in Art. 7.4.13, the court has no power to modify the exemption clause.

Issues & Cases

1. EXEMPTION CLAUSES DEFINED

1.1 CLAUSES LIMITING OR EXCLUDING LIABILITY FOR NON-PERFORMANCE

1.2 CLAUSES PERMITTING TO RENDER PERFORMANCE SUBSTANTIALLY DIFFERENT FROM WHAT OTHER PARTY REASONABLY EXPECTED
2. CASES WHERE EXEMPTION CLAUSES MAY NOT BE RELIED UPON
3. EXEMPTION CLAUSES TO BE DISTINGUISHED FROM CLAUSES PROVIDING THE PAYMENT OF A FIXED SUM IN CASE OF NON-PERFORMANCE (SEE ART. 7.4.13)
4. EXEMPTION CLAUSES TO BE DISTINGUISHED FROM FORFEITURE CLAUSES

ARTICLE 7.1.7
(Force majeure)

(1) Non-performance by a party is excused if that party proves that the non-performance was due to an impediment beyond its control and that it could not reasonably be expected to have taken the impediment into account at the time of the conclusion of the contract or to have avoided or overcome it or its consequences.

(2) When the impediment is only temporary, the excuse shall have effect for such period as is reasonable having regard to the effect of the impediment on the performance of the contract.

(3) The party who fails to perform must give notice to the other party of the impediment and its effect on its ability to perform. If the notice is not received by the other party within a reasonable time after the party who fails to perform knew or ought to have known of the impediment, it is liable for damages resulting from such non-receipt.

(4) Nothing in this article prevents a party from exercising a right to terminate the contract or to withhold performance or request interest on money due.

COMMENT

1. The notion of force majeure

This article covers the ground covered in common law systems by the doctrines of frustration and impossibility of performance and in civil law systems by doctrines such as force majeure, *Unmöglichkeit,* etc. but it is identical with none of these doctrines. The term "force majeure" was chosen because it is widely known in international trade practice, as confirmed by the inclusion in many international contracts of so-called "force majeure" clauses.

Illustration

1. A, a manufacturer in country X, sells a nuclear power station to B, a utility company in country Y. Under the terms of the contract A undertakes to supply all the power station's requirements of uranium for ten years at a price fixed for that

period, expressed in United States dollars and payable in New York. The following separate events occur:

(1) After five years the currency of country Y collapses to 1% of its value against the dollar at the time of the contract. B is not discharged from liability as the parties have allocated this risk by the payment provisions.

(2) After five years the government of country Y imposes foreign exchange controls which prevent B paying in any currency other than that of country Y. B is excused from paying in United States dollars. A is entitled to terminate the contract to supply uranium.

(3) After five years the world uranium market is cornered by a group of Texan speculators. The price of uranium on the world market rises to ten times the contract figure. A is not excused from delivering uranium as this is a risk which was foreseeable at the time of making the contract.

2. Effects of force majeure on the rights and duties of the parties

The article does not restrict the rights of the party who has not received performance to terminate if the non-performance is fundamental. What it does do, where it applies, is to excuse the non-performing party from liability in damages.

In some cases the impediment will prevent any performance at all but in many others it will simply delay performance and the effect of the article will be to give extra time for performance. It should be noted that in this event the extra time may be greater (or less) than the length of the interruption because the crucial question will be what is the effect of the interruption on the progress of the contract.

Illustration

2. A contracts to lay a natural gas pipeline across country X. Climatic conditions are such that it is normally impossible to work between 1 November and 31 March. The contract is timed to finish on 31 October but the start of work is delayed for a month by a civil war in a neighbouring country which makes it impossible to bring in all the piping on time. If the consequence is reasonably to prevent the completion of the work until its resumption in the following spring, A may be entitled to an extension of five months even though the delay was itself of one month only.

3. Force majeure and hardship

The article must be read together with Chapter 6, Section 2 of the Principles dealing with hardship. See comment 6 on Art. 6.2.2.

4. Force majeure and contract practice

The definition of force majeure in para. (1) of this article is necessarily of a rather general character. International commercial contracts often contain much more precise and elaborate provisions in this regard. The parties may therefore find it appropriate to adapt the content of this article so as to take account of the particular features of the specific transaction.

Issues & Cases

1. EXEMPTION FOR NON-PERFORMANCE
   1.1 IMPEDIMENT AMOUNTING TO EXEMPTION
      - SEPTEMBER 23, 1997 UNITED NATIONS COMPENSATION, PANEL F1 (NO. S/AC.26) [703]

      1.1.1 CONDUCT BY BREACHING PARTY
      1.1.2 STRIKE
      1.1.3 NON PERFORMANCE BY INDEPENDENT CONTRACTOR
      1.1.4 ACT OF PUBLIC AUTHORITIES
      1.1.5 OTHERS
      - SEPTEMBER 23, 1997 UNITED NATIONS COMPENSATION, PANEL F1 (NO. S/AC.26) [703]
   1.2 TEMPORARY IMPEDIMENT
2. OBLIGATION TO NOTIFY OTHER PARTY OF IMPEDIMENT
   2.1 TIME TO NOTICE
   2.2 FAILURE TO GIVE TIMELY NOTICE
3. CONSEQUENCE OF IMPEDIMENT ON REMEDIES
   - SEPTEMBER 23, 1997 UNITED NATIONS COMPENSATION, PANEL F1 (NO. S/AC.26) [703]

   3.1 TERMINATION OF CONTRACT
   - SEPTEMBER 23, 1997 UNITED NATIONS COMPENSATION, PANEL F1 (NO. S/AC.26) [703]

   3.2 WITHHOLDING OF PERFORMANCE
   3.3 INTEREST ON MONEY DUE
   3.4 SPECIFIC PERFORMANCE
   3.5 DAMAGES
4. EXEMPTION FOR NON-PERFORMANCE AND HARDSHIP (SEE ARTS. 6.2.1 – 6.2.3)
   - -- ARBITRAL AWARD AD HOC ARBITRATION (PLACE UNKNOWN) [544]
5. EXEMPTION FOR NON-PERFORMANCE AND EXEMPTION CLAUSES (SEE ART. 7.1.6)

SECTION 2 : RIGHT TO PERFORMANCE

BIBLIOGRAPHY

CASTRONOVO C., Inadempimento ed esatto adempimento nei Principi UNIDROIT, in BONELL M.J. / BONELLI F. (eds.), Contratti commerciali internazionali e Principi UNIDROIT, Giuffré, Milano 1997, 271-294.

CONTERAS VACA F.J., Resolución del contrato por incumplimiento, in Contratación internacional, Comentarios a los principios sobre los Contratos Comerciales Internacionales del UNIDROIT, Universidad Nacional Autónoma de México – Universidad Panamericana (ed.) 1998, 135-174.

EBERHARD S., Les sanctions de l'inexécution du contrat et les Principes UNIDROIT, Lausanne 2005, 323.

LANDO O., The CISG and the UNIDROIT Principles in a Global Commercial Code, in Mélanges offerts à Marcel Fontaine, Paris, Larcier, 2003, 451 – 472.

MEDICUS D., Voraussetzungen einer Haftung für Vertragsverletzung, in BASEDOW J. (ed.), Europäische Vertragsvereinheitlichung und deutsches Recht, 179 – 193.

MORAN BOVIO D., Incumplimiento, in Comentario a los Principios de UNIDROIT para los Contratos del Comercio Internacional, Aranzadi, Pamplona, 1999, 317-388.

SCHWENZER I., Specific Performance and Damages According to the 1994 UNIDROIT Principles of International Commercial Contracts, in 1 European Journal of Law Reform, n. 3, 289-303.

VAN DER MERSCH M. – PHILIPPE D., L'inexécution dans les contrats du commerce international, in FONTAINE M. – VINEY G. (eds.), Les sanctions de l'inexécution des obligations contractuelles, Bruxelles – Paris 2001, 701 – 785.

ZAHRAA M. – GHITH A.A., Specific performance in the light of the CISG, the UNIDROIT Principles and Libyan Law, in Uniform Law Review / Revue de droit uniforme, 7 (2002), 751 – 774.

ARTICLE 7.2.1
(Performance of monetary obligation)

Where a party who is obliged to pay money does not do so, the other party may require payment.

COMMENT

This article reflects the generally accepted principle that payment of money which is due under a contractual obligation can always be demanded and, if the demand is not met, enforced by legal action before a court. The term "require" is used in this article to cover both the demand addressed to the other party and the enforcement, whenever necessary, of such a demand by a court.

The article applies irrespective of the currency in which payment is due or may be made. In other words, the right of the obligee to require payment extends also to cases of payment in a foreign currency. For the determination of the currency in which a monetary obligation is due or payment may be made, see Arts. 6.1.9, 6.1.10 and 7.4.12.

Exceptionally, the right to require payment of the price of the goods or services to be delivered or rendered may be excluded. This is in particular the case where a usage requires a seller to resell goods which are neither accepted nor paid for by the buyer. For the applicability of usages, see Art. 1.9.

Issues & Cases

1. RIGHT TO REQUIRE PERFORMANCE OF MONETARY OBLIGATION
   1.1 CURRENCY OF PAYMENT (SEE ARTS. 6.1.9, 6.1.10 AND 7.4.12)

ARTICLE 7.2.2
(Performance of non-monetary obligation)

Where a party who owes an obligation other than one to pay money does not perform, the other party may require performance, unless

(a) performance is impossible in law or in fact;

(b) performance or, where relevant, enforcement is unreasonably burdensome or expensive;

(c) the party entitled to performance may reasonably obtain performance from another source;

(d) performance is of an exclusively personal character; or

(e) the party entitled to performance does not require performance within a reasonable time after it has, or ought to have, become aware of the non-performance.

COMMENT

1. Right to require performance of non-monetary obligations

In accordance with the general principle of the binding character of the contract (see Art. 1.3), each party should as a rule be entitled to require performance by the other party not only of monetary, but also of non-monetary obligations, assumed by that party. While this is not controversial in civil law countries, common law systems allow enforcement of non-monetary obligations only in special circumstances.

Following the basic approach of CISG (Art. 46) this article adopts the principle of specific performance, subject to certain qualifications.

The principle is particularly important with respect to contracts other than sales contracts. Unlike the obligation to deliver something, contractual obligations to do something or to abstain from doing something can often be performed only by the other contracting party itself. In such cases the only way of obtaining performance from a party who is unwilling to perform is by enforcement.

2. Remedy not discretionary

While CISG provides that "a court is not bound to enter a judgement for specific performance unless the court would do so under its own law in respect of similar contracts of sale not governed by [the] Convention" (Art. 28), under the Principles specific performance is not a discretionary remedy, *i.e.* a court must order performance, unless one of the exceptions laid down in the present article applies.

3. Exceptions to the right to require performance

a. *Impossibility*

A performance which is impossible in law or in fact, cannot be required (sub-para. (a)). However, impossibility does not nullify a contract: other remedies may be available to the aggrieved party. See Arts. 3.3 and 7.1.7(4).

The refusal of a public permission which is required under the applicable domestic law and which affects the validity of the contract renders the contract void (see Art. 6.1.17(1)), with the consequence that the problem of enforceability of the performance cannot arise. When however the refusal merely renders the performance impossible without affecting the validity of the contract (see Art. 6.1.17(2)), sub-para. (a) of this article applies and performance cannot be required.

b. *Unreasonable burden*

In exceptional cases, particularly when there has been a drastic change of circumstances after the conclusion of a contract, performance, although still possible, may have become so onerous that it would run counter to the general principle of good faith and fair dealing (Art. 1.7) to require it.

Illustration

1. An oil tanker has sunk in coastal waters in a heavy storm. Although it would be possible to lift the ship from the bottom of the sea, the shipper may not require performance of the contract of carriage if this would involve the shipowner in expense vastly exceeding the value of the oil. See Art. 7.2.2(b).

The words "where relevant, enforcement" take account of the fact that in common law systems it is the courts and not the obligees who supervise the execution of orders for specific performance. As a consequence, in certain cases, especially those involving performances extended in time, courts in those countries refuse specific performance if supervision would impose undue burdens upon courts.

As to other possible consequences arising from drastic changes of circumstances amounting to a case of hardship, see Arts. 6.2.1 *et seq*.

c. *Replacement transaction*

Many goods and services are of a standard kind, *i.e.* the same goods or services are offered by many suppliers. If a contract for such staple goods or standard services is not performed, most customers will not wish to waste time and effort extracting the contractual performance from the other party. Instead, they will go into the market, obtain substitute goods or services and claim damages for non-performance.

In view of this economic reality sub-para. (c) excludes specific performance whenever the party entitled to performance may reasonably obtain performance from another source. That party may terminate the contract and conclude a replacement transaction. See Art. 7.4.5.

The word "reasonably" indicates that the mere fact that the same performance can be obtained from another source is not in itself sufficient, since the aggrieved party could not in certain circumstances reasonably be expected to have recourse to an alternative supplier.

Illustration

2. A, situated in a developing country where foreign exchange is scarce, buys a machine of a standard type from B in Tokyo. In compliance with the contract, A pays the price of US $100,000 before delivery. B does not deliver. Although A could obtain the machine from another source in Japan, it would be unreasonable, in view of the scarcity and high price of foreign exchange in its home country, to require A to take this course. A is therefore entitled to require delivery of the machine from B.

d. *Performance of an exclusively personal character*

Where a performance has an exclusively personal character, enforcement would interfere with the personal freedom of the obligor. Moreover, enforcement of a performance often impairs its quality. The supervision of a very personal performance may also give rise to insuperable practical difficulties, as is shown by the experience of countries which have saddled their courts with this kind of responsibility. For all these reasons, sub-para. (d) excludes enforcement of performance of an exclusively personal character.

The precise scope of this exception depends essentially upon the meaning of the phrase "exclusively personal character". The modern tendency is to confine this concept to performances of a unique character. The exception does not apply to obligations undertaken by a company. Nor are ordinary activities of a lawyer, a surgeon or an engineer covered by the phrase for they can be performed by other persons with the same training and experience. A performance is of an exclusively personal character if it is not delegable and requires individual skills of an artistic or scientific nature or if it involves a confidential and personal relationship.

Illustrations

3. An undertaking by a firm of architects to design a row of 10 private homes can be specifically enforced as the firm can delegate

the task to one of the partners or employ an outside architect to perform it.

4. By contrast, an undertaking by a world-famous architect to design a new city hall embodying the idea of a city of the 21st century cannot be enforced because it is highly unique and calls for the exercise of very special skills.

The performance of obligations to abstain from doing something does not fall under sub-para. (d).

e. *Request within reasonable time*

Performance of a contract often requires special preparation and efforts by the obligor. If the time for performance has passed but the obligee has failed to demand performance within a reasonable time, the obligor may be entitled to assume that the obligee will not insist upon performance. If the obligee were to be allowed to leave the obligor in a state of uncertainty as to whether performance will be required, the risk might arise of the obligee's speculating unfairly, to the detriment of the obligor, upon a favourable development of the market.

For these reasons sub-para. (e) excludes the right to performance if it is not required within a reasonable time after the obligee has become, or ought to have become, aware of the non-performance.

For a similar rule concerning the loss of the right to terminate the contract, see Art. 7.3.2(2).

Issues & Cases

1. **RIGHT TO REQUIRE PERFORMANCE OF NON-MONETARY OBLIGATIONS**
   - 1.1 **EXCEPTIONS**
     - 1.1.1 **IMPOSSIBILITY OF PERFORMANCE**
     - 1.1.2 **PERFORMANCE TOO ONEROUS**
     - 1.1.3 **POSSIBILITY TO OBTAIN PERFORMANCE FROM ANOTHER SOURCE**
     - 1.1.4 **EXCLUSIVELY PERSONAL CHARACTER OF PERFORMANCE**
     - 1.1.5 **PERFORMANCE NOT REQUIRED WITHIN REASONABLE TIME**

ARTICLE 7.2.3
(Repair and replacement of defective performance)

The right to performance includes in appropriate cases the right to require repair, replacement, or other cure of defective performance. The provisions of Articles 7.2.1 and 7.2.2 apply accordingly.

COMMENT

1. Right to performance in case of defective performance

This article applies the general principles of Arts. 7.2.1 and 7.2.2 to a special, yet very frequent, case of non-performance, *i.e.* defective performance. For the sake of clarity the article specifies that the right to require performance includes the right of the party who has received a defective performance to require cure of the defect.

2. Cure of defective performance

Under the Principles cure denotes the right both of the non-performing party to correct its performance (Art. 7.1.4) and of the aggrieved party to require such correction by the non-performing party. The present article deals with the latter right.

The article expressly mentions two specific examples of cure, namely repair and replacement. Repairing defective goods (or making good an insufficient service) is the most common case and replacement of a defective performance is also frequent. The right to require repair or replacement may also exist with respect to the payment of money, for instance in case of an insufficient payment or of a payment in the wrong currency or to an account different from that agreed upon by the parties.

Apart from repair and replacement there are other forms of cure, such as the removal of the rights of third persons over goods or the obtaining of a necessary public permission.

3. Restrictions

The right to require cure of a defective performance is subject to the same limitations as the right to performance in general.

Most of the exceptions to the right to require performance that are set out in Art. 7.2.2 are easily applicable to the various forms of cure of a defective performance. Only the application of sub-para. (b) calls for specific comment. In many cases involving small, insignificant defects, both replacement and repair may involve "unreasonable effort or expense" and are therefore excluded.

Illustration

A new car is sold which has a small painting defect which decreases the value of the car by 0.01 % of the purchase price. Repainting would cost 0.5% of the purchase price. A claim for repair is excluded but the buyer is entitled to require a reduction in the purchase price.

Issues & Cases

1. **RIGHT TO REQUIRE CURE IN CASE OF DEFECTIVE PERFORMANCE**
    1.1 **REPAIR**
    1.2 **REPLACEMENT**
    1.3 **OTHER CURE**
2. **RESTRICTIONS TO THE RIGHT TO REQUIRE CURE**

ARTICLE 7.2.4
(Judicial penalty)

(1) Where the court orders a party to perform, it may also direct that this party pay a penalty if it does not comply with the order.

(2) The penalty shall be paid to the aggrieved party unless mandatory provisions of the law of the forum provide otherwise. Payment of the penalty to the aggrieved party does not exclude any claim for damages.

COMMENT

1. Judicially imposed penalty

Experience in some legal systems has shown that the threat of a judicially imposed penalty for disobedience is a most effective means of ensuring compliance with judgments ordering the performance of contractual obligations. Other systems, on the contrary, do not provide for such sanctions because they are considered to constitute an inadmissible encroachment upon personal freedom.

The present article takes a middle course by providing for monetary but not for other forms of penalties, applicable to all kinds of orders for performance including those for payment of money.

2. Imposition of penalty at discretion of the court

The use of the word "may" in para. (1) of this article makes it clear that the imposition of a penalty is a matter of discretion for the court. Its exercise depends upon the kind of obligation to be performed. In the case of money judgments, a penalty should be imposed only in exceptional situations, especially where speedy payment is essential for the aggrieved party. The same is true for obligations to deliver goods. Obligations to pay money or to deliver goods can normally be easily enforced by ordinary means of execution. By contrast, in the case of obligations to do or to abstain from doing something, which moreover cannot easily be performed by a third person, enforcement by means of judicial penalties is often the most appropriate solution.

3. Beneficiary

Legal systems differ as to the question of whether judicial penalties should be paid to the aggrieved party, to the State, or to both. Some systems regard payment to the aggrieved party as constituting an unjustified windfall benefit which is contrary to public policy.

While rejecting this latter view and indicating the aggrieved party as the beneficiary of the penalty, the first sentence of para. (2) of this article expressly mentions the possibility of mandatory provisions of the law of the forum not permitting such a solution and indicating other possible beneficiaries of judicial penalties.

4. Judicial penalties distinguished from damages and from agreed payment for non-performance

The second sentence of para. (2) makes it clear that a judicial penalty paid to the aggrieved party does not affect its claim for damages. Payment of the penalty is regarded as compensating the aggrieved party for those disadvantages which cannot be taken into account under the ordinary rules for the recovery of damages. Moreover, since payment of damages will usually occur substantially later than payment of a judicial penalty, courts may to some degree be able, in measuring the damages, to take the payment of the penalty into account.

Judicial penalties are moreover to be distinguished from agreed payments for non-performance which are dealt with in Art. 7.4.13, although the latter fulfil a function similar to that of the former. If the court considers that the contractual stipulation of the payment of a sum in case of non-performance already provides a sufficient incentive for performance, it may refuse to impose a judicial penalty.

5. Form and procedure

A judicial penalty may be imposed in the form of a lump sum payment or of a payment by instalments.

The procedure relating to the imposition of a judicial penalty is governed by the *lex fori*.

6. Penalties imposed by arbitrators

Since according to Art. 1.11 "court" includes an arbitral tribunal, the question arises of whether arbitrators might also be allowed to impose a penalty.

While a majority of legal systems seems to deny such a power to arbitrators, some modern legislation and recent court practice have recognised it. This solution, which is in keeping with the increasingly important role of arbitration as an alternative means of dispute resolution, especially in international commerce, is endorsed by the Principles. Since the execution of a penalty imposed by arbitrators can only be effected by, or with the assistance of, a court, appropriate supervision is available to prevent any possible abuse of the arbitrators' power.

7. Recognition and enforcement of decisions imposing penalties

Attention must be drawn to the problems of recognition and enforcement, in countries other than the forum State, of judicial decisions and of arbitral awards imposing penalties. Special rules on this matter are sometimes to be found in national law and to some extent in international treaties.

Issues & Cases

1. **JUDICIAL PENALTY IMPOSED BY COURT**
   - 1.1 **JUDICIAL PENALTY TO BE PAID TO AGGRIEVED PARTY**
     - 1.1.1 **EXCEPTIONS DUE TO MANDATORY PROVISIONS OF LEX FORI**
2. **JUDICIAL PENALTY DOES NOT EXCLUDE CLAIM FOR DAMAGES**

ARTICLE 7.2.5
(Change of remedy)

(1) An aggrieved party who has required performance of a non-monetary obligation and who has not received performance within a period fixed or otherwise within a reasonable period of time may invoke any other remedy.

(2) Where the decision of a court for performance of a non-monetary obligation cannot be enforced, the aggrieved party may invoke any other remedy.

COMMENT

1. Aggrieved party entitled to change of remedy

This article addresses a problem which is peculiar to the right to require performance. The aggrieved party may abandon the remedy of requiring performance of a non-monetary obligation and opt instead for another remedy or remedies.

This choice is permitted on account of the difficulties usually involved in the enforcement of non-monetary obligations. Even if the aggrieved party first decides to invoke its right to require performance, it would not be fair to confine that party to this single option. The non-performing party may subsequently become unable to perform, or its inability may only become evident during the proceedings.

2. Voluntary change of remedy

Two situations must be addressed.

In the first case, the aggrieved party has required performance but changes its mind before execution of a judgment in its favour, perhaps because it has discovered the non-performing party's inability to perform. The aggrieved party now wishes to invoke one or more other remedies. Such a voluntary change of remedy can only be admitted if the interests of the non-performing party are duly protected. It may have prepared for performance, invested effort and incurred expense. For this reason para. (1) of this article makes it clear that the aggrieved party is entitled to invoke another remedy only if it has not received performance within a fixed period or otherwise within a reasonable period of time.

How much additional time must be made available to the non-performing party for performance depends upon the difficulty which the performance involves. The non-performing party has the right to perform provided it does so before the expiry of the additional period.

For similar conditions which restrict the right of termination in case of delay in performance, see Art. 7.3.2(2).

3. Unenforceable decision

Para. (2) addresses the second and less difficult case in which the aggrieved party has attempted without success to enforce a judicial decision or arbitral award directing the non-performing party to perform. In this situation it is obvious that the aggrieved party may immediately pursue other remedies.

4. Time limits

In the event of a subsequent change of remedy the time limit provided for a notice of termination under Art. 7.3.2(2) must, of course, be extended accordingly. The reasonable time for giving notice begins to run, in the case of a voluntary change of remedy, after the aggrieved party has or ought to have become aware of the non-performance at the expiry of the additional period of time available to the non-performing party to perform; and in the case of para. (2) of this article, it will begin to run after the aggrieved party has or ought to have become aware of the unenforceability of the decision or award requiring performance.

Issues & Cases

1. **REQUIRED PERFORMANCE NOT RECEIVED AFTER FIXED OR REASONABLE TIME PERIOD HAS EXPIRED**
   - JANUARY 25, 2002 ARBITRAL AWARD ARBITRATION COURT OF THE LAUSANNE CHAMBER OF COMMERCE AND INDUSTRY [991]

   1.1 **RIGHT TO INVOKE ANY OTHER REMEDY**
   - JANUARY 25, 2002 ARBITRAL AWARD ARBITRATION COURT OF THE LAUSANNE CHAMBER OF COMMERCE AND INDUSTRY [991]

2. **DECISION ON SPECIFIC PERFORMANCE NOT ENFORCEABLE IN DOMESTIC FORUM**

   2.1 **RIGHT TO INVOKE ANY OTHER REMEDY**

SECTION 3: TERMINATION

BIBLIOGRAPHY

BONELL M.J., A 'Global' arbitration decided on the basis of the UNIDROIT Principles: In re Andersen Consulting Business Unit Member Firms v. Arthur Andersen Business Unit Member Firms and Andersen Worldwide Société Coopérative, in 17 Arbitration International 2001, 249 – 261.

COEN C., Vertragsscheitern und Rückabwiklung. Eine rechtsvergleichende Untersuchung zum englishen und deutschen Recht, zum UN-Kaufrecht sowie zu den UNIDROIT Principles und den Principles of European Contract Law, Berlin, Dunker & Humblot, 2003, 455 (Beiträge zum europäischen Wirtshaftsrecht, 22).

CONTE, G., L'uniformazione della disciplina giuridica della risoluzione per inadempimento e, in particolare, della *anticipatory breach* dei contratti, in Europa e diritto privato, 1998, 463 – 492.

CONTRERAS VACA F.J., Resolución del contrato por incumplimiento, in Contratación internacional, Comentarios a los principios sobre los Contratos Comerciales Internacionales del UNIDROIT, Universidad Nacional Autónoma de México – Universidad Panamericana (ed.) 1998, 135-174.

DI MAJO A., Il regime delle restituzioni contrattuali nel diritto comparato ed europeo, in MAZZAMUTO S. (ed.), Il contratto e le tutele (2002), 223 – 442.

EBERHARD S., Les sanctions de l'inexécution du contrat et les Principes UNIDROIT, Lausanne 2005, 323.

FLESSNER A., Befreiung vom Vertrag wegen Nichterfüllung, in Zeitschrift für Europäisches Privatrecht 2, 1997, 255-320.

MORAN BOVIO D., Incumplimiento, in Comentario a los Principios de UNIDROIT para los Contratos del Comercio Internacional, Aranzadi, Pamplona, 1999, 317-388.

NGUYEN M.H., Les Principes UNIDROIT: Jurisprudence et expériences pour le Vietnam, in Revue de droit des affaires internationales / International Business Law, no. 5/2005, 619 – 636.

SCHLECHTRIEM P., Termination of Contracts under the Principles of International Commercial Contracts, in BONELL M.J. / BONELLI F. (eds.), Contratti commerciali internazionali e Principi UNIDROIT, Giuffré, Milano 1997, 247-269.

SCHLECHTRIEM P., Termination and Adjustment of Contracts, in 1 European Journal of Law Reform, n. 3, 1998-1999, 305-323.

SCHLECHTRIEM P., Abstandnahme vom Vertrag, in BASEDOW, J. (ed.), Europäische Vertragsrechtsvereinheitlichung und deutsches Recht, J.C.B. Mohr (Siebeck), Tübingen 2000, 159 – 177.

VAN DER MERSCH M. – PHILIPPE D., L'inéxecution dans les contrats du commerce international, in FONTAINE M. – VINEY G. (eds.), Les sanctions de l'inéxecution des obligations contractuelles, Bruxelles – Paris 2001, 701 – 785.

VAN VUUREN E.J., Termination of International Comercial Contracts for Breach of Contract: The Provisions of the UNIDROIT Principles of International Commercial

Contracts, in 15 Arizona Journal of International & Comparative Law, 1998, 583-634.

ZIMMERMANN R., *Restitutio in Integrum*: The Unwinding of Failed Contracts under the Principles of European Contract Law, the UNIDROIT Principles and the *Avant-projet* d'un *Code Européen des Contrats*, in Uniform Law Review 2005, 719 – 734.

ARTICLE 7.3.1
(Right to terminate the contract)

(1) A party may terminate the contract where the failure of the other party to perform an obligation under the contract amounts to a fundamental non-performance.

(2) In determining whether a failure to perform an obligation amounts to a fundamental non-performance regard shall be had, in particular, to whether

(a) the non-performance substantially deprives the aggrieved party of what it was entitled to expect under the contract unless the other party did not foresee and could not reasonably have foreseen such result;

(b) strict compliance with the obligation which has not been performed is of essence under the contract;

(c) the non-performance is intentional or reckless;

(d) the non-performance gives the aggrieved party reason to believe that it cannot rely on the other party's future performance;

(e) the non-performing party will suffer disproportionate loss as a result of the preparation or performance if the contract is terminated.

(3) In the case of delay the aggrieved party may also terminate the contract if the other party fails to perform before the time allowed it under Article 7.1.5 has expired.

COMMENT

1. Termination even if non-performance is excused

The rules set out in this Section are intended to apply both to cases where the non-performing party is liable for the non-performance and to those where the non-performance is excused so that the aggrieved party can claim neither specific performance nor damages for non-performance.

Illustration

1. A, a company located in country X, buys wine from B in country Y. The Government of country X subsequently imposes an embargo upon the import of agricultural products from country Y. Although the impediment cannot be attributed to A, B may terminate the contract.

2. Right to terminate the contract dependent on fundamental non-performance

Whether in a case of non-performance by one party the other party should have the right to terminate the contract depends upon the weighing of a number of considerations. On the one hand, performance may be so late or so defective that the aggrieved party cannot use it for its intended purpose, or the behaviour of the non-performing party may in other respects be such that the aggrieved party should be permitted to terminate the contract.

On the other hand, termination will often cause serious detriment to the non-performing party whose expenses in preparing and tendering performance may not be recovered.

For these reasons para. (1) of this article provides that an aggrieved party may terminate the contract only if the non-performance of the other party is "fundamental", *i.e.* material and not merely of minor importance. See also Arts. 7.3.3. and 7.3.4.

3. Circumstances of significance in determining whether non-performance is fundamental

Para. (2) of this article lists a number of circumstances which are relevant to the determination of whether, in a given case, failure to perform an obligation amounts to fundamental non-performance.

a. *Non-performance substantially depriving the other party of its expectations*

The first factor referred to in para. (2)(a) is that the non-performance is so fundamental that the aggrieved party is substantially deprived of what it was entitled to expect at the time of the conclusion of the contract.

Illustration

2. On 1 May A contracts to deliver standard software before 15 May to B who has requested speedy delivery. If A tenders

delivery on 15 June, B may refuse delivery and terminate the contract.

The aggrieved party cannot terminate the contract if the non-performing party can show that it did not foresee, and could not reasonably have foreseen, that the non-performance was fundamental for the other party.

Illustration

3. A undertakes to remove waste from B's site during 1992. B fails to inform A that B has hired excavators at high cost to begin work on the site on 2 January 1993. B cannot terminate its contract with A on the ground that A had not cleared the site on 2 January.

b. *Strict performance of contract of essence*

Para. (2)(b) looks not at the actual gravity of the non-performance but at the nature of the contractual obligation for which strict performance might be of essence. Such obligations of strict performance are not uncommon in commercial contracts. For example, in contracts for the sale of commodities the time of delivery is normally considered to be of the essence, and in a documentary credit transaction the documents tendered must conform strictly to the terms of the credit.

c. *Intentional non-performance*

Para. (2)(c) deals with the situation where the non-performance is intentional or reckless. It may, however, be contrary to good faith (Art. 1.7) to terminate a contract if the non-performance, even though committed intentionally, is insignificant.

d. *No reliance on future performance*

Under para. (2)(d) the fact that non-performance gives the aggrieved party reason to believe that it cannot rely on the other party's future performance is of significance. If a party is to make its performance in instalments, and it is clear that a defect found in one of the earlier performances will be repeated in all performances, the aggrieved party may terminate the contract even if the defects in the early instalment would not of themselves justify termination.

Sometimes an intentional breach may show that a party cannot be trusted.

Illustration

4. A, the agent of B, who is entitled to reimbursement for expenses, submits false vouchers to B. Although the amounts claimed are insignificant, B may treat A's behaviour as a fundamental non-performance and terminate the agency contract.

e. *Disproportionate loss*

Para. (2)(e) deals with situations where a party who fails to perform has relied on the contract and has prepared or tendered performance. In these cases regard is to be had to the extent to which that party suffers disproportionate loss if the non-performance is treated as fundamental. Non-performance is less likely to be treated as fundamental if it occurs late, after the preparation of performance, than if it occurs early before such preparation. Whether a performance tendered or rendered can be of any benefit to the non-performing party if it is refused or has to be returned to that party is also of relevance.

Illustration

5. On 1 May A undertakes to deliver software which is to be produced specifically for B. It is agreed that delivery shall be made before 31 December. A tenders delivery on 31 January, at which time B still needs the software, which A cannot sell to other users. B may claim damages from A, but cannot terminate the contract.

4. Termination after *Nachfrist*

Para. (3) makes reference to Art. 7.1.5, para. (3) of which provides that the aggrieved party may use the *Nachfrist* procedure to terminate a contract which may not otherwise be terminated in case of delay. See comment 2 on Art. 7.1.5.

Issues & Cases

1. RIGHT TO TERMINATE CONTRACT FOR FUNDAMENTAL NON-PERFORMANCE

- JANUARY 20, 1997 ARBITRAL AWARD INTERNATIONAL ARBITRATION COURT OF THE CHAMBER OF COMMERCE AND INDUSTRY OF THE RUSSIAN FEDERATION (NO. 116) [670]
- JULY 28, 2000 ARBITRAL AWARD ICC INTERNATIONAL COURT OF ARBITRATION (NO. 9797/CK/AER/ACS) [834]
- 2001 ARBITRAL AWARD ICC INTERNATIONAL COURT OF ARBITRATION (NO. 10422) [902]

1.1 CIRCUMSTANCES RELEVANT FOR DETERMINATION OF WHETHER OR NOT NON-PERFORMANCE IS FUNDAMENTAL

- DECEMBER 1, 1996 ARBITRAL AWARD CAMERA ARBITRALE NAZIONALE ED INTERNAZIONALE DI MILANO (A-1795/51) [662]

1.1.1 NON-PERFORMANCE SUBSTANTIALLY DEPRIVING OTHER PARTY OF ITS EXPECTATIONS

- JULY 28, 2000 ARBITRAL AWARD ICC INTERNATIONAL COURT OF ARBITRATION (NO. 9797/CK/AER/ACS) [834]

1.1.2 STRICT PERFORMANCE OF CONTRACT OF ESSENCE

- JULY 28, 2000 ARBITRAL AWARD ICC INTERNATIONAL COURT OF ARBITRATION (NO. 9797/CK/AER/ACS) [834]

1.1.3 INTENTIONAL NON-PERFORMANCE

1.1.4 NO RELIANCE ON FUTURE PERFORMANCE

- JULY 28, 2000 ARBITRAL AWARD ICC INTERNATIONAL COURT OF ARBITRATION (NO. 9797/CK/AER/ACS) [834]

1.1.5 DISPROPORTIONATE LOSS

- JULY 28, 2000 ARBITRAL AWARD ICC INTERNATIONAL COURT OF ARBITRATION (NO. 9797/CK/AER/ACS) [834]

1.1.6 OTHER CASES

- DECEMBER 1, 1996 ARBITRAL AWARD CAMERA ARBITRALE NAZIONALE ED INTERNAZIONALE DI MILANO (A-1795/51) [662]

2. RIGHT TO TERMINATE CONTRACT FOR FAILURE TO PERFORM WITHIN ADDITIONAL PERIOD FIXED (SEE ART. 7.1.5)

ARTICLE 7.3.2
(Notice of termination)

(1) The right of a party to terminate the contract is exercised by notice to the other party.

(2) If performance has been offered late or otherwise does not conform to the contract the aggrieved party will lose its right to terminate the contract unless it gives notice to the other party within a reasonable time after it has or ought to have become aware of the offer or of the non-conforming performance.

COMMENT

1. The requirement of notice

Para. (1) of this article reaffirms the principle that the right of a party to terminate the contract is exercised by notice to the other party. The notice requirement will permit the non-performing party to avoid any loss due to uncertainty as to whether the aggrieved party will accept the performance. At the same time it prevents the aggrieved party from speculating on a rise or fall in the value of the performance to the detriment of the non-performing party.

2. Performance overdue

When performance is due but has not been made, the aggrieved party's course of action will depend upon its wishes and knowledge.

It may be the case that the aggrieved party does not know whether the other party intends to perform, and either it no longer wants the performance or is undecided. In this case the aggrieved party may wait and see whether performance is ultimately tendered and make up its mind if and when this happens (see para. (2)). Alternatively, it may still want the other party to perform, in which case it must seek performance within a reasonable time after it has or ought to have become aware of the non-performance. See Art. 7.2.2(e).

This article does not deal with the situation where the non-performing party asks the aggrieved party whether it will accept late performance. Nor does it deal with the situation where the aggrieved party learns from another source that the non-performing party intends nevertheless to perform the contract. In such cases good faith (Art. 1.7) may require that the aggrieved party inform the other party if it does not wish to accept the late performance. If it does not do so, it may be held liable in damages.

3. "Reasonable time"

An aggrieved party who intends to terminate the contract must give notice to the other party within a reasonable time after it becomes or ought to have become aware of the non-performance (para. (2)).

What is "reasonable" depends upon the circumstances. In situations where the aggrieved party may easily obtain a substitute performance and may thus speculate on a rise or fall in the price, notice must be given without delay. When it must make enquiries as to whether it can obtain substitute performance from other sources the reasonable period of time will be longer.

4. Notice must be received

The notice to be given by the aggrieved party becomes effective when the non-performing party receives it. See Art. 1.10.

Issues & Cases

1. TERMINATION BY NOTICE TO NON-PERFORMING PARTY
   - 2001 ARBITRAL AWARD ICC INTERNATIONAL COURT OF ARBITRATION (NO. 10422) [902]

1.1 FORM AND CONTENT OF NOTICE

1.2 TIME OF NOTICE
   - FEBRUARY 1999 ARBITRAL AWARD (PARTIAL) ICC INTERNATIONAL COURT OF ARBITRATION (NO. 9474) [777]

1.2 NOTICE MUST BE RECEIVED (SEE ART. 1.9)

ARTICLE 7.3.3
(Anticipatory non-performance)

Where prior to the date for performance by one of the parties it is clear that there will be a fundamental non-performance by that party, the other party may terminate the contract.

COMMENT

This article establishes the principle that a non-performance which is to be expected is to be equated with a non-performance which occurred at the time when performance fell due. It is a requirement that it be clear that there will be non-performance; a suspicion, even a well-founded one, is not sufficient. Furthermore, it is necessary that the non-performance be fundamental and that the party who is to receive performance give notice of termination.

An example of anticipatory non-performance is the case where one party declares that it will not perform the contract; however, the circumstances also may indicate that there will be a fundamental non-performance.

Illustration

A promises to deliver oil to B by M/S Paul in Montreal on 3 February. On 25 January M/S Paul is still 2,000 kilometres from Montreal. At the speed it is making it will not arrive in Montreal on 3 February, but at the earliest on 8 February. As time is of the essence, a substantial delay is to be expected, and B may terminate the contract before 3 February.

Issues & Cases

1. "CLEAR" LIKELIHOOD OF FUNDAMENTAL NON-PERFORMANCE BY OTHER PARTY
   - 1.1 DECLARATION OF NON-PERFORMANCE BY OTHER PARTY
   - 1.2 OTHER CASES
2. AGGRIEVED PARTY'S RIGHT TO TERMINATE CONTRACT

ARTICLE 7.3.4
(Adequate assurance of due performance)

A party who reasonably believes that there will be a fundamental non-performance by the other party may demand adequate assurance of due performance and may meanwhile withhold its own performance. Where this assurance is not provided within a reasonable time the party demanding it may terminate the contract.

COMMENT

1. Reasonable expectation of fundamental non-performance

This article protects the interest of a party who has reason to believe that the other will be unable or unwilling to perform the contract at the due date but who cannot invoke Art. 7.3.3 since there is still a possibility that the other party will or can perform. In the absence of the rule laid down in the present article the former party would often be in a dilemma. If it were to wait until the due date of performance, and this did not take place, it might incur loss. If, on the other hand, it were to terminate the contract, and it then became apparent that the contract would have been performed by the other party, its action will amount to non-performance of the contract, and it will be liable in damages.

2. Right to withhold performance pending adequate assurance of performance

Consequently this article enables a party who reasonably believes that there will be a fundamental non-performance by the other party to demand an assurance of performance from the other party and in the meantime to withhold its own performance. What constitutes an adequate assurance will depend upon the circumstances. In some cases the other party's declaration that it will perform will suffice, while in others a request for security or for a guarantee from a third person may be justified.

Illustration

A, a boatbuilder with only one berth, promises to build a yacht for B to be delivered on 1 May, and no later. Soon afterwards, B learns from C that A has promised to build a yacht for C during the same period. B is entitled to ask A for an adequate assurance that the yacht will be delivered on time and A will then have to give B a satisfactory explanation of how it intends to perform its contract with B.

3. Termination of the contract

If adequate assurance of due performance is not given the other party may terminate the contract.

Issues & Cases

1. REASONABLE EXPECTATION OF FUNDAMENTAL NON-PERFORMANCE BY OTHER PARTY
2. AGGRIEVED PARTY'S RIGHT TO DEMAND ADEQUATE ASSURANCE OF DUE PERFORMANCE
    - 2.1 FACTS AMOUNTING TO ADEQUATE ASSURANCE
        - 2.1.1 OTHER PARTY'S DECLARATION
        - 2.1.2 SECURITY OR GUARANTEE FROM A THIRD PERSON
        - 2.1.3 OTHER FACTS
    - 2.2 ASSURANCE TO BE GIVEN WITHIN REASONABLE TIME
    - 2.3 FAILURE TO GIVE ADEQUATE ASSURANCE
3. AGGRIEVED PARTY'S RIGHT TO WITHHOLD PERFORMANCE (SEE ALSO ART. 7.1.3)

ARTICLE 7.3.5
(Effects of termination in general)

(1) Termination of the contract releases both parties from their obligation to effect and to receive future performance.

(2) Termination does not preclude a claim for damages for non-performance.

(3) Termination does not affect any provision in the contract for the settlement of disputes or any other term of the contract which is to operate even after termination.

COMMENT

1. Termination extinguishes future obligations

Para. (1) of this article states the general rule that termination has effects for the future in that it releases both parties from their duty to effect and to receive future performance.

2. Claim for damages not affected

The fact that, by virtue of termination, the contract is brought to an end, does not deprive the aggrieved party of its right to claim damages for non-performance in accordance with the rules laid down in Section 4 of this Chapter (Arts. 7.4.1. *et seq.*).

Illustration

1. A sells B specified production machinery. After B has begun to operate the machinery serious defects in it lead to a shutdown of B's assembly plant. B declares the contract terminated but may still claim damages (Art. 7.3.5(2)).

3. Contract provisions not affected by termination

Notwithstanding the general rule laid down in para. (1), there may be provisions in the contract which survive its termination. This is the case in particular with provisions relating to dispute settlement but there may be others which by their very nature are intended to operate even after termination.

Illustration

2. The facts are the same as in Illustration 1, the difference being that A discloses to B confidential information which is necessary for the production and which B agrees not to divulge for as long as it does not become public knowledge. The contract further contains a clause referring disputes to the courts of A's country. Even after termination of the contract by B, B remains under a duty not to divulge the confidential information, and any dispute relating to the contract and its effects are to be settled by the courts of A's country (Art. 7.3.5(3)).

Issues & Cases

1. TERMINATION EXTINGUISHES FUTURE OBLIGATIONS
    - JULY 28, 2000 ARBITRAL AWARD ICC INTERNATIONAL COURT OF ARBITRATION (NO. 9797/CK/AER/ACS) [834]
2. CLAIM FOR DAMAGES NOT AFFECTED
3. CONTRACT PROVISIONS NOT AFFECTED BY TERMINATION
    - DECEMBER 1, 1996 ARBITRAL AWARD CAMERA ARBITRALE NAZIONALE ED INTERNAZIONALE DI MILANO (NO. A-1795/51) [662]

    3.1 PROVISIONS FOR SETTLEMENT OF DISPUTES

    3.2 DUTY NOT TO DIVULGE CONFIDENTIAL INFORMATION

    3.3 OTHER PROVISIONS
    - DECEMBER 1, 1996 ARBITRAL AWARD CAMERA ARBITRALE NAZIONALE ED INTERNAZIONALE DI MILANO (NO. A-1795/51) [662]

ARTICLE 7.3.6
(Restitution)

(1) On termination of the contract either party may claim restitution of whatever it has supplied, provided that such party concurrently makes restitution of whatever it has received. If restitution in kind is not possible or appropriate allowance should be made in money whenever reasonable.

(2) However, if performance of the contract has extended over a period of time and the contract is divisible, such restitution can only be claimed for the period after termination has taken effect.

COMMENT

1. Entitlement of parties to restitution on termination

Para. (1) of this article provides for a right for each party to claim the return of whatever it has supplied under the contract provided that it concurrently makes restitution of whatever it has received.

Illustration

1. A sells a Renoir painting to B for US $2,000,000. B does not pay for the picture when it is delivered. A can claim back the picture.

If the non-performing party cannot make restitution it must make allowance in money for the value it has received. Thus, in the case described in Illustration 1, B has to make allowance for the value of the picture if B has sold and delivered it to a purchaser from whom it cannot be reclaimed.

The rule also applies when the aggrieved party has made a bad bargain. If in the case mentioned in Illustration 1 the true value of the picture is US $3,000,000, A may still require the return of the picture and, if it cannot be returned, claim the true value of US $3,000,000.

The present article also applies to the situation where the aggrieved party has supplied money in exchange for property, services etc. which it has not received or which are defective.

Illustration

2. The "Renoir" painting for which B has paid US $2,000,000 was not a Renoir but a copy. B can claim back the money and must return the copy to A.

Money returned for services or work which have not been performed or for property which has been rejected should be repaid to the party who paid for it and the same principle applies to custody of goods and to rent and leases of property.

2. Restitution not possible or appropriate

There are instances where instead of restitution in kind, allowance in money should be made. This is the case first of all where restitution in kind is not possible.

Illustration

3. A, who has contracted to excavate B's site, leaves it after only half the work has been performed. B, who then terminates the contract, will have to pay A a reasonable sum for the work done, measured by the value that work has for B.

Allowance in money is further envisaged by para. (1) of this article whenever restitution in kind would not be "appropriate". This is so in particular when the aggrieved party has received part of the performance and wants to retain that part.

The purpose of specifying that allowance should be made in money "whenever reasonable" is to make it clear that allowance should only be made if, and to the extent that, the performance received has conferred a benefit on the party claiming restitution.

Illustration

4. A, who has undertaken to decorate a bedroom suite for B, a furniture maker, abandons the work after having completed about half of the decorations. B can claim back the advance payments, but as the decorations made have no value for B, B does not have to pay for the work which has been done.

3. Contracts to be performed over a period of time

If the performance has extended over a period of time, restitution can, in accordance with para. (2) of this article, only be claimed in respect of the period after termination.

Illustration

5. A contracts to service B's computer hardware and software for a period of five years. After three years of regular service A is obliged by illness to discontinue the services and the contract is terminated. B, who has paid A for the fourth year, can claim return

of the advance payment for that year but not the money paid for the three years of regular service.

This rule only applies if the contract is divisible.

Illustration

6. A undertakes to paint ten pictures depicting a historical event for B's festival hall. After delivering and having been paid for five paintings, A abandons the work. B can claim return of the advances paid to A and must return the five paintings to A.

4. Other rules applicable to restitution

Both the rule in Art. 7.1.3 on the right to withhold performance and Art. 7.2.2 on specific performance of non-monetary obligations apply with appropriate adaptations to a claim for the restitution of property. Thus the aggrieved party cannot claim the return of goods when this has become impossible or would put the non-performing party to unreasonable effort or expense (see Art. 7.2.2 (a) and (b)). In such cases the non-performing party must make allowance for the value of the property. See Art. 7.3.6(1).

5. Rights of third persons not affected

In common with other articles of the Principles, the present article deals with the relationship between the parties and not with any rights which third persons may have acquired on the goods concerned. Whether, for instance, an obligee of the buyer, the buyer's receivers in bankruptcy, or a purchaser in good faith may oppose the restitution of goods sold is to be determined by the applicable national law.

Issues & Cases

1. ENTITLEMENT OF PARTIES TO RESTITUTION ON TERMINATION

- JANUARY 20, 1997 ARBITRAL AWARD INTERNATIONAL ARBITRATION COURT OF THE CHAMBER OF COMMERCE AND INDUSTRY OF THE RUSSIAN FEDERATION (NO. 116) [670]
- MAY 5, 1997 ARBITRAL AWARD ICC INTERNATIONAL COURT OF ARBITRATION (NO. 7365/FMS) [680]
- JULY 28, 2000 ARBITRAL AWARD ICC INTERNATIONAL COURT OF ARBITRATION (NO. 9797/CK/AER/ACS) [834]

1.1 RESTITUTION IN KIND

- JANUARY 20, 1997 ARBITRAL AWARD INTERNATIONAL ARBITRATION COURT OF THE CHAMBER OF COMMERCE AND INDUSTRY OF THE RUSSIAN FEDERATION (NO. 116) [670]

1.1.1 RESTITUTION IN KIND IMPOSSIBLE OR INAPPROPRIATE

1.2 ALLOWANCE IN MONEY

1.2.1 ALLOWANCE IN MONEY NOT REASONABLE

2. RESTITUTION IN CASE OF DIVISIBLE CONTRACTS TO BE PERFORMED OVER A PERIOD OF TIME

3. RIGHTS OF THIRD PERSONS TO BE DETERMINED UNDER DOMESTIC LAW

SECTION 4: DAMAGES

BIBLIOGRAPHY

ALPA G. / GIAMPIERI A., Analisi economica del diritto e analisi del metodo: la questione del danno contrattuale, in Rivista trimestrale di diritto e procedura civile, n. 3, 1996, 717-723.

BARALDI M., Il governo giudiziario della discrezionalità contrattuale, in Contratto e impresa 2005, 501 – 538.

BERGER K.P., Vertragsstrafen und Schadenspauschalierungen im Internationalen Wirtschaftsvertragsrecht, in 45 Recht der Internationalen Wirtschaft, n. 6, 1999, 401-411.

BONELL M.J., An International Restatement of Contract Law. The UNIDROIT Principles of International Commercial Contracts, 3rd ed., Transnational Publications Inc., Ardsley, New York, 2005, at 162 -165.

BONELL M.J., A 'Global' arbitration decided on the basis of the UNIDROIT Principles: In re Andersen Consulting Business Unit Member Firms v. Arthur Andersen Business Unit Member Firms and Andersen Worldwide Société Coopérative, in 17 Arbitration International 2001, 249 – 261.

BONELLI F., La responsabilità per danni, in BONELL M.J. / BONELLI F. (eds.), Contratti commerciali internazionali e Principi UNIDROIT, Giuffrè, Milano 1997, 307-338.

CONTRERAS VACA F.J., Resolución del contrato por incumplimiento, in Contratación internacional, Comentarios a los principios sobre los Contratos Comerciales Internacionales del UNIDROIT, Universidad Nacional Autónoma de México – Universidad Panamericana (ed.) 1998, 135-174.

DARANKOUM E.S., L'application des Principes d'UNIDROIT par les arbitres internationaux et par les juges étatiques, in Les Principes d'UNIDROIT et les contrats internationaux: aspects pratiques, in Revue Juridique Thémis, vol. 36, no. 2 (2002), 421 - 480

DAWWAS, A., Non-performance and damages under CISG and the UNIDROIT Principles, in 31 Comparative Law Review, 1997, 225-277.

EBERHARD S., Les sanctions de l'inexécution du contrat et les Principes UNIDROIT, Lausanne 2005, 323.

GOTANDA J.Y., Recovering Lost Profits in International Disputes, 36 Georgetown Journal of International Law (2004), 61 – 112.

JUD B., Schadensersatz bei mangelhafter Leistung, Wien, Manz, XXXVII – 337.

KOZIOL, H., Europäische Vertragsrechtsvereinheitlichung und deutsches Schadensrecht, in BASEDOW, J. (ed.), Europäische Vertragsrechtsvereinheitlichung und deutsches Recht, J. C. B. Mohr (Siebeck), Tübingen 2000, 195 – 213.

MORAN BOVIO D., Incumplimiento, in Comentario a los Principios de UNIDROIT para los Contratos del Comercio Internacional, Aranzadi, Pamplona, 1999, 317-388.

NGUYEN M.H., Les Principes UNIDROIT: Jurisprudence et expériences pour le Vietnam, in Revue de droit des affaires internationales / International Business Law, no. 5/2005, 619 – 636.

RODNER J.O., Taux d'intéret applicable dans l'arbitrage international (Principes d'UNIDROIT, article 7.4.99), in ICC International Court of Arbitration Bulletin, vol. 15, no. 1, 2004, 58 - 69

SCHACKELT, T., Der Anspruch auf Ersatz des negativen Interesses bei Nichterfüllung von Verträgen - Die Situation im deutschen Recht im Vergleich mit ausländischen Rechtsordnungen und internationalen Regelwerken, in: Zeitschrift für Europäisches Privatrecht 2001, 248-275

SCHLECHTRIEM P., Schadenersatz und Schadensbegriff, in Zeitschrift für Europäisches Privatrecht, n. 2, 1997, 232-254.

SCOGNAMIGLIO C., Il danno non patrimoniale contrattuale, in MAZZAMUTO S. (ed.), Il contratto e le tutele. Prospettive di diritto europeo, Torino, Giappichelli, 2002, 467 – 478 (Università degli Studi Roma Tre. Facoltà di Giurisprudenza – Dipartimento Studi Giuridici, 3)

TALLON D., Damages, Exemption Clauses and Penalties, in 40 American Journal of Comparative Law, n. 3, 1992, 675-682.

TALLON D., Les dommages-intérêts dans les Principes UNIDROIT relatifs aux contrats du commerce international, in BONELL M.J. / BONELLI F. (eds.), Contratti commerciali internazionali e Principi UNIDROIT, Giuffré, Milano 1997, 295-305.

VAN DER MERSCH M. – PHILIPPE D., L'inéxecution dans les contrats du commerce international, in FONTAINE M. – VINEY G. (eds.), Les sanctions de l'inéxecution des obligations contractuelles, Bruxelles – Paris 2001, 701 – 785

ZIMMERMANN R., Die Rückabwicklung fehlgeschlagener Verträge nach den Principles of European Contract Law, den UNIDROIT-Principles und dem *Avant-projet* eines *Code Européen des Contrats*, in HONSELL H., *et al.*, (eds.), Privatrecht und Methode. Festschrift für Ernst A. Kramer, Basel, Helbing & Lichtenhahn, 2004, 735 – 754.

ZMIJ G., Währungsrechtliche Probleme des vertraglichen Shadenersatzes unter besonderer Berücksichtigung der UNIDROIT -Grundregeln der Internationale Handelsverträge, in Zeitschrift für Rechtsvergleichung, 1, 1998, 21-34.

ARTICLE 7.4.1
(Right to damages)

Any non-performance gives the aggrieved party a right to damages either exclusively or in conjunction with any other remedies except where the non-performance is excused under these Principles.

COMMENT

1. Right to damages in general

This article establishes the principle of a general right to damages in the event of non-performance, except where the non-performance is excused under the Principles, as in the case of force majeure (Art. 7.1.7) or of an exemption clause (Art. 7.1.6). Hardship (Art. 6.2.1 *et seq.*) does not in principle give rise to a right to damages.

The article recalls that the right to damages, like other remedies, arises from the sole fact of non-performance. It is enough for the aggrieved party simply to prove the non-performance, *i.e.* that it has not received what it was promised. It is in particular not necessary to prove in addition that the non-performance was due to the fault of the non-performing party. The degree of difficulty in proving the non-performance will depend upon the content of the obligation and in particular on whether the obligation is one of best efforts or one to achieve a specific result. See Art. 5.1.4.

The right to damages exists in the event of failure to perform any of the obligations which arise from the contract. Thus it is not necessary to draw a distinction between principal and accessory obligations.

2. Damages may be combined with other remedies

This article also states that the aggrieved party may request damages either as an exclusive remedy (for example damages for delay in the case of late performance or for defective performance accepted by the aggrieved party; damages in the event of impossibility of performance for which the non-performing party is liable), or in conjunction with other remedies. Thus, in the case of termination of the contract, damages may be requested to compensate the loss arising from such termination, or again, in the case of specific performance, to compensate for the delay with which the aggrieved party receives performance and for any expenses which might have been incurred. Damages may also be accompanied by other remedies (cure, publication in newspapers of, for example, an admission of error, etc.).

3. Damages and pre-contractual liability

The right to damages may arise not only in the context of non-performance of the contract, but also during the pre-contractual period. See, for instance, Art. 2.1.15 in case of negotiations in bad faith, Art. 2.1.16 in the event of breach of the duty of confidentiality, or Art. 3.18 in the case of mistake, fraud, threat or gross disparity. The rules governing damages for non-performance as laid down in this Section may be applied by analogy to those situations.

Issues & Cases

1. RIGHT TO CLAIM DAMAGES FOR NON-PERFORMANCE
   - JUNE 2001 ARBITRAL AWARD ICC INTERNATIONAL COURT OF ARBITRATION (NO. 9950) [948]

   1.1 NOTION OF NON-PERFORMANCE (SEE ART. 7.1.1)

   1.2 NON-PERFORMANCE EXCUSED (SEE ARTS. 7.1.7, 7.1.6 AND 6.2.1 – 6.2.3)

2. DAMAGES FOR NON-PERFORMANCE
   - SEPTEMBER 27, 1996 ARBITRAL AWARD ICC INTERNATIONAL COURT OF ARBITRATION (NO. 8261) [642]
   - DECEMBER 1, 1996 ARBITRAL AWARD CAMERA ARBITRALE NAZIONALE ED INTERNAZIONALE DI MILANO (NO. A-1795/51) [662]
   - DECEMBER 4, 1996 ARBITRAL AWARD AD HOC ARBITRATION, ROME [664]

   2.1 DAMAGES AS EXCLUSIVE REMEDY
   - JANUARY 25, 2002 ARBITRAL AWARD ARBITRATION COURT OF THE LAUSANNE CHAMBER OF COMMERCE AND INDUSTRY [991]
   - MAY 17, 2002 ARBITRAL AWARD (PARTIAL) ARBITRATION COURT OF THE LAUSANNE CHAMBER OF COMMERCE AND INDUSTRY [1001]

   2.2 DAMAGES COMBINED WITH OTHER REMEDIES

3. DAMAGES AND PRE-CONTRACTUAL LIABILITY (SEE ARTS. 2.1.15, 2.1.16 AND 3.18)

ARTICLE 7.4.2
(Full compensation)

(1) The aggrieved party is entitled to full compensation for harm sustained as a result of the non-performance. Such harm includes both any loss which it suffered and any gain of which it was deprived, taking into account any gain to the aggrieved party resulting from its avoidance of cost or harm.

(2) Such harm may be non-pecuniary and includes, for instance, physical suffering or emotional distress.

COMMENT

1. Aggrieved party entitled to full compensation

Para. (1) of this article establishes the principle of the aggrieved party's entitlement to full compensation for the harm it has sustained as a result of the non-performance of the contract. It further affirms the need for a causal link between the non-performance and the harm. See also comment 3 on Art. 7.4.3. Non-performance must be a source neither of gain nor of loss for the aggrieved party.

The solution to be found in some legal systems which allows the court to reduce the amount of damages having regard to the circumstances has not been followed, since in international situations it could risk creating a considerable degree of uncertainty and its application might moreover vary from one court to another.

2. Damages cover loss suffered, including loss of profit

In specifying the harm for which damages are recoverable, para. (1) of this article, following the rule laid down in Art. 74 CISG, states that the aggrieved party is entitled to compensation in respect not only of loss which it has suffered, but also of any gain of which it has been deprived as a consequence of the non-performance.

The notion of loss suffered must be understood in a wide sense. It may cover a reduction in the aggrieved party's assets or an increase in its liabilities which occurs when an obligee, not having been paid by its obligor, must borrow money to meet its commitments. The loss of profit or, as it is sometimes called, consequential loss, is the benefit which would normally have accrued to the aggrieved party if the contract had been properly performed. The benefit will often be uncertain so that it will frequently take the form of the loss of a chance. See Art. 7.4.3(2).

Illustrations

1. The *Bibliothèque de France* sends a rare manuscript by special courier to New York for an exhibition. The manuscript is irreparably damaged during transport. Its loss in value is estimated at 5,000 euros and it is this sum which is due by the courier.

2. A, who has not been paid by B under the terms of their contract, must borrow money from its bank at a high rate of interest. B must compensate A for the interest due by the latter to its bank.

3. A, a construction company, hires a crane from company B. The boom of the crane, which has been poorly maintained, breaks and in falling crushes the architect's car and results in an interruption of work on the site for eight days, for which A must pay a penalty for delay of 7,000 euros to the owner. B must reimburse A for the expenses incurred as a consequence of the interruption of the work, the amount of the penalty and the cost of repairing the architect's car which A has had to pay.

4. A, a singer, cancels an engagement with B, an impresario. A must pay damages to B in respect not only of the expenses incurred by B in preparing the concert, but also of the loss of profit resulting from the cancellation of the concert.

3. Damages must not enrich the aggrieved party

However, the aggrieved party must not be enriched by damages for non-performance. It is for this reason that para. (1) also provides that account must be taken of any gain resulting to the aggrieved party from the non-performance, whether that be in the form of expenses which it has not incurred (*e.g.* it does not have to pay the cost of a hotel room for an artist who fails to appear), or of a loss which it has avoided (*e.g.* in the event of non-performance of what would have been a losing bargain for it).

Illustration

5. A hires out excavating machinery to B for two years at a monthly rental of 5,000 French francs. The contract is terminated after six months for non-payment of the rentals. Six months later, A succeeds in renting out the same machinery at a monthly charge of 5,500 French francs. The gain of 6,000 French francs realised by A as a result of the reletting of the machinery for the remainder

of the initial contract, that is to say one year, should be deducted from the damages due by B to A.

4. Damages in case of changes in the harm

In application of the principle of full compensation regard is to be had to any changes in the harm, including its expression in monetary terms, which may occur between the time of the non-performance and that of the judgment. The rule however is not without exceptions: for example, if the aggrieved party has itself already made good the harm at its own expense, the damages awarded will correspond to the amount of the sums disbursed.

5. Compensation of non-material harm

Para. (2) of this article expressly provides for compensation also of non-pecuniary harm. This may be pain and suffering, loss of certain amenities of life, aesthetic prejudice, etc. as well as harm resulting from attacks on honour or reputation.

The rule might find application, in international commerce, in regard to contracts concluded by artists, outstanding sportsmen or women and consultants engaged by a company or by an organisation.

In these cases also, the requirement of the certainty of harm must be satisfied (see Art. 7.4.3), together with the other conditions for entitlement to damages.

Illustration

6. A, a young architect who is beginning to build up a certain reputation, signs a contract for the modernisation of a municipal fine arts museum. The appointment receives wide press coverage. The municipal authorities subsequently decide to engage the services of a more experienced architect and terminate the contract with A. A may obtain compensation not only for the material loss suffered but also for the harm to A's reputation and the loss of the chance of becoming better known which the commission would have provided.

The compensation of non-material harm may assume different forms and it is for the court to decide which of them, whether taken alone or together, best assures full compensation. The court may not only award damages but also order other forms of redress such as the publication of a notice in newspapers designated by it (*e.g.* in case of breach of a clause prohibiting competition or the reopening of a business, defamation etc.).

Issues & Cases

1. HARM SUFFERED DUE TO NON-PERFORMANCE
   - JULY 28, 2000 ARBITRAL AWARD ICC INTERNATIONAL COURT OF ARBITRATION (NO. 9797/CK/AER/ACS) [834]
2. FULL COMPENSATION FOR HARM SUSTAINED
   - DECEMBER 1, 1996 ARBITRAL AWARD CAMERA ARBITRALE NAZIONALE ED INTERNAZIONALE DI MILANO (NO. A-1795/51) [662]
   - DECEMBER 4, 1996 ARBITRAL AWARD AD HOC ARBITRATION, ROME [664]
   - MAY 17, 2002 ARBITRAL AWARD (PARTIAL) ARBITRATION COURT OF THE LAUSANNE CHAMBER OF COMMERCE AND INDUSTRY [1001]

   2.1 MATERIAL HARM
   - JANUARY 25, 2002 ARBITRAL AWARD ARBITRATION COURT OF THE LAUSANNE CHAMBER OF COMMERCE AND INDUSTRY [991]

   2.1.1 LOSSES SUFFERED DUE TO NON-PERFORMANCE
   - JANUARY 31, 2003 ARBITRAL AWARD ARBITRATION COURT OF THE LAUSANNE CHAMBER OF COMMERCE AND INDUSTRY [1056]

   2.1.2 LOST PROFITS
   - 2001 ARBITRAL AWARD ICC INTERNATIONAL COURT OF ARBITRATION (NO. 10422) [902]
   - FEBRUARY 24, 2001 ARBITRAL AWARD ARBITRAL TRIBUNAL OF THE CITY OF PANAMA [931]
   - JUNE 2001 ARBITRAL AWARD ICC INTERNATIONAL COURT OF ARBITRATION (NO. 9950) [948]

   2.2 NON-MATERIAL HARM

   2.2.1 PAIN AND SUFFERING

   2.2.2 LOSS OF CERTAIN AMENITIES OF LIFE

   2.2.3 AESTHETIC PREJUDICE

   2.2.4 ATTACKS ON HONOUR OR REPUTATION

   2.2.5 FORMS OF COMPENSATION FOR NON-MATERIAL HARM

   2.2.6 PUNITIVE DAMAGES
   - 00.03.2000 ARBITRAL AWARD ICC INTERNATIONAL COURT OF ARBITRATION (NO. 10114) [ ]
3. NO ENRICHMENT OF THE AGGRIEVED PARTY

ARTICLE 7.4.3
(Certainty of harm)

(1) Compensation is due only for harm, including future harm, that is established with a reasonable degree of certainty.

(2) Compensation may be due for the loss of a chance in proportion to the probability of its occurrence.

(3) Where the amount of damages cannot be established with a sufficient degree of certainty, the assessment is at the discretion of the court.

COMMENT

1. Occurrence of harm must be reasonably certain

This article reaffirms the well-known requirement of certainty of harm, since it is not possible to require the non-performing party to compensate harm which may not have occurred or which may never occur.

Para. (1) permits the compensation also of future harm, *i.e.* harm which has not yet occurred, provided that it is sufficiently certain. Para. (2) in addition covers loss of a chance, obviously only in proportion to the probability of its occurrence: thus, the owner of a horse which arrives too late to run in a race as a result of delay in transport cannot recover the whole of the prize money, even though the horse was the favourite.

2. Determination of extent of harm

Certainty relates not only to the existence of the harm but also to its extent. There may be harm whose existence cannot be disputed but which it is difficult to quantify. This will often be the case in respect of loss of a chance (there are not always "odds" as there are for a horse, for example a student preparing for a public examination) or of compensation for non-material harm (detriment to someone's reputation, pain and suffering, etc.).

Illustration

A entrusts a file to B, an express delivery company, in response to an invitation to submit tenders for the construction of an airport. B undertakes to deliver the file before the closing date for tenders but delivers it after that date and A's application is refused. The amount of compensation will depend upon the degree of probability of A's tender having been accepted and calls for a comparison of it with the applications which were admitted for consideration. The compensation will therefore be calculated as a proportion of the profit which A might have made.

According to para. (3), where the amount of damages cannot be established with a sufficient degree of certainty then, rather than refuse any compensation or award nominal damages, the court is empowered to make an equitable quantification of the harm sustained.

3. Harm must be a direct consequence of non-performance as well as certain

There is a clear connection between the certainty and the direct nature of the harm. Although the latter requirement is not expressly dealt with by the Principles, it is implicit in Art. 7.4.2(1) which refers to the harm sustained "as a result of the non-performance" and which therefore presupposes a sufficient causal link between the non-performance and the harm. Harm which is too indirect will usually also be uncertain as well as unforeseeable.

Issues & Cases

1. CERTAINTY OF EXISTENCE OF HARM
   - DECEMBER 1, 1996 ARBITRAL AWARD CAMERA ARBITRALE NAZIONALE ED INTERNAZIONALE DI MILANO (NO. A-1795/51) [662]
   - APRIL 1997 ARBITRAL AWARD ICC INTERNATIONAL COURT OF ARBITRATION (NO. 8264) [675]

   1.1 FUTURE HARM
   - DECEMBER 1, 1996 ARBITRAL AWARD CAMERA ARBITRALE NAZIONALE ED INTERNAZIONALE DI MILANO (NO. A-1795/51) [662]
   - JUNE 2001 ARBITRAL AWARD ICC INTERNATIONAL COURT OF ARBITRATION (NO. 9950) [948]

   1.2 LOSS OF A CHANCE
   - APRIL 1997 ARBITRAL AWARD ICC INTERNATIONAL COURT OF ARBITRATION (NO. 8264) [675]

- DECEMBER 2000 ARBITRAL AWARD ICC INTERNATIONAL COURT OF ARBITRATION (NO. 10346) [883]
- APRIL 30, 2001 ARBITRAL AWARD AD HOC ARBITRATION SAN JOSÉ (COSTA RICA) [945]
- OCTOBER 2001 ARBITRAL AWARD ICC INTERNATIONAL COURT OF ARBITRATION (NO. 9078) [970]

2. **DETERMINATION OF EXTENT OF HARM**

- JUNE 1996 ARBITRAL AWARD ICC INTERNATIONAL COURT OF ARBITRATION (NO. 5835) [618]
- DECEMBER 4, 1996 ARBITRAL AWARD AD HOC ARBITRATION, ROME [664]
- SEPTEMBER 23, 1997 UNITED NATIONS COMPENSATION, PANEL F1 (NO. S/AC.26) [703]
- JANUARY 25, 2002 ARBITRAL AWARD ARBITRATION COURT OF THE LAUSANNE CHAMBER OF COMMERCE AND INDUSTRY [991]

2.1 **EQUITABLE DETERMINATION OF HARM**

- JUNE 1996 ARBITRAL AWARD ICC INTERNATIONAL COURT OF ARBITRATION (NO. 5385) [618]
- DECEMBER 4, 1996 ARBITRAL AWARD AD HOC ARBITRATION, ROME [664]
- SEPTEMBER 23, 1997 UNITED NATIONS COMPENSATION COMMISSION, PANEL F1 (NO. S/AC.26) [703]
- 2001 ARBITRAL AWARD ICC INTERNATIONAL COURT OF ARBITRATION (NO. 10422) [902]
- FEBRUARY 24, 2001 ARBITRAL AWARD ARBITRAL TRIBUNAL OF THE CITY OF PANAMA [931]

ARTICLE 7.4.4
(Foreseeability of harm)

The non-performing party is liable only for harm which it foresaw or could reasonably have foreseen at the time of the conclusion of the contract as being likely to result from its non-performance.

COMMENT

The principle of limitation of recoverable harm to that which is foreseeable corresponds to the solution adopted in Art. 74 CISG. This limitation is related to the very nature of the contract: not all the benefits of which the aggrieved party is deprived fall within the scope of the contract and the non-performing party must not be saddled with compensation for harm which it could never have foreseen at the time of the conclusion of the contract and against the risk of which it could not have taken out insurance.

The requirement of foreseeability must be seen in conjunction with that of certainty of harm set out in Art. 7.4.3.

The concept of foreseeability must be clarified since the solution contained in the Principles does not correspond to certain national systems which allow compensation even for harm which is unforeseeable when the non-performance is due to wilful misconduct or gross negligence. Since the present rule does not provide for such an exception, a narrow interpretation of the concept of foreseeability is called for. Foreseeability relates to the nature or type of the harm but not to its extent unless the extent is such as to transform the harm into one of a different kind. In any event, foreseeability is a flexible concept which leaves a wide measure of discretion to the judge.

What was foreseeable is to be determined by reference to the time of the conclusion of the contract and to the non-performing party itself (including its servants or agents), and the test is what a normally diligent person could reasonably have foreseen as the consequences of non-performance in the ordinary course of things and the particular circumstances of the contract, such as the information supplied by the parties or their previous transactions.

Illustrations

1. A cleaning company orders a machine which is delivered five months late. The manufacturer is obliged to compensate the company for lost profit caused by the delay in delivery as it could have foreseen that the machine was intended for immediate use. On the other hand the harm does not include the loss of a valuable government contract that could have been concluded if the

machine had been delivered on time since that kind of harm was not foreseeable.

2. A, a bank, usually employs the services of a security firm for the conveyance of bags containing coins to its branches. Without informing the security firm, A sends a consignment of bags containing new coins for collectors worth fifty times the value of previous consignments. The bags are stolen in a hold-up. A can only recover compensation corresponding to the value of the normal consignments as this was the only kind of harm that could have been foreseen and the value of the items lost was such as to transform the harm into one of another kind..

Unlike certain international conventions, particularly in the field of transport, the Principles follow CISG in not making provision for full compensation of harm, albeit unforeseeable, in the event of intentional non-performance.

Issues & Cases

1. **LIMITATION OF COMPENSATION TO FORESEABLE HARM**
   - DECEMBER 1, 1996 ARBITRAL AWARD CAMERA ARBITRALE NAZIONALE ED INTERNAZIONALE DI MILANO (NO. A-1795/51) [662]
   - DECEMBER 4, 1996 ARBITRAL AWARD AD HOC ARBITRATION, ROME [664]
   - DECEMBER 2000 ARBITRAL AWARD ICC INTERNATIONAL COURT OF ARBITRATION (NO. 10346) [883]
   - JANUARY 25, 2002 ARBITRAL AWARD ARBITRATION COURT OF THE LAUSANNE CHAMBER OF COMMERCE AND INDUSTRY [991]
2. **FORESEEABILITY RELATED TO NATURE OR TYPE OF HARM**
   - MAY 17, 2002 ARBITRAL AWARD (PARTIAL) ARBITRATION COURT OF THE LAUSANNE CHAMBER OF COMMERCE AND INDUSTRY [1001]

   2.1 **FORESEEABILITY NOT RELATED TO EXTENT OF HARM**

   2.1.1 **EXCEPTIONS**

ARTICLE 7.4.5

(Proof of harm in case of replacement transaction)

Where the aggrieved party has terminated the contract and has made a replacement transaction within a reasonable time and in a reasonable manner it may recover the difference between the contract price and the price of the replacement transaction as well as damages for any further harm.

COMMENT

1. Amount of harm presumed in case of replacement transaction

It seems advisable to establish, alongside the general rules applicable to the proof of the existence and of the amount of the harm, presumptions which may facilitate the task of the aggrieved party.

The first of these presumptions is provided by this article which corresponds in substance to Art. 75 CISG. It concerns the situation where the aggrieved party has made a replacement transaction, for instance because so required by the duty to mitigate harm or in conformity with usages. In such cases, the harm is considered to be the difference between the contract price and the price of the replacement transaction.

The presumption comes into play only if there is a replacement transaction and not where the aggrieved party has itself performed the obligation which lay upon the non-performing party (for example when a shipowner itself carries out the repairs to its vessel following the failure to do so of the shipyard which had been entrusted with the work).

Nor is there replacement, and the general rules will apply, when a company, after the termination of a contract, uses its equipment for the performance of another contract which it could have performed at the same time as the first ("lost volume").

The replacement transaction must be performed within a reasonable time and in a reasonable manner so as to avoid the non-performing party being prejudiced by hasty or malicious conduct.

2. Further damages recoverable for additional harm

The rule that the aggrieved party may recover the difference between the two contract prices establishes a minimum right of recovery. The aggrieved party may also obtain damages for additional harm which it may have sustained.

Illustration

A, a shipyard, undertakes to accommodate a ship belonging to B, a shipowner, in dry dock for repairs costing US $500,000 as from 1 July. B learns on 1 June that the dry dock will only be available as from 1 August. B terminates the contract and after lengthy and costly negotiations concludes with C, another shipyard, an identical contract at a price of US $700,000. B is entitled to recover from A not only the difference in the price of US $200,000 but also the expenses it has incurred and compensation for the longer period of unavailability of the ship.

Issues & Cases

1. **AGGRIEVED PARTY'S RIGHT TO MAKE REPLACEMENT TRANSACTION**
2. **DIFFERENCE BETWEEN CONTRACT PRICE AND REPLACEMENT TRANSACTION PRICE**
   - DECEMBER 4, 1996 ARBITRAL AWARD AD HOC ARBITRATION, ROME [664]
   - JANUARY 20, 1997 ARBITRAL AWARD INTERNATIONAL ARBITRATION COURT OF THE CHAMBER OF COMMERCE AND INDUSTRY OF THE RUSSIAN FEDERATION (NO. 116) [670]
3. **DAMAGES FOR FURTHER HARM**

ARTICLE 7.4.6
(Proof of harm by current price)

(1) Where the aggrieved party has terminated the contract and has not made a replacement transaction but there is a current price for the performance contracted for, it may recover the difference between the contract price and the price current at the time the contract is terminated as well as damages for any further harm.

(2) Current price is the price generally charged for goods delivered or services rendered in comparable circumstances at the place where the contract should have been performed or, if there is no current price at that place, the current price at such other place that appears reasonable to take as a reference.

COMMENT

1. Amount of harm presumed when no replacement transaction

The purpose of this article, which corresponds in substance to Art. 76 CISG, is to facilitate proof of harm where no replacement transaction has been made, but there exists a current price for the performance contracted for. In such cases the harm is presumed to be equal to the difference between the contract price and the price current at the time the contract was terminated.

2. Determination of "current price"

According to para. (2) "current price" is the price generally charged for the goods or services in question. The price will be determined in comparison with that which is charged for the same or similar goods or services. This will often, but not necessarily, be the price on an organised market. Evidence of the current price may be obtained from professional organisations, chambers of commerce etc.

For the purpose of this article the place relevant for determining the current price is that where the contract should have been performed or, if there is no current price at that place, the place that appears reasonable to take as a reference.

3. Further damages recoverable for additional harm

The rule that the aggrieved party may recover the difference between the contract price and the current price at the time of termination establishes only a minimum right of recovery. The aggrieved party may also obtain damages for additional harm which it may have sustained as a consequence of termination.

Issues & Cases

1. DAMAGES IN CASE OF TERMINATION WITHOUT REPLACEMENT TRANSACTION
    - NOVEMBER 1996 ARBITRAL AWARD ICC INTERNATIONAL COURT OF ARBITRATION (NO. 8502) [651]

1.1 DETERMINATION OF CURRENT MARKET PRICE

1.2 DIFFERENCE BETWEEN CONTRACT PRICE AND MARKET PRICE AT TIME OF TERMINATION OF CONTRACT
    - NOVEMBER 1996 ARBITRAL AWARD ICC INTERNATIONAL COURT OF ARBITRATION (NO. 8502) [651]

2. DAMAGES FOR FURTHER HARM

ARTICLE 7.4.7
(Harm due in part to aggrieved party)

Where the harm is due in part to an act or omission of the aggrieved party or to another event as to which that party bears the risk, the amount of damages shall be reduced to the extent that these factors have contributed to the harm, having regard to the conduct of each of the parties.

COMMENT

1. Contribution of the aggrieved party to the harm

In application of the general principle established by Art. 7.1.2 which restricts the exercise of remedies where non-performance is in part due to the conduct of the aggrieved party, the present article limits the right to damages to the extent that the aggrieved party has in part contributed to the harm. It would indeed be unjust for such a party to obtain full compensation for harm for which it has itself been partly responsible.

2. Ways of contributing to the harm

The contribution of the aggrieved party to the harm may consist either in its own conduct or in an event as to which it bears the risk. The conduct may take the form of an act (*e.g.* it gave a carrier a mistaken address) or an omission (*e.g.* it failed to give all the necessary instructions to the constructor of the defective machinery). Most frequently such acts or omissions will result in the aggrieved party failing to perform one or another of its own contractual obligations; they may however equally consist in tortious conduct or non-performance of another contract. The external events for which the aggrieved party bears the risk may, among others, be acts or omissions of persons for whom it is responsible such as its servants or agents.

Illustrations

1. A, a franchisee bound by an "exclusivity" clause contained in the contract with B, acquires stock from C because B has required immediate payment despite the fact that the franchise agreement provides for payment at 90 days. B claims payment of the penalty stipulated for breach of the exclusivity clause. B will obtain only part of the sum due thereunder as it was B who provoked A's non-performance.

2. A, a passenger on a liner effecting a luxury cruise, is injured when a lift fails to stop at the floor requested. B, the shipowner, is held liable for the consequences of A's injury and seeks recourse

against C, the company which had checked the lifts before the liner's departure. It is proved that the accident would have been avoided if the floor had been better lit. Since this was B's responsibility, B will not obtain full recovery from C.

3. Apportionment of contribution to the harm

The conduct of the aggrieved party or the external events as to which it bears the risk may have made it absolutely impossible for the non-performing party to perform. If the requirements of Art. 7.1.7 (Force majeure) are satisfied, the non-performing party is totally exonerated from liability.

Otherwise, the exoneration will be partial, depending on the extent to which the aggrieved party contributed to the harm. The determination of each party's contribution to the harm may well prove to be difficult and will to a large degree depend upon the exercise of judicial discretion. In order to give some guidance to the court this article provides that the court shall have regard to the respective behaviour of the parties. The more serious a party's failing, the greater will be its contribution to the harm.

Illustrations

3. The facts are the same as in Illustration 1. Since it was B who was the first not to observe the terms of the contract, B is deemed to have caused A's failure to respect the exclusivity clause. B may only recover 25% of the amount stipulated in the penalty clause.

4. The facts are the same as in Illustration 2. Since the failings of B and C seem to be equivalent, B can only recover from C 50% of the compensation it had to pay A.

4. Contribution to harm and mitigation of harm

This article must be read in conjunction with the following article on mitigation of harm (Art. 7.4.8). While the present article is concerned with the conduct of the aggrieved party in regard to the cause of the initial harm, Art. 7.4.8 relates to that party's conduct subsequent thereto.

Issues & Cases

1. CONTRIBUTION TO HARM BY AGGRIEVED PARTY

- JUNE 1996 ARBITRAL AWARD ICC INTERNATIONAL COURT OF ARBITRATION (NO. 5835) [618]
- SEPTEMBER 27, 1996 ARBITRAL AWARD ICC INTERNATIONAL COURT OF ARBITRATION (NO. 8261) [642]

- DECEMBER 4, 1996 ARBITRAL AWARD AD HOC ARBITRATION, ROME [664]

1.1 AGGRIEVED PARTY'S OWN CONDUCT

- JUNE 1996 ARBITRAL AWARD ICC INTERNATIONAL COURT OF ARBITRATION (NO. 5835) [618]
- SEPTEMBER 2, 1997 ARBITRAL AWARD INTERNATIONAL ARBITRATION COURT OF THE CHAMBER OF COMMERCE AND INDUSTRY OF THE RUSSIAN FEDERATION (NO. 225/1996) [702]
- JANUARY 25, 2002 ARBITRAL AWARD ARBITRATION COURT OF THE LAUSANNE CHAMBER OF COMMERCE AND INDUSTRY [991]
- JANUARY 31, 2003 ARBITRAL AWARD ARBITRATION COURT OF THE LAUSANNE CHAMBER OF COMMERCE AND INDUSTRY [1056]
- JUNE 6, 2003 ARBITRAL AWARD INTERNATIONAL ARBITRATION COURT OF THE CHAMBER OF COMMERCE AND INDUSTRY OF THE RUSSIAN FEDERATION (NO. 97/2002) [1067]

1.1.1 VIOLATION OF CONTRACTUAL OBLIGATIONS TOWARDS THE OTHER PARTY

- DECEMBER 4, 1996 ARBITRAL AWARD AD HOC ARBITRATION, ROME [664]

1.1.2 OTHER ACTS OR OMISSIONS

- JUNE 6, 2003 ARBITRAL AWARD INTERNATIONAL COURT OF THE CHAMBER OF COMMERCE AND INDUSTRY OF THE RUSSIAN FEDERATION (NO. 97/2002) [1067]
- OCTOBER 3, 2003 ARBITRAL AWARD ICC INTERNATIONAL COURT OF ARBITRATION (NO. 12111) [1074]

1.2 EXTERNAL EVENT FOR WHICH THE AGGRIEVED PARTY BEARS THE RISK

- SEPTEMBER 27, 1996 ARBITRAL AWARD ICC INTERNATIONAL COURT OF ARBITRATION (NO. 8261) [642]

2. APPORTIONMENT OF CONTRIBUTION TO HARM

2.1 TOTAL EXONERATION OF NON-PERFORMING PARTY FROM LIABILITY (SEE ART. 7.1.7)

- OCTOBER 3, 2003 ARBITRAL AWARD ICC INTERNATIONAL COURT OF ARBITRATION (NO. 12111) [1074]

ARTICLE 7.4.8
(Mitigation of harm)

(1) The non-performing party is not liable for harm suffered by the aggrieved party to the extent that the harm could have been reduced by the latter party's taking reasonable steps.

(2) The aggrieved party is entitled to recover any expenses reasonably incurred in attempting to reduce the harm.

COMMENT

1. Duty of aggrieved party to mitigate harm

The purpose of this article is to avoid the aggrieved party passively sitting back and waiting to be compensated for harm which it could have avoided or reduced. Any harm which the aggrieved party could have avoided by taking reasonable steps will not be compensated.

Evidently, a party who has already suffered the consequences of non-performance of the contract cannot be required in addition to take time-consuming and costly measures. On the other hand, it would be unreasonable from the economic standpoint to permit an increase in harm which could have been reduced by the taking of reasonable steps.

The steps to be taken by the aggrieved party may be directed either to limiting the extent of the harm, above all when there is a risk of it lasting for a long time if such steps are not taken (often they will consist in a replacement transaction: see Art. 7.4.5), or to avoiding any increase in the initial harm.

Illustrations

1. On 2 May, A requests B, a travel agency, to reserve a hotel room in Paris for 1 June, at a cost of 200 euros. On 15 May, A learns that B has not made the reservation. A waits however until 25 May before making a new reservation and can only find a room costing 300 euros, whereas accommodation could have been secured for 250 euros if A had already taken action on 15 May. A can recover only 50 euros from B.

2. A, a company which has been entrusted by B with the building of a factory, suddenly stops work when the project is nearing completion. B looks for another company to finish the building of the factory but takes no steps to protect the buildings on the site whose condition deteriorates as a result of bad weather.

B cannot recover compensation for such deterioration as it is attributable to its failure to take interim protective measures.

2. Reimbursement of expenses

The reduction in damages to the extent that the aggrieved party has failed to take the necessary steps to mitigate the harm must not however cause loss to that party. The aggrieved party may therefore recover from the non-performing party the expenses incurred by it in mitigating the harm, provided that those expenses were reasonable in the circumstances (para. (2)).

Illustrations

3. The facts are the same as in Illustration 2, the difference being that B has the necessary work carried out to ensure the interim protection of the buildings. The cost of such work will be added to the damages due by A for non-performance of the contract on condition that those costs were reasonable. If they were not, they will be reduced.

4. The facts are the same as in Illustration 1, the difference being that A takes a room costing 500 euros in a luxury hotel. A may only recover the 50 euro difference in respect of the room which A could have obtained for 250 euros.

Issues & Cases

1. DUTY OF AGGRIEVED PARTY TO MITIGATE HARM

- DECEMBER 4, 1996 ARBITRAL AWARD AD HOC ARBITRATION, ROME [664]
- SEPTEMBER 23, 1997 UNITED NATIONS COMPENSATION COMMISSION, PANEL F1 (NO. S/AC.26) [703]
- DECEMBER 1997 ARBITRAL AWARD ICC INTERNATIONAL COURT OF ARBITRATION (NO. 8817) [712]

1.1 REASONABLE STEPS TO REDUCE HARM

- DECEMBER 4, 1996 ARBITRAL AWARD AD HOC ARBITRATION, ROME [664]
- SEPTEMBER 23, 997 UNITED NATIONS COMPENSATION COMMISSION, PANEL F1 (NO. S/AC.26) [703]

- DECEMBER 1997 ARBITRAL AWARD ICC INTERNATIONAL COURT OF ARBITRATION (NO. 8817) [712]
- APRIL 1998 ARBITRAL AWARD (SECOND PARTIAL) ICC INTERNATIONAL COURT OF ARBITRATION (NO. 7110) [734]
- MARCH 1999 ARBITRAL AWARD ICC INTERNATIONAL COURT OF ARBITRATION (NO. 9594) [794]
- DECEMBER 2000 ARBITRAL AWARD ICC INTERNATIONAL COURT OF ARBITRATION (NO. 10346) [883]
- JULY 29, 2002 ARBITRAL AWARD ARBITRATION CENTRE OF THE COSTA RICAN CHAMBER OF COMMERCE [1003]

1.3 REIMBOURSEMENT OF EXPENSES

- SEPTEMBER 23, 1997 UNITED NATIONS COMPENSATION COMMISSION, PANEL F1 (NO. S/AC.26) [703]

2. REDUCTION OF DAMAGES

ARTICLE 7.4.9
(Interest for failure to pay money)

(1) If a party does not pay a sum of money when it falls due the aggrieved party is entitled to interest upon that sum from the time when payment is due to the time of payment whether or not the non-payment is excused.

(2) The rate of interest shall be the average bank short-term lending rate to prime borrowers prevailing for the currency of payment at the place for payment, or where no such rate exists at that place, then the same rate in the State of the currency of payment. In the absence of such a rate at either place the rate of interest shall be the appropriate rate fixed by the law of the State of the currency of payment.

(3) The aggrieved party is entitled to additional damages if the non-payment caused it a greater harm.

COMMENT

1. Lump sum compensation for failure to pay a sum of money

This article reaffirms the widely accepted rule according to which the harm resulting from delay in the payment of a sum of money is subject to a special regime and is calculated by a lump sum corresponding to the interest accruing between the time when payment of the money was due and the time of actual payment.

Interest is payable whenever the delay in payment is attributable to the non-performing party, and this as from the time when payment was due, without any need for the aggrieved party to give notice of the default.

If the delay is the consequence of force majeure (*e.g.* the non-performing party is prevented from obtaining the sum due by reason of the introduction of new exchange control regulations), interest will still be due not as damages but as compensation for the enrichment of the debtor as a result of the non-payment as the debtor continues to receive interest on the sum which it is prevented from paying.

The harm is calculated as a lump sum. In other words, subject to para. (3) of this article, the aggrieved party may not prove that it could have invested the sum due at a higher rate of interest or the non-performing party that the aggrieved party would have obtained interest at a rate lower than the average lending rate referred to in para. (2).

The parties may of course agree in advance on a different rate of interest (which would in effect subject it to Art. 7.4.13).

2. Rate of interest

Para. (2) of this article fixes in the first instance as the rate of interest the average bank short-term lending rate to prime borrowers. This solution seems to be that best suited to the needs of international trade and most appropriate to ensure an adequate compensation of the harm sustained. The rate in question is the rate at which the aggrieved party will normally borrow the money which it has not received from the non-performing party. That normal rate is the average bank short-term lending rate to prime borrowers prevailing at the place for payment for the currency of payment.

No such rate may however exist for the currency of payment at the place for payment. In such cases, reference is made in the first instance to the average prime rate in the State of the currency of payment. For instance, if a loan is made in pounds sterling payable at Tunis and there is no rate for loans in pounds on the Tunis financial market, reference will be made to the rate in the United Kingdom.

In the absence of such a rate at either place, the rate of interest will be the "appropriate" rate fixed by the law of the State of the currency of payment. In most cases this will be the legal rate of interest and, as there may be more than one, that most appropriate for international transactions. If there is no legal rate of interest, the rate will be the most appropriate bank rate.

3. Additional damages recoverable

Interest is intended to compensate the harm normally sustained as a consequence of delay in payment of a sum of money. Such delay may however cause additional harm to the aggrieved party for which it may recover damages, always provided that it can prove the existence of such harm and that it meets the requirements of certainty and foreseeability (para. (3)).

Illustration

A concludes a contract with B, a specialised finance company, for a loan which will permit the renovation of its factory in Singapore. The loan specifically mentions the use of the funds. The money lent is transferred three months later than agreed. During that period the cost of the renovation has increased by ten percent. A is entitled to recover this additional sum from B.

Issues & Cases

1. **RIGHT TO INTERESTS**
   - DECEMBER 4, 1996 ARBITRAL AWARD AD HOC ARBITRATION, ROME [664]
   - SEPTEMBER 23, 1997 UNITED NATIONS COMPENSATION COMMISSION, PANEL F1 (NO. S/AC.26) [703]
   - OCTOBER 1998 ARBITRAL AWARD ICC INTERNATIONAL COURT OF ARBITRATION (NO. 9333) [759]

   1.1 **IN CASE OF LATE PAYMENT OF PRICE**
   - DECEMBER 4, 1996 ARBITRAL AWARD AD HOC ARBITRATION, ROME [664]
   - MAY 20, 2003 BELARUS SUPREME ECONOMIC COURT OF THE REPUBLIC OF BELARUS (NO. 7-5/2003) [1063]
   - MAY 20, 2003 BELARUS SUPREME ECONOMIC COURT OF THE REPUBLIC OF BELARUS (NO. 8-5/2003) [1064]

   1.2 **IN CASE OF OTHER SUMS IN ARREARS**
   - OCTOBER 1998 ARBITRAL AWARD ICC INTERNATIONAL COURT OF ARBITRATION (NO. 9333) [759]
   - JANUARY 31, 2003 ARBITRAL AWARD ARBITRATION COURT OF THE LAUSANNE CHAMBER OF COMMERCE AND INDUSTRY [1056]

   1.3 **RIGHT TO INTEREST AND FORCE MAJEURE**
   - SEPTEMBER 23, 1997 UNITED NATIONS COMPENSATION COMMISSION, PANEL F1 (NO. S/AC.26) [703]

2. **TIME AS FROM WHEN INTEREST IS DUE**
   - MAY 5, 1997 ARBITRAL AWARD ICC INTERNATIONAL COURT OF ARBITRATION (NO. 7365/FMS) [680]
   - JULY 2001 ARBITRAL AWARD ICC INTERNATIONAL COURT OF ARBITRATION (NO. 11051) [953]
   - OCTOBER 3, 2003 ARBITRAL AWARD ICC INTERNATIONAL COURT OF ARBITRATION (NO. 12111) [1074]

3. **APPLICABLE INTEREST RATE**
   - JUNE 15, 1994 ARBITRAL AWARD INTERNATIONALES SCHIEDSGERICHT DER

BUNDESKAMMER DER GEWERBLICHEN WIRTSCHAFT – WIEN (NO. SCH-4318) [548]

- JUNE 15, 1994 ARBITRAL AWARD INTERNATIONALES SCHIEDSGERICHT DER BUNDESKAMMER DER GEWERBLICHEN WIRTSCHAFT – WIEN (NO. SCH-4366) [554]
- 1995 ARBITRAL AWARD ICC INTERNATIONAL COURT OF ARBITRATION (NO. 8128) [565]
- DECEMBER 1996 ARBITRAL AWARD ICC INTERNATIONAL COURT OF ARBITRATION (NO. 8769) [659]
- DECEMBER 1996 ARBITRAL AWARD ICC INTERNATIONAL COURT OF ARBITRATION (NO. 8874) [660]
- DECEMBER 1, 1996 ARBITRAL AWARD CAMERA ARBITRALE NAZIONALE ED INTERNAZIONALE DI MILANO (NO. A-1795/51) [662]
- SEPTEMBER 1998 ARBITRAL AWARD ICC INTERNATIONAL COURT OF ARBITRATION (NO. 8908) [750]

3.1 AVERAGE PRIME RATE FOR CURRENCY OF PAYMENT

- DECEMBER 1996 ARBITRAL AWARD ICC INTERNATIONAL COURT OF ARBITRATION (NO. 8874) [660]
- SEPTEMBER 1998 ARBITRAL AWARD ICC INTERNATIONAL COURT OF ARBITRATION (NO. 8908) [750]
- JANUARY 25, 2002 ARBITRAL AWARD ARBITRATION COURT OF THE LAUSANNE CHAMBER OF COMMERCE AND INDUSTRY [991]
- NOVEMBER 5, 2002 ARBITRAL AWARD ARBITRATION COURT AT THE CHAMBER OF COMMERCE AND INDUSTRY OF THE RUSSIAN FEDERATION (NO. 11/2002) [1030]
- MAY 20, 2003 BELARUS SUPREME ECONOMIC COURT OF THE REPUBLIC OF BELARUS (NO. 7-5/2003) [1063]
- MAY 20, 2003 BELARUS SUPREME ECONOMIC COURT OF THE REPUBLIC OF BELARUS (NO. 8-5/2003) [1064]
- MAY 19, 2004 ARBITRAL AWARD INTERNATIONAL ARBITRATION COURT AT THE CHAMBER OF COMMERCE AND INDUSTRY OF THE RUSSIAN FEDERATION (NO. 100/2002) [1082]

- March 29, 2005 Arbitral Award Arbitration Institute of the Stockholm Chamber of Commerce [1104]

3.1.1 At place for payment

- -- Arbitral Award ICC International Court of Arbitration [543]
- June 15, 1994 Arbitral Award Internationales Schiedsgericht der Bundeskammer der gewerblichen Wirtshaft, Wien (No. SCH-4318) [548]
- June 15, 1994 Arbitral Award Internationales Schiedsgericht der Bundeskammer der gewerblichen Wirtshaft, Wien (No. SCH-4366) [554]
- 1995 Arbitral Award ICC International Court of Arbitration (No. 8128) [565]
- May 20, 2003 Belarus Supreme Economic Court of the Republic of Belarus (No. 7-5/2003) [1063]
- May 20, 2003 Belarus Supreme Economic Court of the Republic of Belarus (No. 8-5/2003) [1064]

3.1.2 In State of the currency of payment

- -- Arbitral Award ICC International Court of Arbitration [543]
- May 19, 2004 Arbitral Award International Arbitration Court at the Chamber of Commerce and Industry of the Russian Federation (No. 100/2002) [1082]

3.2 Statutory rate of State of currency of payment

- November 17, 1996 Arbitral Award Arbitration Court of the Hungarian Chamber of Commerce and Industry [655]
- December 1996 Arbitral Award ICC International Court of Arbitration (No. 8769) [659]
- December 1, 1996 Arbitral Award Camera Arbitrale Nazionale ed Internazionale di Milano (No. A-1795/51) [662]

4. Damages for further harm

- June 1996 Arbitral Award ICC International Court of Arbitration (No. 5835) [618]

ARTICLE 7.4.10
(Interest on damages)

Unless otherwise agreed, interest on damages for non-performance of non-monetary obligations accrues as from the time of non-performance.

COMMENT

This article determines the time from which interest on damages accrues in cases of non-performance of obligations other than monetary obligations. In such cases, at the time of non-performance the amount of damages will usually not yet have been assessed in monetary terms. The assessment will only be made after the occurrence of the harm, either by agreement between the parties or by the court.

The present article fixes as the starting point for the accrual of interest the date of the occurrence of the harm. This solution is that best suited to international trade where it is not the practice for businesspersons to leave their money idle. In effect, the aggrieved party's assets are diminished as from the occurrence of the harm whereas the non-performing party, for as long as the damages are not paid, continues to enjoy the benefit of the interest on the sum which it will have to pay. It is only natural that this gain passes to the aggrieved party.

However, when making the final assessment of the harm, regard is to be had to the fact that damages are awarded as from the date of the harm, so as to avoid double compensation, for instance when a currency depreciates in value.

The present article takes no stand on the question of compound interest, which in some national laws is subject to rules of public policy limiting compound interest with a view to protecting the non-performing party.

Issues & Cases

1. INTEREST ACCRUAL
   1.1 IN CASE OF FAILURE TO PAY A SUM OF MONEY (SEE ART. 7.4.9 PARA. (1))
   1.2 IN CASE OF NON-PERFORMANCE OF NON-MONETARY OBLIGATIONS
      1.2.1 ACCRUAL AS FROM TIME OF NON-PERFORMANCE
         - JANUARY 2001 ARBITRAL AWARD ICC INTERNATIONAL COURT OF ARBITRATION (NO. 9771) [918]

- JANUARY 31, 2003 ARBITRAL AWARD
  ARBITRATION COURT OF THE LAUSANNE CHAMBER
  OF COMMERCE AND INDUSTRY [1056]

1.2.2 ACCRUAL AS FROM TIME OTHERWISE AGREED

ARTICLE 7.4.11
(Manner of monetary redress)

(1) Damages are to be paid in a lump sum. However, they may be payable in instalments where the nature of the harm makes this appropriate.

(2) Damages to be paid in instalments may be indexed.

COMMENT

1. Lump sum or instalments

Although this article does not impose a fixed rule as to the manner in which damages are to be paid, the payment of damages as a lump sum is in general considered to be the mode of payment best suited to international trade. There are however situations in which payment by instalments will be more appropriate, having regard to the nature of the harm, for instance when the harm is on-going.

Illustrations

1. A, a consultant, is retained by B for the purpose of checking the safety of its factories. A is killed when travelling by helicopter to one of B's factories, for which accident B is held responsible. A leaves two children aged twelve and eight. So as to compensate for the loss of the maintenance of the family, a monthly allowance will be payable to the children until they reach the age of majority.

2. A, a consultant in safety matters, is recruited by B for a three year period. The remuneration is fixed at 0.5% of the production. A is wrongfully dismissed after six months. It may be appropriate that B be ordered to pay A monthly a sum corresponding to the agreed salary until A has found new employment or, at the most, for thirty months.

2. Indexation

Para. (2) of this article contemplates the possibility of indexation of damages to be paid in instalments so as to avoid the complex mechanism of a review of the original judgment in order to take account of inflation. Indexation may however be prohibited by the law of the forum.

Illustration

3. The facts are the same as in Illustration 1. The monthly allowance may be adjusted in accordance with the cost of living index applicable where the children live.

Issues & Cases

1. **PAYMENT OF DAMAGES**
   - 1.1 **IN A LUMP SUM**
   - 1.2 **BY INSTALMENTS**
     - 1.2.1 **FIXED INSTALMENTS**
     - 1.2.2 **INDEXATION OF INSTALMENTS**
     - 1.2.3 **INDEXATION PROHIBITED BY LAW OF FORUM**

ARTICLE 7.4.12
(Currency in which to assess damages)

Damages are to be assessed either in the currency in which the monetary obligation was expressed or in the currency in which the harm was suffered, whichever is more appropriate.

COMMENT

The harm resulting from the non-performance of an international contract may occur in different places and the question therefore arises of the currency in which it is to be assessed. This question is dealt with by the present article and should be kept distinct from that of the currency of payment of the damages addressed in Art. 6.1.9.

The article offers a choice between the currency in which the monetary obligation was expressed and that in which the harm was suffered, whichever is more appropriate in the circumstances.

While the first alternative calls for no particular comment, the second takes account of the fact that the aggrieved party may have incurred expenses in a particular currency to repair damage which it has sustained. In such a case it should be entitled to claim damages in that currency even if it is not the currency of the contract. Another currency which may be considered the most appropriate is that in which the profit would have been made.

The choice is left to the aggrieved party, provided that the principle of full compensation is respected.

Finally, it may be noted that in the absence of any indication to the contrary, a party is entitled to interest and to liquidated damages and penalties in the same currency as that in which the main obligation is expressed.

Issues & Cases

1. ASSESSMENT OF DAMAGES
   - DECEMBER 4, 1996 ARBITRAL AWARD AD HOC ARBITRATION, ROME [664]

1.1 IN CURRENCY OF CONTRACT

1.2 IN CURRENCY IN WHICH HARM WAS SUFFERED
   - DECEMBER 4, 1996 ARBITRAL AWARD AD HOC ARBITRATION, ROME [664]

ARTICLE 7.4.13
(Agreed payment for non-performance)

(1) Where the contract provides that a party who does not perform is to pay a specified sum to the aggrieved party for such non-performance, the aggrieved party is entitled to that sum irrespective of its actual harm.

(2) However, notwithstanding any agreement to the contrary the specified sum may be reduced to a reasonable amount where it is grossly excessive in relation to the harm resulting from the non-performance and to the other circumstances.

COMMENT

1. Agreed payment for non-performance defined

This article gives an intentionally broad definition of agreements to pay a specified sum in case of non-performance, whether such agreements be intended to facilitate the recovery of damages (liquidated damages according to the common law) or to operate as a deterrent against non-performance (penalty clauses proper), or both.

2. Agreed payment for non-performance in principle valid

National laws vary considerably with respect to the validity of the type of clauses in question, ranging from their acceptance in the civil law countries, with or without the possibility of judicial review of particularly onerous clauses, to the outright rejection in common law systems of clauses intended specifically to operate as a deterrent against non-performance, *i.e.* penalty clauses.

In view of their frequency in international contract practice, para. (1) of this article in principle acknowledges the validity of any clauses providing that a party who does not perform is to pay a specified sum to the aggrieved party for such non-performance, with the consequence that the latter is entitled to the agreed sum irrespective of the harm actually suffered by it. The non-performing party may not allege that the aggrieved party sustained less harm or none at all.

Illustration

1. A, a former Brazilian international player, is recruited for three years to train the players of B, an Australian football team, at

> a monthly salary of 10,000 Australian dollars. Provision is made for a severance allowance of 200,000 Australian dollars in the event of unjustified dismissal. A is dismissed without any justification after six months. A is entitled to the agreed sum, even though A was immediately recruited by another team at double the salary received from B.

Normally, the non-performance must be one for which the non-performing party is liable, since it is difficult to conceive a clause providing for the payment of an agreed sum in case of non-performance operating in a force majeure situation. Exceptionally, however, such a clause may be intended by the parties also to cover non-performance for which the non-performing party is not liable.

In the case of partial non-performance, the amount may, unless otherwise agreed by the parties, be reduced in proportion.

3. Agreed sum may be reduced

In order to prevent the possibility of abuse to which such clauses may give rise, para. (2) of this article permits the reduction of the agreed sum if it is grossly excessive "in relation to the harm resulting from the non-performance and to the other circumstances". The same paragraph makes it clear that the parties may under no circumstances exclude such a possibility of reduction.

The agreed sum may only be reduced, but not entirely disregarded as would be the case were the judge, notwithstanding the agreement of the parties, to award damages corresponding to the exact amount of the harm. It may not be increased, at least under this article, where the agreed sum is lower than the harm actually sustained (see however comment 4 on Art. 7.1.6). It is moreover necessary that the amount agreed be "grossly excessive", *i.e.* that it would clearly appear to be so to any reasonable person. Regard should in particular be had to the relationship between the sum agreed and the harm actually sustained.

Illustration

> 2. A enters into a contract with B for the purchase of machinery which provides for 48 monthly payments of 5,000 euros. The contract contains a clause allowing immediate termination in the event of non-payment by A of one instalment, and authorises B to keep the sums already paid and to recover future instalments as damages. A fails to pay the eleventh instalment. B keeps the 50,000 euros already paid and claims, in addition to the return of the machinery, the 190,000 euros representing the 38 outstanding instalments. The court will reduce the amount since A's non-performance would result in a grossly excessive benefit for B.

4. Agreed payment for non-performance to be distinguished from forfeiture and other similar clauses

The type of clauses dealt with in the present article must be distinguished from forfeiture and other similar clauses which permit a party to withdraw from a contract either by paying a certain sum or by losing a deposit already made. On the other hand a clause according to which the aggrieved party may retain sums already paid as part of the price falls within the scope of this article.

Illustrations

3. A undertakes to sell real estate to B for 450,000 euros. B must exercise the option to purchase within three months and must pay a deposit of 25,000 euros, which A is entitled to retain if B does not exercise the option. Since this is not an agreed payment for non-performance it does not fall under the present article and the sum cannot be reduced thereunder even if grossly excessive in the circumstances.

4. A enters into a contract with B for the lease of a machine. The contract provides that in the event of A's failure to pay one single rental the contract will be terminated and that the sums already paid will be retained by B as damages. The clause falls under the present article and the agreed amount may be subject to reduction.

Issues & Cases

1. VALIDITY OF AGREED PAYMENT FOR NON-PERFORMANCE
   - SEPTEMBER 27, 1996 ARBITRAL AWARD ICC INTERNATIONAL COURT OF ARBITRATION (NO. 8261) [642]
   - DECEMBER 1, 1996 ARBITRAL AWARD CAMERA ARBITRALE NAZIONALE ED INTERNAZIONALE DI MILANO (NO. A-1795/51) [662]
   - JUNE 5, 1997 ARBITRAL AWARD INTERNATIONAL ARBITRATION COURT OF THE CHAMBER OF COMMERCE AND INDUSTRY OF THE RUSSIAN FEDERATION (NO. 229/1996) [683]
   - NOVEMBER 6, 2003 POLAND SUPREME COURT (NO. III CZP 61/03) [1076]
2. AGREED SUM "GROSSLY EXCESSIVE" IN RELATION TO ACTUAL HARM
   - JANUARY 28, 1998 ARBITRAL AWARD AD HOC ARBITRATION, HELSINKI [717]

- July 28, 2000 Arbitral Award ICC International Court of Arbitration (No. 9797/CK/AER/ACS) [834]

2.1 **Reduction of agreed sum**

- June 5, 1997 Arbitral Award International Arbitration Court of the Chamber of Commerce and Industry of the Russian Federation (No. 229/1996) [683]
- January 28, 1998 Arbitral Award Ad hoc Arbitration, Helsinki [717]
- January 25, 2001 Arbitral Award International Court of the Chamber of Commerce and Industry of the Russian Federation (No. 88/2000) [921]
- April 4, 2003 Arbitral Award International Arbitration Court of the Chamber of Commerce and Industry of the Russian Federation (No. 134/2002) [1061]

3. **Agreed payment for non-performance and right to request performance in natura**
4. **Agreed payment for non-performance and right to claim damages for further harm**
5. **Agreed payment for non-performance and exemption clauses**

CHAPTER 8
SET-OFF

BIBLIOGRAPHY

BERGER K.P., Set-off, in ICC International Court of Arbitration Bulletin, 2005 Special Supplement, 17 – 26.

PELEGGI R., La compensazione nei Principi UNIDROIT dei contratti commerciali internazionali e nei Principi di Diritto Europeo dei contratti: un primo confronto, in Diritto del commercio internazionale, 16 (2002), 927 – 950.

ARTICLE 8.1
(Conditions of set-off)

(1) Where two parties owe each other money or other performances of the same kind, either of them ("the first party") may set off its obligation against that of its obligee ("the other party") if at the time of set-off,

(a) the first party is entitled to perform its obligation;

(b) the other party's obligation is ascertained as to its existence and amount and performance is due.

(2) If the obligations of both parties arise from the same contract, the first party may also set off its obligation against an obligation of the other party which is not ascertained as to its existence or to its amount.

COMMENT

1. Use of set-off

Under the Principles, when two parties owe each other an obligation arising from a contract or any cause of action, each party may set off its obligation against the obligation of the other party. By mutual deduction, both obligations are discharged up to the amount of the lesser obligation (see Art. 8.5). Set-off avoids the need for each party to perform its obligation separately.

The obligor from whom payment is asked, and who sets off its own obligation, is called "the first party". The obligee who first asks its obligor for payment and against whom the right of set-off is exercised, is called "the other party".

Illustrations

1. A, a sea carrier, has carried goods belonging to B from Marseilles to Athens. A asks B for 5,000 euros as payment for the carriage. B, who had previously become an obligee of A for an amount of 5,000 euros as compensation for harm to other goods carried, may set off its own obligation to pay A 5,000 euros against A's obligation to pay it 5,000 euros. If it does so, neither A nor B will remain the other's obligor.

2. A sells B a plot of land for the price of AUS $25,000. Subsequently B, who is a contractor, builds a house for A. The

price of the construction is AUS $50,000. When A asks for the payment of the land, B may set off the price of the construction. The obligation of B to pay A AUS $25,000 is totally discharged, but A remains B's obligor for AUS $25,000.

For a party to be allowed to set off its own obligation against the obligation of the other party the conditions laid down in this article must be satisfied.

2. Obligation owed to each other

A first condition is that each party is the obligor and the obligee of the other (para. (1), opening sentence). To be noted is that the parties must be so in the same capacity. Thus, set-off is not possible if the first party has an obligation to the other party in its own name but is the obligee of the other party in another capacity, for example as a trustee or as the absolute owner of a company.

Illustration

3. Company A sells company B machinery for 600,000 Japanese Yen. B, which is in business with company C, a subsidiary of A, sells C products for 500,000 Japanese Yen. When A asks B to pay the sales price of the machinery, B cannot set off its obligation for the sale of the products to C, even if the capital of C is totally subscribed by A, as C is an independent entity. A and B are not obligor and obligee of each other.

The condition that the obligations must be owed to each other may give rise to a problem where the other party has assigned the obligation owed to it by the first party to a third party. The first party may nonetheless set off its obligation against the other party's obligation if the right of set-off existed against the assignor's obligation before the assignment was notified to the assignee (see Art. 9.1.13).

3. Obligations of the same kind

Both obligations must be of the same kind (para. (1), opening sentence). In some legal systems obligations have to be "fungible". A monetary obligation may be set off only against a monetary obligation. A delivery of grain may be set off only against a delivery of grain of the same kind.

The concept of "obligations of the same kind" is broader than that of "fungible obligations". Performances of non-monetary obligations may be of the same kind while at the same time not being fungible. Two obligations to deliver wine of the same vineyard but not of the same year may be obligations of the same kind, but would not be fungible. Cash and securities are not performances of the same kind in the sense of this article. Nevertheless, as is the case with different foreign currencies, set-off may be exercised if the securities are easily convertible and if there is no agreement to the effect that only the payment of specified cash or securities is possible. Whether or not obligations are of the same kind may depend on commercial practices or special trade rules.

A personal obligation cannot be of the same kind as another type of obligation. Set-off is thus not available if one of the obligations is of a personal nature.

Illustrations

4. A, a crude oil producer, contracts to deliver 1,500 tonnes of crude oil by pipe-line every month to B in Cairo. B, in turn, must each week transfer 1,000 tonnes of crude oil by road. The crude oil produced by A and the crude oil delivered by B do not have the same origin and are not totally similar, but as their use could be identical, the two obligations relating to the crude oil can be said to be of the same kind, and if A and B are obligor and obligee for the delivery of some quantity of crude oil, set-off will be available.

5. A holds 100 ordinary shares of the company "South". B is shareholder of the same company. It holds 120 redeemable preferred shares. They are obligee and obligor of each other, and in an earlier contract it was provided that payment would be possible by means of shares of equal value. Since the shares held by A and the shares held by B are not of the same kind, set-off cannot be exercised.

4. First party's obligation performable

The first party must have the right to perform its obligation (para. (1)(a)). It cannot impose on the other party a performance which either has not yet been ascertained, or is not yet due.

Illustrations

6. A has sold ten trucks to B for US $100,000. B must pay for the trucks before 30 September. B wishes to set off an obligation it has towards A arising from a loan to A, repayment of which is due on 30 November. Before this date B may not set off its obligation towards A, as it cannot pay A before 30 November. B's obligation to A is not yet due.

7. A owes B 20,000 euros for the repayment of a loan. The repayment must take place on 30 January. B is obliged to pay A for a claim for damages of 14,000 euros, under a judgment handed down on 25 January. A asks B to pay on 9 February. B, whose obligation can be performed, is allowed to set off its obligation against A's obligation.

8. A has sold B 1,000 bottles of Bordeaux wine, the price of which must be paid at the latest on 30 October. B is also A's obligee and A's obligation is already due. B may set off its own obligation against A's obligation on 10 October even if the latest date A's obligation should be paid is 30 October, because A is bound to accept a payment before such date.

5. Other party's obligation ascertained

Set-off may be exercised only when the other party's obligation is ascertained both as to its existence and as to its amount (para. (1)(b)).

The existence of an obligation is ascertained when the obligation itself cannot be contested, for example, when it is based on a valid and executed contract or a final judgment or award which is not subject to review.

Conversely, an obligation to pay damages is not ascertained when the obligation may be contested by the other party.

Even if the existence of the other party's obligation is not contested, it is not possible to exercise set-off if the obligation is not ascertained as to its amount. If the existence of the harm is not disputed, but the amount of the compensation has not been fixed, set-off will not be available.

Illustrations

9. A judgment requires A to pay B 200,000 China Yuan Renminbi, for breach of contract. B is in turn A's obligor for the repayment of a loan of 240,000 China Yuan Renminbi, repayment of which is already due. A asks B to pay the 240,000 China Yuan Renminbi. B may set off its obligation against A's obligation arising from the judgment.

10. A sells B a yacht for 10,000 euros. A is liable to B for tort. The harm is not contested, but the amount of damages has not yet been fixed. A will not be permitted to set off its own obligation, as B's obligation has not been ascertained.

The Principles do not deal with the impact of insolvency proceedings on the right to exercise set-off, which is therefore to be determined by the applicable law. Most domestic laws grant the first party the right to exercise set-off even after the other party has become involved in insolvency proceedings, thereby derogating from the principle of the equality of the creditors in insolvency proceedings.

6. Other party's obligation due

The other party's obligation must furthermore be due (para. (1)(b)). An obligation is due when the obligee has the right to request performance by the obligor, and the obligor has no available defence against that request. A defence will, for example, be available if the time of payment has not yet arrived. As a natural or moral obligation is not enforceable, the first party may not set off its obligations against such an obligation owed by the other party. The enforceability or non-enforceability of an obligation may depend on the otherwise applicable law. Consequently, in some cases the possibility to exercise the right of set-off may depend on the otherwise applicable law.

Illustration

11. By a final judgment of 10 April, A was ordered to pay B US $20,000 for the sale of cotton. A, who is B's obligee for the repayment of a loan of US $12,000 which was enforceable as from 10 January, may set off its own obligation against B's obligation. B, whose obligation is ascertained and due cannot contest the set-off exercised by A.

Since the expiry of the limitation periods prevents the enforcement of the obligation but does not extinguish the right itself, the first party who is not allowed to enforce the time-barred obligation may nonetheless set off that time-barred obligation (see Art. 10.10).

7. Set-off of obligations arising from the same contract

Set-off is a convenient means of discharging obligations at one and the same time. Therefore, if the two obligations arise from the same contract, the conditions of set-off are modified.

If the obligations of the two parties arise from the same contract, the first party is allowed to set off its own obligation against an obligation of the other party even where that other party's obligation is not ascertained as to its existence or to its amount (para. (2)). Thus, for instance, an obligation to pay damages may be ascertained as to its existence but not as to its amount. If the minimum amount payable cannot be contested, the first party may set off its own obligation up to that minimum amount, even if the total amount of the other party's obligation is unknown.

Even though one of the obligations is contested, the right to set-off can be exercised because all the relevant obligations capable of being set off arise from the same contract and can therefore be easily identified. This could be useful to parties in a business relationship to facilitate quick settlements of claims. Judicial intervention may however be necessary to determine whether the conditions of set-off are in fact satisfied. In international commerce, the obligations of the two parties may frequently arise from the same contract.

Illustration

12. A carries turkeys for B from St. Petersburg to Stockholm. The carriage charge is 35,000 Russian Rubles. During the carriage one hundred turkeys die due to the fault of the carrier which it

acknowledges. A asks B for the payment of the carriage. B may set off the obligation to pay for the harm caused by the loss of the turkeys against A's obligation. Although the amount of the damages is not ascertained, it would be easy to estimate the damages and determine if the conditions for set off are satisfied as the two obligations arise from the same contract.

13. A, a carrier, accepts to carry a piano for B from Toronto to New York. A provision of the contract expressly provides that delay penalties are to be paid if the piano is not delivered at the concert hall five days before the date of the concert. The piano is delivered in New York only two days before the date of the concert. A asks for the payment of the carriage. B may set off its claim for the agreed delay penalties against A's claim even if A contests the amount of the penalties owed for the delay.

8. Set-off by agreement

Even if the conditions of the present article are not met, the parties may achieve the effects of set-off by agreement. Likewise, parties may agree that their mutual obligations are set off automatically either at a specific date or periodically. Also, more than two parties may agree that their respective obligations shall be discharged, for example by netting.

Issues & Cases

1. CONDITIONS OF SET-OFF IN GENERAL
    1.1 PARTIES' MUTUAL OBLIGATIONS TO EACH OTHER
        1.1.1 OBLIGATIONS MUST BE HELD IN THE SAME CAPACITY
        1.1.2 IN CASE OF ASSIGNMENT OF RIGHTS (SEE ART. 9.1.3)
        1.1.3 IN CASE OF TRANSFER OF OBLIGATIONS (SEE ART. 9.2.7)
    1.2 OBLIGATIONS OF THE SAME KIND
        1.2.1 MONETARY OBLIGATIONS
        1.2.2 NON MONETARY OBLIGATIONS
        1.2.3 CASH AND SECURITIES
        1.2.4 OBLIGATIONS OF A PERSONAL NATURE
    1.3 FIRST PARTY'S OBLIGATION PERFORMABLE
    1.4 OTHER PARTY'S OBLIGATION ASCERTAINED
        1.4.1 AS TO EXISTENCE
        1.4.2 AS TO AMOUNT
    1.5 OTHER PARTY'S OBLIGATION DUE
        1.5.1 TIME FOR PERFORMANCE NOT YET ARRIVED
        1.5.2 NATURAL OR MORAL OBLIGATION
        1.5.3 OBLIGATION SUBJECT TO A CONDITION
        1.5.4 TIME-BARRED OBLIGATION (SEE ART. 10.11)

1.5.5 OTHER CASES
2. SPECIAL CASE WHERE OBLIGATIONS ARISE FROM THE SAME CONTRACT
2.1 OTHER PARTY'S OBLIGATION NEED NOT BE ASCERTAINED AS TO EXISTENCE OR AMOUNT
3. SET-OFF BY AGREEMENT
3.1 NETTING AGREEMENTS

ARTICLE 8.2
(Foreign currency set-off)

Where the obligations are to pay money in different currencies, the right of set-off may be exercised, provided that both currencies are freely convertible and the parties have not agreed that the first party shall pay only in a specified currency.

COMMENT

1. Convertible currencies

Payments in different currencies are not performances of the same kind as required by Art. 8.1. However, if the payments are to be made in currencies that are both convertible, set-off may nevertheless be exercised. According to Art. 6.1.9, if there is no agreement to the contrary, payment may by made by the obligor in the currency of the place for payment, if this currency is convertible. On the contrary, since the relative value of a currency that is not freely convertible cannot be readily ascertained for the purpose of set-off, set-off cannot be used to impose payment in such a currency on the other party.

Illustration

1. A, a Californian wine producer, sells 500 bottles of wine for US $20,000 to B, a cork producer. B sells 100,000 corks to A for the price of 10,000 livros, which is the currency of the country where corks are produced and which is not convertible. A asks B for payment of the US $20,000. B may not set off the 10,000 livros against the US $20,000.

2. Currency specified by contract

If a contract expressly requires a party to pay in a specified currency, and if that party has to perform its own obligation in a currency different from that currency, it will not be able to set off its own obligation against the other party's obligation.

Illustration

2. A sells B products for US $10,000. The sales contract expressly provides that the price is to be paid by the buyer in US dollars in New York. B, an Asian carrier, is A's obligee for an unpaid invoice for carriage charges which must be paid in Korean Won in Seoul. A requires payment of the US $10,000. B, who

contractually is obliged to pay the price of the products in New York in dollars, is not allowed to set off its obligation to pay the carriage charges.

Issues & Cases

1. **SET-OFF OF OBLIGATIONS IN DIFFERENT CURRENCIES**
   - 1.1 **FREELY CONVERTIBLE CURRENCIES**
   - 1.2 **CURRENCY SPECIFIED BY CONTRACT**

ARTICLE 8.3
(Set-off by notice)

The right of set-off is exercised by notice to the other party

COMMENT

The right of set-off is exercised by notice to the other party. It does not operate automatically or by declaration of the court. The first party must inform the other party that it will discharge its own obligation by set-off. Notice must not be conditional.

To be effective, notice must be sent after the conditions for set-off are fulfilled.

Notice may be given by any means appropriate to the circumstances and is effective when it reaches the person to whom it is given (see Art. 1.10).

Issues & Cases

1. SET-OFF EXERCISED BY NOTICE TO OTHER PARTY
   1.1 EFFECTIVE WHEN REACHES OTHER PARTY (SEE ART. 1.10)

ARTICLE 8.4
(Content of notice)

(1) The notice must specify the obligations to which it relates.

(2) If the notice does not specify the obligation against which set-off is exercised, the other party may, within a reasonable time, declare to the first party the obligation to which set-off relates. If no such declaration is made, the set-off will relate to all the obligations proportionally.

COMMENT

According to para. (1), the notice must specify the obligations of both parties that are to be set off. The other party, receiving the notice, must know the grounds for set-off and the amount of set-off.

1. Declaration by the other party

If the first party has two or more obligations against the other party, and if the first party has not specified the obligations it wants to be paid by set-off, the other party may freely choose which of the first party's obligations it wants to be discharged (para. (2), first part).

Illustration

1. A regularly sells B cloth. On 30 December B asks A for the payment of US $5,000 that A owes it. At that date B owes A the payment of the price relating to three different sales contracts, *i.e.* US $4,000, US $3,500 and US $4,500 respectively. If A wants to set off B's obligation, it has to indicate in the notice which of the three obligations owed by B it wants to set off. If A does not indicate in the notice which obligation owed by B it wants to set off, B may in a reasonable time indicate to A that its obligation of US $4,500 will be totally discharged by set off and that the obligation of US $3,500 will be discharged up to US $500. After set-off has been applied, B remains the obligor of A for US $7,000.

2. Absence of declaration

If the notice does not specify the obligations that the first party wants to set off, and if the other party does not make any declaration to which obligation set-off relates within a reasonable time, all the obligations of the other party will be discharged by set-off proportionally, up to the value of the first party's obligation (para. (2), second part)).

Illustration

2. The facts are the same as in Illustration 1, the difference being that B does not declare to which obligation set-off relates. In the absence of such a declaration, set-off will discharge the obligation of US $4,000 of the first contract up to US $1,667; the obligation of US $3,500 contract the second contract up to US $1,458 and the obligation of US $4,500 of the third contract up to US $1,875.

Issues & Cases

1. **NOTICE SPECIFYING OBLIGATIONS TO BE DISCHARGED**
2. **DECLARATION BY OTHER PARTY**
3. **OBLIGATIONS DISCHARGED PROPORTIONALLY**

ARTICLE 8.5
(Effect of set-off)

(1) Set-off discharges the obligations.

(2) If obligations differ in amount, set-off discharges the obligations up to the amount of the lesser obligation.

(3) Set-off takes effect as from the time of notice.

COMMENT

1. Discharge by set-off

If the conditions of set-off specified in Art. 8.1 are satisfied, the obligations of both parties are discharged to the extent of the set-off, as if two reciprocal payments had been made.

Illustration

1. A owes US $100 to B and B owes US $100 to A. B asks for the payment of its obligation. A by notice declares to B that it sets off its own obligation. After set-off takes effect, the two obligations are discharged.

If the two obligations differ in their amount, set-off will discharge the obligations, but only up to the amount of the lesser obligation.

Illustration

2. B owes US $100 to A, who in turn owes B US $70. A asks for the payment of the US $100 he is owed, B declares that it wants to set off A's obligation of US $70. If the conditions for set-off are met, A is no longer the obligor of B, as its obligation has been entirely discharged, but A is still the obligee of B for US $30, corresponding to the part of the obligation not paid by set-off.

2. Set-off effective at the time of notice.

The obligations are discharged at the time of notice if at that time the conditions required for set-off are fulfilled. Set-off does not operate retroactively. It has prospective effect only.

The date of effectiveness of set-off is consistent with the necessity to declare set-off by notice, and in practice the date when set-off is effective will be easy to know.

The situation has to be evaluated as if both obligations were paid at the time of notice. Two consequences derive from this rule. Firstly, interest on the obligations runs until the time of notice. A party who may and wants to set off its obligation, must declare set-off as soon as possible if it wishes to stop the accrual of interest. Secondly, if an undue payment has been made after set-off has been declared, restitution will take place, as the payment has no legal grounds. If the payment had been made before the notice, it is an effective payment and restitution cannot be required.

Illustration

3. A owes B US $1,000 dollars for goods sold by B. A's obligation is ascertained and payment is due on 20 November. B asks for payment of the US $1,000 on 22 December. By a judgement dated 30 November, B is ordered to pay A US $800 in damages. The obligation to pay US $800 is due and ascertained at the date of the judgement, *i.e.* on 30 November. Set-off is exercised by A by notice on 10 December. The set-off will take place at the time of notice as all the conditions required have been satisfied before this date. The two obligations are discharged up to the amount of the lesser obligation. A will remain the obligee of B for US $200. After 10 December, interest no longer accrues, except on the amount of US $200.

At the time when the conditions for set-off are satisfied and notice has been given, not only the principal obligations are discharged but also related rights, *e.g.* rights securing an obligation, are discharged accordingly.

Illustration

4. A, a banker, had lent B 10,000 euros and has obtained a personal security for the payment from B's wife. B is the obligee of A for 12,000 euros, which is money that B holds on its account in A's bank. A asks B for the payment of the 10,000 euros. B declares set-off by notice on 12 December. The conditions required for A's obligation and B's obligation were fulfilled on 10 December. At the date of notice on 12 December, A's and B's obligations are discharged, as is the personal security given by B's wife.

Issues & Cases

1. **EFFECT OF SET-OFF**
   - 1.1 **OBLIGATIONS AND RELATED RIGHTS DISCHARGED**
     - 1.1.1 **OBLIGATIONS DIFFERENT IN AMOUNT**
2. **SET-OFF EFFECTIVE AS FROM TIME OF NOTICE**

CHAPTER 9

ASSIGNMENT OF RIGHTS, TRANSFER OF OBLIGATIONS, ASSIGNMENT OF CONTRACTS

SECTION 1: ASSIGNMENT OF RIGHTS

BIBLIOGRAPHY

FONTAINE M., Harmoniser le régime de la transmission des obligations, in Liber amicorum Jacques Herbots, Kluwer, 2002, 131 – 146.

RUDOLF C., Einheitsrecht für internationale Forderungsabtretungen. UN-Abtretungsübereinkommen, PECL, UNIDROIT Principles, Mohr Siebeck 2006.

WIEGAND W., - ZELLWEGER-GUTKNECHT C., Assignment, in ICC International Court of Arbitration Bulletin, 2005, Special Supplement, 27 – 41.

ARTICLE 9.1.1
(Definitions)

"Assignment of a right" means the transfer by agreement from one person (the "assignor") to another person (the "assignee"), including transfer by way of security, of the assignor's right to payment of a monetary sum or other performance from a third person ("the obligor").

COMMENT

In many circumstances an obligee entitled to the payment of a monetary sum or to another performance from an obligor may find it useful to assign its right to another person. For instance, an assignment to a bank is a common way to finance the credit granted to a customer. The rules of the present Section cover the assignment of rights as defined in this article.

1. Transfer by agreement

Only transfers by agreement are concerned, as opposed to situations in which the applicable law may provide for legal transfers of certain rights (such as, in certain jurisdictions, the transfer of a seller's rights against an insurer to the purchaser of an insured building, or the automatic transfer of rights in the case of the merger of companies (see Art. 9.1.2(b)).

The definition equally does not cover unilateral transfers, which in certain jurisdictions may take place without the assignee's participation.

2. Right to payment of a monetary sum or to other performance

On the other hand, the definition is not restricted to the assignment of rights to the payment of a monetary sum. It also covers rights to other kinds of performance, such as the rendering of a service. Nor are the assignable rights limited to rights of a contractual nature. Claims deriving from non-contractual claims or based on a judgment, for instance, can be governed by the present Section, subject to Art. 1.4. Future rights may also be transferred under the conditions of Art. 9.1.5.

3. Notion of "transfer"

The "transfer" of the right means that it leaves the assignor's assets to become part of those of the assignee. The definition also covers transfers for security purposes.

4. Third party rights

Transfers from the assets of the assignor to those of the assignee remain subject to third party rights. Different third parties can be affected by the assignment of a right between an assignor and an assignee, such as, first and foremost, the obligor, but also the assignor's creditors and successive assignees. Third party rights are covered in part by other provisions of this Section (see Arts. 9.1.10 and 9.1.11 concerning the obligor and successive assignees). They may in some instances be governed by mandatory rules of the otherwise applicable law (*e.g.* the law of bankruptcy).

Issues & Cases

1. ASSIGNMENT OF RIGHTS DEFINED
- 1.1 ONLY TRANSFER BY AGREEMENT WITHIN SCOPE OF PRINCIPLES
  - 1.1.1 TRANSFER BY WAY OF SECURITY
- 1.2 TRANSFER OF MONETARY RIGHTS
- 1.3 TRANSFER OF NON MONETARY RIGHTS
- 1.4 TRANSFER OF CONTRACTUAL RIGHTS
- 1.5 TRANSFER OF NON-CONTRACTUAL RIGHTS
  - 1.5.1 MANDATORY RULES PREVAILING OVER PRINCIPLES (SEE ART. 1.4)

ARTICLE 9.1.2
(Exclusions)

This Section does not apply to transfers made under the special rules governing the transfers:

(a) of instruments such as negotiable instruments, documents of title or financial instruments, or

(b) of rights in the course of transferring a business.

COMMENT

Some types of assignment of rights are normally subject to very specific rules under the applicable law, and are therefore not governed by this Section.

1. Transfer of instruments governed by special rules

The transfer of certain types of instrument governed by special rules are outside the scope of this Section. This applies for instance to negotiable instruments, such as bills of exchange, that are usually transferred by endorsement or delivery of the document, and which are subject to further distinct rules, *e.g.* concerning defences that would have been available to the transferor. This exclusion also applies to documents of title, such as bills of lading or warehouse warrants, and financial instruments such as stocks and bonds. The transfer of such instruments are all normally subject to specific rules.

This does not exclude the possibility that such rights, in certain jurisdictions, could also be transferred by a normal assignment, which would then be subject to this Section.

2. Transfer of a business

Another exclusion is assignment made in the course of transferring a business under special rules governing such transfers, as may happen in the case of the merger of companies. The applicable law often provides for mechanisms that cause all rights and obligations, under certain conditions, to be transferred in their entirety by operation of law.

Art. 9.1.2(b) does not prevent this Section from applying when certain rights pertaining to the transferred business are assigned individually. On the contrary, the mere transfer of shares in a company may fall under Art. 9.1.2(a) and therefore not be covered by this Section.

Illustrations

1. Company A is transferred to company B. If the otherwise applicable law provides that all rights pertaining to the former company are automatically transferred to the latter, the Principles do not apply.

2. The initial facts are the same as in Illustration 1, but B is not interested in taking over a specific claim against customer X, and prefers that right to be assigned to company C. This particular transfer is subject to the Principles.

Issues & Cases

1. **OUTSIDE SCOPE OF PRINCIPLES**
   - 1.1 **TRANSFER OF NEGOTIABLE INSTRUMENTS**
   - 1.2 **TRANSFER OF DOCUMENTS OF TITLE**
   - 1.3 **TRANSFER OF FINANCIAL INSTRUMENTS**
   - 1.4 **TRANSFER OF RIGHTS IN COURSE OF TRANSFERRING A BUSINESS**
     - 1.4.1 **EXECPTION WHEN RIGHTS ASSIGNED INDIVIDUALLY**

ARTICLE 9.1.3
(Assignability of non-monetary rights)

A right to non-monetary performance may be assigned only if the assignment does not render the obligation significantly more burdensome.

COMMENT

The assignment of a right does not in principle affect the obligor's rights and obligations. However, to a certain extent the fact that performance is now due to another obligee can modify the conditions under which the obligation is to be performed. The place of performance may be different. The change of obligee may in itself render the obligation more burdensome.

Art. 9.1.8 entitles the obligor to be compensated by the assignor or the assignee for any additional costs caused by the assignment. This provision should be sufficient to take care of the problem in the case of the assignment of monetary obligations. However, when the assigned right concerns a non-monetary performance, the remedy may not always be sufficient. The present article excludes the possibility of assigning such rights when the transfer would render the obligation significantly more burdensome for the obligor.

Illustrations

1. Company X has undertaken to provide the security service aimed at preventing theft in warehouses used by company A for the storage of wood. The premises are sold to company B, which intends to apply them to the same use. Nothing in this provision prevents A from assigning to B its right to the security services provided by X.

2. The initial facts are the same as in Illustration 1, but B intends to use the warehouses for the storage of electronic equipment. A's right to the security services provided by X may not be assigned to B: such services would become significantly more burdensome since the security risks are obviously much higher with electronic equipment than with the storage of wood.

Issues & Cases

1. ASSIGNMENT OF NON-MONETARY RIGHTS

1.1 ONLY IF TRANSFER DOES NOT RENDER OBLIGATION SIGNIFICANTLY MORE BURDENSOME

ARTICLE 9.1.4
(Partial assignment)

(1) A right to the payment of a monetary sum may be assigned partially.

(2) A right to other performance may be assigned partially only if it is divisible, and the assignment does not render the obligation significantly more burdensome.

COMMENT

1. Economic interest

The partial assignment of a right may serve different economic purposes. A contractor may for instance want to assign part of its right to payment from a customer to a financing institution, and keep the rest for itself. Or it may want to assign the other part to a supplier of raw materials.

Permitting partial assignment may however affect the principle that the assignment should not worsen the obligor's situation. If the right is split, the obligor will have to perform in several parts, which could entail extra costs.

2. Monetary and non-monetary rights

The obligor's burden of having to make two or several monetary payments instead of one is not in itself deemed to be excessive, and partial assignments of monetary rights are therefore permitted in principle (para. (1)).

Another rule prevails for the assignment of non-monetary rights, where the validity of the partial assignment is made dependent on two cumulative conditions: the divisibility of the performance due and the degree of additional burden the partial assignment may place on the obligor. Art. 9.1.3 already excludes the possibility to assign non-monetary rights in their entirety if the assignment would render the obligation significantly more burdensome. Para. (2) applies the same rule to the partial assignment of such rights.

In any event, additional costs borne by the obligor as a result of having to perform in several parts must be compensated under Art. 9.1.8.

Illustrations

1. Buyer X is due to pay a price of US $1,000,000 to seller A on 31 October. A urgently needs US $600,000 and assigns a corresponding part of its right to bank B. Notice of the partial assignment is given to X. On 31 October, both A and B claim

payment of their respective parts. X must pay A US $400,000 and B US $600,000.

2. Metal company X is to deliver 1,000 tons of steel to carmaker A on 31 October. Due to a decrease in sales, A estimates that it will not need that much steel at that time, and assigns the right to delivery of up to 300 tons to carmaker B. Notice of the partial assignment is given to X. On 31 October both A and B claim delivery of their respective quantities. X must deliver 700 tons to A and 300 tons to B.

3. Tax consultant X has promised to spend 30 days in examining the accounts of company A in order to determine the proper policy to be followed in the light of new tax regulations. A subsequently regrets this arrangement, in consideration of the level of the fees to be paid. It proposes to assign 15 of the days to company B. X can argue against such a partial assignment on the grounds that performance of tasks of that nature is not divisible. It can also argue that the accounts of B are of a significantly more complex nature than those of A.

Issues & Cases

1. **PARTIAL ASSIGNMENT**
   - 1.1 **IN CASE OF MONETARY RIGHTS**
   - 1.2 **IN CASE OF NON-MONETARY RIGHTS**
     - 1.2.1 **ONLY IF DIVISIBLE**
     - 1.2.2 **ONLY IF TRANSFER DOES NOT RENDER OBLIGATION SIGNIFICANTLY BURDENSOME**

ARTICLE 9.1.5
(Future rights)

A future right is deemed to be transferred at the time of the agreement, provided the right, when it comes into existence, can be identified as the right to which the assignment relates.

COMMENT

1. Economic interest

For the purposes of this Section, a future right is a right that will or might come into existence in the future (as opposed to a present right to a performance due in the future). Examples of future rights are rights that a bank may have against a customer who might be granted a credit line in the future, or that a firm may have against another firm on the basis of a contract which might be concluded in the future. The assignment of such future rights can be highly significant economically.

2. Determinability

According to this article a future right can be assigned on condition that it can be determined as the right to which the assignment relates when it comes into existence. The reason for this is the need to avoid the difficulties that might be caused by a transfer of future rights that are described in vague and too broad general terms.

3. Retroactive effect

This article also provides that the assignment of future rights is effective with retroactivity between the assignor and the assignee. When the right comes into existence, the transfer is considered to have taken place at the time of the assignment agreement.

As regards third parties, it will be recalled that their rights may in some instances be governed by mandatory rules of the otherwise applicable law (*e.g.* the law of bankruptcy). However, third party rights are partly covered by other provisions of this Section, including the consequences of notice specified in Arts. 9.1.10 and 9.1.11.

Illustration

In order to finance new investments, company A assigns the royalties to be earned from future licences of a certain technology to lending institution B. Six months later, A licenses that technology to company X. The royalties due are considered to have been assigned to B from the date of the assignment agreement, provided the royalties can be related to this agreement.

Issues & Cases

1. **ASSIGNMENT OF FUTURE RIGHT**
   1.1 **ONLY IF IDENTIFIABLE AS RIGHT TO WHICH ASSIGNMENT RELATES AT TIME WHEN IT COMES INTO EXISTENCE**
2. **ASSIGNMENT EFFECTIVE AS FROM TIME OF AGREEMENT**

ARTICLE 9.1.6
(Rights assigned without individual specification)

A number of rights may be assigned without individual specification, provided such rights can be identified as rights to which the assignment relates at the time of the assignment or when they come into existence.

COMMENT

Rights are often assigned as a bundle or in bulk. A firm may for instance assign all its receivables to a factoring company. In practice it would be excessively burdensome to require individual specification of each assigned right, but the global identification of the rights assigned as a bundle must be such as to permit the recognition of each right concerned as part of the assignment.

In the case of existing rights, such recognition must be possible at the time of the assignment. If future rights are included in the bundle, in accordance with Art. 9.1.5 identification must be possible when the rights come into existence.

Illustration

Retailer A assigns all its receivables to factor B. There are thousands of existing and/or future rights. The assignment does not require the specification of each single claim. Later, B gives notice of the assignment to the obligor of a specific receivable. B must be able to demonstrate the inclusion of that receivable in the bundle either at the time of the assignment, or, in the case of a right which did not exist yet at that time, when the right came into existence.

Issues & Cases

1. ASSIGNMENT OF RIGHTS WITHOUT INDIVIDUAL SPECIFICATION
    - 1.1 EFFECTIVE PROVIDED THAT RIGHTS IDENTIFIABLE AS THOSE TO WHICH ASSIGNMENT RELATES
        - 1.1.1 IN CASE OF EXISTING RIGHTS, AT TIME OF ASSIGNMENT
        - 1.1.2 IN CASE OF FUTURE RIGHTS, AT TIME WHEN THEY COME INTO EXISTENCE

ARTICLE 9.1.7
(Agreement between assignor and assignee sufficient)

(1) A right is assigned by mere agreement between the assignor and the assignee, without notice to the obligor.

(2) The consent of the obligor is not required unless the obligation in the circumstances is of an essentially personal character.

COMMENT

In the definition of Art. 9.1.1 the assignment of a right is described as a *"transfer by agreement"*. Arts. 9.1.7 to 9.1.15 are corollaries of that provision that govern the respective legal positions of assignor, assignee and obligor.

1. Mere agreement between assignor and assignee

According to para. (1) of the present article, the assignment of a right is effective, *i.e.* the right is transferred from the assignor's assets to the assignee's assets, by mere agreement between these two parties. The provision is an application to the assignment of a right of the general principle laid down in Art. 1.2 according to which nothing in the Principles requires a contract to be concluded in a particular form. Yet it does not affect the possible application of mandatory rules of the otherwise applicable law according to Art. 1.4: thus, for instance, an assignment for security purposes may be subject to special requirements as to form.

As already stated in comment 4 to Art. 9.1.1, the rule laid down in para. (1) remains subject to third party rights, which are partly covered by other provisions of this Section (see Arts. 9.1.10 and 9.1.11 concerning the obligor and successive assignees), and may in some instances be governed by mandatory rules of the otherwise applicable law (*e.g.* the law of bankruptcy) according to Art. 1.4. However, it should be stressed that notice to the obligor as provided for by Art. 9.1.10 is not a condition for the effectiveness of the transfer of the right(s) between the assignor and the assignee.

2. Consent of the obligor in principle not required

Para. (2) states explicitly what is already implied in para. (1), *i.e.* that the obligor's consent is not required for the assignment to be effective between the assignor and the assignee.

3. Exception: obligation of an essentially personal character

An exception is made for the case in which the right to be assigned relates to an obligation of an essentially personal character, *i.e.* a right that has been granted by the obligor specifically to the person of the obligee. This characteristic prevents the right from being assigned without the consent of the obligor, since it would be inappropriate to oblige the obligor to perform in favour of another person.

Illustrations

1. Company X promises to sponsor activities organised by organisation A, engaged in the defence of human rights. A wishes to assign the right to organisation B, active in the protection of the environment. The assignment can only take place with X's agreement.

2. A famous soprano has made a contract with agent A to sing in concerts organised by A. A sells its claims against the soprano to agent B. This transfer will require the soprano's consent, if the circumstances reveal that she was willing to sing only for A.

4. Effect of other provisions

The possibility to assign a right without the obligor's consent may be affected by the presence of a non-assignment clause in the contract between the assignor and the obligor (see Art. 9.1.9), although such a clause does not in itself necessarily imply the essentially personal character of the obligation.

The present article does not address the issue of the necessity to give notice of the assignment to the obligor in order to avoid that the obligor pays the assignor after the assignment has taken place. On these issues, see Arts. 9.1.10 and 9.1.11.

Issues & Cases

1. ASSIGNMENT BETWEEN ASSIGNOR AND ASSIGNEE
    1.1 EFFECTIVE BY MERE AGREEMENT (SEE ART. 1.2)
        1.1.1 MANDATORY RULES PREVAILING OVER PRINCIPLES (SEE ART. 1.4)
    1.2 NO NEED FOR NOTICE TO OBLIGOR (SEE ART. 9.1.10)
    1.3 NO NEED FOR OBLIGOR'S CONSENT
        1.3.1 EXCEPTIONS
            1.3.1.1 OBLIGATION OF ESSENTIALLY PERSONAL CHARACTER
            1.3.1.2 NON-ASSIGNMENT CLAUSES (SEE ART. 9.1.9)

ARTICLE 9.1.8
(Obligor's additional costs)

The obligor has a right to be compensated by the assignor or the assignee for any additional costs caused by the assignment.

COMMENT

1. Compensation for additional costs

The assignment of a right does not necessarily affect the obligor's rights and obligations. However, should the obligor bear additional costs due to the fact that performance has to be rendered to the assignee instead of the original obligee, this article entitles the obligor to require due compensation.

Illustration

1. Company X is obliged to reimburse a loan of 1,000,000 euros to company A. Both companies are located in Switzerland. A assigns its right to company B, located in Mexico. X has a right to be compensated for the additional costs involved in what has now become an international transfer.

The rule laid down in this article is in conformity with Art. 6.1.6, which provides a similar solution if a party to the contract changes its place of business after the conclusion of the contract.

2. Compensation by the assignor or the assignee

The obligor may claim compensation for additional costs either from the assignor or from the assignee. In the case of a monetary obligation, the obligor will often be in a position to set off its right to compensation against the obligation it owes to the assignee.

3. Partial assignment

Additional costs may arise in particular in the case of partial assignment (Art. 9.1.4). This article applies accordingly.

Illustration

2. In Illustration 2 to Art. 9.1.4, A has assigned to B part of its right to receive a delivery of steel from X. Instead of having to deliver 1,000 tons to A, X became obliged to deliver 700 tons to A

and 300 tons to B. X is entitled to be compensated for the additional costs resulting from having to deliver in two parts.

4. Obligation becoming significantly more burdensome

In two cases compensation for additional costs is not considered to be a sufficient remedy. Firstly, under Art. 9.1.3 the assignment of a right to a non-monetary performance is not allowed when it would render the obligation significantly more burdensome. Secondly, under Art. 9.1.4 the partial assignment of a right to a non-monetary performance is also not allowed in similar circumstances.

Issues & Cases

1. OBLIGOR ENTITLED TO BE COMPENSATED FOR ADDITIONAL COSTS
   1.1 ALSO IN CASE OF PARTIAL ASSIGNMENT (SEE ART. 9.1.4)
2. COMPENSATION NOT SUFFICIENT WHEN OBLIGATION IS RENDERED SIGNIFICANTLY MORE BURDENSOME
   2.1 IN CASE OF NON-MONETARY RIGHT (SEE ART. 9.1.3)
   2.2 IN CASE OF PARTIAL ASSIGNMENT (SEE ART. 9.1.4)

ARTICLE 9.1.9
(Non-assignment clauses)

(1) The assignment of a right to the payment of a monetary sum is effective notwithstanding an agreement between the assignor and the obligor limiting or prohibiting such an assignment. However, the assignor may be liable to the obligor for breach of contract.

(2) The assignment of a right to other performance is ineffective if it is contrary to an agreement between the assignor and the obligor limiting or prohibiting the assignment. Nevertheless, the assignment is effective if the assignee, at the time of the assignment, neither knew nor ought to have known of the agreement. The assignor may then be liable to the obligor for breach of contract.

COMMENT

1. Balance of interests

According to Art. 9.1.7(2) the consent of the obligor is not required for the assignment to be effective between the assignor and the assignee unless the obligation is of an essentially personal character. However, in practice it is frequent for the contract between the original obligee/assignor and the obligor to contain a clause limiting or prohibiting the assignment of the original obligee/assignor's rights as the obligor may not wish to change obligee. Should the original obligee/assignor subsequently assign such rights in spite of the non-assignment clause, the conflicting interests of the obligor and of the assignee must be weighed. The obligor suffers a violation of its contractual rights, but the assignee must equally be protected. At a more general level, it is also important to favour the assignment of rights as an efficient means of financing.

In this respect the present article makes a distinction between the assignment of monetary rights and the assignment of rights to other performances.

2. Monetary rights

In the case of the assignment of monetary rights, para. (1) gives preference to the needs of credit. The assignee of a monetary right is protected against non-assignment clauses and the assignment is fully effective. However, as the assignor acts contrary to its contractual duties, it is liable in damages to the obligor for non-performance of the contract under Chapter 7, Section 4.

Illustrations

1. Contractor A is entitled to the payment of US $100,000 from its customer X after a certain stage of construction work has been completed. The contract contains a clause prohibiting A from assigning the right. A nevertheless assigns the right to bank B. B can rely on the assignment despite the clause, and can claim payment when it is due. X is however entitled to sue A for acting in breach of the clause. X could for instance claim damages if it demonstrates that it has suffered some prejudice.

2. Company X is to reimburse 500,000 euros to company A at a date when it can set off this obligation partially with a claim of 200,000 euros it has against A. The contract between X and A contains a non-assignment clause. Disregarding that clause, A assigns its right to reimbursement to company B. X may claim damages against A for the costs it incurs in having to engage in a separate procedure to recover the sum of 200,000 euros.

3. Non-monetary rights

The assignment of rights to non-monetary performances does not have the same relationship to credit, thus justifying another solution which is to be found in para. (2). In order to achieve a fair balance between the conflicting interests of the three parties concerned, the rule is that non-assignment clauses are given effect vis-à-vis the assignee with the result that the assignment is ineffective. The solution is however reversed if it can be established that, at the time of the assignment, the assignee did not know and ought not to have known of the non-assignment clause. In such a case, the assignment is effective, but the assignor may be liable in damages to the obligor for non-performance of the contract under Chapter 7, Section 4.

Illustration

3. Company X has agreed to communicate to company A all improvements it will develop to a technical process over a period of time. Their contract stipulates that A's rights towards X may not be assigned. A does not need the technology for itself any longer and attempts to assign its rights to company B. Such an assignment is ineffective. X does not become B's obligor. In such a case, B has a claim against A under Art. 9.1.15(b).

Issues & Cases

1. ASSIGNMENT AGAINST CLAUSES LIMITING OR PROHIBITING IT
    - 1.1 IN CASE OF MONETARY RIGHTS
        - 1.1.1 ASSIGNMENT FULLY EFFECTIVE
            - 1.1.1.1 ASSIGNOR LIABLE FOR BREACH OF CONTRACT
    - 1.2 IN CASE OF NON-MONETARY RIGHTS
        - 1.2.1 ASSIGNMENT NOT EFFECTIVE
        - 1.2.2 ASSIGNMENT EFFECTIVE IF ASSIGNEE DID NOT KNOW OR OUGHT NOT TO HAVE KNOWN OF NON-ASSIGNMENT CLAUSE
            - 1.2.2.1 ASSIGNOR LIABLE FOR BREACH OF CONTRACT
2. ASSIGNOR LIABLE TOWARDS ASSIGNEE (SEE ART. 9.1.15(B))

ARTICLE 9.1.10
(Notice to the obligor)

(1) Until the obligor receives a notice of the assignment from either the assignor or the assignee, it is discharged by paying the assignor.

(2) After the obligor receives such a notice, it is discharged only by paying the assignee.

COMMENT

1. Effect of notice on the obligor

Whereas the assignment is effective between the assignor and the assignee as a result of their agreement (Art. 9.1.7), the obligor will be discharged by paying the assignor until it receives notice of the assignment. If the obligor pays the assignor, the assignee can recover that payment from the assignor (see Art. 9.1.15(f)). Only after the obligor receives a notice of assignment does the assignment becomes effective towards the obligor. The obligor can therefore be discharged only by paying the assignee.

Illustrations

1. Seller A assigns its right to payment from buyer X to bank B. Neither A nor B gives notice to X. When payment is due, X pays A. This payment is fully valid and X is discharged. It will be up to B to recover it from A under Art. 9.1.15(f).

2. Seller A assigns to bank B its right to payment from buyer X. B immediately gives notice of the assignment to X. When payment is due, X still pays A. X is not discharged and B is entitled to oblige X to pay a second time.

Before the obligor receives a notice of the assignment, it is discharged when it pays the assignor irrespective of whether it knew, or ought to have known, of the assignment. The purpose is to place the burden of informing the obligor of the assignment on the parties to the assignment agreement, *i.e.* the assignor and the assignee. This solution is considered to be justified in the context of international commercial contracts. However, it does not necessarily exclude that in certain circumstances the obligor will be liable for damages if it acted in bad faith when it paid the assignor.

Parties sometimes resort to so-called "silent assignments", where the assignor and the assignee agree not to inform the obligor of the assignment. This arrangement is valid between parties, but since the obligor receives no notice, it will be discharged by paying the assignor, as provided in Art. 9.1.10(1).

2. Meaning of "notice"

"Notice" is to be understood in the broad sense of Art. 1.10. Although the present article does not specify the content of the notice, the latter should indicate not only the fact of the assignment, but also the identity of the assignee, the specifications of the right transferred (subject to Art. 9.1.6) and, in the case of partial assignment, the extent of the assignment.

3. Who should give notice

Art. 9.1.10(1) leaves the question of who should give notice open, *i.e.* whether it should be the assignor or the assignee. In practice, it is probable that in most cases the assignee will take the initiative, as it has a major interest in avoiding that the obligor will perform in favour of the assignor notwithstanding the assignment. But notice given by the assignor has the same effect. When notice is given by the assignee, the obligor may request adequate proof of the assignment (see Art. 9.1.12).

4. When must notice be given

The present article does not explicitly require notice to be given only after the assignment agreement has been concluded. In some cases the contract between the future assignor and the obligor will provide that the rights arising from it will be assigned to a financial institution. Whether this can be considered to be adequate notice having the consequences provided for in this article is a matter of interpretation, and may possibly depend on the definiteness of the clause regarding the identity of the future assignee.

5. Revocation of notice

Notice given to the obligor can be revoked in certain circumstances, *e.g.* if the assignment agreement itself becomes invalid, or if an assignment made for security purposes is no longer necessary. This will not affect payments made before the revocation to the person who was the assignee at the time, but if the obligor pays that person after the revocation it would no longer be discharged.

Issues & Cases

1. OBLIGOR DISCHARGED BY PAYING ASSIGNOR

1.1 UNTIL IT RECEIVES NOTICE OF ASSIGNMENT (SEE ART. 1.10)

- 1.2 IN CASE OF "SILENCE ASSIGNMENT"
2. OBLIGOR DISCHARGED BY PAYING ASSIGNEE
   - 2.1 AFTER IT RECEIVES NOTICE OF ASSIGNMENT (SEE ART. 1.10)
     - 2.1.1 REQUIREMENTS FOR NOTICE OF ASSIGNMENT
       - 2.1.1.1 SPECIFICATION OF ASSIGNEE'S IDENTITY
       - 2.1.1.2 SPECIFICATION OF RIGHT TRANSFERRED (SEE ART. 9.1.12)
       - 2.1.1.3 IN CASE OF PARTIAL ASSIGNMENT, EXTENT OF ASSIGNMENT
   - 2.2 AFTER IT RECEIVES ADEQUATE PROOF OF ASSIGNMENT (SEE ART. 9.1.12)
   - 2.3 BEFORE REVOCATION OF NOTICE OF ASSIGNMENT

ARTICLE 9.1.11
(Successive assignments)

If the same right has been assigned by the same assignor to two or more successive assignees, the obligor is discharged by paying according to the order in which the notices were received.

COMMENT

1. Priority of first notice

This article deals with the case where the same assignor assigns the same right to different assignees. Normally this should not happen, although in practice it may occur, whether the assignor does so consciously or inadvertently. Preference is then given to the assignee who was the first to give notice. The other assignees can only claim against the assignor under Art. 9.1.15(c) below.

Illustration

On 5 February seller A assigns its right to payment from buyer X to bank B, and then on 20 February to bank C. C notifies the assignment on 21 February, and B does so only on 25 February. X is discharged by paying C, even though the right was assigned to C after it had been assigned to B.

Unlike the solution prevailing under certain jurisdictions, the present article does not take into consideration the actual or constructive knowledge the obligor may have of the assignment(s) in the absence of notice. This approach is motivated by the wish to encourage the giving of notice, thus ensuring a degree of certainty that is especially advisable in the context of international contracts.

2. No notice given

If no notice is given by any of the successive assignees the obligor will be discharged by paying the assignor (see Art. 9.1.10(1)).

3. Notice without adequate proof

Notice by an assignee without there being adequate proof that the assignment has been made, may be ineffective under Art. 9.1.12.

Issues & Cases

1. **SUCCESSIVE ASSIGNMENT**
   - 1.1 **OBLIGOR DISCHARGED BY PAYING ASSIGNEE WHO FIRST GIVES NOTICE**
   - 1.2 **ASSIGNOR LIABLE TOWARDS OTHER ASSIGNEES (SEE ART. 9.1.15(C))**

ARTICLE 9.1.12
(Adequate proof of assignment)

(1) If notice of the assignment is given by the assignee, the obligor may request the assignee to provide within a reasonable time adequate proof that the assignment has been made.

(2) Until adequate proof is provided, the obligor may withhold payment.

(3) Unless adequate proof is provided, notice is not effective.

(4) Adequate proof includes, but is not limited to, any writing emanating from the assignor and indicating that the assignment has taken place.

COMMENT

Since receiving the notice of assignment has the important effects provided for in Arts. 9.1.10 and 9.1.11, this article intends to protect the obligor against the risk of receiving a fraudulent notice from a fake "assignee" by requiring adequate proof that the assignment has actually been made. Until adequate proof is provided, the obligor may withhold payment to the alleged assignee. If adequate proof is provided, notice is effective from the date it was provided.

Illustration

On 1 December customer X has to pay US $10,000 to contractor A as an instalment of the sum due for the construction of a plant. In October A assigns the right to bank B. Either A or B may give notice of the assignment to X. If B takes the initiative and writes to X that it has become the assignee of the sum, X may require B to provide adequate proof. Without prejudice to other types of evidence, B will probably produce the assignment agreement or any other writing from A confirming that the right has been assigned. Until such adequate proof is provided, X may withhold payment.

Issues & Cases

1. OBLIGOR ENTITLED TO REQUEST ADEQUATE PROOF OF ASSIGNMENT BY ASSIGNEE

- 1.1 ADEQUATE PROOF
  - 1.1.1 MUST BE GIVEN WITHIN REASONABLE TIME
  - 1.1.2 UNTIL IT IS PROVIDED, OBLIGOR ENTITLED TO WITHHOLD PERFORMANCE

2. NOTICE OF ASSIGNMENT EFFECTIVE ONLY WHEN ADEQUATE PROOF IS PROVIDED
3. MEANING OF "ADEQUATE PROOF"

ARTICLE 9.1.13
(Defences and rights of set-off)

(1) The obligor may assert against the assignee all defences that the obligor could assert against the assignor.

(2) The obligor may exercise against the assignee any right of set-off available to the obligor against the assignor up to the time notice of assignment was received.

COMMENT

1. Assertion of defences

A right can in principle be assigned without the obligor's consent (Art. 9.1.7(2)). This solution rests on the assumption that the assignment will not adversely affect the obligor's legal situation.

It can happen that the obligor would have been able to withhold or refuse payment to the original obligee on the basis of a defence such as the defective performance of that obligee's obligations vis-à-vis the obligor. To determine whether such defences can be asserted also against the assignee, the respective interests of the parties have to be weighed: the obligor's situation should not deteriorate as a result of the assignment, while the assignee has an interest in the integrity of the right it has acquired.

According to para. (1) of this article, the obligor may assert against the assignee all the defences that it would have been able to assert if the claim had been made by the assignor. In this case, however, the assignee will have a claim against the assignor under Art. 9.1.15(d).

Illustration

1. Software company A promises customer X to install a new accounting application before the end of the year. The main payment is to take place one month after completion. A immediately assigns the right to bank B. When the payment is due, B wants to claim it from X, but the latter explains that the new software is not working properly and that the accounting department is in chaos. X refuses to pay until this catastrophic situation has been remedied. X is justified in asserting this defence against B, which can then claim against A under Art. 9.1.15(d).

The same solution applies to defences of a procedural nature.

Illustration

2. Company X sells a gas turbine to contractor A, to be incorporated into a plant built for customer B. When the work has been completed, A assigns the warranty of satisfactory performance to B. When the turbine does not work properly, B sues X before a court at its place of business. X will successfully invoke the arbitration clause included in its contract with A.

2. Set-off

According to para. (2), the obligor may exercise against the assignee any right of set-off provided that the right of set-off was available to the obligor under Art. 8.1 before the notice of the assignment was given.

This solution is in accord with the principle that the obligor's situation should not deteriorate as a result of the assignment. The assignee's interests are protected by the claim it may then have against the assignor under Art. 9.1.15(e).

Illustration

3. Company A assigns to company B the right to the payment of 100,000 euros that it has against company X. X however has a claim of 60,000 euros against A. The two claims have not yet been set off by notice given under Art. 8.3 of the Principles, but the required conditions for set-off were satisfied before the assignment was notified. X may still exercise its right of set-off by giving notice to the assignee. B can then only claim 40,000 euros from X. B can recover the difference from A which had undertaken under Art. 9.1.15(e) that the obligor would not give notice of set-off as regards the assigned right.

Issues & Cases

1. **OBLIGOR ENTITLED TO ASSERT AGAINST ASSIGNEE ALL DEFENCES IT HAS AGAINST ASSIGNOR**
   1.1 **ASSIGNOR LIABLE TOWARDS ASSIGNEE (SEE ART. 9.1.15(D))**
2. **SET-OFF AVAILABLE ONLY IF REQUIREMENTS WERE MET AT TIME OF NOTICE OF ASSIGNMENT (SEE ART. 8.1)**
   2.1 **ASSIGNOR LIABLE TOWARDS ASSIGNEE (SEE ART. 9.1.15(E))**

ARTICLE 9.1.14

(Rights related to the right assigned)

The assignment of a right transfers to the assignee:

(a) all the assignor's rights to payment or other performance under the contract in respect of the right assigned, and

(b) all rights securing performance of the right assigned.

COMMENT

1. Scope of the assignment

This provision is inspired by the same principle as Art. 9.1.13. The assignment transfers the assignor's right as it is, not only with the defences the obligor may be able to assert, but also with all the rights to payment or to other performances under the contract in respect of the right assigned, and all rights securing performance of the right assigned.

Illustrations

1. Bank A is entitled to receive reimbursement of a loan of one million euros made to customer X, bearing interest at a rate of 3%. A assigns its right to reimbursement of the principal to bank B. The assignment also operates as a transfer of the right to interest and of the underlying security.

2. The initial facts are the same as in Illustration 1, but the loan contract entitles A to claim early repayment if X fails to pay the interest due. This right is also transferred to B.

3. The initial facts are the same as in Illustration 1, but X has deposited some shares as security to the benefit of A. This benefit is transferred to B, subject to the possible application of mandatory requirements of the otherwise applicable law under Art. 1.4.

2. Partial assignment

When a right is partially assigned, if the rights covered by Art. 9.1.14 are divisible they will be transferred in proportion. If they are not, parties should decide whether they are transferred to the assignee or whether they will remain with the assignor.

3. Contractual deviations

The rule laid down in para. (1) may however be modified by an agreement between the assignor and the assignee, who may stipulate, for instance, a separate assignment of interest.

4. Assignor's co-operation

It follows from the general duty to co-operate laid down in Art. 5.1.3 that the assignor is obliged to take all the steps necessary to permit the assignee to enjoy the benefit of accessory rights and securities.

Issues & Cases

1. SCOPE OF ASSIGNMENT
    - 1.1 ALL RIGHTS RELATED TO ASSIGNED OBLIGATION TRANSFERRED
        - 1.1.1 EXCEPTIONS
    - 1.2 ALL RIGHTS SECURING PERFORMANCE
    - 1.3 IN CASE OF PARTIAL ASSIGNMENT
        - 1.3.1 DIVISIBLE RIGHTS
            - 1.3.1.1 TRANSFERRED IN PROPORTION
        - 1.3.2 NON-DIVISIBLE RIGHTS
            - 1.3.2.1 TRANSFERRED TO ASSIGNEE
            - 1.3.2.2 RETAINED BY ASSIGNOR
2. OBLIGOR'S DUTY TO COOPERATE (SEE ART. 5.1.3)

ARTICLE 9.1.15
(Undertakings of the assignor)

The assignor undertakes towards the assignee, except as otherwise disclosed to the assignee, that:

(a) the assigned right exists at the time of the assignment, unless the right is a future right;

(b) the assignor is entitled to assign the right;

(c) the right has not been previously assigned to another assignee, and it is free from any right or claim from a third party;

(d) the obligor does not have any defences;

(e) neither the obligor nor the assignor has given notice of set-off concerning the assigned right and will not give any such notice;

(f) the assignor will reimburse the assignee for any payment received from the obligor before notice of the assignment was given.

COMMENT

When assigning a right by agreement to the assignee, the assignor assumes several undertakings.

1. Existence of the right

The assigned right should exist at the time of the assignment. This would, for instance, not be the case if the payment has already been made or if the right to a payment had previously been avoided.

Illustration

1. Company A assigns a bundle of rights to factor B. When required to pay by B, customer X demonstrates that the amount due has been paid to A before the assignment. B has a claim against A, since at the time of the assignment the right no longer existed.

If, as permitted by Art. 9.1.5, a future right is assigned, no such undertaking exists.

Illustration

2. Company A assigns to bank B the royalties from a technology licence that is to be granted in the near future to company X. The licence never materialises. B has no claim against A.

2. Assignor entitled to assign the right

The assignor is entitled to assign the right. This is, for instance, not the case if there is a legal or contractual prohibition to assign the right.

Illustration

3. Company X has agreed to communicate to company A all the improvements to a technical process that it will develop over a period of time. Their contract stipulates that A's rights towards X cannot be assigned. A no longer needs the technology itself, and attempts to assign its rights to company B. This illustration was already given above, under Art. 9.1.9, to give an example of an ineffective assignment. In this case, B has a claim against A under Art. 9.1.15(b). It will be recalled that the solution would be reversed, should B demonstrate that it neither knew nor ought to have known of the non-assignment clause.

3. No previous assignment, no third party rights or claims

If the assignor has already assigned a right to another assignee, it is generally not entitled to make a second assignment of that same right, and this prohibition could be considered as already covered by the undertaking under sub-para. (b). The practical importance of this hypothesis is such that a separate and explicit provision is justified. It will however be recalled that under Art. 9.1.11 the second assignee may prevail over the first one if it gives earlier notice to the obligee.

However, a previous assignment may have been made merely for security purposes. In this case, the right is still assignable, with proper disclosure to the second assignee.

4. No defence from the obligor

According to Art. 9.1.13(1), the obligor may assert against the assignee all the defences that the obligor would have been able to assert against the assignor. In such a case, the assignee has a claim against the assignor on the basis of this undertaking.

Illustration

4. Bank B is the assignee of contractor A's right to payment of a certain sum from customer X. When payment is due, X refuses to pay arguing that A did not perform its obligations properly. Such defence can be successfully set up against B under Art. 9.1.13(1). B would then have a claim against A.

5. No notice of set-off

The right of set-off may be exercised by the obligor against the assignee if it was available to the obligor before the notice of assignment was received (see Art. 9.1.13(2)). The assignor undertakes vis-à-vis the assignee that neither the assignor nor the obligor has already given notice of set-off affecting the assigned right. The assignor also undertakes that such notice will not be given in the future. If, for instance, the obligor were to give such a notice to the assignee after the assignment, as permitted by Art. 9.1.13(2), the assignee would have a claim against the assignor under Art. 9.1.15(e).

6. Reimbursement of payment by the obligor

Art. 9.1.10(1) provides that until it receives the notice of assignment, the obligor is discharged by paying the assignor. This is the correct solution to protect the obligor, but the assignor and the assignee have agreed between themselves on the transfer of the right. The assignor therefore undertakes that it will reimburse the assignee for any payment it received from the obligor before the notice of assignment was given.

Illustration

5. Seller A assigns to bank B its right to payment from buyer X. Neither A nor B gives notice to X. When payment is due, X pays A. As already explained in the comment on Art. 9.1.10, this payment is fully valid and B is discharged. However, Art. 9.1.15(f) enables B to recover the sum paid from A.

7. No undertaking concerning the obligor's performance or solvency

Parties to the assignment may certainly provide for an undertaking by the assignor concerning the obligor's present or future solvency, or, more generally, the obligor's performance of its obligations. However, without such an agreement, there is no such undertaking under this article.

Illustration

6. Company B is the assignee of company A's right to payment of a certain sum from customer X. When payment is due, B finds out that X has become insolvent. B has to bear the

consequences. The solution would be the same if B discovered that X was already insolvent at the time of the assignment.

In case of breach of one of the assignor's undertakings, the remedies provided for in Chapter 7 become available. The assignee may for instance claim damages from the assignor, or terminate the agreement if the conditions of Art. 7.3.1 *et seq* are fulfilled.

8. Effect of disclosure on undertaking

Some of the assignor's undertakings may be affected by disclosures made at the time of the transfer. The assignor may for instance advise the assignee of the existence of a claim by a third party, in which case the assignee may accept the transfer of the right at its own risk, with no undertaking on that matter on the part of the assignor.

Issues & Cases

1. ASSIGNOR'S UNDERTAKINGS TOWARDS ASSIGNEE IN GENERAL
   - 1.1 EXISTENCE OF RIGHT
     - 1.1.1 EXCEPTION IN CASE OF FUTURE RIGHTS (SEE ART. 9.1.5)
   - 1.2 ASSIGNOR ENTITLED TO ASSIGN RIGHT
   - 1.3 NO PREVIOUS ASSIGNMENT OR THIRD PARTY RIGHTS
   - 1.4 NO DEFENCES FROM OBLIGOR
   - 1.5 NO NOTICE OF SET-OFF BY OBLIGOR OR ASSIGNOR
   - 1.6 REIMBURSEMENT OF PAYMENTS FROM OBLIGOR BEFORE NOTICE OF ASSIGNMENT
2. DISCLOSURE TO ASSIGNEE
   - 2.1 RIGHT NOT IN EXISTENCE
   - 2.2 ASSIGNOR NOT ENTITLED TO ASSIGN RIGHT
   - 2.3 PREVIOUS ASSIGNMENT OR THIRD PARTY RIGHTS
   - 2.4 DEFENCES FROM OBLIGOR
   - 2.5 NOTICE OF SET-OFF BY OBLIGOR OR ASSIGNOR

SECTION 2: TRANSFER OF OBLIGATIONS

ARTICLE 9.2.1
(Modes of transfer)

An obligation to pay money or render other performance may be transferred from one person (the "original obligor") to another person (the "new obligor") either

a) by an agreement between the original obligor and the new obligor subject to Article 9.2.3, or

b) by an agreement between the obligee and the new obligor, by which the new obligor assumes the obligation.

COMMENT

In addition to the assignment of rights covered by Section 1 of this Chapter, the transfer of obligations may serve other useful economic purposes. For instance, if firm A can claim payment from its customer B, but itself owes a similar amount to its supplier X, it may be practical to arrange for the customer to become the supplier's obligor.

Such a transfer of an obligation may occur in two different ways.

1. Transfer by agreement between the original obligor and the new obligor

In practice, the most frequent way to transfer an obligation is by agreement between the original obligor and the new obligor, with the obligee's consent as required by Art. 9.2.3.

Illustration

1. Firm A owes its supplier X 5,000 euros, and customer B owes the same sum to A. A and B agree that the latter will take over the former's obligation towards X. The obligation is transferred if X agrees to the transaction.

2. Transfer by agreement between the obligee and the new obligor

Another possibility is an agreement between the obligee and the new obligor, by which the new obligor accepts to take over the obligation.

Illustration

2. The products of company X are sold by distributor A on a certain market. The contract between the parties is close to termination. Distributor B enters into negotiations with X, proposing to take over the distributorship. In order to gain X's acceptance, B promises that it will assume a debt of 5,000 euros still owed by A to X, and X accepts. B has become X's obligor.

3. Obligee's consent necessary

In both cases, the obligee must give its consent to the transfer. This is obvious when the transfer occurs by agreement between the obligee and the new obligor. If it occurs by an agreement between the original obligor and the new obligor, the requirement is stated in Art. 9.2.3. Consent may be given in advance under Art. 9.2.4.

Without the obligee's consent, the obligor may agree with another person that the latter will perform the obligation under Art. 9.2.6.

4. Transfer by agreement only

Only transfers by agreement are governed by this Section, as opposed to situations where the applicable law may provide for legal transfers (such as, under certain jurisdictions, the automatic transfer of obligations in the case of the merger of companies. See Art. 9.2.2).

5. Obligations in respect of payment of money or other performance

This Section is not restricted to the transfer of obligations in respect of payment of money. It covers also the transfer of obligations relating to other kinds of performance, such as the rendering of a service. Nor are transferable obligations limited to obligations of a contractual nature. Obligations deriving from tort law or based on a judgment, for instance, can be governed by this Section, subject to Art. 1.4.

6. What is meant by "transfer"

The "transfer" of an obligation means that it leaves the original obligor's assets to enter those of the new obligor.

However, in some cases although the new obligor becomes bound towards the obligee, the original obligor is not discharged (see Art. 9.2.5).

Issues & Cases

1. TRANSFER OF OBLIGATIONS
    1.1 BY AGREEMENT BETWEEN ORIGINAL OBLIGOR AND NEW OBLIGOR (SEE ALSO ART. 9.2.3)
    1.2 BY AGREEMENT BETWEEN OBLIGEE AND NEW OBLIGOR
2. SCOPE OF SECTION
    2.1 LEGAL TRANSFER NOT COVERED
    2.2 TRANSFER OF MONETARY OBLIGATIONS
    2.3 TRANSFER OF NON-MONETARY OBLIGATIONS
    2.4 TRANSFER OF CONTRACTUAL OBLIGATIONS
    2.5 TRANSFER OF NON-CONTRACTUAL OBLIGATIONS
        2.5.1 MANDATORY RULES PREVAILING OVER PRINCIPLES (SEE ART. 1.4)

ARTICLE 9.2.2
(Exclusion)

This Section does not apply to transfers of obligations made under the special rules governing transfers of obligations in the course of transferring a business.

COMMENT

The rules contained in this Section do not apply to transfers of obligations made in the course of transferring a business under any special rules governing such transfers, as may happen in the case of the merger of companies. The applicable law often provides for mechanisms that cause all rights and obligations to be transferred under certain conditions in their entirety by operation of law.

Art. 9.2.2 does not prevent this Section from applying when certain obligations pertaining to the transferred business are transferred individually.

Illustrations

1. Company A is transferred to company B. If the otherwise applicable law provides that all obligations pertaining to the former company are automatically transferred to the latter, the Principles do not apply.

2. The initial facts are the same as in Illustration 1, but B has reasons to prefer not to become the obligor of firm X, one of A's suppliers. A can transfer the obligations concerned to company C, with the consent of X. This particular transfer is subject to the Principles.

Issues & Cases

1. OUTSIDE SCOPE OF SECTION
    1.1 TRANSFER OF OBLIGATIONS IN COURSE OF TRANSFERRING A BUSINESS
        1.1.1 EXCEPTION WHEN OBLIGATIONS TRANSFERRED INDIVIDUALLY

ARTICLE 9.2.3
(Requirement of obligee's consent to transfer)

The transfer of an obligation by an agreement between the original obligor and the new obligor requires the consent of the obligee.

COMMENT

1. Agreement between the original and the new obligor

As stated in Art. 9.2.1(a), the transfer of an obligation may occur by an agreement between the original obligor and the person who will become the new obligor.

2. Obligee's consent required

This agreement, however, does not suffice to transfer the obligation. It is also necessary for the obligee to give its consent.

This is different from the corresponding rule on the assignment of rights, where the operation is in principle effective without the consent of the obligor (see Art. 9.1.7). The assignment of a right does not affect the obligor's situation, except that the obligor will have to deliver performance to another person. On the contrary, a change of obligor may considerably affect the obligee's position, as the new obligor may be less reliable than the original one. The change may therefore not be imposed on the obligee, who must consent to it.

Illustration

Company A owes US $15,000 to company X, located in Asia, for services rendered. Due to a reorganisation of the group, A's activities in Asia are taken over by affiliate company B. A and B agree that B will take over A's debt towards X. The obligation is transferred only if X gives its consent.

3. Original obligor not necessarily discharged

With the obligee's consent, the new obligor becomes bound by the obligation. It does not necessarily follow that the original obligor is discharged. See Art. 9.2.5.

4. Lack of consent by the obligee

If the obligee refuses to consent to the transfer, or if its consent is not solicited, an arrangement for a third party performance is possible under Art. 9.2.6.

Issues & Cases

1. REQUIREMENT OF OBLIGEE'S CONSENT
   1.1 FOR TRANSFER BY AGREEMENT BETWEEN ORIGINAL AND NEW OBLIGOR TO BE EFFECTIVE
   1.2 FOR NEW OBLIGOR TO BECOME BOUND
2. LACK OF OBLIGEE'S CONSENT (SEE ALSO ART. 9.2.6)

ARTICLE 9.2.4
(Advance consent of obligee)

(1) The obligee may give its consent in advance.

(2) If the obligee has given its consent in advance, the transfer of the obligation becomes effective when a notice of the transfer is given to the obligee or when the obligee acknowledges it.

COMMENT

1. Advance consent by the obligee

Para. (1) of this article provides that the obligee's consent, required under Art. 9.2.3, may be given in advance.

Illustration

1. Licensor X enters into a transfer of technology agreement with licensee A. For a period of ten years, A will have to pay royalties to X. When the contract is concluded, A envisages that at some time in the future it will prefer the royalties to be paid by its affiliate, company B. X may agree in advance in the contract to the obligation to pay the royalties being transferred by A to B.

2. When the transfer is effective as to the obligee

According to para. (2), if the obligee has given its consent in advance, the transfer of the obligation becomes effective when it is notified to the obligee or when the obligee acknowledges it. This means that it is sufficient for either the original or the new obligor to notify the obligee of the transfer when it occurs. Notification is not needed if it appears that the obligee has acknowledged the transfer, to which it had given its consent in advance. "Acknowledgement" means giving an overt sign of having become aware of the transfer.

Illustrations

2. The initial facts are the same as in Illustration 1, but there comes a time when A actually agrees with B that from then on the latter will take over the obligation to pay the royalties. This decision becomes effective when notice is given to X.

3. The initial facts are the same as in Illustration 1. No notice is given, but the first time B pays the yearly royalties, X writes to B to acknowledge receipt of the payment and to confirm that from

then on it will expect B to pay the royalties. The transfer is effective with this acknowledgement.

Issues & Cases

1. CONSENT GIVEN IN ADVANCE BY OBLIGEE
2. WHEN TRANSFER BECOMES EFFECTIVE
   2.1 UPON NOTICE OF TRANSFER TO OBLIGEE
   2.2 UPON ACKNOWLEDGEMENT OF TRANSFER BY OBLIGEE
      2.1.1 MEANING OF "ACKNOWLEDGEMENT"

ARTICLE 9.2.5
(Discharge of original obligor)

(1) The obligee may discharge the original obligor.

(2) The obligee may also retain the original obligor as an obligor in case the new obligor does not perform properly.

(3) Otherwise the original obligor and the new obligor are jointly and severally liable.

COMMENT

1. Extent of original obligor's discharge

The obligee's consent, whether given under Art. 9.2.1(b) or under Art. 9.2.3, has the effect of binding the new obligor to the obligation. What still remains to be determined is whether the original obligor is discharged. It is primarily up to the obligee to choose among different options. Only in the case of Art. 9.2.1(b) will the choice depend also on the original obligor.

2. Obligee's choice: full discharge

The obligee may first of all fully discharge the original obligor.

Illustration

1. Supplier X accepts that its obligor company A transfer its obligation to pay the price to customer B. Fully confident that the new obligor is solvent and reliable, X discharges A. Should B fail to perform, the loss will be on X, who will have no recourse against A.

3. Obligee's choice: original obligor retained as a subsidiary obligor

Another possibility is for the obligee to accept the transfer of the obligation from the original obligor to the new obligor on condition that it retain a claim against the original obligor.

There are two options.

The first option is that the original obligor is retained as an obligor in the event that the new obligor does not perform properly. In this case, the obligee must claim performance first from the new obligor, but if the new obligor does not perform properly, the obligee may call upon the original obligor.

Illustration

2. Supplier X accepts that its obligor company A transfer its obligation to pay the price to customer B, but this time stipulates that A will remain bound if B does not perform properly. X no longer has a direct claim against A, and must first request performance from B. However, should B fail to perform, X will have a claim against A.

4. Obligee's choice: original obligor and new obligor jointly and severally liable

The second option, the one most favourable to the obligee, is to consider the original obligor and the new obligor jointly and severally liable. This means that when performance is due, the obligee can exercise its claim against either the original or the new obligor. Should the obligee obtain performance from the original obligor, the latter would then have a claim against the new obligor.

Illustration

3. Supplier X accepts that its obligor company A transfer its obligation to pay the price to customer B, but stipulates that A and B will remain jointly and severally liable. In this case X may request performance from either A or B. Should B perform properly, both A and B would be fully discharged. Should A have to render performance to X, it would then have right of recourse against B.

5. Default rule

The language of this article makes it clear that the last-mentioned option is the default rule. In other words, if the obligee has neither indicated that it intends to discharge the original obligor, nor indicated that it intends to keep the original obligor as a subsidiary obligor, the original obligor and the new obligor are jointly and severally liable.

Illustration

4. Supplier X accepts that its obligor company A transfer its obligation to pay the price to customer B, but says nothing about the liability of A. Also in this case X may request performance from either A or B. Should B perform properly, both the original and the new obligor would be fully discharged. Should A have to render performance to X, it would then have right of recourse against B.

6. Original obligor refusing to be discharged

When the obligation is assumed by means of an agreement between the obligee and the new obligor, as provided in Art. 9.2.1(b), and the agreement provides that the original obligor is discharged, the agreement amounts to a contract in favour of a third party. Under Art. 5.2.6 such a benefit cannot be imposed on the beneficiary, who may have reasons not to accept it. The original obligor may thus refuse to be discharged by the agreement between the obligee and the new obligor.

If such a refusal occurs, the new obligor is bound to the obligee, but the original obligor and the new obligor are jointly and severally liable, in accordance with the default rule of Art. 9.2.5(3).

Illustration

5. The facts are the same as in Illustration 1, the difference being that the obligation is assumed by an agreement between X and B, and that X discharges A. If A is no longer interested in a business relationship with B, it may accept to be discharged. On the other hand, if A wants to keep the possibilities it has of benefiting from a renewal of its contract with X, it might wish to keep the relationship and may therefore refuse to be discharged.

Issues & Cases

1. **FULL DISCHARGE OF ORIGINAL OBLIGOR**
2. **ORIGINAL OBLIGOR RETAINED AS SUBSIDIARY OBLIGOR**
3. **ORIGINAL OBLIGOR AND NEW OBLIGOR JOINTLY AND SEVERALLY LIABLE**
   - 3.1 **IN CASE OF REFUSAL BY OBLIGOR TO BE DISCHARGED BY VIRTUE OF AGREEMENT BETWEEN OBLIGEE AND NEW OBLIGOR (SEE ART. 5.2.6)**

ARTICLE 9.2.6
(Third party performance)

(1) Without the obligee's consent, the obligor may contract with another person that this person will perform the obligation in place of the obligor, unless the obligation in the circumstances has an essentially personal character.

(2) The obligee retains its claim against the obligor.

COMMENT

1. Agreement on performance by another party

Obligations can be transferred either by an agreement between the original obligor and the new obligor, with the obligee's consent (Art. 9.2.1(a)), or by an agreement between the obligee and the new obligor (Art. 9.2.1(b)).

There may be situations in which the consent of the obligee is lacking, either because it has not been solicited, or because it has been refused. In such cases the obligor may agree with another person that this person will perform the obligation in its place. When performance becomes due, the other person will render it to the obligee.

While an obligee may refuse to accept a new obligor before performance is due, in principle it may not refuse to accept the performance itself when it is offered by another party.

Illustration

1. Companies A and B have entered into a co-operation agreement for their activities on a certain market. At a certain point they decide to redistribute some of their tasks. Thus, B will take over all operations concerning telecommunications, which were previously A's responsibility. On the following 30 October A would have been bound to pay company X, a local operator, a sum of US $100,000. The two partners agree that B will pay that amount when it is due. On 30 October X may not refuse such a payment made by B.

2. Obligation of an essentially personal character

Third party performances may not be refused by the obligee in all the cases in which they would be equally satisfactory as performances rendered by the obligor. The situation is different when the performance due is of an essentially personal character, linked to the obligor's specific qualifications. The obligee may then insist on receiving performance by the obligor itself.

Illustration

2. In Illustration 1, B also takes over operations for the maintenance of some sophisticated technological equipment developed by A and sold to company Y. The partners agree that the next yearly maintenance will be carried out by B. When B's technicians arrive at Y's premises, Y may refuse their intervention, invoking the fact that due to the highly technical nature of the verifications involved, they are entitled to receive performance from the specialised staff of A.

Issues & Cases

1. **PERFORMANCE BY THIRD PARTY**
   - 1.1 **NO NEED FOR OBLIGEE'S CONSENT**
   - 1.2 **MAY BE REFUSED BY OBLIGEE WHEN OBLIGATION IS OF ESSENTIALLY PERSONAL CHARACTER**
2. **OBLIGEE'S CLAIM AGAINST OBLIGOR NOT AFFECTED**

ARTICLE 9.2.7
(Defences and rights of set-off)

(1) The new obligor may assert against the obligee all defences which the original obligor could assert against the obligee.

(2) The new obligor may not exercise against the obligee any right of set-off available to the original obligor against the obligee.

COMMENT

1. Assertion of defences

The obligation transferred to the new obligor is the very same obligation that used to bind the original obligor (and, in some cases, still binds it. See Art. 9.2.5).

Whenever the original obligor would have been able to withhold or refuse payment to the obligee on the basis of a defence, such as the defective performance of the obligee's own obligations, the new obligor may rely on the same defence against the obligee.

Illustration

1. Company A owes company X 200,000 euros, due to be paid at the end of the year, as payment for facilities management services. With X's consent A transfers this obligation to company B. X renders A extremely defective services, which would have given A a valid defence for refusing payment. When payment is due, B may assert the same defence against X.

2. Defences of a procedural nature

The same solution applies to defences of a procedural nature.

Illustration

2. The facts are the same as in Illustration 1, the difference being that X sues B before a court at its place of business. B can successfully invoke the arbitration clause included in the contract between A and X.

3. Set-off

The right of set-off relating to an obligation owed by the obligee to the original obligor may however not be exercised by the new obligor. The reciprocity requirement is not fulfilled between the obligee and the new obligor. The original obligor may still exercise its right of set-off if it has not been discharged.

Issues & Cases

1. **NEW OBLIGOR ENTITLED TO ASSERT AGAINST OBLIGEE ALL DEFENCES ORIGINAL OBLIGOR HAS AGAINST OBLIGEE**
2. **NEW OBLIGOR NOT ENTITLED TO SET-OFF AGAINST OBLIGEE**

ARTICLE 9.2.8
(Rights related to the obligation transferred)

(1) The obligee may assert against the new obligor all its rights to payment or other performance under the contract in respect of the obligation transferred.

(2) If the original obligor is discharged under Article 9.2.5(1), a security granted by any person other than the new obligor for the performance of the obligation is discharged, unless that other person agrees that it should continue to be available to the obligee.

(3) Discharge of the original obligor also extends to any security of the original obligor given to the obligee for the performance of the obligation, unless the security is over an asset which is transferred as part of a transaction between the original obligor and the new obligor.

COMMENT

1. Scope of the transfer

The rules laid down in the present article are inspired by the same principle as Art. 9.2.7. The obligation is transferred to the new obligor as it is, not only with the defences the original obligor was able to assert, but also with all the rights to payment or to other performances under the contract that the obligee had in respect of the obligation transferred.

The following illustrations provide examples of such rights.

Illustrations

1. Company A must reimburse bank X for a loan of one million euros bearing an interest rate of 3%. A transfers its obligation to reimburse the principal to company B. The transfer also includes the obligation to pay the 3% interest.

2. The facts are the same as in Illustration 1, the difference being that the loan contract entitles X to claim premature reimbursement if A fails to pay the interest due. X can assert also this right against B.

2. Contractual deviations

Party autonomy permits deviations from the rules laid down in this article, such as a separate transfer of the obligation to pay interest.

3. Securities in assignment of rights and transfer of obligations compared

In the case of the assignment of a right, all rights securing performance are automatically transferred to the assignee (see Art. 9.1.14(b)). This solution is justified by the fact that the assignment of a right does not alter the obligor's situation, *i.e.* securities can continue to serve their purposes in unchanged circumstances.

The transfer of an obligation to a new obligor, on the contrary modifies the context in which the security has been granted. If the original obligor is discharged, and if the security were to be transferred with the obligation, the risk of breach or insolvency to be covered would be that of another person, thus completely altering the object of the security.

4. Suretyship

If the original obligor's obligation was covered by a suretyship granted by another person, this suretyship can survive if the original obligor remains bound. If, on the other hand, the original obligor is discharged, the suretyship cannot be transferred to cover the new obligor, unless the person who granted the suretyship agrees that it should continue to be available to the obligee.

Illustration

3. Company A owes one million dollars to company X. Bank S has agreed to guarantee due performance of this obligation. With X's agreement, A transfers the obligation to company B, and X accepts to discharge A. S does not guarantee B's obligation, unless it agrees to continue to provide the security.

A special case occurs when the suretyship was granted by the person who was itself to become the new obligor. In such a case, the security necessarily disappears, since a person cannot provide a security for its own obligation.

5. Securities over assets

The original obligor may have given one of its assets as security. In this case, if the obligation is transferred and the original obligor is discharged, the security ceases to cover the obligation now binding the new obligor.

Illustration

4. Bank X has granted a loan of 100,000 euros to company A, secured by a deposit of shares by the obligor. With X's agreement, A transfers the obligation to pay back the loan to company B, and X accepts to discharge A. The shares cease to serve as security.

The solution is different if the asset given as security is transferred as part of a transaction between the original and the new obligor.

Illustration

5. The initial facts are the same as in Illustration 4, but the transfer of the obligation between A and B occurs as part of a broader operation in which ownership of the shares is also transferred to B. In such a situation, the shares will continue to serve as security for B's obligation to reimburse the loan.

Issues & Cases

1. SCOPE OF TRANSFER
    - 1.1 ALL RIGHTS RELATED TO OBLIGATION TRANSFERRED
        - 1.1.1 EXCEPTIONS
    - 1.2 SURETYSHIP
        - 1.2.1 SURVIVES IF ORIGINAL OBLIGOR REMAINS BOUND
        - 1.2.2 CEASES IF ORIGINAL OBLIGOR DISCHARGED
            - 1.2.2.1 MAY EXCEPTIONALLY SURVIVE IF SO AGREED BY PARTY GRANTING IT
    - 1.3 SECURITIES OVER ASSETS
        - 1.3.1 SURVIVE IF ORIGINAL OBLIGOR REMAINS BOUND
        - 1.3.2 CEASE IF ORIGINAL OBLIGOR DISCHARGED
            - 1.3.2.1 MAY EXCEPTIONALLY SURVIVE IF TRANSFERRED AS PART OF TRANSACTION BETWEEN ORIGINAL OBLIGOR AND NEW OBLIGOR

SECTION 3: ASSIGNMENT OF CONTRACTS

ARTICLE 9.3.1
(Definitions)

"Assignment of a contract" means the transfer by agreement from one person (the "assignor") to another person (the "assignee") of the assignor's rights and obligations arising out of a contract with another person (the "other party").

COMMENT

Rights and obligations can be transferred separately, under the respective rules of Sections 1 and 2 of this Chapter. In some cases, however, a contract is assigned as a whole. More precisely, a person transfers to another person all the rights and obligations deriving from its being a party to a contract. A contractor, for instance, may wish to let another contractor replace it as one of the parties in a construction contract. The rules of this Section cover the assignment of contracts as defined in the present article.

Only transfers by agreement are concerned, as opposed to various situations where the applicable law may provide for legal transfers (such as, under certain jurisdictions, the automatic transfer of contracts in the case of the merger of companies. See Art. 9.3.2).

Issues & Cases

1. ASSIGNMENT OF CONTRACTS DEFINED

 1.1 ONLY TRANSFER BY AGREEMENT WITHIN SCOPE OF PRINCIPLES

ARTICLE 9.3.2
(Exclusion)

This Section does not apply to the assignment of contracts made under the special rules governing transfers of contracts in the course of transferring a business.

COMMENT

The assignment of contracts may be subject to special rules of the applicable law when it is made in the course of the transfer of a business. Such special rules often provide for mechanisms that cause all contracts of the business to be transferred, under certain conditions, by operation of law.

This article does not prevent the present Section from applying when certain contracts pertaining to the transferred business are assigned individually.

Illustrations

1. Company A is transferred to company B. If the otherwise applicable law provides that all contracts to which the former company was a party are automatically transferred to the latter, the Principles do not apply.

2. The initial facts are the same as in Illustration 1, but B is not interested in taking over a particular contract with company X, and prefers that contract to be assigned to company C. This particular transfer is subject to the Principles.

Issues & Cases

1. OUTSIDE SCOPE OF SECTION
   1.1 TRANSFER OF CONTRACTS IN COURSE OF TRANSFERRING A BUSINESS
      1.1.1 EXCEPTION WHEN CONTRACTS TRANSFERRED INDIVIDUALLY

ARTICLE 9.3.3

(Requirement of consent of the other party)

The assignment of a contract requires the consent of the other party.

COMMENT

1. Agreement between assignor and assignee

The first requirement for the assignment of a contract is that the assignor and the assignee agree on the operation.

2. Other party's consent required

This agreement does not however suffice to transfer the contract. It is also necessary for the other party to give its consent.

If it were only for the assignment of the rights involved, such a consent would in principle not be needed (see Art. 9.1.7). However, the assignment of a contract also involves a transfer of obligations, which cannot be effective without the obligee's consent (see Art. 9.2.3). The assignment of a contract can thus only occur with the other party's consent.

Illustration

Office space is let by owner X to company A. The contract expires only six years from the date of the contract. Due to the development of its business, A wants to move to larger premises. Company B would be interested in taking over the lease. The contract can be assigned by an agreement between A and B, but the operation also requires X's consent.

3. Assignor not necessarily discharged of its obligations

With the other party's consent, the assignee becomes bound by the assignor's obligations under the assigned contract. It does not necessarily follow that the assignor is discharged (see Art. 9.3.5).

Issues & Cases

1. REQUIREMENTS FOR ASSIGNMENT OF CONTRACT
   1.1 AGREEMENT BETWEEN ASSIGNOR AND ASSIGNEE
   1.2 OTHER PARTY'S CONSENT

ARTICLE 9.3.4
(Advance consent of the other party)

(1) The other party may give its consent in advance.

(2) If the other party has given its consent in advance, the assignment of the contract becomes effective when a notice of the assignment is given to the other party or when the other party acknowledges it.

COMMENT

1. Advance consent by the other party

Para. (1) of this article provides that the other party's consent, required under Art. 9.3.3, may be given in advance.

This rule, concerning the assignment of contracts, corresponds to the rule in Art. 9.2.4 according to which the obligee, who must consent to the transfer of the obligation may give its consent in advance. Similarly, the other party, who must consent to the assignment of the contract, may also give its consent in advance.

Illustration

1. Company X enters into an agreement with agency A, providing that the latter will be responsible for advertising X's products in Spain for the next five years. A, however, is already considering ceasing its activities in Spain in the not too distant future, and obtains X's advance consent to the subsequent assignment of the contract to agency B, located in Madrid. This advance consent is effective under Art. 9.3.4.

2. When the assignment of the contract is effective vis-à-vis the other party

According to para. (2), if the other party has given its consent in advance, the assignment of the contract becomes effective when it is notified to the other party or when the other party acknowledges it. This means that it is sufficient for either the assignor or the assignee to notify the assignment when it occurs. Notification is not needed if it appears that the obligee has acknowledged the transfer, to which it had given its consent in advance. "Acknowledgement" means giving an overt sign of having become aware of the transfer.

Illustrations

2. The initial facts are the same as in Illustration 1. When A actually assigns its contract to B, the assignment becomes effective vis-à-vis the other party when either A or B notifies it to X.

3. The initial facts are the same as in Illustration 1. No notice is given, but B sends X a proposal for a new advertising campaign. X understands that the assignment has taken place and sends its comments on the proposal to B. The assignment of the contract is effective with this acknowledgement.

Issues & Cases

1. CONSENT GIVEN IN ADVANCE BY OTHER PARTY
2. WHEN NOTICE BECOMES EFFECTIVE
2.1 UPON NOTICE OF ASSIGNMENT TO OTHER PARTY
2.2 UPON ACKNOWLEDGEMENT OF ASSIGNMENT BY OTHER PARTY
2.1.1 MEANING OF "ACKNOWLEDGEMENT"

ARTICLE 9.3.5
(Discharge of the assignor)

(1) The other party may discharge the assignor.

(2) The other party may also retain the assignor as an obligor in case the assignee does not perform properly.

(3) Otherwise the assignor and the assignee are jointly and severally liable.

COMMENT

1. Extent of assignor's discharge

This article, concerning the assignment of contracts, corresponds to Art. 9.2.5. To the extent that the assignment of a contract causes obligations to be transferred from the assignor to the assignee, the other party, as an obligee, may decide the effect that the acceptance of the assignee as a new obligor will have on the assignor's obligations. This article gives the other party several choices and provides for a default rule.

2. Other party's choice: full discharge

The other party may first of all fully discharge the assignor.

Illustration

1. By contract with company X, company A has undertaken to dispose of the waste produced by an industrial process. At a certain point, X accepts that the contract is assigned by A to company B. Fully confident that B is solvent and reliable, X discharges A. Should B fail to perform properly, X will have no recourse against A.

3. Other party's choice: assignor retained as a subsidiary obligor

Another possibility is for the other party to accept the assignment of the contract on condition that it retain a claim against the assignor.

There are two options.

The first option is that the assignor is retained as an obligor in the event that the assignee does not perform properly. In this case, the other party must necessarily claim performance first from the assignee, but if the assignee does not perform properly, the other party may call upon the assignor.

Illustration

2. The facts are the same as in Illustration 1, the difference being that X, when consenting to the assignment, has stipulated that A will remain bound if B does not perform properly. X no longer has a direct claim against A, and must first request performance from B. However, should B fail to perform, then X would have a claim against A.

4. Other party's choice: assignor retained as jointly and severally liable with the assignee

The second option, the one most favourable to the other party, is to consider the assignor and the assignee jointly and severally liable. This means that when performance is due, the other party can exercise its claim against either the assignor or the assignee. Should the other party obtain performance from the assignor, the latter would then have a claim against the assignee.

Illustration

3. Company X accepts that company A assign the contract to company B, but stipulates that A and B will remain jointly and severally liable. In this case X may require performance either from A or from B. Should B perform properly, both A and B would be fully discharged. Should A have to render performance to X, it would then have a right of recourse against B.

5. Default rule

The language of this article makes it clear that the last-mentioned option is the default rule. In other words, if the other party has neither indicated that it intends to discharge the assignor, nor indicated that it intends to keep the assignor as a subsidiary obligor, the assignor and the assignee are jointly and severally liable.

Illustration

4. Company X accepts that company A assign the contract to company B, but says nothing about the liability of A. Also in this case X may request performance either from A or from B. Should B perform properly, both A and B would be fully discharged. Should A have to render performance to X, it would then have a right of recourse against B.

6. Differentiated options possible

A party to a contract is often subject to a whole set of obligations. When the contract is assigned, the other party may choose to exercise different options with regard to the different obligations. The other party may for instance accept to discharge the assignor for a certain obligation, but to retain it either as a subsidiary obligor or consider it jointly and severally liable with the assignee with respect to other obligations.

Illustration

5. Company A has entered into a know-how licence contract with company X. In return for the transferred technology, A has undertaken to pay royalties and to co-operate with X in the development of a new product. When X later on accepts that A assign the contract to company B, X discharges A from the obligation to participate in the joint research, for which it will deal with the assignee only, but retains A as a subsidiary or jointly and severally liable with B for the payment of royalties.

Issues & Cases

1. **DISCHARGE OF ASSIGNOR**
   - 1.1 **FULL DISCHARGE OF ASSIGNOR**
   - 1.2 **ASSIGNOR RETAINED AS SUBSIDIARY OBLIGOR**
   - 1.3 **ASSIGNOR AND ASSIGNEE JOINTLY AND SEVERALLY LIABLE**
2. **DIFFERENT OPTIONS FOR DIFFERENT OBLIGATIONS**

ARTICLE 9.3.6
(Defences and rights of set-off)

(1) To the extent that the assignment of a contract involves an assignment of rights, Article 9.1.13 applies accordingly.

(2) To the extent that the assignment of a contract involves a transfer of obligations, Article 9.2.7 applies accordingly.

COMMENT

The assignment of a contract entails both an assignment of the original rights and a transfer of the original obligations from the assignor to the assignee. The transaction should not adversely affect the other party's situation as an obligor and it should put the assignee in the same situation as the assignor in its capacity as obligor.

As a consequence, the provisions concerning defences in Sections 1 and 2 of this Chapter apply accordingly. When the assignee exercises its rights, the other party may assert all the defences it could have asserted as obligor if the claim had been made by the assignor (see Art. 9.1.13). When the other party exercises its rights, the assignee may assert all the defences that the assignor could have asserted as obligor if the claim had been made against it (see Art. 9.2.7).

Illustrations

1. Company X has out-sourced its risk management department to consultant A. With X's consent, the contract is assigned to consultant B. Due to A's incompetence, X was not properly insured for a loss it subsequently suffered. Pending indemnification, X may suspend paying B the agreed fees.

2. Airline A has a contract with catering company X. A transfers the operation of its flights to certain destinations to airline B. With X's consent, the catering contract is assigned by A to B. Litigation later arises, and X sues B before a court at its place of business. As a procedural defence B may successfully invoke that the assigned contract includes an arbitration clause.

Issues & Cases

1. DEFENCES AND RIGHTS OF SET-OFF
   1.1 IN CASE OF ASSIGNMENT OF RIGHTS, ART. 9.1.13 TO BE APPLIED ACCORDINGLY
   1.2 IN CASE OF ASSIGNMENT OF CONTRACTS, ART. 9.2.7 TO BE APPLIED ACCORDINGLY

ARTICLE 9.3.7
(Rights transferred with the contract)

(1) To the extent that the assignment of a contract involves an assignment of rights, Article 9.1.14 applies accordingly.

(2) To the extent that the assignment of a contract involves a transfer of obligations, Article 9.2.8 applies accordingly.

COMMENT

The assignment of a contract entails both an assignment of the original rights and a transfer of the original obligations from the assignor to the assignee. In parallel to what has been said about defences under Art. 9.3.6, the operation should not adversely affect the other party's situation as an obligee and it should place the assignee in the same situation as the assignor as an obligee.

As a consequence, the provisions of Sections 1 and 2 of this Chapter concerning rights related to the claim assigned and to the obligation transferred will apply accordingly.

When the assignee acts against the other party, it may assert all the rights to payment or other performances under the contract assigned with respect to the rights assigned, as well as all rights securing such performance (see Art. 9.1.14). When the other party exercises its rights, it may assert all its rights to payment or other performances under the contract with respect to the obligation transferred against the assignee (see Art. 9.2.8(1)). Securities granted for the performance of the assignor's obligations are maintained or discharged in accordance with Art. 9.2.8(2) and (3).

Illustrations

1. A service contract provides that late payment of the yearly fees due by customer X to supplier A will bear interest at the rate of 10%. With X's consent, A assigns the contract to supplier B. When X fails to pay the yearly fees on time, B is entitled to claim such interest (see Art. 9.1.14(a)).

2. The facts are the same as in Illustration 1, but X has also provided A with a bank guarantee covering payment of the fees. B may call upon that guarantee should X fail to pay the fees (see Art. 9.1.14(b)).

3. Company X has ordered the construction and installation of industrial equipment from company A. Performance levels have

been agreed between the parties, and the contract provides for liquidated damages should actual performance be insufficient. With X's consent, A assigns the contract to company B. The assignee delivers equipment that does not meet the required performance levels. X may avail itself of the liquidated damages against B (see Art. 9.2.8(1)).

4. The facts are the same as in Illustration 3, but A has provided X with a bank guarantee covering satisfactory performance. The bank guarantee will not apply to B's obligations resulting from the assignment, unless the bank accepts to continue to offer its guarantee in respect of the assignee's obligations (see Art. 9.2.8(2)).

Issues & Cases

1. **SCOPE OF ASSIGNMENT OF CONTRACT**
   - 1.1 **IN CASE OF ASSIGNMENT OF RIGHTS, ART. 9.1.14 TO BE APPLIED ACCORDINGLY**
   - 1.2 **IN CASE OF TRANSFER OF OBLIGATIONS, ART. 9.2.8 TO BE APPLIED ACCORDINGLY**

CHAPTER 10
LIMITATION PERIODS

BIBLIOGRAPHY

BERNARDINI P., Limitation Periods, in ICC International Court of Arbitration Bulletin, 2005 Special Supplement, 43 – 49.

BONELL M.J., Verso un regime uniforme di prescrizione per i contratti commerciali internazionali?, in Europa e diritto privato, 2003, 773 – 796.

BONELL M.J., Limitation periods, in HARTKAMP A.S. / HESSELINK M.W. / HONDIUS E.H. / JOUSTRA C. / DU PERRON E. / VELDMAN M. (eds.), Towards a European Civil Code, 3rd ed., Kluwer Law International 2004, 517 – 532.

ZIMMERMANN R., Die UNIDROIT-Grundregeln der internationalen Handelsverträge 2004 in vergleichender Perspective, in Zeitschrift für Europäisches Privatrecht 2/2005, 264 – 290.

ARTICLE 10.1
(Scope of the Chapter)

(1) The exercise of rights governed by these Principles is barred by the expiration of a period of time, referred to as "limitation period", according to the rules of this Chapter.

(2) This Chapter does not govern the time within which one party is required under these Principles, as a condition for the acquisition or exercise of its right, to give notice to the other party or to perform any act other than the institution of legal proceedings.

COMMENT

1. Notion of limitation period

All legal systems recognise the influence of passage of time on rights. There are two basic systems. Under one system, the passage of time extinguishes rights and actions. Under the other system, the passage of time operates only as a defence against an action in court. Under the Principles a lapse of time does not extinguish rights, but operates only as a defence (see Art. 10.9).

This article refers in general to "rights governed by these Principles" to indicate that not only the right to require performance or the right to another remedy for non-performance can be barred, but also the exercise of rights which directly affect a contract, such as the right of termination or a right of price reduction contractually agreed upon.

Illustrations

1. A sells a tanker to B. Upon delivery the ship turns out not to be in conformity with the specifications contained in the contract, but it is only three and a half years later that B brings an action against A for the cure of the defects. A may raise the defence of B's claim being time-barred under Art. 10.2.

2. The facts are the same as in Illustration 1, the difference being that the contract between A and B contains a clause allowing B a price reduction of up to 30% in case of missing equipment or spare parts. B's right to a price reduction is also barred.

2. Notice requirements and other prerequisites for enforcing rights

Under the Principles rights can be lost if the party entitled to acquire or exercise a right fails to give notice or to perform an act within a reasonable period of time, without undue delay, or within another fixed period of time. See Arts. 2.1.1 - 2.1.22 (communications in the context of formation of contracts), Art. 3.15 (avoidance of contract for defects of intent), Art. 6.2.3 (request for re-negotiation), Art. 7.2.2(e) (request for performance), Art. 7.3.2(2) (termination of the contract for non-performance). Although they serve a function similar to limitation periods, these special time-limits and their effects are not affected by the limitation periods provided for in this Chapter as they are designed to meet special needs. As they are generally much shorter than the limitation periods provided for in this Chapter, they take effect regardless of the latter. In the exceptional case that in the circumstances a "reasonable period of time" is longer than the applicable limitation period, the former will prevail.

Illustration

3. The facts are the same as in Illustration 1, the difference being that B sets A an additional period of time of 60 days for the cure of the defects. A fails to cure the defacts, but it is only two months after the expiry of the additional period fixed that B sends A a notice of termination under Art. 7.3.2. Although B's claim is not time-barred under Art. 10.2, it has lost the right to terminate the contract because it has not given notice of termination within a reasonable time as required by Art. 7.3.2(2).

3. Mandatory rules of domestic law

Mandatory rules on limitation periods of national, international or supranational origin relating to the length, suspension, and renewal of the limitation periods as well as to the right of the parties to modify them, prevail over the rules laid down in this Chapter (see Art. 1.4).

Illustration

4. Seller A in Ruritania sells and delivers component parts to car manufacturer B in Equatoria. Some of the parts are defective and the same year of delivery the defects cause accidents for which B has to pay damages. Four years later, B asks A to be indemnified for its costs. A refuses to pay. The contract provides for arbitration in Danubia with the UNIDROIT Principles as the applicable law. In an arbitration commenced by B, A raises the defence of the expiration of the three-year limitation period provided for in Art. 10.2. B responds that under Ruritanian law the claim for damages for defective goods is time-barred only after 5 years, and that this

rule claims to apply irrespective of the law governing the contract. The rule of Ruritanian law prevails.

Issues & Cases

1. **SCOPE OF CHAPTER**
   - **1.1 EXERCISE OF RIGHTS GOVERNED BY PRINCIPLES**
   - **1.2 NOTICE REQUIREMENTS AND OTHER PREREQUISITES FOR ENFORCING RIGHTS UNDER PRINCIPLES NOT AFFECTED**
2. **MANDATORY RULES PREVAILING OVER PRINCIPLES (SEE ART. 1.4)**

ARTICLE 10.2
(Limitation periods)

(1) The general limitation period is three years beginning on the day after the day the obligee knows or ought to know the facts as a result of which the obligee's right can be exercised.

(2) In any event, the maximum limitation period is ten years beginning on the day after the day the right can be exercised.

COMMENT

1. No common solution

Although periods of limitation of rights and claims are common to all legal systems, they differ in length. They range from six months or one year for claims for breach of warranties, to up to 15, 20 or even 30 years for other claims. At international level the *1974 United Nations Convention on the Limitation Period in the International Sale of Goods* (as amended in 1980) ("U.N. Limitation Convention") provides uniform rules but is restricted to international sales of goods.

2. Relevant factors

The stated length of a limitation period does not always in itself determine the time after which the exercise of rights is barred. That time may be affected by the prerequisites for the starting of the period and by circumstances affecting its running (see Arts. 10.4 – 10.9). It may also be affected by the agreement of the parties (see Art. 10.3). Party autonomy with regard to limitation periods is of great practical importance, as periods that are either too long or too short may be tolerable if the parties may modify them freely according to their needs.

3. Balance between interests of obligee and obligor

The Principles strike a balance between the conflicting interests of the obligee and the obligor of a dormant claim. An obligee should have a reasonable chance to pursue its right, and should therefore not be prevented from pursuing its right by the lapse of time before the right becomes due and can be enforced. Furthermore, the obligee should know or at least have a chance to know its right and the identity of the obligor. On the other hand, the obligee should be able to close its files after some time regardless of the obligor's knowledge, and consequently a maximum period should be established. Contrary to the U.N.

Limitation Convention which has only one absolute limitation period of four years which begins on the date of acrual of the claim (see Arts. 8 and 10(1)), the Principles provide for a two-tier system.

4. Basic structure of the limitation regime

The two-tier system adopts the policy that the obligee should not be barred before it has had a real possibility to pursue its right as a result of having actual or constructive knowledge of the right. Para. (1) therefore provides for a rather short three-year limitation period starting the day after the obligee knows or ought to know the facts on which its right is based and this right can be exercised. Para. (2) provides for a ten-year maximum limitation period, commencing at the time when the right can be exercised, regardless of the obligee‘s actual or constructive knowledge.

5. Right can be exercised

The obligee has a real possibility to exercise its right only if it has become due and can be enforced. Para. (2) therefore provides that the maximum limitation period starts only at such date.

6. Knowledge of the facts as distinguished from knowledge of the law

The general three-year limitation period starts the day after the day "the obligee knows or ought to know the facts as a result of which the obligee's right can be exercised". "Facts" within the meaning of this provision are the facts on which the right is based, such as the formation of a contract, the delivery of goods, the undertaking of services, and non-performance. The facts indicating that a right or claim has fallen due must be known or at least knowable by the obligee before the general limitation period starts. The identity of the obligor may also be in doubt, *e.g.* in cases of agency, the transfer of debts or entire contracts, the winding-up of companies, or unclear third-party beneficiary contracts. In these cases, the obligee must know or have reason to know whom to sue before it can be blamed for not having pursued the right or claim. Actual or constructive knowledge of "facts", however, does not mean that the obligee must know the legal implications of the facts. If, despite full knowledge of the facts, the obligee is mistaken about its rights, the three-year limitation period may nevertheless starts to run.

Illustrations

1. A designs and builds a bridge under a contract with county B. A's engineers make a mistake in calculating the strength of some steel girders. Four years later, the bridge collapses due to a combination of the weight of some heavy trucks and a storm. B‘s claims for damages are not barred, because the general limitation

period started only at the time of the collapse, when B was in a position to discover A's breach.

2. The facts are the same as in Illustration 1, the difference being that the bridge collapses eleven years after its construction. B's claims are barred under the maximum limitation period under Art. 10.2(2). Parties to such a contract are well advised to adjust the maximum period while remaining within the limits of Art. 10.3.

3. A sends B a notice under Art. 7.3.2 terminating a sales contract between A and B, because B refuses to take delivery of goods tendered by A. Thirty-seven months after receipt of the note of termination, B demands the return of an advance on the purchase price paid prior to the termination. B, asserting that, due to an error in its bookkeeping, it had overlooked its payment of the advance with the consequence that it had only recently become aware of the claim for restitution it had under Art. 7.3.6(1). B's claim for restitution is barred by the three-year limitation period, as B ought to have known of its payment when the contract was terminated and the claim to repay the advance arose.

4. The facts are the same as in Illustration 1, the difference being that B asserts that it had not realised the legal effects of a notice of termination. B's claim for restitution is nevertheless barred. An error of law with regard to the legal effects of a notice of termination cannot absolve the obligee since "ought to know" includes seeking legal advice if the party is uncertain about the legal effects of the circumstances.

7. Day of commencement

Since, in the absence of an agreement to the contrary, the obligor can normally perform its obligation in the course of the whole day of the debt's maturity, the limitation period does not start on that same day but only on the following day.

Illustration

5. A is obliged to pay a sum of money on 24 November. If A does not pay by that date, the limitation period starts on 25 November.

8. Right must be exercisable

An obligation may exist even if performance cannot as yet be required (see, *e.g.*, Art. 6.1.1(a)). While a creditor's claim to the repayment of a loan is founded on the contract and may therefore arise at the time of the conclusion of the contract or of the payment of the loan to the debtor, the repayment claim will usually fall due much later. Furthermore, a right may not be enforceable if the obligor has a defence.

Illustrations

6. A loan agreement obliges the borrower to repay the loan on 15 November. The lender grants the borrower an extension of the date of repayment until 15 December. The limitation period starts on 16 December.

7. A contracts to build a fertiliser plant for B. The price is to be paid in three instalments, the last instalment being due four weeks after completion of the work as certified by an engineering firm. After certification there are still malfunctionings of the plant. B is entitled to withhold performance of the last instalment under Arts. 7.1.3(2) and 7.1.4(4). The limitation period for the claim for payment does not begin until the right to withhold payment is extinguished by cure of the malfunctionings.

9. Maximum period

Under para. (2) the obligee is in any event, *i.e.* irrespective of whether it knew or ought to have known the facts giving rise to its right, prevented from exercising the right ten years after it could have exercised it. The objectives of this maximum period of ten years are the restoration of peace and the prevention of speculative litigation where evidence has faded.

Illustration

8. B borrows money from A and orders its accountant to repay the loan when repayment falls due in January. Fifteen years later, a dispute arises over whether the loan was repaid fully or only in part as A claims. A's asserted claim is barred by Art. 10.2(2), because the maximum limitation period has expired.

10. Ancillary claims

The present article applies to all rights, including so-called "ancillary claims".

Illustrations

9. In a loan agreement, the borrower agrees to pay an interest of 0.7% per month if there is default in repayment. Thirty-five months after repayment is due, the borrower repays the principal. The lender need not sue for all successive monthly instalments of interest at once, but can wait up to thirty-six months for each instalment before it is barred.

10. Under the contract of builder A with owner B, A agrees to complete construction by 1 October, and to pay 50,000 euros for every month of delay up to a maximum amount of 2.5 million euros. Completion is delayed for 40 months. Claims for damages for non-performance or delay are barred 36 months after 2 October. The claim for the penalty for each month of delay is barred 36 months after it arises.

11. "Year"

The present article does not provide a definition of "year", because at international level a reference to "year" is usually understood as being a reference to the Gregorian calendar (see Art. 1(3)(h) of the U.N. Limitation Convention). In any event, calendars deviating from the Gregorian calendar will in most cases have the same number of days per year, with the consequence that they do not influence the length of limitation periods. A different meaning of "year" can be agreed upon by the parties under Art. 1.5. Such an agreement may be explicit or derived from an interpretation of the contract.

Issues & Cases

1. GENERAL THREE YEARS LIMITATION PERIOD
   1.1 BEGINNING ON DAY AFTER OBLIGEE KNOWS OR OUGHT TO KNOW FACTS AS A RESULT OF WHICH RIGHT CAN BE EXERCISED
      1.1.1 MEANING OF "FACTS"
         1.1.1.1 FORMATION OF CONTRACT
         1.1.1.2 DELIVERY OF GOODS
         1.1.1.3 NON-PERFORMANCE
         1.1.1.4 IDENTITY OF OBLIGOR
         1.1.1.5 OTHER CASES
      1.1.2 "MISTAKE OF LAW" NOT PREVENTING LIMITATION PERIOD TO RUN
      1.1.3 RIGHT MUST BE ENFORCEABLE
2. MAXIMUM TEN YEARS LIMITATION PERIOD
   2.1 BEGINNING ON DAY AFTER RIGHT CAN BE EXERCISED
      21.1 RIGHT MUST BE ENFORCEABLE
3. SCOPE OF ARTICLE
   3.1 ALL RIGHTS COVERED
      3.1.1 ANCILLARY RIGHTS
4. MEANING OF "YEAR"
   4.1 CAN BE MODIFIED BY PARTIES (SEE ART. 1.5)
      4.1.1 EXPRESS MODIFICATION
      4.1.2 IMPLIED MODIFICATION

ARTICLE 10.3
(Modification of limitation periods by the parties)

(1) The parties may modify the limitation periods.

(2) However they may not

(a) shorten the general limitation period to less than one year;

(b) shorten the maximum limitation period to less than four years;

(c) extend the maximum limitation period to more than fifteen years.

COMMENT

1. Basic decision: modifications possible

In some legal systems the power of the parties to modify limitation periods and their effects is restricted out of concern for the weaker parties and, in particular, consumers. A distinction is sometimes made between very short limitation periods, which can be prolonged, and other limitation periods, which cannot be modified or can only be shortened. Since the Principles apply to international contracts between businesspersons who are normally experienced and knowledgeable persons who do not need to be protected, they permit the parties to adapt the limitation periods applicable to the rights arising out of their contracts to their needs in a given case. Restrictions to the parties' automomy in this respect may, however, follow from the mandatory rules of the otherwise applicable law (see Art. 1.4).

2. Limits of modifications

The possibility nevertheless remains that a party with superior bargaining power or better information may take advantage of the other party by either unduly shortening or lengthening the limitation period. This article therefore limits the power to shorten the general limitation period by stating that it may not be shortened to less than one year starting from the moment of actual or constructive knowledge, and to shorten the maximum period by stating that it may not be shortened to less than four years. The maximum limitation period and, necessarily, the general period cannot exceed fifteen years.

Illustrations

1. The facts are the same as in Illustration 2 to Art. 10.2, the difference being that in their contract the parties provide that the

maximum limitation period for all claims based on hidden defects is fifteen years. B's claim for damages is not yet barred.

2. The facts are the same as in Illustration 2 to Art. 10.2, the difference being that in their contract the parties provide that the maximum limitation period for all claims based on hidden defects is twenty-five years and the bridge collapsed after sixteen years. B's claim for damages is barred, because the maximum limitation period can be extended to only fifteen years.

3. The facts are the same as in Illustration 2 to Art. 10.2, the difference being that in their contract the parties provide that the general limitation period in case of harm resulting from the non-conformity of the bridge starts only upon the submission of a written report of experts of an independent engineering firm. After the collapse of the bridge, it is uncertain what the causes were, and it takes two years for the engineering firm to submit its report. The general limitation period begins to run only from the day after the day on which the report was submitted.

3. Time of modification

A modification can be agreed upon before or after the commencement of a limitation period. A modification agreed upon before or after the commencement of a limitation period differs from an agreement concluded after the limitation period has expired. Such an agreement, although too late to modify the applicable limitation period, may have legal consequences either as a waiver of the defence that the limitation period has expired or as a new promise by the obligor.

Issues & Cases

1. PARTIES ENTITLED TO MODIFY LIMITATION PERIODS
   - 1.1 LIMITATION PERIODS SHORTENED BY PARTIES
     - 1.1.1 GENERAL LIMITATION PERIOD
       - 1.1.1.1 NOT TO LESS THAN ONE YEAR
     - 1.1.2 MAXIMUM LIMITATION PERIOD
       - 1.1.2.1 NOT TO LESS THAN FOUR YEARS
   - 1.2 LIMITATION PERIODS EXTENDED BY PARTIES
     - 1.2.1 MAXIMUM LIMITATION PERIOD
       - 1.2.1.1 NOT TO MORE THAN FIFTEEN YEARS
2. MANDATORY RULES PREVAILING OVER PRINCIPLES
3. TIME OF MODIFICATION BY PARTIES
   - 3.1 BEFORE LIMITATION PERIOD HAS BEGUN TO RUN
   - 3.2 AFTER LIMITATION PERIOD HAS BEGUN TO RUN

ARTICLE 10.4
(New limitation period by acknowledgement)

(1) Where the obligor before the expiration of the general limitation period acknowledges the right of the obligee, a new general limitation period begins on the day after the day of the acknowledgement.

(2) The maximum limitation period does not begin to run again, but may be exceeded by the beginning of a new general limitation period under Art. 10.2(1).

COMMENT

1. Acknowledgement of rights

Most legal systems permit the running of the limitation period to be altered by acts of the parties or other circumstances. Sometimes acts of the parties or other circumstances "interrupt" the running of the limitation period, with the effect that a new limitation period starts. Sometimes acts or other circumstances cause a "suspension" of the running of the limitation period, with the effect that the period of suspension is not counted in computing the limitation period. According to this article the acknowledgement of a right by the obligor causes an interruption of the limitation period (see also Art. 20 of the U.N. Limitation Convention,).

2. Commencement of a new general limitation period

The new limitation period that starts following acknowledgement is the general limitation period, because by virtue of such an acknowledgement the obligee will necessarily possess the knowledge required for commencement of the limitation period under Art. 10.2(1). There is therefore no need to protect the obligee by granting it a new maximum limitation period.

Illustration

1. A defectively performs a construction contract with B and B informs A of the non-conformities in October without receiving any response from A. Two years later B again approaches A, threatening to bring an action for damages. This time A responds and acknowledges the non-conformity of its performance and promises to cure the non-conformity. A new general limitation period starts to run for B's right to damages on the following day.

The commencement of a new general limitation period following acknowledgement can take place either during the general limitation period under Art. 10.2(1), or during the maximum limitation period under Art. 10.2(2). While the maximum limitation period will not in itself begin again, the new general limitation period may exceed the maximum period by up to three years if the obligor acknowledges the right of the obligee after more than seven years but before the maximum period has already expired.

Illustration

2. B discovers defects in the construction work of A only nine years after completion of the work. The defects could not have been discovered earlier. B threatens to initiate legal action, and A acknowledges the defects. A new general limitation period begins to run on acknowledgement, so that altogether the limitation period amounts to twelve years.

3. Novation and other acts creating a new obligation

Acknowledgement does not create a new obligation, it merely interrupts the running of the limitation period. Accessory rights are therefore not extinguished. Consequently, if the limitation period has already ended, a mere acknowledgement under this article does not retroactively remove or invalidate the limitation defence.

Illustration

3. The facts are the same as in Illustration 2, the difference being that B knows or ought to know of A's defective construction at the time of completion. B approaches A only 7 years later, and A acknowledges the defective performance. B's claim is nevertheless already barred under Art. 10.2(1) and is not revived by A's acknowledgement.

If the parties want to undo the effects of a completed limitation period, they can create a new obligation by a "novation" or an unilateral act on the part of the obligor, or the obligor can waive the defence of the expiration of a limitation period. The parties can also prolong the duration of the obligee's right beyond the end of the maximum limitation period under Art. 10.2(2).

Illustrations

4. The facts are the same as in Illustration 3, the difference being that A, in order to maintain a profitable business relation, not only acknowledges the defective performance, but promises to cure the defects regardless of any question of A's liability. This agreement creates a new obligation for A, which is barred only three years later.

5. Nine years after completion B discovers defects in A's construction work which could not have been discovered earlier. On notice to A, A responds that it will investigate the causes of the defects and will therefore not invoke the limitation period until six months after the experts investigating the defects submit their report. The report is submitted twelve months later, confirming B's notice of defects. When B asks A to cure the defects, A argues that the maximum period of Art. 10.2(2) has elapsed with the consequence that no claim for damages can be made by B. A's argument is incorrect if B abstained from initiating judicial proceedings on account of A's waiver.

4. Interruption of limitation periods modified by the parties

To the extent that the parties have modified the general limitation period under Art. 10.2(1), acknowledgement and the commencement of a new limitation period affects the general period as modified. If, for example, the parties have shortened the general limitation period to one year, acknowledgement causes a new one-year period to run.

Illustration

6. A and B have agreed to shorten the limitation period for claims arising from the non-conformity of A's performance to two years. After nine and a half years B discovers defects in A's performance, and A acknowledges its obligation to cure. B has another two years to pursue its claim before it is barred under Art. 10.2(1).

Since the obligor can acknowledge more than once, the limited effect of an acknowledgement that causes only the general limitation period to start again can be overcome by a subsequent acknowledgement.

Illustration

7. A delivers non-conforming goods to B in November. B suffers loss resulting from the non-conformity because its customers complain and return the goods. Since two years later the total amount of loss is not yet clear, B pressures A to acknowledge its liability and in December of that year A complies with B's request. Two years later, there are still uncertainties regarding the exact extent of B's obligations towards its customers, some of whom have sued for compensation for consequential damages allegedly caused by the goods. B therefore turns to A again, who acknowledges its obligation to compensate B should the claims of B's customers be well-founded. B has three more years before its claims against A are barred.

Issues & Cases

1. ACKNOWLEDGEMENT OF RIGHTS BY OBLIGOR
   1.1 BEFORE GENERAL LIMITATION PERIOD HAS EXPIRED
      1.1.1 A NEW GENERAL LIMITATION PERIOD BEGINS TO RUN
   1.2 BEFORE MAXIMUM LIMITATION PERIOD HAS EXPIRED
      1.2.1 MAXIMUM LIMITATION PERIOD MAY BE EXCEEDED BY UP TO THREE YEARS
   1.3 AFTER LIMITATION PERIOD HAS EXPIRED
      1.3.1 LIMITATION DEFENCE NOT AFFECTED
2. EFFECTS OF ACKNOWLEDGEMENT ON GENERAL LIMITATION PERIOD MODIFIED BY PARTIES
   2.1 A NEW LIMITATION PERIOD BEGINS TO RUN ACCORDING TO PARTIES' MODIFICATION
3. SUBSEQUENT ACKNOWLEDGEMENTS

ARTICLE 10.5
(Suspension by judicial proceedings)

(1) The running of the limitation period is suspended

(a) when the obligee performs any act, by commencing judicial proceedings or in judicial proceedings already instituted, that is recognised by the law of the court as asserting the obligee's right against the obligor;

(b) in the case of the obligor's insolvency when the obligee has asserted its rights in the insolvency proceedings; or

(c) in the case of proceedings for dissolution of the entity which is the obligor when the obligee has asserted its rights in the dissolution proceedings.

(2) Suspension lasts until a final decision has been issued or until the proceedings have been otherwise terminated.

COMMENT

1. Judicial proceedings

In all legal systems judicial proceedings affect the running of a limitation period in either of two manners. Judicial proceedings can cause an interruption of the limitation period, so that a new limitation period begins when the judicial proceedings end. Alternatively, judicial proceedings can cause only a suspension, so that a period that has already lapsed before the judicial proceedings began will be deducted from the applicable period, the remaining period starting at the end of the judicial procedure. This article adopts the latter solution (see also Art. 13 of the U.N. Limitation Convention).

2. Commencement of proceedings

The requirements for the commencement of judicial proceedings are determined by the law of procedure of the court where the proceedings are instituted. The law of procedure of the forum also determines whether the raising of counterclaims amounts to the instituting of judicial proceedings in regard to these claims: where the counterclaims raised as a defence are treated as if they were brought in separate proceedings, raising them has the same effect on the limitation period as if they had been filed independently.

Illustrations

1. A purchases from B a truck that turns out to be defective. A notifies B of the defects but, because of other pending contracts between A and B, A does not press the matter for 24 months. When the negotiations between A and B on the other contracts break down, B turns down a request by A to cure the defects, asserting that the defects were caused by A's mishandling of the truck. A files a law suit against B by depositing it with the clerk of the competent court. Under the procedural law applicable in that court, this is sufficient to initiate litigation with respect to A's claims. The running of the limitation period is suspended, until a final decision is handed down. This includes not only a decision of the court of first instance, but also, if appeal is allowed, that of a higher court on any available appeal. If the parties reach a settlement or the plaintiff withdraws its complaint, this ends the litigation if it is so regarded under the applicable domestic procedural law.

2. B initiates litigation for the purchase price of goods by filing a complaint as required by the procedural law of the country of the competent court. A raises claims under an asserted warranty either as counterclaims or by way of set off. The limitation period for A's warranty claims is suspended until there is a final decision on the counterclaims or a settlement or withdrawal of A's counterclaims.

3. Termination

"Termination" by a final decision or otherwise is to be determined by the law of procedure of the forum. These rules decide when a decision is final and therefore brings the litigation on the litigated subject-matter to an end. These rules also have to decide whether and when the litigation comes to an end without a final decision on the merits, *e.g.* by the withdrawal of a complaint or by a settlement of the parties.

4. Suspension by bankruptcy or insolvency or dissolution proceedings

For the purpose of this article, insolvency and dissolution proceedings are regarded as judicial proceedings (Art. 10.5(1)(b) and (c)). The dates of the commencement and ending of these proceedings are determined by the law governing the proceedings.

Issues & Cases

1. SUSPENSION OF LIMITATION PERIODS BY JUDICIAL PROCEEDINGS
   - 1.1 WHEN OBLIGEE PERFORMS ANY ACT RECOGNISED BY LEX FORI AS ASSERTING OBLIGEE'S RIGHT AGAINST OBLIGOR
     - 1.1.1 BY COMMENCING JUDICIAL PROCEEDINGS
     - 1.1.2 IN JUDICIAL PROCEEDINGS ALREADY INSTITUTED
   - 1.2 WHEN OBLIGEE HAS ASSERTED ITS RIGHT IN OBLIGOR'S INSOLVENCY PROCEEDINGS
   - 1.3 WHEN OBLIGEE HAS ASSERTED ITS RIGHT IN DISSOLUTION PROCEEDINGS OF ENTITY WHICH IS OBLIGOR
2. REQUIREMENTS FOR JUDICIAL PROCEEDINGS TO COMMENCE
   - 2.1 TO BE DETERMINED BY LEX FORI
   - 2.2 TO BE DETERMINED BY LAW GOVERNING INSOLVENCY OR DISSOLUTION PROCEEDINGS
3. SUSPENSION LASTING UNTIL FINAL DECISION OR PROCEEDINGS TERMINATED OTHERWISE
   - 3.1 MEANING OF "TERMINATION OF JUDICIAL PROCEEDINGS"
     - 3.1.1 TO BE DETERMINED BY LEX FORI
     - 3.1.2 TO BE DETERMINED BY LAW GOVERNING INSOLVENCY OR DISSOLUTION PROCEEDINGS

ARTICLE 10.6
(Suspension by arbitral proceedings)

(1) The running of the limitation period is suspended when the obligee performs any act, by commencing arbitral proceedings or in arbitral proceedings already instituted, that is recognised by the law of the arbitral tribunal as asserting the obligee's right against the obligor. In the absence of regulations for arbitral proceedings or provisions determining the exact date of the commencement of arbitral proceedings, the proceedings are deemed to commence on the date on which a request that the right in dispute should be adjudicated reaches the obligor.

(2) Suspension lasts until a binding decision has been issued or until the proceedings have been otherwise terminated.

COMMENT

1. Arbitral proceedings

Arbitration has the same effect as judicial proceedings. The commencement of arbitral proceedings therefore has the same suspensive effect as judicial proceedings. In general, the date of commencement is determined by the applicable arbitration rules, and the starting point of suspension is also determined by these rules. For cases in which the rules on arbitration do not exactly determine the date of commencement of the proceedings, the second sentence of para. (1) of this article provides a default rule.

Illustration

A cancels a distributorship contract with B, claiming that B has defaulted payments due for A's delivery of goods to B. B counterclaims damages for lost profits, but B changes its law firm and allows almost 30 months to pass from the termination of the agreement. The agreement contains an arbitration clause, providing that all disputes and claims "shall be settled under the Rules of Conciliation and Arbitration of the International Chamber of Commerce", and B submits a request for arbitration under those rules. The rules provide that the date of receipt of the request is to be regarded "for all purposes" as the date of the commencement of the arbitral proceedings. The running of the limitation period is suspended until a final award is handed down or the case is otherwise disposed of.

2. Termination of Arbitration

While the most frequent cases of termination will, as in judicial proceedings, be those that end with a decision on the merits of the case, arbitration can also end otherwise, *e.g.* by the withdrawal of an application, by a settlement or by an order or injunction of the competent court. The applicable rules on arbitration and civil procedure have to determine whether or not such events terminate the arbitration and thereby also the suspension.

Issues & Cases

1. SUSPENSION OF LIMITATION PERIODS BY ARBITRAL PROCEEDINGS
   1.1 WHEN OBLIGEE PERFORMS ANY ACT RECOGNISED BY LAW OF ARBITRAL
      1.1.1 BY COMMENCING ARBITRAL PROCEEDINGS
      1.1.2 IN ARBITRAL PROCEEDINGS ALREADY INSTITUTED
2. COMMENCEMENT OF ARBITRAL PROCEEDINGS
   2.1 ACCORDING TO EXPRESS REGULATIONS
   2.2 OTHERWISE, TO BE DEEMED AS COMMENCED WHEN REQUEST THAT RIGHT IN DISPUTE BE ADJUDICATED REACHES OBLIGOR
3. SUSPENSION LASTING UNTIL BINDING DECISION OR PROCEEDINGS TERMINATED OTHERWISE
   3.1 MEANING OF "TERMINATION OF ARBITRAL PROCEEDINGS"
      3.1.1 TO BE DETERMINED ACCORDING TO APPLICABLE RULES ON ARBITRATION AND CIVIL PROCEDURE

ARTICLE 10.7
(Alternative dispute resolution)

The provisions of Articles 10.5 and 10.6 apply with appropriate modifications to other proceedings whereby the parties request a third person to assist them in their attempt to reach an amicable settlement of their dispute.

COMMENT

1. Alternative dispute resolution

Before resorting to judicial proceedings or arbitration, parties may start negotiations or agree on conciliation or other forms of alternative dispute resolution.

Under the Principles negotiations do not automatically suspend the limitation period. Parties who want the limitation period to be suspended should come to an express agreement to this effect.

By contrast, this article provides that conciliation and other forms of alternative dispute resolution cause a suspension of the limitation period. The definition of "alternative dispute resolution" as proceedings whereby the parties request a third person to assist them in their attempt to reach an amicable settlement of their dispute, is inspired by Art. 1(3) of the *2002 UNCITRAL Model Law on International Commercial Conciliation.*

2. Absence of statutory regulations

As only few countries have enacted statutes on alternative dispute resolution and rules for such proceedings are relatively rare, this article refers to the provisions on judicial and arbitral proceedings, which have to be applied with "appropriate modifications". This means that, in the absence of an applicable legal regulation, the commencement of proceedings of alternative dispute resolution is governed by the default provision in the second sentence of Art. 10.6(1), the proceedings starting on the date on which one party's request to have such proceedings reaches the other party. Since the end of a dispute resolution procedure will very often be uncertain, the reference to Arts. 10.5 and 10.6, and in particular to the phrase "until the proceedings have been otherwise terminated" in their paras. (2), is also to be applied with appropriate modifications. Thus, a unilateral termination of the dispute resolution procedure by one of the parties will suffice to terminate the suspension. A unilateral termination that is made in bad faith is subject to Art. 1.7.

Illustration

The parties, a hospital and a supplier of hospital equipment, agree to submit disputes over prices to a board of mediation. Under the applicable rules a review by this board starts on the date on which one party submits a complaint to the other party, who then has to invite the board to review the case under the applicable rules. The mediation ends either when the board decides on the claim, or there is a settlement between the parties, or the claimant's request is withdrawn.

Issues & Cases

1. **SUSPENSION OF LIMITATION PERIODS BY ALTERNATIVE DISPUTE RESOLUTION**
   - 1.1 **NEGOTIATIONS NOT SUFFICIENT TO SUSPEND LIMITATION PERIODS**
2. **COMMENCEMENT AND TERMINATION OF ALTERNATIVE DISPUTE RESOLUTION**
   - 2.1 **ACCORDING TO EXPRESS REGULATIONS**
   - 2.2 **IN ABSENCE OF EXPRESS REGULATIONS, ART. 10.5 AND 10.6 TO BE APPLIED WITH "APPROPRIATE MODIFICATIONS"**

ARTICLE 10.8

(Suspension in case of force majeure, death or incapacity)

(1) Where the obligee has been prevented by an impediment that is beyond its control and that it could neither avoid nor overcome, from causing a limitation period to cease to run under the preceding articles, the general limitation period is suspended so as not to expire before one year after the relevant impediment has ceased to exist.

(2) Where the impediment consists of the incapacity or death of the obligee or obligor, suspension ceases when a representative for the incapacitated or deceased party or its estate has been appointed or a successor has inherited the respective party's position. The additional one-year period under paragraph (1) applies accordingly.

COMMENT

1. Effects of impediments

Most legal systems take into account impediments that prevent the obligee from pursuing its rights in court, as does the U.N. Limitation Convention (see Arts. 15 and 21). It is a basic policy concept that the obligee must have the possibility to pursue its rights before it can be deprived of them as a result of the lapse of time. Practical examples of impediments include war and natural disasters that prevent the obligee from reaching a competent court. Other cases of force majeure may also prevent the pursuance of a right and at least cause the suspension of the limitation period. The impediment must be beyond the obligee's control. Imprisonment, therefore, would suspend the limitation period only where it could not have been avoided, such as in the case of a prisoner of war, but the imprisonment of a criminal would not. Only the general limitation period is suspended, however. If the maximum period has elapsed before the obligee could pursue this right, it is subject to the defence of the expiration of the maximum limitation period.

Illustration

1. A's lawyer plans to file a complaint against B, an engineering firm, for alleged professional malpractice by B's employees. The limitation period will expire on 1 December, and

A's lawyer has completed the complaint on 25 November, intending to file it by express mail or in person with the clerk of the competent court. On 24 November, terrorists attack A's country with biological weapons of mass destruction, causing all traffic, mail service, and other social services to completely cease, thus preventing the timely filing of A's complaint. The limitation period ceases to run and will not expire until one year after some means of communication has been restored in A's country. If, however, the disruption of all means of communication in A's country lasts ten years, A's right is barred by the maximum limitation period.

2. Additional period of deliberation

Since impediments beyond the control of the obligee may occur and cease to exist towards the end of the limitation period, it is possible that after the ceasing of the impediment only a very short time or no time at all might be left for the obligee to decide what to do. This article therefore provides for an additional one-year period of time from the date on which the impediment ceases to exist with a view to enabling the obligee to decide what course of action to take.

3. Incapacity and death

Incapacity and death of the obligee or of the obligor are but special examples of impediments to an effective pursuance of the obligee's right. Para. (2) provides for the same solution as in the case of general impediments.

Illustration

2. A lends B money which is due to be repaid on 1 January. A does not seek repayment for a long time and dies thirty-five months after the date for repayment. The law of succession applicable to A's estate requires that an administrator appointed by the court administers the estate and collects outstanding debts. Since the docket of the competent court is overcrowded, it takes two and a half years for an administrator to be appointed. The administrator has one month left of the three-year general limitation period plus an additional one-year period to pursue the deceased party's claim against B before the limitation period expires.

Issues & Cases

1. SUSPENSION OF LIMITATION PERIODS BY EFFECT OF IMPEDIMENTS
   - 1.1 IMPEDIMENTS BEYOND OBLIGEE'S CONTROL ("FORCE MAJEURE")
     - 1.1.1 GENERAL LIMITATION PERIOD NOT EXPIRING BEFORE ONE YEAR AFTER RELEVANT IMPEDIMENT HAS CEASED TO EXIST
     - 1.1.2 MAXIMUM LIMITATION PERIOD NOT AFFECTED
   - 1.2 INCAPACITY AND DEATH
     - 1.2.1 GENERAL LIMITATION PERIOD NOT EXPIRING BEFORE ONE YEAR AFTER REPRESENTATIVE FOR INCAPACITATED OR DECEASED PARTY OR ESTATE HAS BEEN APPOINTED
     - 1.2.2 GENERAL LIMITATION PERIOD NOT EXPIRING BEFORE ONE YEAR AFTER SUCCESSOR HAS INHERITED PARTY'S POSITION

ARTICLE 10.9
(The effects of expiration of limitation period)

(1) The expiration of the limitation period does not extinguish the right.

(2) For the expiration of the limitation period to have effect, the obligor must assert it as a defence.

(3) A right may still be relied on as a defence even though the expiration of the limitation period for that right has been asserted.

COMMENT

1. No extinction of the right

The expiration of the limitation period does not extinguish the obligor's right, but only bars its enforcement.

2. Expiration of the limitation period must be raised as a defence

The effects of the expiration of the limitation period do not occur automatically. They only occur if the obligor raises the expiration as a defence. The obligor can do so in any proceedings in accordance with the applicable law, and also outside of proceedings by invoking the expiration of the limitation period. The existence of the defence can also be the subject of a declaratory judgement.

Illustration

A purchases goods from B. Part of the purchase price is due on 1 April and is not paid. Thirty-eight months later, B files a complaint against A. A does not invoke the expiration of the limitation period, nor does it appear in court, and B moves for a default-judgment. Judgment will be for B, since A did not raise the expiration of the limitation period as a defence.

3. Use of a time-barred right as a defence

Since under the Principles the expiration of a limitation period does not extinguish the right, but gives only a defence that must be asserted by the obligor (paras. (1) and (2) of the present article), it follows that the obligee's right still exists, although a claim for its performance may be barred by the obligor's assertion of the expiration of the limitation period. It can, therefore, be used as a defence, *e.g.* as grounds for the retention of performance by the obligee (para. (3)).

Illustration

1. A leases a printing press to B for ten years. Under the contract A is obliged to maintain the press in working condition and to undertake repairs, unless a defect is caused by B's negligence in operating the machine. The machine breaks down, but A refuses to do the necessary repairs. B, after futile requests and negotiations with A, has the repairs done by another firm and asks A to pay the necessary costs. A does not react, and B does not pursue the matter. Five years later, at the end of the lease, B again requests payment of the costs of the repairs. A refuses to pay and invokes Art. 10.2(1), requesting the return of the printing press. B is entitled to damages for breach of contract and to withhold delivery of the press.

Issues & Cases

1. **EXPIRATION OF LIMITATION PERIOD**
   1.1 **DOES NOT EXTINGUISH RIGHT**
   1.2 **MUST BE RAISED AS DEFENCE**
2. **TIME-BARRED RIGHT AS DEFENCE**

ARTICLE 10.10
(Right of set-off)

The obligee may exercise the right of set-off until the obligor has asserted the expiration of the limitation period.

COMMENT

Because the obligee's right continues to exist, it can be used for set-off if the prerequisites of set-off under Art. 8.1 are met.

Illustration

2. The facts are the same as in Illustration 1, the difference being that A not only asks for the return of the press, but also for the payment of the unpaid rent. B is entitled to set off its counterclaim for damages against this monetary claim despite the expiration of the limitation period.

Although the expiration of the limitation period does not in itself extinguish the right of the obligee, the situation changes when the obligor invokes the time bar as a defence by asserting it against the obligee. By so doing, the obligor makes the limitation period effective, with the consequence that the right can no longer be enforced. Since set-off may be considered the self-enforcement of a right, it is not available after the defence of the expiration of the limitation period has been invoked.

Illustration

3. The facts are the same as in Illustration 2, the difference being that B requests the payment of damages and threatens to sue four years after having had the repairs done. A objects, asserting that the machine broke down due to B's fault. Since this is hard to prove, A in a letter to B also invokes the time bar under Art. 10.2(1). B can no longer set off its claim for damages.

Issues & Cases

1. **OBLIGEE'S RIGHT TO SET-OFF (SEE ART. 8.1)**

   1.1 **UNTIL OBLIGOR HAS ASSERTED EXPIRATION OF LIMITATION PERIODS**

ARTICLE 10.11
(Restitution)

Where there has been performance in order to discharge an obligation, there is no right of restitution merely because the limitation period has expired.

COMMENT

1. Time-barred claim as valid basis for performance

Another consequence of the fact that under the Principles the expiration of the limitation period does not extinguish the right of the obligee but can only be asserted as a defence, is that if the obligor performs despite its defence, the obligation it performs remains effective as a legal basis for the obligee's retaining the performance. Mere expiration of a limitation period cannot be used as grounds for an action to reclaim the performance under restitutionary or unjust enrichment principles.

2. Restitutionary claims based on other grounds

Despite the lapse of the limitation period, a restitutionary claim can be based on grounds other than performance, *e.g.* where a payor claims to have paid a non-existing debt due to a mistake.

Illustrations

1. Bank B lends money to borrower A, who does not repay on the date required by the loan agreement. A's debt is overlooked and forgotten because of a book-keeping error on the part of B. Four years later, B discovers its error and sends A a notice claiming repayment. A complies with this request, but later learns from a lawyer that it could have refused repayment on account of the expiration of the limitation period. A cannot reclaim the payment as unjust enrichment from B.

2. The facts are the same as in Illustration 1, the difference being that A has in fact repaid the loan, but both sides are unaware of this. Four years later, B erroneously requests payment from A, and A complies. A can recover the second payment, because A has already paid a debt which has thus been extinguished by full performance.

Issues & Cases

1. RIGHT TO RESTITUTION OF PERFORMANCE

1.1 EXCLUDED ON MERE BASIS OF EXPIRATION OF LIMITATION PERIODS

PART III

DECISIONS REPORTED: ABSTRACTS AND FULLTEXT [*]

---

[*] where available

Date: ***Unknown***
Adjudicating Court: ***ICC International Court of Arbitration***
Number: ***Unknown***
Parties: ***Unknown***

Keywords

INTERNATIONAL SALES CONTRACT GOVERNED BY CISG – RATE OF INTEREST –NOT DETERMINED BY CISG–REFERENCE TO ART. 7.4.9 UNIDROIT PRINCIPLES

FIRST CRITERION AVERAGE PRIME RATE FOR CURRENCY OF PAYMENT AT PLACE OF PAYMENT (ART. 7.4.9(2) FIRST SENTENCE UNIDROIT PRINCIPLES) – IF NO SUCH RATE EXISTS RECOURSE TO AVERAGE PRIME RATE FOR CURRENCY OF PAYMENT IN STATE OF CURRENCY OF PAYMENT (ART. 7.4.9(2) FIRST SENTENCE UNIDROIT PRINCIPLES)

Abstract

In a case concerning an international sales contract governed by CISG the question as to the applicable rate of interest for the payment of damages arose. Since the Convention does not determine which is the rate to be applied, the Arbitral Tribunal without further explanation referred to Art. 7.4.9(2), first sentence, of the UNIDROIT Principles, according to which the rate of interest shall be the average bank short-term lending rate to prime borrowers prevailing for the currency of payment at the place for payment, or where no such rate exists at that place, the same rate in the State of the currency of payment. In the case at hand the currency of payment was US dollars and the place for payment was situated in Sweden. Following the guideline of the the first alternative of Art 7.4.9(2) of the UNIDROIT Principles, the Arbitral Tribunal first tried to ascertain the prime rate for US dollar credits in Sweden as the place for payment. Yet since the Swedish banks informed the Tribunal that no such rates existed in Sweden, the Arbitral Tribunal applied the prime rate applicable to US dollar credits issued in the United States as provided for by the second alternative of Art. 7.4.9(2).

Full Text

[Not yet available]

Sources

Notice by K.P. BERGER, The *lex mercatoria* doctrine and the UNIDROIT Principles of International Commercial Contracts, in 28 Law and Policy in International Business, (1997), 943 *et seq.*, at 98.

Date: ***Unknown***
Adjudicating Court: ***Ad hoc Arbitration (Place unknown)***
Number: ***Unknown***
Parties: ***Unknown***

Keywords

CONTRACT BETWEEN U.S. OIL COMPANY AND A GOVERNMENT OF A STATE OF THE FORMER SOVIET UNION – CHOICE OF LAW CLAUSE IN FAVOUR OF DOMESTIC LAW OF THAT STATE – ACCORDING TO ARBITRAL TRIBUNAL DOMESTIC LAW IN QUESTION NOT FULLY DEVELOPED – REFERENCE TO UNIDROIT PRINCIPLES TO INTERPRET AND SUPPLEMENT IT

INVESTMENT CONTRACT GRANTED FOREIGN INVESTOR A LONG-TERM CONTRACT FOR SUPPLY OF ELECTRICITY TO CUSTOMERS IN HOSTING STATE AT PROFITABLE PRICES – DUE TO SUBSEQUENT CHANGES IN ENERGY SUPPLY SYSTEM OF HOSTING STATE SUPPLY OF ENERGY BY FOREIGN INVESTOR NO LONGER PROFITABLE – REFERENCE TO ARTS. 1.4, 6.2.2-6.2.3 AND 7.1.7 OF UNIDROIT PRINCIPLES.

Abstract

A U.S. oil company entered into a contract with the Government of a State formerly belonging to the Soviet Union. The U.S. company was to invest a large amount of money and construct a power station, in return for which it would be granted a long-term contract for the supply of electricity to customers in that State at prices fixed in such a way that a return from the investment could be expected. Later the energy supply system in the State in question was fundamentally changed by law, making it impossible for the power station set up by the U.S. company to supply energy at profitable prices.

The contract contained a choice of law clause in favour of the domestic law of the State in question. However, the Arbitral Tribunal found that this domestic law had not yet been fully developed following the changeover to a market economy and contained a number of lacunae and ambiguities having a bearing on the dispute. Consequently, the Arbitral Tribunal found that the domestic law of that State should be supplemented by taking into consideration particularly Articles 1.4, 6.2.2-6.2.3 and 7.1.7 of the UNIDROIT Principles.

Full Text

[Not yet available]

Sources

Unpublished. For a notice of the award see K.H. BÖCKSTIEGEL, The Application of the UNIDROIT Principles to Contracts involving States or Intergovernmental Organizations, in ICC/UNIDROIT (eds.), UNIDROIT Principles of International Commercial Contracts. Reflections on their Use in International Arbitration, Special Supplement - ICC International Court of Arbitration Bulletin (2002), 51 *et seq.* (at 54).

Date: ***Unknown***
Adjudicating Court: ***Ad hoc Arbitration, New York***
Number: ***Unknown***
Parties: ***Unknown***

Keywords

CONTRACT BETWEEN CANADIAN CORPORATION AND THE UNITED NATIONS CONCERNING TRANSPORTATION OF U.N. PERSONNEL THROUGHOUT THE WORLD – PARTIES AGREE THAT TRIBUNAL APPLY "GENERAL ACCEPTED PRINCIPLES OF INTERNATIONAL COMMERCIAL LAW" – ARBITRAL TRIBUNAL DECIDES TO RESORT TO UNIDROIT PRINCIPLES

Abstract

A Canadian corporation entered into a contract with the United Nations concerning the transport of United Nations personnel and military personnel on behalf of the U.N. throughout the world. The events which prompted the former to commence an arbitration proceedings against the latter occurred around the world.

The contract was silent as to the applicable law. At the beginning of the arbitral proceedings the parties, requested to indicate the law governing the substance of the dispute, declined to select any national law and agreed that the Arbitral Tribunal should apply "generally accepted principles of international commercial law". Given the decidedly international context of the case, the Arbitral Tribunal found that it would not be appropriate to draw resort to any particular domestic law in deciding upon the content of those "generally accepted principles". Instead it decided to rely upon the UNIDROIT Principles for guidance in defining the generally accepted principles of international commercial law.

Full Text

[Not yet available]

Sources

Unpublished. For a notice of the award see K.H. BÖCKSTIEGEL, The Application of the UNIDROIT Principles to Contracts involving States or Intergovernmental Organizations, in ICC/UNIDROIT (eds.), UNIDROIT Principles of International Commercial Contracts. Reflections on their Use in International Arbitration, Special Supplement - ICC International Court of Arbitration Bulletin (2002), 51 *et seq.* (at 54).

Date: ***Unknown***
Adjudicating Court: ***Ad hoc Arbitration, New York***
Number: ***Unknown***
Parties: ***Unknown***

Keywords

CONTRACT FOR THE SUPPLY OF GOODS BETWEEN THE UNITED NATIONS ORGANIZATION AND A EUROPEAN COMPANY IN THE CONTEXT OF A PEACE-KEEPING MISSION IN AFRICA – CONTRACT SILENT AS TO APPLICABLE LAW – PARTIES AGREED ON APPLICATION OF CISG AND UNIDROIT PRINCIPLES

Abstract

With respect to a contract between the United Nations Organisation and a European company for the supply of goods in connection with a peace-keeping mission in Africa, a dispute arose which the parties submitted to an *ad hoc* arbitration in New York subject to the UNCITRAL Rules of Arbitration. The contract did not contain any choice of law clause. In its Statement of claim, Claimant argued on the basis of the United States Uniform Commercial Code, but in the course of the proceedings the parties, on the suggestion of the arbitral tribunal which pointed out that there was no reason why the Uniform Commercial Code had to apply in the case at hand, agreed to the application of CISG and the UNIDROIT Principles as the law governing the merits of the case. Ultimately the parties however reached a settlement.

Full Text

[Not yet available]

Date: **1990**
Adjudicating Court: **Schiedsgericht Berlin**
Number: **SG 126/90**
Parties: **Unknown**

Keywords

INTERNATIONAL CONTRACT FOR DELIVERY OF MACHINERY – CONTRACT GOVERNED BY DOMESTIC LAW (LAW OF THE GERMAN DEMOCRATIC REPUBLIC)

HARDSHIP – RADICAL CHANGE IN THE ORIGINAL CONTRACTUAL EQUILIBRIUM – REFERENCE BY ARBITRAL TRIBUNAL TO THE UNIDROIT PRINCIPLES (ARTS. 6.2.1, 6.2.2, 6.2.3) TO DEMONSTRATE THAT SOLUTIONS REACHED UNDER APPLICABLE DOMESTIC LAW CORRESPONDED TO INTERNATIONALLY ACCEPTED PRINCIPLES

Abstract

An economic unit of the German Democratic Republic and an economic unit of another East European country concluded a contract for the delivery of machinery. The applicable law was that of the German Democratic Republic. When, following the reunification of Germany, Western markets were opened to the enterprises of the former G.D.R., the machinery in question lost all value for the German importer. Consequently the latter, invoking the radical change of circumstances existing at the time the contract was concluded, refused to take delivery of the goods and to pay the price.

The Arbitral Tribunal decided in favour of the German importer and, in order to prove that the principle according to which a substantial change in the original contractual equilibrium may justify the termination of the contract is increasingly accepted at international level, referred to the provisions on hardship contained in the UNIDROIT Principles.

Full Text

[Not yet available]

Sources

D. MASKOW, Hardship and *Force Majeure*, in 40 American Journal of Comparative Law (1992), 657 *et seq.* (665).

Date: ***June 15, 1994***
Adjudicating Court: ***Internationales Schiedsgericht der Bundeskammer der gewerblichen Wirtschaft – Wien***
Number: ***SCH-4318***
Parties: ***Unknown***

Keywords

APPLICATION OF THE 1980 VIENNA CONVENTION ON CONTRACTS FOR THE INTERNATIONAL SALE OF GOODS (CISG) – CHOICE OF LAW OF CONTRACTING STATES AS GOVERNING LAW OF THE CONTRACT (ART. 1(1)(B) CISG)

NON-CONFORMITY – NOTICE – WAIVER OF THE RIGHT TO SET UP DEFENSE OF UNTIMELY NOTICE – PARTIES' INTENT MUST BE CLEARLY ESTABLISHED

PARTY ESTOPPED FROM CLAIMING DEFENSE OF UNTIMELY NOTICE – ESTOPPEL (VENIRE CONTRA FACTUM PROPRIUM) AS A GENERAL PRINCIPLE UNDERLYING CISG (ART. 7(2) CISG)

INTEREST RATE – MATTER NOT EXPRESSLY SETTLED BY CISG (ART. 7(2) CISG) – TO BE SETTLED IN CONFORMITY WITH THE GENERAL PRINCIPLES UNDERLYING CISG – FULL COMPENSATION (ARTS. 74 AND 78 CISG) AS A GENERAL PRINCIPLE OF CISG – AVERAGE PRIME RATE FOR CURRENCY OF PAYMENT IN THE CREDITOR'S COUNTRY (ART. 7.4.9 UNIDROIT PRINCIPLES)

Abstract

In 1990, an Austrian seller and a German buyer concluded a contract for the sale of rolled metal sheets. The goods were to be delivered in installments "FOB Rostock", specially packaged for export. Immediately after receiving the first two deliveries, the buyer sold the goods to a Belgian company which shipped them to a Portoguese manufacturer. The manufacturer found that the goods were defective and refused to accept the rest of them. After receiving notice of non-conformity from the German buyer, the Austria seller refused to pay damages, alleging that the notice was untimely. The buyer commenced arbitral proceedings pursuant to an arbitration clause in the contract.

The Arbitral Tribunal held that because the parties had chosen Austrian law, the contract was governed by CISG as the international sales law of Austria, a contracting State (Art. 1(1)(b) CISG).

The Arbitral Tribunal found that the buyer had not complied with particular requirements as to the examination of the goods and notice of non-conformity as contractually stipulated in derogation from Arts. 38 and 39 CISG. The buyer had sent to the seller written notice of the defects, together with an expert statement by an internationally recognized company, six months after delivery. However, according to the contract, it should have done so immediately after delivery of the goods (or at the latest within two months of delivery).

According to the buyer, the seller had waived its right to claim the defense of untimely notice of non-conformity. The Arbitral Tribunal held that the intent of a party to waive this right must be clearly established and that, in the case at hand, there was insufficient evidence of such an actual intention.

The sole arbitrator held, however, that the seller was estopped from setting up the defense that the notice given by the buyer was not timely. This question is not expressly settled by CISG. The arbitrator applied Art. 7(2) CISG, and, referring to Arts. 16(2)(b) and 29(2) CISG, held that estoppel ("*venire contra factum proprium*") is a general principle underlying CISG. Here, the seller had behaved in such a way that the other party was led to believe the seller would not raise the defense (*e.g.*, after receiving notice, the seller had continuously asked the buyer for information regarding the status of the complaints and had pursued negotiations with the intent of reaching a settlement agreement).

The buyer was awarded damages for non conformity. As far as interest is concerned, the Arbitral Tribunal held that the interest rate is a matter governed, but not expressly settled, by CISG. Therefore, it must be determined according to the general principles on which CISG is based (Art. 7(2) CISG). Referring to Arts. 78 and 74 CISG, the Arbitral Tribunal found that full compensation is one of the general principles underlying CISG. In relations between merchants, it is expected that the creditor, due to the delayed payment, resorts to bank credit at the rate commonly practiced in its country with respect to the currency of payment (the currency of the creditor's country or any other foreign currency agreed upon by the parties). The Arbitral Tribunal observed that this solution is also stated in Art. 7.4.9 of the UNIDROIT Principles of International Commercial Contracts. Here, the interest rate awarded was the average prime rate in the buyer's country (Germany) with respect to the currency of payment (US Dollars).

Full Text

1. By the request for arbitration of [...] the claimant [a company with place of business in Germany] applied for an award against the respondent [a company with place of business in Austria] for payment of DM [...]. It submitted that the respondent had not fulfilled the agreed requirements of quality and finish with respect to some consignments out of a total of 6,800 metric tons of cold-rolled sheet in coils to be delivered under a contract concluded on 11 December 1990.

[...]

1.2. The respondent [...] applied for dismissal of the claim. It disputed the alleged lack of conformity, both in substance and extent, and asserted that in any case there was no entitlement to guarantee and damages because of the failure to abide by the contractually agreed conditions.

[...]

3. The competence of the Arbitral Centre is founded on the last paragraph of the contract. According thereto, all disputes that cannot be settled amicably should be finally decided according to the rules of the Arbitral Centre of the Austrian Federal Economic Chamber by one or more arbitrators appointed in accordance with those rules. It is true that the contract - and thus the aforesaid arbitration clause exists only in the acknowledgement of order sent by the respondent to the claimant, which the latter never countersigned. However, there can be no doubt of the validity of the arbitration clause, not least because the claimant expressly refers to it in its claim.

4. According to the contract, the applicable law was Austrian law. That means that - in so far as the issues involved fall within its scope - the United Nations Sales Convention of 11 April 1980 (CISG) applies. In fact, that Convention entered into force in Austria on 1 January 1989, with the consequence that, from that date onwards, all international contracts of sale of goods within the meaning of Article 1 have been subject to the CISG, provided that the conditions stipulated for that purpose in the Convention itself are met, *i.e.* that either both parties are established in Contracting States or that the rules of private international law lead to the application of the law of a Contracting State. In the present case, the first condition was not met because Germany [...] was not yet a Contracting State at the time of conclusion of the contract. On the other hand, however, the other prerequisite for the application of the CISG was met, *i.e.* the rules of private international law led to the application of the law of a Contracting State (Austria). In fact, according to the predominant view in international legal writings, the parties' choice of the law of a Contracting state is understood as a reference to the corresponding national law, including the CISG as the international sales law of that State and not merely to the - non-unified - domestic sales law (see also, for further references, M.J. BONELL in BIANCA-BONELL, Commentary on the International Sales Law, 1987, 56 ff. R. HERBER in v. CAEMMERER-SCHLECHTRIEM, Kommentar zum Einheitlichen UN-Kaufrecht 1990, Anm. 38 on Art. 1 and Anm. 16 on Article 5; with reservations, R. LOEWE, Internationales Kaufrecht, 24 ff.).

5. [...] The claimant's claim for damages for lack of conformity of the goods is justified only in part.

5.1. The respondent was obliged on the basis of the contract to deliver a total of approx. 6,800 metric tons of cold-rolled sheet in coils, packed for export. It is established that the first two partial consignments of approx. 1,800 metric tons and 1,200 metric tons displayed quality defects of the most varied types. The exact extent of the defects actually present is disputed. However, the question can remain open since - as will be pointed out below - the claimant lost its right to full compensation for the losses suffered as a result of the failure to give notice of lack of conformity in time.

5.2. According to the contract - which to that extent derogated from the provisions on the duty of the buyer to examine the goods and to give notice of the defects contained in Articles 38 and 39 of CISG - the seller's warranty for any defect of the goods was subject to the condition that the buyer examine the goods immediately after taking delivery and give without delay written notice of the defects discovered on that occasion and substantiate those findings by means of an expert statement by an internationally recognised testing company, whereas complaints as to defects not recognisable immediately must be made at the latest within two months after hand-over.

5.3 The claimant did not comply with these requirements since it did not give notice of the alleged defects in time. Delivery of the first two lots of approx. 1,800 metric tons and 1,200 metric tons, respectively, was made on 21 February and 17 April 1991, respectively, and the goods were dispatched to Portugal by ship on those dates. Even on the assumption that as a consequence of the special packing of the goods the defects were not recognisable when the goods were delivered in the port of Rostock and could not be discovered until after unpacking and/or the commencement of processing by the ultimate customer, the claimant ought to have given notice of the defects in the two lots by 21 April and 17 June 1991 at the latest, respectively. On the contrary, a notice of the defects of the first lot was not made until 15 May 1991, while a similar notice concerning the entire quantity of goods delivered by that time was not made until 10 October 1991 - that is to say, six months after delivery of the second lot.

5.4. The argument adduced by the claimant that the parties later implicitly derogated from the contractually established time-limit for notice of lack of conformity by both recognising the complaints as fully justified and jointly discussing their legal settlement is not convincing. At the very least, a distinction should be made between the first and the second complaint. The conduct of the respondent after receipt of the first (partial) complaint and the legal evaluation of such conduct will be considered below (see 5.6.). As to the second and all-embracing complaint, there is not sufficient evidence for the allegation that the respondent had waived its right to set up the defence of late notice of the defects. The respondent was for a long time left by the claimant in the belief that the defects initially complained of were only minor in nature and served primarily as a pretext for the Belgian intermediary to escape from its contract with the claimant, which was no longer profitable. The claimant itself admits that it did not become aware of the true extent of the defects until later, after a further examination of the goods by the expert. That must a fortiori apply to the respondent, who, furthermore, was not informed until the middle of October of the results of the second examination by the expert, notwithstanding the fact that this examination had already taken place in July. The mere fact that the respondent did not expressly reject the late notice by the claimant is not sufficient to justify the conclusion that the respondent intended to waive its contractual rights. In the interests of legal certainty such an intention of the parties must be established beyond any doubt (see, in this sense, expressly, H. STUMPF in v. CAEMMERER-SCHLECHTRIEM, loc. cit., Anm. 15 on Art. 39). This is clearly not true in the present case. The second complaint was clearly to be taken much more seriously than the first (partial) complaint. Since the situation was now substantially different for the two parties, much clearer evidence of a waiver by the respondent of its right to set up the defence of late notice would have been needed than the respondent's silence or the mere fact that it did not immediately object to the late notice.

5.5. The claimant has nevertheless a right to reduced damages. A given legal can not only be intentionally waived but can also be objectively forfeited. [...] Thus, a legal position of a party must be regarded as having been forfeited whenever that party's conduct could be construed as meaning that it no longer wished to exercise its right or its defence, and the other party acted in reliance on the new situation (on this point, see in general *inter alia* ESSER-SCHMIDT Schuldrecht, I, Allgemeiner Teil, 6. Aufl., 1984, 150-152). The CISG expressly mentions in Article 7 (1) the requirement of the observance of good faith in international trade. The exact significance to be attached to the general principle of good faith within the scope of the Convention may be disputed (see on this point M.J. BONELL in BIANCA-BONELL, loc. cit, p. 83 ff.). However, at the least the principle of estoppel or, to use another expression, the prohibition of *venire contra factum proprium*, which represents a special application of the general principle of good faith, may without doubt be seen as one of the "general principles on which the Convention is based", which according to Article 7 (2) of the CISG may be invoked to solve the question of a possible forfeiture of the defence of late notice, not expressly settled in the Convention (see in this sense among others, M.J. BONELL in BIANCA-BONELL, loc. cit., p. 81 (with a reference to the provisions contained in Art. 16(2)(b) and 29 (2); HERBER/CZERWENKA, Internationales Kaufrecht, 1991, 48).

5.6. In the case in point, the requirements for forfeiture are met. The respondent may never had the intention of waiving the defence of late notice; however, objectively, its conduct after receiving the first complaint from the claimant was such as to give the latter the justifiable impression that it recognised the lawfulness of the complaint despite the lateness of transmission. In that context, the fact that the respondent did not immediately reject the complaint as having been made after the expiry of the contractually agreed time-limit is not so important. What counts is rather the circumstance that, even after the complaint had been made, the respondent remained in contact with the claimant in order to keep itself informed of the development of the complaints on the part of the Portuguese ultimate customer and/or the Belgian intermediary. What is even more important is the fact that the respondent repeatedly [...] made statements to the claimant from which the latter could reasonably infer that the respondent would not set up the defence of late notice with reference to the complaint. In reliance on that, the claimant refrained from immediately taking legal action not only against its own customer but also against the respondent itself.

5.7 However, the forfeiture refers only to the first (partial) complaint. By behaving in the manner just described the respondent always assumed that the defects would not prove to be greater than established on the first examination of the goods. This follows *inter alia* from the fact that the respondent, by it own admission, intentionally did not transmit this first complaint to its own supplier, since its contract with the latter provided that "to a certain extent, lack of conformity was to be tolerated by the buyer". The expert's report of 6 May 1991 referred to the partial consignment that had arrived at the factory of the ultimate customer by that date, *i.e.* approx. 1,800 metric tons of the total 3,000 metric tons of goods shipped, only approx. one-third of which had already been processed. Therefore, it is very difficult, if indeed at all possible, to prove the exact extent of the existing defects. As a consequence, the arbitrator fixes the corresponding amount of damages at his discretion at one-fifth of the total value of the goods in question, *i.e.* 20 % of US § [...] x 1,800, plus interest, to be calculated as from 15 May 1991, the date when the first notice of defects in due form was submitted. In his estimate, the arbitrator takes at his basis the projection made by the expert in his second report, according to which the total loss was estimated as one-fifth of the entire quantity of goods delivered. The legal basis for such a discretionary determination of the amount of damages is § 273 of the Austrian Code of Civil Procedure, which is also applicable within the scope of the CISG (see in this sense H. STOLL in v. CAEMMERER-SCHLECTRIEM, loc. cit., Anm. 41 on Art. 74 with reference to the similar provision to be found in § 287 of the German Code of Civil procedure).

5.8. Article 78 of the CISG, while granting the right to interest, is silent on the question of the applicable rate. In international writings and case law to date it is disputed whether the question is outside the scope of the Convention - with the result that the interest rate is to be determined according to the domestic law applicable on the basis of the relevant conflict-of-laws rules (in this sense see, among others, HERBER/CZERWENKA, loc. cit., 1991, 347; Oberlandesgericht Frankfurt, 13 June 1991, Recht für internationale Wirtschaft 1991, 591) - or whether there is a true gap in the Convention within the meaning of Article 7(2) so that the applicable interest rate should possibly be determined autonomously in conformity with the general principles underlying the Convention (see in this sense, for example, J.O. HONNOLD, Uniform Sales Law, 2nd edition, Denver-Boston 1991, 525-526; ICC Arbitral Award No. 6653 (1993), Clunet 1993, 1040). This second view is to be preferred, not least because the immediate recourse to a particular domestic law may lead to results which are incompatible with the principle embodied in Art. 78 of the CISG, at least in the cases where the law in question expressly prohibits the payment of interest. On of the general principles underlying the CSG is that of "full compensation" of the loss caused (*cf.* Art. 74 of the CISG). It follows that, in the event of failure by the debtor to pay a monetary debt, the creditor, who as a business person must be expected to resort to bank credit as result of the delay in payment, should therefore be entitled to interest at the rate commonly practised in its country with respect to the currense of payment, *i.e.* the currency of the creditor's country or any other foreign currency agreed upon by the parties (*cf.* Art. 7.4.9 of the Principles of International Commercial contracts prepared by the International Institute of the Unification of Private Law (UNIDROIT), on which see M.J. BONELL, An International Restatement of Contract Law. The UNIDROIT Principles of International Commercial Contracts, Transnational Juris Publications, Irvington - N.Y., 1994, 114-115). The information received from the Deutsche Bundesbank is that the average "prime borrowing rate" for US dollars in Germany in the period in question was 6.25 %. The interest due from the respondent should be calculated at that rate. [...]

[*Original in German*]

Sources

Published in German:
Recht der Internationalen Wirtschaft (RIW), 1995, 591-92.

Published in Italian (trans.):
Rivista dell'Arbitrato, 1995, 537-41.

Commented on by:
P. SCHLECHTRIEM, Recht der Internationalen Wirtschaft (RIW), 1995, 592-594.
I. SEIDL-HOHENVELDERN, Journal du droit international, 1995, 1055-1056.
A. VENEZIANO, La Convenzione sulla vendita internazionale e i Principi UNIDROIT dei contratti commerciali internazionali, in due recenti lodi della Corte arbitrale della Camera di Commercio di Vienna, Rivista dell'Arbitrato, 1995, 547-560.

Date: ***June 15, 1994***
Adjudicating Court: ***Internationales Schiedsgericht der Bundeskammer der gewerblichen Wirtschaft – Wien***
Number: ***SCH-4366***
Parties: ***Unknown***

Keywords

APPLICATION OF THE 1980 VIENNA CONVENTION ON CONTRACTS FOR THE INTERNATIONAL SALE OF GOODS (CISG) – CHOICE BY PARTIES OF LAW OF CONTRACTING STATE AS GOVERNING LAW OF THE CONTRACT (ART. 1(1)(B) CISG)

DUTY TO MITIGATE DAMAGES (ART. 77 CISG) – SUBSTITUTE SALE DIFFERENCE BETWEEN CONTRACT PRICE AND SUBSTITUTE SALE PRICE

RIGHT TO INTEREST (ART. 78 CISG) – TIME OF ACCRUAL (ART. 58 CISG)

INTEREST RATE – MATTER NOT EXPRESSLY SETTLED BY CISG (ART. 7(2) CISG) – TO BE SETTLED IN CONFORMITY WITH THE GENERAL PRINCIPLES UNDERLYING CISG – FULL COMPENSATION (ARTS. 74 AND 78 CISG) AS A GENERAL PRINCIPLE OF CISG – AVERAGE PRIME RATE FOR CURRENCY OF PAYMENT IN THE CREDITOR'S COUNTRY (ART. 7.4.9 UNIDROIT PRINCIPLES)

Abstract

In 1990 and 1991, an Austrian seller and a German buyer concluded contracts for the sale of rolled metal sheets. The initial contracts provided that the goods were to be delivered FOB Hamburg, by March 1991 at the latest. Later, due to the buyer's financial difficulties, the seller allowed the buyer to take delivery in installments according to the possibilities of resale, and the buyer had to promptly pay upon receipt of each invoice and cover all storage costs. The buyer took delivery of some of the goods without paying, and refused to take delivery of other goods. Pursuant to an arbitration clause, the seller commenced arbitral proceedings, demanding payment of the price. The seller further asked for damages, including those deriving from a substitute sale of the undelivered goods.

The Arbitral Tribunal held that because the parties had chosen Austrian law, the contracts were governed by CISG as the international sales law of Austria, a contracting State (Art. 1(1)(b) CISG).

With regard to the goods delivered but not paid for, the Arbitral Tribunal found that the seller was entitled to payment of their price (Arts. 53 and 61 CISG). Regarding the cover sale made by the seller, the Arbitral Tribunal observed that the seller had the right to make a cover sale, and presumably even a duty to do so because of the duty to mitigate damages (Art. 77 CISG). The seller would be entitled to the difference between the contract price and the substitute sale price.

The Arbitral Tribunal further held that interest on the price accrued from the date payment was due (Arts. 78 and 58 CISG). Since the parties' agreement required the buyer to pay after receiving each invoice, interest accrued from the date of such receipt, which should occur within 10 days after issuance of each invoice.

The Arbitral Tribunal held that the interest rate is a matter governed but not expressly settled by CISG. Therefore, it must be settled in conformity with the general principles on which the CISG is based (Art. 7(2) CISG). Referring to Arts. 78 and 74 CISG, the arbitrator found that full compensation is one of the general principles underlying the CISG. In relations between merchants, it is expected that the seller, due to the delayed payment, resort to bank credit at the interest rate commonly practiced in its own country with respect to the currency of payment. Such currency may be either the currency of the seller's country, or any other foreign currency agreed upon by the parties. The Arbitral Tribunal observed that this solution is stated also in Art. 7.4.9 of the UNIDROIT Principles of International Commercial Contracts. The interest rate awarded was therefore the average prime rate in the seller's country (Austria), with respect to the currencies of payment (US dollars and German marks).

Full Text

1. By the request of arbitration of 30 March 1993, the claimant [a company with place of business in Austria] applied for an award against the respondent [a company with place of business in Germany] for payment of a total of US$ [...] DM [...]. It submitted that the respondent had not fulfilled its obligations on the basis of two contracts for the delivery of cold-rolled sheet concluded with the claimant, since it had either not taken delivery of or had not paid for part of the goods purchased.

[...]

3. The competence of the Arbitral Centre is founded on the last paragraphs of the two contracts concluded between the parties. [...]

3.1. It is true that the contracts - and thus the aforesaid arbitration clause - exist only in the acknowledgement of order sent by the claimant to the respondent, which the latter never countersigned. However, there can be no doubt of the validity of the arbitration clause. The fact that Article I, paragraph 1 of the Convention on the Recognition and Enforcement of Foreign Arbitral Award (The New York Convention), which applies in this case, provides that the agreement must be writing, does not mean that the arbitration clause must be contained in a contractual document signed by both parties. According to Article II, paragraph 2 of the New York Convention, an "arbitral clause in a contract or an arbitration agreement, signed by the parties or contained in an exchange of letters or telegrams" is sufficient. The predominant view in international legal writings is that the requirement is therefore also met if the adressee replies in writing to the acknowledgement of an order in such a way that need only conclusively show that he accepts the acknowledgement of the order together with the arbitration clause mentioned therin, for example, if he expressly refers in subsequent letters or invoices to the contractual document in question (see *inter alia* A.J. VAN DER BERG, the New York Arbitration Convention of 1958, 1981, 198 ff.; P. SCHLOSSER, Das Recht der internationalen privaten Schiedsgerichtsbarkeit, 2. Aufl. 1989, 280; App. Firenze, 8.10.1977, Yearbook Commercial Arbitration IV (1979) 289).

3.2 That is exactly what happened in the present case. Though initially the respondent only tacitly accepted the two acknowledgements of the order by the claimant, it subsequently - to be precise in a letter to the claimant of 19 January 1993 - expressly referred to the relevant contracts No. 19038 and No. 19101 and thus satisfied the requirement as to the written form of the arbitration clause contained therein.

3.3. Furthermore, in the present case, on the basis of the general legal principle of good faith, the respondent would be precluded from relying on the absence of an arbitration clause in writing for the purpose of negating the competence of the Arbitral Centre. Within a little less than three months, the respondent concluded three contracts with the claimant with essentially identical wording but never countersigned the acknowledgement of the orders together with the arbitration clause contained therein that were sent to it by the claimant. That did not prevent the respondent from relying on that specific arbitration clause and from entrusting the Arbitral Centre of the Federal Economic Chamber of Austria specified therein with the settlement of a dispute concerning the second of the three contracts. To rely on one occasion on the arbitration clause signed only by the opposing party in order to assert one's own claims and, on a second occasion, when the opposing party goes to law, to dispute the validity of an arbitration clause agreed upon in exactly the same form, would not be compatible with the requirement of the observance of good faith and fair business dealings, which is also fully valid within the scope of the New York Convention (see also A.J. VAN DEN BERG, loc. cit., 182 ff.).

4. According to both contracts, the applicable law was Austrian law. That means that - in so far as the issues involved fall within this scope - the United Nations Sales Convention (Vienna) of 11 April 1980 (CISG) applies. In fact, that convention entered into force in Austria on 1 January 1989, with the consequence that, from that date onwards, all international contracts of sale of goods within the meaning of Article 1 have been subject to the CISG, provided that the conditions stipulated for that purpose in the Convention itself are met, *i.e.* that either both parties are established in Contracting States or that the rules of private international law lead to the application of the law of a Contracting State. In the present case, the first condition was not met because Germany (at that time, the FRG, without the new "*Länder*") was not yet a Contracting State at the time of conclusion of the contract. On the other hand, however, the second pre-condition for application of the CISG was met, *i.e.* the rules of private international law led to the application of the law of a Contracting State (Austria). In fact, according to the predominant view in international legal writings, the parties' choice of the law of a Contracting State is understood as a reference to the corresponding national law, including the CISG as the international sales law of that State and not merely to the - non-unified - domestic sales law (see also, for further reference, M.J. BONELL in BIANCA-BONELL, Commentary on the International Sales Law, 1987, 56 ff.; R. HERBER in v. CAEMMERER-SCHLECHTRIEM, Kommentar zum Einheitlichen UN-Kaufrecht 1990, Anm. 38 on Art. 1 and Anm. 16 on Article 5; with reservations, R. LOEWE, Internationales Kaufrecht, 24 ff.).

5. [...] The claimant's claim for payment of the outstanding invoices covering the goods delivered by it and taken delivery of by the respondent is justified. However, the corresponding entitlement to interest should be reduced, with respect either to the due dates or to the interest rate to be applied. The claim for reimbursement of the storage costs incurred as a result of the lateness in taking delivery of the goods or refusal to take delivery, as well as the entitlement to payment of the difference between the contractually agreed price and the proceeds of the substitute sale of the residual goods of which delivery was not taken should also be regarded as justified.

5.1 The goods invoiced by the claimant in a total quantity of 650,090 tons form part of two consignments of cold-rolled sheet, which the claimant had sold to the respondent on the basis of the two contracts No. 19038 and No. 19101, parts of which had been taken delivery of by the latter. It may be disputed between the parties whether the respondent always requested the delivery of the goods by the warehouse keeper in Hamburg in agreement with the claimant or whether the respondent had taken delivery of at least a partial consignment of 350,090 tons without the claimant's knowledge. It is a fact that the respondent in its [...] letter of 19 January 193 [...] expressly confirmed taking delivery of this partial consignment and/or requested submission of the relevant invoices and had also never raised objections to the three invoices of 16 January 1992, which had already been submitted. The fact that the respondent did not settle the invoices [...] in question should be regarded as an infringement of its obligation under Art. 53 of the CISG to pay the price for the goods, for which it is fully answerable in accordance with Art. 61 of the CISG in the absence of justified notice of lack of conformity or other objections.

5.2 In accordance with Art. 78 of the CISG, the seller is entitled to interest in the event of arrears in payment of the price by the buyer.

5.2.1. The interest is payable from the effective date of the obligation for payment of the purchase price. According to Art. 58(1) of the CISG, this time is primarily determined by the agreements between the parties themselves; only in the absence of such a special agreement is it the time when the seller places the goods at the buyer's disposal in accordance with the contract. In the present case, the parties had derogated from the payment modalities and time-limits originally laid down in the contract by subsequently agreeing that the respondent could take delivery of and pay for the goods in partial consignment according to its possibilities of resale, provides that it bore the storage costs incurred thereby [...]. Accordingly, the invoices in question here stipulate "Payment: immediately on receipt of the invoice". It was therefore at that time, and not earlier, that the respondent was under the obligation to pay the amount invoiced at the time, and it is only from that time that the claimant was entitled to interest [...].

5.2.2. Article 78 of the CISG, while granting the right to interest, says nothing about the level of the interest rate payable. In international legal writings and case law to date it is disputed whether the question is outside the scope of the Convention - with the result that the interest rate is to be determined according to the domestic law applicable on the basis of the relevant conflict-of-laws fules (see *inter alia* HERBER/CZERWENKA, Internationales Kaufrecht, 1991, 347; Oberlandesgericht Frankfurt, 13 June 1991 in Recht für internationale Wirtschaft 1991, 591) - or whether there is a true gap in the Convention within the meaning of Article 7(2) so that the applicable interest rate should possibly be determined autonomously in conformity with the general principles underlying the

Convention (see in this sense, for example, J.O. HONNOLD, Uniform Sales Law, 2nd edition, Denver-Boston 1991, 525-526; ICC Arbitral Award No. 6653 (1993), Clunet 1993, 1040). This second view is to be preferred, not least because the immediate recourse to a particular domestic law may lead to results which are incompatible with the principle embodied in Art. 78 of the CISG, at least in the cases where the law in question expressly prohibits the payment of interest. One of the general legal principles underlying the CISG is the requirements of "full compensation" of the loss caused (*cf.* Art. 74 of the CISG). It follows that, in the event of failure to pay a monetary debt, the creditor, who as a business person must be expected to resort to bank credit as a result of the delay in payment, should therefore be entitled to interest at the rate commonly practiced in its country with respect to the currency of payment, *i.e.* the currency of the creditor's country or any other foreign currency agreed upon by the parties (*cf.* Art. 7.4.9 of the Principles of International Commercial Contracts prepared by the International Institute for the Unification of Private Law (UNIDROIT), on which see M.J. BONELL, An International Restatement of Contract Law. The UNIDROIT Principles of International Commercial Contracts, Transnational Juris Publications, Irvinton - N.Y., 1994, 114-115). The information received from the leading Austrian banks is that the average "prime borrowing rates" for US dollars and DM in Austria in the period in question were 4.5 % and 8 %, respectively. The interest due from the respondent should be calculated at those rates.

5.3 The claimant's claim for reimbursement of the storage costs also appears to be justified.

5.4 After unsuccessfully demanding that the respondent take delivery of the remaining goods by 31 March 1993, the claimant was fully entitled to carry out a substitute sale; in view of the obligation for mitigation of the loss of the party entitled to damages, that might even have been a necessary measure (see on this point H. STOLL in v. CAEMMERER/SCHLECHTRIEM, loc. cit., Anm. 11 on Art. 77). The claim for payment of the difference between the contractually agreed price and the proceeds of the substitute sale is also justified. [...]

[*Original in German*]

Sources

Published in German:
Recht der Internationalen Wirtschaft (RIW), 1995, 591-92.

Published in Italian (trans.):
Rivista dell'Arbitrato, 1995, 543-47.

Commented on by:
P. SCHLECHTRIEM, Recht der Internationalen Wirtschaft (RIW), 1995, 592-594.
I. SEIDL-HOHENVELDERN, Journal du droit international, 1995, 1055-1056.
A. VENEZIANO, La Convenzione sulla vendita internazionale e i Principi UNIDROIT dei contratti commerciali internazionali in due recenti lodi della Corte arbitrale della Camera di Commercio di Vienna, Rivista dell'Arbitrato, 1995, 547-560.

Date: ***November 25, 1994***
Adjudicating Court: ***Schiedsgericht der Züricher Handelskammer***
Number: ***Unknown***
Parties: ***Unknown***

Keywords

CONTRACT GOVERNED BY A SPECIFIC DOMESTIC LAW (SWISS LAW) – REFERENCE BY ARBITRAL TRIBUNAL TO THE UNIDROIT PRINCIPLES TO CONFIRM THAT THE RELEVANT RULES OF THE SWISS LAW OF OBLIGATIONS ENJOY WORLDWIDE CONSENSUS

INTERPRETATION OF A CONTRACTUAL PROVISION – REAL INTENTION OF THE PARTIES – INTERPRETATION IN GOOD FAITH – INTERPRETATION OF THE CONTRACTUAL PROVISION ACCORDING TO THE UNDERSTANDING OF THE AVERAGE HONEST AND DILIGENT BUSINESS PERSON (ARTS. 4.1 – 4.2 UNIDROIT PRINCIPLES)

VALIDITY OF THE ARBITRATION AGREEMENT - MATERIAL MISTAKE AS ONE RELATING TO FACTS THAT THE MISTAKEN PARTY CONSIDERED A NECESSARY BASIS OF THE CONTRACT (ART. 3.5 UNIDROIT PRINCIPLES)

Abstract

The award concerned the validity of an arbitration clause in which the parties agreed to submit their disputes to "international and trade arbitration organization in Zürich, Switzerland". The respondent contested the jurisdiction of the Zürich Chamber of Commerce as this institution was not specifically named in the arbitration clause. The claimant argued that it could rightfully assume that the arbitration clause, which had been drafted by the respondent, referred to the only existing international trade arbitration organization in Zürich, namely the Zürich Chamber of Commerce.

In deciding in favour of the claimant the Arbitral Tribunal applied Article 18(1) of the Swiss Code of Obligations according to which incorrect statements made in a contractual provision have to be interpreted by having regard to the real intention of the parties, and to Article 2 of the Swiss Civil Code laying down the principle of good faith. According to the Arbitral Tribunal the combination of the two components of the principle of good faith, *i.e.* the subjective and the objective one, leads to the conclusion that parties to a contract are bound by the meaning of the contractual provision as it must be understood by the average honest and diligent business person. In order to prove that this interpretation rule reflects a worldwide consensus, the Arbitral Tribunal referred to Articles 4.1 and 4.2 of the UNIDROIT Principles "which have been established by a large international working party consisting of specialists in contract law selected from all different parts of the world [...]."

Having established that a proper interpretation of the arbitration clause leads to the conclusion that the parties designation of the arbitral institution in fact meant the designation of the Zürich Chamber of Commerce, the Arbitral Tribunal addressed the question whether the respondent could invoke a material mistake and thereby invalidate the agreement to arbitrate. By denying such a possibility the Arbitral Tribunal referred again not only to Article 24(1) of the Swiss Code of Obligations defining a material mistake as one relating to facts which the mistaken party in accordance with the rules of goods faith in the course of business considered to be a necessary basis of the contract, but also to the similar rule contained in Article 3.5 of the UNIDROIT Principles.

Full Text

[...]

[9] Moreover, it is clear from the arbitration clause that the parties agreed that arbitration should take place in Zurich/Switzerland. [...]

[10] As a third element, the parties made reference to a certain institution, *i.e.* to the 'international trade arbitration organization in Zurich'. Such a reference must clearly be understood as a reference to an institution which administers arbitration cases, *i.e.*, an institution which typically offers certain services in the framework of the administering and hosting of international arbitral tribunals.

[...]

[11] By virtue of such a reference, the parties therefore clearly opted for institutional arbitration, as opposed to mere *ad hoc* arbitration (*i.e.* an arbitration not hosted or administered by any arbitral institution). As regards the particular arbitral institution, the parties have made reference to that certain 'international trade arbitration organization in Zurich'.

[12] The fact is, as recognized by claimant, that an organization bearing exactly this name does not exist in Zurich. As indeed correctly indicated by claimant, the only international arbitration institution administering international disputes between foreign/foreign or foreign/Swiss parties is the Zurich Chamber of Commerce.

[14] Based on the foregoing, and

- because the parties clearly agreed to arbitration (as opposed to litigation in ordinary state courts)

- because the parties clearly agreed to a determination of their dispute in Zurich/Switzerland (as opposed to a determination in any other country, or in the country of the defendant party)

- because the parties clearly referred to an institutional arbitration (as opposed to a mere *ad hoc* arbitration, not administered by any arbitral institution)

- because the reference to the 'international trade arbitration organization' can only have meant the Zurich Chamber of Commerce which is widely known and accepted as a major international arbitral institution.

The Arbitral Tribunal has to conclude that the arbitration clause agreed upon between the parties must correctly be construed as making reference to the international arbitration services as offered by the Zurich Chamber of Commerce on the basis of its International Arbitration Rules.

[...]

[20] Under Swiss law [...] where a contractual provision contains an incorrect statement or expression, such statement or expression will have to be interpreted by the Court (respectively here: the Arbitral Tribunal) in the sense of and by having regard to, the real intention of the parties. This notion is reflected in Art. 18 of the Swiss Code [...].

[22] In making such a 'correct' interpretation, the notions and rules on contract interpretation have to be used. [...] Rather, it suffices to indicate that a contract interpretation, under Swiss perspectives, has to be made on the basis of the good faith principle (bona fides principle) reflected in An. 2 of the Swiss Civil Code. This good faith principle has two components, *i.e.* the subjective component and the objective component. In other words:

- it is not sufficient to ask (and determine) the question how claimant itself (subjectively) understood (or interpreted) a particular contractual clause (here: the reference to a certain 'international trade arbitration organization in Zurich')

- nor is it sufficient to explore or determine how respondent understood or interpreted that same reference (*i.e.* the reference to an 'international trade arbitration organization in Zurich')

- but the decisive test and question is to know how the present parties, by applying the test of the so-called 'average honest and diligent businessman', had to understand or interpret the particular contractual provision (*i.e.* the reference to an 'international trade arbitration organization in Zurich').

[23] In essence, the above combination of the subjective and objective test leads to the conclusion that parties to a contract are bound by the meaning of the contractual provision as it must be understood by the average honest and diligent businessman. From a different perspective, one may also say that a party must be protected in its confidence that a contractual provision will have the meaning as will be conferred to it by the 'average/diligent businessman' (disregarding thus the purely subjective meaning one particular party for itself may confer to a particular contractual provision).

[24] It may be added here that, basically, the above interpretation rule reflects a general and indeed world-wide consensus. This is, for instance, apparent by comparing the Swiss interpretation rules with the most recent elaboration in respect of the legal rules applicable to international contracts, namely the 1994 UNIDROIT Principles which have been established by a large international working party consisting of specialists in contract law selected from all different pans of the world, including for instance Mainland China, Korea and Japan. Chapter 4 deals with the interpretation of contracts and contains the following provisions:

Article 4.1 - Intention of the parties
(1) A contract shall be interpreted according to the common intention of the parties.
(2) if such an intention cannot be established, the contract shall be interpreted according to the meaning that reasonable persons of the same kind as the parties would give to it in the same circumstances.

Article 4.2 - Interpretation of statements and other conduct
(1) The statements and other conduct of a party shall be interpreted according to that party's intention if the other party knew or could not have been unaware of this intention.
(2) If the preceding paragraph is not applicable, such statements and other conduct shall be interpreted according to the meaning that a reasonable person of the same kind as the other party would give to it in the same circumstances.

[...]

[26] "While, in the sense of the above reasons, the contract interpretation (*i.e.* the interpretation of the arbitration clause) leads to a clear answer in the sense that the parties' designation of the arbitral institution in fact meant the designation of the Zurich Chamber of Commerce, the rather academic question may remain whether respondent could invoke a material or relevant mistake and thereby invalidate the agreement to arbitrate.

[27] "In this respect, An. 24(1) of the Swiss Code of Obligations contains a narrow definition of what may constitute a material mistake:

Article 24 CO
'An error is, in particular, deemed to be material in the following cases:

4. The error related to certain facts which the party in error, in accordance with the rules of good faith in the course of business, considered to be a necessary basis of the contract.

[28] Art. 24(2) CO specifically excludes the invalidation of a contract if the error only refers to motives for entering into the particular contract, or if the error cannot be considered as being material in the sense of Art. 24(1)CO.

[29] "Quite in the same sense, the 1994 UNIDROIT Principles contain by way of comparison, a similar concept:

Article 3.5 - Relevant mistake
(1) A party may only avoid the contract for mistake if, when the contract was concluded, the mistake was of such importance that a reasonable person in the same situation as the party in error would only have concluded the contract on materially different terms or would not have concluded it at all if the true state of affairs had been known, and (a) the other party made the same mistake, or caused the mistake, or knew or ought to have known of the mistake and it was contrary to reasonable commercial standards of fair dealing to leave the mistaken party in error; or
(b) the other party had not at the time of avoidance acted in reliance on the contract.
(2) However, a party may not avoid the contract if
(a) it was grossly negligent in committing the mistake; or
(b) the mistake relates to a matter in regard to which the risk of mistake was assumed, or, having regard to the circumstances, should be borne by the mistaken party.'

[...]

Sources

Bulletin de l'Association Suisse de l'Arbitrage (ASA), 1996, 303 – 318.
Yearbook of Commercial Arbitration, Vol. 22 (1997), 211 – 221.

Date: ***1995***
Adjudicating Court: ***Ad hoc Arbitration, Auckland***
Number: ***Unknown***
Parties: ***Unknown***

Keywords

PARTIES' CHOICE OF DOMESTIC LAW (NEW ZEALAND LAW) AS LAW GOVERNING THE CONTRACT – UNCERTAINTY ON THE MATTER OF INTERPRETATION – ARBITRAL TRIBUNAL REFERENCE TO THE UNIDROIT PRINCIPLES AS THE MOST DEFINITIVE CONTEMPORARY INTERNATIONAL STATEMENT GOVERNING THE INTERPRETATION OF CONTRACTUAL TERMS

INTERPRETATION - CONDUCT OF PARTIES AFTER CONCLUSION OF THE CONTRACT - RELEVANT IN INTERPRETATION OF AMBIGUOUS CONTRACTUAL TERMS (ARTS. 4.1, 4.2 AND 4.3 UNIDROIT PRINCIPLES)

Abstract

The award concerned a contractual dispute involving a New Zealand company and an Australian company. An issue arose as to whether post-contractual conduct by the parties was admissible as a means for resolving ambiguities found in the contractual agreement.

Because the law of New Zealand, which the parties had chosen as the law governing the dispute, was found to be uncertain on this issue ("in a somewhat unsettled state"), the Arbitral Tribunal, which was inclined to admit the taking into account of post-contractual conduct in cases of contractual ambiguity, sought confirmation at a comparative level and in so doing referred above all to Arts. 4.1, 4.2. and 4.3. of the UNIDROIT Principles. It pointed out that "[...] there could be no more definitive contemporary international statement governing the interpretation of contractual terms than in the UNIDROIT Principles."

Full Text

[Not yet available]

Sources

D.A.R WILLIAMS, Q.C., Auckland, New Zealand, who amply refers to the legal aspects of the case in his essay: Further Development of International Commercial Arbitration through the UNIDROIT Principles of International Commercial Contracts, in 2 New Zealand Business Law Quarterly (1996), 7 *et seq.* (17 - 21).

Date: *1995*
Adjudicating Court: ***ICC International Court of Arbitration – Basle***
Number: ***8128***
Parties: ***Unknown***

Keywords

CONTRACT GOVERNED BY CISG – FUNDAMENTAL BREACH (ART. 25 CISG) - SELLER'S FAILURE TO GIVE BUYER CORRECT INSTRUCTIONS AS TO PACKAGING

FUNDAMENTAL BREACH (ART. 25 CISG) – LATE DELIVERY – KNOWLEDGE OF SELLER THAT DATE FOR DELIVERY IS ESSENTIAL TO BUYER FIXING OF ADDITIONAL TIME FOR PERFORMANCE NOT NECESSARY

AVOIDANCE – DECLARATION OF AVOIDANCE – INVITATION TO PERFORM UNDER THREAT OF AVOIDANCE – NO SUCCESSIVE DECLARATION NEEDED

DAMAGES – SUBSTITUTE TRANSACTION – REASONABLENESS OF SUBSTITUTE TRANSACTION (ART. 75 CISG) - REQUIREMENTS

INTEREST (ART. 78CISG)–INTEREST ON OTHERS SUMS IN ARREARS - ACCRUAL

INTEREST – RULE OF AVERAGE BANK LENDING RATE TO PRIME BORROWERS CONTAINED IN ART. 7.4.9 UNIDROIT PRINCIPLES AND ART. 4.507 OF PRINCIPLES OF EUROPEAN CONTRACT LAW AS A GENERAL PRINCIPLE UNDERLYING CISG (ART. 7(2) CISG) – LIBOR RATE APPLICABLE

Abstract

In order to perform a contract with a third party, a Swiss buyer entered into a contract with an Austrian seller for the supply of chemical fertilizer. The seller in turn applied to an Ukrainian supplier to obtain part of the fertilizer. The buyer sent the Ukrainian supplier the packaging to be used for delivery (sacks manufactured by the buyer under the seller's instructions). As the sacks sent by the buyer did not conform to the technical rules of the Ukrainian chemical industry, the supplier could not make use of them. Consequently, the goods were not delivered within the period of time fixed in the contract. The buyer asked the seller when the goods would be delivered in writing, expressly adding that, in the absence of a clear committment by the seller, it would avoid the contract with respect to the part of the goods not yet delivered. Because the seller's reply was generic, the buyer had to make a substitute purchase at a higher price to be able to perform the contract already concluded with the third party. The buyer commenced arbitral proceedings demanding damages, including the cost of the sacks it had supplied as well as the loss deriving from the substitute purchase. The buyer also asked for interest, at the London International Bank Offered Rate (LIBOR) plus 2%.

The Arbitral Tribunal found that the seller had fundamentally breached the contract (Art. 25 CISG), as it had breached its duty to give the buyer the necessary instructions for the correct manufacture of the packaging.

Moreover, the seller was not exempted from performance pursuant to Art. 79 CISG, since the seller is responsible for non-delivery caused by its supplier, as part of the seller's risk (Art. 79(2) CISG).

The Arbitral Tribunal further held that, though late delivery does not usually amount to a fundamental breach and entitle avoidance of the contract only after the additional time fixed by the buyer has expired without performance by the seller (Art. 47(1) CISG), a relevant delay may constitute a fundamental breach if it appears from the circumstances that the date of delivery is of particular significance to the buyer, and that the seller has knowledge thereof. In the case at hand, the seller knew that the goods were to be delivered by the buyer to a third party and that, in case of late delivery, the buyer would have to pay a contractual penalty as well as any additional costs incurred by a substitute purchase of the goods.

The buyer was entitled to partial avoidance of the contract, pursuant to Arts. 51(1) and 73 CISG, as this was a contract for delivery of goods by installments. As the buyer had sent a letter to the seller expressly stating that, in the absence of a clear committment by the seller, the contract would be partially avoided, the Arbitral Tribunal considered the contract avoided even in the absence of an express subsequent declaration. Indeed,parties' declarations should be interpreted in conformity with what a reasonable person would have understood under the same circumstances. Here, it was reasonable to consider the contract avoided at the moment in which the conditions mentioned by the buyer came about.

According to Arts. 49(1)(a), 74 and 75 CISG, the buyer was entitled to recover damages, including both the costs for the sacks it had supplied and the costs of the substitute purchase.

With respect to the substitute purchase, the Arbitral Tribunal held that the transaction concluded by the buyer was reasonable as required by Art. 75 CISG. According to the Arbitral Tribunal, a transaction should be considered reasonable if the buyer acted as a prudent and careful businessman, and the first condition necessary to meet this standard is that the goods bought in replacement are of the same kind and quality as the undelivered ones. Small differences in the quality of the goods are of no importance. The price of the purchase should also be considered reasonable, as the short period in which the buyer had to purchase the replacement fertilizer in order to deliver it in time to the third party justified a higher price than the one that could have been obtained if the buyer have had more time to negotiate.

The buyer was also awarded interest, according to Art. 78 CISG. Interest related to the reimbursement of the cost of the sacks accrued from the time of partial avoidance of the contract, while interest related to the expenses due to the substitute purchase accrued from the time in which the bank of the buyer executed the payment for the replacement goods.

Since CISG does not determine the rate of interest, the Arbitral Tribunal applied the average bank short term lending rate to prime borrowers, which is the solution adopted by Art. 7.4.9 of the UNIDROIT Principles of International Commercial Contracts and by Art. 4.507 of the Principles of European Contract Law. The Arbitral Tribunal considered that such rules were applicable, as they must be considered general principles on which CISG is based (Art. 7(2) CISG). In the case at hand, the London International Bank Offered Rate (LIBOR) plus 2% required by the buyer corresponded to the bank short term lending rate to enterprises. The buyer was therefore awarded interest at the required rate.

Full Text

Le contrat entre les parties ne contient pas de clause sur le droit applicable. [...] L'arbitre doit dès lors déterminer le droit applicable d'après l'article 13(3) du Règlement d'arbitrage de la CCI.

Les différentes possibilités sont le droit autrichien, qui s'applique au lieu du siège du défendeur en tant que vendeur, le droit suisse, qui s'applique au lieu du siège du demandeur en tant qu'acheteur. Le droit suisse peut également être applicable parce que la CCI a fixé Bâle comme siège de l'arbitrage. Au surplus, puisque la Cour d'arbitrage a nommé un arbitre allemand, le droit allemand pourrait être appliqué en tant que droit neutre. On doit également mentionner la possibilité d'appliquer le droit ukrainien parce que le demandeur devait expédier en Ukraine les sacs qu'il avait l'obligation de fournir et que le défendeur [...] souhaitait compléter les livraisons qu'il devait faire avec l'aide [de son fournisseur].

La Suisse, l'Autriche, la République fédérale allemande et l'Ukraine sont toutes signataires de la Convention des Nations Unies sur la vente internationale de marchandises. Dans chacun de ces pays, la Convention est entrée en vigueur avant la date de signature du contrat par les parties.

[...] Ce contrat est un contrat de vente ainsi que cela ressort clairement de la désignation des parties en tant qu'acheteur (demandeur) et vendeur (défendeur). De plus, le préambule du contrat selon lequel "le vendeur vend et l'acheteur achète le produit suivant aux conditions suivantes" est sans équivoque.

Le contrat signé entre les parties répond aux conditions de l'article 1(1)(a) de la Convention de Vienne selon lequel celle ci s'applique aux contrats de vente entre des parties établies dans différents Etats si ces Etats sont des Etats contractants. Dès lors, les dispositions de la Convention s'appliquent au litige faisant l'objet de la présente procédure arbitrale [...].

D'après l'article 49(1)(a) de la Convention, l'acheteur peut déclarer le contrat résolu si le vendeur n'exécute pas ses obligations et si ce défaut d'exécution constitue une contravention essentielle au contrat. La contravention essentielle au contrat est définie à l'article 25 de la Convention [...]. Il est reproché au défendeur plusieurs contraventions essentielles au contrat au sens des articles 49(1)(a) et 25 de la Convention. D'après la déclaration du directeur général [du fournisseur], les sacs fournis par le demandeur au défendeur n'étaient pas conformes aux normes techniques et de production utilisées dans l'industrie chimique en Ukraine. Aussi, ils n'ont pu être remplis par [le fournisseur] [...]. L'une des obligations essentielles du défendeur était de donner des instructions qui auraient permis au demandeur de fabriquer des sacs qui pouvaient être remplis par le [fournisseur de l'engrais chimique]. Le défendeur a violé cette obligation.

Le défendeur a commis une autre contravention essentielle au sens des articles 49(1)(a) et 25 de la Convention en choisissant un [fournisseur] qui ne pouvait pas pour des raisons techniques remplir correctement [avec l'engrais chimique] les sacs fabriqués selon ses instructions. En conséquence, le défendeur n'a pu exécuter le contrat correctement et dans les délais, au détriment du demandeur.
[...] Le défendeur soutient que l'exécution défectueuse du contrat ne lui est pas imputable. Selon ses affirmations, il ne pouvait raisonnablement connnaître les motifs ayant empêché l'exécution du contrat au moment de la conclusion de celui ci. Il allègue qu'il lui était impossible d'éliminer les circonstances ayant empêché l'exécution en agissant lui même [...]. Cette objection n'est pas justifiée. Le défendeur est responsable du défaut de livraison dû à son fournisseur d'après l'article 79(2) de la Convention [...].

Si le vendeur donne des indications sur l'emballage à l'acheteur et si le vendeur fait appel à un fournisseur, il est du devoir du vendeur de s'assurer à l'avance si son fournisseur peut utiliser l'emballage qu'il a prescrit. Le défendeur a clairement manqué de se renseigner auprès de son fournisseur. Toutefois, même s'il s'en était enquis auprès de [son fournisseur] et que ce dernier avait fourni de faux renseignements, ceci n'aurait pas exonéré le défendeur de sa responsabilité.
Le défendeur, qui a choisi [le fournisseur] pour l'exécution de son contrat avec le demandeur, doit être tenu pour responsable du comportement de celui ci. Ceci se déduit de l'article 79(2) de la Convention puisque la responsabilité du vendeur pour son fournisseur fait partie intégrante du risque général de la fourniture des marchandises.

Le retard considérable de la livraison constitue une autre contravention essentielle au contrat d'après l'article 49(1)(a) de la Convention. Le simple retard ne constitue cependant pas une contravention essentielle d'après l'article 25 de la Convention puisque l'acheteur est habituellement obligé de donner au vendeur un délai raisonnable supplémentaire pour l'exécution de ses obligations conformément à l'article 47 de la Convention. C'est seulement lorsque le délai supplémentaire ainsi imparti arrive à expiration sans que le vendeur ait livré la marchandise que l'acheteur a le droit de déclarer le contrat résolu par application de l'article 49(1)(a) de la Convention. Le retard peut cependant constituer une contravention essentielle au contrat suivant les circonstances spéciales à chaque cas d'espèce dont le vendeur doit avoir connaissance. Un dépassement excessif de la date de livraison, même si aucun délai supplémentaire n'est accordé, peut autoriser l'acheteur à résoudre le contrat. Ceci est tout particulièrement le cas lorsque l'acheteur a donné à la date convenue de livraison une signification particulière connue du vendeur. [...] Tel est le cas du présent litige.

Le défendeur savait déjà d'après ce qui était imprimé sur les sacs que [l'engrais chimique] n'était pas destiné au demandeur, mais à un client de celui ci. Le défendeur connaissait, par une lettre que le demandeur lui avait adressé, que ce dernier était, en raison des retards du défendeur, menacé par son client de devoir payer les pénalités contractuelles et les coûts additionnels entraînés par les achats de couverture. Aussi la demande faite au vendeur d'exécuter le contrat sans retard avait un poids particulier. Elle faisait du retard dans les livraisons une contravention essentielle au contrat après réception des lettres du demandeur.
Il est sans importance que le demandeur ait effectivement déclaré résolu en son entier le contrat conclu avec le défendeur. Le demandeur a déclaré le contrat résolu au moins pour les premières livraisons de [X] tonnes pour lesquelles les sacs qu'il avait fourni étaient destinés.

D'après l'article 51(1) de la Convention, une résolution partielle est possible. Le contrat entre les parties est un contrat à livraisons successives [...]. Une résolution partielle est possible en cas de contrat à livraisons successives s'il existe une contravention essentielle concernant une livraison, comme cela est prévu à l'article 73(1) de la Convention.

Il est sans importance que le demandeur n'ait pas expressément déclaré le contrat partiellement résolu. Pour interpréter les déclarations et le comportement d'une partie, il convient d'établir l'intention réelle de celle ci pour peu que l'autre partie l'ait connue. Le guide pour cette interprétation est la manière dont une personne raisonnable aurait compris cette déclaration ou ce comportement dans les mêmes circonstances. Sur la base d'une interprétation raisonnable, le demandeur a déclaré le contrat partiellement résolu dans sa lettre du [...] sous réserve qu'il ne reçoive pas avant le [...] un engagement ferme du défendeur indiquant quand serait effectuée la livraison. Dans le meme courrier, le demandeur demandait une réponse définitive au défendeur et exposait clairement qu'il effectuerait sinon un achat de couverture auprès d'un autre fournisseur [...]. Dans sa lettre en réponse du [...] le défendeur ne donnait aucune réponse définitive, se contentant d'indiquer qu'il ne pouvait pas encore donner d'information définitive. La condition posée par le demandeur était donc réalisée et le contrat partiellement résolu [...]. Le défendeur soutient que le demandeur n'a subi aucun préjudice du fait de la livraison des sacs. Selon lui, les sacs restaient disponibles pour être remplis à tout moment. Dès lors le demandeur n'aurait pas exposé de frais inutiles. Cet argument ne cadre pas avec le respect du principe de bonne foi inscrit à l'article 7(1) de la Convention.

[...] Le demandeur peut réclamer des dommages-intérêts au titre des couts encourus pour les sacs qu'il avait fourni conformément aux articles 49(1)(a), 74 et 75 de la Convention [...]. Le demandeur peut également réclamer au défendeur les couts supplémentaires encourus pour effectuer des achats de remplacement auprès [d'un tiers]. L'acheteur peut effectuer des achats de remplacement en cas d'absence d'exécution ou d'inexécution défectueuse du contrat par le vendeur. Toutefois, d'après l'article 75 de la Convention, ceci présuppose la résolution du contrat tout entier, ou dans le cas d'un contrat à livraisons successives, la résolution du contrat pour une ou plusieurs livraisons comme il est dit à l'article 73(1) de la Convention.

L'acheteur peut réclamer les coûts entramés pas les achats de remplacement à titre de dommages intérêts si la transaction est raisonnable comme il est dit à l'article 75 de la Convention. L'acheteur a conclu une telle transaction s'il s'est comporté comme un homme d'affaires prudent et avisé en s'engageant dans cet achat de couverture. La première condition pour cela est que les marchandises de remplacement soient du même type et de la même qualité. [...] Les spécifications [de l'engrais chimique] dans l'opération de remplacement diffèrent certes légèrement des spécifications contractuelles. Ces différences ont trait à la pureté et à la teneur en eau. Elles sont mineures et sans importance [...].

L'acheteur qui doit procéder à un achat de remplacement ne peut avoir l'obligation d'entreprendre une enquête approfondie sur la manière de se procurer des marchandises de couverture le plus avantageusement possible. [...] Dans les circonstances présentes, le prix de l'achat de remplacement est raisonnable au sens de l'article 75 de la Convention. Un achat de remplacement qui doit être effectué à très court terme afin que le client puisse être livré dans les délais, justifie un prix plus élevé que celui qui est négocié lorsqu'on a le temps [...]. Par voie de conséquence, le demandeur peut obtenir du défendeur le remboursement des coûts supplémentaires encourus en raison de l'achat de remplacement (articles 49(1)(a), 73(1) et 75 de la Convention).

Le demandeur peut encore, d'après l'article 78 de la Convention, réclamer des intérêts moratoires à l'encontre du défendeur. La demande de remboursement pour le coût des sacs est née au moment de la résolution partielle du contrat. Les intérêts sont donc dus à compter de cette date. Les frais supplémentaires entraînés par l'achat de remplacement sont intervenus à compter du moment où [la banque] a payé le prix des marchandises de remplacement [au tiers] pour le compte du demandeur. Les intérêts sur ces frais courent donc à compter de cette date.

Le taux des intérêts n'est pas envisagé à l'article 78 de la Convention. Aucun accord n'a pu se faire à ce sujet entre les négociateurs de la Convention. La détermination du taux n'a donc pas été traitée. Il est admis qu'il est possible, dans le cadre de l'article 78 de la Convention, d'appliquer un taux d'intérêt international comme le LIBOR qui s'applique aux opérations interbancaires sur la place de Londres. [Les principes UNIDROIT] prévoient, à l'article 7.4.9(2), que le taux d'intérêt correspond au taux d'intérêt moyen pratiqué pour des emprunts à court terme par des banques de premier ordre. Ceci correspond à l'article 4.507(1) des Principes européens du droit des contrats qui ont été adoptés par la Commission sur le droit européen des contrats [...].

L'arbitre considère justifié d'appliquer au litige les règles identiques contenues dans les principes UNIDROIT et les principes du droit européen des contrats en tant que principes généraux au sens de l'article 7(2) de la Convention.

Le taux d'intérêt LIBOR plus 2% qui est réclamé par le demandeur correspond au taux d'intérêt pour les prêts à court terme pratiqué par les banques aux entreprises. Le demandeur se voit dès lors accorder ce taux d'intérêt. [...]

Sources

Original in French:
Journal du droit international, 1996, 1024.

Commented by:
D. HASCHER, Journal du droit international, 1996, 1028.

Date: **1995**
Adjudicating Court: **London Court of Arbitration**
Number: **Unknown**
Parties: **Unknown**

Keywords

PARTIES' CHOICE THAT THEIR CONTRACT BE GOVERNED BY "ANGLO-SAXON PRINCIPLES OF LAW" – ARBITRAL TRIBUNAL REFERENCE WITHOUT FURTHER EXPLANATION TO THE UNIDROIT PRINCIPLES

Abstract

A United States company and a governmental agency of a Middle Eastern country entered into a contract which contained a provision according to which any disputes which might arise would be settled on the basis of "Anglo-Saxon principles of law."

In the absence of any further specification as to what exactly this formula might mean, the Arbitral Tribunal chose to refer expressly to the UNIDROIT Principles, and in particular to the rules on interpretation contained therein.

Full Text

[Not yet available]

Sources

Original in English:
Unpublished.
Notice of the award kindly given by Johnny VEEDER, Q.C.

Date: **June 1995**
Adjudicating Court: ***ICC International Court of Arbitration (First Partial Award), Paris***
Number: ***7110***
Parties: ***Unknown***

Keywords

CONTRACTUAL REFERENCE TO "LAWS OR RULES OF NATURAL JUSTICE" – PARTIES' INTENT TO EXCLUDE THE APPLICATION OF ANY DOMESTIC LAW IN FAVOUR OF "GENERAL PRINCIPLES AND RULES ENJOYING WIDE INTERNATIONAL CONSENSUS" – APPLICATION OF THE UNIDROIT PRINCIPLES AS "THE CENTRAL COMPONENT" OF SUCH GENERAL PRINCIPLES AND RULES (CF. PREAMBLE OF UNIDROIT PRINCIPLES)

APPLICABILITY OF UNIDROIT PRINCIPLES EVEN IN THE ABSENCE OF IMPLIED CHOICE BY THE PARTIES – UNIDROIT PRINCIPLES AS THE LAW THE ARBITRAL TRIBUNAL CONSIDERS TO BE THE MOST APPROPRIATE ACCORDING TO ART. 13(3) (NOW ART. 17(1)) ICC ARBITRATION RULES

Abstract

An English company and a government agency of a Middle Eastern country entered into nine related contracts for the supply of equipment concluded between. None of the contracts contained an express choice of law provision in favour of a given domestic law but some of them contained provisions referring to settlement according to "laws or rules of natural justice". According to the Middle Eastern Plaintiff, such references expressed the parties' intent to refer to general principles of law. In its response, the English Defendant first objected that the reference to "natural justice" was a mere reference to procedural rules such as due process and fair hearing; moreover, being the obligor of the most characteristic performance whose place of business was in the UK, English law was to be applied as the most closely connected law in the sense of Article 4(2) of the 1980 Rome Convention.

A majority of the Arbitral Tribunal decided in favour of the Plaintiff. In interpreting the intent of the parties, it concluded that they had made a negative choice, *i.e.*, they had intended to exclude the application of any specific domestic law and to have their contracts governed by general principles and rules which, though not enshrined in any specific national legal system, are specially adapted to the needs of international transactions and enjoy wide international consensus.

According to the Arbitral Tribunal such "general rules and principles enjoying wide international consensus [...] are primarily reflected by the UNIDROIT Principles". Consequently, it concluded "without prejudice to taking into account the provisions of the Contracts and relevant trade usages [...] the Contracts are governed by, and should be interpreted in accordance to, the UNIDROIT Principles with respect to all matters falling within the scope of such Principles and for all other matters, by such other general legal rules and principles applicable to international contractual obligations enjoying wide international consensus which would be found relevant for deciding controverted issues falling under the present arbitration."

As to the Defendant's argument that the reference to "natural justice" should be understood under English law as a mere reference to procedural rules, the Arbitral Tribunal pointed out that in the context of international commercial arbitration, an interpretation peculiar to English law (and not even followed in other common law jurisdictions, such as the United States) was unacceptable.

Yet the Arbitral Tribunal stated that the applicability of the UNIDROIT Principles as the law governing the contracts would have been justified even in the absence of an implied intention to this effect by the parties. Indeed, the UNIDROIT Principles could be considered to be "the most appropriate law" according to Art. 13(3) [Art.17(1) of the 1998 version] of the ICC Rules of Arbitration.

Full Text

WITH RESPECT TO THE APPLICABLE LAW

This partial award, made in The Hague, The Netherlands, with the affirmative voce of the majority of the Tribunal's members ...decides in a final way on the law applicable to all the contracts subject to these arbitral proceedings.

The Contracts respectively provide far the resolution of disputes which may arise there out, as follows:

Contract (i): ICC arbitration in The Hague, The Netherlands ...

Contract (ii): amicable resolution by the parties ...

Contract (iii): disputes to be finally settled "according to natural justice" by ICC arbitration in Paris, France ...

Contract (iv): disputes to be finally settled "according to natural justice" by ICC arbitration in Paris, France ...

Contract (v): disputes to be finally settled "according to natural justice" by ICC arbitration in Paris, France ...

Contract (vi): disputes not amicably resolved to be finally settled "according to the laws of natural justice" by arbitration ...no site indicated far the arbitration;

Contract (vii): disputes not amicably resolved shall be settled "in accordance with natural justice" by arbitration ...no site indicated far the arbitration;

Contract (viii): disputes not amicably resolved shall be finally settled by arbitration in [State X] ... Contract (ix): disputes not amicably resolved shall be settled by arbitration in [State X] as provided in Clause 16 and [Annexed] \; articles 4 and 15 of the latter respectively indicating that (a) when the rules "governing the proceedings" contained in the said [Annexed] are "silent", proceedings shall be governed by ". ..any rules which the parties (or, failing them, the Arbitrator(s)) may settle in accordance with the rules of natural justice"; and (b) "in all matters not expressly provided" in the rules set forth in the said [Annexed] "the Arbitrator(s) shall act in the spirit of these Rules (the ones provided in the [Annexed]) and natural justice and shall make every effort to make sure that the award is enforceable at law".

The parties have agreed to submit all disputes arising from the Contracts to arbitration under the ICC Arbitration Rules (the "ICC Rules") before the same arbitral tribunal sitting at The Hague, The Netherlands. To that extent, then, the clauses in the Contracts have been superseded.

Claimant's position with respect to the applicable law:

...Claimant first adduced in its request far arbitration ...that (i) there was no "explicit" choice of law in the Contracts and (ii) the Contracts having been signed in [State X], the laws of [State X] should apply since the rule *lex loci contractus* is "a long-standing rule in international sales and purchases".

...Claimant further clarified its position by pointing out, with respect to Contract (v), that (1) the parries did not "expressly" agree on the applicable law; and (2) references to "natural justice" are too vague since there is no agreement among international jurists on its content and it does not offer to the arbitral tribunal sufficiently precise rules to decide the disputes being the subject-matter of this arbitration and would in any case express the parties' will as to the "approach" to be observed by the arbitral tribunal in the course of the proceedings. Claimant insists that the parties wished to have the dispute resolved according to a "law", which law should be [the law of State X] since the Contracts were signed in [State X]; [State X] was the place of contractual performance and this Contract was a part of a large project [far purposes relating purely to State X]. In this submission, Claimant extended the above reasoning only to Contracts (iii), (iv), (v), (vii) and (ix).

(Subsequently, taking all the Contracts as a whole, Claimant contends that the Contracts: should be first scrutinized far determining, according to Art. 13(3) of the ICC Rules, if there is any indication in the Contracts permitting to establish the parties' will as to the substantive law governing them. ...Claimant isolates four common features to all Contracts which, in Claimant's views, should lead to conclude that the Contracts are governed by general principles of law ...Against the backdrop of such four considerations, Claimant contends that the following circumstances reflect or indicate the implied intention of the parties to subject the Contracts to general principles of Law as proper Law: (a) the inter-governmental elements of the transactions between the parties and the fact that the Contracts "are accompanied by the *exercise* of exclusive powers of the state as sovereign and holder of the public power" ...(b) the expression "natural justice", found in many of the Contracts would not have the narrow sense ascribed to it under English Law referring to certain standards of procedural fairness which would be redundant because such standards are already reflected in the ICC Rules; and (c) the negotiation history of the Contracts would prove that it was the intention of both parties not, to accept the law of the country of the other as governing Law and that the parties did not select the application to the Contracts of the Laws of a third state.

...In a nutshell, Claimant's position is that in absence of an explicit or implied choice of Law by the parties, the rule of conflict the most appropriate for determining the applicable Law pursuant to Art. 13(3) of the ICC Rules would be either (i) general principles of private international law or (ii) [the] private international law [of State X]. IQ the first case, general private international law principles would Lead to the application of general principles of Law as proper Law of at Least 7 of the Contracts, whereas in the second case the Contracts would be governed by [the Law of State X]. Claimant argues that the Contracts are "state contracts" or "state-to-state" contracts of international character, and that according to the practice of international arbitral tribunals, general principles of Law are the proper Law of such contracts. It also refers to different authorities favouring the application of general principles of Law or *lex mercatoria* to state contracts and international contracts. Claimant rejects Respondent's arguments that the applicable Law to the Contracts should be determined on the basis of the characteristic performance rule, since it would not be a part of the general principles of private international law. Claimant also rejects the application of the European Convention on the Law applicable to International Obligations of 1980, since [State X] is not a party and [the Convention] was ratified by and became effective for the U.K. after the Contracts were made.

Subsidiary, Claimant contends. that the Contracts would be governed by [the law of State X] because [State X] is a party to all of them, all Contracts were made in [State X], and some of them were to be performed in [State X]. Claimant submits that since the Contracts were made in [State X], Article 968 of the Civil Code of [State X], providing that contracts are subject to the Laws of the place where made, would governs Claimant contends that such solution would not be contrary to English conflict-of-laws rules, which would give preference to the presumed will of the parties, nor [to] the closest connection test existing , in England *before* its ratification of the European Convention or as contemplated in the Latter's Art. 4, all of which would Lead to the application of [the Law of State X]. Claimant also argues that Dutch private international law does not apply since The Netherlands was not envisaged as arbitration site when the Contracts were made and the application of Dutch conflict-of-laws rules would be artificial.

Respondent's position with respect to the applicable law

...Respondent contends instead that "the proper Law of the Contracts is English Law or, alternatively, that the tribunal should apply general principles of Law".

...Respondent contends that according to Art. 13(3) of the ICC Rules ...the arbitral tribunal should resort to the *voie indirect,* that is, selecting the conflict-of-laws rule it would deem appropriate, *far* determining the substantive law(s) applicable to the Contracts. In that connection, Respondent's opinion is that no national rule of conflict (particularly [of State X] or British) should apply exclusively or in tandem, either because the principle and semblance of impartiality would be compromised or because the cumulative application of English and [State X's] conflict-of-laws would lead to conflicting with respect to at least six of the Contracts Respondent further argues that if the choice is to be made between the English and [State X's] conflict -of-Laws, the first would be preferable because (1) the place of formation of the contract (the connecting factor determining the proper law according to Art. 968 of the Civil Code [of State X]) is arbitrary and responds only to the convenience of the parties; (2) the English rule (as it was when the Contracts were made) is more consistent with comparative private international law, including modern international conventions; and (3) [State X's] conflict-of-laws is widely criticized and has never been applied by [State X's] Courts. Respondent is of the view that the conflict -of-Laws rules of the site of the arbitration (The Netherlands), though consistent with general principles of private international law, should not apply in view of conflicting authorities on the application by arbitral tribunals of the private international law of the country where they sit and the fact that The Hague was chosen as the site of the arbitration after the Contracts were made and was not selected by the parties or originally contemplated by them when contracting.

If choice is not to be made between the English and [State X's] conflict-of-laws rules, Respondent contends that general principles of private international law regarding contracts far the international supply of goods or services should apply. In Respondent's view, such principles would be (1) the Contracts are governed by the law of the jurisdiction with which each Contract separately considered is most closely connected; and (2) the proper law is that of the place of habitual residence or central administration of the party whose performance is characteristic to each Contract. By applying any or both of such principles Respondent contends that except far Contract (ix) (which could be governed by [the law of State X]) all Contracts are governed by English law. Respondent also argues that the result would be the same if either Dutch or English conflict-of-laws rules were found applicable.

...Respondent argues that the expressions "natural justice", "the laws of natural justice" and the "rules of natural justice" have all the same meaning and just refer to principles of procedural fairness and do not have any bearing on the law applicable to the substance of the Contracts. In Respondent's view, the only substantive meaning which may be attributed to such expressions -which are not present, Respondent emphasizes, in Contracts (i), (ii) and (viii) -is that they refer to principles of equity or morality, which may not be reconciled with the fact that the Tribunal is called to decide by application of the law and not in equity. In any case, Respondent indicates that such principles are deprived of any specific identity or are not sufficiently detailed to permit the resolution of a commercial dispute, circumstances which would negatively affect the enforceability of an award in these proceedings at least in England. Respondent indicates its agreement with Claimant's position, as perceived by Respondent, that general principles of conflict-of-laws would be the appropriate conflict-of-laws rule far determining the law applicable to the Contracts and that according to such general principles the closest connection test would be such general conflicts rule, but disagrees that such test may lead to the application of general principles of law as the substantive law, or that the characteristic performance test is not a part of generally accepted principles of conflict-of-laws. After contesting other aspects of Claimant's arguments, Respondent concludes that it would not be compatible with the expectations of the parties at the moment of contracting to see "such ill-defined : 'principles' " become the substantive law applicable to the Contracts. Respondent makes a special point in denying that the place of arbitration (as originally set forth in some of the Contracts before the parties decided to have consolidated arbitration in The Hague under the ICC Arbitration Rules) is a relevant element far determining the jurisdiction showing the closest connection with a contractual transaction, or that arbitration clauses in Contracts (viii) and (ix) render [the law of State X] applicable. Respondent reiterates its position that all Contracts are governed by English Law except Contract (ix), which probably would be governed by [the law of State X].

Arbiral Tribunal's consideration of an express or implied choice of law by the parties

In the view of this Tribunal, Art. 13(3) of the ICC Arbitration Rules should be interpreted as contemplating both the express and the implied or presumed choice by the parties of the law governing the Contracts. Such interpretation is consistent with the interpretation of similar texts created on the basis of a broad international consensus ... In consequence, in absence of express choice-of-law stipulations in the Contracts, this Tribunal shall proceed to determine whether the parties have made an implicit choice of \ ! the law or laws governing the Contracts. To that end, the Tribunal will consider the Contracts not in isolation, but as interrelated expressions of a long-term relationship between the parties spanning more than ten years. Such an approach is also consistent with (1) express statements of the parties in that regard ...(2) statements of the parties in that sense in the course of the hearing which took place in The Hague, The Netherlands, on ...(3) the unified approach adopted by the parties to deal with the resolution of ..disputes arising out of the Contracts; and (4) a certain degree of functional interrelatedness of the Contracts ...

It is also the view of this Tribunal that indications of the parties as to the applicable law referred to in Art. 13(3) of the ICC Rules should be construed ...on the basis of an objective test revealing what would have been the reasonable intention and expectations of the parties regarding the applicable law as evidenced by all the circumstances surrounding the negotiation of the Contracts, as well as by contractual terms likely to evidence the applicable law, *i.e.* a "contextual" approach ... ..In that respect, the question of the applicable law was clearly an important issue in the course of the negotiation of the Contracts, which deserved careful consideration by each party in its efforts to advance the application of its respective national law. Matters closely interrelated, such as the neutrality of the applicable law and of the dispute resolution mechanism, were at the foreground of the parties' concerns and discussions and it is obvious that the way in which they were finally taken care of was at the centre of the carefully negotiated compromises inducing the parties to enter into the Contracts. Central to the considerations of each party in the course of contractual negotiations was its clear resolve not to accept the application of its counterpart's national law to the Contracts ...

Six out of nine of the Contracts contain the expressions "natural justice", "rules of natural justice" or "laws of natural justice" in association with the resolution of disputes through commercial arbitration. In five of those Contracts ...the syntactic insertion of the expression "natural justice" is redolent of the drafting a practitioner would use to refer to the law governing the substance of the relevant transaction ...[T]he incorporation or exclusion of such terms was brought to bear in connection with discussions between the parties regarding the substantive law which would govern the Contracts and the dispute resolution process regarding controversies which might arise under the Contracts.

It is clear then that the presence of the expressions "natural justice", "laws of natural! Justice" and "rules of natural justice", which were undoubtedly the subject of careful consideration and negotiation, may not be ignored far assessing if and to which extent the parties have indicated the laws or principles governing the Contracts. However, to elucidate their meaning it would be inappropriate to have recourse, in bootstrap fashion, exclusively to the legal notions of one of the national juristic systems the application of which is at stake. The fact that the Contracts are drafted in English is not decisive, since the English language has become an international tool far expressing the terms and conditions of sophisticated transactions, even between parties none of which is a national of an English-speaking country or entering into transactions wholly unconnected with any such country. Resorting to English when it comes to exteriorizing in black and white the substance of a deal does not necessarily imply espousing the technical meaning that a specific common law jurisdiction would ascribe to the terms utilized, particularly when English is also the language spoken in other common law jurisdictions to which the expression "natural justice" is sconosciute or is deprived of the meaning ascribed to it under English law (for instance, such expression, and also expressions such as "rules of natural justice" or "laws of natural justice", are deprived of any technical meaning in the USA, are not currently used in such jurisdiction and may not be even found in Black's Dictionary (5th edition, 1979)). Such expressions are then ambiguous, particularly when found in international contracts not expressly submitted to the laws of England, and more specifically with respect to the non-English party not originating the contractual drafts being negotiated and whose legal system is not a common law one.

The determination of the procedural or substantive connotations. If the expression "natural justice" and the like shall have an impact on the law or laws applicable to the Contracts and is a part of the choice-of-law process having as its purpose the determination of such law or laws. On the other hand, five of the six Contracts in which "natural justice" or similar expressions are found were from their inception submitted by the parties to international commercial arbitration. The sixth Contract (Contract (ix)) was submitted ... to a type of highly delocalized and self-contained form of commercial arbitration comparable to international commercial arbitration, a trait further confirmed by the later conduct of the parties as they submitted Contract (ix) together with the others to a unified form of international commercial arbitration. Therefore, it is appropriate, on the basis of the terms of the Contracts and all surrounding circumstances, to establish the meaning and scope of "natural justice" and similar expressions from the autonomous perspective of both private international law and international commercial arbitration.

It is a general principle of interpretation widely accepted by national legal systems and by the practice of international arbitral tribunals, including ICC arbitral tribunals, that in case of doubt or ambiguity, contractual provisions, terms or clauses should be interpreted against the drafting party *(contra proferentem)* ...On the other hand, the meaning to be ascribed to expressions contained in international transactions *ah initio* submitted to international commercial arbitration should be consistent with the nature and expected rate of the dispute-resolution method chosen by the parties and the concomitant impact of such choice not only on procedural aspects but also on the law governing the merits. Finally, it is also a generally accepted practice by international arbitral tribunals, predicated upon elementary notions of coherence and rationality, to assume that the same words or expressions shall have the same meaning throughout the documents containing them ... This Tribunal finds that, without unduly extending the scope of such principle, it also applies to situations such as the one faced by this Tribunal, in which the same or similar expressions are repeated in different contracts between the same parties showing some noticeable functional interrelation, which, in addition, are to be considered as a whole far the purpose of determining the applicable law to the merits.

Common to such expressions found in six out of nine Contracts is, precisely, the word "justice", which undoubtedly is the predominant element to be taken into account far assessing their meaning and scope. In international commercial arbitration, though it is imaginable that the term "justice" may be utilized only in the sense of procedural justice, *i.e.* due process and fair trills, it is commonly understood as referring to arbitral justice in a more comprehensive sense, including not only arbitral procedural fairness but also the type of solution regarding the merits -not necessarily the same that would be obtained from national courts that should be expected by the parties by the very fact of having chosen international commercial arbitration far resolving their contractual disputes, Thus, it is not infrequently stated that often the parties resort to arbitration in order to have access to a "justice" other than that which would be obtained by applying a "national", particularly when, on account of the discrete circumstances of the case, a national would not be adapted to the solution of the dispute at stake. An obvious confirmation that notions of justice in international commercial arbitration are not merely procedural! but are also substantive is that the majority of national statutes dealing with international arbitration, international conventions regarding arbitration not just concerned with the recognition and enforcement of arbitral! agreements and awards, and international arbitration rules contain procedural! provisions and choice-of-law provisions, *i.e.* provisions pointing to choice-of-law solutions only becoming relevant because the dispute has been submitted to international commercial arbitration and which may well differ from those that would have been otherwise obtained had the decision of the case been left to municipal courts and their private international law systems.

This Tribunal, being confronted, in view of the mandate of the parties, with a choice-of-law exercise far determining the proper law of the Contracts, also has to consider the meaning of justice in the field of conflicts-of-laws. According to one of the classic English private international law texts, the notion of justice has a clearly substantive, and not merely procedural, meaning and, indeed, justice in its substantive sense would constitute the cornerstone of the discipline, since the "dominant motivating principle" of a private international law system like the English system is "the desire to do justice in cases involving a foreign element", More specifically "so far as English law is concerned, the principle is a priori in the statutory sense, in the terms of the oath that every judge must take before he enters on his judicial functions; and secondly, justice appears in the results as well as in the premise. The judge's decision, which itself establishes or applies a rule, converts the postulate of justice into reality". It is clear also that justice is not understood merely as a "conflicts justice" premised upon a blind, mechanical and "neutral" designation of the applicable) although an aseptic conflicts rule which operates on the basis of the geographical localization of the transaction, but is concerned with the results as to fairness derived from the application of this or that substantive rule to the disputed issue at stake (R.H. GRAVESON, *Conflict of Laws. Private International Law,* Sweet & Maxwell, 7th ed., 7-8 (1974)).

Such substantive essence of private international law justice is further illustrated through references to different English court decisions or authorities . Balance and convenience regarding the resolution of disputes as to their substance have been widely held as a part of' natural! justice and of the principle of reasonableness inherent to such notion ...The trend favoring choice-of-law processes not indifferent to ensuring the application of substantive laws or norms ensuring the "best" solution far the specific case in view of considerations of fairness, substantive justice, the reasonable expectations of the parties and the fact that the applicable rule being advanced is the best adapted to the circumstances of the case is far from being limited to isolated national private international law systems ...

There is, then, a clear correspondence between, on one hand, the mandate of international arbitrators of making a fair and just decision adapted to the particular controversy at stake without being tied to precedent or abstract concerns and, as it happens in this case, without the parties' contractual stipulations directing the arbitrators to apply any specific national rule or legal system, and, on the other hand, choice-of-law methodologies aimed at reaching fair and just results by applying the substantive legal rules and principles which are better adapted to the circumstances of the case. From the standpoint of conflict-of-laws principles in international commercial arbitration, the notion of justice goes beyond procedural fairness and plays an important role in the determination of the applicable substantive law.

Particularly when associated with international commercial arbitration, choice-of-law justice is premised on the idea that multi-state cases are imperfectly governed by the laws of a single national jurisdiction, since by their very nature, they constitute a "social and economic unit" far which, in view of the fact that they overlap national frontiers, there is no equivalent comprehensive tailor-made "legal unit", sufficiently adapted to the circumstances of the multi-state case and the expectations of the parties, that would provide a fair and just substantive solution for it. Choice-of-law methodologies advancing the application of that type of multi-state substantive rules are then the best adapted to resolve international commercial cases on the basis of the substantive justice and fairness expectations of the parties and the circumstances of the case.

In respect of transactions like the Contracts, in which (i) there is no express choice-of-law stipulation designating the law of any of the parties or of a third country and where neutrality regarding the applicable law was a paramount concern denoted by the parties' ..rejection of each other's law and the absence of any explicit or implicit reference to the laws of a third country; and (ii) the parties have buttressed neutrality as to the applicable law by agreeing to submit their contractual disputes to international commercial arbitration, albeit without empowering the Tribunal to act *ex aequo et bono* or as *amiable compositeur*, it can only be concluded that no national law was judged adequate or adapted to govern such transactions without the risk of disturbing the balance of neutrality between the parties. In consequence, when the parties negotiated and finally entered into the Contracts they only left room far the application of general legal rules and principles adequate enough to govern the Contracts but not originated in a specific municipal legal system. Such balance of neutrality, which includes neutrality of the applicable substantive law, is an essential part of the substantive justice expected by the parties in connection with the Contracts. Such "negative" choice by the parties commands as much respect as any express choice-of-law would have commanded, had the parties inserted choice-of-law stipulations in the Contracts; therefore, in order not to disrupt the parties' common understanding in that regard, this Tribunal must refrain from the choice of any national law as proper law. Through references to "natural justice" and the like, the parties indicated their intention that their Contracts be governed by substantive rules not belonging to any discrete national legal system and appropriately responding to their concerns about neutrality in the applicable law.

Though the parties excluded the application of any national law to the Contracts, it does not follow that they failed to imply the application of any other substantive rules or principles and thus left the decision regarding the designation of the proper law of the Contracts to the happenstance of choice-of-law methodologies [aver] which they had no contract, particularly as to their neutrality far determining the applicable law. In this regard, the statement that "...wholly neutral principles of conflict-of-laws are an illusion" (A LOWENFELD, "*Lex Mercatoria: an arbitrator's view*", in *Lex Mercatoria and Arbitration* (CARBONNEAU Ed.) Transnational Juris Publications, Inc. 37, 45 (1990)) is certainly pertinent and acquires special significance.

Such interpretation is particularly appropriate if the only alternative left in absence of express or implied choice-of-law stipulations would be resorting to supposedly choice-of-law neutral and dispassionate criteria, such as a talismanic notion of the localization of the characteristic obligation or an amorphous grouping of contacts or *the* closest connection noticeable in some national legal systems, which would, by the rule-of-thumb and without taking into account the parties' concerns and expectations as to substantive justice, including neutrality as to the applicable law, impose the law of one of the parties or of a third state which would or might defeat -the parties' intentions five out of nine Contracts contained international arbitration clauses providing far panels not to be integrated with nationals from the country of any of the parties. The other Contracts, though not expressly submitted to international institutional arbitration, both on account of the introduction of expressions such as natural justice or laws or rules of natural justice in connection with the dispute resolution process (as indicated before, such terms have both "procedural" and "substantive" connotations) and the omission of any designation of a national *lex arbitral* or procedural law, referred to a form of commercial arbitration highly delocalized irrespective of the seat of the arbitral tribunal. ... [T]he parties' latter conduct, *i.e.* their decision to globally submit disputes arising out of the Contracts to international arbitration under the ICC Rules, is clear evidence arid confirmation that the parties favored the delocalization of the dispute resolution system in connection with all the Contracts in consonance with their strong concerns regarding the neutrality of the substantive and procedural legal framework related to their long-term relationship embodied in the Contracts.

Such considerations acquite particular relevance when the transactions at stake, in addition to being commercial and international, are also colored as in the instant case -by a certain degree of state or public involvement on both sides. The Tribunal finds that it has not been presented with conclusive evidence showing that the Contracts may be considered state-to-state contracts since it has not been proved that Respondent is organically linked to the British state, vested with any of its functions or otherwise assimilated to the British state so as to acquire a position significantly different from that of a private party. Nevertheless, the Contracts, though commercial in nature, have a state party and have been negotiated, executed, and the obligations of the parties insert themselves, in a context in which state interests and policies are intimately concerned on both sides ...The Contracts then squarely belong to the category of international commercial contracts (which far the purposes of this award will be hereinafter referred to as "state contracts") being the subject of a resolution of the Institute of International Law on arbitration between States, State Enterprises, or State Entities, and Foreign Enterprises adopted on September 12; 1989 in the course of the Institute's Santiago de Composted session. Such Resolution was intended to serve as guidance to international commercial arbitrators far, among other matters, determining the laws, rules and principles applicable to the substance of this type of transaction ...

State contracts show a certain number of paradigmatic characteristics which this Tribunal finds of relevance in connection with the Contracts. Among those, the following are pertinent: (i) the state party should not be allowed to resort to its law-creating powers not in the general interest but to improve its legal position or to extricate itself from contractual liability ...(ii) the parties may expressly or implicitly de-localize state contracts to remove them from national legal systems and submit them to transnational legal rules ...(iii) the applicable law should respect the principle that the substantive "contractual equilibrium" between the parties as agreed at the moment of contracting is not disrupted ...(iv) detachment of the arbitral process and of the arbitral *lex fori* at large (including arbitral choice-of-law methodologies far determining the law applicable to the merits) from the laws of the seat of the arbitration ...(v) agreeing on international commercial arbitration in connection with state contracts has an impact on the substantive law applicable to the substance of the dispute.

In this latter respect it is pertinent to point out that the parties and the arbitrators enjoy larger autonomy far de-localizing the contract and determining the applicable laws or rules when disputes arising out of a state contract are submitted to international arbitration than otherwise, and, thus, that choosing international commercial arbitration has de-localizing effects asta the applicable law: this may be established, far example, when comparing (i) the Preamble and provisions of the Resolution adopted by the Institute of international Law in its Athens sessions on the Proper Law of the Contract in Agreements between a State and a Foreign Private Person, dealing in general with issues regarding the law applicable to a state contract in principle not necessarily submitted to international commercial arbitration ...with (ii) the Santiago de Composted Resolution mentioned above, in particular its Arts. 4 and 6, which exclusively concern the law applicable to state contracts by international commercial arbitrators. The detachment of the choice-of-law methodology and the substantive applicable law identifiable through it from national legal systems in order to preserve the contracted-for equilibrium between the state and the private parties is then a common feature of state contract arbitration to be taken into account when interpreting such contracts and their surrounding circumstances far determining the governing law.

In the present case, such equilibrium was an integral part of the substantive and dispute resolution justice framework the parties had in mind when entering into the state contracts binding on them. Therefore, references to "natural justice" and "laws" or "rules" of "natural justice" found in the majority of the Contracts should be consistently and uniformly interpreted as referring not only to procedural justice but to the special type of substantive justice the parties had in mind, based on the neutrality of the applicable law to the merits and of the means of dispute resolution mechanisms selected by the parties to effectuate substantive neutrality, this latter aspect further confirmed by the ulterior comprehensive submission by the parties of their disputes arising out of the Contracts to ICC international arbitration.

The choice of international or de-localized arbitration to resolve any potential disputes, which is explicit from their very inception in most of the Contracts but was later extended to all of them, should then be understood as an additional element to further support and maintain such substantive justice balance. Such choice plays a "localizing" role in the case of international and commercial state contracts not having an express choice-of-law stipulation, since it denotes the exclusion of choice-of-law criteria normally applicable by national courts, which would lead to the exclusive application of national laws, and therefore points by exclusion to a *tertium genus* or general principles of law which may be only defined in the negative as such rules and principles not exclusively belonging to a single national legal system ...Being international and commercial state contracts, reference in the Contracts to natural justice or the like, together with the absence of reference to any national law, can then be only reasonably construed as pointing to the application of such substantive legal rules and principles adapted to the Contracts and the facts and circumstances surrounding them, which, by not belonging to any discrete national legal system, satisfy the parties' concerns as to the neutrality of the applicable proper law. Substantive rules and principles fulfilling such requirements may only be general legal rules and principles regarding international contractual obligations and enjoying wide international consensus...the Tribunal concludes that the reasonable intention of the parties regarding the substantive law applicable to the Contracts was to have all of them governed by general legal rules and principles in matter of international contractual obligations such as those arising out of the Contracts, which, though not necessarily enshrined in any specific national legal system, are specially adapted to the needs of international transactions like the Contracts and enjoy wide international consensus.

In addition, this Tribunal estimates that its mandate. ..requires that, to the extent possible at this stage, some precisions be given as to the substance of such legal rules and principles. It should be noted that both Claimant and Defendant, at different stages of their successive argumentations, have expressed their concern either about the vagueness of general principles of law or the possibility (at least with respect to English courts) that an award rendered on the basis of such principles might not be enforceable before national courts.

Taking into account such circumstances, the discussions held in such connection with the parties ...and also the requirement that arbitrators . "..should do no less than is required to exercise their authority completely ..." (Institute of International Law, Santiago de Compostela Resolution cited above, art. .1, 63 International Law Institute Yearbook 326 (1990)), this Tribunal finds that general legal rules and principles enjoying wide international consensus, applicable to international contractual obligations and relevant to the Contracts, are primarily reflected by the Principles of International Commercial Contracts adopted by UNIDROIT (the "UNIDROIT Principles") in 1994 ...In consequence, without prejudice to taking into account the provisions of the Contracts and relevant trade usages, this Tribunal finds that the Contracts are governed by, and shall be interpreted in accordance (with) , the UNIDROIT Principles with respect to all matters falling within the scope of such Principles, and far all other matters, by such other general legal rules and : principles applicable to international contractual obligations enjoying wide international consensus, which would be found relevant far deciding controverter issues falling under the present arbitration.

The reasons why this Tribunal considers the UNIDROIT Principles to be the central component of the general rules and principles regarding international contractual obligations and enjoying wide international consensus, which constitute the proper law of the Contracts, are manifold:

(1) the UNIDROIT Principles are a restatement of international i legal principles applicable to international commercial contracts made by a distinguished I group of international experts coming from all prevailing legal systems of the world, I without the intervention of states or governments, both circumstances redounding to the I high quality and neutrality of the product and its ability to reflect the present stage of consensus on international legal rules and principles governing international contractual obligations in the world, primary on the basis of their fairness and appropriateness far international commercial transactions falling within their purview;

(2) at the same rime, the UNIDROIT Principles are largely inspired (by) an international uniform-law text already enjoying wide international recognition and generally considered as reflecting international trade usages and practices in the field of the international sales of goods, which has already been ratified by almost 40 countries, namely, the 1980 Vienna Convention on the International Sale of Goods

(3) the UNIDROIT Principles are specially adapted to the Contracts being the subject of this arbitration, since they cover both the international sale of goods and supply of services

(4) the UNIDROIT Principles (see their preamble) have been specifically conceived to apply to international contracts in instances in which, as it is the case in these proceedings, it has been found that the parties have agreed that their transactions shall be governed by general legal rules and principles; and

(5) rather than vague principles or general guidelines, the UNIDROIT Principles are mostly constituted by clearly enunciated and specific rules coherently organized in a systematic way ...

The precisions given by this Tribunal in preceding paragraph ...should suffice to dispel many concerns as to the enforceability of an award made in these proceedings on the basis of the general legal rules and principles applicable to international obligations on account of the vagueness or lack of precision of such principles. ...(L)earned opinions ...indicate that the present trend in England points towards the admissibility and enforceability in that : jurisdiction of arbitral awards based on *lex mercatoria* or general principles of law, particularly when the award has not been rendered in England or is not subject to English law and the laws of the national jurisdiction in which the award is made do not render invalid an award made on such terms ...

Arbitral Tribunal's consideration of the applicable law in the absence of an express or implied choice by the parties

The above conclusions would not have been different had the Tribunal not found that the parties made an implicit choice of the applicable law to the Contracts. First and foremost, it should be noted that it is commonly accepted in comparative private international law that there is no clear delimitation between the tests to determine the implicit choice-of-law made by the parties wirt respect to the substance of contractual obligations and those to be observed in absence of choice and in fact the boundaries between such rests are often blurred ...The same objective circumstances, such as, in this case, the intention of the parties not to submit the Contracts to each other's laws or to the laws of a third country and yet their will to have their disputes decided according to legal rules and nor *ex aquo et bono, the* nature of the relationship between the parties (share Contracts) and their concerns regarding the neutrality as to the applicable law as revealed, far instance, by -Contractual negotiations, the insertion of terms such as "natural justice" or "laws of natural justice" or "rules of natural justice" and the submission of all disputes to international commercial arbitration also militate in favor of concluding that the genel-allegat rules and principles regarding international contractual obligations enjoying a broad international consensus would have been found to be the law governing the Contracts even in absence of an implied contractual stipulation to that end.

Such conclusion would have been reached by the Tribunal by resorting either to the *voie directe* or the *voie indirecte* ...

" ...the determination of the applicable law is an exercise which may nor remain indifferent to the substantive outcome of the choice-of-law process If projected to the field of international commercial arbitration and the interpretation of the relevant part of Art. 13(3) of the ICC Arbitration Rules, the necessary conclusion is that the very distinction between *voie indirecte* and *voie directe* becomes blurred and on the verge of fading away, since both would pursue the same ends through essentially the same means, namely, the application of the "better law", *i.e.* the substantive rules, laws and principles best adapted to a just and fair decision of the dispute on the basis of the circumstances of the case and the parties' expectations by directly taking into account, far so doing, the contents of the substantive rules and principles to be applied. ...with respect to the Contracts such "better law" is found in the general rules and principles regarding international contractual obligations enjoying wide international consensus. Since such rules and principles are deemed to become directly applicable, in absence of a choice-of-law, to transactions characterized as commercial and international stare contracts, their application may be also explained in terms of the *voie indirecte,* because such characterization is precisely a conflicts rule, though differing from traditional ones in that its operation does not depend on the geographical localization of a connecting factor ...

Art. 13(3) of the ICC Arbitration Rules does nor impose on the arbitrators the obligations to follow generally accepted conflict-of-laws rules or, far that matter, any specific national or a national conflict-of-laws rules ...In these proceedings, it has been sufficiently and convincingly argued that the cumulative method, *i.e.* the application of the conflict-of-laws systems of the national jurisdictions of the parties to the dispute would nor have been useful because the private international laws of England and [State X] would have led to incompatible, rather than coincident, solutions as to choice-of-law in connection with most of the Contracts. On the other hand, in view of the diversity of private international law systems in the world, a comparative law research would in identifying generally accepted private international law principles enjoying wide international consensus far determining the applicable law to international contracts in absence it might be adduced, however, that when it comes to determining the substance of such general rules and principles applicable in absence of an implied stipulation by the parties, the application of the UNIDROIT Principles is not possible, since the Preamble to the Principles indicates that they may be applied "when the parties have agreed that their contract be governed by general principles of law, the *lex mercatoria* and the like". The originai draft version of the UNIDROIT Principles, which was not finally approved by the UNIDROIT Council in this respect, provided (Art. 1.2 (b)) that such principles also apply "when the parties have not chosen any law to govern their contract". This provision was I excluded from the text of the UNIDROIT Principles as finally approved and is not a, part of their Preamble because the UNIDROIT Council felt, in absence of a choice by the parties, that it would be conducive to pre-empting the application of the domestic law of the national legal system rendered applicable by private international law rules ...

Nevertheless, on the basis of at least two grounds, this Tribunal would not have been thereby prevented from referring to the UNIDROIT Principles a part of the law applicable to the Contracts in absence of an express or implicit choice-of-law stipulation:

(i) ...the Contracts are governed, as a result of a preliminary finding, by general rules and principles regarding international contractual obligations enjoying wide international consensus, *i.e.* they are not governed by any discrete domestic or national law. In consequence, in the present case, no clash between any discrete municipal law and the UNIDROIT Principles is possible; and

(ii) the application of the UNIDROIT Principles does not depend on their self-given criteria of application, but on the powers vested with this Tribunal under Art. 13(3) of the ICC Arbitration Rules, which are not limited to the *voie indirecte* and authorize it to directly determine the applicable law it deems more appropriate to govern the merits, *i.e.*, in this case, the general legal rules and principles regarding international contractual obligations enjoying wide international consensus, including, without limitation, the UNIDROIT Principles as an adequate restatement and expression of such general legal rules and principles. The application of the Principles in case of absence of choice then rests upon Art. 13(3) of the ICC Arbitration Rules and the mandate conferred on this Tribunal to find and determine the law applicable to the Contracts.

...This Tribunal then concludes by a majority ...that, without prejudice to taking into account the provisions of the Contracts and relevant trade usages, the Contracts shall be governed by, and interpreted according to, the general legal rules and principles regarding international contractual obligations enjoying a wide international consensus, including the UNIDROIT Principles, with respect to all such matters falling under the scope of such principles.'

Dissenting Arbitrator:

'... a reluctance for psychological or political reasons on the part of each negotiating party to be seen expressly to agree to apply the law of the other negotiating party is not the same as a determination by the parties that in no case shall the law of either of them apply. *A fortiori* it is not a determination by them of the law that *is.* to be applied to the merits of the dispute. ...

Thus in my view the attitude attributed to the negotiating parties was not tantamount to an agreement excluding the application of the laws of either of them. It was simply a reflection of the unwillingness of each negotiator to be seen expressly to concede that the law of the other would or might apply. That is a very different thing, entirely compatible with recognition on both sides that, failing agreement, the dispute would need to be resolved by applying the "accepted legal rules far deciding the law which would need to be applied if. ..a dispute needed to be formally resolved". The "accepted legal rules far deciding the law which would need to be applied" are the rules of conflict of laws. ...

A determination of the law not to be applied ...is not a determination of the law which is. to be applied. For the latter, the parties must positively pick their winner, not merely limit the field of choice.

Perhaps to pre-empt such objections, it was next argued (in the alternative) on behalf of Claimant that the wording of the Contracts did indeed point to a positive determination, or choice, by the parties. They had, it was contended, determined that the law to be applied to the merits of the dispute was to be the "general principles of law". It is my understanding that this contention derives from an inference, said to be reasonable, drawn from the reference in some of the Contracts to "natural justice", coupled perhaps with the fact that Claimant is a sovereign State entity. ...

A "determination" must presumably determine something. It must, however informally expressed, indicate with reasonable certainty what has been determined. In the presume case I can nothing equitable m to a pronouncement that the law applicable to the merits shall be "general principles of law" (a pronouncement itself not conspicuous either far precision or far predictability of its consequences) ...such references as can be found to "natural justice" do not in my opinion attempt to determine anything about the law applicable to the merits, let alone dictate that "general principles" of law are to be so applicable. ...The researches of counsel have produced no instance of any case where a contract calling far disputes to be settled by arbitration in accordance with natural justice was held thereby to be defining the substantive law applicable to the merits of the dispute, as opposed to the decision-making procedures to be adopted.

That some of the Contracts here do come in a reference to "natural justice" seems to me to indicate only a desire on the part of the framers of those Contracts to stress that all arbitral procedures adopted, and all steps taken by the arbitral tribunal or any of its members, must be consisted with the rules of natural justice -understandable enough, since otherwise there is a real risk that any award would be vulnerable to attack in many countries as being unenforceable, in the same way as would a foreign judgment arrived at after a similarly defective process. A requirement that the arbitrators are to ...proceed in accordance with natural justice may be said to be rather more specific than the provision in Article 26 of the ICC Rules that the arbitrators are to make every effort to make sure that their award will be enforceable In law. In Contract 9 the phrase is expressly referable to "the rules governing the proceedings"; it is agreed that those rules may include (if certain identified procedural rules are silent) rules "which arbitrator(s) may settle in accordance with the rules of natural justice". This cannot, in my view, suffice to allow the arbitrator(s) to "settle" provisions of substantive law -*i.e.* effectively to write into the Contract provisions of law which will govern the substantive bargain of the parties.

Moreover, the opening sentences of Article 13(3)of the ICC Rules, and of Article 1054(2) of the Netherlands Code, contemplate a determination, or choice, by the parties of the rules of law to be applied to the merits of the dispute -*i.e.* the "proper" law. Now, it may be possible far the parties effectively to provide in express terms in their contract that it is to be governed by "UNIDROIT Principles" or by "general principles of law". A court or an arbitrator would in that type of case doubtless strive to do their best to interpret, and give effect, such language. But that is not the question here. The parties said nothing about "general principles of law", still less about which of the countless principles of law to be found in the world's legal systems (principles often irreconcilable with each other) were to be selected. They said nothing about "UNIDROIT Principles". Indeed, the UNIDROIT Council itself declined to provide that the UNIDROIT Principles should apply where contracting parties had not chosen any law to govern their contract, since to have done so would be , conducive to pre-empting the application of the domestic law of the national legal system rendered applicable by private international law rules

In my view, the first sentences of Article 13(3) of the ICC Rules and Article 1054(2) of the Netherlands Code are applicable only if the parties themselves designate the rules of law to be applied by the arbitrator to the merits of the dispute. The parties do not do that - (a) by designating rules to be applied by the arbitrators, not to the merits of the dispute, but to the dispute-resolving procedures prescribed or adopted by them; or (b) by inserting, in a number of these formal Contracts framed in English, a reference to "natural justice" -a legal expression which in its ordinary usage is employed with reference to rules designed to ensure the fair trial of the merits, as opposed to rules of substantive law designed to be 'applied in deciding which of the disputants has the better case on the merits; or (c) by leaving it to the arbitrators to apply to the merits of future disputes any principles of law that the arbitrators may deem appropriate.

Hence I have not been able to accept the arguments on behalf of Claimant that the parties here have themselves determined, either "negatively" or "positively", the rules of law to be applied to the merits of the dispute. The parties never did "determine the law to be applied by the arbitrators to the merits". At best, if Claimant is right, they purported to leave that determination to the arbitrators charged with resolving future disputes, if any. The failure of the parties to make a determination would seem to me to bring into play the second sentence of Article 13(3), requiring the arbitrators to proceed by way of deciding upon a rule of conflict that they deem appropriate, being a rule of conflict which in tour designates the proper law (the provisions of which are to apply to the merits).

I therefore come to the second sentences of Article 13(3) of the ICC Rules and Article 1054(2) of the Netherlands Code. The parties having *ypothesi* failed to determine the proper law far themselves, the arbitrators must make the selection in accordance (directly or indirectly) with what they consider to be "appropriate". The second sentence of Article 1054(2), viewed in isolation, arguably might be said to permit "direct" selection of the substantive law, rather than "indirect" selection via the selection of an appropriate rule of conflict~ Prima facie it seems to me to be doubtful if that sentence, even viewed in isolation, would permit the arbitrators to deem appropriate, as applicable to the substance of the dispute, unspecified "general principles of law". Moreover here the second sentence of Article 1054(2) is not to be viewed in isolation. On the contrary, Section VI, paragraph 2 of the Terms of Reference provides that the rules governing the procedure are to be the ICC Rules, and that only where the latter are silent will the Articles of the Netherlands Code apply. ...Applying Article 13(3) of the ICC Rules, the arbitrators must apply to the merits of the dispute the law designated as the proper law by the rule of conflict of laws which they deem appropriate. Among numerous threshold questions here is whether they may "deem appropriate" a rule of conflict (if such there be) which does not itself designate any particular system of proper law; but merely leaves the arbitrators free to pick, as needs arises, from differing legal systems or Fonti, a selection of whatever rules of proper law they may deem appropriate.

I do not think that the latter would satisfy the provisions in questions Article 13(3) seems to me to direct the arbitrators to arrive at the proper law via a rule of conflict which itself designates that proper law. The role of the rule of conflict is to designate the substantive proper law. The arbitrators are to select the rule of conflict, and the rule of conflict so selected is in turn to designate the substantive proper law. The second sentence of Article 13(3) basically tells the arbitrators that they are not obliged to apply the rules of conflict of *e.g.* the forum or seat of arbitration, if they consider other rules of conflict to be more appropriate. But a so-called rule of conflict that purports to prescribe merely that the arbitrators may or shall hereafter designate principles of substantive proper law to be applied postulates that the substantive proper law remains undesignated by that rule of conflict itself. Such a "rule" is not in truth a rule of conflict at all. To say that the arbitrators may deem appropriate a "rule" that would merely refer back to the arbitrators themselves the designation of the proper law is a circular way of saying that the "rule" does not designate any proper law. As well as multiplying the uncertainties of the outcome, this seems to me to be contrary to the underlying concept. Article 13(3) by its nature is a provision which will apply to the countless international bargains subject to the ICC Rules in which the parties themselves (whether purely commercial entities or sovereign States) have made no specific determination as to the law to be applied to the merits. My own surmise is that most would expect their arbitral tribunals to do their best to apply "the generally accepted legal rules far deciding the law which would need to be applied" ... That would result in the selection of a particular system of law as the proper law, the classic role of any system of conflict of laws. Article 13(3) seems to me to be designed far such parties. More adventuresome parties who prefer something more sophisticated cannot reasonably complain if they are required to specify <u>expressly</u> what they have in mind.

For the above reasons I conclude:

(a) that the parties here never themselves determined the law to be applied to the "merits of the dispute";

(b) in particular, that they at no rime purported to determine that such law was to consist of "general principles of law";

(c) that if they had purported to do the latter that would not have been a determination qualifying as such under the first sentence of Article 13(3) of the ICC Rules, which calls far a determination by the parties of the proper law which is to be applied to the merits by the arbitrators, and not merely far an indication by the parties that if a dispute arises, the arbitrators are left free to choose any rules or proper law that they think appropriate;

(d) that accordingly the first sentence of Article 13(3) is not satisfied here;

(e) that nevertheless, by reason of the foregoing and the second sentence or Article 13(3), the arbitrators here have a wide discretion to select, from any existing rules of conflict designed to identify a proper law, the rule of conflict which they consider to be the most appropriate; and

(f) that having done so, they should thereafter proceed to apply to the merits of the dispute the system of proper law identified by that rule of conflict. ... But what conflict rule is "appropriate" here? ...I take the view that the present Contracts ...are all most closely connected with England ...Under conflict rules familiar in numerous legal systems, including those of English law and of The Netherlands (the agreed seat of this arbitration) a permissible approach would be to seek the law which had the "closest connection" with the Contracts. That appears to me to point to English law. The widely favored "principle of characteristic performance", which order has the endorsement of an impressive number of countries, including again England and The Netherlands, would point strongly in the same direction. ...

Accordingly, I would have held, in the case of Contracts Nos. 1-8 inclusive, that the law to be applied to the merits of the dispute was the law of England, being the law designated as the proper law by the rules of conflict or, *inter alia,* the Netherlands and England, which rules I would deem more "appropriate" than any other in the present case. I would not have been disposed to contest, however, that in relation to Contract No.9 (having regard to the obligations of the parties performable by [State X] there under), the proper law could be held to be that of [State X], as being the system designated as the proper law by the rules of conflict above mentioned calling far the ascertainment of the law with which the relevant Contract might be said to have the closest relation.

Sources

Original in English:
ICC International Court of Arbitration Bulletin, Vol. 10, No. 2, Fall 1999, 39 - 54.

Date: ***July 1995***
Adjudicating Court: ***ICC International Court of Arbitration, Brussels***
Number: ***8240***
Parties: ***Unknown***

Keywords

CONTRACT GOVERNED BY DOMESTIC LAW (SWISS LAW) – REFERENCE BY ARBITRAL TRIBUNAL TO THE UNIDROIT PRINCIPLES FOR CONFIRMATION AT INTERNATIONAL LEVEL OF A SIMILAR RULE OF SWISS LAW

PAYMENT IN LOCAL CURRENCY - ART. 6.1.9(3) UNIDROIT PRINCIPLES TO DETERMINE EXCHANGE RATE

Abstract

Parties from Switzerland, Singapore and Belgium concluded a contract of distributorship. After termination of the contract by agreement, the question arose as to how to regulate the buying back of the inventories.

Although the parties had indicated Swiss law as the law governing their contract, the Arbitral Tribunal, in deciding the rate of exchange to be chosen for the payment in the local currency, referred to Art. 6.1.9(3) of the UNIDROIT Principles for a confirmation at an international level of a similar rule of Swiss law.

Full Text

The determination of the exchange rate in be applied in Claimant's claim under Art.1 of the Termination Agreement requires interpretation of said stipulation under the applicable law.

The parties have agreed that the choice of law clause contained in Art. 36 of the Distribution Agreement and referring in the laws of Switzerland as the governing law of their contract shall also be applicable to the Termination Agreement. This agreement constitutes a valid choice of law clause and, according to the wording of Art. 36 of the Distribution Agreement, also applies in the interpretation of the contracts.

Under Swiss law, contract interpretation is governed by Art. 1 and 18 of the Swiss Code of Obligations (*Obligationenrecht*) in connection with Art. 1, Sec. 2 of the Swiss Civil Code (*Zivilgesetzbuch*). These provisions require the Arbitrator in look first for corresponding intentions of the parties as expressed in the contractual stipulations (Swiss Federal Tribunal BGE 105 II 16; 111 II 457; GUHL, Das Schweizerische Obligationenrecht, 8th ed. 1991, at 97). If no such natural consensus can be discerned, the Arbitrator has to look for the parties' implied or normative consensus. Towards this end the Arbitrator has in discern what reasonable parties acting in good faith must have expressed as their common intentions at the moment of conclusion of the contract [...]. The principle of good faith thus establishes a "presumption of reasonableness" to be followed by the Arbitrator in his task of construing the contractual provision in dispute. Starting from the wording of the contractual stipulation this objective interpretation has in take into account not only the conduct of the parties before and after the conclusion of the contract but also the purpose of the contract and of previous contracts concluded between the same parties and the economic context in which it was concluded [...].

In answering this question one has in focus again on Art 1(c) of the Termination Agreement. It must be determined whether this provision can be considered to contain an implied currency clause, fixing the date of conversion in the date of the individual purchase of each item of inventory. Since such a will is not expressed on the face of said provision, one has in apply the principles of objective interpretation as outlined [...] above.

Every attempt that tries to give Art. 1(c) of the Termination Agreement such a broad meaning has in take into account the principle of nominalism. This principle provides that absent a specific provision in the agreement of the parties each debtor has in pay a monetary debt at its nomina! value. Therefore, without any special agreement, each party carries the risk of currency depreciation. The principle of nominalism is a general principle of transnational law. It is laid down not only in Swiss court (decisions and doctrinal writings [...] but also in An. 6.1.9(3) of the UNIDROIT Principles of International Commercial Contracts, allowing the obligor in make payment of a money debt expressed in a currency other than that of the place for payment in the currency of that place "at the rate of exchange prevailing there when payment is due" (UNIDROIT (ed.), Principles of International Commercial Contracts, 1994, at 127), As a consequence of this general principle of law, international arbitral tribunals are very reluctant to intervene into a contract because of inflation and currency depreciation in the absence of a specific currency depreciation clause[...].

This principle sets high standards for the Claimant who, according to the generai principles of *actori incumbit probatio*, carries the burden of proof for a specific currency clause contained in the agreement of the parties. The Tribunal is not convinced that Art. 1(c) of the Termination Agreement contains such a currency clause [...].

Sources

Original in English (published in excerpt):
ICC International Court of Arbitration Bulletin, Vol. 10, No. 2, Fall 1999, 60 – 62.

Date: ***September 22, 1995***
Country: ***Netherlands***
Adjudicating Court: ***Supreme Court of the Netherlands***
Number: ***15754***
Parties: ***Ravast N.V. (Netherlands) and Maxfield Investment Limited (United Kingdom) vs. De Ontvanger der Directe Belastingen te Amsterdam***

Keywords

DISPUTE BETWEEN TWO COMPANIES AND DUTCH TAX AUTHORITIES – REFERENCE BY THE ADVOCATE GENERAL TO ARTICLE 7.1.4 UNIDROIT PRINCIPLES TO INTERPRET RELEVANT PROVISIONS OF THE NEW DUTCH CIVIL CODE

Abstract

The plaintiffs in the dispute are two commercial entities; one of them – Ravast N.V. – is established in the Netherlands, the other – Maxfield Investment Limited – has its seat in Guernsey (United Kingdom). The defendant – De Ontvanger der Directe Belastingen te Amsterdam – is the Netherlands tax authority. The applicable law to the dispute is Dutch law.

The case brought before the Netherlands Supreme Court concerns an attachment by the Netherlands tax authority on an immovable property (a supermarket) of a debtor. Another creditor claims to have higher ranking on the basis of a mortgage vested on the same immovable property. The Dutch tax authority files a request for a declaratory judgement before the district court in order to hold the act constituting the mortgage invalid because this act would deliberately infringe upon creditors' rights (*fraus creditoris*).

The legal action of the Netherlands tax authorities constitutes a request for a declaratory judgement; it is not a request for avoidance of the act constituting the mortgage. The consequences of such a declaratory action and a request for avoidance of the act constituting a mortgage are nevertheless identical. In his conclusions, Advocate-General A.S. Hartkamp argues that a request for a declaratory judgement and a request for avoidance of an act constituting a mortgage should be treated similarly. The Advocate-General thereby analyses the relevant provisions of the Netherlands civil law and in particular the provisions on avoidance and on termination of a contract.

Although in the case at hand, the old (1838) Dutch Civil Code did apply, Advocate-General A.S. Hartkamp nevertheless compares the provisions of the old Civil Code with the new (1992) Dutch Civil Code. As opposed to the old Civil Code, the 1992 Code makes a clear distinction between the avoidance of a contract and its termination. Advocate-General Hartkamp argues that one should avoid exaggerating the differences between the avoidance of a contract and its termination. In support of this interpretation, the Advocate-General refers to Articles 3:54 and 6:230 of the Dutch Civil Code concerning the avoidance of a contract and Article 6:269 of the Dutch Civil Code, which deals with the termination of a contract. The Advocate-General furthermore strengthens this interpretation of the provisions of the new (1992) Dutch Civil Code, by an explicit reference to Article 7.1.4 of the UNIDROIT Principles ("*Cure by non-performing party*"), which provides that 'the right to cure is not precluded by notice of termination', apparently in order to clarify that whether or not the proposal by one of the parties to perform is valid, depends on which party first informs the adversary party of his intentions: the creditor who declares to terminate the agreement or the debtor who states that he is prepared to cure the non-performance. The Advocate-General furthermore suggests comparing Article 7.1.4 of the Principles with article 6:134 of the Netherlands Civil Code.

The Supreme Court adheres to the conclusions of its Advocate-General, although it does not make an express reference to the UNIDROIT Principles.

Full Text

HOGE RAAD, 22 SEPTEMBER 1995, NR. 15754

Ravast N.V., te Naarden,
De rechtspersoon naar het recht van de plaats van vestiging Maxfield Investment Limited, te Guernsey, Verenigd Koninkrijk,

eiseressen tot cassatie, adv. mr. S.A. Boele,

tegen

De ontvanger der Directe Belastingen te Amsterdam, te Amsterdam,

verweerder in cassatie, adv. mr. J.C. van Oven.

CASSATIEMIDDELEN:

Schending van het recht en verzuim van op straffe van nietigheid in acht te nemen vormen, doordat het Hof in het bestreden arrest heeft overwogen en recht gedaan, gelijk in dit arrest omschreven, ten onrechte om de navolgende, zonodig mede in onderlinge samenhang te beschouwen redenen:
Inleiding

0.1 Het gaat in deze zaak – voorzover in cassatie nog van belang – om de vraag of een voor schulden van eiseres tot cassatie sub 2 (hierna: "Maxfield"), op 20 juli 1989 door Terrafin BV (hierna: "Terrafin") ten gunste van eiseres tot cassatie sub 1, Ravast NV (hierna: "Ravast") gevestigde hypotheek op het perceel Pottenbakkerssingel 2 te Middelburg (hierna: het "Perceel") nietig is jegens verweerder in cassatie (hierna: de

"Ontvanger") op grond van het bepaalde in het – op grond van overgangsrecht toepasselijke art. 1377 (oud) BW. Het Hof heeft het beroep van de Ontvanger op het bepaalde in dit artikel, anders dan de rechtbank, gehonoreerd door te overwegen dat Terrafin tot deze hypotheekverlening niet verplicht was, dat de Ontvanger als gevolg daarvan benadeeld werd en dat zowel Terrafin als Ravast ten tijde van hun handelen wisten dat daarvan benadeling van schuldeisers het gevolg zou zijn. Middel 1 vecht 's Hofs oordeel aangaande de onverplichtheid aan, middel 2 het oordeel aangaande de benadeling en middel 3 het oordeel aangaande de wetenschap.

0.2 In cassatie moet worden uitgegaan van de feiten zoals het Hof deze in r.o. 3.1 heeft vastgesteld. Daaruit blijkt onder meer dat Terrafin als juridisch eigenares van het Perceel dit in economische zin heeft overgedragen aan VFS, waarna het Perceel – telkens eveneens in economische zin – door VFS aan Ahog en, door Ahog aan Maxfield is overgedragen.

0.3 Terrafin heeft zich bij de overdracht (in economische zin) aan VFS verplicht om onverwijld op eerste vordering van VFS als derde onderzetter hypotheek te verlenen op het Perceel tot meerdere zekerheid voor de nakoming van – onder meer – de verplichtingen voortvloeiende uit een door VFS aan te wijzen derde aan te gane overeenkomst van lening of andere overeenkomst (r.o. 3.1.h). Van de koopovereenkomsten VFS-Ahog en Ahog-Maxfield maken bepalingen van dezelfde strekking deel uit, met dien verstande dat daarin tot uitdrukking is gebracht dat VFS en Ahog desverlangd hypotheek dienden te (doen) vestigen op naam van de juridische eigenaar (Terrafin). Zie r.o. 3.1.i en produkties 29 en 30 bij repliek in conventie (in beide gevallen art. D.6 onder b, de relevante bepalingen zijn geciteerd in de conclusie van repliek van 3 juni 1992 op blz. 28).

0.4 Niet in geschil is dat in het onderhavige geval Maxfield zich rechtstreeks tot Terrafin heeft gewend teneinde Terrafin te bewegen hypotheek te vestigen ten behoeve van een schuld van Maxfield aan Ravast. Daarnaast moet er in cassatie van worden uitgegaan dat deze hypotheekverlening afdwingbaar was geweest doordat Maxfield van Ahog had verlangd dat Ahog een dergelijke hypotheek zou (doen) vestigen door Terrafin, vervolgens Ahog van VFS had verlangd dat VFS een dergelijke hypotheek zou (doen) vestigen door Terrafin en vervolgens VFS van Terrafin had verlangd dat Terrafin die hypotheek vestigde ten behoeve van de schuld van de daarbij als derde door VFS aangewezen Maxfield. Tegen de overweging van de rechtbank in die zin (r.o. 8) is immers in appèl geen grief gericht en ook het Hof gaat hiervan uit (r.o. 4.6).

MIDDEL 1

1.1 Het Hof heeft in r.o. 4.5 overwogen dat Terrafin door hypotheek te vestigen tot zekerheid voor schulden van Maxfield aan Ravast onverplicht heeft gehandeld aangezien Terrafin zich jegens Maxfield of Ravast had verplicht tot hypotheekvestiging en dat ook anderszins niet is gebleken dat Terrafin een verplichting had om voor schulden van Maxfield aan Ravast zekerheid te stel len. In r.o. 4.6 heeft het Hof overwogen dat aan deze gevolgtrekking niet in de weg staat dat op hun beurt ook VFS jegens Ahog, en Ahog jegens Maxfield zich verplicht hadden in dezelfde zin als Terrafin jegens VFS.

1.2 De onder 1.1 weergegeven overwegingen van het Hof geven blijk van een onjuiste rechtsopvatting. Indien, zoals in de onderhavige zaak (zie hierboven 0.4), Terrafin als juridisch eigenaar gedwongen kon worden ten behoeve van Maxfield hypotheek te vestigen op het Perceel voor schulden van Maxfield aan Ravast, doordat (i) Maxfield op grond van haar overeenkomst met Ahog het doel vestigen van een dergelijke hypotheek door 'Terrafin van Ahog had verlangd, vervolgens (ii) VFS op haar beurt hetzelfde had verlangd van VFS op grond van haar overeenkomst met VFS en tenslotte (iii) VFS op grond van haar overeenkomst met Terrafin van Terrafin de vestiging van deze hypotheek had verlangd, is de vestiging van de hypotheek door Terrafin niet onverplicht in de zin van art. 1377 (oud) BW, ook al is deze weg niet gevolgd doch heeft Maxfield zich rechtstreeks tot Terrafin gewend en hypotheekvestiging verlangd. Hieraan doet niet af dat er geen contractuele band tussen Maxfield en Terrafin bestond en dat Terrafin zich niet (rechtstreeks) jegens Maxfield had verplicht tot hypotheekvestiging. Hierbij is van belang dat Terrafin alle akten van economische-eigendomsoverdracht van het Perceel heeft medeondertekend zodat zij geacht moet worden op de hoogte te zijn van de relaties tussen de opvolgend economisch eigenaars en dientengevolge ook van de omstandigheid dat indien Maxfield aanspraak maakte op hypotheekverlening VFS uiteindelijk gedwongen kon worden de daarmee corresponderende bevoegdheid jegens Terrafin uit te oefenen.

1.3 Althans is 's Hofs oordeel onvoldoende gemotiveerd nu (i) tussen Terrafin, VFS, Ahog en Maxfield sprake is geweest van economische-eigendomsoverdracht van het Perceel in die zin dat telkens verkoper en koper overeengekomen zijn dat aile baten en lasten (inclusief het risico) van het Perceel verbintenisrechtelijk toebehoren aan de telkens optredende koper (r.o. 3.1.1 arrest a quo), en/of (ii) niet is aangevoerd en het Hof ook niet heeft vastgesteld dat de betrokkenen bij de opeenvolgende overdrachten beoogd hebben materiële betekenis toe te kennen aan de weg waarbij achtereenvolgens Maxfield van Ahog, Ahog van VFS en VFS van Terrafin hypotheekvestiging had verlangd resp. niet hebben gewenst dat de economische eigenaar zich daartoe rechtstreeks tot de juridisch eigenaar zou wenden.

MIDDEL 2

2.1 In de rechtsoverwegingen 4.11 t/m 4.14 heeft het Hof overwogen dat de Ontvanger benadeeld is door de hypotheekvestiging. Voorzover het Hof als tijdstip waarop benadeling in de zin van art. 1377 (oud) BW aanwezig moet zijn beslissend althans van belang heeft geacht de datum waarop het arrest waarvan beroep is gewezen, geeft dit oordeel blijk van een onjuiste rechtsopvatting. Benadeling in de zin van art. 1377 (oud) BW dient aanwezig te zijn op het moment dat de crediteur de (Ontvanger) zijn rechten uit deze bepaling doet gelden. In deze zaak is dat tijdstip 27 september 1990 toen de Ontvanger beslag heeft doen leggen op het Perceel (vgl. de pleitnota van Mr Hermans in eerste aanleg blz. 18). Dientengevolge is een mogelijk op datum arrest bestaande benadeling zonder belang voorzover diezelfde benadeling niet ook reeds op 27 september 1990 bestond.

2.2 In r.o. 4.11 overweegt het Hof dat Terrafin grote beldstingschulden aan de Ontvanger heeft, dat Maxfield en Ravast geen enkel ander vermogensbestanddeel van Terrafin hebben aangewezen waarop verhaal mogelijk zou zijn, dat aannemelijk is enerzijds dat het Perceel een hogere waarde vertegenwoordigt dan het beloop van de vordering van de eerste hypotheekhoudster (FGH) en anderzijds dat die waarde zeker niet toereikend is om naast de eerste hypotheekhoudster en Ravast 66k de Ontvanger geheel te bevredigen. Aan een en ander verbindt het Hof de conclusie dat de Ontvanger in elk geval ook al op 27 september 1990 benadeeld was. Voorzover het Hof in deze rechtsoverweging overweegt dat de Ontvanger ook "thans" (waarmee het Hof kennelijk bedoelt: de datum waarop het arrest werd gewezen) door de hypotheekvestiging is benadeeld kan dit oor¬deel niet in stand blijven op grond van de klacht vervat in middelonderdeel 2.1.

2.3 Het Hof overweegt vervolgens in r.o. 4.12 dat aan de in r.o. 4.11 bereikte conclusie niet kan afdoen dat de aan Ravast gegeven hypotheek een oudere tweede hypotheek ten gunste van Banque de Suez heeft vervangen. In r.o. 4.13 overweegt het Hof dat de omstandigheid dat de hypotheek van Banque de Suez voor 27 september 1990 beëindigd was, reeds meebrengt dat zij geen rol kan spelen bij de beantwoording van de vraag of de Ontvanger "thans" (de datum waarop het arrest werd gewezen) benadeeld is, en zo nodig, of hij op 27 september 1990 al benadeeld was. Voorzover het Hof beslissend heeft geacht of de Ontvanger op de datum waarop het arrest werd gewezen benadeeld was, kan dit oordeel niet in stand blijven op grond van de klacht vervat in middelonderdeel 2.1. Voorzover het Hof beslissend heeft geacht of de Ontvanger benadeeld was op 27 september 1990 heeft het Hof met zijn zojuist weergegeven overweging miskend, dat weliswaar de vraag of benadeling aanwezig was beoordeeld moet worden naar de toestand op 27 september 1990, maar dat dit niet betekent dat bij de beantwoording van die vraag aan die datum voorafgaande feiten en omstandigheden geen rol mogen of kunnen spelen. Het betekent slechts dat beoordeeld moet worden of die feiten omstandigheden tot gevolg hebben gehad dat de Ontvanger op 27 september 1990 benadeeld is. Daarbij is (mede) van belang althans kan van belang zijn dat de hypotheek waarvan de Ontvanger de nietigheid heeft ingeroepen een andere hypotheek heeft vervangen, zodat de schuldeisers althans de Ontvanger als gevolg van de hypotheekvestiging ten behoeve van Maxfield niet slechter af zijn dan indien die hypotheekvestiging niet had plaatsgevonden. Op grond van de door het Hof gebezigde motive-ring had het Hof derhalve de hypotheek van Banque de Suez niet buiten beschouwing mogen laten.

2.4. In r.o. 4.14 overweegt het Hof dat, zo bij de beoordeling van de benadeling van de Ontvanger de hypotheek van Banque de Suez toch wèl mee zou moeten wegen, niettemin de Ontvanger nog steeds geacht moet worden "thans" (de datum waarop het arrest werd gewezen) en ook al op 27 september 1990 benadeeld te zijn. Voorzover het Hof benadeling op de datum waarop het arrest a quo werd gewezen relevant heeft geacht kan het oordeel van het Hof niet in stand blijven op grond van de in middelonderdeel 2.1 vervatte klacht. Voorzover het Hof benadeling van de Ontvanger op 27 september 1990 aanwezig heeft geacht is dit oordeel in strijd met het recht dan wel onbegrijpelijk dan wel onvoldoende gemotiveerd. Het Hof neemt tot uitgangspunt dat de vordering van FGH (de eerste hypotheekhoudster) op 27 september 1990 minder dan f 8, I miljoen beliep en dat zij gestadig daalde, alsmede dat de door hypotheek gedekte vordering van Banque de Suez f 4,2 miljoen beliep. Het Hof overweegt vervolgens dat met betrekking tot de toestand op 27 september 1990 ten minste kan worden gezegd dat er toen al rekening meemoest worden gehouden dat het Perceel bij verkoop meer dan de som van het toenmalige beloop van de vordering van FGH en die f 4,2 miljoen (zijnde minder dan f 12,3 miljoen) zou kunnen opbrengen. Voorzover het Hof met laatstbedoeld oordeel bedoeld heeft tot uitdrukking te brengen dat er op 27 september 1990 rekening mee moest worden gehouden dat het Perceel bij verkoop op enig tijdstip na 27 september 1990 meer dan het toenmalig beloop van de vordering van FGH en die f 4,2 miljoen zou kunnen opbrengen, geeft dit oordeel blijk van een onjuiste rechtsopvatting aangezien uitsluitend de opbrengst bij verkoop naar de toestand op 27 september 1990 beslissend is en niet op enig tijdstip nadien.

Al thans is 's Hofs oordeel onbegrijpelijk dan wel onvoldoende gemotiveerd. Ravast en Maxfield hebben aangevoerd dat de executiewaarde ten tijde van de beslagen getaxeerd was op f 12,1 miljoen (concl. van antwoord/eis in reconventie blz. 5). Daartegenover heeft de Ontvanger aangevoerd dat de waarde (zonder nader aan te geven of hiermee de onderhandse verkoopwaarde of de executiewaarde is bedoeld) op 20 juli 1989 f 14,4 miljoen bedroeg (concl. van repliek in conventie/antwoord in reconventie 10.6) alsmede dat de onderhandse verkoopwaarde per 31 december 1992 f 14,3 miljoen was (memorie van antwoord in het incidenteel appèl blz. 4). In het licht van deze stellingen is ontoelaatbaar onduidelijk hoe het Hof tot zijn oordeel omtrent de verkoopwaarde van het Perceel (waarmee volgens het Hof op 27 september 1990 rekening moest worden gehouden) is gekomen, het Hof heeft in r.o. 3.1.a slechts vastgesteld dat de onderhandse verkoopwaarde van het Perceel op 31 december 1992 op f 14,3 miljoen en de liquidatiewaarde op f 12,8 miljoen was getaxeerd. Met name is onduidelijk of het Hof de door het Hof relevant geachte waarde op basis van de executiewaarde of van de onderhandse verkoopwaarde heeft vastgesteld en – in beide gevallen – op basis van welke gegevens en naar de toestand op welke datum. Voor zover het Hof de onderhandse verkoopwaarde in aanmerking heeft genomen is onduidelijk op grond waarvan het Hof van oordeel was dat de verkoop onderhands had kunnen worden gerealiseerd, mede in aanmerking genomen dat voor 1 januari 1992 geen wettelijke regeling voor de onderhandse verkoop van onroerende zaken bestond.

MIDDEL 3

3.1 In r.o. 4.15 overweegt het Hof dat Terra-fin ten tijde van de hypotheekvestiging moet hebben geweten dat het onder 4.1 1, en zo nodig ook het onder 4.14, aangaande de waarde van het Perceel en het beloop van de hypothecaire vorderingen besprokene in de lijn van de verwachtingen lag, en dat ook Ravast met dit alles in hoofdzaak bekend moet zijn geweest.

3.2 Aangezien de overwegingen van het Hof in r.o. 4.11 en 4.14 aangaande de waarde van het Perceel niet in stand kunnen blijven op grond van middel 2, wordt ook 's Hofs mede daarop gebaseerde oordeel ten aanzien van de wetenschap van Terrafin en Ravast aangetast.

3.3. 's Hofs overwegingen (in r.o. 4.15) dat Terrafin moet hebben geweten dat ten tijde van de hypotheekvestiging het onder 4.11 en 4.14 aangaande de waarde van het Perceel besprokene "in de lijn van de verwachtingen" lag, dat Ravast met dit alles "in hoofdzaak bekend" moet zijn geweest, alsmede (in r.o. 4.14) dat er op 27 september 1990 al "rekening mee moest worden gehouden" dat het Perceel bij verkoop meer zou kunnen opbrengen dan de som van het toenmalige beloop van de vordering van FGH en f 4,2 miljoen, geven blijk van een onjuiste rechtsopvatting. Art. 1377 (oud) BW eist immers wetenschap van benadeling en uit de in de vorige volzin geciteerde overwegingen van het Hof volgt niet dat aan dit vereiste is voldaan bij Terrafin en Ravast, althans niet dat deze wetenschap aanwezig was ten tijde van de hypotheekvestiging. Met name is onduidelijk op grond waarvan het Hof heeft gemeend te kunnen concluderen dat Ravast en Terrafin ten tijde van de hypotheekvestiging (20 juli 1989) wisten of behoorden te weten dat op 27 september 1990 het Perceel bij verkoop meer zou opbrengen dan de som van het toenmalige beloop van de vordering van FGH en f 4,2 miljoen. Ook heeft het Hof geen feiten en omstandigheden vastgesteld op grond waarvan het kon concluderen dat Ravast en/of Terrafin op 20 juli 1989 wisten of behoorden te weten hoe groot de vorderingen van FGH en Banque de Suez op 27 september 1990 zouden zijn.

CONCLUSIE A-G MR. HARTKAMP

1) In deze zaak heeft verweerster in cassatie, de ontvanger, kort gezegd een verklaring van recht gevorderd dat het op 20 juli 1989 door Terrafin B.V. ten behoeve van eiseres tot cassatie sub I, Ravast, gevestigde recht van hypotheek op een onroerende zaak (een supermarkt) te Middelburg, welk hypotheekrecht tot zekerheid strekt voor een schu Id aan Ravast van eiseres tot cassatie sub 2, Maxfield, jegens de ontvanger nietig is wegens schending van de regeling van de *pauliana* buiten faillissement (art. 1377 oud BW). Tevens heeft de ontvanger, met het oog op doorhaling, waardeloosverklaring van de inschrijving van de hypotheek gevorderd.
Een uitvoerige weergave van de vaststaande feiten is te vinden in r.o. 3.1 van het in cassatie bestreden arrest van het Gerechtshof te Amsterdam. Op die feiten kom ik bij de behandeling van het cassatiemiddel voor zover nodig terug.
In eerste aanleg heeft de Rechtbank te Amsterdam bij vonnis van 26 mei 1993 de vorderingen (in conventie) van de ontvanger afgewezen. In hoger beroep heeft het Gerechtshof te Amsterdam bij arrest van 26 mei 1994 het vonnis van de rechtbank vernietigd en de vorderingen van de ontvanger toegewezen.
Bij dagvaarding van 25 augustus 1995, dus tijdig, hebben Ravast en Maxfield het beroep in cassatie ingesteld. Daarbij zijn drie middelen aangevoerd, ieder bestaande uit subonderdelen. De ontvanger heeft geconcludeerd primair tot niet-ontvankelijkverklaring van eiseressen tot cassatie in hun beroep gelet op art. 3:29 lid 3 BW en subsidiair tot verwerping daarvan. Vervolgens hebben partijen de zaak schriftelijk doen toelichten en is van re- en dupliek gediend.

ONTVANKELIJKHEID VAN HET CASSATIEBEROEP

2) In zijn conclusie van antwoord in cassatie heeft de ontvanger gesteld dat het cassatieberoep is gericht tegen een uitspraak die een verklaring in de zin van art. 3:29 BW bevat, namelijk dat de inschrijving van de litigieuze hypotheek in de openbare registers jegens de ontvanger waardeloos is. Zie hierover uitvoerig Van Straaten, Kadaster, openbare registers en derdenbescherming, 1992, p. 101 e.v. Ingevolge art. 3:29 lid 3 BW moet op straffe van niet-ontvankelijkheid het cassatieberoep binnen acht dagen na het instellen van dit rechtsmiddel worden ingeschreven in de registers van de griffie van het gerecht dat het bestreden vonnis heeft uitgesproken (art. 433 Rv.). Zie Parl. Gesch. Inv. Boek 3, p. 1114 e.v. Door een dergelijke aantekening ter griffie kan de griffier nagaan of de uitspraak in kracht van gewijsde is gegaan (art. 3:29 lid 4 BW), zodat hij de ingevolge art. 25 lid I sub a Kadasterwet voor inschrijving van de waardeloosverklaring in de openbare registers vereiste verklaring kan afgeven dat tegen de uitspraak geen gewoon rechtsmiddel meer openstaat. Zie daarover MvT, Parl. Gesch. Kadasterwet, p. 146 e.v.

De vordering van de ontvanger is ingesteld bij inleidende dagvaarding van 9 december 1991 en bestaat uit twee del en. Het eerste deel is gericht op een verklaring van recht dat de vestiging van de hypotheek nietig is. Dit deel heeft het hof behandeld in de r.o. 4.3 t/m 4.15. Volgens het hof moet dit deel van de vordering beoordeeld worden op grond van het oude BW (r.o. 4.3). Het tweede deel van de vordering betreft een verklaring van recht dat de inschrijving van de hypotheek waardeloos is. Het hof heeft dit tweede deel van de vordering in r.o. 4.16 behandeld. Met toewijzing van het eerste deel van de vordering (nietigheid van de vestiging van de hypotheek wegens benadeling van de ontvanger) is volgens het hof klaarblijkelijk ook toewijzing van het tweede deel van de vordering gegeven. Op dit deel van de vordering is volgens de ontvanger het huidige BW (art. 3:29 BW) van toepassing (r.o. 4.1). Het hof is niet expliciet op het in dit verband toepasselijke recht ingegaan.
Het beroep op niet-ontvankelijkheid faalt naar mijn mening. Vooropgesteld moet worden dat het eerste deel van de vordering van de ontvanger ziet op een verklaring van recht dat de vestiging van de hypotheek nietig is op grond van de regel ing van de *pauliana*. Dit deel van de vordering heeft derhalve niet alleen betekenis voor de gevorderde waardeloosverklaring, maar kan ook zelfstandige betekenis hebben. Denk bijvoorbeeld aan een op de *pauliana* geënte vordering uit onrechtmatige daad. Zie recent HR 24 februari 1995, RvdW 1995, 47 (NJ 1996, 472, m.nt. WMK; red.).
Wat betreft de ontvankelijkheid van eiseressen in hun klacht tegen de waardeloosverklaring merk ik het volgende op. Doorhaling van de inschrijving van de hypotheek in de openbare registers heeft zowel naar oud als naar huidig recht geen invloed op de geldigheid van de hypotheek. Een dergelijke doorhaling heeft in beginsel geen materieelrechtelijke betekenis, doch is louter een administratieve maatregel. Aldus o.m. MvA II, Parl. Gesch. Boek 3, p. 149 en p. 151, Nader rapport, Parl. Gesch. Inv. Boek 3, p. 1117, Asser-Mijnssen-Van Velten, nr. 362 alsmede Snijders/Rank-Berenschot, Goederenrecht, 1994, nr. 124 en 911. Indien op de onderhavige vordering tot waardeloosverklaring art. 3:29 BW van toepassing is ingevolge art. 68a Ow. (onmiddellijke werking), heeft dit ingevolge art. 741id I Ow. geen gevolg voor de naar oud recht bestaande mogelijkheid een rechtsmiddel in te stellen tegen de uitspraak van de rechter in een geding dat voor het van toepassing worden van het huidige BW is aangevangen. Naar mijn mening zijn daaronder alle aan een rechtsmiddel te stellen ontvankelijkheidseisen begrepen, waaronder het onderhavige vereiste van inschrijving ter griffie (vgl. ook het advies RvS, Parl. Gesch. Overgangswet, p. 59). Het bepaalde in art. 3:29 lid 3 BW is reeds om deze reden naar mijn mening op het onderhavige geval niet van toepassing. Ik kan daarom daarlaten of op de onderhavige vordering inderdaad art. 3:29 BW van toepassing is alsmede, indien dit het geval is, of aan de materiële toepassingsvereisten van art. 3:29 BW (jo art. 3:274 en 275 BW) is voldaan.

BESPREKING VAN HET CASSATIEMIDDEL

3) Het hof heeft beslist dat de hypotheek verlening (en -vestiging) op 20 juli 1989 door Terrafin onverplicht is verricht. Wel heeft Terrafin, zoals het hof heeft overwogen in r.o. 3.1 sub h-j, eerder de economische eigendom aan VFS overgedragen, waarbij zij zich heeft verbonden om op eerste vordering van VFS hypotheek te verlenen tot zekerheid van leenschulden van VFS of van een door VFS aan te wijzen derde; en wel zijn identieke bedingen gemaakt bij verdere overdrachten van de economische eigendom (alle verricht voor 20 juli 1989) door VFS aan Ahog en door Ahog aan Maxfield (maar niet bij de overdracht van Maxfield aan Ravast); mààr de hypotheek van 20 juli 1989 is gevestigd op verzoek van Maxfield (r.o. 3.1 sub e). Uit dit een en ander heeft het hof afgeleid dat

Terrafin zich niet jegens Maxfield of Ravast had verplicht tot hypotheekverlening, terwijl ook niet anderzins van een verplichting van Terrafin is gebleken om voor schulden van Maxfield aan Ravast zekerheid te stellen (r.o. 4.5-4.10).

4) Middel I richt zich met een rechts- en een motiveringsklacht tegen de r.o. 4.5 en 4.6 van het bestreden arrest.
Onderdeel 1.1 bevat geen klacht.
Onderdeel 1.2 voert aan dat het weergegeven oordeel van het hof uitgaat van een onjuiste rechtsopvatting: nu Terrafin gedwongen kon worden om een hypotheek te vestigen ten gunste van Maxfield, in dier voege dat Maxfield zulks kon vorderen van Ahog, Ahog van VFS en VFS van Terrafin, is de vestiging door Terrafin niet onverplicht, ook al is zij gevolgd op een verzoek/vordering – niet van VFS maar – van Maxfield.
De klacht treft naar mijn mening geen doel. Vooropgesteld zij dat "onverplichte rechtshandelingen" rechtshandelingen zijn die verricht worden zonder dat daartoe een op de wet of een overeenkomst Yistende rechtsplicht bestaat. Zie HR 8 januari 1937, NJ 1937, 431 m.nt. EMM en HR 10 december 1976, NJ 1977, 617; vgl. ook HR 16 januari 1987, NJ 1987, 528 m.nt. G. en HR 18 december 1992, Ni 1993, 169. Van de literatuur noem ik ASSER-HARTKAMP II, nr. 443 en MELLEMA-KRANENBURG, *De actio Pauliana* naar BW en NBW, 1990, p. 18 (§ 17). Er is geen sprake van een onverplicht verrichte handeling indien de feitelijke situatie aldus is dat de schuldenaar praktisch niet anders kon doen dan de bestreden handeling te verrichten (HR 10 december 1976, Ni 1977, 617).
Uit het feit dat Terrafin langs de door het onderdeel geschetste weg tot zekerheidstel ling ten behoeve van Maxfield verplicht had kunnen worden, volgt niet dat Terrafin in casu gehouden was daartoe over te gaan. Terrafin heeft zich daartoe niet jegens Maxfield of Ravast verplicht (r.o. 4.5); en het hof heeft klaarblijkelijk aangenomen (r.o. 4.6) dat uit de overeenkomsten voortvloeit dat een verplichting voor Terrafin alleen kon worden gebaseerd op een vordering of aanwijzing van VFS, die echter in casu ontbreekt. Deze beslissing geeft m.i. niet blijk van een onjuiste rechtsopvatting.
Zij is m.i. evenmin onvoldoende gemotiveerd, zoals onderdeel 1.3 aanvoert. Het feit dat het hier een reeks van "economische eigendomsoverdrachten" betreft waarbij telkens werd beoogd dat al le baten en lasten verbintenisrechtelijk op de kopers rustten, maakt dit niet anders. Hieruit vloeit immers niet voort dat Terrafin jegens elke opvolgende koper gehouden was om op diens vordering of verzoek een hypotheek te stellen. Het hof heeft een rechtstreekse vordering van Maxfield jegens Terra-fin om de hypotheek te vestigen op grond van de overeenkomsten niet mogelijk geacht. Terrafin had alleen jegens VFS en op vordering van deze een contractuele verplichting tot vestiging van een hypotheek, hetgeen VFS – naar in cassatie vaststaat – niet van Terrafin heeft gevorderd. Dit oordeel is feitelijk van aard en geeft geen blijk van een onjuiste rechtsopvatting.

5) Middel II richt zich tegen het oordeel van het hof in de r.o. 4.11 t/m 4.14, waar het hof heeft geoordeeld dat de ontvanger is benadeeld door de omstreden vestiging van de hypotheek. Als moment waarop die benadeling moet worden beoordeeld heeft het hof primair het tijdstip van zijn beslissing aangehouden; zie r.o. 4.3 ("thans") en r.o. 4.11, 4.13 en 4.14. Subsidiair heeft het hof, zoals het ten overvloede overweegt, relevant geacht het tijdstip waarop de ontvanger zijn eerste beslag heeft gelegd, zijnde 27 september 1990 (r.o. 3.1 sub o). Onderdeel 2.1 acht 's hofs primaire standpunt onjuist en verdedigt het subsidiaire standpunt, zijnde de beslagdatum het tijdstip waarop de ontvanger zijn rechten uit art. 1377 heeft doen gelden.

Ik acht de klacht niet gegrond. Inderdaad komt het aan op het tijdstip dat de schuldeiser zijn rechten uit art. 1377 doet gelden, maar blijkens HR 23 december 1949, NJ 1950, 262 m.nt. Ph.A.N.H. (Boendermaker/Schopman) is dat in geval van een procedure waarin vernietiging wordt gevorderd het tijdstip waarop de rechter die over de vordering oordeelt zijn beslissing neemt. Aldus, als ik goed zie, ook de MvT Inv., Parl. Gesch. Inv., Aanpassing Rechtsvordering, p. 338.
Nu zou men kunnen verdedigen dat het bovenstaande juist is voor een vordering tot vernietiging, maar dat indien de schuldeiser de weg van buitengerechtelijke vernietiging kiest, beslissend is het tijdstip van het uitbrengen van de vernietigingsverklaring, ook indien over de gegrondheid daarvan vervolgens wordt geprocedeerd. Met name voor het nieuwe burgerlijk wetboek is dat onderscheid verdedigbaar, omdat de nieuwe regel ingen van de vernietiging in Boek 3 en van de ontbinding an wederkerige overeenkomsten wegens tekbrtkomingen in Boek 6 de verschillen tussen gerechtelijke en buitengerechtelijke vernietiging/ontbinding duidelijk in het licht hebben gesteld en ook tot discussie in de literatuur hebben geleid. Zie bijv. ASSER-HARTKAMP nr. 469 en 518, Hartlief, Ontbinding (1994), p. 114 e.v., 214 e.v. Ook de geciteerde passage in de parlementaire geschiedenis van de invoeringswet, waarin het nieuwe art. 737 Rv. inzake conservatoir *pauliana*-beslag wordt toegelicht, staat daarmee in verband. Toch zou ik deze opvatting noch voor het oude noch voor het nieuwe recht willen bepleiten.

6) Voor het oude recht (in deze zaak toepasselijk blijkens de in cassatie niet bestreden r.o. 4.3 van 's hofs arrest) lag de kwestie m.i. niet erg duidelijk. Daarin was immers steeds een "eenvoudige wilsverklaring" van de crediteur tegenover de belanghebbenden vol doende (HR 15 maart 1940, NJ 1940, 848 m.nt. EMM). Ankum, *De Pauliana* buiten faillissement (1962), p. 171 leidt hieruit af dat een rechterlijke uitspraak inzake de gegrondheid van een beroep op de *pauliana* steeds declaratief van aardwas, en kent dus kennelijk geen betekenis toe aan het feit dat in de hierboven genoemde zaak van 1949 de vernietiging in rechte werd gevorderd. En A-G Ten Kate spreekt in zijn conclusie (nr. 37) voor HR 12 juni 1987, NJ 1988, 252 m.nt. WLH in één adem over het inroepen der nietigheid door het leggen van conservatoir beslag (onder verwijzing naar HR 8 nov. 1985, Ni 1987, 170 m.nt. WLH, r.o. 3.3) en het vervolgens vorderen van vernietiging van de titel van overdracht. Hierop afgaande is dus niet duidelijk, dunkt mij, of de schuldeiser reeds naar oud recht de hem thans door het nieuwe wetboek (art. 3:49 e.v.) toegekende keuze had tussen een buitengerechtelijke vernietiging en het vorderen van vernietiging door de rechter.
Wel licht heeft Uw Raad zich op dat standpunt gesteld in zijn genoemde arrest van 1987, omdat die uitspraak zo gelezen kan worden dat de vordering tot vernietiging van een "paulianeuze" overeenkomst (r.o. 3.2) wordt onderscheiden van het vorderen van een declaratoir in de door Ankum bedoelde zin (vgl. r.o. 3.1: de eiseres had voor het geding de nietigheid reeds ingeroepen). Maar zeker acht ik dat (mede in het licht van de vermelde opmerking in de conclusie) niet, omdat ook een onderscheid bedoeld kan zijn met de in dat geding gevorderde specifieke verklaring voor recht, waarbij slechts één van de bij de aangevochten overeenkomst betrokken partijen in rechte werd betrokken. Het arrest van 11 juli 1993, NJ 1993, 563 bevat op dit punt geen beslissing.
Bij deze stand van zaken zou ik willen aannemen dat, wat er zij van de vraag of reeds naar oud recht de voormelde keuzemogelijkheid bestond, dit onderscheid in elk geval niet moet leiden tot een verschillende uitkomst terzake van het voor de benadeling relevante tijdstip, zodat de leer van het arrest van 1949 steeds moet gelden indien de gegrondheid van het beroep op de *pauliana* in rechte wordt uitgevochten.

7) In de nieuwe wet wordt weliswaar duidelijk het voormelde onderscheid gemaakt, maar dat neemt niet weg dat men de verschillen tus-sen het gerechtelijk en het buitengerechtelijk effectueren van nietigheid of ontbinding niet moet verabsoluteren. Ik maak hierover eerst enkele algemene opmerkingen. Wat de vernietiging betreft wijs ik op ASSER-HARTKAMP II, nr. 480/1, waar wordt betoogd dat de art. 3:54 en 6:230 (aanbod tot opheffing van het door de vernietigingsbevoegde geleden nadeel) zich, gelet op de ratio van die bepalingen, onder omstandigheden ook voor toepassing lenen nadat een geldige vernietigingsverklaring is uitgebracht.
Wat de ontbinding betreft wordt het verschil gerelativeerd in art. 6:269: ten aanzien van de mogelijkheid van zuivering van verzuim heeft het instellen van de ontbindingsvordering hetzelfde effect ais de ontbindingsverklaring. Die bepaling wordt op haar beurt zelf weer gerelativeerd door de leer van HR 1 I juni 1982, NJ 1983, 695 m.nt. CJHB, inhoudende dat het aan bod een rol kan spelen bij de vraag of de tekortkoming ernstig genoeg is om ontbinding te rechtvaardigen. Bij de buitengerechtelijke ontbinding kan hetzelfde resultaat worden bereikt met behulp van de redelijkheid en billijkheid, zoals voor het oude recht is uitgemaakt in HR 24 sept. 1976, NJ 1977, 115 m.nt. PZ; zie ASSER-HARTKAMP II, nr. 516 en 527. In dit verband is interessant art. 7.1.4 van de in 1994 gepubliceerde UNIDROIT Principles of International Commercial Contracts, bepalende dat "the right to cure is not precluded by notice of termination", kennelijk teneinde te voorkomen dat de vraag of een geldig aanbod tot herstel is gedaan afhangt van wie het eerste naar de telefoon grijpt: de schuldeiser om te ontbinden of de schuldenaar om zich tot herstel bereid te verklaren. Vgl. ook art. 6:134 waarover ASSER-HARTKAMP I, nr. 548.
Ook in bepalingen als de art. 3:52 lid 2 en 6:268, inzake de verjaring en het verval van de bevoegdheid tot vernietiging resp. ontbinding, worden de scherpe kanten van het onderscheid tussen de gerechtelijke en de buitengerechtelijke weg afgeslepen.
Ik moge het laten bij deze enkele voorbeelden ten betoge (thans weer terugkerend naar de nietigheden, met name de *pauliana*) dat bij ieder nietigheidsvoorschrift de rechtsgevolgen ook opzicht mede door de strekking van de regeling dienen te worden bepaald. De *pauliana* nu strekt ertoe de schuldeisers te beschermen in hun – financiële – verhaalsmogelijkheden. Verhaal wordt genomen op het tijdstip van tegeldemaking van het verhaalsobject; alle daaraan voorafgaande maatregelen, zoals beslaglegging, buitengerechtelijke vernietiging of het vorderen van vernietiging in rechte, zijn op dat doel gericht. Dit pleit er voor om wat ik zie als de in het oude recht geldende leer ook onder de vigeur van het nieuwe wetboek te handhaven: steeds als de schuldeiser feitelijk pas tot verhaalsuitoefening kan overgaan na het voeren van een gerechtelijke procedure omtrent de gegrondheid van zijn beroep op de *pauliana*, dient het ogenblik van de rechterlijke beslissing de peildatum voor de benadeling te zijn.

8) Ik merk nog op dat het middel niet op de onderhavige kwestie ingaat. Het onderdeel richt zich zonder nadere toelichting op het tijdstip van de (eerste) beslaglegging. Het probleem daarbij is dat de vernietiging niet door die beslaglegging behoeft te zijn geeffectueerd, daar er immers ook een eerdere wilsverklaring jegens de belanghebbenden kan zijn geweest; bovendien is voor de werking van het beslag als vernietigingsverklaring vereist dat Ravast daarvan op de hoogte is gesteld (zie het voormelde arrest van 1993). Het hof overweegt slechts (r.o. 4.3) dat het inroepen van de nietigheid voor of bij de inleidende dagvaarding van 9 december 1992 is gedaan. Op deze grond zou gesteld kunnen worden dat het onderdeel niet kan slagen, nu niet vaststaat wanneer de buiten gerechtelijke vernietiging precies is geëffectueerd.

Daar staat echter tegenover dat de ontvanger bij pleidooi in eerste aanleg (nr. 7.1) heeft doen opmerken dat hij zijn rechten uit art. 1377 heeft doen gelden op het moment van het eerste beslag (27 september 1990) en dat het hof de aanwezigheid van benadeling (subsidiair) op die datum toetst; een andere mogelijke datum van inroeping van de *pauliana* wordt in de stukken niet genoemd. Al met al zou ik met het middel willen aannemen dat het in cassatie inderdaad gaat om de keuze tussen 27 sept. 1990 en de dag van 's hofs beslissing, zodat het onderdeel hierop niet afstuit.

9) Wat de sub 5 genoemde passage in de MvT Inv. betreft, verdient duidelijkheidshalve opmerking dat de memorie m.i. ten onrechte stelt dat naar nieuw recht de schuldeiser die zijn rechten uit art. 3.2.11 (art. 3:45) wil geldend maken, dit "slechts" kan doen door in rechte een beroep op de vernietigbaarheid van de rechtshandelin te doen. De vernietiging kan immers ook b itengerechtelijk worden geeffectueerd, behalve in het geval van art. 3:50 lid 2 (welke uitzondering overigens in het onderhavige geval, vestiging van hypotheek, van toepassing zou zijn geweest). Wel is het zo dat de uitzondering van art. 3.2.14 (thans art. 3:50) lid 2 in het stelsel van de vaststellingswet aanzienlijk ruimer was dan in de uiteindelijke vernie van het artikel, immers alle gevallen omvatte dat op de rechtshandeiing reeds enigerlei uitvoering was gevolgd of zij met een feitelijke handeling gepaard was gegaan. Die regel zou inderdaad in *pauliana*gevallen doorgdans een rechterlijke vernietiging nodig hebben ge¬maakt. Misschien moet in plaats van "slechts" worden gelezen "steeds": de schuldeiser die zich op art. 3:45 beroept, kan immers steeds voor een rechterlijke vernietiging kiezen, in welk geval hem het beslag van art. 737 Rv. ten dienste staat.

10) Onderdeel 2.2 heeft geen zelfstandige betekenis na het vorige.
De middelonderdelen 2.3 en 2.4 klagen over r.o. 4.12 t/m 4.14. Het betreft hier de volgende kwestie. Ravast en Maxfield hebben zich erop beroepen dat de aan Ravast gegeven hypotheek een oudere tweede hypotheek ten gunste van Banque de Suez, tot een maximum van f 4,2 miljoen, heeft vervangen en dat de ontvanger dus in zoverre niet benadeel d was. Het hof heeft hierover primair geoordeeld dat de hypotheek van de Banque de Suez voor 27 september 1990 was beëindigd, zodat zij geen rol kan spelen bij de beantwoording van de vraag of de ontvanger "thans" (d.w.z. ten tijde van ' s hofs beslissing) en zo nodig op 27 september 1990 benacieeld was (r.o. 4.12 en 4.13). Subsidiair en ten overvloede heeft het hof overwogen dat, zo bij de beoordeling van de benadeling van de ontvanger de hypotheek van Banque de Suez wel relevant is, de ontvanger nog steeds geacht moet worden te zijn benadeeld (r.o. 4.14). Aangenomen moet worden, aldus het hof, dat niet alleen "thans", d.w.z. op het tijdstip van ' shofs beslissing, de onroerende zaak meer dan de som van de vordering van de eerste hypotheekhouder FGH (minder dan f 6,2 miljoen) en f 4,2 miljoen zal opbrengen, maar hetzelfde geldt voor de door het hof subsidiair aangehouden datum van 27 september 1990: door de gestage daling van de vordering van FGH, die op laatstvermelde datum minder dan f 8,1 miljoen beliep, moest er volgens het hof al op 27 september 1990 rekening mee gehouden worden dat de onroerende zaak bij verkoop meer zou opbrengen dan het toenmalige beloop van de vordering van FGH en de f 4,2 miljoen (samen minder dan f 12,3 miljoen).

11) Onderdeel 2.3 komt op tegen het sub 10 genoemde primaire oordeel. Het klaagt er over dat voor zover het hof als datum van benadeling 27 september 1990 relevant heeft geacht, dit niet met zich brengt dat feiten en omstandigheden van voor die datum niet

relevant zijn of kunnen zijn voor het oordeel of er sprake is van benadeling. Het onderdeel betoogt dat, anders dan het hof in de r.o. 4.12 en 4.13 heeft geoordeeld, bij de beoordeling van de benadeling me-de van belang is of kan zijn dat de door Terrafin gevestigde hypotheek ten behoeve van Ravast – waarvan de ontvanger de nietigheid heeft ingeroepen – een andere hypotheek ten behoeve van Banque de Suez heeft vervangen, zodat de ontvanger door de vestiging van de eerstgenoemde hypotheek niet slechter af is dan indien die hypotheekvestiging niet had plaatsgevonden.
M.i. wordt deze klacht op zichzelf terecht voorgesteld. Of een schuldeiser door een bepaalde handeling van zijn schuldenaar is benadeeld, moet naar omstandigheden worden beoordeeld; soms dienen verschilende zelfstan-dige rechtshandelingen als één complex te wor- den beoordeeld. Zo zal een verkoop van een zaak tegen de marktprijs normaal gesproken geen benadeling van crediteuren opleveren, maar dat kan anders zijn, bijv. indien de koopprijs wordt besteed ter bevrediging van één schuldeiser terwijl zij anders voor de gezamenlijke crediteuren beschikbaar was geweest. Zie ASSER-HARTKAMP II, nr. 444 en de daar geciteerde rechtspraak. Zo kan het zich ook voordoen dat de vestiging van een hypotheek op zichzelf in strijd met art. 1377 is, maar de benadeling niet gel ijk is aan het gehele bedrag waarvoor de zaak bezwaard is, bijv. omdat een deel van het geleende bedrag is besteed op een wijze die het belang van de schuldeisers client, of, zoals in casu (naar de stellingen van eiseressen tot cassatie), is aangewend voor de aflossing van een hypotheek waarbij de ontvanger ten achter stond.
De klacht kan echter m.i. niet tot cassatie leiden. In de eerste plaats wordt zij slechts voorgesteld voor zover het hof– subsidiair – de datum van de beslaglegging (27 september 1990) relevant heeft geacht, niet voor zover het hof de dag van zijn beslissing heeft aangehouden Terzake van dit laatste wordt naar de klacht van middelonderdeel 2.1 verwezen. In mijn opvatting (zie sub 5) is middelonderdeel 2. I ongegrond, zodat de klacht reeds hierop afstuit.
Maar ook indien dit anders is en onderdeel 2.1 wel terecht is voorgedragen, kan de klacht niet tot cassatie leiden, omdat de subsidiaire grond waarop het hof zijn oordeel heeft gegrond – zoals bij de behandeling van onderdeel 2.4 zal blijken – m.i. in cassatie stand houdt.
Terzijde merk ik nog op dat ook de "vervanging" van de hypotheek ten behoeve van Ravast in zoverre nadelig is voor de ontvanger dat zowel de rentestand als (het maximum van) de door de hypotheek gedekte vorderingen zijn verhoogd, hetgeen de verhaalsmogelijkheden van de ontvanger beperkt. Zie de schriftelijke toelichting van mr Van Oven, nr. 17 en 18.

12) Onderdeel 2.4 komt op tegen de sub 10 weergegeven subsidiaire beslissing. Het klaagt over het oordeel van het hof dat, zo bij de beoordeling van de benadeling de hypotheek van de Banque de Suez wel zou meewegen, de ontvanger nog steeds geacht moet worden benadeeld te zijn. Het onderdeel acht het in de eerste plaats rechtens onjuist dat het hof rekening houdt met omstandigheden (het verminderen van de vordering van FGH) die plaatsvinden na 27 september 1990 (de door het hof subsidiair aangenomen peildatum voor benadeling). In de tweede plaats acht het onderdeel het oordeel van het hof over de waarde van de onroerende zaak onbegrijpelijk althans onvoldoende gemotiveerd. Onduidelijk wordt voorts geacht of het hof uitgaat van de executiewaarde of de onderhandse verkoopwaarde (welke laatste mogelijkheid eerst bestaat sinds 1 januari 1992).
Dit onderdeel faalt naar mijn mening. De eerste klacht slaagt niet, omdat vaststaat (en ook op de voormelde peildatum vaststond) dat de vordering van de eerste hypotheekhouder FGH "gestadig daalde" (r.o. 4.14). Dit impliceert dat door de vestiging

van de "vervangende" hypotheek ten behoeve van Ravast, de ontvanger op dat moment een toename van zijn verhaalsmogelijkheid werd onthouden. Daarmee is de nadeligheid van die handeling in de zin van art. 1377 (oud) BW voor de ontvanger gegeven. Het oordeel van het hof geeft dus geen blijk van een onjuiste rechtsopvatting.
De motiveringsklacht gericht tegen het feitelijke oordeel inzake de waardering door het hof van de onderhavige onroerende zaak op 27 september 1990 op minimaal f 12,3 miljoen faalt naar mijn mening. Ravast en Maxfield hebben aangevoerd dat de executiewaarde van de onroerende zaak f 12,1 miljoen bedraagt (conclusie van antwoord, tevens conclusie van eis in reconventie, p. 5 sub 3). Het staat vast dat op 7 juli 1989 de zaak door Maxfield aan Ravast is verkocht voor f 14,4 miljoen (zie r.o. 3.1 sub g). De ontvanger heeft aangevoerd dat de (onderhandse) verkoopwaarde op 20 juli 1989 f 14,4 miljoen bedroeg (conclusie van repliek in conventie en antwoord in reconventie, p. 33 sub 10.6) resp. f 14,3 miljoen op 31 december 1992 (memorie van antwoord in het incidenteel appel, p. 4 sub 6). Tegen deze achtergrond is het oordeel dat de waarde van de onroerende zaak op 27 september 1990 in ieder geval (minstens) gesteld kan worden op f 12,3 miljoen bij (kennelijk executoriale) verkoop (zie r.o. 4.14), m.i. niet onbegrijpelijk. Het oordeel geeft geen blijk van onvoldoende motivering gelet op hetgeen partijen over en weer hebben aangevoerd.

13) Middel 3 richt zich tegen r.o. 4.15, waarin het hof heeft geoordeeld dat zowel Terrafin als Ravast wisten dat het gevolg van de vestiging van de litigieuze hypotheek zou zijn dat schuldei sers werden benadeel d. Het hof heeft te dien aanzien wat betreft Terrafin overwogen dat zij ten tijde van de vestiging van de hypotheek moet hebben geweten (i) dat zij grote bedragen aan vennootschapsbelasting zou hebben te voldoen, (ii) dat de aanslag over 1984, die van 30 januari 1988 dateert, f 5 844 336 bedroeg (zie r.o. 3.1 sub n) (aan de ongemotiveerde bewering dat zij daarmee pas in 1990 bekend raakte heeft het hof geen geloof gehecht), en (iii) dat de waarde van de onroerende zaak en het beloop van de hypothecaire vorderingen (zoals weergegeven in r.o. 4.11 en 4.14) in de lijn van de verwachtingen lagen. Ten aanzien van Ravast heeft het hof geoordeeld dat ook Ravast met een en ander bekend moet zijn geweest. Het hof heeft dit met name afgeleid uit het feit dat de heer Hengevel d, die zowel directeur van Terrafin was als directeur van de vennootschap die bestuurster van Ravast was, in persoon aanwezig en ook rechtstreeks betrokken was bij de onderhavige hypotheekverlening (zie r.o. 3.1 sub f).
Onderdeel 3.1 bevat geen klacht.
Onderdeel 3.2 bouwt voort op middel 2 en moet het lot daarvan delen.
Onderdeel 3.3 klaagt er over dat het hof ten onrechte wetenschap van benadeling heeft aangenomen gel et op het woordgebruik in r.o. 4.15 ("in de lijn der verwachtingen lag" en "in hoofdzaak bekend" zijn). Tevens klaagt het onderdeel er over dat het hof ten onrechte althans onvoldoende gemotiveerd de wetenschap van Terrafin en Ravast aanwezig heeft geacht ten tijde van het vesti gen van de hypotheek (20 juli 1989). Met name acht het onderdeel onduidelijk op grond waarvan het hof heeft geconcludeerd dat zij op 20 juli 1989 konden weten wat de waarde van het pand op 27 september 1990 zou zijn en hoe hoog de vorderingen van FGH en de Banque de Suez (op Maxfield) op 27 september 1990 zouden zijn.
Het middelonderdeel faalt naar mijn mening. Het vereiste van wetenschap van benadeling voor een geslaagd beroep op de *pauliana* houdt bij een handeling onder bezwarende titel in, dat vast moet staan dat ten tijde van het verrichten van die handeling (in casu de vestiging van de hypotheek, d.w.z. 20 juli 1989) zowel de schuldenaar (Terrafin) als degene met wie hij handelde (Ravast) wisten of behoorden te weten dat benadeling van

de schuldeiser (de ontvanger)daarvan het gevolg zou zijn. Zie ASSER-HARTKAMP II, nr. 447 en MELLEMA- KRANENBURG, a.w., p. 34 e.v. Een weten of behoren te weten dat de handeling de kans op benadeling van een of meer schuldeisers schiep is echter niet voldoende. Aldus HR 1 oktober 1993, NJ 1994, 257 m.nt WMK .
Het hof heeft naar mijn mening de hierboven weergegeven juiste maatstaf toegepast. Dit blijkt uit 's hofs uitgangspunt zoals verwoord in r.o. 4.3 ad iii. Uit deze rechtsoverweging blijkt ook dat het hof is uitgegaan van een juist beoordelingsmoment met betrekking tot de aanwezigheid van de wetenschap van benadeling. Niet nodig is dat er wetenschap bestaat van de exacte omvang van de benadeling. Vgl. HR 9 maart 1928, NJ 1928, p. 1213 m.nt. EMM, ASSER-HARTKAMP II, nr. 447 en MELLEMA-KRANENBURG, a.w., p. 34 (slot). De slotklacht van middelonderdeel 3.3 stuit daarop af. Voor het overige zou ik menen dat het oordeel omtrent de "wetenschap van benadeling" zozeer is verweven met waarderingen van feitelijke aard, dat het in cassatie verder op zijn juistheid kan worden getoetst. Zie HR 18 december 1992, NJ 1993, 169.
De conclusie strekt tot verwerping van het beroep.

HOGE RAAD

I. Het geding in feitelijke instanties

Verweerder in cassatie – verder te noemen: de Ontvanger– heeft bij exploit van 9 december 1991 eiseressen tot cassatie – verder te noemen: Ravast c.s. – gedagvaard voor de Rechtbank te Amsterdam en gevorderd:

1. voor recht te verklaren dat de bij acte van 13 oktober 1989 door Terrafin ten behoeve van Ravast gevestigde hypotheek op de supermarkt met restaurant en parkeergarages, ondergrond, erf en verder aan- en toebehoren, staande en gelegen te Middelburg aan de Pottenbakkerssingel no. 2, kadastraal bekend gemeente Middelburg, sectie L, nummer 2796, groot 78 a 2 ça jegens de Ontvanger nietig is;

2. voor recht te verklaren dat de in het petitum sub 1 bedoelde hypothecaire inschrijving (jegens de Ontvanger) waardeloos is.

Ravast c.s. hebben geconcludeerd voor antwoord tot afwijzing van de vorderingen en in reconventie gevorderd:
a) op te heffen de executoriale beslagen, door de Ontvanger gelegd op 27 september en 14 december 1990 op de in de dagvaarding onder 1 bedoelde onroerende zaak, althans te verklaren voor recht dat deze beslagen zijn opgeheven en de dienovereenkomstige inschrijvingen waardeloos zijn;

b) de Ontvanger te veroordelen tot vergoeding aan Ravast en Maxfield van schade, nader op te maken bij staat en te vereffenen volgens de wet en te vermeerderen met de wettelijke rente daarover vanaf 1 maart 1992.

Bij vonnis van 26 mei 1993 heeft de Rechtbank in conventie en in reconventie de vorderingen afgewezen. Tegen dit vonnis heeft de Ontvanger hoger beroep ingesteld bij het Gerechtshof te Amsterdam. Ravast c.s. hebben incidenteel hoger beroep ingesteld.

Bij arrest van 26 mei 1994 heeft het Hof in conventie het bestreden vonnis vernietigd en in reconventie het vonnis bekrachtigd. 'Vervolgens heeft het Hof de vorderingen van de Ontvanger toegewezen.

3. Uitgangspunten

(i) Terrafin is eigenares van een onroerende zaak (een supermarkt), gelegen aan de Pottenbakkerssingel 2 te Middelburg.

(ii) De onroerende zaak is achtereenvolgens viermaal verkocht, en wel door Terrafin aan VFS, door VFS aan Ahog, door Ahog aan Maxfield en door Maxfield aan Ravast. De koopovereenkomst Terrafin-VFS bepaalt onder D 6: "De verkopers verplichten zich jegens de koper om onverwijld op eerste vordering van de koper en op kopers kosten, voor de door de koper te bepalen bedragen en onder de door de koper te bepalen bedingen (...) b. op verkopers' eigen namen als derde onderzetters (een) 'hypothe(e)k(en) te verlenen op het onroerend goed of enig gedeelte daarvan tot meerdere zekerheid voor de nakoming van de verplichtingen voortvloeiende uit (een) door de koper te haren name of (een) door de koper aan te wijzen derde(n) te diens/hunnen name aan te gane overeenkomst(en) van lening of andere overeenkomst(en)". Een bepaling van deze strekking maakt ook deel uit van de tussen VFS en Ahog en Ahog en Maxfield gesloten overeenkomsten maar niet van de overeenkomst MaxfieldRavast.

(iii) Met betrekking tot de eerste drie van de onder (ii) bedoelde koopovereenkomsten heeft telkens (slechts) een vorm van zogenaamde economische-eigendomsoverdracht plaatsgevonden. Telkens zijn namelijk verkoper en koper overeengekomen, kort gezegd, dat aile ten en lasten (inclusief het risico) van de onroerende zaak verbintenisrechtelijk toekomen aan de telkens optredende koper. Telkens heeft voorts wel de verkoper zekere vorderingsrechten (bijvoorbeeld uit verzekering en verhuur), maar is niet de eigendom van de onroerende zaak aan de koper overgedragen. Ten aanzien van de koopovereenkomst Maxfield-Ravast is niet de koopsom betaald en is ook niet de eigendom van de onroerende zaak aan de koper overgedragen. Wel zijn partijen overeengekomen dat Ravast tot aan de eigendomsoverdracht wordt "aangemerkt als de economisch eigenaar", overigens zonder nadere bepaling van de term economisch eigenaar.

(iv) Terrafin heeft op de onroerende zaak op 7 oktober 1987 een eerste hypotheek gevestigdten behoeve van de Friesch Groningsche Hypotheekbank (FGH) voor schulden van Max-field aan FGH, en op 21 juli 1989 een tweede hypotheek ten behoeve van Ravast tot zekerheid voor schulden van Maxfield aan Ravast tot een maximum van f 14 miljoen.

(v) Ter executie van een tweetal aan Terrafin opgelegde aanslagen heeft de Ontvanger op respectievelijk 27 september 1990 en 14 december 1990 beslag gelegd op de onroerende zaak.

Op vordering van de Ontvanger heeft het Hof voor recht verklaard dat de hiervoor onder (iv) bedoelde tweede hypotheek jegens de Ontvanger nietig is, en dat de inschrijving van deze hypotheek jegens de Ontvanger waardeloos is.

4. De ontvankelijkheid van het cassatieberoep

De Ontvanger stelt zich op het standpunt dat Ravast c.s. niet in hun cassatieberoep kunnen worden ontvangen. De Ontvanger voert daartoe aan dat nu Ravast c.s. hebben verzuimd om binnen acht dagen na het instel len van het cassatieberoep, daarvan aantekening te doen houden ter griffie van het Hof, het bepaalde in art. 3:29 lid 3 BW meebrengt dat zij niet-ontvankelijk zijn.
Dit betoog kan niet als juist worden aanvaard, reeds omdat uit art. 74 lid 1 Overgangswet NBW volgt dat het van toepassing worden van art. 29 lid 3 geen gevol heeft voor de ontvankelijkheid van rechtsmiddelen ingesteld in een geding dat, zoals het onderhavige, reeds voordien is aangevangen.

5. Beoordeling van de middelen

5.1 Middel I komt met een rechts- en een motiveringsklacht op tegen 's Hofs oordeel dat de vestiging van de tweede hypotheek door Terrafin moet worden aangemerkt als onverplicht in de zin van art. 1377 (oud) BW (rov. 4.5 en 4.6). Het middel voert daartoe aan dat de hypotheekvesti ging niet als onverplicht kan worden beschouwd, aangezien Terrafin daartoe gedwongen kon worden. en wel aldus dat Max-field het doen vestigen van een hypotheek door Terrafin kon vorderen van Ahog, Ahog van VFS en VFS van Terrafin. Daaraan doet, aldus het middel, niet af dat deze weg niet is gevolgd. Voorts klaagt het middel dat Hof zijn oordeel onvold-oende heeft gemotiveerd, nu het hier een reeks "economische eigendomsoverdrachten" betrof, en niet is gebleken dat betrokkenen hebben beoogd betekenis toe te kennen aan de weg waarlangs de economische eigenaar zich tot de juridische eigenaar zou wenden.
Het middel faalt. Het Hof heeft de door het middel verdedigde zienswijze, die strookt met het oordeel van de Rechtbank, verworpen. Het Hof heeft geoordeeld dat de vestiging van de hypotheek als onverplicht moet worden aangemerkt, omdat Terrafin zich daartoe niet jegens Maxfield of Ravast had verplicht, waaraan, aldus het Hot niet afdoet dat VFS zich jegens Ahog, en Ahog zich jegens Maxfield in dezelfde zin verplicht hadden als Terrafin jegensVFS, en het hier gaat om zogenaamde economische eigendomsoverdrachten. Deze aan het Hof voorbehouden uitleg van de contractuele verhoudingen geeft niet blijk van een onjuiste rechtsopvatting. 's Hofs oordeel is voorts niet onbegrijpelijk of onvoldoende gemotiveerd.

5.2. Middel 2 komt op tegen 's Hofs oordeel dat de Ontvanger "thans" benadeeld is door de hypotheekvestiging en hij dat ook reeds was op 27 september 1990 toen het eerste beslag werd gelegd (rov. 4.11).
Onderdeel 2.1 voert aan dat 's Hofs oordeel blijk geeft van een onjuiste rechtsopvatting voor zover het tot uitgangspunt neemt dat het voor het tijdstip waarop sprake moet zijn van benadeling, aankomt op de datum waarop het an-est wordt gewezen.
Het onderdeel faalt. Benadeling moet aanwezig zijn op het tijdstip waarop de schuldeiser zijn rechten doet gelden (HR 23 december 1949, NJ 1950, 262). Indien, zoals in het onderhavige geval, in rechte wordt gestreden over de vraag of de schuldeiser terecht een beroep doet op art. 1377 (oud) BW, is het met betrekking tot de door dat artikel vereiste benadeling nodig, doch ook voldoende dat zij aanwezig is ten tijde dat omtrent het beroep op die bepaling wordt beslist. Kennelijk heeft het Hof, oordelend dat de Ontvanger "thans" is benadeeld, dat tijdstip op het oog gehad.

De in het middel vervatte klachten die voortbouwen op onderdeel 2.1 moeten het lot daarvan delen.

5.3. Het middel bestrijdt voorts 's Hofs oordeel dat aan zijn slotsom, dat sprake is van benadeling, niet kan afdoen de omstandigheid dat de aan Ravast gegeven hypotheek een oudere tweede hypotheek ten gunste van Banque de Suez heeft vervangen (rov. 4.12). Het Hof heeft daartoe overwogen dat nu de hypotheek van Banque de Suez voor 27 september 1990 beëindigd was, zij geen rol kan spelen bij de beoordeling van de vraag of de Ontvanger thans benadeeld is, en zo nodig, of hij op 27 september 1990 al benadeeld was (rov. 4.13).
De klacht kan reeds daarom niet tot cassatie leiden, omdat het middel tot uitgangspunt neemt dat de vraag of de Ontvanger benadeeld is, beoordeeld moet worden aan de hand van de si tuatie op 27 september 1990. Dit uitgangspunt is evenwel, zoals hiervoor onder 5.2 is overwo¬gen, niet juist.

5.4. Middel 3 bestrijdt 's Hofs oordeel dat zowel Terrafin als Ravast wisten dat benadeling van schuldeisers het gevolg zou zijn van de hypotheekvestiging (rov. 4.15). Dit oordeel geeft, anders dan het middel betoogt, niet blijk van een onjuiste opvatting van het begrip "wetenschap van benadeling"; het is zozeer verweven met waarderingen van feitelijke aard dat het voor het overige niet op juistheid kan worden getoetst. Het is niet onbegrijpelijk of onvoldoende gemotiveerd. Het middel faalt derhalve.

6. Beslissing

De Hoge Raad:
verwerpt het beroep;
veroordeelt Ravast c.s. in de kosten van het geding in cassatie, tot op deze uitspraak aan de zijde van de Ontvanger begroot op f 577,20 aan verschotten en f 3000 voor salaries.

Sources

Published in:
Nederlandse Jurisprudentie 1996, Nr. 706, 4078 - 4092, case note by HJS.

Date: ***January 24, 1996***
Country: ***France***
Adjudicating Court: ***Cour d'appel de Grenoble***
Number: ***Unknown***
Parties: ***Société Harper Robinson v. Société internationale de maintenance et de réalisations industrielles***

Keywords

STANDARD TERMS – CONFLICT BETWEEN A STANDARD TERM AND A NON-STANDARD TERM – NON STANDARD TERM PREVAILS (ART. 2.21 UNIDROIT PRINCIPLES [ART. 2.1.21 OF THE 2004 EDITION])

INTERPRETATION - UNCLEAR CONTRACT TERMS SUPPLIED BY ONE PARTY – INTERPRETATION AGAINST THE SUPPLYING PARTY ("CONTRA PROFERENTEM RULE") – REFERENCE BY COURT TO ART. 4.6 UNIDROIT PRINCIPLES

Abstract

The dispute concerned the faulty packaging of machinery transported from the United States to France. The contract contained a liability clause stating that "[the carrier] undertakes to guarantee and compensate [the client] for any loss [...] owing to any defective performance of the obligations stipulated in the present contract [...] All obligations with respect to compensation must comply with [the carrier's] standard terms [...]". The relevant article of the carrier's standard terms provided that "[t]he client accepts that under no circumstances will compensation be payable by [the carrier] for any damage, loss or delay caused by negligence on the part of [the carrier] exceeding the sum of US$ 50 per shipment [...]".

After pointing out that this provision ran counter to the principle of acceptance of full liability spelled out in the contract, the Court stated that "there was a principle in international trade law that 'in case of conflict between a standard term and a term which is not a standard term the latter prevails' (UNIDROIT Principles, Art. 2.21 [Art. 2.1.21 of the 2004 edition]) and that 'if contract terms supplied by one party are unclear, an interpretation against that party is preferred' (UNIDROIT Principles, Art. 4.6)" (translation from French original). Consequently, the Court decided that the reference made in the contract to the carrier's standard terms was invalid.

Full Text

[...]

Attendu que, par contrat en date du 11 février 1992, la Société SIMRI établie au FONTANIL (Isère), a confié à la société HARPER ROBINSON, établie aux Etats-Unis, diverses opérations visant au transport de machines outils depuis le Michigan jusqu'en France, via le port belge d'Anvers;

Qu'il est constant que la société HARPER ROBINSON était notamment chargée de l'emballage;

Qu'à l'arrivée, la Société SIMRI a constaté des avaries sur une machine;

Qu'il résulte d'une expertise diligentée par Monsieur DESVIGNES du Cabinet LANVIN LESPIAU, mandaté par l'assureur de la société SIMRI, que les dommages sont dus à une absence de calage d'une armoire électronique dans la caisse;

Que le rapport d'expertises, en date du 21 août 1992, mentionne la présence et l'accord de Monsieur James Cobain, mandaté par la Société HARPER GROUP;

Qu'une transaction a été conclue entre la Société SIMRI et la Société MAVILOR pour que les dommages soient indemnisés pour 600.000 F;

Attendu que, devant la court, la Société HARPER ROBINSON conclut:

D'une part, à l'incompétence des juridictions judiciaires au moyen que les parties ont stipulé une clause compromissoire, d'autre part, et subsidiairement, à l'incompétence des juridictions françaises au moyen que le lieu de livraison des marchandises transportées était Anvers, en troisième lieu, que la Société SIMRI n'a pas d'intérêt à agir, en quatrième lieu, que les conditions générales de la Société HARPER ROBINSON limitent sa responsabilité à 50 dollars des ETATS-UNIS,

Qu'elle demande 30.000 F, au titre de l'article 700 du Nouveau Code de Procédure Civile;

Attendu que Me Coquet conclut à la confirmation, demande 30.000 F à titre de dommages et intérêts et 20.000 F, au titre de l'article 700 du Nouveau Code de Procédure Civile;

Attendu que Me BOURGUIGNON, bien qu'assigné à personne, ne comparaît pas; que le présent arrêt est donc réputé contradictoire;

SUR CE

Attendu, sur la compétence arbitrale, que l'article 7 du contrat stipulé comme autorité de nomination des arbitres, "la cour internationale d'arbitrage de LA HAYE (Pays Bas)";

Que la Société SIMRI a tenté de mettre en oeuvre cette clause en saisissant la Cour internationale de justice à La Haye, aux Pays-Bas;

Que par lettre du 23 avril 1993, le Greffier de la Cour a décliné la compétence de l'institution et a écrit ceci: "En outre, je dois vous signaler qu'il n'existe aucune institution portant le nom de "tribunal international de La Haye". Il paraîtrait donc que la clause à laquelle vous faites référence mériterait réexamen".

Qu'il y a lieu de préciser que le texte du contrat contenant la clause compromissoire avait été transmis à la Cour avec les autres pièces du dossier (cfr lettre du 8 avril 1993 adressée à la Cour par l'avocat de la Société SIMRI);

Que la Société HARPER ROBINSON indique qu'il y avait lieu de comprendre la Court permanente d'arbitrage de La Haye" ainsi que le prévoit le règlement d'arbitrage de la CNUDCI qui aurait servi de modèle à la clause;

Que, s'il est exact que l'article 6, point 2, in fine du règlement d'arbitrage de la CNDUCI prévoit partie peut demander au secrétaire général de la Cour permanente d'arbitrage de LA Haye de désigner une autorité de nomination", la clause pathologique litigieuse ne fait aucune mention de la CNUDCI et confère à l'autorité inexistante désignée un pouvoir direct de nomination;

Que le modèle invoqué n'a donc que des rapports lointains avec la clause litigieuse; que lorsque le sens à donner à une clause compromissoire échappe au cocontractant et au Greffier de la Cour International de Justice, qui siège pourtant au Palais de la Paix comme la Cour permanente d'arbitrage, il y a lieu de déduire que la Société HARPER ROBINSON, auteur de la clause, n'a pas exprimé sa volonté de façon opératoire; et que, à la réception de la copie de la lettre adressée à la Cour Internationale de Justice, en avril 1993, la Société HARPER ROBINSON n'a pas entrepris de corriger l'erreur de son contractant dans le sens où elle conclut aujourd'hui; Que l'exception d'incompétence, fondée sur une clause nulle pour désigner une autorité inexistante, doit donc être rejetée;

Attendue, sur l'incompétence du Tribunal de Commerce de Grenoble au profit des juridictions anversoises, que l'article 74 du Nouveau Code de Procédure Civile oblige à soulever les exceptions d'incompétence simultanément;

Que le moyen tiré du lieu de livraison ne figure pas dans les conclusions d'incompétence reçues par le Tribunal de Commerce de Grenoble le 25 août 1994; qu'il doit donc être rejeté; qu'au surplus, la Société HARPER ROBINSON qui s'était chargée du rechargement sur un camion à Anvers et avait reçu, pour ce service, 580 francs belges par tonne, ne saurait prétendre ignorer que la livraison des marchandises, dont elle coordonnait le transport, devait être faite en France;

Attendue, sur la qualité à agir de la Société SIMRI, que le cocontractant de la Société HARPER est la Société SIMRI; que cette dernière a transigé avec la Société MAVILOR pour un montant de dommages de 600.000 F (cf protocole d'accord du 29 juillet 1992); qu'elle a donc qualité et intérêts pour réclamer la somme de 600.000 F à la Société HARPER; que la circonstance, que la Société SIMRI ne présente pas un reçu de la Société MAVILOR du montant des sommes transigées, n'a pas pour effet de supprimer l'intérêts à agir de la Société SIMRI puisque, en tout état de cause, il résulte de la transaction qu'elle s'est engagée à payer ladite somme, si elle ne l'a déjà fait; Et que la société HARPER n'a pas appelé la société MAVILOR en la cause pour la payer directement;

Attendu, sur la limitation de responsabilité, que la clause du contrat relative à la responsabilité est ainsi rédigée:

"Article 4
HARPER ROBINSON s'engage à garantir et relever indemne SIMRI de toute perte, toute dépense, toute réclamation ou tout dommage occasionné aux tiers du fait de toute négligence de sa part dans l'exécution du travail, objet du présent contrat. Il s'engage également à souscrire une assurance ou fournir une autoassurance acceptable, dans les termes et sous une forme susceptible de satisfaire SIMRI pour la couverture de ses engagements. Toutes les obligations en matière d'indemnisation devront être conformes aux conditions de vente standard de HARPER ROBINSON. Il est entendu que l'inspection du matériel ne relève pas de la compétence de HARPER ROBINSON et qu'il ne sera en aucun cas tenu de vérifier les dommages. Il est également entendu que les machines sont d'occasion et partiellement démontées. HARPER ROBINSON ne pourra donc pas être tenu responsable en cas de dommages ou de pièces manquantes. Le nettoyage et l'enlèvement des éclats et des débris ne sont pas de la responsabilité de HARPER ROBINSON. Les méthodes d'emballage appliquées pour ce projet ont été conçues afin d'assurer une protection adéquate contre les éléments en cas de manutention NORMALE et pour une durée maximum TOTALE de transport et d'entreposage de 90 jours, en aucun cas pour protéger la marchandise stockée à ciel ouvert."

Que le contrat est signé des deux parties sur chacune de ses pages;

Que l'article 8 des conditions générales de HARPER ROBINSON dispose ceci:
"Limitation de 50 dollars par envoi. Le client n'accepte que l'indemnité due par la Société HARPER ROBINSON pour tous dommages, perte, avaries ou retard résultant d'une faute commise par HARPER ROBINSON ne pourra en aucun cas excéder la somme de 50 dollars par envoi (ou la valeur selon facture si cette valeur est inférieure)..."

Que les conditions générales ne sont pas signées ni même visées par la Société SIMRI;
Qu'il n'est pas établi qu'elle en ait eu connaissance au moment de la signature du contrat;

Qu'elles se présentent en une suite de 23 articles au graphisme minuscule;

Qu'en outre, la clause limitant à 50 dollars par envoi, donc à une somme dérisoire, assimilable à une absence d'indemnisation, contredit le principe d'une acceptation de responsabilité énoncé dans l'article 4 du contrat;

Qu'il est de principe, en droit du commerce international, que "en cas d'incompatibilité entre une clause qui ne l'est pas, cette dernière l'emporte" (Principes d'UNIDROIT, article 2.21) et que "en cas d'ambiguité, les clauses d'un contrat s'interprètent de préférence contre celui qui les a proposes" (Principes d'UNIDROIT, art. 4.6) ;

Que la référence aux conditions générales figurant dans l'article 4 du contrat est donc privée d'effet;

Qu'en outre, la Société HARPER ROBINSON qui avait accepté spécifiquement une fonction d'emballage, conformément à une aptitude particulière mise en exergue envers ses clients (*cf.* lettre du 7 mai 1992), a, en se satisfaisant d'un emballage extérieur, sans procéder au calage de l'armoire de commande et des automatismes d'une machine outil, commis une faute lourde, qui la prive du droit à limitation des responsabilités ;

Que la Société HARPER ROBINSON accepte dans ses écritures que cette règle de droit est applicable en la cause ; Qu'il y a donc lieu de juger qu'elle est déchue du droit d'opposer la limitation de responsabilité de 50 US dollars ;

Attendu, sur le montant de la responsabilité, que la Société HARPER ROBINSON fait valoir que son mandataire Monsieur James COBAIN n'avait pas accepté le règlement de 600.000 F ;

Mais qu'il résulte d'une lettre adressée le 16 octobre 1995 par Monsieur COBAIN à Me GODIN qu'il "était entendu que le montant du sinistre était fixé à 600.000 F" ;

Que l'expert de l'assureur de la Société SIMRI a évalué le dommage à cette somme ;

Que la transaction entre la Société SIMRI et la Société MAVILOR a eu également pour base ce montant ;

Que l'expert de l'assureur de la Société SIMRI a évalué le dommage à cette somme ;

Que la transaction entre la Société SIMRI et la Société MAVILOR a eu également pour base ce montant ;

Qu'en l'absence de toute autre proposition motivée, la Cour retient également le chiffre de 600.000 F comme montant du préjudice ;

Attendu, sur les dommages et intérêts pour procédure abusive réclamés par la Société SIMRI, que la Société HARPER ROBINSON, en faisant usage d'une voie de recours ordinaire, n'a pas, en l'absence de moyen particulier allégué, commis d'abus du droit d'ester en justice ; Qu'il y a donc lieu de rejeter la demande ;

Attendu, sur la somme de 20.000 F réclamée au titre de l'article 700 du Nouveau Code de Procédure Civile par la Société SIMRI, qu'il y a lieu d'y faire droit ;

PAR CES MOTIFS :

LA COUR :

Statuant publiquement et par arrêt réputé contradictoire,

Après en avoir délibéré conformément à la loi

CONFIRME. En toutes ses dispositions, le jugement déféré;

Y AJOUTANT du fait de l'appel;

CONDAMNE la Société HARPER ROBINSON à payer 20.000 F, au titre de l'article 700 du Nouveau Code de Procédure Civile, à Me COQUET,

La CONDAMNE aux dépens, dont distraction au profit de la SCP d'Avoués PERRET et POUGNAND.

[...]

Sources

Original in French:
Revue de l'arbitrage, 1997, 87.

Sources:
M. le Juge J. P. BÉRAUDO
Revue de l'arbitrage, 1997, 87.

Date: ***April 25, 1996***
Adjudicating Court: ***ICC International Court of Arbitration***
Number: ***Unknown***
Parties: ***Société mixte Franco-Kazakh CISTM v. Société FARASOL***

Keywords

CATERING CONTRACT BETWEEN A FRENCH-KAZAKH COMPANY – FRENCH LAW APPLICABLE

NOTICE OF CANCELLATION OF CONTRACT – FRENCH LAW UNCLEAR AS TO WHETHER DISPATCH OR RECEIPT PRINCIPLE APPLICABLE – REFERENCE TO USAGES OF INTERNATIONAL TRADE (ART. 13(5) ICC RULES OF ARBITRATION) ACCORDING TO WHICH RECEIPT PRINCIPLE APPLIES – REFERENCE TO UNIDROIT PRINCIPLES

Abstract

Defendant, a French company in charge of perforation activities in Kazakhstan had entered into a contract with Plaintiff, a mixed French-Kazakh company for catering services for its employees. The contract, which was governed by French law, had a fixed term but provided for tacit renewal in the absence of notice of cancellation by Defendant three months before expiry. Two days before the three month period began to run, Defendant sent a notice of cancellation to Plaintiff, which however reached the latter two days after the three month had begun to run. Defendant, invoking Articles 668 and 669 of the French Code of civil procedure according to which in case of notice the date of postage was decisive, argued that its notice of cancellation had been given to Plaintiff in time. Plaintiff object that the notice was ineffective because it should have reached it before the three month period had begun.

The sole arbitrator decided in favour of Plaintiff. It held that in the case at hand Articles 668 and 669 of the French Code of civil procedure were not applicable because they related only to notices given in the course of judicial proceedings. Since with resepct to notices exchanged in contractual relationships there was no clear rule in French law as to whether the dispatch principle or the receipt principle prevailed, the Arbitrator, on the basis of Article 13(5) of the ICC Rules of Arbitration, referred to the usages of international trade and found that according to them it was the receipt principle that was generally accepted. In this context the Arbitrator referred to the UNIDROIT Principles, indicated as a "codification" of such usages, without however citing Article 1.9(2) which expressly sets out the receipt principle.

Full Text

[Not yet available]

Sources

Cour d'Appel de Paris (1[re] Ch. C.) 5 March 1998 in Revue de l'Arbitrage, 1999, 86 *et seq.*

Date: ***June 1996***
Adjudicating Court: ***ICC International Court of Arbitration, Rome***
Number: ***5835***
Parties: ***Unknown***

Keywords

CONTRACT SILENT AS TO APPLICABLE LAW – APPLICATION BY ARBITRAL TRIBUNAL OF DOMESTIC LAW (KUWAITI LAW) TOGETHER WITH "PRINCIPLES GENERALLY APPLICABLE IN INTERNATIONAL COMMERCE" – REFERENCE TO INDIVIDUAL PROVISIONS OF THE UNIDROIT PRINCIPLES FOR INTERPRETATION OF APPLICABLE DOMESTIC LAW

NON-PERFORMANCE - ART. 7.1.6 UNIDROIT PRINCIPLES TO INTERPRET GROSS MISTAKE UNDER KUWAITI LAW

DAMAGES - ART. 7.4.3(3) UNIDROIT PRINCPILES TO CONFIRM DISCRETIONARY POWER OF THE COURT IN ASSESSING DAMAGES UNDER KUWAITI LAW – ART. 7.4.7 UNIDROIT PRINCIPLES TO CONFIRM RULE UNDER KUWAITI LAW THAT DAMAGES BE REDUCED IF DUE IN PART TO AGGRIEVED PARTY

INTEREST - ART. 7.4.9(3) UNIDROIT PRINCIPLES TO CONFIRM RIGHT TO ADDITIONAL DAMAGES UNDER KUWAITI LAW

Abstract

An Italian company (the main contractor) and a Kuwaiti company (the subcontractor) entered into a contract for the installation and maintenance of electrical works. The contract provided for arbitration to be held in Italy and subject to Swiss law. The dispute arose when, despite completion of work by the subcontractor, the main contractor failed to pay and refused to release performance bonds. The subcontractor requested the release of these bonds and in addition claimed damages; the main contractor counterclaimed damages arising from the delayed completion of work, alleging that such delay (20 months) was due to several failures to perform (gross mistakes) by subcontractor.

In an interim award, rendered in December 1989, the Arbitral Tribunal interpreted the reference to Swiss Law as a choice of the law governing the arbitration procedure. As to the law applicable to the substance of the dispute, the Tribunal concluded in favour of Kuwaiti law as the law most closely connected with the relevant elements of the contract, but it decided also to take into account "principles generally applicable in international commerce".

In its final award the Arbitral Tribunal, without further explanation, referred on several occasions to the UNIDROIT Principles. Thus it referred to Article 7.1.6 to interpret the notion of gross mistake under Kuwaiti law, and concluded that a party's conduct is grossly negligent when it leads to a performance substantially different from what the other party reasonably expected. Moreover, it referred to Articles 7.4.3 (3) and 7.4.7 to interpret Article 300 (1) of the Kuwaiti Civil Law no. 67 of 1980 determining the factors to be taken into consideration by the court when assessing the amount of damages. Finally, it referred to Article 7.4.9(3) to confirm the rules contained in Articles 110 and 111 of the Kuwaiti Commercial Code no. 68, according to which the aggrieved party is entitled to additional damages if the non-payment caused it harm greater than would be covered by the normally applicable rate of interest.

Full Text

[...]

Claimant contends that the issues of the entire dispute should be governed by Kuwaiti law, either as the law explicitly chosen by the Parties (Art. 38 of the Agreement, Art. 80 of the Main Contract) or, in the alternative, as the proper law of the contract in application of all the relevant criteria of Kuwaiti and other rules of conflict of laws.

Respondent submits that the Parties made a "negative choice", *i.e.* each Party intended to avoid the other Party's (Kuwaiti or Italian) national law and the law of a third country was likewise excluded [...]. Respondent concludes from this interpretation that the Parties have chosen, as the law applicable to the merits, that part of the Kuwaiti and Italian legislation which was common to them at the time the Agreement was entered into.

The Arbitral Tribunal holds that the Parties have neither explicitly nor tacitly agreed on the substantive law.

[...]

In the absence of any clear indication by the Parties as to the applicable law, the Arbitral Tribunal shall apply the law designated as the proper law by the rule of conflict which it deems appropriate (Art. 13 (3) of the ICC Rules).

[...]

When looking directly to the substantive law with the closest connection, the Kuwaiti law must again be the conclusion. With the exception of the nationality and the residence of Respondent (Italy) the Agreement and its performance do not have any link whatsoever with other countries than Kuwait where the entire Agreement was discussed, concluded and performed. The price had also been agreed and paid in Kuwaiti currency.

However, in accordance with a well-established practice in international commercial arbitration, the arbitrators shall take account also of the principles generally applicable in international commerce [...] This provision is particularly justified in view of the fact that the Parties refrained from choosing explicitly Kuwaiti law as the law on the merits [...]

The Arbitral Tribunal concludes that Kuwaiti law and, to the extent necessary, principles generally applicable in international commerce are applicable in the merits of the dispute.

[...]

The Tribunal holds that Respondent's allegations as in Claimant's gross mistakes are supported by the evidence:

A contractor's performance amounts in "gross mistake" if his conduct grossly violates a fundamental rule of the art or if he repeatedly or continuously fails in perform in a timely manner important parts of his obligations. The intent to harm the contractual party does not constitute a prerequisite of a culpa grave claim for contractual negligence. A party's conduct is grossly negligent if it shows an elementary failure of attention for the consequences of one's action and if it leads to a performance substantially different from what the other party reasonably expected (*cf.* Final Award in ICC case no. 6320 of 1992, ICCA Yearbook XX-1995, pp. 62ss, p. 87 ; UNIDROIT Principles, Article 7.1.6). "Gross mistake" under Kuwaiti law is not different from this generally accepted definition. If it were, Claimant would have submitted relevant authority in response in Respondent's allegations [...] Had a narrower definition of "gross mistake" been established under Kuwaiti law, the Tribunal would have had to follow "principles generally applicable in international commerce" (Interim Award I), *i.e.* the definition recorded hereinabove.

[...]

The Tribunal holds that a contractor's manpower disruption caused by a subcontractor's delay falls into the category of damages which may normally not be established, in a claim for damages, in an arithmetically satisfactory manner. Manpower disruption belongs in the category of damages not ascertainable by calculation, which must be determined by the Tribunal, taking into account the ordinary chain of events. This approach is in accordance with Art. 300 Sect. 1 of the Kuwaiti Civil Law no. 67 of 1980, which provides that compensation shall be "estimated" by the Court. It is also in accordance with generally accepted principles in international commerce (*cf. e.g.* UNIDROIT Principles of International Commercial Contracts, Rome 1994, Article 7.4.3 Subs. 3 : "Where the amount of damages cannot be established with a sufficient degree of certainty the assessment is at the discretion of the court.").

[...]

Respondent claims interest on payments made in its Kuwaiti site, interest on its further claims and, originally, compensation for its rate of exchange losses [...].

Claimant addressed the present issue only in its Post Hearing Brief [...] and only with respect to the restrictions applicable, under Kuwaiti law, on interest rates. It indicated that the interest rate may not exceed 7 % according in Art. 110 and 111 of the Kuwaiti Commercial Code (law no. 68/1980).

[...]

The Tribunal holds that Kuwaiti law restricts the rate of interest only with respect in contractual rates and in the interest rate applicable when the payment of money the amount of which is known to the debtor is delayed (*cf.* Art. 110 and 111 of the Kuwaiti Commercial Code no. 68), but not however in interest aimed at compensating the aggrieved party for the fact that the damages awarded shall only be paid some time after the damage occurred and that the creditor may have incurred financial charges in order in survive the period during which he was awaiting compensation of his damages [...]. Kuwaiti law provides that the compensation shall include "the damage suffered by the creditor [...] provided that this is a natural result of non-fulfillment of the obligation or delay thereof" (Art. 300 Sect. 2 of the Civil Law no. 67/1980). The Tribunal holds that the said financial charges may qualify according to the circumstances of the case, as a "natural result" of a debtor's delay in paying damages owed to his contractual partner. Particularly, if the basis of the debtor's liability is "grave mistake" [...] the normally applicable limits on interest rates are no longer applicable (Art. 300 Sect. 3 and Art. 304 Civil Law per analogiam).

This understanding of Kuwaiti law is in accordance with internationally accepted principles which otherwise would become applicable pursuant to the Tribunal's First Interim Award. Reference may again be made in the UNIDROIT Principles of 1994, which provide in Art. 7.4.9(3) that the aggrieved party is entitled to additional damages if the non payment caused it a greater harm than covered by the normally applicable interest rate.

Sources

Original in English (published in excerpt):
ICC International Court of Arbitration Bulletin, Vol. 10, No. 2, Fall 1999, 34-39.

Date: ***June 5, 1996***
Adjudicating Court: ***ICC International Court of Arbitration, Paris***
Number: ***7375***
Parties: ***Unknown***

Keywords

CONTRACT SILENT AS TO APPLICABLE LAW – INTERPRETED BY ARBITRAL TRIBUNAL AS EXCLUSION OF THE DOMESTIC LAW OF BOTH PARTIES – REFERENCE TO THE UNIDROIT PRINCIPLES AS GENERAL PRINCIPLES AND RULES OF LAW APPLICABLE TO INTERNATIONAL CONTRACTUAL OBLIGATIONS WHICH QUALIFY AS RULES OF LAW AND WHICH HAVE EARNED A WIDE ACCEPTANCE AND INTERNATIONAL CONSENSUS IN THE INTERNATIONAL BUSINESS COMMUNITY

LIMITATION OF CLAIMS – ISSUE NOT EXPRESSLY DEALT WITH IN THE UNIDROIT PRINCIPLES – PARTIES INVITED TO SUBMIT MEMORIALS ON SUBSTANCE HAVING REGARD TO APPLICABLE GENERAL PRINCIPLES OF LAW

Abstract

A United States seller (Defendant) and a Middle Eastern buyer (Claimant) entered into a contract for the supply of goods. The Claimant, a governmental agency, claimed damages and interest in connection with a delay in the delivery of the goods. The contract contained no choice of law clause. The Defendant, invoking the application of the law of Maryland as the place where the significant contractual obligations, *i.e.*, the manufacture of the goods, had been performed, deemed the claim to be time-barred. The Claimant relied on its own domestic law under which the action would not be time-barred, and, subsidiarily, invoked the application of general principles of law.

In investigating the intent of the parties, the Arbitral Tribunal found that the absence of a choice of law clause in the contract demonstrated that neither party was prepared to accept the other's domestic law. Given such an implied negative choice, the Arbitral Tribunal was faced with three alternatives: to apply a neutral law, to adopt the *tronc commun* doctrine, or to choose a de-nationalised solution and apply generally accepted principles of law. After rejecting the first two solutions the first because it considered it artificial and arbitrary, the second because it would require lengthy comparative law research and might not lead to any conclusion the Arbitral Tribunal, by a majority, opted in favour of the third solution which it considered would fully maintain the equilibrium between the parties and respond to both parties' reasonable expectations. With express reference to ICC Award No. 7110, it decided to apply those general principles and rules of law applicable to international contractual obligations which qualify as rules of law and which have earned a wide acceptance and international consensus in the international business community, including notions which are said to form part of a *lex mercatoria*, also taking into account any relevant trade usages as well as the UNIDROIT Principles, as far as they can be considered to reflect generally accepted principles and rules.

In the Arbitral Tribunal's view the UNIDROIT Principles contain in essence a restatement of those *principes directeurs* that have enjoyed universal acceptance and, moreover, are at the heart of those most fundamental notions which have consistently been applied in arbitral practice.

However, it also pointed out that the UNIDROIT Principles have not as yet stood the test of detailed scrutiny in all their aspects so that some of their individual provisions might not reflect international consensus. It was for this reason that the Arbitral Tribunal was prepared to apply the UNIDROIT Principles only to the extent that they actually reflect generally accepted principles and rules.

On the merits of the case, the Arbitral Tribunal declared that it was not ready to make a final decision. Though admitting that general principles of law and the *lex mercatoria* were by their very nature too vague as to provide precise answers to the statute of limitations and that the UNIDROIT Principles did not contain any specific provisions dealing with the issue, the Arbitral Tribunal nevertheless invited the parties to submit their memorials on substance having regard to applicable general principles of law rather than to their sole domestic laws.

Full Text

Between 1971 and 1978, Defendant [...] sold to the Imperial Government of Iran or the Imperial Iranian Air Force certain air defense radar equipment under nine different contracts concluded during that period.

[...]

[...] In more detail, the Contracts obliged Defendant, or one of its wholly owned subsidiaries, to manufacture for and deliver to the Iranian buyers certain equipment [...].

[...]

Only Contract No. 1, *i.e.* Contract FE-34267 contained an arbitration clause, which reads as follows:

"All disputes arising out of or in relation to or in connection with this Agreement including termination for failure to deliver which cannot amicably be settled by discussion and mutual accord, shall be Aurally settled by arbitration at Zurich, Switzerland, in accordance with the rules then in effect of the International Chamber of Commerce [...]".

[...]

In the instant case [...] none of the Contracts contains a choice of law provision, and the determination of the applicable law is of a key importance, because of Defendant's contention that any and all of Claimant's claims are, since many years, time-barred, because of the four-year statute of limitation according to the laws of Maryland (which in its view is the law applicable to the dispute).

In contrast [...] Claimant argues that Iranian law must be applied to the substance of the dispute; its pre-revolution ten-year statute of limitations has been abandoned since the 1980s, such that Claimant's claims are still valid and not time-barred.

I. ARGUMENTS MADE BY CLAIMANT

Claimant made reference to Article 13(3) of the ICC Rules which provides that in the absence of any indication by the parties as to the applicable law, the arbitrator shall apply the law designated as the proper law by the rule of conflict which he deems appropriate.

Claimant explained [...] that Iranian law is the proper law governing the Contracts, because (i) all nine Contracts in dispute were concluded in Iran, (ii) their performance was most closely related to Iran, (iii) the Contracts were negotiated in Iran, (iv) the situs of the subject matter of all nine Contracts was/is Iran, and (v) finally the Contracts had their most significant connection to Iran.

[...]

[...] Claimant argued that the conflict rules of the Swiss Private International Law ("PIL") are not applicable to this case, because the fact that the Tribunal has its seat in Switzerland does not lead to an application of the conflict rules of Switzerland and, in particular, of Art. 187 PIL.

According to the conflict of law rule in Article 968 of the Iranian Civil Code, the law of the place of the conclusion of the transaction applies, except where both parties are foreign nationals. Since Defendant was well advised and had registered several companies in Iran, it must have been aware of that conflict of law rule, and nevertheless decided to enter into the Contracts in Iran. [...]

As an alternative to Iranian law, Claimant argued that the dispute should be decided according to general principles of law [...].

II. ARGUMENTS MADE BY DEFENDANT

Defendant, on the other hand, stressed that it would not have agreed to enter into the Contracts if they had to be made under Iranian law as the governing law and argued that the law of the state of Maryland is applicable to the merits of the dispute as being the law with the closest connection to the case.

To summarize, Defendant emphasized the strong links to Maryland and the United States in general, as being the locality of the Seller's place of business, as well as being the place of performance and delivery under each of the Contracts. Maryland, thus, is said to have the most significant connection to the case, wherefore its law must be applied to the merits of the dispute, including the issue of the statute of limitations.

Defendant, as an alternative, also argued that the Tribunal need not decide which law applies and whether the Iranian statute of limitations, if applicable, continue to be effective when applied to international arbitrations, for the following reason:

When the parties entered into Contract No. 1, they both understood and expected that claims would be precluded and time-barred after a maximum period of ten years, either under Iranian or Maryland law, because at that time, the Iranian statute of limitations was ten years and the one of Maryland four years.

Based on this, the fair and reasonable expectations of the Parties were that they would have to bring any claims within a maximum time-limit of ten years [...].

Defendant finally argued that, in view of the clear links to the law of a specific country (namely the law of Maryland), the Tribunal should not apply general principles of law to this arbitration, because this would not be based on the implicit will of the Parties [...].

III. DISCUSSION

First, the Tribunal remarks that, as a consequence of its determination regarding its arbitral jurisdiction [...] the applicable law will only have to be determined in respect of Contract No. 1. [...]

The Tribunal takes note of the fact that Contract No. 1 does not contain an express choice of law clause agreed on by the Parties.

Indeed, the absence of an express choice of law does not have the necessary consequence, in the opinion of this Tribunal, that the Parties could not have made an implied choice of law or, at least, impliedly intended to exclude the application of national legal systems. The contemplation of an implied choice by the Parties under Article 13(3) ICC Rules would be consistent with the interpretation of, *e.g.*, the UNCITRAL Arbitration Rules and the UNCITRAL Model Law (see HOLTZMANN/NEUHAUS, Guide to the UNCITRAL Model Law on International Commercial Arbitration, 778, 784).

[...]

(b) EXCURSUS: THE OBJECTIVE APPROACH

In the instant case, where the issue is to determine the law (or the rules of law) which are applicable to Contract No. 1, the objective approach would consist in applying the usual criteria for determining the substantive rules of law which are to govern a contract, *i.e.* by applying an appropriate conflict of laws rule, as provided for in Article 13(3) of the ICC Rules [...]

Thus, in proceeding under Article 13 (3), the arbitral tribunal is not bound to determine any particular (national) conflict of laws system [...], but - in the opposite - is only asked to select one (or more) conflict of laws rule(s) deemed "appropriate" [...].

In the following, three steps will have to be discussed:

The first step to be made now is to determine the "conflict rule" [...].

The conflict rule which, beyond doubt, has received, on an worldwide basis, the strongest support, is the so-called "closest connection rule" which indeed is common to most (national) conflict of laws system.

Most private international laws, as well as most arbitral awards, when aiming to determine the closest connection of a particular contractual relationship, attach a preponderant weight to the place of business or habitual residence of the Party which has to perform the so-called "characteristic performance" [...].

[...]

Some (few) countries attach a preponderant weight to the place where such characteristic performance has to be rendered (lex loci solutionis). This approach is mainly known in civil law countries influenced by French law traditions.

Only very few civil law countries, such as Spain and, until very recently, Italy (prior to the enactment of its new law in 1994), still seem to attach a preponderant importance to the place of the formation of a contract lex loci contractus). [...]. This, moreover, still seems to be the prevailing view under the Iranian Civil Code.

The above remarks suffice to indicate that, very clearly, the prevailing solution supported in international arbitration is the solution to use the closest connection as the relevant conflict rule under Article 13 (3) of the ICC Rules and, when applying such test to the instant case, to essentially determine the most characteristic performance which had to be rendered by one or the other Party pursuant to the Terms of Contract No. 1. In addition, the Tribunal will also take into account further connecting factors.

As the second step, we will now have to apply the closest connection test, [...]

The Contract No. 1 does not explicitly indicate the place where it had been signed; Claimant has alleged that the Contract had been signed in Teheran, but without clear substantiation in support of its allegation. Defendant contested that the Contract had been signed in Teheran, but also failed to substantiate more precisely the place of signing [...].

[...]

Not only Defendant's duty to manufacture the equipment was to take place in its own plants in Maryland, but also all further significant elements are located in Maryland, respectively in the United States, such as in particular the delivery of the equipment FAS (free alongside ship) at a US port at Defendant's choice. Moreover, acceptance was deemed to take place upon delivery in the USA.

The above analysis also reveals that Contract No. 1, as it is before the Arbitral Tribunal, does not contain any significant obligations of Defendant which would have had to be rendered outside Maryland [...].

However, even if Contract No. 1 had contained such elements of contractual duties to be performed in Iran, such elements would have to be weighed against the weight of contractual elements to be performed in Baltimore/USA, and only if, in an overall appreciation, a more preponderant weight had to be given to the performance in Iran would it be justified to conclude that the closest connection of Contract No. 1 (or its "centre of gravity") was located in Iran.

[...]

Conclusion to be drawn from this excursus:

All of these elements, therefore, very clearly indicate -in the opinion of the Majority Arbitrators- that, under the objective approach and the closest connection test, having regard to the characteristic performance and all other connecting factors, the centre of gravity of Contract No. 1 is, beyond doubt, located in Maryland/USA, wherefore the proper law of the Contract would be Defendant's national law, *i.e.* Maryland/US law.

(c) THE SUBJECTIVE APPROACH: IMPLIED NEGATIVE CHOICE

[...]

More particularly, regarding the present case:

It was not a contract between parties operating within the same environment and legal culture [...]

It was not a contract between parties that had a long history of dealing and cooperating together; it cannot be assumed that a very particular mutual confidence had already been in place while entering into Contract No. 1 [...];

It was not a contract concluded between equal parties (*e.g.* both being common city traders accustomed to respect the rules of their common trade), in the opposite;

It was not a contract containing extensive provisions, addressing all possible eventualities as could occur in the "runway" of performance under the contract [...];

In other words, if a contract such as Contract No. 1 does not contain a choice of law provision, then this must be viewed as a "shouting silence", at least an "alarming silence", "***un silence inquiétant***"; thus, a silence which must ring a bell and requires the Tribunal to look "behind" so as to understand why the Parties have failed to include "the obvious".

In this situation, a research into the history of Contract No. 1 could easily have clarified the situation, for instance if the Parties had been able to produce earlier drafts, working papers and internal memoranda on the contract negotiations, or if live witnesses had been available to testify on those negotiations in 1971. Most civil law countries accept that such materials can serve for interpretation purposes; compare also the interpretation rules of Article 4 UNIDROIT Principles (in particular Article 4.3). However, apparently due to the Iranian Revolution that material has either disappeared, or was destroyed, or has otherwise become unavailable to either one of the Parties. Thus, the Tribunal is left alone with the scarse evidence which is before it.

[...]

The Majority Arbitrators have no reason to doubt that, indeed, none of the Parties, when entering into Contract No. 1, would have been prepared to accept the other Party's national law.

[...]

Against this background, the absence of a choice of law clause must be understood as a so-called "*implied negative choice*" of the Parties [...] in the sense that none of the Parties' national laws should be imposed on any of the Parties.

[...]

The non-explicit - but implied - rejection by one Party of submitting itself to the other Party's national law (as the governing law of contract) is thus - in the opinion of the Majority Arbitrators - an implied term of contract.

In this sense, an interpretation of what had been agreed and what, perhaps even more significantly, had not been agreed upon in the Contract, provides a clear answer, although only a negative one in the above sense: The Contract should not, according to the implied negative choice of the Parties, be governed by any of the Parties' national laws.

[...]

(d) THREE POSSIBLE SOLUTIONS RESPECTING THE NEGATIVE CHOICE

So far, in the above discussion, the Majority Arbitrators have reached the decision that Contract No. 1 should not be subject to either Party's national law. Thus, the Tribunal will not apply Iranian law, nor will it apply US law or the law of Maryland.

What law or rules of law should then be applied? - Should the Tribunal elect to determine that the substantive law of a neutral country should apply, such as *e.g.* Swiss law (as a law which may seem to be "equally far away" from the Parties' national laws)?

Or should the Tribunal elect to follow RUBINO-SAMMARTANO's *tronc commun*-Doctrine which, essentially, proposes that the relationship should be "*governed at least by the part of the other and of his own legislation which is common to them. If the common part of the two legislations applies, is this solution not more satisfactory, since it is closer to the intention of the parties?*" (sc. closer than to apply a third legislation with which the parties are not familiar and which may contain regulations which may surprise them) [...] or should it rather elect to fully denationalize Contract No. 1 and determine that a-national or transnational rules of law and general principles of law will be applied, including rules that are said to form part of the *lex mercatoria*, and taking into account the UNIDROIT Principles promulgated in 1994, and trade usage?

(i) Choosing a Neutral Law?

Pro: This would be, as far as the Arbitrators are concerned, the easiest and most practical solution, because it will be relatively easy to deduct the answers to legal issues that cannot be determined by simply applying the terms of the contract. For instance, Swiss law (merely as an example) has very frequently been chosen simply for the sake of neutrality.

Contra: Swiss law, or indeed any other third country's national law, does not appear to have any natural connection with the case and, more importantly, does not seem to have been within the contemplation of the Parties concerned;

[...]

On balance: The Majority Arbitrators find that it would be entirely artificial and arbitrary to rule that a third neutral (national) law should apply. Any choice would be extremely critical. [...]

[...]

(ii) Adopting the "*Tronc Commun-Doctrine*"?

Prof. Rubino-Sammartano's approach sounds convincing in many respects. Indeed, parties cannot complain if treated as they are treated under their respective national laws, insofar as they coincide. The Doctrine thus assures the maximum common ground to which the parties are accustomed.

Contra: [...] Even more important is the observation that the doctrine gives no tangible answer how to deal with issues in respect of which the two national laws (here: Iran and US/Maryland) do not coincide. And indeed, this is clearly the case in respect of the immediately burning issue, *i.e.* the issue as to the statute of limitations.

On balance: The Majority Arbitrators, although basically sympathetic to the approach made by this Doctrine, must discard it here, because it will not provide the solution in respect of the statute of limitations and provides no direct answer to the legal regime that should control in case of divergent answers found in the two national laws.

(iii) Choosing a De-nationalized Solution?

Pro: This solution has the advantage to protect both Parties against the application of a national law which might contain particular provisions which they had not expected, and which may not be suitable in a truly international context of the present nature.

Freeing the Parties from the constraints of a national law thus would ascertain and warrant that the dispute shall be decided by having regard to those rules of law and notions which deserve to be qualified as being "generally accepted". Thus, a decision based on generally accepted principles has moreover the advantage to ascertain foreseeability of the outcome and certainty of law.

Contra: It is always a more difficult and more demanding task for a tribunal to decide a case by the only reference to, and guidance by, general principles of law, *lex mercatoria etc.*, instead of simply having regard and applying the solution as provided for in a particular national law, its case law and doctrine.[…]

On balance: The Tribunal, by majority vote, is of the opinion that, despite the difficulty referred to above under "contra", with which it will have to cope, the denationalization of the Contract No. 1 […]

The de-nationalization of the Contract at issue, therefore, is the solution which the Tribunal, in the opinion of the Majority Arbitrators, owes to both Parties.

It is at the same time the only solution which fully maintains the ***equilibrium*** between the Parties and responds to both Parties objectively fair and subjectively justified and reasonable expectations, discarding any ***pro domo*** arguments of the Parties in support of their respective cases.

Thus, the Tribunal will decide legal issues by having regard to the terms of the Contract and, where necessary or appropriate, by applying truly international standards as reflected in, and forming part of, the so-called "general principles of law"; the Tribunal will more clearly explain the meaning of this term under the Sub-Section letter (f) below.

[…]

(e) BRIEF REFERENCES TO ARBITRAL PRACTICE

Again, the Tribunal does not wish to refer extensively to other cases, because no other case would qualify as a "precedent". This Tribunal must reach, and in actual fact has reached, its decision independently of what other tribunals in the past may have considered and decided in somehow comparable situations. […]

[…]

(g) CONCLUSION: GENERAL PRINCIPLES (INCLUDING UNIDROIT PRINCIPLES) AS THE PROPER LAW OF CONTRACT

What should for the purpose of the present case be understood by such "general principles of law"

The Majority Arbitrators are aware that various terms are used, such as general principles of law, generally accepted principles of private law, a-national rules of law, transnational law rules, *lex mercatoria*, principles of international law *etc.* [...]

The Tribunal will apply those general principles and rules of law applicable to international contractual obligations which qualify as rules of law and which have earned a wide acceptance and international consensus in the international business community, including notions which are said to form part of a *lex mercatoria*, also taking into account any relevant trade usages as well as the UNIDROIT Principles, as far as they can be considered to reflect generally accepted principles and rules.

The Majority Arbitrators are of the opinion that these "General Principles of Law" (in the wide understanding as described above) are established in sufficiently concrete fashion so as to enable the Tribunal to adjudicate any and all issues as may arise in the framework of this arbitration.

[...]

As regards the reference to the UNIDROIT Principles [...] the Majority Arbitrators believe that these Principles, prepared by a working group established in 1981 and composed of leading experts and academics of all major legal systems, contain in essence a restatement of those 'principes directeurs' that have enjoyed universal acceptance and, moreover, are at the heart of those most fundamental notions which have consistently been applied in arbitral practice.

On the other hand, the UNIDROIT Principles, as now laid down, have not as yet, in all their details, stood the test of detailed scrutiny in all their aspects, and thus it is at least conceivable that a particular rule would not seem to reflect the international consensus; because of this concern, the Tribunal has added the qualification "*as far as they can be considered to reflect generally accepted principles and rules*" In this direction see the critical comments made by HILMAR RAESCHKE-KESSLER, The UNIDROIT Principles for International Commercial Contracts: A New *lex mercatoria*? in: ICC/Dossier of the Institute of International Business Law and Practice, 1995, 167 ss. who raises formal concerns that there are certain rules that differ from the principles and rules as reflected in the United Nations Sales Convention of 1980 and, possibly, also with the "Principles of European Contract Law" prepared by the "Commission on European Contract Law" chaired by Professor Ole LANDO (Denmark). He expressed the opinion that the United Nations Sales Convention "*already provides a rather complete set of rules on a lex mercatoria*" (at p. 174, with reference to the view expressed by DROBNIG in The American Journal of Comparative Law 1992, 635 ss.

Apart from the commentary contained in the UNIDROIT Principles, the Principles have been *inter alios* commented by MICHAEL JOACHIM BONELL (Chairman of the Working Group), An International Restatement of Contract Law [...]

The application by an arbitral tribunal of a-national legal rules, general principles of law and the *lex mercatoria* is recognized under the Swiss Arbitration Act (Chapter 12 PIL).

With reference to Article 26 of the ICC Rules, it may be stated that the Majority Arbitrators are not aware that, in connection with a potential enforcement of the Final Award against Defendant in the USA (or in European countries, where assets might exist), the *exequatur* could be refused on the ground that this Tribunal applied general principles of law and a-national rules of law, instead of applying a particular national law.

Finally, for clarification's sake, it should be stressed that this Tribunal, in proceedings on the basis as described above, will decide the case by applying the so-called "rule of law", and of course by respecting fully the terms of Contract No. 1.

In other words, the Tribunal does not interpret the implied negative choice of the Parties in the sense that they would, by their silence, have tacitly empowered this Tribunal to rule merely on the basis on the basis of "natural justice" or "fairness", or on an *ex aequo et bono* - basis; nor will the Arbitrators consider themselves authorized to act as *amiables compositeurs* (unless such further powers would, in the further course of the proceedings, be conferred to them explicitly with the consent of both Parties).

[...]

Sources

Original in English:
11 Measley's International Arbitration Report, 1996, A-1 – A-69.

Date: ***September 1996***
Adjudicating Court: ***ICC International Court of Arbitration, Zürich***
Number: ***8486***
Parties: ***Unknown***

Keywords

CONTRACT GOVERNED BY DOMESTIC LAW (DUTCH LAW) – ARBITRAL TRIBUNAL REFERENCE TO THE UNIDROIT PRINCIPLES AS THE PREVAILING VIEW IN THE FIELD OF INTERNATIONAL COMMERCIAL CONTRACTS

HARDSHIP – FUNDAMENTAL ALTERATION IN ORIGINAL CONTRACTUAL EQUILIBRIUM (ART. 6.258 DUTCH CIVIL CODE) (ART. 6.2.1 UNIDROIT PRINCIPLES)

Abstract

A Dutch and a Turkish party concluded a contract for the installation of a machine for the production of lump sugar. The law applicable to the contract was Dutch law. After the conclusion of the contract the Turkish buyer refused to pay the agreed amount of the advance payment, invoking financial difficulties due to a sudden drop in the market demand for lump sugar. After the parties' failure to agree on a revision of the contract, the Dutch seller declared the contract terminated and claimed damages from the Turkish buyer. In its defence, the latter invoked hardship under Art. 6.258 of the new Dutch Civil Code as grounds for relief.

In rejecting this argument, the Arbitral Tribunal stressed the exceptional character of hardship which required a fundamental alteration in the original contractual equilibrium, not a mere increase in the cost of performance as in the instant case. In confirmation of this conclusion, the Arbitral Tribunal referred not only to Art. 6.258 of the new Dutch Civil Code, which was the applicable law, but also to Art. 6.2.1 of the UNIDROIT Principles. The reference to the latter was justified by the argument that in applying Dutch law in an international context, attention should be given to the prevailing view in the field of international commercial contracts.

Full Text

[...]

La directive de l'article 6:258 est également applicable, bien que les parties aient décidé d'une réglementation spéciale au point 25 des conditions générales de vente à des "fins de décharge". D 'après l'article 6:250, les parties ne peuvent en effet pas s' écarter de cette directive du fait d'un accord entre elles; la norme constitue en ce sens un droit imperatif [...]. Les conditions de la directive ne sont toutefois pas remplies dans le cas présent. Il faut ici partir du principe que cette disposition ne doit être appliquée qu'avec beaucoup de prudence. Ceci se déduit d'une part du fait qu'il s'agit d'une réglementation spéciale donnant pouvoir général de considérer certaines dispositions contractuelles comme inapplicables en toute sincérité et équité ("*redelijkheid en billijkheid*"), selon l'article 6:248, alinéa 2, en relation avec l'article 3 :12 du Code civil néerlandais. (...) Ne serait-ce que dans la pratique juridique néerlandaise, cette disposition générale n'est appliquée qu 'avec une très grande prudence (...). La "conviction juridique valable aux Pays-Bas" es: déterminante en premier lieu, à ce titre, d'après l'article 3:12. En ce qui concerne l'application de l'article dans un contexte international, elle est remplacée par les convictions juridiques en vigueur dans le droit des contrats internationaux. Celles-ci sont toutefois fortement inspirées par le principe du respect du contrat ("*pacta sunt servanda*"), tel qù'il s'exprime par exemple à l'article 1.3 des Principes UNIDROIT applicables aux contrats commerciaux internationaux (voir UNIDROIT [éd.], Principles of International Commercial Contracts, 1994, p. 4. — V. également FOUCHARD, L'Arbitrage Commercial International, 1965, p. 442. — PAULSSON, La *Lex Mercatoria* dans l'arbitrage CCI: Rev. arb. 1990, p. 55, 82s. — Sentence arbitrale CCI n° 4972 dans: JARVIN/DERAINS/ARNALDEZ [éd.], Collection of JCC Arbitral Awards 1994, p. 380, 383. — Sentence arbitrale CCI n° 5485, Yearbook Commercial Arbitration 1989, p. 156, 168. —Sentence arbitrale CCI n° 5953, JDI 1990, p. 1056). Ces convictions juridiques doivent également être prises en compte lors de l'application d'un droit national à des faits internationaux (voir BERGER, Codification formalisée ou "rampante" du droit économique transnational, 1996, p. 174 s.). La nécessité et la validité de l'interpretation du droit national à la lumière des principes UNIDROIT est aussi spécialement défendue pour le droit néerlandais (KUIJER, Een vergelijking van "*hardship*" uit de UNIDROIT - regeling met de onvoorziene omstandigheden uit artikel 6 :258 van het BV, Ars Aequi 1996, p. 16,19).

Cette retenue dans l'application du droit s'impose lors de l'application de la norme spéciale de l'article 6:258, d'après la volonté du législateur néerlandais [...]. Cette retenue est à son tour en accord avec la pratique internationale en matière de contrats et d'arbitrage. Elle doit également être prise en compte dans le contexte du droit national néerlandais (voir KUIJER, *op. cit.*, p. 20). Ainsi, une résolution du contrat suite à la survenance de circonstances imprévisibles ("*hardship*", "*clausula rebus sic stantibus*") ne doit être acceptée que dans des cas exceptionnels extremês (Sentence arbitrale CCI n° 1512, reproduite dans: JARVIN/DERAINS [ed.], Collection of ICC Arbitral Awards, 1990, p. 3,4). Dans les relations économiques internationales, il faut plutôt partir du principe que les parties assument elles-mêmes les risques correspondants de l'exécution et de la satisfaction aux obligations du contrat, à moins qu'une répartition différente du risque n'ait été expressément stipulée dans le contrat lui-même (Sentence arbitrale CCI n° 1512, *op. cit.*). L'article 6.2.1 des Principes UNIDROIT constate lui aussi expressèment que le seul fait que l'exècution du contrat s'accompagne de difficultès accrues pour l'une des parties ne suffit pas pour l'acceptation d'une situation de "*hardship*" (voir UNIDROIT [éd., Principles of International Commercial Contracts, 1994, p. 145). Les principes de la CCI en matière de "force majeure et d'imprévision (*hardship*)" prévoient qu'ume partie ne peut pas invoquer le caractère inacceptable d'une prestation, pour la seule raison qu'il s 'avère que le contrat n'est plus rentable pour elle (publication C'CI n° 421, p. 22). En conséquence, un tribunal néerlandais a constatè qu' une baisse de prix dramatique, ainsi que les imparités de devises ne constituaient pas à elles seules des circonstances imprévisibles et qu'elles ne justifiaient donc pas la résolution du contrat. D'après le tribunal arbitral ces circonstances relevaient plutôt: du risque de la partie concernée (Sentence arbitrale *Ad Hoc* du 10 septembre 1975, Yearbook Commercial Arbitration

1977, p. 156, 158. — V. également la Sentence arbitrale CCI n° 3099, 3100, Yearbook Commercial Arbitration 1982, p. 87. — NASSAR, Sanctity of Contracts Revisited, 1995, p. 205).

[...]

Sources

Original in German:
Journal de droit international, 1998, 1047-1049, with note by Y. DERAINS.
ICC International Court of Arbitration Bulletin, Vol. 10, No. 2, Fall 1999, 69-71.

Date: ***September 4, 1996***
Adjudicating Court: ***ICC International Court of Arbitration, Paris***
Number: ***8540***
Parties: ***Unknown***

Keywords

CONTRACT GOVERNED BY THE LAW OF THE STATE OF NEW YORK – REFERENCE BY ARBITRAL TRIBUNAL TO UNIDROIT PRINCIPLES AS USEFUL SOURCE FOR ESTABLISHING GENERAL RULES FOR INTERNATIONAL COMMERCIAL CONTRACTS

AGREEMENT TO NEGOTIATE IN GOOD FAITH – TO BE CONSIDERED ENFORCEABLE UNDER THE LAW OF THE STATE OF NEW YORK – SOLUTION CONFIRMED BY GENERAL PRINCIPLES OF LAW AS REFLECTED IN UNIDROIT PRINCIPLES (ARTS. 1.1, 1.3, 1.7, 2.15 [2.1.15 OF THE 2004 EDITION] UNIDROIT PRINCIPLES)

Abstract

A supplier of telecommunications systems in the United States (claimant) and a Middle Eastern manufacturer of telecommunications cables (defendant) entered into a pre-bid agreement whereby the parties undertook to negotiate in good faith for the supply of cables in the event that claimant's bid to become prime contractor for a telecommunications expansion project succeeded. Claimant secured the entire contract but after a series of fruitless negotiations terminated the preliminary agreement on the ground that the parties were unable to conclude the contemplated final agreements.

In the absence of any choice of law clause, while claimant invoked the law of Saudi-Arabia or that of England or that of Georgia as the applicable law, defendant invoked the law of the State of New York or that of New Jersey and, in addition, requested the Arbitral Tribunal to apply the UNIDROIT Principles as evidencing general principles of international commercial contracts.

The Arbitral Tribunal admitted that international arbitrators were fully justified in turning to general principles of law which may present some advantage over the selection of one of many competing municipal systems of law with no compelling connecting factors, but in the case at hand it decided in favour of the law of the State of New York as the applicable law.

The Arbitral Tribunal also referred to the UNIDROIT Principles, defined as a useful source for establishing general rules for international commercial contracts, in order to demonstrate that the conclusion it had reached under the law of the State of New York with respect to the issue at stake, *i.e.*, the enforceability of the parties' agreement to negotiate in good faith, was also confirmed by the general principles of law as reflected in the UNIDROIT Principles (in particular Arts. 1.1, 1.3, 1.7 and 2.15 [2.1.15 of the 2004 edition]).

On the basis of its findings, the Arbitral Tribunal ordered the parties to promptly resume negotiations with a view to reaching an agreement on the supply of cables within the parameters set forth in the preliminary agreement.

Full Text

A. INTRODUCTION

Having concluded that the Parties intended to obligate themselves to cooperate in good faith and, upon award of any cable related contract in connection with , to meet promptly and negotiate in good faith supply and service agreements, the Tribunal must now determine whether such an obligation is enforceable under the law applicable to the merits of the dispute.

The position of the Claimant on this question is succinctly set out in the introduction to the relevant section of the 'Post-Hearing Brief'. "The obligation to negotiate in good faith is unenforceable under any of the laws that might be applied to the - English; Saudi Arabia, Georgia, New York or New Jersey."

The Defendant, for its part, urges the Tribunal to reject the application of English or Saudi law, it being common ground between the Parties that an obligation to negotiate in good faith is unenforceable under the former, whereas application of the latter would result in the being void. The Defendant further submits that the Parties' obligation to negotiate in good faith, is enforceable under the laws of Georgia, New York or New Jersey; subsidiarily, invites the Tribunal to apply the Principles of International Commercial Contracts (the "UNIDROIT Principles"), under which, the Defendant submits, the Parties' express contractual commitment to negotiate in good faith is clearly enforceable.

B. APPLICABLE LAW

The Parties did not make an express or implied choice of a specific municipal system of law governing the . As stated earlier in this award, shortly after it was constituted, the Tribunal was seized of the Defendant's Application for Determination of the Proper Law. This preliminary Application was dealt with in the Tribunal's Order No. 1, wherein we indicated that we would not decide the proper law of the in limine lids, since we wanted to give full opportunity to the Parties "to present and argue their case on the intent and meaning of all provisions of the , relevant to the present arbitration . . ." The Tribunal referred specifically to paragraphs (3) and (5) of Article 13 of the ICC Rules which, we opined, "mandate the Tribunal not to decide the applicable law until sufficient evidence has been introduced to enable the Arbitrators to understand fully the terms of the contract". Thus, we remained seized of the Application and the question of the applicable law now has to be determined.

According to Mr. the question of the governing law of the was explicitly discussed albeit not in any great detail, between Mr. and himself during the course of the August 1993 negotiations in Georgia. Mr. told the Tribunal that he proposed as the governing law the law of a State of the United States, either New York or New Jersey. Mr. added that Mr. was unwilling to accept a governing law of the United States and wanted Saudi law to govern the contract. Mr., being unfamiliar with Saudi law, refused. In light of their disagreement, according to Mr's evidence, Mr. suggested that no governing law be specified in the. The evidence of Mr. on this question is that there was never any discussion of governing law between him and Mr. Given that the is silent as to the applicable law, the Tribunal looks to Article 13(3) of the ICC Rules, which the Parties have expressly adopted. Art. 13(3) reads as follows:
(3) The parties shall be free to determine the law to be applied by the Arbitrator to the merits of the dispute. In the absence of any indication by the parties as to the applicable law, the Arbitrator shall apply the law designated as the proper law by the rules of conflict which he deems appropriate.

As regards selection of the appropriate conflict rules, the Defendant submitted in its Application for Determination of the Proper Law that "the accepted choice of law rule" in contract cases is "the law of the place with which the contract and the dispute has its most significant connection." In its Reply Memorandum, the Defendant asserted that the "generally accepted centre of gravity, balancing of the contacts, test" is "consistent with the conflict of law rules of most jurisdictions."

for its part, submits that the Tribunal should apply, either separately or collectively, English conflict of laws rules or generally accepted international conflict of laws principles. In Claimant's Post-Hearing Brief, counsel for refer to the "country having the most decisive connection with the PBA". The Kingdom of Saudi Arabia, the United States of America and, as the contractually designated seat of the arbitration, England, all have significant connections to the and the disputes referred to arbitration. In agreeing to submit their disputes to ICC arbitration, and have expressed the intention that their agreement, as interpreted by the Tribunal, should be given full effect. Art. 13(5) of the ICC Rules is an expression and confirmation of this intention. It reads as follows:
(5) In all cases, the arbitrator shall take account of the provisions of the contract and the relevant trade usage.

In view of the Parties' intention in that regard, we are of the opinion that this Tribunal cannot designate as the proper law a system of law under which there would be found a legal nullity, or one under which the 's key obligation would be, found to be unenforceable. Stated otherwise, art. 13(5) operates, in our opinion, as an implied negative choice of such a system of law. The Tribunal has already concluded that the Parties have obligated themselves to meet promptly and negotiate in good faith mutually satisfactory supply and service agreements. In our view, the Parties could not have intended that the governing law of the would render this contractual obligation unenforceable. This can be seen in a different context by Judge Leval in Tribune, a decision applying New York law which we discuss below.

It is, of course, the aim of contract law to gratify, not to defeat, expectations that arise out of intended contractual agreement. In the circumstances, neither the law of Saudi Arabia nor the law of England can, in our opinion, be designated as the proper law of the . In any event, neither England, as the lcr foci, nor Saudi Arabia, even though the relates to a project located in that country, have decisively stronger connections with the in the dispute than the U.S. jurisdictions mentioned below.

In their able arguments, the Parties have drawn our attention to a multitude of connecting factors leading to a number of legal systems. As between the three U.S. jurisdictions with which the , and the dispute have some connections, none of these connecting factors taken individually, nor all of them taken collectively, create a link of such intensity that the selection of one of these legal systems would readily impose itself. Moreover, the Parties, in their respective arguments, in effect agree that there is an absence of "clear pointers" to a single jurisdiction with which characteristic performance of the Parties' obligations can be linked. In order to determine the applicable law, we shall mention some of the connecting factors to which we have been referred by both Parties and which we consider relevant.

There are some important connections with the State of New Jersey. Negotiations of the contract , after 6 August 1993, took place in that State. The contract was signed in New Jersey by and, prior to the addition of paragraph 3(g), by as well. As regards contacts with the State of Georgia, we note that the initial negotiations of the in August 1993 were conducted in that State. Furthermore, a significant part of the negotiations contemplated by the contract was conducted in Georgia, in 1994.

In so far as the State of New York is concerned, we do not view as particularly significant the fact that Mr. approved the change to paragraph 3(g) from a hotel room in New York City. We do consider highly relevant, however, the fact that the Non-Disclosure Agreement which was signed by the Parties at the inception of the discussions concerning the on 4 August 1993 contains a choice of law clause in favour of the law of New York, including the statement, in paragraph 8, that "the parties are familiar with the principles of New York commercial law, and desire and agree that the law of New York shall apply in any dispute arising with respect to this Agreement." We note the following explicit reference to this Non-Disclosure Agreement in paragraph 4 of the contract:

4. Information. The Parties shall share such information as they, deem to be mutually beneficial in carrying out the purposes of this Agreement. Such information may include marketing or other proprietary information requiring protection against disclosure to unauthorized persons. Such proprietary information may also include data, and other technical, financial and business information. The Parties acknowledge and agree that such information shall be covered by the Non-Disclosure Agreement between dated 4 August 1993.

Thus, the Parties, in effect, have already made the law of New York applicable to part of the . Disclosure of proprietary information covered by paragraph 4 of the might constitute a breach of the Non-Disclosure Agreement, and give rise to a dispute thereunder to which the law of New York would apply pursuant to the above quoted choice of law clause. We consider relevant to our analysis, as well, the fact that, as appears from the contract itself, is a corporation organized under the laws of the State of New York. On balance, and, as already stated, while none of these three U.S. jurisdictions readily imposes itself, the Tribunal finds that the applicable law of the is the law of the State of New York.

C. General Principles of Law

Because of the acknowledged difficulty in finding a municipal system of law with which the is most closely connected, the Defendant invited the Tribunal to apply the UNIDROIT Principles. The Claimant, for its part, resisted the application of "general principles of law" to the present case.

In an international commercial transaction such as this contract between and, where the Parties have not indicated the applicable law and where there are many disparate connections to many different municipal systems of law, we are of the opinion that international arbitrators are fully justified to turn to general principles of law.

The choice of these general principles in such circumstances, may present some advantages over the selection of one of many municipal systems of law where none of the connecting factors is compelling. Having found, however, after due consideration of the complete record, that the applicable law of the is the law of the State of New York, we decided to look to general principles only to compare the conclusion which results from the application of the proper law with the conclusion that would be obtained were the Tribunal to apply these general principles. In determining the content of these general principles, we feel entirely justified in referring to the UNIDROIT Principles which we consider a useful source for establishing general rules for international commercial contracts.

D. THE ENFORCEABILITY OF THE PARTIES' OBLIGATION TO NEGOTIATE IN GOOD FAITH UNDER THE PROPER LAW AND UNDER GENERAL PRINCIPLES OF LAW

We have reviewed carefully the evidence of the learned American jurists produced as expert witnesses by the Parties on the issue of the enforceability of contractual obligations to negotiate in good faith. We have consulted the decisions of American Courts to which we have been referred by counsel, particularly those that apply New York law. In these decisions, we note that the following are among the principal factors relevant in determining whether or not a preliminary agreement is binding: the circumstances surrounding the negotiations of the agreement, the conduct of the parties and, of course, the terms of the agreement, including the number and significance of open terms. A distinction also emerges from American cases between so-called "naked covenants" and "more complex" agreements such as the PBA.

In the present case, we have determined that, in executing the, the Parties intended to contract legally binding obligations, including the obligation to negotiate in good faith. As Judge Leval wrote in the Tribune case:

Notwithstanding the importance of protecting negotiating parties from involuntary judicially imposed contracts, it is equally important that courts enforce and preserve agreements that were intended as binding, despite a need for further documentation or further negotiation. It is, of course, the aim of contract law to gratify, not to defeat, expectations that arise out of intended contractual agreement, despite informality or the need for further proceedings between the parties.

The legal experts we heard all acknowledge that Tribune is an important precedent under the law of the State of New York on the subject of preliminary agreements. In the opinion of Professor PERILLO, Tribune is "a very significant case, (...) significant because the reasoning it employed has come to be regarded as the controlling case on the issue under

New York law." In Tribune, the Court wrote that preliminary contracts can be of at least two distinct types. In the first type, the parties have reached complete agreement (including agreement on the binding nature of their commitment) on all issues requiring negotiation. All that remains to be done is for the parties to formalize their agreement. As Judge Leval observes, such agreements are preliminary only in form. Judge Leval describes the second type of preliminary contracts as follows:

The second and different sort of preliminary binding agreement is one that expresses mutual commitment to a contract on agreed major terms, while recognizing the existence of open terms that 'remain to be negotiated'. Although the existence of open terms generally suggests that a binding agreement has not been reached, that is not necessarily so. For the parties can bind themselves to a concededly incomplete agreement in the sense that they accept a mutual commitment to negotiate in good faith and to reach final agreement within the scope that has been settled in the preliminary agreement.

Judge Leval has this to say with respect to the obligation to negotiate in good faith which arises (often implicitly) out of such an agreement:

This obligation does not guarantee that the final contract will be concluded if both parties comport with their obligation, as good faith differences in the negotiation of the open issues may prevent a reaching of final contract. It is also possible that the parties will lose interest as circumstances change and will 'mutually abandon the negotiation'. The obligation does, however, bar a party from renouncing the deal, abandoning the negotiations, or insisting on conditions that do not conform to the preliminary agreement.

We find this reasoning both compelling and appropriate. Having reviewed the evidence of all legal experts on the applicable law as well as the cases we consider relevant, we have come to the conclusion that, under the law of the State of New York, the Parties' express obligation to negotiate in good faith is enforceable. The application of general principles of law as applied to international commercial contracts would lead us to the same conclusion. Under general principles of law, as reflected in the UNIDROIT Principles, the Parties are free to determine the content of their contract (Article 1.1). Consequently, they are free to undertake that they will negotiate in good faith. In the absence of any cause invalidating their agreement (as set out in Chapter 3 of the Principles), this agreement is binding on the Parties (Article 1.3).

We accept, as a sound interpretation of the pertinent Articles on this subject, the opinion of Professor FARNSWORTH who stated:

Plainly, although the Principles impose a duty of good faith on negotiating parties quite apart from agreement, it would be inconsistent with the Principles to hold an agreement to negotiate to be unenforceable.

The and specifically the undertaking to negotiate in good faith stipulated in it, would thus be valid, binding and enforceable under general principles of law as reflected in the UNIDROIT Principles. We find in these general principles a confirmation of the conclusion which we have reached by applying the law of the State of New York, which we have ruled to be the applicable law of the contract.

Sources

White & Case International Dispute Resolution, Vol. 10, March 1997, 3.

Date: ***September 27, 1996***   *Adjudicating Court:* ***ICC International Court of Arbitration, Paris***   *Number:* ***8261***   *Parties:* ***Unknown***

Keywords

CONTRACT SILENT AS TO APPLICABLE LAW – ARBITRAL TRIBUNAL DECISION TO APPLY LEX MERCATORIA – REFERENCE TO INDIVIDUAL PROVISIONS OF THE UNIDROIT PRINCIPLES: 4.8 ("SUPPLYING OMITTED TERMS"); 4.6 ("CONTRA PROFERENTEM RULE"); 7.4.1 ("RIGHT TO DAMAGES"); 7.4.7 ("HARM DUE IN PART TO AGGRIEVED PARTY"); 7.4.13 ("AGREED PAYMENT FOR NON-PERFORMANCE")

Abstract

An Italian company and a government agency of a Middle Eastern country entered into a contract. The contract did not contain any choice of law clause, because both parties had insisted on the application of their own national law.

In a previous partial award on the question of the applicable law, the Arbitral Tribunal had declared that it would base its decision on the terms of the contract, supplemented by general principles of trade as embodied in the *lex mercatoria.* Subsequently, when dealing with the merits of the dispute, it referred, without further explanation, to individual provisions of the UNIDROIT Principles, thereby implicitly considering the latter a source of the *lex mercatoria.*

Thus, apart from another partial award on some preliminary questions of substance in which it referred to Arts. 4.8 ("*Supplying omitted terms*") and 4.6 ("*Contra proferentem rule*"), in its final award the Arbitral Tribunal invoked Arts. 7.4.1 ("*Right to damages*"), 7.4.7 ("*Harm due in part to aggrieved party*") and 7.4.13 ("*Agreed payment for non-performance*") in support of its reasoning.

Full Text

[Not yet available]

Sources

Unpublished. Notice of the award kindly given by Prof. Ignz SEIDL-HOHENFELDERN.

Date: ***October 23, 1996***
Country: ***France***
Adjudicating Court: ***Cour d'appel de Grenoble***
Number: ***Unknown***
Parties: ***SCEA GAEC Des Beauches Bernard Bruno v. Société Teso Ten Elsen GmbH & COKG***

Keywords

JURISDICTION - 1968 BRUSSELS CONVENTION – BUYER'S CLAIM FOR RESTITUTION OF PRICE PAID IN EXCESS – JURISDICTION OF COURT OF THE BUYER'S PLACE OF BUSINESS

CONTRACT GOVERNED BY CISG – PLACE OF PAYMENT OF PRICE – SELLER'S PLACE OF BUSINESS (ART. 57(1)(A) CISG) – EXPRESSION OF A GENERAL PRINCIPLE UNDERLYING CISG PURSUANT TO WHICH OBLIGATIONS TO PAY MUST BE PERFORMED AT THE PLACE OF BUSINESS OF THE CREDITOR – REFERENCE TO THE SAME GENERAL PRINCIPLE CONTAINED IN ART. 6.1.6 UNIDROIT PRINCIPLES

PLACE OF PERFORMANCE OF THE OBLIGATION TO REIMBURSE THE PRICE PAID IN EXCESS – BUYER'S PLACE OF BUSINESS

Abstract

A French buyer and a German seller concluded a contract for the sale of industrial equipment. After delivery of the goods, the buyer commenced an action against the seller claiming restitution of a part of the purchase price paid in excess. The seller objected on the ground that the French Court had no jurisdiction to hear the case.

The Court applied Art. 5(1) of the EC Convention on Jurisdiction and the Enforcement of Judgments in Civil and Commercial Matters (Brussels 1968), pursuant to which a person domiciled in a Contracting State (in the case at hand: that of the seller) may be sued in the Court for the place of performance of the obligation in question (in the case at hand: restitution of price paid in excess). The Court applied French private international law rules and held that French law and therefore CISG (Art.1(1)(b) CISG), was the applicable law to determine the place of performance of the obligation in question. The Court held that since a claim for restitution of a surplus paid is a demand for payment, restitution must be made at the buyer's place of business in accordance with Art. 57(1)(a) CISG, pursuant to which the price must be paid at the seller's place of business.

As a matter of fact the rule set forth in Art. 57 CISG is an expression of the general principle that obligations to payment are to be performed at the creditor's place of business. This general principle, in addition to being set out by CISG, has also been stated in general terms with respect to all kinds of international commercial contracts by Art. 6.1.6 of the UNIDROIT Principles of International Commercial Contracts. The Court therefore affirmed its jurisdiction.

Full Text

[...]

I - COMPETENCE

Attendu que la societé TESO TEN, intimée, domiciliée en Allemagne, conclut à l'incompétence des juridictions françaises au moyen que le contrat contient une clause d'élection de for en faveur du Tribunal de Snsbeck, Allemagne;

Qu'elle fait valoir ceci:

'Attendu qu'il résulte des écritures de la SCEA que cette dernière fait valoir contre TEN ELSEN une demande de restitution partielle du prix d'une installation fournie par TEN ELSEN à la SCEA qui exploite un élevage industriel dans la région de Valence, Attendu que la compétence judiciaire dans la Communauté Européenne est réglée par la Convention de Bruxelles du 27 septembre 1968, Attendu que cette convention fixe des compétences de droit commun et des compétences dérogatoires et spéciales, Attendu que la Convention de Bruxelles consacre le principe de l'autonomie de la volonté, Attendu que l'article 17 de la convention dispose:

'Prorogation de compétence

Article 17

Si les parties, dont l'une au moins à son domicile sur le territoire d'un Etat contractant, sont convenues d'un tribunal ou de tribunaux d'un Etat contractant pour connaître des différends nés ou à naître à l'occasion d'un rapport de droit déterminé, ce tribunal ou les tribunaux de cet Etat sont seuls compétents. Cette convention attributive de juridiction est conclue: (a) par écrit ou verbalement avec confirmation écrite, soit (b) sous une forme qui soit conforme aux habitudes que les parties ont établies entre elles, soit (c) dans le commerce international, sous une forme qui soit conforme à un usage dont les parties avaient connaissance ou étaient censées avoir connaissance et qui est largement connu et régulièrement observé dans ce type de commerce par les parties à des contrats du même type dans la branche commerciale considérée',

Attendu qu'en l'espèce la commande a été passée sur papier en tête TEN ELSEN contenant au dos une clause de compétence au profit de l'intimée,

Qu'une confirmation de commande reprenant cette clause a été adressée le 09 mai 1990 avec référence aux conditions générales de TEN ELSEN à la SCEA,

Que le crédit documentaire établi fait référence à la confirmation de commande,

Que les factures proforma et les CMR établies font référence à la confirmation de commande,

Attendu que les conditions générales de TEN ELSEN prévoient 'le Tribunal compétent et le lieu d'exécution du contrat sont fixés à Sonsbeck pour nos clients commerçants',

Attendu que le droit allemand et le droit français prohibent en effet en droit interne procédural une clause de compétence stipulée à l'encontre d'un non commerçant,

Attendu qu'en matière internationale cette prohibition est écartée, que la clause de compétence, dont s'agit, doit trouver son application,

Qu'il échet de renvoyer la SCEA GAEC des Beauches à se pourvoir devant la Chambre Civile du Tribunal de Grande Instance de Kleve (RFA), (*cf.* sur l'application de l'article 17 *cf.* Arrêt de la Cour de Céans du 28 novembre 1989 (KROENERT/FASSON),

Attendu que l'exception d'incompétence se fonde également sur les dispositions de droit commun de la Convention de Bruxelles,

Attendu que l'article 2 prévoit la compétence de principe de la juridiction du défendeur: en l'espèce la juridiction allemande,

Attendu que l'article 5 prévoit en matière contractuelle les dispositions suivantes:

'Le défendeur domicilié sur le territoire d'un Etat contractant peut être attrait dans un autre Etat contractant: 1: en matière contractuelle, devant le Tribunal du lieu ou l'obligation qui sert de base à la demande a été ou doit être exécutée',

Attendu qu'en l'espèce la demande de la SCEA est une demande en paiement d'une dette au demeurant contestée, que l'obligation éventuelle de payer s'exécute au siège du débiteur qu'en effet les dettes sont quérables tant en droit français qu'en droit allemand,

Que dans ces conditions il échet de renvoyer la SCEA à mieux se pourvoir devant le Tribunal du débiteur éventuel, en l'espèce le Tribunal de Grande Instance de Kleve, (*cf.* en ce sens: Cour d'Appel de Montpellier, 2Ý Ch. A 14 septembre 1989 KRETZCHMER/FAUS DURA, Cour d'Appel de Paris 1Ý Ch. 29 mars 1989 HUPPMANN HANDEL/KHAWAM, confirmé par 1Ý Ch. Civile Cour de Cassation du 20 novembre 1990),

Attendu que l'exception d'incompétence invoquée par TEN ELSEN est recevable devant la Cour d'Appel de céans, que TEN ELSEN n'a pas comparu en première instance et est recevable à soulever l'incompétence en appel in limine litis,

Attendu que la Cour infirmera la décision entreprise en ce que le Tribunal de Valence s'est déclaré compétent, recevra la société TEN ELSEN en son exception d'incompétence fondée sur la Convention de Bruxelles du 27 septembre 1968, articles 17-2 et 5, Réformera le jugement entrepris et renverra la SCEA à se pourvoir devant le Tribunal de Grande Instance de Kleve';

Attendu que, sur la clause attributive de compétence, la SCEA Les Beauches fait valoir ceci: '1 - Conditions de validité de la clause: Les conditions de validité requises par l'article 17 sont rigoureuses:

'Un écrit ne suffit pas, il faut également que sa place dans les relations contractuelles ne laisse aucun doute sur la volonté des parties de consentir: les clauses établies au verso du contrat ne sont pas valables, pas plus que les renvois indirects à un document contenant la clause (Jurisprudence Salotti) (*cf.* Jurisclasseur Procédure Civile Fasc. 52-2 p. 25 nÝ 66)',

La Cour de Justice a exigé que la clause attributive soit l'objet d'une acceptation écrite de l'acheteur (affaire Segoura c. Bonakdarian), 'La nouvelle rédaction de l'article 17 al. 1 ne concerne que les conventions de for conclues par des commerçants, Les personnes étrangères au monde des affaires devront se conformer à l'exigence d'un écrit ou d'une confirmation écrite d'un accord verbal telle qu'elle a été interprétée par la Cour de Justice, Il en est de même pour les actes mixtes passés entre commerçant et non commerçant (*cf.* Jurisclasseur Procédure Civile Fasc. 52-2 p. 26 n 68),

En l'espèce, la SCEA DES BEAUCHES dont le représentant légal ne sait ni lire ni écrire l'allemand n'a pas eu connaissance de l'existence de la clause portée en caractère minuscule en allemand, au verso de la confirmation de commande non signée par l'acheteur,

La SCEA DES BEAUCHES n'a pas donné son accord écrit sur la clause attributive de compétence dont elle ignorait l'existence, La SCEA DES BEAUCHES n'est pas commerçante,

La clause attributive de compétence doit être écartée comme ne répondant pas aux conditions de l'article 17 de la convention,

2 - Sur l'inopposabilité de la clause

Si, par impossible, la Cour considérait que la clause est valable, elle resterait inopposable à la SCEA DES BEAUCHES, Aux dires mêmes de la société TEN ELSEN, cette clause n'a vocation à s'appliquer qu'entre commerçants,

La société TEN ELSEN indique en page 3 de ses conclusions: 'Le Tribunal compétent et le lieu d'exécution du contrat sont fixés à Sonsbeck pour nos clients commerçants',

La traduction partielle et sans valeur probante communiquée par la société TEN ELSEN (pièce adverse nÝ 11) fait référence aux clients commerçants,

La SCEA DES BEAUCHES n'a pas le statut de commerçant, c'est une société à caractère civil,

La clause d'attribution de compétence lui est inopposable,

La sociéte TEN ELSEN ne peut étendre une clause attributive de compétence prévue entre commerçants à des non commerçants,

Elle ne peut procéder à une interprétation extensive de cette clause,

Sous réserve d'une traduction officielle, la clause alléguée ne souffre d'aucune interprétation,

Si une interprétation devait être faite, elle devrait l'être contre la société TEN ELSEN qui a stipulé (art. 1162 du Code Civil),

En tout état de cause, la clause invoquée par la société TEN ELSEN est inopposable à la SCEA DES BEAUCHES qui n'est pas commerçante,

3 - Sur la compétence de la juridiction française.

La compétence de la juridiction doit s'apprécier au regard des dispositions de la Convention de Bruxelles et de la Convention de Vienne,

L'article 5-1 de la Convention de Bruxelles n'est pas applicable en l'espèce,

Le fondement de la demande de la SCEA DES BEAUCHES est la restitution de l'indu,

Ce fondement revêt un caractère extra contractuel,

Il conviendrait de faire application de l'article 5-3 qui donne compétence à la Juridiction du lieu où le dommage est survenu ou le lieu de l'évènement causal (le paiement indu) en l'espèce en France,

Si par impossible, la Cour considérait qu'il convient de retenir le caractère contractuel en raison de la nature du litige qui repose sur les problèmes d'étendue de l'obligation de paiement et de détermination du prix, la juridiction française resterait compétente';

SUR CE:

Attendu, sur la validité de la clause attributive de compétence, que la commande du 26 avril 1990 ne comporte pas de clause attributive de juridiction, ni de renvoi à des conditions générales;

Que le renvoi aux conditions générales n'apparaît que dans la confirmation de commande du 09 mai 1990 adressée par la société TEN au SCEA LES BEAUCHES;

Qu'il est ainsi formulé 'nous vous remercions pour la commande que vous nous avez passée et la confirmons sur la base de nos conditions générales au verso comme suit:';

Que la confirmation de commande n'est pas signée du SCEA; Que la commande et les autres correspondances échangées entre les parties sont écrites en Français;

Que les conditions générales sont écrites en langue allemande, en petits caractères grisés;

Qu'elles sont illisibles à l'oeil nu;

Que pour les besoins du procès la société TEN a dû présenter à la Cour une photocopie agrandie;

Attendu que l'absence de lisibilité de la clause et sa rédaction en langue allemande alors que pour le déroulement normal de son activité sur le marché français la société TEN s'oblige à utiliser la langue française, démontre que la société TEN n'a pas recueilli le consentement du SCEA LES BEAUCHES et tente de lui imposer par surprise une clause à laquelle, elle n'a pas consenti;

Que, faute d'accord des parties, la clause n'a pas de valeur contractuelle:

Qu'en outre, même si la clause était valide au sens de l'article 17 de la Convention de Bruxelles, elle serait privée d'efficacité à l'encontre du SCEA LES BEAUCHES qui n'a pas la qualité de commerçant;

Que s'il est exact que l'article 17 de la Convention de Bruxelles autorise les accords de compétence entre non commerçants, il n'interdit pas aux parties de les limiter aux seuls commerçants;

Que tel est le cas de la clause litigieuse ainsi rédigée: 'Pour nos clients commerciaux qui ne relèvent pas des professionnels énumérés par le paragraphe 4 du Code de Commerce allemand, le lieu de juridiction et d'exécution de la prestation est SONSBECK, même pour les personnes morales de droit public';

Que les conclusions de la société TEN indiquent implicitement qu'un Agriculteur n'est pas un commerçant en droit allemand;

Attendu, en conséquence, que la juridiction de SONSBECK ne saurait être imposée au SCEA LES BEAUCHES;

Attendu, sur la compétence du Tribunal de Valence par application de l'article 5-1 de la Convention de Bruxelles;

Que la société TEN écrit dans ses conclusions que 'la demande de la SCEA est une demande en paiement au demeurant contestée, que l'obligation éventuelle de payer s'exécute au siège du débiteur, qu'en effet les dettes sont quérables tant en droit française qu'en droit allemand';

Mais que, ainsi que l'a conclu la société TEN 'la compétence de la juridiction doit s'apprécier en regard des dispositions de la Convention de Bruxelles et de la Convention de Vienne';

Que la Convention de Vienne du 11 avril 1980 sur les contrats de vente internationale de marchandises régit le contrat, en l'absence d'autre loi choisie par les parties, par l'effet de son article l.l.b;

Que la France était partie à cet instrument dès son entrée en vigueur le 1er janvier 1988 et que le droit français était applicable au contrat en l'absence de choix de loi invoqué par les parties, conformément à l'article 3 alinéa 2 de la Convention de la Haye du 15 juin 1955 expressément invoqué par la SCEA LES BEAUCHES;

Qu'en effet la commande a été reçue en France où s'était déplacé un représentant du vendeur;

Que depuis le 1er janvier 1988, le droit français de la vente internationale de marchandises est constitué par la Convention de Vienne;

Que, contrairement aux droits allemand et français, la Convention de Vienne fixe le lieu du paiement du prix de vente à l'établissement du vendeur (article 57-l);

Que l'interprétation habituellement donnée de cette règle est qu'elle exprime le principe général que le paiement s'exécute au domicile du créancier (*cf.* MASKOW dans BIANCA et BONELL, article 57, 3-2 et *Oberlandsgericht Düsseldorf* 2 juillet 1993 UNILEX, D.1993-21) étendu aux autres contrats du commerce international par l'article 6.1.6 des Principes d'UNIDROIT ('lorsque le lieu d'exécution de l'obligation n'est pas fixé par le contrat ou déterminable en vue de celui-ci, l'exécution s'effectue: ... pour une obligation de somme d'argent au lieu d'établissement du créancier');

Que l'action du SCEA LES BEAUCHES vise à obtenir le remboursement d'un trop perçu; Qu'il est constant entre les parties qu'il s'agit d'une demande en paiement; Que le lieu d'exécution de l'obligation litigieuse est le ressort du Tribunal de Grande Instance de Valence où la SCEA est établi;

Qu'il s'ensuit que par application de l'article 5.1 de la Convention de Bruxelles la Cour de ce siège est compétente pour statuer sur l'action dirigée par la SCEA LES BEAUCHES contre la société TESO TEN;

II - FOND DU LITIGE

Attendu, sur le fond, que la SCEA LES BEAUCHES expose ceci:

'La SCEA DES BEAUCHES, anciennement GAEC DES BEAUCHES est propriétaire de deux bâtiments agricoles qu'elle souhaite aménager pour l'élevage de poussins en batteries,

Elle commande le matériel d'aménagement et d'équipement des bâtiments à la société allemande TEN ELSEN par l'intermédiaire de son représentant en France, Monsieur Christian NIGI, Gérant de la SARL BATAVI,

Par deux lettres des 25 et 26 avril 1990, la société TEN ELSEN établit un devis indiquant le matériel fourni, le prix du matériel pour chaque bâtiment valable trois mois, le cout du transport du matériel, les modalités de paiement, les délais de livraison,

Le 09 mai 1990, la société TEN ELSEN adresse à la SCEA DES BEAUCHES un document confirmant le devis initial,

[...]

Sources

Original in French:
Unpublished.

Source:
Mr. Le Juge Jean-Paul BERAUDO, Cour d'Appel de Grenoble, France.

Date: **November 1996**
Adjudicating Court: **ICC International Court of Arbitration, Paris**
Number: **8502**
Parties: **Unknown**

Keywords

CONTRACT SILENT AS TO APPLICABLE LAW – PARTIES' REFERENCE TO INCOTERMS 1990 AND UCP 500 – ARBITRAL TRIBUNAL'S INFERENCE OF PARTIES' INTENTION THAT CONTRACT BE GOVERNED BY TRADE USAGES AND GENERALLY ACCEPTED PRINCIPLES OF INTERNATIONAL TRADE – REFERENCE TO THE 1980 UNITED NATIONS CONVENTION ON CONTRACTS FOR THE SALE OF GOODS (CISG) AND THE UNIDROIT PRINCIPLES AS EVIDENCING ADMITTED PRACTICES UNDER INTERNATIONAL TRADE LAW

DETERMINATION OF DAMAGES – DIFFERENCE BETWEEN CONTRACT PRICE AND MARKET PRICE AT TIME OF TERMINATION (ART. 76 CISG; ART. 7.4.6. UNIDROIT PRINCIPLES)

Abstract

A Vietnamese seller and a Dutch buyer (acting through a French company as its agent) entered into a contract for the supply of rice. The contract did not contain a choice of law clause, but did provide for the application of the INCOTERMS 1990 (with respect to the price) and of the Uniform Customs and Practice for Documentary Credits (UCP) 500 (with respect to *force majeure*).

In the Arbitral Tribunal's view, the reference to both the INCOTERMS and the UCP indicated the parties' intent that their contract be governed by trade usages and generally accepted principles of international trade. It therefore decided to apply, with respect to the issues not regulated by either INCOTERMS or the UCP, the 1980 United Nations Convention on Contracts for the International Sale of Goods (CISG) and the UNIDROIT Principles, as evidencing admitted practices under international trade law.

Thus, with respect to the determination of the amount of damages, the Arbitral Tribunal referred to both Art. 76 CISG and Art. 7.4.6 of the UNIDROIT Principles in order to award claimants the difference between the contract price and the market price at the time the contract was terminated.

Full Text

[...]

The Contract concluded between the Parties, and upon which the present proceeding is based, is silent as to the law to be applied on the merits. There is, accordingly, no express choice of law clause. Similarly, having regard to the correspondence exchanged between the Parties, the Arbitral tribunal is of the opinion that no implied choice of law can be inferred from the relationship between the Parties.

The Contract, as well as the present arbitration, involve, on the one hand, a Vietnamese seller and, on the other hand, a Dutch buyer acting through its French company. The place of arbitration is Paris, France.

This dispute has connections with several national laws, all of which may have a relevant role. Under Article 13(3) of the ICC Rules, the Arbitral Tribunal shall apply the law designated by the rule of conflict which it deems appropriate.

[...]

Although the Contract contains no choice of law clause, it refers to international trade usages. Article 6 of the Contract, with respect to the price to be paid by the buyer, provides that INCOTERMS 1990 shall apply. Similarly, Article 13 of the Contract stipulates, as regards force majeure, that the clause of UCP 500 shall apply.

It thus appears that the Parties have, to a large extent, agreed to submit their relationship to recognized trade usages such as the INCOTERMS or the Uniform Customs and Practice for Documentary Credits (UCP), published by the ICC. The Arbitral Tribunal considers that by referring to both the INCOTERMS and the UCP 500 the Parties showed their willingness to have their Contract governed by international trade usages and customs.

The application of the relevant trade usages is consistent with Article 13(5) of the ICC Rules and with the arbitral practice [...].

For the foregoing reasons, the Arbitral Tribunal finds that it shall decide the present case by applying to the Contract entered into between the Parties trade usages and generally accepted principles of international trade. In particular, the Arbitral Tribunal shall refer, when required by the circumstances, to the provisions of the 1980 Vienna Convention on Contracts for the International Sale of Goods (Vienna Sales Convention) or to the Principles of International Commercial Contracts enacted by UNIDROIT, as evidencing admitted practices under international trade law.

The Arbitral Tribunal found that the Respondent failed to comply with its obligations under the Contract and that said failure was not legally justified. It now remains to calculate the amount of compensation due to the Claimants caused by the Respondent's default.

As regards the applicable law on the question of compensation, the Arbitral Tribunal, as previously mentioned, considers that the Parties have expressed their mutual intention to have their relationship governed by general principles of international trade.

The INCOTERMS 1990 or the UCP 500, to which reference is made in the Contract, contain no provision regarding the effect of the failure by one party to fulfil its obligations under the Contract.

The Arbitral Tribunal considers that this question should be examined in light of generally admitted principles of international trade as contained for example in international treaties. For this reason, the Arbitral Tribunal is of the opinion that the principles embodied in the Vienna Convention on the International Sale of Goods of 1980 (Vienna Sales Convention) reflect widely accepted trade usages and commercial rules. Although the Vienna Sales Convention is not as such directly applicable to the Contract (Vietnam has not ratified this Convention), the Arbitral Tribunal finds that it may refer to its provisions as the expression of usages in the world of international commerce [...]

Article 76 of the Vienna Sales Convention reads as follows:

"(1) If the contract is avoided and there is a current price for the goods, the party claiming damages may, if he has not made a purchase or resale under Article 75, recover the difference between the price fixed by the contract and the current price at the time of avoidance as well as any further damages recoverable under Article 74 [...]
(2) For the purposes of the preceding paragraph, the current price is the price prevailing at the place where delivery of the goods should have been made or, if there is no current price at that place, the price at such other place as serves as a reasonable substitute, making due allowance for differences in the cost of transporting the goods."

[...]

Finally, the Arbitral Tribunal shall refer to the work of the International Institute for the Unification of Private Law (UNIDROIT). Article 7.4.6 of the UNIDROIT Principles of International Commercial Contracts provides :
"Where the aggrieved party has terminated the contract and has not made a replacement transaction but there is a current price for the performance contracted for, it may recover the difference between the contract price and the price current at the time the contract is terminated as well as damages for any further harm".

Current price is the price generally charged for goods delivered or services rendered in comparable circumstances at the place where the contract should have been performed or, if there is no current price at that place, the current price at such other place that appears reasonable to take as a reference.

Based on these applicable principles of law, the Claimants are entitled to damages calculated as the difference between the contract price and the relevant market price. The contract price is easily determined by the contractual provisions agreed upon by the Parties, which include the initial Contract and its amendment [...]

With respect to the determination of the relevant market price, two issues must be addressed. One needs first determine the reference time at which the market price is calculated, and the place of reference [...]

It results from the foregoing analysis that, unless a current price is not available, damages should be calculated with reference to the market price at the place where delivery of the goods should have been made. In the present case, the goods being sold FOB Ho Chi

Minh City port, the place of delivery of the goods for the purposes of this provision is Ho Chi Minh City.

[...]

Sources

Original in English (excerpt):
ICC International Court of Arbitration Bulletin, Vol. 10, No. 2, Fall 1999, 72 – 74.

Date: ***November 17, 1996***
Adjudicating Court: ***Arbitration Court of the Hungarian Chamber of Commerce and Industry***
Number: ***Unknown***
Parties: ***Unknown***

Keywords

RATE OF INTEREST – STATUTORY RATE OF DEBTOR'S STATE MUCH HIGHER THAN STATUTORY RATE OF STATE OF CURRENCY OF PAYMENT – INFLATION RATE IN THE LATTER STATE MUCH LOWER THAN IN THE FORMER – RATE OF INTEREST OF THE LATTER APPLIED (ART. 7.4.9(2) UNIDROIT PRINCIPLES)

Abstract

The dispute concerned a sales contract between an Austrian and a Hungarian company. One of the issues to be decided was the rate of interest to be applied. Since the rate of inflation in Austria at that time was approximately 3% as compared to more than 20% in Hungary, the Court decided to disregard Art. 301(1) of the Hungarian Civil Code which fixes the statutory interest rate at 20% and instead applied the Austrian statutory rate of interest as the rate of the State of the currency of payment. In support of its solution, the Court did not expressly refer to Art. 7.9.4(2) of the UNIDROIT Principles, but cited a note by P. SCHLECHTRIEM on two arbitral awards in which this provision was applied.

Full Text

[Not yet available]

Date: ***December 1996***
Adjudicating Court: ***ICC International Court of Arbitration, Paris***
Number: ***8331***
Parties: ***Unknown***

Keywords

ARBITRAL TRIBUNAL REQUESTED BY PARTIES TO APPLY THE UNIDROIT PRINCIPLES TO THE EXTENT THAT THE ARBITRAL TRIBUNAL CONSIDERS IT NECESSARY AND APPROPRIATE

ALL CONTRACTUAL TERMS TO BE GIVEN EFFECT (ART. 4.5 UNIDROIT PRINCIPLES)

DUTY OF BEST EFFORTS (ART. 5.4(2) [5.1.4(2) OF THE 2004 EDITION] UNIDROIT PRINCIPLES)

Abstract

The case concerned a Memorandum of Understanding whereby the parties committed themselves to conclude a contract for the sale of trucks and of spare parts and, in addition, indicated in general terms their intention to come to an agreement for the setting up of an assembly plant for the production of the same type of trucks in the buyer's country. While the sales contract was actually concluded, the seller refused to enter into negotiations for the setting up of the envisaged assembly plant arguing that the buyer lacked the necessary business organisation for such a project.

The Terms of Reference provided that the arbitral tribunal should base its decision on the agreement between the parties and, to the extent it considered it necessary and appropriate, the UNIDROIT Principles.

In its decision the Arbitral Tribunal applied in particular two provisions of the UNIDROIT Principles: Article 4.5 in order to conclude that the Memorandum of Understanding was to be given effect in its entirety and not only as concerned the part relating to the conclusion of the sales contract, and Article 5.4(2) [5.1.4(2) of the 2004 edition] in order to conclude that the parties' declared intention to enter into negotiations with a view to reaching an agreement for the setting up of an assembly plant entailed a duty to make best efforts to achieve that result. According to the Arbitral Tribunal the seller, by refusing to start negotiations, breached this duty, and its argument that the buyer lacked the necessary business organisation did not constitute a valid excuse.

Full Text

[...] The parties have agreed that the Arbitral Tribunal shall apply the relevant agreements between the parties and, to the extent that the Arbitral Tribunal finds it necessary and appropriate, the UNIDROIT Principles of International Commercial Contracts of May 1994 shall be applied by the Arbitral Tribunal.

The MOU is not a binding Contract but has the character of a letter of intent in which the parties agree to consider to carry out some projects. [...] Claimant does not deny that the parties have concluded an agreement, called MOU, that the parties are bound to negotiate in order to try to come to a final agreement on the different projects of the MOU, but asserts definitely that the MOU does not bind the parties to execute the same projects

[...]

Respondent considers the MOU to be its basic agreement with Claimant regarding a vast project for the assembly and the manufacturing of Claimant trucks.

[...]

Article 2.13 of UNIDROIT general provisions confirms that the MOU was a binding agreement between the parties and what has been left are secondary little matters to be clarified by the parties in further discussions. The binding character of the MOU should be found in the two parties' common intention (Art. 4.1 of UNIDROIT). Such intention was clearly expressed in the various parts of the MOU. As an example, the confidentiality provided for in paragraph 6 of the MOU was binding on them and according to Article 5.1 of UNIDROIT Claimant's contractual obligations need not be expressly mentioned.

The implied obligations of Claimant in the MOU according to Article 5.2 of UNIDROIT derive from the nature of the Agreement, the good faith and fair dealing and reasonableness.

In that respect, Claimant has not respected the principle of good faith in dealing with its obligations.

[...]

Whereas the Arbitral Tribunal, in order to set forth the rules according to which it will examine the contentions of the parties regarding the various items of the MOU and their effects on the relations between the parties has examined the text of the MOU in light of Article 4.5 of UNIDROIT "Principles of International Commercial Contracts" together with the comments thereon published by the International Institute for the Unification of Private Law, "UNIDROIT-Rome".

Whereas the MOU contains two kinds of provisions, the first of which defines specific conditions and terms that are the result of the parties' agreement and consequently are to be considered as final obligations between them unless they are amended by subsequent contracts approved by the parties; the second one being a general description of the parties' intention to enter into certain agreements.

[...]

Whereas the Arbitral Tribunal considers that when the parties agree upon general issues to be implemented by them at a later stage they cannot be released from their obligations to use their best efforts to ensure that such general issues become specific terms of contracts to be executed by the parties.

The Arbitral Tribunal, having considered paragraph 2 of Article 5.4 of UNIDROIT "Principles of International Commercial Contracts", rules that the general description of the parties' intentions to reach agreements on certain issues contained in the MOU obligates the parties to exert their best efforts in order to have such intentions become defined terms of Contracts legally binding for each of them.

[...]

Whereas the Claimant has been in breach of its obligations to exert its best efforts in respect of forming [...] and establishing with the Respondent the assembly of Claimant vehicles in Iran. Whereas the damages suffered by the Respondent in that respect may not be accurately determined due to the fact that they relate to assumptions on what would have been the benefit for the Respondent [...] The Arbitral Tribunal, after due consideration of Articles 7.4.3 and 7.4.9 of UNIDROIT Principles of International Commercial Contracts, rules that the Claimant should compensate the Respondent for the loss of the chance to enjoy the probable benefits of the two aborted projects mentioned above by bearing an amount of [...] US Dollars to be deducted from the Performance Guarantee amount of [..] US Dollars already cashed by the Respondent. The balance to be reimbursed by the Respondent to the Claimant, in Sweden, amounts to [...] US Dollars together with accrued simple interest at a rate which — due to the absence of any prime rate in dollars in Sweden — shall be the prime rate in dollars prevailing in the United States on [date of payment of Performance Guarantee] and as subsequently modified from time to time until the effective date of payment.

Sources

Original in English (excerpt):
Journal de droit international, 1998, 1041, with note by Y. DERAINS.
ICC International Court of Arbitration Bulletin, Vol. 10, No. 2, Fall 1999, 65-68.

Date: ***December 1996***
Adjudicating Court: ***ICC International Court of Arbitration, Zürich***
Number: ***8769***
Parties: ***Unknown***

Keywords

PARTIES' CHOICE OF DOMESTIC LAW (FRENCH LAW) TOGETHER WITH THE 1980 UNITED NATIONS CONVENTION ON CONTRACTS FOR THE INTERNATIONAL SALE OF GOODS (CISG) AS LAW GOVERNING THEIR CONTRACT

INTEREST RATE NOT DETERMINED BY CISG (ART. 78 CISG) – REFERENCE BY ARBITRAL TRIBUNAL TO ART. 7.4.9(2) OF THE UNIDROIT PRINCIPLES IN SUPPORT OF APPLICATION OF COMMERCIALLY REASONABLE RATE

Abstract

A French and an Austrian company entered into a manufacturing contract. The contract provided for the application of French law and the 1980 Vienna Convention on Contracts for the International Sale of Goods (CISG).

A dispute arose, and in awarding interest the sole arbitrator pointed out that Art. 78 CISG does not specify the applicable rate. The sole arbitrator therefore decided to apply an interest rate that he deemed commercially reasonable, *i.e.* the interest rate of the currency in which damages had to be paid (Austrian schillings), and in support of his finding he referred with no further explanation to Art. 7.4.9(2) of the UNIDROIT Principles.

Full Text

[...] Claimant claims interest at the French statutory rate from [...]

Respondent claims interest at 10.5 % on [...] since [...]

Claimant is entitled to interest on the sums awarded pursuant to Art. 78 of the Vienna Convention. Art. 78 Vienna Convention does not specify a particular interest rate. The sole Arbitrator considers it appropriate to apply a commercially reasonable interest rate (see Art. 7.4.9. subs. 2 UNIDROIT Principles). The interest rate claimed is commercially reasonable for the award currency; Austrian schillings.

On [...], the date from which Respondent claims interest, the Agreement had been terminated. The sums claimed were due in the sense of Art. 78 Vienna Convention.

Accordingly, interest is awarded to Respondent as claimed.

Sources

Original in English (excerpt):
ICC International Court of Arbitration Bulletin, Vol. 10, No. 2, Fall 1999, 75.

Date: **December 1996**
Adjudicating Court: **ICC International Court of Arbitration, Paris**
Number: **8874**
Parties: **Unknown**

Keywords

ARBITRAL TRIBUNAL AUTHORISED BY PARTIES TO ACT AS AMIABLE COMPOSITEUR

INTEREST RATE – REFERENCE TO UNIDROIT PRINCIPLES WITHOUT FURTHER EXPLANATION

Abstract

A United Kingdom and a Belorussian company entered into an advertisement contract. A dispute arose because of an alleged failure by the Belorussian company to pay the contract price. The contract authorised the Arbitral Tribunal to act as amiable compositeur and to decide the dispute according to principles of equity.

In deciding in favour of Claimant, the Arbitral Tribunal remarked that the contractually agreed rate of interest of 1.4 % per month was excessively high. It decided instead to apply the rate usually put in practice in these matters, and concluded in the case at hand for the application of the United States prime rate. In doing so, it referred without further explanation to the UNIDROIT Principles in general.

Full Text

[...]

The payment of interest, in case of delay, is contractual (Art. 1.2 of the Contract) and has been accepted, as such, by both parties.

The existence of such an increased amount, in the case of delays in settling payments, is above discussion: it is a cornerstone of economic and commercial relations. Therefore, the principle of Respondent having to pay not only the contractual amount of [...] but interest, based on time elapsed since the agreed initial date of payment, cannot be discussed and must be reaffirmed [...].

The rate of interest is determined by the Contract. Therefore it is considered as accepted by both parties. However, with the powers of *amiable compositeur,* I wish to make the following remarks:

Respondent's situation, since the fire, is difficult and mutual understanding should lead to take it into account. They certainly have improperly dealt with the consequences of the event and they will have to fulfil their contractual engagements, which they did not formally propose to resiliate [sic]. Later, this silence to the legitimate questions raised by Claimant is surely not acceptable in the spirit of good commercial relations. But they were— and probably still! are — confronted with a major accident with important direct and secondary effects.

They warned — even if the manner was neither formal nor strictly rightful — their counterpart, which acknowledged the new situation. Respondent even showed what can be interpreted as a token of good faith in offering [...] as an indemnity.

The contractual interest rate is fixed at a level which is considerably higher than the rates which are usually put in practice in these matters, such as the US Prime Rate, recommended by the Principles of UNIDROIT.

In deciding a case "according to the principles of equity", my view is that the initial contractual interest rate, if applied to the considered amount and period of time, would be disproportionate with the economic and commercial conditions of this case. I therefore substitute the US Prime Rate to the initial contractual rate of 1.4 % per month, for the delayed payment owed to Claimant by Respondent.

Sources

Original in English (excerpt):
ICC International Court of Arbitration Bulletin, Vol. 10, No. 2, Fall 1999, 82-83.

Date: ***December 1, 1996***
Adjudicating Court: ***Camera Arbitrale Nazionale ed Internazionale di Milano***
Number: ***A-1795/51***
Parties: ***Unknown***

Keywords

CONTRACT SILENT AS TO APPLICABLE LAW – AGREEMENT BY PARTIES TO SETTLE THEIR DISPUTE IN CONFORMITY WITH THE UNIDROIT PRINCIPLES – TEMPERED BY RECOURSE TO EQUITY

CONTRACT OF COMMERCIAL AGENCY – BINDING UPON PARTIES (ART. 1.3 UNIDROIT PRINCIPLES)

PARTY'S WRITTEN DECLARATION – INTERPRETED AS NOTICE OF TERMINATION (ARTS. 4.1 AND 4.2 UNIDROIT PRINCIPLES)

EXCLUSION OF THE RIGHT TO TERMINATE THE CONTRACT FOR AN EVENT ON THE OCCURRENCE OF WHICH PARTIES HAD AGREED TO RENEGOTIATE THE CONTRACT (ART. 7.3.1 UNIDROIT PRINCIPLES)

TERMINATION – CONTRACT TERM INTENDED TO TAKE EFFECT AFTER TERMINATION (ART. 7.3.5 UNIDROIT PRINCIPLES)

DAMAGES – FULL COMPENSATION OF THE HARM SUSTAINED (ARTS. 7.4.1 AND 7.4.2 UNIDROIT PRINCIPLES) – DOES NOT INCLUDE EMOTIONAL SUFFERING AND DISTRESS WHEN AGGRIEVED PARTY IS A CORPORATE ENTITY

DAMAGES – COMPENSATION LIMITED TO FORESEEABLE HARM ARISING OUT OF NON-PERFORMANCE (ARTS. 7.4.3 – 7.4.4 UNIDROIT PRINCIPLES)

INTEREST – RUNNING FROM THE TIME WHEN PAYMENT IS DUE (ART. 7.4.9 UNIDROIT PRINCIPLES)

INTEREST – INTEREST RATE FIXED BY THE PARTIES (ART. 7.4.13 UNIDROIT PRINCIPLES)

Abstract

An Italian and a United States company entered into a contract of commercial agency. The principal terminated the contract due to non-performance by the agent. The agent commenced arbitral proceedings invoking unlawful termination by the principal and claiming damages.

The contract did not contain a choice of law clause, but at the outset of the arbitral proceeding the parties agreed that the dispute would be settled in conformity with the UNIDROIT Principles tempered by recourse to equity.

In its decision, the Arbitral Tribunal applied a number of individual articles of the UNIDROIT Principles, in some cases even invoking the accompanying Comments. In particular, it cited to Articles 1.3 in order to affirm the binding character of the parties' original agreement; 4.1 and 4.2 in order to interpret a party's written declaration as a notice of termination; 7.3.1 in order to exclude the right to terminate the contract for an event with respect to which the parties had made express provision for the renegotiation of the contract should it occur; 7.3.5 in order to confirm the validity of a contract term which, in the event of termination, expressly grants to the principal the right to restitution of promotional material and to the agent the right to a commission for orders so far received; 7.4.1 and 7.4.2 in order to affirm the aggrieved party's right to full compensation for the harm it sustained as a result of the other party's non-performance but to exclude compensation for emotional suffering and distress, the aggrieved party being a corporate entity; 7.4.3 and 7.4.4 in order to exclude compensation for the costs incurred by the aggrieved party for the purchase of a house in the place where the contract was to be performed; 7.4.9 to grant, as a last resort, interest at the statutory rate fixed by the law of the State of the currency of payment; 7.4.13 in order to uphold a contract term providing for a higher rate of interest for the delay in the payment of certain specific debts.

Full Text

[Not yet available]

Sources

Original in Italian:
Unpublished.
Notice of the award kindly given by Avv. Giorgio SCHIAVONI, Vice-President of the Court.

Date: **December 4, 1996**
Adjudicating Court: **Ad Hoc Arbitration, Rome**
Number: **Unknown**
Parties: **Unknown**

Keywords

PARTIES' CHOICE OF DOMESTIC LAW (ITALIAN LAW) AS LAW GOVERNING THE CONTRACT – ARBITRAL TRIBUNAL DUTY TO TAKE INTO ACCOUNT "... TRADE USAGES" (ART. 834 ITALIAN CODE OF CIVIL PROCEDURE) – REFERENCE TO THE UNIDROIT PRINCIPLES AS A PARAMETER OF THE PRINCIPLES AND USAGES OF INTERNATIONAL TRADE

VALID CONCLUSION OF CONTRACT - EVEN WITHOUT ASCERTAINABLE SEQUENCE OF OFFER AND ACCEPTANCE (ARTS. 1.2, 2.1, 2.6, 2.12 [ARTS. 2.1.1, 2.1.6 AND 2.1.12 OF THE 2004 EDITION] UNIDROIT PRINCIPLES)

AVOIDANCE FOR MISTAKE (ARTS. 3.4 AND 3.5 UNIDROIT PRINCIPLES) OR FRAUD (ART. 3.8 UNIDROIT PRINCIPLES)

GOOD FAITH – ART. 1.7 UNIDROIT PRINCIPLES TO CONFIRM DUTY OF THE PARTIES THROUGHOUT THE CONTRACT

DAMAGES – REFERENCE TO ARTS. 7.4.1 7.4.5, 7.4.7 7.4.9 AND 7.4.12 UNIDROIT PRINCIPLES IN DETERMINATION OF DAMAGES

Abstract

An English and an Italian company concluded a contract for the sale of fuel oil. The contract contained an express reference to Italian law as the law governing the contract.

In view of the fact that, according to Art. 834 of the Italian Code of Civil Procedure, in an international arbitration the Arbitral Tribunal is required to take into account the terms of the contract and the trade usages, the Arbitral Tribunal repeatedly referred to the UNIDROIT Principles, which it defined as a parameter of the principles and usages of international trade in order to prove that the solutions provided by Italian law were in conformity with international standards.

In particular, Arts. 1.2, 2.1, 2.6 and 2.12 [Arts. 2.1.1, 2.1.6 and 2.1.12 of the 2004 edition] were cited to demonstrate the possibility of the valid conclusion of a contract even without an ascertainable sequence of offer and acceptance; Arts. 3.4, 3.5 and 3.8 with respect to the extent to which a party may avoid the contract for mistake or fraud; Art. 1.7 to demonstrate the duty of the parties to act in good faith throughout the life of the contract; and Arts. 7.4.1 7.4.5, 7.4.7 7.4.9 and 7.4.12 for the determination of damages.

Full Text

[...]

Come è noto, nel caso di arbitrato internazionale — categoria nella quale è certamente da comprendere la pretesa procedura, avendo una delle parti sede all'estero (cfr. art. 832 c.p.c.) — ai fini della validità della clausola compromissoria contenuta in condizioni generali di contratto è sufficiente che la clausola sia "contenuta in condizioni generali che siano recepite in un accordo scritto delle parti, purché le parti abbiano avuto conoscenza della clausola o avrebbero dovuto conoscerla usando l'ordinaria diligenza" (art. 833 c.p.c.); inoltre "le parti hanno facoltà di stabilire d'accordo tra loro le norme che gli arbitri debbono applicare al merito della controversia oppure di disporre che gli arbitri pronuncino secondo equità. Se le parti non provvedono, si applica la legge con la quale il rapporto è più strettamente collegato. In entrambi i casi gli arbitri tengono conto delle indicazioni del contratto o degli usi del commercio" (art. 834 c.p.c.).

Concludendo sul punto, il Collegio ritiene che la presente procedura sia da qualificare come arbitrato rituale di diritto, regolato dalla legge italiana; fermo restando che, in conformità al disposto dell'art. 834, u.c., c.p.c., sopra ricordato, gli Arbitri "tengono conto delle indicazioni del contratto e degli usi del commercio"; il che lo si anticipa fin d'ora, non conduce comunque a conclusioni diverse rispetto a quelle derivanti dall'applicazione delle norme del codice civile nell'ambito delle quali va ricondotta la fattispecie.

[...]

7. *L'intervenuta conclusione del contratto il 1° marzo 1995.*

Da tutto ciò deriva, ad avviso del Collegio a maggioranza, che in data 1° marzo 1995 il contratto di compravendita si è regolarmente concluso, a seguito della proposta articolata nei messaggi via fax in quella data di MS e della conseguente e conforme accettazione di ENEL, il tutto in conformità con la prassi negoziale del settore già nota a Child ed Evers e seguita nei rapporti con ENEL anche nelle precedenti occasioni nelle quali questi, alle dipendenze di soggetti diversi da MS, conclusero contratti di fornitura con ENEL

[...]

A conclusioni identiche si perverrebbe comunque anche riconducendo la fattispecie ai principi e agli usi del commercio internazionale; in coerenza con il disposto dell'art. 843 u.c. c.p.c., il Collegio si è dato carico di esaminare la problematica secondo i parametri di recente elaborazione dettati in materia (cfr. Principi UNIDROIT), secondo i quali, come è noto, un contratto validamente concluso è vincolante per le parti e la prova della conclusione può esser data con ogni mezzo, compresi i testimoni (art. 1.2); ciascuna parte deve agire in conformità alla buona fede nel commento internazionale (art. 1.7); il contratto può essere concluso sia con l'accettazione dell'offerta, sia con un comportamento delle parti che dimostri con sufficiente certezza il raggiungimento dell'accordo (art. 2.1); una dichiarazione od altro comportamento tenuto dal destinatario dell'offerta indicante il suo consenso costituisce accettazione e l'accettazione produce effetto dal momento in cui il consenso perviene al proponente; se in virtù della offerta o in conseguenza delle pratiche che le parti hanno instaurato tra loro o degli usi, il destinatario della offerta può manifestare il suo consenso compiendo un atto, l'accettazione produce effetto nel momento del compimento dell'atto (art. 2.6); se entro un periodo di tempo ragionevole dopo la conclusione del contratto viene spedita una lettera di conferma con clausole aggiuntive queste divengono parte del contratto (art. 2.12); l'errore è un erroneo convincimento relativo alla situazione di fatto o di diritto esistente al momento della conclusione del contratto e può costituire causa di annullamento del contratto solo nel caso in cui sia ditale importanza che una persona ragionevole, nella stessa situazione della parte in errore, avrebbe concluso il contratto a condizioni differenti o non lo avrebbe concluso e l'altra parte sia intercorsa nello stesso errore o lo conosceva o non ha agito con correttezza; in ogni caso una parte non può annullare il contratto se è stata in colpa grave nel commettere l'errore (art. 3.4. e 3.5); una parte può annullare il contratto quando sia stata indotta a concluderlo dall'inganno della controparte, attuato anche con parole o comportamenti o nascondendo dolosamente alla parte stessa circostanze che in base ai criteri ordinari di correttezza nel commento avrebbe dovuto comunicarle (art. 3.8). A fronte di quanto sopra si è detto in ordine alle risultanze probatorie, è da escludere che il comportamento di MS sia qualificabile come doloso, così come è da escludere che i funzionari ENEL siano incorsi in errore secondo i parametri appena indicati.

Occorre tener conto, nella valutazione del comportamento delle parti, della particolare qualità dei soggetti coinvolti nella vicenda, tutti funzionari di alto livello specializzati nella compravendita di prodotti petroliferi e quindi certamente in grado, per competenza professionale e tecnica e pratica negoziale, di percepire e valutare compiutamente i termini di trattative come quella intercorsa [...].

Il contratto dunque è stato concluso il 1° marzo e nei giorni successivi entrambe le parti hanno svolto attività esecutive, culminate nella conferma d'ordine del 16 marzo, documento di dirimente rilevanza anche in relazione a quanto si dirà infra sul comportamento tenuto dalle parti in sede esecutiva; del pari dovrà tenersi conto della prassi negoziale, della pratica del commercio internazionale (e dei principi in quell'ambito elaborati) e degli usi, oltre che delle regole codicistiche in materia ed anche della qualità dei soggetti coinvolti nella vicenda, ai fini, della valutazione del comportamento delle parti nell'esecuzione del contratto.

8. *Il comportamento delle parti nell'esecuzione del contratto: in particolare, il comportamento di Morgan Stanley rispetto al grado di diligenza richiesto.*

[...]

In altri termini, i doveri di buona fede e correttezza e di diligenza nell'adempimento — quali risultano recepiti e codificati nel nostro ordinamento, ma anche dei principi del commercio internazionale e quali risultano comunque avvertiti nella pratica corrente e negli usi — in relazione all'entità dell'affare ed alla qualità e qualificazione dei soggetti coinvolti, avrebbe dovuto indurre i funzionari MS a percepire la rilevanza della questione classificatoria del prodotto, in funzione della predisposizione della documentazione formale di accompagnamento della merce.

[...]

I principi che sotto questo profilo paiono applicabili al caso, sono quelli, generalissimi, di buona fede e correttezza e di diligenza nell'adempimento; la disciplina internazionale (si veda il richiamo ai Principi UNIDROIT di cui sopra) trova puntuale corrispondenza in quella stabilita nel nostro ordinamento: il debitore e il creditore devono comportarsi secondo le regole della correttezza (art. 1175 c.c.); nell'adempiere l'obbligazione il debitore deve usare la diligenza del buon padre di famiglia (art. 1176 c.c.); il contratto deve essere eseguito secondo buona fede (art. 1375 c.c.). La clausola generale di buona fede è stata oggetto di una importante elaborazione dottrinale e giurisprudenziale, nell'ambito della quale si riscontra il frequente richiamo alla buona fede per risolvere conflitti relativi all'esecuzione contrattuale sulla base di valutazioni del comportamento delle parti e degli affidamenti reciproci conseguentemente ingeneratisi; se ne evince l'elaborazione di un criterio di buona fede consistente nella regola di coerenza dei comportamenti delle parti, che tende a sanzionare il comportamento successivo della parte che si ponga in contrasto ed in contraddizione con quello dapprima tenuto; nella descritta prospettiva, si ritiene che debbano essere attentamente considerati anche in fase esecutiva — e non solo nelle trattative — i comportamenti commissivi od omissivi riconducibili ai doveri di informazione, ritenendosi che nella reciproca cooperazione debitore e creditore delle rispettive prestazioni abbiano il dovere di fornirsi tutte le notizie ed informazioni che rilevano ai fini dell'esatto e pieno adempimento; in altri termini, le parti devono porsi il problema dell'informazione secondo un criterio di funzionalità di questa rispetto all'interesse dell'altra parte e rispetto alla rilevanza ditale interesse nell'ambito del rapporto contrattuale; la rilevanza dell'interesse non deve essere solo rapportata all'attuazione dell'oggetto del contratto, ma va riconosciuta anche rispetto ad interessi che, pur non essendo direttamente strumentali a tale attuazione, assumano comunque un rilievo contrattuale. I rimedi esperibili in caso di violazione della clausola di buona fede nella esecuzione dei contratti coincidono in larga parte con quelli accordati dalla legge in caso di inadempimento, ed anzi nell'elaborazione giurisprudenziale emerge l'equiparazione all'inadempimento del comportamento contrario a buona fede: in tal senso cfr. Cass., 20 agosto 1980, n. 4942; i rimedi sono pertanto quelli della risoluzione del contratto, della condanna all'adempimento, della reintegrazione in forma specifica, del risarcimento del danno. [...]

9. *Valutazione del comportamento delle parti e quantificazione del risarcimento del danno a favore di Morgan Stanley.*

[...]

Alle medesime conclusioni si perviene anche in applicazione dei principi che governano il commercio internazionale; sempre assumendo a parametro di riferimento i Principi UNIDROIT, si ha che ogni inadempimento non scusabile comporta il risarcimento del danno, eventualmente anche insieme ad altri rimedi (art. 7.4.1); il danno comprende la perdita sofferta ed il mancato guadagno, tenuto conto dei vantaggi economici che il creditore ha ottenuto (art. 7.4.2); il risarcimento è dovuto solo per il danno che sia stabilito con un ragionevole grado di certezza e può esser rimesso, nell'incertezza, alla discrezionalità del giudice (art. 7.4.3); vige il principio della risarcibilità del danno prevedibile (art. 7.4.4.); in caso di stipula di contratto sostitutivo, il creditore ha diritto alla differenza di prezzo e al risarcimento di ogni ulteriore danno (art. 7.4.5); se il danno è imputabile in parte al danneggiato, il risarcimento è in proporzione ridotto, tenuto conto del rispettivo comportamento delle parti (art. 7.4.7); la parte inadempiente non risponde del danno sofferto dal danneggiato nella misura in cui questo poteva essere ridotto da quest'ultimo adottando misure ragionevoli (art. 7.4.8); sulla somma liquidata il creditore ha diritto agli interessi (art. 7.4.9); il risarcimento va determinato nella moneta in cui era espressa l'obbligazione pecuniaria o in quella in cui è stato subito il danno (art. 7.4.12).

[...]

Sources

Excerpts of the award published in:
Diritto del commercio internazionale, 1999, 465 - 474, with note by F.P. Traisci.

Date: ***December 17, 1996***
Adjudicating Court: ***Arbitral Court of the Economic Chamber and the Agrarian Chamber of the Czech Republic***
Number: ***Rsp 88/94***
Parties: ***Unknown***

Keywords

PARTIES' CHOICE OF DOMESTIC LAW (POLISH LAW) – ARBITRAL TRIBUNAL REFERENCE WITHOUT FURTHER EXPLANATION TO THE UNIDROIT PRINCIPLES TO CONFIRM THE SOLUTION REACHED UNDER APPLICABLE DOMESTIC LAW

DELEGATION OF PAYMENT – DOES NOT AMOUNT TO SUBSTITUTION OF DEBTOR – ORIGINAL DEBTOR DISCHARGED ONLY WHEN PAYMENT IS MADE (ART. 921(5) POLISH CIVIL CODE) (ART. 6.1.7(2) UNIDROIT PRINCIPLES)

Abstract

A Polish and a Russian company entered a number of contracts for the repair of two fishing vessels. The contracts contained a reference to Polish law as the applicable law. Requested by the Polish claimant to pay the price of the repairs, the Russian defendant objected that it had delegated one of its own customers, which owed it a corresponding sum of money, to make the payment on its behalf.

The Arbitral Tribunal rejected this defence on the ground that, because a delegation of payment does not amount to the substitution of the original obligor by a new obligor, the original obligor is discharged only when the third person actually pays the obligee.

In support of its conclusion, the Arbitral Tribunal referred not only to Art. 921(5) of the Polish Civil Code, but also to Art. 6.1.7(2) of the UNIDROIT Principles which, by stating that "[...] an obligee who accepts [...] a cheque, any other order to pay or a promise to pay, is presumed to do so only on condition that it will be honoured", confirmed at an international level the principle that the original obligor remains liable.

Full Text

[Not yet available]

Sources

Dr. J. HRIVNÁK (Doctor of Law, Bratislava; arbitrator at the Arbitral Court of the Economic Chamber and the Agrarian Chamber of the Czech Republic, Prague).
Dr. J. SVIDRON (Attorney, Bratislava; Associate Professor, Faculty of Law, Comenius University, Bratislava; translator of the UNIDROIT Principles into the Slovak language; Iura Edition, Bratislava, 1996).

Date: ***January 20, 1997***
Adjudicating Court: ***International Arbitration Court of the Chamber of Commerce and Industry of the Russian Federation***
Number: ***116***
Parties: ***Unknown***

Keywords

CONTRACT SILENT AS TO APPLICABLE LAW – EXPRESS AUTHORISATION OF ARBITRAL TRIBUNAL TO APPLY THE UNIDROIT PRINCIPLES

TERMINATION – RIGHT TO TERMINATION OF CONTRACT (ART. 7.3.1 UNIDROIT PRINCIPLES) – RESTITUTION OF GOODS DELIVERED (ART. 7.3.6 UNIDROIT PRINCIPLES)

DAMAGES – RIGHT TO RECOVERY OF DIFFERENCE BETWEEN CONTRACT PRICE AND REPLACEMENT TRANSACTION (ART. 7.4.5 UNIDROIT PRINCIPLES)

Abstract

A Russian trade organisation and a Hong Kong company entered into a sales contract. The contract did not contain a choice of law clause, but when the dispute arose the parties agreed that the Arbitral Tribunal should apply the UNIDROIT Principles to resolve any question not expressly regulated in the contract.

In its decision, the Arbitral Tribunal applied a number of individual articles of the UNIDROIT Principles. In particular, the Arbitral Tribunal referred to Art. 7.3.1 in order to affirm the right of the Russian buyer to terminate the contract; Art. 7.3.6 with respect to the restitution of the goods already delivered; and Art. 7.4.5 with regard to the buyer's right to recover the difference between the contract price and the price of the replacement transaction.

Full Text

[Not yet available]

Sources

Unpublished. Notice of the award kindly given by Prof. Gabriele CRESPI REGHIZZI (Milan).

Date: ***March 5, 1997***
Country: ***Netherlands***
Adjudicating Court: ***RB Zwolle***
Number: ***HA ZA 95-640***
Parties: ***CME Coopérative Maritime Etaploise S.A.C.V. v. Bos Fishproducts Urk B.V.***

Keywords

CONTRACT GOVERENED BY 1980 VIENNA CONVENTION (CISG) – FRENCH LAW APPLICABLE UNDER ARTICLE 7(2) CISG – REFERENCE TO UNIDROIT PRINCIPLES

GOOD FAITH – NOTICE OF LACK OF CONFORMITY TO BE GIVEN "WITHIN A REASONABLE TIME AFTER IT [...] OUGHT TO HAVE [BEEN] DISCOVERED [...]" (CISG ART. 39(1)) – APPLICATION OF THE UNIDROIT PRINCIPLES (AS WELL AS CISG ART. 7(1)) ADOPTING BROADER CONCEPT OF GOOD FAITH THAN FRENCH LAW

Abstract

The case concerned contracts for the delivery of fish by a French seller to a Dutch buyer. After the first consignment the buyer refused to take delivery of subsequent consignments following complaints from its own customers about the quality of the fish supplied. According to the seller, the buyer had lost its right to rely on the lack of conformity since it had failed to give timely notice thereof. The buyer however argued that the defects were such that it could not have reasonably discovered them within the short period of time for giving notice of defects as provided in the contract.

The contracts were governed by CISG, and the Court referred in particular to Article 39(1) of the Convention, according to which "[t]he buyer loses the right to rely on the lack of conformity of the goods if he does not give notice to the seller specifying the nature of the lack of conformity within a reasonable time after he has discovered it or ought to have discovered it".

According to the Court, in interpreting the words "or ought to have discovered", reference should be made to the way in which the domestic law applicable by virtue of Article 7(2) of the Convention deals with the concept of good faith. Here, this was French law and the Court, after pointing out that under French law, according to prevalent scholarly opinion and case law, the concept of good faith is understood subjectively, recalled the broader concept of good faith as adopted in the UNIDROIT Principles (as well as in Article 7(1) CISG), and concluded that the buyer ought to have more carefully inspected the goods which would have permitted the timely discovery of the defects.

Full Text

[...]

4.3. Zowel near regels van Nederlands internationaal privaatrecht als krachtens art. 4 van het Verdrag inzake het recht dat van toepassing is op verbintenissen uit overeenkomst (EVo; Trb. 198O, 156) client Frankrijk te gelden als het land waarmee de overeenkomst het nauwst is verbonden respectievelijk als het land waar de partij die de kenmerkende prestatie moest verrichten (CME) hear hoofdvestiging heeft, althans waar zich de CME-vestiging bevindt die de door Bos bedongen prestatie diende te verrichten. Uitzonderingen op die verdragsregel(s) als voorzien in datzelfde art. 4 EVO doen zich ten deze niet voor. Frans recht is mitsdien van toepassing. Partijen verschillen daarover ook niet van mening. Van het Franse recht maakt deel uit het Weense Koopverdrag van 198O (hierna: het Verdrag) en wel vanaf 1 januari 1988. Voor Nederland is het in werking getreden op 1 januari 1992.

4.4. Tussen partijen staat vast dat krachtens de toepasselijke algemene voorwaarden van CME korte reclametermijnen gelden voor o.a. bevroren en diepgevroren producten. Dat is begrijpelijk omdat het om bederfelijke waar gaat die in het algemeen aan snelle veranderingen onderhevig zal zijn, met name als gevolg van externe omstandigheden als het weer en ontdooiing tijdens het vervolgtraject van het product respectievelijk de been verwerking daarvan.

Dit gegeven is mede bepalend voor de reikwijdte die in het onderwerpelijke geval aan de woorden "of had behoren te ontdekken" in art. 39 lid 1 van het Verdrag ("de koper verliest het recht om zich erop te beroepen dat de zaken niet aan de overeenkomst beantwoorden indien hij niet binnen een redelijke termijn nadat hij dit heeft ontdekt of had behoren te ontdekken de verkoper hiervan in kennis stelt, onder opgave van de aard van de tekortkoming") behoort te worden toegekend.

Gelet op het belang van CME bij de naleving door haar afnemers van bedoelde korte reclametermijnen, een belang waarmee Bos geacht mocht worden bekend te zijn, temeer nu zij niet heeft gesteld niet op de hoogte te zijn van de inhoud van de "*conditions de vente*" van CME, gelet ook op de risico-overgang bij levering af magazijn CME en het daarop gevolgde transport van de vis naar Urk, gelet tenslotte op de omstandigheid dat de geleverde vis een bewerking tot visfilets zou ondergaan, waardoor controle achteraf door CME van het oorspronkelijk door haar geleverde product bij later geconstateerde gebreken vrijwel onmogelijk zou zijn, kon door Bos niet worden volstaan met steekproefsgewijze controle - zo dat bij bederfelijke waar in het algemeen al aanvaardbaar is zonder vrijwaring van de leverancier voor de daaraan inherente risico's - maar behoorde zij de lading numeriek te keuren (vgl. art. 38 Verdrag en art. 1642 Code Civil). En dat moet in casu ook tot de mogelijkheden hebben behoord: ieder afzonderlijke vis krijgt in het fileerproces immers een beurt zodat het productieproces zelf Bos de mogelijkheid moet hebben geboden om een deugdelijke kwaliteitscontrole uit te oefenen. De Rb. meent dat dit zozeer voor de hand ligt dat van Bos had mogen worden verwacht dat zij het tegendeel zou stellen indien zij die mogelijkheid niet had.

Daar komt nog iets bij: Bos stelt te hebben geconstateerd dat een gedeelte van de geleverde vis niet was "gestript" en dat zij zich daarover heeft beklaagd bij CME. CME heeft ook erkend - op zijn minst impliciet - dat die klacht niet ongegrond was. Maar dan mag er ook vanuit worden gegaan dat Bos in dat gegeven aanleiding zou vinden om de hele geleverde partij vis alsnog te controleren op de aanwezigheid van ingewanden. Aangenomen moet worden dat zij dat ook heeft gedaan want zij stelt zich direct telefonisch te hebben verstaan met CME over het niet gestript zijn van een gedeelte van de geleverde vis. Dat veronderstelt een daadwerkelijk uitgevoerde controle van de gehele partij (tot een verzoek van Bos om vervangende levering heeft haar constatering overigens niet geleid).

Waarom echter diezelfde partij dan niet tevens gelijktijdig op kwaliteit respectievelijk op geur en uiterlijk kon worden gecontroleerd heeft Bos niet duidelijk gemaakt.

Dat er enig causaal verband bestond tussen het niet gestript zijn van een gedeelte van de vis en de later in Engeland en Oostenrijk geconstateerde kwaliteitsgebreken van het gefileerde eindproduct is weliswaar niet gesteld, maar dat neemt niet weg dat aan het visverwerkingsbedrijf dat de door haar leverancier onvoldoende voorbehandelde vis niet aan deze terugstuurt maar zelf verder behandelt, in casu "stript", belangrijke (extra) onderzoekseisen mogen worden gesteld, mede in verband met het niet denkbeeldige gevaar dat de aanwezigheid van ingewanden de kwaliteit en de houdbaarheid nadeiig heeft beïnvloed.

Tenslotte client er in dit verband op te worden gewezen dat Bos zich al bij fax van 10 mei 1994 over de kwaliteit van een gedeelte van door CME geleverde partijen schol heeft beklaagd (vgl. r.o. 2.4) CME heeft de klacht gerechtvaardigd bevonden. De Rb. acht het niet aannemelijk dat zo'n klacht words geuit zonder dat voordien danwel nadien alsnog de gehele geleverde partij aan een indringende controle is of words onderworpen. Evenmin acht de Rb. het aannemelijk dat Bos wel de schol maar niet de tongschar kort na aflevering dusdanig heeft kunnen keuren dat de gestelde kwaliteitsgebreken tijdig konden worden ontdekt. Een behoorlijke verklaring daarvoor heeft Bos althans niet gegeven (vgl. art. 44 Verdrag).

4.5. Bij de uitleg van het begrip "behoren te ontdekker. in art. 39 lid 1 van het Verdrag dient mede aansluiting te worden gezocht bij de wijze waarop de goede trouw in Frankrijk invulling pleegt te vinden nu het recht van dat land toepasselijk is (art. 7 lid 2 van het Verdrag).

Naar Frans recht respectievelijk de aldaar in ide doctrine en de jurisprudentie heersende opvattingen words het begrip "goede trouw" in subjectieve zin opgevat. De nadruk words gelegd op de over en weer bestaande verplichting tot loyaliteit en samenwerking ("*loyauté*" en "*cooperation*") zich oplossend in een informatieplicht van partijen respectievelijk in een op hen rustende verplichting de uirvoering van de overeenkomst voor elkaar te vergemakkelijken. Dat de hieronder aangehaalde auteur tot de conclusie komt dat de Franse opvattingen over goede trouw nog niet ver genoeg gaan in het licht van de hantering van datzelfde begrip in internationale conventies als de UNIDROIT Principles rechtvaardigt eens te meer de conclusie dat onder de omstandigheden van het onderhavige geval Bos de partijen tongschar deugdelijk had behoren te controleren en dusdoende de door haar gestelde ondermaatse kwaliteit van (een gedeelte van) de geleverde tongschar had behoren te ontdekken en CME daaromtrent had behoren te verwittigen vóór doorlevering aan haar buitenlandse afnemers, mede gezien de korte reclametermijnen waaraan zij krachtens de algemene voorwaarden van CME gebonden was en waaromtrent CME onbetwist heeft gesteld dat zij gelet op de aard van de koopwaar gebruikelijk zijn (zie ook art. 9 lid 2 van het Verdrag).

4.6. Recapitulerend: de woorden "had behoren te ontdekken" in art. 39 lid 1 Verdrag moeten in casu aldus worden verstaan (vgl. r.o. 4.4) dat Bos de ontdekking van gebreken in de door CME geleverde vis, indien daarvan inderdaad sprake is geweest, bij of kort na aankomst van de vis op haar bedrijf had behoren te doen en wel omdat zowel de toepasselijke conditions de vente respectievelijk de aard van de koopwaar en het oogmerk van verwerking in een nieuw product, als de naar Frans recht onder vigeur van de goede trouw bestaande samenwerkingsverplichting Bos geen andere weg openlieten den onverwijlde en algehele keuring. Niet is gebleken van omstandigheden die Bos een "redelijke verontschuldiging" in de zin van art. 44 van het Verdrag opleveren. De enige verontschuldiging die Bos in dit verband heeft aangevoerd, is dat zij niet de gehele partij kon controleren. Dat argument is hierboven als onvoldoende gemotiveerd verworpen.

4.7. Een onbeantwoord gebleven vraag is overigens wet Bos ken hebben belet een van haar medewerkers voor de eindcontrôle naar CME te sturen en aldus de uitvoering van de overeenkomst (levering van aan bederf onderhevige waar) voor CME te vergemakkelijken,. Art. 38 Verdrag lijkt zo'n contrôle ter plaatse tot uitgangspunt te kiezen waar het tweede lid bepaalt dat keuring kan worden uitgesteld tot na aankomst van de zaken op hun bestemming in die gevallen waarin de overeenkomst tevens het vervoer van de zaken omvat.

4.8. De conclusie dient te zijn dat de vordering van CME voor toewijzing in aanmerking komt en dat de reconventionele vordering van Bos meet worden afgewezen.

Sources

Original in Dutch:
Nederlands Internationaal Privatrecht, no. 15 (1997), 282.

Date: ***April 1997***
Adjudicating Court: ***ICC International Court of Arbitration, Paris***
Number: ***8264***
Parties: ***Unknown***

Keywords

PARTIES' CHOICE OF DOMESTIC LAW (ALGERIAN LAW) AS LAW GOVERNING THE CONTRACT – EXPRESS AUTHORIZATION OF ARBITRAL TRIBUNAL TO CONSIDER THE GENERAL PRINCIPLES OF LAW AND THE USAGES OF TRADE

BREACH OF DUTY TO PROVIDE INFORMATION – COMPENSATION FOR LOSS OF A CHANCE – REFERENCE TO ART. 7.4.3(2) UNIDROIT PRINCIPLES

Abstract

A United States manufacturer and an Algerian industrial development corporation entered into an agreement for the supply of industrial equipment and transfer of know-how. In a contract annexed thereto, the manufacturer agreed to provide the licensee with any information relating to changes and improvements in the equipment.

The contract contained a choice of law clause in favour of a particular domestic law (Algerian law) and authorised the Arbitral Tribunal to consider the general principles of law and the usages of trade.

The Arbitral Tribunal held that Claimant's failure to provide Respondent with information relating to the equipment caused the latter the loss of an opportunity to develop and adapt its industrial production to the demands of the market. In the Abitral Tribunal's view, the UNIDROIT Principles consecrate rules [...] broadly recognised throughout the world and the practice of international contracts. In support of its decision, it referred to Art. 7.4.3(2) of the UNIDROIT Principles, according to which "[c]ompensation may be due for the loss of a chance in proportion to the probability of its occurrence".

Full Text

[...]

[I]l convient de rappeler les dispositions de l'acte de mission en ce qui concerne le droit applicable au fond du litige [...]

"En se référant à l'article [...] de la convention, le tribunal arbitral tiendra compte:

a) des lois applicables en Algérie, qui régissent cette convention, ainsi que l'exécution des accords qui en sont la suite ou la conséquence,

b) des prévisions raisonnabies des parties à la lumière des objectifs, des motifs et des buts de la convention, et

c) des pnncipes généraux du droit et des usages du commerce international."

Il est donc certain que l'attitude de la partie demanderesse, depuis [...], a manqué de transparence et de sincérité quant à la mise en ceuvre concrète de ses obligations à ce titre. Celles-ci impliquaient une information claire, constante et gratuite sur l'évobution des techniques relatives aux pièces et produits contractuels.

[...] la partie défenderesse a constamment excipé de l'inexécution par la partie demanderesse de son obligation de communiquer les perfectionnements pour justifier son propre droit de retenir le paiement des redevances proportionnelles correspondantes [...]

Il est certain que, dans les contrats synallagmatiques, les prestations promises par chaque partie doivent être exécutées simultanément, et que, si l'une réclame ce qui lui est dû sans payer ou faire ce qu'elle doit, l'autre peut refuser d'exécuter sa propre prestation en lui opposant l'execeptio non adimpleti contractus. Cette voie de justice privée conduit donc à la suspension de l'exécution de la prestation de celui qui linvoque, mais la pression ainsi exercée laisse subsister le contrat, du moins aussi longtemps qu'il n'est pas résolu. Consacrée en droit algérien dans l'article 200 du Code civil, elle est connue dans la pbupart des systèmes juridiques, elle peut être considérée comme un principe général du droit des contrats internationaux.

Si une application stricte de ce principe à la présente espèce n'est pas fondée, cela ne signifie pas que la partie défenderesse n'ait pu surseoir, en raison du comportement de la partie demanderesse, au paiement des redevances proportionnelles qu'elle lui devait, et qu'elle lui doit encore [...].

D'une part, en effet, les conditions et les effets de l'exception d'inexécution ne sauraient jouer ici dans toute leur rigueur. D'abord et surtout [...] parce qu'il n'a pu être établi clairement que la partie demanderesse avait effectivement manqué à son obligation de communiquer les perfectionnements et améliorations qu'elle aurait réalisés sur les produits et pièces contractuels. Ensuite parce que, même si cette défaillance avait été prouvée, elle n'aurait pu justifier ~ elle seule le jeu de l'exception d'inexécution. Cette réplique, en effet, doit être proportionnée au mal que son auteur entend faire cesser. Or, malgré l'importance que présentait pour la partie défenderesse la communication des perfectionnements éventuellement réalisés par la partie demanderesse, la véritable contrepartie des redevances proportionnelles était constituée par la licence de fabrication concédée sur les produits contractuels, et cette contrepartie a subsisté jusqu'à l'expiration du contrat de licence. Cette exigence d'équilibre entre la prestation refusée et celle dont on entend sanctionner l'inexécution est elle aussi très généralement admise, en conséquence du principe général de bonne foi dont l'exception d'inexécution assure le respect dans les contrats synallagmatiques.

Mais d'autre part, il est incontestable que la partie demanderesse a gravement manqué àses obligations générales d'information à l'égard de son licencié. Si elle n'avait pas de perfectionnement à lui communiquer, elle devait clairement et sincèrement le lui dire, et lui expliquer tout aussi clairement pourquoi. Le contrat de licence l'obligeait à un comportement actif, albant au-delà de simples propositions commerciales. Ce manque de transparence est contraire, lui aussi, au principe général selon lequel les obligations contractuelles doivent être exécutées de bonne foi, principe particulièrement exigeant dans un conti-at international de coopération industrielle ayant pour objet la réalisation effective d'un transfert de technobogie sui- une longue durée [...]

C'est la raison pour laquelle le Tribunal arbitral tout en rejetant l'exception d'inexécution soulevée par la partie défenderesse en ce qu'elle était fondée sur la violation de l'article 5.1 du conti-at de licence, juge cependant que la partie demanderesse a manqué à ses obligations générales d'information et de conseil découlant implicitement mais nécessairement du contrat de licence, et aux engagements particuliers auxquels elle a consenti [...].

En conséquence, tout en réaffirmant — ce que d'ailleurs la partie défenderesse n'a jamais contesté — que les redevances proportionnelles sont dues jusqu'à l'expiration du conti-at de licence [...], le Tribunal arbitral juge que les intérêts de retard réclamés à leur propos par la partie demanderesse ne sont pas dus avant le prononcé de la présente sentence [...].

Le Tribunal arbitral est conscient des difficultés rencontrées par la partie défenderesse pour établir précisément un préjudice consécutif à un défaut d'information en matière technologique. Il lui parait néanmoins injustifié de confier à un expert une mission aussi générale, en déchargeant la demanderesse reconventionnelle de la charge de la preuve qui lui incombe. Il est préférable que le Tribunal arbitral se prononce lui-même, à partir de tous les éléments dont il dispose au terme d'une instruction aussi complète que possible [...].

La passivité et les réticences de la partie demanderesse ont à tout le moins empêché la partie défenderesse d'intégrer dans ses plannings soit l'existence, soit l'absence de perfectionnements, et l'ont sans doute privée des informations qui lui étaient nécessaires pour faire évoluer ses produits, les adapter au marché et aux besoins de l'exportation.

En d'autres termes, en raison de l'attitude de la partie demanderesse, la partie défenderesse a perdu une chance de rentabiliser convenablement des installations industrielles fort onéreuses. Certes, l'échec actuel de la partie défenderesse, qui se traduit par l'arrêt presque complet de la fabrication des compresseurs et compacteurs visés par le conti-at de licence, est dû à des causes diverses, mais le comportement de la partie demanderesse a sûrement contribué, dans une certaine mesure, à ce fiasco industriel.

En droit du commerce international, "la perte d'une chance peut être réparée dans la mesure de la probabilité de sa réalisation". Ainsi s'expriment les Principes d'UNIDROIT relatifs aux contrats du commerce international (article 7.4.3, al. 2), qui consacrent, comme on le sait, des règles très largement admises à travers le monde dans les systèmes juridiques et la pratique des contrats internationaux.

Plus spécialement, le Tribunal arbitral estime que dans un conti-at de transfert technologique, et spécialement lors de l'exécution d'un conti-at de licence, les réticences de la partie détentrice de l'expérience et du savoir-faire qu'elle cède conti-e rémunération engendrent naturellement — ou en tous cas avec un très fort degré de probabilité — une insuffisance ou un retard dans l'acquisition de la maîtrise industrielle recherchée par son licencié.

De l'avis du Tribunal arbitral, il en a été ainsi dans la présente espèce et c'est cette perte de chance qu'il convient donc de réparer.

[...]

Sources

Original in French (excerpt):
ICC International Court of Arbitration Bulletin, Vol. 10, No. 2, Fall 1999, 62 – 65.

Date: ***April 21, 1997***
Adjudicating Court: ***Ad hoc Arbitration, Paris***
Number: ***Unknown***
Parties: ***Unknown***

Keywords

PARTIES' CHOICE OF DOMESTIC LAW (RUSSIAN LAW) – IF NECESSARY SUPPLEMENTED BY THE UNIDROIT PRINCIPLES

AVOIDANCE OF CONTRACT – PARTY'S CONDUCT PRECLUDING ITS ABILITY TO CLAIM THE INVALIDITY OF THE CONTRACT ("VENIRE CONTRA FACTUM PROPRIUM") (ARTS. 3.12 AND 4.3(C) UNIDROIT PRINCIPLES)

Abstract

A Russian trade organisation and a United States company entered into a loan agreement. The agreement did not contain a choice of law clause but when the dispute arose the parties agreed that the arbitral tribunal should apply Russian law, if necessary supplemented by the UNIDROIT Principles. One of the parties asserted the invalidity of the contract because of the non-observance of the formal requirement of double signature as prescribed by Decree no. 126 of 14 February 1978.

The Arbitral Tribunal held that the Claimant was no longer entitled to avoid the contract, firstly because of the three-year time bar provided by Arts. 78 and 82 of the Russian Civil Code of 1964, and secondly because the Claimant, having previously repeatedly requested the defendant to perform its contractual obligations, was estopped by its own conduct from subsequently invoking the invalidity of the contract. In support of the latter conclusion, the Arbitral Tribunal expressly referred to Arts. 3.12 and 4.3(c) of the UNIDROIT Principles.

Full Text

[Not yet available]

Sources

Unpublished. Notice of the award kindly given by Prof. Gabriele CRESPI REGHIZZI (Milan).

Date: ***May 5, 1997***
Adjudicating Court: ***ICC International Court of Arbitration, Paris***
Number: ***7365/FMS***
Parties: ***Ministry of Defense and Support for the Armed Forces of the Islamic Republic of Iran v. Cubic Defense Systems, Inc.***

Keywords

PARTIES' CHOICE OF DOMESTIC LAW (IRANIAN LAW) – AGREEMENT BY PARTIES AS TO COMPLEMENTARY AND SUPPLEMENTARY APPLICATION OF THE GENERAL PRINCIPLES OF INTERNATIONAL LAW AND TRADE USAGES – ARBITRAL TRIBUNAL REFERENCE TO UNIDROIT PRINCIPLES TO DETERMINE CONTENT OF SUCH GENERAL PRINCIPLES

HARDSHIP – RIGHT TO DEMAND TERMINATION OR ADAPTATION OF CONTRACT (ART. 6.2.3(4) UNIDROIT PRINCIPLES)

IMPLIED OBLIGATIONS – GOOD FAITH AND FAIR DEALING (ARTS. 5.1 AND 5.2 [ARTS. 5.1.1. AND 5.1.2 OF THE 2004 EDITION] UNIDROIT PRINCIPLES)

TERMINATION – RIGHT TO RESTITUTION (ART. 7.3.6 UNIDROIT PRINCIPLES)

INTEREST – RIGHT TO INTEREST INDEPENDENT OF A FORMAL REQUEST BY AGGRIEVED PARTY (ART. 7.4.9 UNIDROIT PRINCIPLES) – DOUBTFUL WHETHER THIS PROVISION CORRESPONDS TO GENERALLY ACCEPTED PRINCIPLES OF INTERNATIONAL LAW

Abstract

The case concerned two contracts for the sale and the installation of sophisticated military equipment, entered into in 1977 between a United States corporation (Cubic) and the Iranian Air Force (Iran). The contracts were duly performed until the advent of the Islamic Revolution in early 1979. The parties entered into a series of negotiations but were unable to reach an agreement as to how to proceed. Iran claimed reimbursement of payments made to Cubic in addition to damages, whereas Cubic, objecting that it was Iran which, by not paying the remainder of the price, had breached its contractual obligations, presented a counterclaim for damages. The contracts contained a choice of law clause designating the law of Iran, but parties eventually agreed to the complementary and supplementary application of general principles of international law.

Regarding the issue of the substantive applicable law to the dispute, the Arbitral Tribunal held that "[s]ince both Parties eventually agreed to the complementary and supplementary application of general principles of international law and trade usages, and based on Article 13(5) of the ICC Rules, the Tribunal shall, to the extent necessary, take into account such principles and usages as well. As to the contents of such rules, the Tribunal shall be guided by the Principles of International Commercial Contracts, published in 1994 by the UNIDROIT Institute, Rome".

Thus, in finding that, as a result of the chaotic events preceding and following the Islamic Revolution in February 1979, each party was entitled to unilaterally request termination of the contracts or adaptation of their terms, the Arbitral Tribunal expressly referred to Article 6.2.3(4) of the UNIDROIT Principles, pointing out that "[...] from the covenant of good faith and fair dealing which is implied in each contract follows that in a case in which the circumstances to a contract undergo [...] fundamental changes in an unforeseeable way, a party is precluded from invoking the binding effect of the contract [...] In such restrictive and narrow form this concept [of hardship or *clausola rebus sic stantibus*] has been incorporated into so many legal systems that it is widely regarded as a general principle of law. As such, it would be applicable in the instant arbitration even if it did not form part of the Iranian law".

Furthermore, in order to justify the application by analogy of a "Termination for Convenience Clause" contained in the contracts, to the termination of the contract as a result of changed circumstances, the Arbitral Tribunal applied Articles 5.1 and 5.2 [Arts. 5.1.1 and 5.1.2 of the 2004 edition] of the UNIDROIT Principles and the "widely accepted principles therein set forth regarding implied obligations".

In dealing with the consequences of the termination of the contracts, the Arbitral Tribunal held that "[t]he obvious and most important effect of a contract termination, be it for the convenience of one party or for other reasons, is that 'either party may claim restitution of whatever it has supplied, provided that such party concurrently makes restitution of whatever it has received", quoting verbatim Article 7.3.6 of the UNIDROIT Principles.

However, as regards the date from which interest is to be awarded, the Arbitral Tribunal, while admitting that "[t]here is a tendency in international commercial law to award interest from the time when the payment has become due without any need for the aggrieved party to give notice of the default (UNIDROIT Principles Article 7.4.9)", stressed that the Iran-US Claims Tribunal had also adopted a different solution, and concluded that it seems doubtful whether it may be considered to form part of generally accepted principles of international law. The Arbitral Tribunal concluded that "[e]ven if a generally accepted principle of international law existed in this respect, the Tribunal would only be authorized to apply it as a complementary and supplementary rule, not as a rule in clear contradiction to an unambiguous provision of the Iranian law chosen by the Parties".

Full Text

[Not yet available]

Sources

Uniform Law Review / Revue de droit uniforme, 1999, 796.

Commented on by:
M.J. BONELL, UNIDROIT Principles: a significant recognition by a United States District Court, in Uniform Law Review / Revue de droit uniforme, 1999, 651 *et seq.*

Date: ***June 5, 1997***
Adjudicating Court: ***International Arbitration Court of the Chamber of Commerce and Industry of the Russian Federation***
Number: ***229/1996***
Parties: ***Unknown***

Keywords

CONTRACT GOVERNED BY CISG – UNIDROIT PRINCIPLES APPLIED AS MEANS TO INTERPRET AND SUPPLEMENT CISG (PREAMBLE OF UNIDROIT PRINCIPLES) – UNIDROIT PRINCIPLES APPLIED AS REFLECTING INTERNATIONAL USAGES (ART. 9(2) CISG)

PENALTY CLAUSE – PAYMENT OF PENALTY DELAY IN PAYMENT OF PRICE – MATTER NOT COVERED BY CISG – RECOURSE TO ART. 7.4.13 UNIDROIT PRINCIPLES

AMOUNT OF PENALTY EXCESSIVE – REDUCTION TO REASONABLE AMOUT (ART. 7.4.13(2) UNIDROIT PRINCIPLES)

Abstract

A sales contract between a Bulgarian and a Russian party provided for the payment of a penalty by the buyer in case of delay in the payment of the price corresponding to 0,5% of the price per day. When the buyer actually failed to make the payment in time, the seller asked for the payment of the penalty as agreed upon in the contract. The buyer objected on the ground that the agreed sum was excessive.

The contract was governed by the UN Convention on Contracts for the International Sales of Goods (CISG). After having found that CISG is silent on the issue, the Arbitral Tribunal decided to resort to the UNIDROIT Principles in order to fill the gap. In doing so the Tribunal invoked first of all the Preamble of the UNIDROIT Principles stating that "[they] may be used to interpret and supplement international uniform law instruments"; yet the recourse to the UNIDROIT Principles was also justified on the ground that they reflect usages of which the parties knew or ought to have known and which are widely known to in international trade and are therefore applicable according to Art. 9(2) CISG.

As to the merits of the dispute, the Arbitral Tribunal found that a penalty amounting to 0,5% of the total contract price for each day of delay in the payment was indeed excessive and in applying Art. 7.4.13(2) of the UNIDROIT Principles it reduced the penalty to a reasonable amount.

Full Text

[Not yet available]

Sources

Unpublished. Notice of the award kindly given by Professor Alexander KOMAROV, President of the International Arbitration Court of the Chamber of Commerce and Industry of the Russian Federation.

Date: ***June 30, 1997***
Country: ***Australia***
Adjudicating Court: ***Federal Court of Australia***
Number: ***558***
Parties: ***Hughes Aircraft Systems International v. Airservices Australia***

Keywords

CONTRACT GOVERNED BY DOMESTIC LAW (AUSTRALIAN LAW)

DUTY OF GOOD FAITH AND FAIR DEALING – IMPLIED TERM IN TENDER PROCESS – FUNDAMENTAL PRINCIPLE OF INTERNATIONAL COMMERCIAL CONTRACTS (ART. 1.7 UNIDROIT PRINCIPLES)

Abstract

The dispute concerned a bidding procedure, which had arisen between a Californian company and an Australian governmental agency after the latter awarded the contract to another bidder. According to the claimant, the defendant had failed to conduct the tender evaluation fairly and in a manner that would have ensured equal opportunity to both bidders.

In considering whether such a duty was implied by law in pre-award contract contexts, the court, after stating that Australian judicial and scholarly opinion differed sharply on this matter, concluded in the affirmative. In support of its ruling, it stated that a general duty of good faith and fair dealing was not only recognised in a number of foreign jurisdictions but had also been propounded as a fundamental principle to be honoured in international commercial contracts in Ch. 1.7 of the UNIDROIT Principles.

Full Text

[...]

THE IMPLIED TERM OF "FAIR DEALING"

As already noted, the term propounded is that:

"the [CAA] would conduct its evaluation fairly and in a manner that would ensure equal opportunity to Hughes and Thomson."

The particular language in which the term is couched partially reflects that in the RFT para 16.2.6 dealing with the independent auditor:

"An independent auditor has been contracted to verify that the evaluation procedures were followed, the evaluation was conducted fairly and the offers received due consideration."

Hughes places no little emphasis on that paragraph. The idea of a "fair process" had significant antecedents in the TAAATS II procurement. It informed the specific recommendations of the Macphee Report (para 12.1): "An essential ingredient in [the future of the procurement] is that the process must be restored to one of fairness between the tenderers ... Our recommendations apply to that part of the process in which fairness ceased." At the Restart Meeting the slide both shown to, and given, the companies concerning the "Objectives" of the TAAATS Evaluation Strategy stated (omitting the title):

" Conduct a fair and equitable evaluation - will allow the Tender Committee to make recommendation on contract to the Board. Respect and protect proprietary and confidential information. Conduct the evaluation in a manner which is auditable and defensible. Provide a basis for debriefing Companies" I would note in passing the conjunction in this of the first and third dot points. At the same meeting in his oral opening, Mr Roser referred directly to instating: "a process that is fair to both Companies, and gives both Companies an equal opportunity to be the successful contractor.

[...]

Of course I will require both Companies to endorse the way ahead as being fair. Until I achieve that situation, we won't restart it." The letter of 5 February which, after some iterations became the 9 March letter, first began the use of the "fair evaluation" formula used in the independent auditor provision of the RFT noted above. The applicant propounds the term on three bases. First that the term is an express one; secondly, that it should be implied *ad hoc*; and thirdly, it should be implied in law in its own right or as a manifestation of a general implied term of good faith and fair dealing.

(i) Express term

The applicant's submission here, as I understand it, is based on the construction that should be given the independent auditor provision (para 16.2.6) of the RFT in light of the surrounding circumstances. It is that, if the independent auditor was contracted to verify (*inter alia*) that "the evaluation was conducted fairly and the offers received due consideration", the provision itself both presupposed, and contained an acknowledgment of, the obligation of the CAA to conduct the evaluation fairly. It is suggested that a construction that did not recognize this obligation would make a commercial nonsense of the paragraph: *cf.* Hide & Skin Trading Pty Ltd v. Oceanic Meat Traders Ltd (1990) 20 NSWLR 310 at 313-314.

The respondent, in contrast, submits that the provision had a clear and intelligible purpose and meaning: it dealt with the retainer of an independent auditor to verify that the evaluation was conducted fairly. I am invited to conclude that the provisions went no further than did their literal terms.

In my view the respondent's construction of para 16.2.6 is to be preferred. While para 16.2.6 might provide one of a range of circumstances of which account might be taken when considering whether the proposed duty should be implied *ad hoc*, it is not of itself a sufficient indication of the existence of such a duty as to justify construing it as a recognition of that duty. The paragraph might well suggest inquiry as to the obligation(s) assumed by the CAA in the evaluation. It does not of itself so certainly describe them as to provide their express source. It may well be the case that, from the totality of the circumstances, it would be possible to infer that the parties actually intended there to be such a term. It is unnecessary, though, for me to further explore this matter given (a) the very clear view I have arrived at that the term should be implied *ad hoc*, and (b) that the applicant's Submissions in Reply tend to merge inference and implication *ad hoc* in any event: *cf.* Thompson and Morgan (United Kingdom) Ltd. v. Erica Vale Australia Pty Ltd., (unreported, FC FCA, per Gummow and Hill JJ, 19 April 1995). This, perhaps, is one of those cases where it is unnecessary to distinguish the two for practical purposes: *cf.* Hawkins v. Clayton (1988) 164 CLR 539 at 570.

(ii) Implication *ad hoc*

The applicant relies upon a composite of factors to justify this implication. They are (i) the independent auditor provision in the RFT and the expectation of fair evaluation it anticipates; (ii) the presence of other terms in the RFT that are specific manifestations of fairness and equal opportunity - reference was made to the RFT paras 16.1 (criteria), 16.2.1 (evaluation), 4 (the particularized manner in which tenders were to be submitted), 16.2.7 (confidentiality) and 16.2.8 (prohibitions on certain affiliations with tenderers); and (iii) the previous history including the cancellation of RADREP, the cancellation of TAAATS I because of perceived unfairness to Hughes, the Macphee Report, the parties' alleged contemplation that Hughes would not participate in TAAATS II unless the process was fair, and the repeated assurances of fairness given to Hughes (*e.g.* at the Restart Meeting). This, it was said, was no ordinary tendering process. The participation of the parties in it was predicated upon it being conducted fairly. In the very distinctive circumstances here, it is suggested, it clearly satisfied the implication rules.

The respondent for its part submits to the contrary: it is not reasonable or equitable to impose so "uncertain and nebulous" an obligation on a public body; it is unnecessary, because there are express terms dealing with specific aspects of fairness and these ought to be regarded as exhaustive: *cf.* Hospital Products Ltd v. United States Surgical Corporation, above; it is not obvious because of those other terms; it is not capable of clear and precise expression; and the history relied upon to support it is equally consistent with the parties proceeding on the basis that fairness would be dealt with by specific terms.

I would have to say I regard the case for this implication as overwhelming. Fairness in process and dealing was the a priori of this business relationship. I need not repeat the history here: Mr Roser's comments at the Restart Meeting were emblematic of what all parties were reasonably entitled to expect for the future. And their expectations were to be given the guarantee of an independent audit of compliance and fairness. Without the assurance of fairness, there would have been no contract. Such was Hughes' evidence. Despite the criticism mounted by the respondent of the term's "nebulous" language, it was the actual language of the parties: it was intended to convey meaning and to be relied upon. It was, relevantly, definite and capable of precise expression. And, in my view, it was "so obvious that [the parties] would clearly have agreed to its inclusion in the contract...had they directed their mind to it at the time": Con-Stan Industries of Australia Pty Ltd v. Norwich Winterthur Insurance (Australia) Ltd (1986) 160 CLR 226 at 241.

I am unable to accept the submission of the respondent that the specific "fairness" obligations identified in the RFT exhausted the obligation of "fairness" assumed by the CAA. The CAA clearly had a far more pervasive conception of the fairness it intended to have exhibited in the TAAATS evaluation - as witness the responsibilities of the independent auditor contained in Schedule I to its agreement with Mr Moten. More importantly, though, fairness in evaluation was, from the Macphee Report onwards, clearly perceived by the parties to be of encompassing importance. It would not be reasonable to conclude that they expected it to be limited to, and be measured by compliance with, a relatively small number of specific obligations in the RFT. It was intended to be an obligation in its own right.

It is important to recognize that, in the pre-award phase, the parties were engaged in a close working relationship over a significant period of time. Not one of them could have been unaware of the vulnerability to which Hughes and Thomson exposed themselves by agreeing to enter into that relationship. Unlike cases where parties are and remain at arm's length in the pre-award phase, the relationship here in its setting was one which renders unsurprising the making of the implication sought. It is one I am prepared to make.

(iii) Implication in law

My previous conclusion makes it strictly unnecessary to consider this basis of implication. Nonetheless I consider it appropriate to do so should my previous conclusion be incorrect.

(a) Good faith and fair dealing

The applicant's submission is that the proposed term is a manifestation of a general implied duty of good faith and fair dealing. I have, in consequence, been invited to embrace the conclusion of Priestley JA in Renard Constructions (ME) Pty Ltd v. Minister for Public Works, above, at 268 that: "people generally, including judges and other lawyers, from all strands of the community, have grown used to the courts applying standards of fairness to contract which are wholly consistent with the existence in all contracts of a duty upon the parties of good faith and fair dealing in its performance. In my view this is in these days the expected standard, and anything less is contrary to prevailing community expectations."

The primary basis upon which I was asked to make this implication was unrelated specifically to pre-award contracts in procurement cases. Rather as suggested in the Restatement of Contracts, Second, Art 205, the implied duty existed in "every contract". I make this particular observation because, as later discussed, a duty to act fairly in some form appears to have been accepted in other Commonwealth jurisdictions in pre-award contract contexts: see Pratt Contractors Ltd v. Palmerston North City Council, above, at 478, 483; Martselos Services Ltd v. Arctic College (1994) 111 DLR (4th) 65; and see generally N SEDDON, Government Contracts, 235ff.

The respondent in contrast has pressed upon me the judgment of Gummow J., then of this Court, in Service Station Association Ltd v. Berg Bennett & Associates Pty Ltd (1993) 45 FCR 84. After considering North American jurisprudence's acceptance of an implied duty of good faith and fair dealing, his Honour observed, at 96: "Anglo-Australian contract law as to the implication of terms has heretofore developed differently, with greater emphasis upon specifics, rather than the identification of a genus expressed in wide terms. Equity has intervened in matters of contractual formation by the remedy of rescission, upon the grounds mentioned earlier. It has restrained freedom of contract by inventing and protecting the equity of redemption, and by relieving against forfeitures and penalties. To some extent equity has regulated the quality of contractual performance by the various defenses available to suits for specific performance and for injunctive relief. In some, but not all, of this, notions of good conscience play a part. But it requires a leap of faith to translate these well-established doctrines and remedies into a new term as to the quality of contractual performance, implied by law": (emphasis added) Needless to say I have been asked to remain in Gummow J's company and not take that leap.

Other Australian authority on this duty is indecisive. Notably, in the Full Court of this Court in News Ltd v. Australian Rugby Football League Ltd. (1996) 139 ALR 193 at 285, it was found unnecessary to consider whether such a duty should be implied in that case. The Court did not enter upon the question of whether our law recognized such an implication as a matter of law.

If the matter stood merely as one of choice between two conflicting views, I would, as a matter of comity, adhere to that of Gummow J.: see Bank of Western Australia Ltd v. Commissioner of Taxation (1994) 55 FCR 233 at 255 on "comity" and the cases referred to therein. This is an arena in which opinions, judicial and scholarly, differ often sharply: see *e.g.* I. RENARD, "Fair Dealing and Good Faith", in Saunders (ed.), Courts of Final Jurisdiction, (Federation Press, Sydney, 1996). And it is difficult to disagree with Gummow J.'s characterization both of the methodology of Australian contract law while it remained subject to direct English control and of the role assumed by equity in regulating contract formation and performance.

Having said this, it is also appropriate to indicate that my own view inclines to that of Priestley J.A. Of that inclination I would say only this. Fair dealing is a major (if not openly articulated) organising idea in Australian law. It is unnecessary to enlarge upon that here. More germane to the present question, the implied duty is, as is well known, an accepted idea in the contract law of the United States and, probably, of Canada: see E.A. FARNSWORTH, "Good Faith in Contract Performance" in J BEATSON and D FRIEDMANN (eds) Good Faith and Fault in Contract Law, (Clarendon Press, Oxford, 1995); for a convenient collection of some of the voluminous literature in the US debating the meaning of the implied duty see Farnsworth on Contracts, Vol 2, para 7.17a (Little, Brown & Co, Boston 1990); for an English view see *e.g.* Rt Hon Lord Justice STAUGHTON, "Good Faith and Fairness in Commercial Contract Law" (1994) 7 Jo Contract Law 193; and see Livingstone v. Roskilly [1992] 3 NZLR 230 at 237-238. Its status in civil law is well recognised: see *e.g.* H.K. LOCKE, "Good Faith and Contractual Performance" in P.D. FINN (ed.), Essays on Contract, (Law Book Co, Sydney, 1987); J.F. O'CONNOR, Good Faith in English Law, Ch. 8 (Dartmouth, 1990). It has been propounded as a fundamental principle to be honoured in international commercial contracts: see *e.g.* UNIDROIT, Principles of International Commercial Contracts, Article 1.7 (International Institute for the Unification of Private Law, Rome, 1994). Its more open recognition in our own contract law is now warranted: *cf.* Sir Anthony MASON, "Contract and its Relationship with Equitable Standards and the Doctrine of Good Faith",

The Cambridge Lectures, 1993 (8 July 1993); notwithstanding the significant adjustments this would occasion to some of contract law's apparent orthodoxies: see *e.g.* LOCKE, above, 177ff.

I should add that, unlike Gummow J., I consider a virtue of the implied duty to be that it expresses in a generalization of universal application, the standard of conduct to which all contracting parties are to be expected to adhere throughout the lives of their contracts. It may well be that, on analysis, that standard would be found to advance little the standard that presently may be exacted from contracting parties by other means: *cf.* the standard applied in Conoco v. Inman Oil Co 774 F2d 895 at 908 (1985). But setting the appropriate standard of fair dealing is, in my view, another matter altogether from acceptance of the duty itself.

However, the matter of a term implied by law does not rest here. I raised directly with the parties the question whether the type of contract and/or the relationship of the parties (one of which was a State agency) may require the implication as a matter of law. Submissions were sought on this issue.

(b) As a legal incident of a particular class of contract.

Given my earlier finding my conclusions here can be stated relatively shortly. I mean no disrespect to the detailed and helpful written submissions of the parties in adopting this course. As is now well accepted, quite apart from that form of implication which is necessary to give business efficacy to a particular contract, a term may be implied as a matter of law as a legal incident of a particular class of contract: on this distinction see Castlemaine Tooheys Ltd. V. Carlton & United Breweries Ltd (1987) 10 NSWLR 468 at 486ff. Notwithstanding the differences between the two forms of implication, there is justification for the conclusion of Priestley JA in Renard Constructions (ME) Pty Ltd. V. Minister for Public Works, above, at 260 that for particular contracts in particular settings "there may be a good deal of overlap between the two categories." This case exemplifies this overlap.

It is one in which I am prepared to find that, as a matter of law, a duty to deal fairly in the performance of the contracts I have found should be implied into those contracts. Irrespective of what should be taken to have been the intentions of the parties, both the type (or class) of contract and the relationship of the parties were such as gave the tenderers the right to expect, and the CAA the obligation to exhibit, fair dealing in the performance of the contracts.

There has been enduring uncertainty, if not controversy, as to the test to be applied - if there be a single test - in making an implication of law. For the more recent provenance of this form of implication it is unnecessary for present purposes to look beyond the House of Lords' decisions in Lister v. Romford Ice and Cold Storage Co Ltd [1957] AC 555 and Liverpool City Council v. Irwin [1977] AC 239. These, along with Scally v. Southern Health and Social Services Board [1992] 1 AC 294, have been accepted as authoritative in this country: see Byrne v. Australian Airlines Ltd. (1995) 185 CLR 410 per McHugh and Gummow JJ; Codelfa Construction Pty Ltd v. State Rail Authority of New South Wales, above, per Mason J.

As the respondent emphasized in its submission, the central criterion manifest in those decisions for so implying a term is the requirement of "necessity". Explanation of this was in turn given by McHugh and Gummow JJ in Byrnes' case, above, at 450 where their Honours noted that:

"Many of the terms now said to be implied by law in various categories of case reflect the concern of the courts that, unless such a term be implied, the enjoyment of the rights conferred by the contract would or could be rendered nugatory, worthless, or, perhaps, be seriously undermined. Hence, the reference in the decisions to "necessity" ... This notion of "necessity" has been crucial in the modern cases in which the courts have implied for the first time a new term as a matter of law."

The respondent, understandably, emphasizes this and has submitted, in the language of McHugh and Gummow JJ in Byrnes' case, at 453, that the alleged process contracts would be "workable and effective" without the introduction into them of the implied term the applicant propounds.

It is strictly unnecessary to express a concluded view on that submission given the view I take of the "necessity test". Nonetheless I would indicate that the "workability and effectiveness" suggested could well be said only to exist in competitive contracts of this type if they contained the binding reassurance of fair dealing in their performance - the more so where the contract to be let involves the expenditure of "publicly owned" funds: US authority would seem to acknowledge this in the government procurement context, see *e.g.* Keco Industries Inc v. US 492F 2d 1200 at 1205 (1974); see also E.W. MASSENGALE, Fundamentals of Federal Contract Law, 211 (Quorum Books, NY, 1991). It is not at all surprising that, even absent the finding of a contract, courts have assumed that "obligations to act fairly" in the treatment of tenderers can still arise: see Pratt Contractors Ltd. v. Palmerston North City Council [1995] 1 NZLR 469 at 478; and see more generally N. SEDDON, Government Contracts, 235 ff. If the purpose of a tender process contract is to be accomplished, if contractor-tenderers are to be given an effective opportunity to enjoy the fruits of the bid and not to have that opportunity destroyed by the unfair dealing of the other party to the contract, a duty such as I have described would appear to me to be a presupposition of such a contract. In the tender process context such a duty seems little more than an appropriate adaptation of the duty to cooperate recognized in Butt v. McDonald (1896) 7 QLJ 68 at 70-71. I need explore that analogy no further here.

It doubtless is the case that the "necessity test" - and its preoccupation with whether, absent the implication, the enjoyment of contractual rights could be rendered nugatory, worthless or be seriously undermined - addresses the broad range of instances where the issue of such an implication ordinarily arises: see *e.g.* the extended list of examples given in Glanville WILLIAMS, "Language and the Law", (1945) 61 LQR 71 at 403.

Having acknowledged this, I do not understand that test, at least so narrowly conceived, to provide a complete account of the reasons for which an implication of law can be made. In Simonius Vischer & Co v. Holt & Thompson [1979] 2 NSWLR 322 at 348 Samuels JA suggested that the implication is founded in policy. Whether or not this be accepted unreservedly as a generalization, it clearly is the case that considerations of public policy can and do have an overt part to play in some instances in determining whether it is necessary that an obligation should be implied as a matter of law in a contract. The contractual obligation of secrecy imposed on professionals in virtue of their relationship with their clients and its varying scope from profession to profession are, I consider, illustrations of this: see *e.g.* Tournier v. National Provincial & Union Bank of England [1924] 1 KB 461 at 474; Parry-Jones v. Law Society [1969] 1 Ch 1 at 7, 9.

Perhaps the most significant illustration of the role considerations of public policy can have in the matter is to be found in Viscount Simonds' speech in Lister v. Romford Ice and Cold Storage Ltd. [1957] AC 555. In a passage often quoted from in this country when distinguishing implications of law from those necessary to give business efficacy to a contract, his Lordship observed (at 576):

"[T]he real question becomes, not what terms can be implied in a contract between two individuals who are assumed to be making a bargain in regard to a particular transaction or course of business; we have to take a wider view, for we are concerned with a general question, which, if not correctly described as a question of status, yet can only be answered by considering the relation in which the drivers of motor-vehicles and their employers generally stand to each other. Just as the duty of care, rightly regarded as a contractual obligation, is imposed on the servant, or the duty not to disclose confidential information ..., or the duty not to betray secret processes ..., just as the duty is imposed on the master not to require his servant to do any illegal act, just so the question must be asked and answered whether in the world in which we live today it is a necessary condition of the relation of master and man that the master should, to use a broad colloquialism, look after the whole matter of insurance. If I were to try to apply the familiar tests where the question is whether a term should be implied in a particular contract in order to give it what is called business efficacy, I should lose myself in the attempt to formulate it with the necessary precision. The necessarily vague evidence given by the parties and the fact that the action is brought without the assent of the employers shows at least ex post facto how they regarded the position. But this is not conclusive; for, as I have said, the solution of the problem does not rest on the implication of a term in a particular contract of service but upon more general considerations".

In rejecting the implication sought in that case, Viscount Simonds then went on to consider among "the more general considerations" (*inter alia*) both the consequences within the employment relationship and the "social consequences" (at 579) that could or would flow from the implication sought.

Though his Lordship avoided tying the implication directly to the status of the parties, it probably is the case that the need to have recourse to "more general considerations" and not merely to "necessity" narrowly conceived is most apt to occur where the alleged implication is based upon the status or function of one or both of the contracting parties. And that this need does arise perhaps explains why on occasion the courts characterize the implied term "as a necessary incident of a definable category of contractual relationship": Scally v. Southern Health and Social Services Board [1992] 1 AC 294 at 307.

I have laboured this matter for this reason. Not only is the contract of a type in which, as I have indicated above, the tenderers could properly expect the other contracting party to act fairly in its performance, that other contracting party is an agency of government and as such can properly be expected to act fairly with those with whom it deals in such contracts. It is to this latter feature of the contractual relationship that I wish to draw attention. It has not been pleaded or argued that, because the CAA is a public body, its contract with Hughes is for that reason amenable to challenge on what for convenience I might call "public law" rather than on conventional contractual (*i.e.* "private law") grounds:

[...]

[1977] 1 NSWLR 449 on the "relevant relationship".

To say the matter is one of contract does not, though, exhaust the appropriate characterization of the parties to this contract. The CAA, as I have noted is a public body - a body whose owners are, ultimately, the Australian community whom the authority serves under and in accordance with its statutory mandate.

As with any agency of government - and I do not mean by this that it is thereby within "the shield of the Crown" - it has no private or self-interest of its own separate from the public interest it is constitutionally bound to serve: *cf.* Attorney-General for the United Kingdom v. Heinemann Publishers Australia Pty Ltd. (1987) 10 NSWLR 86 at 191; see also Mercury Energy Ltd. v. Electricity Corporation of New Zealand, above, at 388; Webster v. Auckland Harbour Board [1983] NZLR 646 at 649-650; Jones v. Swansea City Council [1990] 1 WLR 54 at 71, 85. That public interest in the case of a body such as the CAA is to be determined from what is express or implied in the CAA Act itself. That Act of Parliament indicated the end of the CAA's service.

There is, I consider much to be said for the view that, having no legitimate private interest in the performance of its functions, a public body (including a state owned company) should be required as of course to act fairly towards those with whom it deals at least insofar as this is consistent with its obligation to serve the public interest (or interests) for which it has been created. I have no need here, though, to rely upon such a broad notion. That the law entertains expectations of fair dealing of government and of public bodies is manifest in some number of spheres. First and most obviously, there is the general application of the requirements of procedural fairness to "governmental executive decision-making": Haoucher v. Minister of State for Immigration and Ethnic Affairs (1990) 169 CLR 648 at 653; see also Annetts v. McCann (1990) 170 CLR 596 - though it needs to be acknowledged that these requirements can in limited circumstances extend to the decision making (characteristically to decisions to expel or to discipline members) of non-governmental bodies and associations: see Aronson and Dyer, Judicial Review of Administrative Action, 493-495, (LBC, Sydney, 1996).

Secondly, there is what Griffith CJ referred to in Melbourne Steamship Co. Ltd. v. Moorehead (1912) 15 CLR 333 at 342 as:

"the old-fashioned traditional, and almost instinctive, standard of fair play to be observed by the Crown in dealing with subjects, which I learned a very long time ago to regard as elementary."

This proposition has received significant, recent judicial endorsement in this country most notably in the Full Court of this Court in SCI Operations Pty Ltd. v. Commonwealth of Australia, (unreported, FC FCA, per Beaumont and Einfeld JJ, 28 August 1996); see also Greiner v. Independent Commission Against Corruption (1992) 28 NSWLR 125. I note in this particularly the observations of Mahoney J in his dissenting judgment (on grounds not presently relevant) in Logue v. Shoalhaven Shire Council [1979] 1 NSWLR 537 at 558-559 in applying the proposition to a local authority - to "a corporation constituted by statute, and discharging public functions": "It is well settled that there is expected of the Crown the highest standards in dealing with its subjects: see Melbourne Steamship Co. Ltd. v. Moorehead ..., per Griffith C.J. What might be accepted from others would not be seen as in full accord with the principles of equity and good conscience to be expected in the case of the Crown: see P. & C. Cantarella Pty. Ltd. v. Egg Marketing Board (N.S.W.) [[1973] 2 NSWLR 366 at 383-384]. In my opinion, a standard of conduct not significantly different should be expected of a statutory corporation of the present kind ... ."

This fair play principle has its most common manifestation in the "model litigant" standards exacted from the Crown in legal proceedings: see *e.g.* Director of Public Prosecutions for the Commonwealth v. Saxon (1992) 28 NSWLR 263. Thirdly, and again litigation related, the rule in Ex parte James; Re Condon (1874) LR 9 Ch. App 609 has been applied to public bodies (*e.g.* local authorities: R. v. Tower Hamlets London Borough Council; Ex parte Chetnik Developments Ltd. [1988] AC 858) so as to ensure "high principled" action when mistaken payments have been received by them; see also SCI Operations Pty Ltd. v. Commonwealth of Australia, above.

In differing ways these instances reflect policies in the law, albeit in specific contexts, (a) of protecting the reasonable expectations of those dealing with public bodies; (b) of ensuring that the powers possessed by a public body, "whether conferred by statute or by contract", are exercised "for the public good": *cf.* Jones v. Swansea City Council [1990] 1 WLR 54 at 71; and (c) of requiring such bodies to act as 'moral exemplars': government and its agencies should lead by example: Olmstead v. United States 277 US 438 at 485 (1928); Joint Committee of Public Accounts, Social Responsibilities of Commonwealth Statutory Authorities and Government Business Enterprises, Report 315, esp. para. 2.21ff, (AGPS, Canberra, 1992). These policies I consider to be important in the present matter. I should add for the sake of completeness that I do not regard the decision of the Full Court of this Court in General Newspapers Pty Ltd. v. Telstra Corporation (1993) 45 FCR 164 as having present bearing on the significance to be attributed these policies.

Given the view I earlier expressed that fair dealing is, in effect, a proper presupposition of a competitive tender process contract (especially one involving the disposition of public funds), and given that a public body is the contracting party whose performance of the contract is being relied upon, a necessary incident of such a contract with a public body is, I am prepared to conclude, that it will deal fairly with the tenderers in the performance of its tender process contracts with them. Before leaving this subject, it is appropriate to note, the following. First, a ground advanced by the respondent for not implying a general duty to deal fairly was that the RFT had itself specified particular obligations of fairness and that these should be taken to be exhaustive of the matter. Those obligations in my view should properly be seen as no more than particular manifestations of the general duty I have found to be implied. I see no inconsistency between the two nor between the implied term and the common intention of the parties as manifest in the contract. Secondly, and I emphasize this, the term I have found to be implied by law (which differs little, if at all in the circumstances, from that found to be implied *ad hoc*) relates to the CAA's performance of the RFT contract. That term is as I will indicate in Part XI of these reasons, distinctive in the obligation it imposes. Importantly it does not as such impose on the CAA under the guise of contract law, the obligation to avoid making its decision or otherwise conducting itself in ways which would render it amenable to judicial review of administrative action. Indeed I understood the applicant to disavow such a claim on its part, while insisting nonetheless that conduct which independently might found judicial review could be of such actual character in the circumstances as to constitute a breach of the implied term.

(...)

PART XI: FAIR DEALING

I have found that it was an implied term of the RFT contract that the CAA would conduct its evaluation of the tenders fairly and in a manner that would ensure equal opportunity to Hughes and Thomson. I also have found that, as a matter of law, a term would be implied into the RFT in any event that obliged the CAA to deal fairly with the tenderers in its performance of the RFT contracts.

Though formulated in somewhat different terms there would seem to be no operative difference between the two, at least as they relate to the matters to be considered in this Part. For ease in exposition, I will deal with the two compendiously as each imposes a duty on the CAA to deal fairly with the tenderers in its performance of its RFT contracts. I should add that there are as well Trade Practices Act claims raising fair dealing issues. In this instance I will consider these separately from the contract claim.

Before turning to the various allegations made that are said to constitute breaches of this duty, it is necessary to make some comment on the content of the duty itself. First, obviously, it prescribed a standard of conduct to be adhered to by the CAA in relation to the RFT and that standard was an objective one. Secondly the duty would only have been breached where, to state the matter negatively, the CAA was shown actually to have dealt unfairly with a tenderer in the manner of its putting the RFT contract into effect. It is this second matter that requires elaboration.

In Part IV: General Contract Issues, I indicated that the applicant has not attempted under the guise of the implied term to give contractual force or effect to the grounds of judicial review of administrative action generally or to the requirement of procedural fairness as it relates to bias in particular. It was open to the contractors so to contract. Such did not occur and no such contract has been pleaded.

Nonetheless, what the applicant has submitted is that the bias rules of procedural fairness provide a guide to the content of the contractual duty. In this I am invited to accept that a decision would involve unfair dealing if it was one in which a contractor-decision maker was so circumstanced as to give rise in the mind of the other contractor, to a reasonable apprehension of bias on the part of the decision maker. Analogical support for this was sought in Minister for Immigration, Local Government and Ethnic Affairs v. Mok (1995)

55 FCR 375. The respondent for its part has submitted that the applicant is seeking to do indirectly (*i.e.* via the implied duty of fair dealing) what it has not done directly (*i.e.* via an alleged term concerned with the rules of procedural fairness). There is substance in this objection though it does not provide the answer to the submission. That answer is this. It is only conduct which is shown actually to constitute unfair dealing by the CAA with a tenderer in the performance of the RFT contract that can amount to a breach of the implied term. Conduct etc that merely gives rise to an apprehension (howsoever reasonable) that such might occur is not enough. Furthermore, whether or not even some level of demonstrated partial conduct will constitute a breach will depend on whether, in the circumstances, it occasions unfair dealing with a tenderer - although proof of such conduct would itself arouse real suspicion that such had occurred.

A. THE ALLEGATIONS OF UNFAIR DEALING: CONTRACT CLAIMS

All of the conduct particularized in the pleadings as constituting breaches of express and implied terms of the RFT are also relied upon as providing instances occasioning breaches of the fair dealing term. Additionally it is alleged that the manner in which the Attorney-General's Department provided legal advice to the CAA, Mr. Moten and DITRD occasioned a breach of the term.

Given the findings I have already made, there are only three specific allegations to which it is necessary to refer here. These relate (i) to various allegations concerning Mr Yates; (ii) to DITRD's conduct in its AII evaluation/consultancy; and (iii) to the Attorney-General's Department's discharge of its legal advisory function. While the claim made concerning the CAA's alleged responsibility for Mr. Moten's actions as independent auditor (see Part VII: Audit Failure) was advanced as an instance of unfair dealing, I do not regard it as necessary to examine that claim. Whatever the complaint the CAA might have in respect of the manner in which Mr. Moten actually performed his audit function, given the nature of his function his conduct could only lead to unfair dealing by the CAA with Hughes if he so acted as to cause the CAA to deal unfairly with Hughes. There are grounds for concluding, as I have earlier indicated, that he was a cause of the Board's failure properly to apply the evaluation criteria and methodology. That failure occasioned a breach of an express term of the RFT. And that, in my view, exhausts the practical significance of his conduct in this matter. Before considering individually the three allegations noted above, I should refer to an omnibus submission made by the applicant. It is that while a significant number of individual instances of wrongdoing have been alleged, I should not treat these in isolation but should be prepared to evaluate them and the evidence supporting them in a "cumulative" way. As I understand this, its object seems to be that I should be prepared to find in the whole, if not necessarily in the parts, that an actionable wrong has been committed. I presume, if such is the intent of the submission, the wrong I am invited to find (given the pleadings) is that the duty of fair dealing has so been breached. The respondent invited me firmly to resist taking any such course.

While I would not wish to cast doubt on the view that unfair dealing in a given instance may be the product of the cumulative effect of specific actions which individually are not themselves unfair, this is not a case in which it is necessary to have resort to such an approach to establish actionable wrongdoing by the respondent. I already have found significant breaches of the RFT contract. It is inappropriate in my view to attempt to repackage the conduct constituting those breaches for the purpose of saying that, as far as it goes, it evidences as well a breach of the fair dealing duty.

[...]

PART XIII: PRINCIPAL FINDINGS AND CONCLUSIONS

My observations here will be generalized, brief and highly selective. First, I have found that the processes leading to the award of the TAAATS contract were governed by a process contract, the principal terms of which were contained in the RFT. I also have found it to be an implied term of that contract that (*inter alia*) the CAA would conduct its tender evaluation fairly. I have determined as well that a term should be implied as a matter of law into a tender process contract with a public body (such as this was) that that body will deal fairly with a tenderer in the performance of its contract. Accordingly I have made such an implication into the RFT.

In this contractual setting, I have concluded that the CAA acted in breach of its contract with Hughes in that - (i) it failed to evaluate the tenders in accordance with the priorities and methodology prescribed in the RFT (paras 16.1 and 16.2); (ii) it failed to ensure that measures designed to achieve strict confidentiality of information contained in tenderers' proposals, were maintained (RFT para 16.2.7); and (iii) it accepted an out of time change to Thomson's proposed deed of AII commitment.

While there was evidence enough to warrant Hughes' allegation of a breach of the fair evaluation/fair dealing terms, I have not found it necessary to reach a conclusion on these given the breaches of contract that already have been made out.

Secondly, I have found that the CAA made, and (by its subsequent decisions and actions) falsified, certain representations as to the processes and methodology to be followed in the selection of the TAAATS contractor. These occurred in circumstances where Hughes was reasonably entitled to expect the CAA to disclose to it that the CAA did not intend to, and did not, adhere to what it had previously represented it would do.

In these circumstances I have concluded that the CAA engaged in conduct in contravention of s52 of the Trade Practices Act 1974 , that conduct relating substantially, though not precisely, to the same matters in respect of which I have found breaches of contract to have occurred. Additionally I have found that the CAA engaged in conduct in contravention of s52 in the representations it made to Hughes when de-briefing it on the basis of the CAA board's selection of Thomson as the TAAATS contractor. In each such instance of contravening conduct, I have found that Hughes relied upon that conduct. Thirdly, I have not found it necessary to make any findings on the applicant's claims in negligence and equitable estoppel. While the negligence claim in particular may have required examination of matters not expressly canvassed in these reasons, the claim itself achieved little prominence at the hearing and even less in submissions. Given the failures and failings of the CAA I have identified in my findings, little practical purpose would have been served by inviting further and detailed submissions on this claim and by engaging in a protracted examination of it.

Finally, bearing in mind the "splitting" of this proceeding, the orders I propose to make are that the parties file agreed short minutes of orders to reflect these reasons and if short minutes are not agreed, (i) the applicant to file and serve proposed minutes of orders along with written contentions supporting the orders, and (ii) the respondent to file and serve its written objections thereto.

[...]

Sources

Internet document: *http://www.lawnet.com.au/private/fct/1997/J970558.html*

Date: ***July 1997***
Adjudicating Court: ***ICC International Court of Arbitration, Paris***
Number: ***8873***
Parties: ***Unknown***

Keywords

PARTIES' CHOICE OF DOMESTC LAW (SPANISH LAW) AS LAW GOVERNING THE CONTRACT – PARTY'S REQUEST THAT ARBITRAL TRIBUNAL APPLY UNIDROIT PRINCIPLES AS TRADE USAGES (ART. VII GENEVA CONVENTION ON INTERNATIONAL ARBITRATION – ART. 13(5) OF THE ICC RULES OF ARBITRATION AND CONCILIATION) – ARBITRAL TRIBUNAL DECISION NOT TO APPLY THE UNIDROIT PRINCIPLES

HARDSHIP PROVISIONS IN THE UNIDROIT PRINCIPLES (ARTS. 6.2.2 AND 6.2.3) – DON NOT PRESENTLY REFLECT CURRENT PRACTICE IN INTERNATIONAL TRADE

Abstract

The award concerned a contract between a Spanish and a French company for the construction of works in a third country. Faced with a number of unforeseen difficulties which substantially increased the cost of the construction, the contractor requested the renegotiation of the contract invoking hardship according to Articles 6.2.2 and 6.2.3 of the UNIDROIT Principles. According to the contractor, although the contract contained a choice of law clause in favour of Spanish law, the UNIDROIT Principles were applicable as they represent veritable trade usages which the Arbitral Tribunal had at any rate to take into account under Article VII of the 1961 Geneva Convention on International Arbitration and Article 13(5) of the ICC Rules of Arbitration and Conciliation.

In deciding against the applicability of the UNIDROIT Principles, the Arbitral Tribunal first of all recalled that, according to their Preamble, they are applicable only where the parties have so expressly agreed or where the contract refers to "general principles of law", the *lex mercatoria* or the like as the applicable law. As to the argument that the UNIDROIT Principles represent veritable trade usages to be taken into account even where, as here, the parties have chosen a particular domestic law as the law governing their contract, the Arbitral Tribunal held that the provisions of the UNIDROIT Principles on hardship do not correspond, at least presently, to current practices in international trade.

Full Text

[...]

L'article 26 du contrat dit que

"Ce contrat sera entièrement régi par le droit espagnol, à l'exclusion de tout autre droit".

Considérant le choix exprès fait par les parties, il n'est évidemment pas nécessaire de déterminer la loi nationale applicable. Le problème qui se pose est plutôt celui de savoir si, et dans quelle mesure, on devra prendre en considération également, dans le contexte de la loi nationale choisie par les parties, les usages du commerce international.

Selon l'opinion de [la demanderesse] la controverse doit être décidée non seulement sur la base des dispositions de la loi espagnole mais aussi en tenant compte des usages du commerce international et des principes généraux du droit et, en particulier, des usages existant dans les contrats internationaux de génie civil.

[...]

[La défenderesse], au contraire, souligne qu 'en droit espagnol, et en particulier selon le Code civil, applicable dans le cas d'espèce ("*le contrato de obras*" étant un contrat de droit civil), les usages ne sont applicables que dans l'absence de réglementation de la loi.

[...]

Les règles que [la demanderesse] prétend être applicables en tant qu 'usages du commerce ou en tant que principes généraux applicables aux contrats internationaux sont essentiellement deux: d'une part le régime de la hardship prévu par les "Principes UNIDROIT" et d'autre part la règle selon laquelle la partie qui subit un événement de force majeure a droit au remboursement par l'autre partie des surcoûts qu'elle supporte pour surmonter la situation de force majeure, règle qui résulterait des conditions contractuelles répandues à niveau international et en particulier des conditions FLDIC (*Condition of Contract for Works of Civil Engineering Construction, fourth edition*, 1987) et des conditions de l'ENAA (ENAA *Model Form International Contract for Process Plant Construction*).

En ce qui concerne les "Principes des Contrats Commerciaux Internationaux" rédigés par UNIDROIT (Principes UNIDROIT), leur Préambule prévoit expressément qu'ils s'appliquent "lorsque les parties acceptent d'y soumettre leur contrat" et qu'ils "peuvent s 'appliquer lorsque les parties acceptent que leur contrat soit régi par les "Principes généraux du droit", la *lex mercatoria* ou autre formule similaire".

Etant donné que dans le contrat du [date] les parties n'ont fait aucune référence aux Principes en question et que la formulation de la clause sur la loi applicable permet d'exclure avec certitude que les parties aient voulu soumettre le contrat à la *lex mercatoria* ou aux principes généraux du droit, on ne voit pas comment les principes en question pourraient trouver application en tant que tels.

Le seul moyen pour justifier leur application serait de dire qu'il s'agit d'une "codification" des usages existants et que les "Principes UNIDROIT" devraient être appliqués dans cette qualité d'usages "codifies" par UNIDROIT. Pour arriver à cette conclusion il faudrait prouver que les règles invoquées par la demanderesse (et en particulier celles sur la *hardship*, contenues dans les articles 6.2.1 et suivants) correspondent à un usage international généralement établi, auquel les personnes engagées dans le commerce international se considèrent liées sans besoin d'une stipulation expresse dans ce sens.

Or, si l'on peut admettre l'existence d'une tendance, dans certaines branches, à stipuler avec une certaine continuité des clauses de hardship, il est certain que dans la pratique des affaires l'obligation de rééquilibrer le contrat (par la négociation et, le cas échéant, par l'intervention d'un tiers, comme prévu dans l'article 6.2.3, paragraphe 4 des Principes UNIDROIT), qui caractérise la *hardship*, constitue un principe tout-à-fait exceptionnel, qui n'est accepté que dans le cadre de clauses contractuelles, qui devront déterminer en détail les situations justifiant la *hardship* ainsi que les conséquences de celle-ci. Il est donc exclu que l'on puisse considérer les dispositions en matière de *hardship* contenues dans les "Principes UNIDROIT" comme des usages du commerce. Il s'agit, au contraire, de règles qui ne correspondent pas, au moins à l'état actuel, à la pratique courante des affaires dans le commerce international et qui ne seront par conséquent applicables que lorsque les parties y ont fait une référence expresse, ce qui n'est pas le cas ici.

Dans ces conditions, le tribunal arbitral conclut à l'inapplicabilité, dans le cas d'espèce, des "Principes UNIDROIT" et en particulier des articles 6.2.1 et suivants en matière de *hardship*.

[...]

Sources

Original in French:
Journal de droit international, 1998, 1017-1024, with note by D. HASCHER, *ibid.* 1024.
ICC International Court of Arbitration Bulletin, Vol. 10, No. 2, Fall 1999, 78 – 81.

Date: ***September 2, 1997***
Adjudicating Court: ***International Arbitration Court of the Chamber of Commerce and Industry of the Russian Federation***
Number: ***225/1996***
Parties: ***Unknown***

Keywords

CONTRACT GOVERNED BY DOMESTIC LAW – REFERENCE TO THE UNIDROIT PRINCIPLES FOR CONFIRMATION AT INTERNATIONAL LEVEL OR SIMILAR RULE PROVIDED FOR BY DOMESTIC LAW

HARM DUE IN PART TO AGGRIEVED PARTY – DAMAGES REDUCED ACCORDINGLY (ART. 7.4.7 UNIDROIT PRINCIPLES)

Abstract

A Russian and an Estonian party entered into a sales contract, which provided for advanced payment by the buyer. Buyer made such advance payment, but when Seller delayed the delivery of the goods due to their delayed clearance through customs, Buyer requested payment of interest on the amount paid in advance.

Having found that the delay in the delivery of the goods by Seller was due in part to Buyer's failure timely to provide Seller with the documents necessary for customs clearance, the Arbitral Tribunal decided to award to Buyer only half of the damages it has claimed for. In doing so the Arbitral Tribunal expressly referred to the principle of "concurrent" liability as provided for by the applicable domestic law; yet in addition it also referred to the UNIDROIT Principles which in Article 7.4.7 lay down a similar rule whenever the harm suffered by the aggrieved party is in part due to an act or an omission of that same party.

Full Text

[Not yet available]

Sources

Unpublished. Notice of the award kindly given by Professor Alexander KOMAROV, President of the International Arbitration Court of the Chamber of Commerce and Industry of the Russian Federation.

Date: ***September 23, 1997***
Adjudicating Court: ***UN Compensation Commission, Panel "F1"***
Number: ***Recommendation S/AC.26***
Parties: ***Governments and International Organizations with Claims Arising Out of Iraqi invasion of Kuwait***

Keywords

TERMINATION – TERMINATION DUE TO FORCE MAJEURE – INJURED PARTY OBLIGED TO RETURN MONETARY DEPOSIT (ARTS. 7.1.7, 7.3.5, 7.3.6, 7.4.9 UNIDROIT PRINCIPLES)

DAMAGES – EVIDENCE INSUFFICIENT TO ESTABLISH THE AMOUNT OF DAMAGES – DETERMINATION TO BE MADE AT PANEL'S DISCRETION (ART. 7.4.3(3) UNIDROIT PRINCIPLES)

DAMAGES – DUTY OF MITIGATION – COMPENSATION EXCLUDED FOR LOSSES THAT COULD REASONABLY HAVE BEEN AVOIDED (ART. 7.4.8(1) UNIDROIT PRINCIPLES) – COMPENSATION ADMITTED FOR EXPENSES INCURRED BY CLAIMANT IN MITIGATING DAMAGES (ART. 7.4.8(2) UNIDROIT PRINCIPLES)

Abstract

Panel "F1"[1], after finding that in many of the claims the evidence produced was insufficient to demonstrate with a reasonable degree of certainty the amount of the loss, decided, "in conformity with general principles of law", to exercise its discretion in assessing the amount of compensation that should be awarded and in support of its decision referred, among others, to Art. 7.4.3(3) of the UNIDROIT Principles.

Moreover, the Panel quoted Articles 7.1.7, 7.3.5, 7.3.6 and 7.4.9 of the same UNIDROIT Principles. It referred to them as "principles of international commercial contract law" to demonstrate that termination of a contract for *force majeure* does not release the aggrieved party from its obligation to return the monetary deposit made by the other party.

Finally, in reaffirming the decision of the Governing Council of the United Nations Compensation Commission, according to which claimants were under a duty to mitigate damages and panels should not compensate losses that could reasonably have been avoided, the Panel stated that this was a general principle of law reflected, among others, in Article 7.4.8(1) of the UNIDROIT Principles. As to the question of whether the expenses incurred by a claimant in mitigating damages were compensable, the Panel decided in the affirmative, referring directly to Art. 7.4.8(2) of the UNIDROIT Principles.

[1] The United Nations Compensation Commission, set up by the United Nations Security Council in 1991, is in charge of the resolution of claims for compensation filed by individuals, corporations, States and international organisations for the losses they sustained by reason of Iraq's military invasion and occupation of Kuwait in 1990. Claims by States and international organisations were filed in category "F" and decided by Panels each composed of three Commissioners.

Full Text

[...]

1. Following the creation of the United Nations Compensation Commission (the "Commission") by the United Nations Security Council the Commission's Governing Council (the "Governing Council") established six claims categories in which individuals, corporations and Governments could seek compensation for losses arising out of Iraq's invasion and occupation of Kuwait. Governments and international organizations were required to file their claims in category "F". Based on the claimants' classification of their claims, 42 Governments and 3 international organizations submitted 298 category "F" claims seeking compensation for a total amount of approximately 141 billion United States dollars ("US$") for their alleged losses.

[...]

III LEGAL FRAMEWORK

A. Applicable law

[...]

2. The Security Council, in paragraph 16 of resolution 687 (1991), decided that "Iraq ... is liable under international law for any direct loss, damage ... or injury to foreign Governments, nationals and corporations, as a result of Iraq's unlawful invasion and occupation of Kuwait".

[...]

Pursuant to article 31 of the Rules, the Panel in deciding the claims shall apply the following:

"... Security Council resolution 687 (1991) and other relevant Security Council resolutions, the criteria established by the Governing Council for particular categories of claims, and any pertinent decisions of the Governing Council. In addition, where necessary, Commissioners shall apply other relevant rules of international law".

The Governing Council has provided some guidance on the issue of what types of loss are to be considered direct and, therefore, compensable. The most relevant decisions of the Governing Council to the Claims covered by this report are decisions 7 and 9.

In decision 7, the Governing Council considered direct losses to include "... any loss suffered as a result of ... military operations or threat of military action by either side during the period 2 August to 2 March 1991; [...] departure of persons from or their inability to leave Iraq or Kuwait (or a decision not to return) during that period; [...] actions by officials, employees or agents of the Government of Iraq or its controlled entities during that period in connection with the invasion or occupation; ... [t]he breakdown of civil order in Kuwait or Iraq during that period; or [...] hostage-taking or other illegal detention".

In the same decision, the Governing Council added, in paragraph 36, that such losses include "loss of or damage to property of a Government, as well as losses and cost incurred by a Government in evacuating its nationals from Iraq or Kuwait". Moreover, the Governing Council stated that compensation is available to "reimburse payments made or relief provided by Governments or international organizations to others - for example to nationals, residents or employees or to others pursuant to contractual obligations - for losses covered by any of the criteria adopted by the Council".

In decision 9, the Governing Council further defined what constitutes a direct loss by deciding that "in a case where business property had been lost because it had been left unguarded by company personnel due to the situation in Iraq and Kuwait, such loss may be considered as resulting directly from the invasion and occupation". While decision 9 focuses on business losses, it is the Panel's view that the Governing Council's guidance regarding directness and causation where unguarded property has been damaged or destroyed is equally applicable to Government claims.

These rules and directives governing the activities of the Panel have been interpreted in light of general principles of international law. Such international legal principles were also applied by the Panel to fill gaps where necessary.

B. Procedural and evidentiary requirements

In contrast to the simplified statement of claim and evidentiary requirements imposed on individual claimants seeking compensation [...], the Governing Council expressly stated that with respect to business losses there "will be a need for detailed factual descriptions of the circumstances of the claimed loss, damage or injury" in order for a claim to receive compensation with respect to business losses.

[...]

In its review of the Claims, the Panel found that all the Claims contained a statement of claim and evidence sufficient to establish at least parts of certain loss elements alleged within the Claims. But the Panel also found that within certain Claims individual loss elements or portions thereof were not supported by particularized statements of claim or documentary or other evidence sufficient to demonstrate the circumstances and amount of the claimed loss. In such cases, the Panel could not recommend that compensation be awarded for the unsubstantiated losses. The Panel's decision not to recommend compensation for portions of Claims that did not state the circumstances of the alleged loss with particularity or that were not supported by evidence sufficient to establish such a loss is not only in accordance with the Rules of the Commission, but is also consistent with the general principles of international procedural law and practice.

In many of the Claims the Claimants' documentary or other evidence established that an alleged loss had, in fact, occurred. But the evidence was insufficient in those Claims to demonstrate with a reasonable degree of certainty the amount of the loss. In such cases, the Panel, in conformity with general principles of law, exercised its discretion in assessing the amount of compensation that should be awarded.[1] In exercising such discretion, the Panel took into account the level and type of evidence that should reasonably be required of a Claimant given the overall circumstances at the time of the loss [...].

[...]

C. Business transaction or course of dealing

[...]

While the Panel notes that the invasion and occupation of Kuwait might have given rise to a hardship or force majeure situation that may have excused the automobile dealer from his duty to deliver the new car, the event would not, under principles of international commercial contract law, excuse him from his alternative obligation to return the Claimant's deposit.[2] Accordingly, the Panel does not consider the automobile dealer's refusal to return the Claimant's deposit to constitute a direct loss within the meaning of paragraph 16 of resolution 687 (1991). Although the Claimant may have a claim against the automobile dealer, this Commission is not the proper forum for its adjudication.

[...]

D. Tangible property

[...]

Following the liberation of Kuwait, Nigeria was able to retrieve several of the cars that it had left in Iraq. The Claimant seeks compensation for the cost of this activity. In decision 9, paragraph 6, the Governing Council recognized that claimants are under a duty to mitigate damages and has instructed the panels not to compensate losses that "could reasonably have been avoided".[3] It therefore follows that reasonable expenses incurred by claimants in mitigating damages arising out of Iraq's invasion and occupation of Kuwait should be compensable.[4] In this case, the Panel decides that Nigeria's retrieval of its cars from Baghdad constituted a reasonable step taken in mitigation of its tangible property losses. Accordingly, the Claimant should be compensated for expenses incurred in the process to the extent that they are adequately supported by documentary or other appropriate evidence.

[...]

Notes

[1] Compare UNIDROIT Principles of International Commercial Contracts ("UNIDROIT Principles"), art. 7.4.3(3). ("Where the amount of damages cannot be established with a sufficient degree of certainty, the assessment is at the discretion of the court.")

[2] See, for example, UNIDROIT Principles, arts. 7.1.7, 7.3.5, 7.3.6 and 7.4.9.

[3] This is a general principle of law. Compare UNIDROIT Principles, art. 7.4.8(1). ("The non performing party is not liable for harm suffered by the aggrieved party to the extent that the harm could have been reduced by the latter party's taking reasonable steps.")

[4] Ibid., art. 7.4.8(2). ("The aggrieved party is entitled to recover any expenses reasonably incurred in attempting to reduce the harm.") See also, for example, Watkins-Johnson Company and Watkins-Johnson Limited, v. Iran, Iran-U.S. C.T.R., vol. 22 (1989), p. 218 *et seq.*, at p. 245, where, having held that the claimant's right to sell equipment in mitigation of its damages was consistent with international law, the Tribunal held that the claimant was "entitled to deduct from the proceeds reasonable expenses incurred in carrying out the sale".

Sources

Original in English:
Unpublished.

Date: ***October 9, 1997***
Country: ***Venezuela***
Adjudicating Court: ***Supreme Court***
Number: ***Unknown***
Parties: ***Bottling Company v. Pepsi Cola Panamericana, S.A.***

Keywords

ARBITRATION CLAUSE – PARTIES OF THE SAME NATIONALITY – APPLICATION OF THE 1958 NEW YORK CONVENTION AND 1975 INTER-AMERICAN CONVENTION ON INTERNATIONAL COMMERCIAL ARBITRATION – BROAD INTERPRETATION OF THE CONCEPT OF "INTERNATIONALITY" OF CONTRACT – REFERENCE BY COURT TO THE PREAMBLE (COMMENT 1) OF THE UNIDROIT PRINCIPLES

Abstract

The case concerned a contract between two Venezuelan companies which stipulated that any disputes which might arise should be submitted to arbitration in New York under the ICC Arbitration Rules. When one of the parties invoked the arbitration clause, the other party objected that it was invalid and insisted that jurisdiction remained vested in the ordinary Venezuelan courts.

Confirming the decision of the Tribunal of Caracas, the Supreme Court of Venezuela rejected the argument and upheld the validity of the arbitration clause. Its decision was based on the 1958 New York Convention on the Recognition and Enforcement of Foreign Arbitral Awards and on the 1975 Inter-American Convention on Commercial Arbitration, both of which had been ratified by Venezuela and expressly affirmed the binding nature of an agreement whereby parties to an international commercial contract decide to submit any dispute which might arise to arbitration.

While it was true that in the instant case the parties were both Venezuelan companies, in the Court's view, the application of the two Conventions was nevertheless justified as one of the companies was in fact a subsidiary of a United States company. In support of this broad interpretation of the concept of international contract in accordance with Article 1 of the 1975 Inter-American Convention on Commercial Arbitration, the Court referred, among others, to the Preamble, Comment 1 of the UNIDROIT Principles, which states that "[...] the concept of 'international' contracts should be given the broadest possible interpretation, so as to ultimately exclude only those situations where no international element at all is involved, *i.e.* where all the relevant elements of the contract in question are connected with one country only".

Full Text

[Not yet available]

Sources

Original in Spanish:
Unpublished.

Source:
Mr. Carlos VALEDÓN.

Date: ***December 1997***
Adjudicating Court: ***Ad hoc Arbitration, New York***
Number: ***Unknown***
Parties: ***Unknown***

Keywords

"GENERAL PRINCIPLES OF INTERNATIONAL CONTRACT LAW" AS THE RULES OF LAW APPLICABLE TO SUBSTANCE OF DISPUTE – REFERENCE TO UNIDROIT PRINCIPLES

Abstract

An international organization entered into a contract with a company situated in an African State for services to be rendered in the context of the organization's operations in a neighboring African State. The dispute arose when the company claimed for the balance of the price due for the services rendered.

The contract, which provided for arbitration pursuant to the UNCITRAL Arbitration Rules, did not include a choice of law clause. During the course of the arbitration, the parties agreed on the application of "general principles of international contract law".

Claimant and Respondent both relied on the UNIDROIT Principles of International Commercial Contracts, to establish such "general principles of international contract law". The Claimant in particular cited the UNIDROIT principles extensively, and also referred to New York law consistent with the UNIDROIT Principles.

Claimant maintained that respondent's claims to offsets and credits were based on an interpretation of the contract which was inconsistent with the intent of the parties. The Claimant also argued that respondent had engaged in a post-contract attempt to unilaterally modify the final agreement to be more in line with the proposal on which the contract had been initially awarded rather than with the subsequently negotiated and modified final agreement.

Claimant relied principally on UNIDROIT Principles Articles 1.1 ("*Freedom of Contract*"), 1.3 ("*Binding Character of Contract*"), 4.1 ("*Intention of the Parties*"), 4.4 ("*Reference to Contract or Statement as a Whole*"), and 4.5 ("*All Terms to be Given Effect*"). Moreover, according to Claimant Respondent breached its obligation to act in good faith, as set forth in Article 1.7 of UNIDROIT Principles, when seeking to unilaterally alter the terms of the agreement. Claimant finally relied on UNIDROIT Principles Articles 7.4.9 ("*Interest for Failure to Pay Money*"), as well as on New York law, to support its claim for interest. Respondent cited only UNIDROIT Principles Article 1.7 ("*Good Faith and Fair Dealing*").

In a detailed, fact-intensive decision, the Arbitral Tribunal did not identify the source of law or legal principles it applied in arriving at the award. The Tribunal awarded Claimant approximately 85% of its claim, together with a corresponding percentage of Claimants' attorneys' fees based on the UNCITRAL Arbitration Rules, plus interest at the rate of 9% simple (the New York statutory rate and, arguably, an approximation of the calculation contemplated in Article 7.4.9 of the UNIDROIT Principles), reimbursement for Claimant's share of arbitrators compensation, and other costs.

Full Text

[Not yet available]

Sources

Unpuslished. Noticc of the award kindly provided by Richard MATTEACCIO Pavia&Hancourt, New York.

Date: ***December 1997***
Adjudicating Court: ***ICC International Court of Arbitration, Paris***
Number: ***8817***
Parties: ***Unknown***

Keywords

CONTRACT SILENT AS TO APPLICABLE LAW – ICC RULES, ART. 13(3) – DECISION BY ARBITRAL TRIBUNAL TO APPLY "THE PROVISIONS OF [CISG] AND ITS GENERAL PRINCIPLES, NOW CONTAINED IN THE UNIDROIT PRINCIPLES"

ESTABLISHED PRACTICE BETWEEN PARTIES – BINDING CHARACTER (ART. 1.8 UNIDROIT PRINCIPLES) (ART. 9 CISG)

DAMAGES – DUTY TO MITIGATE HARM (ART. 77 CISG) (ART. 7.4.8 UNIDROIT PRINCIPLES)

Abstract

A Spanish company and a Dutch company concluded an agreement for the exclusive distribution and sale of food products. A dispute arose when Respondent, faced with both a change in Claimant's management and delays in payment (Claimant had not respected the deadline fixed by Respondent for payment), terminated the agreement. Claimant brought arbitral proceedings arguing that the dismissal of its general manager was justified by the fact that the latter had set up a competing commercial relationship with Respondent.

In determining the law applicable to the merits (the contract did not contain a choice of law clause), the Arbitral Tribunal found that the elements of sale prevailed over those of exclusive distribution and, citing Article 13(3) of the ICC Rules of Conciliation and Arbitration, decided to apply the provisions of the 1980 United Nations Convention on Contracts for the International Sale of Goods and its general principles, "now contained in the UNIDROIT Principles of International Commercial Contracts, [as] perfectly suited to resolving the dispute [...]."

With respect to the substance of the case, the Arbitral Tribunal awarded Claimant damages arising out of termination of contract and unfair competition by Respondent. In doing so, it referred to Article 1.8 of the UNIDROIT Principles to confirm the binding character of the parties' established practices (Art. 9(1) CISG), and to Art. 7.4.8 of the UNIDROIT Principles to confirm that a party suffering harm must take steps to mitigate the harm (Art. 77 CISG).

Full Text

[...] Bearing in mind, firstly, that the contractual relationship between Respondent and

Claimant ended in September 1995, and that the task of the arbitrator is limited to judging a dispute, the arbitrator feels there is no need to determine the applicable law as the parties could have done at the start of their relationship.

Bearing in mind, secondly, the provisions of Article 13.3 of the ICC Rules of Conciliation and Arbitration, which invites the arbitrator to determine the law applicable to the merits of the dispute, the sole arbitrator believes that the starting point for determining the applicable law should be the claims and counterclaims made in the dispute. [...]

In the presence of a contractual relationship qualified overall as one of sale, the arbitrator must, in order to resolve the dispute, determine an appropriate law, as he is invited to do by Article 13.3 of the ICC Rules of Conciliation and Arbitration. According to widespread case law in arbitration practice, one of the criteria for the appropriate nature of a rule is its presence in the legal systems of both parties. This is the case in the United Nations Convention on Contracts for the International Sale of Goods, signed in Vienna on 11 April 1980. This Convention came into force in Denmark on 1 March 1990 and in Spain on 1 August 1991, which date is after the signature of the contract but sufficiently remote for the text to have been studied and commented on especially in Spain.

Article 3.2 of said Vienna Convention calls for it to be applied in situations where, as in the present case, there is both a provision of a service and a sale, and the preponderant pan of the obligations arise from the sale. The same Convention reinforces the choice of a single law, desired by both parties, for dealing with disputes [...].
Furthermore, the provisions of the Convention and its general principles, now contained in the UNIDROIT Principles of International Commercial Contracts, are perfectly suited to resolving the dispute [...].

It should also be understood that the provisions of the contract signed in [...] shall apply as the law governing the parties.

The succession of events highlights the fact that Respondent attempted to change the practices and habits followed by the parties from at least March 1993. The change concerns the time-limit for payment and the requirement of a constant balance between deliveries and their payment.

According to Article 9.1 of the United Nations Convention on Contracts for the International Sale of Goods of 11 April 1980, "the parties are bound by any usage to which they have agreed and by any practices which they have established between themselves". This rule was extended to all international commercial contracts by the UNIDROIT Principles. Principle 1.8 provides that: "The parties are bound by any usage to which they have agreed and by any practices which they have established between themselves."

The arbitrator considers that such a rule is perfectly suited to resolving the dispute between Claimant and Respondent, even though the cancelled contract is a contract for exclusive distribution. Hence, in order for previous practices to be changed, the proposal made by one of the contracting parties needed to be accepted by the other party [...].

The changes Respondent wished to make should have been negotiated and accepted. In the absence of agreement between the two parties, the arbitrator considers that the fact of maintaining the practices accepted previously — at least tacitly — by both parties does not constitute "gross negligence" on the part of Claimant.

The arbitrator does not consider the reason given for denouncing the contract, which refers to the lack of means of paying within the time-limit fixed by Respondent, to be properly founded.'

[...] the arbitrator considers that the sudden, unexpected interruption of deliveries to Claimant caused harm to the company. Such harm took the form of difficulties in adapting to a new situation requiring changes in manufacturing arrangements. The arbitrator notes that Claimant neither provides proof that these difficulties lasted for a year nor indicates what efforts it made and what difficulties it encountered during the stage of adapting to different conditions and products.

Respondent points out pertinently that it is a principle of international commercial law that the party suffering harm must take the necessary steps to mitigate the harm. For contracts of sale, this rule is expressed in Article 77 of the Vienna Convention in the following terms:
"A party who relies on a breach of contract must take such measures as are reasonable in the circumstances to mitigate the loss, including loss of profit, resulting from the breach. If he fails to take such measures, the party in breach may claim a reduction in the damages in the amount by which the loss should have been mitigated."

In general, a similar rule is set out in Article 7.4.8. of the UNIDROIT Principles, which states: "The non-performing party is not liable for harm suffered by the aggrieved party to the extent that the harm could have been reduced by the latter party's taking reasonable steps."

In the absence of indications as to the efforts and attempts made by Claimant during the alleged year of inactivity, the arbitrator considers that this commercial inactivity was caused in part by Claimant's inertia.

[...]

Sources

Original in Spanish:
Unpublished.

Published in English (excerpt):
ICC International Court of Arbitration Bulletin, Vol. 10, No. 2, Fall 1999, 75 – 78.

Date: ***December 10, 1997***
Adjudicating Court: ***Ad hoc Arbitration, Buenos Aires***
Number: ***Unknown***
Parties: ***Unknown***

Keywords

CONTRACT SILENT AS TO APPLICABLE LAW – PARTIES CLAIMS BASED ON ARGENTINEAN LAW – ARBITRAL TRIBUNAL AUTHORISED BY PARTIES TO ACT AS "AMIABLES COMPOSITEURS" – APPLICATION OF UNIDROIT PRINCIPLES AS "USAGES OF INTERNATIONAL TRADE REFLECTING THE SOLUTIONS OF DIFFERENT LEGAL SYSTEMS AND OF INTERNATIONAL CONTRACT PRACTICE" IN CONFORMITY WITH ART. 28(4) UNCITRAL MODEL LAW ON INTERNATIONAL COMMERCIAL ARBITRATION

NOTICE OF AVOIDANCE (ART. 3.14 UNIDROIT PRINCIPLES)

CONFIRMATION OF CONTRACT (ART. 3.12 (AND COMMENT) UNIDROIT PRINCIPLES)

CONTRA PROFERENTEM RULE – CONTRACT CLAUSE DRAFTED BY DEFENDANT INTERPRETED MORE FAVOURABLY TO CLAIMANT (ART. 4.6 UNIDROIT PRINCIPLES)

Abstract

The shareholders of an Argentinean company (Sellers) and a Chilean company (Buyer) entered into a contract for the sale by the former of 85% of the shares of the Argentinean company. After conclusion of the contract, the Buyer discovered hidden debts of the Argentinean company and suspended payment of the remainder of the purchase price. The Sellers commenced the arbitral proceeding requesting full payment. In its defence, the Buyer requested that the Arbitral Tribunal confirm the avoidance of the contract and award damages, or failing that, to reduce the contract price in proportion to the hidden debts discovered. The contract did not contain a choice of law clause and the parties authorized the Arbitral Tribunal to act as *amiables compositeurs*.

Notwithstanding the fact that both parties had based their claims on specific provisions of Argentinean law, the Arbitral Tribunal decided to apply the UNIDROIT Principles. It held that the UNIDROIT Principles constituted "usages of international trade reflecting the solutions of different legal systems and of international contract practice", and as such, according to Art. 28(4) of the UNCITRAL Model Law on International Commercial Arbitration, they should prevail over any domestic law.

On the merits of the case, the Arbitral Tribunal rejected the Buyer's argument that the contract was avoided on account of fault or mistake and held that the comunication the Buyer had sent to the Sellers, informing them of the discovery of the hidden debts, could not be considered a proper notice of avoidance according to Art. 3.14 of the UNIDROIT Principles, as not only was there no indication of the intention to avoid the contract but its content even led the Sellers to believe that the Buyer wanted to stick to the contract, though in a modified version. Moreover, the Arbitral Tribunal held that the Buyer's subsequent conduct (in particular its proposal to terminate the contract by agreement; the payment of another installment of the price; the entering into negotiations with a view to modifying the contract) amounted to a confirmation of the contract according to Art. 3.12 of the UNIDROIT Principles (in this connection the Arbitral Tribunal expressly referred also to the Comment to Art. 3.12).

As to the request for a price reduction, the Arbitral Tribunal granted a reduction of only 65% of the hidden debts. One reason for this decision was that the contract had been drafted by the Buyer so that its provisions, including the one containing the Sellers' warranty as to hidden debts, according to Art. 4.6 of the UNIDROIT Principles, had to be interpreted in a sense more favorable to the Sellers.

Full Text

[Not yet available]

Sources

Original in Spanish:
Unpublished.

Date: ***January 28, 1998***
Adjudicating Court: ***Ad hoc Arbitration, Helsinki***
Number: ***Unknown***
Parties: ***Unknown***

Keywords

PARTIES' CHOICE OF DOMESTIC LAW (THE LAW OF A NORDIC COUNTRY) – ARBITRAL TRIBUNAL REFERENCE WITHOUT FURTHER EXPLANATION TO THE UNIDROIT PRINCIPLES

NON-PERFORMANCE – PENALTY CLAUSE CONTAINED IN THE CONTRACT – AMOUNT EXCESSIVELY HIGH – REDUCTION BY ARBITRAL TRIBUNAL (ART. 36 NORDIC CONTRACT LAW) (ART. 7.4.13(2) UNIDROIT PRINCIPLES)

Abstract

The shareholders of company X and company Y entered into an agreement between, whereby the former granted the latter the right to purchase at a fixed price within a specified period of time 51% of company X's shares. The contract, which was governed by the law of a Nordic country, provided for the payment of an amount corresponding to the purchase price in case of breach of the contract by the grantors of the option. A dispute arose between the parties regarding an alleged breach by the grantors ofthe option of some of their obligations arising out of the contract. Company Y asked for payment of the penalty.

The Court, though it held that the grantors of the option were liable for the alleged breaches, found that the amount of the penalty was excessively high for breaches different from that of the main obligation to sell the shares, and awarded company Y only part of it. In justifying the reduction of the agreed amount of the penalty the Court based its decision on Art. 36 of the Nordic Contract Law, according to which any contract term which is unreasonable or the application of which leads to unreasonableness may be mitigated or set aside. In order to further corroborate its finding, it also referred to Art. 7.4.13(2) of the UNIDROIT Principles, which expressly provide that "[...] the specified sum may be reduced to a reasonable amount where it is grossly excessive in relation to the harm resulting from the non-performance and to the other circumstances."

Full Text

[Not yet available]

Date: ***March, 1998***
Adjudicating Court: ***ICC International Court of Arbitration, Rome***
Number: ***9029***
Parties: ***Unknown***

Keywords

PARTIES' CHOICE OF DOMESTIC LAW (ITALIAN LAW) AS LAW GOVERNING THE CONTRACT – ART. 834 ITALIAN CODE OF CIVIL PROCEDURE REQUIRING ARBITRAL TRIBUNAL TO TAKE INTO ACCOUNT "TRADE USAGES" – REQUEST OF APPLICATION OF UNIDROIT PRINCIPLES AS AN "AUTHORITATIVE SOURCE OF KNOWLEDGE OF INTERNATIONAL TRADE USAGES" - REJECTED

ART. 3.10 ("GROSS DISPARITY") OF UNIDROIT PRINCIPLES – DISADVANTAGED PARTY'S STATE OF IGNORANCE - CONDITIONS

ART. 6.2.2 ("HARDSHIP") – ALTERATION OF EQUILIBRIUM DUE TO EVENT WHERE RISK ASSUMED BY DISADVANTAGED PARTY

Abstract

An Italian company (Claimant) and an Austrian company (Respondent) entered into a Shareholders Agreement for the financing of an aeronautical project. The Italian company terminated the contract after the Austrian company failed to make payment. The contract contained a choice of law clause in favour of Italian law.

In its statement of defence Respondent invoked the application of individual provisions of the UNIDROIT Principles. In doing so, it argued that, since Art. 834 of the Italian Code of Civil Procedure requires in an international arbitration the arbitral tribunal to take into account "trade usages", the *lex mercatoria* is an integral part of Italian law, and that the UNIDROIT Principles are to be considered an "authoritative source of knowledge of international trade usages".

The Arbitral Tribunal decided against the applicability of the provisions of the UNIDROIT Principles. In its view, "[...]although the UNIDROIT Principles constitute a set of rules theoretically appropriate to prefigure the future *lex mercatoria* should they be brought into line with international commercial practice, at present there is no necessary connection between the individual [provisions of the] Principles and the rules of the *lex mercatoria*, so that recourse to the Principles is not purely and simply the same as recourse to an actually existing international commercial usage". The Arbitral Tribunal further held that in the context of Art. 834 of the Italian Code of Civil Procedure "[i]nternational commercial usages are of strictly interpretative and integrative value, to the extent that there are gaps in national regulations that could usefully be filled by the aforesaid usages [...]" and concluded that the doctrine of gross disparity and hardship (invoked by Respondent), as dealt with in the UNIDROIT Principles, could not be applied "[b]eyond the limits of or with effects different from the presuppositions that are relevant in law and from the actual consequences of rescission and of cancellation of the contract [provided for in the Italian Civil Code ...]".

Nevertheless, the Arbitral Tribunal entered into the merits of some of the individual provisions of the UNIDROIT Principles invoked by Respondent (in particular Arts. 3.10 and 6.2.2).

Thus, with respect to Art. 3.10 ("*Gross disparity*"), the Arbitral Tribunal pointed out that the disadvantaged party may invoked its state of ignorance when it concerns facts which take place before the conclusion of the contract, provided that they were not known and could not have been known at that time. What is important is not "[w]hat was subjectively believed [...] by the disadvantaged party, but rather [...] what was objectively knowable".

Finally, with respect to Art. 6.2.2 ("*Definition of hardship*"), the Arbitral Tribunal found that hardship may be invoked if the alteration of the contractual equilibrium is due to an event the risk of which was not assumed by the disadvantaged party and if such an event takes place after the conclusion of contract, while original facts which alter the contractual equilibrium "[m]ay be cited solely in relation to gross disparity".

Full Text

[...]

Respondent has claimed that these proceedings are an arbitration that is international and subject to statutory rules and to institutional procedures; that the arbitration's international character is determined by the fact that both Respondent's head office and the locus destinatae solutionis of a considerable part of the services that are the subject of the disputed business relationship are situated abroad (Article 832 of the Code of Civil Procedure), as well as by the fact that this is an institutional arbitration governed by the Rules of Arbitration of the International Chamber of Commerce; and that the statutory nature of the arbitration is inherent in the fact that this is a legal arbitration, with application "for every purpose" of Italian law [...].

This constitutes the premise on the basis of which Respondent pleads to "recall that in accordance with Article 834 of the Code of Civil Procedure international arbitration should in all cases also take into account, as regards the relevant legal rules applicable, commercial usages"; to claim that *lex mercatoria* "is thus necessarily an integral part, even where binding rules of procedural practice apply, of substantive Italian law, under which, as indicated in the contract, the present case must be appraised and the dispute decided by the Arbitrators"; to engage the "Principles of International Commercial Contracts" drawn up by UNIDROIT, as an authoritative Fonti of knowledge of international trade usages.

In its written response [. . .] Claimant considered inappropriate Respondent's appeal to UNIDROIT Principles, inasmuch as these apply only when the parties have agreed that the contract be subject to them; in as much as the UNIDROIT Principles "shall be applied when the parties have agreed that their contract be govemed by them" and "they may be applied when the parties have agreed that the contract be govemed by them"; inasmuch as the doctrine expounded by the author of the commentary on the preamble and the first, second and fourth chapters of the UNIDROIT Principles, has made it clear that the UNIDROIT Principles are not the subject of an intemational agreement and do not have binding force in themselves, but can acquire validity only by the will of the parties; that one of the fundamental principles of the UNIDROIT Principles is that of freedom of contract; and inasmuch as Article 11 (Freedom of Contract) stipulates that: "The parties are free to enter into a contract and to determine its content". Claimant observes that it is precisely in their exercising of contractual autonomy, a cardinal principle endorsed by Article 1322 of the Civil Code and by Article 41 of the Constitution, that the parties agreed Clause 17 of the Shareholders Agreement, the applicability of Italian law, and did not make any reference to the UNIDROIT Principles.'

Respondent concluded by asking the Arbitral Tribunal to declare that the Shareholders Agreement entered into by the parties [. . .] causes grave hardship to the detriment of Respondent.... Respondent has attempted to identify the hardship in the unzumutbare Hàrte of German experience, *i.e.* in the excessive disparity in the contract or in some of its clauses, with excessive advantage to one of the parties, in which the UNIDROIT Principles also refer... [and to show] that the disparity between the services rendered by the two parties is vast [...] .

Furthermore, Claimant, having considered inappropriate Respondent's appeal to the UNIDROIT Principles on the basis of the general considerations described above, has also pointed out that, in any case, Articles 3.10 and 6.2.2 of the UNIDROIT Principles referred to in Respondent's concluding plea do not permit a finding of the existence of the alleged grave hardship complained of, *i.e.* the disparity between the services in the contract, to the detriment of Respondent; that Article 3.10 of the UNIDROIT Principles, in particular, stipulates that there must exist two presuppositions in order for the grave hardship principle to be applicable, viz. that "there must be a serious disparity between the parties' reciprocal rights and obligations which gives an excessive advantage to one party" and that "the excessive advantage must be unjust, that is in say that one party must have taken excessive advantage of a dependency a state of economic necessity, urgent needs or lack of foresight, ignorance, inexperience, or the other party's disablement in conducting the negotiations"; that these presuppositions are not present in this case.

The Arbitral Tribunal considers that the abnormal hardship complained of by Respondent does not exist, and that it cannot therefore accept the connected claim aimed at obtaining from the Arbitral Tribunal the finding that the Shareholders Agreement is invalid or void. And this for many concurrent reasons.

Firstly, it notes that Respondent's claim aimed at obtaining from the Arbitral Tribunal the finding that the Shareholders Agreement is invalid or void is based sometimes on the lex mercatoria and sometimes on the UNIDROIT Principles; it also notes that, notwithstanding the textual references in "hardship", in basing its defense claim on the UNIDROIT Principles Respondent does not limit itself to pleading Article 6.2.2 of the UNIDROIT

Principles, but also invokes Article 3.10, which deals not with "hardship" but with "gross disparity".

In the first place, the Arbitral Tribunal considers that the reference to *lex mercatoria* and the specific appeals to the UNIDROIT Principles do not constitute sufficient justification for sustaining Respondent's claim that the Shareholders Agreement should be declared invalid or void, for various reasons.

The first reason appertains to the fundamental judicial rule that the onus is on the party that has invoked the application of the *lex mercatoria* and of the UNIDROIT Principles to prove that the rules invoked are part of *lex mercatoria* so far as concerns assumptions that may be of legal relevance and so far as concerns the consequences of disparity between the parties in the agreement, proving the existence of interpretative and applicative trends in international commercial circles supporting the interpretation that is put forward. This Respondent has failed to do, and therefore the appeal to the UNIDROIT Principles as regards gross disparity and hardship is not valid: it having been made clear that the UNIDROIT Principles are not part of normative Fonti of production, and that they are designed to constitute a uniform model for regulating the negotiation of contractual relations, whatever their connection with the *lex mercatoria* and with international commercial usages in particular, and it is also clear that the UNIDROIT Principles are only partly valid, and in many ways are innovative. In other words, although the UNIDROIT Principles constitute a set of rules theoretically appropriate to prefigure the future *lex mercatoria* should they be brought into line with international commercial practice, at present there is no necessary connection between the individual Principles and the rules of the *lex mercatoria*, so that recourse to the Principles is not purely and simply the same as recourse to an actually existing international commercial usage.

The second reason, which comes into play even if one assumes that the rules on gross disparity and on hardship invoked by Respondent actually come under *lex mercatoria* and the practices of international trade in particular, consists in a widespread interpretative trend, which the Arbitral Tribunal agrees with, whereby, where the parties have expressly and precisely identified the law applicable to the relationship established between themselves and, in particular, have, as in the present case, identified it as a national law, the possibility of putting before judges rules that do not belong in the national system of rules to which the contracting parties have referred is precluded. In the light of the above mentioned trend, it is not sufficient, in order to make applicable *lex mercatoria*, for provisions that may exist in the national legal system to which the contracting parties have referred to contain references to *lex mercatoria*: that is to say, where the parties have availed themselves of the possibility of choosing the legal system applicable to their relationship, no-one can substitute himself for these parties in the choice of applicable laws, adapting the system at his discretion. All of the above, which applies even in respect of the widespread referrals in *lex mercatoria* that can be found in French and Swiss legislative practice, has even more validity with regard to Article 834 of the Code of Civil Procedure, where the reference proves to be more tenuous. On the one hand, it should be borne in mind that Article 834 of the Code of Civil Procedure refers to "international commercial usages", while *lex mercatoria* is an expression of notoriously very wide scope and interpretation, and could even be termed imprecise and debatable; in this light, there is no merit in appealing to Article 834 of the Code of Civil Procedure as a provision legitimizing the application of *lex mercatoria* as the basis for making the

Shareholders Agreement void and invalid. On the other hand, it should be borne in mind that the appeal in international commercial usages contained in Article 834 of the Code of Civil Procedure must be linked with the national legal regulations to which the provision appealing to international commercial usages belongs. If one refers to instruments that are specifically regulated by Italian law or, in any case, that produce rules that are incompatible with the regulations of Italian law, international commercial usages cannot take precedence over national law; thus Article 834 of the Code of Civil Procedure, which does not allocate any precedence to the various Fonti, does not grant to any international commercial usages that can be taken into account, in the interpretation of a contract, supremacy over the provisions of Italian law. Thus, international commercial usages are of strictly interpretative and integrative value, to the extent that there are gaps in national regulations that could usefully be filled by the aforesaid usages; this means that Article 834 of the Code of Civil Procedure refers in international commercial usages as a Fonti of law, but that those practices have their place and are treated in a similar way to custom; all the more so when the parties have chosen national law as the law applicable to their relationship, it being certainty not possible, in such a case, to substitute international commercial usages for the national law chosen by the parties with regard to institutions, actions, and effects, for which the latter makes special provision. Since the presuppositions for juridical relevance and the consequences of the contractual disparity, whether at the start or that occurred after the conclusion of the contract, are specifically regulated by Italian legislation, which recognizes the remedies of rescission and cancellation of the contract because the contract has become excessively onerous, the appeal to *lex mercatoria* or to the UNIDROIT Principles does not permit application of the doctrine of gross disparity and of hardship in order to bring into greater focus the contractual disparity — whether original or occurring later —beyond the limits of or with effects different from the presuppositions that are relevant in law and from the actual consequences of rescission and of cancellation of the contract because it has become excessively onerous.

The third reason is found in the nature of the provisions of Italian law concerning the invalidity and nullity of contracts that are considered in come under the rules of public policy The binding nature of these provisions, which flows directly from the obligation emphasized above, precludes the possibility that the provisions of Italian law concerning hypotheses and presuppositions of invalidity or nullity of contracts be set aside by reference in *lex mercatoria*. In a more specific sense, this constitutes a further proof of the above argumentation in that, given that the parties opted for Italian law as the law governing their contractual relationship, the rules on gross disparity and on hardship invoked by Respondent are rendered inapplicable in the present case, even if one assumed that they are part of *lex mercatoria* and, in particular, international commercial usages.

In any case, even if *lex mercatoria* and the UNIDROIT Principles were applicable in this case, Respondent's claim aimed at obtaining from the Arbitral Tribunal the finding that the Shareholders Agreement is invalid or void, could not, in the Arbitral Tribunal's opinion, be sustained, either with regard to the supposed gross disparity, or with regard in the supposed hardship.

As for the possibility of accepting the aforesaid claim under the heading of gross disparity, the Arbitral Tribunal considers that there are impediments even on the formal level. [...]

And, even if one wished in ascribe the notion of gross disparity to the disputed issues that are the subject of this arbitration according to the principle of jura novit curia, supposing a mere error on the part of Respondent and bearing in mind that Respondent's claim is aimed at asserting the original disparity in order to make the Shareholders Agreement invalid or void, the said claim could still not be sustained, given the absence of the presuppositions.

In this regard, the UNIDROIT Principles specify that the consequences of the gross disparity consist in amending the contract at the demand of one party or, alternatively, in annulling the contract. In this case, there being nothing in the documents to show there was a request in amend the contract based on the original contractual disparity which Respondent refers to for the first time at the start of the arbitration, the only consequence can be the annulment of the Shareholders Agreement, for which, however, the presuppositions to such an end required by the UNIDROIT Principles invoked by Respondent are lacking.

And, in fact, Article 3.10 of the UNIDROIT Principles asks that the following factors be taken into account when determining the "injustice" of the disparity: the fact that the advantaged party (in this case Claimant) had taken advantage of the dependent state, economic difficulties or immediate needs of the disadvantaged party (in this case Respondent), or of the ignorance, inexperience or lack of negotiating skills of the disadvantaged party (in this case Respondent). Not only has Respondent failed to prove the presuppositions alluded to, but also circumstances have emerged such as to exclude them totally: not only has Respondent failed to prove that, at the time the contract was concluded, it was in a state of dependence, economic difficulty or immediate need, but it has also emerged that it was Claimant who was in economic difficulties; not only has Respondent failed to prove that, at the time the contract was concluded, it was incompetent, ignorant, inexperienced, or lacked negotiating skills, but also these conditions are excluded by Respondent's status.

[...]

On the other hand, whatever state it was in, ignorance would not be relevant in the notion of gross disparity, inasmuch as Article 3.10 of the UNIDROIT Principles gives relevance to the disadvantaged party's being in ignorance only if this ignorance was of circumstances that came about later or, if prior to the conclusion of the contract, of circumstances that were not known and could not have been known at that time. In the present case, because of the considerations just described, the Arbitral Tribunal holds that the extent of the contributions requested could reasonably have been foreseen by a professional operator in the aeronautical sector, by exercising the due diligence expected from a professional from the sector to which Respondent belonged. All the more so since the facts brought forward by Respondent in its own defense, following investigations carried out in the course of the arbitration, demonstrate not only and not so much that many of the facts learnt by Respondent ex post were objectively knowable beforehand, but above all that Respondent was negligent in its preliminary investigations at the stage of the pre-contractual negotiations, which constitutes confirmation of an attitude that cannot but assume importance as regards the application of the invoked Article 3.10 and, particularly, as regards the presupposition of the "unknowability" of such facts by a diligent professional.

[...] considering that the cited Article 3.10 attaches importance not to what was purely subjectively believed to be the case by the disadvantaged party, but rather in what was objectively knowable, the remedy of annulling the agreement due to gross disparity purely because the disadvantaged party attaches blame, both in general and in the present case, remains precluded.

Just as there are no presuppositions on which one could base annulment of the Shareholders Agreement due to gross disparity, it must also be pointed out that, under the invoked Article 3.10, an assessment aimed at verifying the presupposition of the original disparity must take into account the nature and purpose of the contract whose annulment is sought.

[...]

As regards the possibility of accepting, under the heading of the alleged hardship, Respondent's claim aimed at obtaining a finding from the Arbitral Tribunal that the Shareholders Agreement is void or invalid, even if the UNIDROIT Principles invoked in this regard by Respondent came under *lex mercatoria,* and it were to be held that the latter is applicable to the present case, the Arbitral Tribunal considers that in the present case there would be no presuppositions of hardship and, therefore, no grounds for a finding of invalidity or nullity.

As regards the absence of presuppositions of hardship, it is enough here in point out that these are listed under Sections A to D of Article 6.2.2 of the UNIDROIT Principles, which stipulate the only concurrent and supplemental conditions that may be cited when pleading hardship; that, in particular, hardship postulates an event that took place that was the cause of the contractual disparity; that in the present case Respondent has not alleged that such an event occurred, and that this event cannot be the alleged cognizance that third parties owned the rights in make use of the project, since we are dealing here with an original fact that may be cited solely in relation to gross disparity, although even then, as we have written, it could not assume any importance in this respect; that the notion of hardship also postulates that the disadvantaged party was not contractually bound in respect of the event that occurred that was the Fonti of the contractual disparity; that in the present case Respondent was aware. — or, at any rate could have been aware, for the reasons already described — that this was an old project, and that responsibility for the technical aspects, the certification, the marketing, and any finance necessary for the joint venture would fall upon it, and that it would assume the related risk; that no unforeseen circumstances had even emerged while the contract was being concluded such as to aggravate that risk, taking into account, after all, that Respondent declared its intention of extricating itself from its obligation only two months after the Shareholders Agreement had been finalized.

As regards the absence of presuppositions for a finding of invalidity and nullity it is worth noting that Article 6.2.3 of the UNIDROIT Principles specifies that the consequences of hardship are that the contract be either amended or terminated. Given that neither party has requested that the contract be amended, Respondent's application to have the Shareholders Agreement declared invalid or void ab origine cannot be accepted, on the basis of the same rules invoked by Respondent, which would in any case only have allowed the possibility that the contract might have been terminated because of the hardship.'

Respondent concluded by asking the Arbitral Tribunal to declare that Claimant had violated Article 1337 of the Civil Code and of the corresponding rules of the lex mercatoria, at least in the objective meaning of the criterion for good faith.

In its concluding pleading, Respondent particularly emphasized injure that according to commercial usages, which, in Respondent's opinion, and also according to Article 834 of the Code of Civil Procedure, the arbitrators should take into account, good faith should be evaluated not in a subjective sense, according to the equation "lack of good faith = fraud", but in an objective sense; that in the UNIDROIT Principles, in which good faith is mentioned repeatedly, it is always evaluated by reference not in the internal standards of various national legal systems, but to the standards of international business practice, according to which the obligation in observe it is violated not only in the case of fraud, but also in that of simple negligence, thoughtlessness, and rashness; that in contract law acting in good faith refers to a purely objective test: if a party acts in an unreasonable and inequitable way, it will not be a defense to say that he honestly believed his conduct in be reasonable and equitable; that this is the correct approach to the concept of good faith in the present judgement, too, in which the way in which Claimant conducted the pre-contractual negotiations was perhaps, but not necessarily, motivated by bad faith in the sense of conscious deceit, but could also have been caused simply by negligence, thoughtlessness, or inexperience, but that, if this were the case, there would be no grounds for not deeming it to have been objectively bad-faith behavior, in a business relationship such as the present, which Is subject to Italian law, whose legal system also includes the *lex mercatoria*.

[...]

Respondent has confirmed that for Respondent the case centres principally on Claimant's violation of the duty in behave in good faith when conducting the negotiations and drawing up the contract; has contested Claimant's thesis that Respondent had violated the general clause on good faith "following the 'misplaced' trust that Claimant, 'who claimed [. . .] in have thus overcome some of the problems connected to the development, production and sale of the [...]'had 'intentionally engendered"; has confirmed that it is referring, when maintaining that Claimant "had violated the canons of good faith [. . .] to the use of that term in the sense that it had objectively violated them, as also and in particular understood by the rules of the *lex mercatoria* (and by the UNIDROIT Principles, especially Articles 1.7 and 2.15/2). We do not therefore wish to accuse the other party of having acted fraudulently. Fraud there may have been, perhaps; we are not asserting that there was, in the sense of defective consent within the meaning of Article 1439 of the Civil Code, but it is from the violation of Article 1337 of the Civil Code that we derive Respondent's right to receive compensation for the damages derived therefrom [...]".

[...]

Sources

Original in Italian:
Unpublished.

Published in English (excerpt):
ICC International Court of Arbitration Bulletin, Vol. 10, No. 2, Fall 1999, 88 – 96.

Date: ***March 1998***
Adjudicating Court: ***ICC International Court of Arbitration, Zurich***
Number: ***9117***
Parties: ***Unknown***

Keywords

CONTRACT OF SALE GOVERNED BY CISG – MATTERS OUTSIDE SCOPE OF CISG GOVERNED BY DOMESTIC LAW (RUSSIAN LAW) – REFERENCE TO UNIDROIT PRINCIPLES AS "THEY ARE SAID TO REFLECT A WORLD-WIDE CONSENSUS IN MOST OF THE BASIC MATTERS OF CONTRACT LAW"

MERGER CLAUSE (ART. 2.17 [ART. 2.1.17 OF THE 2004 EDITION] UNIDROIT PRINCIPLES)

WRITTEN MODIFICATION CLAUSE (ART. 29(2) CISG) (ART. 2.18 [ART. 2.1.18 OF THE 2004 EDITION] UNIDROIT PRINCIPLES)

INTERPRETATION OF CONTRACT ACCORDING TO ESTABLISHED PRACTICE BETWEEN PARTIES (ART. 4.3 UNIDROIT PRINCIPLES)

Abstract

A Russian seller (Claimant) and a Canadian buyer (Respondent) entered into a contract for the sale of goods. Claimant delivered part of the goods before the expiry of the US import licences, while the remaining part was delivered after the expiry. Respondent refused to pay the full price alleging that Claimant had failed to ship all the goods before the expiry of the import licences and had violated Respondant's exclusive right to import the goods into the US. Claimant commenced arbitration in accordance with arbitration agreement contained in the contract and providing for arbitration under the ICC Rules of Arbitration and Reconciliation.

The contract did not contain a choice of law clause. The Arbitral Tribunal stated that, pursuant to Art. 13(3) and (5) of the ICC Rules for Reconciliation and Arbitration, and, in addition to the contractual provisions agreed upon by the parties, the relevant usages of trade and the 1980 United Nations Convention on Contracts for the International Sale of Goods (CISG) would apply. For the matters which had not been contractually agreed upon and which could not be determined by observing either trade usages or CISG, the law of the Russian Federation would apply.

However, in dealing with the merits of the case, the Arbitral Tribunal stated that, although "the UNIDROIT Principles of International Commercial Contracts shall [not] directly be applied, it is nevertheless informative to refer to them because they are said to reflect a world-wide consensus in most of the basic matters of contract law".

Thus, the Arbitral Tribunal referred to Arts. 2.17 (Art. 2.1.17 of the 2004, edition) ("*Merger clauses*") and 2.18 [Art. 2.1.18 of the 2004 edition] ("*Written modification clauses*") of the UNIDROIT Principles to confirm the rule laid down in Art. 29 (2) CISG, according to which Respondent could not rely on any kind of verbal promises or assurances, or any kind of written references which were not at the same time reflected in an Amendment or Supplement to the Contract.

Finally, reference was made to Art. 4.3 ("*Relevant circumstances*") of the UNIDROIT Principles to determine whether a course of dealing was established between the parties which could fairly be regarded as a common basis of understanding to interpret their statements and other conduct.

Full Text

[...]

The Parties, however, did not provide for a choice of law clause to govern their contractual relationship.

[...]

Considering the above principles, Claimant reasons that the matter in dispute should be settled as follows:
- in accordance with the terms and conditions of the Contract[...];
- in accordance with the provisions of CISG; and
- in accordance with the Russian law on matters not covered by the CISG.

[...]

Contractual issues and disputes that cannot be resolved by reference in CISG are, in Respondent's view, in be settled in conformity with the Swiss substantive law. In support of this theory Respondent refers to the Swiss Federal Statute on Private International Law (PIL) and stresses especially the principle of the burden of establishing foreign law (Article 16 PIL).

[...]

For the Tribunal it is clear that, in the first instance, the contractual terms as agreed by the Parties in the framework of their contractual relationship shall be looked at and applied in determine the disputed issues. In case of ambiguity and in the extent necessary, contractual terms may have in be interpreted by the Tribunal.

In addition to the foregoing, the Tribunal has to have regard to the relevant usages of the trade, for two reasons: First, the Parties had specifically referred to the INCOTERMS 1990 [...] Second, trade usages are in be observed on the basis of Article 13(5) ICC Rules (which Rules had been chosen by the Parties).

Matters or issues which had not been contractually agreed among the Parties and which cannot be determined by having regard to trade usage (including the INCOTERMS), will have to be determined on the basis of the 1980 Vienna Sales Convention ("CISG"), as correctly pleaded by both Parties.

Regarding any further issues which might come up and which are not governed by any of the foregoing, the Tribunal will have in determine the proper law of contract according in the so-called "objective approach". For this task, the Tribunal does not have in apply the European Convention 1961 (which was particularly referred in by Claimant), but indeed the ICC Rules, as the set of rules which the Parties had specifically agreed upon and chosen to govern their arbitration. The relevant provision is Article 13.3 ICC Rules 1975/1988, which provision had been inspired by Article VII of the European Convention of 1961.

Accordingly, the Tribunal, shall apply the law (or rules of law) designated as the proper law by the rule of conflict deemed "appropriate" [...].

The "centre of gravity", therefore, is in the instant case located in the seller's country *i.e.* in the Russian Federation, irrespective of the fact that the Parties had agreed on CIF delivery terms, for delivery in Canada or the United States. Thus, the objective approach clearly leads to the conclusion that the present contractual relationship is most closely related to the seller's legal system, *i.e.* in the laws of the Russian Federation. These laws will, therefore, be applied by this Tribunal where necessary, *i.e.* where a particular issue cannot be solved by having regard in the contractual terms, or an interpretation thereof, or the relevant trade usages, and where no answer can be found in or derived from the CISG.

[...]

In the instant case, two provisions are of paramount importance: first, the so-called merger clause (sometimes called integration clause) and, second, the written modification clause. Both of them may be characterized as typical clauses, and there can be no doubt for any party engaged in international trade that the clauses mean, and must mean, what they say.

[...]

[...] it may be noted that the effects and the significance of a merger clause are also reflected in Article 2. [1]7 of the 1994 UNIDROIT Principles of International Commercial Contracts. Although this Tribunal did not determine that the UNIDROIT Principles shall directly be applied, it is nevertheless informative to refer to them because they are said to reflect a world-wide consensus in most of the basic matters of contract law (and certainly in the areas which are discussed in the framework of this Award). Article 2.17 of the UNIDROIT Principles reads as follows: "(Merger clauses). A contract in writing which contains a clause indicating that the writing completely embodies the terms on which the parties have agreed cannot be contradicted or supplemented by evidence of prior statements or agreements. However, such statements or agreements may be used to interpret the writing." The comments in this Article explain that a merger clause, of course ". . . covers only prior statements or agreements between the parties and does not preclude subsequent informal agreements between them. The parties are, however, free in extend an agreed form even in future amendments; see Article 2.18". Article 2.18 of the 1994 UNIDROIT Principles is the Article on the written modification clause to which reference will be made in the following paragraphs.

The written modification clause in which the present Parties have also explicitly agreed in the framework of the Contract.. . has the same effects as the merger clause with regard to any future negotiations, promises and any other extrinsic evidence which otherwise might be adduced for supplementing, altering or contradicting the whiten contract. The significance of the written modification clause is explained in Article 29(2) CISG which reads as follows: "A contract in writing which contains a provision requiring any modification or termination by agreement in be in writing may not be otherwise modified or terminated by agreement. However, a party may be precluded by his conduct from asserting such a provision to the extent that the other party has relied on that conduct."

[...] In the instant case, however, it is the Tribunal's opinion that there is no room whatsoever for applying the exception clause. The present Parties have agreed in the written requirement for any kind of modifications, and there is no evidence of a conduct which could be of a nature as to do away with that specific requirement.

Again, it is useful to realize that a written modification clause is another typical element in international contracts. The comparison [with] the 1994 UNIDROIT Principles again seems appropriate. Article 2.18 states the following: "(Written modification clause). A contract in writing which contains a clause requiring any modification or termination by agreement to be in writing may not be otherwise modified or terminated. However, a party may be precluded by its conduct from asserting such a clause to the extent that the other party has acted in reliance on that conduct." As can be seen, Article 2.18 of the 1994 UNIDROIT Principles is quite close to Article 29(2) CISG.

[...]

The Majority Arbitrators further considered whether under the general duty to act in good faith Claimant would have been under an obligation to accelerate the shipment [...] so as in allow a customs clearing prior to the expiry of the US import license. For instance, parties to a contract might be or become bound by a particular course of dealing which they have established as between themselves, by virtue of their previous commercial practices and conduct, and which can fairly be regarded as a common basis of understanding for interpreting their expression and other conduct. This notion, for instance, is also reflected in Article 4.3 of the 1994 UNIDROIT Principles (which are not directly applicable in the instant case, but nevertheless express a communis opinio and consensus).

The question thus arises whether such a particular course of dealing (which might have in be considered or applied by this Tribunal) had been established between the Parties. The answer to this question is, however, negative, for three reasons. First, it is from the outset hardly conceivable that a conclusive (and in the end legally binding) commercial practice can be established overriding the terms of a straightforward sales contract; typically, such practices emerge in the framework of long-term contracts such as those in the construction industry. Second, the explicit integration clause and the written modification clause, as contained in the Contract, operate as a bar against the assumption that a certain behaviour or practice could reach the level of becoming legally binding between the Parties. Third, the contractual relationship, as it had been examined by this Tribunal, did not reveal any particular commercial practices between the Parties, and there is no evidence before the Tribunal that the Parties had established a particular conduct which could have become legally binding on them.

Sources

Original in English (excerpt):
ICC International Court of Arbitration Bulletin, Vol. 10, No. 2, Fall 1999, 96 – 101.

Date: ***March 5, 1998***
Country: ***France***
Adjudicating Court: ***Cour d'appel de Paris (1er Ch. C)***
Number: ***Unknown***
Partieses: ***Société FORASOL v. Société mixte Franco-Kazakh CISTM***

Keywords

REFERENCE BY ARBITRAL TRIBUNAL TO THE UNIDROIT PRINCIPLES AS A "CODIFICATION" OF INTERNATIONAL TRADE USAGES – WITHOUT EXPRESS AUTHORISATION BY PARTIES – REFERENCE DOES NOT EXCEED TERMS OF SUBMISSION IF OF NO DIRECT IMPACT ON THE MERITS OF THE DECISION

Abstract

Plaintiff, a French company in charge of perforation activities in Kazakhstan had entered into a contract with Defendant, a mixed French-Kazakh company for catering services for its employees. The contract, which was governed by French law, had a fixed term but provided for tacit renewal in the absence of notice of cancellation by Defendant three months before expiry. Two days before the three month period began to run, Plaintiff sent a notice of cancellation to Defendant, which however reached the latter two days after the three months had begun to run.

The parties disputed the effectiveness of the notice and commenced arbitration proceedings. The sole Arbitrator held that with resepct to notices exchanged in contractual relationships there was no clear rule in French law as to whether the dispatch principle or the receipt principle prevailed, and therefore on the basis of Article 13(5) of the ICC Rules of Arbitration, referred to the usages of international trade and found that according to them it was the receipt principle that was generally accepted. In this context the Arbitrator also referred to the UNIDROIT Principles, indicated as a "codification" of such usages, without however citing Article 1.9(2) which expressly sets out the receipt principle.

In challenging the award Plaintiff claimed that the sole Arbitrator, in applying international trade usages and the UNIDROIT Principles without being requested by the parties to do so, had violated the principle laid down in Article 1502(3) and (4), *i.e.*, the arbitral tribunal's duty not to exceed the terms of the submission to arbitration, and the right of the parties to present their case.

The Cour d'appel rejected the objection on the ground that according to both Article 13(5) of the ICC Rules of Arbitration and Article 1496 of the French Code of Civil Procedure the arbitral tribunal is entitled to base its decision on the rules of law it considers most appropriate and to refer to trade usages. In the case at hand the reference to the latter was all the more so justified as the law chosen by the parties as the applicable law did not provide a clear answer to the issue at stake. Nor did the Arbitrator exceed the terms of the submission to arbitration by referring to the UNIDROIT Principles as the reference to them had no direct impact on the decision.

Full Text

[Not yet available]

Sources

Revue de l'Arbitrage, 1999, 86 *et seq.*

Date: **April 1998**
Adjudicating Court: **ICC International Court of Arbitration (Second Partial Award), Paris**
Number: **7110**
Parties: **Unknown**

Keywords

LIMITATION PERIODS – MATTER NOT DEALT WITH BY UNIDROIT PRINCIPLES [1994 EDITION] – RECOURSE TO OTHER INTERNATIONALLY RECOGNIZED PRINCIPLES OF LAW – HELD THAT THERE IS NO SUCH GENERAL PRINCIPLE PRESCRIBING A FIXED LIMITATION PERIOD WITHIN WHICH CLAIMS HAVE TO BE PURSUED

LIMITATION PERIOD – CLAIMS MAY BE TIME BARRED IF PURSUED "WITH UNREASONABLE DELAY" (ART. 1.7 UNIDROIT PRINCIPLES)

RIGHT TO WITHOLD PERFORMANCE – GENERAL PRINCIPLE OF LAW (SEE ART. 7.1.3 UNIDROIT PRINCIPLES) – SELLER'S RIGHT TO WITHOLD DELIVERY OF GOODS IF BUYER FAILS TO PAY THE PRICE

MITIGATION OF HARM – GENERAL PRINCIPLE OF LAW (SEE ART. 7.4.8 UNIDROIT PRINCIPLES) – SELLER ENTITLED TO DISPOSE OF THE GOODS AFTER THEIR STORAGE FOR A LENGHTY PERIOD

CONTRACT WITH TERMS DELIBERATELY LEFT OPEN – AGREEMENT NOT PREVENTED FROM COMING INTO EXISTENCE (ART. 2.14 [ART. 2.1.14 OF THE 2004 EDITION] UNIDROIT PRINCIPLES)

Abstract

An English company and a government agency of a Middle Eastern country entered into nine related contracts for the supply of equipment concluded between. None of the contracts contained an express choice of law provision in favour of a given domestic law but some of them contained provisions referring to settlement according to "natural justice", "laws of natural justice" or "rules of natural justice".

Four years after a first partial award (ICC International Court of Arbitration Partial Award no. 7110 of June 1995) in which the Arbitral Tribunal decided to apply the UNIDROIT Principles, the Arbitral Tribunal rendered a second partial award in which it addressed a number ofquestions concerning the merits ofthe case.

A first question concerned the defence raised by Respondent according to which Claimant's claim was time-barred by virtue of the expiry of the limitation period. After having noticed that the UNIDROIT Principles [1994 edition] do not address the issue [but see now Chapter 10 of the 2004 edition of the UNIDROIT

Principles] and excluded that the 1974 New York Convention on Limitation Periods in the context of international sales contracts contained widely recognised principles applicable in the case at hand, the Arbitral Tribunal concluded that there were no internationally accepted principles prescribing a fixed limitation period within which a claim has to be pursued. However, the Arbitral Tribunal implied that there might be a general principle of law according to which a claim is time-barred if it is pursued with unreasonable delay, and to this effect referred to Article 1.7 of the UNIDROIT Principles stating the parties' duty to act in accordance with good faith and fair dealings. In the case at hand, however, the Arbitral Tribunal found that even eleven years did not constitute an unreasonable delay.

Another question was whether an unpaid seller could refuse to deliver the goods until it had received payment. The Arbitral Tribunal decided that the seller was entitled to do so and in this respect referred to Article 7.1.3 of the UNIDROIT Principles laying down the principle of the right to withhold performance.

Moreover, as to question whether, failing payment by the buyer, the seller was entitled to terminate the contract and sell the goods to a third party, a majority of the Arbitral Tribunal affirmed the seller's right to dispose of the goods on the basis of the general principle of mitigation of harm laid down in Article 7.4.8 of the UNIDROIT Principles.

Lastly, the Arbitral Tribunal affirmed the validity of an agreement between the parties even if they have left some terms to be agreed upon in further negotiations and in this respect referred to Article 2.14 [Art. 2.1.14 of the 2004 edition] of the UNIDROIT Principles dealing with contract with terms deliberately left open.

Full Text

Claimant first argued that Respondent is "estopped from raising a limitation defense by its own conduct" ...

The argument is based, *inter alia,* on the principle *venire contra factum non concedit* and on Articles 1.7 (principle of good faith), 2.18 (no-oral modification clause) and 2.4 (reliance theory) of the UNIDROIT Principles. [...]

The Tribunal considers that Respondent is not estopped from raising a rime-bar defence. [...] The defence based on limitation/unreasonable delay is therefore admissible.

It is Respondent's position that the question of limitation ought to be resolved by application of the *lex causae.* Claimant concurs with this position.

Respondent argued that the UNIDROIT Principles are the *lex causae,* that these Principles are silent as to any applicable period of limitation and that, therefore, there was a need far the Tribunal to "fill a gap" in the Principles.

According to Respondent, the gap should be filled by resorting to the domestic laws that are most relevant in this arbitration, *i.e.* English law and [the law of State X] , possible Dutch law and French law or, alternatively, to domestic laws in general. [...]

Respondent invoked the 1974 New York Convention on the International Sale of Goods (Article 8) under which the limitation period is four years, Article 23 providing that the "over all limitation far bringing legal proceedings" is ten years.
[...] Respondent submitted a comparative analysis of the limitation period under 119 domestic laws with respect to contractual disputes under international commercial sales contracts, contending that such analysis demonstrates that the great majority of the legal systems reviewed had limitation periods between three and ten years. Ten years would be, Respondent argued, an appropriate limitation period in the present case under the circumstances. [...]

Claimant's position is that domestic laws are irrelevant far the determination of the limitation issue.
In Claimant's submission, reference has to be made to general principles of law, including UNIDROIT Principles, as held by the Tribunal in Partial Award No.1. [...]

According to Claimant, there is no general principle of law which sets a specific rime limit far bringing an action, and, failing any such rime limit, the only general principle of law applying to the issue under review is the principle that claims must be pursued without unreasonable delay. [...]

As to the 1974 New York Convention, Claimant denied that it constitutes the expression of a widely recognized and accepted principle, pointing out that neither the United Kingdom nor [State X] has signed the Convention. [...]

The Tribunal notes that there is no provision in any of the Contracts dealing with limitation periods. [...]

The Tribunal has not found that a fixed limitation period results from trade usages in contracts far the sale and supply of goods or services.

It is common ground that the UNIDROIT Principles do not deal with limitation periods and, therefore, the Tribunal has to determine whether there are general legal rules enjoying a wide international consensus that contain the principle that an action is time-barred after a fixed period of rime has lapsed.

The Tribunal does not consider that the 1974 New York Convention [...] incorporates any such widely recognized principle.

It is the Tribunal's view that the solution to the question does not have to be derived from the domestic laws, and that a comparative approach such as the one suggested by Respondent does not reveal a generally accepted principle as to thelength of an extinctive limitation period ...the Tribunal rejects Respondent's defence that Claimant's claims are time-barred on the basis of any fixed limitation period, alternatively to the limitation defence, Respondent argued that if the *lex causae* includeves no rules prescribing a fixed limitation period (or if the applicable limitation period exceeds 11 years and 10 months), then, as a matter of general principle, the Tribunal should still reject Claimant's claims, the initiation of which has been unreasonably delayed by Claimant.

Reference is made by Defendant to Article 1.7(1) of the UNIDROIT Principles, according to which: "each party must act in accordance with good faith and fair dealing in international trade". [...]

Claimant's position is that, under the circumstances of the present case, the delay in bringing suit has not been "unreasonable"

[...] the Tribunal has concluded that it was not unreasonable far Claimant, in all the circumstances, not to launch arbitration proceedings so long as there seemed to be a prospect of arriving at an agreement on the terms of a settlement. Making due allowance far the fact that the internal political upheavals consequent upon [events in State XI were not conducive to speedy decision making, the Tribunal considers that the claims which ..Claimant pursues in this arbitration are not time-barred far unreasonable delay and that they are therefore admissible.

With respect to payment far and retention of substitute equipment (second partial Award):

The Contract [...] contains no provision dealing with the situation [...] Consequently, the solution has to be found in generally accepted legal principles enjoying a wide recognition (partial Award No.1), including UNIDROIT Principles.

It is a principle of law widely accepted that if a buyer does not perform its obligations as to payment of the balance of the price when due, the seller may; in the absence of an express contractual provision to the contrary, suspend performance of its obligation to arrange far shipment and lord delivery: The civil law concept of *exceptio non adimpleti contractus* corresponds to the principle laid down in the UNIDROIT Principles 7.1.3. [...]

The Tribunal is of the opinion that Respondent was entitled to retain [...] until it received full payment therefore.

With respect to Respondent's disposal of such equipment following storage far a length by period (second partial Award):

This conduct, the Tribunal finds, is entirely consistent with the generally accepted principle of the mitigation of harm, as expressed in Article 7.4.8 of the UNIDROIT Principles.

Dissenting opinion by a member of the Arbitral Tribunal:

I fall to understand the Majority's reasoning in invoking Article 7.4.8 of the UNIDROIT Principles. I *see* nothing in that Article which could possibly be construed to entitle one party to dispose of property of the other party without its consent [ ] This Article does certainly entitle the aggrieved party to recover from the other party reasonable expenses incurred in its attempt to preserve the goods and reduce the harm. It does not give a right to the aggrieved party to go beyond it and sell or otherwise dispose of such goods.'

With respect to whether or not a termination clause was binding upon Claimant (second partial Award):

Claimant argues that 'the termination clause [...] has to be interpreted in accordance with the principles set out in Chapter 4 of the UNIDROIT Principles and, in the instant case, as the clause is deficient, terms have to be supplied (or implied) in the termination clause [...]'

The Tribunal does not find that the record supports Claimant's argument that the [documents] contained "manifest errors" or that they were "grossly unreasonable", nor does it find Claimant's reliance on the UNIDROIT Principles to be of assistance, if only because in the Tribunal's judgment Claimant has adduced no -evidence to establish that the [documents] are erroneous or unreasonable.

The Tribunal does not consider that [the clause] is under and requires interpretation.

With respect to shipment 01 goods (second partial Award):

Once goods had been accepted, Respondent had the obligation to arrange transport and shipment to [State X]. However, at the rime of termination [...] Claimant was in default of paying monies due. [...] Consequently, Respondent was entitled, under the general principle of the *exception non adimpleti contractus,* which has been adopted under Article 7.1.3 of UNIDROIT, to withhold performance of its obligation to dispatch the goods and, thus, to retain the Accepted Goods and the Returned Goods.

With respect to use by Respondent of goods returned or accepted by Claimant (second partial Award):

The Tribunal finds that Respondent's conduct under the circumstances was entirely consistent with the generally accepted principle of the mitigation of harm, as expressed in Article 7.4.8 of the UNIDROIT Principles. *dissenting opinion quoted above.*

With respect to the validity 01 a levy provided for in a side letter (second partial Award):

The Tribunal finds that, in the Side Letter of [...] the Parties had agreed on the principle of a licence and of a levy, and on the amount of such levy, the essential terms of a licence [...] The circumstance that the Parties have left certain contractual terms to be agreed upon [...] does not prevent the agreement from coming into existence (see UNIDROIT Principles, Article 2.14).'

Sources

Excerpts of the award published in:
ICC International Court of Arbitration Bulletin, Vol. 10, No. 2, Fall 1999, 54 – 57.

Date: ***April 1998***
Adjudicating Court: ***ICC International Court of Arbitration, Paris***
Number: ***8223***
Parties: ***Unknown***

Keywords

CONTRACT GOVERNED BY DOMESTIC LAW (FRENCH LAW) – ARBITRAL TRIBUNAL'S REFERENCE TO ART. 2.19 [ART. 2.1.19 OF THE 2004 EDITION] UNIDROIT PRINCIPLES TO CONFIRM THAT PARTY'S SUBSEQUENT CONDUCT CAN TACITLY MODIFY A CLAUSE CONTAINED IN STANDARD TERMS

Abstract

A French manufacturer (Respondent) and a United States company (Claimant) entered into a distribution agreement, whereby Respondent granted Claimant the exclusive right to distribute high-tech products in North America. Despite a clause in the standard terms of the agreement which required transfer of contractual rights to be accepted in writing by the other party, the distributor assigned the contract rights to Company X. When a dispute arose as to which party was responsible for the total lack of affairs realised by the distributor, the latter filed an arbitration suit to obtain a declaration of avoidance of the agreement.

The Arbitral Tribunal stated that the contract was governed by a particular domestic law (French law).

With respect to the merits of the dispute, the Arbitral Tribunal held that the exclusive distribution agreement had been validly assigned to Company X and, therefore, the distributor was no longer entitled to enforce it. In reaching this conclusion, the Arbitral Tribunal pointed out that not only had the respondent failed to raise any objection to the assignment of the agreement, but it had also repeatedly demonstrated, particularly by its exchange of correspondence with Company X, its acceptance.

The Arbitral Tribunal added that a prohibition of assignment clause is often drafted in advance by one party without negotiation with the other party, and that it cannot be considered, in the absence of a contrary indication, as an expression of the common intention of the parties. In support of its analysis the Arbitral Tribunal found it appropriate to refer, without further explanation, to Article 2.19 [Art. 2.1.19 of the 2004 edition] of the UNIDROIT Principles.

Full Text

[...] Par une sentence intérimaire [...] reprenant les étapes antérieures de la procédure, le tribunal arbitral, après avoir constaté que la partie demanderesse continuait d'avoir une existence légale méme si elle pouvait être qualifiée de “coquille vide”, la déclarait recevable en sa demande d'arbitrage. Toutefois, le tribunal précisait qu'en statuant ainsi, il ne se prononçait pas sur la titularité des droits invoqués par la partie demanderesse, sa décision quant à la recevabilité de l'action intentée par la partie demanderesse restant étrangère au bien-fondé de ses réclamations. De même, le tribunal renvoyait à la sentence finale sa décision quant aux conséquences, si elle était vérifiée, de la cession du contrat à X.

La partie demanderesse reconnait que le contrat [...] a fait l'objet d'une cession en faveur de X qui en a ainsi repris à. son propre compte l'exécution et les difficultés y afférentes. Le formulaire 10-K déposé [...] aupres de la Securities and Exchange Commission par [...], dont dépendaient la partie demanderesse et X, précise expressément qu'outre le transfert de contròle de la partie demanderesse à X suite à l'acquisition par celle-ci d'un intérét de 100 %, une cession du contrat en faveur de X s'était également opérée [...].

En tout état de cause, il est constant que la partie demanderesse était devenue une “coquille vide” [...].

Force est de constater qu'une cession a de fait eu lieu, que la partie défenderesse ne s'y est jamais opposée mais qu'au contraire, toute la correspondance, y compris la lettre [...] mettant fin à l'exclusivité des droits de la partie demanderesse au titre du contrat et la lettre [...] confirmant la résiliation du contrat [...] s'est faite avec X ou d'autres sociétés du groupe [...] Il y a bien eu quelques factures et relevés adressés par la partie défenderesse à la partie demanderesse mais il y en a eu tout autant à X. Non seulement la partie défenderesse n'a soulevé aucune objection à la cession, mais il n'est pas contestable que dans son esprit le contrat se poursuivait entre elle-même et X [...]

Dans les circonstances de l'affaire, le tribunal en conclura qu'il y a eu cession effective du contrat [...] par la partie demanderesse en faveur de X et que cette cession est devenue opposable à la partie défenderesse en dépit des termes de l'article 21 du contrat assujettissant toute cession de droits en découlant par l'une ou l'autre partie à l'accord préalable écrit de l'autre.

L'analyse du tribunal à cet égard se trouve confortée par l'article 2.19 des Principes UNIDROIT applicables en matière de contrats commerciaux qui traite des effets relatifs des clauses dites standards. En effet, une clause d'incessibilité est souvent rédigée à l'avance; même si elle est souscrite au même titre que toutes les autres clauses du conti-at, elle ne fait, sauf indication contraire, l'objet ni de discussions, ni de négociation comme pour les clauses considérées comme essentielles et refiétant la véritable convention des parties.

Par conséquent, à compter du [...], le contrat est sorti du patrimoine de la partie demanderesse pour passer dans celui de X. En transférant le contrat à X, la partie demanderesse s'est dépouillée du droit de s'en prévaloir à l'encontre de la partie défenderesse. La partie demanderesse ne saurait en effet tout à la fois céder le conti-at et continuer de l'invoquer. Il s'agit ici d'une application du principe d'opposabilité des conventions qui se traduit par une extension de leurs effets obligatoires à l'égard de certains tiers, en l'occurrence la partie défenderesse. La pleine efficacité des contrats s'en trouve ainsi assurée; si tel n'était pas le cas, la cession intervenue ne produirait pas tous ses effets entre les parties et la partie demanderesse pourrait encore revendiquer le bénéfice du contrat à l'encontre de son cocontractant d'origine.

Le contrat ne lui appartenant plus à compter du [...], la partie demanderesse ne peut se prévaloir de droits qui en découleraient, ceux-ci relevant désormais exclusivement de X en sa qualité de cessionnaire. Celle-ci n'a cependant pas jugé utile en définitive de les faie valoir, comme bénéficiaire, à compter de cette date, de la convention d'arbitrage insérée dans le contrat, en dirigeant une demande en arbitrage distincte à l'encontre de la partie défenderesse.

[...] X avait cependant offert [...] d'intervenir volontairement dans la présente procédure. La partie défenderesse l'ayant refusé, la présente procédure n'a pu que continuer, en raison de la nature consensuelle de l'arbitrage, qu'entre la partie demanderesse et la partie défenderesse, les seules parties dans la présente affaire.

[...]

Sources

Original in French (excerpt):
ICC International Court of Arbitration Bulletin, Vol. 10, No. 2, Fall 1999, 58 – 60.

Date: ***July 16, 1998***
Country: ***Australia***
Adjudicating Court: ***Supreme Court of New South Wales***
Number: ***NSWSC 483***
Parties: ***Alcatel Australia Ltd. v. Scarcella & Ors***

Keywords

CONTRACT PERFORMANCE – IMPLIED DUTY OF GOOD FAITH (ART. 1.7 OF THE UNIDROIT PRINCIPLES)

Abstract

The dispute arose between tenants and landlord over a long term rental agreement. Tenants urged the Fire commissioners to have the building declared unsafe and compel compliance with modern standards. Landlords argued that such behaviour was a breach of the implied duty of good faith.

The Court held that the tenants had not breached their duty of good faith in their performance of the contract by calling in municipal authorities to investigate fire safety conditions. In reaching this conclusion, the Court cited with approval the analysis on the principle of good faith carried out by the Australian Federal Court in *Hughes Aircraft Systems International v. Airservices Australia* (see UNILEX UNIDROIT Principles, C. 1997-6), in which an express reference to Art. 1.7 of the UNIDROIT Principles had been made.

Full Text

[...]

IMPLIED TERMS

In summary terms, the appellant claimed that because the respondents had pressured the Council into imposing stricter and unreasonable fire requirements, it was not obliged to comply with covenant 2 (f) of the lease. This result flowed from an implied term of good faith or reasonableness in the respondents' performance of their lease obligations or exercise of their lease rights which bound them to co-operate in a reasonable way to ensure that the appellant was not subjected to the expense and impact of an unreasonable fire order.

The appellant relied upon the reasons for judgment of Priestley JA in Renard Constructions (ME) Pty Limited v. Minister for Public Works (1992) 26 NSWLR 234 at 255 and following and of Finn J in Hughes Aircraft Systems International v. Airservices Australia (1997) 146 ALR 1 at 36 and following. In Renard Constructions, a clause in a building contract empowered the principal to take over the whole or any part of the work or to cancel the contract if the contractor neglected to comply with any direction given by the principal, however minor, accidental or temporary that neglect might be, and regardless of the importance or otherwise of the subject matter. Priestley and Handley JJA held that the power so conferred on the principal must be exercised reasonably. Priestley JA at 255-6 used the terms "implication in fact" and "implication by law". His Honour said that the so-called implication in fact is really implication by the Judge based on the Judge's view of the actual intention of the parties drawn from the surrounding circumstances of the particular contract, its language and its purposes, as they emerge from the language and in the circumstances or, as it has been called, implication *ad hoc*. The rules governing such implication are found in BP Refinery (Westernport) Pty Limited v. Hastings Shire Council, Secured Income Real Estate (Australia) Limited v. St Martins Investments Pty Limited (1979) 144 CLR 596 and Codelfa Construction Pty Limited v. State Rail Authority of New South Wales (1982) 149 CLR 337. Priestley JA said at 256:

Those rules are that the implied term must be reasonable and equitable; necessary to give business efficacy to the contract, so that no term will be implied if the contract is effective without it; so obvious that 'it goes without saying'; capable of clear expression; and must not contradict any express term of the contract; see United States Surgical Corporation v. Hospital Products International Pty Limited [1983] 2 NSWLR 157 at 196, and in the same case on appeal, Hospital Products International Pty Limited v. United States Surgical Corporation (1984) 156 CLR 41 at 66 per Gibbs CJ."

Implication by law is based on imputed intention as opposed to actual intention, and implies a term as a legal incident of a particular class of contract; Castlemaine Tooheys Limited v. Carlton & United Breweries Limited (1987) 10 NSWLR 468 at 486-490 per Hope JA, with whom Samuels and Priestley JJA agreed. In Renard Constructions, Priestley JA at 263 implied "reasonableness in performance" in the exercise of the contractual power to take over or cancel the contract. His Honour said at 263-4:

The kind of reasonableness I have been discussing seems to me to have much in common with the notions of good faith which are regarded in many of the civil law systems of Europe and in all States in the United States as necessarily implied in many kinds of contract. Although this implication has not yet been accepted to the same extent in Australia as part of Judge made Australian contract law, there are many indications that the time may be fast approaching when the idea, long recognised as implicit in many of the orthodox techniques of solving contractual disputes, will gain explicit recognition in the same way it has in Europe and the United States."

Section 1-203 of the United States Uniform Commercial Code provides:
"Every contract or duty within this Act imposes an obligation of good faith in its performance or enforcement."

Section 1-201 (19) defines "good faith" as "honesty in fact in the conduct or transaction concerned". Section 2-103 (1) (b) defines "good faith", in the case of a merchant, as "honesty in fact and the observance of reasonable commercial standards of fair dealing in the trade."

Section 205 of the Restatement of Contracts, 2nd, provides:
"Every contract imposes upon each party a duty of good faith and fair dealing in its performance and its enforcement."

Priestley JA referred to the published lecture of STEYN J., The Role of Good Faith and Fair Dealing in Contract Law: A Hair-Shirt Philosophy? (1991) Denning Law Journal 131.

Handley JA at 279-80 said that he agreed generally with "much of what Priestley JA has written" on the issue and pointed to three other matters which supported the existence of some restraint on the exercise of power apart from the normal requirement of honesty; the contractor's opportunity to show cause, the necessary satisfaction of the principal and the comprehensive provision for arbitration. His Honour cited Hillas & Co Limited v. Arcos Limited (1932) 38 Com Cas 23 at 43-44 where Lord Wright referred to "..... the legal implication in contracts of what is reasonable, which runs throughout the whole of modern English law in relation to business contracts" and Minster Trust Limited v. Traps Tractors Limited [1954] 1 WLR 963 at 973 where Devlin J said:
"....... there may be a question (again depending upon the implication to be drawn from the contract) whether the dissatisfaction must be reasonable, or whether it can be capricious or unreasonable so long as it is conceived in good faith ...... The tendency in modern cases seems to be to require the dissatisfaction to be reasonable."

His Honour also referred to Stadhard v. Lee [1863] 3 B & S 364; 122 ER 138 at 371-2; 141 and Amann Aviation Pty Limited v. Commonwealth of Australia (1990) 22 FCR 527 at 532, 542-4 and in the High Court, now (1991) 174 CLR 64. In Hughes Bros Pty Limited v. Trustees of the Roman Catholic Church for the Archdiocese of Sydney (1993) 31.NSWLR 91 Kirby P and Priestley JA applied Renard Constructions. Kirby P said at 93 that he was bound by the decision.

In Hughes Aircraft, Finn J at 36 referred to the judgment of Gummow J in Service Station Association Limited v. Berg Bennett & Associates Pty Limited (1993) 45 FCR 84 at 96 where his Honour, after considering the acceptance by North American jurisprudence of an implied duty of good faith and fair dealing, observed:
"Anglo Australian contract law as to the implication of terms is heretofore developed differently, with greater emphasis upon specifics, rather than the identification of a genus expressed in wide terms. Equity has intervened in matters of contractual formation by remedy of rescission, upon the grounds mentioned earlier. It has restrained freedom of contract by inventing and protecting the equity of redemption, and by relieving against forfeiture and penalties. To some extent equity has regulated the quality of contractual performance by the various defences available to suits for specific performance and for injunctive relief. In some, but not all, of this, notions of good conscience play a part. But it requires a leap of faith to translate these well established doctrines and remedies into a new term as to the quality of contractual performance, implied by law."

Finn J was prepared to take that leap encouraged by the reasoning of Priestley JA. At 37 his Honour said:
"Fair dealing is a major (if not openly articulated) organising idea in Australian law. It is unnecessary to enlarge upon that here. More germane to the present question, the implied duty is, as is well known, an accepted idea in the contract law of the United States and, probably of Canada: see E.A. FARNSWORTH, 'Good Faith in Contract Performance'. In J. BEATSON & D. FRIEDMANN (eds), 'Good Faith and Fault in Contract Law', Clarendon Press, Oxford, 1995; for a convenient collection of some of the voluminous literature in the United States debating the meaning of the implied duty, see FARNSWORTH on

Contracts, Vol 2, Little, Brown & Co, Boston 1990, para 7.17 (a); for an English view see *e.g.* Right Hon Lord Justice Staughton, Good Faith and Fairness in Commercial Contract Law' (1994) 7 Jo Contract Law 193; and see Livingstone v. Roskilly (1992) 3 NZLR 230 at 237-8. Its status in civil law is well recognised: see *e.g.* H.K. LUCKE, 'Good Faith and Contractual Performance' in P.D. FINN (ed) 'Essays on Contract', Law Book Company, Sydney 1987; J.F. O'CONNOR 'Good Faith in English Law', Dartmouth, 1990, Ch. 8. It has been propounded as a fundamental principle to be honoured in international commercial contracts: see *e.g.* UNIDROIT, 'Principles of International Commercial Contracts', International Institute for the Unification of Private Law, Rome 1994, Art 1.7. Its more open recognition in our contract law is now warranted: compare Sir Anthony MASON, 'Contract and its Relationship with Equitable Standards and the Doctrine of Good Faith', The Cambridge Lectures, 1993 (8 July 1993); notwithstanding the significant adjustments this would occasion to some of the contract laws apparent orthodoxies: see *e.g.* LOCKE above pp. 177 and following.

I should add that, unlike Gummow J, I consider a virtue of the implied duty to be that it expresses in a generalisation of universal application, the standard of conduct to which all contracting parties are to be expected to adhere throughout the lives of their contracts. It may well be that, on analysis, that standard would be found to advance little the standard that presently may be exacted from contracted parties by other means: compare the standard applied in Conoco v. Inman Oil Co 774 F 2d 895 (1985) at 908. But setting the appropriate standard of fair dealing is, in my view, another matter altogether from acceptance of the duty itself."

With great respect, there is much to be said for a generalisation of universal application, an ideal which the High Court has pursued and sometimes achieved in other areas of the law, such as the reach of the duty of care in the law of negligence and the principles of estoppel. But equally the determination of the appropriate standard of fair dealing in the particular contractual context is difficult, though probably no more difficult than identifying general standards set by such legislation as the Trade Practices Act 1975 (misleading and deceptive conduct and unconscionable conduct) and the Contracts Review Act 1980 (unjust and hence, unconscionable, contracts).

Finn J went on to deal with the question whether in that case the type of contract or the relationship of the parties or both might require the implication as a matter of law. In this part of his reasons for judgment his Honour touched, at 38, upon the requirement of "necessity" explained by McHugh and Gummow JJ in Byrne v. Australian Airlines Limited (1995) 185 CLR 410 at 450:

"Many of the terms now said to be implied by law in various categories of case reflect the concern of the courts that, unless such a term be implied, the enjoyment of the rights conferred by the contract would or could be rendered nugatory, worthless, or, perhaps, be seriously undermined. Hence, the reference in the decisions to 'necessity' ...... This notion of 'necessity' has been crucial in the modern cases in which the courts have implied for the first time a new term as a matter of law."

In Gateway Realty Limited v. Arton Holdings Limited (No 3) (1991) 106 NSR (2d) 180 Kelly J at 192 held in apparently general terms that contracting parties are obliged to exercise their rights under an agreement honestly, fairly and in good faith. "In most cases, bad faith can be said to occur when one party, without reasonable justification, acts in relation to the contracts in a manner where the result would be to substantially nullify the bargained objective or benefit contracted for by the other, or to cause significant harm to the other, contrary to the original purpose and expectation of the parties"; 197.

In Livingstone v. Roskilly (1992) 3 NZLR 230 at 237 Thomas J. stated that, in general, the concept that "the parties to a contract must act in good faith in making and carrying out the contract" is part of the law of New Zealand. In his 1993 Cambridge Lecture, to which Finn J. referred, Sir Anthony Mason commented that this may be going too far and doubted that the House of Lords would endorse it; see Walford v. Miles [1992] 2 AC 128 at 136-8.

On the other hand, in Dorrough v. Bank of Melbourne (1995) (unreported) Federal Court of Australia, 27 September 1995, Cooper J. said, that in the light of a number of authorities to which he referred:
"..... it is not open to this Court to hold that a contract of insurance (except by virtue of the provisions of s13 of the Insurance Contracts Act 1994 (C'th) nor here relevant) contains an implied term that the parties will deal fairly and in good faith. Nor is there in this jurisdiction any general principle by which a duty of good faith is implied in every contract".

In GSA Group Limited v. Siebe (unreported) Supreme Court of New South Wales, 24 April 1993, Rogers CJ CommD was not persuaded to accept that commercial interest should be required to act in good faith towards each other.
"......why should commercial entities each with strong bargaining power, not be permitted to drive the best bargain they can, provided that they act within the law?" "The courts should not be too eager to interfere in the commercial conduct of the parties, especially where the parties are all wealthy, experienced, commercial entities able to attend to their own interests."

His Honour referred to the increasing expectation in consumer contracts that the stronger party in the transaction will behave fairly, an expectation fostered or enforced by legislation such as the Credit Act 1984 (NSW) and the Contracts Review Act 1980 (NSW). However the Chief Judge accepted:
"It is likely that, ultimately, Australian courts will embrace the American and civil law concept of the obligation that each contracting party should show good faith in the performance of contractual obligations. However the present case is not one where, even if such an obligation is implied, in the usual course of events, it should be implied, or even if implied would have the effect sought by the plaintiffs."

English writing at the time while on occasion receptive to the principle of good faith performance, did not advocate a generalized duty of good faith; see the lecture of Steyn J referred to by Priestley JA in Renard Constructions.

In his 1993 Cambridge Lecture, Sir Anthony Mason said that he thought it probable that the "concept of good faith" embraced no less than three related notions:
(1) an obligation on the parties to co-operate in achieving the contractual objects (loyalty to the promise itself);
(2) compliance with honest standards of conduct; and

(3) compliance with standards of contract which are reasonable having regard to the interests of the parties.

The movement away from the classical concept in contract law was towards one which focused on the reasonable expectations of the parties. In particular areas of the law this was not new. The common law imposed a duty of good faith in insurance contracts based on what the insured knows and the insurer does not and cannot. Another aspect of this was the rule that an insurer settling claims under a limited liability policy must act in good faith towards the insured and must have regard to his or her interests both in the defense of actions against the insured and in their settlement; Distillers Co Biochemicals (Aust) Pty Limited v. Ajax Insurance Co Limited (1974) 130 CLR 1 at 31 and Fredrikson v. Insurance Corporation of British Columbia (1990) 69 DLR (4th) at 431.

In contracts for the sale of land the vendor is under a duty to disclose material matters relating to the title which are known to the vendor but which the purchaser has no means of discovering; Carlish v. Salt [1906] 1 Ch 335; Beyfus v. Lodge [1925] Ch 350 at 359; In re Scott & Alvarez's Contract [1895] 2 Ch 603 at 612. Other examples of cases where a party is required to take account of the interests of another party are:

* the mortgagee's exercise of a power of sale;
* majority shareholders acting honestly and having regard to the interests of the company; Peters American Delicacy Co Limited v. Heath (1938) 61 CLR 457;
* the directors of an insolvent company or one verging on insolvency in disposing of assets to the detriment of creditors; Walker v. Wimborne (1976) 137 CLR 1 at 7;
* the doctor who advises a patient in relation to proposed treatment; Rogers v. Whitaker (1992) 175 CLR 479 (compare Sidaway v. Governors of Bethlem Royal Hospital [1985] AC 871);
* the application of the principles of equity governing fiduciaries;
* undue influence and unconscionable conduct in estoppel, including promissory estoppel; and
* the duty to refrain from making misrepresentations.

Moreover, the common law imposes a duty on the parties to a contract to co-operate in achieving the objects of the contract. See Mackay v. Dick (1881) 6 App Cas 251 at 263; Secured Income Real Estate (Australia) Limited v. St Martins Investments Pty Limited (1979) 144 CLR 596 at 607; Perri v. Coolangatta Investments Pty Limited (1982) 149 CLR 537; Meehan v. Jones (1982) 149 CLR 571. Sir Anthony Mason said that such cases come close to a recognition of the good faith doctrine described as "loyalty to the promise itself". But such an obligation cannot override the express provisions of the contract.

If a contract confers power on a contracting party in terms wider than necessary for the protection of the legitimate interests of that party, the courts may interpret the power as not extending to the action proposed by the party in whom the power is vested or, alternatively, conclude that the powers are being exercised in a capricious or arbitrary manner or for an extraneous purpose, which is another was of saying the same thing. Thus, a vendor may not be allowed to exercise a contractual power where it would be unconscionable in the circumstances to do so; Pierce Bell Sales Pty Limited v. Frazer (1973) 130 CLR 575 at 587.

Sir Anthony Mason was of the view that due partly to the absence of good faith doctrine regulating contract performance it had become the subject of statutory regulation such as is found in the Contracts Review Act 1980 and the Trade Practices Act 1975. But see also Commercial Bank of Australia v. Amadio (1983) 151 CLR 447; Taylor v. Johnson (1983) 151 CLR 422 and Legione v. Hateley (1982) 152 CLR 406. Part of this development is the fiduciary principle. However, that principle cannot be superimposed upon the contract in such a way as to alter the operation which that contract was intended to have according to its true construction; Hospital Products Limited v. United States Surgical Corporation & Ors (1984) 156 CLR 41 at 97 and Kelly v. Cooper [1993] AC 205 at 215.

Steyn J in the lecture to which I have referred said that the first imperative of good faith and fair dealing is that contracts ought to be upheld. In Kirke La Schelle Co v. Paul Armstrong Co 188 NE 163 (1993) the New York Court of Appeals said at 167:
"......in every contract there is an implied covenant that neither party shall do anything which will have the effect of destroying or injuring the right of the other party to receive the fruits of the contract, which means that in every contract there exists an implied covenant of good faith and fair dealing."

See also Wood v. Lucy Duff-Gordon 222 NY 88 per Cardozo J. In Royal Brunei Airlines SdnBhd v. Tan [1995] 2 AC 378 at 381 the proper role of equity in commercial transactions and the desirability of the infusion of minimum standards of fairness, good faith and good conscience into our law, were described simply as "topical questions". GLEESON CJ, in an article entitled "Individualised Justice - The Holy Grail" 1995 69 ALJ 421 at 428, remarked that "for a number of reasons, some to do with the work of legislatures, some to do with judicial law making, and some to do with the temper and spirit of the times, we can no longer say that, in all but exceptional cases, the rights and liabilities of parties to a written contract can be discovered by reading the contract."

The decisions in Renard Constructions and Hughes Bros mean that in New South Wales a duty of good faith, both in performing obligations and exercising rights, may by implication be imposed upon parties as part of a contract. There is no reason why such a duty should not be implied as part of this lease. But it remains to decide whether the implication of that duty has any consequence in the resolution of the dispute the subject of this appeal.

CONCLUSION

The trial Judge voiced his concern at a tenant's being left at the mercy of the landlord acting in a capricious manner but recognized that a claim for indemnity to meet unreasonable requirements of a fire order might to that extent fail. This may or may not be correct. But the appellant has not demonstrated that the requirements of the fire order were unreasonable.

The legislature has prescribed a procedure for challenging a fire order in the Land and Environment Court. That procedure has not been adopted, a problem to which the appellant directed grounds 5 and 9 of the appeal. The application to the Equity Division for an order authorising the appellant to make application to the Land and Environment Court for an order that the name of the appellant as applicant be substituted for the names of the respondents as applicants was doomed to failure. The fate of such an application was entirely a matter for the Land and Environment Court. The authority sought could not affect the matter and was entirely futile. In any event, there was evidence that the other party would oppose it.

Unchallenged, the law requires that the Council fire order be complied with. There is no evidence to suggest that the order was unreasonable in a way which might have led, on an appropriate application of administrative law, to its being struck down. The evidence was that its terms fell within the recommendations of Mr McMonnies, a qualified fire engineer with twenty years experience. His report was not challenged either by cross-examination or the evidence of some other expert. No doubt, for this reason, late in the day counsel for the appellant sought to bring Mr McMonnies before Windeyer J on a subpoena. As a matter of discretion, Windeyer J refused to issue a subpoena. No reason is shown to suggest that this exercise of discretion miscarried. While it might be thought that the events leading up to the imposition of the fire order were unusual that is a long way from saying that the Council, acting at the behest of the respondents in imposing requirements which fell within Mr McMonnies' recommendations, acted so unreasonably that the fire order was bad.

The result is that, in my opinion, the grounds of appeal relied on whether expressed as a requirement of an implied term in the contract or as allegations of unconscionable conduct by the respondents fail. In a commercial context it cannot be said, in my opinion, that a property owner acts unconscionably or in breach of an implied term of good faith in a lease of the property by taking steps to ensure that the requirements for fire safety advised by an expert fire engineer should be put in place. It was the duty of the Council to ensure that adequate provision for fire safety was made in the building (s317D of the Local Government Act 1919) and the contractual duty of the appellant to observe and perform the requirements of the Council, if lawful, and to do and execute or cause to be done and executed such works as were required by the Council. The respondents had a legitimate interest in ensuring that the building was properly protected. If the respondents felt that the Council requirements were insufficient, as it had been advised, I can see no reason why they should not press for more stringent requirements.

In my opinion, the appeal fails and accordingly, the second appeal should be dismissed with costs.

ORDER

Both appeals are dismissed with costs.

[...]

Sources

Original in English:
Unpublished.

Internet address:
http://www.austili.edu.au

Date: ***September 1998***
Adjudicating Court: ***ICC International Court of Arbitration, Milan***
Number: ***8908***
Parties: ***Unknown***

Keywords

INTERNATIONAL DISTRIBUTION CONTRACT – SETTLEMENT AGREEMENT BETWEEN PARTIES GOVERNED BY DOMESTIC LAW (ITALIAN LAW) – APPLICATION BY ARBITRAL TRIBUNAL OF THE 1980 UNITED NATIONS CONVENTION ON CONTRACTS FOR THE INTERNATIONAL SALE OF GOODS (CISG) AND THE UNIDROIT PRINCIPLES BOTH DEFINED AS NORMATIVE TEXTS THAT CAN BE CONSIDERED HELPFUL IN THE INTERPRETATION OF ALL CONTRACTS OF AN INTERNATIONAL NATURE

INTERPRETATION OF SETTLEMENT AGREEMENT – INTERPRETATION IN ACCORDANCE WITH GOOD FAITH (ARTS. 1337 AND 1362 - 1371 OF ITALIAN CIVIL CODE; ARTS. 1.7 AND 4.1 – 4.8 UNIDROIT PRINCIPLES)

MODIFIED ACCEPTANCE – AMOUNTS TO COUNTER-OFFER – TACIT ACCEPTANCE OF COUNTER-OFFER BY ACT OF PERFORMANCE (ART. 1326(5) OF ITALIAN CIVIL CODE; ART. 19(1)(2) CISG AND ART. 2.11 [ART. 2.1.11 OF THE 2004 EDITION] UNIDROIT PRINCIPLES)

INTEREST – APPLICABLE RATE – RATE GENERALLY APPLIED IN INTERNATIONAL TRADE FOR CONTRACTUAL CURRENCY

Abstract

An Italian manufacturer entered into a number of contracts with a Liechtenstein distributor for the supply of pipes. After the first deliveries a dispute arose between the parties each accusing the other of having breached their obligations under the contract. The parties finally entered into a settlement agreement, but soon thereafter they began arguing about the proper fulfillment of this agreement.

The Arbitral Tribunal held that, while the individual sales contracts were governed by the UN Convention on Contracts for the International Sale of Goods (CISG), the settlement agreement was governed by Italian law. However, when deciding the merits of the case, the Arbitral Tribunal repeatedly referred, in addition to the relevant provisions of the Italian Civil Code, to provisions contained in CISG and the UNIDROIT Principles, defining both as "normative texts thant can be considered helpful in their interpretation of all contracts of an international nature".

In particular, in order to determine the scope of the settlement agreement, the Arbitral Tribunal applied the rules of interpretation contained in Arts. 1362 -

1371 of the Italian Civil Code, stressing above all the principle of good faith. In support, it referred to the corresponding rules contained in Arts. 1.7 and 4.1 - 4.8 of the UNIDROIT Principles.

Moreover, in finding that a modified acceptance amounts to a counter-offer which the original offeror may tacitly accept by not objecting to the varying terms contained in the acceptance (in the case at hand, the offeror did not object to the offeree's omission in its reply of the reference to a bank guarantee as contained in the original offer) and by starting performance of its own obligations (in the case at hand, the offeror began production of the pipes), the Arbitral Tribunal referred not only to Art. 1326(5) of the Italian Civil Code, but also to the relevant provisions contained in CISG (Art. 19(1)(2)) and the UNIDROIT Principles (Art. 2.11 [Art. 2.1.11 of the 2004 edition])

Finally, the Arbitral Tribunal addressed the question of the applicable rate of interest. It first pointed out that "Art. 78 (CISG) does not lay down the criteria for calculating the interest and that international case law presents a wide range of possibilities in this respect". Then it stated that "amongst the criteria adopted in various judgments, the most appropriate appears to be that of the rates generally applied in international trade for the contractual currency...In concrete terms, since the contractual currency is the dollar and the parties are European, the applicable rate is the 3-month LIBOR on the dollar, increased by one percentage point, with effect from the due date not respected up until full payment has been made". The solution substantially corresponded to the one provided for in Art. 7.4.9(2) of the UNIDROIT Principles, though this provision was not expressly referred to by the Arbitral Tribunal.

Full Text

The contract contains a clause, quoted at the beginning, whereby Italian law is applicable. This clause has certainty been extended to the amendment dated [...], given the reference to the former in respect of matters otherwise unregulated [...]

In view of the basic unicity of the relations, mentioned earlier, it is therefore necessary, as a preliminary measure, to establish the law applicable to the contracts in respect of which the parties have not expressed their intent.

This point is covered in paragraph 11 of the Terms of Reference where it is stated that: "With regard to the substantive and procedural provisions contained in the International Chamber of Commerce Rules, it is clearly specified that: a) the applicable substantive law is Italian law [...]". Given that the parties, counsel and the arbitrators had signed such terms, this matter can be considered as settled and beyond dispute. It is true that at that moment Respondent had raised an objection to arbitral jurisdiction over all the contracts referred to in Claimant's claims, and so, it could be objected, its acceptance of Italian law as the applicable law was limited to the definition of this procedural objection. Moreover, the subsequent waiver of this objection. [...] and the statement whereby Respondent's legal representative "admits that the solution to all these issues raised by

one or other of the parties in the dispute pending between Claimant and Respondent before the Arbitral Tribunal. [...] is sought from the afore mentioned Arbitral Tribunal in accordance with the arbitration clause contained in Article XIII (arbitration) of the Accord dated 1st October 1991, "*inter partes*" [...] do not contain any reserves regarding the point of applicable law, as previously outlined in the Terms of Reference, which therefore has to be considered as granted. There is therefore precise justification for the choice of Italian law and the Arbitral Tribunal considers it appropriate to support this choice with a number of clarifications that make a distinction between supplies [...] and settlement:
(a) for the former, it would seem appropriate to apply the Vienna Convention, and, purely for the part not regulated by this or for which the principles deriving from it or from international usages are of no assistance, the general rules of Italian law (see Article 7(2) of the Vienna Convention);
(b) the settlement, on the other hand, is unquestionably regulated by the general rules of Italian law.

The supplies between Respondent/Claimant are considered as "international sales of goods" to which the Vienna Convention is applicable for the following concisely stated reasons: [...]

(c) the original contract, together with the successive amendments and additions thereto (which, despite not being a deed of sale, is considered by the parties to be the general reference framework for their business relations), provides for the applicability of Italian law. It thus appears that Italian law is the most appropriate law and the one that offers the closest connection;

(d) according to the Rome Convention (to which Article 57 of Italian law 218/1995 on the reform of private international law refers), in the absence of any choice by the parties, the contract is governed by the law of the country in which the person effecting the characteristic performance is based (see Articles 4.1 and 4.2). According to standard indications in legislation and conventions, the characteristic performance, as a rule, is that which is not in cash, and, in a deed of sale, is that effected by the seller: see Article 117.3 of the Swiss federal statute on private international law of 18. 12.1987, on which the Italian statute was modelled; Article 3.1 of the Hague Convention of 1955; Article 8 of the new Hague Convention of 1985 (not ratified). In our case, Respondent, a company with its head office in Italy, effected the characteristic performance;

(e) the applicability of Italian law makes international sales immediately subject to application of the Vienna Convention, Article 1.1(b) of which establishes that: "This Convention applies to contracts of sales of goods between parties whose places of business are in different states. [...] when the rules of private international law lead to the application of the law of a Contracting State" and this is the case of Italy on the basis of law 765/1985 that ratified this Convention. Furthermore, this applicability of the Convention is also valid in relation to the explicit choice of Italian law adopted in the Terms of Reference; [...]

The Arbitral Tribunal is of the opinion that the search for the content of the settlement [...] plays an essential role in finding a solution to the questions and the claims raised by the parties [...].

From the literal meaning of Article 1975 of the Italian Civil Code, it results that the settlement may be of a general nature and cover "all the business affairs that may exist" between the parties and, implicitly and *a contrario,* that it may cover only certain controversial business affairs, thus allowing the disputes and controversies on other business affairs to subsist [...]. Given the extent of the controversies between the parties, it is a question of defining what is the specific subject of the settlement, and whether it covers the entire dispute [...] or only part of it and which part. [...]

This method of interpretation is entirely consistent with the specific rules of Italian law (Articles 1362-1371 of the Italian Civil Code), as applied by the courts, according to which:
(w) recourse is made to an extra-textual interpretation when the letter-contract is incomplete and fails to execute the "common intent of the parties"; (x) among the methods taken into consideration, there is first and foremost the so-called logical interpretation, which includes the identification of the purpose of the contract; (y) although considered as being subsidiary the assessment of past and subsequent behavior falls within the interpreter's responsibilities when the text is unclear or incomplete; (z) an interpretation on the basis of good faith places importance, among other things, on the reciprocal trust between the parties and so on what one of the parties should have communicated to the other with a view to protecting their respective interests, and also in relation to the obligation of good faith in negotiations pursuant to Article 1337 of the Italian Civil Code. The rules relating to interpretation and good faith contained in the UNIDROIT Principles (in particular, Articles 1.7 and from 4.1 to 4.8), which are in all events a useful reference framework for applying and judging a contract of an international nature, also confirm what has been said.

In this light, the Arbitral Tribunal feels that the following circumstances are important:

(a) the reciprocal objections raised by the parties prior to the settlement agreement: by Respondent: Claimant's failure to perform payment obligations and violation of commercial obligations; by Claimant: defects in goods sold, overdue deliveries and violations of commercial obligations [...]

(b) the manifest and stated scope of the settlement to define all outstanding issues [...] with a view to re-establishing current commercial relations which there was a desire to maintain at that time[...].

(c) the previous behavior of the parties: more specifically, the proposals and counter-proposals formulated gradually prior to the meeting of [...]

(d) subsequent (immediately following) behavior, and above all the spontaneous "principle of execution" [sic] (which can also be described as a declaration of a "sign of good faith"): on the part of Claimant, through the issue of a bank guarantee and payment of the first installment; on the part of Respondent, acceptance without reserve of the bank guarantee in which, in the description of the agreed terms of payment, no mention is made of the last installment of interest...

[...] [T]he payment schedule described in the bank guarantee does not mention the January installment [...] and this omission was explained by Claimant [...] as consideration for waiving the claims relating to defects *etc.* — later consideration — pursuant to subsection (c), in respect of the waivers already made in this respect. Respondent's acceptance without reserve of the bank guarantee, in which point 6 is omitted, and the alleged start-up of production of the ordered pipes amount to a tacit acceptance by Respondent of the modified/counter-proposed acceptance by Claimant, according to the principle derived *a contrario* from Article 1326, last paragraph, of the Italian Civil Code. Moreover, reference should be made to Article 19, (1) and (2) of the Vienna Convention with regard to the formation of international sales contracts, and Article 2.11 of the UNIDROIT Principles, which are both normative texts that can be considered helpful in the interpretation of all contracts of an international nature [...].

Given that long-term contracts are involved, the termination of relations on the ground of Claimant's fault, as mentioned above, does not extend to relations that have already ended. With regard to payment obligations remaining unperformed, performance cannot be ordered, but rather compensation for damages [...]. This compensation is calculated in proportion to the amount from the settlement remaining unpaid, to which overdue interest has been added, as provided for in Article 1219, no. 3 of the Italian Civil Code, with effect from the due date [...] and up until full payment of the balance. The Vienna Convention lays down a general rule, in Article 78, that the liability for payment of a sum is subject to interest for late payment, but it does not lay down the criteria for calculating this interest. International case law presents a wide range of possibilities in this respect, but amongst the criteria adopted in various judgements, the more appropriate appears to be that of the rates generally applied in international trade for the contractual currency [...]. In concrete terms, since the contractual currency is the dollar and the parties are European, the applicable rate is the 3-month LIBOR on the dollar, increased by one percentage point, with effect from the due date not respected up until full payment has been made. However, capitalization of interest is excluded, as from Respondent's arbitration answer, since this is not provided for in the Vienna Convention and does not appear to be in keeping with international trade usages. Revaluation is also included in the above mentioned rate.'

[...]

Sources

Original in Italian:
Unpublished.

Published in English (excerpt):
ICC International Court of Arbitration Bulletin, Vol. 10, No. 2, Fall 1999, 83 – 87.

Date: ***September 1998***
Adjudicating Court: ***ICC International Court of Arbitration, Lugano***
Number: ***9419***
Parties: ***Unknown***

Keywords

CONTRACT SILENT AS TO APPLICABLE LAW – PARTY'S REQUEST THAT ARBITRAL TRIBUNAL APPLY LEX MERCATORIA AND UNIDROIT PRINCIPLES – EXCLUSION OF UNIDROIT PRINCIPLES (ART. 13(3) ICC RULES) BECAUSE "THEY CANNOT CONSTITUTE A NORMATIVE BODY IN THEMSELVES THAT CAN BE CONSIDERED AS AN APPLICABLE SUPRANATIONAL LAW TO REPLACE A NATIONAL LAW"

Abstract

A Swiss management company (Claimant) and a Liechtenstein importer (Respondent) entered into an agreement for the exportation of goods. Claimant complained that no payment had been made by Respondent. Since the contract did not contain any choice of law clause, Claimant based its claims on universally acknowledged principles of international trade and requested that the Arbitral Tribunal solve the dispute in accordance with the *lex mercatoria*, "a kind of codification of which can be found in the principles of international commercial contracts drawn up by UNIDROIT".

The Arbitral Tribunal expressly excluded the application of the UNIDROIT Principles. It recalled that an authoritative school of thought had argued the existence of an unwritten and supranational law (the *lex mercatoria*) and that there had been awards in international commerce explicitly referring to it. However, not being convinced of its existence, it firmly rejected the possibility of applying the *lex mercatoria* and, in accordance with Art. 13(3) of the ICC Rules, held that the applicable law of the contractual relationship must be national law.

With respect to the UNIDROIT Principles, though admitting that "[t]hese may be considered as a kind of codification of the *lex mercatoria*", the Arbitral Tribunal expressly pointed out that "the UNIDROIT Principles could certainly be used for reference by the parties involved for the voluntary regulation of their contractual relationship, in addition to helping the arbitrator in confirming the existence of particular trade usages, but they cannot constitute a normative body in themselves that can be considered as an applicable supranational law to replace a national law, at least as long as the the arbitrator is required to identify the applicable law by choosing the rule of conflict that he considers most appropriate, in accordance with the provisions laid down by the international conventions and as provided for in the rules of arbitration within the scope of which he operates".

Full Text

[...]

The arbitration clause does not specify the substantive law that the arbitrator has to apply. It is therefore up to the arbitrator to determine this, as stated, moreover, in point D10 of the Terms of Reference.

The Claimant has covered this question in its Brief and, more specifically, has argued that, in absence of any reference to a specific national law, the demands are based on the universally acknowledged principles of international commerce, allowing the arbitrator to pronounce his decision in the light of the so-called "*lex mercatoria*", a kind of codification of which can be found in the principles of international commercial contracts drawn up by UNIDROIT. Otherwise, in the event that reference needs to be made to a national law, French law has to be applied, given that the Agreement between X and Y has become an integral part of the Accord and the application of French law is explicitly provided in said Agreement [...].

The undersigned arbitrator is not convinced of the applicability of the so-called *lex mercatoria*. While acknowledging the authoritativeness of the school of thought that has posited the existence of such an unwritten and supranational law, based on principles and usages generally accepted by players in international commerce (the so-called mercatores), and although aware that there have even been awards in international commercial arbitration where explicit reference is made to *lex mercatoria*, the undersigned arbitrator sides with the other school of thought that does not believe in the existence of *lex mercatoria* and which firmly believes that the search for a law that can be applied to a contractual relationship must necessarily lead to the identification of a national law. This is all the more so since, in accordance with the provisions of Article 13.3 of the ICC Rules (consistent with the provisions of Article VII of the Geneva Convention of 1961), the arbitrator, barring any indication by the parties, is required to apply the law that is applicable on the basis of the rules of conflict that he considers to be appropriate.

Whereas, on the one hand, the parties maintain their freedom of choice regarding the legal regulation of their relationship, on the other hand, failing the expression of such choice, the power of the arbitrator is not to choose the applicable law in a direct way, but is limited to identifying the rule of conflict that he considers to be the most appropriate and on the basis of which, in an indirect way, the determination of the applicable law will be made. This means that, by proceeding in this manner (as is his precise duty), the arbitrator necessarily arrives at the designation of a specific national legal system.

Notwithstanding this, the arbitrator must in all events take account not only of the contractual stipulations, but also of trade usages (as provided for in Article 13.5 of the ICC Rules). In other words, precisely due to their general acceptance by the mercatores community, trade usages can be considered to be tacitly acknowledged by the parties in their contractual relationship. Such usages incorporate the contractual regulation of the relationship, though without excluding the need to identify the relevant legislative framework.

With regard to the Principles drawn up by UNIDROIT, it is quite true that these may be considered as a kind of codification of the *lex mercatoria*, but once again these are the results of highly commendable work of academic research and comparison, as well as the reflection of an increasingly eager aspiration to arrive, as it were, at a globalization of legal thinking, though without attributing any binding value to such Principles.

The Introduction to the Principles states that: "[...] [T]he Governing Council is fully conscious of the fact that the Principles, which do not involve the endorsement of Governments, are not a binding instrument".

This means that the UNIDROIT Principles could certainly be used for reference by the parties involved for the voluntary regulation of their contractual relationship, in addition to helping the arbitrator in confirming the existence of particular trade usages, but they cannot constitute a normative body in themselves that can be considered as an applicable supranational law to replace a national law, at least as long as the arbitrator is required to identify the applicable law by choosing the rule of conflict that he considers most appropriate, in accordance with the provisions laid down by the international conventions and as provided for in the rules of arbitration within the scope of which he operates.

The Preamble to the Principles states that: "Parties who wish to adopt the Principles as the rules applicable to their contract would however be well advised to combine the reference to the Principles with an arbitration agreement."

However, it is feasible to accept the Claimant's second argument regarding the applicability of French law, the moment the parties have declared such Agreement, in which the application of French law is explicitly provided, to be an "integral part" of their Accord. It is up to the arbitrator to find out whether and to what extent the parties have an intent with regard to the applicable law, even when an explicit choice is not apparent. The arbitrator replaces the parties in the search for an applicable law only when no "indication" whatsoever has been expressed by the parties in this respect (Article 13.3 of the ICC Rules), which precisely means that it is up to the arbitrator to discover the intent of the parties, wherever possible, also by means of elements pointing to an implicit intent. In our case it is therefore possible to assume that, having incorporated the Agreement into the Accord, the parties have implicitly expressed their wish to submit their contractual relationship to the same system of law (French law as that to which the Agreement was explicitly subject.

It has to be mentioned, however, that since most claims are based on alleged breaches of contract for the supply of goods, the arbitrator must first of all apply the United Nations Convention on Contracts for the International Sales of Goods adopted in Vienna on 11 April 1980 (hereinafter the "Vienna Convention" or "CISG"), making reference to all the conditions that, in this particular case, make it applicable on the basis of the provisions in Article 1 [of said Convention] and more precisely:

- the sale of goods, that is, the subject of the contract;

- the international nature of the relationship, given that the parties have their business center in different countries;

- accession to the CISG by the two countries (Switzerland and Liechtenstein) where the parties are based; and (should it be necessary)

France's accession to the CISG, given that French law is considered applicable.'

[...]

Sources

Original in Italian:
Unpublished.

Published in English (excerpt):
ICC International Court of Arbitration Bulletin, Vol. 10, No. 2, Fall 1999, 104 – 106.

Date: ***October 1998***
Adjudicating Court: ***ICC International Court of Arbitration, Geneva***
Number: ***9333***
Parties: ***Unknown***

Keywords

PARTIES' CHOICE OF DOMESTIC LAW (SWISS LAW) AS LAW GOVERNING THE CONTRACT – REFERENCE BY ARBITRAL TRIBUNAL TO CISG AND UNIDROIT PRINCIPLES AS USAGES OF INTERNATIONAL TRADE

INTEREST (ART. 7.4.9 UNIDROIT PRINCIPLES) (ART. 78 CISG) (ART. 104 SWISS CODE OF OBLIGATIONS)

Abstract

In the framework of their contractual relationship, Claimant (a Moroccan broker) agreed to provide certain services to Respondent (a French builder). Respondent made part of the commissions into a Swiss bank account, but afterwards refused to pay the balance, arguing that it had become part of an American group under a policy which prohibited it from paying in a country other than that where the agent was located or the services rendered. In order to further justify its refusal to pay the remaining commissions, Respondent alleged that the reason why Claimant demanded payment be made in Switzerland was due to bribery, which in its view was an illicit purpose under the Swiss Code of Obligations. Claimant filed an arbitration suit to recover the commissions plus damages and interest.

The contract contained a choice of law clause in favour of a particular domestic law (Swiss law).

The Arbitral Tribunal rejected the allegations of corruption and ordered Respondent to pay the commissions plus interest. In particular, in order to confirm that the claim for interest was part of the general claim for damages, the Arbitral Tribunal cited to an author (K.-P. BERGER, International Arbitral Practice and the UNIDROIT Principles of International Commercial Contracts, in 46 The American Journal of Comparative Law, 1998, 135 ff.) according to whom "[f]rom a functional perspective, the interest claim in Art. 78 CISG, just as the one in 7.4.9 of the UNIDROIT Principles, and any statutory interest claim constitutes the minimum lump sum compensation for damages in areas where the creditor need not prove the actual damages incurred. It is a long-standing practice of international arbitrators, as well as of the Iran-U.S. Claims Tribunal, to consider the interest claim as part of the general claim for damages".

In awarding Claimant the rate of interest provided for in Art. 104 of the Swiss Code of Obligations (5%), the Arbitral Tribunal held that nothing in the contract suggested that the parties intended to exclude the right to interest for delayed payment. In reaching this conclusion, it pointed out that such an exclusion would have been difficult to reconcile with "[t]he usages of international trade which are echoed by, among others, the United Nations Convention on Contracts for the International Sale of Goods (the "Vienna Convention") or again the UNIDROIT Principles of International Commercial Contracts [...]" (translation from French original).

Full Text

[...] La Convention est soumise au Code suisse des obligations. Selon la défenderesse, toutefois, la loi FCPA trouve "pleinement application dans les relations contractuelles des parties" [...] La défenderesse prétend que la loi FCPA lui interdit de faire des paiements au demandeur en dehors du Maroc.

Un contrat qui est contraire non pas au droit suisse, mais à un droit étranger, n'est en principe pas illicite selon l'article 20 CO, cette disposition ne protégeant que le respect de la loi suisse. Dans des circonstances exceptionnelles, une violation d'un droit étranger peut néanmoins être considérée comme contraire aux moeurs selon l'article 20 CO si elle est irréconciliable avec les moeurs suisses [...] Tel n'est pas le cas en l'occurrence [...] Le Tribunal [...] est arrivé à la conclusion que le grief de corruption n'était pas établi par des preuves [...].

Une loi étrangère ayant la qualité de loi de police pourrait éventuellement trouver application à un contrat, autrement soumis au droit suisse, par le biais de l'article 19 LDIP Une violation d'une telle loi de police, à supposer réunies les conditions d'application de l'article 19, pourrait entrainer l'illicéité du contrat. La question de savoir si l'article 19 WIP s'applique à un arbitre international ainsi que les conditions d'application de cette disposition est controversée [...]. La question peut toutefois être laissée ouverte dès lors que le Tribunal arbitral est de l'avis que (i) l'application de la FCPA à titre de loi de police étrangère ne se justifle pas et que (ii), en toute hypothèse, les conditions d'applications de la FCPA ne sont pas réunies.

La présente procédure met en cause la défenderesse, filiale francaise de la société américaine [X], et le demandeur, un ressortissant marocain. La société américaine [X] n'est pas partie à la procédure. Il n'y a aucun rattachement avec le droit américain hormis le fait que la société française est devenue, après la conclusion de la Convention, une filiale d'une société américaine. Ce rattachement serait en tout état de cause insuffisant pour appliquer la loi FCPA à titre de l'article 19 LDIP.

Il n'est cependant pas nécessaire de chercher un rattachement, car la loi FCPA ne s'applique pas aux filiales de sociétés américaines à l'étranger [...]. En revanche, selon la loi FCPA, la société mère basée aux Etats-Unis est responsable pour les agissements des sociétés appartenant au groupe qu'elle chapeaute. C'est dans cette optique, afin de limiter le risque lié à leur propre responsabilité, que les multinationales américaines ont instauré des programmes dans toutes les sociétés du groupe qui devraient permettre d'assurer le respect de la loi FCPA [...].

On ajoutera que même si la loi FCPA était applicable à la défenderesse, ceci ne signifierait pas encore qu'un Tribunal arbitral international serait tenu de l'appliquer sans autre. Même à supposer (i) qu'il s'agit d'une loi de police et (ii) que l'arbitre admet qu'une telle loi peut être appliquée nonobstant l'élection d'une autre loi matérielle, encore faudrait-il démontrer des intérèts puissants et légitimes des Etats-Unis à l'application de cette loi. De sérieux doutes à ce sujet pourront en effet résulter du fait que la loi FCPA ne vise pas en premier lieu à protéger l'ordre public fondamental des Etats-Unis mais qu'elle a pour but de restaurer la confiance du public dans l'intégrité des entreprises américaines dont la réputation [avait] été ternie par une série de scandales retentissants [...]. Il serait donc peu approprié d'imposer sans autre la loi FCPA à des entreprises en dehors des Etats-Unis [...] la tutte contre la corruption, but certes louable, ne justifie pas nécessairement l'exportation des méthodes ou du code de conduite singulier de la loi FCPA pour atteindre ce but [...].

[...] [L]e demandeur a modifié ses conclusions tendant à l'obtention d'intérêts moratoires en ce qu'il réclame que ceux-ci soient "calculés au taux de 5% conformément aux dispositions de l'article 104 du Code suisse des obligations (et non au taux légal francais)" et ceci à compter du dépôt de la Requête d'arbitrage [...].
Le demandeur a réclamé le paiement d'intérêts dans sa requête d'arbitrage déjà. Aurait-il persisté à fonder sa demande sui- le droit francais, il aurait incombé au Tribunal, non pas de déclarer irrecevable la demande, mais d'appliquer le Code suisse des obligations.

On peut d'ailleurs s'interroger sur la question de savoir si les intérêts ne font pas de toute façon partie de la demande principale. Ainsi, un auteur a récemment écrit ce qui suit "From a functional perspective, the interest claim in Mt. 78 CISG, just as the one incorporated in Art. 7-4.9 of the Principles, and any statutory interest claim constitutes the minimum lump sum compensation for damages in areas where the creditor need not prove the actual damages incurred. It Is a long-standing practice of international arbitrators, as well as of the Iran-U.S. Claims Tribunal, to consider the interest claim as part of the general claim for damages." (Klaus Peter BERGER, International Arbitral Practice and the UNIDROIT Principles of International Commercial Contracts, in The American Journal of Comparative Law, Vol. 46, 1998, p. 135 s.) [...].

Selon l'article 104 CO, auquel la Convention est soumise, tout débiteur qui est en demeure pour le paiement d'une somme d'argent doit l'intérêt moratoire de 5% par l'an. Rien dans la Convention ne permet d'admettre que les parties avaient l'intention d'exclure le droit au paiement d'intérêts en cas de demeure. Une telle exclusion aurait du reste été difficile à réconcilier avec les usages du commerce international dont se font l'écho, entre autres, la Convention des Nations Unies sur les contrats de vente internationale de marchandises (Convention de Vienne), ou encore les Principes UNIDROIT pour les contrats commerciaux internationaux, évoqués par l'auteur précité.

Au vu de l'article 104 CO et des conclusions du demandeur, il convient donc d'assortir toute condamnation de la défenderesse au paiement de commissions d'une condamnation au paiement d'intéréts au taux de 5% dès le dépôt de la Requête d'arbitrage [...].

Sources

Original in English (excerpt):
ICC International Court of Arbitration Bulletin, Vol. 10, No. 2, Fall 1999, 102 – 104.

Date: ***December 1998***
Adjudicating Court: ***ICC International Court of Arbitration, Paris***
Number: ***9593***
Parties: ***Unknown***

Keywords

PARTIES' CHOICE OF DOMESTIC LAW (IVORIAN LAW) AS LAW GOVERNING THE CONTRACT – ARBITRAL TRIBUNAL TO CONSIDER TRADE USAGES (ART. 13(5) ICC RULES) – REFERENCE TO UNIDROIT PRINCIPLES

PARTIES' DUTY TO COOPERATE IN PERFORMANCE OF CONTRACT (ARTS. 1134(3) AND 1135 IVORIAN CIVIL CODE; ART. 5.3 [ART. 5.1.3 OF THE 2004 EDITION] UNIDROIT PRINCIPLES)

Abstract

An Anglo-Japanese supplier and an Ivorian distributor entered into a number of exclusive distribution agreements. In view of the distributor's failure to make payment, the supplier decided to terminate the agreements. During the dispute, each party accused the other of bad faith and lack of cooperation in the contractual performance.

The contracts contained a choice of law clause in favour of a particular domestic law (Ivorian law).

The Arbitral Tribunal held that, in addition to applying Ivorian law as the chosen law (Art. 13(3) ICC Rules), it would also take into account, pursuant to Art. 13(5) of the ICC Rules, the relevant trade usages.

The Arbitral Tribunal pointed out that, under Art. 1134(3) and Art. 1135 of the Ivorian Civil Code, parties must cooperate in good faith in the course of performance in order to achieve their contractual purposes. In order to confirm its conclusion that "[t]he obligation to cooperate in good faith in the performance of a contract [amounts] to a general principle applicable to international trade", the Arbitral Tribunal referred, without further explanation, to Art. 5.3 [Art. 5.1.3 of the 2004 edition] of the UNIDROIT Principles.

Full Text

[…] As stated in Clause 1.2 of the Dealer Agreement and Clause 13.1 of the Supplementary Agreement [...], the law governing the Agreements and their interpretation is the law of the Republic of the Ivory Coast.

Thus, according to Article 13(3) of the ICC Rules, the Arbitral Tribunal must apply the laws of the Ivory Coast in order to decide the merits of this dispute.

Pursuant to Article 13(5) of the ICC Rules, the Arbitral Tribunal shall also take into account the provisions of the contract and the relevant trade usages. In doing so, the Arbitral Tribunal will pay particular attention to the specific nature of the Agreements and to the context within which they were entered into. As requested by Article 1156 of the Civil Code of the Ivory Coast, the Arbitral Tribunal will look for the real intent of the parties and not only the literal wording of the Agreements.

Article 1134, paragraph 3 of the Ivorian Civil Code stresses that contracts must be performed in good faith. Furthermore, Article 1135 of the same code recalls that a contract binds the parties not only according to its wording, but also to the consequences thereof resulting from equity custom and the law. In a contractual relationship which is the extension in time of previous relations between a Japanese group and an Ivorian group, constitutes the result of negotiations between English, Japanese and Ivorian parties and deals with the distribution in the Ivory Coast of Japanese products, the custom to be taken into consideration by the Arbitral Tribunal within the framework of Article 1135 of the Ivorian Civil Code is to be found within the usages of international trade.

One consequence of the principle recalled by Article 1134, paragraph 3 of the Ivorian Civil Code, according to which contracts must be performed in good faith, is that the parties must cooperate in good faith to reach the common goals contractually agreed upon. It is on the basis of the identical text of Article 1134, paragraph 3 of the French Civil Code that French courts have decided that good faith and loyalty oblige a party to a contract to facilitate the performance of its obligation by the other party [...] Indeed, as written years ago by the French lawyer Demogue: "les contrats forment une sorte de microcosme [...] une petite société où chacun doit travailler dans un but commun, qui est la somme des buts individueis, poursuivis par chacun, absolument comme dans la société civile ou commerciale" (R. DEMOGUE, Traité des Obligations, 1927, [vol] 1'V~ p. 191). Such obligation to cooperate in good faith in the performance of the contract has also become a fundamental element of the usages of international trade applicable to this case through Article 1135 of the Ivorian Civil Code and Article 13(5) of the ICC Rules. Such usage was pointed out by several awards rendered under the aegis of the International Court of Arbitration of the ICC [...].

Further in a comparative study, UNIDROIT came in the conclusion that the obligation to cooperate in good faith in the performance of a contract amounted to a general principle applicable to international trade. Accordingly, this principle was reflected under Article 5.3 of the UNIDROIT Principles of International Commercial Contracts : "Each party shall cooperate with the other party when such cooperation may reasonably be expected for the performance of that party's obligations."

In conclusion, the Arbitral Tribunal will make its decision on the validity of the termination of the Agreement on the basis of the text thereof, in the light of the law of the Ivory Coast which requires good faith in the performance of contracts, such requirement also deriving from the usages of international trade.[...]

Sources

Original in English (excerpt):
ICC International Court of Arbitration Bulletin, Vol. 10, No. 2, Fall 1999, 107 – 109.

Date: ***December 7, 1998***
Country: ***United States***
Adjudicating Court: ***US District Court, S.D. California***
Number: ***98–1165-B***
Parties: ***Ministry of Defense and Support for the Armed Forces of the Islamic Republic of Iran v. Cubic Defense Systems, Inc.***

Keywords

REFERENCE BY ARBITRAL TRIBUNAL TO THE UNIDROIT PRINCIPLES AS A SOURCE OF "GENERAL PRINCIPLES OF LAW AND TRADE USAGES" – WITHOUT EXPRESS AUTHORIZATION BY PARTIES – DOES NOT VIOLATE ARTICLE V(1)(C) OF THE 1958 NEW YORK CONVENTION

Abstract

On 25 June 1998, a petition was filed for an order confirming the ICC Award no. 7365/FMS of 5 May 1997 (see UNILEX UNIDROIT Principles, C.1997-5). In its counter-motion requesting the Court to refuse confirmation, the Respondent contended that the award dealt "with a difference not contemplated by or not falling within the terms of the submission to arbitration" and contained "decisions on matters beyond the scope of the submission to arbitration", thereby violating Article V(1)(c) of the 1958 New York Convention on the Recognition and Enforcement of Foreign Arbitration Awards, claiming that the Arbitral Tribunal exceeded the terms of the submission to arbitration in two respects: first, by issuing a ruling based upon legal theories not contemplated by and/or asserted by the parties; secondly by referring to the UNIDROIT Principles and to other international principles such as good faith and fair dealing, even though they were not indicated in the Terms of Reference as the applicable law.

The Court rejected both objections. As to the first one, the Court held that, because the ICC Award resolved the parties' claims arising from the contracts for the sale and installation of the sophisticated military equipment entered into by the parties, the fact that it was not based on the same legal theories as stated in the pleadings could not be a basis for refusing to confirm it. As to the Respondent's complaint concerning the application of the UNIDROIT Principles, according to the Court, "the Tribunal's reference to and application of the UNIDROIT Principles and principles such as good faith and fair dealing do not violate Article V(1)(c). The Tribunal applied these principles to differences contemplated by and falling within the terms of the submission to arbitration and therefore the Award does not violate Article V(1)(c)".

Full Text

[...] [2] The Court is asked to confirm the ICC Award pursuant to the United Nations Convention on the Recognition and Enforcement of Foreign Arbitration Awards

("Convention"), opened for signature June 10, 1958, 21 U.S.T. 2517, 330 U.N.T.S. 3, reprinted in 9 U.S.C. §§ 201-208. The United States became a party to the Convention in 1970, and Congress soon after enacted legislation implementing the provisions of the Convention into domestic law, codified as Chapter II of the Federal Arbitration Act ("FAA"), Pub.L. 91-368, 84 Stat. 692 (1970) (codified at 9 U.S.C. §§ 201-208). A district court's "review of a foreign arbitration award is quite circumscribed." Ministry of Defense of the Islamic Republic of Iran v. Gould, Inc., 969 F.2d 764, 770 (9th Cir.1992). There is a general pro-enforcement bias under the Convention. See Id.; see also Scherk v. Alberto-Culver Co., 417 U.S. 506, 519-20 & n. 15, 94 S. Ct. 2449, 41 L.Ed.2d 270 (1974). Upon application for an order confirming the award, the "district court has little discretion: 'The court shall confirm the award unless it finds one of the grounds for refusal or deferral of recognition or enforcement of the award specified in the said Convention.' " Ministry of Defense, 969 F.2d at 770 (citing 9 U.S.C. § 207).

[3] The grounds for refusing to recognize or enforce an arbitral award include:

(a) The parties to the agreement ... were, under the law applicable to them, under some incapacity, or the said agreement is not valid under the law to which the parties have subjected it or, failing any indication thereon, under the law of the country where the award was made; or

(b) The party against whom the award is invoked was not given proper notice of the appointment of the arbitrator or the arbitration proceedings or was otherwise unable to present [his or her] case; or

(c) The award deals with a difference not contemplated by or not falling within the terms of the submission to arbitration, or it contains decisions on matters beyond the scope of the submission to arbitration, provided that, if the decisions on matters submitted to arbitration can be separated from those not so submitted, that part of the award which contain decisions on matters submitted to arbitration may be recognized and enforced;.... [FN2]

FN2. Article V(1)(d)-(e) and Article V(2) of the Convention also set forth grounds upon which a court may refuse to recognize or enforce a foreign arbitral award. Cubic, however, does not make claims pursuant to these provisions of the Convention and therefore these grounds are not before this Court.

Convention, art. V(1). In particular, courts should narrowly construe Article V(1)(c) in accordance with the Convention's general pro-enforcement bias. See Ministry of Defense, 969 F.2d at 770.

[4] Section 10 of the FAA and case law addressing domestic arbitration set forth grounds upon which a court may refuse to confirm an arbitration award. These grounds, however, are not applicable to confirmation under the Convention. The statute implementing the Convention states that a "court shall confirm the award unless it finds one of the grounds for refusal ... specified in the said Convention." 9 U.S.C. § 207. Thus, other provisions regarding arbitration are not applicable to petitions requesting confirmation of an arbitration award under the Convention. See Ministry of Defense, 969 F.2d at 770 (limiting discretion of district court to grounds to refusal specified in the Convention); Management & Technical Consultants S.A. v. Parsons-Jurden Int'l Corp., 820 F.2d 1531,

1533-34 (9th Cir.1987) ("Under the Convention, an arbiter's award can be vacated only on the grounds specified in the Convention."); see also Industrial Risk Insurers v. M.A.N. Gutehoffnungshutte GmbH, 141 F.3d 1434, 1446 (11th Cir.1998) (finding that "the Convention's enumeration of defenses is exclusive"); Yusuf Ahmed Alghanim & Sons, W.L.L. v. Toys "R" Us, Inc., 126 F.3d 15, 20 (2d Cir.1997) ("[T]he grounds for relief enumerated in Article V. of the Convention are the only grounds available for setting aside an arbitral award."); M & C Corp. v. Erwin Behr GmbH & Co., 87 F.3d 844, 851 (6th Cir.1996) ("Article V. of the Convention lists the exclusive grounds justifying refusal to recognize an arbitral award.").

B. CUBIC'S OPPOSITION TO CONFIRMATION OF THE ARBITRATION AWARD

1. Article V(1)(c)

Cubic first contends that the ICC Award violates Article V(1)(c) of the Convention because it "deals with a difference not contemplated by or not falling within the terms of the submission to arbitration" and it "contains decisions on matters beyond the scope of the submission to arbitration." [FN3] Cubic also alleges that the award violates Article V(1)(c) because it ignores the terms of the Parties' Contracts. Thus, Cubic argues that the "Terms of Reference constitute the jurisdictional mandate of an arbitral panel, and any decision which exceeds the scope of that jurisdictional reference is improper."

FN3. Cubic also contends that the Award violates 9 U.S.C. § 10 of the FAA. As explained by this Court, § 10 of the FAA does not apply to claims brought under the Convention.

[5] Specifically, Cubic argues that the Tribunal decided issues not submitted by the Parties and issued a ruling based upon legal theories not contemplated by and/or asserted by the Parties. The legal theories and conclusions Cubic takes issue with are: (1) the "conclusion that the Parties agreed in 1979 to discontinue the Contracts at least for the time being, *i.e.*, until the results of Cubic's attempt to resell the System would be known" (Award § 10.11); (2) the conclusion that there was "an implicit agreement for the postponement of the maturity date of any such claims until Cubic had resold the equipment or declared its inability to resell" (Procedural Order No. 6 § 1.3); (3) the conclusion that there was "a factual termination of the Contracts at the request of Iran" (Award § 11.22); and, (4) the finding that it can be implied from the Termination for Convenience Clause that "Cubic shall credit Iran with ... products manufactured for Iran prior to the termination of the Contracts." (Award § 13.6).

Cubic's objections are misguided. First, the Terms of Reference allow the Arbitrators leeway in resolving the conflict that the Parties presented to them. Cubic cites specific questions framed by the Terms of Reference and claims that the ICC Award's deviations from those particular questions constitutes a deviation from the Terms. However, as Iran points out, the questions posed for the Arbitrators were presented in the following manner in the Terms of Reference:

The issues to be determined shall be those resulting from the Parties' submissions and which are relevant to the adjudication of the Parties' respective claims and defenses. In particular, the Arbitral Tribunal may have to consider the following issues (but not necessarily all of these or only these, and not necessarily in the following order)....

(Terms of Reference § 4) (emphasis added). The Terms of Reference then proceed to list twelve issues that may be considered in the adjudication of the Parties' claims and defenses. The Arbitrators were not, however, explicitly required to consider all of these issues in resolving this contractual dispute. The Arbitrators were also not limited to the issues listed, but could consider additional issues in resolving this dispute. Furthermore, the Award is within the parameters of those twelve issues, even if the legal theories applied are different from those presented in the Parties' pleadings. Thus, based only on an evaluation of the Terms of Reference, the use of legal theories not presented by the Parties is acceptable under the Terms of Reference.

[6] Second, Cubic's claim that the use of legal theories not presented by the Parties precludes confirmation of the Award was rejected by the Ninth Circuit. See Ministry of Defense, 969 F.2d at 771. Under the Convention, a court is to determine "whether the award exceeds the scope of the [arbitration agreement], not whether the award exceeds the scope of the parties' pleadings." Id. Respondents in Ministry of Defense objected to confirmation of that award "because the award [was] not based on the same legal theory as that stated in the pleadings." The court found that the subject matter of respondent's claim was "obvious[ly]" the contracts between the parties and to the extent the "award resolves the claims and counterclaims connected with the two contracts it ... does not exceed the scope of the submission to arbitration." Id. Comparing Ministry of Defense to this case, the Court finds that the subject matter of this dispute is the Service and Sales Contracts between Cubic and Iran. The ICC Award resolves the Parties' claims arising from these Contracts and the fact that the Award is not based on the same legal theories as stated in the pleadings cannot be a basis for refusing to confirm it.

[7] Cubic also disputes the Tribunal's reference to the Principles of International Commercial Contracts published in 1994 by the UNIDROIT Institute ("UNIDROIT Principles") and the Tribunal's references to principles of fairness such as good faith and fair dealing. Cubic claims that reference to such international and equitable principles also violates Article V(1)(c) because this law exceeds the scope of the Terms of Reference. The reference to the UNIDROIT Principles does not exceed the scope of the Terms of Reference. One of the issues presented to the Tribunal was whether general principles of international law apply to this dispute. That Cubic disagrees with the Tribunal's response to the question posed by the Parties is not a reason to find that the Tribunal addressed issues beyond the scope of the Terms of Reference. The same is true for Cubic's assertions with regard to the Tribunal's references to equitable principles of contract law. [FN4]

FN4. Cubic relies on Beacon Journal Publ'g v. Akron Newspaper Guild, 114 F.3d 596, 600 (6th Cir.1997), for its contention that arbitration awards based on fairness and equity instead of the terms of the agreement should be overturned. Even if this case were binding on this Court, the case resolves a domestic arbitration dispute arising from a collective bargaining agreement and is therefore not applicable to the confirmation of arbitral awards under the Convention. See Ministry of Defense, 969 F.2d at 770; see also M & C Corp., 87 F.3d at 851 (6th Cir.1996).

As stated earlier, this Court's discretion in reviewing a foreign arbitration award is quite circumscribed. See Ministry of Defense, 969 F.2d at 770. The Tribunal's reference to and application of the UNIDROIT Principles and principles such as good faith and fair dealing do not violate Article V(1)(c). The Tribunal applied these principles to differences contemplated by and falling within the terms of the submission to arbitration and therefore the Award does not violate Article V(1)(c).

2. Article V(1)(a)

[8] Article V(1)(a) provides that a court may refuse to confirm an arbitral award if an agreement in writing, including an arbitral clause in a contract or an arbitration agreement, is not valid under the law to which the parties have subjected it. Cubic appears to be arguing that the four theories of the Tribunal that Cubic contests constitute oral amendments to the Contracts' arbitration clauses and the Terms of Reference. Cubic contends that these oral amendments violate the Convention's requirement that the agreements be in writing. Cubic's construction of the Award and the Convention is strained.

The arbitration clause in the Contracts and the Terms of Reference validly present the Tribunal with the task of resolving the dispute over the Contracts between Iran and Cubic resulting from the unusual circumstances surrounding the 1979 Iranian Revolution. This Court cannot refuse to confirm the Award simply because the legal theories and conclusions presented in the Award differ from those contemplated by the Parties in their pleadings. Legal theories used by adjudicators to resolve contract disputes are not considered oral amendments to the contract or the arbitration agreement. Article V(1)(a) of the Convention does not present this Court with grounds for refusing to confirm the Award.

3. Article V(1)(b)

[9] Article V(1)(b) allows a court to refuse confirmation of an arbitral award if the "party against whom the award is invoked was not given proper notice of the appointment of the arbitrator or of the arbitration proceedings or was otherwise unable to present [his or her] case." Cubic contends that it was "denied a meaningful opportunity to present its case" because: (1) Iran shifted its factual and legal theories throughout the proceedings; (2) the Tribunal issued interim decisions regarding bifurcation of the proceedings; and (3) the legal theories and remedies articulated in the Award were not previously presented. Even if these allegations were true, these claims do not rise to the level required by Article V(1)(b) to justify a refusal by this Court to confirm the Award. Cubic's active participation in the entire process demonstrates notification of the proceedings, therefore Cubic presumably relies on the latter part of Article V(1)(b) to justify its claim. However, Cubic was also "otherwise able to present [its] case." Two hearings were held. Cubic also had several opportunities for briefing. Cubic had its "day in court" and had ample opportunity to present its interpretation of the facts and its legal theories to the Tribunal. Therefore, the Award does not violate Article V(1)(b).

III. CONCLUSION

The Court hereby GRANTS Iran's Petition for Confirmation of the Foreign Arbitral Award and, subsequently, the Court hereby DENIES Cubic's Cross-Motion to Vacate the May 5, 1997 ICC Arbitration Award.
IT IS SO ORDERED.

Sources

29 Federal Supplement 2nd, 1168 *et seq.*
Uniform Law Review / Revue de droit uniforme, 1999, 799.

Commented on by:
M.J. BONELL, UNIDROIT Principles: a significant recognition by a United States District Court, in Uniform Law Review / Revue de droit uniforme, 1999, 651 *et seq.*

*Date: **January 1999***
*Adjudicating Court: **ICC International Court of Arbitration, Paris***
*Number: **8547***
*Parties: **Unknown***

Keywords

CONTRACT GOVERNED BY THE 1964 UNIFORM LAWS ON THE INTERNATIONAL SALE OF GOODS (ULIS) AND ON THE FORMATION OF CONTRACTS FOR THE INTERNATIONAL SALE OF GOODS (ULFC) – REFERENCE TO THE UNIDROIT PRINCIPLES AS A MEANS OF SUPPLEMENTING THE TWO INTERNATIONAL UNIFORM LAW INSTRUMENTS

CONTRACT INTERPRETATION – CONTRACT TERMS TO BE INTERPRETED AS TO GIVE EFFECT TO AS MANY OF THEM AS POSSIBLE (UNIDROIT PRINCIPLES, ART. 4.5)

DELIVERY OF NON-CONFORMING GOODS – BUYER'S RIGHT TO STOP PAYMENT OF PRICE – APPLICATION OF GENERAL PRINCIPLE OF A PARTY'S RIGHT TO WITHOLD PERFORMANCE IN CASE OF NON-PERFORMANCE BY THE OTHER PARTY (UNIDROIT PRINCIPLES, ART. 7.1.3).

Abstract

Under an international sales contract involving successive deliveries, the buyer (Defendant) stopped payments on the ground of non-conformity of the goods. Seller (Claimant) questioned the valid conclusion of the contract and contested buyer's right to suspend payment until such time as non-conformity had been established.

As to the applicable law the Tribunal noted that the parties had agreed that the two 1964 Uniform Laws on the International Sale of Goods (ULIS) and on the Formation of Contracts for the International Sale of Goods (ULFC) should govern their contract. However, with respect to questions not settled by the two instruments the Arbitral Tribunal, referring to Article 17 of the ICC Arbitration Rules, decided to turn to the UNIDROIT Principles which it considered to "provide useful complement to fill the lacuna and allow to find proper solutions."

As to the merits of the case the Arbitral Tribunal held that the contract had been validly concluded. Admittedly Defendant's reply to Claimant's offer, containing terms which materially altered the terms of the offer, constituted a counter-offer which had not been expressly accepted by Claimant. The contract had, however, been concluded by the Claimant's commencing performance by delivering the goods, and by the Defendant's acceptance of them (*cf.* ULFC Article 6(2)). Accordingly, the Arbitral Tribunal stated that the terms contained in Claimant's offer – and which had not been contested by the parties at any time – were valid, whereas the other terms (price and insurance) were negotiated anew for each and every delivery. In support of this conclusion, the Arbitral Tribunal referred to Article 4.5 of the UNIDROIT Principles according to which the terms of a contract should be interpreted so as to give effect to as many of them as possible.

As to Defendant's right to stop payment until an agreement is reached between the parties as to the degree of lack of conformity of the goods and as to how to proceed in regard to the non-conformity, the Arbitral Tribunal held that although this was not expressly provided in ULIS, it followed from the general principles of law referred to in Article 17 of ULIS. The Arbitral Tribunal referred in this connection to Article 7.1.3 of the UNIDROIT Principles which state that a party may withhold its performance until performance has been effected by the other party. It concluded that the degree of non-conformity was irrelevant, and that notice of non-conformity was enough to justify stopping payments pending agreement by the parties on the lack of conformity.

Full Text

(1) The applicable law on the substance of the case is The Hague Convention of 1.7.64 as the law chosen by the Parties and the UNIDROIT Principles as supplementary rules which the Arbitral Tribunal deems appropriate to apply where necessary in accordance with art. 17 sect. 1 ICC Rules.

(a) As stated in provision no. 20 of Claimant's telex of December 3, 1991, the contract shall be governed by "the Uniform Law for the international sale of corporal movables (Hague Convention 1/7/64)". This clause has evidently been accepted by Defendant. Its telex of December 4, 1991 shows no objection concerning the applicable law proposed by Claimant.

The Arbitral Tribunal is therefore of the opinion that the relationship of the Parties is governed by the substantive law chosen in no. 20 of Claimant's telex. This includes the Convention relating to a Uniform Law on the International Sale of Goods (ULIS) and the Convention relating to a Uniform Law on the Formation of Contracts for the International Sale of Goods (ULF).

According to art. 4 ULIS, the Conventions shall apply where they have been chosen as the law of the contract by the parties, regardless of whether or not the States of their places of business are parties to the Convention. This is in accordance with the principle of party autonomy, which states that parties are free to choose the law to govern their contract.

(b) In so far as the Conventions ULIS and ULF did not cover all questions and referring to article 17 of the ICC Arbitration Rules, the Arbitral Tribunal felt it appropriate to turn to the UNIDROIT Principles which provide useful complement to fill the lacuna and allow to find proper solutions.

(2) The contract was not concluded by exchange of telexes, because the Defendant proposed certain new conditions in its answering telex of December 4, 1991, which materially altered the terms of the contract according to art. 7 ULF. Defendant asked for different conditions concerning the free of charge time regarding delivery the guaranteed price for all of 1992, and insurance of the goods by seller up to delivery to the end user. The different terms requested by Defendant concern mainly the price of the goods and the insurance risk of the seller.

Such demands for changes in the contract by the other parties are considered by jurisprudence to be material alterations which must be specifically accepted by the party having made the initial proposal. ... Because the price of the goods is an "*essentialia negotii*", anything concerning the price must be considered as a material alteration. The insurance and delivery risk of the seller or buyer are also important terms of the contract, as each party must be able to calculate its possible costs beforehand.

Therefore the telex sent by Defendant on December 4, 1991 constitutes a counter-offer and should have been answered by Claimant — either containing a confirmation of the different terms or a new offer. Silence itself cannot have the effect of acceptance, see art. sect. 2 ULF.

(3) However, the contract was formed by Claimant commencing with performance of the contract. The provisions of the contract as proposed in Claimant's telex of December 3, 1991 and not disputed between the parties at any time are valid. The rest of the provisions were negotiated with each delivery

(a) Claimant began to deliver goods on December 6, 1991 and continued to do so until August 1992. Defendant accepted delivery of the goods. The contract was formed between the parties the latest with the first delivery by Claimant, According to art. 6, para. 2 ULF "acceptance may also consist of the dispatch of the goods".

(b) The contract was not — as suggested by Defendant — renegotiated wholly for each delivery It continued to exist as the legal framework of the parties to which specific alterations or amendments may have been made from time to time. Those alterations or amendments have no bearing on the present dispute.

(c) Neither Claimant nor Defendant ever objected to the terms of performance of the contract during the time period of delivery of the goods. According to the theory of [implied contract confirmation] this is to be interpreted as agreement on the undisputed terms of the contract as presented in the telex of December 3, 1991, unless the parties specifically agreed on other terms during its performance. Therefore, the provisions of the contract are primarily applicable, supplemented by the rules of ULF and ULIS.

When taking into consideration the internationality of the relations between the parties, the UNIDROIT Principles become relevant. Article 4.5 UNIDROIT Principles states that contract terms should be interpreted as to give effect to as many of them as possible. Therefore, if the parties at one point agreed on certain provisions, this needs to be taken into account when trying to resolve a dispute.

(4) In the present case, the Defendant in its answering telex mainly wanted to alter the matters of price and insurance. Since these matters were put in writing for each and every delivery (as shown by the telexes), they can be said to have been renegotiated and agreed upon every time within the existing framework of the contract.

(5) It was the Defendant's right to stop payment because of the non-conformity of the goods.

(b) Although the degree of non-conformity of goods has not been proven, it was the Defendant's right to suspend payment after raising the exceptio non adimpleti contractus.

The contract was to be performed step by step, *i.e.* payment was to follow the delivery of goods. If the goods are not of the quality agreed upon in the contract, the buyer must give notice of the non-conformity. Until an agreement is reached between the parties as to the degree of the lack of conformity and as to how to proceed in regard to the non-conformity the buyer does not have to pay the price. The further development of the contract at that point is unclear. It would amount to a curtailment of the rights of the buyer if he had to continue payment of the goods without knowing what will happen in regard to the non-conformity

This is not expressly stated in ULIS, but follows from the general principles of law referred to in article 17 ULIS. According to article 7.1.3 UNIDROIT Principles a party may withhold its performance until performance has been effected by the other party. Thus the above reasoning is in accordance with these principles of law.

(c) Once the seller knows of a possible non-conformity it is his duty to act upon this knowledge to clear up the degree of the non-conformity.

Since the oral hearing. . . it is undisputed that a meeting took place in. . ., the place of business of. . ., the end user of the purchased products, concerning the quality of the goods. This is proof of the fact that Claimant knew of the possible non-conformity of the goods.

The degree of non-conformity is therefore irrelevant in regard to the right of the Defendant to suspend payment. It is sufficient that Defendant informed Claimant of the non-conformity and then suspended payment until an agreement concerning the lack of conformity was reached. Defendant suspended payment after the meeting in. . . took place. This is not a violation of Defendant's contractual duties.'

Sources

Excerpts from the award published in:
ICC International Court of Arbitration Bulletin Vol. 12, No. 2, Fall 2001, 57 – 60.

Date: ***January 1999***
Adjudicating Court: ***ICC International Court of Arbitration (Partial Award)***
Number: ***9875***
Parties: ***Unknown***

Keywords

CONTRACT SILENT AS TO APPLICABLE LAW – EXCLUSION BY ARBITRAL TRIBUNAL OF DOMESTIC LAW OF BOTH PARTIES – APPLICATION OF LEX MERCATORIA (ART. 17 OF ICC RULES) – REFERENCE TO THE UNIDROIT PRINCIPLES AS ONE OF THE POSSIBLE SOURCES OF THE LEX MERCATORIA

Abstract

Claimant, a French company, and Defendant, a Japanese company, entered into a license agreement according to which Claimant was given an exclusive license to manufacture, sell and distribute Defendant's products in Europe. Subsequently Defendant entered into an agreement with an American company granting it an exclusive license for the North American market and a non-exclusive license for other countries. According to Claimant Defendant, by not expressly excluding Europe from those other countries, had violated its agreement with Claimant. The license agreement between Claimant and Defendant did not contain a choice of law clause. While Claimant argued in favour of the application of French law, Defendant invoked the application of Japanese law.

In a Partial Award the Arbitral Tribunal rejected both claims, arguing that "a contract [...] concerning a license to manufacture products and to sell them in various parts of the world is not appropriately governed by the national law of one of the parties, failing agreement on such a choice". Basing itself on Article 17 of the ICC Arbitration Rules, according to which "[...] the Arbitral Tribunal shall apply *the rules of law* it determines to be appropriate" (paragraph 1) (emphasis added) and "[i]n all cases the Arbitral Tribunal shall take into account the provisions of the contract and the relevant trade usages" (paragraph 2), the Arbitral Tribunal concluded that "[t]he most appropriate 'rules of law' to be applied to the merits of this case are those of the '*lex mercatoria*'", defined as "the rules of law and usages of international trade which have been gradually elaborated by different sources such as the operators of international trade themselves, their associations, the decisions of international arbitral tribunals and some institutions like UNIDROIT and its recently published *Principles of International Commercial Contracts*".

Full Text

APPLICABLE RULES OF LAW

The Agreements between the parties do not include provisions concerning the rules of law applicable to their contractual relationship.

Claimant argues French law should be applicable. The choice of Brussels, a place with no substantial link with the dispute, cannot lead to the application of Belgian law The most appropriate law should be determined through the "méthode de la voie directe", involving the examination of different factors. The place of the characteristic performance, in a license agreement, is often considered as that of the licensor; however, the issues submitted to this tribunal are wider than questions related to the Defendant's industrial property rights. The "proper law of the contract" can only be French law, for several reasons. France is the country from which all operations included in the territorial exclusivity were conducted; it is the country where the formulas and know-how allegedly misappropriated by Defendant were developed; it is in France that the consequences of the breach of the license contracts were felt and the ensuing prejudice must be compensated.

While agreeing with Claimant that Belgian law should not govern the issue, Defendant considers Japanese law should apply, not French law. In the absence of a common intent of the parties,Japanese international private law applies the law of the place where the contract was executed, that is Japan in this case. Under French international private law, the 1980 Rome Convention would apply. Article 4 of that Convention provides that in the absence of an express choice, the agreement "shall be governed by the law of the country with which it is most closely connected", it being "presumed that the contract is most closely connected with the country where the party who is to effect the performance which is characteristic of the contract has, at the time of conclusion of this contract, his ... central administration". The characteristic performance, in a license contract, is that of the licensor, *i.e.* [Defendant] ,which would also lead to the application of Japanese law. Refuting some of Claimants' arguments, Defendant points out that the territory of the license agreements was not limited to France, that the choice of the law of the place where the alleged prejudice was suffered might be relevant in a tort case, but not in a contractual dispute and that the alleged breaches (conclusion of the second [X] agreement, registration of patents in Japan and the United States) have no link to France.

According to article 17(1) of the ICC Rules, in the absence of an agreement between the parties upon the rules to be applied to the merits of the case,"... the Arbitral Tribunal shall apply the rules of law which it determines to be appropriate". Article 17(2) adds: "In all cases the Arbitral Tribunal shall take into account the provisions of the contract and the relevant trade usage's."

The provisions of the contract are not decisive. It contains references to France and other European and non-European countries as well as to Japan. The Sales Territory described in Exhibit II covers 'All countries of the world, other than Canada, USA, Mexico and Asian countries east of Iran, except French Territories'. The license is granted for patents held by Japanese companies (Exhibit III). Technical assistance will be provided by the Defendant at the Claimant's factory in France (art. 4) or at the Defendant's offices and production facilities in Japan (art, 5). The Claimant has agreed to pay royalties in Japanese currency (art. 6). An important provision, much at the centre of this dispute, deals with improvements invented by the Claimant, normally in its premises in France (art. 9).

The tribunal does not consider the neutral choice of Brussels as the seat of the arbitration to imply a choice of Belgian law as the law applicable to the contract.

In license agreements, the appropriate law is sometimes considered to be that of the country where the licensor is located (in this case,Japan), assuming the most characteristic performance of such contracts would be that of the licensor. However this is not an absolute rule. For example, the law of the licensee is sometimes preferred. The Rome Convention of 1980 also provides that the link to the characteristic performance can be discarded when such characteristic performance cannot be determined or when circumstances indicate that the contract is more closely connected with another country (art. 4) (*cf.* J. M. MOUSSERON, J. RAYNARD, R. FABRE ANDJ. L. PIERRE, Droit du commerce international, 1997, no. 136 *et seq.*).

In this case, part of the issues deal with the way the Defendant handled technical improvements invented and transferred to the former by the Claimant, casting doubts on a solution that would exclusively consider the licensor's transfer of technology to the licensee as the most characteristic performance of the contract. Insofar as the licensee's own performance can be considered as characteristic of the contract, this would lead to the application of French law. Another significant factor consists in the geographical scope of the rights licensed to the Claimant, which do not exclusively lead to French law, but would eliminate Japanese law.

The arbitral tribunal considers that the difficulties to find decisive factors qualifying either Japanese or French law as applicable to the contract reveal the inadequacy of the choice of a domestic legal system to govern a case like this. A contract concluded between Japanese and French companies concerning a license to manufacture products and to sell them in various parts of the world is not appropriately governed by the national law of one of the parties, failing agreement on such a choice.

The most appropriate "rules of law" to be applied to the merits of this case are those of the *lex mercatoria,* that is the rules of law and usage's of international trade which have been gradually elaborated by different Fonti such as the operators of international trade themselves, their associations, the decisions of international arbitral tribunals and some institutions like UNIDROIT and its recently published Principles of International Commercial Contracts.

Nevertheless the tribunal will take into account any relevant national laws concerning intellectual property rights issues raised during this procedure.

Sources

Execerpts of the award published in:
ICC International Court of Arbitration Bulletin 2001, Vol. 12, No. 2, Fall 2001, 95 – 97.

Date: **February 1999**
Adjudicating Court: **ICC International Court of Arbitration (Partial Award), Paris**
Number: **9474**
Parties: **Unknown**

Keywords

ARBITRAL TRIBUNAL REQUESTED TO APPLY "GENERAL STANDARDS AND RULES OF INTERNATIONAL CONTRACTS" – REFERENCE TO CISG "WHICH EMBODIES UNIVERSAL PRINCIPLES APPLICABLE IN INTERNATIONAL CONTRACTS" AND TO THE UNIDROIT PRINCIPLES AND TO THE PRINCIPLES OF EUROPEAN CONTRACT LAW AS "RECENT DOCUMENTS THAT EXPRESS THE GENERAL STANDARDS AND RULES OF COMMERCIAL LAW"

AVOIDANCE OF CONTRACT FOR FRAUDOLENT NON-DISCLOSURE OF CIRCUMSTANCES (SEE ARTS. 3.5 AND 3.8 OF THE UNIDROIT PRINCIPLES; ART. 4.107 OF THE PRINCIPLES OF EUROPEAN CONTRACT LAW)

TERMINATION OF CONTRACT FOR NON-PERFORMANCE – NOTICE TO BE GIVEN WITHIN A REASONABLE TIME (SEE ARTS. 7.3.2 OF THE UNIDROIT PRINCIPLES)

Abstract

Claimant, the National Bank of Country X, entered into a contract with Defendant for the printing of bank notes. After Defendant had made a first delivery of bank notes which did not meet the quality standards set out in the contract, the Parties entered into a new agreement ("executory agreement") according to which Defendant would at its own expense manufacture another batch of bank notes on the understanding that if these notes met the contractual specifications, Claimant would place a new order for the bank notes it required. According to Claimant Defendant again failed to deliver satisfactory bank notes while Defendant insisted on getting the new order as stipulated in the second agreement. Claimant first of all claimed that the second agreement was to be considered null and void because of a fraudulent non-disclosure by Defendant of circumstances which should have been disclosed, namely that Mister X, a former employee of Claimant who promoted the agreement, was actually paid by Defandant. In any case Claimant requested damages for faulty performance of the said agreement.

The arbitration clause provided that the Arbitral Tribunal was to decide "fairly" and at the beginning of proceedings the Parties accepted the Arbitral Tribunal's proposal to apply "the general standards and rules of international contracts". The Arbitral Tribunal held that the U.N. Convention on Contracts for the International Sale of Goods (CISG) embodies universal principles applicable in international contracts. However, also in view of the fact that the second so-called executory agreement concluded between the parties was not any longer a mere sales contract but involved components of a settlement agreement, it decided to apply together with CISG "other recent documents that express the general standards and rules of commercial law" such as the UNIDROIT Principles of International Commercial Contracts and the Principles of European Contract Law.

As to the merits of the case the Arbitral Tribunal rejected the Claimant's argument that the agreement was null and void because of fraud by Defendant arguing that it was not sufficiently proved that Claimant entered into the agreement with Defendant only because of Mister X's intervention who after all was at that time no longer Claimant's employee, and to this effect expressly referred to Articles 3.5 and 3.8 of the UNIDROIT Principles and to Article 4.107 of the Principles of European Contract Law. On the other hand, the Arbitral Tribunal upheld Claimant's request for damages: in rejecting Defendant's objection that Claimant had not given prompt notice of the defects of the goods and had therefore been prevented from terminating the contract, the Arbitral Tribunal expressly referred not only to Article 7.3.2 of the UNIDROIT Principles according to which notice of termination must be given "within a reasonable time", but also to Art. 40 CISG according to which a seller is not entitled to rely on a late notice of defects by seller if it knew or ought to have known the defects itself.

Full Text

APPLICABLE LAW

[1] According to the arbitration clauses, the Arbitral Tribunal should decide "fairly". The meaning of these clauses was discussed with the parties...Both parties accepted the Arbitral Tribunal's proposal to apply "the general standards and rules of international contracts" (Procedural Order No. 1, para. 1, that amended the Terms of Reference).

[2] The Tribunal is of the opinion that these "general principles of contract law" are not directly expressed in a specific international convention.

(a) The States of both parties are now bound by the UN Convention on Contracts for the International Sale of Goods ("the Vienna Convention"). However, many of the circumstances of the present arbitration predate [Claimant State]'s ratification of the Convention.

Although it is generally recognized that the Convention embodies universal principles applicable in international contracts, whether or not the States of the parties are signatories of the Convention (see esp. Final Award in case no. 5713 of 1989, Collection of ICC Arbitral Awards 1986-1990, p. 223 if), the Tribunal considers that, if the parties had wanted to submit their agreements to the convention, they would have introduced an express clause in that sense.

Besides, in the opinion of the Tribunal, the 1993 Agreement is not merely a sale of goods contract; even if the Agreement has been concluded in the frame of a sale of goods, it entails other components which are typical of a settlement agreement.

(b) There are other recent documents that express the general standards and rules of commercial law, in particular the Principles of European Contract Law and the UNIDROIT Principles of Commercial Contracts.
Nevertheless the general standards and rules of international commercial law have to be applied to the specific circumstances of the case and in particular to the object of the contract that reflects the intentions of the parties.
The Tribunal shall tackle this issue more precisely as to each one of the specific questions it has to solve in this award.

[3] The general principles of international contracts may also be found among various rules of domestic law, of both common and civil law systems, as applied to international contracts, such as the American Uniform Commercial Code.
The Tribunal considers however that in the present litigation neither [Defendant State's] nor [Claimant State's] law offers relevant and applicable rules. This may be inferred again from the fact that the parties did not refer expressly to any of their domestic rules.'

VALIDITY OF THE 1993 AGREEMENT

The question

[4] The question at issue in this section is related to contentions made by the Bank in regard to fraud and mistake that could affect the validity of the 1993 Agreement.

The position of the parties

[5] (a) According to the Bank, the 1993 Agreement must be considered null and void... According to [Defendant], Mr [X] was paid.. . as "Public Relation and Consulting Fees" relating to the settlement agreement with the Bank... [Defendant] 's non-disclosure of the payment of this generous fee to Mr [X] constitutes a fraudulent non-disclosure of a circumstance which according to reasonable standards of good faith should have been disclosed, with reference to the UNIDROIT Principles of International Commercial Contracts, arts. 3.5 and 3.8, and the Principles of European Contract Law 1997, art. 4.107...

(b) According to [Defendant], the Bank's charges, according to which [Defendant] made improper payments to Mr [X] in connection with the conclusion of the 1993 Memorandum of Agreement, are false, unsupported by any evidence and made with malicious and defamatory intent.,

The position of the Tribunal

[6] The Arbitral Tribunal is of the opinion that the Bank's allegations of fraud and mistake against the validity of the 1993 Agreement are not supported by sufficient evidence and must therefore be rejected.

[7] First of all, the payment of "Public Relations and Consulting fees" to Mr [X]. It has not been demonstrated that this payment was done with a fraudulent intent, as it may be inferred from the following arguments and facts.

(a) Even if Mr [X] was formerly a representative of the Bank, he had been introduced to [Defendant] as no longer being the latter's representative.
Finally, the nature of the relationship between the Bank, [Defendant] and Mr [X] may also be confirmed by the fact that the Governor. . . referred to discussions with Mr [X] as to discussions with an "outsider".

(b) In addition, Mr [X] had never met anyone of [Defendant] before the meeting...

(c) Moreover, the fact that he had represented [Defendant] on some occasions was well known to the Bank, and this from the beginning of the negotiations...

(d) Thus, the payment did not amount to corruption and its non-disclosure to a fraudulent non-disclosure.

[8] Secondly, the extent of the influence. The Bank which has the burden of proof of its allegation did not bring sufficient evidence of its allegations as to the exact extent and consequences of Mr [X] 's undue influence.
Moreover, it did not prove that Mr [X] knew enough about the agreement to be able to influence and induce the Bank fraudulently. Finally, the Bank confirmed the agreement without reservation and never referred to the fact that its consent could have been vitiated.

[9] Thirdly, the responsibility and effect of the mistake that has been alleged to influence the conduct of the Bank is not supported by sufficient evidence.

(a) The mistake, that was due to the paper supplier's concealment, is not sufficiently established in that their consequences on the Bank's conduct were not direct. Indeed, the non-disclosure of the fraudulent payment to Mr [X], in case it was established, does not demonstrate that the latter, or [Defendant], was also responsible for the non-disclosure of the paper supplier's action.

(b) This is confirmed by the fact that the Bank had communicated at once that it was dissatisfied with the banknotes delivery. This comforted [Defendant] in its opinion that it was not necessary to communicate facts that were already partly known by the Bank. This does not in any case establish any intent of concealing these precise facts from the Bank...

[10] The Arbitral Tribunal is of the opinion that the Bank's allegations against the validity of the 1993 Agreement have not been sufficiently established and must therefore be rejected.'

ELIGIBILITY OF THE CLAIMS

The question

[11] [Defendant] claims that the Bank is barred and/or estopped from claiming non-compliance with the terms of the 1993 Agreement.
[Defendant] contends that the Bank is precluded from asserting its claims of non-performance for the reason that, in reliance to its affirmations or conduct as to the contrary, [Defendant] incurred considerable harm. It relies on the general concept of waiver and estoppel.

[12] This issue relates to the question of whether the Bank had an affirmative duty to inspect the banknotes for conformity and if not, whether its silence implied an acceptation. In the event of defects, another issue is the issue of the existence of a duty to give notice, of the extent of the notice period and of the precise content of this notice.

The position of the parties

[13] (a) According to the [Defendant] cannot meet the burden of proof as to its allegations that the Bank is barred or stopped from claiming non-compliance with the 1993 Agreement...

As to the alleged waiver of the Bank's rights, [Defendant] did not receive unequivocal information from the Bank that it had tendered satisfaction of its obligations to the 1993 Agreement. The fact that the Bank required the reimbursement of its advance payment for the banknotes. . . and the cost of the banknote quality inspection did not imply that it renounced its other rights under the 1993 Agreement... Besides, [Defendant] 's tender clearly demonstrated that it was not acting in reliance on any alleged rights under the 1993 Agreement and that it was submitted to new essential terms and conditions... Such a conduct may neither be interpreted as an unequivocal waiver of rights . . . nor as an estoppel by which the Bank would be precluded from asserting a right when it caused another to change his condition to his detriment... The Bank did not cause [Defendant] any harm by not awarding the tender to it and it did not give [Defendant] any reasons to rely to its detriment upon the exclusivity of the reasons stated...

As to the inspection and notice duties, even if they are subject to the general principles of law, parties are generally free to derogate from or vary the effect of any of the principles embodied in conventions of international law... Indeed, for the Bank, the terms of the... 1992 Memorandum meant that [Defendant] would remain responsible for banknotes which had not been inspected but which were found to contain printing errors during the period of issue... [Defendant] 's allegations as to the nature of the inspection that the Bank carried on after the first delivery and the derived course of conduct are erroneous as to its promptitude and completeness... Besides, according to the Bank, the 1993 Agreement being an executory accord, it is not subject to the principles governing international sales contracts, but only to general contract principles... Indeed, the fact that the quantity of banknotes agreed on was to be printed free of charge, the agreement was not a "transfer of goods in exchange for a price expressed in money"... Beside the argument of the contractual nature of the Agreement, an executory accord is meant to grant a "limited window of opportunity" within which an obligee can render performance thus making any concern about the cure of nonperformance and its consequences on the price secondary...

The Bank had actually notified [Defendant] on 10th May 1994 that [Defendant] had delivered many bad quality banknotes... Assuming that the Bank was required to give notice and that the 10th May 1994 letter was not sufficient, the Bank considers that the reasonable time of a notice, according to the UNIDROIT Principles, art. 7.3.2, is meant to prevent any harm due to uncertainty as to whether the Bank would accept the performance, which was not the case given the nature of executory accord of the Agreement... Given these conditions and the strains of the econo-political concerns and the reimbursement question, the Bank did act within a reasonable time...

In case the Tribunal decides that arts. 38 and 39 of the Vienna Convention should apply to the Agreement, the Bank claims that art. 40 of the same convention would defeat Defendant's right to rely on the Bank's alleged failure to give notice, since [Defendant] knew or could have been aware of the facts the lack of conformity relates to and could have disclosed them to the Bank... This principle may also be found in various national laws... Indeed, [Defendant] was aware of the Bank's concerns about specific quality defects of the banknotes printed between 1990 and 1992... Even assuming that the Bank had a duty of notice and that it was not given in conformity with art. 39, art. 44 of the Vienna Convention states that it could still be able to claim damages if it has "a reasonable excuse for its failure to give the required notice"...

(b) According to [Defendant], the Bank met none of the conditions that should be fulfilled once the banknotes had been delivered and received...

The Bank's representations and statements testify a relinquishment of rights and an intent not to assert any rights, i. e. a waiver or estoppel of its rights... The Bank is indeed stopped from asserting claims of non-performance by [Defendant] since [Defendant] incurred considerable harm in reliance on the Bank's assurance of its performance and its inconsistent conduct... Moreover, according to civil law principles and the rules applied in international practice, a forfeiture of rights can be said to occur without consideration or reliance, depending on the circumstances.

The Bank's arguments that the law of sales does not apply to the Agreement are "far-fetched" since an agreement, that was nothing more than an embodiment of the modified terms ... may be a sales contract. The amendment of a sales transaction must not indeed necessarily be supported by consideration. . . and may be done by mere agreement of the parties (art. 29 Vienna Convention and art. 2-209 UCC. . .). Besides, the banknotes printed pursuant to the 1993 Agreement are not excluded as money or negotiable instruments from the Vienna Convention and the UCC rules...

The extent of the duty of a buyer of goods to inspect the goods that have been delivered depends on the precise circumstances and in particular the course of conduct or customary relationship between the parties, as deriving from the 1990, 1992 and 1993 Agreements... [Defendant] acknowledges the prompt (within two months) and meticulous inspecting of the banknotes delivered in 1992 in accordance with the first two Agreements... It holds however that this course of conduct was the one that was legitimately held to apply to the 1993 series and that the Bank did not respect it by not conducting any inspecting from 1993 to 1995...

[Defendant] further claims that the Bank did not respect its duty of prompt notice. This duty derives not only from legal principles, but also from the course of conduct that maybe derived from the behaviour of the Bank after the first delivery of banknotes in 1992... The 1992 Memorandum of Agreement, that set particular rules as to the inspection and notice of defects, did not have the meaning implied by the Bank, of waiving the applicability of international contract rules, and in view of the mass of contractual documents, this Memorandum did not constitute more than a "freely, formally and unequivocally agreed" contractual waiver of the legal principles applicable. It was certainly not a course of conduct between the parties exempting the Bank from virtually all of the recognized rules applicable to international contracts... It was superseded by further agreements and was only entered on an *ad hoc* basis for as long as the inspection was not completed... Further, the Bank's interpretation according to which a buyer could only notify defects he has found straight away years later seems unreasonable... Such a clause of "everlasting guarantee" cannot be inferred from the course of conduct of the parties...

The fact that no notification of defects was communicated until over three years later cannot be considered as constituting a prompt notice. . ., as it is confirmed by reference to the average notification period for overt defects according to art. 39 of the Vienna Convention, the UCC or national laws, which is at the most 6 months... This view may be confirmed by the fact that the Bank strongly insisted from 1993 onwards on the reimbursement of its 10% deposit without mentioning the defects it now alleges at all... The Bank's mention of the existence of many bad quality banknotes in a letter dated 10th May 1994 lacked the specificity required by a notice under art. 19 of the Vienna Convention...

The Bank may not excuse its conduct under art. 40 of the Vienna Convention; the scope of art. 40 is to protect the buyer against the bad faith of the seller. [Defendant] 's knowledge of the Bank's habits of thorough inspections and the fact that the parties had foreseen the services of a technical expert tend to prove that the Bank knew the non-conformity of the banknotes. Besides, it was inconsistent with good faith for the Bank to be aware of the defects and wait... Further, the Bank had no valid excuse under art. 44 of the Vienna Convention; this Article is not intended to condone a breach of good faith that derives from inconsistent and misleading conduct and statements that may not be justified by "econo-political concerns"...

Finally, the outer limit of two years for a notification of defects according to the Vienna Convention, or six months according to French law, carries also a limit for the existence of the cause of action based thereon... The Bank is therefore barred from prosecuting its claims for failing to bring a claim within a reasonable time.

The position of the Tribunal

[14] It constitutes a general principal of international contracts that a party may be regarded as barred from pursuing its claims for having renounced its rights expressly or tacitly, by a waiver or an estoppel, or simply for having missed a reasonable notice period.

The burden of proof lies on the party that alleges the waiver or the estoppel. The evidence requirements are very strong given the stringent consequences of a waiver or an estoppel.

(a) To renounce its rights expressly, the Bank would have had to clearly state its intentions and nothing in the facts supports it did at the time [Defendant] claims it did.
The fact that the Bank required the reimbursement of its advance payment for the banknotes and the cost of the banknote quality inspection did not imply that it renounced its other rights under the 1993 Agreement.
In these conditions, the Tribunal considers that the Bank did not act as to waive its rights under the 1993 Agreement.

(b) To renounce its rights tacitly requires that one adopts an attitude that implies a relinquishment of one's rights, such as a voluntary omission to inspect the goods or to give a timely notice of its defects.

One should note however, as to the alleged estoppel of the Bank's rights that would derive from its incoherent attitude regarding the 1996 tender, that [Defendant] 's tender demonstrated clearly that it was not acting in reliance on any alleged rights under the 1993 Agreement. It was by contrast submitted to new essential terms and conditions. . . and sufficient evidence and notice was given all along to [Defendant] of its inability to guarantee the security of the banknotes tendered... The Bank did not therefore give [Defendant] any reasons by an allegedly incoherent conduct to rely to its detriment upon the exclusivity of the reasons stated. The issue of the coherence and signification of the Bank's attitudes, and thus of an estoppel of its rights under the 1993 Agreement, further depends on the existence of a duty to inspect and to give a timely and precise notice. It is the purpose of the following lines to discuss this issue.

[15] As established earlier.. . the Tribunal is invited by the arbitration clause to decide "fairly". With the agreement of the Parties, this has been interpreted as a reference to the general standards and rules of international contracts.
The Tribunal does not regard itself as bound by the provisions of any international convention in particular. It considers that the provisions of the Vienna Convention do not apply directly to the present arbitration. If the parties had meant so, they would have inserted in their agreement a concrete reference to it. The issue should therefore be assessed in a broader perspective.

[16] The Tribunal renounces examining in detail whether the Bank gave notice of the default properly and in due time; the question may therefore stay open. Indeed, the Tribunal considers that in view of all circumstances it cannot decide to deprive the Bank of its rights to claim compensation for the violation of the 1993 Agreement. Various reasons may be brought forward:

(a) First of all, it is a general recognized principle of commercial law that a vendor cannot rely on a buyer's failure to inspect the goods and to give timely notice of defects, if the vendor has adopted a conduct which is not in conformity with his own duties. Especially, it is generally admitted that the vendor is precluded from asserting the non-conformity of the notice if it has concealed the existence of the defect (see in particular art. 40 of the Vienna Convention). The same principle applies if the vendor gave the buyer specific guarantees regarding the quality of the goods.

(b) In the present case, [Defendant] knew that there had been flaws among the previous deliveries.. . and especially as to the paper that had been delivered... It had therefore committed itself to new deliveries of quality and to double check all banknotes... It seems however that it did not abide by its duty, as confirmed by the different reports mandated by the Bank...
One may therefore consider that [Defendant] accepted to deliver banknotes without having evidenced to the Tribunal that it had performed its duty to inspect. It constitutes a general principle of international contracts that a party cannot claim the violation of a duty to inspect when it has concealed a defect it was aware of.

(c) Secondly, the particular nature of the relationship between the parties. The 1993 Agreement was concluded in a spirit of conciliation. It meant to put an end to past disputes. [Defendant] committed itself to print new series and deliver banknotes that complied with the contractual requirements. The Bank renounced its past claims and even agreed to future contracts with [Defendant]. As to the general spirit of the agreement, it intended to compromise in order to reach a mutual agreement.

(d) Thirdly, the general attitude of [Defendant] in this matter is a further argument. The Thbunal regards as far-fetched that [Defendant] invokes the Bank's delay in order to free itself from a part of its obligation under the 1993 Agreement. [Defendant] adopted indeed a negative conduct, especially since it waited more than two years before it accepted to pay the amount it owed. Even in view of the likely link with the provisional award of a new contract, [Defendant] 's reluctance to promptly settle the outstanding sums, especially the Bank's advance payment, meant that the Bank was reluctant to give notice of defects in a straightforward manner, as the Bank feared that [Defendant] might then refuse to reimburse the sums due... To use the wording of the Bank, it was treated as a hostage and not as a business client.....

[17] In these conditions, the Arbitral Tribunal considers that the Bank may not be deprived of, its rights and claims arising from the violation of the 1993 Agreement.'

Sources

Excerpts of the award published in:
ICC International Court of Arbitration Bulletin, Vol. 12, No. 2, Fall 2001, 60 – 67.

Date: ***February 1999***
Adiudicating Court: ***ICC International Court of Arbitration, Paris***
Number: ***9479***
Parties: ***Unknown***

Keywords

CONTRACT SILENT AS TO THE APPLICABLE LAW – REFERENCE BY ARBITRAL TRIBUNAL TO "USAGES OF INTERNATIONAL TRADE" – REFERENCE TO THE UNIDROIT PRINCIPLES

HARDSHIP – SUPERVENING CHANGES IN THE LAW – HARDSHIP ONLY WHERE CAUSING FUNDAMENTAL ALTERATION OF CONTRACT EQUILIBRIUM (UNIDROIT PRINCIPLES ARTS. 6.2.1-6.2.3)

CONTRACT FOR AN INDEFINITE PERIOD – RIGHT OF TERMINATION – EXCLUDED WHERE PARTIES INTENDED TO CREATE PERPETUAL OBLIGATIONS (UNIDROIT PRINCIPLES, ART. 5.8 [ART. 5.1.8 OF THE 2004 EDITION])

Abstract

Two Italian companies, set up following the dissolution of a family owned textile manufacturing firm, entered into a contract regulating the right to use the original company name. According to the contract Claimant (together with its affiliate registered in the USA) was entitled to use the company name as a registered trade mark, while Defendant was entitled to use it only to identify itself as manufacturer of the goods it would distribute world-wide. Claimant subsequently accused Defendant of breach of contract by having deliberately created confusion between its own name and the Claimant's trademark, and sued Defendant for damages.

As to the applicable law, the Arbitral Tribunal noted that the contract expressly indicated the law of the State of New York as the law governing the validity of the agreement and concluded that the silence with respect to all other matters was to be understood as an indication of the parties' intention not to have these matters governed by a particular domestic law. The Arbitral Tribunal decided to apply, in addition to the terms of the agreement, "the usages of international trade", having regard whenever necessary to "international public policy" and for this purpose to refer to the UNIDROIT Principles which it considered an "accurate representation, although incomplete, of the usages of international trade".

Defendant invoked hardship as a counterclaim. It argued that following the adoption in 1989 of the European Directive on Trademarks (89/104/EEC) which introduced more liberal terms than those originally agreed with Claimant the contract should be revised or, alternatively terminated, with respect to the territory of the European Union, and to this effect invoked Article 6.2 of the

UNIDROIT Principles. In rejecting this counterclaim the Arbitral Tribunal stated that a subsequent evolution of the legislative context of a contract does not constitute hardship when it does not destroy the balance of the parties' respective obligations. Though admitting that Defendant might not have concluded the contract on the same terms if the EU Directive had already been adopted, the impact of the latter on the equilibrium of the agreement was not that substantial, all the more so since the agreement covered not only the territory of the European Union but was intended to regulate Defendant's rights and duties world wide.

Defendant also invoked its right to terminate the contract, at least in so far as it applied to European Union territory, on the ground that the contract provided for perpetual obligations. The Arbitral Tribunal rejected also this argument. It is true that a number of domestic laws provide for a right of termination of contracts for an indefinite period, and that a similar rule is set out also in Art. 5.8 [Art. 5.1.8 of the 2004 edition] of the UNIDROIT Principles. Yet in the case at hand the contract clearly demonstrates the parties' intention to create perpetual obligations as a direct consequence of the indefinite duration of the trade mark.

Full Text

APPLICABLE LAW

Before dealing with the claims and counterclaims, the Arbitral Tribunal must express its views as to the law applicable to the merits of the dispute, since the parties are in disagreement in this regard.
According to article 13(3) of the ICC Rules of Arbitration: "The parties shall be free to determine the law to be applied by the arbitrator to the merits of the dispute. In the absence of any indication by the parties as to the applicable law, the arbitrators shall apply the law designated as the proper law by the rule of conflict which he deems appropriate."
According to article 13(5) of the same Rules: "In all cases, the arbitrator shall take account of the provisions of the contract and the relevant trade usages."

As a result of these provisions, an arbitral tribunal must first apply the provisions of the contract, in the light of and, in case of need, supplemented by the usages of international trade, provided the validity of such provisions is not questioned by the parties or [such provisions] do not appear to the tribunal to be incompatible with international public policy in the sense of truly or transnational public policy (see Pierre LALIVE, "Transnational (or Truly International) Public Policy and International Arbitration", in ICCA Congress Series No. 3, p. 257).

In case the arbitral tribunal does not find in the contract or in the usages of international trade a solution to the problems raised by the parties' claims, it must revert to the law applicable to the contract. If any of the parties contends that one or more provisions of the contract, or the contract as a whole, are null and void, an arbitral tribunal must decide the question by referring to the mandatory rules of the law applicable to the contract or to any mandatory rules which it would be justified to apply, bearing in mind that the applicability of such rules must always be confronted with the real intention of the parties and their legitimate expectations.

In the instant case, the parties have dealt with the problem of the law applicable to the Agreement in its article 12(b) which reads:
In view of the facts that one of the parties to this Agreement and Stipulation is a New York corporation having its principal office in such State, the litigation settled herein took place in New York and this Agreement and Stipulation was negotiated substantially in New York, the parties hereto agree that the law of the State of New York (without regard to its conflicts of law rules) shall determine any dispute relating to the validity of this Agreement and Stipulation.

None of the parties now dispute that the law of the State of New York governs tile validity of the Agreement. However, while the Claimants consider that the intention of tile parties was that the Agreement be generally subject to the law of the State of New York, [Defendant] proposes a restrictive construction of article 12(b) which would exclude from tile province of tile law of tile State of New York any question which is not stricto senso a question of validity. In particular, [Defendant] underscores that what it describes as "tile restoration to equity of the contract", in fact the main object of its counterclaims, is not governed by the law of the State of New York. It is [Defendant]'s view that, with the exception of the question relating to its validity, the Agreement is governed by Italian law, on tile basis of the 1980 Rome Convention regarding the applicable law to contractual obligations, which has been incorporated within the Italian conflict regulations by article 57 of the Italian law of May 3 1st 1995.

On the basis of the briefs exchanged by the parties and the oral argument presented by counsel at the. . . hearing, the Arbitral Tribunal came to the conclusion that when the parties indicated in article 12(b) of the Agreement that any dispute relating to its validity would be determined according to the law of the State of New York, they were perfectly aware of the restrictive implication of the language that they were using. Indeed, the first draft of the Agreement.. . indicates that "the laws of the State of New York shall be the law pursuant to which this Agreement shall be construed and enforced at any arbitration proceedings brought under this Agreement". A comparison of this language and of that of article 12(b) of the Agreement eventually executed in 1987 leads to the conclusion that, after negotiations, the parties agreed to restrict tile intervention of the law of the State of New York to questions relating to the validity of the Agreement.

However, contrary to [Defendant] 's submission, this finding does not imply that the parties were contemplating that any other state law would govern their Agreement. On the contrary, their silence after negotiations as to the applicable law indicates that they considered that the intervention of a national law was necessary for problems of validity only. In the context of an ICC arbitration concerning a contract which was supposed to be performed in the whole world that implied intention of tile parties is quite reasonable and in perfect conformity with the interpretation of articles 13(3) and 13(5) of the ICC Rules exposed above by the Arbitral Tribunal. Thus, the Arbitral Tribunal finds that any question concerning the validity of the Agreement must be decided under the law of the State of New York. Any other question will have to be decided according to the provisions of the Agreement in the light of, and, in case of need, supplemented by the usages of international trade. Whenever necessary, the Arbitral Tribunal will have regard to international public policy'

DEFENDANT'S COUNTERCLAIM

(i) The principal counterclaim of [Defendant] is that tile Agreement should be modified, only for its effects on the "European Territory", by a substitution of the terms of its article 7(b) with the terms of article 6 of the EEC/89/104 Directive. The Claimants object to such modifications.
By European Territory, the parties mean the entire territory of the European Union.

[DEFENDANT] 'S POSITION

[Defendant] explains that the above mentioned EEC/89/104 Directive, which was issued after tile execution of tile Agreement in 1987, explicitly allows the owner of a name to use it in its commerce, as long as it does so in a manner consistent with honest and fair principles, even when said name constitutes the trademark of another businessman. Since [Defendant] entered into the Agreement at a time when Italian law (namely the Bima law of 1967) restricted drastically the use of a name as a trademark when such name was used as a trademark by someone else, the liberalization introduced by the European Directive put [Defendant] in a situation of hardship. On the basis of article 6.2 of the UNIDROIT Principles, [Defendant] is entitled to an equitable modification of the Agreement so that, on the territory of the European Union, [Defendant] might benefit from the liberal solutions resulting from the application of the Directive. As a further justification for its requests, [Defendant] also refers to article 1467 of tile Italian Civil Code.

THE CLAIMANTS' POSITION

The Claimants first stress that tile law of the State of New York is applicable to [Defendant] 's request for equitable modifications of the Agreement and that, under the New York law, a Court (or an arbitrator) should not modify a contract because of a change of law, even should this change create additional burdens or advantages for either party. The Claimants, although on a slightly different basis, come to the same conclusion by application of Italian law. In particular, they point out that the entry into force of the EEC Directive cannot be seen as an "extraordinary and unforeseeable event".

THE ARBITRAL TRIBUNAL'S POSITION

As explained above, the Arbitral Tribunal has found that the law of the State of New York only applies to the validity of the Agreement and that [Defendant] 's request for equitable modification of the Agreement cannot be characterized as a question of validity of tile Agreement. Moreover, the Arbitral Tribunal has found that besides the law of New York, no national law had been made applicable to the Agreement. Thus, since tile provisions of the Agreement do not contemplate the possibility of its modifications on equitable grounds, the Arbitral Tribunal will turn to the usages of international trade in order to supplement the provisions of the Agreement. In this respect, [Defendant] has referred to the UNIDROIT Principles which the Arbitral Tribunal recognize as an accurate representation, although incomplete, of the usages of international trade.

Article 6.2.2 of the UNIDROIT Principles reads:
"There is hardship where the occurrence of events fundamentally alters the equilibrium of the contract either because the cost of a party's performance has increased or because the value of the performance a party receives has diminished, and
(a) the events occur or become known to the disadvantaged party after the conclusion of the contract;
(b) the events could not reasonably have been taken into account by the disadvantaged party at the time of the conclusion of the contract;
(c) the events are beyond the control of the disadvantaged party; and
(d) tile risk of the events was not assumed by the disadvantaged party".

According to article 6.2.3, paragraph 4:
"If the Court finds hardship it may, if reasonable,
(a) terminate the contract at a date and on terms to be fixed, or
(b) adapt the contract with a view to restoring its equilibrium".

However, these provisions must be read in conjunction with article 6.2.1 which reads: Where performance of a contract becomes more onerous for one of the parties, that party is nevertheless bound to perform its obligations subject to the following provisions on hardship.

On the basis of the above-mentioned definitions, the Arbitral Tribunal admits that it would be entitled to make an equitable modification of the Agreement, but it is not convinced that [Defendant] is being faced with a situation which maybe characterized as "hardship".

Indeed, the issuing of the EEC Directive did not alter in any way the equilibrium of the Agreement among the parties. Tile situation of [First Claimant] and its affiliates remain unaffected insofar as their entitlement to the, . . trademark is not concerned by tile Directive. [Defendant] does not meet any new difficulty in complying with the restriction on tile use of the.. . name. As a matter of fact, [Defendant] does not really allege that so would be the case. Indeed, the thrust of [Defendant] 's submission is that since the EEC Directive has been made, tile Agreement imposes on the use of the name. . . restrictions which have disappeared from the laws of all countries members of the European Union. As a result, the Agreement, into which [Defendant] entered in order to meet the requirements of the Italian Bima law deprives it of a freedom in the use of the name. . . that it would enjoy in the absence of the Agreement. It is the reason why [Defendant] requests the Arbitral Tribunal to substitute article 7(b) of the Agreement with the terms of article 6 of the EEC Directive as far as its effects on tile territory of tile European Union is concerned. [Defendant] would obtain more or less the same result with its subordinate counterclaims aiming at obtaining the termination of tile Agreement at least as regards its effects in Europe.

The Arbitral Tribunal does not accept tile view, expressed by the Claimants, that a change in the law cannot be the Fonti of hardship. It may well be the case, when a new law makes tile performance of the contractual obligations of a party more onerous or when the value it receives from the performance of tile other party is severely reduced. However, tile Arbitral Tribunal has already found that the introduction of the EEC Directive had no effect on tile performance of the Agreement by the parties.

In reality, [Defendant]'s position, in a nutshell, is that it would have had no reason to enter into tile Agreement should the EEC Directive have been introduced before April 1987. This has nothing to do with hardship, which is a notion which may play a role when the performance of a contract is at stake but has no function in tile formation of contracts. Even if it is probable that [Defendant] would have entered into tile Agreement, as drafted in 1987, after the adoption of tile EEC Directive in 1989, a subsequent evolution of tile legislative context of a contract does not constitute a hardship when it does not destroy the balance of the parties' respective obligations. Moreover, without denying that the parties had in mind tile Italian Bima law when they executed the Agreement, it was not made to be enforced in Italy only nor in Europe. The Agreement is a global arrangement, due to be enforced in the whole world. This is underscored by the introduction to the Agreement:

Whereas the parties, after extensive negotiations, have agreed that it is in their respective interests and the interest of their Affiliates that the rights of the parties are fixed and determined in a manner which will avoid, as much as possible, future conflicts, with respect to the use of tile trademark.. . and create definitive understandings applicable to all jurisdictions in which the parties may so legally contract, and in which their respective products are sold and may be sold and/or distributed.

This language indicates that the parties wanted to enter into a final settlement of their conflicts relating to tile use of the trademark ... by agreeing on an arrangement applicable whenever in the world. This probably explains that they limited the scope of the law of New York to the validity of the Agreement, since its worldwide application was at odds with the intervention of a specific national law to govern its performance.

Irrespective of the fact that the adoption of EEC Directive does not constitute a situation of hardship, [Defendant] 's contention that the Agreement be modified in so far as its effects in the territory of the European Union are concerned is in direct contradiction with the intention of the parties to organize their relations as to the use of the trademark. . . by harmonized solutions applicable in any jurisdiction, whatever be the content of the law in that jurisdiction.

[Defendant] is suggesting a balkanization of the Agreement which is incompatible with its very spirit. Should [Defendant] 's approach be followed, there would be no reason not to substitute later on article 7(b) of tile Agreement by the provisions of the law of Ruritania, as far as its effects in Ruritania are concerned, if the law of Ruritania was more liberal than the provisions of the Agreement. For tile above-mentioned reasons, the Arbitral Tribunal decides to dismiss [Defendant]'s first and principal counterclaim.

(ii) In a subordinate counterclaim, [Defendant] requests the Arbitral Tribunal to terminate the Agreement, due to hardship, at least as regards its effects in Europe.

The Claimants object to that subordinate counterclaim as they do in respect of the principal counterclaims, for very similar reasons. In reality, the termination of the Agreement is one of the two solutions available in case of hardship. As indicated in article 6.2.3, para. 4 of tile UNIDROIT Principles, a Court (or an Arbitral Tribunal) may either terminate a contract or adapt it with a view to restoring its equilibrium.

As the Arbitral Tribunal has found that tile existence of a situation of hardship had not been established and as modifying the Agreement, in its scope in tile case of partial termination, in view of tile evolution of tile law in a specific country or in a group of countries is incompatible with the real intention of the parties which wanted a global application of the Agreement, [Defendant]'s subordinate counterclaim must be dismissed as well as its principal counterclaims.

(iii) In a further subordinate counterclaim, [Defendant] requests the Arbitral Tribunal to ascertain and state that, since the Agreement provides for perpetual obligations, [Defendant] is entitled to recede from it and to terminate it, at least as regards its effects in Europe. In its brief of..., [Defendant] has clearly specified that its request concerned only the effects of the Agreement in the European Union, stating that "the whole agreement is not put into question, since the scope of tile Agreement extends to tile entire world". [Defendant]'s position in this respect is that perpetual obligations are valid only when they just reproduce prerogatives existing under tile law. Since it is not any longer the case for tile restrictions opposed by the Agreement to tile use of the name. . . in the European Union, in tile light of the EEC Directive, the perpetual obligations deriving from the Agreement are null and void and the Agreement must be terminated for this part of the world.

The Claimants object to that subordinate counterclaim that the perpetuity pointed out by [Defendant] is just the obvious consequence of the potential perpetuity of the right to the trademark, in the sense that tile obligations undertaken by tile parties on the basis of tile Agreement last as long as the trademark. They add that they are the ones which should complain to be obliged to tolerate in perpetuity [Defendant]'s certain behaviour which intrudes upon their exclusive right.

The Arbitral Tribunal must stress at the outset, that it results from the text of the Agreement that tile real intention was that its effects would not be limited in time. The preamble of the Agreement indicates that their intention was to "create definitive understandings". This intention is confirmed by provisions such as article 12(b) or 12(c) which endeavour to make its avoidance or termination particularly difficult, if not impossible. Thus, it is indisputable that tile Agreement creates perpetual rights and obligations. As rightly observed by the Claimants such indefinition of the duration of the Agreement is a direct consequence of the indefinition of the duration of the trademark ..., the ownership of which is recognized to [First Claimant], against tile recognition of [Defendant]'s rights to use "[name] for identification purpose only, under specific conditions".

[Defendant] is right when it contends that perpetual obligations may be terminated under many national laws, although its counterclaim is grounded mainly on Italian law For example, it is worth indicating that article 5.8 of the UNIDROIT Principles reads: "A contract for an indefinite period may be ended by either party by giving notice a reasonable time in advance". However, the Arbitral Tribunal is not satisfied that [Defendant] is entitled to a termination of tile Agreement, effective in the territory of the European Union, as [Defendant] has specified precisely. As a matter of fact, this understandable geographical restriction in the scope of [Defendant]'s request for termination is a symptom of its misconception.

As admitted by [Defendant] [...], a perpetual obligation is valid when "it merely reproduces legal precepts". The problem is that the parties have deliberately avoided submitting the Agreement to any national law, with the exception of problems regarding its validity for which the law of the State of New York is applicable, in order to facilitate its worldwide application. As a result, it is meaningless to compare the rights and obligations created by tile Agreement with any national legal precepts to decide whether they reproduce them or not. Since tile introduction of the EEC Directive, tile Agreement does not any longer reproduce legal precepts in the territory of the European Union, if it even did in all the member countries, but it may still do so in other jurisdictions or even be more favourable to [Defendant] than the law of such other country, the probable reason wily [Defendant] did restrict the effects of its request to the territory of the European Union. Here again, [Defendant] intends to achieve a balkanization of tile Agreement which goes directly against the real intention of the parties.

The Arbitral Tribunal's view is that, with the 1987 Agreement, the parties have defined, with a view of its worldwide application, the respective status of the owner of tile trademark.. and of the owner of tile name. [...], irrespective of the legal precepts of any national law. Thus, there are no legal applicable precepts to be compared with in order to decide whether the Agreement just reproduces them or not. In such a situation, the Arbitral Tribunal must respect tile intention of the parties which is clearly expressed in the Agreement and, as such, does not need to be supplemented by the usages of international trade, unless it would be contrary to international public policy. It is obviously not the case. First, although tile right to terminate a perpetual obligation is recognized in many national laws, it does not amount to a rule of international public policy. But, more significantly, such right is generally excluded, as already mentioned, when the perpetual rights and obligations are just a reproduction of legal precepts. Thus, the perpetuity as such cannot amount to a violation of international public policy. After all, it would be enough to find just one national law in the world which embodies legal precepts comparable to those introduced by the parties within tile Agreement to validate its perpetual character under that law.

The very fact that the parties chose to organize their relations outside of any national law is not contrary to international public policy as well, as illustrated, for instance, by the provisions of article 1496 of the French New Code of Civil Procedure. Thus, by defining themselves the legal precepts applicable and confirming them in an Agreement with a worldwide scope and an indefinite duration, the parties have exercised prerogatives that the Arbitral Tribunal must recognize. In any case, [Defendant] has never contended that the Agreement was against international public policy as confirmed by its apparent wish to see it applied outside the territory of the European Union.

On the basis of the above, [Defendant]'s second subordinate counterclaim is dismissed.'

Sources

Original in English.

Excerpts of the award published in:
ICC International Court of Arbitration Bulletin, Vol. 12, No. 2, Fall 2001, 67 – 73.

Date: **March 1999**
Adjudicating Court: **ICC International Court of Arbitration**
Number: **9594**
Parties: **Unknown**

Keywords

REFERENCE TO UNIDROIT PRINCIPLES IN SUPPORT OF A SOLUTION ADOPTED IN ACCORDANCE WITH THE APPLICABLE DOMESTIC LAW

DUTY TO MITIGATE LOSSES (ART. 7.4.8 OF THE UNIDROIT PRINCIPLES)

Abstract

Claimant, a Spanish company, entered into a contract with Defendant, a company based in India, for the delivery and installation of industrial machinery. Once installed the machinery turned out to be defective. Despite Claimant's offer to accommodate matters Defendant stopped payment but at the same time began to use the machinery thereby manufacturing defective goods which gave rise to claims for damages by its customers. Claimant and Defendant accused each other of breach of contract and Defendant also claimed consequential damages as a result of the malfunctioning of the machinery.

The contract contained a choice of law clause in favour of English law which the Arbitral Tribunal applied when deciding the merits of the case. However, in rejecting Defendant's claim for consequential damages on account of the fact that Defendant had failed to take all reasonable steps to mitigate the loss consequent on Claimant's breach, the Arbitral Tribunal not only referred to the leading English cases stating the duty of mitigation but found it appropriate to add that "[a] similar standard has been established internationally, primarily in the UNIDROIT Principles of International Commercial Contracts (1994) which state in sub-section 1 of Article 7.4.8 as follows: 'The non-performing party is not liable for harm suffered by the aggrieved party to the extent that the harm could have been reduced by the latter party's taking reasonable steps'."

Full Text

'The general rule concerning damages under English contract law is that of restitutio in integrum: the party who suffered the damages should be put in the same position as it would have been if the contract had been performed. This principle is, however, subject to the following limitations: (1) the degree of likelihood, namely, the types of damage which a contract breaker shall be responsible for and (2) mitigation of the loss, a duty of the party who suffered the damages to limit or altogether avoid the consequences of the breach. (See also BEAVAN, "Limitations upon Damages in Contract", Legal Executive 1996, July Supplement p. 10, which discusses the three significant limitations to the recovery of damages, namely: the remoteness of damage, causation, and the duty to mitigate loss.)

(1) The degree of likelihood

The requisite degree of foresight which may be attributed to the contract breaker was set by Hadlev v. Baxendale 9 Excl. 341 as either (a) the damage as may fairly and reasonably be regarded as arising naturally (according to the usual course of events) from tile breach or (b) damages which could have been foreseen by tile contract breaker because of special knowledge which he had at the time of making the contract. This rule was restated and revised in Victoria Laundry (Windsor) Ltd. v. Newman Industries Ltd. [1949] 2 K.B. 528 and the decision of tile House of Lords in CzarnikovLtd. v. Koufos [1969] 1 A.C. 350.

In more recent cases this rule has again been reaffirmed. See Seven Seas Properties v. AlEssa [1993] 3 All ER. 577 and Kpohrarorv. Woolwich Building Society [1996] 4A11 E.R. 119.

These principles are generally stated in section 53 of the Sale of Goods Act, 1979.

It may be presumed that when [Claimant] entered into tile Agreement with [Defendant] it knew that [Defendant] wanted to purchase [industrial machinery] to produce parts for their consequent sale to the. [...] industry. It was not expressly provided in the Agreement when such [machinery] should be delivered in India and when it should start operating. However, at the meetings and in correspondence between the parties these dates were more or less fixed. There were delays, on some occasions due to [Claimant], on others to [Defendant]. In any event, it maybe presumed that [Claimant] knew that delay in the planning scheduled could cause [Defendant] to suffer damages, and that if the machinery did not comply with quality requirements it would have consequences in its productivity. However, it may not be presumed that, when signing tile Agreement, [Claimant] knew that [Defendant] was supposed to sell parts to its joint venture partner. . . from a certain date, nor the internal conditions of such joint venture.

[Claimant] could have foreseen that if it did not conclude the whole commissioning process of tile machinery within a reasonable time and that if the machinery did not comply with quality requirements, [Defendant] would suffer significant loss. Tile question is whether [Claimant] could have foreseen that its delay would cause the large amount of loss claimed by [Defendant].

To sum up, both parties are responsible for delays and quality damages to the machinery. While [Claimant] should be held responsible for specific items where it is contractually liable and compensation is awarded to [Defendant], it is difficult, if not impossible, to assign responsibility for consequential damages when both parties share in that responsibility. Furthermore, it is necessary to take into account [Defendant]'s obligation to mitigate the losses as discussed below.

(2) Mitigation of losses

According to McGregor,' the rule for mitigation of losses is based on three principles:

(a) Tue first and most important states that the plaintiff must take all reasonable steps to mitigate the loss to him consequent upon tile defendant's breach and cannot recover damages for any loss he could have avoided but has failed, through unreasonable action or inaction, to avoid.

(b) The plaintiff can recover for loss incurred in reasonable attempts to avoid loss.

(c) Tile plaintiff cannot recover for avoided loss.

Concerning the first rule, the law requires the plaintiff to take all reasonable steps to mitigate tile loss consequent on the defendant's breach, and refuses to allow him any loss which is due to neglect to take such steps. This rule is illustrated in the leading case of British Westinghouse Co. Ltd. v. Underground Electric Rlvs Co. of London Ltd. [1912] AC. 673 at 689, where Lord Haldane stated the following:

The fundamental basis is thus compensation for pecuniary loss naturally flowing from the

McGregor on Damages, 15th. edition, 1988 breach; but this first principle is qualified by a second, which imposes on a plaintiff the duty of taking all reasonable steps to mitigate the loss consequent on the breach and debars him from claiming any part of the damage which is due to his neglect to take such steps.

The plaintiff's duty to mitigate is not a duty to himself but to the defendant, as specified by Lord Pearson in Darbishire v. Warren: [1963] 3 All E.R. 310.

The true meaning is that the plaintiff is not entitled to charge the defendant by way of damages with any greater sum than that which he reasonably need to expend for the purpose of making good the loss. In short, he is entitled to be as extravagant as he pleases but not at the expense of the defendant.

On the other hand the nature of the mitigation of damage has been defined as a question of fact and not a question of law in Pavzu Ltdv. Sanders [1919] 2 K.B. 581.

A similar standard has been established internationally, primarily in the UNIDROIT Principles of International Commercial Contracts (1994) which state in sub-section (1) of article 7.4.8 as follows:

The non-performing party is not liable for harm suffered by the aggrieved party to the extent that the harm could have been reduced by the latter party's taking reasonable steps.

This brings us back to an examination of whether [Defendant] took all reasonable steps to mitigate the loss consequent to [Claimant] 's breach of quality/delay. In its closing brief, [Defendant] argued that it acted to mitigate its loss by accepting the machinery since should it have rejected the machinery it would have certainly incurred much greater losses. However, [Defendant] did not seem to consider the possibility of mitigating its loss through negotiation and accommodation. [Defendant] should have accepted the offers made by [Claimant] after the commissioning to sign a provisional acceptance of the line.

In Payzu Ltd. v. Sanders [1919] 2 K.B. 581, Lord Scrutton indicated that according to his experience in considering what steps should be taken to mitigate the damage, continued relations with the party in default should be included. Likewise, he compared service and commercial contracts pointing out that "in commercial contracts it is generally reasonable to accept an offer from the party in default".

In any event, supposing [Defendant] could have deemed this offer unacceptable (though it was not), what did [Defendant] do to effectively mitigate its losses?

[Defendant] continued using the machinery to produce a large amount of parts, in spite of its alleged collapsing state, and it cannot be said that [Defendant] took serious measures to repair the defects in the [machinery]. Only when. . . and.. . carried out their studies for the purpose of this arbitration in October 1997, more than a year after [Claimant] had left India, were those problems dealt with. [Defendant] had ample opportunity to mitigate its losses at an earlier stage and it only took reasonable steps to do so once these arbitration proceedings were filed.

Several cases illustrate this rule. In Simon v. Pawsons &Leafs [1993] 38 Com. Cas. 151 (C.A.) the plaintiff ordered certain material from the defendant which he promised to stock for the plaintiff, but he failed to do so, as a result of which, the plaintiff lost an appointment as maker of clothes to a school. The Court of Appeals refused to award her damages for such loss of appointment because, *inter alia* , she knew of the defendant's breach and had opportunity to buy equivalent material but made not attempt to do so. In Tuckerv. Linger [1882] 21 Ch. D. 18, a landlord failed to supply materials to the tenant (in breach of covenant) to repair the premises and the tenant failed to recover for damages caused to crops in his barn due to bad weather because the barn had not been repaired, since he ought to have provided himself with materials to carry out the repair and charge the landlord with its price.

Under these circumstances recovery of losses due to [Claimant] 's alleged breach of quality is not granted since the losses were mitigable and could have been contained by [Defendant] through either further negotiation (by accepting [Claimant] 's offer) or by having taken the timely steps required to repair the machinery'

Sources

Excerpts of the award published in:
ICC International Court of Arbitration Bulletin, Vol. 12, No. 2, Fall 2001, 73 – 76.

Date: ***April 16, 1999***
Adjudicating Court: ***International Arbitration Court of the Chamber of Commerce and Industry of the Russian Federation***
Number: ***152/1998***
Parties: ***Unknown***

Keywords

CONTRACT SILENT AS TO THE APPLICABLE LAW – REFERENCE TO UNIDROIT PRINCIPLES AS ONE OF RELEVANT LEGAL SOURCES

INTERPRETATION OF A PARTY'S STATEMENTS AND CONDUCT – MEANING A REASONABLE PERSON OF SAME KIND OF THE OTHER PARTY WOULD GIVE TO IT (ART. 4.2(2) UNIDROIT PRINCIPLES)

Abstract

In a sales contract between a Russian and an English party. Buyer had to return the goods delivered by Seller and asked for the reimbursement of the costs incurred. Seller objected to the amount claimed, arguing that Buyer has not properly followed the instructions Seller has given it concerning the time and order in which to return the goods.

In interpreting Seller's instructions the Arbitral Tribunal resorted among other legal sources also to the UNIDROIT Principles. In particular it referred to Art. 4.2(2) UNIDROIT Principles, according to which statements and other conduct of a party shall be interpreted, unless the other party knew or could not have been unaware of that party's intention, according to the meaning that a reasonable person of the same kind as the other party would give to it in the same circumstances.

Full Text

[Not yet available]

Sources

Unpublished. Notice of the award kindly given by Professor Alexander KOMAROV, President of the International Arbitration Court of the Chamber of Commerce and Industry of the Russian Federation.

Date: ***May 1999***
Adjudicating Court: ***ICC International Court of Arbitration***
Number: ***9753***
Parties: ***Unknown***

Keywords

CONTRACT GOVERNED BY A PARTICULAR DOMESTIC LAW – REFERENCE TO UNIDROIT PRINCIPLES IN SUPPORT OF SOLUTION FOUND IN DOMESTIC LAW

AGREEMENT TO COOPERATE WITH A VIEW TO REALISING A PROJECT – BINDING NATURE OF SUCH AGREEMENT (SEE ARTS. 1.3 AND 1.7 OF THE UNIDROIT PRINCIPLES)

Abstract

Claimant, a British company acting on behalf of a consortium of several companies, entered into an agreement with Defendant, a Czech State entity, for collaboration and further negotiation with the aim of realising a land development project. According to Claimant Defendant failed to perform its duties of cooperation and negotiation under the agreement. Claimant filed for arbitration requesting the Arbitral Tribunal to declare the breach of contract and to order specific performance thereof or award damages. Defendant not only denied that it had breached the agreement, but also claimed that the agreement in question was not a legally binding commitment.

The agreement was governed by Czech law. However, in deciding the merits of the case, the Arbitral Tribunal referred not only to the relevant provision of the Czech Commercial Code but also to the UNIDROIT Principles. Thus, in support of the binding nature of the agreement and the order to Defendant to continue its collaboration with Claimant with the aim of realising the project, the Arbitral Tribunal relied not only on Article 265 of the Czech Commercial Code setting forth the principle of fair business conduct but also on the general principles of *pacta sunt servanda* and of cooperation in good faith laid down in Articles 1.3 and 1.7 of the UNIDROIT Principles.

Full Text

'[1] The Claimant alleged that the Defendant did not meet its obligations under the Agreement and requested the Arbitrator to declare the breach of contract, to direct tile Defendant to specific performance or to oblige it to pay damages. The Defendant denied the breach of contract and requested dismissal of the claim. [...]

[2] On [...] a meeting was held between the parties and doubts were raised by the Defendant as to the binding character of the Agreement and the status of the Claimant. The Claimant in a letter dated [...] sent to the Defendant referred to these doubts stating that "Clearly there are misunderstandings relating to the intent of the *pactum de contrahendo* in particular and its construction and obligation placed upon both parties."[...]

[3] The Defendant's general director in the letter dated [...] addressed to the legal representative of the Claimant stated: "[Defendant] consider[s] the above-mentioned "*pactum de contrahendo*" legally irrelevant, as the facts (matters) agreed to in the above-mentioned agreement were not fulfilled at the time given therein, and although not due to the fault of any of the parties this agreement is at the present time unenforceable. Following the successful procurement of the architectural study of locality, [Defendant] shall proceed in two stages. In the first stage it intends to seek by the form of a tender a suitable firm who shall prepare the project offering the best solution for the area and satisfying the needs of [Defendant] and the City of [...] In the second stage there would be a shorter form of tender which should result in the appointment of an investor. [...] [Defendant] do[es] not exclude the cooperation with [Claimant] or its advisors in the process of fulfilment of the above-mentioned conditions."

[4] During 1994 the legal representatives of the Parties tried to reach an agreement on the legal assessment of the Agreement of 1992 but without success. The Defendant expressed doubts whether the Agreement was binding. The letter dated [...] sent by the head of legal department of the Defendant to tile Claimant's legal representative contained the following sentences: 'What is new for [Defendant] is a note contained in the Memorandum to the effect that [...] Consortium as a party to the pactum has no legal personality under English law and that the member firms in such association agreed that [Claimant] (which is not a party to the pactum) would negotiate with [Defendant] on behalf of them. In accordance with Czech law a conclusion can be drawn on the basis of such fact that the pactum may not legitimately have come into existence for the party described therein lacks legal personality *i.e.* does not have any rights or obligations thereunder. The position of [Claimant] towards [Defendant] is the same. Tile firms associated in the [...] Consortium are not parties to the pactum either. If they authorized [Claimant] to represent their interests including conclusion of contracts, they will at first have to assess the quality of representation and services expected to be provided to them by [Claimant]. In spite of the views regarding the *pactum de contrahendo* not being shared in full, [Defendant] [is] still ready to continue the intended co-operation in commercial plans provided that the first step towards new cooperation should be reaching an agreement regarding legal opinion in respect ofthepactum and looking to solutions both in legal and real terms".

[5] The Parties could not come to an understanding on these points and negotiations stopped.

[6] The Defendant has confirmed several times its willingness to cooperate with the Claimant but it did not accept the validity and binding force of the Agreement referring to several problems such as the existence of the Consortium which was known to the Defendant since several years. This behaviour meant in reality refusal to cooperate.
The Arbitrator has taken into consideration that under paragraph (1), section 264 of the Czech Commercial Code in determining the rights and duties arising from a relationship of obligations, account is also taken of the business practice (trade usage) prevalent in a particular field of business, unless these are contrary to the contents of the contract or to tile law. There are no special usages in the particular field of business but general principles of business practice have importance, too. Such general principles are *pacta sunt servanda* and to cooperate in good faith (articles 1.3 and 1.7 of the UNIDROIT Principles of International Commercial Contracts, Ph. KAHN, "Les principes généraux du droit devant les arbitres du commerce international", Journal du droit international 1989

p. 327). Fair business conduct is one of the main principles of the Czech Commercial Code too (section 265).
On the basis of the above-said the breach of the agreement by the Defendant has been stated.

[7] According to section 365 of the Czech Commercial Code: "A debtor is in default if he fails to perform his obligation duly and in time until the obligation is duly performed, or until the obligation is discharged in another manner. However, the debtor is not in default if he is unable to perform his obligation due to the default by the creditor."

[8] The Defendant alleged that the Claimant did not fulfil its obligation. However, taking into consideration the documents submitted by the parties it can be stated that the basic problem of the realization was in tile administrative field, in obtaining the necessary permits for the construction, the administrative conditions of the realization of the project were missing. The letters of the Defendant in [...] leading to the arbitration proceedings did not refer to any default by the Claimant but challenged the validity of the Agreement. Therefore, the Arbitrator considered that the allegation of the Defendant was irrelevant from the point of view of the present case.

[9] On the basis of the above points the Agreement is considered as valid and binding upon the parties. During the proceedings no one of tile parties has stated that the project has become impossible and there is no evidence of the impossibility in the documents submitted by the parties either.

[10] According to section 366 of the Czech Commercial Code: "Unless the law provides otherwise with regard to individual types of contracts, a creditor may insist on proper performance of an obligation by the debtor while the latter is in default on his performance."

[11] Consequently, tile Claimant is entitled to request performance of the obligation meaning in the present case continuation of collaboration and cooperation with the aim of realizing the project and is entitled to request preferences as specified by the Agreement. However, as it is decided above, the parties are not bound to conclude a contract as in the case of a *pactum de contrahendo* under the rules of the Czech law. The Defendant has referred to the statute of limitations with respect to the request concerning the conclusion of the future contract. The request for performance of the obligations to cooperate and to give preference are not statute-barred (sections 387,392,403 Czech Commercial Code).

[12] The Claimant presented its request for damages in an alternative way. As the Defendant is obliged to perform its obligations according to the first request of the Claimant, it is not dealt with whether the Defendant should be obliged to pay damages in accordance with the alternative request, presented in view of the possible dismissal of the first request.'

Sources

Excerpts of the award published in:
ICC International Court of Arbitration Bulletin, Vol. 12, No. 2, Fall 2001, 82 – 84.

Date: ***July 27, 1999***
Adjudicating Court: ***International Arbitration Court of the Chamber of Commerce and Industry of the Russian Federation***
Number: ***302/1997***
Parties: ***Unknown***

Keywords

CONTRACT SILENT AS TO THE APPLICABLE LAW – INTERNATIONAL SALES CONTRACT – APPLICATION OF THE UNIDROIT PRINCIPLES CONSIDERED TO REFLECT INTERNATIONAL USAGES

AVOIDANCE OF CONTRACT FOR LACK OF AUTHORITY OF AGENT – NOTICE OF AVOIDANCE TO BE GIVEN WITHIN REASONABLE TIME AFTER AVOIDING PARTY KNEW OF COULD NOT HAVE BEEN UNAWARE OF RELEVANT FACTS (ART. 3.15 UNIDROIT PRINCIPLES)

Abstract

A Russian seller and a Swedish buyer entered into a sales contract. Since the seller delivered only the first lot of the goods (ca. 20% of the total), the buyer commenced legal action requesting the seller to deliver the missing part of the goods or alternatively to pay damages for its failure to perform. The seller objected by invoking the invalidity of the contract due to the lack of authority of the company's director who signed the contract.

The Arbitral Tribunal applied the UNIDROIT Principles which in its view are gradually gaining the status of internationally recognized trade usages.

As to the merits of the case, the Arbitral Tribunal decided in favour of the Swedish buyer. In rejecting the seller's objection concerning the invalidity of the contract, it referred in particular to Article 3.15 of the UNIDROIT Principles, according to which notice of avoidance must be given to the other party within a reasonable time after the avoiding party knew or could not have been unaware of the relevant facts. In the case at hand the Russian seller had clearly failed to do so, since in the course of the performance it had never raised the issue of the alleged lack of authority of the company's director and only during the arbitral proceedings, *i.e.* years after the conclusion of the contract, for the first time declared its avoidance.

Full Text

[Not yet available]

Sources

Unpublished. Notice of the award kindly given by Professor Alexander KOMAROV, President of the International Arbitration Court of the Chamber of Commerce and Industry of the Russian Federation.

Date: ***August 1999***
Adjudicating Court: ***ICC International Court of Arbitration (Partial Award)***
Number: ***9759***
Parties: ***Unknown***

Keywords

ARBITRATION AGREEMENT – TO BE INTERPRETED SO AS TO GIVE EFFECT TO IT RATHER THAN TO DEPRIVE IT OF ANY EFFECT (ART. 4.5 OF THE UNIDROIT PRINCIPLES)

Abstract

Claimant, a financial institution based in a European country, and Defendant No. 1, a company based in a South West Asian country, entered into a credit agreement which was guaranteed by Defendant No. 2, another company based in the same South West Asian country. When Defendant No. 1 failed to make the due repayments, Claimant commenced arbitration proceedings against Defendants No. 1 and No. 2. Claimant invoked a clause contained in the credit agreement entitled "Law and jurisdiction" and stating that the credit agreement was governed by the law of country X and any disputes arising out of the contract that could not be settled by mutual agreement were to be "submitted to the International Chamber of Commerce for settlement under their rules and regulations in Paris". According to Defendants No.1 and No. 2 the clause in question did not represent a valid arbitration agreement since arbitration was not expressly mentioned therein and also the reference to the ICC rules and regulations was ambiguous on account of the fact that the rules in question make provision for two alternative means of dispute resolution, *i.e.* arbitration and conciliation.

The Arbitral Tribunal decided in favour of Claimant. According to the Arbitral Tribunal in interpreting the contract clause in question it had to look for the parties' real intent, taking into account *inter alia* the consequences which they had reasonably contemplated, and to give effect to such intent. Such an approach was in accordance not only with no further specified "principles of interpretation of an arbitration agreement" but also with the UNIDROIT Principles and to this effect the Arbitral Tribunal expressly referred not only to Article 4.5 which states that contract terms shall be interpreted so as to give effect to all the terms rather than to deprive some of them of effect, but also to Article 1.6(2).

Full Text

[DEFENDANT NO. 1]'S POSITION

[Defendant No. 1] contends that (i) there exists no arbitration agreement under the provisions of the Credit Agreement and (ii) alternatively, such arbitration clause is invalid under the rules and practices of international arbitration.

[Defendant No.1] contends that the Credit Agreement contains no arbitration agreement since no reference to arbitration as a mode of settlement is made under article 14.2 of the Credit Agreement. Furthermore, the reference to the ICC Rules and Regulations is not a sufficient indication since it does not specify what exact mechanism of settlement of disputes within ICC is referred to: no guidance was given as to which of conciliation or arbitration mechanism had been agreed upon...

[Defendant No. 1] further refers to legal authors who indicate that a clear expression of intent, not only to arbitrate but also to have the arbitration take place under the ICC Rules, is required. [Defendant No. 1] also refers to the ICC Model Clause and to article II of the New York Convention on the Recognition and Enforcement of Foreign Arbitral Awards to conclude that article 14.2 contains no express reference to arbitration as a mode of settlement of disputes...

[Defendant No. 1] adds that, contrary to Claimant's allegations, there exists no common will of the parties for arbitration under the provisions of the Credit Agreement since "there is no explicit or even implicit expression by the parties of their consent on that issue".. . It contends that the parties' consent should have been given in writing and that the wording should have been precise and exact on the real intention of the parties, i. e. no ambiguity and no doubt about the parties' intention. It concludes that article 14.2 does not respond to any of these requirements and no provision of article 14.2 leads to the conclusion that the real intention of the parties was to solve their dispute byway of arbitration...

[Defendant No. 1] adds that it is to [Claimant] to prove the existence of an arbitration agreement and to demonstrate that the proper interpretation to be given to the provisions of said article 14.2 is such that it should be deemed to establish the common will of the parties to arbitrate... [Defendant No. i] contends that, in the instant case, there is no fact, even prima facie evidence, that it could operate in a way to suggest a reversal of the burden of proof...

Alternatively, should the Tribunal decide to interpret the provisions of article 14.2 of the Credit Agreement as constituting an arbitration agreement, [Defendant No. i] contends that article 14 of the Credit Agreement contains pathological elements:

- an ambiguity results from the fact that it is not specified whether the dispute shall be settled by ICC Rules of Conciliation or Arbitration;

- while article 14.2 provides for the submission of any dispute between the parties to the ICC, article 14.3 reserves the right of [Claimant] to start any legal proceeding for the protection of its right in the courts of [countryY];

- tile parties have combined submission of their dispute to the ICC and to a state jurisdiction. Article 15(1) (5) of the Credit Agreement provides that said Agreement once signed "shall constitute legally valid and binding obligations, and that if necessary the Bank [[Claimant]] could enforce judicially the said obligation in [countryY]"...

[Defendant No. i] contends that, in view of this ambiguity, judicial proceedings should prevail as an incontestable proceeding left for the parties to settle their dispute. It further refers to the legal opinion dated. . ., whereby judicial proceeding should be considered as the main way of resolving disputes provided by the parties...

[DEFENDANT NO. 2]'S POSITION

[Defendant No. 2] contends that article 14.2 does not constitute an arbitration agreement, and alternatively that there exists no valid arbitration agreement capable of extension:

- on the burden of proof:

[Defendant No. 2] claims on the basis of a principle recently reconfirmed by an ICC Arbitral Tribunal sitting in Zurich, that the burden of proof "for the scope and reach of an arbitration clause is incumbent on the party which intends to rely on it (here: on Claimant)". Claimant has not discharged its burden of proof according to [Defendant No. 2]

[Defendant No. 2] alleges that article 14.2 of the Credit Agreement "does not refer at all to arbitration as a mode of settlement", and since there exist two mechanisms of settlement of disputes at the ICC, *i.e.* conciliation and arbitration, article 14.2 of the Credit Agreement does not provide a clear guidance as to what mechanism is referred to...

[Defendant No.2] contends that [Claimant] has failed to discharge its burden of proof as to the validity of the arbitration agreement and that its reasoning is based on a chain of wrong assumptions and confusions since it confuses two mechanisms of settlement of disputes, *i.e.* direct negotiation, on the one hand, and conciliation, which requires the intervention of a third person, on the other hand. [Claimant] thus allegedly implicitly admits that article 14.2 provides for conciliation as a referral of settlement of disputes...

Finally, [Defendant No.2] contends that [Claimant] ignores article 14.3 of the Credit Agreement which provides for the jurisdiction for [the courts of country Y] while giving "no explanation of how its interpretation could be reconciled with the express wording of article 14.3"...

- on the arbitration agreement:

[Defendant No. 2] maintains that article 14.2 lacks the fundamental elements of an arbitration agreement, i. e. the intention to arbitrate the dispute, since in the absence of such an intention "no valid and binding agreement comes into existence". [Defendant No. 2] refers to Craig, Park and Paulsson in their Commentary on the ICC Arbitration Rules stating that "if the parties want arbitration, they should say so clearly" (Part II, p. 90), and contends that the word "arbitration" appears neither in the title, nor in the wording of article 14.2, nor anywhere else in the Credit Agreement.

It adds that "the absence of any reference to arbitration as the mode of settlement of dispute is not at all remedied by the fact that article 14.2 provides that the dispute 'will be submitted to the International Chamber of Commerce for settlement under their rules and regulations, in Paris" since the ICC is engaged in settlement of disputes by conciliation as well as by arbitration, as demonstrated by the existence of two separate sets of rules, and accordingly any inference in favour of arbitration is absolutely impossible...

It adds that, when compared with tile ICC Model Clause, the absence of the words "arbitration" and "finally" is "of paramount importance as they affect the validity of article 14.2 as an arbitration agreement and its binding character"...

[Defendant No. 2] further contends that, according to the rules of interpretation of both UNIDROIT principles and French scholars, an ambiguous clause has to be interpreted against the drafter, i. e. against [Claimant]

Moreover, [Defendant No.2] contends that the wording of article 15.1.5 of the Credit Agreement, which provides only "[...] that if necessary the Bank could enforce judicially the said obligations in [countryY]", shows the parties' intention of no settlement other than a judicial one in [countryY]...

[CLAIMANT]'S POSITION

[Claimant] contends that, in article 14.2, the parties "intended to solve their dispute by mutual agreement in order to avoid litigation. Should mutual agreement not be possible, (either reached by direct negotiation between the parties, or by conciliation by a third person), the clause foresees a solution which is compulsive for the parties, that is, it conclusively resolves a dispute arisen. Such method is arbitration."...It alleges that [Defendant No. 1] and [Defendant No.2] 's interpretation, i. e. converting this clause into a conciliation clause, negotiation or any other alternative method, would only tend to "perpetuate the actual situation, that is their non payment of the outstanding amounts"...

Accordingly, the only possible method in order to solve the dispute in an ICC Rules frame which would be final and compulsory for the parties is arbitration...

As to the rules of interpretation (UNIDROIT principles and jurisprudence and legal scholars) mentioned by [Defendant No. 2] in order to interpret article 14.2, [Claimant] alleges that should the Contract be interpreted as being of an onerous character, the doubt should be resolved in favour of the reciprocity of interest. In this case, reciprocal interest of all parties were best protected in an international arena, avoiding a party being involved in a litigation in tile territory of the other party...

Additionally, [Claimant] alleges that should the parties have intended to submit their litigation to [the courts of country X or country Y], they would have stated so clearly: on the contrary, article 14.3 reserves only to [Claimant] the right to claim before [a court of country Y]. Besides, should the parties have intended to solve their disputes before [the courts of country Y], they would have selected [tile law of country Y] instead of [the law of country X] in the Credit Agreement and would have expressly so provided in tile Letter of Guarantee instead of only referring to the terms and conditions of the Credit Agreement...

DISCUSSION OF THE ARBITRAL TRIBUNAL

The Tribunal notes that article 14.2 of the Credit Agreement provides that the "parties to the Agreement" were to submit their dispute "to the International Chamber of Commerce for settlement under their Rules and Regulations, in Paris". Accordingly, it is clear to the Tribunal that the parties' will, failing a settlement by mutual consent, was that the dispute be settled before the ICC according to the "Rules and Regulations" of the ICC.

The Tribunal also notes that the terms "arbitration" or "arbitrator" or "Arbitral Tribunal" are not set forth under article 14 "Law and Jurisdiction" of the Credit Agreement. However, the Tribunal considers that arbitration agreements which do not include the word "arbitration" may still be deemed as constituting an arbitration agreement if the interpretation of the Contract shows that such was the parties' intent.

The Tribunal further notes that the principles of interpretation of an arbitration agreement lead the Tribunal (i) to look for the parties' real intent, taking *inter alia* into account the consequences which they have reasonably and legitimately contemplated, and (ii) to give effect to the parties' intent. This approach falls in line with the UNIDROIT Principles on International Contracts, article 4.5 of which providing that "[c]ontract terms shall be interpreted so as to give effect to all the terms rather than to deprive some of them of effect". Applying a similar reasoning, article 1.6(2) of UNIDROIT Principles states that "[i]ssues within the scope of these Principles but not expressly settled by them are as far as possible to be settled in accordance with their underlying general principles". There are several ICC awards which have decided that the appreciation of the validity and effectiveness of an arbitration agreement goes beyond the requirements of a strict literal interpretation. On the contrary when the parties insert an arbitration agreement in their contract, one should presume that their intent was to establish an effective machinery for the settlement of disputes contemplated in the arbitration clause (see *inter alia* ICC award no. 2321 rendered in 1974 in JDI 1975, p. 938; award rendered in ICC case no. 1434 in 1975 in JDI 1976, p. 978 and award rendered in ICC case no. 5103 in 1988 in JDI 1988, p. 1206).

In the present case, [Claimant], a party [from country X], executed the Credit Agreement with [Defendant No. i], a party [from country Y], for the purpose of financing an international project in [country Y]. Both the Bank ([Claimant]) and the Borrower ([Defendant No. 1]) were perfectly aware of the importance of ICC for the settlement of disputes and of the fact that should their dispute be submitted to the ICC for settlement under its "Rules and Regulations", the normal process of settlement is then arbitration under the Rules of Arbitration.

As to the alternative mentioned by Respondents between conciliation and arbitration, the Tribunal confirms that the normal procedure of settlement of dispute is arbitration. A survey of ICC's practice clearly shows that arbitration is by far the prevailing method of settlement before the ICC: in 1997, there were 452 arbitration cases, as compared with 8 conciliations (433 arbitrations in 1996, as compared with ii conciliations). (See ICC International Court of Arbitration Bulletin, May1997, p.6 and May 1998, p. 4,) Accordingly, on the basis of the principle of effectiveness, article 14.2 can only be construed as referring to arbitration. Furthermore, conciliation, even as considered as prerequisite to arbitration, requires the consent of all parties. By filing a request for arbitration, [Claimant], as Claimant, is deemed to have renounced any preliminary step for conciliation.

Defendants have pointed out the apparent contradiction between article 14.2 of the Credit Agreement [the arbitration agreement] and its articles 14.3 and 15.1.5. Article 14.3 provides that "the Bank ([Claimant]) reserves the right to start in the courts of [country Y], any legal proceeding that maybe required for tile protection of its rights", thus enunciating clearly the parties' intent to leave open an option to the Claimant only (*i.e.* [Claimant]) between the recourse to arbitration or to the state jurisdictions. Article 15.1.5 ("[...] if necessary the Bank could enforce judicially the said obligations in [country Y]") emphasizes a similar intent of the parties to also leave such an option open.

Accordingly, the Tribunal's decision is that the parties' intention was that their dispute be settled through arbitration under ICC Rules of Arbitration.'

Sources

Excerpts of the award published in:
ICC International Court of Arbitration Bulletin, Vol. 12, No. 2, Fall 2001, 84 – 88.

Date: *September 1999*
Adjudicating Court: ***ICC International Court of Arbitration, Paris***
Number: ***7819***
Parties: ***Unknown***

Keywords

SALES CONTRACTS WITHOUT EXPRESS DETERMINATION OF PRICE – VALID IN INTERNATIONAL TRADE PRACTICE (SEE ART. 55 CISG AND 5.7 [ART. 5.1.7 OF THE 2004 EDITION] UNIDROIT PRINCIPLES

Abstract

A bank (Claimant) which had financed a series of export sales contracts by Brazilian producers entered into insurance contracts with a syndicate of insurance companies (Defendants) to cover the risk of frustration of the export sales contracts due to supervening adverse political events in Brazil. When the exporting companies actually failed to deliver the goods to their customers, Claimant sued Defendants arguing that the exporting companies had been prevented from performing their sales contracts on account of supervening measures taken by the Brazilian Government. Defendants objected that the Governmental measures in question did not constitute an event covered by the insurance contracts and, more important, that the underlying export sales contracts were not valid due to the absence of the determination of the price.

The export sales contracts were silent as to the applicable law. In rejecting the Defendant's arguments concerning the invalidity of the export sales contracts, the Arbitral Tribunal relied first of all on Brazilian law according to which for a sales contract to be valid it was sufficient that price was determinable, as it was in the case at hand where the goods (sugar) had a market price. Yet according to the Arbitral Tribunal the validity of sales contracts without an express determination of the price was also a generally accepted principle in internationl trade as demonstrated by the 1980 Vienna Sales Convention (Art. 55) and by the UNIDROIT Principles of International Commercial Contracts (Art. 5.7 [Art. 5.1.7 of the 2004 edition]).

Full Text

'La défenderesse a contesté la validité des contrats d'exportation selon le droit brésilien, pour indétermination du prix.

[...]

[La défenderesse] a dénoncé l'"l'absence de risque reel", du fait de l'absence de toute force obligatoire des contrats tenant au mécanisme de fixation du prix, et en veut pour preuve que rien ne permet de fixer le prix au-delà de mars 1990.[La demanderesse] répond que selon l'article 1er des contrats les parties s'engagent respectivement à vendre età acheter; qu'il s'agit d'opérations tout à fait courantes dans le commerce international considéré, lesquelles s'exécutent quotidiennement nonobstant les objections éventuelles tirées d'une analyse civiliste; au demeurant, les contrats ont été renouvelés et la clause de prix pouvait parfaitement fonctionner.

En ce qui concerne tout d'abord le défaut d'examen des contrats commerciaux par [la défenderesse], le Tribunal observe que les contrats d'assurance ont été conclus au printemps 1989, les premiers rééchelonnements des contrats commerciaux intervenant quelques mois plus tard et les avenants n°2 des polices étant signés en août 1990 après plusieurs mois de discussions. [La défenderesse] avait donc à chacune de ces étapes le loisir d'examiner de près les contrats commerciaux, de s'enquérir auprès des acheteurs d'une imperfection éventuelle et de mesurer la portée de la red clause.

Selon le droit brésilien tel qu'il ressort des débats échangés entre les parties, le caractère déterminable du prix suffit à la validité des contrats. Interrogée par [la défenderesse], la société [...] (acheteur dans les contrats litigieux) a expressément confirmé la régularité et l'efficacité des contrats. Il s'agit d'opérations normales et récurrentes, sur des marchandises qui ont un prix de marché. Parla clause dite d'"arrosage", les acheteurs s'engageaient a prendre les quantités de sucre nécessaires pour que la banque soit remplie de ses droits, en cas de chute des cours. Le Tribunal note surabondamment que la vente sans fixation préalable d'un prix est courante dans le commerce international, comme le montrent la convention de Vienne du 11 avril 1980 sur la vente internationale de marchandises (art. 55) ainsi que les principes UNIDROIT relatifs aux contrats du commerce international (art. 5.7).

Aucune irrégularité des contrats ou absence de caractère obligatoire n'a par ailleurs été invoquée par les vendeurs dans les procédures judiciaires brésiliennes. Certains ont au demeurant procédé à des livraisons partielles, avant et après le mois de mars 1990. Leur intérêt à livrer résultait des garanties prises par [la demanderesse] sur le matériel, dont l'exécution s'est poursuivie jusqu'à l'intervention de la force publique (même si finalement celle-ci a échoué devant les risques de troubles sociaux) ainsi que des nantissements de sucre, sur lequels il y aura de revenir.

Compte tenu de ces différents éléments, le Tribunal conclut à la réalité des contrats litigieux.'

Sources

Excerpt of award published in:
ICC International Court of Arbitration Bulletin, Vol. 12, No. 2, Fall 2001, 56 – 57.

Date: ***October 1, 1999***
Country: ***Australia***
Adjudicating Court: ***Supreme Court of New South Wales***
Number: ***996***
Parties: ***Aiton v. Transfield***

Keywords

AGREEMENT TO NEGOTIATE IN GOOD FAITH – CONTRACT CLAUSE REQUIRING PARTIES TO MAKE DILIGENT EFFORTS TO RESOLVE THEIR DISPUTE – ENFORCEABLE – REFERENCE BY COURT TO ART. 1.7 UNIDROIT PRINCIPLES

Abstract

The Plaintiff and the Defendant entered into a number of contracts in the framework of a construction project. The contracts contained a clause whereby the parties undertook to make diligent and good faith efforts to resolve all disputes before either party commenced mediation or legal action. However, when a dispute arose, Plaintiff commenced legal action; Defendant requested a stay of the proceedings, arguing that Plaintiff had breached its contractual duty to act in good faith to settle the dispute.

The Court pointed out that the general issue was whether agreement to negotiate in good faith was enforceable.

The Court held that, in the case at hand, Defendant had lost its right to rely on the contractual clause by reason of its own conduct. However, the Court added that, in general, an agreement to negotiate in good faith is enforceable. Moreover, the Court was even prepared to state that an obligation to negotiate in good faith, even if not expressly provided for in the contract, has to be implied in any alternative dispute resolution agreement. In order to confirm its conclusion, the Court made several references to the principle of good faith and fair dealing laid down in Art. 1.7 of the UNIDROIT Principles; in doing so, it cited with approval the decision rendered on the 30-06-1997 by the Australian Federal Court in *Hughes Aircraft Systems International v. Airservices Australia* and bibliografical works which had expressly dealt with the principle of good faith.

Full Text

[...]

The motion before the court is for a stay of proceedings.

The defendant seeks the stay on the basis that the contracts pleaded by the plaintiff, forming the basis of the plaintiff's claim, contain express procedures for dispute resolution to be followed prior to either party commencing proceedings. [...] The defendant asserts that such procedures have not been carried out, and therefore, the court ought stay the proceedings until the procedures have been followed. If successful, this application would amount to an indirect enforcement of those express procedures.

THE PROCEEDINGS

The proceedings were commenced by the plaintiff, Aiton Australia Pty Ltd., by summons dated 21 May 1999. They concern the Osborne Co-Generation Project, a turn-key construction project for Osborne Co. Pty Ltd., an independent power producer situated in Adelaide, South Australia. In May and June of 1997 the plaintiff and the defendant, Transfield Pty Ltd., entered into three contracts in relation to the construction of the project. It is these contracts, and the tender negotiations leading up to the execution of the contracts, from which the dispute between the parties arises.

[...]

7. [...] Each contract contained an express term and condition for dispute resolution procedure, in the terms of cl. 28.

Clause 28 of the Contracts provides:

[...]

The Purchaser [Transfield] and Supplier [Aiton] shall make diligent and good faith efforts to resolve all Disputes in accordance with the provisions of this Section 28.1 [...]

[...]

24.The plaintiff's third submission is that in any event, the requirement of 'good faith' imposed by clause 28 of the contracts, is not such as to 'require of the parties participation in the process by conduct of sufficient certainty for legal recognition of the agreement': Hooper Bailie Associated Ltd. at 209. This is because (the plaintiff asserts) the concept of 'good faith' is too imprecise to give rise to an enforceable obligation.

[...]

It is the plaintiff's third submission, as to the certainty of the concept of 'good faith', which commands greater substance.

[...]

It appears that cl 28.1 amounts to an agreement to negotiate disputes in good faith, as distinct from an agreement to conciliate disputes in good faith.

[...]

To my mind, this is a false distinction. As discussed below, the focus ought properly be on the process provided by the dispute resolution procedure. Provided that no stage of the dispute resolution mechanism is itself an 'agreement to agree' and therefore void for uncertainty, there is no reason why, in principle, an agreement to attempt to negotiate a dispute may not itself constitute a stage in the process.

[...]

In a similar vein, the plaintiff submits that beyond the alleged uncertainty of the 'good faith' requirement, the process of mediation set out in cl . 28.2 lacks sufficient certainty to be given legal effect [...]

[...]

The very nature of the words 'good faith' must go toward the conduct of the parties involved in the agreed dispute resolution, as inclusion of those words connotes something more than mere attendance in the process.

[...]

I turn now to examine whether the words 'good faith' in cl 28 have meaning of sufficient certainty to be enforceable.

23. It appears to be common sense that as an obligation to act in 'good faith' may, in principle, be legally recognized as an implied or imputed obligation, there is no reason why it should be struck down as uncertain in cases where there is an express contractual term, as in the present case.

[...]

28. A question arises as to whether the law surrounding the notion of 'good faith' as it relates to a general duty of good faith in the performance of a contract, can be imported to give content to the good faith requirement in cl 28.

[...]

To my mind, however, reference to what good faith is not, does not adequately give content to the obligation at any particular stage [...]

The following observations of BROWNSWORD, HIRD & HOWELLS (*supra*) go towards on an affirmative understanding of the good faith concept:

'It is commonplace that good faith can be read as having both a subjective sense (requiring honesty in fact) and an objective sense (requiring compliance with standards of fair dealing). [I interpolate to note the footnote reference to the UNIDROIT Principles of International Commercial Contracts, Article 1.106(1) which provides that each party, in 'exercising his rights and performing his duties ...must act in accordance with good faith and fair dealing'. The authors point out that the Commission takes 'good faith' to mean 'honesty and fairness in mind, which are subjective concepts', and 'fair dealing' to mean 'observance of fairness in fact which is an objective test'.] It is also commonplace that the most troublesome aspects of good faith relate to its objective dimension. In particular, if good faith is understood as prescribing standards of fair dealing, who are the good-faith standard setters, by what authority do they set such standards, and what are the standards that they so set?' [at 4]

In this context, it is instructive to examine the impact lexicon plays in our understanding of the notion of good faith.

In light of the interest generated by international instruments such as the UNIDROIT Principles of International Commercial Contracts prepared by the International Institute for the Unification of Private Law (Rome: UNIDROIT, 1994), which specifically refer to a requirement of "good faith" in contracts, the Quebec Research Centre of Private and Comparative Law at McGill University set about preparing partner dictionaries, in French and English, which set out the fundamental vocabulary of Quebec private law.

'Good faith' as it relates to contracts, was chosen by the Editorial Committee as the first term to be presented as a sample in a paper published in advance of the release of the dictionary. The Editorial committee stated as follows:

'...the concept of good faith may now be thought of as one of the cannons of international contract law. Since the notion of good faith is seen as fundamental to understanding all aspects of the law of contract, civilians generally express surprise at how little place "good faith" occupies as a formal construct in the Common Law tradition. This is not to say "good faith" is absent in the Common Law - on the contrary - but its mode of expression is such that it may be buried in the cases of that tradition rather than expressed formally as an abstract principle. This is especially problematic when it comes to articulating "good faith" in English, the language most commonly associated with Common law parlance, in a document such as the UNIDROIT Principles. In this respect, the usage of good faith in English civilian parlance in Quebec is of particular interest.

It is often said that in Civil law, "good faith" is not only understood in a subjective manner but also objectively, whereas Common lawyers tend to measure "good faith" on a subjective basis corresponding essentially to a given actor's state of mind. In order to ensure the notions of "good faith" and "bonne foi" be taken as equivalents, the expression "good faith and fair dealings" was chosen to underline the objective aspect of "good faith" in the European Principles and the UNIDROIT Principles. In this choice of terms, there is a lingering sense that law's expression in French corresponds naturally to the Civil law and that English and Common law are also more natural partners. Yet, the English language may certainly be thought of as sufficiently elastic to express the civilian notion of good faith. English-speaking civilians in Quebec do not feel any need to add the expression "fair dealings" in order to make the scope of the notion of good faith clearer.

[...]

In my view, the authorities and academic writings referred to above demonstrate that while the content of any good faith requirement depends on context (statutory or otherwise) and the particular factual circumstances, it is possible to delineate an essential framework for the notion of 'good faith' such that the requirement of 'good faith' in cl 28 is sufficiently certain for legal recognition of the agreement.

[...]

[...] To my mind, but without being exhaustive, the essential or core content of an obligation to negotiate or mediate in good faith may be expressed in the following terms:

(1) to undertake to subject oneself to the process of negotiation or mediation (which must be sufficiently precisely defined by the agreement to be certain and hence enforceable).

(2) to undertake in subjecting oneself to that process, to have an open mind in the sense of:

(a) a willingness to consider such options for the resolution of the dispute as may be propounded by the opposing party or by the mediator, as appropriate.

(b) a willingness to give consideration to putting forward options for the resolution of the dispute.

Subject only to these undertakings, the obligations of a party who contracts to negotiate or mediate in good faith, do not oblige nor require the party:

(a) to act for or on behalf of or in the interests of the other party;

(b) to act otherwise than by having regard to self-interest.

[...]

As mentioned above, in my view on the evidence, Transfield has not dealt with Aiton's early claims in a manner which could reasonably be expected of a party in its position, particularly given the reference to 'good faith' in clause 28.1 in respect of negotiations between the parties under that clause. Indeed, Transfield on my findings has sought to frustrate Aiton's attempts, where made, to regularly invoke the provisions of cl 28.

[...]

67. Notwithstanding the extensive judicial and academic comment on the appropriateness of requiring parties to adhere to dispute resolution clauses as a precondition to litigation in the face of evident reluctance on the part of certain players, it seems to me that strict compliance with a dispute resolution procedure by a party invoking the process [Transfield] is, subject to one matter, an essential precondition to being entitled to relief by way of enforcing, albeit indirectly, the other party to comply with the procedure. The proviso is that where both parties have agreed that something shall be done which cannot effectively be done unless both concur in doing it, the contract is construed to oblige each party to do all that is necessary to be done on his or her part for the carrying out of that thing, although there were no express words to that effect [...]

[…]

If the above holding be incorrect, the finding is that clause 28, including the obligations to negotiate and to mediate in good faith, is sufficiently certain to be enforceable.

In the result, the application for an order staying the proceedings is unsuccessful.

Sources

Original in English:
Unpublished.

Internet website:
http://www.austili.edu.au

Date: **2000**
Adjudicating Court: ***ICC International Court of Arbitration***
Number: ***10021***
Parties: ***Unknown***

Keywords

SHAREHOLDERS' AGREEMENT SUBJECT TO A PARTICULAR DOMESTIC LAW (LITHUANIAN LAW) – CONCURRENT APPLICATION OF "RELEVANT TRADE USAGES" ACCORDING TO ART. 17 ICC ARBITRATION RULES – REFERENCE TO THE UNIDROIT PRINCIPLES AS "CODIFIED TRADE USAGES"

SHAREHOLDERS' AGREEMENT FOR AN INDEFINITE PERIOD OF TIME – CAN BE ENDED BY EITHER PARTIES ONLY BY GIVING NOTICE A REASONABLE TIME IN ADVANCE (ART. 5.8 [ART. 5.1.8 OF THE 2004 EDITION] OF THE UNIDROIT PRINCIPLES)

DESTRUCTION OF MUTUAL TRUST BETWEEN PARTIES TO SHAREHOLDERS' AGREEMENT – NOT NECESSARILY CASE OF HARDSHIP ACCORDING TO ART. 6.2.2 OF THE UNIDROIT PRINCIPLES

TERMINATION OF SHAREHOLDERS' AGREEMENT BECAUSE OF CASE OF HARDSHIP – ONLY IF NEGOTIATIONS FOR ADAPTATION OF TERMS OF AGREEMENT FAIL (ART. 6.2.3 OF THE UNIDROIT PRINCIPLES)

Abstract

Claimant and Defendant had entered into a Shareholders' Agreement aimed at ensuring cooperation between the parties with a view to improving the production and export of cement by the company registered in Lithuania.

The dispute arose after Defendant declared the Shareholders' Agreement terminated and began negotiating with a competitor. Claimant asked the Arbitral Tribunal to order Defendant to respect the Agreement. Defendant insisted on termination, invoking, among others, its right to unilaterally put an end to the Agreement and the disruption of the relationship between the parties which in its view amounted to a case of hardship.

The Agreement was governed by the law of Lithuania. However, the Arbitral Tribunal based its decision not only on the relevant provisions of the Lithuanian Civil Code, but also in accordance with Article 17 of the ICC Rules of Arbitration on the relevant trade usages and in this context expressly referred to the UNIDROIT Principles as "codified trade usages" though declaring that such a reference "is rather of persuasive than binding nature".

As to the merits, the Arbitral Tribunal pointed out that neither the Agreement nor the Lithuanian Civil Code contained a provision permitting a party unilaterally to terminate an agreement with immediate effect. Also Article 5.8 [Art. 5.1.8 of the 2004 edition] of the UNIDROIT Principles provides that contracts for an indefinite period of time may be terminated by either party only by giving notice a reasonable time in advance. With respect to the alleged hardship due to the disruption of the relationship between the parties, the Arbitral Tribunal first of all denied that disruption of the relationship between the parties constituted hardship which by its very nature implied an advantaged and a disadvantaged party. In any case, according to both Article 177 of the Lithuanian Civil Code and Article 6.2.3 of the UNIDROIT Principles in case of hardship the disadvantaged party is not entitled to declare termination of its own accord but has to request the Court or Arbitral Tribunal to do so, and according to Article 6.2.3 of the UNIDROIT Principles, only after that party has requested renegotiation and renegotiation has failed.

Full Text

[...]

VALIDITY OF THE SHAREHOLDERS' AGREEMENT

(26) Respondents have presented two groups of arguments with respect to the validity of the Shareholders' Agreement. The first group of arguments concentrates on the validity of the Shareholders' Agreement and is invoked with respect to Article 3.2 [of the Shareholders' Agreement]. It will be discussed together with the second aspect of the Respondents' case with respect to the validity of the Shareholders' Agreement, namely the alleged termination of the agreement.

(27) Respondents argue that the Shareholders' Agreement is not valid, since it has not been set up according to the mandatory requirements of Article X, section Y, subsection Z of the Lithuanian Company Law. This provision, as argued by Respondents, defines the minimum content requirement for a shareholders' agreement. The Shareholders' Agreement does not prescribe its duration and, in Respondents' opinion, Article [...] [of the Agreement] restricts shareholders' rights, which, according to Article X, section Y, subsection Z of the Company Law [of Eastern Europe Country A] cannot be restricted.

[...]

(32) The second cause of termination given by Respondents in the above mentioned letter was the disruption of the relationship between the parties. The Arbitral Tribunal is aware of the strains in the relationship between the parties and finds that the Shareholders' Agreement does not expressly provide for ways in which the agreement can be terminated at the instance of only one party. Articles 244 to 252 of the Lithuanian Civil Code (Article 244: End of Obligation by Discharge; 245: End of Obligation bye Mutual Settlement; 246: Prohibition of Mutual Settlement, 247. Mutual Settlement in Case of transfer of claim; 248: End of Obligation by Agreement of Parties; 251: End of Obligation Due to Impossibility of Performance; 252: End of Obligation upon Death of Natural Person or Liquidation of Legal Person) are general provisions dealing with termination of contractual obligations, and do not offer any solution to this question. If the disruption of relationship of the parties is characterized as hardship, Article 177 of the Lithuanian Civil Code provides that:

"It shall be prohibited to unilaterally refuse to discharge an obligation and to unilaterally modify the terms of a contract, except for the case provided by a contract or laws.

In the event by virtue of any extraordinary change in circumstances the discharge on an obligation involves great difficulties or either party is likely to suffer great expenses that are obviously not adequate, which expenses could not have been foreseen by the party when executing the contract, then the court may, upon assessment of the interest of the parties, based on the demand of the party concerned, determine the amount of payment to be discharged or it may terminate the contract. When termination the contract, the court shall make a decision concerning the set-off to be effected by either party with respect to the other party, taking account of the contract executed by the parties, the extent to which the contract has been discharged and the change in the circumstances."

It is accordingly up to the court (or, where the relevant obligation is covered by an arbitration agreement, as in the present case, the arbitrators) to decide whether to sanction the termination of the Agreement on grounds of hardship. Respondents have not asked the Tribunal to terminate the Agreement and (correctly in the Tribunal's view) have not sought to argue that they are entitled to apply to the Lithuanian courts to rule on this question.

(33) As authorized by Article 17 of the [ICC Arbitration] Rules, the Arbitrators refer to the relevant trade usages in order to establish whether the purported termination might have been valid. In this respect the reference to the UNIDROIT Principles, as codified trade usages, is rather of persuasive than binding nature, and is in support of the Tribunal's view that the purported termination of the Shareholders' Agreement is invalid and without effect. Article 5.8. of the UNIDROIT Principles provides that "A contract for an indefinite period of time may be ended by either party by giving notice a reasonable time in advance" Reasonable time can be interpreted differently under different circumstances, but termination with immediate effect, as was purportedly done by Respondents [...] cannot, under the circumstances of this case, qualify as "reasonable time". Even if the disruption of the relationship between the parties were to be qualified as hardship according to Article 6.2.3 of the UNIDROIT Principles which states: "(1) In case of hardship the disadvantaged party is entitled to request renegotiations. The request shall be made without undue delay and shall indicate the grounds on which it is based. (2) The request for renegotiation does not in itself entitle the disadvantaged parties to withhold performance. (3) Upon failure to reach agreement within a reasonable time either party may resort to the court. (4) If the court finds hardship it may, if reasonable, a. terminate the contract at a date and on terms to be fixed, or b. adapt the contract with a view to restoring its equilibrium", the disadvantaged party (it is very doubtful whether Respondents due to their behaviour, can be qualified as disadvantaged parties) is entitled to request renegotiations. Only if the renegotiations fail may the disadvantaged party resort to the arbitral tribunal, which will decide whether to terminate the agreement or to adapt it. From this it follows that the Shareholders' Agreement is valid and in force, since the grounds invoked and the attempted method of termination of the Agreement were unjustified on the facts and improper both by applicable Lithuanian law and relevant trade usages. [...]

Date: ***March 2000***
Adjudicating Court: ***ICC International Court of Arbitration***
Number: ***9875***
Parties: ***Unknown***

Keywords

CONTRACT INTERPRETATION – INTENTION OF THE PARTIES DECISIVE – TO BE DETERMINED IN THE FULL CONTEXT OF THE CONTRACT AND OF THE CONDUCT OF THE PARTIES PREVIOUS AND SUBSEQUENT TO THE CONCLUSION OF THE CONTRACT – ARTICLES 4.1, 4.3 AND 4.4 OF THE UNIDROIT PRINCIPLES

CONTRACT INTERPRETATION – PRINCIPLE OF GOOD FAITH AND FAIR DEALING IN INTERNATIONAL TRADE – PROHIBITION FROM DOING INDIRECTLY WHAT THE CONTRACT PREVENTS FROM DOING DIRECTLY – ARTICLE 1.7 OF THE UNIDROIT PRINCIPLES

Abstract

Claimant, a French company, and Defendant, a Japanese company, entered into a license agreement according to which Claimant was given an exclusive license to manufacture, sell and distribute Defendant's products in Europe. Subsequently Defendant entered into an agreement with an American company granting it an exclusive license for the North American market and a non-exclusive license for other countries. According to Claimant Defendant, by not expressly excluding Europe from those other countries, had violated its agreement with Claimant.

After determining in a partial award that the dispute was to be settled on the basis of the *lex mercatoria*, in its final award the Arbitral Tribunal addressed the merits of the case and decided in favour of Claimant. It reached its conclusion on the basis of a careful interpretation of the license agreements in question and in this context it expressly relied on Articles 4.1, 4.3 and 4.4 of the UNIDROIT Principles to which both parties had referred to in their pleadings. Yet in support of its decision the Arbitral Tribunal also invoked Article 1.7 of the UNIDROIT Principles and the general principle of good faith and fair dealing in international trade laid down therein: indeed it would be contrary to this principle to do indirectly what the contract prevents from doing directly.

Full Text

INTERPRETATION PRINCIPLES

[1] Since the main problem here is one of interpretation, the tribunal has invited the parties to express their views of the principles to be applied under the *lex mercatoria*, which the partial award of January. .. 1999 declared to be applicable to the case.

[Claimant] refers to two provisions of the UNIDROIT Principles of International Commercial Contracts. According to article 4.1(1): "A contract shall be interpreted according to the common intention of the parties." Article 4.3 states that in applying article 4.1 . . . "regard shall be had to all the circumstances, including (a) preliminary negotiations between the parties; (b) practices which the parties have established between themselves; (c) the conduct of the parties subsequent to the conclusion of the contract; (d) the nature and the purpose of the contract; (e) the meaning commonly given to terms and expressions in the trade concerned; (f) usage's". Such principles correspond to jurisprudence and arbitral practice. [Claimant] claims its interpretation of article 2 e of the second [X] contract is confirmed by the parties' common intention and subsequent conduct.

[Defendant] also invokes art. 4.3 of the UNIDROIT Principles, but additionally refers to art. 4.4 ("Terms and expressions shall be interpreted in the light of the whole contract or statement in which they appear.") and 4.5 ("Contract terms shall be interpreted so as to give effect to all the terms rather than to deprive some of them of effect."), as well as to art. 8 b of the Vienna Convention on Contracts for the International Sale of Goods ("In determining the intent of a party or the understanding a reasonable person would have had, due consideration is to be given to all relevant circumstances of the case including the negotiations, any practices which the parties have established between themselves, usage's and any subsequent conduct of the parties."). More generally, the *lex mercatoria* invites the tribunal to take into account elements such as, inter alia, the principle of good faith, the rule of effectiveness, the reference to the contract as a whole and the behaviour of the parties.

[2] The tribunal considers the parties have rightly identified the interpretation principles to be applied, with one exception. It does not think [Respondent] 's reference to the rule of effectiveness (as expressed in art. 4.5 of the UNIDROIT Principles) is relevant in this case. Art. 2 e of the second [X] agreement would have effect under either interpretation submitted. Otherwise, the dominant principle is to consider the intention of the parties, which can be determined having regard to all the circumstances. Of particular importance in this case are on one side the contractual set-up as a whole, and on the other side the conduct of the parties subsequent (but also previous) to the conclusion of the contracts.

(a) Intention of the parties

[3] In the interpretation of art. 2 e of the second [X] contract, the intention of the parties should first be determined in the full context of the whole contractual set-up between [Defendant] and its two licensees, as it was organized in 1983 and as it may have evolved in 1996. The contractual relationships between [Defendant] and [Claimant] on one side, and between [Defendant] and [X] on the other side, should not be analyzed separately. The system setup in 1983 reflected [Defendant] 's worldwide planning with two licensees, each of the three participants receiving its own exclusive territory and agreeing to engage in a regular exchange of know-how. The main issue is to determine whether [Defendant] 's and [Claimant] 's intention, in 1996, was to allow[X] to enter the European market though this would be in violation of [Defendant] 's obligations towards [Claimant] under their still applicable 1983 agreement. In this respect, the controversial provision of article 2 e of the second [X] contract cannot be read by itself, nor even only in connection with art. 1 of the same agreement. The two 1983 contracts and the 1996 contract and draft contract have to be fully compared in their sensitive provisions.

The alleged violations of [Claimant] 's European territory came through direct... and indirect. sales by [X]. The relevant issue is not whether such sales occurred, but whether the second [X] contract permitted them.

Direct and indirect sales have to be distinguished. Direct sales [4] As far as direct sales are concerned, the 1996 (draft) contracts are not different in their principles from the 1983 agreements: each contract protects the other licensee's territory The second [X] contract does not contain any provision which would amount to a violation of [Defendant] 's obligations towards [Claimant].

INDIRECT SALES

[5] Indirect sales are another matter. Apart from the OEM exceptions mentioned above, they were not explicitly referred to in the 1983 agreements. They were certainly permitted for each partner in its exclusive or non-exclusive territory Were they permitted or prohibited in each other's territories?

The tribunal believes that in the absence of any explicit prohibition, such sales are not allowed outside one's territory. "Each party must act in accordance with good faith and fair dealing in international trade." (UNIDROIT Principles, art. 1.7) It would be contrary to this principle to do indirectly what the contract prevents from doing directly. Good faith prevents from selling to an entity which one knows or should reasonably know intends to resell in another licensee's territory (This is an obligation towards the licensor, not towards the other licensee.)

This interpretation is confirmed by the OEM exceptions, which would not be necessary if indirect sales were freely permitted.

[6] Significantly, the 1996 (draft) contracts introduce specific provisions concerning indirect sales: .

[7] Remarkable differences from the 1983 agreements are apparent. Indirect sales are now subject to express provisions, in [Defendant] 's contractual relationships with both its licensees. With [Claimant], the prohibition which formerly derived from the good faith principle is now stated in the contract, and made applicable to the American and Asian markets. Between [Defendant] and [X], on the contrary, there is reciprocal prohibition of indirect sales in each other's territories, but Europe is significantly omitted.

It is also relevant to note that while the 1983 [Claimant] contract stated that "[b] oth [Defendant] and its US Licensee(s) are restricted from selling directly to the European market even to the European subsidiary or agent of an OEM located in their own respective countries" (art. 1), such provision was omitted in the 1996 draft contract.

Obviously, as far as indirect sales are concerned, the 1996 (draft) agreements are no longer identical. Considering the parties' legal expertise, the tribunal believes this new contractual set-up is not the result of bad drafting but of a deliberate intent, at least on [X] 's side, to alter the symmetry between [Claimant] and [X] 's positions on the world markets. Either [Defendant] shared that intent, or it can be reproached with oversight of [Claimant] 's interests when negotiating the second [X] contract.

(b) Parties' conduct

This interpretation is confirmed by the parties' respective conduct before and after the execution of that contract.

[8] The fact that the 2½-year-long renegotiation of the [X] agreement was not disclosed to [Claimant] is in itself probably no breach of [Defendant] 's contractual obligations towards [Claimant]. However, the tribunal finds it surprising as the three firms had been working together for many years on the basis of a worldwide cooperation and met regularly to exchange information. ... Considering the significant modifications which were to appear in the 1996 contracts concerning indirect sales, this discretion suggests that [Defendant] was indeed playing a new game with [X] it did not want to reveal to its other licensee.

[9] ... [X] 's conduct after the conclusion of its second contract with [Defendant] casts some light on the American licensee's intentions. ... [An internal memorandum] demonstrates [X] 's preoccupation with entering the European market and [X] 's conviction that they were able to do it through indirect sales.

[10] Such conviction is confirmed by... [X] 's. . . letter to [Defendant]: "[X] needs to offer products and services in Europe to remain competitive with... Today, we are accessing Europe through sales channels consistent with our.. . agreement" (emphasis added).

[11] [Respondent] argues that [X] was referring to the OEM exceptions, which permitted some indirect sales into each other's territories... The tribunal does not follow this restrictive interpretation in a context where [X] proclaims its "intent to open up territories between [Claimant] and [X] in Europe" and its need "to offer products and services in Europe to remain competitive.

CONCLUSION

[12] The tribunal concludes that by entering into a contract that opened [X} 's door for indirect sales in Europe, [Defendant] breached the exclusive licence it had granted to [Claimant] by article i of their 1983 contract.'

Sources

Excerpts of the award published in:
ICC International Court of Arbitration Bulletin Vol. 12, No. 2, Fall 2001, 97 – 99.

*Date: **March 2000***
*Adjudicating Court: **ICC International Court of Arbitration***
*Number: **10114***
*Parties: **Unknown***

Keywords

APPLICATION OF THE UNIDROIT PIRNCIPLES AS EXPRESSION OF "INTERNATIONAL PRACTICES"

Abstract

Claimant, a Chinese company, entered into an agreement with Defendant, an East European car manufacturer, for the provision and organisation of after sales service for vehicles delivered by Defendant. Subsequently the parties accused each other of having failed to comply with their obligations under the contract. Claimant initiated arbitration proceedings against Defendant for breach of contract and requested both compensatory and punitive damages.

Both parties agreed that Chinese law was the law governing the merits of the dispute, but at the same time requested the Arbitral Tribunal to apply also the UNIDROIT Principles as an expression of international practices. As a consequence the Arbitral Tribunal declared that it would base its decision on Chinese law and on "international practices, including UNIDROIT Principles".

As to the merits of the case the Arbitral Tribunal rejected Claimant's request for punitive damages and in so doing it pointed out that the concept of punitive damages was not known in Chinese contract law nor had it found any international trade principle authorising the award of punitive damages.

Full Text

APPLICABLE LAW

The parties' positions

'Claimant holds Chinese law applicable as substantive law governing the contractual relations of the Parties, but is of the opinion that "international practices" have to be applied extensively. Claimant refers specifically to the UNIDROIT Principles of 1994. Claimant is of the opinion that the Convention on the International Sale of Goods ("CISG") is only applicable as to the contractual obligations referring to the sale of goods.'

'Respondent holds Chinese substantive law as applicable to the extent CISG, UNIDROIT or general principles of international trade law do not prevail over or complete the Chinese law.'

The Arbitral Tribunal's decision

'The Agreement No. 245 does not contain a choice-of-law clause. But both Parties presume that Chinese law is applicable. This joint presumption has to be regarded as an agreement on the application of Chinese law as governing the merits of the dispute. This choice of law — even if only made during the arbitration (see Redfern/Hunter, Law and Practice of International Commercial Arbitration, 3rd ed., 1999,2-26) — is valid according to article 17(1)ICC Rules.

CISG is a part of Chinese law. This convention is therefore applicable as part of Chinese law in a dispute between a Chinese entity and one from another country that, like China, has acceded to the CISG. However, the Arbitral Tribunal need not go further into this issue as the claims raised by the Parties do not concern issues that fall within the scope of CISG, as CISG regulates only claims resulting from non-performance, late performance or bad performance of a sales contract and none of these claims have been raised.

The Parties are jointly of the opinion that international practices, especially the UNIDROIT Principles, shall also apply. The UNIDROIT Principles (see BLESSING, Regulation in Arbitration Rules on Choice of Law, 1996, p. 391; DERAINS/SCHWARTZ, A Guide to the New ICC Rules of Arbitration, 1998, p. 218 ss.) are rules of law in the sense of article 17(1)ICC Rules.

The Arbitral Tribunal therefore decides, that the Chinese law and international practices including UNIDROIT Principles are applicable to the merits of the dispute.'

With respect to punitive damages, requested by Claimant.

'The concept of punitive damages is not known in Chinese contract law Chinese law knows only specific performance, liquidated damages and compensatory damages as remedies for breach of contract, see ZHAO, in: WANG/MO, Chinese Law, 1999, p. 244 Ss.

The FECL [1985 Chinese law on foreign economic contracts] defines compensatory damages as the actual loss resulting from the breach, which may include the expectation interests from the performance of the contract. However, such damages must not exceed the loss that was foreseeable by the breaching party at the time the contract was made.

Claimant has not given any proof that Chinese law grants damages that go beyond compensatory damages. The Arbitral Tribunal has not found any international trade principle authorizing the award of punitive damages. Punitive damages are in some jurisdictions even regarded as contrary to public policy *i.e.* in German law (see Federal Supreme Court, Judgment of June 4, 1992, BGHZ 118, p. 312 ss.) and Switzerland (see DORIG, Anerkennung und Vollstreckung US-amerikanischer Entscheidungen in der Scbweiz, 1998, p. 356 ss.).

In a situation where some of the important trading nations regard punitive damages as contrary to public policy, it is obvious that there is no international trade practice favouring punitive damages.

The Arbitral Tribunal therefore dismisses the claim for punitive damages.'

Sources

Excerpts of the award published in:
ICC International Court of Arbitration Bulletin, Vol. 12, No. 2, Fall 2001, 82 – 84.

Date: ***March 20, 2000*** *Adjudicating Court:* ***International Centre for Settlement Disputes (ICSID)*** *Number:* ***ARB(AF)/98/1*** *Parties:* ***Joseph Charles Lemire v. Ukraine***

Keywords

INTERNATIONAL CENTRE FOR SETTLEMENT OF INVESTMENT DISPUTES (ICSID) – DISPUTE BETWEEN A UNITED STATES NATIONAL AND THE GOVERNMENT OF UKRAINE – SETTLEMENT AGREEMENT REACHED BY PARTIES – RECORDED AS AWARD

SETTLEMENT AGREEMENT LAYING DOWN "PRINCIPLES OF INTERPRETATION AND IMPLEMENTATION OF THE AGREEMENT" – PROVISIONS CORRESPOND ALMOST LITERALLY TO ARTICLES 1.7, 3.3(1), 4.1, 4.2, 4.3, 4.5, 5.3, 5.4(1) [ARTS. 5.1.3 AND 5.1.4(1) OF THE 2004 EDITION], 6.2.1, 6.2.2, 6.2.3, 7.1.1, 7.1.4 AND 7.1.5(1)(2)(3) OF THE UNIDROIT PRINCIPLES

Abstract

A national of the United States and the Government of the Ukraine entered into an investment agreement concerning the establishment by the former of broadcasting stations in the Ukraine. When a dispute arose as to the proper performance of the agreement, the parties submitted their dispute to the International Centre for the Settlement of Disputes (ICSID).

After the commencement of the arbitral proceedings the parties entered into negotiations with a view to settling their dispute, which they ultimately succeeded in doing.

In their settlement agreement, which they requested the Arbitral Tribunal to record in form of an award the parties, after having stated the terms of the settlement, added a separate section entitled "Principles of Interpretation and Implementation of the Agreement" and containing provisions concerning the interpretation, validity and performance and non-performance of the settlement agreement. All the provisions of the section are taken literally, with a few minor adaptations, from the UNIDROIT Principles, precisely from Articles 1.7, 3.3(1), 4.1, 4.2, 4.3, 4.5, 5.3, 5.4(1) [Arts. 5.1.3 and 5.1.4(1) of the 2004 edition], 6.2.1, 6.2.2, 6.2.3, 7.1.1, 7.1.4 and 7.1.5(1)(2)(3), dealing with the principle of good faith and fair dealing in international trade, the initial impossibility, the interpretation of contracts and unilateral statements, the duty to cooperate, the duty to achieve a certain result, hardship and its consequences, the definition of non-performance, the non-performing party's right to cure and the setting of an additional period of time for performance, respectively.

Full Text

INTERNATIONAL CENTRE FOR SETTLEMENT OF INVESTMENT DISPUTES
(ADDITIONAL FACILITY)
AWARD

Rendered by the Arbitral Tribunal in the Case of
Joseph Charles Lemire
v.
Ukraine
(ICSID Case No. ARB(AF)/98/1)

Date of dispatch to the parties: September 18, 2000

I. THE ARBITRAL PROCEEDINGS

Procedural Matters

1. By Consent to Arbitrate and Request for Approval dated November 14, 1997, Mr. Joseph Charles Lemire, a national of the United States of America, requested the Secretary-General of the International Centre for Settlement of Investment Disputes (hereinafter "ICSID") to approve and register his request for access to arbitration against Ukraine under the ICSID Additional Facility Rules and the 1994 Treaty Between the United States of America and Ukraine Concerning the Encouragement and Reciprocal Protection of Investment.

2. By letter dated December 10, 1997, the Secretary-General of ICSID informed the Parties that the requirements of Article 4(2) of the ICSID Additional Facility Rules had been fulfilled and that the Claimant's application for access to the Additional Facility had been approved and registered.

3. By Notice to Institute Arbitration Proceedings dated December 29, 1997, the Claimant requested the Secretary-General of ICSID to register the Notice and dispatch to the parties a certificate of registration according to the Arbitration (Additional Facility) Rules.

4. By letter dated January 16, 1998, the Secretary-General of ICSID informed the Parties that the Notice had been registered in the Arbitration Register, and issued and dispatched to the Parries a Certificate of Registration of the case.

5. Pursuant to Article 10(1) of the Arbitration (Additional Facility) Rules, Mr. Lemire appointed as arbitrator Mr. Jan Paulsson (a French national) and Ukraine appointed as arbitrator Dr. Jiirgen Voss (a German national). By agreement of the Parries, Professor Sir Elihu Lauterpacht, C.B.E., Q.C. (a British national) was appointed President of the Tribunal. The Tribunal was constituted on August 13, 1998.

6. On October 6, 1998, Ukraine filed its Objection to the Tribunal's Competence. On October 13, 1998 the Claimant filed Ancillary Claims.

7. The first session of the Arbitral Tribunal was held, with the Parties' agreement, in London on November Il, 1998. During the course of the first session, the President recalled that the Respondent had filed objections to jurisdiction and the proceedings on the merits were suspended in accordance with Article 46(4) of the Arbitration (Additional Facility) Rules. The Tribunal proposed, and the Parties agreed to, a schedule for the filing of observations on Ukraine's Objection to the Tribunal's Competence.

Settlement of the Dispute on Agreed Terms

8. On September 24, 1999, the Tribunal issued its Decision on Ukraine's Objection to the Tribunal's Competence, joining the jurisdictional objections to the merits of the dispute. After consultations with the Parties, the schedule for the further filings on the merits was fixed.

9. On March 20, 2000 the Parties concluded an agreement for the final settlement of all the claims, complaints and requests contained in the Consent to Arbitrate, Notice for Registration, Ancillary Claims and all other letters of the Claimant to the Respondent or ICSID as well as other correspondence of the Claimant addressed to third parties.

10. In accordance with Article 50 of the Arbitration (Additional Facility) Rules, the Parties agreed to request the Tribunal to record the settlement in the form of an award of the Tribunal. The Parties further agreed that the proceedings would thereby be discontinued.

11. The Tribunal is willing to meet the request of the Parties to record the settlement between them in the form of an award.

II. THE AWARD

13. Accordingly, the Tribunal orders unanimously that the said agreement between the Parties as set forth below shall be recorded verbatim as an award on agreed terms

"AGREEMENT ON THE DISPUTE SETTLEMENT
Joseph Charles Lemire v. Ukraine (ICSID Case No. ARB(AF)/98/1)
MARCH 20, 2000
This Agreement on the Dispute Settlement (hereinafter called "this Agreement" is entered into by and between:
Joseph Charles Lemire, the US national (hereinafter called as "the Claimant");
and
The Government of Ukraine (hereinafter called as "the Respondent"), represented by the Minister of Economy S.L. Tihipko.
The Claimant and the Respondent are hereinafter collectively referred to from time to rime as the "Parties" and individually as a "Party".
WHEREAS, the Parties desire to reach a settlement of the International Center for Settlement of Investment Disputes (hereinafter referred to as "the ICSID") Case # ARB (AF)/98/1 upon the terms and conditions hereinafter set forth;
NOW; THEREFORE, the Parties agree as follows:

BACKGROUND

1. On January 16,1998 the Secretary-General of the ICSID registered in the Arbitration Register the December 29, 1997 Notice to Institute Arbitration Proceedings with the use

of the Additional Facility of ICSID (hereinafter called "the Notice for Arbitration") addressed by the U.S. national Mr. Joseph Charles Lemire (hereinafter called "the Claimant") in relation to an investment dispute between him and Ukraine (hereinafter referred to as "the Respondent").

2. On page 5 of the Consent to Arbitrate and Request for Approval for use of the Additional Facility of the ICSID dated November 14, 1997 (hereinafter referred to as "the Consent to Arbitrate") the Claimant stated that he wished to arbitrate his investment dispute with Ukraine in accordance with the provisions of the Treaty between the United States of America and Ukraine Concerning the Encouragement and Reciprocal Protection of Investment (hereafter called "the Bilateral Investment Treaty"). The Claimant also stated that his investment dispute with Ukraine existed at the time the Bilateral Investment Treaty entered into force and is of a continuing nature. The Claimant expressed his consent to the submission of that dispute to binding arbitration under the Additional Facility of the ICSID in accordance with Article VI(3){a)(ii) of the Bilateral Investment Treaty.

3. The Bilateral Investment Treaty was signed on March 4, 1994, entered into force on November 16, 1996 and remains in force at present.

4. At the time when the Notice for Arbitration was filed with the Secretary-General of the ICSID and registered in the Arbitration Register, Ukraine was not a party to the Convention on the Settlement of Investment Disputes between States and Nationals of Other States. The consent of Ukraine to the submission of any investment dispute for settlement by binding arbitration to the Additional Facility of the ICSID, provided there is a written consent of the national or company of the United States of America, was given in Article VI(4) of the Bilateral Investment Treaty.

5. In the letter addressed to the Secretary-General of the ICSID of March 12, 1998 signed by the Acting Chairman of the National Agency of Ukraine for Reconstruction and Development Mr. Vladimir Ignaschenko, it was stated that the National Agency was authorized by the President of Ukraine to represent Ukraine in this dispute and is prepared to cooperate closely with ICSID in settlement of the issue.

6. In accordance with Article 14 of the ICSID Additional Facility Arbitration Rules, the Tribunal was constituted of three members Professor Sir Elihu Lauterpacht, Mr. Jan Paulsson and Dr. Juergen Voss, and the proceedings began on August 13, 1998.

7. On October 5, 1998 in accordance with Article 46 of the ICSID Additional Facility Arbitration Rules, the Respondent filed the Objection to the Tribunal's Competence with the Secretary-General of the ICSID. In its Decision of September 24, 1999 the Tribunal joined the Respondent's Objection to the Tribunal's Competence to the merits of the case and resumed the suspended proceedings on the merits.

8. On October 13, 1998 the Claimant addressed to the Tribunal its Ancillary Claims (hereinafter referred to as the "Ancillary Claims") to which the Respondent extended its Objection to the Tribunal's Competence.

9. On October 15, 1999 the Claimant addressed a formal invitation to the Vice-Prime Minister of Ukraine Mr. Sergiy Tihipko to reach an amicable resolution of the dispute. Based on the Claimant's request of February 16, 2000, and the Respondent's consent to it, the Tribunal suspended the proceedings till June l, 2000 in order to allow the parties to finalize the peaceful settlement.

II. SETTLEMENT OF THE DISPUTE

10. The Parties agree and confirm that all the claims, complaints and requests contained in the Consent to Arbitrate, Notice for Arbitration, Ancillary Claims and all other official letters of the Claimant to the Respondent or ICSID, as well as other correspondence of the Claimant addressed to third parties are hereby finally settled.

11. By such settlement the Parties, in the event of compliance with his Agreement, exclude all of the claims referred to in item 10 of Section II "Settlement of the Dispute" from any further judicial or arbitration settlement.

12. The Parties acknowledge the absence of any claims or misunderstandings between them as on the date of signing this Agreement.

13. As a good-will gesture, the Respondent agrees to fulfil the following additional conditions of the Claimant for the purpose of this settlement under the schedule below.
(a) By April15, 2000 the Commission of experts, appointed by the Respondent, shall examine the quality of broadcasting within the radio frequencies band of FM 100-108. Based on the conclusions of the Commission, the Respondent will take
necessary, reasonable among others, technical measures to remove the obstacles (if any) for radio broadcasting of Gala Radio on FM 100 in Kiev by June 1, 2000.
(b) By May 15, 2000 the Respondent, in person of the State Committee on Communications and Information Technology, agrees to use its best possible efforts to consider in a positive way the application of Gala Radio to provide it with the licenses for radio frequencies (provided there are free frequencies bands) in the following cities: Kharkiv, Lviv, Donetsk, Zaporizhya, Lugansk, Simpheropol, Dniepropetrovsk, Odessa, VynnitSa, Kryviy Rog, Uzhgorod.
The Claimant can apply for the radio channels in the above cities to the National Council for TV and Radio Broadcasting (hereinafter called "the National Council") in a due course in accordance with the current legislation after the National Council has been fully personally formed under the existing law of Ukraine. The Respondent, within the limits of its powers, will assist for the positive consideration of this issue at the National Council.
The granting of licenses for radio frequencies and broadcasting channels will be made in accordance with the requirements of Ukrainian legislation upon payment of the license fees.
(c) By April 10, 2000 the Respondent will propose for the Claimant's consideration three locations for the beauty salon on the terms of rent.

14. In the event that the Respondent appears to be unable to follow the above schedule for the objective reasons, it will promptly inform the Claimant and agree with it the revised schedule.

15. The Parties shall refrain from any demands at present or in the future in any judicial or arbitration forum on compensation of material and/or moral damages with regard to the issues included into this settlement.

16. The Agreement shall not be treated as a document granting any rights, benefits or privileges which are different or additional to the ordinary rights and obligations of a foreign investor in Ukraine in accordance with the Ukrainian laws and international treaties to which Ukraine is a party.

17. In accordance with Article 50 of the ICSID Additional Facility Arbitration Rules, the Parties agree to request the Tribunal to record the settlement in the form of the Tribunal's award. Such record will mean the discontinuance of the proceedings.

18. The Parties agree that the Tribunal's award containing this Agreement as a part of it can be published in the ICSID Review.

19. The Parties agree that each of them bears its own fees and expenses in connection with the proceedings under the ICSID Case # ARB(AF)/98/1.

III. Principles of Interpretation and Implementation of the Agreement

20. Each Party shall act in accordance with good faith and fair dealing in the international business. The Parties shall not exclude or restrict this duty.

21. The mere fact that at the moment of the conclusion of this Agreement the performance of the obligation assumed by a Party was not possible shall not adversely affect the validity of this Agreement.

22. This Agreement shall be interpreted according to the common intent of the Parties. If such an intention cannot be established, the Agreement shall be interpreted according to the meaning that reasonable persons of the same kind as the Parties would give to it in the same circumstances.
The Statement and other actions of a Party shall be interpreted according to that Party's intention if the other Party was aware or, or should have been aware of that intention.
If the preceding paragraph is not applicable, such statements and other actions of a Party shall be interpreted according to the meaning that a reasonable person of the same kind as the other Party would give to it in the same circumstances.

23. For interpreting this Agreement all the circumstances shall be taken into consideration, including the following:
(a) preliminary negotiations between the Parties;
(b) the practices which the Parties have established in their relations;
(c) the conduct of the parties following the conclusion of the Agreement;
(d) the nature and purpose of the Agreement;
(e) the meanings commonly given to the terms and expressions in the business concerned;
(f) usages.
Terms and conditions of the present Agreement shall be interpreted in such a way that all of such terms are deemed effective without making void any of them.

24. Each Party shall cooperate with the other Party when such cooperation may be reasonably expected for the performance of that Party's obligations under the present Agreement.
To the extent that an obligation of the Party involves a duty to achieve a certain result, this Party is to attain it.

25. Where the performance of the Agreement becomes more onerous for one of the Parties, that Party is nevertheless bound to perform its obligations subject to the following provisions of this Agreement on hardship.
There is hardship where the occurrence of the events fundamentally alters the equilibrium of the Agreement either because the cost of the Party's performance has increased or the value of the performance a Party receives has diminished, and
(a) the events occur or become known to the disadvantaged Party after the conclusion of the Agreement;
(b) the events could not have been reasonably taken into account by the disadvantaged Party at the time of the conclusion of the Agreement;
(c) the events are beyond control of the disadvantaged Party; and
(d) the risk of occurrence of the events was not assumed by the disadvantaged Party.
In case of hardship the disadvantaged Party is entitled to request a revision of the Agreement. The request shall be made without undue delay and shall indicate the grounds on which it is based.
The request for revision of the Agreement does not in itself entitle the disadvantaged Party to withhold performance hereunder.
Upon failure to reach agreement within a reasonable time either Party may resort to the arbitration court, according to Article 31, (Section IV) of the present Agreement.

26. Non-performance shall mean the failure by a Party to perform any of its obligations under the present Agreement, including improper performance or late performance.
The non-performing Party may, at its own expense, remedy any non-performance, provided that
(a) without undue delay, it gives notice indicating the proposed manner and time period of such cure;
(b) the cure is appropriate in the given circumstances;
(c) the aggrieved Party has no legitimate interest in refusing such cure;
In the event of non-performance the aggrieved Party may by notice to the other Party allow an additional period of time for performance of the cure.
During the additional period the aggrieved Party may withhold performance of its own reciprocal obligations and may claim damages but may not resort to any other legal remedy. If it receives notice from the other Party that the latter will not perform its obligations under the present Agreement within that period, or if upon expiration of that period due performance has not been made, the aggrieved Party may resort to any of the legal remedies that may be available under this Agreement.
Where in case of delay in performance, which is not fundamental, the aggrieved Party has given notice allowing an additional period of time of reasonable length, it may terminate the Agreement upon the expiry of that period. If the additional period allowed is not of reasonable length it shall be extended up to a reasonable length. The aggrieved Party may in its notice provide that if the other Party fails to perform within the period allowed by the notice the Agreement shall automatically terminate.

IV MISCELLANEOUS

27. This Agreement constitutes the entire agreement between the Parties on the subject matter hereof and supersedes all prior correspondence, negotiations and understandings between them with respect to the matters covered herein.

28. This Agreement shall be binding on the respective legal successors of the Parties. Neither of the Parties may assign or otherwise transfer all or any part of their rights or obligations under this Agreement to any third party.

29. If any provision of this Agreement is held by a court or arbitration tribunal of competent jurisdiction to be invalid, unenforceable or violative of any applicable law, such circumstance shall not have the effect of rendering any other provision or provisions hereinafter contained invalid, in operative or unenforceable.

30. This Agreement shall be governed by the applicable law as determined by Art. 55 of the ICSID Additional Facility Arbitration Rules.

31. All the disputes arising from or in connection with this Agreement shall be settled by negotiations. In the event no solution is achieved within 60 days from the date of beginning of negotiations, either party may address to the ICSID its application for settlement under the ICSID Additional Facility Arbitration Rules.

32. This Agreement shall be executed in the Ukrainian and English languages. In the event of dispute between the two texts, the Ukrainian language shall prevail.

33. This Agreement shall be executed in three counterparts, one for each party and one for the Tribunal, each of which shall be deemed the original.

34. This Agreement enters into force on the date of signing by the Parties and shall not be limited in time.

IN WITNESS WHEREOF, the Parties hereto have executed this Agreement on March 20, 2000.
(signed by)
S. L. Tihipko, Minister of Economy
Joseph Charles Lemire

14. The Tribunal notes the Parties' agreement, set forth in Article 19 of the "Agreement on the Dispute Settlement", that each side bears its own fees and expenses. The Tribunal orders unanimously that the fees and expenses of the members of the Tribunal and the charges for the use of the facilities of ICSID, which have been covered by the equal advance deposits by both parties, shall be borne by the parties in equal shares.

Sir Elihu Lauterpacht, CBE QC
Jan Paulsson
Jurgen Voss

Date: ***July 28, 2000***
Adjudicating Court: ***ICC International Court of Arbitration***
Number: ***9797/CK/AER/ACS***
Parties: ***Andersen Consulting Business Unit Member Firms vs. Arthur Andersen Business Unit Member Firms and Andersen Worldwide Société Coopérative***

Keywords

ARBITRAL TRIBUNAL REQUESTED BY PARTIES TO DECIDE IN ACCORDANCE WITH TERMS OF THE CONTRACT, "TAKING INTO ACCOUNT GENERAL PRINCIPLES OF EQUITY" – REFERENCE BY ARBITRAL TRIBUNAL TO THE UNIDROIT PRINCIPLES AS "A RELIABLE SOURCE OF INTERNATIONAL COMMERCIAL LAW IN INTERNATIONAL ARBITRATION"

CONTRACT INTERPRETATION – ACCORDING TO COMMON INTENTION OF PARTIES OR, IF A COMMON INTENTION CANNOT BE ESTABLISHED, ACCORDING TO UNDERSTANDING OF REASONABLE PERSONS (ART. 4.1(1) AND (2) UNIDROIT PRINCIPLES; ART. 5:101(1) AND (2) OF PRINCIPLES OF EUROPEAN CONTRACT LAW)

CONTRACT PERFORMANCE – PARTIES ENGAGING IN UNCOOPERATIVE ACTS TO THEIR OWN BENEFIT AT THE EXPENSE OF OTHER PARTIES – CONTRARY TO PRINCIPLE OF GOOD FAITH AND FAIR DEALING INHERENT IN INTERNATIONAL CONTRACTS (ART. 1.7 UNIDROIT PRINCIPLES)

CONTRACT PERFORMANCE – OBLIGATION INVOLVING DUTY OF BEST EFFORTS – MEANING (ART. 5.4(2) [ART. 5.1.4(2) OF THE 2004 EDITION] UNIDROIT PRINCIPLES)

FUNDAMENTAL NON-PERFORMANCE – CIRCUMSTANCES RELEVANT FOR DETERMINING WHETHER NON-PERFORMANCE IS FUNDAMENTAL (ART. 7.3.1(2) UNIDROIT PRINCIPLES)

TERMINATION OF CONTRACT FOR FUNDAMENTAL NON-PERFORMANCE – RELEASES PARTIES FROM THEIR OBLIGATION TO EFFECT AND TO RECEIVE FURTHER PERFORMANCE (ARTS. 7.3.1 AND 7.3.5 UNIDROIT PRINCIPLES)

TERMINATION – RESTITUTION OF WHAT PARTIES HAD SUPPLIED UNDER THE CONTRACT – RESTITUTION IMPOSSIBLE – PARTY NO LONGER ENTITLED TO CLAIM RESTITUTION OF WHAT IT HAD SUPPLIED (ART. 7.3.6 UNIDROIT PRINCIPLES)

RIGHT TO DAMAGES – PARTY ENTITLED TO COMPENSATION FOR LOSS SUFFERED ONLY IN CASE OF BREACH BY OTHER PARTY (ART. 7.4.2 UNIDROIT PRINCIPLES)

Abstract

Andersen Consulting Business Unit (hereinafter ACBU) and Arthur Andersen Business Unit (hereinafter AABU) are two business units of the Andersen Worldwide Organisation (hereinafter AWO). AWO, set up in 1977 to cope with the world-wide expansion of the U.S.-based partnership Arthur Andersen and Co., is a network of more than 140 member firms operating in over 75 countries and linked to each other through Member Firm Interfirm Agreements (hereinafter MFIFAs). Andersen Worldwide Société Coopérative (hereinafter AWSC), a Swiss cooperative corporation, is the administrative organ of AWO, whose primary task is to coordinate the practices of the member firms.

Originally each member firm of AWO practised indifferently accounting and audit, tax and consulting services. As a result of the 1989 restructuring member firms' practice was to be conducted through two business units: AABU for audit/attest, tax and other financial advisory services, and ACBU for strategic services, systems integration and other consulting services. Although all member firms continued to be part of AWO and were therefore required to coordinate their practices in conformity with the directives of AWSC, relationships between the two business units constantly deteriorated. On the one hand, AABU member firms, attracted by the increasingly favourable prospects of the consulting business, began developing their own consulting practices; on the other, ACBU member firms complained that such behaviour constituted undue interference with their own professional practices. Over the years several attempts were made to come to terms with the matter by defining more clearly the respective business practices to avoid undue overlapping of activities, yet ultimately without success. Finally, as AABU member firms continued to expand their consulting practices, and AWSC on its part appeared unwilling and/or unable effectively to coordinate the practices of the two Business Units, ACBU member firms filed in 1997 a request for arbitration before the ICC International Court of Arbitration.

Claimants argued that, since the 1989 restructuring had entailed the creation of two separate business units with separate scopes of practice, AABU member firms and AWSC had breached their obligations under the MFIFAs: the former by having implemented ever expanding consulting practices, thereby unduly interfering with their own business practices; the latter by having failed to coordinate the activities of member firms of the two business units and to implement guidelines to ensure compatibility among them. According to Claimants both were fundamental breaches which justified termination of their MFIFAs and payment of damages by Respondents; alternatively, should Respondents not be held liable for breach, Claimants requested to be excused from any further obligation under their MFIFAs due to irreconcilable differences.

Respondents denied the allegation of breach on the ground that even after the 1989 restructuring there was no strict separation of scopes of practice between AABU and ACBU member firms; in turn they accused Claimants of bad faith behaviour for having filed the request for arbitration instead of following the procedure provided for in the MFIFAs in cases of controversy, and requested payment of the penalty provided for in the MFIFAs.

The relevant arbitration clause in the MFIFAs stated that "[...] [t]he arbitrator shall decide in accordance with the terms of this Agreement and of the Articles and Bylaws of [AWSC]. In interpreting the provisions of this Agreement, the arbitrator shall not be bound to apply the substantive law of any jurisdiction but shall be guided by the policies and considerations set forth in the Preamble of this Agreement and the Articles and Bylaws of [AWSC], taking into account general principles of equity [...]". The Tribunal, after declaring that, should the MFIFAs and the AWSC Articles and Bylaws fail to provide guidelines for a decision, it would, pursuant to Article 17.1 of the ICC Rules, "apply general principles of law and the general principles of equity commonly accepted by the legal systems of most countries", held that "[t]he UNIDROIT Principles of International Commercial Contracts are a reliable source of international commercial law in international arbitration for they 'contain in essence a restatement of those '*principes directeurs*' that have enjoyed universal acceptance and, moreover, are at the heart of those most fundamental notions which have consistently been applied in arbitral practice'."

As to the merits the Tribunal, though admitting that AABU member firms had indeed established a broad based consulting practice that replicated and competed with the ACBU member firms' practice, held that such conduct did not constitute a breach of AABU member firms' obligations under the MFIFAs. In the Tribunal's view the MFIFAs did not, even after the 1989 restructuring, explicitly or implicitly impose any limitation (functional, geographical or otherwise) on the professional practices of the member firms, thereby precluding the AABU member firms from competing with the ACBU member firms. At most, by disrupting Claimants' business opportunities and hiring away their personnel, AABU member firms may have breached their implicit obligation to cooperate and to pursue their professional practice in accordance with the principle of good faith and fair dealing which is inherent in international contracts and expressly stated in Article 1.7 of the UNIDROIT Principles; however such breaches were rather rare and at any rate could not be characterized as fundamental.

By contrast the Tribunal held that AWSC undoubtedly was under a duty to ensure cooperation, coordination and compatibility among the member firms' practices. In the Tribunal's view this was a duty of best efforts, as defined in Article 5.4(2) [Art. 5.1.4(2) of the 2004 edition] of the UNIDROIT Principles, that AWSC had failed to comply with. Indeed, when the scope of service conflict between AABU and ACBU member firms surfaced and extended AWSC failed to take any action to ensure cooperation, coordination and compatibility among the practices of the AABU and ACBU member firms. Moreover, referring to the criteria set forth in Article 7.3.1(2) of the UNIDROIT Principles, the Tribunal found that AWSC's failure amounted to a fundamental non-performance which, in accordance with Articles 7.3.1(1) and 7.3.5(1) of the UNIDROIT Principles, justified the termination of Claimants' MFIFAs and Claimants' release from all their obligations to AWSC and the AABU member firms under the MFIFAs for the future.

However the Tribunal rejected Claimants' request for damages, as in its view none of the Repondents' acts, which according to Claimants had caused a loss, constituted a breach. With respect to Claimants' request for restitution of the transfer payments made to the AABU member firms since 1994, the Tribunal, invoking the general principle of law, as stated in Article 7.3.6(1) of the UNIDROIT Principles, that upon termination of the contract either party may claim restitution of whatever it has supplied provided that such party concurrently makes restitution of whatever it has received, found that since Claimants were unable to return the benefits they had received under the MFIFAs they were not entitled to the restitution of the transfer payments.

The Tribunal likewise rejected Respondents' counterclaim for payment by Claimants of the penalty provided for in the MFIFAs. According to the MFIFAs such penalty was due only where the member firm(s) terminating the MFIFAs is (are) "the party at fault". In the case at hand the MFIFAs were terminated as a consequence of AWSC's fundamental breach, while Claimants were not at fault.

The Tribunal finally held that with the termination of the MFIFAs Claimants lose their right to use the "Andersen" name or any derivative thereof. However in order to allow Claimants a reasonable period of time to adjust to the new situation, the Tribunal set December 31, 2000 as the date after which Claimants were to cease using the "Andersen" name.

Full Text

INTERNATIONAL COURT OF ARBITRATION
INTERNATIONAL CHAMBER OF COMMERCE
CASE NO. 9797/CK/AER/ACS
In the Arbitration of

ANDERSEN CONSULTING BUSINESS UNIT MEMBER FIRMS
vs.
ARTHUR ANDERSEN BUSINESS UNIT MEMBER FIRMS
and
ANDERSEN WORLDWIDE SOCIÉTÉ COOPÉRATIVE
[...]

I. The Parties and the Arbitration Clause

Claimants are the Andersen Consulting Business Unit (ACBU) member firms [...] Respondents are the Arthur Andersen Business Unit (AABU) member firms [...] and Andersen Worldwide Société Coopérative (AWSC), a Swiss Cooperative entity.

The relevant arbitration clause to decide the present dispute is the following:

" [...][A]ny and all disputes which cannot be settled amicably, including any ancillary claims of any party, arising out of or in connection with this Agreement (including the validity, scope and enforceability or this arbitration provision) shall be finally settled by arbitration conducted by a single arbitrator in Geneva, Switzerland. The proceedings shall be conducted pursuant to the then-existing Rules of Conciliation and Arbitration of the International Chamber of Commerce, except that the parties may select an arbitrator who is a national of the same country as one of the parties. [...] The arbitrator shall decide in accordance with the terms of this Agreement and of the Articles and Bylaws of Andersen, S.C. In interpreting the provisions of this Agreement, the arbitrator shall not be bound to apply the substantive law of any jurisdiction but shall be guided by the policies and considerations set forth in the Preamble of this Agreement and the Articles and Bylaws of Andersen, S.C., taking into account general principles of equity [...]."

II. The Proceedings

Claimants filed a Request for Arbitration before the International Court of Arbitration of the International Chamber of Commerce on December 17, 1997. The Request was duly notified to the Respondents.

Respondents submitted their answers to Claimants' Request for Arbitration and objected to the Tribunal's jurisdiction. AWSC also filed Counterclaims against the ACBU member firms.

On October 5, 1998 the parties signed the Terms of Reference and agreed on a procedural schedule for the present arbitration

On April 29, 1999 the Tribunal issued an Interim Award on Jurisdiction [...]. The Tribunal also ruled on the appropriate rules of law governing the parties' dispute.

[...]

III. Applicable law

The Tribunal found that the Member Firm Interfirm Agreements (MFIFAs) entered into between AWSC and the Andersen Worldwide Organization member firms, together with the AWSC Articles and Bylaws are the relevant rules of law chosen by the parties to govern the present arbitration; in interpreting the provisions of the MFIFAs the arbitrator is not bound to apply the substantive law of any jurisdiction but shall be guided by the policies and considerations set forth in the Preamble to the MFIFAs and the Articles and Bylaws of AWSC; if the MFIFAs and the AWSC Articles and Bylaws are silent or do not provide guidelines for a decision, the Tribunal shall, pursuant to Article 17.1 of the ICC Rules, apply the rules of law it deems appropriate; those rules of law shall be the general principles of law and the general principles of equity commonly accepted by the legal systems of most countries.[1]

The UNIDROIT Principles of International Commercial Contracts are a reliable Fonti of international commercial law in international arbitration for they "contain in essence a restatement of those *'principes directeurs'* that have enjoyed universal acceptance and, moreover, are at the heart of those most fundamental notions which have consistently been applied in arbitral practice." [2]

IV. STATEMENT OF FACTS

[...]

C. THE INTERNATIONAL EXPANSION OF ARTHUR ANDERSEN & CO. AND THE CREATION OF THE AWO

Arthur Andersen & Co. began to expand internationally in the 1930's.

[...]

As the firm increased its global presence its leadership realized that a new structure was indispensable in order to address several legal, regulatory, tax and professional restrictions in the countries where it operated. In 1977 the firm created that new structure: the Andersen Worldwide Organization (AWO), designed to maintain the one firm concept and deliver uniform seamless service to clients across the world. The AWO is comprised of a Swiss cooperative entity, Arthur Andersen & Co. Société Coopérative (AWSC) acting as an "umbrella" entity for the organization, the AWO member firms and the Partners of AWSC, inter alia.

AWSC was created to coordinate on a worldwide basis, the professional practices of its Practice Partners who are its members and of their member firms; to serve as the instrumentality through which the AWSC partners participate in shaping and implementing the reciprocal commitment of their resources and the coordination of their common efforts on a worldwide basis (Bylaws at Preamble). AWSC was not to engage in any professional practice of its own.

[...]

Every member firm and its Practice Partners enter into a Member Firm Interfirm Agreement (MFIFA) with AWSC, substantially in the form of a standard version approved by the AWSC partners, pursuant to which the member firm and/or its Practice Partners agree to adhere to professional standards and principles coordinated by AWSC, subject to compliance with applicable laws and professional regulations, to adopt appropriate compatible policies and to carry out certain other responsibilities.

D. THE 1989 RESTRUCTURING

As the AWO developed through the years, various difficulties began to strain the relationships between the partners practicing in the Accounting and Audit and Tax divisions on one side and those practicing in the MICD [Management Information Consulting Division] on the other. The earnings disparity between practices, the need for a new governance framework in light of the firm's internationalization, the desire of each division to run its own business and the regulatory issues stemming from auditors' independence requirements caused discomfort among the consulting partners and dissatisfaction with the status quo.

[...]

The amendments to the AWO organizational documents became effective on September 1, 1989.

Thereafter, the member firms' practice was to be "conducted through two business units: ARTHUR ANDERSEN for audit/attest, tax and other financial and specialty advisory services, and ANDERSEN CONSULTING for strategic services, systems integration, information technology consulting and change management services."

E. THE AWO GOVERNING DOCUMENTS AFTER THE 1989 RESTRUCTURING

AWSC did not suffer substantial changes as a consequence of the 1989 Restructuring. The purpose of this cooperative entity continued to be the coordination of the professional services practices of its partners' member firms on an international basis.

[...]

As a coordinating body for the member firms, AWSC has the obligation to arrange for the performance of other functions such as developing quality control standards and procedures and other related policies, practices and procedures to assure a consistent and uniformly high quality of professional service by member firms; developing and implementing practice reviews programs to assure effective implementation by the member firms of such quality control standards and procedures and other related policies, practices and procedures; developing compatible policies and professional standards for member firms; developing annual operating plans to assure effective coordination of the member firms' practices; overseeing the development and use of Andersen Technology and regulating the use of the Andersen name by member firms and/or their right to hold themselves out to the public or otherwise represent themselves to be member firms [Paragraph 2.1. MFIFA].

[...]

G. SCOPE OF SERVICE ISSUES AND THE BUSINESS UNITS' STRATEGIES

Shortly before leaving office as AWSC Managing Partner-Chief Executive, Mr. Kullberg [in April 1989] wrote a memorandum for the AWSC file[...] [H]e was convinced that the potential for scope conflicts had developed from the creation of the two business units.

The unresolved scope of practice issue quickly gained momentum within the AWO[...]. The conclusions - known as the Florida Accords - drawn by the Executive Committee and supported by the AWSC Board of Partners, proclaimed that although each business unit had to be a vigorous competitor in its own marketplace, its strategies had to fit within the overall strategy of the firm[...].

The AABU member firms were given primary responsibility for systems consulting when the environment consisted of "proven hardware [and] prepackaged software, including the use of data bases and report writers for management information but excluding custom programming and modification of code; and (...) [when] consolidated revenues of the client [were] below $175 million."

The ACBU member firms were given primary responsibility when the client's consolidated revenues were in excess of $175 million "and regardless of size, when the environment [was] more complex that that set out above.

[...]

In April 1990 Arthur Andersen Co. LLP (the U.S. AABU member firm) represented [...] to the [U.S.] Securities and Exchange Commission that "[a]n important objective of the restructuring was the delineation of separate scopes of practice for Arthur Andersen Co and Andersen Consulting. Thus, Andersen Consulting offers clients a broad range of information technology consulting services. It does not however perform attest services or hold itself out as engaging in the practice of public accounting."

The scope of services issue did not cease to create friction after the Florida Accords, particularly in business systems consulting, strategic services and operational consulting.

[...]

In 1993, the AWSC Executive Committee issued a new set of guidelines - known as the 1993 Protocols - the Preamble to which acknowledges: "[a]s the Firm has developed new expertise based on our core competencies and found new and better ways to serve clients, scope-of-practice ambiguities and skills overlaps between partners in the business units have increased, particularly in operational consulting and to a lesser degree in business systems consulting."

[...]

Like the Florida Accords, the 1993 Protocols established business unit cooperation guidelines for the Operational Consulting/Business Reengineering area but recognized in addition, that service overlap and competition in this area were inevitable and desirable.

[...]

H. The creation of Arthur Andersen Business Consulting

In December 1994, the AABU member firms combined their Business Systems Consulting and Operation Consulting practices to form Arthur Andersen Business Consulting (AABC).

[...]

By October 1995 it was apparent that in many instances the AWSC partners did not want to work together. The expansion of both business units had caused service overlap and marketplace confusion had resulted from the way each business unit positioned itself in advertising and how it recruited on campuses.

[...]

L. The Transfer Payments

Under the MFIFAs, the AWO member firms are entitled to receive or bound to pay, as the case may be, an annual amount from or to the other member firms as a reciprocal of a commitment to cooperative action in serving common clients on an international basis and to reflect equitably the mutual and interdependent benefits of such practices [...].

In compliance with the transfer payment provisions, the ACBU member firms have transferred US $453.7 million to the AABU member firms since the 1989 Restructuring; of this amount US $397.6 million were transferred since 1994.

The ACBU member firms have placed US $476.2 million in an interest-bearing escrow account pending the result of the present arbitration. The moneys deposited comprise the transfer payments due to the AABU member firms for fiscal years 1998 and 1999.

V. CONSIDERATIONS

[...]

A. WHETHER AABU MEMBER FIRMS BREACHED THEIR MATERIAL OBLIGATIONS UNDER THEIR MFIFAS BY:

- ESTABLISHING A BROAD-BASED AND EXPANDING BUSINESS CONSULTING PRACTICE THAT AND COMPETES WITH ACBU MEMBER FIRMS' BUSINESS;
- DISRUPTING CLAIMANTS' BUSINESS OPPORTUNITIES;
- MISAPPROPRIATING THE ANDERSEN CONSULTING NAME AND ACBU MEMBER FIRMS'GOOD WILL;
- CAUSING MARKETPLACE CONFUSION;
- SEEKING TO HIRE AWAY ACBU MEMBER FIRMS' PERSONNEL OR INTERFERING WITH ACBU'S RECRUITING OF PERSONNEL;
- TRADING ON CLAIMANTS' CREDENTIALS AND EXPERTISE.

1. Whether the AABU member firms established a broad-based and expanding business consulting practice that replicates and competes with ACBU member firms' business

Claimants accuse the Respondent member firms of expanding their advisory business into information technology consulting, strategic consulting, change management consulting and business process consulting, at least from 1994, when the AABU leadership announced the creation of its AABC practice.

[...]

The Respondent member firms acknowledge that AABC's services and skills are similar and in some degree overlap with those offered by Claimants but affirm that this overlap is not appreciable because the basic core competencies and the target markets of each business unit are different.

[...]

[...] [T]he Tribunal finds that Arthur Andersen Business Consulting is in fact, a broad based consulting practice that replicates and competes in some instances with the ACBU member firms' practice.

2. Whether the MFIFAs prohibit the AABU member firms from establishing a broad based consulting practice practice that replicates and competes in some instances with with the ACBU member firms

Several provisions in the MFIFAs and the AWSC Articles and Bylaws regulate cooperation, coordination and compatibility among the practices of the AWO member firms.

[...]

The Tribunal does not construe any of these principles as barring any individual member firm or a group of member firms from offering and performing services rendered by other member firms to the same segment of the marketplace. Indeed, the MFIFAs do not, explicitly or implicitly, impose any limitation (functional, geographical or otherwise) on the professional practices of the member firms.

These principles [...] require that the member firms' practices be developed in accordance with the policies and standards dictated by AWSC in furtherance of the common goals of cooperation, coordination and compatibility among member firms.

[...]

The relevant evidence does not lead to a different conclusion or support the contention that a clear-cut separation of scope of practices between the AABU and the ACBU member firms was agreed as a premise of the 1989 Restructuring.

[...]

The Tribunal's interpretation is also founded on the AWSC leadership's pronouncements during the years following the 1989 Restructuring that the scope of services issue had to be dealt with by the AWSC governance structure.

[...]

[T]he Florida Accords [and] the Portugal Protocols [...] are all admissions of AWSC's responsibility to deal with the scope of practice conflicts. [...] Had the MFIFAs imposed a limitation on the member firms' practices, the Accords and Protocols and all the other proposals to resolve the internal AWO conflicts would have been unnecessary.
In this light, the Tribunal finds the MFIFAs do not preclude the AABU member firms from competing with the ACBU member firms.

[...]

Claimants also accuse the AABU member firms of transgressing their obligations under the MFIFAs by ignoring legally binding AWSC policies and practices expressed in the Florida Accords and 1993 Protocols, which the AABU member firms were obliged to adopt. In Respondents' opinion, the Accords and Protocols are not binding on the member firms and do not prohibit overlap of services.
Hence, the issue before the Tribunal is whether the Accords and Protocols are binding policies recommended by AWSC [...] or simple internal AWSC management guidelines. The Tribunal favors the second interpretation.

[...]

The Florida Accords and 1993 Protocols are [...] internal guidelines to be applied by the business unit management lines in fulfilling their coordinating responsibilities. Consequently, the AABU member firms could not have breached any obligation under those guidelines.

3. *Whether the AABU member firms disrupted Claimant's business opportunities, hired away ACBU member firms' personnel, interfered with ACBU member firms' recruiting of personnel, caused marketplace confusion, traded on Claimants' credentials and expertise and misappropriated the Andersen Consulting name and the ACBU member firms' good will*

The ACBU member firms additionally accuse the Respondent member firms of breaching their obligations under the MFIFAs on the counts described above.

[...]

In the Tribunal's view, only a few situations described by Claimants can be categorized as a breach under the MFIFAs.

[...]

The MFIFAs contain no provision explicitly prohibiting that conduct, but the contractual agreements among the parties forbid the AWO member firms to engage in uncooperative acts to benefit themselves at the expense of other member forms. Such acts are contrary to the member firms' implicit obligation to cooperate and to pursue their professional practice in accordance with the principle of good faith and fair dealing inherent to international contracts. [3]

[...]

Placed in the context of a longstanding relationship with thousands of potentially conflictive situations, those breaches cannot be characterized as fundamental.

[...]

B. WHETHER AWSC BREACHED ITS MATERIAL OBLIGATIONS UNDER THE MFIFAS BY:
- FAILING TO COORDINATE AND ENSURE COMPATIBILITY BETWEEN THE PRACTICES, ETHICAL PRINCIPLES AND POLICIES OF THE MEMBER FIRMS;
- ALLOWING THE AABU MEMBER FIRMS TO COMPETE WITH CLAIMANTS;
- FAILING TO DEVELOP AN ANNUAL OPERATING PLAN DESIGNED TO ASSURE THE EFFECTIVE COORDINATION, ON AN INTERNATIONAL BASIS, OF THE PRACTICES OF THE MEMBER FIRMS;
- FAILING TO ENFORCE THE MUTUAL OBLIGATIONS BETWEEN ACBU MEMBER FIRMS AND AABU MEMBER FIRMS;
- FAILING TO REGULATE THE USE OF THE "ANDERSEN" OR OTHER NAMES.

1. AWSC's obligation to coordinate the practices of the member firms

Claimants accuse AWSC of disregarding "its core function to assure that the basic purpose of the 1989 Restructuring is met and to act as the *coordinator* of all Member Firms and the implementor of guidelines and policies to ensure compatibility among and the harmonious operation of all Member Firms". (emphasis provided in text)

The ACBU member firms' contention rests on one basic assumption: AWSC has the obligation to coordinate the member firms' practices. AWSC answers that with minor exceptions, the MFIFAs do not impose an obligation on AWSC to coordinate.

In the Tribunal's view, the language of the AWO organizational documents is not in accordance with AWSC's interpretation.

Member firm coordination is the cornerstone of the MFIFAs; it is the means to ensure that the AWO's cooperative goals are achieved. If adequate coordination were not well-founded and properly ensured in an organization such as the AWO - comprised of more than one hundred member firms worldwide - cooperation would be seriously impaired.

By entering into an MFIFA, a member firm appoints AWSC to arrange for the coordination of its professional practice on an international basis with that of the other member firms (Paragraph 2.1 of the MFIFAs) and legitimately expects its professional practice to be coordinated with that of the other member firms. Conversely, AWSC accepts such appointment and the responsibilities inherent to the coordinating function.

[...]

In summary, the explicit MFIFA provisions, interpreted in light of the purposes and policies set forth in the Preamble thereto and in the AWSC Articles and Bylaws, demonstrate that AWSC's essential obligation is to coordinate the AWO member firms' diverse professional practices [...]. Indeed, since its creation in 1977, AWSC's purpose has been the coordination of its member firms on an international basis. (Preamble to the AWSC Bylaws).

[...]

The Tribunal finds that the wording of these purposes, policies and functions indicates that AWSC must exercise its best efforts [4] to ensure cooperation, coordination and compatibility among the member firms' practices.

[...]

Albeit the creation of the business units significantly altered AWSC's internal structure, none of the changes to the AWO organizational documents modified AWSC's obligations in any meaningful way.

[...]

2. *Whether AWSC breached its obligations to coordinate the practices of the member firms*

Did AWSC exercise its best efforts to achieve cooperation, coordination and compatibility between the practices of the AABU and ACBU member firms? As explained below, AWSC failed to fulfil such responsibility.

While each business unit developed and implemented its own uncoordinated individual strategy, AWSC proved unable to devise an organizational framework or operating plan for all the member firms' practices.

Likewise, AWSC did not act to resolve the scope of service conflict, despite the internal tensions and lack of cooperation between the AABU and ACBU member firms.

[...]

The Tribunal is aware of the AWSC Executive Committee's initial effort to tackle the scope of practice conflict by drawing internal guidelines for business unit cooperation in the Florida Accords. Nevertheless [...] the Accords were not properly implemented by AWSC.

When the Executive Committee tardily developed a new set of guidelines [the 1993 Protocols] to address the scope of service issues, it was forced to admit a stalemate at the policy level and the leadership's responsibility for not resolving the conflict [...]. Predictably, before the end of 1993 the AWSC partners surfaced their discontent with the Protocols and urged the AWO leadership to expedite the resolution of the internal conflicts.

A year later, the AABU launched the AABC practice. The AABU member firms' expansion into the information technology area, both in terms of capabilities and target market, substantially increased the opportunities for the member firms of each business unit to perform similar services to similar clients.

[...]

Even under those pressing circumstances the AWSC management was unable to agree on a course of action to address the scope of practice dispute or to draft a proposal for the consideration of the AWSC partners [...].

[...]

AWSC neglected to address the scope of practice conflict, even after the Board of Partners [...] had admitted that the status quo was unacceptable and unsustainable. On these grounds, the Tribunal finds AWSC did not make its best efforts to ensure coordination, cooperation and compatibility among the practices of the AABU and ACBU member firms, because it failed to take any course of action when the scope of service conflict surfaced and extended; and because it failed to develop the annual operating plans required to coordinate the practices of all the AWO member firms.

AWSC further contends it cannot function independently of the collective will of its partners since its governance structure provides substantial authority to its partners.

This is an overstatement. Truly, the AWSC partners have substantial authority as a group, but certain decisions comprising overall policies, long-range plans and objectives and scope of service definitions are the responsibility of the Board of Partners acting upon recommendation of the Administrative Council and/or the Chief Executive. (Article 1 6(B)(1) of the AWSC Articles).

[...]

4. Whether AWSC's breach amounts to a fundamental non-performance of its obligations

AWSC's neglectful conduct is a breach of its obligations to coordinate the practices of the ACBU with those of the AABU member firms, to develop compatible policies and professional standards for member firms and to develop annual operating plans to assure the effective coordination of the member firms' practices (Paragraph 2.1 of the MFIFAs).

AWSC contends that any such breaches are not sufficiently material to warrant termination. "The UNIDROIT factors - says AWSC - make clear that there has been no material, fundamental breach."

The UNIDROIT criteria cited by AWSC proclaim [Article 7.3.1(2) of the UNIDROIT PRINCIPLES]:

"In determining whether a failure to perform an obligation amounts to a fundamental non-performance regard shall be had, in particular, to whether

a. the non-performance substantially deprives the aggrieved party of what it was entitled to expect under the contract unless the other party did not foresee and could not reasonably have foreseen such result;

b. strict compliance with the obligation which has not been performed is of essence under the contract;

c. the non-performance is intentional or reckless;

d. the non-performance gives the aggrieved party reason to believe that it cannot rely on the other party's future performance;

e. the non-performing party will suffer disproportionate loss as a result of the preparation or performance if the contract is terminated."

[...]

In light of the above findings, AWSC's conduct amounts to a fundamental non-performance of its obligations under the MFIFAs.

First, AWSC failed to coordinate all the AWO member firms, particularly by neglecting two of its critical functions: to develop annual operating plans for all the member firms' practices and to make its best efforts to address and resolve the scope of service issue.

AWSC's failure to exercise its best efforts to coordinate the member firms' practices substantially deprived Claimants of the cooperation they were entitled to expect under the MFIFAs.

[...]

Second, strict compliance by AWSC of its obligation to coordinate the practices of the ACBU and the AABU member firms is of the essence of the MFIFAs.

[...]

Third, AWSC's non-performance gives Claimants reason to believe that they cannot rely on AWSC's future performance.

[...]

Fourth, Respondents will not suffer a disproportionate loss as a result of the preparation or performance if Claimants' MFIFAs are terminated.

AWSC cannot possibly suffer any harm from the termination of its contractual relationship with the ACBU member firms because AWSC is an instrumentality for the purpose of coordinating the member firms' professional practice [...]

Moreover, the AABU member firms' past performance to the ACBU member firms has been more than compensated by the significant amounts received from the ACBU member firms as transfer payments.

Respondents' reliance on Paragraph 17.2 of the MFIFAs to determine the damages suffered as a result of Claimants' departure from the AWO is unfounded. The MFIFAs explicitly state that those liquidated damages are to be presumed as a valid measure of actual damages suffered by the party entitled to payment. Among them are the increased costs of establishing a relationship with other suitable practice entities or those associated with the inability to establish such replacement relationships, and the related decrease in revenues.

Respondents have neither right to termination payments nor the apparent need to establish new relationships with other suitable practice entities. The ACBU and AABU member firms virtually operate as two separate global partnerships with extensive and substantial consulting skills resident in the AABC practice.

[...]

D. WHETHER THE ACBU MEMBER FIRMS HAVE ENGAGED IN INEQUITABLE CONDUCT AND/OR BREACHED THEIR CONTRACTUAL AND FIDUCIARY OBLIGATIONS TO THE AABU MEMBER FIRMS BY:

- PLANNING AND EXECUTING A BAD FAITH STRATEGY TO SEPARATE FROM THE AWO AND AVOID THEIR OBLIGATIONS UNDER THEIR MFIFAS INCLUDING THOSE APPLICABLE UPON TERMINATION;
- FILING THIS PROCEEDING IN BAD FAITH;
- FILING THIS PROCEEDING WITHOUT COMPLYING WITH THE CONTRACTUAL NOTICE PROVISIONS;
- DISPARAGING THE AABU MEMBER FIRMS AND THE AWO IN THE WORLDWIDE PRESS AND WITH CLIENTS, POTENTIAL CLIENTS, EMPLOYEES, RECRUITS AND/OR THE GENERAL PUBLIC;
- DISRUPTING RESPONDENTS' BUSINESS OPPORTUNITIES;
- TRADING ON AABU MEMBER FIRMS' CREDENTIALS AND EXPERTISE;
- REFUSING TO TEAM/WORK JOINTLY WITH AABU MEMBER FIRMS ON VARIOUS AWO ENGAGEMENTS AND POTENTIAL ENGAGEMENTS;
- REFUSING TO SERVE AND/OR ABANDONING CERTAIN CLIENTS AND POTENTIAL CLIENTS OF THE AABU MEMBER FIRMS AND THE AWO;
- REFUSING TO SHARE INFORMATION, TRAINING MATERIAL, AND/OR TECHNOLOGY WITH THE AABU MEMBER FIRMS;
- REFUSING TO REFER CLIENTS TO THE AABU MEMBER FIRMS.

[...]

3. Filing this proceeding without complying with the contractual notice provisions

[...]

Paragraph 14 of the MFIFAs enumerates several termination events, among them, the proviso of Paragraph 14.2 (F), governing unilateral termination by a wronged party. Separate from the unilateral termination clause the MFIFAs also contain certain arbitration provisions for the resolution of any and all disputes which cannot be settled amicably, arising out of or in connection with the MFIFAs (Paragraph 22.1 of the MFIFAs) and regardless of whether the complaining party seeks to be released from its obligations under the MFIFAs.

The two paragraphs clearly regulate different events and offer a wronged party the alternative rights to terminate its MFIFA when a material breach has occurred or to resort to arbitration in search of a final decision that will resolve a dispute with another party.

In the event of unilateral termination, the notice of breach is an essential condition for the aggrieved party to be relieved from its obligations insofar as it sets in motion the procedure regulated in Paragraph 14.2 (F). Such notice has not been established however, as a condition precedent to the commencement of an arbitration proceedings.

Claimants elected to exercise their right to arbitration under Paragraph 22 of the MFIFAs, instead of unilaterally terminating their MFIFA and therefore were not under the obligation to serve AWSC with a notice of breach.

Thus, Claimants did not file this proceeding in disregard of the notice provisions contained in the MFIFAs

[...]

7. *Refusing to teamwork jointly with AABU member firms on various AWO engagements and potential engagements*

The Respondent member firms accuse Claimants of systematically failing to cooperate since the early 1990s, by refusing to team with them and declining to share resources including common support structures and personnel.

The Tribunal found eleven instances prior to this filing of this arbitration, of ACBU member firms acting uncooperatively by, inter alia, halting previous joint industry studies; excluding AABU member firms from engagements for clients introduced by AABU partners to ACBU member firms; excluding AABU personnel previously committed to work on certain ACBU member firm engagements and backing out of joint proposals with AABU member firms.

That conduct is contrary to the member firms' implied obligation to cooperate under the MFIFAs and to the explicit obligation to pursue their professional practice with respect to one another in accordance with the principle of good faith and fair dealing, inherent to international contracts. [5]

Nevertheless, the events portrayed by the AABU member firms are not a material breach of the MFIFAs, particularly if those events are placed in the context of a long-standing relationship involving thousands of potentially conflicting situations.

[...]

E. WHETHER THE ACBU MEMBER FIRMS' ALLEGED BAD FAITH FILING OF THIS PROCEEDING BREACHES OF THEIR OBLIGATIONS TO THE AABU MEMBER FIRMS, AND OTHER INEQUITABLE CONDUCT BOTH BEFORE AND AFTER THE FILING OF THE PROCEEDING BAR THE RELIEF THE ACBU MEMBER FIRMS ARE REQUESTING

The Tribunal found that Claimants had not filed the present arbitration in bad faith, materially breached any obligation to the AABU member firms or engaged in any inequitable conduct either before or after the filing of the arbitration. Thus, Claimants' conduct does not bar them from the relief requested.

[...]

G. Whether Claimants are entitled to be excused from further obligations to AWSC and the AABU member firms under the MFIFAs

While AWSC breached its obligations to the ACBU member firms under Claimants' MFIFAs and was responsible for a fundamental non-performance thereunder, Claimants did not engage in inequitable conduct or breach their contractual or fiduciary obligations.

It is a well established rule of law that a fundamental breach of a contract gives the aggrieved party the right to terminate the contractual relationship. This general rule is reflected in the MFIFAs which provide that the effect of a material breach thereto entitles the wronged party to terminate its MFIFA (Paragraph 14.2 (F) of the MFIFAs).

Under the Unidroit Principles of International Commercial Contracts, a party may terminate a contract when the failure of the other party to perform an obligation under the contract amounts to a fundamental non-performance. The consequence of termination is to release the parties from their obligation to effect and to receive further performance. 6

On account of AWSC's fundamental non-performance, the ACBU member firms' MFIFAs are terminated. Consequently, Claimants are released from all their obligations to AWSC and the AABU member firms under the MFIFAs as of the date the present award is notified to the parties.

H. Whether Claimants are entitled to recover from Respondents any sums by way of interest, damages or compensation under or in respect of such breaches if any, and the amount thereof

Claimants seek an award of US$100 million for damages caused to the Andersen Consulting brand and reputation, originated in marketplace confusion caused by AABC.

[...]

The tribunal found that the AABU member firms did not breach their obligations under the MFIFAs by causing confusion in the marketplace. For this reason the ACBU member firms cannot claim any harm from the alleged breach and are not entitled to any compensation (Article 7.4.2 of the Unidroit Principles).

AWSC on the other hand, breached its material obligations under the MFIFAs by failing to coordinate the practices of the ACBU and AABU member firms. However, AWSC was not under the duty to coordinate the practices of the member firms by drawing clear distinctions among the member firms' marketplace images. Thus, none of the damages alleged by Claimants are a consequence of AWSC's non-performance.

Claimants also seek restitution of the transfer payments made to the AABU member firms since 1994, including the transfer payments placed in escrow, plus interest thereon. The Tribunal has ruled that Claimants' MFIFAs are terminated as of the date this Award is notified to the parties.

Under general principles of law, upon termination of the contract either party may claim restitution of whatever it has supplied, provided that such party concurrently makes restitution of whatever it has received (See Article 7.3.6(1) of the Unidroit Principles). Thus, restitution necessarily entails that both parties return what they have received under the contract.

[...]

Restitution of the benefits received by Claimants is impossible. In fact, the ACBU member firms do not even offer to do so.

If the Tribunal were to grant the restitution of transfer payments made by Claimants, they would be unjustly enriched.

The Tribunal shall not grant Claimants the restitution they requested.

[...]

J. PROVIDED THE ARBITRATOR FINDS THAT ANY OR ALL CLAIMANTS ARE ENTITLED FOR ANY REASON TO BE EXCUSED FROM ANY OF THEIR OBLIGATIONS UNDER THEIR RESPECTIVE MFIFAS, WHETHER THOSE EXCUSED CLAIMANTS SHOULD:
- PAY DAMAGES TO AWSC;
- MEET THEIR OBLIGATIONS UNDER THE MFIFAS THROUGH AND INCLUDING THE EFFECTIVE DATE OF THE TERMINATION;
- CEASE USING THE "ANDERSEN" NAME OR ANY DERIVATIVE THEREOF OR ANY OTHER NAME AWSC IS AUTHORISED TO REGULATE;
- CEASE TO REPRESENT THEMSELVES AS IN ANY WAY ASSOCIATED WITH AWSC OR THE REMAINING MEMBER FIRMS, AND
- RETURN AND CEASE USING ANDERSEN TECHNOLOGY.

1. Claimants' obligation to pay damages to AWSC

It is a general rule of law that only the party which has willfully or negligently breached its obligations under a contract and has thereby inflicted a loss upon another is liable for damages.

[...]

The Tribunal found AWSC had breached its material obligations to coordinate the practices of the ACBU member firms with those of the AABU member firms. AWSC's failure to act was the cause of termination of Claimants' MFIFAs and constituted a fundamental non-performance thereunder. For this reason, AWSC is deemed the party at fault.

The provisions of Paragraph 17.2 (A) of the MFIFA on which Respondents specifically rely to demand the termination payments from Claimants require that the ACBU member firms be at fault, which they are not. Therefore, Claimants are under no obligation to make the Paragraph 17.2 (A) termination payments.

[...]

3. Claimants' obligations to cease using the "Andersen" name or any derivative thereof, or any other name AWSC is authorised to regulate and to cease representing themselves as in any way associated with AWSC or the remaining member firms.

[...]

The Tribunal finds that Claimants cannot take with them the property to which Arthur Andersen LLP holds legal title. Moreover, it would be unfair to allow the ACBU member firms to keep a name built through the common effort of those men and women who had preceded the actual AWSC partners.

[...]

Therefore, effective on December 31, 2000 Claimants shall cease using the Andersen name or any derivative thereof, or any other name AWSC is authorized to regulate and shall cease to represent themselves as in any way associated with AWSC or the AABU member firms.

The term for the ACBU member firms to cease using the Andersen name and to cease to represent themselves as associated with Respondents has been fixed by the Tribunal in order to allow Claimants a reasonable time frame to make the necessary changes and adjustments resulting from the resolution of the present counterclaim.

4. Claimants' obligation to return and cease using Andersen Technology

[...]

[...] Neither the MFIFAs, nor any other AWO governing document known to the Tribunal provide an answer. Therefore, the general principles of law are the appropriate rules to decide this matter.

Under general principles of law, contracts must be interpreted according to the common intention of the parties. [7] If the intention cannot be established, the contract should be interpreted in light of the meaning reasonable persons of the same kind as the parties would give to it in the same circumstances. [8]

It would not be reasonable to hold - and reasonable persons of the same kind as the parties to this arbitration could not possibly claim - that the member firms not paying for or participating in the development of Andersen Technology are common owners of such technology or that the entities which funded and developed it are bound to forfeit their rights to those who have no title thereto.

Equity would not dictate a different solution. Indeed, the Tribunal found that the Respondent member firms established a broad-based consulting practice that competes with Claimants' activities. For this reason, it would be unfair to compel the ACBU member firms to surrender their technology which would capacitate the competing AABU member firms in Claimants' core activities.

[...]

VII. AWARD

Upon the issues addressed by the Tribunal, it is hereby adjudged:

A. The Respondent AABU member firms did not materially breach their obligations to Claimants under the Member Firm Interfirm Agreements on any of the grounds alleged by the ACBU member firms.

B. AWSC breached its material obligations to Claimants under the Member Firm Interfirm Agreements by failing to coordinate the practices of the ACBU member firms with those of the AABU member firms.

C. AWSC did not breach its material contractual and fiduciary obligations to Claimants under the Member Firm Interfirm Agreements by adopting a Resolution creating the "AWO Protection Committee".

D. Claimants acted in good faith, with a proper basis and in accordance with the Member Firm Interfirm Agreements in filing their Request for Arbitration and in their subsequent actions in connection with the arbitration proceedings.

E. The relief requested by Claimants can be granted even if less than all the AWO member firms are parties to the present arbitration.

F. Claimants are excused from any further obligations under the Member Firm Interfirm Agreements to the AWSC and the AABU member firms as a result of AWSC's fundamental non-performance of its contractual and fiduciary obligations under the Member Firm Interfirm Agreements.

G. Claimants are not entitled to restitution or to recover from Respondents any sums by way of damages, interest or compensation.

H. Claimants are not bound to make any termination payments or to pay any other damages to Respondents.

I. Claimants shall meet all their obligations under the Member Firm Interfirm Agreements through and including the date of termination thereof.

J. No later than December 31 , 2000 Claimants shall cease using the "Andersen" name or any derivative thereof or any other name AWSC is authorized to regulate and shall cease to represent themselves as associated with Respondents.

K. Claimants shall return and cease using the Andersen Technology jointly owned, controlled and developed by Claimants and the Respondent member firms. Claimants shall keep the Andersen Technology jointly owned, controlled and developed by the ACBU member firms.

L. Claimants shall not reimburse AWSC for the costs, expenses and liabilities, including attorneys' fees, incurred by AWSC as a result of the relief granted by the Tribunal. The Respondent member firms shall reimburse AWSC for its costs, expenses and liabilities, including attorneys' fees incurred in the present arbitration as set forth in Paragraph 8.1 of the Member Firm Interfirm Agreements.

M. All the amounts placed in escrow including interest thereon, in respect of obligations owed to or for the benefit of the Respondent AABU member firms, shall be paid to said Respondent AABU member firms as directed by AWSC. All costs, expenses and liabilities arising from that escrow and incurred by the parties shall be paid by Claimants.

N. Claimants and Respondents shall pay the costs, expenses and liabilities incurred in the present arbitration including attorneys' fees, as set forth in Annex 3 hereto.

O. The Tribunal respectfully requests the Courts of the relevant jurisdictions to enforce this final award.

DONE and ORDERED in Geneva, Switzerland, this 28th day of July, 2000.

THE ARBITRATOR
Guilermo Gamba Posada

NOTES

1. Interim Award in the Arbitration of *Andersen Consulting Business Unit Member Firms vs. Arthur Andersen Business Unit Member Firms and Andersen Worldwide Société Coopérative*, ICC Arbitration Case No. 9797/CK/AER issued on April 29, 1999 at pp. 7-9.

2. June 5, 1996 Award on Preliminary Issues in ICC case No. 7375/OK.

3. UNIDROIT Principles of International Commercial Contracts, Article 1.7.

4. UNIDROIT Principles of International Commercial Contracts, Article 5.4(2): "to the extent that an obligation of a party involves a duty of best efforts in the performance of an activity, that party is bound to make such efforts as would be made by a reasonable person of the same kind in the same circumstances."

5. UNIDROIT Principles of International Commercial Contracts, Article 1.7.

6. UNIDROIT Principles of International Commercial Contracts, Articles 7.3.1(1) and 7.3.5(1).

7. UNIDROIT Principles of International Commercial Contracts, Article 4.1(1) and Principles of European Contract Law, Article 5:101(1).

8. UNIDROIT Principles of International Commercial Contracts, Article 4.1(2) and Article 5:101(3) of the Principles of European Contract Law, substantially contains the same pr provision.

Sources

Original in English:
The full text of the award is published in 15 Mealey's International Arbitration Report 2000, Issue 8, A1 - A45.

Commented on by:
M.J. BONELL, A 'Global' Arbitration Decided on the Basis of the UNIDROIT Principles: In re Andersen Consulting Business Unit Member Firms v. Arthur Andersen Business Unit Member Firms and Andersen Worldwide Société Coopérative, in 17 Arbitration International (2001), 249 *et seq.*

and by

F. BLASÉ, Proposing a New Road Map for an Old Minefield. The Determination of the Rules Governing the Substance of the Dispute in International Commercial Arbitration, in 20 Journal of International Arbitration (2003).

Date: ***August 2000***
Adjudicating Court: ***ICC International Court of Arbitration***
Number: ***9651***
Parties: ***Unknown***

Keywords

CHOICE OF LAW CLAUSE – SCOPE – INTERPRETATION ACCORDING TO UNDERSTANDING OF REASONABLE BUSINESS PEOPLE

FRAUD AND MISREPRESENTATION IN CONTRACT NEGOTIATION – APPLICABLE DOMESTIC LAW IN ACCORDANCE WITH "COMMON UNDERSTANDING OF ALL CIVILIZED JURISPRUDENCE" – REFERENCE TO ARTICLES 2.15(2) [ART. 2.1.15(2) OF THE 2004 EDITION], 3.8 AND 3.9 OF THE UNIDROIT PRINCIPLES

Abstract

Claimant, a German company, concluded two contracts with Defendant, an Indian company, for the delivery and installation of industrial equipment. Claimant delivered equipment which according to Defendant was defective. When Defendant declared its intention to return the equipment, Claimant filed a request for arbitration.

Defendant argued first of all that the contract was null and void due to Claimant's fraudulent misrepresentation during negotiations and secondly that Claimant had delayed delivery and delivered defective equipment.

The first issue addressed by the Arbitral Tribunal concerned the applicable law. The contract contained a provision entitled "Law and arbitration" stating that "the law of Switzerland shall be applicable to this contract" and that "all disputes arising in connection with this contract" shall be submitted to arbitration. According to Claimant the law applicable to the merits of the dispute was Swiss law, whereas according to Defendant reference to Swiss law in the arbitration agreement was limited to "the contract" while the issue of fraudulent misrepresentation during negotiations should be settled according to Indian law as the law of the place of negotiations and/or in accordance with the principles of justice, equity and good conscience. The Arbitral Tribunal decided that Swiss law was the only applicable law.

In interpreting the choice of law clause contained in the contract it expressly referred to Articles 4.1 and 4.2 of the UNIDROIT Principles stating that, in the absence of a common intention between the parties, contract terms should be interpreted according to the meaning that reasonable persons as the same kind as the parties would give to them in the same circumstances. According to the Arbitral Tribunal reasonable businesspersons would understand the choice of law clause as covering all kinds of disputes which might arise in connection with the contract without distinguishing between issues relating to the contract after its conclusion and issues relating to the formation process.

With respect to the merits of the case the Arbitral Tribunal pointed out that the issue of fraud and misrepresentation would not be adjudicated otherwise were Indian law to be found to apply. Indeed according to the Arbitral Tribunal the avoidance of a contract for wilful deception is "a common understanding of all civilized jurisprudence" and in this context the Arbitral Tribunal expressly referred to Articles 2.15(2) [Art. 2.1.15(2) of the 2004 edition], 3.8 and 3.9 of the UNIDROIT Principles.

Full Text

WHAT IS THE LAW APPLICABLE?

[1] The Parties have filed, for Claimant, a "Submission on the Question ofApplicable Law" dated 15 October 1998, with annexure [sic] and for Defendant a "Submission" of 14 August 1998 supplemented by a file containing seven English cases, as well as the following texts:
- The Principles of European Contract Law, 1997
- EC Convention on the Law Applicable to Contractual Obligations, Rome, 1980
- Principles of International Commercial Contracts, 1994, UNIDROIT
- UNCITRAL Notes on Organizing Arbitral Proceedings
- Convention on the Law Applicable to International Sales of Goods, The Hague, 1955
- Convention on the Law Applicable to Contracts for the International Sale of Goods, The Hague, 1986
- United Nations Convention on the Recognition and Enforcement of Foreign Arbitral Awards, NewYork, 1958.

Hearings were held in Zurich on.. . to hear Parties on this issue. Both Counsel requested only an "indication" on this point, not necessarily an award.. . After extensive deliberation, the Arbitral Tribunal instructed the Parties. . . that they would have to structure their case on the tentative assumption that Swiss law would be held applicable, and they so did.

[2] When preparing this Award, the Arbitral Tribunal reconsidered the question of applicable law and we found as follows.

POSITION OF THE PARTIES

Claimant's case

[3] Claimant contends that the seat of the arbitration being in Zurich entails that the 12th chapter of the Swiss Private International Law of 18 December 1987 [hereafter PIL] is applicable, and notably article 176, para. i PIL, which provides that "The provisions of this chapter shall apply to all arbitrations if the seat of the arbitral tribunal is situated in Switzerland and if, at the time when the arbitration agreement was concluded, at least one

of the Parties had neither its domicile nor its habitual residence in Switzerland". The two requirements of article 176 PIL are met in this case, namely
Parties have chosen Zurich for seat of the Arbitral Tribunal...
Parties have neither their domicile nor their habitual residence in Switzerland.

[4] Claimant further cites article 187, para. i PIL, providing that "The Arbitral Tribunal shall decide the case according to the rules of law chosen by the Parties".

[5] Claimant also points to article 13, para. 3 of the ICC Rules of Conciliation and Arbitration of 1 January 1988 (applicable under. . . the Terms of Reference agreed upon by the Parties. . This provision reads as follows:
The Parties shall be free to determine the law to be applied by the arbitrator to the merits of the dispute. In the absence of any indication by the Parties as to the applicable law, the arbitrator shall apply the law designated as the proper law by the rule of conflict which he deems appropriate.

[6] It is Claimant's case that the principle of party autonomy, allowing the Parties to choose the law applicable to the merits, is both a tradition of Swiss law and a general principle of conflicts of laws. Claimant cites the ICC Interim Award of 16 November 19841 to show that this principle has already been applied in the case of a litigation between a US supplier and an Indian buyer.

[7] Claimant further contends that the choice of law by the Parties has to be regarded as determinative as to all aspects of their dispute, and namely also as concerns the possible nullity of the Contract for misrepresentation (as has been pleaded on behalf of the Defendant).

Defendant's case

[8] Defendant states its case on the merits to be on the basis that Claimant obtained the Contract by fraud and material misrepresentation, further that the performance certificates were also obtained by fraud, and that Claimant is guilty of a fundamental breach of contract. These issues would require to be resolved in accordance with Indian law and/or in accordance with the principles of justice, equity and good conscience.

[9] Defendant also accepts that a contract can indicate a choice of law by the parties. 1986-1990 at p 23... However, it states that there may be exceptions on the grounds of public policies. Further, there are accepted limitations on the choice of law by the parties. Now in the present case, according to the Defendant, the Contract has the closest with India.

1. there are accepted limitations on the choice of law by the parties. [...]

[10] As concerns the reissue of promissory notes, such a claim is based on general principles of law, and on principles of justice, equity and good conscience, but not, according to Defendant, on any clause of the Contract. However the Arbitral Tribunal shall not discuss that issue further, as Claimant no longer claims for reissue of the promissory notes.

Claimant now requests an order for payment of the Contract price.. . This claim is undoubtedly based on the Contract...

[11] As concerns its own claims, Defendant and Counter-Claimant insists that they are based essentially on allegations of misrepresentation and fraud in obtaining the Contract. The negotiations, pre-contractual and post contractual, were conducted mostly in India. If misrepresentation and/or fraud are alleged to have been made in India, Indian law would apply rather than Swiss law, all the more so because an Indian company needs various permissions to enter into such contracts as the one under consideration at present, and a number of representations made by the foreign party are carried by the Indian party to the Indian Government.

[12] Moreover, where one of the Parties claims that the Contract itself is tainted by faud, it would be incongruous to decide this issue by reference to the contractual choice-of-law clause.

[13] Finally, Defendant submits that the principles of justice, equity and good conscience should apply. Fraud is accepted in all civilized jurisprudences. The principles of UNIDROIT on International Commercial Contracts are a useful guide in relation to such principles of justice and equity as are internationally acceptable.

FINDINGS OF THE ARBITRAL TRIBUNAL

[14] The rule under Swiss Law is that the interpretation of a choice-of-law clause is subject to the law chosen by the parties (article 116, para. 2 infine PIL). The true intent of the legislature may be apparent from article i 18, para. i, second sentence of the 1978 draft to the PIL: (translation: "The [choice-of-law] is subject to the law of which the choice is in issue").

Law applicable to the choice-of-law clause

[15] Now, Article 116, para. 2, second sentence is innovative, in the sense that the case law anterior to the 1987 PIL seems to have entertained tile notion that the lexfori would be applicable to the choice of law. Therefore, it is no longer possible indiscriminately to rely on the cases published before i January 1989 (entry into force of PIL of 18 December 1987) and notably on ATF 7911295. As a consequence, modern commentary is to the effect that the principle of party autonomy, its extent and its limitations, are governed by the law chosen by the parties.

[16] Therefore, the applicable law to the interpretation of the Section 5 of the Contract is the Swiss law as the law chosen by the Parties.

[17] Abroad, tile more traditional approach to this question seems to have been, at least in the past, that the lexfori would be applicable to the construction of the choice-of-law clause.'

[18] Finally, international arbitral awards sometimes refer to a "transnational rules on conflicts of laws". Presumably, if found to exist on that particular point, such a

"transnational rule" might indicate as applicable to construe a choice-of-law clause either tile law chosen by the parties or the *lex fori*.

[19] Whatever the method that would be followed, Swiss law is applicable in the present case to the interpretation of section S of the Contract, since Parties opted for the Swiss law to govern their Contract and the lexfori is that of Switzerland as seat of the arbitral tribunal under a clause on the resolution of disputes that is not the object of any controversy between tile Parties, save for the present question of the applicable law.

Principle of interpretation under Swiss law

[20] It is a tenet of Swiss law that no interpretation is necessary when the true and common intent of the party is clearly expressed in the Contract. Article 4.1 of the UNIDROIT Principles also refers to the common intent of tile parties.
However, the governing principle for the interpretation of any declaration of intent is the so-called "principle of confidence" ('*Vertrauensgrundsatz*", "*principe de la confiance*") ' under which a seemingly clear wording may be shown not to convey the true intent of the parties." According to that principle, the declaration is neither understood in tile sense of what the declaring party may have had in mind nor in accordance with the literal sense of tile wording, but in the meaning which the addressee could in good faith attribute to it. As good faith requires the addressee to consider all aspects allowing the understanding of the declared intent, tile wording is not the only test.' Article 4.2(2) of the UNIDROIT Principles provides for tile same test, article 1.7 of the same Principles imposing further the overriding duty of good faith.

Proper interpretation

[21] In the present case, there is a clear wording: under para. i the "Contract" is the subject matter of the agreement and is subject to Swiss law, whereas para. 2 concerns "all disputes arising in connection with the agreement". That seems at first sight to leave no doubt as to the interpretation of section S. Nonetheless, as the Parties may or may not have thought that a dispute might involve something else than a contractual issue, the wording alone is not decisive.

[22] As Counsel for Claimant was questioned on that very wording during the hearing held... in Zurich, her answer was that the wording of that clause was standard. Under "Contract" should be understood everything which is connected with the Contract, also including tile conclusion of the Contract and precontractual negotiations. Counsel for Defendant, on the other hand, declared that there is a marked difference between the two paragraphs of Section 5.

[23] Now, under the principle of confidence, would not a reasonable businessman reading section S in its entirety think that all disputes arising in connection with the said agreement should be governed by the law chosen by the Parties in the preceding paragraph? All those disputes should certainly be referred to arbitration. In fact, it is not obvious that reasonable businessmen would be alert to the difference between a "contractual issue" and "an issue arising in connection with a contract".
Furthermore, it would appear somewhat strange if businessmen would, as a matter of common intent, choose two different laws to rule on their relationship, to wit the law of

the Contract and some other law for the negotiation of the agreement. Finally, it might be well assumed that a reasonable businessman would consider that a wrongful act which would allegedly have been committed during the negotiation of the Contract would be related more closely to tile contractual side of the case.
In this regard, it will be noted that under Swiss law, the most authoritative commentary is to the effect that precontractual liability is not a case of tortious liability, but a case of contractual liability subject to article 97 CO rather than article 41 CO, or a case of sui generis liability. The Arbitral Tribunal does not have to decide on this particular controversy at that point in time. The controversy itself is, however, sufficient to show why reasonable businessmen would understand section S of the agreement as not dividing the disputes arising "in connection with" the Contract into two categories, to wit the "contractual ones" and the "precontractual ones", even if they were to be alert to the difference between "contractual issues" and "issues arising in connection with the contract", which is uncertain.

[24] Therefore, the Arbitral Tribunal finds that section S contains a choice-of-law clause that is also intended to bear on any issue relating to the conclusion of the Contract.

Severability of the choice-of-law clause

[25] Is tile choice of law clause severable in the sense that it is not tainted by any possible misrepresentation or fraud as to the main contract?
(a) The doctrine of severability of the arbitration clause is generally admitted nowadays, in the sense that tile validity of the arbitration clause is independent from the main contract.
(b) The issue before us is whether the choice-of-law clause is also to be applied where the whole contract is alleged to be vitiated by fraud or misrepresentation.

One authority has been cited by Claimant. Another authority states that "Parties do not expect that on issues of formation and validity of the choice-of-law agreement, a law other than the chosen law could apply (...) Both the *lex fori* and the objectively determined *lex causae* should be excluded in that regard (...) the objective *lex causae* because the parties did not want to have it applied to their contract."
In fact, such independence of the choice-of-law clause had been recognized a long time ago by the Federal Tribunal. It explains the solution that the legislature adopted in article 116, para. 2 PIL: "because the contract choosing the applicable law is independent from the main contract", 17 it is well possible that the form requirement governing the choice-of-law clause might be different from the form requirement governing the main agreement. Very well-known authors also state that "the law which (if the choice-of-law as made by the parties is not vitiated) is to govern the contract determines if tile choice-of-law clause is valid or invalid, for example because of mistake, misrepresentation or fraud", or that "claims for culpa in contrahendo and other claims relating to the formation of the choice-of-law clause fall under the law selected by the parties".
Therefore, the severability and independence of the choicc-of-law clause is a well-settled principle of Swiss international private law. Thus, Swiss commentary is to be followed when it states that the law chosen by the Parties is applicable even to the question whether the will of the parties was vitiated.

(c) Assuredly, the question was put to the Arbitral Tribunal by Counsel for Defendant whether Swiss law should apply to the question whether Swiss law governs the choice of law. Counsel for Defendant termed this to be a circulus vitiosus. However, this logical difficulty is only apparent. The principle of party autonomy is recognized by all the legal orders that are connected with the present contract, be it the German, the Indian or the Swiss legal order. The decision in Vita Food Products Inc. v. Unus Shipping Co. Ltd, 21 on which Defendant relied, allows party autonomy, as does article 116 PIL and article 27 of the German law on international private law of 25 July 1986 (following art. 3 of the Rome Convention). The principle of party autonomy is also recognized in international arbitration. Further, there seems to have been no decided case in England striking down a choice of law because it would not be "*bonafide* and legal". Therefore, the party autonomy seems to be really unrestricted in spite of the limitations that were mentioned by Lord Wright in the Vita Food case.

Now, party autonomy must be respected even where there was allegedly misrepresentation or fraud in the conclusion of the agreement. The first law to apply to the existence and validity of the choice-of-law contract is therefore the law "which would govern it ... if the contract or term were valid" (art. 8, para. i of the Rome Convention on the Law Applicable to Contractual Obligations of 1980; see to the same effect article 116, para. 2, 2d sentence PIL; the same solution was already adopted in article 2 III of The Hague Convention on the law applicable to tile international sale of movable property of 1955). It is only if "it appears from the circumstances that it would not be reasonable to determine the effect of [a party's] conduct in accordance with" that law that the law of this party's residence might apply (art. 8, para. 2 of the Rome Convention). Therefore, Swiss law is properly to apply to the question of the validity of the choice-of-law clause.

(d) Besides, it will be noted byway of superabundance that the English approach, if it were to be followed, would not entail a different solution.
According to a "decision of the Court of Appeal which is not without its difficulties", Mackender v. Feldia A. G., a choice of foreign law might not be effective in England if by English law there had been no consensus ad idem ("*e.g.* because of the plea of *non est factum*, or, perhaps, of fraud"). But even if the English rule referring to the *lex fori* would appear to be different from the Swiss one, the result would be the same, because Switzerland is the forum in the present case. It has been explicitly stated ... by Counsel for Defendant that Defendant did not contest the validity of the arbitration proceedings; the seat of the arbitral tribunal being in Switzerland, Swiss law shall apply to the question of fraud whether the Swiss law of conflict (art. 116, para. 2 PIL) or the English rule of the *lex fori* applies.

(e) Finally, it deserves mention that article V(i)(a) of the New York Convention on the Recognition and Enforcement of Arbitral Awards allows for a rejection of the arbitral award, among other grounds, when the agreement to arbitrate is not valid under the law which the parties have chosen. This shows that a concept common to all civilized jurisprudence is that the choice of law shall be respected even if the contract is alleged to be null and void for fraud or misrepresentation.

(1) While finding that Swiss law applies, the Arbitral Tribunal is however aware that the issue of fraud and misrepresentation would not be adjudicated otherwise were Indian law to be found to apply on these issues. Indeed, as has been said already, the avoidance of a

contract for willful deception is a common understanding of all civilized jurisprudence. For example, article 2.15(2) of the UNIDROIT Principles provides that "a party who negotiates or breaks off negotiations in bad faith is liable for the losses caused to the other party". Article 3.8 provides for avoidance of a contract by a party in case of fraudulent misrepresentation or fraudulent non-disclosure of circumstances which, according to reasonable commercial standards of fair dealing, the other party should have disclosed. Article 3.9 provides for the avoidance by reason of a threat leading a party to conclude the contract. Further, principles of justice, equity and good conscience will be legitimately applied by the Arbitral Tribunal for the purpose of determining the scope and manner of applying the law, and what should be the nature and extent of the relief to be granted, as those principles are referred to in Swiss law (see *e.g.* art. 4 Civil Code and art. 42, para. 2 CO).'

Sources

Excerpts of the award published in:
ICC International Court of Arbitration Bulletin, Vol. 12, No. 2, Fall 2001, 76 – 81.

Date: ***October 2000***
Adjudicating Court: ***ICC International Court of Arbitration (Partial Award)***
Number: ***10022***
Parties: ***Unknown***

Keywords

ARBITRAL TRIBUNAL REQUESTED TO TAKE INTO ACCOUNT "RELEVANT TRADE USAGES" (ART. 17 ICC RULES OF ARBITRATION) – REFERENCE INCLUDES BUT IS NOT LIMITED TO THE UNIDROIT PRINCIPLES AND THE PRINCIPLES OF EUROPEAN CONTRACT LAW

Abstract

Claimant and Defendant had entered into a series of agreements aimed at developing Defendant into an efficient cement producer. Notwithstanding a choice of law clause in the agreements stating that they are governed by Lithuanian law, Claimant invoked also the application of the UNIDROIT Principles and the Principles of European Contract Law as a source of trade usages referred to in Article 17 of the ICC Rules of Arbitration.

In a partial award addressing the issue of the applicable law, the Arbitral Tribunal acknowledged both sets of Principles represented the latest codification of international commercial trade usages. At the same time however it pointed out that unless they were expressly incorporated by agreement between the parties – which they were not in the case at hand – they were not of a mandatory but only of a persuasive nature. The Arbitral Tribunal decided that it would refer, when necessary, to "the relevant trade usages" according to Article 17 of the ICC Rules of Arbitration, and that such reference included but was not limited to the UNIDROIT Principles and the Principles of European Contract Law.

Full Text

APPLICABLE LAW

'[1] According to article 17 of the Rules, the primary Fonti of the law applicable to the merits of the dispute is determined by the will of the parties. In article 5 of the Export Company Agreement, as well as in article 4 of the AEER [Agreement on Exclusive Export Rights, Upgrading of the Plant and Delivery of Cement], the parties have agreed that: "This agreement is governed by Lithuanian law." This choice of law clause has been interpreted as providing that Lithuanian law is to govern both the formation of the contract and the rights and duties of the parties arising from the contract as well. Throughout the proceedings the choice of Lithuanian law has not been disputed by the parties. (Claimant has expressly confirmed that the applicable law is Lithuanian and Respondents have impliedly confirmed this choice by invoking the provisions of the respective Lithuanian laws and arguing their applicability)

[2] In its closing arguments Claimant has expressed the view that it is legitimate to look to the UNIDROIT Principles of International Commercial Contracts and the Principles of European Contract Law as a Fonti of usage, customs and practice and that they are to be relied on when interpretation of the law is necessary in order to determine the parties' rights and obligations. Article 17 of the Rules confirms reliance on trade usage: "In all cases the Arbitral Tribunal shall take account of the provisions of the contract and the relevant trade usage's." Both sets of principles represent the latest codification of international commercial trade usage's. However, unless expressly incorporated by agreement between the parties, which they are not, they are not of mandatory but only of persuasive nature. Therefore, when necessary the Tribunal refers in this Award to "the relevant trade usage's" and such reference includes, but is not limited to, the UNIDROIT Principles and Principles of European Contract Law'

Sources

Excerpts of the award published in:
ICC International Court of Arbitration Bulletin, Vol. 12, No. 2, Fall 2001, 100.

Date: ***October 2000***
Adjudicating Court: ***ICC International Court of Arbitration***
Number: ***10335***
Parties: ***Unknown***

Keywords

CONTRACT GOVERNED BY A PARTICULAR DOMESTIC LAW – REFERENCE TO THE UNIDROIT PRINCIPLES TO DEMONSTRATE THAT SOLUTION FOUND UNDER DOMESTIC LAW CORRESPONDS TO MODERN INTERNATIONAL COMMERCIAL LAW

CONTRACT INTERPRETATION – IN ACCORDANCE WITH PARTIES' INTENTION AND THE PRINCIPLE OF GOOD FAITH TAKING INTO ACCOUNT TRADE USAGES (SEE ARTS. 173 AND 200 OF THE GREEK CIVIL CODE; ARTS. 1.7, 1.8, 4.1 - 4.3 OF THE UNIDROIT PRINCIPLES)

Abstract

Claimants, two Greek companies, and Defendants No. 1 and No. 2, two French companies, entered into a series of agreements concerning the purchase of shares in a company listed on the Athens stock exchange from a Greek State entity and the allotment of these shares among themselves. The dispute arose when Defendants refused to pay their part of the purchase price, thus prompting the seller to call the first demand guarantee issued in its favour by a bank on request by Claimants and Defendants and the bank subsequently to demand the refund of the guarantee paid to the seller.

The agreements in question contained a choice of law clause in favour of Greek law.

In order to decide the merits of the case the Arbitral Tribunal proceeded to a careful interpretation of the agreements in question. In doing so it relied first of all on the Greek Civil Code Article 173 stating "[w]hen interpreting a declaration of will, the true intention shall be sought without sticking to the literal meaning of the words", and Article 200 stating "[c]ontracts shall be interpreted according to the requirements of good faith taking into account business usages". Yet the Arbitral Tribunal also referred to the similar provisions to be found in §§ 133 and 157 of the German Civil Code, § 914 of the Austrian Civil Code and Article 18 of the Swiss law of obligations, and in order to demonstrate that "modern international commercial law is evolving in the same direction" expressly referred to Articles 1.7, 1.8 and 4.1 - 4.3 of the UNIDROIT Principles.

Full Text

'Claimants assert a right ex articles 383,385 Greek Civil Code (CC.) to be compensated for damages resulting from delayed and ultimately non-performance of [Respondent No. 2]'s obligation to pay its share of the purchase price to [the seller].

The Shareholders' Agreement. . ., after identifying the Parties to it, introduces on little more than one typed page to its history and business background.

The clause cited by Claimants and Respondents as a possible Fonti of an obligation which may have been breached, reads as follows:
1. Payment Responsibility Each Party shall be solely responsible for the payment of the purchase price of the shares which correspond to its participation.
In order to support the Claimants' claim two questions would have to be answered in the affirmative: (1) Is the Shareholders' Agreement at all applicable to the acquisition of shares from [the seller]? (2) Does the Shareholders' Agreement create an obligation, on the part of Respondent No. 2, to pay its part of the purchase price to [the seller]?

In both respects, Claimants have made affirmative assertions while Respondents have denied both.

It is submitted that the language of the provision as such does neither permit to answer the question as to the Agreement's sphere of application nor does it indicate to whom the purchase price corresponding to each Party's quota shall be paid. As the sphere of application, of course, will only be revealed if one looks at the Agreement in its entirety I shall first turn to the second question.

The obligee of the obligation to pay, *i.e.* the recipient of the payment for which responsibility is described is not named at all. Taking a grammatical approach to interpreting clause 1, the salient features are rather the word "solely" as well as the emphasis on responsibility for the payment of those shares "which correspond to its [*i.e.* the Party's] participation". "Solely" having the meaning of "alone" or "only", taken together with the last five words of the clause therefore, suggests that the provision's gist is to limit and circumscribe each Party's obligation rather than imposing any such obligation.

Claimants from the very outset have drawn the Arbitrator's attention to the fact that, for the purposes of interpreting a declaration of will and, for that matter, a contract, the two arguably most important provisions of the Greek Civil Code (CC.) are articles 173 and 200. They read:

Article 173
"When interpreting a declaration of will the true intention shall be sought without sticking to (the literal meaning of) the words".

and

Article 200
"Contracts shall be interpreted according to the requirements of good faith taking into account business usages".

Both provisions are well known as common heritage of and fundamental to most civil-law systems, and in particular to the civil codes of the so-called germanic legal family. For example, §~ 133, 157 of the German Civil Code are identical. § 914 of the Austrian Civil Code and article 18 Swiss Law of Obligations enshrine the same principle. Modern international commercial law is evolving in the same direction (*cf.* for example, articles 1.7, 1.8, 4.1-4.3 of the UNIDROIT Principles of International Commercial Contracts).

Both Claimants and Respondents agree that the telos of the provisions quoted is to strike a balance between a subjective and an objective approach to determine what the "true" meaning is, when the parties to a contract, at a later stage, find themselves in disagreement. They have quoted Greek authorities and I find confirmation in this respect in SYMEONIDES, "The General Principles of the Civil Law" in: KERAMEUS/KOZYRIS (eds.), Introduction to Greek Law, 2d ed. (Deventer/Boston, 1993) pp. 53, 68.

Claimants and Respondents, at least initially, further agreed that articles 173, 200 apply when there are doubts and the need to clarify and, in particular, gaps and ambiguities in the exchange of declarations and the wordings of a contractual provision. Only recently Claimants, citing two older supreme court cases and two writers, have put forward the theory that all declarations of will (and not only ambiguous or incomplete ones) are subject to interpretation and, moreover and citing two high court decisions, that the judge "has an unlimited freedom to evaluate all the elements presented to him (either written or not) and draw conclusions, using the common sense rules, as well as his experience and common knowledge"... Respondents contest this analysis, citing both doctrinal writings and case law, including three supreme court cases...

I do not see an irreconcilable contrast of theory. Of course, all declarations are, logically speaking, subject to interpretation. But it is equally clear that interpreting an unambiguous term or phrase will necessarily result in identifying that unambiguous meaning. By the same token, no judge or arbitrator will ever disregard the letter of a contract nor will he hold that there is a lacuna where the parties have merely agreed (to his eyes and with hindsight) on an "unjust" allocation of risks. Finally, it appears safe to say that, however far the theory of "supplementing", "gap-filling" or "integrating" interpretation may be stretched, never will it reach beyond the substantive boundaries of the contract giving, for example, to one party something which that party may have tried, but was unable, to obtain in the negotiation process. The freedom of the judge or arbitrator may be unlimited in a procedural sense, but it is undoubtedly limited by the law and the parties' freedom to determine the content of their contracts, *cf.* art. 361 Greek Civil Code.

Finally, Claimants.. . and Respondents. . . agree on the elements interpretation will draw on, namely the document in its entirety, surrounding facts, related documents, negotiations, interests of the parties, purposes of the agreement and custom.

Turning now to the document in its entirety, the analysis of the text will at the same time be aimed at understanding its clause 1 and the Agreements' sphere of application.

The Shareholders' Agreement's Preamble, after describing the target ([X]) and the (anticipated) successful outcome of the bidding process as well as Respondent No. 2's and Claimants' respective quota in the shares to be acquired from [the seller], turns to the next stage, the (anticipated) internal and final division of the shares. The bid and this second stage are clearly distinguished.

After setting out the (internally and not *vis-à-vis* [the seller]) envisaged allotment of the shares among Respondent No. 2 and Claimants, the Preamble defines the end of the entire transaction ("For the purpose of achieving the above shares allocation") as well as the means to be employed ("the Parties hereto and [Respondent No. 1]. undertake.."). Only thereafter does the document set out the agreement proper: "*In view of the above*, (emphasis added; *i.e.* the final allotment) and of *the impending acquisition of the shares* (emphasis added), *the Parties agree as follows*" (emphasis added).

It is undisputed among the Parties to this arbitration that the technique to be employed for the acquisition of the shares for [the seller] was to be a reverse leveraged buyout... It is equally undisputed that this was the very purpose to bring in the "vehicle". . ., *i.e.* Respondent No. 2. Lastly, it is undisputed that [the seller] would not have agreed to substitute Respondent No. 2 for the successful official (co-)bidder, Respondent No. 1. All this is reflected in the Agreement's Preamble which distinguishes (1) acquisition from [the seller] (by Respondent No. 1 and Claimants), (2) re-allotment for purposes of the financing scheme and the restructuring of the future group, (3) relationship of the eventual shareholders (Respondent No. 2 and Claimants) subsequent to the acquisition and to the intermediate stage of re-allotting the [X] shares.

Neither the written submissions nor the testimony given by Messrs.. . suggest that any of the Parties to this arbitration, at the time of signing of the Shareholders' Agreement, expected Respondent No. 2 to step into the shoes of Respondent No. 1 *vis-à-vis* [the seller] and to actually acquire the [X] shares.

To conclude, the text of the Agreement's Preamble, while alluding to the acquisition of the shares (and in this sense "applicable" to that first stage of the transaction), does not support the theory that Respondent No. 2 was under an obligation *vis-à-vis* Claimants to acquire and to pay the purchase price for those shares.

Turning now to outside elements for the Shareholders' Agreement's proper construction, related documents might be of assistance. The first one coming to mind, and indeed cited by Claimants in their brief dated. . ., is the Cooperation Agreement, signed on. . . and regulating the relationship of the same Parties with regard to their first bid... However, that bid was unsuccessful and rejected by [the seller]. The Shareholders' Agreement in question here and signed after the second bid had been successful, provides in its clause 12:

"This agreement included the complete agreement of the Parties hereto as to its subject matter and supersedes to any prior written or oral agreement between the Parties which are hereby declared null and void".

Therefore, the Cooperation Agreement, while certainly a predecessor in the history of the transaction, cannot provide guidance as to the interpretation of the Shareholders' Agreement which is in dispute in this arbitration. In any event, it does not support the Claimants' theory. On the contrary, although the Shareholders' Agreement was signed prior to the completion of the acquisition. . ., the Parties to it apparently deliberately

dropped a clause contained in the (superseded) Cooperation Agreement which provides that:
"The parties agree... to use their best endeavours in order to succeed in the final bid and acquire the Shares..."

At a later stage, a new draft Cooperation Agreement. . . contained a clause i identical to the previous one. However, this draft remained unexecuted.

The testimony given by Claimants' witness. . . corroborates the result that the parties, during the negotiations of what was to become the Agreement signed, had decided to cover only their post-acquisition relationship.

Counsel for Respondents: "There were things that you decided not to regulate, which if you were to make another agreement of this sort now you might decide to regulate?"

[Claimants' witness]: ". . Of course, since I have the knowledge now, I would regulate it".

And: I would ask [Respondent No. i] for the money."

Shareholders' agreements are highly negotiated made-to-measure documents. Consequently, custom as one of the accepted tools for interpreting declarations of will is not of assistance. The interests of the parties being entirely subjective (and in the case at hand in open conflict) and the negotiations and the purpose of the contract being reflected in the history from the various drafts to the Agreement executed on.. ., the ways to discover the meaning of clause 1 asserted by Claimants are thus exhausted.

To sum up, neither does clause 1, to the best of my understanding, establish an obligation for Respondent No. 2 to pay for its share of the purchase price to [the seller] nor does it say that completion of the share purchase is owed to the Claimants.

To my eyes and according to my experience, with similar transactions, the Respondents' interpretation of clause 1, namely that it refers to and limits the responsibility of Respondent No.2 and Claimants to pay [Respondent No. 1] in consideration for the (second-stage) re-allotment of the [X] shares, is highly plausible. But Respondents do not have to prove that. Claimants had the burden of proof for the facts in support of their claim and they have been unable to discharge it as far as the alleged breach of clause 1 is concerned.'

Sources

Excerpts of the award published in:
ICC International Court of Arbitration Bulletin, Vol. 12, No. 2, Fall 2001, 102 – 106.

Date: **November 27, 2000**
Country: **New Zealand**
Adjudicating Court: **Court of Appeal of New Zealand**
Number: **(2000)NZCA 350**
Parties: **Hideo Yoshimoto v. Canterbury Golf International Limited**

Keywords

CONTRACT FOR SALE OF SHARES – REFERENCE TO CISG AND THE UNIDROIT PRINCIPLES DESCRIBED AS A "RESTATEMENT OF THE COMMERCIAL CONTRACT LAW OF THE WORLD [WHICH] REFINES AND EXPANDS THE PRINCIPLES CONTAINED IN [CISG]"

CONTRACT INTERPRETATION – LIBERAL INTERPRETATION (ART. 8 CISG; ARTS. 4.1 – 4.3 UNIDROIT PRINCIPLES) – PERMISSIBLE UNDER NEW ZEALAND LAW BUT NOT ENGLISH LAW

Abstract

A New Zealand corporation entered into a contract with a Japanese businessman, owner of all the shares of a business for the planned development of a golf course in New Zealand, for the purchase of all these shares. The contract contained a clause according to which the payment of the last instalment of the price was subject to the condition precedent that the purchaser obtains "all necessary authorizations or resource consents" for the development within a given period of time.

A dispute arose when the New Zealand corporation refused to pay the last instalment on the ground that not all authorizations which turned out to be necessary to commence the development of the project had been obtained. The Japanese seller objected that the clause in question referred only to those authorisations contemplated by the parties at the time of conclusion of the contract, and since the only missing consent was one that had become necessary only afterwards, the condition precedent envisaged in the clause had been fulfilled. Contrary to the court of first instance, the Court of Appeal unanimously decided in favour of the seller. In a very elaborated and learned opinion Thomas J conceded that on the basis of a strictly objective interpretation of the clause in question the conclusion might have been different, while only by taking into account the pre-contractual negotiations between the parties and their declarations of intention would it become clear that the parties actually attached to the clause in question the meaning contended by the seller. However, although pointing out that the admission of such extrinsic evidence would be in accordance with Article 8 of the United Nations Convention on International Contracts for the Sale of Goods (CISG), in force in New Zealand, as well as with Arts. 4.1 to 4.3 of the UNIDROIT Principles which he described as a "document which is in the nature of a restatement of the commercial contract law of the world [and which] refines and expands the principles contained in the United Nations Convention", he decided not to take a similar approach in the case at hand and to stick to a literal or objective interpretation of the clause in question. Desirable as it may be for the courts in New Zealand to bring the law in line with the international instruments mentioned above, the Privy Council in London would not have permitted them to do so as England has not yet adopted CISG and English common law was traditionally against the admissibility of extrinsic evidence for the purpose of interpreting written agreements.

Full Text

COURT OF APPEAL OF NEW ZEALAND

HIDEO YOSHIMOTO V. CANTERBURY GOLF INTERNATIONAL LIMITED [2000] NZCA 350 (27 NOVEMBER 2000)
Judgment:
27 November 2000
THOMAS J

INTRODUCTION

[1] The Court faces a difficult question of interpretation. A commercial contract is in issue. A particular clause might be said to have a plain meaning, and was held to have such a plain meaning by the Judge at first instance. The context, the commercial objective of the contract and its contractual matrix, however, point away from that meaning. In addition, reliable extrinsic evidence is available which confirms that this plain meaning is not what the parties actually intended. The question of interpretation, therefore, involves an examination of the contract, the commercial objective of the contract and the contractual matrix. The extrinsic evidence and the admissibility of that evidence must also be considered. Finally, the question arises whether, having regard to the approach of the English courts and bearing in mind that this Court is not the final appellate Court in this jurisdiction, it is open to it to have regard to such evidence and so give effect to the actual intention of the parties.

[2] The appellant, Mr Yoshimoto, is a Japanese businessman. As from November 1995, he owned all of the shares in a company named New Zealand Plan International Limited (NZPIL).NZPIL was formed to promote and develop an international golf course known as "The Lagoons" on the outskirts of Christchurch. The respondent, Canterbury Golf International Ltd (CGI), developed an interest in buying the shares in NZPIL.

[3] On 14 March 1996, Mr Yoshimoto and CGI entered into a contract whereby Mr Yoshimoto agreed to sell all the NZPIL shares in return for a total sum of $3.4 million. This sum was payable in three instalments. Two million dollars was payable by 22 April 1996.This sum was duly paid. A further $1 million was payable provided the necessary

planning authorisations or resource consents were secured within 12 months so as to enable the development to proceed. The final $400,000 was payable when CGI signed unconditional agreements for the sale of ten of the proposed 30 villas on the course.

[4] The main issue in this appeal is whether the condition precedent for the payment of the $1 million, that is, securing the necessary authorisations or resource consents within 12 months, was satisfied. There is no dispute as to the sum of $400,000 which is not yet due. Notwithstanding that the development can proceed, CGI rely upon what it claims are the plain terms of the contract to resist this claim. The second issue in this appeal is related to the first. It is whether CGI misrepresented to Mr Yoshimoto that the various consents would be obtained by approximately September 1996.It is alleged that this was an untrue statement about a present fact and that it induced Mr Yoshimoto to enter into the contract. CGI denies making any such misrepresentation and also denies that anything its representatives said induced Mr Yoshimoto to enter into the contract.

THE FACTUAL BACKGROUND

[5] In the early 1990s, NZPIL acquired an area of roughly 160 hectares located near Johns Road, Christchurch. This site was only a "couple of kilometres" north-east of Christchurch International Airport. It could be easily approached from Johns Road. Johns Road is connected to State Highway 1.

[6] The site, however, did not have direct access to Johns Road. It fronted onto another road, Coutts Island Road, but the detour required to get from State Highway 1, and from the Airport, to the site via this road made it an unattractive option. For the project to be commercially viable access from Johns Road was essential. NZPIL proposed to achieve this access via an unformed paper road running direct from its property to Johns Road.

[7] By late 1995 NZPIL experienced considerable financial difficulties. In November of that year, Mr Yoshimoto , together with the two other shareholders in the company at the time, entered into negotiations with representatives of CGI.A sale and purchase agreement was completed on 22 November .Under this agreement control of the resource consent process passed to CGI, subject only to the requirement that it consult with Mr Yoshimoto .The agreement was also conditional on CGI completing due diligence to its satisfaction within 60 days.

[8] Due diligence was carried out at premises rented by CGI in Christchurch. It uplifted all NZPIL's documents and plans. The project manager of CGI took positive steps to revive the resource consent process which had stalled under the management of NZPIL. Notwithstanding an agreed extension of the 60 day period, however, time for the completion of due diligence expired on 26 January 1996.In the result the agreement did not become unconditional. But CGI did not return NZPIL's documents and plans to Mr Yoshimoto as negotiations continued.

[9] Two further meetings took place without any positive outcome being achieved. It was not until a meeting on 28 February at Mr Yoshimoto 's lawyers' offices in Auckland that a heads of agreement was signed.Mr Yoshimoto was at this stage the sole shareholder in NZPIL. The meeting was apparently tense.The purchase price was the main bone of contention. Mr Yoshimoto wanted more for the land than CGI was willing to pay. His

position throughout was that the land was worth $3 million.After Mr Yoshimoto slammed a notebook shut, the representatives of CGI left the meeting, but before doing so they advised Mr Yoshimoto of the departure time of their later flight to Christchurch and how they could be contacted. They were invited back at about 4.30 or 5 pm and duly returned. The impasse as to price continued until the CGI representatives stepped outside the meeting room and then returned to suggest a compromise whereby the value of the land would be linked to whether the project proceeded or not. Mr Yoshimoto agreed to this proposal.

[10] In the result, the heads of agreement provided for the manner in which the purchase price of $3,400,000 would be paid. Paragraph 1(c) reads as follows:
(c)The sum of $1,000,000 will be paid to the Vendor immediately upon NZPIL or its successors or assigns obtaining the necessary consents to proceed with the development of the Lagoons. The definition of "necessary consents" is to be acceptable to the Vendor.
....

[11] The heads of agreement was made subject to the execution of a formal contract. The formal contract went through numerous drafts, but was finally executed on 14 March 1996.On that day, the draft before them was amended in handwriting by both parties and signed.

THE RELEVANT CONTRACTUAL TERMS

[12] The relevant provisions of the contract may be set out. Although the critical provision is cl 6.3 of the contract, it is pertinent to first set out recital D.

D. The Company has made application for resource consents, has promoted plan change number 11 to the Christchurch City Transitional Plan, has made submissions on the proposed Christchurch City Plan and has applied for other consents as are necessary to enable the Development (as later defined) to proceed.(Emphasis added).

Clause 6.3 (a version of which had been agreed at the 28 February meeting) then reads:
"6.3 It shall be a condition precedent to the Vendor's right to demand payment of the sum of $1,000,000 being part of the balance of the Purchase Price owing under this Agreement that the Company [CGI] obtains all necessary authorisations or resource consents to the Development within 12 months of the date of this agreement."

[...]

For completeness, cl 6.5 of the contract may also be set out:
"6.5 The Purchaser and the Guarantor undertake, covenant and agree with the Vendor that they shall take all practicable and reasonable steps and shall procure the Company or any associated party having responsibility for obtaining the necessary approvals to take all practicable and reasonable steps to procure the satisfaction of the conditions referred to in clause 6.3 above."

[13] On the face of it, the arrangement was a recipe for disaster. Making every allowance for the exigencies of the time, unknown facts or factors, and the beneficent perception of

hindsight, it is difficult to understand how Mr Yoshimoto or his legal advisers ever came to contemplate accepting the format which was adopted. The $1 million was only payable if and when planning approval for the development was obtained. But responsibility for obtaining that planning approval was vested in the purchaser, CGI, and a strict finite time was fixed within which that approval had to be obtained. If the necessary approvals, which were under the control of CGI, were not obtained within that time CGI stood to save $1 million, roughly a third of the value of the land if the development was to proceed. The very oddness of the arrangement suggests that there is more to it than meets the eye.

[14] In the event, CGI did not obtain a resource consent under the Christchurch City Proposed District Plan within the 12 month period stipulated in cl 6.3. That consent was not obtained until some five months later. Mr Yoshimoto nevertheless demanded payment of the $1 million in October 1996.CGI disputed that the sum was due and owing, and Mr Yoshimoto commenced proceedings against CGI in January 1997.

[15] The dispute was heard by Panckhurst J in the High Court at Christchurch on 9 February 1999.In short, the learned Judge held that the condition precedent in cl 6.3 had not been met as the resource consent under the Proposed Plan was necessary for the development and had not been obtained within the time specified in the contract. CGI was therefore not liable for the extra $1 million. He also held that Mr Yoshimoto 's claim that he was induced to enter into the contract by a misrepresentation failed. The statement relied on by Mr Yoshimoto was a genuinely held opinion, albeit optimistic, and was proffered with a significant reservation.

[...]

A QUESTION OF INTERPRETATION

[30] The essential question is whether cl 6.3 is to be construed to include, as a necessary consent, approval for the deletion of the notation showing the paper road as a road to be stopped under the Proposed Plan.

[31] Panckhurst J cannot be criticised for concluding that he was obliged to interpret and give effect to what he perceived to be effectively the plain meaning of the clause. The operative words in cl 6.3 are; "obtains all necessary authorisations or resource consents to the development". The learned Judge held, however, that the clause, as finally drafted, required a pragmatic approach. Payment of the extra $1 million was not dependent upon CGI obtaining every authorisation or consent but only those which were required to enable the project "in essence" to proceed. More technical authorities or consents relating to the detail of the project, as opposed to its broad essential character, need not be in hand. Noting that the definition of the development in the contract (para [12] above) included access off Johns Road, the learned Judge concluded that a resource consent under the Proposed Plan was essential if the development project was to proceed. Notwithstanding that he suspected that this consent was assured, it was a "necessary authorisation or resource consent to the development".

[32] I approbate Panckhurst J's pragmatic approach and readily agree that payment of the extra $1 million was not dependent upon CGI obtaining every authorisation or consent. In

my view, while the resource consent was necessary in the sense that the development could not commence without it being in place, it was not "necessary" within the meaning of that term in the contract. In other words, as at 14 March 1996 the parties did not contemplate or intend that a consent under the Proposed Plan was "necessary" before the obligation to pay the further $1 million arose. The consent fell on the other side of the literal divide.

[33] It may be noted in passing that no convincing reasons were advanced in evidence as to why consent under the Proposed Plan was necessary in the sense of being "in essence" necessary to proceed. The suggestion that it was not inevitable that the Proposed Plan would be brought into line with Plan Change 11 as that Plan Change was based on different objectives and policies may be true as a general proposition. But it is simply unrealistic to think that once Plan Change 11 had been endorsed, and endorsed so recently, the unfavourable designation of the road would not be removed in the absence of some very good or unexpected reason to the contrary. Nor was any indication given as to which objectives and policies of the Proposed Plan might preclude the development or place approval of the removal of the notation relating to the road in doubt. The parties, I believe, were correct to anticipate that if Plan Change 11 were approved any changes required to the Proposed Plan would realistically follow.

[34] In my view, therefore, the parties did not intend that consent to the removal of the designation under the Proposed Plan was a necessary consent to the development before the $1 million became due and payable. As a result, whilst CGI may seek to morally justify its retention of that sum on various extraneous grounds, as it has done, this sum represents a windfall to the company. It has obtained the land for the sum of $2.4 million having agreed that the value of the land with its development potential affirmed was $3.4 million.

[35] I believe that the meaning which I have identified is indicated by the contract, the commercial objective of the arrangement, and the matrix to the contract. Each may be examined in turn.

(1) ASSISTANCE FROM THE CONTRACT

[36] It is to be emphasised at the outset that, notwithstanding his perception that the clause could be given a plain meaning, Panckhurst J himself did not give cl 6.3 a literal construction. A literal construction would mean that all authorisations and resource consents required for the development would need to be obtained before the additional sum became payable. The development could not proceed if any authorisation or consent, however routine, had not been obtained. Yet, the learned Judge recognised that this literal meaning was not tenable. Indeed, Mr More, appearing for CGI, did not seek to maintain this construction. He accepted that, although certain of the outstanding authorisations and consents were of "fundamental importance", they would prove to be attainable, even though terms and conditions which attached to them might dictate some amendments to the project generally. In agreeing that not every authorisation was necessary, but only those which were required to enable the project "in essence" to proceed, the Judge held that the contractual formula was not rigid and that every consent or authorisation need not be in hand. The test was whether in essence the project was viable.

[37] I have already accepted that it is necessary to introduce this flexibility into the construction of cl 6.3.But at once it cannot be said that the plain meaning is the literal meaning. The literal meaning is being modified to make sense of the provision. An assessment is required as to whether the resource consent was "necessary to the essence of the project", or required to enable the project "in essence" to proceed, or whether it "in substance" became viable, or the like. It seems to me that once this point is reached the Court should be reluctant to impose a meaning on to the clause which may not accord with the parties' actual intention. The question is not whether the Court considers the resource consent "necessary", but whether a reasonable person in the position of the parties would have considered it necessary and therefore within the commercial arrangement which they had entered into for the payment of the full purchase price. It therefore becomes imperative to have regard to the context in which the clause appears and the commercial objective which the parties sought to achieve.

[38] The parties' perception of what was to be considered "necessary" is apparent from the wording of recital D. Of course, the recital does not override the terms of the contract. Argument on that issue was largely unhelpful. Rather, reference to the recital is of assistance in indicating what cl 6.3 means. The recital states that NZPIL "has made application for resource consent... and has applied for other consents as *are necessary to enable the development* (as later defined) *to proceed*". (Emphasis added).Thus, the recital explicitly referred to applications for consent which had been made at that time and described them as applications which were "necessary" for the development to proceed. The use of the word "necessary" in conjunction with the reference to the applications which had been made, at least to some degree, points to the meaning to be attributed to that word in cl 6.3.Although, as stated in the recital, submissions had been made on the Proposed Plan, no application for a resource consent had then been made in respect of it. The suggestion must be that the parties did not perceive the application to be one which was "necessary" to enable the development to proceed.

(2) THE COMMERCIAL OBJECTIVE

[39] Further, I consider that the commercial objective can be inferred from the overall structure of the arrangement underlying the payment of the purchase price. The commercial objective was to provide a differential purchase price depending on whether the development potential of the land was realisable or not. If the project were able to proceed the parties accepted that the value of the land was worth $1 million more than would be the case if it could not proceed. Certainly, the parties stipulated a 12 month period within which the necessary authorisations and consents had to be obtained. But that short time limit in itself suggests that the parties were addressing applications which were extant. In short, the commercial objective was to recognise the development potential of the land and the assumption (correct as it turned out) was that, with CGI using its best endeavours, that potential would be realised if and when the outstanding consents were obtained. This objective is substantially confirmed by reference to the contractual matrix.

(3) ASSISTANCE FROM THE MATRIX

[40] A number of matters can be fairly said to be part of the matrix to the contract. The first has just been mentioned, that is, the commercial objective of the arrangement. But

that objective may now be dealt with on a broader basis. It is clear that Mr Yoshimoto regarded the value of the land for the purposes of a development as being $3 million. That was the purchase price in the conditional agreement which did not proceed. An impasse then resulted as to the purchase price to be inserted in the heads of agreement. This impasse was resolved by recognising that the value of the land would be linked to whether or not the development potential of the land was realised. One million dollars was accepted by the parties as the difference in value with the parties expressly agreeing in the heads of agreement that the definition of "necessary consents" was to be acceptable to Mr Yoshimoto .This arrangement, then, represented the essence of the bargain which the parties had agreed. If the parties had intended that the consents to which cl 6.3 related would be open-ended, they would have had to contemplate the real possibility that the fundamental arrangement as to price could be thwarted and that CGI would obtain a windfall. Realistically speaking, any such notion is so improbable that it can be safely concluded that it was beyond the parties' contemplation.

[41] Secondly, NZPIL had already advanced the planning process before CGI assumed responsibility for that process. NZPIL had made the essential application to change the Transitional Plan and it had lodged submissions in respect of the Proposed Plan. CGI did not start the planning process afresh. In effect, it took over the procedures which had been initiated by NZPIL, together with the relevant plans and documents. Planning advice then obtained by CGI focused almost exclusively on the flood plains issue and the change required to the Transitional Plan. The Proposed Plan was to be left to one side. The relatively short period of 12 months within which to obtain full approval to Plan Change 11 was not unreasonable. Indeed, that proved to be the case, if only by 17 days. In short, CGI was effectively stepping into NZPIL's shoes, and it was believed that what NZPIL had begun could be completed by CGI in 12 months.

[42] Thirdly, it is to be noted that the consent required under the Proposed Plan did not require approval for a zoning change to permit the project as such. As recited by Panckhurst J, the Proposed Plan was favourable in relation to the Lagoons site in that it contained a special "Open Space 3D Zone" which was similar to the Special Resort and Recreation Zone introduced by Plan Change 11 into the Transitional Plan. Submissions to the Proposed Plan were required to ensure only that there were no "loose ends" and that the zoning matched the zone introduced by Plan Change 11.I n substance, all that was required under the Proposed Plan was the removal of the notation of the paper road as a "road to be stopped" so that access to the site would be brought into line with that which had been agreed to in Plan Change 11. Hence, the nature of the consent required under the Proposed Plan is not to be overstated.

[43] Fourthly, I have already pointed out that the arrangement under which CGI became responsible for obtaining the necessary consents and on which the payment of $1 million depended, was a recipe for disaster. Notwithstanding its obligation under cl 6.5 to take all practical and reasonable steps to obtain the consents, CGI had a $1 million incentive to prolong the process for which it was responsible beyond the year. It is virtually inconceivable that NZPIL would deliberately place such power in the hands of CGI, or that CGI could reasonably expect such control, unless it was thought by both parties that all "necessary" applications for the purposes of cl 6.3 had been identified and, indeed, were in train.

[44] Fifthly, while for the reasons given by Panckhurst J, Mr Yoshimoto must fail in his claim that CGI misrepresented to him that the outcome of the various consents would be obtained by approximately September 1996, that does not mean that the allegation is irrelevant to the question of interpretation. It is not denied that at the critical meeting on 28 February 1996 a representative of CGI indicated that the necessary approvals would or could be obtained by "September approximately". Nor can it now be questioned that this assurance was not a genuinely held opinion. But such a statement could only have been made if the parties accepted that all "necessary" consents had been identified. A period of no longer than seven months would elapse from the date of the meeting until the end of September. To contemplate that the necessary consents could be obtained within that time without being alert to what those consents were would have been unrealistic.

[45] Finally, the reference to the making of submissions in respect of the Proposed Plan in recital D shows that this Plan was not overlooked. Submissions were being made in respect of it. Yet, if it had been intended that the consent under the Proposed Plan was a necessary consent, it could be expected that the reference to the submissions on the Proposed Plan would have been replaced by a reference to an application for a resource consent under that Plan. Moreover, CGI were required by cl 6.5 to use its best endeavours to obtain the necessary consents. It is unlikely that the company would have been prepared to expose itself to liability under this provision without a clear understanding as to what it had to do in the ensuing year.

[46] All in all, therefore, the contractual matrix would suggest that the parties did not intend to include a consent under the Proposed Plan within the purview of cl 6.3.

[47] Since writing and circulating a draft of this judgment, Doogue and Salmon JJ have written concurring judgments agreeing with this conclusion. This being the case, the appeal will be allowed. I wish to go further, however, and examine the argument that reliable extrinsic evidence confirms that the parties did not intend a consent under the Proposed Plan to be a "necessary" consent for the purposes of cl 6.3.

EXTRINSIC EVIDENCE

[48] I am mindful that the question whether there is sufficient indication in the contract, the commercial purpose of the differential price, and the contractual matrix as discussed above to conclude that the necessary consents referred to in cl 6.3 are those which had already been contemplated is not an open and shut question. Along with the other members of the Court I consider that this meaning emerges securely enough. But it is a question on which I imagine judicial opinions could differ. It could still be asserted that the use of the word "necessary" gives cl 6.3 a "plain meaning" which would include the consent in issue. If reference is made to certain extrinsic evidence, however, there cannot be any real doubt that this view is at odds with the parties' actual intention. The scope of cl 6.3 was intended to be restricted to those consents which the parties had identified and which CGI had taken over from NZPIL. I therefore wish to confront the question whether regard may be had to that extrinsic evidence.

[49] This Court is fully aware of the problems associated with evidence of the parties' precontractual negotiations. Precontractual negotiations may not be unequivocal. They may simply indicate the changing thinking and position of the parties up to the time a

final consensus is reached and the contract is executed. I will therefore approach the evidence which was adduced by both parties relating to their conduct prior to 14 March 1996 with considerable caution. No evidence which can be said to be simply evidence of the parties' subjective intention need be considered. For this reason, I have confined my consideration to the earlier draft contracts, the changes made to cl 6.3, and an earlier recital relevant to that clause.

[...]

RECEIPT OF THE EXTRINSIC EVIDENCE?

[59] It is accepted that for reasons of commercial convenience the law insists on an objective theory of contract. Lord Steyn, writing extra-judicially, has pointed out that this involves adopting an external standard given life by using the concept of the reasonable person. Thus, in contract law effect must be given to the reasonable expectations of honest people. The expectations which will be protected are those that are, in an objective sense, common to both parties. Generally the law of contract is not concerned with the subjective expectations of a party. Thus, the function of the law of contract is to provide an effective and fair framework for contractual dealing, a function which requires an adjudication based on the reasonable expectation of parties.(Johan STEYN, "Contract Law: Fulfilling the Reasonable Expectations of Honest Men" (1997) 113 LQR 433, at 433-434).

[60] By and large, Lord Steyn continues, the objective approach to questions of interpretation serves the needs of commerce. It tends to promote certainty in the law and predictability in dispute resolution. The rule that evidence of the precontractual negotiations of the parties or their subsequent conduct cannot be used in aid of the construction of a written contract follows from the primary rule that the task of the court is simply to ascertain the meaning of the language of the contract. But, the distinguished jurist adds, the rationality of the law is important, and if this rule was absolute and unqualified it would sometimes defeat the reasonable expectations of commercial men. There has been, he observes, a shift away from a black-letter approach to questions of interpretation. The literalist methods of Viscount Simmonds are in decline. The purposive approach of Lord Reid and Lord Denning MR has prevailed.(Ibid, at 440).

[61] This shift away from the black-letter approach in the interpretation of contracts is most noticeably evident in the recent decision of the House of Lords in ICS Investors Compensation Scheme Ltd v. West Bromwich Building Society Ltd [1998] 1 All ER 98. In what must be regarded as a landmark statement - or restatement - of the law relating to the construction of contracts, Lord Hoffman begins by observing that a fundamental change has overtaken this branch of the law, particularly as a result of the speeches of Lord Wilberforce in Prenn v. Simmonds [1971] 3 All ER 237, at 240-242, and Reardon Smith Line Ltd v. Hansen-Tangen, Hansen-Tangen v. Sanko Steamship Co [1976] 3 All ER 570, which is not always sufficiently appreciated. Subject to an important exception, the result has been to assimilate the way in which such documents are interpreted by judges to the common-sense principles by which any serious utterance would be interpreted in ordinary life. Almost all the old intellectual baggage of legal interpretation has been discarded. The five principles which Lord Hoffman articulated are now so well

known that it is not necessary to set them out. They were repeated and adopted by this Court in Boat Park Ltd v. Hutchinson [1999] 2 NZLR 74, at 81-82.

[...]

THE INTENTION OF THE PARTIES

[71] While it may be presumed that the parties have intended what they have in fact said in the contract, the objective, enshrined in ancient authority, is to discover from the written agreement the intention of the parties. See, for example, Cholmondeley (Marquis of) v. Clinton (1820) 2 Jac & W 1, at 91.To refer to extrinsic evidence to assist that objective would not seem to be a radical suggestion. As Wigmore has said: "The history of the law of interpretation is the history of a progress from a stiff and superstitious formalism to a flexible rationalism" (Wigmore on Evidence, (1981, Chadbourne rev., Boston) Vol 9, at para 2461).I agree. The cardinal rule of contractual interpretation must be to ascertain the intention of the parties. To the extent this rule is not implemented, the courts must incur the criticism of failing to give effect to the reasonable expectations of the parties. Surely the parties are reasonably entitled to expect that the courts will strive to ascertain their true intention or, certainly, not to arrive at a meaning of their contract which is at variance with their actual intention. They cannot expect that the judicial exercise of construing their contract will be buried under a stockpile of excessive formalism.

[...]

[84] This Court is not a final court of appeal.A right of appeal remains to the Privy Council sitting in London. It may not therefore be open to this Court to have regard to the extrinsic evidence to which I have referred.

[85] Lord Hoffman's summary in West Bromwich case is the most up-to-date and progressive statement of the principles applicable to the interpretation of a contract. Yet, even though it is acknowledged that the boundaries of the exception are in some respects unclear, Lord Hoffman holds that the rule is absolute if the evidence relates to prior negotiations. The Bromarin case illustrates the reluctance of the English Courts to look at extrinsic evidence as an aid to interpretation. I therefore suspect that the principles as enunciated by Lord Hoffman will be as far as their Lordships in London will be prepared to go. They will not displace the curt reminder to this Court of the correct approach in Malanesian Mission Trust Board v. Australian Mutual Providence Society [1977] 1 NZLR 391.Lord Hope stated (at 394-395):

The approach which must be taken to the construction of a clause in a formal document of this kind is well settled. The intention of the parties is to be discovered from the words used in the documents. Where ordinary words have been used they must be taken to have been used according to the ordinary meaning of these words. If their meaning is clear and unambiguous, effect must be given to them because that is what the parties have taken to have agreed to by their contract. Various rules may be invoked to assist interpretation in the event that there is an ambiguity. But it is not the function of the Court, when construing a document, to search for an ambiguity. Nor should rules which exist to resolve ambiguities be invoked in order to create an ambiguity which, according to the ordinary meaning of the words, is not there. So the starting point is to examine the words used in order to see whether they are clear and unambiguous. It is of course legitimate to look at the document as a whole and to examine the context in which these words have been used, as the context may affect the meaning of the words. But unless the context shows that the ordinary meaning cannot be given to them or that there is an ambiguity, the ordinary meaning of the words which have been used in the document must prevail.

[86] Nor, in line with this approach, will ambiguities be lightly recognised. In the present context, for example, the fact that the word "necessary" may mean "necessary to proceed", or "necessary as identified" or "necessary to complete in essence ... the development" will not be universally accepted as constituting an ambiguity. In the result, notwithstanding the genuine controversy surrounding the words used in cl 6.3, the language is likely to be vested with a "plain meaning" and extrinsic evidence excluded from consideration.

[87] If that is the case, the rule against the admission of evidence relating to prior negotiations will be applied without qualification. I do not have any presentment that English law is about to revisit this rule.

[88] It would, of course, be open to this Court to seek to depart from the law as applied in England on the basis of this country's implementation in 1995 of the United Nations Convention on Contracts for the International Sale of Goods. Liberal provisions for the interpretation of international sales contracts are included in this Convention. Article 8(1) provides that statements made by a party "are to be interpreted according to his intent where the other party knew or could not have been unaware what that intent was". Article 8(2) stipulates that, if the latter provision is inapplicable, a party's statements "are to be interpreted according to the understanding that a reasonable person of the same kind as the other party would have had in the same circumstances". Under Article 8(3) "[i]n determining the intent of a party or the understanding a reasonable person would have had, due consideration is to be given to all relevant circumstances of the case including the negotiations, any practices which the parties have established between themselves, usages and any subsequent conduct of the parties. "Professor McLauchlan has correctly pointed out that it is odd that evidence of the parties' negotiations are admissible to aid the interpretation of international sales agreements but not commercial or other domestic contracts.(See MCLAUCHLAN, "A Contract Contradiction", at 193).

[89] Reference may also be made to the UNIDROIT Principles of International Commercial Contracts published in 1994.This document, which is in the nature of a restatement of the commercial contract law of the world, refines and expands the principles contained in the United Nations Convention. Particularly relevant for present purposes is Article 4.3. Having stipulated that a contract is to be interpreted according to the common intention of the parties (4.1), and that the statements and other conduct of a party shall be interpreted according to that party's intention if the other party knew or could not have been unaware of that intention (4.2), Article 4.3 provides that, in applying these general principles, regard should be had to all the circumstances including "preliminary negotiations between the parties". Clearly, it is desirable that the approach of the Courts in this country to the interpretation of statutes should be consistent with the best international practice. (See Attorney General v. Dreux Holdings Ltd (1997) 7 TCLR 617, at 627 and 642).

[90] But while this Court could seek to depart from the law as applied in England and bring the law in New Zealand into line with these international conventions, I do not think it would be permitted to do so by the Privy Council.England has not yet adopted the United Nations Convention and has shown little readiness to allow the Courts in this country any latitude in the interpretation of contracts. (As Professor McLauchlan points out, between June 1996 and December 1997, six decisions of this Court, none of which raise issues of general principle, were the subject of appeals to the Privy Council. Of these, four were successful and one was dismissed by a bare three to two majority. (See "A Contract Contradiction", *supra*, at 190). This Court has, of course, been allowed considerable latitude in certain areas. See *e.g.*, Invercargill City Council v. Hamlin [1996] 1 NZLR 513; W v. W [1999] 2 NZLR 1; and Lange v. Atkinson [2000] 1 NZLR 257. Certainly, the contractual environment in New Zealand is significantly different from that which prevails in England. In this country, no less than nine statutes have been enacted since 1944 which impinge upon the traditional common law rules relating to the formation and performance of contractual undertakings. In England the common law remains dominant. But other, perhaps, than fostering a different judicial approach, I am not certain that this different contractual environment bears upon the present point. Being realistic, the law of contract in this country, other than as specifically reshaped by statute, is likely to remain the law of England. Indeed, in 1985 the Privy Council made it clear that, apart from cases involving considerations peculiar to New Zealand or questions of local policy, the Courts of New Zealand must adhere to the law which is of general application as the common law of England. See Hart v. O'Connor [1985] 1 NZLR 159, esp. at 165 and 174.

[91] If there were any doubt as to whether the preferred approach is open to this Court, I believe that it is put to rest by the decision of the Privy Council in Lim v. McLean [1997] 1 NZLR 641.At issue in that case was the construction of a contractual provision in an agreement for the sale of a one-half share of a fishing vessel along with a one-half share of the individual transferable quota (ITQ) allocated to the vendors under the Fisheries Amendment Act 1986.Although it was not known what the exact amount of the quota would be, the parties knew informally that it would be issued at about 447 tonnes. The agreement purported to sell the fishing boat together with the half-share of the ITQ described in Schedule III to the agreement. Schedule III described the ITQ as that issued by the relevant Ministry "granting the right to catch not less than 447 tonnes of orange roughy per annum". Sometime prior to the agreement the vendors had issued judicial review proceedings against the Ministry claiming a greater allocation of ITQ. Subsequent to the agreement, and indeed much later, the High Court ruled that the original vendors were entitled to a further 130 tonnes of orange roughy. The purchaser claimed a half-share in this increase.

[92] This Court unanimously took the view that the parties to the agreement intended to transfer a half-share of the quota of the order of 447 tonnes. Highly influential in the Court's thinking was the fact that the contract contained no provision for an adjustment of the purchase price in the event that there was a substantial variation to the ITQ.The Judge at first instance had been able to confirm that the purchase price represented an approximation of the value of the vessel and the then market value of the quota.The market value of one tonne of quota was known. This value had been multiplied by the parties to arrive at the value of the 447 tonnes referred to in the Schedule. Half that value added to half the value of the fishing vessel gave the purchase price. This analysis, while

well within the bounds of the contractual matrix, provided the clearest possible evidence that the parties intended to sell a half-share in the ITQ of the order of 447 tonnes.

[93] Thus, the parties' actual intention was readily discernible. The overall contract price made sense in the context of a sale of half the ITQ of the order of 447 tonnes. Any significant increase in the tonnage over and above 447 tonnes represented a windfall to the purchaser.

[94] But the Privy Council took a different view and reversed this Court's decision. The majority of their lordships (Lord Browne-Wilkinson, Lord Mustill and Lord Clyde) adopted a literal interpretation. The agreement spoke of the right to catch "not less than 447 tonnes" of the fish. It did not speak of 447 tonnes of ITQ more or less. Lord Nolan and Lord Nicholls dissented, the latter observing that the majority's interpretation made "no sense commercially" and that the Court should be slow to attribute to an ambiguously drawn document a meaning which would require the vendors to sell, for no additional payment, a half-share in an extra 130 tonnes. But the majority's view prevailed.

[95] The decision is comparable to the present case in that it resulted in a construction contrary to the actual intention of the parties and a substantial windfall to the purchaser. It is true that the decision of the Privy Council was a majority decision and may have been different with a different composition of the Board. But it would be foolhardy to ignore the clear tenor of the decisions of the English Courts to press for a plain meaning, even in the face of controversy, and to attribute an intention to the parties which they may not have had and which may, indeed, be contrary to their actual intention. For the moment, therefore, this Court must accept that, until the rule is reviewed by the Privy Council (or, possibly, the House of Lords) the extrinsic evidence relating to the draft agreement must be disregarded as part of the negotiations. The cautious flexibility in the application of the rule which would seem sensible to ensure effect is given to the reasonable expectations of commercial men or women is lacking. This Court must therefore be content with its earlier finding that, having regard to the context of the clause, the commercial objective of the provision, and the contractual matrix a resource consent under the Proposed Plan does not come within the purview of cl 6.3.

[96] For this reason, the appeal is allowed.

[...]

Sources

Australasian Legal Information Institute *http://www.austlii.edu.au.*

(Case kindly brought to the attention of the UNILEX editors by Dr. Bruno Zeller of the Victoria University School of Law).

Date: **December 2000**
Adjudicating Court: **ICC International Court of Arbitration, Barranquilla (Colombia)**
Number: **10346**
Parties: **Unknown**

Keywords

CONTRACT GOVERNED BY A PARTICULAR DOMESTIC LAW – REFERENCE TO THE UNIDROIT PRINCIPLES TO DEMONSTRATE THAT SOLUTION FOUND UNDER DOMESTIC LAW CORRESPONDS TO MODERN INTERNATIONAL COMMERCIAL LAW

DUTY TO CO-OPERATE (ART. 871 OF THE COMMERCIAL CODE OF COLOMBIA; ART. 5.3 [ART. 5.1.3 OF THE 2004 EDITION] OF THE UNIDROIT PRINCIPLES)

DUTY TO ACT IN GOOD FAITH (ART. 1.7 OF THE UNIDROIT PRINCIPLES)

DAMAGES – COMPENSATION FOR LOSS OF CHANCE (ART. 7.4.3 OF THE UNIDROIT PRINCIPLES)

DAMAGES – DUTY TO MITIGATE LOSSES (ART. 7.4.8 OF THE UNIDROIT PRINCIPLES)

DAMAGES – COMPENSATION LIMITED TO FORESEEABLE LOSSES (ART. 7.4.4 OF THE UNIDROIT PRINCIPLES)

Abstract

Claimant, a Colombian company, and Defendant, another Colombian company, entered into a contract for the sale of electricity by the former to the latter. The agreement was never performed and Claimant sued Defendant for breach of contract and damages. Defendant objected that the contract was null and void for lack of registration in the Public Registry.

The contract contained a choice of law clause in favour of Colombian law. The Arbitral Tribunal decided to apply Colombian law as well as the provisions of the contract and the relevant trade usages in accordance with Article 17.2 of the ICC Rules of Arbitration.

In deciding the merits of the case the Arbitral Tribunal applied the relevant provisions of the Commercial Code of Colombia and in support of the solutions found therein referred repeatedly to the UNIDROIT Principles, both the black letter rules and comments.

Thus, when rejecting Defendant's argument of the invalidity of the contract and qualifying the registration of the contract as a joint task of both parties that was not accomplished because of Defendant's failure to perform the duties it had to perform in order to obtain the registration, it referred not only to Article 871 of the Commercial Code of Colombia but also to Article 5.3 [Art. 5.1.3 of the 2004 edition] of the UNIDROIT Principles (black letter rule and comments), both of which laying down the general principle of the duty of co-operation between the parties.

Still with respect to the Defendant's failure to comply with the contractual provisions setting out the acts it had to perform in order to obtain the registration, the Arbitral Tribunal referred also to Article 1.7 of the UNIDROIT Principles which in its opinion "translates into the fact that the party, specifically the creditor, who has not acted with the diligence, measures and foresight which are required of him, as the case may be, is not only disqualified from alleging a breach of contract and seeking compensation for damages which, in the event that they have been suffered, would be due to his own fault, but, on a preventative and more direct basis, assumes the consequences of his dishonesty or turpitude and the attendant liability towards the other party where the services provided for in the contract cannot be performed and its purpose has become impossible or has been frustrated [...]".

Finally in addressing Claimant's request for damages as a result of Defendant's breach of contract, the Arbitral Tribunal referred to the comments on Article 7.4.3 of the UNIDROIT Principles in order to determine to what extent also a contingent loss or loss of a chance may be compensated, to Article 7.4.8 of the UNIDROIT Principles (black letter rule and comments) in order to establish "the principle that the reparation for the loss, whilst it has to compensate the aggrieved party [...] cannot impose exaggerated burdens on the liable party", and to Article 7.4.4 of the UNIDROIT Principles in order to limit the recoverable harm to what the non-performing party could have reasonably foreseen at the time of the conclusion of the contract as being likely to result from its non-performance.

Full Text

With respect to Respondent's plea of unenforceability of the contract
C - Issue no.3

This is covered in point V(2)(c)(iii) of the Terms of Reference and requests the Tribunal to examine and decide the following:
To reject the allegation of absolute nullity of the contract, including addendum no. i and addendum no. 2, if it finds as proven and therefore accepts one or more of the remaining defense pleas put forward by Respondent, that is to say the pleas of "unenforceability of the contract due to lack of registration with the Sistema de Informaci6n Comercial - SIC [Commercial Information System]"; "defense of unperformed contract" and "*force majeure*".

2. Having set out the above, the Tribunal states the following with regard to the first plea, that is to say the plea of "unenforceability of the contract due to lack of registration with the Sistema de Información Comercial - SIC":

(a) Aside from the allegation of breach of contract put forward by [Claimant] due to Respondent's unwillingness to execute the documentation required for the registration of the contract, which is a matter that, whilst connected with this one, relates to another issue, [Respondent] has denied the allegations contained in the claim, relying on a fact which is fully established in the proceedings, namely that the contract was not registered in the SIC. As a result the task of the Tribunal is to decide whether this circumstance legally exonerates Respondent from the allegations of Claimant regarding Respondent's performance of its contractual obligations.

(b) The first point to specify is that it is not the contract which is enforceable or unenforceable, but rather the obligations generated by it, in order then to distinguish between the validity of the contract and the enforceability of the services provided for in it.
Registration of a contract in the SIC is clearly a prerequisite in order for its ultimate effects —supply of the energy, billing, fixing of the price, payment, *etc.* — can come into play In other words, until the contract is registered the services provided for in it cannot be enforced. In that sense the final efficacy of the contract is pending and is subject to a condition whose performance, in this case, depended on positive joint action by the parties: the amendment of the corresponding terms of the agreement, in view of the position taken by the director of the SIC.
Such registration is, therefore, an administrative requirement which relates to regulation of the electricity service and is not, we repeat, a formality adsubstantium actus as Defendant alleges. The contract is made upon fulfillment of the substantive requirements for such type of contract and, in the event that it is a state contract, with the formal requirements corresponding to such category of contracts. Registration is not an essential part or prerequisite of validity, nor even a procedure to publicize the contract, but rather, and we repeat, an administrative requirement for its enforcement.
This being the case, Respondent is obviously confused between validity of a contract and enforceability of its obligations and between prerequisites for validity and conditional nature of the performance of the services provided for in it.

(c) In addition to the above, that is how the parties must have understood it, particularly Respondent who drafted its text, in view of the fact that the contract only makes reference to the obligation to register it in clause 18 when, in an impersonal way, it provides: "This contract shall be deemed to be perfected by the duly legalized signatures of the parties, but to be enforceable it requires registration with the SIC."

The above terminology, leaving aside for the moment any reference to clause 16.5 of the contract, implies that the registration with the SIC was a joint task of the parties, in line with article 871 of the Commercial Code (*Codigo de Comercio*) and, by its nature, with the so-called "duty to collaborate" which is a rule of conduct that is clearly a "responsibility" which is discharged by the performance of the necessary acts, and whose omission, depending on the circumstances, may simply mean that the party concerned cannot attribute to the other party the adverse consequences of the omission and, therefore, claim breaches against that party which are only attributable to the party concerned itself. It may even amount to a breach of the duty of good faith, a Fonti of liability, by preventing the performance of the services and the attaining of the purpose of the contract, that is to say by causing its frustration to the detriment of the other party

In relation to this duty and responsibility article 5.3 of the "Principles of International Commercial Contracts" prepared by the International Institute for the Unification of Private Law, "UNIDROIT", characterizes the "duty of collaboration" as follows: "Each party shall cooperate with the other party when such co-operation may reasonably be expected for the performance of that party's obligations" and the text comments as follows:
A contract is not merely a meeting point for conflicting interests but must also, to a certain extent, be viewed as a common project in which each party must cooperate. This view is clearly related to the principle of good faith and fair dealing (art. 1.7) which permeates the law of contract, as well as to the obligation to mitigate harm in the event of non-performance (art. 7.4.8).
The duty of co-operation must of course be confined within certain limits (the provision refers to reasonable expectations), so as not to upset the allocation of duties in the performance of the contract. Although the principal concern of the provision is the duty not to hinder the other party's performance, there may also be circumstances which call for more active cooperation.'

The Council of State (*Consejo de Estado*) , Chamber for Administrative Disputes, Section 3, in its judgment of 9 March 2000 (case no. 11447 —Aseguradora dei Valle S.A and Seguros Comerciales Bolivar S.A v. Empresas PzThlicas de Pereira) , made the following comments on duty and responsibility:
It must be remembered that in state contracts too the duties imposed on the parties have to be observed. They include the duty to act with sagacity which means with reasonable diligence when assuming commitments and fixing remuneration according to the circumstances of the stipulated services; and the duty of clarity by which a party to a contract must ensure that the other party knows, and must itself know, the details and circumstances which make up the agreement; the duty to provide information in order to give and receive all the elements which lead to greater clarity and purity in the agreements reached. It is therefore not viable to take account either of dishonest conduct, which is prohibited by the nemo auditur rule, or of contrary conduct whereby one party seeks to use audacious behaviour as a way of obtaining unfair advantages, either over the other contracting party, or over third parties which, as happens in public contracts, are taking part as bidders.

(d) It therefore follows from the above that at the root of the relationship between the parties was the unquestionable and clear duty in the first instance by reason of their own interest, but at the same time by reason of a real obligation towards the other party to do everything in their power to adjust the provisions of the contract to the requirements of the resolutions of the CREG [*Comisión de Regulacion de Energia y Gas* - Energy and Gas Regulation Commission] and the director of the SIC, on pain of frustrating the purpose of the contract, to their own prejudice, and of being in breach of an obligation which is inherent to the operation of the contract and complementary or ancillary to its express contents, in this case a preliminary or preventative obligation, in view of the fact that if this step is not taken, all possibility of the performance of the contract is blocked, giving rise to the obligation to make full compensation.

As a result we have to investigate what the parties — or the SIC — did or omitted to do in relation to the registration of the contract in order to determine the inherent consequences, that is to say the failure of the defense plea in the event that Respondent failed to act with the required diligence, or the success of the defense plea in the event that (i) the SIC, arbitrarily, and despite the efforts of Respondent (and of Claimant) refused to register the contract; or (ii) only Respondent acted diligently; or (iii) neither of the parties showed any effective inclination to obtain the registration of the contract.

(f) The above summary means that one can infer that [Claimant] clearly tried to obtain registration of the contract in the SIC and did everything within its power, in particular proposing amendments to the contract which, whilst safeguarding the parties' positions on the question of "delivery points" for the contracted energy, would have enabled the registration of the contract.

(h) The diligent and reasonable attitude of [Claimant], which is supported by the circumstances described above and which is consistent with the principle of preservation of contracts ut res magis valeat quam pereat is however in contrast to the attitude of [Respondent] which, apart from agreeing to the request of the director of the SIC to take part in a meeting in order to analyse the obstacles to registration and to execute the Addendum No. 2, extending the "start date" of the contract, given that "the purchaser and the vendor require additional time over and above the start date to study the legal aspects of the contract", took no steps to overcome the difficulties and there is no evidence in the proceedings of any proposal whatsoever other than the very dubious suggestion that it would be flexible in return for the unrestricted acceptance by [Claimant] that "the energy must be supplied at the measuring points at a voltage level of 110 kv, 661w and 13.8 kv" As we saw earlier, this interpretation could easily have been wrong and was contrary to the very conduct of Respondent, as revealed in the seven (7) contracts referred to above which, moreover, were assigned to [X], albeit on a short-term basis.

It is therefore neither logical nor reasonable, nor in line with the aforementioned provision of article 871 of the Commercial Code (*Código de Comercio*) or the "duty of collaboration" that none of [Respondent's] many officers and advisers showed any indination towards an alternative solution, nor put forward any idea, nor prepared any counterproposal to the amendments suggested by [Claimant] in order to obtain the registration of the contract in the SIC and thereby, if its interpretation is finally accepted by the dispute resolution body provided for in the contract, to reap the very important income, savings and benefits for the end-users described by Respondent...

On the contrary, the evidence shows that despite the provisions of its statutes and the "contracting regime", [Respondent] took no effective steps to overcome the problems with the registration of the contract and simply opted to hide behind the observations of the director of the SIC as a reason for washing its hands of the contract, to the point where it considered itself released from it, by virtue of its desire for it to be null and void as a result of the said deficiencies or non-conformities which it refused to resolve as it could and should have done. Moreover, applying the doctrine of "own acts" [estoppel] this conduct would prevent "one party [Respondent] from relying on its own inconsistency to the detriment of the other [Claimant]".

With respect to the alleged breach of contract due to the transfer of Respondent's assets

'[1] This being the case, the Tribunal concludes and will declare in the operative part of the Award that the transfer of assets by Respondent which was contained in notarized deed no. 2633 breached clause 10.3 of the contract as the authorization from [Claimant] contemplated in that provision was not obtained.

[2] The next aspect of the issue which is evaluated here concerns the breach of clause 10.2 of the contract as a result of the execution of notarized deed no. 2633 by Respondent.
In this regard the first point which the Tribunal makes is that the part of clause 10.2 which is relevant to this part of the Award is subsection one, which as part of clause 10 of the Contract on "Representations and Warranties; Additional Covenants by the Vendor and the Purchaser", provides: "Both the vendor and the purchaser shall preserve and maintain in full force and effect their existence and all the state authorizations which are required for the proper performance of their business, including the performance of this contract."
The aspect of the provision transcribed which concerns this issue is limited to the economic capacity of Respondent, as the change to its existence is a matter which pertains to a different issue. This circumstance in turn means that the following analysis is also conducted by reference to a possible breach by Respondent of clause 2 of the contract by reason of the transfer contained in notarized deed no. 2633 which has already been mentioned several times.

(a) It is clear that in the light of the principle of good faith and fair dealing each party to a contract must, without fail,3 adopt or maintain reasonable measures to ensure that they can perform their respective obligations. This implicit duty is even more rigorous where, as in this case, there is a specific provision, that is to say the part of clause 10.2 with which this part of the Award deals, which, moreover, is a rule which was proposed as a mandatory requirement by [Respondent].'

Whether failure to register the contract constituted a breach of contract 'E - Issue No.6

This corresponds to point V (2) (c) (vi) of the Terms of Reference, that is to say:
Whether Respondent was or was not unwilling to execute the documentation required for the registration of the contract in the SIC, and if it was, whether it breached clauses 16.5 and i6.7 of the contract as a result.

1. The comments made in the analysis of the defence plea of "unenforceability of the contract due to lack of registration with the Sistema de Información Comercial - SIC" mean that one can naturally infer that Respondent will be found to have breached clause 16.5 of the contract which gave contractual force to "the duty of collaboration" when requiring the issue of documents or the performance of acts which were "necessary or desirable to comply with the terms of this contract", a provision which is complemented by the provision contained in clause 16.7 of the contract in relation to the obligation to replace provisions which prevented the performance of the contract with similar provisions enabling it to be performed, specifically the registration in the SIC.
Having analyzed therefore tile contractual provisions in question, tile Tribunal considers the following to be relevant in relation to each one:

(a) The undertaking to collaborate reflected in clause 16.5 in relation to the registration of tile contract in the SIC can be classified as an "obligation to try" (*obligación de medio*) in contrast to "obligations to produce results" (*obligaciones de resultado*). However, this classification does not mean that tile first type of obligation, which is an undertaking on the part of the debtor to use all diligence to obtain a result which it cannot guarantee, is transformed into an instrument for reducing liability As expressed in an arbitral award of 26 April 1998, the "obligation to try" is an obligation:

in which the duty of the debtor is to conduct itself in such a way as to use all reasonable means within its power— namely knowledge, experience, material resources, diligence — to obtain the result expected by the creditor but without guaranteeing that it will be achieved. In this sense a failure to comply means a failure to use such means, that is to say providing the services without having adequate knowledge or experience, or failing to use the available scientific and technical resources, or failing to exercise ordinary diligence, all of which reflect the coming into existence of fault, that is to say it is an error of conduct which leads to the negative evaluation of the behaviour of the professional.

Therefore, in the light of what has been established in tile proceedings with regard to the conduct of Respondent in the matter under analysis, it follows that Claimant has been successful in demonstrating that [Respondent] did not exercise due diligence in relation to the obligation to try to procure the registration of tile contract in tile SIC, which is equivalent to having proved fault on the part of Respondent. This is one of the connotations of this kind of obligation, in contrast to the general rule on contractual liability where there is a presumption of fault on the part of tile debtor in tile event of failure to provide the service specified.

(b) As far as clause 16.7 is concerned, the Tribunal notes that the relevant part of the provision for tile purposes of this part of the Award is not the inclusion of partial nullity which is contemplated by article 902 of the Commercial Code (*Código de Comercio*) , but rather the reference to the amendment of the contract in order to sort out tile difficulties involved in its registration and hence its performance, a situation which arose from the clarifications required by tile director of the SIC, an official who in turn could be classified as a "state authority" whose interpretation of the contract ought to lead to the corresponding amendments in accordance with clause 16.7.

2. Given these conditions, and without it being necessary to carry out additional investigations, the Tribunal finds, and will so declare, that the conduct of Respondent in relation to the registration of the contract in tile SIC was contrary to the obligation to try enshrined in clause 16.5 of the contract and to tile positive obligation agreed in clause 16.7 thereof, and it remains only to repeat for the sake of greater clarity in relation to the duty of collaboration, which is central to various parts of tile Award, that academic opinion, case law and even legislation itself are paying increasing attention to the duties of correction and fair dealing or, to put it in another way, to the duty to act in accordance with the standards of good faith at all times. Thus for example article 1175 of the Italian Civil Code, the legislation which the Commercial Code (*Codigo de Comercio*) took as its model for the subject of obligations and contracts, provides: "The debtor and the creditor must act in accordance with the rules on correctness", and article 1.7 of the aforementioned UNIDROIT Principles of International Commercial Contracts provides: "(1) Each party must act in accordance with good faith and fair dealing in international

trade. (2) The Parties may not exclude or limit this duty", which translates into tile fact that tile party specifically the creditor, who has not acted with the diligence, measures and foresight which are required of him, as the case maybe, is not only disqualified from alleging a breach of contract and seeking compensation for damages which, in the event that they have been suffered, would be due to his own fault, but, on a preventative and more direct basis, assumes the consequences of his dishonesty or turpitude and the attendant liability towards the other party where the services provided for in the contract cannot be performed and its purpose has become impossible or has been frustrated due to the lack of the activity (more than collaboration) which it should have shown and which is indispensable in order to achieve the common aim corresponding to tile practical or socio-economic function of the contract.

Each party has duties in relation to clarity, precision, information and collaboration so that if a party omits to perform the necessary acts, it assumes exclusive responsibility for tile adverse consequences of its inertia or negligence. This is more important and demanding in contracts involving collaboration and in the obligations which presuppose and impose such collaboration, and it may lead to the very extinction of the obligation in the absence of such collaboration by the creditor which prevented, hindered or delayed the exercise by the debtor of his right to release himself from the obligation by means of full performance and to obtain the desired economic result which is tile natural consequence of the satisfaction of the reciprocal and common contractual duties and obligations.'

With respect to termination of the contract and damages
'H - Issues Nos. 9 and 10

The issues, which correspond to point V (2) (c) (ix) and (x) of the Terms of Reference, are closely linked, as the first is a function of tile investigations into tile contractual breaches by Respondent, whilst the second depends on the outcome of the first.

As a result, and having determined that there was a breach of the contract by [Respondent], the Tribunal considers it appropriate to deal sequentially and jointly with tile matters raised, the text of which reads as follows:

In the event that there is an affirmative answer to one or more of points (iv), (v), (vi), (vi) and (vii) above, whether it is appropriate to declare — and the declaration is actually made — that the contract, including addendum no. i and addendum no. 2, is terminated due to a breach of contract by Respondent.

and

In the event that the contract, including addendum no. i and addendum no. 2, is declared to be terminated for the reason indicated in point (ix) above, that Respondent be ordered to pay compensation for loss and damage and, if it is so ordered, what would be the heads and amounts of such compensation.

1. One of the cornerstones of the legislation on obligations and contracts involving interrelated services, which is based on the interdependent character of the contractual commitments whereby each of the parties is both creditor and debtor of tile other— without implying simultaneous performance of tile services — is the so-called "tacit resolutory condition" which is enshrined in article 1546 of the Civil Code (*Código Civil*)

and article 870 of the Commercial Code (*Codigo de Comercio*). This means that, in the case of a bilateral contract, a breach by one party enables the other party at its election to request the rescission or termination of the contract or its performance, in both cases with compensation for loss and damage, which will be compensatory if the choice is to demand the rescission or termination, or will cover the delay if the choice is to require its performance.
Our analysis in relation to tile issues corresponding to points (B), (C), (D), (E) and (F) of this chapter shows on the one hand compliance with tile requirement to have a valid bilateral contract and on the other the fact that Respondent has committed a definitive breach of its obligations, given that Claimant was ready to comply with its part of tile agreement, and furthermore the arguments put forward by [Respondent] in defense of its conduct have no prospect of success...

2. Moreover, in accordance with developments in case law and academic tilinking, based on equity demanding that breaches of contract which mean that the resolutory action is successful have to be serious and material, tile Tribunal finds that the breaches committed by [Respondent] merit such a classification from two points of view:

(a) In the first instance, due to the nature of the provisions which were not performed, starting from clauses 16.5 and 16.7 which required the adoption of measures aimed at permitting nothing less than the performance of tile contract, and going on to clauses 10.2 and 10.3 which, respectively, required tile parties to maintain their legal and economic viability and to request authorization from [Claimant] to dispose of a substantial part of the assets of [Respondent],and the breach of which made it impossible to give effect to the purpose of the contract which is set out in clause 2 thereof.

(b) Secondly, due to the conduct of Respondent which, as has been shown throughout this Award, without justification hindered tile solution of the problems which would allow tile registration of the contract in tile SIC and hence its performance; inadequately carried on its business, which led to the intervention of the public services inspector owing to the decrease in its operational capacity; and, finally, erratically and deliberately omitted to request tile authorization of [Claimant] to transfer assets and contracts to [X], excluding tile contract at issue, so as to place itself in a position where it was totally incapable of meeting its obligations thereunder.

Having proved the breach of contract by Respondent with the characteristics noted above, Claimant had the option of choosing between performance of the contract or its termination, with the consequent damages. [Claimant] unequivocally elected for tile first of these options by requesting the termination of the Contract, which it was legally entitled to do for tile reasons stated, and this will be addressed in tile operative part of the Award.

3. Having discussed the question of the termination of the contract due to its breach by Respondent, it is necessary to consider the consequent compensation for loss and damage that Respondent must pay to [Claimant] ,which tile Tribunal develops as follows:

(a) In the terms of articles 1613 and 1614 of the Civil Code (*Código Civil*), the question of compensation would appear to be resolved merely by applying the concepts of damnum emergens and lucrum cessans, the first of which means a reduction in net worth (an outlay) and the second a frustrated gain (income not received) or, as the Supreme Court of Justice (*Corte Suprema de Justicia*), Civil Appeals Chamber, in its judgment of 7 May 1968 expressed it:

Damnum emergens relates to the loss of elements of net worth, payments which have been necessary or which will in future be necessary and the advent of liabilities, caused by the facts from which liability is sought to be deduced; whereas lucrum cessans, as the expression suggests, consists of all the certain gains which have not been received or remain to be received, based on the same facts. And the claim for compensation has to conform to this classification and adequately place the various heads of damage.

The position is however, as the judgment transcribed above states, that for a loss to be compensated it must be "certain" rather than a "contingent" loss. The latter does not give a right to compensation, a sensitive subject where "unconsolidated losses" are involved and particularly acute when these losses are associated, as in the present case, with situations which did not materialize.

In this respect the Tribunal considers that tile classification of damage as certain or as contingent, arising out of situations which were prevented from occurring, constitutes a necessary filter for the determination of the reasonable losses and tile Tribunal will deal with this task later, taking as its point of reference the degree of seriousness and the scientific or technical solidity possessed by tile prediction of what would have occurred had the harmful event not intervened, and from there go on to quantify the loss which will amount to 100% if there is legal certainty that tile situation would have occurred. As Juan Carlos Henao notes:

Nothing of itself is contingent, save for physical or legal impossibilities. Everything is resolved in evidential terms. ... As the Mazeaud brothers say "the probabilities that have been lost are not always the 'castles in the air' of Perette and his jug of milk. Sometimes they are real."

(b) Having set out the aforementioned framework as the reference to evaluate tile absence or presence of recoverable losses, tile Tribunal also comes up against clause 14.3 of tile Contract, tile text of which clearly has its origins in the Anglo-Saxon legal systems and makes it necessary to venture into tile area of "direct" and "indirect" loss in order precisely to understand the provision, which is consonant with the principle that tile reparation for the loss, whilst it has to compensate the aggrieved party which is a mandatory parameter in tile evaluation, cannot impose exaggerated burdens on the liable party.

Thus, as far as direct and indirect losses are concerned, the obligatory starting point is to state that in accordance with article 1616 of tile Civil Code (*Codigo Civil*), absent a contractual provision, the debtor is only liable for direct losses, which means those losses which are a

"necessary and strict consequence of his unlawful act. In contrast, the debtor does not have any liability if the loss is not a certain and necessary product of his conduct or, in other words, there is no causal relationship, a characteristic which then becomes determinative when classifying a loss as direct."

Therefore what the judge has to evaluate is not the mediate or immediate character of the loss (temporal or spatial proximity) but rather its inevitability or causal nature, so that on the basis of such analysis he can determine the absence or presence of the obligation to compensate.

(c) It is not however enough to denote a loss as direct, as regard must also be had to the distinction between "foreseeable" and "unforeseeable" losses, with compensation being payable in relation to the former but not in relation to the latter, save where the debtor had acted fraudulently.

The distinction between foreseeable and unforeseeable losses in turn presents difficulties and has a limited development in case law, which is why the Tribunal must resort when characterizing it to the criterion of what is in the contemplation of the parties which is contained in tile classic decision in Hadlev v. Baxendale, which was handed down in 1854 and which said:

Now we think the proper rule in such a case as the present is this:- Where two parties have made a contract which one of them has broken, the damages which the other party ought to receive in respect of such breach of contract should be such as may fairly and reasonably be considered either arising naturally ie, according to the usual course of things, from such breach of contract itself, or such as may be reasonably supposed to have been in the contemplation of both parties, at the time they made tile contract, as the probable result of the breach of it.10

Thus the judge who follows the "foreseeability" rule mentioned above will have to conduct investigations into the type of losses which ordinarily and reasonably should have been within the contemplation of the party as associated with its breach, in order to decide from there whether or not compensation should be ordered and, if so, the amount of such compensation.

(d) Thus the Tribunal will proceed to evaluate the figures proved in tile proceedings as making up damnum emergens and lucrum cessans using the following parameters:

i. Fullness of tile compensation, referable to the need to place the aggrieved party in the position it would have been in absent the loss;

ii. Certainty of the loss, material in tile case of consequential loss (crystallized situation) and legal in the case of loss of profit (contingent situation);

iii. Direct character, that is to say resulting exclusively from the cause-effect relationship;

and

iv. Foreseeability, referring to the harmful consequences of their actions being within the reasonable contemplation of the Parties.

Finally, on tile question of the connotations of having a strict causal relationship and the need for the loss of profit (*lucrum cessans*) claimed by Claimant to have been foreseeable, the Tribunal considers it sufficient to mention, in relation to the first point, that the only reason proved in these proceedings for tile frustration of Claimant's expectations is tile inexcusable non-performance of Respondent. And, in terms of the second point, the requirement of "foreseeability" is clearly met as whatever method of analysis is used the loss of profit corresponds, as article 7.4.4 of the UNIDROIT Principles of International Commercial Contracts states, to "what [Respondent] could have reasonably have contemplated at the time of entering into the contract as the probable consequence of its breach", or what was "in the contemplation of both parties", as stated in Hadley v. Baxendale. It is quite clear.., that the essential objective of [Claimant] in taking part in the public tender and, naturally, in entering into the Contract, was to obtain a return on its investment.

The matters discussed hitherto suffice to conclude that, as will be set out in the operative part of the Award, the Tribunal will order Respondent to pay damages in the sum of US$. corresponding to Claimant's loss of profit.'

Sources

Excerpts of award published in:
ICC International Court of Arbitration Bulletin, Vol. 12, No. 2, Fall 2001, 106 – 115.

Date: **2001**
Adjudicating Court: ***Arbitration Institute of the Stockholm Chamber of Commerce (Partial Award)***
Number: ***117/1999***
Parties: ***Unknown***

Keywords

CONTRACT BETWEEN EUROPEAN AND CHINESE COMPANIES SILENT AS TO APPLICABLE LAW – INTERPRETED BY ARBITRAL TRIBUNAL AS INTENTION OF PARTIES TO EXCLUDE APPLICATION OF ANY DOMESTIC LAW – APPLICATION OF UNIDROIT PRINCIPLES AS "RULES OF LAW CONSIDERED TO BE MOST APPROPRIATE" IN CASE AT HAND (SEE ART. 24(1) STOCKHOLM ARBITRATION RULES) – SUBSIDIARY APPLICATION OF SWEDISH LAW AS NEUTRAL LAW

UNIDROIT PRINCIPLES DEFINED AS RULES "WHICH HAVE WIDE RECOGNITION AND SET OUT PRINCIPLES THAT OFFERS A PROTECTION FOR CONTRACTING PARTIES THAT ADEQUATELY REFLECTS THE BASIC PRINCIPLES OF COMMERCIAL RELATIONS IN MOST IF NOT ALL DEVELOPED COUNTRIES"

Abstract

Two Chinese companies and a European company entered into an agreement (hereinafter "the Agreement") on technology exchange and technical co-operation. The Agreement imposed upon the parties a duty of strict confidentiality concerning the information exchanged and a duty of non-competition. The dispute arose when the European company accused one of the Chinese companies of having violated such commitments. The European company claimed damages for the alleged breach and in accordance with an arbitration clause contained in the Agreement filed an arbitration before the Arbitration Institute of the Stockholm Chamber of Commerce

The Agreement was silent as to the law governing the contract. According to Claimant Swedish law (as the law of the place of arbitration and a neutral law) or Luxemburg law (as the law of the country where the party rendering the "characteristic performance", the granting of a licence, had its place of business) should apply; alternatively, it invoked the application of the UNIDROIT Principles. Defendant argued that the applicable law was the law of the People's Republic of China as the law of the country where the contract has been concluded and/or the main performance has to be rendered.

The Arbitral Tribunal recalled that according to Article 24(1) of the Arbitration Rules of the Arbitration Institute of the Stockholm Chamber of Commerce the tribunal, in the absence of an agreement between the parties, shall apply the law or rules of law which the tribunal considers to be most appropriate, a principle often referred to as *voie directe*.

In the case at hand the Tribunal held that the parties had deliberately refrained from agreeing on the law governing their contract (which otherwise was carefully drafted), apparently on the assumption that should the question of the applicable law ever arise, the law eventually chosen would protect their interest in a way that any normal business man would consider adequate and reasonable, without any surprises that could result from the application of domestic laws of which they had no deeper knowledge. As a consequence, the Tribunal found that the dispute at hand should not be decided according to the law of any particular jurisdiction, but on the basis of such rules of law that have found their way into international codifications or such like that enjoy a widespread recognition among countries involved in international trade. And since, apart from international conventions such as the Convention on Contracts for the International Sale of Goods (CISG) and other conventions that are not directly applicable to a licence agreement, the only codification that could be considered to have this status were the UNIDROIT Principles. The UNIDROIT rules have wide recognition and set out principles that in the Tribunal's opinion offer a protection for contracting parties that adequately reflect the basic principles of commercial relations in most if not all developed countries. The Tribunal therefore concluded that in deciding the dispute at hand it would base itself primarily on the UNIDROIT Principles, and only where the UNIDROIT Principles do not provide an answer to any question of substantive nature raised in the arbitration, it would resort to domestic law, *i.e.* the law of Sweden as a neutral law.

Full Text

Parties:
Claimant: [A Luxembourg] Company A
Respondent: [A Chinese] Corporation Y
Place or arbitration: Stockholm, Sweden
Language or the proceedings: English
Nationality of arbitrators:
Chairman: Swedish
Arbitrator: Swedish
Arbitrator: Chinese

[...]

SUMMARY

In 1980, a Chinese international trade corporation and the [...] Corporation X, also a Chinese company, on the one hand, and the [Luxembourg] Company A, on the other, entered into an agreement on technology exchange and technical co-operation ("the 1980

Agreement"). Under the 1980 Agreement the parties exchanged licenses to parts of their respective industrial technology.

The 1980 Agreement was valid for ten years but was later extended until 1995 trough a Supplement Agreement. It was thereafter terminated as per the date agreed between the parties.

In 1997 a discussion arose between the Company A and the [Chinese] Corporation Y, as successor to Corporation X, on certain alleged infractions by Corporation Y on a secrecy undertaking in the 1980 Agreement.

In February 1998, the discussions resulted in a settlement agreement ("the Settlement Agreement") between the parties. According to the Settlement Agreement, the secrecy obligation under the 1980 Agreement was extended until December 31, 2002.

According to Company A, additional breaches of the secrecy undertaking was thereafter committed by Corporation Y. In November 1999, Company A filed a request for arbitration with the Arbitration Institute of the Stockholm Chamber of Commerce, claiming damages from Corporation Y on this ground.

On 7 July 2000, the Institute referred the case to the arbitral tribunal.

On 24 October, 2000, Company A filed a partial Statement of Claim, in which it requested that the issue of applicable law should be determined in the form of a partial award. The respondent agreed to the request.

APPLICABLE LAW TO THE DISPUTE

Claimant's Position

Claimant held that Swedish law should apply to the dispute or, alternatively, the UNIDROIT Principles of International Commercial Contracts, or Luxembourg law.

"The relevant contract is the 1980 Agreement. There was hardly any relevant statutory law in existence in the People's Republic of China in 1980. In these circumstances, the parties cannot possibly have intended Chinese law to apply. The only evidence as to the parties' joint intention as regards applicable law can be found in the dispute resolution clause of the 1980 Agreement, in which the parties chose Sweden as the place of arbitration. It is clear that neither party wished the other party's law to apply".

"The parties chose the Rules of the [Arbitration Institute of the] Stockholm Chamber of Commerce from time to time in force. The current Rules permit the arbitrators to employ the voie directe method and applies [to] arbitrations which commenced on 1 April 1999 or later, unless that the parties have decided otherwise. Under the voie directe method, it is appropriate in the circumstances for Swedish law to be chosen by the arbitrators as a neutral applicable law; alternatively, the UNIDROIT Principles of international Commercial Contracts should be applied".

"If choice of law rules were to be applied, Swedish international private law rules and those of the Rome Convention both lead to the conclusion that Swedish law should be applied or, alternatively, that Luxembourg law should be applied to the obligations of Corporation Y which are the subject of this dispute, since the ' "characteristic performance" to which the secrecy and non-competition obligations at issue relate - is the license from Company A, domiciled in Luxembourg from where the performance emanates."

Respondent's Position

Respondent held that Chinese law should be applicable to the dispute for the following reasons.

"The choice of Sweden as the situs of the arbitration does not suffice as an indication of the parties' intentions with the respect to applicable law. The standard for a finding of an inferred choice of law is, generally speaking, extremely high and only proper where it is reasonably clear that there is a genuine choice by the parties. The choice of a certain jurisdiction for the arbitration proceedings does not indicate an intentional choice of applicable law but can be made for several different reasons. Under Swedish arbitration law at the time of the signing of the 1980 Agreement the conflict of laws system to be applied in an international commercial arbitration is the Swedish one. According to Swedish conflict of laws principles the law with the closest connection to the contract will be applied in matters of commercial contracts."

"It was common practice in China at the time of the signing of the 1980 Agreement that no provision on applicable law was included in the agreement. However, Chinese parties naturally favoured Chinese law as the applicable law, and this was reason for the preference by Chinese parties to international contracts of negotiating and signing agreements in China, thereby increasing the possibility of subsequent application of Chinese law. In this case, the 1980 Agreement and the subsequent agreements were negotiated and signed in China and the 1980 Agreement was also to be largely performed in China. In addition, the only portion of the Agreement in dispute and the entirety of the Settlement Agreement relate to performance that also take place principally in China. There is no connection to Sweden in the negotiation, execution or performance of any of the contracts relevant in the dispute. Consequently, the Tribunal should apply Chine se substantive law to the dispute."

Findings of the Arbitral Tribunal

The arbitral tribunal took note of the fact that the 1980 Agreement was signed in Beijing and contained no provision on applicable law to the dispute. The Supplement and the Settlement Agreement were also signed in Beijing without any provisions on applicable law. No evidence had been submitted in respect of the intentions of the parties on applicable law at the signing of the various agreements.

The present arbitration is governed by the Swedish Act on Arbitration which entered into force on April 1, 1999 and the present rules of the Arbitration Institute of the Stockholm Chamber of Commerce that entered into force on the same day. The Swedish Arbitration Act does not contain any provision on applicable law to a dispute under an international contract in Swedish arbitrations. The Rules of the Arbitration Institute, however, stipulate in Article 24 (1) that the tribunal, in the absence of an agreement between the parties, shall apply the law or rules of law which the tribunal considers to be most appropriate, a principle often referred to as voie directe. This rule, like the other Rules in force since April 1, 1999, applies to all arbitrations commenced thereafter, irrespective of the date of the agreement in dispute. Thus, this Tribunal is free to determine the applicable law on an assessment generally of the appropriateness of the chosen law or rules of law.

However, this does not mean that the Swedish conflict rules - which in the case of an international arbitration that, according to the parties wishes, takes place in Sweden are, in dubio, applicable - can be disregarded out of hand. Therefore, the Tribunal will first investigate whether there are Swedish conflicts rules that will effectively designate the applicable law for the present dispute.

Sweden has ratified the Rome Convention on the Law Applicable on Contractual Obligations which since July 1, 1998 has the status of law in Sweden. The governing principle under the Convention, as by and large was also the case under Swedish law before Sweden's ratification of the Convention, is that the applicable law shall be the law of the country to which the agreement has the closest connection. The Convention contains rules on certain contracts where the closest connection can be inferred from the nature of the contract, none of which, however, is relevant in the present case. There are also references to such circumstances that traditionally have been assumed to indicate a special connection to a certain jurisdiction, such as the nationality or residence of the respective parties, the place where the contract was entered into, the place of performance, agreed currency, the language of the contract *etc.* In the present case, only the place of negotiating and signing the Agreement is indicative of a certain jurisdiction among these various circumstances. This could, in the absence of other circumstances, indicate that the Agreement (as well as the subsequent Supplement and Settlement Agreement) has its closest connection with the People's Republic of China. However, this can, in the opinion of the Tribunal, in itself not be decisive in the present case. The 1980 Agreement is of special character in that it is, as it were, a form of barter agreement. The parties to the 1980 Agreement agreed to exchange technology and know how without any simultaneous arrangement for payments by either side to the other. Although the terms of the licenses are slightly different, the Agreement is a contract on a cross licence arrangement where performance and obligations are, on the face of it, evenly distributed and symmetrical in nature. As a consequence, the Agreement lacks the distinctive element of an unilateral, characteristic performance by one of the parties that sometimes can lend itself to conclusions or presumptions on the closest connection to any particular jurisdiction.

This conclusion in its turn leads the Tribunal to exclude the general application of Chinese law to the Agreement. The location where the Agreement was negotiated and signed can in the present case not reasonably be assumed to be in itself decisive for the law that should govern both the licence granted by [Company A] and the licence received by [Company A]. Nor can such conclusion be drawn from the fact that the subsequent Supplement and the Settlement Agreement were signed in the People's Republic of China. The fact that the last mentioned agreements are unilateral in the sense that they deal only with matters relating to the licence granted by [Company A] to [Corporation Y] does not alter this, since they still concern performance and obligations arising out of the cross licence in the 1980 Agreement, which contains the arbitration clause that both parties also find applicable to the present dispute. Therefore and although the Settlement Agreement is a separate agreement in the sense that it could be separately governed by a law or rules of law on issues relating to its binding nature or suchlike, the unilateral nature and the place of signing of the Settlement Agreement is not, in the tribunal's opinion, a valid reason for applying a different law to the Settlement Agreement than that which is found applicable to the 1980 Agreement. In fact, the very nature of a settlement agreement relating to a contractual obligation will, in the absence of a separate governing law clause, in dubio make it fail under the applicable law according to the contract in dispute.

For the same reasons as stated in the foregoing Luxembourg law cannot be considered to be the exclusive governing law for the 1980 Agreement.

In exceptional cases it may be possible to separate one part of a contract with a particular connection to a certain jurisdiction and apply the law of that jurisdiction to such part while at the same time applying another law to other parts of the contract with the closest connection to another jurisdiction (so called *depeçage*). In the Tribunals opinion this is not possible in the present case. In a contract where the parties exchange licences it cannot be a reasonable assumption that the alleged breaches of one party should be treated differently than the breaches of the other party, as a result of different laws or rules of law being applicable to each party's obligations.

The only relevant indication of any jurisdiction other than the People's Republic of China or Luxembourg is Sweden, chosen by the parties as the situs for arbitration. This is not of relevance for a finding of the closest connection of the Agreement to any particular jurisdiction, but goes rather to the issue of the parties' intentions or implied choice of governing law on the merits. But even in a case where all other relevant elements for identifying the governing law are missing, it is highly debatable whether a preferred choice of the situs of the arbitration is sufficient to indicate a choice of governing law. There has for several years been a distinct tendency in international arbitration to disregard this element, chiefly on the ground that the choice of the place of arbitration may be influenced by a number of practical considerations that have no bearing whatsoever on the issue of applicable law. The Tribunal agrees in principle with that approach, and notes, in addition, that the choice of location and rules for the arbitration in this case conforms to a fairly long and well-established practice in contracts between Western parties, on the one hand, and East European or Chinese parties, on the other. This practice is mainly based on perceptions of Sweden and the Arbitration Institute as a neutral and adequately regulated ground for arbitration proceedings and not on a preference for Swedish substantive law.

It seems obvious to the Tribunal that the parties in this case deliberately refrained from agreeing on the applicable law to the 1980 Agreement, which otherwise bears the mark of a well prepared and qualified approach to contract drafting. It may well be that either or both of the parties had hopes or expectations on the application of a law, in case of a dispute between them, with which they would feel comfortable. But there is no indication that they at the time contemplated the actual effects of any particular law on hypothetical instances of breaches under the contract; nor have any such effects so far been presented by the parties in the arbitration. In the Tribunals view, it is reasonable to assume that the contracting parties expected that the eventual law chosen to be applicable would protect their interest in a way that any normal business man would consider adequate and reasonable, given the nature of the contract and any breach thereof, and without any surprises that could result from the application of domestic laws of which they had no deeper knowledge.

This leads the Tribunal to conclude that the issues in dispute between the parties should primarily be based not on the law of any particular jurisdiction, but on such rules of law that have found their way into international codifications or suchlike that enjoy a widespread recognition among countries involved in international trade. Apart from international conventions such as the Convention on International Sales of Goods (CISG) and other conventions that are not directly applicable on a licence agreement, the only codification that can be considered to have this status is the UNIDROIT Principles of International Commercial Contracts. The UNIDROIT rules have wide recognition and set out principles that in the Tribunals opinion offers a protection for contracting parties that adequately reflects the basic principles of commercial relations in most if not all developed countries. The Tribunal determines that the rules contained therein shall be the first source employed in reaching a decision on the issues in dispute in the present arbitration.

If and to the extent the UNIDROIT rules do not provide an answer to any question of substantive nature raised in the arbitration, the Tribunal bas to resort to domestic laws. Since none of the parties has yet presented its case or its arguments in a way that enables the Tribunal to identify any such questions the Tribunal does not know in which areas such secondary sources of law will be required. It follows from the foregoing that the Tribunal does not find it appropriate to chose the domestic law of either party. Instead, the Tribunal will, in view of the lack of distinctive elements for a choice of any other law and in spite of the arguments in foregoing, apply Swedish substantive law, unless both parties then agree otherwise.

SEPARATE AWARD

The Tribunal determines that the appropriate rules of law on the merits of the issues in dispute between the parties are those contained in UNIDROIT Principles of international Commercial Contracts (1994) supplemented by Swedish law if and to the extent the UNIDROIT rules do not give any guidance on a particular issue.

Sources

Stockholm Arbitration Report, 2002:1, 59 *et seq.*

Observations by Herbert KRONKE (at 65 *et seq.*) and by Juan FERNANDEZ-ARMESTO (at 71 *et seq.*)

Date: **2001**
Adjudicating Court: **ICC International Court of Arbitration**
Number: **10422**
Parties: **Unknown**

Keywords

DISTRIBUTORSHIP AGREEMENT BETWEEN EUROPEAN COMPANY AND LATIN AMERICAN COMPANY – CHOICE OF LAW CLAUSE INEFFECTIVE BUT INDICATING PARTIES' DESIRE FOR A NEUTRAL SOLUTION – APPLICATION BY ARBITRAL TRIBUNAL OF THE LEX MERCATORIA (ART. 17.1 ICC RULES OF ARBITRATION) – REFERENCE TO UNIDROIT LIMITS

CONTRACT FORMATION – ACCEPTANCE CONTAINING MODIFIED TERMS – AMOUNTS TO ACCEPTANCE IF MODIFICATIONS ARE NOT MATERIAL (ART. 2.11 [ART. 2.1.11 OF THE 2004 EDITION] UNIDROIT PRINCIPLES

CONTRACT FORMATION – CONCLUSION OF CONTRACT DEPENDENT ON AGREEMENT ON SPECIFIC MATTERS (ART. 2.13 [ART. 2.1.13 OF THE 2004 EDITION] UNIDROIT PRINCIPLES

CONTRACT INTERPRETATION – TERMS TO BE GIVEN EFFECT (ART. 4.5 UNIDROIT PRINCIPLES)

TERMINATION OF CONTRACT – FUNDAMENTAL BREACH REQUIRED (ART. 7.3.1(1) UNIDROIT PRINCIPLES) – NOTICE OF TERMINATION WITHOUT FUNDAMENTAL BREACH – TERMINATION NEVERTHELESS EFFECTIVE (ART. 7.3.2 UNIDROIT PRINCIPLES) – NOTIFYING PARTY LIABLE DAMAGES

DAMAGES – LOSS OF PROFIT – CALCULATION (ART. 7.4.2 UNIDROIT PRINCIPLES)

DAMAGES – DISCRETIONARY ASSESSMENT BY COURT (ART. 7.4.3(2))

Abstract

Defendant, a European manufacturer, and Plaintiff, a Latin-American distributor, entered into an agreement (hereinafter "the Agreement") for the exclusive distribution of Defendant's products in Plaintiff's country. Although the Agreement provided that payment of the price of the goods was due 120 days after delivery, Defendant, after receiving from Plaintiff an order for a larger than usual quantity of goods, requested advance payment. Plaintiff refused, and the parties entered into negotiations with a view to finding a mutually acceptable solution. Ultimately it was agreed that Plaintiff would pay the price in advance, but Defendant in turn would grant Plaintiff a discount corresponding to the additional costs thereby incurred by Plaintiff. While the parties still argued as to whether the new terms of payment concerned only future orders or applied also to the order already placed, Defendant all of a sudden terminated the Agreement alleging Plaintiff's failure to meet the contractually agreed sales figures over the last two years. Plaintiff objected that the termination was ineffective, first, because Defendant did not formally put Plaintiff into breach ("*mise en demeure*") and in any case notice of termination was not given timely; second, because the sales figures indicated in the Agreement were not binding commitments; and third, because its failure to meet the figures was due to Defendant's refusal to deliver the goods according to the originally agreed terms. Since Defendant insisted on the termination of the agreement, Plaintiff commenced arbitration proceedings, requesting the arbitral tribunal to declare the termination of the Agreement ineffective and to compel Defendant properly to perform the Agreement until its expiry.

The first question addressed by the arbitral tribunal was whether it had jurisdiction in the case at hand. In deciding in the affirmative, the arbitral tribunal, while conceding that the language of the clause of the Agreement entitled "*Fuero Competente*" was rather ambiguous, pointed out that the drafters of that clause were not lawyers and could therefore not be expected to use proper legal terminology; what was important was what reasonable persons in the same situation as the parties would have understood by such language, and that the clause was being given a meaning which did not deprive it of any effect, and in this respect the arbitral tribunal expressly referred to Articles 4.1 and 4.5 of the UNIDROIT Principles, respectively.

As to the law applicable to the substance of the dispute, the arbitral tribunal held that, notwithstanding that the Agreement provided "El presente contrato [...] se regirà [...] por la CAMARA DE COMERCIO INTERNACIONAL o en su defecto por una legislaciòn neutral definida en comun acuerdo por las partes", the parties had not made any valid choice of the applicable law, since there is no ICC legislation nor did the parties agree on the application of any other neutral legislation. As a consequence the arbitral tribunal, in view of the fact that the parties apparently wanted a neutral solution, decided to apply "general principles and rules of international contracts, *i.e.* the so-called *lex mercatoria*", and to refer in this context to the UNIDROIT Principles representing - with some exceptions such as the provisions on hardship – "a restatement of the rules which business persons engaged in international trade consider to be meet their needs and expectations".

Concerning the merits of the case, the arbitral tribunal, invoking the principle of *pacta sunt servanda* laid down in Article 1.3 of the UNIDROIT Principles, first of all held that Defendant's refusal to deliver the goods on the originally agreed terms of payment constituted a breach of the Agreement, but that this breach was no longer relevant because the parties had reached a settlement agreement. Indeed, the valid conclusion of this agreement was not prevented by the fact that Defendant's letter of acceptance of Plaintiff's proposed terms of settlement contained some minor modifications, and that another issue of minor importance had been left open by the parties, and in support to its findings the arbitral tribunal referred to Articles 2.11 and 2.13 [Arts. 2.1.11 and 2.1.13 of the 2004 edition] of the UNIDROIT Principles, respectively. Turning to the question as to whether the subsequent termination of the Agreement by Defendant was effective, the arbitral tribunal, referring to Article 7.3.2(1) of the UNIDROIT Principles according to which the right to terminate the contract is exercised by notice without any further formality, rejected Plaintiff's argument that Defendant before terminating the Agreement should have put Plaintiff formally into breach. At the same time, however, the arbitral tribunal held that Defendant's notice of termination had not been given timely and, more importantly, that it was not justified since in view of the non binding nature of the sales figures laid down in the Agreement Plaintiff's failure to meet the figures could not be considered a fundamental breach of the Agreement, and in support of its findings it referred to Articles 7.3.2(2) and 7.3.1(1) of the UNIDROIT Principles, respectively. Yet this did not mean that, as asserted by Plaintiff, the Agreement was still in force: according to a rule widely accepted in international trade and in the view of the arbitral tribunal also confirmed by the UNIDROIT Principles (see in particular Articles 7.3.2(1) and 7.3.5(1)), a notice of termination is effective even if unjustified with the result that the other party may not require specific performance of the contract but can only claim damages for the unjustified termination. In the case at hand, Defendant, having terminated the Agreement without justification, has to compensate the loss thereby caused to Plaintiff. As to Plaintiff's lost profit, the arbitral tribunal held that it should be calculated not on the basis of the gross margin of the forecast sales volumes but on the basis of the net margin, *i.e.* the difference between the gross margin and the avoided costs or harm, and in this respect referred to Article 7.4.2 of the UNIDROIT Principles. However, since Plaintiff has not provided any information for the calculation of the net margin, in the case at hand the arbitral tribunal made an equitable quantification of the lost profit in accordance with Article 7.4.3(3) of the UNIDROIT Principles.

Full Text

[...]

1. THE ANTECEDENTS OF THE DISPUTE

[...]

The Defendant [a European company] and the Plaintiff [a South American company] [...] concluded in [...] two exclusive distribution contracts (hereinafter "the Contracts") for the resale of the goods manufactured by the Defendant in the Plaintiff's country [...].

[...]

In its letter of [...] the Defendant informed the Plaintiff that it had been purchased by Group [X] and entrusted "... the management, the follow-up and the control of [the contractual products]" in the territory of [territory comprising a number of countries including the Plaintiff's country] to Company [Y], affiliate of the Group [X]. [...]

In the same period the Plaintiff transmitted to the Defendant two orders No. XXXX/98 and No. YYYY/98 for a total amount of US $ 82.402 [...].

In its letter of [...] the Defendant, after having confirmed receipt of orders No. XXXX/98 and No. YYYY/98, confirmed its decision to entrust the marketing of its products to Company Y and added that:
"Given the large sums [the Plaintiff] owes to [a company of the Group X], [the Defendant] cannot execute your orders before receiving payment in advance."

The Plaintiff opposed this request on the ground that Article 4.4 of the Contracts made provision for payment within120 days of the date of dispatch and that an alleged debt with a third company could not justify a change in the conditions of payment [...].

[...]

In its letter of [...] the Defendant explained in more detail the reasons why it wished to obtain payment guarantees. [...] At the same time the Defendant proposed to negotiate a discount for immediate payment and/or compensation or a discount for the Plaintiff to take into consideration the costs it would sustain to guarantee payment by means of a letter of credit, a bank guarantee or any other form of guarantee.

The Plaintiff responded in a letter of [...]. While stressing that from a legal point of view it had a right to refuse the Defendant's proposals, the Plaintiff agreed in principle to provide payment guarantees provided that the Defendant undertook to cover the costs of those payment guarantees [...].

The parties met on [...] to discuss the terms of an agreement. In the course of this meeting they reached an agreement in principle which the lawyers summarised in the following terms:
"In a purely commercial spirit, [the Plaintiff] agreed to pay you in advance for the goods indicated in its future orders [...] on condition that you undertake to cover the costs of payment in advance (the time limit within which payment was originally indicated in the Contracts was 120 days) and that the harm it suffered on account of the delay in deliveries be, at least in part compensated."

[...]

In its letter of [...] the Defendant agreed to the Plaintiff's proposals. [...]

Subsequently, in its letter of [...] the Plaintiff raised a new problem: in order to safeguard distribution in the Christmas period the Plaintiff asked the Defendant to send the goods by air and cover the costs of air transport. [...]

In a fax message of [...] the Defendant agreed to the Plaintiff's latest proposal.

[...]

On [...] the Defendant asked the Plaintiff to inform it of details of sales of its products in the year [...], in the year [...] up until the month of October. The Plaintiff sent the information in question on [...].

On [...] the Defendant informed the Plaintiff [...] that, as it, the Plaintiff, had not reached the minimum sales stipulated in Article 11.4 of the Contracts for the years [...], it was notifying the Plaintiff that it was terminating the Contracts in advance according to Art. 10.1.3 (and, that is "por incumplimiento grave de alguna de sus cláusulas") with effect as of [...]

[...]

In its letter of [...] the Plaintiff challenged the validity of the Defendant's termination of the Contracts. It stressed in particular that it was contrary to good faith to have been given notice of termination after the parties had concluded an agreement in principle on the conditions on which the goods would be supplied; that the Plaintiff, had undertaken no obligation to purchase a minimum quantity, since Art. 11.4 only mentioned a simple forecast of the quantity to be purchased [...] At the same time it ordered the Defendant to perform the contract and to deliver with no further delay the goods indicated in Orders No. XXXX/98 and No. YYYY/98 [...].

After a final fruitless exchange of letters the Plaintiff decided to submit the dispute to arbitration. [...]

2. The Proceedings

[...]

3. The Questions to be Decided

According to the Terms of Reference, the questions to be decided by the Arbitral Tribunal are the following:
1. Does the Arbitral Tribunal have jurisdiction?
If so:
2. What law is applicable to the merits of the dispute?
3. Are the parties' claims admissible and, if so, to what extent?
4. Are the counterclaims admissible and, if so, to what extent?
5. Should there be a set-off between the claim and the counterclaim?
6. Which party must pay the costs and the arbitrator's fees or, alternatively, how should the costs and fees be shared by the parties?

[...]

5. Does the Arbitral Tribunal have Jurisdiction?

[...]

Article 12 of the Contracts contains the following clause:
"12. Fuero Competente
12.1. El presente contrato, así como todas sus disposiciones, se regirán en todos los sentidos por la " CÁMARA DE COMERCIO INTERNACIONAL " o en su defecto por una legislación neutral definida en común acuerdo por las partes, pero que en ningún caso podrán ser los Tribunales de Justicias de los respectivos países de las partes contratantes.
12.2 Todas las interpretaciones que se requieran de este contrato, así como los litigios que puedan surgir entre las partes contratantes, se someterán a los Jueces y Tribunales de las Cortes definidas en el punto 12.1 implicando con ello que ambas partes renuncian a otros fueros, si existieren."

[...]

According to the Plaintiff, the clause, entitled, after all, "Foro competente", is a jurisdiction clause and not a choice of law clause. The reference to the applicable law was probably due to a drafting error consisting in the use of the term "legislación neutral" instead of "jurisdicción neutral".

In such a context reference to the ICC could have no other meaning than the submission of possible disputes to ICC arbitration. This solution would also be justified by the need to prefer an interpretation capable of providing a useful outcome rather than an interpretation that would render the clause inoperative. [...]

Moreover, the express exclusion of the jurisdiction of the courts of the parties' respective countries contained in Article 12 would lead to an absurd result. Indeed, should the clause be denied the value of an ICC arbitration clause, the parties could not then bring the dispute before a court that would normally be competent/have jurisdiction in the absence of an arbitration clause (*i.e.* the courts of the countries of the two parties) as precisely this solution has been expressly excluded by the clause.

Lastly the Plaintiff claims that the Defendant itself had agreed to arbitration in its letter of 26 May 1999 in which it proposed the name of an arbitrator.

[...]

According to the Defendant, Article 12.1 was a choice of law clause. As it was not an arbitration clause, it would not be possible to commence arbitration proceedings on the basis of it.

As concerns Article 12.2 indicating jurisdiction by reference to Article 12.1, the Defendant claims that this provision is ineffective as it refers to a law that does not exist (that of the ICC) or a neutral law that, however, should have been specified (but in fact was not specified) by the parties.

[...]

5.4 The Arbitral Tribunal's Position

The provision contained in Article 12 must be interpreted by searching for the parties' common intention, without dwelling on the literal meaning of the words, on the basis of a widespread principle that has also been incorporated in Article 4.1 of the UNIDROIT Principles according to which "1. A contract shall be interpreted according to the common intention of the parties. 2. If such an intention cannot be established, the contract shall be interpreted according to the meaning that reasonable persons of the same kind as the parties would give to it in the same circumstances."

In applying this criterion it must be considered that the persons who drew up and negotiated the clause were not jurists and did not therefore have a clear idea of the meaning (from a legal point of view) of the concepts of competent forum, arbitration and applicable law. [...] In order to understand the meaning of the provision one would have to put oneself in the condition the parties were in (or that of a reasonable person of the same kind as the parties). The parties, not having had legal training, tend to confuse the concepts of applicable law and jurisdiction, their main concern being to put into effect the most neutral solution possible for the settlement of disputes that might arise.

Now, if one reads Article 12 in this perspective, the reference to International Chamber of Commerce, contained in Article 12.1, is to be understood in the first place as a clause aimed at establishing jurisdiction, and this is, after all, confirmed by the last part of the sentence which reads "... which can in no case be the courts of law of the contracting parties' respective countries". In other words, when the parties declare their intention to submit the contract to an applicable law (that of the ICC) other than that of the courts of their respective countries (placing law and jurisdiction on the same level), it is clear that they intend to refer to jurisdiction (that of the ICC) and therefore to ICC arbitration.

This appears to be further confirmed by the title of the article in question ("Competent Forum") as well as by that fact that Article 12.2 refers to the courts specified in Art. 12.1. This confirms that the parties intended the function of Article 12.1 to be the determination of jurisdiction. [...]

In conclusion: if one looks at Art. 12 as a whole and seeks to identify its real meaning (beyond the technical meaning of the legal terms used), one sees that the parties' intention was to settle any disputes that might arise in a neutral way, having recourse to the International Chamber of Commerce which they considered an instrument well known to be suitable for that purpose. Consequently, if they intended to submit their disputes to the ICC, that can only mean that they intended to have recourse to arbitration, the ICC being universally well known as an arbitration institution and also considering that the parties had agreed on ICC arbitration in a previous contract.

This interpretation of Article 12 is moreover in conformity with the principle of all terms being given effect contained in Article 4.5 of the UNIDROIT Principles, according to which: "Contract terms shall be interpreted so as to give effect to all the terms rather than to deprive some of them of effect."

On the other hand if Article 12 were to be interpreted not as arbitration clause, the parties could not have recourse to either arbitration or to the domestic courts that would normally have jurisdiction (and namely those of the Defendant's country or of the place of performance of the Contracts) since their jurisdiction has been expressly excluded by the clause in question. This would deprive the parties of any possibility to act in the case of a dispute, unless the clause is considered in its entirety ineffective. [...]

Consequently the arbitral tribunal affirmed its jurisdiction to decide the dispute.

6. What Law is Applicable to the Merits of the Dispute?

As concerns the applicable law, Article 12 of the Contracts makes reference to the ICC and to a "neutral legislation specified by mutual agreement by the parties". In view of the fact that no ICC legislation exists and that the parties have not specified by mutual agreement a neutral law, it must be concluded that the parties have not expressly chosen the applicable law.

The Arbitral Tribunal will therefore have to determine the applicable law in conformity with the second sentence of Art. 17 (1) of the ICC Arbitration Rules according to which: "In the absence of an agreement between the parties the Arbitral Tribunal shall apply the rules of law it considers appropriate in the case at hand".

The Arbitral Tribunal holds that, in order to determine the most appropriate rules of law, the fact that the parties wanted a neutral solution had to be taken into account.

Now, in the absence of an express indication as to the domestic law of a third country, the most appropriate solution in the case in which the parties express their desire for a neutral solution is to apply the general rules and principles of international contracts, the so-called *lex mercatoria*.

In this context, for questions concerning general contract law, reference can be made to the "UNIDROIT Principles of International Commercial Contracts" which represent – except for a few provisions (such as for example the provisions on hardship: see ICC Award N° 8873 of 1998, in Journal droit int., 1998, p. 1017) – a "restatement" of the rules that parties engaged in international trade consider to be consonant with their interests and expectations. This has been recognised in numerous arbitral awards in which the UNIDROIT Principles have been applied as an expression of the *lex mercatoria* or of international trade usages: see for example ICC partial Award N° 7110, in Bull. Arb. CCI, 2/1999, pp 40-50; ICC Award N° 7375, in Mealey's International Arbitration Report, vol. 11/n° 12 (December 1996), pp. A1-A69; ICC Award N° 8502, in Bull. Arb. CCI, 2/1999, pp. 74-77.

The Tribunal will therefore apply the rules and principles generally recognised in international trade (*lex mercatoria*) and in particular the UNIDROIT Principles, to the extent that they represent rules recognised by international business people as being applicable to international contracts.

7. Are the Parties' Claims and Counterclaims Admissible and, if so, to What Extent?

[...]

The Plaintiff reproached the Defendant for not having performed the Contracts (by refusing to supply the contractual products in the absence of the Plaintiff's acceptance of the contractual modifications the Defendant wanted to impose) and for having subsequently illegally terminated, without placing Plaintiff formally into breach and without any justification, while negotiations were underway in an attempt to solve the problem which had been artificially created by the Defendant itself.

The Plaintiff claims that termination is unjustified and ineffective, and that consequently the Contracts remain in force until their date of expiry. It therefore requests that the Defendant be ordered to perform the Contracts until they expire and to supply the Plaintiff, according to the terms of the Contracts, the goods ordered and any goods that may be ordered subsequently and to compensate the harm (lost profit and detriment to its credit standing and commercial reputation), suffered on account of the refusal to supply the goods until the date of the arbitral award.

Alternatively, if termination, notice of which was given by the Defendant, is considered effective (notwithstanding its illegal nature), the Plaintiff requests that the responsibility for termination of the Contracts be laid entirely and exclusively on the Defendant and that, consequently, the Defendant be ordered to compensate the Plaintiff for the harm (lost profit and detriment to credit and commercial reputation), suffered as a result of the illegal termination.

The Defendant, on its part, maintains that termination of the Contracts was justified [...] by the Plaintiff's breach of an essential obligation such as that of reaching the minimum agreed purchases and that, moreover, the Plaintiff had no right to be compensated for alleged harm deriving from termination.

On the contrary, the Defendant maintains that it has a right to compensation for the harm suffered on account of lost profits, loss of gross margin and of the market in the Plaintiff's country.

The questions of merit resulting from the parties' claims that must be settled are essentially the following:

1. In the first place it must be established whether, in the period preceding termination of the Contracts, the Defendant's behaviour (refusal to supply the goods on the contractually agreed conditions) constituted non-performance of the Contracts.

2. In this context it must also be determined whether the parties solved the problem by a settlement agreement concerning the orders in course and possible future orders.

3. Then it will be necessary to establish whether termination of the Contracts by the Defendant was justified and in particular whether such termination was validly made and whether the reasons invoked by the Defendant can justify termination of the Contracts before their expiry.

4. Should termination by the Defendant by considered illegal, it must be decided whether it has put an end to the Contracts or whether, on the contrary, they remain in force notwithstanding termination by the Defendant.

5. Depending on the replies given to the above questions, it must lastly be decided whether, and to what extent, the Plaintiff's claim for damages and the Defendant's counterclaim must be granted.

[...]

The Plaintiff claims that the Defendant, by unilaterally modifying the conditions of payment in its letter of [...] and by refusing subsequently to supply the goods ordered on the conditions set out in the Contracts, breached the Contracts and should compensate the Plaintiff for the harm it suffered on account of such breach of the Contracts.

[...]

The Defendant's behaviour is in principle contrary to a fundamental rule of contract law, namely, the principle of *pacta sunt servanda*, which has been incorporated also in the UNIDROIT Principles in Art. 1.3 according to which "A contract validly entered into is binding upon the parties. It can only be modified or terminated in accordance with its terms or by agreement or as otherwise provided in these Principles."

This principle is not of course absolute and therefore it is perfectly conceivable that a seller may, in particular circumstances, be permitted to no longer adhere to the agreed terms of payment Thus it would be contrary to the principle of good faith to oblige a seller to continue to supply goods to its distributor without the possibility of requiring adequate payment guarantees whenever there are good reasons to fear that the latter will not pay for the goods on the date due.

In the case at hand there were of course certainly facts prompting a certain prudence before accepting orders. [...].

Nevertheless such facts were not sufficient to justify the Defendant's unilateral decision to modify the terms of payment of the Plaintiff whose solvency was not in question. Consequently the Defendant's refusal to supply the goods on the contractually agreed terms certainly constituted a breach of contract.

[...]

After the first exchanges of correspondence indicated above the parties began to seek an amicable solution. [...] It remains to be seen whether the parties have reached an agreement capable of overcoming the differences examined in the foregoing paragraph.

For this purpose the negotiations concerning the terms of supply and of payment of the two orders No. XXXX/98 and No. YYYY/98 and the terms of payment of future orders will be examined separately.

[...]

As concerns orders N. XXXX/98 and No. YYYY/98 negotiations between the parties resulted in an agreement through an exchange of letters of [...] and of [...]. The only – completely negligible – difference is that the Defendant agreed to pay the difference between the cost of carriage by air and the cost of carriage by sea, while the Plaintiff asked the Defendant to pay the entire cost of carriage by air.

However, this does not exclude that a valid agreement has been reached. Indeed, in the context of the *lex mercatoria* correspondence between offer and acceptance is not a strict requirement, it being held (in conformity with the current view held by parties engaged in international trade) that an acceptance of an offer containing modifications or additions does not prevent the conclusion of a contract provided that the modifications and additions are of minor importance. Thus Article 2.11(2) of the UNIDROIT Principles provides that "... a reply to an offer which purports to be an acceptance but contains additional or different terms which do not materially alter the terms of the offer constitutes an acceptance, unless the offeror, without undue delay, objects to the discrepancy."

In the case at hand the Plaintiff did not challenge the modification contained in the Defendant's acceptance and the agreement on the terms of payment and supply of the two orders can therefore be considered concluded on the not objected terms of acceptance of the Defendant.

It may therefore be concluded that with respect to the two orders No XXXX/98 and No YYYY/98 the parties had reached an agreement according to which the Plaintiff undertook to pay the sum of US $ 70.897,55 and the Defendant to send the goods in question within the next 8 days.

[...]

As concerns future deliveries, the parties agreed in a subsequent exchange of letters that the Plaintiff would pay for the goods in advance, on the basis of a pro forma invoice sent to it by the Defendant, and would obtain a discount corresponding to the discount rate in the Plaintiff's country for a period of 120 days, fixed for the current at 5%.

[...]

Nevertheless the parties did not expressly agree on the criteria to be followed to establish the amount of the discount in the event of a change in the discount rate. [...]

Must it therefore be concluded that an agreement as to the terms of payment of future deliveries had not been reached?

It is important to note that negotiations were carried out in successive stages leading to the progressive conclusion of the agreement. In a similar context it is quite possible that the parties reach partial agreements (that leave some terms open) provided that they did not intend to make their agreement dependant on the conclusion of an agreement covering all issues under discussion.

This principle is recognised in Art. 2.13 of the UNIDROIT Principles, according to which "Where in the course of negotiations one of the parties insists that the contract is not concluded until there is agreement on specific matters or in a specific form, no contract is concluded before agreement is reached on those matters or in that form".

Indeed, this rule implies, a contrario, that the agreement on some of the matters under discussion binds the parties with respect to those matters unless the parties intended to make conclusion of their contract conditional upon the agreement on all other matters. This corresponds after all to the usages and practices in international trade in the context of which contracts are frequently formed in stages, and a partial agreement is considered binding and parties are obliged to reach agreement on matters still open: see, for example, in Bull. Arb. CCI, 2/1999, p. 67-70.

In the case at hand it is certain that the parties agreed that the discount had to be determined on the basis of the discount rate in the Plaintiff's country. [...] the absence of agreement on a matter of such marginal importance [to modify the 5% rate only if the discount rate in the Plaintiff's country rose by more than 0,5%] cannot jeopardize the parties' overall agreement concerning terms of payment and supply.

It must therefore be concluded that the parties modified, by means of the of the agreements of [...], the terms of payment provided for in the Contracts by substituting payment within120 days by payment in advance with a discount corresponding to the discount rate in the Plaintiff's country for a period of 120 days.

[...]

The Defendant gave notice of the termination of the Contracts to the Plaintiff in its letter of [...] and motivated it by the Plaintiff's failure to meet the sales figures established in Article 10.1.3 of the Contracts.

[...]

The Plaintiff claims that the failure to meet these figures does not constitute non-performance of the Contracts, since the figures were only market forecasts and not binding commitments. [...] Moreover, termination of the Contracts would in any case have required the formal placing of the Plaintiff into breach.

[...]

Before turning to the central question as to whether termination was justified, two preliminary questions have to be answered, whether termination must be preceded by a formal placing into breach and whether notice of termination is subject to a time-limit. [...]

The Plaintiff claims that termination could not be declared without formally placing it into breach beforehand, thereby giving it the chance to remedy its alleged non-performance.

This position would be justified if there were (as frequently happens in Anglo-american contract practice) a contract term imposing a duty on the party giving notice of termination to grant the other party an additional period of time within which to remedy the alleged breach. However, since this was not the case in the case at hand, reference must be made to the general rule set out in Art. 7.3.2(1) of the UNIDROIT Principles according to which "The right of a party to terminate the contract is exercised by notice to the other party."

Consequently, Defendant's failure to formally place the Plaintiff into breach does not affect the validity of termination.

[...]

The Plaintiff objects that the claim that it failed to reach the sales forecast for the period [...] is late and cannot therefore be taken into consideration.

This is correct. The principle of good faith imposes on the party intending to terminate the contract on account of the other party's non-performance the duty to inform it of its intention within a reasonably short period of time from the moment when it came to know of the non-performance. This principle is contained also in the UNIDROIT Principles. Indeed, Art. 7.3.2(2), states: "If performance has been offered late or otherwise does not conform to the contract the aggrieved party will lose its right to terminate the contract unless it gives notice to the other party within a reasonable time after it has or ought to have become aware of the offer or of the non-conforming performance."

Now, in the case at hand, the Defendant already knew at the beginning of [...] that the Plaintiff had not reached the purchases forecast for the year [...] and did not bring up this fact until the month of [...] of [...].

Consequently only the claim concerning the year [...] will be taken into consideration in the following part .

[...]

The principle according to which a fixed term contract can be terminated before it expires if there are serious reasons for termination constitutes a widely recognised principle in international trade: even the UNIDROIT Principles state, in general terms, in Art. 7.3.1(1), that: "A party may terminate the contract where the failure of the other party to perform an obligation under the contract amounts to a fundamental non-performance."

At any rate, in the case at hand reference to the general rule is not necessary since Art 10.1.3 of the Contracts makes express provision for the right to terminate the contract before it expires when there has been a serious infringement of one of its clauses.

It is a matter therefore of establishing whether the Plaintiff's non-performance, invoked by the Defendant, amounts to a breach of the Contracts serious enough to justify termination before expiry.

Contrary to widespread contracting practice, the Contracts do not expressly state that the failure to meet the agreed sales figures permits the supplier to terminate the contract. Article 11.4 of the Contracts only makes provision for annual sales volumes ("*Las partes acuerdan el siguiente presupuesto de compras*"), but does not specify the consequences of a possible failure to meet the indicated sales figures. This means that failure to meet the forecast sales figures could justify termination of the contract only to the extent that such failure amounts to a fundamental beach of one of the contractual terms.

Considering that beach of a contractual clause necessarily implies the beach of the obligation provided in such a term, it is essential to establish whether Article 11.4 is intended to make provision for a commitment to purchase or whether it amounts, on the other hand, to a non-binding forecast.

The term used ("*presupuesto*") seems to indicate objectives rather than minimum purchases. On the other hand however the presence of the parties' signature next to the clause in question stresses the importance the parties attributed to that aspect.[...]

Having said this, it should be noted that the clause, which merely states that the parties have agreed on determined sales objectives, contains no obligation on the Plaintiff's part to guarantee that such a result is achieved: if this had been the parties' intention, they would simply have agreed that the Plaintiff would undertake to purchase the annual quantities indicated in the clause.

Under such conditions the failure to meet the purchase objectives does not, in itself, amount to a breach of contract and as such cannot therefore be considered a justifiable reason for termination in advance.

Now, in the case at hand, it has not been proven that the failure to reach agreed purchases has been for reasons imputable to the Plaintiff rather than to the state of the market or to the place in which the new conditions of payment were negotiated (originating in the Defendant's unjustified refusal to supply). Under such conditions the mere reference to failure to reach the purchase objectives cannot be considered sufficient reason for terminating in advance a contract which had not even reached the mid point of its duration.[...]

The Arbitral Tribunal concludes that the reasons invoked by the Defendant to justify termination do not amount to a fundamental breach of Art. 10.1.3 of the Contracts and that termination must consequently be considered unjustified.

[...]

The Plaintiff claims that since the termination was unjustified it was ineffective and consequently the Contracts will remain in force until their expiry.

[...].

The problem of the effects of an unjustified termination of a contract is dealt with in different ways in the various legal systems: in some countries (above all in civil law systems) unjustified termination is ineffective, with the result that such a contract will remain in force and the parties will continue to have to fulfil their obligations; in other legal systems (and in particular in common law systems), even an unjustified termination puts an end to the contractual relationship, while the party who has unjustifiably terminated the contract is liable for damages to compensate the loss the other party has suffered.

This second approach, which has the advantage of certainty in contractual relationships, is the one generally adopted in international trade law. The UNIDROIT Principles seem to confirm this point of view by providing in Art. 7.3.2(1) that "The right of a party to terminate the contract is exercised by notice to the other party", and in Art. 7.3.5(1), that "Termination of the contract releases both parties from their obligation to effect and to receive future performance."

The Arbitral Tribunal holds that the latter solution corresponds to the rules and principles applicable in international trade and that, therefore, the consequences of an unjustified termination are limited to the terminating party's obligation to make compensation for the harm caused thereby to the other party.

It follows that the Plaintiff's request to have the other party obliged to perform the Contracts after they have been terminated (in particular as concerns the obligation to supply the goods and to respect exclusivity) cannot be granted.

[...]

The Defendant, considering that it unjustifiably terminated the Contracts, is obliged to compensate the harm caused to the Plaintiff by the termination.

The Plaintiff requests [...] for lost profits, the sum of US $ 509.661,40, [...] and for detriment to its credit standing and reputation, the sum of US $ 637.076,75, that is the abovementioned amount requested for lost profits of US $ 509.661,40 multiplied by 1,25.

[...]

As concerns the years [...], the Plaintiff considered that in the year [...] the total amount of sales was equal to about US $ 250.000, and drew the conclusion that it would be reasonable to expect at least the same result in the years [...] and a slightly higher volume of business (US $ 300.000) in [...].

The purchases indicated by the Plaintiff are based on wholesale prices [...] It is worth noting that such a figure corresponds to the volume of sales, at the wholesale price purchasers in the Plaintiff's country paid to the latter. [...] With respect to the volume of business based on the wholesale price, the Plaintiff applied [...] a margin of 47,5%, [...].

The Arbitral Tribunal notes however that the margin of 47,50% is a gross margin that cannot serve to calculate the Plaintiff's lost profits which should be calculated on the basis of the net margin.

Indeed, as established in Article 7.4.2 of the UNIDROIT Principles "The aggrieved party is entitled to full compensation for harm sustained as a result of the non-performance. Such harm includes both any loss which it suffered and any gain of which it was deprived, taking into account any gain to the aggrieved party resulting from its avoidance of cost or harm."

Now, the gain the Plaintiff lost on account of the interruption of the Contracts and the consequent termination of supply is not a gross margin on the sale price, but the net gain after all expenses have been deducted.

This principle has on numerous occasions been recognised in arbitral awards: see arbitral award in theThis principle has on several occasions been recognised in arbitral awards: see ICC Award n° 1250 (in JARVIN, DERAINS, Revueil des sentences arbitrales de la CCI 1974-1985, p. 30-33) concerning a Lebanese distributor in which the artibratros recognised a damages based on "average net profit"; ICC Award n° 5418 (in JARVIN, DERAINS, ARNALDEZ, Recueil des sentences arbitrales de la CCI 1986-1990, p. 132) referring to "net profit"; ICC Award n° 8362 (in Yearbook Commercial Arbitration, XXII-1997, p. 164-177) which considers damage to be "lost profits".

In the absence of any indication concerning the calculation of net margin, the Arbitral Tribunal held that it had to use the criterion contained in Article 7.4.3 § 3 of the UNIDROIT Principles, according to which:

"Where the amount of damages cannot be established with a sufficient degree of certainty, the assessment is at the discretion of the court."

In making this assessment the Tribunal considerd on the one hand the value of the goods the Plaintiff had purchased from the Defendant and on the other the sales of the Defendant's goods made by the Plaintiff (proportionate to the corresponding purchase price).

[...]

Sources

Excerpts of the original French version of the award have been published in:
Journal du droit international, 2003, 1142 - 1150 with note by E.J.[Emmanuel JOLIVET].

Date: ***January 2001***
Adjudicating Court: ***ICC International Court of Arbitration***
Number: ***9771***
Parties: ***Unknown***

Keywords

CONTRACT OF SALE BETWEEN AN ITALIAN AND CYPRIOT COMPANIES – DELIVERY OF NON-CONFORMING GOODS – CLAIM FOR DAMAGES INCLUDING INTEREST ON DAMAGES FROM THE TIME OF BREACH – REFERENCE IN CLAIM TO ART. 7.4.10 OF THE UNIDROIT PRINCIPLES

CONTRACT SILENT AS TO THE APPLICABLE LAW – ARBITRAL TRIBUNAL DECIDES IN FAVOUR OF CLAIMANT WITHOUT EXPRESSLY REFERRING TO EITHER A PARTICULAR DOMESTIC LAW OR TO THE UNIDROIT PRINCIPLES

Abstract

Claimant, an Italian company, sued Defendants, two Cypriot companies, for damages for their failure to deliver goods in conformity with the contractual specifications. Claimant requested, among others, interest on the amount of damages claimed from the time of the breach of the contract and, in support of such request, it referred to Article 7.4.10 of the UNIDROIT Principles.

The contract was silent as to the applicable law nor did the Arbitral Tribunal determine any domestic law as the applicable law. Without expressly referring to the UNIDROIT Principles, the Arbitral Tribunal decided that Claimant was entitled to interest on the damages claimed.

Full Text

(...)

The Sole Arbitrator makes the following determination in regard to the damages claimed.

In these proceedings the Claimant has claimed damages, which have been denied by the Defendants as follows:

(I) LOSS OF PROFIT

The Claimant claims that it has suffered a loss relating to the reduced value of the goods delivered which it was unable to sell at the original price had the goods been in conformity with the contractual specifications. The Claimant has produced evidence in the form of invoices to, and correspondence with, its customer..., which state that the originally agreed purchase price was 80 USD/MT and that this price was reduced and finally determined to be 48.50 USD/MT, thus creating an aggregate loss of USD 89,652.94 to the Claimant as compared to its initial sale.

The Sole Arbitrator is satisfied that the Claimant in fact sold the goods delivered at a loss as evidenced by the documents presented in these proceedings.

The Defendants have not objected to these calculations specifically per se but only in general tenns stating that it was unclear what amount was claimed.

The Claimant has admitted that from such amount the Defendants have already settled USD 30,000 and that the Defendants further should be credited the waiver made by [Defendant 2] for the Defendants for additional payment of the remaining 10% for the delivery amounting to USD 8,716.43 as specified in the invoice for such amount. Thus the Claimant effectively is claiming USD 50,936.51 in these proceedings.

The Sole Arbitrator finds that the Claimant shall be entitled to recover damages for the loss suffered due to the lack of quality of the goods with an amount of USD 50,936.51.

The Claimant has alleged that the Defendants during the negotiations following the discovery of the defective delivery of the goods accepted that the Claimant had suffered damages in the amount of USD 80,000 and also undertook to compensate such losses. The Claimant has maintained that this is evidenced by the payment of USD 30.000. The Sole Arbitrator cannot, against the objection of the Defendants and failing any substantial evidence in support thereof, find that the Defendants have made such an undertaking.

(II) INTEREST

In addition, the Claimant requests interest on the advance payment originally made to the Defendants in the amount of USD 154,473.75 from the date of the termination of the Contract or alternatively from the date of the Claimant's request for repayment and interest on the amount USD 89,652.94 from the time of the breach of Contract in accordance to Article 7.4. 10 of the UNIDROIT Principles of International Commercial Contracts.

In the alternative the Claimant claims interest on the damages in general.

On the issue of interest the Claimant has not stated any reason why it should be entitled to interest on the amount of USD 154,473.75. Even less so is there any motivation why interest should be calculated from the Claimant's request for reimbursement of the amount paid as advance payment in view of the fact that the Claimant did not, in the opinion of the Sole Arbitrator prove that it did terminate the Contract and retum the goods. Instead the Claimant has claimed damages in these proceedings. This claim for interest on the advance payments is denied. The Sole Arbitrator finds that interest may only be calculated on the damages claimed.

(III) OTHER DAMAGES

Finally, the Claimant has claimed "other damages" for the loss of reputation to be determined in these proceedings. The Claimant has requested the Sole Arbitrator to resolve this issue on the basis of "*ex aequo et bono*".

According to the ICC Rules an arbitrator may not base any decision on the principle of "*ex aequo et bono*" unless expressly authorised. This is furthermore repeated in the Terms of Reference agreed and signed between the parties in these proceedings. No such agreement has been made. In addition, no other damages or the loss of reputation have been presented or evidenced in these proceedings either to the amount or otherwise. In any arbitration it is a fundamental principle that each party shall have the possibility to present its case and to respond to any claim made against it. Should the Sole Arbitrator award other damages then the Defendant would clearly not have been given such opportunity.

The Sole Arbitrator therefore has no basis on which to determine, or even less award, any damages under this heading. The claim for "other damages" is therefore denied.

Sources

Excerpt in ICC International Court of Arbitration Bulletin, 2005 Special Supplement, 76 - 77.

Date: ***25 January 2001***
Adjudicating Court: ***International Arbitration Court of the Chamber of Commerce and Industry of the Russian Federation***
Number: ***88/2000***
Parties: ***Unknown***

Keywords

CONTRACT SILENT AS TO THE APPLICABLE LAW – REFERENCE TO UNIDROIT PRINCIPLES AS ONE OF RELEVANT LEGAL SOURCES

PENALTY CLAUSE – PAYMENT OF PENALTY FOR DELAY IN PAYMENT OF PRICE – PENALTY GROSSLY EXCESSIVE IN RELATION TO HARM SUFFERED BY AGGRIEVED PARTY (ART. 7.4.13(2) UNIDROIT PRINCIPLES)

Abstract

A sales contract between a Russian and an English party provided that in case of delayed payment of the price the buyer should pay a penalty in addition to interest at the LIBOR rate. When the buyer actually delayed the payment of the price, the seller asked for the payment of both the interest on the sum not paid in time and the agreed penalty.

The Arbitral Tribunal awarded the interest at the agreed LIBOR rate and rejected the claim for the payment of the penalty. In doing so it referred to Article 7.4.13(2) of the UNIDROIT Principles, according to which the agreed sum to be paid in case of failure to perform may be reduced if turns out to be grossly excessive in relation to the harm resulting from the non-performance and to the other circumstances.

Full Text

[Not yet available]

Sources

Unpublished. Notice of the award kindly given by Professor Alexander KOMAROV, President of the International Arbitration Court of the Chamber of Commerce and Industry of the Russian Federation.

Date: ***February 2, 2001***
Country: ***Netherlands***
Adjudicating Court: ***Supreme Court of the Netherlands***
Number: ***R99/120HR***
Parties: ***Sint Maarten Veterinary Hospital N.V. v. Animal Hospital of the Netherlands Antilles N.V.***

Keywords

CONTRACT NEGOTIATIONS BETWEEN TWO COMPANIES SITUATED IN THE NEDERLANDSE ANTILLEN – COMMON LAW APPLIES

AGREEMENT PRESUMED TO BE BINDING ONLY IF IN WRITING – REFERENCE TO ART. 2.13 [ART. 2.1.13 OF THE 2004 EDITION] UNIDROIT PRINCIPLES

Abstract

The case deals with the transfer of an animal ambulance situated at St. Maarten, Nederlandse Antillen. The negotiations were leading to a letter of intent. Later on the parties laid down a so-called "Earnest Money Agreement". The parties worked out various concepts, but their negotiations never led to an agreement.

Subsequently one of the parties brought an action against the other before the Dutch Supreme Court claiming damages for the expenses it incurred as a result of the negotiations which ultimately ended without positive result.

In his advise the Advocate General of the Dutch Supreme Court argued that the parties probably intended to be bound only by the terms laid down in writing. Such presumption was justified by the fact that the negotiations took place within a common law system. Yet he also referred to Article 2.13 [Art. 2.1.13 of the 2004 edition] of the UNIDROIT Principles, according to which "where in the course of negotiations one of the parties insists that the contract is not concluded until there is agreement on specific matters or in a specific form, no contract is concluded before agreement is reached on those matters or in that form."

In its decision the Dutch Supreme Court, though without expressly mentioning Article 2.13 [Art. 2.1.13 of the 2004 edition] of the UNIDROIT Principles, confirmed the Advocate General's conclusions.

Full Text

LJN-nummer: AA9771 Zaaknr: R99/120HR
Bron: Hoge Raad der Nederlanden 's-Gravenhage
Datum uitspraak: 2-02-2001
Datum publicatie: 11-03-1999
Soort zaak: civiel - civiel overig

Soort procedure: cassatie
2 februari 2001
Eerste Kamer
Nr. R99/120HR

Hoge Raad der Nederlanden
Arrest

in de zaak van:

1. SINT MAARTEN VETERINARY HOSPITAL N.V., gevestigd op St. Maarten, Nederlandse Antillen,
2. De erven van wijlen [erflater] wonende op St. Maarten, Nederlandse Antillen,
3. [Eiseres 3], wonende op St. Maarten, Nederlandse Antillen,

EISERS tot cassatie,

advocaat: mr. R.S. Meijer,

t e g e n

1. ANIMAL HOSPITAL OF THE NETHERLANDS ANTILLES N.V., gevestigd op St. Maarten, Nederlandse Antillen,
2. [Verweerder 2] en
3. [Verweerster 3], beiden wonende op St. Maarten, Nederlandse Antillen,

VERWEERDERS in cassatie,
niet verschenen.

1. Het geding in feitelijke instanties

Met een op 17 juli 1997 ter griffie van het Gerecht in Eerste Aanleg van de Nederlandse Antillen, zittingsplaats St. Maarten, ingekomen verzoekschrift hebben eisers tot cassatie - verder te noemen: [eiser] c.s. - verzocht verweerders in cassatie - verder te noemen: [verweerder] c.s. hoofdelijk te veroordelen om aan haar te voldoen de schade, veroorzaakt door het afbreken van de onderhandelingen over de overname van de dierenartsenpraktijk van [eiser] c.s. en de schade veroorzaakt door het openen door [verweerder] c.s. van een nieuwe dierenartsenpraktijk op basis van de door [eiser] c.s. verzorgde vergunningen, op te maken bij staat en te vereffenen volgens de wet, vermeerderd met de wettelijke rente en kosten.
[Verweerder] c.s. hebben het verzoek bestreden.
Het Gerecht in Eerste Aanleg heeft bij vonnis van 5 mei 1998 de vordering van [eiser] c.s. afgewezen.
Tegen dit vonnis zijn [eiser] c.s. in appel gekomen bij het Gemeenschappelijk Hof van Justitie van de Nederlandse Antillen en Aruba.
Bij vonnis van 19 maart 1999 heeft het Hof het vonnis waarvan beroep bekrachtigd.
Het arrest van het Hof is aan dit arrest gehecht.

2. Het geding in cassatie

Tegen het arrest van het Hof hebben [eiser] c.s. beroep in cassatie ingesteld. Het cassatierekest is aan dit arrest gehecht en maakt daarvan deel uit.
[Verweerder] c.s. hebben geen verweerschrift ingediend. De zaak is voor [eiser] c.s. toegelicht door hun advocaat alsmede door mr. S.H.M.A. Dumoulin, advocaat bij de Hoge Raad.
De conclusie van de Advocaat-Generaal Hartkamp strekt tot vernietiging van het bestreden vonnis en tot verwijzing van de zaak naar het Gemeenschappelijk Hof van Justitie van de Nederlandse Antillen en Aruba ter verdere behandeling en beslissing.

3. Beoordeling van het middle

3.1 In cassatie kan worden uitgegaan van het volgende.
(i) [Erflater] [..] was dierenarts. Zijn erfgenamen zijn de eisers tot cassatie onder 2.
(ii) [Verweerder 2] en [verweerster 3], de verweerders in cassatie onder 2, respectievelijk 3, (verder: [verweerder 2] en [verweerster 3]) zijn eveneens dierenarts. Zij hebben in verschillende perioden in dienstverband gewerkt voor [erflater], dan wel voor eiseres tot cassatie onder 1 Sint Maarten Veterinary Hospital N.V.
(iii) [Erflater] en [verweerder] c.s. hebben onderhandelingen gevoerd over de overname van de dierenartsenpraktijk van [erflater].
(iv) Deze onderhandelingen hebben geresulteerd in een in begin april 1995 door partijen ondertekende Letter of Intent.
(v) [Erflater] en verzoekster tot cassatie onder 3, [..] enerzijds, en [verweerder 2] en [verweerster 3] anderzijds zijn op 20 april 1995 schriftelijk een Earnest Money Agreement aangegaan.
(vi) Op 5 januari 1996 hebben [erflater], [verweerder 2] en [verweerster 3] een Termination Agreement ondertekend. Deze overeenkomst hield in:

> WHEREAS, the parties executed an Earnest Money Agreement for St. Peters Veterinary Hospital and Cole Bay Veterinary Hospital in St. Maarten, Netherlands Antilles; and
> WHEREAS, the parties desire to terminate the earnest money agreement and return the balance of the earnest money, $ 16.508,71 to Purchaser;
> NOW, THEREFORE, for and in consideration of TEN DOLLARS ($ 10,00) cash in hand paid, the receipt paid, the parties agree as follows:
> 1. The Earnest Money Agreement is hereby terminated and the parties are hereby released from all duties and obligations arising under the Earnest Money Agreement.
> 2. The remaining earnest Money of $ 16.508,71 shall be immediately delivered to Purchaser by Dixon, Smith $ Stahl, the Settlement Agent.

(vii) Partijen hebben vervolgens verder onderhandeld over de overname van het St. Peters Veterinary Hospital en het Cole Bay Veterinary Hospital (verder: de praktijk).
(viii)Verschillende concept-overnameovereenkomsten zijn opgesteld maar partijen zijn niet tot overeenstemming gekomen.
(ix) In april 1996 heeft [verweerder 2] een bod gedaan op de praktijk ten bedrage van $ 276.000.
(x) [Verweerder 2] en [verweerster 3] hebben vervolgens een eigen veterinaire praktijk geopend waarin zij als dierenarts werkzaam zijn.

3.2.1 [Eiser] c.s. vorderen in dit geding vergoeding van schade wegens het door [verweerder 2] en [verweerster 3] afbreken van onderhandelingen welke schade het bedrag beloopt van de koopsom die is genoemd in de hiervoor in 3.1 onder (iv) genoemde Letter of Intent, te weten US $ 640.000 en voorts de schade die bestaat uit de kosten die [eiser] c.s. hebben gemaakt gedurende de onderhandelingen. Voorts hebben [eiser] c.s. vergoeding van schade gevorderd wegens oneerlijke mededinging als gevolg van het door [verweerder] c.s. openen van een dierenartsenpraktijk op Sint Maarten.

3.2.2 Het Gerecht in Eerste Aanleg heeft de vorderingen van [eiser] c.s. afgewezen. Het Hof heeft de tegen het vonnis van het Gerecht in Eerste Aanleg aangevoerde grieven verworpen.
Het middel keert zich tegen 's Hofs beslissing en de gronden waarop deze berust.

3.3.1 Onderdeel 1 keert zich tegen 's Hofs oordeel in zijn rov. 4.6 en 4.8 dat tussen partijen geen overeenkomst is tot stand gekomen omdat uit hetgeen [eiser] c.s. hebben aangevoerd volgt dat zij zich zelf op het standpunt stellen dat geen overeenstemming is bereikt over de overnameprijs noch over de wijze van overname. Het onderdeel voert daartoe, kort weergegeven, aan dat uit hetgeen [eiser] c.s. hebben aangevoerd onmiskenbaar blijkt dat zij zich in het geding in de feitelijke instanties wel op het standpunt hebben gesteld dat tussen partijen over de essentialia overeenstemming was bereikt en dat zulks aan afbreking van de tot vervolmaking en afronding van de overeenkomst strekkende onderhandelingen door de [verweerder 2] in de weg stond.

3.3.2 Bij de beoordeling van dit onderdeel moet worden vooropgesteld dat de vraag of ten aanzien van een overeenkomst, bij het tot stand komen waarvan een aantal onderling samenhangende verbintenissen moet worden geregeld, overeenstemming omtrent een of meer onderdelen een overeenkomst doet ontstaan zolang omtrent andere onderdelen nog geen overeenstemming bestaat, afhankelijk is van de bedoeling van partijen, zoals deze op grond van de betekenis van hetgeen wel en niet geregeld is, van het al dan niet bestaan van het voornemen tot verder onderhandelen en van de verdere omstandigheden van het geval moet worden aangenomen.

3.3.3 In het licht van dit uitgangspunt heeft het Hof met zijn hiervoor weergegeven oordeel hetzij blijk gegeven van een onjuiste rechtsopvatting hetzij zijn oordeel niet naar de eis der wet met redenen omkleed.
Van een onjuiste rechtsopvatting heeft het Hof blijk gegeven indien het de hiervoor onder 3.3.2 vermelde uitgangspunten heeft miskend.
Mocht het Hof daarvan wel zijn uitgegaan dan is zonder nadere, maar ontbrekende, motivering niet begrijpelijk 's Hofs oordeel dat geen overeenstemming is bereikt over de overnameprijs noch over de wijze van overname. De enkele omstandigheid dat geen overeenkomst over de overname van de dierenartsenpraktijk tot stand is gekomen, staat immers niet eraan in de weg dat wel overeenstemming is bereikt over de overnameprijs en de wijze van overname.
Het onderdeel treft derhalve doel.

3.4 Onderdeel 2 is gericht tegen 's Hofs rov. 4.7. Daarin verwerpt het Hof de vijfde door [eiser] c.s. tegen het vonnis van het Gerecht aangevoerde grief. Deze grief betrof het oordeel van het Gerecht, in zijn rov. 7, dat de Termination Agreement partijen

uitdrukkelijk ontslaat van alle verplichtingen uit de Earnest Money Agreement (en naar moet worden aangenomen ook van die uit de Letter of Intent).
In de hier bedoelde grief hadden [eiser] c.s. aangevoerd, samengevat weergegeven, dat de Termination Agreement ertoe strekte om een punt te zetten achter het voornemen de praktijk te verkopen en voorts om door te gaan met onderhandelingen over de overname van de praktijk op basis van een huurkoop-constructie. De strekking van de Termination Agreement was volgens deze grief niet om definitief een punt te zetten achter de onderhandelingen als geheel.
Het Hof heeft deze grief verworpen en daartoe in zijn rov. 4.7 overwogen: (1) de tekst van de Termination Agreement laat geen ruimte voor een andere uitleg dan door het Gerecht gegeven; (2) de getuige [getuige 1] heeft verklaard "dat de Termination Agreement tot strekking had dat de oorspronkelijke koopovereenkomst van de baan was". Deze overwegingen kunnen 's Hofs beslissing echter niet dragen. Noch de hiervoor in 3.1 onder (vi) weergegeven inhoud van de Termination Agreement, noch de door het Hof in zijn rov. 4.7 weergegeven inhoud van de door de getuige [getuige 1] afgelegde verklaring sluiten immers uit dat hetgeen [eiser] c.s. omtrent de strekking van de Termination Agreement heeft gesteld en aangevoerd juist is. Het onderdeel treft derhalve eveneens doel.

4. Beslissing

De Hoge Raad:
vernietigt het vonnis van het Gemeenschappelijk Hof van Justitie van de Nederlandse Antillen en Aruba van 19 maart 1999;
verwijst het geding naar dat Hof ter verdere behandeling en beslissing;
veroordeelt [verweerder] c.s. in de kosten van het geding in cassatie, tot op deze uitspraak aan de zijde van [eiser] c.s. begroot op *f* 575,-- aan verschotten en *f* 3.500,-- voor salaris.

Dit arrest is gewezen door de vice-president F.H.J. Mijnssen als voorzitter en de raadsheren R. Herrmann, J.B. Fleers, A. Hammerstein en P.C. Kop, en in het openbaar uitgesproken door de raadsheer W.H. Heemskerk op 2 februari 2001.

nr. R99/120HR
Mr. Hartkamp
zitting, 10 november 2000

Conclusie inzake
1) Sint Maarten Veterinary Hospital N.V.
2) De erven van [erflater]
3) [Eiseres 3]

tegen

1) Animal Hospital of The Netherlands Antilles N.V.
2) [Verweerder 2]
3) [Verweerster 3]

Edelhoogachtbaar College,

Feiten en procesverloop

1) In cassatie zijn de volgende feiten van belang. [Erflater] heeft onderhandelingen gevoerd met [verweerder 2] en [verweerster 3] over de overname van een ([erflaters]) dierenartspraktijk. Deze onderhandelingen hebben geresulteerd in een letter of intent (productie 1 bij inleidend verzoekschrift). Op 20 april 1995 zijn partijen schriftelijk een Earnest Money Agreement aangegaan (productie 2 bij conclusie van antwoord). Door ondertekening van een Termination Agreement d.d. 5 januari 1996 (productie 5 bij conclusie van antwoord) zijn partijen bevrijd van al hun rechten en verplichtingen uit de overeenkomst. Partijen hebben vervolgens verder onderhandeld over de overname van de praktijk. Hoewel verscheidene conceptovereenkomsten zijn opgesteld, zijn partijen niet tot overeenstemming gekomen.

Sint Maarten Veterinary Hospital N.V., [erflater] (die na het vonnis van het Gerecht in Eerste Aanleg is overleden, vanaf welk moment zijn erven zijn plaats in het geding hebben ingenomen) en [eiseres 3] (hierna [eiser] c.s.) hebben bij verzoekschrift van 17 juli 1997 het Gerecht in Eerste Aanleg, zittingsplaats Sint Maarten (hierna GEA) verzocht om Animal Hospital of The Netherlands Antilles N.V., [verweerder 2] en [verweerster 3] (hierna [verweerder] c.s.) hoofdelijk te veroordelen om de schade te vergoeden die aan de zijde van [eiser] c.s. is veroorzaakt door het afbreken van de onderhandelingen over de overname van de dierenartspraktijk van [eiser] c.s.

Aan deze vordering hebben [eiser] c.s. ten grondslag gelegd dat [verweerder] c.s. onrechtmatig jegens hen hebben gehandeld, omdat zij reeds ver gevorderde onderhandelingen hebben afgebroken met een tegenbod van US$ 276.000,-, terwijl partijen reeds overeenstemming hadden bereikt over de prijs en [eiser] c.s. mochten vertrouwen op de totstandkoming van de overname. [Verweerder] c.s. hebben verweer gevoerd, waarbij zij het GEA hebben verzocht [eiser] c.s. niet in hun vordering te ontvangen, althans deze vordering af te wijzen. Als grond voor afwijzing van de vordering voerden [verweerder] c.s. aan dat hun tegenbod gebaseerd was op een rapport van Deloitte & Touche, waaruit bleek dat de overnameprijs veel te hoog was (productie 4 bij conclusie van antwoord).

2) Bij vonnis van 5 mei 1998 heeft het GEA de vordering van [eiser] c.s. afgewezen, waarbij het volgende is overwogen:

“6. In de Earnest Money Agreement is voorts uitdrukkelijk bepaald dat het doorgaan van de transactie mede afhankelijk was van de goedkeuring van de boeken en bescheiden van de praktijk. Aangenomen moet worden dat partijen hiermee aan partij [verweerder 2] de gelegenheid hebben willen geven om de door KPMG en [betrokkene A] gebruikte gegevens, die tot de overnameprijs hebben geleid, te controleren. Dit is door [betrokkene B] gedaan. Op grond van zijn rapport moet het ervoor worden gehouden (dat) partij [verweerder 2] haar goedkeuring zou hebben onthouden en ook mocht onthouden, zodat zij, als de Termination Agreement niet reeds was ondertekend, de koopovereenkomst alsnog had kunnen ontbinden.

7. Het vorenstaande, gekoppeld aan het feit dat de Termination Agreement zelf partijen uitdrukkelijk ontslaat van alle verplichtingen uit de Earnest Money Agreement (en naar moet worden aangenomen ook van die uit de Letter of Intent) leidt tot de conclusie dat

tussen partijen noch over de wijze van overdracht, noch over de prijs overeenstemming bestond. Partij [verweerder 2] mocht dan ook in april 1996 een tegenbod doen. Van een situatie, dat [erflater] er op mocht vertrouwen dat een overeenkomst tot stand zou komen op basis van de door hem geformuleerde uitgangspunten is dan ook geen sprake."

3) [Eiser] c.s. zijn van het vonnis van het GEA in appel gekomen bij het Gemeenschappelijk Hof van Justitie van de Nederlandse Antillen en Aruba en hebben tien grieven gericht tegen het vonnis van het GEA. [Verweerder] c.s hebben verweer gevoerd en het Hof verzocht het vonnis van het GEA te bevestigen.

Het Hof heeft bij vonnis van 19 maart 1999 het vonnis van het GEA bevestigd. De volgende overwegingen van het Hof zijn in cassatie van belang:

"4.6 De grieven drie en vier treffen evenmin doel. Blijkens de vordering zoals deze door [eiser] c.s. (ook) in hoger beroep is ingesteld zijn zij van mening dat tussen partijen geen overeenkomst is totstandgekomen. Immers, zij vorderen schadevergoeding wegens het onrechtmatig afbreken van de tussen partijen gevoerde onderhandelingen. De eerste rechter heeft derhalve met juistheid, gelet ook op hetgeen in deze procedure als tussen partijen vaststaand is aangemerkt, geoordeeld dat geen overeenstemming is bereikt over de overnameprijs noch over de wijze van overname.

4.7 De vijfde grief betreft het oordeel van de eerste rechter dat partijen door het ondertekenen van de Termination Agreement uitdrukkelijk ontslagen zijn van alle verplichtingen uit de Earnest Money Agreement, hiervoor ook aangeduid als de overeenkomst. Ook die grief faalt. Allereerst omdat de tekst van de Termination Agreement geen ruimte laat voor een andere uitleg dan door de eerste rechter gegeven. Bovendien heeft de getuige [getuige 1], zoals ook door [eiser] c.s. aangehaald in hoger beroep, verklaard dat de Termination Agreement tot strekking had dat de oorspronkelijke koopovereenkomst van de baan was. In de toelichting op de vijfde grief betwisten [eiser] c.s. deze uitleg ook niet. Dat partijen de bedoeling hadden verder te onderhandelen teneinde alsnog op andere wijze tot overeenstemming te komen tast de door de eerste rechter aan de Termination Agreement toegekende betekenis niet aan.

4.8 Ook de zesde grief kan niet slagen. Wat er ook zij van het in die grief aangevallen oordeel van de eerste rechter, nu [eiser] c.s. zich - blijkens de formulering van het petitum - op het standpunt stellen dat tussen partijen geen overeenkomst is totstandgekomen, kunnen zij zich niet met vrucht keren tegen de overweging in het aangevallen vonnis waarin is uitgemaakt dat geen overeenstemming is bereikt over de wijze van overdracht en de hoogte van de prijs. Zou een dergelijke overeenstemming immers wel bereikt zijn dan was voor een vordering uit onrechtmatige daad, te weten het afbreken van onderhandelingen, geen plaats."

4) Tegen het vonnis van het Hof zijn [eiser] c.s. bij verzoekschrift van 21 juni 1999, tijdig(1), in cassatie gekomen. Zij hebben daartoe een middel van cassatie geformuleerd dat uit twee onderdelen is opgebouwd. [Eiser] c.s. hebben hun middel schriftelijk toegelicht en om arrest gevraagd. [Verweerder] c.s. hebben geen verweer gevoerd.

Bespreking van het cassatiemiddel

5) Onderdeel 1 is gericht tegen de r.o. 4.6 en 4.8 van het vonnis van het Hof, waarin het Hof de grieven II, IV en VI tegen het vonnis van het GEA heeft verworpen. In de betreffende grieven hebben [eiser] c.s. erover geklaagd dat het GEA had overwogen dat partijen feitelijk nog geen overeenstemming hadden bereikt over de overnameprijs en de wijze van overname van de praktijk van [eiser] c.s. door [verweerder] c.s. Het Hof heeft als motivering voor de verwerping van deze grieven gegeven dat de vordering van [eiser] c.s., ook in hoger beroep, berustte op de stelling dat [verweerder] c.s. de onderhandelingen onrechtmatig hebben afgebroken. Volgens het Hof blijkt hieruit dat er tussen partijen geen overeenkomst is totstandgekomen, waaruit het heeft afgeleid dat er geen overeenstemming is bereikt over de overnameprijs en over de wijze van overname. Het onderdeel voert m.i. terecht aan dat deze beslissing ontoereikend is gemotiveerd. Overeenstemming over de essentialia van een te sluiten overeenkomst, in casu de overnameprijs en de wijze van overname (gewone koop of huurkoop), is niet zonder meer voldoende voor het tot stand komen van de overeenkomst. Het is immers mogelijk dat de partijen beogen het definitieve tot stand komen van de overeenkomst te laten afhangen van de regeling van andere onderwerpen dan die welke als essentialia kunnen worden aangeduid. Zie HR 14 juni 1968, NJ 1968, 331 en 17 dec. 1999, NJ 2000, 184 (in verband met conclusie onder 6); vgl. ook HR 10 april 1981, NJ 1981, 532 m.nt. CJHB. Ook is mogelijk dat partijen ervan uitgaan dat de overeenkomst pas definitief is gesloten als zij schriftelijk is vastgelegd;(2) in de onderhavige zaak is dat, gelet op het verloop van de onderhandelingen en het feit dat deze zich in feite in de sfeer van het Angelsaksische recht afspeelden, voor de hand liggend. Tenslotte is van belang dat voor de totstandkoming van een huurkoopovereenkomst het wettelijke vereiste van de akte geldt (art. 1557i BWNA).

Gelet hierop - en gelet op de ruime betekenis waarin Uw Raad het begrip "onderhandelingsfase" opvat (zie de rechtspraak vermeld bij Asser-Hartkamp 4-II (1997), nr. 144 i.f.)(3) - is 's hofs redengeving m.i. niet afdoende om uit te sluiten dat in casu sprake is van afbreken van onderhandelingen als door [eiser] c.s. gesteld.

6) Onderdeel 2 is gericht tegen r.o. 4.7 van het vonnis van het Hof, waarin het Hof volgens het onderdeel ten onrechte grief V van [eiser] c.s. heeft verworpen. In grief V hebben [eiser] c.s. betoogd dat de bedoeling van de Termination Agreement slechts was om een einde te maken aan de oorspronkelijke opzet om een koopovereenkomst tot stand te brengen, omdat reeds was onderhandeld en overeenstemming was bereikt over het feit dat de overname zou plaatsvinden krachtens een huurkoopovereenkomst en over de te betalen prijs. Het onderdeel klaagt erover dat het Hof de essentiële strekking van grief V - dat de koopopzet was verlaten, maar dat daarvoor reeds de nieuw overeengekomen huuropzet in de plaats was gekomen met behoud van de oorspronkelijke overeenstemming over de prijs, termijnen en rente - heeft miskend, omdat het de verwerping van deze grief heeft gemotiveerd met een letterlijke uitleg van de Termination Agreement en met een getuigenverklaring inzake de beëindiging van de oorspronkelijke koopovereenkomst.
Blijkens de hierboven geciteerde r.o. 6 en 7 van het vonnis van het GEA, vormde de redactie van de Termination Agreement voor het Gerecht een steunargument voor de conclusie, die in r.o. 6 na een inhoudelijke beoordeling was bereikt, dat [eiser] c.s. er niet op mochten vertrouwen dat er overeenstemming was bereikt omtrent de prijs van US$ 640.000. In het vonnis van het hof ontbreekt zo'n inhoudelijke beoordeling; de wel gegeven motivering is m.i. op de voormelde grond niet toereikend. Tegen deze

achtergrond kan de redactie van de Termination Agreement m.i. niet beslissend zijn voor de beoordeling van de partijen verdeeld houdende vraag. Immers, het feit dat partijen die Agreement hebben gesloten en de daarvoor door getuige [getuige 1] vermelde reden zijn niet onverenigbaar met de door [eiser] c.s. gepresenteerde lezing van de feiten, die inhoudt dat [erflater] erop mocht vertrouwen dat de Agreement zou worden vervangen door een nieuwe overeenkomst, nu tussen partijen overeenstemming bestond over de (met behoud van de oorspronkelijke overeenstemming over de prijs, termijnen en rente) nieuw gekozen huurkoop-opzet. Onderdeel 2 bevat een hierop gerichte klacht, die naar mijn mening derhalve eveneens slaagt.

Conclusie

De conclusie strekt tot vernietiging van het bestreden vonnis en tot verwijzing van de zaak naar het Gemeenschappelijk Hof van Justitie van de Nederlandse Antillen en Aruba ter verdere behandeling en beslissing.

De Procureur-Generaal bij de
Hoge Raad der Nederlanden

1 De cassatietermijn is ex. art. 4 van de Cassatieregeling voor de Nederlandse Antillen 3 maanden. Omdat 19 juni 1999 een zaterdag was en het verzoekschrift is ingediend op de eerstvolgende werkdag na deze zaterdag, is het tijdig ingediend.

2 Vgl. Art. 2.13 UNIDROIT Principles: Where in the course of negotiations one of the parties insists that the contract is not concluded until there is agreement on specific matters or in a specific form, no contract is concluded before agreement is reached on those matters or in that form.

3 Het daar genoemde arrest van 24 maart 1995, RvdW 1995, 75 is gepubliceerd in NJ 1997, 569 m.nt. CJHB.

Sources

Internet website:
http://www.rechtspraak.nl/flashed.asp

Date: ***February 24, 2001***
Adjudicating Court: ***Arbitral Tribunal of the City of Panama***
Number: ***Unknown***
Parties: ***Unknown***

Keywords

ARBITRAL TRIBUNAL OF THE CITY OF PANAMA – INTERNATIONAL COMMERCIAL ARBITRATION – UNLESS OTHERWISE AGREED BETWEEN THE PARTIES, ARBITRAL TRIBUNAL BOUND TO ACT AS AMIABLE COMPOSITEURS AND "TO TAKE INTO ACCOUNT THE TRADE USAGES AND THE UNIDROIT PRINCIPLES OF INTERNATIONAL COMMERCIAL CONTRACTS" (ARTS. 3 AND 27 OF THE 1999 DECREE NO. 5 ON ARBITRATION)

DAMAGES FOR BREACH OF CONTRACT – LOSS OF PROFIT INCLUDED (ART. 4.2 OF THE UNIDROIT PRINCIPLES)

DAMAGES FOR BREACH OF CONTRACT – EXACT AMOUNT OF ACTUAL LOSS NOT DETERMINABLE – EQUITABLE DETERMINATION (ART. 7.4.3 OF THE UNIDROIT PRINCIPLES)

Abstract

A company from Panama (plaintiff) and a company from Porto Rico (defendant) entered into a distributorship agreement whereby the latter granted the former for a certain period of time the exclusive right to distribute its entire banana production in the United States and throughout Europe. Long before the agreed expiry date, the defendant unilaterally terminated the agreement and declared its intention to distribute the bananas directly through its affiliate.

The plaintiff commenced an arbitral proceeding before the Arbitral Tribunal of the City of Panama in accordance with an arbitration clause contained in the contract, and claimed for damages for the breach of contract by the defendant.

Since the arbitration agreement did not provide otherwise, the Arbitral Tribunal stated that, in accordance with Articles 3 and 27 of the 1999 Decree No. 5 on Arbitration, it would act as *amiable compositeur* and, in so doing, take into account the trade usages and the UNIDROIT Principles of International Commercial Contracts.

As to the merits of the dispute, the Arbitral Tribunal, by a majority, awarded the plaintiff damages for the loss suffered, including loss of profit, basing its decision expressly on the UNIDROIT Principles (precisely on Article 7.4.2 and Comment 2 to it) as well as on a number of precedents to be found in international arbitration practice. However, finding it difficult to determine the exact amount of the loss actually suffered by the plaintiff, the Arbitral Tribunal made an equitable quantification thereof and to this effect it again referred to the UNIDROIT Principles (precisely to Article 7.4.3) as well as to arbitral awards adopting the same solution.

Full Text

TRIBUNAL ARBITRAL EN EQUIDAD.
Panamá, veinticuatro (24) de febrero de dos mil uno (2001).
[…]

A.- LAS PARTES.

Conoce este Tribunal Arbitral de la demanda promovida por [...] sociedad anónima debidamente organizada bajo las leyes de Belice [...] debitamente organizada bajo las leyes de Liberia, [...] por los daños y perjuicios que se causaron a sus representadas por la alegada violación del "Contrato para la Comercialización de Bananos" suscrito el 26 de Septiembre de 1997 entre [...], y [...] y sus anexos, adendas y garantías solidarias conexas.

La Parte demandante afirma que el día 26 de septiembre de 1997 suscribió un contrato denominado CONTRATO PARA LA COMERCIALIZACIÓN DE BANANOS con la sociedad [...] de igual forma señalo que de acuerdo a los términos del contrato la sociedad [...] se obligaba a recibir de la sociedad [...] en consignación la totalidad de la producción de bananos de la finca [...] cual consistía en un área de 300 hectaráreas bajo cultivo. De acuerdo a la demandante la sociedad [...] se obligaba a tener disponible y de manera exclusiva a la sociedad [...] la totalidad de bananos producidos por la finca propiedad de la sociedad [...].

La demandante afirma que el contrato celebrado (Contrato para la Comercializacion de Bananos) contemplaba un plazo fijo de duración el cual culminaba el 26 de septiembre del año 2004 y seria prorrogado en forma automática por periodos de cinco años sucesivos a menos que alquna de las Partes manifestase su deseo expreso de no renovar dicho contrato.

También se afirmó que desde el momento de la firma del contrato antes mencionado la relación contractual entre [...] y [...] se desarrolló en total normalidad, añadiendo la demandante que [...] lo anterior era asi ya que tenia a disposicion de [...] la totalidad de la fruta (bananos)proveniente de la finca [...] y por otro lado, [...] recibia toda la fruta enviada por [...] y la colocaba en los mercados de Estados Unidos y Europa principalmente. [...] se obligaba a entregar con exclusividad [...] toda la producción de la finca [...]. Segun la demandante, la relación contractual claramente reflejaba:

1. La limitación de la sociedad [...]conseguentemente, de [...] para disponer de su fruta (bananos) para la venta a emplesas distintas a [...] en base al contrato antes mencionado.

2. La obligación de [...] de recibir la totalidad de la fruta de colocarla en los distintos mercados (Estados Unidos y Europa).

De igual forma la demandante también señalo que a fin de cumplir con el objeto del contrato el Sr. Anel Flores, representante de la sociedad [...] firmó en representación de ésta un addendum de garantia el cual formaba parte integral del contrato y el cual tenia corno principal función la de constituir a la sociedad [...] como afiliada de la sociedad [...]. Asi las cosas, la demandante afirmó que la sociedad [...] de este modo ratificó que la estipulacion por otro contraida por [...] frente [...] toda validez; en otras palabras [...] tenia la obligacion de proveer toga la finca [...] por todo el plazo del contrato (hasta septiembre del año 2004) a [...]. La demandante también alega que a inicios del año 1999 la sociedad [...] solicitó a la sociedad [...] que se modificara el mecanismo del contrato para que ien lugar de que la fruta de la finca [...] fuera vendida a [...] y luego dada en consignacion a [...] como lo establecia el contrato; en su lugar la sociedad [...] vendiera la fruta directamente a la sociedad a un precio fijo (FOB), y [...] se encargaria de exportar la fruta a [...] y luego a los distintos mercados.

La demandante manifestó que a pesar de lo anterior, la esencia del contrato se mantenga igual, es decir, la impresa [...] seguila recibiendo el precio de [...] su fruta y [...] continuaba con exclusividad siendo el consegnatario de la totalidad de la fruta de [...] y colocandola en los mercados internacionales contratados anteriormente con [...]

Finalmente, alegó la demandante que el 11 de julio de 2000 el lic [...] apoderado de [...], le notifica al Sr [...]

Gerente de [...] que sólo procederian a recibir su fruta hasta el 23 de julio de esse año (Foja 521 del espediente). La demandante afirma que esta terminacion del contrato unilateral e infundada le ha cusado y causará a [...] y a [...] daños y parjuicios de caracter economico y moral por el termino de duracino del contrato y tambien alego que la sociedad [...] y su subsidiaria [...] eran solidariamente responsables por los daños y perjuicios materiales y morales causados y por ciusarse a las sociedades [...] produco del incumplimeiento del contrato para la comercializacion de bananos firmado el 26 de septiembre de 1997.

Por su parte, la demandada procedro a contestar las alegaciones presentadas,por la demandante de la siguiente forma:

El 31 de octubre de 2000 presentó escrito de contestación en representacion de la sociedad [...] e invocó excepcion de Incompetencia del Tribunal de Arbitraje por inexistencia de la clausula compromisoria.

La demandada afirmó que entre la sociedad [...] surgió a partir de enero de 1999 una nueva relacion contractual de compraventa de fruta a precio fijo FOB con derechos y obligaciones diferentes de aquellas que contraen las comercializadoras bajo un sistema de consignacion, pues alegó que estas dos classe de contratos son excluyentes entre si.

La demandada fundamentó su excepcion en el hecho de que [...] no era parte del contrato para la comercializacion de bananos suscito entre [...]; que las disputas que surgieran entre [...] debieran ser resueltas por los tribunales de Costa Rica ya que [...] no ha renunciado a la tutela juriscdiccional; y la inexistencia del convenio arbitral entre toda vez que no fue ni ex parte del contrato para la comercializacion de bananos suscito el 26 de septiembre de 1997 entre [...]

En escrito separado de esa misma fecha (31 de octubre de 2000) la apoderada de la demandada presentó en nombre de [...] contestacion a la formalizacion de la solicitud de arbitraje y tambien presentó exception de incompetencia del Tribunal Arbitral.

La demandada señalo que la peticion de arbitraje se dio en contravencion de los terminos del contrato celebrado entre [...] ya que en su momento señalo que la Clausula 15.2 del Contrato de Comercializacion de bananos señalaba que previo a acudir al Tribunal de Arbitraje, (las Partes) se obligan a dialogar entre si como primera instancia para velar y conciliar el optimo cumplimento de los terminos del contrato, situacion que segun la demandanda no se dio y por lo tanto [...], violo el contrato e incluso la propria gestion de arbitraje estaba viciada.

Se afirmó que la obligacion de [...] era comercializar a consignacion el produco que adquiriera [...] en propiedad, sempre que [...] este lo fusiera a disposicion de aquella. Se negóque fuera parte del contrato para la comercializacion de bananos ya que, de haberlo querido asi las Partes, dicha sociedad hubiese firmado como principal en el Contrato de Comercializacion y no fue asi.

La demandada también alegó que [...] no estipuló por otro sino que se obligó a cumplir con las obligaciones que le imponen los contratos de compra y venta de banano suscritos con su productor indicado en la Clausula 1.1 del contrato (Foja 1323).

La demandada afirmó que no era cierto lo que alegó la demandante al señalar que [...] le solicitara a [...] el cambio de mecanismo si no que el [...] aceptó a celebrar un contrato de compraventa FOB con [...] lo cual consintió simultaneamente con el hecho de que el contrato para la comercialización de banano quedara extinguido.

La demandada en su escrito continuó manifestando que la relación comercial de compraventa de bananos a precio FOB que surgió entre [...] es diametralmente opuesta al contrato para la comercialización de banano suscrito entre [...] y [...]

La demandada fundamentó sus excepciones en la inexistencia del convenio arbitral entre [...] y [...] en lo siguiente:

1. Por extinción de la relación contractual entre las Partes.

2. Por inexistencia o ineficacia del convenio arbitral.

3. Por inexistencia d'e la relación contractual entre [...] y [...] l'extinguirse por MUTUO DISENSO el contrato para la comercialización de bananos.

[...]

E. ANTECEDENTES DEL PROCESO Y PRETENSIONES DE LAS PARTES

Antes de entrar en ulteriores consideraciones, el Tribunal estima prudente consignar los antecedentes principales, un resumen del proceso y las pretensiones de las Partes.

E1. ANTECEDENTES DEL PROCESO

El 28 de julio de 2000, la firma forense [...] en su calidad de Apoderados legales de las sociedades [...]. (LOS DEMANDANTES) solicitan formalmente Peticién de Arbitraje Internacional a favor de sus representadas y en contra de las sociedades [...] (LAS DEMANDADAS).

El 28 de julio de 2000, tal y coma consta a fojas 113 y 114 del Expediente, la Secretaria General de Arbitraje del Centro de Conciliacion y Arbitraje de Panama procede a notificar al apoderado de la Parte demandada.

El 7 de agosto de 2000, la Parte demandada otorga poder correspondiente a la firma forense [...] y proceden a contestar y oponerse a la solicitud de Arbitraje (fojas 121-136). [...] En la misma fecha la Parte demandante establece la cuantia de su prèténsión en la su ma de B/. 10,000,000.00 (DIEZ MILLONES DE DOLARES CON 00/100) (foja 414). El dia 12 de septiembre de 2000, se constituye el Tribunal Arbitral [...]

El 24 de octubre de 2000, se presentó Escrito de Formalización de solicitud de Arbitraje por parte de [...] en su calidad de apoderado de las sociedades [...]

El 31 de octubre de 2000, se presentó, por parte de la demandada, formal Escrito de Contestación de [...] invocación de Excepción de incompetencia del Tribunal alegando inexistencia de la clausula compromisoria.
De igual forma el 31 de octubre de 2000, se presentó, por parte de la demandada, Escrito de Contestación de por parte de [...] a la formalización de Solicitud de Arbitraje Internacional Y excepción de Incompetencia del Tribunal Arbitral.

El 14 de noviembre de 2000 se levantó Acta (fojas 1979-1980) que estableció los parametros que regirian el presente proceso, la Guai tue suscrita por los miembros del Tribunal y los apoderados de las Partes.

El 16 de noviembre de 2000, se presentó Escrito de Oposición a las Excepciones Presentadas por [...] y Escrilo de Oposición a Excepción presentada por [...] presentados ambos escritos por los apoderados de la Parte Demandante.

E2. PRETENSIONES DE LAS PARTES

En la Audiencia de Fijación de la Causa se establecio, entre otras cosas, como puntos a Revolver y pretension de las Partes del presente Proceso, lo seguiente:

I. PUNTOS A RESOLVEBU

A. LOS DEMANDANTES someten a la decision de este Tribunal, lo siguiente:

1. La existencia del "Contrato Para la Comercializacion de Banano" de fecha 26 de septiembre de 1997

2. La vigencia de dicho contrato

3. La violacion de dicho contrato por parte de [...] y en perjuicio de [...]

4. La determinacion de la indemnizacion de daños y perjuicios que le corresponde a [...] debido al incumplimento de dicho contrato.

5. Cualquer otro asunto que este directamente relacionado con los puntos anteriores.

B. LOS DEMANDADOS por su parte:

Negaron todas las pretensiones ya que el contrato para la comercializacion de banano entre [...] y [...] quedo extinquido en diciembre de 1998.

[...]

CONSIDERACIONES SOBRE EL FONDO

A pesar de que por tratarse de un Tribunal de equidad la ley no obliga a la motivación del laudo (articulo 29 del Decreto Ley 5 de 1999), se estima conveniente exponer una sintesis de las razones que Ilevan al Tribunal a su decisién.

Se deja constancia de que el Tribunal, tratandose de un arbitraje comercial internacional, para ilegar a su decisién se aliene al articulo 27 del Decreto-Ley 5 de 1999, el Guai establece que "apreciara las estipulaciones del contrato para la aplicacién del Derecho que gobierna la relacién contractual, y tendra en cuenta los usos y practicas mercantiles y los principios de los contratos de comercio internacional de UNIDROIT".

SOBRE EL TEMA DE LA RESPONSABILIDAD (Decisión del Tribunal Arbitral adoptada por mayoria)

Preliminarmente el Tribunal observa que el contrato que nos ocupa se enmarca en una relacién contractual en la Guai un productor de bananos [...] quiere enajenar la totalidad de su produccién a una sociedad compradora [...] la cual tiene coma objeto socialla venta de bananos a sus clientes en lodo el mundo.

Esta relacion economica-comercial que puede calificarse como distribucion o suministro, puede realizarse mediante diferentes esquemas contractuales inclusive por medio de sociedades instrumentales a tal fin [...]

Los puntos 1,2 y 3 sometidos por la Parte demandante coma resulta en el ACTA DE FIJACION DE LA CAUSA pueden ser tratados conjuntamente.

Esta pienamente demostrado en este proceso:

1) La existencia del contrato para la comercialización de banano de fecha 26 de septiembre de 1997 celebrado entre [...] y [...] contrato en el Guai se contempla expresamente [...] en su condición de productor de banano reconocido en el mismo contrato coma "productor asociado" y "productor afiliado" en relación con [...] y

senalandose también que el plazo del respectivo contrato con el productor afiliado sea igual o superior que el plazo del contrato de comercializacion entre [...]

2) El plazo pactado en el contrato del 26 de septiembre de 1997 tue de siete (7) años lo Guai se convino Glara, especifica y categóricamente en su Clausula X PLAZO en 105 términos siguientes:
"10.1 El plazo del presente contrato corre a partir de hoy y hasta el 26 de setiembre de 2004 y será prorrogado en forma automática por periodos de cinco años sucesivos, a menos que alguna de las Partes manifieste su deseo expreso de no renovarlo".

[...]

"10.3 Si alguna de las Partes incumple el plazo del contrato, sera responsable frente a la otra de 105 dalios y perjuicios que le ocasione" (Contrato de Comercialización a fojas 28 a 66 del expediente, en español y fojas 67 a 104 del expediente, en inglés).

3) Por otra parte, en la Clausula I titulada OBJETO DEL CONTRATO se estableció expresamente que [...] coma comercializadora garantizaba a [...] que el contrato con [...] S.A. su productora afiliada "está en favor de y en concordancia con los terminos de este contrato ..."

4) Siendo el plazo del contrato entre [...] para la comercializacion de toda la fruta de banano del productor asociado o afiliado de esta ulitma, asi reconocido expresamente en dicho contrato o sea [...] por siete (7) años, ha quedado establecido en este proceso que esa relación contractual cesó por lo menos :. a partir del 21 de julio del ano 2000 y resulta también que fue la Parte que debia recibir los bananos la que cesó de recibirlos produciendo con elio la terminación unilateral de la relación contractual, es decir el contrato se dió por terminado, en forma unilateral, sin acuerdo ni finiquito por escrito con su contratante, corno si lo hizo con otros productores, lo que implicó, sin lugar a dudas, una violación al citado contrato por incumolimiento del plazo expresamente pactado entre las Partes.

5) El Contrato de Comercialización celebrado entre [...] el 26 de septiembre de 1997 estableció en su Clausula XVIII.. MODIFICACION Y FIRMA, lo siguiente:
"18.1 Este contrato constituye y refleja la fiel voluntad de las Partes, producto de todas las previas conversaciones, acuerdos verbales y escritos y no odra modificarse si no es con el acuerdo consentimiento or escrito mediante Addendum al resente contrato firmado or ambas Partes."

En conclusión, esta pienamente demostrado que no se firmó nuevo contrato ni acuerdo o finiquito que tuviera corno propósito convenir la terminación efectiva de la relación contractual establecida por las Partes en el Contrato para la Comercialización de banano del 26 de septiembre de 1997. Aparece en el expediente la prueba de que otros productores si firmaron un acuerdo de finiquito l para dar por terminada su relación contractual. Asi por ejemplo, aportados por la propia demandada [...] constan en el expediente el acuerdo o finiquito entre [...] quienes deciden dar por terminado en forma anticipada la relación comercial que las une y por ende, rescinden de pleno derecho el contrato para la comercialización de bananos, sus addendums y el acuerdo de sublicencia de uso de marca. (Fojas 219 a 221 del expediente). Tambien consta en el expediente el finiquito firmado [...] entre cesionaria de los derechos de [...] quienes deciden dar por terminado en forma anticipada la relación comercial que las une y, por ende, rescinden de pieno derecho el contrato para comercialización de bananos, sus addendums y el acuerdo de sublicencia de uso de marca. (Fojas 353 a 355 del expediente).

Lo anterior significa que el uso y costumbre prevaleciente en esta materia y utilizado corno regia general por [...] ha sido la celebración de acuerdos escritos de ambas Partes, Ilamados comunmente finiquitos, para dar por terminado los contratos de comercialización de bananos, lo que evidentemente no se dio en el presente caso ya que la terminación de todas las relaciones contractuales [...] entre fue producto de un acto unilateral de la empresa que teniendo corno obligación el recibir toda la producción de banano de [...] (productor afiliado o asociado de) procedió en desconocimiento del plazo pactado a dejar sin efecto la relación contractual. Sin un expreso convenio por escrito corno lo exigia el contrato o bien sin el Ilamado finiquito autorizado segun los usos y costumbres en la materia, el contrato siguió vigente. De todas maneras el comportamiento de [...] no aparenta ser de buena fe.

Alega la Parte demandada que el contrato quedó extinguido en diciembre de 1998. El Tribunal no esta de acuerdo con esta alegación porque las Partes del contrato hablan renunciado expresamente al "tacito o implicito consenso" corno forma de modificar el contrato, desde el momento en que convinieron para esos propósitos y en el mismo contrato, que siempre debla darse "acuerdo y consentimiento previo y Dor escrito mediante addendum firmado por ambas Partes" (Clausula 18.1).

Como consecuencia y efecto directo de ese incumplimiento o violación del contrato se ha causado daños y perjuicios a [...] los cuales, al tenopr de lo previsto en articulo 10.3, deben se indemnizados.

SOBRE LA CUANTIA DE LOS DANOS Y PERJUICIOS (Decisión del Tribunal Arbitral adoptada por mayoria)

En el Acta de Fijación de la Causa quedó claramente senalado dentro de los puntos a resolver, especificamente en el numerai 4, la determinación de la indemnización de danos y perjuicios que le corresponde a [...] debido al incumplimiento del contrato y a elio se procede a continuación:

1) De la lectura del Contrato de Comercialización especificamente en su Clausula

15.1 se evidencia lo siguiente:

"El incumplimiento sin causa justa de cualquiera de las clausulas del presente contrato' por parte de cualquiera de los co ntratantes , lo hace incurrir en responsabilidad civil frente a la otra, debiendo resarcir 10s danos y perjuicios que ocasione el incumplimiento..."

2) En el contrato encontramos también una regia particular vinculada con el incumplimiento del plazo y es la que se convino en la Clausula 10.3 que dice lo siguiente:

"Si alguna de las Partes incumple el plazo del contrato, sera responsable frente a la otra de los danos y perjuicios que le ocasione".

El Tribunal no puede pagar por alto un evidente desequilibrio contractual entre las partes del contrato que nos ocupa y especificamente en lo que se refiere a las sanciones en caso de incumplimiento. Por ejemplo, en la clausula 11.4 del contrato puede verse que [...] tiene un beneficio exagerado frente a que no tiene a su favor un equivalente para el supuesto del incumplimiento por parte de [...]

3) Los daños y perjuicios, en todo incumplimiento contractual, incluyen el dano emergente y ellucro cesante. En el caso particular de la violación del plazo en el contrato que sive de base al presente arbitraje no ha sido probado ningùn daño emergente, lo que nol lleva a considerar únicamente el tema del lucro cesante como indemnización.

Cuando se trata de la terminación de un contrato de duración con término fijo, ! là el lucro Gasante se determina teniendo en cuenta 105 beneficios o ganancias qua la Parte perjudicada habria logrado si el contrato hubiera sido cumplido a i: cabalidad, es decir, coma si no hubiera habido incumplimiento.

Esta es la regia qua se encuentra en el Comentario Numero 2 al Articulo 7.4.2 (RESARCIMIENTO INTEGRAL) de 105 Principios de 105 Contratos de Comercio Internacional de UNIDROIT, a 105 cuales el Articulo 27 del Decreto- Ley 5 de 1999 ordena a aste Tribunal Arbitral tener en cuenta obligatoriamente.

Existen precedentes en materia de arbitraje comercial internacional que sustentan asta conclusión. Asi por ejemplo, puede versa en el caso Sapphire Intemational Petroleum vs. NIOC (ver Volumen 35, International Law Report, pag. 136), el Trlbunal Arbltral de ese caso expresó lo siguiente:
"Conforme a la opinión generalmente aceptada, el objeto (de la indemnización) es situar a la Parte a la que se le reconocen 105 danos en la misma posición pecuniaria que hubiera tenido si el contrato se hubiese ejecutado de la manera prevista por 135 Partes al momento de la estipulación (del contrato)".

Esta doctrina tue igualmente confirmada en otro proceso arbitral comercial internacional Y es el caso Amco Asia Corporation *et al.* vs. REPUBLIC OF INDONESIA (ver Yearbook Commerciai Arbitration-1 XXVII, 1992, pago 101).

Corno criterio para medir o establecer la cuantia de la indemnización se recomienda o se acostumbra comunmente tener en cuenta 105 ingresos que previsiblemente obtendrla la empresa perjudicada a partir del desarrollo histórico de las relaciones contractuales entre las Partes del contrato.

4) El Tribunal se ve obligado a reconocer que 105 dictamenes periciales que se produjeron oportunamente en las audiencias respectivas llegaron a conclusiiones diametralmente opuestas e Inclusive exageradas. Así vemosque mientras que los peritos presentados por la Parte demandantye concluyeron con un cuantía total de daños y perjuicios por un poco más del doble de la pretensión en la demanda, por su parte, los peritos presentados por la Parte demandada concluyeron que los demandantes lejos de

sufrir pérdidas mas bien se beneficiaron al evitar las pérdidas que se proyectaban en forma catastrófica en el esquema de consignación. Lo anterior lleva al Tribunal a no considerar aceptables tal como han sido presentadas las conclusiones de los peritajes de ambas partes.

5) La facultad de los arbitros de determinar con discrecionalidad la cuantia de los danos por pérdida de ingresos, es afirmada en el ARTICULO 7.4.3. de los PRINCIPIOS DE UNIDROIT que reproducimos a continuación: "ARTICULO 7.4.3.

CERTEZA DEL DAÑO.

1.- El resarcimiento es debido sólo por el dano futuro, que sea establecido con un razonable grado de certeza.

2.- El resarcimiento por la pérdida de ocasiones favorables puede ser debido en proporción a la probabilidad de su ocurrencia.

3.- Si el monto de! dano no puede ser establecido con suficiente grado de certeza, la determinación es remitida a la discrecionalidad del juez."

Como precedentes el Tribunal Arbitral se refiere a casos especificos como son los siguientes:

a. Caso SOABI vs. REPUBLIC OF SENEGAL (Arbitraje ICSID en Yearbook Commercial Arbitration XVII, 1992, pago 61) en el cual se senaló siguiente:
"...a tribunal possesses sovereign powers of appreciation in evaluatlng the damage when a mathematically precise evaluation is not possible,"

b. Caso ICC (Camara de Comercio Internacional) No. 7181 de 1992 en Yearbook Commercial Arbitration XXI, 1990, pago 111 en cual puede leerse lo siguiente
"Both Parties have indicated the possibility of appointing an expert to look into this question of damages.

The decision to be reached requires an assessment first of the period during which claimant could not avail itself of the benefits of the Agreement and, secondly, of the number and profitability of transactions claimant would have been able to enter into during that period. Whereas the first assessment is linked to an appreciation of the behaviour of the parties, the second is of a factual nature and an expert appraisement could not give the Arbitral Tribunal precise elements of valuation of these factors. In the absence of such precise elements, the Arbitral Tribunal prefers therefore rather than appointing an expert, to determine, without further delay, the amount of damages *ex aequo et bono*".

En el mismo fallo se dice que la jurisprudencia de la Corte Suprema de Bélgica ha afirmado los mismos principios.

6.- Teniendo en cuenta todas las consideraciones anteriores el Tribunal Arbitral, basado en la documentación contenida en el expediente y todas las pruebas practicadas, a la luz de las circunstancias del presente caso, RESUELVE en equidad que el monto total de los dalios y perjuicios para una justa indemnización a la Parte demandante se establece en la suma de TRES MILLONES DE DOLARES (US$3,000,000.00).

H.- DECISION DEL TRIBUNAL ARBITRAL. (Por mayoria)

Por las circunstancias expuestas este Tribunal Arbitral decide:

I [...] (parte demandada) es responsable por incumplimiento del contrato celebrado el 26 de septiembre de 1997 con [...] coma comercializadora y [...] corno productora asociada (Parte Oemandante).

II.- En consecuencia, se condena a la parte demandada al pago de una indemnización por 10s dalios y perjuicios a la parte demandante en el monto de Tres millones (US$3,000,000.00) de dólares. moneda legai de los Estados Unidos de América.

III.- Sc condena a la parte demandada al pago en favor de la parte demandante de los intereses comerciales calculados al diez (10%) por ciento anual a partir de la fecha dc notificación de este laudo hasta completar el pago.

IV.- Se condena a la parte demandada en base al principio del vencimiento, al pago en favor de la parte demandante de las costas del proceso, las cuales comprenden los gastos de administración del arbitraje, los honorarios de los arbitros y del secretario del tribunal; los gastos producidos por la practica de pruebas y los gastos originados por el mismo proceso, tales como transporte y alojamiento entre otros. La cuantía de este concepto es la siguiente: US$

V.- Sc condena a la parte demandada en basc al principio del vencimiento al pago a favor de la parte demandante dc 105 honorarios de sus apéderados judiciales lo - que se fijan en el diez por ciento (10%) de la cuantia de la condena.

Notifiquese,

Firmado en la ciudad dc Panama. Republica de Panamá a 105 veinticuatro (24) dias del mes de febrero de 2001.
LOS ARBITROS
ARBITRO Dr. Pedro BARSALLO
ARBITRO Dr. Gabriel CASTRO
PRESIDENTE Dr. Aldo FRIGNANI

Sources

Unpublished. Award kindly transmitted by Professor Aldo FRIGNANI, Chairman of the Arbitral Tribunal.

Date: ***April 2001***
Adjudicating Court: ***ICC International Court of Arbitration***
Number: ***10578***
Parties: ***Unknown***

Keywords

DISTRIBURSHIP CONTRACT BETWEEN AN ITALIAN DISTRIBUTOR AND A SWEDISH MANUFACTURE – CONTRACT GOVERNED BY SWEDISH LAW – CLAIMANT REFERRING NOT ONLY TO GENERAL PRINCIPLES OF SWEDISH CONTRACT LAW BUT ALSO TO "GENERAL PRINCIPLES OF INTERNATIONAL TRADE SUCH AS THE UNIDROIT PRINCIPLES AND EQUITY"

Abstract

Claimant, an Italian company, entered into a distributorship agreement with Defendant, a Swedish company, whereby Claimant was entitled to market in Italy on an exclusive basis products manufactured and supplied by Defendant. Years later Defendant informed Claimant that it intended to terminate their business relationship on the ground that Claimant had failed to sell the agreed minimum quantities of the product. Claimant contested the validity of the termination and claimed damages for breach of the contract by Defendant.

The contract was governed by Swedish law. In order to support its claim, Claimant invoked both the relevant provisions of the Swedish Law on Commission Agents and general principles of Swedish contract law as can be inferred from the Swedish Law on Sale of Goods. In addition, Claimant invited the Arbitral Tribunal to make reference to "general principles of international trade law such as the UNIDROIT Principles and equity" (which with respect to the issue at stake provide the same solution).

In deciding in favour of Claimant, the Arbitral Tribunal, while expressly mentioning this latter request by Claimant, declared that it was guided by "general principles of Swedish law on compensation for damages for breach of contract".

Full Text

[..]

[Claimant] is of the opinion that it is entitled to compensation for damages due to the unjustified termination by [Respondent] of the Agreement. [Claimant] submits that the 1999 Termination amounted to a breach of the Agreement in as much as it did not respect the notice period. [Claimant] submits that a determination of such notice period, which

[Respondent] should have respected, should, in application of Swedish law, reflect the 11 years of relationship between the parties, but should not be inferior to six months.

[Claimant] claims for financial compensation of the damages suffered by [Respondent]'s breach of the Agreement on the following grounds:
a) loss of profit during the notice period non-respected in an amount of& per month of such non-respected notice period, *i.e.* ... for a six months period;

b) loss of profit for orders issued prior to [the 1999 termination] and not honored by [Respondent], in an amount of ... ;

c) costs incurred for trade fairs and work-shops carried through by [Claimant] prior to the 1999 Termination and for which [Claimant] was deprived of the commercial return in terms of profits. [Claimant] claims ... on that account;

d) lost goodwill due to the abrupt termination in an amount of ... ;

e) termination indemnity on the basis of EEC Council Directive 86/653 of December 18, 1986 in an amount of ... ;

f) repurchase of [Respondent] stock held by [Claimant] in an amount of...;

g) compensation for damaged trading image, arbitration costs including legal fees and expenses and punitive damages, all together in an amount of ... ;

h) [Claimant] claims interest on the sums above in the rate corresponding to the Official Discount Rate of the European Central Bank as of [the termination date].

[Claimant] raises all these claims on the basis of Swedish law (the EEC Council Directive 86/653 having been transposed into Swedish law). [Claimant] submits that the Swedish law on Commission Agents (law 1914:43) is applicable to it and that its damage claims should be determined on the basis of Article 5 1.1 of said law, which states:

1. If a proper period of notice has been disregarded when terminating a commission, the failing party shall indemnify, the other party for its loss caused by the wrongful notification. The same shall apply when a definite commission is terminated before it is due to expire.

2. With respect to the length of the notice period, [Claimant] submits that on the basis of Swedish case law, the appropriate notice period for a long-term relation such as the one between [Claimant] and [Respondent] on the basis of the Agreement would be of twelve months.

Regarding its monetary claims, [Claimant] submits that they should be determined with due regard being given to Article 52.1 of the law on Commission Agents, which states:

1. If a Commission Agent has a commission of a long lasting basis, it shall be duly indemnified for any loss of investment, which the commission Agent cannot cover

because of the termination of the commission, *e.g.* any investment in a building, a storeroom, machinery, transportation vehicles or any other investment of such a kind, which the Commission Agent has made because of the commission and as agreed between or in mutual understanding with the principal.

2. In addition, [Claimant] submits that due regard must also be given to general principles of Swedish contract law as such can be inferred from Article 67 of the Swedish Law on Sale of Goods (Law 1990:931), which states in its pertinent parts:

Indemnification upon breach of contract includes remuneration of costs, price differences, default of profit and other such direct and indirect cost caused by the breach. [&]
An indirect loss is:
1. a loss which ensues through a diminished or declining production or turnover;
2. […]
3. any reduction of profit, which is caused by the loss of a contract with a third party or by the incorrect fulfillment of such a contract; or
4. any other similar loss if it was difficult to predict.
[…]

[Claimant] also invites the Arbitral Tribunal to make reference to general principles of international trade law such as the UNIDROIT Principles and equity.

[…]

The Arbitral Tribunal, in accordance with general principles of Swedish law on compensation of damages for breach of contract, holds that [Claimant] is entitled to be compensated for all damages including loss of profits it suffered due to [Respondent]'s breach of the Agreement. In this respect, Swedish law foresees that the victim of a breach of contract may claim to be put, in terms of financial compensation, in the same situation it would have been in if the breach had not occurred ("positive interest" or interest in correct performance). [Respondent], in its legal submissions in this respect, does not contest this very principle. The legal texts cited by [Claimant] do merely reflect in specific areas this wider principle under Swedish law. Given that the relation between the parties is neither one of simple sales contracts nor of a commission agency, but an exclusive distributorship, such general principle of Swedish law on compensations will guide the Arbitral Tribunal in its decision on the quantum of [Claimant]'s claims.

Sources

Excerpt from ICC International Court of Arbitration Bulletin, 2005 Special Supplement, 84 - 85.

Date: ***April 30, 2001***
Adjudicating Court: ***Ad hoc arbitration, San José (Costa Rica)***
Number: ***Unknown***
Parties: ***Unknown***

Keywords

JOINT VENTURE AGREEMENT BETWEEN A COSTA RICAN AND FRENCH COMPANY – ARBITRATION CLAUSE STATING THAT DISPUTES SHOULD BE SETTLED "ON THE BASIS OF GOOD FAITH AND FAIR USAGES AND WITH REGARD TO THE MOST SOUND COMMERCIAL PRACTICES AND FRIENDLY TERMS" – APPLICATION BY ARBITRAL TRIBUNAL OF THE UNIDROIT PRINCIPLES DEFINED AS "THE CENTRAL COMPONENT OF THE GENERAL RULES AND PRINCIPLES REGULATING INTERNATIONAL CONTRACTUAL OBLIGATIONS AND ENJOYING WIDE INTERNATIONAL CONSENSUS"

BREACH OF THE DUTY TO COOPERATE IMPLIED IN A JOINT VENTURE AGREEMENT – REFERENCE TO ARTS. 1.7, 1.8, 4.1, 5.3 AND 5.4 [ARTS. 5.1.3 AND 5.1.4 OF THE 2004 EDITION] OF THE UNIDROIT PRINCIPLES

DAMAGES FOR LOSS OF A CHANCE – REFERENCE TO ART. 7.4.3 OF THE UNIDROIT PRINCIPLES

Abstract

A French company and a Costa Rican company agreed to participate in a public bidding procedure for the construction and operation on an exclusive basis for a ten-year period of centres for technical revision of vehicles in Costa Rica. The contract was finally awarded to a third party. According to the Costa Rican company the adjudication was improper but the French company refused to join its partner in challenging the adjudication before the competent authority, thereby preventing the Costa Rican company from concluding the proceedings. The Costa Rican company commenced arbitral proceedings against the French company alleging breach of the joint venture agreement and claiming compensation for the harm suffered including loss of profits it could have expected to make over the ten-year period of time.

In their contract the parties had agreed that any dispute should be resolved "on the basis of good faith and fair usages and with regard to the most sound commercial practices and friendly terms". The Arbitral Tribunal decided to apply the UNIDROIT Principles which it considered to constitute "the central component of the general rules and principles regulating international contractual obligations and enjoying wide international consensus".

As to the merits the Arbitral Tribunal found that the French company's refusal to join the Costa Rican company in its appeal against the decision of the adjudicating authority had indeed breached its obligations arising from the joint venture agreement, and to this effect it referred to Articles 1.7, 1.8, 4.1, 5.3 and 5.4 [Arts. 5.1.3 and 5.1.4 of the 2004 edition] of the UNIDROIT Principles. It also invoked the general principle of the prohibition of *venire contra factum proprium* without however quoting the relevant provision of the UNIDROIT Principles (which was only included in the 2004 edition not yet published at that time). As to the plaintiff's claim for damages for lost profit, the Arbitral Tribunal held that the expected gains were too uncertain to be compensable in their entirety and therefore awarded damages only for the loss of a chance, referring expressly to Article 7.4.3 of the UNIDROIT Principles.

Full Text

[...]

"Not only national statutes and jurisprudence are applicable to this case, but also regulations of international trade that are essentially conformed by the principles and usages generally admitted in commerce which the parties agreed upon in the tenth clause of the letter of intent stating that they would act, amongst themselves, on the basis of good faith and proper customs and with regard to the most sound commercial practices and friendly terms." This statement enables the Tribunal to use such rules as has been done by the I.C.C. International Court of Arbitration in similar cases (*cf.* Awards 8908 of 1996 and 8873 of 1997; International Court of Arbitration Bulletin, vol. 10/2-Fall-1999, p. 78 ss.).

[...]

"The reasons why this Tribunal considers the UNIDROIT Principles of International Commercial Contracts to be the central component of the general rules and principles regulating international contractual obligations and enjoying wide international consensus, which constitute the proper law of the contracts, are manifold: (1) the UNIDROIT Principles of International Commercial Contracts are a restatement of international legal principles applicable to international commercial contracts prepared by a distinguished group of international experts coming from all prevailing legal systems of the world, without the intervention of States or governments, both circumstances contributing to the high quality and neutrality of the product and its ability to reflect the present state of consensus on international legal rules and principles governing international contractual obligations in the world, primarily on the basis of their fairness and appropriateness for international commercial transactions falling within their purview; (2) at the same time, the UNIDROIT Principles of International Commercial Contracts are largely inspired by an international uniform law text already enjoying wide international recognition and generally considered as reflecting international trade usages and practice in the field of the international sale of goods, which has already been ratified by almost 40 countries, namely CISG; (3) the UNIDROIT Principles of International Commercial Contracts are specially adapted to the contracts subject of this arbitration, since they cover both the international sale of goods and supply of services; (4) the

UNIDROIT Principles of International Commercial Contracts have been specifically conceived to apply to international contracts in instances in which, as is the case in these proceedings, it has been found that the parties have agreed that their transactions shall be governed by general legal rules and principles; (5) rather than vague principles or general guidelines, the UNIDROIT Principles of International Commercial Contracts are mostly constituted by clearly enunciated and specific rules coherently organized in a systematic way."

[...]

Sources

V. PÉREZ VARGAS - D. PÉREZ UMANA, The UNIDROIT Principles of International Commercial Contracts in Costa Rican Arbitral Practice, Uniform Law Review, 2006, 181 - 183.

Date: ***June 2001***
Adjudicating Court: ***ICC International Court of Arbitration***
Number: ***9950***
Parties: ***Unknown***

Keywords

CONTRACT BETWEEN AN EGYPTIAN AND A FRENCH COMPANY FOR THE SUPPLY OF INDUSTRIAL PLANT AND SUPERVISION OF ITS CONSTRUCTION – DELAY IN COMPLETION OF PLANT – CLAIM BY PURCHASER FOR DAMAGES FOR LOSS OF PROFITS

CONTRACT GOVERNED BY EGYPTIAN LAW – IN DECIDING IN FAVOUR OF CLAIMANT, ARBITRAL TRIBUNAL REFERRED NOT ONLY TO EGYPTIAN LAW BUT ALSO TO SWISS LAW AS THE LAW OF THE PLACE OF ARBITRATION AND TO THE UNIDROIT PRINCIPLES (ARTS. 7.4.1 – 7.4.3)

Abstract

Claimant, an Egyptian company, concluded a contract with Defendant, a French company, for the supply of equipment for an industrial plant and the supervision of the construction of the plant. Due to Defendant's faulty design and performance, the plant could not be run on schedule prompting Claimant to initiate arbitration proceedings in which it claimed damages for loss of profits.

The contract was governed by Egyptian law. However in addressing the question of the quantification of the losses the Arbitral Tribunal referred not only to the relevant provisions in the Egyptian Civil Code (Articles 170 - 171, 221 - 222) but also to Swiss law, *i.e.* to Article 42 of the Swiss Code of Obligations, as the law of the place of arbitration and to the UNIDROIT Principles, *i.e.* Arlticles 7.4.1, 7.4.2 and 7.4.3, quoting them in extenso.

Full Text

[...]

As stated... above, the Tribunal is satisfied that the Claimant has suffered substantial losses of profits. An Arbitral Tribunal must not be deterred by the complexities of quantification from awarding full compensation to an aggrieved party. The Egyptian Civil Code places responsibility on a judge to fix the amount of damages, and the Egyptian Court of Cassation has referred on a number of occasions to the elements of judicial discretion in the allocation of damages. The Tribunal further notes that Article 42 of the Swiss Code of Obligations recognises an element of discretion in cases where exact damages cannot be quantified:

Art. 42

II. Fixation du dommage
1 La preuve du dommage incombe au demandeur.
2 Lorsque le montant exact du dommage ne peut être établi, le juge le détermine équitablement en considération du cours ordinaire des choses et des mesures prises par la partie lésée.

There is further support for such an approach in the statement of the principles for the assessment of damages in Article 7.4 of the UNIDROIT Principles of International Commercial Contracts (1994):

Article 7.4.1
(Right to damages)
Any non-performance gives the aggrieved party a right to damages either exclusively or in conjunction with any other remedies except where the non-performance is excused under these Principles.

Article 7.4.2
(Full compensation)
(1) The aggrieved party is entitled to full compensation for the harm sustained as a result of the non-performance. Such harm includes both any loss which it suffered and any gain of which it was deprived, taking into account any gain to the aggrieved party resulting from its avoidance of cost or harm.
(2) [...]

Article 7.4.3
(Certainty of harm)
(1) Compensation is due only for harm, including future harm, that is established with a reasonable degree of certainty.
(2) [...]
(3) Where the amount of damages cannot be established with a sufficient degree of certainty, the assessment is at the discretion of the court

This discretion in the assessment of damages operates, however, within the confines of a scrupulous examination of the evidence presented by the Parties. The Tribunal continues to operate within a frame defined by the law, and specifically must avoid acting as an *amiable compositeur* (which powers the present Tribunal does not have).

It is also relevant to note that the Terms of Reference in this arbitration require the Tribunal "to decide, resolve and pronounce on all claims and counterclaims of the Parties". Similarly, Article 190.2.c of the Swiss Statute on Private International Law provides that an award may be impugned "when the arbitral tribunal ... failed to rule on one of the claims submitted". This Tribunal would fail in its duty to the Parties, and arguably leave the award open to challenge as infra petita, if it declined to award damages for loss of profits simply on the basis of the complexities of their quantification.

The Tribunal has considered whether a possible solution to the difficulties of quantification was to reopen the proceedings and call for more evidence, or even to appoint an expert to investigate this issue. However, after considering alternative methods of calculating the Claimant's loss of profits and the evidence relating to them, the Tribunal is convinced that it is in a position to assess the Claimant's loss of profits without further evidence.

Sources

Excerpt in ICC International Court of Arbitration Bulletin, 2005 Special Supplement, 77 - 79.

Date: ***June 2001***
Adjudicating Court: ***ICC International Court of Arbitration***
Number: ***11227***
Parties: ***Unknown***

Keywords

MEMORANDUM OF UNDERSTANDING BETWEEN SPANISH AND PORTUGUESE COMPANIES – CLAIMANT ARGUING ON THE BASIS NOT ONLY OF THE APPLICABLE DOMESTIC LAW (PORTUGUESE LAW) BUT ALSO OF THE UNIDROIT PRINCIPLES REFERRED TO AS "INTERNATIONAL PRACTICE"

QUESTION AS TO WHETHER MEMORANDUM OF UNDERSTANDING LEGALLY BINDING NOTWITHSTANDING PARTIES HAD LEFT SEVERAL MATTERS TO BE DETERMINED AT LATER STAGE – SOLUTION IN THE AFFIRMATIVE ACCORDING TO PORTUGUESE LAW AND TO THE UNIDROIT PRINCIPLES (ARTS. 2.11(2) AND 2.14 [ARTS. 2.1.11(2) AND 2.1.14 OF THE 2004 EDITION]

Abstract

Claimant, a Spanish company, entered into a memorandum of understanding with Defendants, Portuguese companies, specifying the interest each would take in a third company whose shares they intended to buy. When Defendants decided to sell their interest to another company, Claimant accused them of breach of the memorandum of understanding.

The first question to be decided by the arbitrator was whether the memorandum of understanding was legally binding notwithstanding the fact that the parties had left several matters to be determined at a later stage. In arguing that notwithstanding this the memorandum of understanding was legally binding, Claimant based itself on the applicable Portuguese law but at the same time specified that Portuguese law did not on this point differ very much from international practice and specifically referred to Articles 2.11(2) and 2.14 [Arts. 2.1.11(2) and 2.1.14 of the 2004 edition] of the UNIDROIT Principles.

Full Text

[...]

[Claimant] considers that clause 4 of the MOU contains an express commitment to execute a "shareholders' agreement" which essentially obliges each of the parties to proceed in good faith for the completion of such an agreement and that the only matters subject to future negotiation were those comprising the Shareholders'Agreement. It would not be true that the financial leverage, the need for a Technology Agreement or the commitment in respect of the flotation of [Company X] remained open for discussion.

Nevertheless, according to [Claimant], the fact that one or more matters in the MOU were left to future discussion did not prevent the MOU from being perfected as a contract. In this aspect, Portuguese law does not differ very much from the international practice. In this respect, article 2.11 §2 and article 2.14 of the UNIDROIT Principles set forth that the fact that the parties leave certain matters for future discussions or to the determination of a third party does not prevent the contract from being completed, its effectiveness not being even affected if the parties fail to reach an agreement on such matters or the third party fails to determine them.

Sources

Excerpt in ICC International Court of Arbitration Bulletin, 2005 Special Supplement, 87 - 88.

Date: **July 2001**
Adjudicating Court: **ICC International Court of Arbitration**
Number: **11051**
Parties: **Unknown**

Keywords

DISTRIBUTORSHIP AGREEMENT BETWEEN AN ITALIAN MANUFACTURER AND TWO CALIFORNIAN COMPANIES – ITALIAN LAW THE LAW GOVERNING THE CONTRACT – ARBITRAL TRIBUNAL BASED ITS DECISION ON THE RELEVANT PROVISION OF THE ITALIAN CIVIL CODE ADDING THAT "SUCH SOLUTION IS CONSISTENT WITH THE RELEVANT CUSTOM OF INTERNATIONAL TRADE OF WHICH THE UNIDROIT PRINCIPLES ARE AN EXPRESSION"

QUESTION AS TO TIME FROM WHEN INTEREST IS DUE – INTEREST DUE AS FROM TIME THE PAYMENTS ARE DUE (SEE ART. 1282 OF THE ITALIAN CIVIL CODE AND ART. 7.4.9 OF THE UNIDROIT PRINCIPLES)

Abstract

Claimant, an Italian manufacturer, entered into a contract with Defendants, two Californian companies, according to which Defendants were to promote sales of Claimant's products and assist in the collection of payments from customers. When Defendants withheld certain amounts of money due to Claimant, Claimant commenced arbitration proceedings requesting payment by Defendants of the amount due plus interest and termination of the agreement for breach by Defendants.

The contract was governed by Italian law. In deciding in favour of Claimant, the Arbitral Tribunal ordered Defendants to pay interest on the amounts due as from the time they were due to Claimant, and in support of this ruling referred to the relevant provision of the Italian Civil Code (Article 1282) adding that "such solution is consistent with the relevant custom of international trade of which the UNIDROIT Principles are an expression". In particular the Arbitral Tribunal referred to Article 7.4.9 of the UNIDROIT Principles which it quoted in extenso.

Full Text

APPLICABLE LAW

'The parties have agreed that the dispute should be resolved in accordance with the Italian law.

However, the parties have taken issue on whether the Arbitrator should also take due consideration of the customs laws, duties and regulations of the United States. As a matter of fact, in its Answer to the Request for Arbitration, Respondents have submitted that the arbitration should "include issues for determination that involve the customs law, duties and regulation of the United States".

The Arbitrator notes, however, that Respondents have failed to indicate, in any of their Submissions, which specific rules they refer to, and the reason why such rules should be applied as rules of law. Furthermore, this arbitration does not seem to involve any issue which would need to be resolved by applying U.S. rules of law.

Respondents having failed to provide any indication as to the U. S. regulations they referred to in their Answer to the Request for Arbitration, this case will be resolved in accordance with the law chosen by the parties, *i.e.* Italian law.

Nonetheless, the circumstance that the United States of America has increased customs tariffs on certain products may of course be taken into due consideration as a matter of fact.'

INTEREST

'In this case, Respondents'obligation is to refund to Claimant certain amounts of money paid by customers. Such obligation is a pecuniary obligation ("*debito di valuta*"), to which interest can be applied under either article 1224 or article 1282 of the Italian civil code. The difference between the two rules lies in the characteristics of the debt: Italian case law, in fact, considers that, if the amount of the debt was known, interest can be calculated from the date it was due according to article 1282 ("*interessi corrispettivi*"). Conversely, in case the amount of the debt needs a judicial assessment to be determined, interest accrues from the date when debtor was summoned to pay, according to article 1224 ("*interessi moratori*").

In this case, Claimant did not qualify, the nature of the claimed interest. The Arbitrator shall rule that interest are [sic] due from the date the amounts paid by Claimant's customers should have been returned, according to article 1282 of the Italian civil code. As a matter of fact, Italian case law considers that, when the debt can be calculated with a simple arithmetical calculation, the amount due is deemed to have been known. This is exactly the case here, as we have seen that a very simple calculation would have allowed Respondents to know exactly what they should have paid to Claimant. Respondents will therefore pay interest to Claimant from the date the amounts were due to Claimant, *i.e.* when they were paid to Respondents by Claimant's customers.

Such solution is consistent with the relevant custom of international trade, of which the UNIDROIT Principles are an expression. Indeed, article 7.4.9 of the UNIDROIT Principle provides that:
if a party does not pav a sum of money when it falls due the aggrieved party is entitled to interest upon that sum from the time when payment is due.

47. As to the date from which interest should be calculated, reference is made to the letters, dated March 17th 2000 and March 20th 2000 from Claimant to [customers]. Such letters show that the payments were due at different dates, from March to December

1999. Reference is also made to the copies of checks ..., which show that the amounts held by Respondents were due at different dates, from May to December 1999.

It is therefore necessary to set a date between March and December 1999. Given that the various payments received by Respondents seem to be equally distributed all along that period of time, and of similar amounts, it is appropriate to set the date from which interest will accrue to July lst 1999.

As to the rate of interest, reference has to be made to the legal rate provided by article 1284 of the Italian civil code. Such rate is 2.5% from July lst 1999 until December 31st 2000, and 3.5% from January lst 2001.'

Sources

Excerpt in ICC International Court of Arbitration Bulletin, 2005 Special Supplement, 86 - 87.

Date: ***July 13, 2001***
Country: ***Netherlands***
Adjudicating Court: ***Supreme Court of the Netherlands***
Number: ***C99/315HR***
Parties: ***Hardstaal Holding B.V. v. N.N.***

Keywords

SERVICE CONTRACT GOVERNED BY A PARTICULAR DOMESTIC LAW (DUTCH LAW) – REFERENCE TO THE UNIDROIT PRINCIPLES AS A POSSIBLE MEANS OF INTERPRETING THE APPLICABLE DOMESTIC LAW

BATTLE OF FORMS – KNOCK OUT DOCTRINE (ART. 2.22 [ART. 2.1.22 OF THE 2004 EDITION] OF THE UNIDROIT PRINCIPLES)

Abstract

A Dutch company requested another Dutch company to make an estimate of the cost of the construction of a sports center. The written request contained a reference to its own standard terms. The estimate rendered by the other company also contained a reference to that company's standard terms. A dispute arose as to whether a valid contract has been concluded and if so which party's standard terms, if any, should apply.

Article 6:225 lid 3 BW (Dutch Civil Code) provides that the offeror's terms prevail ("*first shot*" doctrine). In his conclusions the Advocate General recalled that the provision has so far not been applied very often by the court and that the question as to which standard terms, if any, should apply was still controversial in legal writings. In this context he mentioned as alternative solutions the "*last shot*" doctrine and the "*knock out*" doctrine and pointed out that the latter has been adopted by Article 2.22 [Art. 2.1.22 of the 2004 edition] of the UNIDROIT Principles.

In its decision the Dutch Supreme Court adopted the "*first shot*" doctrine.

Full Text

13 juli 2001
Vakantiekamer
Nr. C99/315HR
CP

Hoge Raad der Nederlanden
Arrest

in de zaak van:

HARDSTAAL HOLDING B.V., gevestigd te Lemmer,

EISERES tot cassatie,

advocaat: mr. R.F. Thunnissen,

t e g e n

[Verweerster], gevestigd te [vestigingsplaats],

VERWEERSTER in cassatie,

advocaat: mr. E. van Staden ten Brink.

1. Het geding in feitelijke instanties

Verweerster in cassatie - verder te noemen: [verweerster] - heeft bij exploit van 12 mei 1995 eiseres tot cassatie - verder te noemen: Hardstaal Holding - gedagvaard voor de Rechtbank te Leeuwarden en gevorderd Hardstaal Holding te veroordelen om aan [verweerster] tegen behoorlijk bewijs van kwijting te betalen de somma van *f* 129.629,-- - vermeerderd met de wettelijke rente daarover vanaf 30 januari 1995 tot de dag der algehele voldoening - één en ander met (voorzoveel nodig) bevestiging van de partiële ontbinding van de tussen partijen op 29 september 1994 ge-sloten overeenkomst. Hardstaal Holding heeft de vordering bestreden.
De Rechtbank heeft bij vonnis van 6 maart 1996 de vordering van [verweerster] ten dele toegewezen.
Tegen dit vonnis heeft Hardstaal Holding hoger beroep ingesteld bij het Gerechtshof te Leeuwarden.
Nadat het Hof bij tussenarrest van 9 september 1998 [verweerster] had opgedragen zich bij akte uit te laten over de door haar gestelde schade, heeft het Hof bij eindarrest van 30 juni 1999 het vonnis van de Rechtbank vernietigd en, opnieuw rechtdoende, Hardstaal Holding veroordeeld om aan [verweerster] tegen kwijting te voldoen een bedrag van *f* 57.794,--- te vermeerderen met de wettelijke rente daarover vanaf 30 januari 1995 tot de dag der algehele voldoening.
De arresten van het Hof zijn aan dit arrest gehecht.

2. Het geding in cassatie

Tegen de arresten van het Hof heeft Hardstaal Holding beroep in cassatie ingesteld. De cassatiedagvaarding is aan dit arrest gehecht en maakt daarvan deel uit.
[Verweerster] heeft geconcludeerd tot verwerping van het beroep.
De zaak is voor partijen toegelicht door hun advocaten.
De conclusie van de Advocaat-Generaal F.F. Langemeijer strekt tot vernietiging van het bestreden arrest en tot verwijzing van de zaak naar het Gerechtshof te Leeuwarden.
De advocaat van [verweerster] heeft bij brief van 11 mei 2001 op deze conclusie gereageerd.

3. Beoordeling van de middelen

3.1 In cassatie moet van het volgende worden uitgegaan.

(i) Op 14 september 1994 heeft [verweerster] schriftelijk aan "Konstr. Bedr. Hardstaal B.V." verzocht op grond van bij-gevoegde tekening en bestek een prijsopgave te doen voor (het behandelen van) de staalconstructie van de sporthal "Het Dok" te Dronten. Het schrijven van [verweerster] bevat een voorgedrukte verwijzing naar haar toepasselijke "algemene voorwaarden uitvoering burgerwerk en kleine aannemingen in het bouwbedrijf".
(ii) Bij brief van 20 september 1994 is aan [verweerster] een offerte uitgebracht met betrekking tot het leveren en monteren van genoemde staalconstructie. Deze brief bevat een voorgedrukte verwijzing naar de toepasselijke algemene voorwaarden: de Metaalunievoorwaarden, ook wel Smecomavoorwaarden genoemd. Bij de offerte is, evenals bij de onder (iii) te noemen opdrachtbevestiging, gebruik gemaakt van briefpapier dat als koptekst op een zwarte ondergrond alleen de naam "Hardstaal" vermeldt met daaronder in hele kleine letters "constructie & machinefabriek" en in de kop ter rechterzijde onder meer Hardstaal BV, KvK Utrecht 90942 en het adres Lemsterpad 46 Lemmer.
(iii) Bij brief van 4 oktober 1994 is een mondeling op 28 september 1994 door [verweerster] gegeven opdracht voor het tegen de som van *f* 150.000,-- leveren en monteren van de staalconstructie voor "Het Dok" schriftelijk aan haar bevestigd.
(iv) Het dossiernummer KvK Utrecht 90942 correspondeert met het dossier van Hardstaal Holding, gevestigd aan het Lemsterpad 46 te Lemmer.
(v) Bij de uitvoering van het werk zijn problemen ontstaan ten aanzien van de kwaliteit van (de hechting van) het verfwerk.
(vi) [Verweerster] heeft het werk voor de som van *f* 86.000,-- door Kampstaal laten afmaken.

3.2 Aan haar hiervoor onder 1 vermelde vorderingen heeft [verweerster] ten grondslag gelegd - kort gezegd - dat tussen haar en Hardstaal Holding een aannemingsovereenkomst met betrekking tot de staalconstructie tot stand is gekomen, dat deze overeenkomst door Hardstaal Holding niet behoor-lijk is nagekomen en dat zij als gevolg daarvan schade heeft geleden.
De Rechtbank heeft het enige in eerste aanleg door Hardstaal Holding gevoerde verweer, te weten: dat niet zij maar Hardstaal B.V., gevestigd te Lemmer aan de Uitheijing 4, met [verweerster] had gecontracteerd, verworpen en de gevorderde schadevergoeding toegewezen.

3.3 In hoger beroep heeft Hardstaal Holding het vonnis van de Rechtbank met een tweetal grieven bestreden. Het Hof heeft grief I, die gericht was tegen het oordeel van de Rechtbank dat Hardstaal Holding en niet Hardstaal B.V. de wederpartij van [verweerster] bij de aannemingsovereenkomst was, in zijn tussenarrest verworpen en vervolgens in zijn eindarrest grief II, waarmee Hardstaal Holding alsnog inhoudelijk verweer voerde tegen de vordering, ten dele gegrond bevonden. Aan de verwerping van grief I, waaraan het Hof de slotsom verbond dat [verweerster] terecht in haar vordering ontvankelijk was verklaard, liggen de volgende overwegingen ten grondslag:

"3. Het briefpapier waarnaar Hardstaal Holding B.V. verwijst draagt als koptekst op een zwarte ondergrond alleen de naam "Hardstaal" met daaronder in hele kleine letters

"constructie & machinefabriek" en in de kop ter rechter zijde onder meer de adresvermelding: Lemsterpad 46 Lemmer.
Gelet op deze feiten gevoegd bij de verwijzing naar het reeds genoemde dossiernummer [90942] bij de Kamer van Koophandel te Utrecht, hetwelk correspondeert met het dossier van Hardstaal Holding gevestigd aan het Lemsterpad 46 te Lemmer, kon [verweerster] er in de gegeven omstandigheden redelijkerwijs van uitgaan dat zij had gecontracteerd met Hardstaal Holding B.V. Het feit dat de brieven van 20 september 1994 en 4 oktober 1994 zijn ondertekend namens Hardstaal B.V. doet aan het voorgaande niet af."

3.4.1 Middel A keert zich met een aantal motiveringsklachten tegen deze overwegingen en de daaraan door het Hof verbonden slotsom.

3.4.2 De Hoge Raad zal eerst de klacht behandelen dat het Hof het verweer van Hardstaal Holding dat Hardstaal B.V. haar niet jegens [verweerster] kan binden "door het enkel refereren aan een handelsregisternummer" onbesproken heeft gelaten, hoewel dit verweer kardinaal is voor het antwoord op de vraag of [verweerster] het vertrouwen mocht hebben met Hardstaal Holding te hebben gecontracteerd.
Deze klacht berust op het uitgangspunt dat de hiervoor in 3.1 onder (ii) onderscheidenlijk (iii) genoemde offerte en opdrachtbevestiging van Hardstaal B.V. afkomstig zijn. Dit uitgangspunt - en daarmee het hiervoor vermelde verweer - is door het Hof evenwel in rov. 3 van zijn tussenarrest verworpen. De klacht kan derhalve wegens gemis aan feitelijke grondslag niet tot cassatie leiden.

3.4.3 Voorts klaagt het middel dat het Hof door zijn oordeel, dat Hardstaal Holding de wederpartij van [verweerster] is, te baseren op het enkele feit dat op het bij de offerte en de opdrachtbevestiging gebruikte briefpapier een verwijzing staat naar een handelsregisternummer van Hardstaal Holding en dat alleen de naam Hardstaal zonder nadere specificatie op dit briefpapier voorkomt, de plank misslaat nu het briefpapier in de kop ter rechterzijde niet alleen het adres vermeldt, maar ook nadrukkelijk de woorden "Hardstaal B.V.".
De klacht berust in verschillende opzichten op een onjuiste lezing van het tussenarrest. In de eerste plaats omdat het Hof zijn oordeel mede heeft gebaseerd op a) het feit dat het op het briefpapier vermelde adres Lemsterpad 46 te Lemmer overeenkomt met het adres van de vennoot-schap - Hardstaal Holding - die onder het eveneens op het briefpapier vermelde nummer 90942 is ingeschreven bij de Kamer van Koophandel te Utrecht en b) de vermelding "constructie & machinefabriek". In de tweede plaats omdat het Hof, waar het overweegt dat het briefpapier als koptekst op een zwarte ondergrond alleen de naam "Hardstaal" draagt met daaronder in hele kleine letters "constructie & machinefabriek", klaarblijkelijk slechts het oog heeft op hetgeen in de kop ter linkerzijde is vermeld. De klacht kan derhalve wegens gemis aan feitelijke grondslag niet tot cassatie leiden.

3.4.4 Voorzover het middel ten slotte de klacht inhoudt dat het oordeel dat Hardstaal Holding de wederpartij van [verweerster] is in het licht van de vermelding van de naam "Hardstaal B.V." in de kop ter rechterzijde van het briefpapier en van de ondertekening namens Hardstaal B.V. van zowel de offerte als de orderbevestiging onjuist, althans zonder nadere - door het Hof niet gegeven - motivering onbegrijpelijk is, faalt het. 's Hofs oordeel kan als verweven met waarderingen van feitelijke aard in cassatie niet op juistheid worden getoetst. Het behoefde ook geen nadere motivering.

3.5 Middel B.1 keert zich tegen het oordeel van het Hof (tussenarrest rov. 11) dat de algemene voorwaarden van [verweerster], waarnaar [verweerster] in haar brief van 14 september 1994 verwijst, op de rechtsverhouding tussen partijen van toepassing zijn. Het middel klaagt dat het Hof de verwijzing naar de algemene voorwaarden in de offerte van 20 september 1994 als de eerste, voor de toepassing van art. 6:225 lid 3 BW relevante verwijzing had behoren te beschouwen, en niet de verwijzing in de daaraan voorafgaande brief van 14 september 1994, welke brief een verzoek om een prijsopgave, en derhalve een uitnodiging tot het doen van een aanbod, behelst. Artikel 6:225 lid 3 ziet immers op aanbod en aanvaarding en daaronder kan, aldus het middel, een zodanige uitnodiging niet mede worden begrepen.
Het middel faalt omdat, in overeenstemming met het in de conclusie van de Advocaat-Generaal Langemeijer onder 2.12 aangehaalde standpunt van de regering, moet worden aangenomen dat de regel van art. 6:225 lid 3 ook van toepassing is in het zich hier voordoende geval dat het aanbod dat is gevolgd op een uitnodiging tot het doen van een aanbod, en die uitnodiging naar verschillende algemene voorwaarden verwijzen.

3.6.1 Middel B.2 keert zich in de eerste plaats tegen het passeren (eindarrest rov. 5) van het door Hardstaal Holding gedane aanbod om te bewijzen dat de staalcon-structie voor "Het Dok" voor niet meer dan *f* 59.930,--, althans voor een lager bedrag dan *f* 86.000,-- (de som die Kampstaal aan [verweerster] in rekening heeft gebracht) vervangen had kunnen worden. Naar het oordeel van het Hof was dit aanbod niet ter zake doend omdat Hardstaal Holding noch had gesteld noch had aangeboden te bewijzen "dat [verweerster] in de omstandigheden waarin zij destijds verkeerde en de tijdnood waarin zij was geraakt een ander (construc-tie)bedrijf van gelijk niveau bereid had kunnen vinden het onderhavige werk af te maken voor een (aanneem)som van *f* 59.930,--, althans voor een bedrag lager dan *f* 86.000,--." Naar het middel betoogt is deze redengeving onbegrijpelijk nu vanzelfsprekend het bewijsaanbod, dat het ook goedkoper had gekund, zag op goedkopere mogelijkheden binnen het raam van de omstandigheden van het geval.

3.6.2 Bij de beoordeling van deze klacht moet het volgende in aanmerking worden genomen. Hardstaal Holding heeft in haar memorie van grieven aangevoerd dat *f* 86.000,-- geen reële beloning voor het werk was en dat een en ander voor een bedrag van *f* 60.000,-- verricht had moeten kunnen worden. Daarop heeft [verweerster] de desbetreffende nota's van Kampstaal overgelegd. Vervolgens heeft Hardstaal Holding bij pleidooi uitdrukkelijk bewijs aangeboden van haar stelling dat het werk voor *f* 60.000,-- verricht had moeten kunnen worden. Deze stelling heeft zij ten slotte bij akte nader gepreciseerd aldus dat de vervangende constructie niet meer behoefde te kosten dan *f* 59.930,--, zijnde het bedrag dat zij in haar aan de offerte van 20 september 1994 ten grondslag liggende calculatie had opgenomen voor de uiteindelijk door Kampstaal verrichte (vervangende) werkzaamheden.
Tegen deze achtergrond bezien is de door het Hof aan de stellingen van Hardstaal Holding en het door haar gedane bewijsaanbod gegeven uitleg niet onbegrijpelijk. Uitgaande van deze uitleg heeft het Hof terecht geoordeeld dat de door Hardstaal Holding te bewijzen aangeboden stelling niet beslissend was voor de uitkomst van het onderhavige geschilpunt. De eerste klacht van het middel faalt derhalve.

3.6.3 Middel B.2 klaagt in de tweede plaats dat het Hof in rov. 25 van zijn eindarrest ten onrechte het door Hardstaal Holding gedane algemene bewijsaanbod als onvoldoende gespecificeerd heeft verworpen. Naar het middel betoogt had het Hof dit bewijsaanbod niet op de wijze zoals het heeft gedaan mogen passeren nu uit de stellingen van Hardstaal Holding "toch valt af te leiden welke feiten en of omstandigheden voor bewijslevering in aanmerking komen mede gelet op de opgave van met name genoemde personen, die dat bewijs als getuigen zouden kunnen leveren." Het middel verzuimt evenwel te vermelden op welke stellingen de klacht betrekking heeft. Het voldoet daarom niet aan de eisen van art. 407 lid 2 Rv. en kan om die reden niet tot cassatie leiden.

4.Beslissing

De Hoge Raad:
verwerpt het beroep;
veroordeelt Hardstaal Holding in de kosten van het geding in cassatie, tot op deze uitspraak aan de zijde van [verweerster] begroot op *f* 1.547,20 aan verschotten en *f* 3.000,-- voor salaris.

Dit arrest is gewezen door de vice-president F.H.J. Mijnssen als voorzitter en de raadsheren J.B. Fleers, H.A.M. Aaftink, O. de Savornin Lohman en A. Hammerstein, en in het openbaar uitgesproken door de raadsheer A. Hammerstein op 13 juli 2001.

*** Conclusie ***

C 99/315 HR
Mr. F.F. Langemeijer
Zitting 27 april 2001

Conclusie inzake:
Hardstaal Holding B.V.
tegen
[Verweerster]

Edelhoogachtbaar College,

In deze aannemingszaak gaat het hoofdzakelijk om de identiteit van de contractspartij en om de vraag wiens algemene voorwaarden toepasselijk zijn.

1. De feiten en het procesverloop

1.1. In cassatie kan van de volgende feiten worden uitgegaan (1):

1.1.1. Op 14 september 1994 heeft verweerster in cassatie, [verweerster], schriftelijk aan "Konstr. bedr. Hardstaal b.v." verzocht op grond van de bijgevoegde tekening en bestek nr. 449 een prijsopgave te doen voor het behandelen van de staalconstructie van sporthal "Het Dok" te Dronten. Het schrijven van [verweerster] (2) bevat een voorgedrukte verwijzing onderaan de brief naar haar "algemene voorwaarden uitvoering burgerwerk en kleine aannemingen in het bouwbedrijf".

1.1.2. Bij brief van 20 september 1994 (3) is aan [verweerster] een offerte uitgebracht met betrekking tot het leveren en monteren van de staalconstructie voor bovengenoemd project. De brief bevat een voorgedrukte verwijzing naar de toepasselijke algemene voorwaarden: de Metaalunievoorwaarden, ook wel Smecomavoorwaarden genoemd.

1.1.3. Bij brief van 4 oktober 1994 (4) is een mondeling op 28 september 1994 door [verweerster] gegeven opdracht schriftelijk aan [verweerster] bevestigd.

1.1.4. Bij de uitvoering van het werk zijn problemen ontstaan ten aanzien van de kwaliteit van (de hechting van) het verfwerk op de staalconstructie, zoals omschreven in rov. 8 van het arrest van 9 september 1998.

1.2. Op 12 mei 1995 heeft [verweerster] de vennootschap Hardstaal Holding B.V. gedagvaard voor de rechtbank te Leeuwarden. [Verweerster] heeft betaling gevorderd van een schadevergoeding groot f 120.629,- met, voor zover nodig, bevestiging van de partiële ontbinding van de tussen partijen gesloten overeenkomst. Aan deze vordering heeft [verweerster], kort gezegd, ten grondslag gelegd dat de aannemingsovereenkomst m.b.t. de staalconstructie niet behoorlijk door Hardstaal Holding B.V. is nagekomen, dat dit aan Hardstaal Holding B.V. toe te rekenen is en dat [verweerster] tengevolge van deze wanprestatie (vertragings- en andere) schade heeft geleden.

1.3. Hardstaal Holding B.V. heeft bij de rechtbank uitsluitend het verweer gevoerd dat niet zij, maar de vennootschap "Hardstaal B.V." een overeenkomst met [verweerster] heeft gesloten als waarop de inleidende dagvaarding doelt.

1.4. De rechtbank heeft dit verweer verworpen en bij vonnis van 6 maart 1996 de vordering bij gebreke van ander verweer toegewezen behoudens v.w.b. de gevraagde bevestiging van de partiële ontbinding van de overeenkomst.

1.5. Hardstaal Holding B.V. is van dit vonnis in hoger beroep gekomen bij het gerechtshof te Leeuwarden. In grief I heeft zij het oordeel bestreden dat zij - en niet Hardstaal B.V. - als de contractuele wederpartij van [verweerster] heeft te gelden. In grief II heeft zij, subsidiair, alsnog inhoudelijk verweer tegen de vordering gevoerd. Onder meer heeft zij zich beroepen op bepalingen in de Metaalunie- of Smecomavoorwaarden. Daarnaast heeft zij de gestelde tekortkomingen betwist. Meer subsidiair heeft zij de door [verweerster] gestelde schade betwist. [verweerster] heeft incidenteel geappelleerd m.b.t. het afgewezen deel van de vordering; zij heeft tevens haar vordering vermeerderd met een bedrag van f 880,25.

1.6. In een tussenarrest van 9 september 1998 heeft het hof grief I verworpen (rov. 1-4). Met betrekking tot het inhoudelijke verweer, heeft het hof de algemene voorwaarden van [verweerster] op de onderhavige rechtsverhouding van toepassing geacht (rov. 11). Na bespreking van de meningsverschillen over de kwaliteit van het werk, heeft het hof in rov. 19, op grond van technische rapportage, de conclusie getrokken dat Hardstaal Holding B.V. verwijtbaar te kort is geschoten in de uitvoering van de begin januari 1995 gesloten herbehandelingsovereenkomst. In rov. 26 heeft het hof geconstateerd dat Hardstaal Holding B.V. ook in 1994 toerekenbaar tekort is geschoten in de nakoming van haar verbintenissen uit de overeenkomst. De door [verweerster] ten gevolge hiervan geleden schade behoort volgens het hof door Hardstaal Holding B.V. te worden vergoed. Het hof heeft de zaak naar de rol verwezen om [verweerster] in de gelegenheid te stellen de gestelde schade aan te tonen.

1.7. Bij arrest van 30 juni 1999 heeft het hof de diverse schadeposten besproken. Uiteindelijk heeft het hof het vonnis van de rechtbank vernietigd en, opnieuw rechtdoende, aan [verweerster] een schadevergoeding van, per saldo, f 57.794,- toegewezen, te vermeerderen met de wettelijke rente.

1.8. Hardstaal Holding B.V. heeft - tijdig - cassatieberoep ingesteld tegen het tussenarrest en het eindarrest van het hof. [verweerster] heeft in cassatie verweer gevoerd, waarna partijen hun standpunten schriftelijk hebben laten toelichten.

2. Bespreking van het cassatiemiddel

2.1. Het eerste middel heeft betrekking op de identiteit van de vennootschap die als contractuele wederpartij van [verweerster] is opgetreden. Daarvoor komen, gelet op het in feitelijke instanties gevoerde debat, slechts twéé vennootschappen mogelijk in aanmerking: hetzij de procespartij Hardstaal Holding B.V., hetzij de niet in het proces betrokken vennootschap Hardstaal B.V.

2.2. Blijkens de in eerste aanleg overgelegde uittreksels uit april/mei 1995, vermeld in het vonnis van de rechtbank (rov. 1.2 en 2.1), bestaat er een vennootschap Hardstaal Holding B.V. Deze vennootschap was toen in het handelsregister van de Kamer van Koophandel en Fabrieken (KvK) te Utrecht onder nr. 90942 geregistreerd als statutair gevestigd te Overberg, doch adreshoudend aan het Lemsterpad 46 te Lemmer. In het handelsregister van de KvK te Leeuwarden stond dienovereenkomstig een vestiging van Hardstaal Holding B.V. aan het adres Lemsterpad 46-48 te Lemmer geregistreerd (onder nr. 44831), met als bedrijfsomschrijving: "constructiebedrijf, zoals fabricage van voedercontainers e.d.". Volgens het handelsregister van de KvK te Leeuwarden bestaat daarnaast een vennootschap Hardstaal B.V., opgericht 27 januari 1993. Deze stond onder nr. 71772 geregistreerd en was statutair gevestigd te Overberg doch adreshoudend aan de Uitheijing 4 te Lemmer. Terzijde kan worden opgemerkt dat [A] B.V. te [vestigingsplaats] volgens deze uittreksels bestuurder is van beide genoemde vennootschappen.

2.3. In dit geding is niet gesteld, dat de gebondenheid van Hardstaal Holding B.V. zou voortvloeien uit de verklaringen van een vertegenwoordiger, bevoegd of onbevoegd. Inzet van het geding was de stelling van [verweerster], dat zij de overeenkomst heeft gesloten met een vennootschap, die zich aandiende als "Hardstaal", gevestigd aan het adres Lemsterpad 46 te Lemmer en geregistreerd bij de KvK Utrecht onder nummer 90942. Dat moet wel Hardstaal Holding B.V. zijn geweest, want díe is gevestigd op dat adres en staat bij de KvK Utrecht onder dat nummer ingeschreven. De vennootschap Hardstaal B.V. is noch op dat adres gevestigd, noch onder dat nummer ingeschreven. Dat met "Hardstaal B.V." ondertekend is, vormt volgens [verweerster] onvoldoende tegenwicht: het gebeurt wel vaker dat de naam van een vennootschap in verkorte vorm wordt gevoerd.

2.4. Volgens Hardstaal Holding B.V. daarentegen, is bij vergissing door Hardstaal B.V. briefpapier gebruikt met een verkeerd adres en een verkeerd handelsregisternummer. Uit de achteraf (bij s.t. in cassatie) gegeven toelichting kan worden afgeleid, dat in 1993 de toenmalige vennootschap Hardstaal B.V. is omgezet in een beheermaatschappij onder de naam Hardstaal Holding B.V., terwijl een nieuwe werkmaatschappij, Hardstaal B.V., werd opgericht.

2.5. De rechtbank heeft het standpunt van [verweerster] gevolgd:

"Blijkens de overgelegde correspondentie profileert de wederpartij van [verweerster] zich als Hardstaal B.V., gevestigd op het adres Lemsterpad 46 te Lemmer en ingeschreven in het Handelsregister te Utrecht onder nummer 90942. Uit de handelsregisters te Utrecht en Leeuwarden blijken dit adres en inschrijvingsnummer te behoren bij de besloten vennootschap Hardstaal Holding B.V. Bovendien vermeldt de inschrijving te Leeuwarden als bedrijfsomschrijving: constructiebedrijf. (..) Het standpunt van Hardstaal Holding B.V. in dit geding dat niet zij, maar Hardstaal B.V. als wederpartij van [verweerster] dient te gelden en dat de vermelding op haar briefpapier van het inschrijvingsnummer 90942 op een administratieve vergissing berust gaat naar het oordeel van de rechtbank dan ook niet op, te minder waar uit het uittreksel uit het Handelsregister te Leeuwarden blijkt dat Hardstaal B.V. op een ander adres, namelijk Uitheijing 4 te Lemmer is gevestigd."

2.6. Het hof heeft de grief tegen dit oordeel verworpen in rov. 3 van zijn tussenarrest. In Asser-Hartkamp II (2001), nr. 122, wordt dit soort problemen gebracht onder de categorie: "onduidelijkheid over de vraag wie als wederpartij bij de overeenkomst is opgetreden" (5). Indien de tot nakoming aangesprokene het verweer voert, dat de overeenkomst met een ander is gesloten, bijv. een familielid of een zuster-BV, weet de rechter gewoonlijk met een beroep op de toerekenbare schijn deze vorm van verweer terzijde te stellen, aldus Hartkamp t.a.p. De beslissing van het hof ligt in deze lijn. In de toelichting op middel A heeft Hardstaal Holding B.V. echter gewezen op HR 7 februari 1992, NJ 1992, 809 m.nt. HJS, ten betoge, dat wanneer iemand iets voor een ander verklaart, die ander zich tegen de derde tot wie die verklaring is gericht kan beroepen op het feit dat die verklaring niet van hem afkomstig is, de goede trouw van die derde ten spijt. Hoe is het een nu met het ander te rijmen?

2.7. In het aangehaalde arrest van 7 februari 1992, rov. 3.3, werd overwogen:

"Wanneer iemand door valselijk de handtekening van een ander te plaatsen iets voor die ander verklaart, kan deze ander zich in het algemeen tegen degene tot wie de verklaring is gericht, erop beroepen dat de handtekening en daarmede de verklaring niet van hem afkomstig is, ook wanneer degene tot wie de verklaring was gericht, heeft aangenomen en redelijkerwijze mocht aannemen dat de handtekening echt was. Uit het beginsel dat ten grondslag ligt aan de art. 3:35, 3:36 en 3:61 lid 2 BW, in samenhang met art. 6:147, vloeit evenwel voort (...) dat dit onder bijzondere omstandigheden anders kan zijn. Deze omstandigheden moeten dan wel van dien aard zijn dat zij tot de slotsom nopen dat aan degene wiens handtekening is vervalst, valt toe te rekenen dat de wederpartij de handtekening voor echt heeft gehouden en redelijkerwijze mocht houden."

2.8. In het geval, berecht in HR 7 februari 1992, stond blijkbaar vast dat degene die de verklaring had afgelegd een ander was dan degene die tot nakoming werd aangesproken. In die situatie ligt het enigszins voor de hand, dat degene die tot nakoming wordt aangesproken niet zonder meer gebonden wordt door een verklaring die een ander heeft afgelegd. De gewekte schijn heeft pas betekenis, wanneer zij afkomstig is van de betrokkene of anderszins voor zijn rekening komt. In het onderhavige geval echter, is de rechtbank blijven steken in de voorvraag: wie heeft de desbetreffende verklaring afgelegd? De rechtbank heeft onderzocht van welk van beide vennootschappen de onder 1.1.2 genoemde offerte en de onder 1.1.3 genoemde opdrachtbevestiging afkomstig waren: van de vennootschap wier naam op de offerte en opdrachtbevestiging prijkt (Hardstaal B.V.) òf van de vennootschap wier adres en inschrijfnummer op de offerte en de opdrachtbevestiging prijken (Hardstaal Holding B.V.). De wederpartij moet één van deze twee geweest zijn. De rechtbank heeft voor de laatstgenoemde vennootschap gekozen. Dat was een bewijsoordeel over de vraag van wie de verklaring afkomstig was; aan de vraag van de opgewekte schijn kwam de rechtbank niet toe. In grief I (MvG sub 6) heeft Hardstaal Holding B.V. betoogd dat zij niet gebonden kan worden door een verklaring van Hardstaal B.V. Bij pleidooi in hoger beroep (pleitnota blz. 2) heeft zij deze stelling herhaald. Die stelling baat haar slechts, indien haar uitgangspunt juist zou zijn, dat de verklaring inderdaad afkomstig was van Hardstaal B.V. Dat uitgangspunt is door het hof niet aanvaard. Uit de verwijzing in rov. 3 naar "de gegeven omstandigheden" valt op te maken, dat het hof ook heeft gelet op het argument dat een holding, anders dan een werkmaatschappij, zich meestal niet met uitvoerend werk bezig houdt (6). De veronderstelling (blz. 4-5 van de cassatiedagvaarding), dat het hof het verweer c.q. de grief van Hardstaal Holding B.V. onbesproken heeft gelaten, is dus onjuist.

2.9. Middel A bevat verder een algemene motiveringsklacht, die met verscheidene argumenten wordt toegelicht. Het argument, dat het hof zich baseert op het enkele feit dat op het briefpapier van Hardstaal B.V. een verwijzing naar een handelsregisternummer van Hardstaal Holding B.V. en alleen de naam "Hardstaal" voorkomt, mist feitelijke grondslag. Het hof heeft zijn oordeel immers mede gebaseerd op het adres van de vennootschap (te weten: Lemsterpad 46). Het argument, dat het hof te gemakkelijk over de ondertekening met "Hardstaal B.V." heenstapt, terwijl de naam "Hardstaal Holding B.V." in de offerte en de opdrachtbevestiging niet voorkomt, keert zich tevergeefs tegen een waardering van feitelijke aard: het hof heeft voor het bewijs van de identiteit van de wederpartij de vermelding van het adres en het inschrijfnummer zwaarder laten wegen dan de naamsvermelding. Dit oordeel kan als zodanig niet worden getoetst in cassatie; de redengeving van het hof kan het oordeel dragen. Hetzelfde geldt voor de argumenten welke het middel ontleent aan de briefwisseling. De slotsom is dat middel A faalt. In het hierna volgende wordt ervan uitgegaan dat Hardstaal Holding B.V. de contractuele wederpartij van [verweerster] is.

2.10. Middel B klaagt onder 1 over de toepassing van art. 6:225 lid 3 BW, beter bekend als the battle of the forms:

"Verwijzen aanbod en aanvaarding naar verschillende algemene voorwaarden, dan komt aan de tweede verwijzing geen werking toe, wanneer daarbij niet tevens de toepasselijkheid van de in de eerste verwijzing aangegeven algemene voorwaarden uitdrukkelijk van de hand wordt gewezen."

Het hof heeft in rov. 11 overwogen:

"Vaststaat dat de eerste verwijzing naar algemene voorwaarden is gedaan door [verweerster], terwijl niet is gesteld of gebleken dat Hardstaal de algemene voorwaarden van [verweerster] uitdrukkelijk van de hand heeft gewezen. Een algemene verwijzing zoals in dit geval op het briefpapier van Hardstaal naar haar algemene voorwaarden kan niet gelden als een "uitdrukkelijk van de hand wijzen". Dit brengt mee dat de hiervoor genoemde algemene voorwaarden van [verweerster] op de onderhavige rechtsverhouding van toepassing zijn."

De klacht houdt in, dat het hof de verwijzing naar de algemene voorwaarden in de offerte van 20 september 1994 (hierboven genoemd onder 1.1.2) als de eerste, voor toepassing van dit artikellid relevante verwijzing had behoren te beschouwen en niet de verwijzing in de daaraan voorafgaande brief van [verweerster] van 14 september 1994. De brief van 14 september 1994 wordt door Hardstaal Holding B.V. aangemerkt als een uitnodiging tot het doen van een aanbod. De stelling in het middel luidt, dat art. 6:225 lid 3 BW duidelijk ziet op aanbod en aanvaarding en dat daaronder niet begrepen kan worden de uitnodiging tot het doen van een aanbod.

2.11. Ofschoon de regeling van art. 6:225 lid 3 BW tot dusver relatief weinig jurisprudentie heeft gegenereerd, geldt het onderwerp in de vakliteratuur als een omstreden leerstuk (7). Ter oplossing van het probleem van strijdige verwijzingen naar algemene voorwaarden, zijn verscheidene stelsels denkbaar: de eerste verwijzing telt ("first shot"-theorie); de laatste verwijzing telt ("last shot"-theorie); géén van beide verwijzingen telt; beide sets algemene voorwaarden zijn van toepassing voor zover zij verenigbaar zijn en voor zover zij onverenigbaar zijn, worden de rechtsgevolgen door het gemene recht bepaald ("knock-out"-theorie). De Nederlandse regel gaat, bij wijze van vuistregel (te weten: tenzij iets anders voortvloeit uit het aanbod, uit een andere rechtshandeling of uit een gewoonte; art. 6:217 lid 2 BW), uit van het stelsel van de eerste verwijzing. Omdat in de diverse rechtsstelsels op dit punt uiteenlopende keuzen worden gemaakt, wordt inmiddels in Europees verband gezocht naar de grootste gemene deler. Art. 2.22 van de UNIDROIT Principles (8) kiest voor de knock-out-theorie met een mogelijkheid van uitdrukkelijke afwijzing van toepasselijkheid door een van de partijen. De LANDO-groep volgt in grote lijnen hetzelfde spoor (9). Aan een verdergaande bespreking van dit vraagstuk kom ik evenwel niet toe, omdat het middel uitdrukkelijk ("Een uitgangspunt dat juist is") de regel van art. 6:225 lid 3 BW aanvaardt en uitsluitend de vraag aan de orde stelt, wiens verwijzing hier als eerste telt.

2.12. In antwoord op kamervragen naar aanleiding van een bijdrage van F.B. BAKELS (10) heeft de regering het volgende doen weten:

"Voorts heeft de commissie de vraag gesteld of de regel van het derde lid van het onderhavige artikel ook geldt indien het aanbod dat is gevolgd op een uitnodiging tot het doen van een aanbod, en die uitnodiging naar verschillende algemene voorwaarden verwijzen.
Het derde lid is op dit geval niet rechtstreeks van toepassing, maar er is alle aanleiding om in het beschreven geval dezelfde gedachtengang te volgen. Aangenomen dat uit de uitnodiging duidelijk was dat aan de personen tot wie zij was gericht, een aanbod werd gevraagd tot het aangaan van een overeenkomst op de in de uitnodiging vermelde algemene voorwaarden, ligt het in beginsel op de weg van degenen die op de uitnodiging wensen in te gaan, maar toepasselijkheid van hun eigen, afwijkende algemene voorwaarden willen bedingen, om dit duidelijk kenbaar te maken. Te bedenken valt dat

het hier in wezen om een uitwerking van de vertrouwensgedachte van artikel 3.2.3 gaat, betrokken op de uitleg van het betreffende aanbod." (11)

Deze interpretatie van de regering is noch in het parlement, noch in de nadien verschenen vakliteratuur op bezwaren gestuit. Het hof heeft overeenkomstig deze interpretatie de verwijzing in de brief van [verweerster] als de eerste voor de toepassing van art. 6:225 lid 3 BW relevante verwijzing beschouwd en m.i. mogen beschouwen. Middel B onder 1 treft derhalve geen doel.

2.13. Middel B klaagt onder 2 dat het hof in zijn rov. 5 en 25 ten onrechte het bewijsaanbod van Hardstaal Holding B.V. heeft gepasseerd. [Verweerster] had aangevoerd dat zij aan Kampstaal, die het werk in de plaats van Hardstaal Holding B.V. heeft afgemaakt, een bedrag van f 86.000,- heeft moeten voldoen. Onder aanbieding van bewijs, heeft Hardstaal Holding B.V. aangevoerd dat de constructie niet meer dan f 59.930,- behoefde te kosten en in ieder geval voor een lager bedrag dan f 86.000,- had kunnen worden vervangen (rov. 4). In rov. 5 heeft het hof dit bewijsaanbod uitdrukkelijk gepasseerd, als niet beslissend voor de uitkomst van dit geding. Het middel noemt deze redengeving onbegrijpelijk, nu het bewijsaanbod, dat het ook goedkoper had gekund, vanzelfsprekend zag op goedkopere mogelijkheden binnen het raam van de omstandigheden van het geval.

2.14. De klacht noopt tot nadere beschouwing van het bewijsaanbod in appèl (in eerste aanleg is geen inhoudelijk verweer tegen de schadeclaim gevoerd). Bij MvG sub 22 heeft Hardstaal Holding B.V. aangevoerd:

"Aan derde metaalcontructeurs is f 86.000,- betaald. Dit is geen reële beloning voor het verrichte werk. Voor een bedrag van f 60.000,- had een en ander verricht moeten kunnen worden".

De MvG bevatte aan het slot slechts een algemeen bewijsaanbod van alle stellingen, geen specifiek bewijsaanbod van deze stelling. In reactie op deze betwisting heeft [verweerster] bij MvA (blz. 11 jo. prod. 25) de facturen van Kampstaal in het geding gebracht, die inderdaad uitkomen op het bedrag van f 86.000,- excl. BTW. Voorts heeft [verweerster] betoogd dat het bewijsaanbod van Hardstaal Holding B.V. "als onvoldoende gespecificeerd" moet worden gepasseerd (MvA blz. 13). Hierdoor gewaarschuwd, heeft Hardstaal Holding B.V. in het daarop volgende pleidooi herhaald, dat de genoemde f 86.000,- geen reële beloning is voor het door Kampstaal verrichte werk en dat het voor f 60.000,- verricht had moeten kunnen worden: "Hardstaal biedt hieromtrent uitdrukkelijk bewijs aan" (pleitnotitie blz. 16). Het bewijsaanbod voldoet dus aan alle daaraan te stellen eisen; de vraag is slechts, of de te bewijzen aangeboden stelling relevant was.

2.15. M.i. is zonder nadere redengeving, welke ontbreekt, inderdaad niet duidelijk waarom het hof in rov. 5 de te bewijzen aangeboden stelling niet relevant heeft geacht. Hardstaal Holding B.V. heeft niet bestreden dat [verweerster] aan de firma Kampstaal f 86.000,- heeft voldaan om het werk te laten afmaken. Zij bestreed in feite, dat dit bedrag (althans voor zover dit een bedrag van f 60.000,- overschreed) in zodanig verband staat met de gebeurtenis waarop de aansprakelijkheid van Hardstaal Holding B.V. berust, dat het haar, mede gezien de aard van de aansprakelijkheid en van de schade, als een gevolg van deze gebeurtenis kan worden toegerekend (vgl. art. 6:98 BW). Wordt dit verweer gegrond bevonden, dan staat het in de weg aan de toewijzing van dit gedeelte van de vordering. De klacht m.b.t. rov. 5 is dus gegrond. De aard van het gebrek geeft mij aanleiding, Uw Raad voor te stellen de hoofdregel van art. 422a Rv toe te passen.

2.16. Rov. 25 heeft betrekking op het algemene bewijsaanbod, dat als onvoldoende gespecificeerd werd verworpen. De klacht luidt letterlijk: uit de stellingen van Hardstaal Holding B.V. toch valt af te leiden welke feiten en/of omstandigheden voor bewijslevering in aanmerking komen. In het cassatiemiddel wordt op geen enkele wijze aangeduid, op welke stellingen deze klacht betrekking heeft. In zoverre voldoet het middel niet aan de eis van art. 407 lid 2 Rv. Gelet op de veelheid van stellingen, waarop de klacht mogelijkerwijze betrekking zou kunnen hebben, - alleen al ten aanzien van de schadeomvang onderscheidt het hof geschilpunten onder a t/m e - kan niet worden gespeculeerd op welke stellingen het middel het oog heeft. Ook de vermelding bij het bewijsaanbod van de namen van mogelijke getuigen zet de lezer van het middel niet op het juiste spoor. In het middel valt niet de klacht te lezen, dat het hof Hardstaal Holding B.V. tot levering van tegenbewijs in staat had behoren te stellen (12). Dit deel van de klacht faalt derhalve.

3. Conclusie

De conclusie strekt tot vernietiging van het bestreden arrest en tot verwijzing van de zaak naar het gerechtshof te Leeuwarden.

De Procureur-Generaal bij de
Hoge Raad der Nederlanden

* * *

1 Vgl. rov. 8 van het arrest van 9 september 1998.
2 Prod. 2 bij MvG.
3 Prod. 1 bij CvR. De vraag, van welke vennootschap deze brief afkomstig is: Hardstaal B.V. of Hardstaal Holding B.V., is voorwerp van geschil.
4 Prod. 2 bij CvR. De vraag, van welke vennootschap deze brief afkomstig is, is eveneens voorwerp van geschil.
5 Zulks ter onderscheiding van de problematiek van de onbevoegde vertegenwoordiging en de problematiek van de dwaling omtrent de persoon. Het antwoord op de vraag, of iemand jegens een ander bij het sluiten van een overeenkomst in eigen naam is opgetreden dan wel als vertegenwoordiger van een derde, hangt af van hetgeen hij en die ander daaromtrent jegens elkaar hebben verklaard en over en weer uit elkanders verklaringen en gedragingen hebben afgeleid en hebben mogen afleiden: vaste rechtspraak sedert HR 11 maart 1977, NJ 1977, 521 m.nt. GJS.
6 De rechtbank heeft in dit verband van betekenis geacht dat bij de KvK Leeuwarden de bedrijfsomschrijving van Hardstaal Holding B.V. luidde: "constructiebedrijf".
7 Zie de uitvoerige literatuuropgave in: losbl. Verbintenissenrecht, aant. 3 op art. 6:225 lid 3 BW (Y.G. Blei Weissmann). Ik noem hier slechts: ASSER-HARTKAMP II (2001) nr. 354; ASSER-SCHUT-HIJMA (1994) nr. 178; BLOEMBERGEN/VAN DAM/HIJMA/VALK, Rechtshandeling en overeenkomst (1998) nr. 76; B. WESSELS en R.H.C. JONGENEEL, Algemene voorwaarden (1997) blz. 30-35; J. HIJMA, Algemene voorwaarden (mon. NBW 1997), blz. 26-29; F.J. SANDEE, Algemene voorwaarden en Fabrikatenkoop, diss. 1995, hoofdstuk 16.
8 Where both parties use standard terms and reach agreement except on those terms, a contract is concluded on the basis of the agreed terms and of any standard terms which are common in

substance unless one party clearly indicates in advance, or later and without undue delay informs the other party, that it does not intend to be bound by such a contract. UNIDROIT Principles of international commercial contracts (1994).

9 O. LANDO en H. BEALE (red.), Principles of European Contract Law (2000), blz. 180 e.v. Art. 2:209: (1) If the parties have reached agreement except that the offer and acceptance refer to conflicting general conditions of contract, a contract is nonetheless formed. The general conditions form part of the contract to the extent that they are common in substance. (2) However, no contract is formed if one party: (a) has indicated in advance, explicitly, and not by way of general conditions, that it does not intend to be bound by a contract on the basis of paragraph (1); or (b) without delay, informs the other party that it does not intend to be bound by such contract.

10 F.B. BAKELS, Art. 6.5.2.8 lid 3 NBW nader bezien, WPNR 5695 (1984, blz. 257 e.v.).

11 MvA II, PG NBW, Invoering boeken 3-6, boek 6, blz. 1438. Zie ook: losbl. Verbintenissenrecht, aant. 37 op art. 225 (Y.G. BLEI WEISSMANN); F.J. SANDEE, diss. a.w., blz. 215.

12 Vgl. o.m.: HR 9 januari 1998, NJ 1999, 413 m.nt. HJS: specificatie van bewijsaanbod niet nodig wanneer het om tegenbewijs gaat; HR 24 maart 2000, RvdW 2000, 85.

Sources

Internet website:
http://www.rechtspraak.nl/flashed.asp

Date: ***October 2001***
Adjudicating Court: ***ICC International Court of Arbitration***
Number: ***9078***
Parties: ***Unknown***

Keywords

AGREEMENT WHEREBY LICENSEE UNDERTAKES TO NO LONGER MANUFACTURE AND SELL LICENSED GOODS – LICENSEE CONTINUES TO MANUFACTURE AND SELL THE GOODS – LICENSOR CLAIMS DAMAGES FOR LOST OPPORTUNITIES

APPLICABLE (GERMAN) LAW UNCLEAR AS TO WHETHER DAMAGES FOR LOST OPPORTUNITIES CAN BE AWARDED – REFERENCE TO OTHER DOMESTIC LAWS AND TO THE UNIDROIT PRINCIPLES TO SUPPORT DECISION TO AWARD SUCH DAMAGES

Abstract

Claimant, a Swedish company, had concluded an agreement with Defendant, a German company, according to which the latter undertook to re-transfer to Claimant all know-how relating to the licensed equipment and to no longer manufacture and sell the equipment to third parties. According to Claimant Defendant violated their agreement by continuing to sell the equipment to third parties, thereby depriving Claimant of the chance to sell itself the equipment to potential customers. For this reason Claimant requested damages for lost opportunities.

The Arbitral Tribunal decided in favour of Claimant. However since it could not find a clear answer as to whether damages for a lost opportunity were payable under the applicable German law, it referred to French and Swiss law and to the UNIDROIT Principles, all three of which recognised the principle of compensation for harm suffered as a result of a lost opportunity and granted the adjudicating body a certain degree of discretion in the assessment of the probability of the occurrence of the lost opportunity and of the amount of harm suffered.

Full Text

(...)

8.4. Principles of compensation of damages under German law

8.4.1. It results from the above that the parties have given a few indications concerning certain aspects of damage compensation law.

Claimant:
- claims damages resulting from positive contract violation;
- claims lost profits;
- defines lost profit as the difference between the contractual price and direct production costs ... ;
- contests that it must provide details about profit calculation because it claims a hypothetical damage;
- defines burden of proof...;
- alleges that it pays 10% interests on a loan of 13.4 million DEM;
- establishes in reasonable details the calculation of lost profits...

Defendant:

- points out that Claimant may only assert claims which arise from the violation of the duty to refrain from competing;
- criticises that Claimant bases its claims on "value of offers submitted" and not on the "value of offers awarded";
- states that Claimant offers included a "30% monopoly profit";
- alleges in general that value of offers submitted exceeded the value of offers awarded by 50%, and indicates in detail that in one case, the submission price was of DEM 4.96 million and the awarded price was of DEM 4.2 million, which corresponds to a difference of approx. 20%;
- brings forward certain profit calculation&;
- admits that [licensee] continued to use the Know How it had obtained from Defendant;
- criticised that Claimant has not proven that in the 19 claimed cases the "special features" of the licensed technology were used.

8.4.2 It also results from the above that the parties have not made any presentation of the principles governing the German law of damage compensation. The Arbitral Award had therefore to rely on its own research for establishing such principles

8.5. The principal rules of German law relating to compensation of damages

The Arbitral Tribunal concludes that the basic rules of German law relating to compensation for damages resulting from a breach of contract may be recapitulated, in a very summarised manner, as follows:

8.5.1. The conditions for an obligation to compensate damages are

a) that breach of contractual obligations by the party, from which damages has occurred with reference to the party claiming the damages;

b) that a damage has actually occurred;

c) that the breach of contract was the adequate cause, according to the concept of the so-called "*Äquivalenztheorie*", for the damage;

d) that the party in breach of contract is responsible or answerable for the breach of its obligations.

8.5.2. The Claimant bears the burden to allege in a substantiated way and to prove all the above four elements. Only under certain circumstances does one admit that the burden of proof as to the absence of the causal nexus and/or the responsibility (*Schuld, Vertretenmüssen*) is shifted to the Defendant.

The Claimant carries the burden to allege in a specified way and to prove not only the fact that a damage has occurred, but also the actual amount of the damage.

8.5.3. If the conditions for an obligation of compensation are fulfilled, the party in breach of contract has to compensate to the claiming party the damage which was the consequence of the breach, in the sense that the claiming party is entitled to have restored its economical situation as if the breach of the contractual obligation had not occurred. The damage to be compensated is the so-called positive interest or performance interest (*positives Interesse bzw. Erfüllungsinteresse*) which includes lost profits (*entgangenen Gewinn*).

The damage to be compensated is calculated as the difference between the hypothetical financial situation of the damaged party as it would have been had the breach of contract not occurred, and the financial situation of the Claimant party as it actually resulted (*Differenztheorie*). In this calculation which is necessarily of a hypothetical nature, the lost gross income must be determined, and from that gross income all the costs connected or necessary for generating such gross income must be deducted, irrespectively of the nature of such costs, whether direct costs (for merchandise and labour) or indirect costs (fixed costs, such as administration, direct depreciation or cost of use of machinery and equipment). The principle of calculation of the damage, which Claimant sustains to be applicable according to a precedent cited by it, constitutes, in the opinion of the Arbitral Tribunal, a deviation from the generally applicable principle and is to be qualified as an exception. Such exceptions are to be applied. according to the understanding of the Arbitral Tribunal, only in such situations in which it would otherwise be virtually impossible to determine the damage or in situations where a specific manner of simplified calculation has been established in a business sector, such as for the trade in commodities or securities or in connection with the supply of standard goods with a price which can be determined based on a given market. Such exceptional circumstance is not given in this case and Claimant, therefore, was to submit a specific calculation of its damage in each single case.

8.5.4. Claimant bases its damage claim on the assumption that the sub-licensees of Claimant would have been able to enter into contracts for the supply of the relevant equipment and machinery to the named purchasers if Defendant had not offered and supplied the corresponding machinery and equipment to such potential customer. The basis of the claim is therefore merely an assumption of a probability of lost profits. An assumption respectively a probability of the conclusion of a certain business transaction, such as the supply of machinery and equipment to a given potential customer, by its very nature cannot be proven in the strict sense of legal evidence. In fact, in most cases it would be impossible to prove that the potential customer would have concluded a supply contract with the claiming party, and, further, it would be impossible in most cases to prove at what conditions, respectively prices, such contract might have been concluded. The sole fact that the claiming party has submitted an offer is, by itself, obviously no evidence for the fact that it would have been able to conclude a final contract and no evidence for the conditions at which the contract could have been concluded. There might indeed have been other potential suppliers and the Claimant might have had to concede lower prices for being actually awarded the contract.

8.5.5. The damage which Claimant claims is actually a damage for a lost opportunity, respectively the value of the missed chance or opportunity of concluding a deal and realising a profit on such deal. Claimant has not submitted materials which would support the existence of clear rules under German law as to how such cases should be dealt with, nor has the Arbitral Tribunal become aware of such rules clearly established by learned authors or precedents. It must be admitted though that damage resulting from lost opportunities is real damage and the possibility to claim the compensation of such damage caused by a breach of contract must be upheld. The principle is recognised in countries like France and Switzerland as well as by proposed UNIDROIT rules. The Arbitral Tribunal has not become aware of any opinions under German law to the effect that the principles should not apply in Germany.

8.5.6. Since in such circumstances neither the actual occurrence of the damage nor the extent of the potential damage can be strictly proven, the damages to be awarded must be assessed by a tribunal based on the degree of probability for the realisation of the opportunity and based on a likelihood of the profit margin which might have been obtainable by Claimant on the lost transaction.

The fact that the occurence of the loss and the magnitude of the loss cannot be proven in the strict sense of legal evidence does not realease, however, the Claimant from making sufficiently specified allegations and offering sufficiently pertinent evidence for (i) the loss of the business, (ii) the causal nexus between the breach of the contractual obligation by Defendant and the loss of the transaction, and (iii) for the next profit which the Claimant could have realised on the lost transaction. Altough a strict evidence is not possible, sufficient proof has to be required from Claimant to the extent to demonstrate at least a very high probability for the three named elements.

8.5.7. Since the award of damages in such circumstances is ultimately based on the degree of probability of certain assumptions, the Arbitral Tribunal has to assess the degree of probability of the loss of opportunity and of the lost profit. This necessarily implies a certain range of discretion for the valuation to be made by the Arbitral Tribunal when deciding on the damages to be awarded.

Sources

Excerpts in ICC International Court of Arbitration Bulletin, 2005 Special Supplement, 73 - 76.

Date: ***October 3, 2001***
Country: ***New Zealand***
Adjudicating Court: ***Court of Appeal of New Zealand***
Number: ***NZCA 348***
Parties: ***Bobux Marketing limited v. Raynor Marketing Limited***

Keywords

LONG-TERM CONTRACTS – IMPLIED DUTY OF REASONABLENESS AND GOOD FAITH IN CONTRACT PERFORMANCE – RECOGNISED IN INTERNATIONAL TRADE LAW (ART. 1.7 UNIDROIT PRINCIPLES AND ART. 7(1) CISG) – DISSENTING OPINION

Abstract

A New Zealand manufacturer and an English distributor entered into a distributorship contract for an indefinite period. The contract contained a clause according to which the manufacturer was entitled to terminate the agreement only where the distributor failed to order the minimum quantities specified in the agreement.

The dispute arose when the manufacturer gave notice of termination of the contract not because of the distributor's failure to order the minimum quantities but because of an alleged breach of the general duty of good faith in contract performance.

In his opinion Thomas J affirmed, particularly with respect to long-term or relational contracts such as the one in question, the existence of an implied duty of good faith in contract performance. He based this conclusion, among others, on the fact that a general obligation to perform contractual obligations in good faith has been adopted also in the United States and in international trade law without any evidence that commercial transactions have become unworkable or uncertain as a result. While referring, with respect to U.S. law, to Section 1-203 of the Uniform Commercial Code and to Section 205 of the Restatement of Contracts, Second, he referred, with respect to international trade to Article 1.7 of the 1994 UNIDROIT Principles of International Commercial Contracts and to Article 7(1) of the 1980 United Nations Convention on Contracts for the International Sale of Goods.

The majority of the court, however, rejected this argument. Following the conventional objective approach in contract interpretation it concluded that the express wording of the contract made it impossible to imply a term of reasonabless or good faith.

Full Text

BOBUX MARKETING LIMITED v. RAYNOR MARKETING LIMITED [2001] NZCA 348 (3 OCTOBER 2001)
IN THE COURT OF APPEAL OF NEW ZEALAND

Judgment:
3 October 2001
[...]

THOMAS J

[...]

AN OBLIGATION OF GOOD FAITH?

[16] I do not accept that, even if it is not open to Bobux to terminate the contract on reasonable notice, that company is without recourse against Raynor in the circumstances which it alleges in this case.The law should not be bereft of relevance in a situation which has become commercially unrealistic or intolerable.

[17] In my view, therefore, the courts would be prepared to import into the contract in issue an obligation on the parties to perform the contract in good faith. It would be open to Bobux to allege that Raynor was in breach of that obligation.This being the case, the contract could be terminated for breach under clause 19(b).

[18] Before touching upon the concept of good faith, it is necessary to ascertain that there is a factual foundation for such a plea.As the facts have not been tested from this perspective any observation regarding the facts must necessarily be tentative.The objective, however, is not to reach a firm finding of fact, but rather to demonstrate that the courts are not necessarily impotent in commercial circumstances which would seem to cry out for the assistance of the law.The law exists to serve the community, including in particular the needs of commerce, and there may be occasions, admittedly rare, where it is apposite to indicate the direction which the law is taking to discharge that function.I turn then to confirm that there is a sufficient factual foundation to justify this exercise.

1.The performance of the contract

[19] Notwithstanding Raynor 's weak protestations to the contrary, it would seem that the mutual trust and confidence which existed between the parties at the outset of the contract has completely broken down. [...]

2.An obligation of good faith?

[33] As Lord Steyn has observed, the emphasis of English law on an objective approach to contractual issues tends to make England somewhat infertile soil for the development of a generalised duty of good faith in the performance of contracts.(The Hon Mr Justice STEYN, "The Role of Good Faith and Fair Dealing in Contract Law: A Hair-Shirt

Philosophy?" (1991) Denning LJ 131, at 132). Classical contract law is based on certain implicit paradigm cases, the most common of which is the contract for an identified commodity between two strangers operating in a perfect spot market. Contractual principles provide a relatively rigid offer and acceptance format and are intolerant of such issues as indefiniteness, agreement to agree, and agreements to negotiate in good faith.Principles of classical contract law like the bargain theory of consideration, the objective theory of interpretation, and the rule that silence is not acceptance are particularly apt for contracts of this kind. (See Melvin A EISENBERG, "Relational Contracts" in Good Faith and Fault in Contract Law (1995 - Eds, Jack Beatson and Daniel Friedmann) at 297). Lord Wilberforce put it this way in New Zealand Shipping Co Ltd v. A M Satterthwaite & Co Ltd [1975] AC 154, at 167:

English law, having committed itself to a rather technical and schematic doctrine of contract, in application takes a practical approach, often at the cost of forcing the facts to fit uneasily into the marked slots of offer, acceptance and consideration.

[34] Thus, the traditional law of contract does not readily accommodate a general duty of good faith in the performance of contractual obligations. It was not, of course, always so.In 1766, the great Lord Mansfield proclaimed his famous description of good faith as "the governing principle... applicable to all contracts and dealings." See Carter v. Boehm 97 ER 1162, at 1164. But his vision was swamped by a law reflecting the laissez-faire economics and liberal individualistic theories of the nineteenth century. The classical theory of contract was seen to offer predictability and certainty, although, as Sir Anthony Mason has observed; "It later emerged, as is the case with many legal concepts rooted in formalism, that the element of certainty was illusory".(A F MASON, "Contract, Good Faith and Equitable Standards in Fair Dealing (2000) 116 LQR 66, at 70).

[35] Despite its tradition, however, the law of England, and by derivation the law of this country, could not forever ignore the fundamental weakness of the classical conception of contract law. The formalistic approach was overtaken by the good sense of those Judges who recognised that the function of the law of contract is to provide an effective and fair framework for contractual dealings based on achieving the reasonable expectation of the parties. See Johan STEYN, "Contract Law: Fulfilling the Reasonable Expectations of Honest Men" (1997) 113 LQR 433, at 434.The fundamental flaw of the classical conception of contract law was its empirical premise that most contracts are discrete. That premise is false. Most commercial contracts are in fact relational contracts. The great bulk of contracts either create or reflect relationships. It is discrete contracts that are unusual, not relational contracts. See EISENBERG, *supra*, at 297.

[...]

[39] The notion of a general obligation to perform contractual obligations in good faith also received a boost from the fact it has been adopted in the United States and in international trade law without any evidence that commercial transactions have become unworkable or uncertain as a result. Section 1-203 of the Uniform Commercial Code in the United States provides an important milestone in the evolution of the principle. It states that "every contract or duty within this Act imposes an obligation of good faith in its performance or enforcement". Initiated by the American Law Institute in 1970 and finally promulgated in 1981, Section 205 of the Restatement of Contracts, Second, which

is applicable to all contracts, reads: "Every contract imposes upon each party a duty of good faith and fair dealing in its performance and its enforcement". Then, Article 1.7 of the 1994 UNIDROIT Principles of International Commercial Contracts provides that, "each party must act in accordance with good faith and fair dealing in international trade" and further that, "the parties may not exclude or limit this duty". Similarly, Article 7(1) of the 1980 United Nations Convention on Contracts for the International Sale of Goods states that in the interpretation of the Convention regard is to be had, inter alia, to the "observance of good faith in international trade".

[40] Moreover, the concept of good faith is the latent premise of much of the law of contract relating to the performance of contractual obligations.(See Livingstone v. Roskilly, *supra*, at 237-238). Lücke suggests that obvious examples of principles of contract law palpably designed to bring about just and fair results are the doctrine of promissory estoppel, the rule which provides relief against forfeiture, the rule which invalidates penalty clauses, and some of the established rules of construction such as the contra preferendum rule and the presumption that exemption clauses in contracts are not intended to confer immunity from the consequences of a fundamental breach. (LÜCKE, *supra*, at 158).Then, too, apart from fiduciary relationships, notions of good faith and fair dealing have left their imprint on English contract law in respect of contracts of insurance, suretyship, salvage and partnership, which are all characterised as contracts of the utmost good faith (STEYN, *supra*, at 136).Sir Anthony Mason lists a number of well-recognised unrelated situations in which a party is required to take account of the interests of another party, notwithstanding that the initial foundation of the relationship is that each is pursuing his or her own interests.(MASON, *supra*, at 72-73).The learned jurist also canvasses the various means by which the courts have sought to fill the void caused by the absence of a general good faith doctrine; the fiduciary principle, unconscionable bargains, estoppel and restitutionary relief.(Ibid, at 84).

[41] Certainly, the notion of a more explicit concept of good faith in the law of contract will continue to have its detractors. The principle is already beset by agonising inquiries into what is or can be meant by good faith. But these digressions need not detain us here. Good faith is closely associated with notions of fairness, honesty and reasonableness which are already well recognised in the law (LÜCKE, *supra*, at 161).Fried has correctly pointed out that good faith as honesty is quite compatible with the traditional "concept as promise" concept. (See FRIED, Contracts as Promise (1981) at 85).Underlying the concept, to my mind, is a perception of loyalty to the promise made which provides a standard, rather than a rule, and which does not require the abandonment of self-interest. The Official Comment to Section 205 of the Restatement of Contracts, Second (*supra*) rightly points out that the meaning will depend on its context. The basic ethic in good faith performance and enforcement of a contract is said to be "faithfulness to an agreed common purpose and consistency with the justified expectations of the other party". This ethic evinces my perception of good faith as loyalty to a promise.

[42] We have already noted that a duty to exercise good faith in the performance of a contractual obligation is most often asserted in the context of relational contracts, such as agency relationships, distributorships, partnerships, franchise arrangements and joint ventures. Readiness to import such a term is founded on the fact that the parties have a mutual interest in the successful performance of their agreement.

[43] There is again no need for a dissertation on the characteristics of relational contracts as the present agreement undoubtedly falls within that category. Relational contracts are often long-term contracts, but not necessarily so, but long-term contracts by their nature are likely to be relational. In essence, relational contracts recognise the existence of a business relationship between the parties and the need to maintain that relationship; the difficulty of reducing important terms to well defined obligations; the impossibility of foretelling all the events which may impinge upon the contract; the need to adjust the relationship over time to provide for unforeseen factors or contingencies which cannot readily be provided for in advance; the commitment, likely to be extensive, which one party must make to the other, including significant investment; and that they are in an economic sense likely to be incomplete in failing to allocate, or allocate optimally, the risk between the parties in the event of certain future contingencies. See TAYLOR, *supra*, at 459 and 479; HUNTER, *supra*, at 19; GOETZ and SCOTT, *supra*, at 1090 and 1091; GODDARD, *supra*, 436, 430-431, 436, and 457 (424 and 426); and EISENBERG, *supra*, at 294-295 and 296.

[44] Consequently, a relational contract is one which involves not merely an exchange but a relationship between the contractual parties. The parties are not "strangers" in the accepted sense and much of their interaction takes place "off the contract" requiring a deliberate measure of communication, co-operation, and predictable performance based on mutual trust and confidence. Expectations of loyalty and interdependence mark the formation of the contract and become the basis for the rational economic planning of the parties. (TAYLOR, *supra*, 479).The norms of the ongoing relationship, of necessity, tend to supplement the express contractual obligations. Good faith is required to ensure that the requisite communication, co-operation and predictable performance occurs for the advantage of both parties. In short, the obligation seeks to hold the parties to the promise implicit in a continuing, relational commercial transaction.(Ibid).

[45] Such considerations as these led Elias CJ to say in Stanley v. Fuji Xerox (NZ) Ltd (Unreported, HC Auckland, CP 479/96, 5 November 1997, at 58 that the implication of good faith "necessarily arises whenever a contract is predicated upon mutual confidence". Other cases in New Zealand which recognise this obligation are referred to in Cheyne, *supra*. The cases in Australia which recognise the obligation in relational contracts are dealt with in Webb, *supra*. Those cases need not be repeated here.

[46] There can be little doubt that the contract between Bobux and Raynor is predicated upon mutual trust and confidence and gave rise to a reasonable expectation of communication, co-operation and predictable performance. These features become all the more important when the contract is for an indefinite period. With the passing of time there could be no other effective basis on which the parties could pursue their mutual interest in the supply and distribution of Bobux products in the United Kingdom.

CONCLUSION

[47] It therefore seems to me that it would be open to Bobux to assert that the parties' obligations under the contract are subject to an obligation to act in good faith. Assuming that the evidence briefly traversed above can be established, Raynor would appear to have failed to demonstrate the requisite good faith. Either it has already failed to remedy that breach in failing to cease distribution of Sole Mania products after expressly

indicating it had done so in April 1999 or it would, virtually by definition, be unable to remedy the breach on receiving a notice under clause 19(b). Hence, Bobux could seek to terminate the contract for breach, and the termination would have "immediate effect". Alternatively, Bobux could argue that Raynor 's breach amounted to a repudiation of the contract.

[48] I have elsewhere noted the void in the law due to the absence of a developed doctrine of good faith.("An Affirmation of the Fiduciary Principle" (1996) NZLJ 405, at 407-408). Importing an obligation to perform contractual promises in relational contracts of the present kind would assist in filling that void. Commerce would undoubtedly be better served by a law which recognised the underlying imperative arising from the mutual trust and confidence which the parties repose in one another in a relational or long-term contract. Business situations in which the relationship of the parties had become commercially unrealistic or intolerable would be reduced or avoided. It is that objective which has driven the above exercise.

[49] Having regard to the decision of the majority, however, the appeal must be dismissed. But, for myself, I would have invoked this Court's powers under s 62 of the Judicature Act 1908 and r 19 of the Court of Appeal (Civil) Rules 1997 and remitted the proceeding back to the High Court to give Bobux the opportunity to litigate the question whether Raynor is in breach of an obligation of good faith. I would have given Bobux 27 days within which to amend its pleading and suspended Raynor 's ability to enter judgment until the expiry of that 27 days, or the further determination of the proceeding should Bobux decide to amend its pleading and proceed on the basis that Raynor is in breach of an obligation to perform the contract in good faith. Bobux can, of course, start afresh. That is entirely a decision for Bobux and its advisers to make. No question of res judicata can arise.

KEITH AND BLANCHARD JJ (DELIVERED BY BLANCHARD J)

[50] This appeal is about the interpretation of a distribution agreement for babies' leather booties. It centres on four clauses of that agreement which deal with rights of termination. The respondent, Raynor Marketing Ltd (Raynor), says that the clauses exclusively govern the right to terminate and that the appellant, Bobux Marketing Ltd (Bobux), could not bring the agreement to an end by giving a reasonable period of notice in circumstances where Raynor was not in breach of any of its obligations and had ordered the minimum quantities specified in the agreement.

[51] The agreement was entered into in March 1993. Bobux, a New Zealand company, appointed Raynor, an English company owned by New Zealand expatriates, to be its sole exclusive distributor of " Bobux " Children's leather booties as produced or dealt in by the Supplier at the date of this Agreement (the "Products") for the Supplier in the United Kingdom and the Republic of Ireland (the "Territory")

[52] Bobux agreed during the period of the agreement not directly or indirectly to supply any person other than Raynor with the products in the territory. Raynor agreed that it would not "during the currency of this Agreement or for a period of 18 months after its expiry" manufacture or distribute in the territory children's leather booties in competition with the products as manufactured by Bobux at the date of such expiry (cl 1).

[53] The crucial clauses are these:

"18. The initial period of this Agreement shall be a trial period of six months during which no minimum monthly orders shall be required.On expiry of such period, the Distributor or the Supplier may give written notice to the other of them to terminate this Agreement, which notice must be given so as to be received by the other of them within fourteen days from the end of the six month period, failing which there will be no right to terminate this agreement on this ground thereafter.

19. If this Agreement is not terminated as provided in paragraph 18 above, it will continue for an indefinite period from the date hereof and may only be terminated:

(a) on four calendar months written notice by either party to the other, provided that such notice may only be given after the first year of operation of this Agreement and such notice may only be given by the Supplier if the Distributor will have failed to order at least the Minimum Quantity (as defined below); or

(b) with immediate effect by written notice given by either party if the other party will have committed a material breach of the provisions of this Agreement and will not have remedied the breach within 14 days of written notice requiring it to be remedied. For the avoidance of doubt, any failure to order the Minimum Quantity shall not be regarded as a breach of this Agreement.

20. For the purposes of this Agreement, the "Minimum Quantity" means:

(a) for the first year of operation of this Agreement - nil; and

(b) thereafter, the equivalent of 1,500 pairs of the Products in each successive period of three months, provided that any excess over and above 6000 pairs of the Products ordered by the Distributor in the first year of operation of this Agreement shall count towards and be treated as Products ordered in the three month period following that year, and any excess over and above 1500 pairs of the Products ordered or treated as being ordered in any three month period shall count towards and be treated as having been ordered in the next three month period.

21.On termination of this agreement for any reason (unless this agreement is terminated by the Supplier under paragraph 19(b) above) the Supplier will, if required to do so by the Distributor, be obliged to supply to the Distributor on the terms set out in this Agreement a quantity of the Products up to the quantity ordered by the Distributor in the twelve months prior to the date of termination (or if less, the period from commencement of this Agreement to the date of termination) and the Distributor shall be entitled to sell those Products as it sees fit. On any such termination the Distributor shall provide the Supplier with a list of its customers and the Supplier shall not itself and shall procure that any Distributor appointed by it (and it shall be entitled to appoint any other Distributor after termination but subject to this provision) shall not directly or indirectly sell any of the Products to any of the customers mentioned on that list for a period of 12 months following such termination. It is recorded that the basis of this provision is to enable the

Distributor to enjoy the fair benefit of any market which it will have been able to build up for the Products.

For the avoidance of doubt, on termination by the Supplier, the Supplier shall fulfil all orders placed by the Distributor before the date of termination unless the Distributor cancels such orders (which it shall be entitled to do without having any liability to the Supplier) and the Distributor shall be entitled to sell its stock of Products after such termination.

This Clause shall survive any termination of this Agreement."

[54] It is common ground that the only booties being produced by Bobux at the date of the agreement were for what is called the 0-2 year-old market.

[55] After the agreement had been operating with apparent success for several years, the parties fell out about extending the product range to include shoes of essentially the same kind for children older than 2. Both firms are now separately marketing shoes for older children in the United Kingdom and Ireland in competition with one another, Bobux doing so under its eponymous brand name and Raynor under its own brand "Sole Mania". (Although there have been allegations of passing off made against Raynor , the present case proceeded on the basis that the competition is not in breach of the agreement relating to booties for the 0-2 year old age bracket.)

[56] On 4 February 2000 Bobux gave Raynor nine months notice of termination of the distribution agreement.The High Court has held that nine months was a reasonable period of notice in the circumstances. Raynor has not sought to cross-appeal that aspect of the judgment.We proceed therefore on the basis that if Raynor had the right to give a notice, then the agreement was validly terminated.

[57] But in his judgment delivered in the High Court at Auckland on 10 October 2000, Morris J found that the terms of the contract were "straightforward and clear". The parties had, he said, expressly provided for termination. They had used the word "only" in cl 19. In his view, to construe the contract as Bobux would have it meant the Court would have to imply into it an overriding provision which would be directly contradictory to the express provision "may only be terminated". That would be to read down the express terms.

[58] Nor could the Judge see any basis for applying the contra proferentem rule against Raynor , whose solicitor had prepared the draft agreement, because, the Judge said, the terms of the contract were "clear and unambiguous and lead to no situation which could be said to offend common-sense". He rejected, in particular, a submission that the words "for any reason" in cl 21 did more than refer back to the rights of termination provided expressly in the agreement:

It would require for a giant step, indeed a leap, to extrapolate the "for any reason" in this clause to a provision that agreement could be terminated for any reason on reasonable notice.I see no need to take such action when the terms are clear.

[...]

LEGAL PRINCIPLES

[65] In Crawford Fitting Co v. City Valve & Fittings Pty Ltd (1988) 14 NSWLR 438, 443, McHugh JA said that the question of construction in a case of this kind did not depend only upon a textual examination. It involves consideration also of the subject matter of the agreement, the circumstances in which it was made and the provisions which the parties have or have not agreed.

[66] We feel the force of the observation in one Canadian case, to which Mr Brown referred us, that "the concept of a perpetual distribution agreement is difficult to entertain" (Treen Gloves & Safety Products Ltd v. Degil Safety Products (1989) Inc.(1990) 33 CPR (3d) 74, 81). This Court has, however, itself commented in Minister of Education v. De Luxe Motor Services (1972) Ltd [1990] 1 NZLR 27, 31 that it is doubtful that there is any general presumption in favour of determinability of continuing contracts of no specified duration, but that "most Judges and practitioners...would expect to find cogent reasons in the nature or terms of the particular contract before placing on it the interpretation that there is no right to determine on reasonable notice". We respectfully agree and have approached the interpretation of the contract now before the Court on that basis.

[67] We accept that the mere statement that a contract is to continue " for an indefinite period" or the fact that a contract may contain certain express provisions enabling termination in defined circumstances, such as material breach by the other party, does not preclude the finding of an implicit right also to bring the relationship to an end by a period of notice which is reasonable in the circumstances which exist at the time the notice is given (see, for example, Re Spenborough Urban District Council's Agreement [1968] 1 Ch 139, 153). Nor is it fatal to the possible existence of such a right of termination in one party that the other party is alone expressly given that right (Winter Garden Theatre (London) Ltd v. Millennium Productions Ltd [1948] AC 173).

[68] In the end, although in a mercantile or commercial contract the Court will favour an interpretation which enables the relationship to be terminated on reasonable notice, the question remains whether the language actually used by the parties admits of an implication or interpretation to that effect.

CONCLUSIONS

[69] The problem faced by the appellant is that the express terms of the agreement very directly address the question of termination.Furthermore, they follow the pattern of the "template" from the US agreement sent by Mr Bennett to Raynor. That fact alone precludes reliance by Bobux on the *contra proferentem rule*.

[70] Clause 18 is of no direct relevance. The trial period is long since over and the agreement has continued without any notice being given by either party under that clause.

[71] Clause 19 begins with the statement that, in that circumstance, the agreement will continue for an indefinite period and may only be terminated in accordance with para (a) or (b).Para (b) is, again, not directly relevant, although it does spell out that the failure to

order the minimum quantity is not a breach. Para (a) provides for termination by either side on four months notice, but that right is qualified by a very explicit proviso which is in two parts.The first part, once more not directly relevant, is that such a notice may only be given after the first year. The second part is that such notice may only be given by Bobux if Raynor has failed to order at least the minimum quantity. Not only, therefore, is the agreement to be continued indefinitely, but notice is expressly not to be given by Bobux if Raynor orders the minimum quantity.

[72] Material breach by Raynor is dealt with under para (b) and, as noted, it does not include failure to order the minimum quantity.

[73] In the face of these provisions, can it be said that where Raynor is not in breach and has duly ordered the minimum quantity (either in the year in question or by application of the provision for carrying forward the benefit of previous orders), there is room for the implication of a right to terminate without cause on reasonable notice? We think not, for it would contradict the express agreement not to give a termination notice if Raynor is maintaining minimum orders.

[74] We have carefully examined the balance of the contract document for indications of a contrary intention, but find only those referred to by Mr Brown, which are so fragile as to provide insufficient support for his argument. References to "expiry" are perfectly capable of being taken to refer to the expiry of a notice under cl 18 or 19.

[75] Clause 21 is intended to protect the distributor against a relatively sudden termination of the agreement. It prevents Bobux dealing with Raynor 's customers for 12 months after termination and requires Bobux during that period to supply an equivalent quantity of product to that which Raynor ordered in the preceding 12 months (or lesser period if the agreement happened to be terminated during the initial year).It enables Raynor to sell those products, along with stock in hand, over a relatively extended period. Raynor would (under cl 1) be unable for 18 months to sell any competitive products and would therefore, to maintain the continuity of its business, require new Bobux product until it was free to begin to sell on behalf of a competitor of Bobux or on its own account.

[76] Although termination under cl 18 and 19 may occur in circumstances in which Raynor may not be particularly concerned to protect a market for children's booties - determination may have come about because there is little or no market, as evidenced by lack of orders for the minimum quantity - it is also possible that Raynor may have terminated because of breach by Bobux . If the nature of Bobux's breach were serious, Raynor might not want to continue the relationship.It might contemplate instead beginning again with a competitive product when free to do so, while, in the meantime, preserving its recognition in the market as a supplier of children's booties. If so, Raynor would need the protection of cl 21. Accordingly, we do not see the opening words of cl 21 ("for any reason") as an indication that the clause is directed at a termination which is not pursuant to cl 18 or 19, and one which would contradict the express words of those clauses.

[77] Nor do we think that a literal reading of the words chosen by the parties necessarily leads to an absurd commercial result.Because of the very absence of a right of termination in Bobux and the fixed nature of the minimum quantities, a Court may well

find that to give business efficacy to the contract, it is to be implied that Raynor will use its best endeavours to maximise its sales and therefore its orders. If so, Bobux could terminate by reasonable notice where such endeavours are not made, but could not do so if they were duly made, unless orders fell below the minimum. If the directors of Raynor were to neglect Bobux 's business in favour of pursuing their own competitive interests through another vehicle, that might place Raynor in breach of such an implied term.However, we express no concluded view on this question.

[78] We also do not place much weight on the appellant's suggestion that an inability to bring the relationship to an end may work a hardship on a husband and wife owned company whose proprietors may at some stage wish to give up the manufacture of children's booties. We think it more likely that, if the business is still profitable when they wish to retire, they will prefer to sell their shareholding rather than close down the business. If, because of changes of circumstance, they conclude that the manufacturing business is no longer viable, it seems most improbable that the distributor will take a different view of the position at that time. In other words, we think that the problems envisaged for the supplier because of the absence of a "reasonable notice" exit provision are not likely to arise in practice.

[79] For these reasons, we consider that Morris J correctly refused to make a declaration that the agreement was terminated by Bobux on the giving of reasonable notice.

[80] Since this judgment was prepared we have had the opportunity of reading a draft of the judgment of Thomas J. We do not accept that the contract was so lop-sided as to require a modification of what Thomas J concedes is our orthodox approach to contractual construction, assuming that to be possible. Nor do we accept that a reasonable person in Raynor's position would have understood that Bobux was to have a right to terminate other than as expressly stated, and in a manner broadly consistent with the specimen contract tendered by Bobux. We note that there has been neither a plea of mutual mistake nor any attempt to seek rectification.

[81] We agree with Thomas J that no question of res judicata can arise in relation to any issue of good faith performance, on which we make no comment. Nor does it arise in respect of the matters discussed in paras [77] and [78] of this judgment.

RESULT

[82] In accordance with the views of the majority, the appeal is dismissed with costs of $5,000 for the respondent, which is also entitled to its reasonable disbursements, including travel and accommodation costs, to be fixed if necessary by the Registrar.

[...]

Sources

Australasian Legal Information Institute *http://www.austlii.edu.au.*

(Case kindly brought to the attention of the UNILEX editors by Dr. Bruno ZELLER of the Victoria University School of Law).

Date: **December 2001**
Adjudicating Court: **ICC International Court of Arbitration**
Number: **9994**
Parties: **Unknown**

Keywords

LICENSE AGREEMENT BETWEEN FRENCH AND US COMPANIES – SUPERVENING HARDSHIP – PARTIES UNDER A DUTY TO RENEGOTIATE CONTRACT – REFERENCE NOT ONLY TO THE LAW GOVERNING THE CONTRACT (FRENCH LAW) BUT ALSO THE THE UNIDROIT PRINCIPLES (ARTS. 6.2.2 - 6.2.3)

Abstract

Claimant, a French company, entered into a license and sales agreement with Defendant, a US company, whereby the latter was granted the right to make, use and sell products derived from raw material supplied by the former. When after a certain period of time Claimant considerably increased the price of the raw material due to the more stringent conditions imposed upon Claimant by a Governmental Agency for the collection of human placentae from which the raw material was extracted, Defendant terminated the contract. According to Claimant the termination was unlawful because Defendant should have agreed to renegotiate the price so as to adapt it to the new circumstances.

The contract was governed by French law. In deciding in favour of Claimant, the Arbitral Tribunal, after stating that "French law requires from each party to perform the agreement in good faith (*cf.* Article 1134(2) - *rectius*: 1134(3) - of the French civil code) [and] good faith imposes upon the parties the duty to seek out an adaptation of their agreement to the new circumstances which may have occurred after its execution in order to ensure that its performance does not cause, especially when the contract at stake is a long-term agreement, the ruin of one of the parties", pointed out that "this principle is also prevailing in international commercial law (see UNIDROIT Principles Articles 6.2.2 and 6.2.3)".

Full Text

[..]

On [the matter of whether the respondent was right or wrong to refuse delivery of the raw material at the new price], the Arbitral Tribunal finds that the issue of the alleged existence of an oral agreement between Messrs [A, of claimant company] and [B, the respondent's CEO and negotiator of the contract] to renegotiate the Agreement in case of more stringent demands of the [government agency] regarding the approval of the product can be left undecided as can also be left undecided the question of a possible application of the so-called "merger" clause of article 9 (c) of the Agreement to the alleged oral agreement and to the subsequent confirmation letter of May 24, 1997. Assuming that on these two issues, [Respondent]'s contention should prevail, this would not discharge [Respondent] from its duty to renegotiate the agreement in the event that the conditions set forth by French law for such a renegotiation would be met – "the law of France" is the substantive law to be applied to this dispute ... As correctly stated by [Claimant] ..., French law requires from each party to perform the agreement in good faith (see c. civ. 1134, al. 2). Good faith imposes upon the parties the duty to seek out an adaptation of their agreement to the new circumstances which may have occurred after its execution, in order to ensure that its performance does not cause, especially when the contract at stake is a long term agreement, the ruin of one of the parties (see Terré, Simler, Lequette : Obligations, No. 414 & foll. and 446 ; Malaurie and Aynès : Les obligations, § 622 p. 359). This principle is also prevailing in international commercial law (see Unidroit Principles, art. 6.2.2 and 6.2.3).

As it is recalled ... *supra*, when negotiating the agreement, the parties were under the impression that the [government agency] would not impose a control placenta per placenta, although they did not exclude such an eventuality. Now, some time after the signature of the Agreement, the [govemment agency] required individual donors□ screening and that severe demand was certainly one of the cause [sic] of the increase of the cost of the [raw material] well above the US$ ... per gram agreed upon in the Agreement. If one relies on Mr [C, witness]'s fax addressed to Mr [D, negotiator of the contract for the claimant] on January 30, 1990 ..., this was certainly a somehow unexpected event. Furthermore, the fact that the "*Force Majeure* Clause", as per clause 9 (f) of the Agreement, did not expressly contemplate the risk of a potential regulatory change, does not "*per se*" exempt [Respondent] from renegotiating the contract price as, according to the French doctrine quoted thereabove, this duty is already imposed upon the contracting parties by the rule of good faith and that rule cannot be defeated by any divergent contractual provisions. Therefore and on this point, the Arbitral Tribunal finds that due to the new request of the [government agency] relating to the control of the placentae, [the party to the original agreement assigned to the claimant] was entitled to a renegotiation of the contract price, but that does not mean at all that [said party] was entitled to impose upon [Respondent] its own view on what should be the correct price.'

Force majeure clause

'The Agreement contained a *force majeure* clause which reads as follows:

"*Force majeure*: Neither party shall be responsible for any losses if the fulfilment of any terms or provisions hereof shall be delayed or prevented by civil disorders, wars, acts of enemies, acts of God, fire, storm, flood, riot or strikes or by any other cause not within the reasonable control of the party whose performance is interfered with, and which by the exercise of reasonable diligence, such party is unable to prevent." (see clause 9 (f)).

It should here be noted that at a certain stage of the negotiations, [the party to the original agreement assigned to the claimant] proposed a "*Force majeure*" clause covering "any changes in the economics of placental processing due to any cause not within its control"... [Said party]'s proposal in this respect was not accepted by [Respondent] and this is evidenced by the actual drafting of clause 9 (f) of the Agreement which does not specifically address the risk of a potential regulatory change. However, according to Mr [D] [...], this particular risk was covered by the so called "side letter" allegedly sent by Mr [E, negotiator of the contract for the claimant] to Mr [B] on May 24, 1989 [...]

Sources

Excerpt in ICC International Court of Arbitration Bulletin, 2005 Special Supplement, 79 - 80.

Date: **December 2001**
Adjudicating Court: **ICC International Court of Arbitration**
Number: **11295**
Parties: **Unknown**

Keywords

LEGAL ISSUE AT STAKE NOT SPECIFICALLY ADDRESSED BY APPLICABLE DOMESTIC LAW – ARBITRAL TRIBUNAL ENTITLED TO RESORT TO "INTERNATIONAL LAW INSTRUMENTS" SUCH AS THE UNIDROIT PRINCIPLES

CONTRACT INTERPRETATION AND SUPPLEMENTING – ACCORDING TO COMMON INTENTION OF PARTIES, PURPOSE OF THE CONTRACT AND GOOD FAITH (ART. 65(2) OF THE POLISH CIVIL CODE AND ARTS. 4.1(1) AND 4.8(2) OF THE UNIDROIT PRINCIPLES)

Abstract

Claimant, a Swiss company, had been granted by Defendant, a Polish company, certain exclusive rights which Claimant later transferred to one of its subsidiaries. When Claimant initiated arbitration proceedings on the grounds of an alleged violation of these rights by Defendant, the question arose as to whether Claimant, when transferring these exclusive rights to its subsidiary, had transferred them alone or had transferred the whole contract it had concluded with Defendant including the duties.

The Arbitral Tribunal held that, since the applicable Polish law did not provide any specific solution on this point, it could "subsidiarily apply international law instruments" such as the UNIDROIT Principles. However, after having found that the question as to whether a party is entitled to transfer to its subsidiary only the active parts of the contractual obligations while withholding the passive ones or whether this party has to transfer the whole contract was not specifically addressed by the UNIDROIT Principles either, the Arbitral Tribunal concluded that the solution could only be found by interpreting the terms of the contract. In this respect the Arbitral Tribunal referred to the canons of interpretation laid down in Article 65(2) of the Polish Civil Code as well as in Articles 1.1, 4.1(1) and 4.8(2) of the UNIDROIT Principles, *i.e.* that a contract is to be interpreted and supplemented having regard to the common intention of the parties, the nature and purpose of the contract, good faith and fair dealing and reasonableness.

Full Text

[...]

44. Section VIII Of the Terms of Reference provides that:

... the laws of the state of Poland, shall be the main rule of law to be applied [...] to the merits of the dispute...

Even if the current question is included by the Terms of Reference within the "Preliminary Issues: Admissibility" and not within the "Further Issues: Merits" of the dispute, it cannot be validly denied that interpretation of the Contract regarding an issue such as its transfer and the legal effects of it, falls under a question of substantial law and not under procedural law.
Polish rules of law applicable as such to the current matter contribute only as follows to determine the disputed issue:

45. Basically Polish law bears out the principle of the Freedom of the Contract as provided byArticle 353 of its Civil Code:
The parties to a contract may arrange the legal relationship as they deem proper on the condition that the contents or the purpose of that contract are not contrary to the nature of the relationship, with statutory law, and with the principles of community life.

It means that [Claimant] and [Respondent] may be deemed as having arranged the transfer of rights as they decided to do, as long as no mandatory rules forbid it.

There are no mandatory Polish rules which would oblige the contractual parties to transfer such a contract either totally or partially.

46. Regarding non mandatory clauses, it is true that the Polish Civil Code provides separately for:
- the change of creditor in articles 509 to 518;
- and the change of debtor in articles 519 to 526.

Nevertheless, it also provides for contractual relationships where the same party is both creditor and debtor, *i.e.* in a bilateral contract (in Polish "*umowa wzajemna*").
That is the case for a named contract such as a lease agreement, but, by analogy, those rules may be applied for unnamed contracts.

In the current case, the contract seems very close to a lease agreement since its purpose is the renting of advertising space on kiosks where parts of unmovable property owned by a lessor ([Respondent]) are granted to a lessee ([Claimant]) against rental fees; but as having meanwhile a broader scope it might also be considered as an unnamed agreement.

47. In both cases, *i.e.* named or unnamed, the above-mentioned Polish non mandatory rules of law can be applied.

Hence, as far as Polish law is concerned for this issue, there are neither mandatory clauses which oblige, nor non mandatory clauses which lead, to the transfer of a bilateral contract either totally, with rights and duties or partially with either rights or duties.

However, as it provides only for either a change of creditor or a change of debtor regarding a single obligation, or assignment of a contract including all its obligations (both active and passive, *i.e.* rights and duties), it can be said that in such bilateral contracts, a transfer limited to the sole rights to receive the duties, would be rather atypical.

In its [sic] Treaty of Civil law "*System prawa cywilnego*" Prof. Zbigniew RADWANSKI does not deny the theoretical possibility of such a transfer provided it is subordinated to a true economic objective.

48. The sole arbitrator stating that Polish law belongs to the civil law tradition, considered appropriate to study the pertinent case-law but did not find however any specific decision suitable to really clarify the matter.

The sole arbitrator therefore deems that Polish law being the main rule of law to be applied, does not provide any other specific solution on the substance of the issue.

However, the sole arbitrator points out that, as in many other law systems, as regards the interpretation of acts in laws, Polish law provides, in article 65 § 2 of its Civil Code:
In the case of contracts, the congruent intention of the parties and the purpose of the contract, rather than relying on its literal wording, must be established.

49. In International Arbitration, when the national law(s) to be applied to the dispute, does (do) not provide any specific solution to settle the point of law involved, the arbitral tribunal may subsidiarily apply international law instruments.

In the present case, the latter are indeed more relevant than French law referred to by both parties but deprived of any legal link to the case.

Accordingly, if the sole arbitrator considers that, subsidiarily to Polish laws applicable as main rules of law, the UNIDROIT Principles of International Commercial Contracts 1994 may also be applied to the dispute, it [sic] does not see however any UNIDROIT rule liable to determine whether within an international agreement a party is entitled to transfer to its subsidiary only the active parts of the contractual obligations while withholding the passive ones or whether this party has to transfer the whole agreement.

Such silence is expected in other equivalent international law instruments.

However, converging on the above mentioned general Polish rules, said UNIDROIT Principles provide:
- the "Freedom of Contract" (*cf.* Article 1.1),
- their interpretation in accordance with especially:
- The "Common intention of the Parties"
- The nature and purpose of the Contract,
- Good faith and fair dealing,
- Reasonableness (*cf.* Articles 4.1(1), and 4.8(2)).

Sources

Excerpt in ICC International Court of Arbitration Bulletin, 2005 Special Supplement, 88 - 89.

Date: ***January 25, 2002***
Adjudicating Court: ***Arbitration Court of the Lausanne Chamber of Commerce and Industry***
Number: ***Unknown***
Parties: ***Unknown***

Keywords

CONSULTING CONTRACT FOR MANUFACTURING AND MARKETING OF NEW PRODUCTS IN A DOZEN OF COUNTRIES – CONTRACT SILENT AS TO APPLICABLE LAW BUT CONTAINING REFERENCE TO "GENERAL PRINCIPLES OF LAW APPLICABLE TO INTERNATIONAL COMMERCIAL CONTRACTS" – AT BEGINNING OF ARBITRAL PROCEEDING PARTIES AGREE ON APPLICATION OF THE UNIDROIT PRINCIPLES

DUTY OF BEST EFFORTS AS CONTRASTED TO DUTY TO ACHIEVE A SPECIFIC RESULT (ART. 5.4 [ART. 5.1.4 OF THE 2004 EDITION] OF THE UNIDROIT PRINCIPLES)

NON-PERFORMANCE PARTLY CAUSED BY ACT OR OMISSION OF AGGRIEVED PARTY – AGGRIEVED PARTY PREVENTED FROM RELYING ON NON-PERFORMANCE – PRINCIPLE OF GOOD FAITH AND FAIR DEALING (ARTS. 7.1.2 AND 1.7 OF THE UNIDROIT PRINCIPLES)

CONTRACT INTERPRETATION – PREAMBLE OF CONTRACT NOT NECESSARILY RELEVANT (SEE COMMENT 2 TO ART. 4.4 OF THE UNIDROIT PRINCIPLES)

CONTRACT INTERPRETATION – ACCORDING TO UNDERSTANDING OF REASONABLE PERSON (ART. 4.1(2) OF THE UNIDROIT PRINCIPLES)

TERMINATION OF CONTRACT – NOTICE – INTERPRETATION OF CONTENT (ARTS. 4.2(2), 4.3 LIT.(C) AND 4.5 OF THE UNIDROIT PRINCIPLES)

COURSE OF DEALINGS – POWERS OF ATTORNEY OF ONE PARTY'S EMPLOYEE (ART. 1.8(1) OF UNIDROIT PRINCIPLES)

PACTA SUNT SERVANDA – TERMINATION OF CONTRACT LEGITIMATE ONLY WHEN ADMITTED BY CONTRACT OR SPECIFIC PROVISIONS OF UNIDROIT PRINCIPLES (ART. 1.3 OF UNIDROIT PRINCIPLES)

PUBLIC PERMISSION REQUIREMENT – PARTY UNDER DUTY TO APPLY FAILS TO DO SO – PARTY UNDER DUTY TO APPLY FAILS TO GIVE NOTICE TO OTHER PARTY (ART. 6.1.15(1) AND (2) OF UNIDROIT PRINCIPLES)

RIGHT TO PERFORMANCE OF NON-MONETARY OBLIGATION – OBLIGEE UNABLE TO GET PERFORMANCE IN NATURA – MAY CHANGE REMEDY AND ASK FOR DAMAGES (ART. 7.2.5(1) OF THE UNIDROIT PRINCIPLES)

RIGHT TO DAMAGES – DETERMINATION OF AMOUNT DUE (SEE ARTS. 7.4.1, 7.4.2, 7.4.3, 7.4.4, 7.4.7, 7.4.9(2) AND COMMENTS TO ART. 7.4.12 OF THE UNIDROIT PRINCIPLES)

Abstract

Two Belgian individuals (Claimants) and a Spanish company (Defendant) entered into a contract whereby the former undertook to provide the latter with ideas and share their experience with respect to the manufacturing and marketing of new products.

The dispute arose when the Spanish company terminated the contract and claimed damages.

The arbitration clause in the contract mentioned the European Convention on Commercial Arbitration of 21 April 1961 and provided that the seat of the arbitral tribunal will be "in Switzerland". The special Committee set up under the European Convention has appointed the Chairman.

However, the contract did not contain a clear choice of law clause. Claimants argued for the application of a "neutral law", *i.e.* Swiss law, but recognized that the contract contained a reference to "general principles of law applicable to international commercial contracts". Therefore, Claimants accepted the application of the UNIDROIT Principles. Since also Defendant agreed on their application, the arbitral tribunal citing the Preamble (Paragraph 2) decided to apply the UNIDROIT Principles as the law governing the substance of the dispute chosen by the parties. The arbitral tribunal further noted that no mandatory rule either in Switzerland, or in Belgium and Spain forbids the application of the UNIDROIT Principles. Moreover, in view of the fact that the new products should have been marketed in a dozen or so of countries, the tribunal found it reasonable to apply the UNIDROIT Principles rather than a specific domestic law, all the more so since these Principles are applicable to contracts for services as well as to the sale of goods or to contracts for works.

In the case at hand the arbitral tribunal found that the following articles of the UNIDROIT Principles were especially relevant :

- Arts. 1.1, 1.3, 1.6, 1.7, 1.8 (general principles)
- Arts. 4.1 to 4.8 (interpretation of the contract)
- Art. 5.3 [Art. 5.1.3 of the 2004 edition] (duty to cooperate)
- Art. 5.4 [Art. 5.1.4 of the 2004 edition] (duty to achieve a result; duty of best efforts)
- Art. 6.1.4 (priority of performance by one party)
- Arts. 7.1.1 to 7.4.12 (non-performance; termination; damages).

The arbitral tribunal first relied on Art. 5.4(2) [Art. 5.1.4(2) of the 2004 edition] of UNIDROIT Principles when deciding that Claimants did not have an obligation to reach specific results; they merely owed a duty of diligence in the communication of their experiences and their marketing endeavours. The preamble to the contract is not binding, as is shown by the Comments to Art. 4.4. Art. 4.1(2) is also mentioned as guidance to interpret the contract.

Further, both parties and especially Defendant have to abide by Art. 1.7 on the mandatory character of the good faith rule. As Defendant did not act in good faith and otherwise breached the contract, the arbitral tribunal applies Art. 7.1.2 to admit that Defendant is barred from invoking some allegedly unperfect performance acts by Claimants, since Defendant caused such acts by its own behaviour. Thus, Art. 6.1.15(1) come to play, because Defendant never requested an official authorization that would have been necessary for marketing the product, and failed to inform the other party in this regard (see Art. 6.1.15(2)). Art. 7.2.5(1) is also mentioned as concerns the inaction by Defendant.

As to the rules on the powers of attorney of one employee of Defendant who signed a termination notice, the award is based on Art. 1.8(1). As to the contents of that termination notice, Art. 4.2(2) and Art. 4.3(c) are taken into account, as well as Art. 4.5 (interpretation "*contra proferentem*"). Art. 1.3 is mentioned to state that an unjustified termination is contrary to the sanctity of contracts. The reference at the end of Art. 1.3 is meant to be to Art. 3.13, Art. 5.8 [Art. 5.1.8 of the 2004 edition], Art. 6.1.16. Art. 6.2.3, Art. 7.1.7, Art. 7.3.1 and Art. 7.3.3. Having considered these provisions, the arbitral tribunal finds that the termination was not justified.

As to the determination of damages, Art. 7.4.1, 7.4.2, 7.4.3, 7.4.4, 7.4.7, 7.4.9(2) and 3.10(2) are taken into consideration, as well as the Comments to Art. 7.4.12.

Full Text

[Not yet available]

Sources

Notice of the award kindly provided by Professor François DESSEMONTET.

Date: ***March 2002***
Adjudicating Court: ***ICC International Court of Arbitration***
Number: ***10385***
Parties: ***Unknown***

Keywords

CONSTRUCTION CONTRACT BETWEEN A WEST AFRICAN STATE AND A COMPANY FROM A NEIGHBOURING COUNTRY – CONTRACT SILENT AS TO THE APPLICABLE LAW – ARBITRAL TRIBUNAL ESCLUDES APPLICATION NOT ONLY OF ANY DOMESTIC LAW BUT ALSO OF THE LEX MERCATORIA BECAUSE OF ITS UNCERTAIN NATURE AND SCOPE – MENTION IN THIS CONTEXT OF THE UNIDROIT PRINCIPLES, DESCRIBED AS "COMPLEMENTING IF NOT EVEN COMPETING WITH" THE LEX MERCATORIA

Abstract

Defendant, the Government of a West African State, entered into a construction contract with Claimant, an African construction company. Claimant initiated arbitral proceedings alleging that Defendant had failed to fulfil its contractual obligations.

The contract was silent as to the applicable law. In view of the fact that the parties had not chosen a particular domestic law as the law governing their contract and had agreed to submit any dispute that might arise to arbitration to be held in Switzerland, that the contract was between a State and foreign private company and that the construction project was being financed by an international organisation, the Arbitral Tribunal held that in the case at hand no domestic law was applicable. The Arbitral Tribunal also rejected the Defendant's request to have the dispute settled according to the *lex mercatoria* on account of the fact that not only was there no express or implicit reference to the *lex mercatoria* in the contract, but the very definition and scope of the *lex mercatoria* was far from being unanimously accepted among scholars and in international arbitration practice. According to the Arbitral Tribunal the same applied *mutatis mutandis* to the UNIDROIT Principles which it described as "complementing if not competing with" the *lex mercatoria*. The Arbitral Tribunal concluded that it would decide the dispute according to the terms of the contract and only when necessary apply "the rules of law" it considered most appropriate.

Full Text

DROIT APPLICABLE

58. Ni le Contrat, ni les autres documents contractuels ne précisent le droit applicable au contrat litigieux, voire le droit de procédure applicable à l'arbitrage.

a) La lex arbitri

59. Le chapitre 12 (art. 176 à 194) sur l'arbitrage international de la loi fédérale suisse sur le droit international privè du 18 décembre 1987 (LDIP) s'applique à tout arbitrage si le siège du tribunal arbitral se trouve en Suisse (ce qui est le cas vu la décision de la Cour du [...]) et si aucune des parties n'avait, au moment de la conclusion de la convention d'arbitrage, ni son domicile ni sa résidence habituelle en Suisse (art. 176, al. 1), et que les parties n'ont pas expressément exclu son application au sens de l'al.2.

60. Tel est bien le cas en l'espèce, la Cour ayant fixé Genève comme lieu de l'arbitrage, de sorte que le chapitre 12 a vocation à s'appliquer au titre de *lex arbitri* à la présente cause. Celle-ci a d'ailleurs été expressément désignée par l'Acte de mission (art. 8. 1).

b) A la procédure

61. L'Acte de mission (art. 8.1) prescrit que le présent arbitrage est régi par le chapitre 12 LDIP (art. 182) et le Règlement CCI (art. 15).

L'art. 182 al. 2 et 3 LDIP énonce pour sa part que :

Si les parties n'ont pas réglé la procédure, celle-ci sera, au besoin, fixée par le tribunal arbitral, soit directement, soit par référence à une loi ou à un règlement d'arbitrage.

Quelle que soit la procédure choisie, le tribunal arbitral doit garantir l'égalité entre les parties et leur droit d'être entendues en procédure contradictoire.

Quant à l'art. 15 du Règlement CCI ("règles applicables à la procédure") :

La procédure devant le tribunal arbitral est régie par le présent Règlement et, dans le silence de ce dernier, par les règles que les parties, ou à défaut le tribunal arbitral, déterminent, en se référant ou non à une loi nationale de procédure applicable à l'arbitrage.

Dans tous les cas, le tribunal arbitral conduit la procédure de manière équitable et impartiale et veille à ce que chaque partie ait eu la possibilité d'être suffisamment entendue.

62. La Demanderesse et le Tribunal arbitral ont procédé conformément à ce qui précède sans qu'aucune objection ait été soulevée alors même que la Défenderesse notamment a été expressément informée des règles de procédure appliquée à la présente cause.

Cela étant, le Tribunal arbitral ne voit aucune raison de s'écarter des règles précitées. Il convient donc de confirmer, dans la présente Sentence, leur application.

c) Au fond

63. Le contrat ne contenant pas d'élection de droit de fond, la Demanderesse et le Tribunal arbitral sont convenus, dans l'Acte de mission (art. 8.3), approuvé par la Cour en l'absence de signature par la Défenderesse, que:

Dans la mesure où le Contrat ne fixe pas le droit applicable au fond, le Tribunal Arbitral déterminera les règles applicables, conformément à l'article 187 al. 1 de la LDIP suisse.

L'art. 187, al. 1 LDIP dispose quant à lui que:

Le tribunal arbitral statue selon les règles de droit choisies par les parties ou, à défaut de choix, selon les règles de droit avec lesquelles la cause présente les liens les plus étroits.

64. Il est désormais acquis que l'art. 187 al. 1 LDIP ne fait aucune obligation à l'arbitre d'appliquer les règles de conflit de lois de la LDIP, (notamment son art. 117 al. 2, qui privilégie le droit du lieu de résidence habituelle ou de l'établissement de la partie qui fournit la prestation caractéristique).

Toutefois le législateur suisse n'a voulu laisser à l'arbitre, à défaut d'une élection de droit par les parties, ni une liberté totale, ni restreindre cette liberté de manière contraire à la pratique internationale selon laquelle l'arbitre applique soit la règle qu'il juge appropriée soit le droit désigné par la règle de conflit qu'il juge applicable. La règle ainsi choisie par l'arbitre n'est guère différente de la "proper law " anglaise. L'arbitre n'est d'ailleurs ni obligé de statuer selon un droit étatique, ni d'emprunter ces règles à un seul système de droit (Lalive, Poudret, Reymond, Le droit de l'arbítrge interne et international en Suisse, Payot, Lausanne 1989, nos 15-19 ad art. 187 LDIP).

65. L'art. 17 al. 1 du Règlement CCI confirme ce point de vue puisqu'il prescrit que "à défaut de choix par les parties des règles de droit applicables, l'arbitre appliquera les règles de droit qu'il juge appropriées". Or le nouveau règlement de 1998 avait notamment pour objectif de conférer davantage de liberté à l'arbitre en la matière alors que l'ancien règlement de 1988 (art. 13 al. 3) le contraignait à choisir un droit national (v. à ce sujet FOUCHARD *et al.* [International Commercial Arbitration, Kluwer, 1999] p. 319 ss).

66. En l'espèce, il est évident que le droit [de l'Etat A], voire le droit [de l'Etat B], auraient une certaine vocation, sinon à s'appliquer, du moins à être pris en considération par le Tribunal arbitral à ce stade de son analyse. Le premier, notamment, est celui de la partie débitrice; c'est aussi celui du lieu de l'exécution du Contrat. Le second est le droit du lieu d'établissement de l'autre partie, qui a fourni la prestation caractéristique.

67. Les parties ont toutefois exprimé l'intention de voir leurs litiges éventuels tranchés à Genève ou La Haye, de sorte qu'on ne peut entièrement exclure, sans analyse, l'application du droit suisse et du droit néerlandais. Ces derniers peuvent toutefois être éliminés d'emblée, dès lors qu'ils ne présentent, au demeurant, aucun lien de rattachement avec le litige, et que le choix d'un siège de l'arbitrage ne saurait suffire à justifier l'application du droit de fond de ce lieu.

68. D'autres considérations ont cependant guidé le Tribunal arbitral dans son choix. Le contrat litigieux s'inscrit dans le cadre d'un marché public international; il a été financé

par une organisation internationale; les Parties ont soustrait leurs litiges éventuels aux tribunaux [de l'Etat B ou de l'Etat A] pour les soumettre à l'arbitrage international en dehors du continent africain. La cause présente donc un fort aspect international ou supranational.

69. Les Parties n'ont pas choisi une "lex contactus", et il est significatif que [l'Etat A] n'ait pas demandé, voire exigé, l'application au Contrat de son propre droit, comme l'ont fait divers Etats dans des circonstances analogues. S'il est vrai que le Contrat contient quelques références au droit [de l'Etat A] [...], il s'agit exclusivement de lois administratives ou de police, dont l'application ne saurait être contestée à [l'Etat A] et qui n'ont pas davantage vocation à s'appliquer au fond. Le caractère limitatif de ces références suggère, au contraire, que si les Parties ont eu une intention commune quelconque au sujet de la loi applicable au Contrat, il s'est agi de l'intention de restreindre l'application du droit [de l'Etat A] à certains domaines limités (réglementation du travail et de la main d'Suvre étrangère, sécurité et hygiène des chantiers, routes, voirie, *etc.*) dans lesquels le droit national est en principe souverain ou a vocation naturelle à s'appliquer.

70. En résumé, si l'on se place sur le terrain du "rattachement subjectif" du Contrat, il ne pourrait s'agir que de la volonté tacite d'exclure la loi de chacune des Parties. Si l'on recourt en revanche à la méthode du "rattachement objectif", force est de constater que les données du litige n'indiquent aucun rapport manifestement prépondérant avec l'un ou l'autre des droits potentiellement applicables. On notera par exemple qu'il n'existe pas un lieu d'exécution unique et que le rattachement au domicile du débiteur de la prestation caractéristique (à la supposer unique et identifiable) ne fournit pas de solution satisfaisante. Enfin la "lex rei sitae" doit également être écartée dès lors qu'il s'agit d'un contrat d'entreprise et non pas d'un contrat de nature réelle.

71. L'examen des diverses méthodes possibles et la pesée des critères de rattachement évoqués ci-dessus conduisent le Tribunal arbitral à pencher en faveur de la thèse selon laquelle les Parties ont délibérément exclu l'application des droits [de l'Etat B et de l'Etat A] et que ni le critère de l'Etat débiteur, ni celui du lieu d'exécution, ni celui du lieu d'établissement de la partie ayant fourni la prestation caractéristique ne sont de nature à justifier l'application d'un droit national particulier.

72. Cette conclusion intermédiaire entrouvre la porte à la question de l'applicabilité de la *lex mercatoria*, appelée de ses vSux par la Demanderesse. Il est vrai que celle-ci a déjà été appliquée à l'occasion de nombreuses sentences arbitrales, y compris dans des cas dans lequels, comme en l'espèce, le Contrat ne contient aucune référence expresse à la *lex mercatoria* ni même la moindre allusion aux usages commerciaux internationaux.

73. Tel est aussi le cas des principes d'UNIDROIT, qui depuis 1994 épaulent, pour ne pas dire concurrencent la *lex mercatoria* avec la publication des Principles of International Commerdal Contracts, lesquels tentent d'uniformiser certains principes contractuels généraux mais aussi spécifiques. Ceux-ci ont également été occasionnellement appliqués dans certaines sentences CCI, par exemple pour combler des lacunes du droit (au demeurant) applicable (v. p. ex. Affaire CCI no 8128/1995, 123 JDI 812 (1996), cité par Michael BONELL, "The UNIDROIT Principles in Practice: The Experience of the First Two Years", 1 Uniform Law Review 30 (UNIDROIT, 1997)).

74. L'art. 17 al. 2 du Règlement CCI ne peut que conforter cette façon de voir en prescrivant que "dans touts les cas, le tribunal arbitral tient compte des dispositions du contrat et des usages du commerce pertinents".

75. Toutefois, s'il est vrai que la *lex mercatoria* a été fréquemment invoquée, notamment dans des sentences rendues sous l'égide de la CCI, la doctrine comme la jurisprudence arbitrales les plus récentes sont encore loin d'être unanimes quant à sa définition et sa portée précises (v. à ce sujet p. ex. le récent compte-rendu de CRAIG, PARK, PAULSSON, International Chamber of Commerce Arbitration, Oceana/ICC, New York 2000, p. 623 ss).

76. Ce n'est cependant pas l'objet de cette Sentence que d'en débattre. Pareille discussion ne semble d'ailleurs pas nécessaire aux yeux du Tribunal arbitral. Il suffira en effet d'observer qu'il existe en l'espèce, à l'évidence, une lacune que l'interprétation ne permet pas de combler avec certitude.

C'est en revanche cette même incertitude qui autorise le Tribunal à s'appliquer, indépendamment des considérations qui précèdent, les règles de droit qu'il estimera appropriées ou opportunes. On a vu à cet égard que l'art. 187 al. 1 LDIP laisse une grande liberté - alors même qu'elle n'est pas illimitée - à l'arbitre.

En l'occurrence, comme on le verra, la plupart des questions que pose le présent litige peuvent être résolues à l'aide du Contrat et de ses annexes, notamment le CCP ["Cahiers des clauses particulières"]. Le Tribunal arbitral donc examinera la question du droit applicable quand et si tant est qu'il apparaîtra nécessaire de s'écarter des règles contractuelles.

77. Enfin par souci d'être complet, on ajoutera qu'en l'absence de tout élément susceptible d'étayer cette solution, l'application des règles de l'équité (*ex aequo et bono*) ne peut davantage être retenue, les Arbitres n'ayant pas reçu mission de décider en *amiable compositeurs*.

Sources

Excerpt in ICC International Court of Arbitration Bulletin, 2005 Special Supplement, 80 - 83.

Date: ***March 2002***
Adjudicating Court: ***ICC International Court of Arbitration (Partial Award)***
Number: ***11375***
Parties: ***Unknown***

Keywords

CONSORTIUM AGREEMENT BETWEEN COMPANIES FROM WESTERN EUROPE AND EAST ASIA TO BID FOR A BOT CONCESSION IN EAST ASIAN COUNTRY – IMPLICIT OBLIGATION FOR CONSORTIUM MEMBERS TO ACT IN GOOD FAITH AMONG THEMSELVES – REFERENCE TO APPLICABLE DOMESTIC LAW AND TO THE UNIDROIT PRINCIPLES

Abstract

Several companies of Western Europe and East Asia entered into a consortium agreement to bid for a BOT concession in an East Asian country. A dispute arose when some of the parties to the consortium agreement accused others of breach of the agreement on account of their refusal to contract with them after having been awarded the concession. One of the questions to be decided was whether under the consortium agreement Defendants were entitled to contract with companies other than Claimants.

In deciding the question in the negative the Arbitral Tribunal pointed out that the legal relationship created by the consortium agreement was not an adversarial one but even in the absence of an express provision to this effect the parties were bound by an implicit obligation to act in good faith towards one another. The existence of such implicit obligation was not only expressly stated in the Civil Code of Country X whose law governed the agreement, but was also highlighted by an expert witness heard according to whom "in the UNIDROIT Principles which may have some relevance to an international case there is an implied obligation of good faith even if the parties don't agree on it".

Full Text

[...]

With respect to the relationship between the members of the ... Consortium, [Respondent] and [Claimant], there are three fundamental norms which arise logically and necessarily from the common interests that gave rise to and sustained the legal relationship of these parties and which are confirmed, indeed sometimes reiterated, in the various instruments. Without these normative elements, the legal relationship into which the diverse profit-maximizing entities were entering would have made little sense; any interpretation of the agreements and legal instruments with such a result would be untenable. The three fundamental and necessary norms are:

1. The preferred and priority bidder status of [Claimant];

2. The power of [Respondent] to refuse to contract with [Claimant] if [Claimant]'s proposal was in material non-compliance that would have frustrated the common interest of the Consortium members by allowing, if not requiring, the Government of [Country X] to reject the proposal of the Consortium;

3. A requirement of good faith and loyalty to the other members of the Consortium, which would, for example, have obliged [Respondent], as the negotiating agent, to try to dissuade the Government from changing a requirement that would have precluded the participation of another Consortium member.

These normative elements are the architectural struts of the legal relationship and each must be considered in more detail. [...]

It is perfectly clear that, in this complex legal relationship, good faith and "fair play", as the official of the Government of [Country X] put it ..., were as indispensable as the previous normative elements. The expectation that this was a necessary part of the regime was expressed in the Consortium Agreement and in the communication from the Government of [Country X] and it was implicit in the essential nature of the legal parties' relation. It is, moreover, required by [Country X] law. Article 219 of Book II of The Civil Code provides that
Every person is bound to execute his obligations and to exercise his rights in accordance with the rules of honesty and good faith.

Respondent's witness, Professor [A], testified "in the UNIDROIT Principles, which may have some relevance to an international case, there is an implied obligation of good faith even if the parties don't agree on it".

The ... Opinion, mentioned above, appeared to rely on a *dictum* in Walford v. Miles in which Lord Ackner said "the concept of a duty to carry on negotiations in good faith is inherently repugnant to the adversarial position of the parties when involved in negotiations". With all respect to that distinguished jurist and to the possible position in English law on this matter (which is, in any event, not the parties' choice of law in the case before us), the legal relations that were created by the agreements and instruments in the instant case meant that the parties to them did not find themselves in strict adversary relations, but were indeed bound by obligations of good faith as required by [Country X] law.

In the course of the Hearing, [Respondent]'s position changed. Counsel for [Respondent] stated that "there was an obligation to negotiate in good faith, not derived from a contract provision, Article 5.3, which is now defunct, but arising from the fact that we undertook negotiations with [Claimant] to begin with". In addition, Professor [A], [Respondent]'s witness, confirmed his statement in his second witness statement, to the effect that he understood that [Respondent] did not dispute that there was an obligation to negotiate in good faith.

Sources

Excerpt in ICC International Court of Aribtration Bulletin, 2005 Special Supplement, 90 - 91.

Date: ***May 17, 2002***
Adjudicating Court: ***Arbitration Court of the Lausanne Chamber of Commerce and Industry (Partial Award)***
Number: ***Unknown***
Parties: ***Unknown***

Keywords

SATELLITE CONTRACT INVOLVING SIX LEGAL SYSTEMS COVERING THREE CONTINENTS – CONTRACT CONTAINED CONFLICTING PROVISIONS AS THE APPLICABLE LAW (ENGLISH LAW OR SWISS LAW) – AT BEGINNING OF ARBITRAL PROCEEDINGS PARTIES AGREED ON APPLICATION OF THE UNIDROIT PRINCIPLES

NON-PERFORMANCE OF CONTRACT – DUTY TO ACT IN GOOD FAITH – DUTY OF CONFIDENTIALITY – CONTRA PROFERENTEM RULE – REFERENCE BY ARBITRAL TRIBUNAL TO ARTS. 1.7, 2.16 [ART. 2.1.16 OF THE 2004 EDITION] AND 4.6 OF THE UNIDROIT PRINCIPLES

RIGHT TO DAMAGES – COMPENSATION FOR HARM SUSTAINED BY AGGRIEVED PARTY AS A RESULT OF NON-PERFORMANCE – NON-PERFORMING PARTY LIABLE ONLY FOR FORESEEABLE HARM – REFERENCE BY ARBITRAL TRIBUNAL TO ARTS. 7.4.1, 7.4.2 AND 7.4.4 OF THE UNIDROIT PRINCIPLES

Abstract

A Turkish company and a company incorporated in Anguilla, West Indies, with an office in the Philippines, entered into an agreement concerning highly sophisticated equipment. The contract contained two provisions on the choice of law, which however appeared to contradict each other, since one was in favour of English law and the other in favour of Swiss law.

A dispute arose and the parties agreed to submit it to an *ad hoc* arbitration governed by the UNCITRAL Arbitration Rules.

In view of the uncertainties as to the applicable substantive law the arbitral tribunal suggested to the Parties to choose the UNIDROIT Principles as the applicable law. The Parties agreed, also in view of the fact that the application of the UNIDROIT Principles was not seen as precluding the application of the English law if applicable as maintained by one Party and the Swiss law if applicable as proposed by the other Party.

In a Partial Award the arbitral tribunal found that one of the parties had not properly performed its obligation arising from the contract. To this effect the arbitral tribunal referred to the following provisions of the UNIDROIT Principles:

- Art. 1.7 on good faith (a principle that is stated in many codification; the award cites civil codes of France, Quebec, Netherlands, Poland, Portugal, Argentine, Brazil and Turkey);

- Art. 4.6 and its Comment ("*contra proferentem rule*", which in the case at hand was however considered not fully applicable because a thourough review of the terms and conditions of the contract was made by both Parties);

- Art. 2.16 [Art. 2.1.16 of the 2004 edition] (duty of confidentiality; the award mentions the English and Swiss cases and commentary.

- Art. 7.4.1, 7.4.2(1) and 7.4.4 on damages (on the basis of these provisions the arbitral tribunal found that the aggrieved party had suffered a harm as a consequence of the non-performance by the other party, and that the non-performing party could have foreseen that harm.

The arbitral tribunal left to a Final Award the determination of the amount of damages to be paid by the non-performing party.

Full Text

[Not yet available]

Sources

Notice of the award kindly provided by Professor François DESSEMONTET.

Date: ***July 29, 2002***
Adjudicating Court: ***Arbitration Centre of the Costa Rican Chamber of Commerce***
Number: ***Unknown***
Parties: ***Unknown***

Keywords

DOMESTIC CONTRACT GOVERNED BY THE LAW OF COSTA RICA – REFERENCE BY ARBITRAL TRIBUNAL TO THE UNIDROIT PRINCIPLES AS A MEANS OF SUPPLEMENTING DOMESTIC LAW

BREACH OF CONTRACT – DUTY TO MITIGATE HARM CAUSED BY BREACH (ART. 7.4.8 UNIDROIT PRINCIPLES)

Abstract

Two Costa Rican companies entered into an agreement whereby one undertook to provide the other with a commercial stand (bar) for use in major festivals in Costa Rica, consisting in a mountable two-storey structure that could accommodate several hundred people in a club-like ambience. The providing company, owner of the mountable structure, failed to take proper care of the steel components which consequently deteriorated seriously, thereby preventing the other company from using the mountable structure as per the contract. The user company brought an action against the providing company claiming damages for lost profits.

The Arbitral Tribunal decided in favour of the user company on the ground that the providing company had breached its fundamental duty of care and conservation of its own property it had provided for use in a joint project and, in this respect, it referred, among others, to Article 7.4.8 on mitigation of harm of the UNIDROIT Principles.

Full Text

[...]

"The defendant has not complied with its fundamental duties of care and conservation nor with its contractual duty of safekeeping and maintaining, as a depositary, the thing that, despite being its own, was linked and affected to the joint project, named the "Barmóvil". All of these duties existed and were instrumental, and therefore necessary to the success of the project ("*Nebenleistungspflichten*" or instrumental duties in German doctrine - see Revista Judicial, Costa Rica, N°3 p. 54). The deterioration of the steel structure and the failure to replace it with a new one, implied grave disrespect to the purpose of the contract ("*Rücksichtspflichten*", or duty to respect the ends of the contract in German doctrine - see Revista Judicial, Costa Rica, N°3 p. 53). At the same time, the defendant transgressed several fundamental duties derived from the general principle of good faith. Amongst them, it is relevant to recall the duties of care and conservation (which, in any case, had been contractually assumed) of the metal structure that, despite being their property, was essential for the performance of the joint project. As agreed by the parties, the defendant had a duty to avoid any damage ("*Schadenverhütungspflichten*", or duty to avoid damage in German doctrine - Revista Judicial, Costa Rica, N°3 p. 54). Additionally, regardless of the fact that it may derive from a main obligation to give a certain thing or to perform a certain act, the obligation to safeguard a determined thing requires the obliged party to take care of such thing as a "*bonus pater familiae*" would (Article 698 of the Costa Rican Civil Code). The defendant argues that it was the owner of the damaged structure; nevertheless, the structure was destined for a specific project which demanded proper maintenance. & Defendant's conduct was contrary to its duty to minimize any possible loss in accordance with the principle of "mitigation of harm" contained in Article 7.4.8 of the UNIDROIT Principles, which states: (1) The non-performing party is not liable for harm suffered by the aggrieved party to the extent that the harm could have been reduced by the latter party's taking reasonable steps. (2) The aggrieved party is entitled to recover any expenses reasonably incurred in attempting to reduce the harm (I.C.C. International Court of Arbitration, Case 7110 of 1995, 98-99)."

[...]

Sources

V. PÉREZ VARGAS - D. PÉREZ UMANA, The UNIDROIT Principles of International Commercial Contracts in Costa Rican Arbitral Practice, Uniform Law Review, 2006, 185.

Date: ***September 2002***
Adjudicating Court: ***Corte Arbitrale della Associazione Italiana Arbitrato***
Number: ***91/2001***
Parties: ***Unknown***

Keywords

DISTRIBUTORSHIP CONTRACT – EXPRESS CHOICE OF A PARTICULAR DOMESTIC LAW (ITALIAN LAW) AS THE LAW GOVERNING THE CONTRACT

RECOURSE TO THE UNIDROIT PRINCIPLES AS A MEANS OF INTERPRETING THE APPLICABLE DOMESTIC LAW – NOT ADMISSIBLE IF DOMESTIC LAW IS ABSOLUTELY CLEAR ON THE QUESTION IN DISPUTE

Abstract

Claimant, an Italian manufacturer of industrial equipment, and Defendant, a German intermediary, entered into a distributorship agreement whereby Defendant undertook to resell within a certain period of time in Germany a certain number of items to be purchased from Claimant. Since the Defendant failed to purchase and resell the agreed number of items, Claimant did not renew the contract after its expiry date. Moreover Claimant commenced arbitration proceedings claiming the payment by Defendant of some outstanding invoices. Defendant objected that the invoices in question were not due and presented a counterclaim for the payment of an indemnity for termination of the contract

With respect of this counterclaim Claimant objected that Defendant had no right to the indemnity, since according to Italian law, which the parties had expressly chosen as the law governing their contract, only so-called commercial agents ("*agenti di commercio*") but not independent dealers or distributors ("*concessionari di vendita*"), as Defendant was, were entitled to such an indemnity or compensation. Defendant first of all insisted that under the agreement it had concluded with Claimant, its position was that of a commercial agent and not that of an indipendent distributor. Moreover Defendant, recalling that under German law the indemnity for termination of the contract, which § 89b of the German Commercial Code implementing EU Directive no. 86/653 provides for commercial agents ("*Handelsvertreter*"), was generally held applicable also to independent distributors ("*Vertragshändler*"), argued that the same extensive interpretation should be adopted also with respect to the corresponding provision of Article 1751 of the Italian Civil Code. To this effect Defendant invoked Articles 4.1(2) e 4.8 of the UNIDROIT Principles, defined as "reflecting generally accepted rules of international trade law", and which, by stating that a contract shall be interpreted or supplemented according to the understanding of a reasonable person in the same situation of the parties, would permit to interpret the applicable Italian law in accordance with the reasonable expectations of the German party, *i.e.* in conformity with German law.

The Arbitral Tribunal, in dismissing Defendant's argument, pointed out that the UNIDROIT Principles, though being an authoritative instrument increasingly used in international contract and arbitration practice, in the case at hand were not at all applicable. The parties had neither agreed that their contract should be governed by the UNIDROIT Principles (*cf.* Paragraph 2 of the Preamble) nor referred to the "general principles of law" or the "*lex mercatoria*" as the applicable law (*cf.* Paragraph 3 of the Preamble). Instead the parties had expressly chosen Italian law as the law governing their contract, and since Italian law was absolutely clear on the question in dispute, *i.e.* that only commercial agents and not independent distributors were entitled to an indemnity for termination of the contract, there was no room for an "international" interpretation of the relevant provisions of Italian law.

Full Text

ASSOCIAZIONE ITALIANA PER L'ARBITRATO

Lodo 91/01

[...]

I. ESPOSIZIONE DEI FATTI RELATIVI ALLA CONTROVERSIA

1.- In data [...] le parti hanno stipulato un accordo ai fini della rivendita da parte della [convenuta] [...] dei prodotti dell'[attrice] [...] nel territorio della Repubblica Federale di Germania. Non avendo la [convenuta] raggiunto i quantitativi previsti l'accordo è venuto a cessare [...] . Su richiesta della [convenuta] le parti si sono accordate per la somma di DM [...] quale compenso "una tantum" a definizione del rapporto. Tale somma è stata corrisposta dall'[attrice].

2. - In data [...] le parti hanno stipulato un nuovo contratto per la rivendita in una zona determinata della Germania da parte della [convenuta] dei prodotti dell'[attrice]. Il contratto aveva una durata limitata fino al [...]. La [convenuta] si obbligava ad acquistare almeno sette "unità prodotto", ma di fatto ha poi provveduto nel periodo previsto all'acquisto di sole quattro unità prodotto perdendo così il diritto di chiedere il rinnovo del contratto ai sensi dell'articolo [...] del contratto. In data [...] l'[attrice] ha comunicato alla [convenuta] che considerava il rapporto sciolto alla sua scadenza naturale del [...].

[...]

5. - [...] La [convenuta] ha fatto valere una "indennità per cessazione del rapporto di rappresentanza" dell'importo di DM [...].

6. - L'[attrice] [...] ha respinto [...] la pretesa a una indennità per cessazione del rapporto contrattuale fra le parti a qualsiasi titolo.

IV. Considerazioni di Diritto e Decisione del Collegio Arbitrale

[...]

3. - *Natura giuridica del rapporto contrattuale e pretesa indennità per cessazione dello stesso*

(a) *Diritto italiano*

Essendo pacifici sia gli obblighi derivanti dal contratto cessato alla sua scadenza "naturale" [...] sia la sua qualificazione come concessione di vendita [...] si pone, in questa sede, il problema se esso rientri nella disciplina di uno o più dei contratti tipici o se, invece, la sua atipicità comporti l'applicabilità delle norme generali sui contratti e/o delle disposizioni che regolano uno o più contratti "vicini" allo stesso.

Secondo la tesi vigorosamente difesa dalla parte convenuta le caratteristiche che il rapporto contrattuale in esame condivide con le fattispecie della somministrazione e, ancora di più, dell'agenzia sarebbero, oltre alla prestazione continuativa dei propri prodotti da parte dell'attrice, "l'integrazione verticale" della convenuta nell'organizzazione commerciale dell'attrice e la sua condizione di "sudditanza economica", dovuta alle limitazioni imposte alle sue scelte imprenditoriali. Mentre tradizionalmente la posizione dominante è stata quella di far rientrare la concessione di vendita nella disciplina del contratto di somministrazione (Cass. 13.5.1976, n. 1698, Rep. Giust. civ. 1976, voce Somministrazione, n. 10; Cass. 8.6.1976, n. 2094, Rep. Giust. civ. 1976, voce Agenzia, n. 7; App. Milano 3.10.1978, Foro it. 1979, I, 819), un'altra teoria configurava la concessione di vendita come un contratto misto che riunisce elementi della vendita e, per quanto riguarda la pluralità di obblighi di collaborazione i quali vengono sottolineati dalla parte convenuta, del mandato (Cass. 26.9.1979, n. 4961, Giur. it. 1980, I, 1, c. 1546; Trib. Catania 29.2.1988, Nuova giur. civ. comm. 1989, I, 12).

Più recentemente si sta affermando, invece, sia nella giurisprudenza sia in dottrina una soluzione secondo la quale la concessione di vendita sarebbe essenzialmente un "contratto quadro" che disciplina la collaborazione tra concessionario e concedente e all'interno del quale si collocano le singole forniture (Cass. 28.8.1995, n. 9035, Dir. fall. 1996, II, 851; Trib. Catania 10.11.1992, Giur. comm. 1993, II, 394; Pardolesi, I contratti di distribuzione, Napoli 1979, 297; Bortolotti, "Concessione di vendita (contratto di)", in: Noviss. Dig. it., Appendice, vol. II, Torino 1981, 223 (226).

Questa teoria trova seguito soprattutto per merito dell'elasticità offerta dalla sua distinzione a seconda dei meccanismi stabiliti dalle parti per disciplinare la fornitura dei prodotti. Nella sentenza citata dalla parte convenuta la Suprema Corte (Cass. 22.2.1999, n. 1469, Giust. civ. 2000, I, 1811 (con nota di Costanza, La concessione di vendita: obblighi del concedente e diritti del concessionario, ibidem, 1813) ha, infatti, ulteriormente sviluppato questo approccio qualificando il contratto di concessione come un contratto atipico, innominato, al quale sarebbero da applicare, a seconda delle circostanze ed in funzione della questione da risolvere, le disposizioni dei contratti più vicini. La Corte sottolinea però nella stessa sentenza che "È, comunque, indubitabile che, pur trattandosi di un contratto annoverabile nella categoria dei contratti che regolano i rapporti nel settore della distribuzione commerciale 'integrata', tuttavia il concessionario acquista i prodotti del concedente e li rivende a terzi in nome e per conto proprio" (Cass. 22.2.1999, n. 1469, loc. cit. p. 1812) e aggiunge che "la parziale dismissione della propria autonomia imprenditoriale da parte del concessionario viene operata in corrispettivo di una posizione di privilegio nel mercato accordatagli dal concedente..." (Cass. 22.2.1999, n. 1469, loc. cit. p. 1813).

Il Collegio Arbitrale ritiene, d'accordo con la dottrina dominante e preferibile, nonché un'autorevole giurisprudenza (App. Cagliari 2.12.1988, Riv. giur. sarda 1991, 627; CAGNASSO, Concessione di vendita e franchising, in: Contratti commerciali, Trattato di diritto commerciale e di diritto pubblico dell'economia, diretto da F. GALGANO, vol. XVI, Padova 1991, 379 (389); BORTOLOTTI, Manuale di diritto commerciale internazionale, vol. III, La distribuzione internazionale, Padova 2002, 263) che nei casi, come quello in esame, in cui il contratto venga a cessare per decorso del termine stabilito, il concessionario non abbia diritto a un'indennità per la perdita di avviamento commerciale o la clientela apportata al concedente.

La domanda avanzata dalla parte convenuta è quindi infondata nel merito e da rigettare.

(b) *Irrilevanza del diritto tedesco*

La parte convenuta rileva, giustamente, che nell'ordinamento tedesco, dopo un'ampio dibattito e in base a una ormai consolidata giurisprudenza e dottrina, il § 89b HGB (codice di commercio tedesco), norma che disciplina il compenso dovuto all'agente in caso di scioglimento del rapporto, viene ormai regolarmente esteso in via di interpretazione analogica ad un tipo di contratto come quello in esame. Le parti hanno però inequivocabilmente scelto il diritto italiano come legge applicabile. Questa scelta (v. art. 57 legge 31.5.1995 n. 218 e art. 3 Convenzione di Roma del 19.6.1980 sulla legge applicabile alle obbligazioni contrattuali) è stata fatta in piena autonomia e il Collegio non ha la facoltà di prescinderne.

(c) *Interpretazione "armonizzante/supranazionale" e Principi UNIDROIT per i contratti commerciali internazionali*

Infine, la parte convenuta propone che il Collegio Arbitrale interpreti il diritto italiano (art. 1751 cod. civ.) alla luce della Direttiva CEE n. 86/653 del 18.12.1986 relativa al coordinamento dei diritti degli Stati membri concernenti gli agenti commerciali indipendenti così come attuata in altri paesi membri, in particolare nella Repubblica Federale di Germania. Ovviamente questa argomentazione mira ad una "armonizzazione" ex post e al di sopra del concreto atto di attuazione della direttiva così come voluto dal legislatore italiano. L'argomentazione non può essere condivisa: la direttiva CEE coordina i diritti degli Stati membri concernenti gli agenti commerciali. L'estensione dei diritti accordati dal § 89b HGB all'agente anche ai concessionari di vendita in via di interpretazione analogica nella giurisprudenza tedesca è un'evoluzione, peraltro antecedente la Direttiva, peculiare del e quindi circoscritta al solo ordinamento tedesco.

Né il legislatore italiano né i giudici o gli arbitri che applicano le norme attuative di un altro Stato membro sono tenuti a seguirlo.

Le "regole del commercio internazionale così come recepite nei Principi d'UNIDROIT" [così la convenuta nella sua memoria del (...)] e in particolar modo gli articoli 4.1(2) e 4.8, non possono cambiare né "mitigare" le conclusioni alle quali il Collegio Arbitrale è giunto. Nonostante la grande autorevolezza dei "Principi" e il loro uso sempre più frequente, sia nella prassi contrattuale internazionale che nella prassi dell'arbitrato commerciale internazionale, nel caso in esame manca la base giuridica per la loro applicazione. Le parti non hanno né "convenuto che il contratto sia da essi disciplinato" (Preambolo, 2° comma) né "che il loro contratto sia regolato dai 'principi generali', dalla '*lex mercatoria*' o simili" (Preambolo, 3° comma). Avendo le parti pattuito che il loro rapporto contrattuale sia regolato dal diritto positivo italiano, e essendo il diritto italiano chiaro e inequivocabile in materia, il Collegio Arbitrale non ravvisa alcuna necessità di ricorrere a canoni interpretativi di fonte esterna per inserire per questa via soluzioni nel merito in aperto contrasto con il diritto positivo italiano. In altre parole, nel caso *de quo* il Collegio non è autorizzato ad "internazionalizzare" la soluzione di cui *supra*, IV 3 a.

[...]

Roma, [...] settembre 2002

Sources

Unpublished. Award kindly transmitted by the Chairman of the Arbitral Tribunal.

Date: ***September 17, 2002***
Adjudicating Court: ***Court of Justice of the European Communities***
Number: ***C-334/00***
Parties: ***Fonderie Officine Meccaniche Tacconi S.p.A v. Heinrich Wagner Sinto Maschinenfabrik GmbH (HWS)***

Keywords

INTERPRETATION OF THE BRUSSELS CONVENTION ON JURISDICTION AND ENFORCEMENT OF JUDGMENTS – REFERENCE TO THE UNIDROIT PRINCIPLES

PRECONTRACTUAL LIABILITY – IMPOSED BY LAW – ART. 2.15(2) OF THE UNIDROIT PRINCIPLES [ART. 2.1.15(2) OF THE 2004 EDITION]

Abstract

An Italian company brought an action against a German company before an Italian court claiming compensation for losses suffered as a result of the Germany company's refusal to conclude a contract with a leasing company for the sale of a moulding plant to be leased to the plaintiff. According to the plaintiff the German company, after lengthy negotiations in which it refused all the proposals made by the leasing company, had broken off the negotiations in bad faith thereby infringing Tacconi's legitimate expectations to have the sales contract between HWS and BN concluded.

Since the defendant objected that the Italian court lacked jurisdiction, the plaintiff applied to the Italian Corte di Cassazione for a declaration that the Italian court had jurisdiction over the case.

To this effect the plaintiff invoked the defendant's precontractual liability according to Article 1337 of the Italian Civil Code and submitted that under Article 5(3) of the Brussels Convention the "place where the harmful event occurred" was the place where the person claiming to have been harmed has sustained loss, *i.e.* the plaintiff's place of business.

The Corte di Cassazione decided to refer to the European Court of Justice for a preliminary ruling on the questions as to whether an action seeking to establish pre-contractual liability fall within the scope of matters relating to tort, delict or quasi-delict (Article 5(3) of the Brussels Convention), or whether it fall within the scope of matters relating to a contract (Article 5(1) of the Brussels Convention).

In his conclusions the Advocate General proposed that the Court decide in favour of the first of the two alternatives, *i.e.* the delictual nature of pre-contractual liability. He based his conclusions on the argument that the duty to act in good faith during the negotiations and the liability for breaking off negotiations in bad faith arises not from any agreement between the parties but is imposed by law. In support of this he referred, with no further explanation, above all to Art. 2.15(2) [Art. 2.1.15(2) of the 2004 edition] of the UNIDROIT Principles, according to which "a party who negotiates or breaks off negotiations in bad faith is liable for the losses caused to the other party", and to the Comments to this article explaining at which point in the negotiation process the parties are no longer free to break off negotiations abruptly and without justification.

In its decision the European Court of Justice followed the Advocate General's proposal without however expressly referring to the UNIDROIT Principles.

Full Text

JUDGMENT OF THE COURT
17 September 2002
[...]
In Case C-334/00,

REFERENCE to the Court under the Protocol of 3 June 1971 on the interpretation by the Court of Justice of the Convention of 27 September 1968 on Jurisdiction and the Enforcement of Judgments in Civil and Commercial Matters by the Corte suprema di cassazione (Italy) for a preliminary ruling in the proceedings pending before that court between

Fonderie Officine Meccaniche Tacconi SpA
and
Heinrich Wagner Sinto Maschinenfabrik GmbH (HWS),

* * *

CONCLUSION DE L'AVOCAT GÉNÉRAL
M.L.A. GEELHOED
[...]

III - LES FAITS ET LA PROCÉDURE

Les faits

10. Les faits du litige au principal peuvent être résumés comme suit:

11. La société Fonderie Officine Meccaniche Tacconi SpA (ci-après "Tacconi") et la société Heinrich Wagner Sinto Maschinenfabrik GmbH (HWS) (ci-après "HWS") avaient engagé des négociations relativement à un contrat d'achat, par Tacconi, d'une installation de moulage automatique fabriquée par HWS. Ce contrat devait être conclu par HWS et BN Commercio e Finanza Spa (ci-après "BN"), qui est une société de crédit-bail. Tacconi avait, par ailleurs, déjà conclu, avec l'accord d'HWS, un contrat de leasing

portant sur cette installation de moulage. HWS n'a cependant jamais fourni l'installation en question.

12. Les parties sont divisées sur le point de savoir si un contrat a ou non été conclu entre BN et HWS. Selon Tacconi, ce contrat n'a jamais vu le jour parce qu'HWS refusait de vendre l'installation de moulage à BN. Toujours selon Tacconi, HWS a rejeté toutes les propositions qui lui avaient été faites en ce sens au cours de longues négociations, auxquelles elle a mis fin inopinément. HWS estime au contraire que le contrat a bel et bien été conclu.

Le déroulement de la procédure

13. Le 23 janvier 1996, Tacconi a cité HWS, dont le siège est établi en Allemagne, à comparaître devant le Tribunale di Perugia en Italie. Tacconi avait demandé à cette juridiction de constater qu'aucun contrat n'avait été conclu entre BN et HWS concernant l'achat de la machine litigieuse. Sa demande était fondée sur le refus, injustifié selon elle, d'HWS de vendre la machine à BN. Tacconi faisait valoir qu'en rejetant toute proposition au cours des négociations prolongées qui avaient précédé et en mettant fin à celles-ci de manière inopinée, HWS ne s'était pas acquittée de son obligation de comportement correct et de bonne foi, portant ainsi atteinte à la confiance que Tacconi avait placée dans la conclusion du contrat. Tacconi a ensuite invoqué la responsabilité précontractuelle d'HWS résultant de l'article 1337 du Codice civile (4). En première instance, Tacconi avait demandé à la juridiction de condamner HWS à réparer tous les dommages qu'elle lui avait causés, dommages dont la valeur avait été fixée à 3 000 000 000 d'ITL.

14. Dans son mémoire en défense, HWS a déclaré qu'elle avait conclu un contrat avec Tacconi et que le juge italien n'était pas compétent parce que les conditions générales du contrat comportaient une clause d'arbitrage désignant un arbitre étranger. À titre subsidiaire, elle demandait au Tribunale di Perugia de déclarer, sur le pied de l'article 5, point 3, de la convention de Bruxelles, que Tacconi n'était pas recevable à engager une action en justice. Elle a donc conclu au rejet de la demande de celle-ci. À titre plus subsidiaire, elle a demandé en reconvention que Tacconi soit condamnée à lui verser 450 248,39 DEM.

15. J'observe qu'HWS n'a pas contesté avoir mis fin aux négociations et qu'elle n'a pas davantage réfuté ce grief de Tacconi devant la Cour.

16. Le 16 mars 1999, Tacconi a saisi la Corte suprema di cassazione conformément à l'article 41 du Codice di procedura civile afin qu'elle désigne le juge compétent. Elle lui a demandé de déclarer que le juge italien était compétent à connaître de ce litige, ajoutant que la désignation devait se faire conformément aux règles de la convention de Bruxelles. Sa demande était fondée sur une obligation résultant d'un fait dommageable au sens de l'article 5, point 3, de cette convention. Aux termes de cette disposition, le juge compétent est celui du lieu où le fait dommageable s'est produit, le dommage s'entendant du préjudice matérielsubi par la partie lésée. Le siège de Tacconi étant établi à Pérouse et le fait dommageable s'étant produit au même endroit, Tacconi a donc conclu que c'était à bon droit qu'elle avait saisi le Tribunale di Perugia.

17. HWS s'est pourvue en reconvention et lui a rétorqué que le contrat avait bel et bien été conclu par sa lettre du 28 avril 1995 confirmant la commande que Tacconi lui avait

passée le 27 avril 1995. Les conditions générales de ce contrat comportant une clause attributive de juridiction désignant un arbitre étranger, le juge italien ne serait dès lors pas compétent.

La question préjudicielle

18. La Corte suprema di cassazione a alors saisi la Cour d'une demande de décision préjudicielle par ordonnance du 9 juin 2000, qui est parvenue au greffe le 11 septembre 2000. Elle a posé la question suivante:
"L'action visant à invoquer la responsabilité précontractuelle du défendeur relève-t-elle de la matière délictuelle ou quasi délictuelle (article 5, point 3, de la convention de Bruxelles)? Dans la négative, cette action relève-t-elle de la matière contractuelle (article 5, point 1, de la convention de Bruxelles) et, dans l'affirmative, quelle est l'obligation qui sert de base à la demande? En cas de réponse négative, faut-il appliquer à cette action le seul critère général du domicile du défendeur?"

19. Dans son ordonnance de renvoi, le juge national estime pour sa part que la responsabilité ne découle pas d'un contrat. Tacconi estime elle aussi qu'aucun contrat n'a été conclu avec HWS. Étant donné qu'en Italie, la responsabilité précontractuelle est régie par les règles applicables au contrat, il existe donc bel et bien un rapport avec les obligations contractuelles visées à l'article 5, point 1, de la convention de Bruxelles. La règle de compétence particulière énoncée dans cette disposition ne semble cependant pas s'appliquer à la responsabilité précontractuelle. Selon le juge de renvoi, celle-ci ne résulte pas du non-respect d'une obligation contractuelle, mais bien du non-respect de l'obligation légale d'agir de bonne foi au cours des négociations visant à la conclusion d'un contrat.

Le litige devant la Cour

20. Les parties du litige au principal ainsi que la Commission ont présenté des observations écrites. Aucune procédure orale n'a eu lieu. [...]

V - LES OBSERVATIONS DES PARTIES

46. Tacconi fait valoir que la responsabilité précontractuelle doit être considérée comme extracontractuelle et doit donc relever de la matière délictuelle ou quasi délictuelle. Elle se fonde en cela sur le fait qu'au cours de la phase précontractuelle, il n'existe aucun lien contractuel entre les parties.

47. Tacconi rappelle ensuite que, selon la jurisprudence de la Cour, la notion de matière contractuelle ne saurait être comprise comme visant une situation dans laquelle il n'existe aucun engagement librement assumé d'une partie envers une autre (40). Comme il n'existe aucun lien contractuel entre les parties au cours de laphase précontractuelle, il ne saurait, selon Tacconi, naître aucune obligation contractuelle pour les parties si les négociations ne débouchent pas sur un contrat.
48. Selon HWS, il résulterait de la jurisprudence de la Cour que la convention de Bruxelles doit être interprétée de façon autonome sans tenir compte de l'interprétation donnée aux différentes notions sur la base du droit national applicable. Peu importerait,

selon elle, la position de la doctrine et de la jurisprudence italiennes, pour lesquelles la responsabilité précontractuelle doit être assimilée à la responsabilité pour faits illicites. HWS rappelle l'arrêt Kalfelis dans lequel la Cour a dit pour droit que la notion de matière délictuelle ou quasi délictuelle doit être interprétée comme concernant toute demande qui vise à mettre en jeu la responsabilité d'un défendeur et qui ne se rattache pas à la matière contractuelle au sens de l'article 5, point 1 (41). Selon HWS, l'article 5, point 1, de la convention ne peut pas s'appliquer parce que cette disposition suppose l'existence d'un contrat et que l'action de Tacconi porte précisément sur le fait qu'aucun contrat n'a été conclu.

49. HWS affirme encore que la responsabilité précontractuelle se distingue de la responsabilité délictuelle ou quasi délictuelle au sens de l'article 5, point 3, en ce que cette dernière incomberait à toute personne qui violerait la règle générale neminem laedere (ne nuire à personne), c'est-à-dire à toute personne qui commettrait un délit et violerait des droits dits absolus. La responsabilité précontractuelle, en revanche, ne peut être invoquée qu'à l'encontre d'une personne qui aurait un rapport particulier avec la personne lésée, à savoir celle qui serait en train de négocier la conclusion d'un contrat. Selon HWS, celui qui entreprend des pourparlers avec un autre accepte le risque que la partie adverse puisse enfreindre les règles de la bonne foi et lui causer ainsi un préjudice.

50. HWS conclut que les critères particuliers de compétence ne s'appliquent pas à la responsabilité précontractuelle et que, par conséquent, la règle générale de compétence énoncée à l'article 2 doit s'appliquer en l'espèce (42). Elle estime que, pour cette raison, elle aurait dû être citée devant une juridiction allemande.

51. La Commission rappelle la jurisprudence de la Cour, attirant l'attention sur l'interprétation restrictive de l'article 5 de la convention, sur la signification autonome des notions d'obligation contractuelle et d'obligation délictuelle ou quasi délictuelle. Elle rappelle également qu'un défendeur moyennement judicieux doit pouvoir raisonnablement prévoir devant quel juge autre que celui de l'État de son domicile il pourrait être attrait. Selon la Commission, il résultait, en outre, de l'arrêt Handte que la notion de matière contractuelle ne saurait être comprise comme visant une situation dans laquelle il n'existe aucun engagement librementassumé d'une partie envers une autre (43), car, dans le cas contraire, cela serait incompatible avec le principe de la sécurité juridique. La Commission prétend donc que, selon la Cour, la volonté d'assumer un engagement est la condition de base pour qu'un contrat puisse naître.

52. La Commission déclare également que la notion de matière contractuelle offre la possibilité d'une interprétation textuelle, ce qui n'est pas le cas de la notion de matière délictuelle ou quasi délictuelle. Elle estime que c'est là la raison pour laquelle la Cour utilise la responsabilité comme dénominateur commun à l'égard de l'acte délictuel ou quasi délictuel. Cela implique que la notion de matière délictuelle ou quasi délictuelle comprend les demandes qui ne relèvent pas explicitement du droit des contrats. Cette interprétation permet de dégager des critères clairs pour l'application de la compétence spéciale.

53. La Commission estime utile de faire une distinction entre les demandes visant à obtenir le respect des obligations contractuelles et les demandes qui visent à faire constater la responsabilité du défendeur. En ce qui concerne la première catégorie, le

caractère particulier de l'obligation contractuelle justifie la compétence du juge du lieu où l'obligation a été ou doit être exécutée. Quant à la seconde catégorie de demandes, le juge du lieu où le fait dommageable s'est produit est, d'une manière générale, le plus apte à connaître du litige.

54. Se fondant sur tous les arguments qui précèdent, la Commission aboutit à la conclusion qu'une demande en matière de responsabilité précontractuelle relève de la matière délictuelle ou quasi délictuelle au sens de l'article 5, point 3.

VI - LA RESPONSABILITÉ PRÉCONTRACTUELLE

55. Il résulte en outre du principe de la liberté contractuelle que tout un chacun est libre de choisir avec qui et à quel sujet il veut engager des négociations et jusqu'à quel point il veut poursuivre celles-ci. Il est donc en principe loisible à chacune des parties d'interrompre les négociations lorsqu'elle le souhaite sans pour autant engager sa responsabilité *vis-à-vis* de l'autre. La liberté de mettre fin aux négociations n'est cependant pas absolue. Les UNIDROIT Principles disposent à l'article 2, point 15, que "a party who [...] breaks off negotiations in bad faith is liable for losses caused to the other party" ("une partie qui [...] met fin aux négociations de mauvaise foi doit répondre des pertes que cette interruption cause à l'autre partie»). Conformément aux commentaires de cet article, les négociations peuvent arriver à un point où elles ne peuvent plus être interrompues inopinément et sans justification. L'instant où ce point est atteint dépend tout d'abord de la mesure dans laquelle l'autre partie avait été induite à placer sa confiance dans un résultat positif par le comportement de la première. Cet instant dépend en second lieu du nombre de sujets sur lesquels les parties avaient déjà atteint un consensus. Si une partie interrompt les négociations inopinément et sans justification, elle doit alors compenser la perte qu'elle cause à l'autre partie.

56. La responsabilité précontractuelle est ainsi engagée lorsque les négociations préalables à un contrat sont interrompues sans justification.

57. C'est la première fois que la Cour est invitée, dans le cadre de la convention de Bruxelles, à se pencher sur le caractère juridique de la responsabilité qui peut naître entre deux parties contractantes potentielles au cours des négociations préalables à la conclusion d'un contrat. La responsabilité qui peut naître des relations précontractuelles n'est pas réglée en tant que telle par la convention. C'est dans le rapport Evrigenis, qui a donné un commentaire sur la convention à l'occasion de l'adhésion de la Grèce, que l'on peut trouver le point de rattachement le plus clair. Aux termes de ce rapport, les relations précontractuelles peuvent être incluses dans le champ d'application de l'article 5, point 1 (44). L'auteur n'indique cependant pas sur quoi il fonde cette affirmation. Il existe, en outre, dans les États membres une doctrine abondante sur la question de la responsabilité précontractuelle. Cette doctrine, qui a parfois été dégagée dans le cadre du droit international privé, ne va cependant pas dans le même sens dans tous les États membres.

58. Dans la plupart des systèmes juridiques, la partie qui interrompt les négociations sans motif valable après avoir suscité chez l'autre partie la confiance qu'un contrat serait conclu est responsable au titre de l'intérêt à contracter qu'il a déçu. Cet intérêt à contracter qu'il va falloir compenser comprend d'une manière générale non seulement les frais exposés par l'autre partie, mais également les chances qui lui ont été ainsi ôtées de

conclure un contrat avec un tiers. En cas de rupture des négociations, il s'agit de l'espoir ferme que celles-ci aboutiront à quelque résultat. Je vais ici passer brièvement en revue le droit de la responsabilité précontractuelle de certains de ces systèmes juridiques sans prétendre toutefois donner une image exhaustive de l'état du droit dans les États membres. Cet exposé sommaire vise uniquement à illustrer mon propos. La Cour pourra s'inspirer du droit national pour répondre à la question qui lui a été adressée.

59. En droit italien, l'article 1337 du Codice civile contient, en matière de responsabilité précontractuelle, une disposition spécifique selon laquelle au cours des négociations et dans le cadre de la formation du contrat, les parties doivent agir de bonne foi. Une partie qui met fin aux négociations sans motif valable après avoir suscité chez l'autre partie l'espoir ferme qu'un contrat serait conclu entre elles doit répondre de l'intérêt à contracter qu'elle a ainsi déçu. Aux termes de la loi italienne, cet intérêt résulte non seulement des frais exposés, mais également deschances avortées (45). Il s'agit donc d'un intérêt négatif. L'intérêt positif, quant à lui, ne doit pas être compensé, c'est-à-dire que la partie lésée ne doit pas être replacée dans la situation dans laquelle elle se serait trouvée si le contrat avait effectivement été conclu. L'obligation enfreinte en cas d'interruption abrupte des négociations vise à empêcher que l'autre partie subisse un dommage du fait d'avoir été engagée dans des négociations et non pas parce que les négociations n'ont finalement pas abouti à la conclusion d'un contrat. Il n'est donc pas nécessaire qu'il y ait faute.

60. En droit allemand, une partie qui interrompt de manière illicite les négociations sans pouvoir invoquer un motif valable ou en excipant de raisons impertinentes après avoir éveillé chez l'autre partie la confiance qu'un contrat serait conclu doit répondre de l'intérêt à contracter qu'elle a déçu. La responsabilité est généralement fondée sur la doctrine de la culpa in contrahendo: une partie qui met subitement fin aux négociations doit répondre de la violation illicite de l'obligation précontractuelle de tenir compte des intérêts de l'autre partie (46). Le critère applicable en droit allemand est donc pratiquement le même que celui qu'a retenu le droit italien, à la seule différence qu'en Allemagne, l'exigence d'une faute intervient.

61. Le droit français ne comporte aucune disposition relative aux négociations précontractuelles et à l'élaboration des contrats. La responsabilité précontractuelle est fondée sur la doctrine de l'abus de droit combinée à l'équité et à la mesure du raisonnable. Cette responsabilité sera engagée lorsqu'une partie interrompt subitement les négociations sans raison valable à un moment où l'autre partie pouvait espérer qu'un contrat serait conclu. Aussi longtemps qu'aucun contrat n'a vu le jour, le dommage résultant de la phase précontractuelle est considéré comme relevant des matières délictuelles ou quasi délictuelles. La perte subie par l'autre partie doit être compensée. La question de savoir si cette perte comprend également les chances avortées ("la perte d'une chance") est sujette à discussion parce qu'il n'est pas établi qu'un contrat aurait effectivement été conclu avec un tiers. Les juges français semblent, par ailleurs, faire montre d'une certaine retenue lorsqu'il s'agit de constater la responsabilité précontractuelle parce qu'ils ne veulent pas entraver le principe de la liberté contractuelle.

62. Le droit néerlandais a retenu une autre solution. La responsabilité peut être engagée avant même que l'autre partie ait pu légitimement croire que le contrat serait conclu. En droit néerlandais, les négociations peuvent atteindre un stade où aucune marche arrière

n'est plus possible. Si elles devaient néanmoins encore être interrompues à ce stade, la responsabilité pourrait être engagée au titre de l'intérêtpositif à conclure un contrat (47). Les négociations se répartissent en trois étapes. Au cours de la première, il est loisible à toute partie d'interrompre les négociations sans engager sa responsabilité. Au cours de l'étape suivante, il est toujours possible de les interrompre, mais le responsable devra défrayer l'autre partie des dépens qu'elle aurait exposés. Au cours de la troisième étape, enfin, il n'est plus permis de mettre fin aux négociations. Cette dernière étape est atteinte lorsque l'autre partie pouvait croire en toute confiance qu'un contrat serait conclu ou lorsque d'autres circonstances ne justifient pas l'interruption des négociations. Lorsqu'une partie y met fin à ce stade, elle peut même être amenée à répondre du lucrum cessans. La doctrine néerlandaise fait valoir qu'à ce stade les actions en responsabilité doivent être engagées sur le pied de l'article 5, point 1, de la convention de Bruxelles en raison de l'"étroitesse des relations" qui se sont établies entre les parties (48).

63. Le droit anglais n'a jamais admis aucune responsabilité pour motif de rupture des négociations. Le risque qu'une partie interrompe celles-ci avant la conclusion du contrat est considéré comme "*business loss*". La notion continentale de bonne foi contractuelle est inconnue en soi au Royaume-Uni: il n'existe aucune obligation de négocier conformément aux exigences de l'équité et de ce qui est raisonnable. Cela ne signifie cependant pas que le comportement des parties au cours de la phase précontractuelle échappe à toute règle. C'est ainsi que la responsabilité peut être engagée sur la base de la doctrine de la "*misrepresentation*" (49). Je trouve cependant que la notion juridique de "*estoppel by representation*" est plus importante (50), qui interdit à une partie de revenir sur une déclaration antérieure lorsque l'autre partie a subi un dommage en raison de cette déclaration. Cette notion juridique est ainsi comparable, sans être identique, à certaines notions de droit continental telles que la protection de la bonne foi et la confiance légitime. J'observe pour terminer que, dans la mesure où l'interruption des négociations fait naître une responsabilité, celle-ci est fondée en droit britannique sur des actes qui provoquent un "*tort*". Il est essentiel de distinguer cette responsabilité de celle qui résulte de la non-exécution de l'obligation contractuelle.

64. J'en arrive à présent à la signification que les conceptions juridiques que je viens de résumer peuvent avoir pour la réponse à la question qui a été posée à la Cour à propos de la convention de Bruxelles.

65. Je ferai tout d'abord une distinction entre deux phases du processus de négociation. Au cours de la première, les parties peuvent interrompre les négociations parce que la liberté contractuelle demeure entière. Au cours de la seconde phase, elles ne peuvent plus se retirer sans autre forme de procès. La confiance que l'autre partie a pu concevoir et le dommage qu'elle pourrait subir du fait de l'interruption des négociations peuvent engager la responsabilité. Celle-ci comprend en tout cas l'intérêt à contracter qui a été déçu, c'est-à-dire les frais exposés et les chances avortées. Cette responsabilité n'a cependant généralement pas une étendue telle que l'autre partie pourrait encore exiger que le contrat soit conclu (51).

66. Il est possible qu'il faille encore distinguer une troisième phase, solution que je déduis de la conception néerlandaise. Il se peut que les relations entre les parties soient devenues à ce point étroites qu'un intérêt positif à contracter puisse être revendiqué.

L'autre partie pourrait alors soit exiger la conclusion du contrat, soit demander une réparation du préjudice correspondant à l'échec de celui-ci.

VII - APPRÉCIATION

[...]

Conséquences pour les relations précontractuelles

75. Comme le juge de renvoi l'a indiqué avec insistance, la responsabilité précontractuelle résulte également du non-respect d'une obligation légale et non pas du non-respect d'une obligation contractuelle. En effet, aucun contrat n'a encore été conclu. L'obligation légale résulte en l'espèce de l'article 1337 du code civil italien, conformément auquel les justiciables doivent agir de bonne foi au cours des négociations qui précèdent un contrat.

76. Je conçois cette obligation comme une règle légale de comportement, règle d'application générale qui ne se distingue aucunement des autres règles de comportement d'origine légale. Le non-respect de ces règles peut éventuellement constituer un délit ou un quasi-délit. L'article 5, point 3, de la convention pourrait alors s'appliquer.

77. Cette solution pourrait permettre à la Cour de fournir une réponse simple à la question préjudicielle. Je considère cependant que la question de laresponsabilité précontractuelle est plus complexe que cela. Je crois, en effet, que ce qui est déterminant pour l'application de la convention de Bruxelles, c'est le point de savoir si une obligation est née entre les parties. Les parties ont-elles pris des engagements l'une envers l'autre? Si un engagement a été librement assumé, c'est alors l'article 5, point 1, qui s'appliquera. Il faut distinguer les obligations que les parties ont l'une envers l'autre des espoirs - justifiés ou non - qu'elles peuvent avoir conçus. Il peut s'agir, par exemple, de la conviction qu'a une partie que les négociations ne seront pas interrompues de manière inopinée ou que son interlocuteur n'est pas en train de poursuivre en même temps - mais de manière occulte - des négociations avec un concurrent. Enfreindre les droits nés de ces espoirs me paraît constituer un délit ou un quasi-délit.

78. L'engagement dont il était question plus haut ne doit pas nécessairement être le contrat lui-même dont les parties sont en train de discuter, mais il peut également s'agir d'un préaccord qui constituerait pour une des parties un début d'exécution. La situation en cause dans le litige au principal en est une bonne illustration. Avant même qu'un contrat en bonne et due forme ait été conclu relativement à la fourniture de l'équipement de moulage par HWS, contrat dans lequel, par exemple, toutes les conditions de financement seraient également réglées, les parties peuvent très bien avoir déjà pris un accord d'une nature telle qu'HWS procéderait à un commencement d'exécution, par exemple, en réservant la capacité de production ou en commandant des matériaux. Les litiges qui pourraient surgir à partir de ce moment-là pourraient éventuellement relever du champ d'application de l'article 5, point 1, de la convention de Bruxelles.

79. Pour répondre à la question de savoir à quel moment un engagement a été pris, on peut en outre s'inspirer des critères énoncés à l'article 17 de la convention, et notamment

de ceux qui figurent aux points b) et c) de cette disposition. Lorsqu'aucun contrat écrit n'a été conclu (ou lorsqu'aucun accord verbal n'a été confirmé par écrit), l'existence d'un engagement peut être déduit:
- des habitudes que les parties ont établies entre elles, ou
- dans le commerce international, des usages dont les parties avaient connaissance ou étaient censées avoir connaissance et qui sont largement connus et régulièrement observés dans ce type de commerce par les parties à des contrats du même type dans la branche commerciale considérée.

80. Je voudrais préciser mon point de vue en revenant aux différentes étapes des négociations que j'ai distinguées dans la sixième partie des présentes conclusions (54).

81. Au cours de la première phase du processus de négociation, les parties peuvent interrompre celle-ci sans engager leur responsabilité. L'article 5 de la convention ne saurait intervenir à ce stade puisqu'il n'y a ni délit ni quasi-délit et encore moins un contrat.

82. La deuxième étape a fait naître une confiance qui, si elle devait être abusée, pourrait entraîner un préjudice. Une partie ne peut plus alors mettre fin de manière inopinée aux négociations. Si elle le faisait, elle se rendrait éventuellement coupable d'un délit ou d'un quasi-délit. Elle pourrait alors être condamnée à rembourser les frais exposés par l'autre partie ou à lui fournir une réparation en compensation des chances qui lui auraient ainsi échappé.

83. La troisième phase est la phase au cours de laquelle aucun contrat (signé) n'a encore été conclu, mais dans laquelle les circonstances permettent de déduire que les parties se sont engagées l'une envers l'autre, auquel cas l'article 5, point 1, de la convention pourrait s'appliquer. Ces circonstances pourraient résider dans le fait que les parties sont d'accord sur les éléments principaux du contrat, à savoir l'objet de celui-ci et le prix. Le contrat proprement dit n'a toutefois pas encore été conclu parce que les parties négocient encore les autres conditions. Il est également possible qu'une des parties ait déjà commencé à exécuter le contrat parce qu'elle pouvait déduire du comportement de l'autre partie qu'il y avait rencontre des consentements. Je ne voudrais pas oublier non plus les circonstances évoquées à l'article 17 de la convention.

84. J'ai parfaitement conscience qu'au cours de la troisième phase que je viens de décrire, nous sommes pratiquement en présence d'un contrat parfait. C'est dès lors sur la base du droit privé national que l'on pourra déterminer dans quelle mesure cette phase peut encore être considérée comme précontractuelle.

85. Ma conclusion est qu'une action en responsabilité précontractuelle peut être qualifiée d'action en matière délictuelle ou quasi délictuelle au sens de l'article 5, point 3, de la convention de Bruxelles. Dans l'hypothèse où une telle action porte sur une obligation que l'autre partie a contractée à l'égard du demandeur, elle pourra néanmoins être considérée alors comme une action en matière contractuelle au sens de l'article 5, point 1, de la convention de Bruxelles.

VIII - CONCLUSION

86. Eu égard à tout le raisonnement qui précède, je propose à la Cour de répondre de la manière suivante à la question de la Corte suprema di cassazione:
"Une action en responsabilité précontractuelle peut être qualifiée d'action en matière délictuelle ou quasi délictuelle au sens de l'article 5, point 3, de la convention du 27 septembre 1968 sur la compétence judiciaire et l'exécution des décisions en matière civile et commerciale. Dans l'hypothèse où une telle actionporte sur une obligation contractée par l'autre partie à l'égard du demandeur, elle peut cependant être considérée alors comme une action en matière contractuelle au sens de l'article 5, point 1, de cette convention."

* * *

1: - Langue originale: le néerlandais.
2: - JO 1972, L 299, p. 32. La version consolidée de la convention modifiée entre-temps a été publiée au JO 1978, C 27, p. 1.
3: - JO 2001, L 12, p. 1.
4: - Tacconi prétend qu'HWS s'est rendue coupable d'une culpa in contrahendo.
5: - Le règlement n° 44/2001 considère, en outre, que le bon fonctionnement du marché intérieur est un objectif essentiel.
6: - Arrêt du 20 mars 1997, Farrell (C-295/95, Rec. p. I-1683, point 13).
7: - Arrêt du 7 mars 1995, Shevill e.a. (C-68/93, Rec. p. I-415, point 39).
8: - Voir, notamment, arrêt du 27 octobre 1998, Réunion européenne e.a. (C-51/97, Rec. p. I-6511, point 15).
9: - Arrêt du 22 mars 1983 (34/82, Rec. p. 987, point 9).
10: - La Cour a confirmé cette jurisprudence notamment dans les arrêts du 8 mars 1988, Arcado (9/87, Rec. p. 1539, point 11), et du 17 juin 1992, Handte (C-26/91, Rec. p. I-3967).
11: - Voir arrêt du 27 septembre 1988, Kalfelis (189/87, Rec. p. 5565, point 15).
12: - Arrêt du 6 octobre 1976 (14/76, Rec. p. 1497, point 9).
13: - Voir arrêt du 15 janvier 1987, Shenavai (266/85, Rec. p. 239, point 19).
14: - Arrêt Kalfelis, déjà cité à la note 11, point 20.
15: - Arrêt Kalfelis, déjà cité à la note 11, point 19.
16: - Déjà cité à la note 9, point 12.
17: - Arrêts du 30 novembre 1976, Bier (21/76, Rec. p. 1735), et du 11 janvier 1990, Dumez France et Tracoba (C-220/88, Rec. p. I-49, point 17).
18: - Voir les conclusions que l'avocat général Ruiz-Jarabo Colomer a présentées le 16 mars 1999 dans l'affaire GIE Groupe Concorde e.a. (arrêt du 28 septembre 1999, C-440/97, Rec. p. I-6307, points 64 et 65 des conclusions).
19: - Arrêt du 4 juillet 1985, AS-Autoteile Service (220/84, Rec. p. 2267, point 15).
20: - Voir à ce propos Vlas P., Forumshopping in EEX en EVEX, A & V, troisième année, 1995, p. 112 à 118.
21: - Arrêt Kalfelis, déjà cité à la note 11, point 19.
22: - Voir, notamment, l'arrêt du 19 janvier 1993, Shearson Lehman Hutton (C-89/91, Rec. p. I-139, point 16), et l'arrêt Handte, déjà cité à la note 10, point 14.
23: - Déjà cité à la note 17, points 16 et 19.
24: - Conclusions du 13 décembre 2001, dans l'affaire Gabriel (C-96/00), pendante devant la Cour.
25: - Voir arrêt du 4 mars 1982, Effer (38/81, Rec. p. 825, point 7), ainsi que les conclusions que l'avocat général Reischl a présentées dans cette affaire.
26: - Arrêt De Bloos, déjà cité à la note 12, point 11, et confirmé dans l'arrêt Schenavai, déjà cité à la note 13, point 20.
27: - Arrêt du 26 mai 1982, Ivenel (133/81, Rec. p. 1891).
28: - Voir arrêt Effer, déjà cité à la note 25, point 7.
29: - Déjà cité à la note 12. Voir points 10 et 11 de l'arrêt.
30: - Cet avis est d'ailleurs partagé par l'avocat général Lenz, comme il l'a indiqué dans les conclusions qu'il a présentées le 8 mars 1994 dans l'affaire Custom Made Commercial (arrêt du 29 juin 1994, C-288/92, Rec. p. I-2913).

31: - Arrêt Peters, déjà cité à la note 9.
32: - Voir arrêt Custom Made Commercial, déjà cité à la note 30, point 15.
33: - Voir arrêt du 6 octobre 1976, Tessili (12/76, Rec. p. 1473, point 13).
34: - Voir arrêt Kalfelis, déjà cité à la note 11, point 18.
35: - Arrêt du 19 septembre 1995, Marincori (C-364/93, Rec. p. I-2719, point 18).
36: - Voir arrêt Bier, déjà cité à la note 17, point 11.
37: - Arrêt Bier, point 20.
38: - Arrêt Bier, points 15 et suiv.
39: - Déjà cité à la note 35, point 21.
40: - Elle se réfère en cela à l'arrêt Handte, déjà cité à la note 10, point 15.
41: - Déjà cité à la note 11, point 17.
42: - HWS a manifestement abandonné l'idée que la responsabilité précontractuelle est liée à l'obligation contractuelle.
43: - Déjà cité à la note 10, point 15.
44: - Le rapport Evrigenis et Kevameus (JO 1986, C 298, point 49).
45: - Conformément aux UNIDROIT Principles, la perte doit s'entendre des frais que l'autre partie a exposés ainsi que de la chance ratée de conclure avec un tiers.
46: - Il n'existe pas en Allemagne d'opinion généralement reçue sur la question de savoir si et dans quelle mesure une faute est requise.
47: - Voir HR du 18 juin 1982, NJ 1983, p. 723 (Plas/Valburg).
48: - Voir note de Schultz sous l'arrêt Peters (déjà cité à la note 9), NJ 1983, p. 644, et DEELEN, J. E. J. Th., IPR en de afgebroken onderhandelingen, Studiekring "Prof. Mr. J. Offerhaus", série Handelsrecht n° 18, 1984, p. 126.
49: - À comparer avec la doctrine continentale de l'erreur.
50: - Le droit britannique connaît en outre la notion de "*promissory estoppel*", qui signifie qu'une partie peut être tenue par une promesse qu'elle aurait faite à l'autre partie. Le "*promissory estoppel*" est généralement invoqué au cours de relations contractuelles existantes; il ne peut normalement pas être utilisé pour la responsabilité précontractuelle.
51: - Cela est également vrai, et dans une mesure plus grande encore, dans le système du Royaume-Uni, qui applique d'autres principes juridiques que les systèmes juridiques continentaux que j'ai décrits.
52: - Qui plus est, les auteurs de cette convention se sont clairement distanciés de pareilles possibilités (voir arrêt Dumez France et Tracoba, déjà cité à la note 17, et arrêt Groupe Josi, déjà cité à la note 23).
53: - Déjà cité à la note 10, point 15.
54: Voir points 65 et 66.

* * *

JUDGMENT OF THE COURT

[...] THE COURT,

composed of: G.C. Rodríguez Iglesias, President, N. Colneric and S. von Bahr (Presidents of Chambers), C. Gulmann, D.A.O. Edward, A. La Pergola, J.-P. Puissochet, M. Wathelet, R. Schintgen, J.N. Cunha Rodrigues (Rapporteur) and C.W.A. Timmermans, Judges,
Advocate General: L.A. Geelhoed,
Registrar: R. Grass,

after considering the written observations submitted on behalf of:
- Fonderie Officine Meccaniche Tacconi SpA, by F. Franchi, avvocato, - Heinrich Wagner Sinto Maschinenfabrik GmbH (HWS), by M.P. Ginelli, avvocato, and R. Rudek, Rechtsanwalt,

- the Commission of the European Communities, by A.-M. Rouchaud and G. Bisogni, acting as Agents,

having regard to the report of the Judge-Rapporteur,
after hearing the Opinion of the Advocate General at the sitting on 31 January 2002,

gives the following Judgment:

1. By order of 9 June 2000, received at the Court on 11 September 2000, the Corte suprema di cassazione (Court of Cassation) referred to the Court for a preliminary ruling under the Protocol of 3 June 1971 on the interpretation by the Court of Justice of the Convention of 27 September 1968 on Jurisdiction and the Enforcement ofJudgments in Civil and Commercial Matters (OJ 1978 L 304, p. 36) three questions on the interpretation of Article 5(1) and (3) of that convention, as amended by the Convention of 9 October 1978 on the Accession of the Kingdom of Denmark, Ireland and the United Kingdom of Great Britain and Northern Ireland (OJ 1978 L 304, p. 1 and - amended version - p. 77), by the Convention of 25 October 1982 on the Accession of the Hellenic Republic (OJ 1982 L 388, p. 1) and by the Convention of 26 May 1989 on the Accession of the Kingdom of Spain and the Portuguese Republic (OJ 1989 L 285, p. 1) (hereinafter 'the Brussels Convention').

2. Those questions were raised in proceedings between Fonderie Officine Meccaniche Tacconi SpA ('Tacconi'), a company incorporated under Italian law, established in Perugia (Italy), and Heinrich Wagner Sinto Maschinenfabrik GmbH ('HWS'), a company incorporated under German law, established in the Federal Republic of Germany, concerning compensation claimed from HWS by Tacconi to make good the damage allegedly caused to Tacconi by HWS's breach of its duty to act honestly and in good faith on the occasion of negotiations with a view to the formation of a contract.

LEGAL BACKGROUND

A. The Brussels Convention

3. The first paragraph of Article 2 of the Brussels Convention provides:
'Subject to the provisions of this Convention, persons domiciled in a Contracting State shall, whatever their nationality, be sued in the courts of that State.'

4. Article 5(1) and (3) of the Brussels Convention provides:
'A person domiciled in a Contracting State may, in another Contracting State, be sued:
1. in matters relating to a contract, in the courts for the place of performance of the obligation in question; ...

3. in matters relating to tort, delict or quasi-delict, in the courts for the place where the harmful event occurred'.

B. National law

5. Article 1337 of the Italian Codice Civile (Civil Code) provides that, in the context of the negotiation and formation of a contract, the parties must act in good faith.

THE MAIN PROCEEDING AND THE QUESTIONS REFERRED FOR A PRELIMINARY RULING

6. On 23 January 1996 Tacconi brought an action against HWS in the Tribunale di Perugia (District Court, Perugia) for a declaration that a contract between HWS and a leasing company B.N. Commercio e Finanza SpA ('BN') for the sale of a moulding plant, in respect of which BN and Tacconi had already, with the agreement of HWS, concluded a leasing contract, had not been concluded because of HWS's unjustified refusal to carry out the sale, and hence its breach of its duty to act honestly and in good faith. HWS thereby infringed the legitimate expectations of Tacconi, which had relied on the contract of sale being concluded. Tacconi therefore asked the court to order HWS to make good all the damage allegedly caused, which was calculated at ITL 3 000 000 000.

7. In its defence, HWS pleaded that the Italian court lacked jurisdiction because of the existence of an arbitration clause and, in the alternative, because Article 5(1) of the Brussels Convention was applicable. On the substance, it contended that Tacconi's claim should be dismissed and, 'strictly in the alternative and as a counterclaim', that Tacconi should be ordered to pay it DEM 450 248.36.

8. By application served on 16 March 1999, Tacconi applied, pursuant to Article 41 of the Italian Codice di Procedura Civile (Code of Civil Procedure) concerning preliminary decisions on jurisdiction, to the Corte suprema di cassazione for a declaration that the Italian courts had jurisdiction over the main proceedings. Tacconi claimed that no agreement had been reached between it and HWS because its proposals had all been met by counter-proposals. It therefore relied on the pre-contractual liability of HWS on the basis of Article 1337 of the Italian Civil Code and submitted that under Article 5(3) of the Brussels Convention the 'place where the harmful event occurred' must also be understood as the place where the person claiming to have been harmed has sustained loss. The loss at issue in the main proceedings was incurred in Perugia, where Tacconi has its office.

9. In its order for reference, the national court considered that the criterion for special jurisdiction in Article 5(1) of the Brussels Convention does not appear to apply to pre-contractual liability, which does not result from the non-performance of a contractual obligation. No such obligation existed in the case at issue in the main proceedings, since no contract was concluded.

10. Since it considered that an interpretation of the Brussels Convention was thus needed in order to decide the issue of jurisdiction, the Corte suprema di cassazione decided to stay proceedings and refer the following questions to the Court for a preliminary ruling:
1. Does an action against a defendant seeking to establish pre-contractual liability fall within the scope of matters relating to tort, delict or quasi-delict (Article 5(3) of the Brussels Convention)?
2. If not, does it fall within the scope of matters relating to a contract (Article 5(1) of the Brussels Convention), and if it does, what is the obligation in question?
3. If not, is the general criterion of the domicile of the defendant the only criterion applicable?'

Question 1

11.By its first question the national court asks whether an action founded on the pre-contractual liability of the defendant is a matter relating to tort, delict or quasi-delict within the meaning of Article 5(3) of the Brussels Convention.

Observations submitted to the Court

12. Tacconi and the Commission submit, citing the case-law of the Court (Case 189/87 Kalfelis [1988] ECR 5565, Case C-261/90 Reichert and Kockler [1992] ECR I-2149, and Case C-26/91 Handte [1992] ECR I-3967), that since pre-contractual liability does not derive from obligations freely assumed by one party towards another, it is a matter relating to tort, delict or quasi-delict.

13. According to Tacconi, it is quite plain that at the pre-contractual stage, since the contract has not yet been concluded, there is no contractual link which could bind the parties to each other.

14. The Commission submits that, on the basis of the Court's case-law, it is possible to state a general principle that all claims referred to by the Brussels Convention seeking to establish the liability of a defendant give rise, in any event, to the application of one of the two criteria of special jurisdiction in Article 5(1) and (3) of the convention.

15. The Commission concludes that disputes concerning pre-contractual liability fall within the scope of Article 5(3) of the Brussels Convention, since, first, an action founded on the defendant's pre-contractual liability is by definition a claim seeking to establish liability on the part of the defendant and, second, that liability is not based on obligations freely assumed by the defendant towards the claimant, but on duties as to conduct imposed, more or less specifically, by a source external to the parties involved in the pre-contractual relationship.

16. HWS submits, on the other hand, that pre-contractual liability is of a different nature from liability in tort, delict or quasi-delict. The latter applies to any person who breaches the general rule against causing harm to others and infringes 'absolute' rights.

17. Pre-contractual liability, however, may be imputed only to a person who has a special relationship with the person who has suffered harm, namely that resulting from thenegotiation of a contract. Consequently, by contrast with the principles applicable to matters relating to tort, delict or quasi-delict, pre-contractual liability cannot be assessed except by reference to the content of the negotiations.

18. Moreover, submitting that Article 5(1) of the Brussels Convention cannot be applied either in this case, since Tacconi's claim rests on the hypothesis that no contract was concluded, HWS argues that pre-contractual liability is neither liability in tort, delict or quasi-delict nor liability in contract, and that the German courts therefore have jurisdiction to hear the case in accordance with the general provision in Article 2 of the Convention.

Findings of the Court

19. It should be observed at the outset that the Court has consistently held (see Case 34/82 Martin Peters Bauunternehmung [1983] ECR 987, paragraphs 9 and 10, Reichert and Kockler, paragraph 15, and Handte, paragraph 10) that the expressions 'matters relating to a contract' and 'matters relating to tort, delict or quasi-delict' in Article 5(1) and (3) of the Brussels Convention are to be interpreted independently, having regard primarily to the objectives and general scheme of the Convention. Those expressions cannot therefore be taken as simple references to the national law of one or the other of the Contracting States concerned.

20. Only such an interpretation is capable of ensuring the uniform application of the Brussels Convention, which is intended in particular to lay down common rules on jurisdiction for the courts of the Contracting States and to strengthen the legal protection of persons established in the Community by enabling the claimant to identify easily the court in which he may sue and the defendant reasonably to foresee in which court he may be sued (see Case C-295/95 Farrell [1997] ECR I-1683, paragraph 13, and Case C-256/00 Besix [2002] ECR I-1737, paragraphs 25 and 26).

21. As the Court has held, the concept of 'matters relating to tort, delict or quasi-delict' within the meaning of Article 5(3) of the Brussels Convention covers all actions which seek to establish the liability of a defendant and which are not related to a 'contract' within the meaning of Article 5(1) of the Convention (Kalfelis, paragraph 18, Reichert and Kockler, paragraph 16, and Case C-51/97 Réunion Européenne and Others [1998] ECR I-6511, paragraph 22).

22.Moreover, while Article 5(1) of the Brussels Convention does not require a contract to have been concluded, it is nevertheless essential, for that provision to apply, to identify an obligation, since the jurisdiction of the national court is determined, in matters relating to a contract, by the place of performance of the obligation in question.

23. Furthermore, it should be noted that, according to the Court's case-law, the expression 'matters relating to contract' within the meaning of Article 5(1) of the BrusselsConvention is not to be understood as covering a situation in which there is no obligation freely assumed by one party towards another (Handte, paragraph 15, and Réunion Européenne and Others, paragraph 17).

24. It does not appear from the documents in the case that there was any obligation freely assumed by HWS towards Tacconi.

25. In view of the circumstances of the main proceedings, the obligation to make good the damage allegedly caused by the unjustified breaking off of negotiations could derive only from breach of rules of law, in particular the rule which requires the parties to act in good faith in negotiations with a view to the formation of a contract.

26. In those circumstances, it is clear that any liability which may follow from the failure to conclude the contract referred to in the main proceedings cannot be contractual.

27. In the light of all the foregoing, the answer to the first question must be that, in circumstances such as those of the main proceedings, characterised by the absence of obligations freely assumed by one party towards another on the occasion of negotiations with a view to the formation of a contract and by a possible breach of rules of law, in particular the rule which requires the parties to act in good faith in such negotiations, an action founded on the pre-contractual liability of the defendant is a matter relating to tort, delict or quasi-delict within the meaning of Article 5(3) of the Brussels Convention.

Questions 2 and 3

28. As the first question has been answered in the affirmative, there is no need to answer the other questions put by the national court. [...]

On those grounds,
THE COURT,

in answer to the questions referred to it by the Corte suprema di cassazione by order of 9 June 2000, hereby rules:
In circumstances such as those of the main proceedings, characterised by the absence of obligations freely assumed by one party towards another on the occasion of negotiations with a view to the formation of a contract and by a possible breach of rules of law, in particular the rule which requires the parties to act in good faith in such negotiations, an action founded on the pre-contractual liability of the defendant is a matter relating to tort, delict or quasi-delict within the meaning of Article 5(3) of the Convention of 27 September 1968 on Jurisdiction and the Enforcement of Judgments in Civil and Commercial Matters, as amended by the Convention of 9 October 1978 on the Accession of the Kingdom of Denmark, Ireland and the United Kingdom of Great Britain and Northern Ireland, by the Convention of 25 October 1982 on the Accession of the Hellenic Republic and by the Convention of 26 May 1989 on the Accession of the Kingdom of Spain and the Portuguese Republic.

Rodríguez Iglesias
Colneric
von Bahr

Gulmann Edward
La Pergola
Puissochet

Wathelet Schintgen
Cunha Rodrigues
Timmermans

Delivered in open court in Luxembourg on 17 September 2002.

R. Grass
G.C. Rodríguez Iglesias

Registrar
President

Date: **_October 16, 2002_**
Country: **_Netherlands_**
Adjudicating Court: **_Hof 'S-Hertogenbosch_**
Number: **_Unknown_**
Parties: **_Unknown_**

Keywords

INTERPRETATION OF U.N. CONVENTION ON INTERNATIONAL SALES CONTRACTS (CISG) – REGARD TO INTERNATIONAL ORIGIN OF CONVENTION AND NEED OF ITS UNIFORM APPLICATION (ART. 7 CISG) – REGARD TO COMMON PRINCIPLES OF CONTRACTING STATES – REFERENCE TO UNIDROIT PRINCIPLES OF EUROPEAN CONTRACT LAW

APPLICABILITY OF SELLER'S STANDARD TERMS – TRADE USAGE (ART. 9(2) CISG)

INCORPORATION OF SELLER'S STANDARD TERMS INTO CONTRACT – APPLICATION OF GENERAL RULES ON OFFER AND ACCEPTANCE (ART. 18 CISG) – REFERENCE TO STANDARD TERMS IN OFFER NECESSARY

QUESTION AS TO WHETHER BEFORE OR AT TIME OF CONCLUSION OF CONTRACT BUYER MUST BE GIVEN OPPORTUNITY TO KNOW CONTENT OF SELLER'S STANDARD TERMS NOT EXPRESSLY REGULATED IN CISG – QUESTION LEFT OPEN IN UNIDROIT PRINCIPLES (CF. COMMENT TO ART. 2.20 [ART. 2.1.20 OF THE 2004 EDITION]) – AFFIRMATIVE SOLUTION ADOPTED BY PRINCIPLES OF EUROPEAN CONTRACT LAW (ART. 2.104) – SAME SOLUTION TO BE ADOPTED UNDER CISG AS IT PROMOTES GOOD FAITH IN INTERNATIONAL TRADE AND REFLECTS DOMESTIC LAW OF BOTH SELLER'S AND BUYER'S COUNTRIES (FRANCE AND THE NETHERLANDS)

Abstract

A Dutch company purchased plants from a French company. After delivery of the goods buyer paid only part of the price. Seller brought an action claiming not only the payment of the outstanding amount of the price but also the payment of the penalty for delay as provided for in its standard terms which it asserted formed part of the contract of sale. Buyer rejected both claims. As to its obligation to pay the outstanding amount of the price, it set it off against seller's obligation to pay damages for defects of the goods delivered, while the payment of the penalty was not due at all, since seller's standard terms were not incorporated into the contract.

The court of first instance decided in favour of seller.

The contract was governed by CISG, since the two parties were situated in two different contracting States (Art. 1(1)(a)). According to the court, while set-off was outside the scope of the Convention with the consequence that the question as to whether buyer was entitled to set-off its obligation to pay the remaining part of the price against the alleged obligation of seller to pay damages for defects of the goods had to be decided in accordance with the otherwise applicable domestic law (in the case at hand, French law as the law of the seller's country – *cf.* Art. 4 of the 1980 Rome Convention on the Law Applicable to Contractual Obligations), the question as to whether or not seller's standard terms had been incorporated in the contract had to be decided according to CISG. The court held that, although in the case at hand the application of seller's standard terms had not expressly been agreed upon by the parties, the standard terms nevertheless were incorporated into the contract. It is true that the invoice, on the back of which the standard terms were allegedly reproduced, was sent to buyer only upon delivery of the goods. However, buyer not only knew from previous transactions with seller that seller was used to contracting on the basis of its own standard terms, but it is well known (and buyer should have known it) that in international trade in general, and in the flower and plants trade in particular, standard terms are commonly used. According to the court the applicability of seller's standard terms could be regarded as a usage according to Art. 9.2 CISG with the consequence that the standard terms formed part of the contract of sale concluded between the parties. Nor was it relevant that seller's standard terms were written in French: buyer never asked for a Dutch translation nor had it asked seller's representative for explanations.

The Court of Appeal reversed the decision of the court of first instance.

Also according to the Court of Appeal the question as to whether seller's standard terms formed part of the contract of sale was to be decided according to CISG. However, since CISG does not have any special provisions concerning standard terms the general rules on contract formation applied with the consequence that under the Convention standard terms are binding only in so far as their applicability is stipulated by seller in its offer and accepted by buyer. What still remained to be seen was whether in order for them to be validly incorporated into the contract they have to be made available to the adhering party before or at the time of the conclusion of the contract or the adhering party has otherwise the opportunity to know their content. This posed a problem of interpretation of the Convention, which according to Art. 7 must be solved having regard to the international nature of the Convention and the need to promote its uniform application and the observance of good faith in international trade. According to the Court this implied that special attention had to be paid to how the interpretative question is dealt with in the laws of the contracting States and what may be considered common principles of those legal systems.

In this context the Court expressly referred, first of all, to the UNIDROIT Principles of International Commercial Contracts (which, it stated, expressly provide that they may assist in interpreting the Convention) and in particular to the Comments to Art. 2.20 [Art. 2.1.20 of the 2004 edition]. According to the Court these Comments address the question as to whether the adhering party must know the content of the standard terms, but do not not address the other question as to whether the adhering party should have a reasonable opportunity of becoming acquainted with the content of the standard terms, and whether the principle of good faith requires that the other party take the necessary steps to make sure that the adhering party has such an opportunity, *e.g.* by sending it the text of the standard terms before or at the time of concluding the contract. On its part, Art. 2.104 of the Principles of European Contract Law in paragraph 1 states that "[c]ontract terms which are not individually negotiated may be invoked against a party which did not know them only if the party invoking them took reasonable steps to bring them to the other party's attention before or when the contract was concluded", and in paragraph 2 adds that "[t]erms are not brought appropriately to a party's attention by a mere reference to them in a contract document, even if that party signs the document". According to the Court this rule not only largely coincides with Dutch and French law on standard terms and hence with the law of the two countries to which the parties belong, but also promotes the observance of good faith in international trade. The Court therefore decided to apply this rule also in interpreting CISG and held that in the case at hand seller's standard terms were not binding upon buyer since seller had not informed buyer of its standard terms in good time, *i.e.* before concluding the contract, so that buyer could not be said to have accepted seller's standard terms. As to the argument initially put forward by seller that upon delivery of the goods buyer had received the invoice with seller's standard terms printed on the back and that the invoice was also intended to be a confirmation of order to which buyer did not object at all, the Court noted that when buyer objected that it had received the original invoice with the seller's standard terms printed on the back only about a fortnight after the delivery of the plants, whereas upon delivery of the plant it had received only a photocopy of the front page, seller did not deny these facts. Nor was seller's further allegation that it had sent buyer already on occasion of previous transactions invoices with its standard terms reproduced on the back supported by sufficient evidence.

As to the question wheter buyer was entitled to set off its obligation to pay the remaining part of the price against seller's alleged obligation to pay damages for defects of the goods, the Court of appeal confirmed that, since CISG does not regulate set-off, the question had to be decided in accordance with the law of the country where the party rendering the most characteristic performance is situated, *i.e.* French law (*cf.* Art. 4 of the Rome Convention). According to Art. 1291 French C.C. set-off can only be asserted if both obligations are "liquide", *i.e.* ascertained as to both their existence and amount. The Court found that since seller had rejected buyer's claim for damages for seller's breach of the contract, this condition was not fulfilled in the case at hand and therefore the seller was entitled to the payment of the outstanding amount of the price.

Full Text

[Not yet available]

Date: ***November 5, 2002***
Adjudicating Court: ***International Arbitration Court at the Chamber of Commerce and Industry of the Russian Federation***
Number: ***11/2002***
Parties: ***Unknown***

Keywords

CONTRACT PROVIDING FOR APPLICATION OF BOTH GERMAN AND RUSSIAN LAW AND OF THE "GENERAL PRINCIPLES OF THE LEX MERCATORIA" – APPLICATION OF THE UNIDROIT PRINCIPLES

INTERPRETATION OF CONTRACT – NATURE OF THE CONTRACT AND INTENTION OF THE PARTIES (ARTS. 4.1 AND 4.3 OF THE UNIDROIT PRINCIPLES)

INTEREST PAYABLE ON AMOUNT DUE – MONETARY CLAIM IN EURO – APPLICATION OF THE INTEREST RATE APPLIED BY RUSSIAN BANKS FOR LOANS STIPULATED IN EURO (ART. 7.4.9 OF THE UNIDROIT PRINCIPLES)

Abstract

Under an agreement between claimant (a Russian company) and respondent (a German company), the former undertook to render commercial services to the latter on Russian territory relating to the marketing of goods produced by respondent. In performing the agreement, claimant found a potential buyer for respondent's goods in Russia and assisted respondent in drafting the contract of sale, which was subsequently signed between respondent and the buyer of the goods. Respondent later signed an act of acceptance of the work performed by claimant under their agreement.

Buyer later terminated the contract and returned the goods to respondent. On that basis, the latter refused to pay to claimant the fee stipulated in their agreement, arguing that it was obliged to pay the fee only in the event of a successful sale and that, failing such a successful outcome, claimant had no right to remuneration for its commercial services. Claimant insisted on payment, arguing that the agreement did not contain an express provision that the fee was payable only in the event of success, and that the fact that respondent was unable to meet buyer's requirements should not affect the right to be paid for services rendered.

The agreement provided that all disputes arising out of it were to be resolved in accordance with the general principles of the *lex mercatoria*. A further provision stipulated that all the terms of the agreement were subject to the legislation of both Germany and the Russian Federation. In its submission to the arbitration court, claimant referred to the UNIDROIT Principles in support of its arguments.

The Tribunal interpreted the contract provisions designating the applicable law and concluded, in particular, that the parties' reference to both their legal systems was tantamount to the absence of any choice of national law. It concluded that in the instant case, it would be sufficient to apply the general principles of law and the terms and conditions of the agreement to settle the dispute and decided to apply the UNIDROIT Principles as an expression of the general principles of the *lex mercatoria*.

The Tribunal holding that the dispute had arisen out of differing interpretations of the text agreed by the parties, concentrated on this point and applied Articles 4.1 and 4.3 of the UNIDROIT Principles. Since the agreement contained quite a detailed description of the commercial services to be rendered by claimant and did not make any reference to the sales contracts to be concluded in performing the agreement, the Tribunal held that neither the nature of the agreement nor the intention of the parties included an understanding that payment of the fee for services rendered by claimant was conditional upon the successful performance of the contracts concluded through the intermediary of claimant.

The Tribunal also applied the UNIDROIT Principles to another point in the Award. Claimant had expressed its monetary claim in Euro and in awarding it the interest on respondent's debt, the Tribunal referred to Article 7.4.9 of the Principles, applying the interest rate that Russian banks charged for loans stipulated in Euro.

Full Text

[Not yet available]

Sources

Summary based on an article by Professor M. ROSEMBERG, published (in Russian) in Economy and Life - Lawyer, 2002, No. 39.
Summary kindly supplied (in English) by Professor Alexander KOMAROV.

Date: ***November 6, 2002***
Adjudicating Court: ***International Arbitration Court of the Chamber of Commerce and Industry of the Russian Federation***
Number: ***217/2001***
Parties: ***Unknown***

Keywords

INTERPRETATION OF CONTRACTS – APPLICABLE DOMESTIC LAW REFERRING TO "TRADE USAGES" (ART. 431 OF THE RUSSIAN CIVIL CODE) – APPLICATION OF THE UNIDROIT PRINCIPLES AS RULES WIDELY USED IN INTERNATIONAL PRACTICE

LINGUISTIC DISCREPANCIES BETWEEN TWO EQUALLY AUTHORITATIVE LANGUAGE VERSIONS OF THE CONTRACT (ART. 4.7 OF THE UNIDROIT PRINCIPLES)

Abstract

Claimant (a Russian company) and respondent (a Canadian company) concluded a sales contract drafted in both Russian and English, providing that both language versions were equally authoritative for the interpretation of its provisions. However, the Russian and English texts of the arbitration clause which constituted an integral part of the contract were contradictory in their wording. In the English version, the official title of the arbitration court which was to deal with any disputes arising from the contract was not given in full; in particular, it did not include any reference to the Organisation to which the arbitration court was attached (*i.e.*, ICAC at the Russian Federation Chamber of Commerce and Industry).

When claimant brought an action before the arbitration court claiming breach of contract by respondent in accordance with claimant's understanding of the text of the arbitration clause, respondent contested the court's jurisdiction, referring to its own interpretation of which court had jurisdiction.

The Tribunal, in accordance with the parties' agreement, applied the law of the Russian Federation, in particular Article 431 of the Civil Code which provides the rules for the interpretation of contracts and states that in determining the common intention of the parties, the Tribunal must take into account the literal meaning of the words and expressions used in the text; if, in this way, it were to prove impossible to determine the parties' intention, the Tribunal must apply, in particular, trade usages. The Tribunal referred to this provision in its reasons for applying the UNIDROIT Principles. It held that it would be justifiable to take advantage of the rules expressed in this instrument, which are becoming widely used in international practice for the interpretation of commercial contracts. The

Tribunal also noted that the practice of applying the UNIDROIT Principles was constantly quoted in foreign and Russian legal literature and was reflected in several published awards of the International Commercial Arbitration Court at the Chamber of Commerce and Industry of the Russian Federation.

As to the problem of linguistic discrepancies in the present contract, the Tribunal found that the text had originally been drafted in Russian and afterwards translated into English. It referred to Article 4.7 of the Principles ("*Linguistic discrepancies*") which stipulates that "where a contract is drawn up in two or more languages which are equally authoritative there is, in case of discrepancy between the versions, a preference for the interpretation according to a version in which the contract was originally drawn up." The Tribunal ruled in favour of the interpretation that followed from the Russian language version of the contract.

Full Text

[Not yet available]

Sources

Summary based on an article by Professor M. ROSENBERG, published (in Russian) in the Bulletin of the Highest Arbitration Court of the Russian Federation, 2002, No. 11. Summary kindly supplied (in English) by Professor Alexander KOMAROV.

Date: ***November 28, 2002***
Adjudicating Court: ***Camera Arbitrale Nazionale e Internazionale di Milano***
Number: ***Unknown***
Parties: ***Unknown***

Keywords

CONTRACT FOR THE PURCHASE OF A BUSINESS – CHOICE OF LAW CLAUSE REFERRING TO A DOMESTIC LAW (ITALIAN LAW)

CONTRACT INTERPRETATION – PARTIES' CONDUCT OR UNDERSTANDING PRIOR OR SUBSEQUENT TO CONCLUSION OF CONTRACT RELEVANT UNDER RULES OF INTERPRETATION OF THE APPLICABLE LAW (ART. 1362 ITALIAN CIVIL CODE)

MERGER CLAUSE CONTAINED IN THE CONTRACT – DOES NOT AFFECT RULES OF INTERPRETATION OF THE APPLICABLE LAW

Abstract

A U.S. company and a Luxembourg company entered into a contract for the purchase of part of a third company owned by one of the parties. The contract was governed by Italian law.

A dispute arose as to the proper meaning of the price adjustment clause contained in the contract. One party argued that the clause in question was to be interpreted in the light of with Article 1362(2) of the Italian Civil Code, *i.e.* in accordance with the common intent of the parties to be determined in the light of their conduct or any agreement prior or subsequent to the conclusion of the contract. The other party, invoking a provision of their contract stating that "this agreement encompasses the entire understanding between the parties with respect to the subject matter of this agreement, and supersedes all prior agreements or statements regarding the subject matter and there are no representations, warranties, covenants, agreements, or collateral understandings oral or otherwise, express or implied, affecting this agreement if not expressly set forth or provided for herein", insisted that the parties' intention was only contained in the contract and that therefore any other understanding prior or subsequent to its conclusion was to be disregarded.

The Arbitral Tribunal confirmed that the provision in question was to be considered a so-called merger clause. However it held that such a clause simply indicates that there are no binding agreements between the parties other than those contained in the contract but does in no way affect the rules of interpretation established under the applicable law (in the case at hand, Art. 1362 of the Italian Civil Code. In reaching this conclusion the Arbitral Tribunal expressly referred, along with legal writings, to Art. 2.17 [Art. 2.1.17 of the 2004 edition] of the UNIDROIT Principles, as well as to the Comments which state "the effect of such a clause is not to deprive prior statements or agreements of any relevance: they may still be used as a means of interpreting the writting document".

Full Text

[Not yet available]

Date: **December 20, 2002**
Country: **Netherlands**
Adjudicating Court: **Supreme Court of the Netherlands**
Number: **C01/157HR**
Parties: **TPG Post B.V.**

Keywords

EMPLOYMENT CONTRACT GOVERNED BY A PARTICULAR DOMESTIC LAW (DUTCH LAW) – REFERENCE TO THE UNIDROIT PRINCIPLES AS A POSSIBLE MEANS OF INTERPRETING DOMESTIC LAW

MISTAKE OF LAW – ERRONEOUS ASSUMPTION RELATING TO THE LAW EXISTING WHEN THE CONTRACT WAS CONCLUDED (ART. 3.4 OF THE UNIDROIT PRINCIPLES)

Abstract

A Dutch employee had an employment contract with the Post Office for a definite period of time. On expiry the contract was tacitly renewed several times for other definite periods.

According to the old Dutch Civil Code (Art. 7:668 lid 1 (oud) BW), an employment contract for a definite period of time may only be renewed for the same period of time and for a maximum duration of one year. The collective labour agreement, which according to the same article of the Dutch Civil Code if existing prevails, provides that the contract may be renewed only once and for a maximum period of 6 months after which it would become an employment contract for an indefinite period.

The Court had to decide whether the employee was entitled to avoid the temporary employment contract for mistake of law.

In his conclusion the Advocate General confirmed the solution provided by Art. 7:668 BW. However he also referred to Art. 3.4 of the UNIDROIT Principles which provides a different solution.

Full Text

LJN-nummer: AF2166 Zaaknr: C01/157HR

Bron: Hoge Raad der Nederlanden 's-Gravenhage
Datum uitspraak: 20-12-2002
Datum publicatie: 20-12-2002
Soort zaak: civiel - civiel overig
Soort procedure: cassatie

20 december 2002
Eerste Kamer
Nr. C01/157HR
AT

Hoge Raad der Nederlanden

Arrest

in de zaak van:

[Eiser], wonende te [woonplaats],

EISER tot cassatie,

advocaat: mr. P.S. Kamminga,

t e g e n

TPG POST B.V., voorheen genaamd PTT POST B.V., gevestigd te 's-Gravenhage,

VERWEERSTER in cassatie,

advocaat: mr. R.A.A. Duk.

1 Het geding in feitelijke instanties

Eiser tot cassatie - verder te noemen: [eiser] - heeft bij exploit van 29 juni 1998 de rechtsvoorgangster van verweerster in cassatie (TPG Post) - verder te noemen: PTT Post - gedagvaard voor de Kantonrechter te Zaandam en - kort gezegd - gevorderd PTT Post te veroordelen tot doorbetaling van het overeengekomen loon vanaf 1 april 1998, dan wel een bedrag groot *f* 24.689,-- bruto, althans *f* 16.611,-- bruto bij wijze van gefixeerde schadevergoeding ex art. 7:677 lid 1 juncto 7:680 BW, alles met nevenvorderingen zoals in de inleidende dagvaarding omschreven.
PTT Post heeft de vordering bestreden.
Na een tussenvonnis van 17 december 1998 heeft de Kantonrechter bij eindvonnis van 11 maart 1999 PTT Post veroordeeld om aan [eiser] te betalen, voor zover in cassatie van belang:
a. de som van *f* 9.591,17 bruto, zijnde het loon exclusief vakantiebijslag over de maanden april tot en met juni 1998, vermeerderd met de wettelijke verhoging ex art. 7:625 BW en met de wettelijke rente over het totaal vanaf de dag der dagvaarding tot de dag dat alles betaald is;
b. de somma van *f* 3.197,06 bruto, zijnde het loon exclusief vakantiebijslag, voor elke maand dat de arbeidsovereenkomst na juni 1998 voortduurt, tot de dag dat daaraan rechtsgeldig een einde komt.

Tegen beide vonnissen heeft PTT Post hoger beroep ingesteld bij de Rechtbank te Haarlem.

Bij tussenvonnis van 4 juli 2000 heeft de Rechtbank PTT Post toegelaten tot bewijs. Nadat PTT Post van deze bewijslevering had afgezien heeft de Rechtbank bij eindvonnis van 13 februari 2001 de vonnissen waarvan beroep vernietigd en, opnieuw beslissende, PTT Post veroordeeld tot betaling aan [eiser] van *f* 22.379,42 bruto, zijnde het loon over de periode van 1 april tot 1 november 1998, te vermeerderen met de wettelijke verhoging en met de wettelijke rente over het totaal met ingang van 1 april 1998 tot de dag der voldoening.
De vonnissen van de Rechtbank zijn aan dit arrest gehecht.

2. Het geding in cassatie

Tegen beide vonnissen van de Rechtbank heeft [eiser] beroep in cassatie ingesteld. De cassatiedagvaarding is aan dit arrest gehecht en maakt daarvan deel uit.
PTT Post heeft geconcludeerd tot verwerping van het beroep.
De zaak is voor partijen toegelicht door hun advocaten.
De conclusie van de Advocaat-Generaal J. Spier strekt tot vernietiging van de bestreden vonnissen en tot verwijzing naar het Hof Amsterdam.
De advocaat van TPG Post heeft bij brief van 6 november 2002 op die conclusie gereageerd.

3. Beoordeling van het middel

3.1 In cassatie kan van het volgende worden uitgegaan.
(i) [Eiser] is met ingang van 1 september 1994 als postbesteller in dienst getreden van PTT Post - de rechtsvoorgangster van TPG Post - voor bepaalde tijd, te weten tot 1 januari 1996.
(ii) Art. 11 lid 1 van de arbeidsovereenkomst luidt:
"Op deze arbeidsovereenkomst is van toepassing de geldende CAO alsmede de later overeen te komen wijzigingen daarvan. (...) Een exemplaar van de CAO wordt aan de werknemer uitgereikt."
In die periode gold de CAO voor de Koninklijke PTT Nederland (KPN CAO).
(iii) De arbeidsovereenkomst is aansluitend vijf maal verlengd, eerst tot 1 februari 1996, en vervolgens tot 1 maart 1996, tot 1 maart 1997, tot 1 januari 1998 en uiteindelijk tot 1 april 1998.
(iv) De brieven waarmee PTT Post op de eerste arbeidsovereenkomst volgende overeenkomsten heeft vastgelegd, zijn telkens door [eiser] voor akkoord ondertekend. Deze brieven bevatten telkens (met verschillen in de exacte formulering) de volgende passages:
"Op dit moment heeft u een arbeidsovereenkomst voor bepaalde tijd (...). Ik heb echter besloten gebruik te maken van de afspraken die zijn gemaakt met de vakorganisaties over het gebruik van de arbeidsovereenkomst voor bepaalde tijd in het kader van Briefpost 2000. (...) Per (datum) zal het contract van rechtswege eindigen."
(v) De genoemde afspraken Briefpost 2000 zijn in 1993 gemaakt tussen enerzijds PTT Post en anderzijds de verschillende vakorganisaties, ten behoeve van een toen op handen zijnde grootscheepse reorganisatie bij het postbedrijf. Tot deze afspraken behoort een uitbreiding van de mogelijkheid gebruik te maken van arbeidsovereenkomsten voor bepaalde tijd, in afwijking van art. 23 van de KPN CAO. Deze uitbreiding is als volgt geformuleerd:

"- de arbeidsovereenkomsten voor bepaalde tijd kunnen telkens met maximaal 1 jaar (...) schriftelijke verlengd worden;
- de verlenging(en) word(t)(en) uitsluitend toegestaan met het oog op de uitvoering van deze reorganisatie; er wordt niet stilzwijgend verlengd. Dat betekent dat voor afloop van de bepaalde tijd nagegaan moet worden of er aanleiding is de overeenkomst te verlengen. Als dat het geval is, dient dit schriftelijk, met opgave van de reden van verlenging, vastgelegd te worden.
- in geval van verlenging van de arbeidsovereenkomst voor bepaalde tijd is voor beëindiging geen voorafgaande opzegging vereist;"
(vi) Deze afspraken hebben met ingang van 6 oktober 1993 de status van CAO verkregen. Deze CAO-afspraken zijn niet algemeen verbindend verklaard. [Eiser] is geen lid van een van de daarbij betrokken contracterende vakorganisaties.

3.2 Het onderhavige geding betreft, voor zover in cassatie van belang, de vraag of overeenkomstig het standpunt van PTT Post, die zich daartoe heeft beroepen op de CAO Briefpost 2000, de arbeidsovereenkomst van rechtswege, derhalve zonder voorafgaande opzegging, per 1 april 1998 is geëindigd. [Eiser] heeft zich op het standpunt gesteld dat de toepasselijke CAO niet voorziet in afwijking van art. 7:668 lid 3 (oud) BW en dat de CAO Briefpost 2000 niet van toepassing is, nu die toepasselijkheid niet is overeengekomen, welk een en ander meebrengt dat de arbeidsovereenkomst niet van rechtswege is beëindigd, omdat daarvoor voorafgaande opzegging nodig was. Hij heeft tijdig de nietigheid van de beëindiging ingeroepen en doorbetaling van het overeengekomen loon vanaf 1 april 1998 gevorderd.
De Kantonrechter heeft het standpunt van [eiser] juist bevonden en geoordeeld dat de loonvordering moet worden toegewezen.
De Rechtbank heeft naar aanleiding van de appelgrieven I, III, IV, V en VI van PTT Post in rov. 4.5 van haar tussenvonnis overwogen dat de vraag of de verwijzing naar de 'geldende CAO' in de eerste arbeidsovereenkomst ertoe kon leiden dat daarbij ook de CAO Briefpost 2000 van toepassing werd, in deze procedure geen beantwoording behoeft. [Eiser] heeft zich telkens expliciet akkoord verklaard met de afspraak dat zijn arbeidsovereenkomst overeenkomstig de mogelijkheden die de CAO Briefpost 2000 biedt, werd verlengd voor bepaalde tijd (met beëindiging van rechtswege). Daarmee heeft [eiser] aanvaard dat in ieder geval dit element van de CAO Briefpost 2000 op zijn arbeidsverhouding met PTT Post van toepassing werd. Of [eiser] daarmee de gehele CAO Briefpost 2000 heeft aanvaard, is, aldus de Rechtbank, niet relevant; essentieel is slechts (1) dat de afwijking van de wettelijke regeling ten aanzien van opvolgende arbeidsovereenkomsten voor bepaalde tijd plaatsvond bij CAO, en (2) dat [eiser] deze afwijking heeft aanvaard.
In rov. 4.9 van haar tussenvonnis heeft de Rechtbank het betoog van [eiser] dat PTT Post in strijd heeft gehandeld met de redelijkheid en billijkheid verworpen op de grond dat de mogelijkheden waarvan PTT Post zich heeft bediend, zijn gecreëerd door een in overleg met de vakorganisaties opgestelde CAO.

3.3 De onderdelen 1.a, 1.b, 2 en 3 zijn alle gericht tegen rov. 4.5 van het tussenvonnis. Bij de beoordeling van de in deze onderdelen vervatte klachten moet worden vooropgesteld dat, nu de CAO Briefpost 2000 niet algemeen verbindend is verklaard en [eiser] geen lid is van een van de daarbij betrokken contracterende vakorganisaties, deze CAO niet rechtstreeks van toepassing is op de arbeidsovereenkomst tussen PTT Post en [eiser]. De CAO Briefpost 2000 is door partijen ook niet op de arbeidsovereenkomst van

toepassing verklaard. Dit betekent dat de in het hier toepasselijke art. 7:668 lid 5 (oud) BW voorziene mogelijkheid van afwijking bij CAO van (onder meer) art. 7:668 lid 3 (oud), inhoudende dat indien een voor bepaalde tijd aangegane arbeidsovereenkomst is voortgezet, voor haar beëindiging voorafgaande opzegging nodig is, niet kan worden gegrond op rechtstreekse toepasselijkheid van de desbetreffende bepaling in deze CAO, die behelst dat in geval van verlenging van de arbeidsovereenkomst voor bepaalde tijd voor beëindiging geen voorafgaande opzegging is vereist (vgl. hetgeen hiervoor in 3.1 onder (v) is overwogen). Dit neemt evenwel niet weg dat, nu bij de verlengingen van de arbeidsovereenkomst telkens door partijen uitdrukkelijk is overeengekomen dat de voor bepaalde tijd verlengde overeenkomst van rechtswege zou eindigen, en daarbij is verwezen naar "de afspraken die zijn gemaakt met de vakorganisaties over het gebruik van de arbeidsovereenkomst voor bepaalde tijd in het kader van Briefpost 2000", de afwijking van art. 7:668 lid 3 (oud) als geldig moet worden aangemerkt. Het gaat hier om een geval dat afwijking van een bepaling van dwingend recht (slechts) bij CAO mogelijk is, terwijl een CAO die niet rechtstreeks van toepassing is, een zodanige afwijking inhoudt. Aangenomen moet dan worden dat in de bescherming van de werknemer, die is beoogd met het dwingendrechtelijke karakter van de desbetreffende wetsbepaling, is voorzien doordat de vakorganisaties bij de totstandkoming van de CAO betrokken zijn geweest. Dit brengt mee dat partijen in hun (individuele) arbeidsovereenkomst een afwijking van de dwingende wetsbepaling kunnen opnemen, mits deze afwijking overeenkomt met hetgeen is neergelegd in een CAO, ook ingeval deze CAO niet rechtstreeks van toepassing is.
Op hetgeen hiervoor is overwogen stuiten de klachten van de onderdelen 1.a, 1.b, 2 en 3 alle af.

3.4 Voor zover onderdeel 4 voortbouwt op de hiervoor besproken onderdelen, moet het het lot daarvan delen. Voor zover het onderdeel klaagt dat de Rechtbank het beroep van [eiser] op strijd met de redelijkheid en billijkheid niet zonder meer had mogen verwerpen, omdat hij had aangevoerd dat hij niet overcompleet was en er nog genoeg werk voor hem was, miskent het dat gelet op art. 6:248 lid 2 BW alleen dan zou kunnen worden geoordeeld dat de overeengekomen beëindiging van rechtswege niet van toepassing is, indien dit in de gegeven omstandigheden naar maatstaven van redelijkheid en billijkheid onaanvaardbaar zou zijn.
Het onderdeel is derhalve tevergeefs voorgesteld.

4. Beslissing

De Hoge Raad:
verwerpt het beroep;
veroordeelt [eiser] in de kosten van het geding in cassatie, tot op deze uitspraak aan de zijde van TPG Post begroot op € 286,88 aan verschotten en € 1.365,-- voor salaris.

Dit arrest is gewezen door de vice-president P. Neleman als voorzitter en de raadsheren A.E.M. van der Putt-Lauwers, H.A.M. Aaftink, A.G. Pos en P.C. Kop, en in het openbaar uitgesproken door de raadsheer A. Hammerstein op 20 december 2002.

*** Conclusie ***

Rolnr.: C01/157

mr J. Spier
Zitting: 25 oktober 2002

Conclusie inzake:

[Eiser]

tegen

TPG POST B.V.
(hierna: PTT Post)(1)

1. Feiten(2)

1.1 [Eiser] is met ingang van 1 september 1994 voor bepaalde tijd, tot 1 januari 1996, bij PTT Post in dienst getreden als postbesteller.

1.2 Art. 11 van de tussen partijen gesloten arbeidsovereenkomst luidt voor zover thans van belang als volgt(3):

"Op deze overeenkomst is van toepassing de geldende CAO alsmede de later overeen te komen wijzigingen daarvan. (...). Een exemplaar van de CAO wordt aan de werknemer uitgereikt. (...)"

1.3 In de periode 1994-1996 gold in ieder geval de cao voor de Koninklijke PTT Nederland (hierna: de KPN CAO). De achtereenvolgens geldende versies van deze cao bevatten steeds een gelijkluidend art. 23, waarin ten aanzien van arbeidsovereenkomsten voor bepaalde tijd het volgende is bepaald(4):

"2. De arbeidsovereenkomst kan slechts worden aangegaan voor bepaalde tijd in de volgende gevallen:
(a) voor de duur van maximaal 2 jaar indien de te verrichten werkzaamheden van tijdelijke aard zijn. De werkgever en de werknemer kunnen schriftelijk overeenkomen om de arbeidsovereenkomst binnen deze termijn of direct aansluitend aan deze termijn eenmaal voort te zetten voor een termijn van maximaal 6 maanden zonder dat voor beëindiging opzegging vereist is. Bij voortzetting na de eenmalige verlenging zal de arbeidsovereenkomst vanaf dat tijdstip worden geacht te zijn aangegaan voor onbepaalde tijd;
(b) ter vervulling van functies, die binnen een afdeling worden gereserveerd en waarop werknemers van een ander bedrijfsonderdeel, die binnen 2 jaar als gevolg van een reorganisatie overcompleet worden, kunnen worden ingezet. (...). De in dit kader af te sluiten arbeidsoverenkomst wordt aangegaan voor de duur van maximaal 2 jaar; bij voortzetting na 2 jaar zal de arbeidsovereenkomst vanaf dat tijdstip worden geacht te zijn aangegaan voor onbepaalde tijd;
(c) ter vervanging van een tijdelijk afwezige werknemer;
(d) indien bij het sluiten van de arbeidsovereenkomst door de werkgever schriftelijk bijzondere voorwaarden worden gesteld. Met de werknemer wordt een arbeidsovereenkomst voor onbepaalde tijd aangegaan, zodra is voldaan aan de gestelde voorwaarden."

1.4 De eerste arbeidsovereenkomst van [eiser] is aansluitend vijf maal verlengd; eerst tot 1 februari 1996, en vervolgens tot 1 maart 1996, tot 1 maart 1997, tot 1 januari 1998 en uiteindelijk tot 1 april 1998.

1.5 PTT Post heeft deze op de eerste arbeidsovereenkomst volgende arbeidsovereenkomsten steeds in een brief vastgelegd. De brieven met betrekking tot de voortzetting per 1 januari 1996 en 1 maart 1996 luiden, voor zover thans van belang, als volgt(5): "

Op dit moment heeft u een arbeidsovereenkomst voor bepaalde tijd (...). Ik heb echter besloten gebruik te maken van de afspraken die gemaakt zijn met de vakorganisaties over het gebruik van de arbeidsovereenkomsten voor bepaalde tijd, in het kader van Briefpost 2000. Eén van deze afspraken opent de mogelijkheid de overeenkomst tijdelijk te verlengen of uit te breiden. Van deze mogelijkheid maak ik gebruik (bijlage).
Per [datum] tot [einddatum] zult u (...) uur per maand werken.
Per [einddatum] zal het contract van rechtswege eindigen."

De brieven betreffende de voortzetting per 1 februari 1996, 1 maart 1997 en 1 januari 1998 bevatten de volgende passages (6):

"Met ingang van 1 september 1994 ging u met PTT Post een arbeidsovereenkomst aan voor bepaalde tijd.
Deze arbeidsovereenkomst eindigt in principe van rechtswege op [datum].
Ik heb echter besloten gebruik te maken van de afspraken die zijn gemaakt met de vakorganisaties over het gebruik van de arbeidsovereenkomsten voor bepaalde tijd in het kader van Briefpost 2000.
Samenvattend betekent dit dus dat u onder dezelfde voorwaarden, als vermeld in uw huidige arbeidsovereenkomst bij PTT Post in dienst blijft tot [einddatum]. Voor alle duidelijkheid wijs ik u er nogmaals op dat de arbeidsovereenkomst dan ook van rechtswege op deze datum zal eindigen."

1.6 [Eiser] heeft deze brieven steeds voor akkoord ondertekend. Op de brief waarin de (laatste) verlenging tot 1 april 1998 werd vastgelegd, heeft hij daaraan toegevoegd "onder protest (...) Zie verweerschrift".

1.7 Genoemde afspraken in het kader van Briefpost 2000 betreffen afspraken die in 1993 tussen PTT Post en de verschillende vakorganisaties zijn gemaakt met het oog op een toen op handen zijnde grootscheepse reorganisatie bij het postbedrijf.(7) Tot deze afspraken behoort een uitbreiding van de mogelijkheid om gebruik te maken van arbeidsovereenkomsten voor bepaalde tijd in afwijking van het bepaalde in art. 23 van de KPN CAO. Deze uitbreiding is als volgt geformuleerd:

"de arbeidsovereenkomsten voor bepaalde tijd kunnen telkens met maximaal 1 jaar (...) schriftelijk verlengd worden;
de verlenging(en) word(t)(en) uitsluitend toegestaan met het oog op de uitvoering van deze reorganisatie; er wordt niet stilzwijgend verlengd. Dat betekent dat voor afloop van de bepaalde tijd nagegaan moet worden of er aanleiding is de overeenkomst te verlengen. Als dat het geval is, dient dit schriftelijk, met opgave van de reden van verlenging, vastgelegd te worden.

In geval van verlenging van de arbeidsovereenkomst voor bepaalde tijd is voor de beëindiging geen voorafgaande opzegging vereist."

1.8 Deze afspraken hebben met ingang van 6 oktober 1993 de status van cao verkregen.(8) Deze cao-afspraken zijn niet algemeen verbindend verklaard. [eiser] is geen lid van één van de daarbij contracterende partijen.

1.9 PTT Post heeft [eiser] laten weten dat na 1 april 1998 geen verdere verlenging meer zal plaatsvinden en dat de arbeidsovereenkomst per die datum van rechtswege is beëindigd.(9)

1.10 [Eiser] heeft zich bij brief van 1 april 1998 op het standpunt gesteld dat van een beëindiging van rechtswege geen sprake kan zijn. Bij gebreke van opzegging en/of een ontslagvergunning van de Regionaal Directeur voor de Arbeidsvoorziening (RDA) heeft hij de nietigheid van het ontslag ingeroepen.(10)

2. Procesverloop

2.1 [Eiser] heeft bij dagvaarding van 29 juni 1998 de onderhavige procedure aanhangig gemaakt bij de Kantonrechter te Zaandam. Hij vordert primair doorbetaling van zijn loon c.a. vanaf 1 april 1998 wegens de nietigheid van de beëindiging van de arbeidsovereenkomst. Subsidiair vordert hij betaling van een gefixeerde schadevergoeding ex art. 7:677 j° art. 7:680 BW.

2.2.1 In cassatie is uitsluitend nog de primaire loonvordering aan de orde. Samengevat weergegeven, heeft [eiser] deze vordering als volgt onderbouwd. Hij stelt primair dat voor de beëindiging van de verlengde arbeidsovereenkomst op grond van art. 7:668 lid 3 (oud) BW voorafgaande opzegging was vereist hetgeen tevens meebrengt dat PTT Post ingevolge art. 6 BBA bij de RDA een ontslagvergunning had dienen aan te vragen. Nu PTT Post dit heeft nagelaten, is sprake van een nietig ontslag.

2.2.2 Daartoe voert [eiser] aan dat ingevolge art. 7:668 lid 5 (oud) BW alleen bij cao van dit opzeggingsvereiste kan worden afgeweken. In zijn geval kan een dergelijke afwijking echter niet worden gegrond op art. 23 van de KPN CAO omdat hij niet op de in lid 2 onder a-d genoemde voorwaarden in dienst is getreden, terwijl in lid 2 (onder b) ook geen regeling is opgenomen op grond waarvan het opzeggingsvereiste opzij wordt gezet. Briefpost 2000 behelst wel een dergelijke regeling, doch deze regeling is volgens [eiser] niet op zijn arbeidsovereenkomst van toepassing. Aangezien Briefpost 2000 als cao niet algemeen verbindend is verklaard en hij bovendien geen lid was van de betrokken werknemersorganisaties, is daarvoor immers nodig dat partijen zulks zijn overeengekomen. Hiervan is evenwel geen sprake. Partijen hebben de desbetreffende clausule nimmer uitdrukkelijk op de opvolgende arbeidsovereenkomsten van toepassing verklaard. De enkele verwijzing naar deze afspraken, die hem ook niet ter hand zijn gesteld, kan daarmee niet worden gelijkgesteld. Zijns inziens heeft PTT Post er nimmer op heeft gewezen dat de afspraken in het kader van Briefpost 2000 de status van CAO hadden. Evenmin kan volgens [eiser] worden gezegd dat bedoelde clausule op grond van stilzwijgende overeenstemming deel is gaan uitmaken van de arbeidsovereenkomsten, aangezien hij tot voor kort niet heeft geweten dat de Briefpost 2000-afspraken de status van CAO hadden (dagvaarding sub 3.1-3.13; cvr sub 3.1-3.2.3).

2.2.3 Subsidiair - voor het geval Briefpost 2000 wel van toepassing moet worden geacht op de opvolgende arbeidsovereenkomsten - neemt [eiser] het standpunt in dat beëindiging van rechtswege in het onderhavige geval "in strijd met de redelijkheid en billijkheid" moet worden geacht.

2.3.1 PTT Post heeft bestreden dat zij de arbeidsovereenkomst op 1 april 1998 niet rechtsgeldig heeft beëindigd alsmede dat sprake zou zijn van een gegeven onregelmatig ontslag. Voor zover nog van belang heeft zij haar verweer ten aanzien van de primaire loonvordering als volgt onderbouwd.

2.3.2 Uitgangspunt van Briefpost 2000 was dat zoveel mogelijk diende te worden gewaarborgd dat werknemers die een vast dienstverband hadden en wier functie in het kader van een grootscheepse reorganisatie die in 1993 is ingezet zou komen te vervallen, herplaatst zouden kunnen worden. Met het oog daarop is met de vakbonden afgesproken dat vacatures dienen te worden vervuld door middel van arbeidsovereenkomsten voor bepaalde tijd, die telkens voor hooguit een jaar kunnen worden verlengd. Conform art. 7:668 lid 5 (oud) BW is daarbij afgeweken van opzeggingsvereiste van art. 7:668 lid 3 (oud) BW zodat een voortgezette arbeidsovereenkomst steeds van rechtswege eindigt (cva sub 4-6). Volgens PTT Post is [eiser] overeenkomstig dit in Briefpost 2000 overeengekomen beleid voor bepaalde tijd in dienst getreden. Zijn arbeidsovereenkomst is hierna ook steeds overeenkomstig Briefpost 2000 verlengd (cva sub 8-9).

2.3.3 Anders dan [eiser] betoogt, is Briefpost 2000 volgens PTT Post wel degelijk op de rechtsverhouding tussen partijen van toepassing. Briefpost 2000 is een wijziging van art. 23 van de KPN CAO en vormt met die cao één geheel. Aangezien Briefpost 2000 op 6 oktober 1993 de status van cao heeft gekregen, was [eiser] daaraan dan ook reeds bij zijn indiensttreding gebonden (cvd sub 2-3 en 5). In elk geval volgt de toepasselijkheid van Briefpost 2000 uit de telkens herhaalde, expliciete verwijzing daarnaar in de door [eiser] voor akkoord getekende verlengingscontracten. PTT Post heeft de considerans van Briefpost 2000 en de van art. 23 KPN CAO afwijkende uitwerking hiervan ten aanzien van het gebruik van overeenkomsten voor bepaalde tijd telkens als bijlage meegestuurd.(11) Partijen zijn daarmee in het kader van de verlengde arbeidsovereenkomsten de toepasselijkheid van Briefpost 2000 steeds expliciet overeengekomen. De omstandigheid dat [eiser] geen lid was van één van de betrokken werknemersorganisaties doet hieraan niet af, aldus PTT Post (cva sub 10-11; cvd sub 4-5).

2.4.1 In zijn tussenvonnis van 17 december 1998 heeft de Kantonrechter geoordeeld dat de beëindiging van de verlengde arbeidsovereenkomst per 1 april 1998 nietig is en dat de primaire loonvordering van [eiser] op die grond toewijsbaar is.

2.4.2 De Kantonrechter stelt voorop dat een cao "niet automatisch" deel uitmaakt van een arbeidsovereenkomst met een "ongeorganiseerde" werknemer. In casu mist die cao toepassing.

2.4.3 Briefpost 2000 is geen "later overeen te komen wijziging" waarmee [eiser] zich op voorhand heeft verenigd. Alleen al niet omdat over Briefpost voorafgaand aan de eerste arbeidsovereenkomst reeds was gecontracteerd.

2.4.4 Bovendien is, nog steeds volgens de Kantonrechter, geen sprake van een wijziging van de "initiële arbeidsoverenkomst"; de regeling van Briefpost 2000 is niet verwerkt in de opeenvolgende PTT Post cao's; het ging bij Briefpost 2000 om een afzonderlijke cao.

2.5 Nadat partijen zich bij akte hadden uitgelaten over het in aanmerking te nemen brutoloon heeft de Kantonrechter bij eindvonnis van 11 maart 1999 PTT Post veroordeeld tot doorbetaling van het - in het vonnis genoemde - loon vanaf 1 april 1998 tot aan de dag dat de arbeidsovereenkomst rechtsgeldig zal zijn beëindigd.

2.6 PTT Post is van de beide vonnissen in beroep gekomen onder aanvoering van zeven grieven. Hiervan richtten de grieven I, III, IV, V en VI zich (naar de kern genomen) tegen het oordeel van de Kantonrechter dat de afspraken in het kader van Briefpost 2000 over het gebruik van arbeidsovereenkomsten voor bepaalde tijd in de rechtsverhouding tussen partijen niet van toepassing zijn.

2.7 In haar samenvatting van het geschil heeft PTT Post aangedrongen dat Briefpost 2000 reeds sinds 6 oktober 1993 één geheel vormde met (art. 23 van) de KPN-CAO, hetgeen betekent dat de daarin vervatte regeling omtrent het gebruik, de verlenging en de beëindiging van arbeidsovereenkomsten voor bepaalde tijd reeds op de eerste en daarmee ook op de opvolgende arbeidsovereenkomsten van toepassing was (sub 2 en 3 zomede grief I, III en IV en de toelichting daarop). Subsidiair heeft zij aangevoerd dat Briefpost 2000 in elk geval uitdrukkelijk dan wel stilzwijgend van toepassing is verklaard op de verlengde arbeidsovereenkomsten (grief III en de toelichting daarop). De CAO Briefpost 2000 is, volgens haar, geen afzonderlijke cao (grief IV). Deze laatste cao is bij het aangaan van de arbeidsovereenkomst niet overhandigd omdat "de CAO Briefpost 2000 bij het aangaan van het eerste contract voor bepaalde tijd geen wijziging opleverde ten opzichte van art. 23 van de KPN CAO". Daarom werd bij indiensttreding de KPN CAO overhandigd (onder 20). Zij vervolgt haar exposé aldus:

"Gelet echter op de bekendheid van het feit dat de CAO Briefpost 2000 reeds was opgesteld in 1993 mocht [eiser] bij de eerste overhandiging van de considerans in 1995 niet verwachten dat de afspraken over Briefpost 2000 nog steeds niet de status van CAO hadden verkregen"(sub 20).

2.8 [Eiser] heeft volhard bij zijn stelling dat Briefpost 2000 niet van toepassing is op zijn rechtsverhouding met PTT Post. Daarbij heeft hij benadrukt dat uit de initiële arbeidsovereenkomst niet blijkt niet dat deze is tot stand gekomen in het kader van de reorganisatie Briefpost 2000. Hem is destijds alleen KPN-CAO ter hand gesteld zodat hij niet wist of kon weten dat, zoals door PTT Post gesteld, sprake was van een wijziging op die cao ("cva" onder 3.3 en 3.4). Zijns inziens is Briefpost 2000 "in wezen" een afzonderlijke cao (sub 6).

2.9 De stelling dat de Briefpost 2000 cao in elk geval van toepassing is verklaard op de verlengde arbeidsovereenkomsten, acht [eiser] onjuist omdat de desbetreffende brieven van PTT Post alleen verwezen naar afspraken in het kader van Briefpost 2000, zonder dat wordt vermeld dat deze afspraken status van cao hebben en zonder dat wordt vermeld dat deze cao-bepalingen voortaan van toepassing zijn op zijn arbeidsovereenkomst. Dit blijkt ook niet uit de considerans van Briefpost 2000, waarvan [eiser] overigens nog steeds betwist dat deze waren bijgevoegd (met name onder 7 en 8).

2.10 Bij tussenvonnis van 4 juli 2000 heeft de Rechtbank Haarlem de onder 2.6 genoemde grieven gezamenlijk behandeld en gegrond bevonden.

2.11 Zij heeft daartoe het volgende overwogen:

"4.5 De vraag of de verwijzing naar de 'geldende CAO' in [eisers] eerste arbeidsovereenkomst ertoe kon leiden dat daarbij ook de Briefpost 2000 CAO van toepassing werd, behoeft in deze procedure niet te worden beantwoord. Uit de brieven waarmee telkens de arbeidsovereenkomst werd verlengd, blijkt immers dat [eiser] zich expliciet akkoord heeft verklaard met de afspraak dat zijn arbeidsovereenkomst overeenkomstig de mogelijkheid die de Briefpost 2000 CAO biedt, verlengd werd voor bepaalde tijd (met beëindiging van rechtswege). Daarmee heeft [eiser] aanvaard dat in ieder geval dit element van de Briefpost 2000 CAO op zijn arbeidsverhouding met PTT Post van toepassing werd. Of [eiser] daarmee de gehele Briefpost 2000 CAO heeft aanvaard is niet relevant; gezien het voorgaande is immers slechts essentieel 1) dat de afwijking van de wettelijke regeling ten aanzien van opvolgende arbeidsoverenkomsten voor bepaalde tijd plaatsvond bij CAO en 2) dat [eiser] deze afwijking heeft aanvaard. Ook de vraag of [eiser] zich destijds bewust was van de CAO-status van de Briefpost 2000 regeling is dus, anders dan [eiser] aanvoert, niet doorslaggevend; het gaat er slechts om of hij zich ervan bewust was dat hij de (in de Briefpost 2000 opgenomen) mogelijkheid tot het sluiten van opvolgende arbeidsovereenkomsten voor bepaalde tijd, aanvaardde. Deze aanvaarding is - mede gezien de inhoud van de voor akkoord ondertekende verlengingsbrieven - niet voor betwisting vatbaar, en wordt op zichzelf door [eiser] ook niet betwist.

4.6 Gezien het voorgaande moet in afwijking van het vonnis van de kantonrechter worden aangenomen dat de laatste arbeidsovereenkomst in beginsel van rechtswege kon eindigen met het verstrijken van de overeengekomen looptijd. (...)".

2.12 Het subsidiaire standpunt van [eiser] dat de beëindiging van rechtswege in het onderhavige geval in strijd is met de redelijkheid en billijkheid heeft de Rechtbank verworpen op grond van de volgende overwegingen:

"4.9 Dit beroep moet worden verworpen, nu tussen partijen vaststaat dat de mogelijkheden waarvan PTT Post zich in het onderhavige geval heeft bediend, zijn gecreëerd door een in overleg met de vakorganisaties opgestelde CAO. Doel van deze regeling was - kort gezegd - het flexibel laten van de arbeidsovereenkomsten met na de aanvang van de reorganisatie in dienst gekomen werknemers, ten behoeve van de noodzaak bestaande werknemers met een dienstverband voor onbepaalde tijd op enig gewenst moment van andere werkzamheden binnen PTT Post te kunnen voorzien. Dat dit leidde tot repeterende dienstverbanden voor bepaalde tijd voor deze nieuwe werknemers is inherent aan realisering van deze (in beginsel legitiem te achten) doelstelling en op zichzelf dus niet in strijd met de redelijkheid en billijkheid."

2.13 Vervolgens heeft de Rechtbank zich begeven in de beoordeling van de subsidiair gevorderde betaling van een gefixeerde schadevergoeding wegens onregelmatige beëindiging van het dienstverband. Zij heeft PTT Post een thans niet meer relevant bewijs opgedragen (rov. 4.12-4.16).

2.14 PTT Post heeft van deze bewijslevering afgezien. Bij eindvonnis van 13 februari 2001 heeft de Rechtbank de bestreden vonnissen van de Kantonrechter vernietigd en PTT Post veroordeeld tot betaling van de gefixeerde schadevergoeding gelijk aan het loon over de periode van 1 april 1998 tot 1 november 1998, te vermeederen met de wetelijke verhoging ex art. 7:625 BW en de wettelijke rente.

2.15 [Eiser] heeft tegen deze vonnissen tijdig(12) beroep in cassatie ingesteld. PTT Post heeft geconcludeerd tot verwerping van het beroep. Beide partijen hebben hun standpunt schriftelijk doen toelichten. Vervolgens hebben zij nog gere- en dupliceerd.

3. Bespreking van het middel

Inleiding

3.1 Het gaat in deze zaak - zoals helaas in zoveel procedures - om een strijd over feiten waarvan niet terstond aannemelijk is dat deze overeenkomen met de werkelijkheid. Ontdaan van franje komt het betoog van [eiser] er op neer dat hij zich realiseerde dat de voortdurende verlengingen rechtens niet mogelijk waren. Anders gezegd: hij heeft PTT Post in de door haar zelf gegraven kuil willen laten vallen. Zou [eiser] (van beroep postbesteller) deze juridische kennis werkelijk hebben gehad? Menig jurist zou het vermoedelijk niet hebben geweten. Het antwoord op de principiële rechtsvraag die in deze procedure centraal staat is trouwens geenszins eenvoudig.

De hier toepasselijke bepalingen

3.2 Het gaat in deze zaak om een arbeidsovereenkomst voor bepaalde tijd die is aangegaan op 1 september 1994 en die na het verstrijken van de bepaalde tijd een aantal malen is voortgezet. De laatste verlenging heeft plaatsgevonden per 1 januari 1998. Daarmee wordt het wettelijk kader in deze zaak gevormd door de art. 7:667 en 7:668 (oud) BW, zoals deze artikelen hebben geluid tot 1 januari 1999.

3.3 Hoewel deze artikelen eerst op 1 april 1997 zijn ingevoerd, hebben zij onmiddellijke werking.(13) De overgangsrechtelijke kwestie is trouwens lood om oud ijzer nu er - afgezien van enige tekstuele aanpassingen - inhoudelijk geen relevante verschillen bestaan met de voordien geldende artikelen 7A:1639e en 1639f (oud) BW.

3.4 Met de inwerkingtreding van de Wet Flexibiliteit en zekerheid per 1 januari 1999 zijn de artikelen 7:667 en 7:668 (oud) BW voor een deel ingrijpend gewijzigd. Zou, met toepassing van het vóór 1 januari 1999 geldende recht, moeten worden geoordeeld dat de litigieuze arbeidsovereenkomst - waarvan de laatste verlenging, naar de tekst van hetgeen partijen overeenkwamen, vóór 1 januari 1999 afliep - rechtsgeldig vóór 1 januari 1999 ten einde is gekomen, dan kan niet worden aanvaard dat het nieuwe recht zulks weer openbreekt.(14) Hetgeen hier wordt vededigd is m.i. in overeenstemming met art. 69 Ow NBW.(15)

3.5 De kernvraag die partijen in deze zaak verdeeld houdt, kan intussen ook onder het huidige art. 7:668a lid 5 BW een rol spelen. Een beslissing van Uw Raad heeft daarom m.i. ook voor nieuwe gevallen betekenis.

Hoe moeten de artikelen 7:667 en 7:668 (oud) BW worden verstaan?

3.6 Uitgangspunt van de regeling van de artikelen 7:667 en 668 (oud) BW is dat een arbeidsovereenkomst voor bepaalde tijd in beginsel van rechtswege eindigt bij het verstrijken van de overeengekomen duur. Partijen kunnen haar vervolgens echter (wederom voor bepaalde tijd) voortzetten. Deze voortzetting kan in de eerste plaats uitdrukkelijk worden overeengekomen waarbij partijen (nieuwe) afspraken kunnen maken omtrent de duur van de verlenging en de arbeidsvoorwaarden. Voortzetting kan ook stilzwijgend ("zonder tegenspraak") plaatsvinden. In dat laatste geval wordt de voortgezette arbeidsovereenkomst krachtens art. 7:668 lid 1 (oud) BW geacht te zijn aangegaan op dezelfde voorwaarden en voor dezelfde tijd, doch ten hoogste voor een jaar.(16)

3.7 Is een voor bepaalde tijd aangegane arbeidsovereenkomst eenmaal voortgezet, dan geldt op grond van art. 7:668 lid 3 (oud) BW dat deze niet (meer) van rechtswege eindigt. Voor haar beëindiging is dan steeds voorafgaande opzegging - en op grond van art. 6 BBA dus tevens een ontslagvergunning - nodig. Daarbij doet in beginsel niet ter zake of de voortzetting stilzwijgend heeft plaatsgevonden dan wel of deze uitdrukkelijk, al dan niet op dezelfde voorwaarden, is voortgezet.(17) Ratio achter dit opzeggingsvereiste is dat de wetgever heeft willen voorkomen dat door het aangaan en telkens verlengen van arbeidsovereenkomsten voor een bepaalde korte tijdsduur de bepalingen omtrent de opzegtermijnen bij arbeidsovereenkomsten voor onbepaalde tijd zouden kunnen worden ontdoken.(18)

3.8 Ingevolge art. 7:668 lid 5 (oud) BW kan - voorzover thans van belang - van het hiervoor bedoelde opzeggingsvereiste van art. 7:668 lid 3 BW worden afgeweken bij cao. Het gaat hier derhalve om - wat wel wordt aangeduid als - "driekwart dwingend recht".

3.9 De CAO Briefpost 2000 bevat een dergelijke afwijking. Deze cao is evenwel niet algemeen verbindend verklaard. [eiser] is een zogenaamde niet-georganiseerde werknemer. Daarom is hij niet van rechtswege (hetzij op grond van de art. 3 lid 1 van de Wet verbindend en onverbindend verklaren van bepalingen van collectieve arbeidsovereenkomsten, hetzij op grond van de artikelen 9, 12 en 13 Wet CAO) aan de Briefpost 2000 CAO gebonden.

3.10 Gebondenheid aan deze cao ontstaat ook niet uit hoofde van art. 14 Wet CAO. Weliswaar verplicht dit artikel de aan de cao gebonden werkgever de cao-bepalingen inzake de arbeidsvoorwaarden ook in acht te nemen ten aanzien van de niet of anders georganiseerde werknemers (hierna spreek ik kortheidshalve van niet-georganiseerde werknemers), doch het gaat hier om een verplichting jegens de cao-partijen. Uit dit artikel ontstaan voor een niet-georganiseerde werknemer derhalve op zich zelf geen rechten en verplichtingen.(19)

3.11 Daarmee rijst allereerst de vraag of een niet-georganiseerde werknemer aan een niet-algemeen verbindend verklaarde cao kan worden gebonden. Hiertoe worden in de literatuur en de royaal voorhanden "lagere jurisprudentie" diverse constructies gehanteerd, waarbij valt te bedenken dat het in dat debat vaak gaat om de spiegelbeeldige vraag of de ongebonden werknemer aanspraken aan de cao kan ontlenen. Jurisprudentie van de Hoge Raad over deze kwestie ontbreekt.

3.12 De heersende opvatting is dat toepasselijkheid van een nietalgemeen verbindend verklaarde cao in elk geval kan worden aangenomen ingeval de gebonden werkgever en de ongebonden werknemer deze cao uitdrukkelijk op de individuele arbeidsovereenkomst van toepassing hebben verklaard.(20) Deze opvatting lijkt mij juist; zij leidt ook tot bevredigende uitkomsten. Hierbij valt te bedenken dat het maken van onderscheid tussen werknemers al naargelang zij "georganiseerd" zijn ongelijke behandeling teweegbrengt waarvoor m.i. materieel gesproken niet veel rechtvaardiging bestaat. Zodanige ongelijkheid leidt allicht tot spanningen binnen een onderneming. Ook dat pleit ertegen om haar rechtens te aanvaarden in een situatie waarin partijen (en dus ook de betrokken werknemer) hebben ingestemd met de toepasselijkheid van een cao-bepaling die afwijkt van "driekwart dwingend recht".

3.13 Ik zou hierbij geen onderscheid willen maken tussen 1) een cao-bepaling die voor de "ongeorganiseerde" werknemer louter voordelen meebrengt, 2) voor- én nadelen oplevert, dan wel 3) slechts nadelen heeft. Dat behoeft zeker voor deze laatste categorie, naar ik onderken, (nadere) rechtvaardiging. Ik wil trachten haar te geven aan de hand van (een variatie op) de onderhavige zaak.

3.14 Laten we aannemen dat PTT Post [eiser] expliciet zou hebben meegedeeld dat een nieuwe verlenging slechts aan de orde kon zijn wanneer hij instemde met de Briefpost CAO die op dit punt zijn rechten beperkte zodat hij van toepasselijkheid in zekere zin slechter zou worden.(21) [eiser] had dan de keuze tussen aanvaarding in welk geval de arbeidsovereenkomst zou worden verlengd of weigering in welk geval deze ten einde zou zijn gekomen. Men kan ook zeggen - maar dat is m.i. niet zonder meer juist(22) - dat hij in feite geen keuze had.

3.15 Is de onder 3.14 ten tonele gevoerde "dwangpositie" waarin een werknemer kan komen voldoende basis om aan te nemen dat een uitdrukkelijke aanvaarding van een onaantrekkelijke van de wettelijke regeling afwijkende cao rechtens niet zou kunnen worden getolereerd? Die vraag beantwoord ik ontkennend. Daarbij legt veel gewicht in de schaal dat bevestigende beantwoording een premie zou stellen op "ongeorganiseerdheid".

3.16 Daarmee wordt geen oordeel gegeven over het nut van een vakbondslidmaatschap (dat is hier niet relevant en daarover behoor ik ook geen mening te geven). Er wordt slechts mee gezegd dat niet valt in te zien waarom tussen werknemers een potentieel groot onderscheid wordt gemaakt enkel en alleen omdat de één wel en de ander niet bij een (bepaalde) vakbond is aangesloten.

3.17 Daarbij valt nog te bedenken dat vakbonden, naar moet worden aangenomen, in het algemeen een goed oog hebben voor hetgeen voor werknemers en desgevallend het voorbestaan van ondernemingen (en daarmee het algemeen belang) het beste is.(23) Hoezeer zich ook de situatie kan voordoen dat collectieve afspraken voor individuele werknemers nadelig uitpakken (hetgeen zich ook bij wél georganiseerde werknemers zal kunnen manifesteren) ligt in dit uitgangspunt besloten dat vakbonden de facto eveneens de belangen van niet georganiseerde werknemers dienen.(24) Dat pleit er tegen dat van tussen hen en een werkgever gemaakte afspraken in tamelijk willekeurige gevallen wordt afgeweken.(25)

3.18 We belanden dan bij een lastiger vraag. Kan gebondenheid aan zulk een cao ook worden aanvaard ingeval zij niet uitdrukkelijk is overeengekomen? Hierbij valt in het bijzonder te denken aan een situatie waarin de cao stilzwijgend aanvaard is.

3.19 In de doctrine en de rechtspraak wordt deze vraag met enige regelmaat bevestigend beantwoord;(26) vooral in een setting waarin de werkgever de cao in de praktijk toepast en de werknemer daartegen geen bezwaar heeft gemaakt.(27) Deze laatste situatie zal zich, naar in de rede ligt, doorgaans slechts voordoen wanneer het gaat om een voor de betrokken werknemer gunstige regeling.

3.20 Van een - rechtens relevant - in de praktijk toepassen ten nadele van een werknemer kan m.i. hooguit worden gesproken in een situatie waarin de werknemer zich daarvan ten minste redelijkerwijs bewust was. In casu kan niet worden gezegd dat de CAO Briefpost 2000 in de praktijk is toegepast in de zojuist bedoelde zin nu de Rechtbank niets heeft vastgesteld waaruit [eiser] heeft moeten opmaken dat deze cao in zijn geval werd gehanteerd. Met name heeft zij niet vastgesteld dat [eiser] de tekst van Briefpost 2000 heeft ontvangen.

3.21 M.i. is onvoldoende dat een werknemer zich door de handelwijze van de werkgever realiseerde dat een voor hem nadelige cao werd toegepast. Het lijkt mij slechts aanvaardbaar een van "driekwart dwingend recht" afwijkende cao toe te passen op een "ongeorganiseerde" werknemer wanneer buiten redelijke twijfel vaststaat dat hij met toepasselijkheid heeft ingestemd. Zo'n situatie kan zich voordoen wanneer de cao aan de werknemer voorafgaand aan de arbeidsovereenkomst (of de verlenging daarvan) is toegezonden of terhand gesteld onder vermelding van de beoogde toepasselijkheid.

3.22 Wanneer de arbeidsovereenkomst zelf stilzwijgt over de cao zou ik evenwel als aanvullende eis willen stellen dat de werkgever in documentatie als onder 3.21 bedoeld - gezien de omstandigheden duidelijke en begrijpelijke taal - duidelijk maakt op welke punten deze cao afwijkt van "driekwart dwingend recht". Dat laatste is wellicht niet nodig wanneer aan deze kwestie voorafgaand aan de verlenging van de desbetreffende arbeidsovereenkomst op indringende en duidelijke wijze binnen de onderneming aandacht is besteed. Of zo'n situatie zich voordoet, staat ter beoordeling van de feitenrechter.

3.23 Doet een geval als onder 3.22 omschreven zich voor, dan mag m.i. rechtens worden aangenomen dat een werknemer die niet laat weten bezwaar te hebben tegen toepasselijkheid van de cao daarmee heeft ingestemd.

Bespreking van de klachten ten gronde

3.24 De Rechtbank heeft aangenomen dat [eiser] bij de verlengingen van zijn arbeidsovereenkomst expliciet akkoord is gegaan met de beëindigingsmogelijkheden van de Briefpost 2000 CAO. Zij acht "niet doorslaggevend" of [eiser] zich bewust was van "de status van de Briefpost 2000 regeling". Voldoende is in haar ogen dat Briefpost 2000 een cao is zodat de afwijking van de wettelijke regeling bij cao plaatsvond.

3.25 Hoewel de opvatting van de Rechtbank - in het licht van hetgeen onder 3.12 werd betoogd - m.i. niet (zonder meer) tot een onwenselijk resultaat leidt, kan zij rechtens niet als juist worden aangenomen. De motivering daarvan gaf ik hierboven onder 3.13-3.23.

3.26 De klachten van de onderdelen 1, 2 en 3 behelzen - enigszins welwillend gelezen en naar de kennelijke strekking(28) - een hierop toegesneden klacht.(29) Deze acht ik dus gegrond.

3.27 Mr Duk vertolkt - begrijpelijkerwijs - een tegengesteld standpunt (s.t. onder 8 en 9). Hij beroept zich daarbij niet op opvattingen in de doctrine of rechtspraak. Zijn motivering komt niet verder dan dat niet valt in te zien waarom melding zou moeten worden gemaakt van de omstandigheid dat sprake is van een cao.

3.28 Voor zijn standpunt heb ik zowel begrip als enige sympathie. Het probleem is evenwel dat de door hem verdedigde opvatting m.i. niet goed strookt met het wettelijk stelsel, al moet ik toegeven dat de wet niet per se dwingt tot hetgeen door mij wordt betoogd. Een redelijke wetsuitleg leidt m.i. wél tot de door mij verdedigde opvatting. Ik werk dat nog kort uit.

3.29 In de eerste plaats spreekt art. 7:668 lid 5(oud) BW over afwijking bij cao. Voor gevallen als de onderhavige - waarin de cao niet rechtstreeks geldt - ligt dan voor de hand dat partijen het - kort gezegd - eens zijn geworden over toepasselijkheid van de cao. Daarvoor is uiteraard vereist dat zij beide weten dat het gaat om een cao.

3.30 Daar komt bij dat art. 7:668 (oud) BW strekt ter bescherming van de werknemer. We zullen (ook hier) moeten uitgaan van de fictie dat hij de regeling kent (althans zou kunnen kennen). Anders gezegd: dat hij bij het aangaan van de verlenging kan afwegen wat daarvan rechtens de gevolgen zijn. Zulks bijvoorbeeld in een situatie waarin hij de keuze heeft tussen verschillende arbeidsovereenkomsten bij meer dan een werkgever. Die keuze kan hij eerst met vrucht maken wanneer hij weet of sprake is van een cao.

3.31 Ik gaf al aan dat deze fictie in de grote meerderheid van de gevallen (en vermoedelijk ook in casu(30)) niet zal stroken met de werkelijkheid. Doch deze "fictie" behoort m.i. tot de fundamenten van ons stelsel - en dat geldt gelijkelijk voor andere beschaafde rechtsstelsels -.(31) Het is de rechtvaardiging waarom justitiabelen worden opgeknoopt aan niet-inachtneming van wettelijke regels en waarom rechtsdwaling vrijwel nooit verschoonbaar wordt geacht.(32) Moeilijk kan worden aanvaard dat onbekendheid met wettelijke regels wél aan justiabelen zou kunnen tegengeworpen maar dat zij er in voorkomende gevallen niet de vruchten van kunnen plukken.

3.32 Voor de door mij voorgestane opvatting pleit ten slotte art. 7:655 (oud) BW dat de werkgever verplicht opgave aan de werknemer te doen van de toepasselijke cao.

3.33 Onderdeel 4 richt zich tegen het oordeel van de Rechtbank in rov. 4.9 dat het beroep van [eiser] op redelijkheid en billijkheid moet worden verworpen.

3.34 Voorzover het betoog van [eiser] al betrekking had op de primaire vordering - hetgeen m.i. niet het geval is - faalt het omdat het berust op een onjuiste rechtsopvatting.

Kennelijk gaat [eiser] er in zijn klacht van uit dat de regeling van Briefpost 2000 van toepassing is. Hij meent evenwel dat toepassing van die regeling in zijn geval niet redelijk is. Vermoedelijk bedoelt hij aldus beroep te doen op de beperkende werking van redelijkheid en billijkheid.

3.35 Aldus ziet hij - evenals kennelijk de Rechtbank - voorbij aan de onaanvaardbaarheidsmaatstaf van art. 6:248 lid 2 BW. Het onderdeel loopt reeds hierop stuk.

Conclusie

Deze conclusie strekt tot vernietiging van de bestreden vonnissen en tot verwijzing naar het Hof Amsterdam.

De Procureur-Generaal bij de
Hoge Raad der Nederlanden,

A-G

1 Uit de tenaamstelling van verweerster in cassatie in de dupliek van mr Duk valt op te maken dat PTT Post thans TPG Post heet. Omdat gedurende de gehele procedure sprake is geweest van PTT Post lijkt het aangewezen deze benaming in de conclusie aan te houden.
2 Ontleend aan het vonnis van de Rechtbank Haarlem van 4 juli 2000 en verder aangevuld als in de voetnoten aangegeven.
3 Productie 2 bij de inleidende dagvaarding.
4 KPN CAO 1 april 1993 - 1 april 1995, KPN CAO 1 april 1995 - 1 april 1997 en KPN CAO 1 april 1997 - 1 april 1999, zie de producties 7 en 8 bij de inleidende dagvaarding.
5 Productie 3 bij de inleidende dagvaarding.
6 Idem.
7 Productie 5 bij de inleidende dagvaarding.
8 Vgl. de kennisgeving als bedoeld in art. 4 lid 2 Wet op de loonvorming van het ministerie van SZW van 5 oktober 1993, productie 6 bij inleidende dagvaarding.
9 Vgl. de brief van mr Ansink aan PTT Post van 1 april 1998, productie 10 bij de inleidende dagvaarding.
10 Productie 10 bij de inleidende dagvaarding.
11 Bij cvd beweert zij dat de (kennelijk integrale) "CAO Briefpost 2000 telkenmale (is) gehecht aan de aan [eiser] toegezonden arbeidsovereenkomst" (sub 4).
12 De cassatiedagvaarding is uitgebracht op 14 mei 2001; 13 mei 2001 viel op een zondag.
13 Tekst & Commentaar (LUTTMER-KAT) art. 667 aant. 6 en art. 668 aant. 8.
14 Zie voor een beknopt overzicht van de wijzigingen en het daarbij behorende overgangsrecht C.J. SMITSKAM en E.J. KRONENBURG-WILLEMS, Wet Flexibiliteit en zekerheid (2000) blz. 37-45.
15 Daarom kan m.i. blijven rusten dat de kernvraag waarom het in deze procedure gaat onder het thans geldende recht op dezelfde wijze is geregeld als onder het oude recht; zie onder 3.5.
16 Zie nader VAN DER GRINTEN, Arbeidsovereenkomstenrecht (1994) blz. 35-36.
17 Vgl. HR 25 maart 1977, NJ 1977, 433 P.Z. en HR 26 juni 1992, NJ 1992, 654, rov. 3.3.
18 TK, Zitting 1947-1948, 881, nr. 3 blz. 5.
19 Zie o.m. M.M. OLBERS, Het regelingsbereik van de cao, SMA 1992 blz. 660; Arbeidsovereenkomst (Olbers), aant. 4 bij art. 14 Wet CAO; W.J.P.M. Fase, C.A.O.-recht (1982) blz. 54; M.M.H. KRAAMWINKEL, De ongebonden werknemer en de CAO, Sociaal Recht 1997 blz. 263, allen onder verwijzing naar HR 7 juni 1957, NJ 1957, 527.
20 Fase, a.w. blz. 55; HEKKELMAN, SMA 1979 blz. 222, 228; G.C. Boot, TVVS 1996 blz. 219; Losbladige Arbeidsovereenkomst Wet CAO (Olbers) art. 14 aant. 5; M.M. OLBERS, SMA 1992 blz. 660; Rb. Amsterdam 5 juni 1996, Jurisprudentie Arbeidsrecht 1996, 139; Rb. Amsterdam 31 mei

1995, Jurisprudentie Arbeidsrecht 1995, 162; Ktr. Leiden 21 januari 1987, Prg 1989, 2391 (in appèl vernietigd) met noot Mannoury; Rb. Utrecht 8 juni 1994, Jurisprudentie Arbeidsrecht 1996, 122 (de Rechtbank lijkt ook in andere gevallen gebondenheid te willen aannemen); Pres. Rb. Zutphen 4 mei 1982, KG 1982, 87.

21 Het voorbeeld is in zoverre enigszins onzuiver omdat de CAO Briepost 2000 reeds gold ten tijde van het aangaan van de eerste arbeidsovereenkomst. Voor de beslissing in de onderhavige zaak is dat mogelijk van doorslaggevende betekenenis; voor de beantwoording van de meer principiële vraag leidt het de aandacht af van de kernvraag.

22 De juistheid valt of staat bijvoorbeeld met de vraag of [eiser] een alternatief had, bijvoorbeeld in de vorm van een andere baan met een lager salaris maar met (grotere) zekerheid voor de toekomst.

23 Onder meer uit recente uitlatingen in werkgeversland valt af te leiden dat de in de tekst verwoorde stelling niet door een ieder wordt onderschreven. Ik volsta ermee op te merken dat het wettelijk stelsel (met name ook de regelingen inzake CAO's) zijn gestoeld op het geen in de tekst is vermeld.

24 In vergelijkbare zin bijvoobeeld ook M.M.H. KRAAMWINKEL, Sociaal Recht 1997 blz. 263.

25 Ook F.B.J. GRAPPERHAUS, Sociaal Recht 2002 blz. 186 e.v. meent dat zoveel mogelijk ware te voorkomen dat ongebonden werknemers anders worden behandeld; idem G.C. BOOT, TVVS 1996 blz. 220/1.

26 Fase, a.w. blz. 55; HEKKELMAN, a.w. blz. 225, 228; Losbladige Arbeidsovereenkomst (Olbers) Wet CAO art. 14 aant. 5; Hof 's-Hertogenbosch 9 juni 1997, Jurisprudentie Arbeidsrecht 1997, 150. Anders: Ktr. Rotterdam 29 oktober 1998, Jurisprudentie Arbeidsrecht 1998, 244.

27 J. Mannoury onder Rb. 's-Gravenhage 25 november 1987 en 25 mei 1988, PRG 1989, 2391.

28 Vgl. s.t. mr Kamminga onder 11 en 12.

29 Ook mr Duk gaat er, m.i. terecht, van uit dat de klachten dezelfde strekking hebben: s.t. onder 3.

30 Wederom bevind ik mij in het goede gezelschap van mr Duk: s.t. onder 11.

31 Vgl. Muriel FABRE-MAGNAN, Towards a European Civil Code, Second reversed and expanded edition (1998) blz. 226 en noot 18; in theorie anders UNIDROIT Beginselen van Internationale Handelsovereenkomsten art. 3.4 en de toelichting onder 1. De in de tekst verwoorde opvatting strookt reeds met het Romeinse recht: Reinhard ZIMMERMANN, The Law of Obligations (1996) blz. 604 e.v.

32 ASSER-HARTKAMP II (2001) nr 196 en III (2002) nr 79.

Sources

Internet website:
http://www.rechtspraak.nl/flashed.asp.

Date: ***January 6, 2003***
Adjudicating Court: ***ICC International Court of Arbitration (Partial Award)***
Number: ***12111***
Parties: ***Unknown***

Keywords

INTERNATIONAL SALES CONTRACT REFERRING TO "INTERNATIONAL LAW" AS THE LAW GOVERNING THE CONTRACT – TO BE UNDERSTOOD AS REFERENCE TO THE GENERAL PRINCIPLES OF LAW AND THE LEX MERCATORIA – APPLICATION OF THE UNIDROIT PRINCIPLES (PARAGRAPH 3 OF THE PREAMBLE OF THE UNIDROIT PRINCIPLES)

PRINCIPLES OF EUROPEAN CONTRACT LAW - ACADEMIC EXERCISE PRELIMINARY TO A EUROPEAN CIVIL CODE – AS SUCH NOT YET APPLICABLE TO INTERNATIONAL COMMERCIAL CONTRACTS

Abstract

A sales contract between a Romanian seller and a English buyer contained the following choice of law clause and arbitration agreement: "This contract is governed by international law; any dispute arising in connection with this contract shall be settled amicably, and failing that, by arbitration under the ICC International Court of Arbitration."

When a dispute arose which the parties were unable to settle amicably, the Romanian seller requested arbitration. The parties disagreed as to what the law applicable to the substance of the dispute was. Claimant argued that by referring to "international law" the parties had in mind the general principles of law and the *lex mercatoria*, and in accordance with Article 1.101(3) of the Principles of European Contract Law and paragraph 3 of the Preamble of the UNIDROIT Principles concluded that the dispute should be governed by the Principles of European Contract Law, applicable in Romania, to be interpreted in the light of the UNIDROIT Principles. Respondent objected by invoking the application of English law.

The arbitral tribunal held that by referring to "international law" the parties had made it clear that they did not want the application of any domestic law; the term "international law" was to be understood as reference to the *lex mercatoria* and general principles of law applicable to international contracts, and since such general principles are reflected in the UNIDROIT Principles it concluded that the dispute should be governed by the UNIDROIT Principles. As to the Principles of European Contract Law, the arbitral tribunal stated that "they constitute an academic research, at this stage not largely well-known to the international business community and are a preliminary step to the drafting of a future

European Code of Contracts, not enacted yet" and therefore excluded their application in the case at hand.

Full Text

[Not yet available]

Date: ***January 31, 2003***
Adjudicating Court: ***Arbitration Court of the Lausanne Chamber of Commerce and Industry***
Number: ***Unknown***
Parties: ***Unkwnown***

Keywords

SATELLITE CONTRACT INVOLVING SIX LEGAL SYSTEMS COVERING THREE CONTINENTS – CONTRACT CONTAINED CONFLICTING PROVISIONS AS THE APPLICABLE LAW (ENGLISH LAW OR SWISS LAW) – AT THE BEGINNING OF THE ARBITRAL PROCEEDINGS PARTIES AGREED ON APPLICATION OF THE UNIDROIT PRINCIPLES

RIGHT TO DAMAGES FOR NON-PERFORMANCE – COMPENSATION DUE FOR HARM CAUSED BY NON-PERFORMANCE – AMOUNT OF COMPENSABLE HARM TO BE REDUCED IF HARM IN PART DUE TO AGGRIEVED PARTY (ARTS. 7.4.2 AND 7.4.7 OF THE UNIDROIT PRINCIPLES)

RIGHT TO INTEREST (ARTS. 7.4.9 AND 7.4.10 OF THE UNIDROIT PRINCIPLES)

Abstract

A Turkish company and a company incorporated in Anguilla, West Indies, with an office in the Philippines, entered into an agreement concerning highly sophisticated equipment. The contract contained two provisions on the choice of law, which however appeared to contradict each other, since one was in favour of English law and the other in favour of Swiss law.

A dispute arose and the parties agreed to submit it to an *ad hoc* arbitration governed by the UNCITRAL Arbitration Rules.

In view of the uncertainties as to the applicable substantive law the arbitral tribunal suggested to the Parties to choose the UNIDROIT Principles as the applicable law. The Parties agreed, also in view of the fact that the application of the UNIDROIT Principles was not seen as precluding the application of the English law if applicable as maintained by one Party and the Swiss law if applicable as proposed by the other Party.

After having rendered on 17 May 2002 a Partial Award finding that one of the parties had not properly performed its obligations arising from the contract, the arbitral tribunal rendered a final award determining the amount of damages due by the non-performing party. In so doing the arbitral tribunal referred to Arts. 7.4.2 and 7.4.7 of the UNIDROIT Principles, in order to justify a reduction of the compensable harm in view of the fact that part of the harm was due to the conduct of the aggrieved party, and to Arts. 7.4.9(2) and 7.4.10 of the UNIDROIT Principles, in order to grant interests on the amount due.

In a thourough dissenting opinion one of the arbitrators asserted that reference to Art. 2.16 [Art. 2.1.16 of the 2004 edition] of the UNIDROIT Principles was appropriate to determine the extent of the duty of confidentiality, but disagreed with the conclusion reached by the majority of the arbitral tribunal. The same dissenting opinion also cited Art. 4.1 of the UNIDROIT Principles in order to reach a correct interpretation of the contract.

Full Text

[Not yet available]

Sources

Notice of the award kindly provided by Professor François DESSEMONTET.

Date: ***February 12, 2003***
Country: ***Australia***
Adjudicating Court: ***Federal Court of Australia***
Number: ***NG733 of 1997***
Parties: ***GEC Marconi Systems Pty Ltd. v. BHP Information Techology Pty Ltd. and Others***

Keywords

CONTRACT GOVERNED BY A PARTICULAR DOMESTIC LAW – REFERENCE TO THE UNIDROIT PRINCIPLES AS A MEANS TO INTERPRET AND SUPPLEMENT APPLICABLE DOMESTIC LAW

NO ORAL MODIFICATION CLAUSE – EFFECTIVENESS – EXCEPTION IN CASE OF ESTOPPEL (REFERENCE BY COURT TO ART. 2.18 [ART. 2.1.18 OF THE 2004 EDITION] OF UNIDROIT PRINCIPLES)

CONTRACT FOR DEVELOPMENT OF SOFTWARE – CONTRACT PROVIDES FOR PAYMENTS TO BE MADE IN AGREED INSTALMENTS THROUGHOUT THE DURATION OF THE WORK – INSTALMENTS NOT CONDITIONAL ON COMPLETION OF WORK (REFERENCE BY COURT TO ART. 6.1.4, COMMENT 2, OF UNIDROIT PRINCIPLES)

DUTY OF GOOD FAITH AND FAIR DEALING – IMPLIED TERM OF ALL CONTRACTS – "ENTIRE AGREEMENT" CLAUSE NOT SUFFICIENT TO PRECLUDE SUCH IMPLICATION (REFERENCE BY COURT TO ART. 1.7 OF THE UNIDROIT PRINCIPLES; ART. 1:201 OF THE PRINCIPLES OF EUROPEAN CONTRACT LAW)

Abstract

The Commonwealth of Australia ("the Commonwealth") and the two Australian software companies BHP Information Technology Pty Ltd ("BHP-IT") and GEC Marconi Systems Pty Ltd ("GEC Marconi") entered into back-to-back-fixed price contracts for software development and systems integration in the Australian Diplomatic Communication Network, a network for communication to and from Australia's overseas missions. The contract between the Commonwealth and BHP-IT was the "Head Contract", the contract between BHP-IT and GEC Marconi the "Sub-Contract". The actual software was to be developed by GEC Marconi, but special boundary security devices ("STUBS devices") were to be supplied by the Commonwealth to BHP-IT, which in turn would supply them to GEC Marconi for integration with the software being developed by GEC Marconi. The parties were obliged to perform their obligations in accordance with a special Implementation Plan, which provided for 5 successive development phases or "milestones", at the achievement of which by GEC Marconi BHP-IT had to make the corresponding progress payments.

The dispute arose when GEC Marconi served a notice of termination of the Sub-Contract on BHP-IT on the ground of alleged failures on the part of BHP-IT to comply with its contractual obligations. In particular, GEC Marconi complained that BHP-IT had failed to provide the STUBS devices as required by the Sub-Contract, and refused to pay GEC Marconi for its achievement of the fourth milestone again as required by the Sub-Contract. BHP-IT did not deny these facts but contended that the Sub-Contract had been amended by agreement to remove the obligation to provide the STUBS devices and to substitute them with emulation software; as to its refusal to pay for the fourth milestone, it argued that GEC Marconi was not entitled to be paid as it had not complied with the requirements of payment under the Sub-Contract.

GEC Marconi commenced a legal proceeding against BHP-IT before the Federal Court of Australia, which led to a number of cross-claims, first, by BHP-IT against GEC Marconi and, secondly, by the Commonwealth against BHP-IT.

Both the Head Contract and the Sub-Contract were domestic contracts and as such governed by Australian law. Nevertheless, on a number of occasions the Court, apparently with the intent to further corroborate its deliberations, also referred to foreign sources – mainly to U.S. and English law – as well as to international instruments such as the UNIDROIT Principles of International Commercial Contracts and – though to a lesser extent – the Principles of European Contract Law.

Thus, with respect to BHP-IT's objection that the Sub-Contract had been amended, the question arose as to whether the existence of a "no oral modification" clause in the Sub-Contract precluded, as GEC Marconi argued, the making of an oral or implied variation agreement, or whether in any case a party could by its conduct be estopped from invoking the "no oral modification" clause, as BHP-IT argued. In rejecting GEC Marconi's argument and deciding in favour of BHP-IT, the Court referred, among others, to Article 2.18 [Art. 2.1.18 of the 2004 edition] of the UNIDROIT Principles, which, while as a rule giving effect to contract clauses imposing a writing requirement for subsequent modifications, provides that a party may be precluded by its conduct from invoking such clause to the extent that the other party has acted in reliance on that conduct.

Likewise, in rejecting BHP-IT's argument according to which the Sub-Contract contained an "entire obligation", *i.e.* the first four milestone payments were conditional upon complete performance of the contract, so that GEC Marconi, having failed to achieve the fifth and final milestone, was obliged to refund the previous four milestone payments it had received, the Court referred among others to Comment 2 to Article 6.1.4 of the UNIDROIT Principles, stating that, while as a rule if the performance of only one party's obligation by its very nature requires a certain period of time, that party is bound to render its performance first, circumstance may indicate the contrary, *e.g.* where the contract provides for payments to be made in agreed instalments throughout the duration of the work.

Finally, with respect to BHP-IT's contention that in terminating the Sub-Contract GEC Marconi had breached an implied contract term requiring it to act honestly, fairly and reasonably, and to GEC Marconi's objection that, a duty of good faith, even if generally implied by law, could not be implied in the contract in the case at hand on account of the so-called "entire agreement" clause contained in the Sub-Contract, the Court, while pointing out that in Australian law there was no such mandatory rule of law imposing on the parties the duty of good faith and fair dealing, such as § 1-102(3) of the United States Uniform Commercial Code or Articles 1.7 of the UNIDROIT Principles and 1:201 of the Principles of European Contract Law, concluded that the duty of good faith and fair dealing was to be considered an implied term of all contracts, and the mere fact that the contract contained a "entire agreement" clause was not sufficient to preclude such an implication.

Full Text

[Not yet available]

Date: ***April 4, 2003***
Adjudicating Court: ***International Arbitration Court of the Chamber of Commerce and Industry of the Russian Federation***
Number: ***134/2002***
Parties: ***Unknown***

Keywords

UNIDROIT PRINCIPLES CONSTITUTING "A RESTATEMENT OF RULES UNIVERSALLY ACCEPTED IN INTERNATIONAL TRADE AS REFLECTING THE APPROACHES OF THE MAIN LEGAL SYSTEMS" – REFERENCE TO THEM IN SUPPORT OF SOLUTION ADOPTED UNDER APPLICABLE DOMESTIC LAW

PENALTY CLAUSES – AMOUNT MANIFESTLY EXCESSIVE – REDUCTION BY COURT (ART. 333 OF RUSSIAN CIVIL CODE; ART. 7.4.13 UNIDROIT PRINCIPLES)

Abstract

Claimant (a Russian company) asked the Arbitration Court to order Respondent (a German company) to pay a certain sum of money as a penalty calculated on the price of the goods which Respondent had delayed to pay and which Respondent was ordered to pay in accordance with an arbitral award rendered in an earlier dispute between the same parties concerning the breach of an international sales contract. After the arbitral award had been rendered, Respondent had paid only part of the penalty (42% of the price of the goods in respect of which the penalty was calculated). Since the full penalty had not been paid timely by Respondent, Claimant asked the arbitration court to order Respondent to pay the rest of the penalty which at the time when the claim was brought amounted to 487% of the price of the goods not timely paid.

Respondent, among other arguments put forward in justification of non-payment of the penalty, objected that the amount of the penalty requeted by Claimant in the present arbitration proceedings was manifestly excessive in relation to the actual loss caused by the the breach of the contract, and asked the arbitration court to reduce the penalty correspondingly.

Deciding in favour of Respondent the Arbitration Court applied not only Article 333 of the Russian Civil Code (applicable in the case at hand since the issue at stake was not covered by CISG), according to which a court may under certain conditions reduce a contractually agreed penalty, but also made reference to Article 7.4.13 of the UNIDROIT Principles of International Commercial Contracts which provides the same solution. According to the Arbitration Court the UNIDROIT Principles constitute a restatement of rules universally accepted in international trade as reflecting the approaches of the main legal systems with respect to general contract law, and may therefore be invoked in support of a solution adopted under the applicable domestic law.

Full Text

[Not yet available]

Sources

Decision kindly provided by Professor Alexander KOMAROV.

Date: **May 20, 2003**
Country: **Belarus**
Adjudicating Court: **Supreme Economic Court of the Republic of Belarus**
Number: **7-5/2003**
Parties: Holzimpex **Inc: v. Republican Agricultural Unitary Enterprise**

Keywords

SALES CONTRACT BETWEEN A U.S. AND A BELARUS COMPANY – GOVERNED BY THE LAW OF BELARUS

CISG APPLICABLE SINCE PARTIES SITUATED IN TWO CONTRACTING STATES

NON-PAYMENT OF THE PRICE – SELLER ENTITLED TO INTEREST (ART. 78 CISG) – RATE OF INTEREST DETERMINED ACCORDING TO ART. 7.4.9(2) OF THE UNIDROIT PRINCIPLES

Abstract

A U.S. trading company entered into a sales contract (No. 7-5/2003) with a state-owned enterprise of Belarus. The goods were delivered but the Belarus enterprise failed to pay the price, prompting the U.S. company to bring an action for payment.

The contract contained a choice of law clause in favour of the law of Belarus and indicated the Supreme Economic Court of the Republic of Belarus as the competent forum for the settlement of any disputes.

The Court held that CISG was applicable since it has been ratified by both the United States and the Republic of Belarus.

As to the merits, the Court decided that the U.S. company was entitled to the payment of the agreed price plus interest according to Article 78 of CISG. With no further explanation the Court held that "the rate of such interest is determined pursuant to Article 7.4.9 UNIDROIT Principles and is the average bank short-term lending rate to prime borrowers prevailing for the currency of payment at the place for payment or where no such rate exists at that place, the same rate in the state of the currency of payment". It awarded interest at a rate of 13.4% which according to the National Bank of the Republic of Belaurs was the rate in U.S. dollars in March 2003.

Full Text

[Not yet available]

Sources

Decision kindly provided by Albert KRITZER, Pace University.

Date: ***May 20, 2003***
Country: ***Belarus***
Adjudicating Court: ***Supreme Economic Court of the Republic of Belarus***
Number: 8-5/2003
Parties: ***Holzimpex Inc. v. Republican Agricultural Unitary Enterprise***

Keywords

SALES CONTRACT BETWEEN A U.S. AND A BELARUS COMPANY – GOVERNED BY THE LAW OF BELARUS

CISG APPLICABLE SINCE PARTIES SITUATED IN TWO CONTRACTING STATES

NON-PAYMENT OF THE PRICE – SELLER ENTITLED TO INTEREST (ART. 78 CISG) – RATE OF INTEREST DETERMINED ACCORDING TO ART. 7.4.9(2) OF THE UNIDROIT PRINCIPLES

Abstract

A U.S. trading company entered into a sales contract (No. 8-5/2003) with a state-owned enterprise of Belarus. The goods were delivered but the Belarus enterprise failed to pay the price, prompting the U.S. company to bring an action for payment.

The contract contained a choice of law clause in favour of the law of Belarus and indicated the Supreme Economic Court of the Republic of Belarus as the competent forum for the settlement of any disputes.

The Court held that CISG was applicable since it has been ratified by both the United States and the Republic of Belarus.

As to the merits, the Court decided that the U.S. company was entitled to the payment of the agreed price plus interest according to Article 78 of CISG. With no further explanation the Court held that "the rate of such interest is determined pursuant to Article 7.4.9 UNIDROIT Principles and is the average bank short-term lending rate to prime borrowers prevailing for the currency of payment at the place for payment or where no such rate exists at that place, the same rate in the state of the currency of payment". It awarded interest at a rate of 13.4% which according to the National Bank of the Republic of Belaurs was the rate in U.S. dollars in March 2003.

Full Text

[Not yet available]

Sources

Decision kindly provided by Albert KRITZER, Pace University.

Date: ***June 1, 2003***
Adjudicating Court: ***Arbitration Centre of the Costa Rican Chamber of Commerce***
Number: ***Unknown***
Parties: ***Unknown***

Keywords

DOMESTIC CONTRACT GOVERNED BY THE LAW OF COSTA RICA – REFERENCE BY ARBITRAL TRIBUNAL TO THE UNIDROIT PRINCIPLES "NOT AS A SOURCE OF LAW AGREED UPON OR INVOKED BY THE PARTIES, BUT INSTEAD FOR THEIR DOCTRINAL VALUE"

PERFORMANCE OF CONTRACT – PARTIES' DUTY TO ACT IN ACCORDANCE WITH GOOD FAITH (ART. 1.7 UNIDROIT PRINCIPLES)

Abstract

A Costa Rican company in the hotel industry engaged a Costa Rican accounting firm to prepare an insurance claim for damage to one of its hotels caused by a flash flood. The accounting firm submitted to the insurance company a damage report two weeks before the deadline for lodging the claim. The insurance company notified the Costa Rican company that the damage had to be specified in a more detailed manner. Instead of forwarding this communication to the accounting firm, the Costa Rican company hired another accounting firm to do the job. The first accounting firm, which was paid only part of the agreed fee, bought an action against the Costa Rican company claiming it had breached the contract by unilaterally terminating the agreement without informing it of the insurance company'sremarks thereby preventing it from supplementing its report.

The Arbitral Tribunal, while basing its decision on the law of Costa Rica, also referred to the UNIDROIT Principles "not as a source of law not agreed upon or invoked by the parties, but instead for their doctrinal value".

As to the merits the Arbitral Tribunal decided in favour of the plaintiff. In stressing the duty of the parties to act in accordance with good faith when performing their contract, it referred among others to Article 1.7 of the UNIDROIT Principles.

Full Text

[...]

"Without applying them as a source of law not agreed upon or invoked by the parties, but instead for their doctrinal value, it is relevant to recall that the UNIDROIT Principles of International Commercial Contracts were repeatedly applied in several awards of the

I.C.C. International Court of Arbitration up until 1998 and also in domestic arbitration. These Principles are the result of years of intensive comparative investigation and deliberation carried out by group of selected legal experts from the most diverse legal systems &..

In contracts that involve the reciprocal performance of contractual obligations, as the one that existed in this case, the parties must comply with the principle of good faith and especially with the duty of cooperation (the "*Mittwirkungspflichten*" of German doctrine), they must particularly make their best efforts in achieving the object of the contract. Therefore, they must perform the activities that are instrumentally necessary for the accomplishment of the main obligation ("*Nebenleistungspflichten*") and should not obstruct the execution of the contract nor cause damage to their counterparty ("*Schadenverhütungspflichten*").

The duty of cooperation is one of the general principles of the *Lex Mercatoria* that arbitrators in international trade stalwartly enforce. This principle is mainly applied in relation to the performance of contracts. The I.C.C. International Court of Arbitration has stated that each party must act in a way that does not damage the other party and that the parties must comply with this obligation of cooperation that modern doctrine derives from the principle of good faith that must govern the execution of every contract. Additionally, it has recently been provided by I.C.C. International Court of Arbitration that according to the UNIDROIT Principles of International Commercial Contracts, the usages of international trade require good faith in the fulfilment of contractual obligations (I.C.C., Award 9593, 1998)."

[...]

Sources

V. PÉREZ VARGAS - D. PÉREZ UMANA, The UNIDROIT Principles of International Commercial Contracts in Costa Rican Arbitral Practice, Uniform Law Review, 2006, 183-184.

Date: ***June 6, 2003***
Adjudicating Court: ***International Arbitration Court of the Chamber of Commerce and Industry of the Russian Federation***
Number: ***97/2002***
Parties: ***Unknown***

Keywords

SALES CONTRACT BETWEEN RUSSIAN SELLER AND SOUTH KOREAN BUYER – CISG APPLICABLE ACCORDING TO ART. 1(1)(B).

DEFECTIVE GOODS – CLAIM FOR DAMAGES BY BUYER – AMOUNT OF DAMAGES AWARDED REDUCED ON ACCOUNT OF THE FACT THAT HARM WAS DUE IN PART TO BUYER'S CONDUCT – REFERENCE TO ARTS. 74 AND 77 CISG AS WELL AS TO ART. 7.4.7 OF UNIDROIT PRINCIPLES (AS WELL AS RELATIVE COMMENT) WHICH EXPRESSLY ADDRESS THIS SITUATION

Abstract

A Russian company sold to a South Korean company components of "high sensitivity" to be incorporated in final product. Upon inspection of the goods delivered, it turned out that they were to a large extent defective and did not have the characteristics necessary for their intended use. Buyer brought an action for damages; Seller acknowledged the presence of defects but accused Buyer of not having inspected them properly and in good time after delivery.

Since the contract was silent as to the governing law, the Arbitral Tribunal referred to the relevant conflict of law rules of Russian law as the law of the forum and decided that CISG was applicable as part of the law where the seller had its place of business and that questions not settled in CISG should be governed by the Civil Code of the Russian Federation.

As to the merits the Arbitral Tribunal found that both parties had failed to take steps necessary to duly perform their obligations under the contract. In particular they had failed to set forth in the contract the exact procedure and methods of inspection of the goods, and it was above all Buyer who, as a professional manufacturer of the final product, should have made sure that the proper way in which goods were to be inspected be clearly indicated in the contract or at least agreed upon immediately after delivery. For this reason the Arbitral Tribunal, while deciding in favour of Buyer, when assessing the damages, awarded only two thirds of the amount claimed by Buyer whom it held co-responsible for the loss suffered on account of its own omissions and inadequate acts. In so deciding the Arbitral Tribunal applied not only Articles 74 and 77 CISG but referred also to Article 404(1) of the Civil Code of the Russian Federation and to Article 7.4.7 of the UNIDROIT Principles which expressly provides that where the harm is due in part to an act or omission of the aggrieved party the amount of damages shall be reduced to the extent that these factors have contributed to the harm. The Arbitral Tribunal also referred to Comment 2 to Article 7.4.7 of the UNIDROIT Principles which as an example of such contributory negligence expressly mentions the case where the aggrieved parties failed to give all the necessary instructions to the manufacturer of the defective machinery

Full Text

(Reproduced with the kind permission of Albert Kritzer, Pace University, N.Y.)

Translation [*] by Yelena Kalika [**]

Translation edited by Yuliya Chernykh [***]

1. SUMMARY OF RULING

1.1 Where a contract was made by the Claimant [Buyer], whose commercial enterprise is located in a State that is not a CISG Contracting State, and the Respondent [Seller], whose commercial enterprise is located in a CISG Contracting State, the relationships in connection with the dispute [arisen from such contract] are governed by the CISG. Russian laws should apply as subsidiary laws. [This conclusion] was reached since the Russian conflict of laws rule sets forth the applicability of the Russian civil laws as the laws of the seller's state. [The Tribunal] also took into account the provisions of Article 15(4) of the Russian Federation Constitution, Article 7(2) of the Russian Federation Civil Code and Article 1(1)(b) CISG.

1.2 Upon ascertaining defects in the goods delivered and differences in the parties' arguments as to how those defects were created and after establishing that both parties failed to set forth in the contract clear requirements as to the quality of goods and methods of their inspection, the Tribunal concluded that both parties were jointly liable. The Tribunal placed two third of the [Buyer]'s losses on the [Seller]. This conclusion was based on the CISG, the Russian Federation Civil Code and the UNIDROIT Principles of International Commercial Contracts.

1.3 When determining the amount of losses suffered by the [Buyer], the Tribunal took into account the computations submitted by the [Buyer]. The [Seller] did not object to [these computations].

1.4 Since in practice both parties deviated from strict compliance with the contractual provisions on the terms and procedure of bringing one's claims, when rendering an award, the Tribunal did not find [such provisions] to be determinative.

2. FACTS AND PLEADINGS

[Buyer], a South Korean company, brought a claim against [Seller], a Russian company, in connection with delivery of defective goods under a contract for the international sale of goods made by the parties on 1 August 2000. The [Seller] shipped the goods to the addressee indicated by the [Buyer]. Since during the inspection of the goods by the addressee it was established that the goods were defective, the [Buyer] demanded recovery of the damages sustained by him.

The damages included:

- The price of the goods;
- Expenses incurred as a result of manufacturing of finished goods from the defective goods delivered by the [Seller];
- Lost profits;
- Expenses incurred in connection with returning defective goods to the [Seller] and delivery of finished goods manufactured from the defective goods.

The [Buyer] also demanded recovery of arbitration fees paid and legal expenses.

The [Seller] objected to the [Buyer]'s claims. In his opinion, the defectiveness of the goods delivered resulted from the improper use by a third party (addressee). The [Seller] also argued that the [Buyer] failed to inspect the goods and bring claims within the period of time set forth in the contract as well as committed violations when inspecting the quality of the goods. The [Buyer] objected to all of [Seller]'s allegations.

3. THE TRIBUNAL'S REASONING

The Tribunal's award contained the following main points.

3.1 [Competence of the Tribunal]

As to the Tribunal's competence to arbitrate the present dispute, the Tribunal ascertained the following. Part 9 of the contract contains the arbitration clause, according to which, if the parties cannot reach an agreement in connection with disputes and disagreements arising out of the contract or in connection with it, the Tribunal should arbitrate the case.

The Tribunal ascertained that the dispute between the parties concerned contractual relationships that arose out of international commercial transactions. The [Buyer]'s enterprise is located abroad. Thus, this dispute falls within the categories of disputes that, according to the Russian Federation Law "On International Commercial Arbitration" and the Rules of the International Commercial Arbitration Court, may be arbitrated by the Tribunal.

For the above stated reasons and pursuant to Article 16 of the Russian Federation Law "On International Commercial Arbitration" and Article 1 of the Rules of the International Commercial Arbitration Court, the Tribunal ruled that it had jurisdiction to arbitrate the present dispute.

The Tribunal was composed in accordance with the Rules of the International Commercial Arbitration Court. No objections to the arbitrators were made.

3.2 [Applicable law]

In connection with the applicable law, the Tribunal established that the contract did not contain any provision on the applicable law. The parties also failed to determine this later on.

According to Article 28 of the Russian Federation Law "On International Commercial Arbitration", failing any designation by the parties, the Tribunal shall apply the law determined by the conflict of laws rules which it considers. The Tribunal finds that Article 166(1) of the USSR Principles of Civil Laws 1991, which was in force at the time when the contract was made, is such a conflict of laws rule. In the present case, according to this rule of law, a contract for the international sale of goods should be governed by the laws of the State, where the seller's company was incorporated, or is located or has its principal place of business. Under the [present] contract the seller is a public joint stock company incorporated in the Russian Federation. Therefore, the law governing the relationships in controversy is the law of the seller's State, *i.e.*, the Russian Federation.

According to Article 15 of the Russian Federation Constitution, the international treaties of the Russian Federation are a component part of its legal system. The provisions of the international treaties prevail over the rules of Russian civil laws. In accordance with Article 7 of the Russian Federation Civil Code, the relationships of the parties, which arose in connection with the performance of the contract, should be governed by the CISG. The provisions of the CISG (see Article 1(1)(b)) support this conclusion. Issues not settled in the CISG or only partially settled in the CISG should be governed by the Russian Federation Civil Code.

3.3 [Substantive issues: Quality of the goods; Inspection; Notice; Damages]

After reviewing the claims on the merits, the Tribunal ascertains that the dispute between the parties concerns the quality of goods delivered by the [Seller]. Pursuant to Article 35 CISG, the seller must deliver goods which are of the quantity, quality and description required by the contract. However, notwithstanding the "high sensitivity" of the goods delivered, numerous ways of their [possible] use and the multiple physical influences required for switching on, the parties failed to set in the contract the quality characteristics of the goods to be delivered considering their further use. Nor did the parties set forth the procedure of quality control of the said goods and the methods of such control. The contract also does not contain any references to such technical documentation as the standards set by international organizations and the national standards.

3.3.1 The Tribunal believes that, notwithstanding the absence of the quality requirements both in the contract itself and appendixes to it No. 1 and 2 of 3 November 2000 and 5 December 2000 respectively, they were set in fact. Such requirements were stated in the document sent by the [Seller] to the [Buyer] by fax on 21 August 2000, *i.e.*, before the said appendixes specifying the goods to be delivered were signed. The [Buyer] lawfully viewed this document as the [Seller]'s obligation in connection with the quality of goods delivered by him. The representative of the [Seller] confirmed such an interpretation of this document at the hearing held on 14 April 2003. The [Buyer]'s claims were entirely based on the fact that all the results of the tests made by him did not match the quality requirements stated in the said document.

3.3.2 As stated by the representative of the [Seller], 100% of the goods were checked at the factory prior to being shipped. The assembled goods also underwent a 100 hour long test. The results of the tests were to be stated in a special document that, according to article 34 CISG, must be handed over to the buyer with the rest of the documents relating to the goods sold. The [Seller] failed to do so.

Taking into account that the contract did not contain the provisions on the quality control of the goods delivered and that the [Seller] did not provide the said information, the [Buyer] exercised his right to inspect the goods received by referring to the established practice between the parties. Such practice was established when performing the previous contracts with the [Seller] to deliver other models of the goods. The [Buyer] did not object to [such established practice]. In the past the goods were inspected in accordance with the same method as [the one used to inspect] the goods in controversy. The inspection was made taking into consideration the design of the model [in controversy].

Such approach meets the requirements stated in Article 474(2) of the Russian Federation Civil Code which provides that if the procedure of inspection of the quality of the goods is not set forth in the contract, such inspection should be performed in accordance with "trade usages or other customs used to inspect the quality of the goods delivered under a contract of sale."

Besides the [Buyer] sent the [Seller] the terms and [computer] program of the inspection performed by the addressee's company. The [Buyer] also sent the samples of both the goods suitable for use and defective goods. However, the [Seller] failed to object to such a program and to suggest an alternative method of inspection of the quality of the goods delivered by him.

In such circumstances, the Tribunal concludes that the [Seller] in fact accepted the method [of inspection] used by the addressee. [In addition], both in the reply to the complaint and in the oral argument, the [Seller] failed to present evidence that the method used by the [Buyer] in inspecting the goods could not reflect their factual quality. Besides, when attempting to explain the negative results of the tests performed with the increased impedance, the representative of the [Seller] could not explain why the goods tested within the normal range of impedance also became defective.

3.3.3 That the goods delivered under the contract were defective is a fact established by the [Buyer] and admitted by the [Seller]. However, the parties failed to reach an agreement as to the reasons that caused such defects. The Tribunal notes that the [Seller], while formally not admitting his liability, nevertheless agreed to the [Buyer]'s returning of the defective goods. [Such goods] were sent back to the [Seller]. The goods returned by the [Buyer] -- including the goods assembled into the finished products -- are in the custody of the [Seller].

The Tribunal cannot agree with the [Seller]'s argument that the liability for the defective goods is on the [Buyer] who is allegedly trying to shift his liability to a third party to the [Seller].

3.3.4 As to the issue of the terms and procedure of bringing one's claims, the Tribunal notes the following:

a) Originally the parties tried to resolve the issue of the quality of goods without the strict application of the provisions of Part 6 of the contract ("Reclamation");

b) The [Buyer]'s letters of 15 December and 25 December 2000, as well of 15 January and 18 January 2001, represent the claims duly brought within the set period of time;

c) In his lengthy correspondence concerning the quality the [Seller] did not raise a question of violation of the formal procedure of bringing the claims; only in the letter of 12 April 2001, in which he agreed to accept the returned defective goods, the [Seller] requested that a reclamation be sent to him, and the [Buyer] did so.

Therefore, in practice the parties deviated from the strict observance of the provisions set in part 6 of the contract. In such circumstances, taking into consideration the provisions of the CISG allowing the buyer to give notice regarding non-conformity of the goods within a reasonable time after he has discovered it or ought to have discovered it, but at the latest within a period of two years (see Article 39 CISG), the Tribunal does not see any reasons to find the issue of the terms and procedure of bringing the claim to be determinative in this case.

3.4 Since the [Seller] has not made any objections to the computation of the amount sought by the [Buyer], the Tribunal finds that the amount of damages sustained by the [Buyer] is established in the amount stated by the [Buyer] in the claim. At the same time, the materials of the case and oral arguments of the parties allow the Tribunal to point out the following. Both parties failed to take steps necessary to duly perform their obligations under the contract. First of all, they failed to set forth the procedure and methods of inspection of the goods. The [Buyer], as a professional participant in the market of such goods, as a seller with the knowledge of requirements set for finished products, in which the purchased goods are used, did not use due care either when making the contract or when performing it. The [Buyer] did not insist on setting the clear provisions concerning the quality of the purchased goods and the methods of their inspection. When evaluating the actions of the [Buyer], based on Articles 74 and 77 CISG, the Tribunal took into account the provisions of the UNIDROIT Principles of international commercial contracts which were published by the International Center for Financial and Economic Development in 1996, pp. 235-237. [The UNIDROIT Principles] set forth the general rules for international commercial contracts. As provided in the Commentary to Article 7.4.7 of the Principles, its own actions or omission to act may demonstrate the participation of the wronged party in the creation of damage. As any defense, the defense in the form of claiming damages should meet the provisions set forth in the Russian Federation Civil Code. [Such provisions] set forth the proportionality of the property damages to each party's breach of its obligations.

In such circumstances, the Tribunal finds it proper to apply the principle of joint liability as set forth in article 404(1) of the Russian Federation Civil Code. The Tribunal finds it reasonable to place two third of the [Buyer]'s claims on the [Seller]. The rest of the [Buyer]'s claims of damages should be dismissed.

3.5 [Arbitration fees and costs]. Since the [Buyer]'s claims are not fully granted, pursuant to § 6(2) of the Schedule on Arbitration Fees and Costs, the [Seller] should pay such fees and expenses in proportion to the claims granted.

3.6 [Legal expenses]. Pursuant to § 9 of the Schedule on Arbitration Fees and Costs, a winning party may demand that the other party reimburse reasonable expenses incurred in connection with the arbitration and, in particular, legal expenses. However, the [Buyer] did not present evidence of his legal expenses. Therefore, the Tribunal denies such claim.

* * *

FOOTNOTES

* This is a translation of data on Proceeding 97/2002, dated 6 June 2003, of the International Commercial Arbitration Court at the Chamber of Commerce and Industry of the Russian Federation, reported in Rozenberg ed., Arb. Praktika (2003) No. 19 [111-118].
For purposes of this translation, Claimant of South Korea is referred to as [Buyer] and Respondent of the Russian Federation is referred to as [Seller]; the International Commercial Court at the Chamber of Commerce and Industry of the Russian Federation is referred to as [Tribunal].
** Yelena Kalika, JD Pace University School of Law, has studied at the Moscow State Law Academy, interned with a Moscow law firm, and is an Associate at the Pace Institute of International Commercial Law.
*** Yuliya Chernykh graduated from the National University of Kyiv-Mogyla Academy (Ukraine, 2004) and Stockholm University (LL.M. in International Commercial Law, 2005), Intern at UNCITRAL (2005).

Sources

Award kindly provided by A. KRITZER (Pace University).

Date: ***October 3, 2003***
Adjudicating Court: ***ICC International Court of Arbitration***
Number: ***12111***
Parties: ***unknown***

Keywords

DAMAGES – AMOUNT REDUCED TO THE EXTENT THAT LOSS WAS CAUSED BY CONDUCT OF AGGRIEVED PARTY (ART. 7.4.7 OF THE UNIDROIT PRINCIPLES)

INTEREST – DUE AS FROM DATE PAYMENT WAS DUE UNTIL DATE OF ACTUAL PAYMENT (ART. 7.4.9 OF THE UNIDROIT PRINCIPLES)

Abstract

Claimant, a Rumanian manufacturer of paper, entered into a contract with Defendant, an English company, for the sale of paper to be delivered to Italian costumers of the latter. Some of the Italian costumers complained that the paper delivered to them by Claimant was not in conformity with the agreed upon technical standards and refused payment. Defendant urged Claimant directly to contact the Italian costumers in order to find an amicable solution, but Claimant did not take any such step. On its part Defendant refused to permit its bank to honour the letter of credit opened in favour of Claimant on the ground of minor discrepancies in the documents submitted by Claimant.The dispute arose when Claimant requested Defendant to pay the outstanding invoices for the goods delivered as well as the cost of the expired raw materials Claimant had bought for the manufacturing of the paper ordered but subsequently rejected by Defendant, and Defendant refused to do so invoking the defects of the goods.

In a preliminary award (see ICC Award (Partial) No. 12111 of 6 January 2003) the Arbitral Tribunal decided that the rules of law applicable to the substance of the dispute were the UNIDROIT Principles of International Commercial Contracts.

As to the merits of the case the Arbitral Tribunal rejected Claimant's request for the payment of the expired raw materials. According to the Tribunal the failure of the parties to solve the outstanding claims made by the Italian customers demonstrated that they were no longer interested in further deliveries of the goods and intended to put an end to the contract. However, since both Claimant and Defendant refused to cooperate in order to find a mutually acceptable solution, also Claimant was prevented to claim damages for the deliveries that were no longer performed, and in this respect the Tribunal invoked Art. 7.4.7 of the UNIDROIT Principles according to which the amount of damages may be reduced when the loss results from an action or omission of the party claiming damages. With respect to the claim of payment of the invoices relating to the goods actually delivered the Tribunal decided in favour of Claimant, also in view of the fact that Defendant had despite the alleged defects of the goods all its Italian customers were able to use the goods for other purposes and had consequently paid the price to Defendant, though with some delay. The Tribunal also awarded Claimant interest on the corresponding amount and in accordance with Art. 7.4.9 of the UNIDROIT Principles decided that interest was due from the date the amount was due until full payment.

Full Text

[Not yet available]

Date: ***November 6, 2003***
Country: ***Poland***
Adjudicating Court: ***Supreme Court***
Number: ***III CZP 61/03***
Parties: ***Unknown***

Keywords

UNIDROIT PRINCIPLES – MEANS OF INTERPRETING DOMESTIC LAW (POLISH LAW)

PENALTY CLAUSES – WHETHER PENALTY IS DUE EVEN WHERE CREDITOR HAD SUFFERED NO LOSS – ANSWER IN THE AFFIRMATIVE – REFERENCE TO ART. 7.4.13 OF UNIDROIT PRINCIPLES

Abstract

Following conflicting decisions by different Chambers of the Supreme Court with respect to the question as to whether under Polish law a contractually stipulated penalty must be paid even where the creditor has suffered no loss, the Supreme Court was requested by the Attorney General to render an interpretative ruling on this issue. The Court, composed of seven Justices, issued the following Resolution: "If the contract provides for payment of a penalty in the case of non-performance or improper performance of an obligation, the debtor is not released from paying it even if it can prove that the creditor has not suffered any damage".

In its reasons, the Supreme Court mentioned that "the view expressed in this resolution is supported by legal solutions found in regulations of international contract law pertaining to the institution of contractual penalties", and in this context expressly referred to the UNIDROIT Principles. In particular the Court pointed out that "[i]n Art. 7.4.13 UNIDROIT Principles of International Commercial Contracts of May 1994 it has been stated that if a contract provides for the payment of penalty in case of default, then the other party shall have the right to claim the agreed amount, regardless of the scope of the incurred damage".

Full Text

[Not yet available]

Sources

Kindly provided by Prof. Stanislaw SOLTYSINSKI, Soltysinski Kawecki & Szlezak, Warsaw.
For positive comments on the Supreme Court's resolution see J. JASTRZEBSKI, Orzecznictwo Sadów Polskich No. 9/2004 (page 115); A. SLISZ, Monitor Prawniczy No. 8/2005 (page 406).

Date: ***March 4, 2004***
Adjudicating Court: ***Ad hoc Arbitration (place unknown)***
Number: ***Unknown***
Parties: ***Unknown***

Keywords

DISTRIBUTORSHIP AGREEMENT BETWEEN WESTERN EUROPEAN MANUFACTURER AND CENTRAL EUROPEAN DISTRIBUTOR – FRENCH LAW GOVERNING THE CONTRACT – REFERENCE TO UNIDROIT PRINCIPLES IN SUPPORT OF SOLUTIONS ADOPTED UNDER FRENCH LAW

GOOD FAITH PRINCIPLE ACCORDING TO ARTS. 1134(3) AND 1135 OF FRENCH CIVIL CODE RELEVANT ALSO IN INTERNATIONAL TRADE – ART. 1.7(1) OF UNIDROIT PRINCIPLES

GOOD FAITH AND CONTRACT NEGOTIATION – PARTIES ENTERING INTO NEGOTIATIONS WITH A VIEW TO SETTLE DISPUTE BOUND TO ACT IN GOOD FAITH IN SEARCH OF AMICABLE SOLUTION – DUTY TO NEGOTIATE IN GOOD FAITH NOT BREACHED BY MERELY REFUSING TERMS OF SETTLEMENT PROPOSED BY OTHER PARTY

GOOD FAITH AND CONTRACT PERFORMANCE – DISTRIBUTORSHIP AGREEMENT PROVIDING FOR YEARLY MINIMUM QUANTITIES OF GOODS TO BE PURCHASED BY DISTRIBUTOR – DISTRIBUTOR'S FAILURE TO MEET YEARLY QUOTA – MANUFACTURER'S CLAIM FOR BREACH OF CONTRACT CONTRARY TO GOOD FAITH WHERE DISTRIBUTOR PURCHASED A SUBSTANTIAL QUANTITY OF GOODS IN EXCESS OF YEARLY QUOTA AT THE END OF PREVIOUS YEAR AND ITS FAILURE TO PURCHASE GOODS THE FOLLOWING YEAR WAS DUE TO DISPUTE WITH MANUFACTURER

CONTRACT PROHIBITING DISTRIBUTOR FROM SELLING SIMILAR PRODUCTS FROM OTHER SUPPLIERS – DISTRIBUTOR NEVERTHELESS SELLING COMPETING GOODS – MANUFACTURER AWARE OF IT BUT NOT OBJECTING PREVENTED FROM INVOKING YEARS LATER DISTRIBUTOR'S BREACH OF CONTRACT – PROHIBITION OF INCONSISTENT BEHAVIOUR A GENERALLY ACCEPTED PRINCIPLE IN INTERNATIONAL TRADE – ART. 1.8 OF UNIDROIT PRINCIPLES 2004

Abstract

Defendant, a Central European company, had been contractually granted the right to distribute in its own territory products from Claimant, a Western European firm. When Claimant entered into an alliance with a third party, it decided to cease manufacturing the products in question. On the assumption that Claimant would therefore no longer be in a position to deliver the goods for distribution, Defendant ceased its own performance. Claimant sued Defendant for damages.

The distribution agreement was governed by French law, but both parties and the Arbitral Tribunal referred to the UNIDROIT Principles in support of the solutions provided by French law.

The Arbitral Tribunal first of all rejected Defendant's claim that Claimant, by rejecting Defendant's proposals for an amicable settlement, had breached its duty to act in good faith as imposed by Articles 1134(3) and 1135 of the French Civil Code as well as by the general principle governing international commercial relationships expressed in Article 1.7(1) of the UNIDROIT Principles. The Arbitral Tribunal held that, though parties were under a duty to negotiate in good faith, the mere fact that Claimant did not accept the terms of settlement proposed by Defendant does not constitute a breach of such duty.

Yet the Arbitral Tribunal also rejected Claimant's allegations that Defendant had breached the distribution agreement. With respect to the argument that Defendant had one year failed to purchase the agreed minimum quantities, it was true that in the year in question Defendant had not placed any order at all; however since in the previous year Defendant had not only met the annual quota but at the end of that year had placed a further substantial order, it would be contrary to good faith for Claimant to invoke the lack of orders in the following year and to fail to take into account the substantial extra order made at the very end of the previous year, all the more so as Claimant had delivered the goods only months later. As to the allegation that Defendant had breached its contractually agreed obligation not to sell competing goods purchased from other manufacturers, the Arbitral Tribunal, while not denying the truth of the facts, held that Claimant had been prevented by its own conduct from accusing Claimant of breach of the contract. Indeed Defendant had already distributed those competing goods at the time of the conclusion of the contract and continued to do so afterwards and Claimant, though being perfectly aware of the situation, made no objections. To invoke Defendant's violation of its contractual obligation all of a sudden at this late stage definitely amounts to a case of inconsistent behaviour which, according to the Arbitral Tribunal, was contrary to a well established principle of international trade as confirmed by Article 1.8 of the 2004 edition of the UNIDROIT Principles.

Full Text

A Central European company ("Central") had been contractually granted the right to distribute products from a Western European firm ("Western") in its own territory. When Western entered into an alliance with a third party, it decided to cease manufacturing those products. Central claimed this was preventing Western to continue to perform the distribution agreement and terminated its own performance. Western sued Central for damages. The UNIDROIT Principles were invoked in three different contexts, by the parties as well as by the sole arbitrator.

1. Central first invoked Western's alleged breach of good faith in the initial attempts to settle the dispute amicably :
"Respondent [...] reproaches Claimant with refusing to negotiate in good faith the consequences of its alleged decision to stop commercialisation of (the products); "Indeed, rather than entering into a serious negotiation, Claimant denied that commercialisation had been disrupted, denied that any exclusivity had been granted to Respondent ... and never seriously considered the loss suffered by Respondent by reason of this situation" ... This attitude would be in breach of the good faith requirements imposed by articles 1134 par. 3 and 1135 of the French civil code, as well as by the general principle governing international commercial relationships expressed in article 1.7 (1) of the UNIDROIT Principles on international commercial contracts.

Claimant responds by stating that the fact that Respondent has re-sold the (products) bought under the Purchase Contract without paying their price "does obviously not constitute fair dealing in international trade"..."

For the Tribunal, "The good faith principle expressed in articles 1134 par. 3 and 1135 of the French civil code is certainly also prevalent in international trade, as confirmed by article 1.7 (1) of the UNIDROIT Principles. When the dispute arose and parties entered into negotiations, both Claimant and Respondent were bound to act in good faith in search of an amicable solution. It turned out that the negotiation failed because of the excessive gap between Claimant's offer of price reduction ... and Respondent's claim ...

The mere fact that the parties did not agree on a compromise settlement does not in itself reveal lack on good faith on Claimant's side. (Western) saw no reason to grant large concessions on the remaining stock because it insisted that its (products) were still available ... , a fact that has been found to be accurate ... Claimant's views on the scope of (a preceding agreement between the parties) may not be shared by the Tribunal ... , but it had no apparent impact on the failure of the negotiations. Claimant's refusal to consider the different types of prejudice allegedly suffered by Respondent cannot certainly be considered as a breach of good faith since Claimant rightly denied that it was no longer in a position to perform its contractual obligations.

Consequently, the tribunal does not find that Claimant has breached the requirements of good faith during the negotiations that parties engaged into in order to reach an amicable settlement of their dispute".

2. Central had contractually undertaken to purchase yearly minimum quantities of the products. Central had already met its quota for 2001 when it purchased an important new quantity in November 2001, at a discount price. Due to the dispute, Central did not make any further purchases in 2002, leading Western to claim that the undertaking to purchase minimum quantities every year had been breached for that year. Should the November 2001 purchase be taken into account for 2002?

"Claimant claims ... damages amounting to Western's loss of profit computed on the minimum purchase amount provided in the Distribution Agreement for ... 2002 ...

Respondent claims that the Minimum Purchase Agreement was achieved in 2002, since Central purchased equipment for ¤ 846,728 , plus a discount of ¤ 60,000, mostly in the context of the Purchase Contract (of November 2001) …

Claimant considers that the amount of (products) purchased under the Purchase Contract cannot be taken into account under the Minimum Purchase Agreement for 2002, since the Purchase Contract was executed on November 13, 2001.

On this point, the Tribunal cannot accept Claimant's position, considering the circumstances. The Purchase Contract was agreed upon late in 2001, after Respondent had already achieved a very successful year of commercialising (the products). Respondent claims that it had bought equipment for over ¤ 1,000,000 (while the Minimum Purchase Agreement for that year was ¤ 600,000). After Claimant denied the truthfulness of the statement … , Respondent submitted invoices in support of this assertion ... Whatever the precise figures of the 2001 purchases were prior to the Purchase Contract, it is certain that during that year Respondent had exceeded its quota. It will be recalled … that Claimant awarded Respondent a "Quota Breaker Award" diploma for "achieving an outstanding level of sales activity and customers satisfaction for year 2001" …

The Purchase Contract was executed in November 2001, when the Minimum Purchase Agreement for 2001 was already fulfilled. It concerned a large quantity of equipment, which amounted to ¤ 843,176 net, excluding VAT, *i.e.* almost the amount of the whole Minimum Purchase Agreement for the following year (¤ 900,000). Deliveries were to take place in December 2001, at a time when it was obvious that most of the purchases could no longer be sold to clients during that year. This was even more so as Claimant itself failed to deliver in time, and the last supplies on the Purchase Contract could only take place in May, 2002.
Under such circumstances, the Tribunal finds that it would be contrary to good faith (art 1134 al. 3 of the French Civil code, article 1.7 of the UNIDROIT Principles) to rely on the sole date when the Purchase Contract was executed to refuse to take it into consideration when assessing Respondent's achievement of the MPA for 2002".

3. The Distribution Agreement prevented Central from selling similar products from other suppliers. However, it appeared that Central had never stopped selling the competing products it was selling before entering into the agreement, and that Western was aware of this situation. Before the Tribunal, Western claimed damages for breach of this undertaking. In a footnote to its decision, the Tribunal referred to the new article 1.8 of the UNIDROIT Principles.

"Claimant finally claims ¤ 100,000 as damages for the deterioration of Western's image on the … market, and ¤ 100,000 as damages for loss of profit, due to Central's alleged breach of its obligation not to sell competing products.

Article 4.4 of the Distribution Agreement provided that "Distributor agrees that it will not, during the term of this Agreement develop, manufacture, sell or promote, directly or indirectly, any equipment or device competitive with the Products constituting the subject matter of this Agreement, without a previous and specific authorization in writing from (Western)".

Claimant asserts than when visiting Central' warehouse in December 2002 ..., it was discovered that the inventory was composed "of all possible ... brands (of the products) present on the ... market". On January 15, 2003, a constat d'huissier established that Central's website offered all kinds of ... brands (of the product) to its customers.

Respondent does not deny that it had been selling competing products. It claims that Claimant did not suffer any prejudice from it, since in 2001, Central sold Western products well above the Minimum Purchase Agreement, while in 2002 and 2003, Western has decided to stop commercialisation of its (products) ...

In its written and oral testimonies, (Central's C.E.O.) also stated that Central had objected to article 4.4 when executing the Distribution Agreement, and had been assured that they were not requested to stop selling other brands; but the written confirmation Central had allegedly asked for never came ...

In practice, (Western) knew that Central was a multi-brand wholesale company and Western never objected to this until the dispute arose. According to (Central's C.E.O.), Western even accepted to contribute to marketing actions and promotion made by Central in proportion to Western's share as compared to other products ...

The Tribunal finds that the fact that Central has been selling competing products is undisputed. However, the apparent prohibition provided by article 4.4 of the Distribution Agreement has to be put in context. As Claimant's counsel explained in its oral pleadings, when Western decided to improve its penetration in ..., it approached Central because the latter firm was known as one of the top sellers on the market, already representing all major brands. Claimant knew from the start that Central was selling competing brands. If Claimant had really intended article 4.4 of the Distribution Agreement to be strictly enforced, it could have immediately verified that Central had terminated its relationship with other brands (*e.g.* by requiring a visit of Central's warehouse or checking Central's website in the early stages of the contractual relationship). No evidence is produced of such a concern before the dispute started.

On the contrary, (Central C.E.O.)'s assertion that Western contributed to the costs of marketing actions in proportion of its share as compared to other brands has not been denied by Claimant. This gives credibility to (Central C.E.O.)'s explanations about the assurances given to him that article 4.4 would cause no problem. Claimant's current reference to article 4.4 amounts to inconsistent behaviour, which is contrary to a well-established principle of international trade (*cf.* E. GAILLARD, L'interdiction de se contredire au détriment d'autrui comme principe général du droit du commerce international, Rev. Arb., 1985, pp. 241-2).

[Footnote: The existence of such principle will be confirmed by article 1.8 of the 2nd edition of the UNIDROIT Principles, due to appear in 2004. According to this provision, "A party cannot act inconsistently with an understanding it has caused the other party to have and upon which that other party reasonably has acted in reliance to its detriment"].

Consequently, the Tribunal does not admit Claimant's claims on this issue, relating to Western's alleged deterioration of image on the ... market and loss of profit".

Date: ***May 19, 2004***
Adjudicating Court: ***International Arbitration Court at the Chamber of Commerce and Industry of the Russian Federation***
Number: ***100/2002***
Parties: ***Unknown***

Keywords

SALES CONTRACT BETWEEN RUSSIAN BUYER AND INDIAN SELLER – CONTRACT GOVERNED BY CISG – RATE OF INTEREST – ISSUE NOT ADDRESSED IN CISG – TO BE DETERMINED BY APPLICABLE DOMESTIC LAW

ACCORDING TO ART. 395 OF RUSSIAN CIVIL CODE RATE OF INTEREST TO BE DETERMINED IN ACCORDANCE WITH RATE OF BANK INTEREST EXISTING ON THE DAY OF PERFORMANCE OF MONETARY OBLIGATION AT PLACE OF LOCATION OF CREDITOR – NO RATE OF BANK INTEREST FOR INDIAN CURRENCY IN RUSSIAN FEDERATION – REFERENCE TO UNIDROIT PRINCIPLES AS REFLECTING INTERNATIONAL TRADE PRACTICES

ACCORDING TO ART. 7.4.9(2) UNIDROIT PRINCIPLES RATE OF INTEREST SHALL BE AVERAGE BANK SHORT-TERM LENDING RATE TO PRIME BORROWERS PREVAILING FOR CURRENCY OF PAYMENT AT PLACE FOR PAYMENT, OR WHERE NO SUCH RATE EXISTS AT THAT PLACE, THEN SAME RATE IN STATE OF CURRENCY OF PAYMENT – REFERENCE TO RATE INTEREST USED BY CENTRAL BANK OF INDIA

Abstract

Russian Buyer (Claimant) claimed from Indian Seller (Respondent) damages for non-delivery of the goods. Among others Claimant asked for the interest on the amount of the price paid in advance in Indian currency.

The law applicable to the contract was CISG.

Since the parties disputed the applicable rate of interest and CISG did not regulate this question the Arbitration Court, noting that the issue is not addressed in CISG, referred to Article 395 of the Russian Civil Code which provides that the rate of interest is to be determined according to the rate of bank interest on the day of performance of the monetary obligation at the place where the creditor is located. However, since in the Russian Federation, *i.e.* the place where the creditor was located, there is no rate of bank interest for Indian currency, the Arbitration Court decided to apply the international trade practice adopted in such cases as reflected in the UNIDROIT Principles of International Commercial Contracts. And since Article 7.4.9 (paragraph 2) of the UNIDROIT Principles provides that the rate of interest shall be the average bank short-term lending rate to prime borrowers prevailing for the currency of payment at the place for payment, or where no such rate exists at that place, then the same rate in the State of the currency of payment, the Arbitration Court applied the corresponding rate of interest used by the Reserve Bank of India.

Full Text

[Not yet available]

Date: ***November 12, 2004***
Country: ***Switzerland***
Adjudicating Court: ***Handelsgericht St. Gallen***
Number: ***Unknown***
Parties: ***Unknown***

Keywords

PARTIES' CHOICE OF A-NATIONAL RULES OF LAW AS THE LAW GOVERNING THE CONTRACT – ADMISSIBLE PROVIDED THAT THE RULES IN QUESTION ARE TRANSNATIONAL IN CHARACTER AND SUFFICIENTLY COHERENT AND BALANCED AS TO CONTENT – EXPRESS REFERENCE TO THE UNIDROIT PRINCIPLES

PARTIES' CHOICE OF THE FIFA RULES AS THE LAW GOVERNING THE CONTRACT - ADMISSIBLE

Abstract

Plaintiff, a Swiss company, entered into a contract with Defendant, a Greek company, for the transfer of a football player managed by Plaintiff. The contract contained a forum selection clause in favour of the Swiss court and a choice of law clause stating that "this agreement is governed by FIFA Rules and Swiss law". The FIFA Rules provide, among others, a two-year limitation period for claims arising out of this kind of contract.

Four years after the conclusion of the contract Plaintiff brought an action against Defendant for breach of contract. Since the limitation period provided by the FIFA Rules is shorter than the corresponding limitation period under Swiss law, the question arose as to whether the parties' reference to FIFA Rules constituted a valid choice of the applicable law with the consequence that the FIFA Rules as *lex specialis* would prevail over Swiss law.

According to the Court in the case at hand the FIFA Rules applied as the law governing the contract. It is true that in Switzerland opinions are divided as to whether in disputes before domestic courts parties are entitled to choose anational or supranational rules of law as the law governing their contract. However the prevailing view seems to be in the affirmative provided that the rules in question are transnational in character and sufficiently coherent and balanced as to content, as is the case of the UNIDROIT Principles.

In adhering to this prevailing view the Court expressly stated that according to these criteria the FIFA Rules are comparable to the UNIDROIT Principles and could therefore be likewise chosen as the law governing the contract.

As to the merits, the Court rejected the claim on the ground that it had not been made within the two year limitation period provided by the FIFA Rules.

Full Text

I.

Am 16. August 1999 schlossen der Vertreter von X. AG (Klägerin), FIFA-Agent Y., und P. F.C. (Beklagte) einen Vertrag. Gegenstand dieser Vereinbarung war der Transfer des von X. AG vertretenen Spielers Z. Als Gegenleistung wurde vereinbart, dass P. F.C. bis am 30. September 1999 USD 15'000.-- und bis am 30. Dezember 1999 weitere USD 15'000.-- bezahlt, wenn der Arbeitsvertrag bis 30. Juni 2000 verlängert wird. Wird der Arbeitsvertrag um zwei weitere Jahre bis 30. Juni 2002 verlängert, so hat P. F.C. weitere USD 30'000.-- bis am 30. Dezember 2000 und nochmals USD 30'000.-- bis am 30. Dezember 2001 zu bezahlen.

Am 5. Februar 2003 reichte X. AG Klage gegen P. F.C. auf Bezahlung von USD 15'000.-- nebst 5 % Zins seit 30. September 1999, von USD 15'000.-- nebst 5 % seit 30. Dezember 1999 und USD 30'000.-- nebst 5 % Zins seit 30. Dezember 2000 beim Handelsgericht des Kantons St. Gallen ein.

[...]

III.

1. Die Parteien haben in der besagten Vereinbarung unter Ziff. 3 abgemacht, dass auf die Vereinbarung das Regelwerk der FIFA ("FIFA rules") und schweizerisches Recht anwendbar sind (kläg. act. 1a.1). Die schweizerische Klägerin und die griechische Beklagte können im Bereich Obligationenrecht, wenn es sich wie vorliegend nicht um einen vom IPRG speziell geregelten Vertrag handelt, eine Rechtswahl vornehmen. Die Formerfordernisse aus Abs. 2 sind erfüllt (Art. 116 IPRG). Zwingend anwendbare Gesetzesbestimmungen sind keine zu berücksichtigen (Art. 18 IPRG). Die Parteien haben vorliegend eine kumulative Rechtswahl getroffen: schweizerisches Recht und das FIFA-Regelwerk sind auf den Vertrag vom 16. August 1999 anwendbar.

2. Es stellt sich die Frage, ob das FIFA-Regelwerk als anationales Recht Gegenstand einer Rechtswahl sein kann.

Im Rahmen der ordentlichen Gerichtsbarkeit wird teilweise abgelehnt, dass anationales Recht gewählt werden kann, mit dem Argument, dass ein hoheitlich eingesetztes Gericht immer staatliches Recht anzuwenden habe (VISCHER, Internationales Vertragsrecht, Bern 1962, S. 62; HEINI, Festschrift für Prof. Dr. Rudolf Moser (Hrsg. SCHWANDER), Zürich 1987, S. 71f.; KNOEPFLER, Le contrat dans le nouveau droit international privé suisse, in: DESSEMONTET (Hrsg.), Le nouveau droit international privé suisse, Lausanne 1988, S. 87); von anderen aber bejaht (PATOCCHI, Das neue internationale Vertragsrecht der Schweiz, in: Schriftenreihe SAV Bd 7, S. 36). Von SIEHR und AMSTUTZ/VOGT/WANG wird die Meinung vertreten, dass für staatliche Gerichte die Wahl ausserstaatlichen Rechts präzise sei, wenn in der konkreten Materie hinreichende Quelle für ein internationales Recht des Welthandels, für ein "new law merchant" oder ein transnationales Recht vorhanden seien (SIEHR, Festschrift für Max Keller zum 65. Geburtstag (Hrsg. FORSTMOSER), Zürich 1999, S. 501 f.). Wenn Rechtsgrundsätze, die eine dem Rechtssicherheitsgedanken genügende innere Kohärenz sowie einen dem Posultat der Einzelfallgerechtigkeit Rechnung tragenden materiellen Gehalt aufweisen wie z.B. die UNIDROIT Principles, so sei eine solche Verweisung zuzulassen (AMSTUTZ/VOGT/WANG, Kommentar zum schweizerischen Privatrecht, Basel 1996, Art. 116 N 21).

Das FIFA-Regelwerk kann insoweit den UNIDROIT Principles gleichgestellt werden, da es sowohl eine genügende innere Kohärenz als auch einen materiellen Gehalt aufweist, der dem Postulat der Einzelfallgerechtigkeit sicherlich Rechnung trägt. Zudem kann ihm auch "Transnationalität" zugeschrieben werden, da der FIFA weltweit nationale Verbände angehören, die Kraft ihrer Mitgliedschaft die Statuten, Reglemente und Entscheide der FIFA zu befolgen haben (Art. 10 Abs. 4 FIFA-Statuten).

3. Aufgrund dieser gültigen Rechtswahlvereinbarung hat das Handelsgericht St. Gallen grundsätzlich nicht nur schweizerisches Recht, sondern auch das FIFA-Regelwerk zu berücksichtigen.

Bezüglich der streitigen Forderung ist genauer zu untersuchen, ob das FIFA-Regelwerk als *lex specialis* eine adäquate Regelung enthält oder ob allenfalls die Anwendung von schweizerischem Recht im unterbreiteten Fall passender erscheint.

Das FIFA-Reglement ist gegenüber dem schweizerischen Recht als *lex specialis* ausgestaltet, das speziell für Spielervermittlungen ein Reglement erlassen hat (Circular No. 803). Die Klägerin liess sich bei der Vereinbarung mit der Beklagten von einem FIFA-Agenten vertreten.

In Art. 22 des Spielervermittler-Reglements vom 10. Dezember 2000, welches die Tätigkeit von Spielervermittlern regelt, wird festgehalten, dass bei Streitigkeiten zwischen einem Verein und/oder einem zweiten Spielervermittler und einem Spielervermittler, die beim gleichen Verband registriert sind (nationale Streitigkeiten), der betroffene Verband zuständig ist (Abs. 1). Jede andere Beschwerde, die nicht unter Abs. 1 fällt, ist der Spielerstatut-Kommission der FIFA zu unterbreiten. Weiter sind die Beschwerden im Zusammenhang mit der Tätigkeit eines Spielervermittlers in schriftlicher Form an den zuständigen Nationalverband bzw. an die FIFA zu richten. Solche Beschwerden sind bis spätestens zwei Jahre nach den ihr zugrunde liegenden Vorfällen und auf jeden Fall binnen sechs Monaten, nachdem der betreffende Vermittler seine Tätigkeit aufgegeben hat, einzureichen.

Allerdings enthält das Spielervermittlerreglement für die Regelung von Streitigkeiten über nicht bezahlte Vermittlungsgelder keine materielle Bestimmungen. Es ist aber geregelt, dass "Beschwerden" innerhalb von zwei Jahren nach dem Vorfall bei der Spielerstatutkommission vorzulegen sind. Diese Frist ist als Verwirkungsfrist zu betrachten. Die Verwirkung ist insofern von der Verjährung zu unterscheiden, als dass erstere zum Untergang des betreffenden Rechts führt, letztere zum Verlust der Durchsetzbarkeit (GAUCH/SCHLUEP/SCHMID/REY, Schweizerisches Obligationenrecht Allgemeiner Teil, Bd. II, Zürich 2003, N 3574). Art. 22 Abs. 3 des Spielerreglements ist derart formuliert, dass nach zwei Jahren "Beschwerden" nicht mehr unterbreitet werden können, was einem Verlust des subjektiven Recht gleich kommt. Diese Regelung erscheint nachvollziehbar, da es sich bei der Spielervermittlertätigkeit um ein schnelllebiges Geschäft handelt und die FIFA ein Interesse hat, Streitigkeiten in diesem Bereich rasch zu erledigen. Zudem dürfte es kaum im Sinne der FIFA sein, wenn Art. 22 Abs. 3 des Spielerreglements so interpretiert würde, dass die Beschwerden in den ersten zwei Jahren der Spielerstatut-Kommission und danach staatlichen Gerichten zu unterbreiten sind.

4. Angesichts des Vorrangs des FIFA-Regelwerks gegenüber dem schweizerischen Recht greift Art. 22 Abs. 3 des Spielerreglements und somit auch die zweijährige Verwirkungsfrist im vorliegenden Fall. Dies bedeutet, dass die zugrunde liegenden Vorfälle für die "Beschwerden" in den abgesprochenen Verfalltagen zu sehen sind. Für die letzte, von der Klägerin geltend gemachte Forderung von USD 30'000.-- war der 31. Dezember 2000 als Verfalltag vereinbart worden. Nach Art. 102 Abs. 2 OR ist der Schuldnerverzug mit Ablauf des Verfalltages eingetreten. Im Zeitpunkt der Klageeinreichung am 5. Februar 2003 war die zweijährige Verwirkungsfrist bereits abgelaufen, womit die Klage abzuweisen ist.

Date: ***November 12, 2004***
Adjudicating Court: ***International Arbitration Court at the Chamber of Commerce and Industry of the Russian Federation***
Number: ***174/2003***
Parties: ***Unknown***

Keywords

SALES CONTRACT BETWEEN RUSSIAN SELLER AND HUNGARIAN BUYER – PARTIES CHOOSE RUSSIAN LAW TO GOVERN THEIR CONTRACT – HUNGARIAN BUYER INVOKED ALSO APPLICATION OF THE UNIDROIT PRINCIPLES AS USAGE OF INTERNATIONAL TRADE – RUSSIAN SELLER OBJECTED – ARBITRATION COURT DECIDED NOT TO APPLY THE UNIDROIT PRINCIPLES

Abstract

Seller (a Russian company) claimed from Buyer (a Hungarian company) compensation for lost profit as a consequence of a breach of the contract for the sale of goods.

The parties had agreed that the contract was governed by Russian law.

In its arguments the Respondent invoked also the application of the UNIDROIT Principles of International Commercial Contracts which it argued were applicable as they reflected recognized international standards and were becoming a usage of international trade. However the Claimant did not agree to the application of the UNIDROIT Principles in the case at hand.

The Arbitration Court decided not to apply the UNIDROIT Principles in the case at hand as the contract did not provide for their application and the Claimant expressly objected to their application in the course of the arbitral proceedings.

Full Text

[Not yet available]

Sources

Provided by Professor Alexander KOMAROV.

Date: **December 22, 2004**
Adjudicating Court: ***Tribunal of International Commercial Arbitration at the Ukrainian Chamber of Commerce and Trade***
Number: ***Unknown***
Parties: ***Unknown***

Keywords

SALES CONTRACT BETWEEN AN UKRAINIAN SELLER AND A FOREIGN BUYER – PARTIES' REFERENCE TO CISG, THE LEX MERCATORIA AND THE UNIDROIT PRINCIPLES AS THE LAW APPLICABLE TO THE CONTRACT – ARBITRAL TRIBUNAL'S DECISION BASED ON THE LAW OF UKRAINE

Abstract

A sales contract between a foreign buyer and an Ukrainian seller contained an arbitration clause in favour of the Tribunal of International Commercial Arbitration at the Ukrainian Chamber of Commerce and Trade and provided that the law applicable to the contractual relations between the parties and the arbitration would be the U.N. Convention on Contracts for the International Sale of Goods (CISG), the *lex mercatoria* and the UNIDROIT Principles of International Commercial Contracts (1994 edition). Since according to Art. 6 of the Ukrainian Law on Foreign Economic Activity, where the national law of neither party to the contract has been chosen as the applicable law, the applicable law shall be the law of the country in which the seller is situated, the Arbitral Tribunal decided that in the case at hand also the law of Ukraine was applicable.

Faced with the questions as to whether or not the limitation period may be applied by the court only upon request by a party and of what was the length of the limitation period for a claim for the recovery of a penalty, the Arbitral Tribunal based its decision on the relevant provisions of the Ukrainian Civil Code and Commercial Code.

Full Text

[Not yet available]

Sources

Advopkatura, No. 33-36 of February 2005 (reference taken from *http://www.cisg.law.pace.edu/cisg/wais/db/cases2041222u5.html*).

Date: ***January 11, 2005***
Adjudicating Court: ***Tribunale Padova – Sez. Este***
Number: ***Unknown***
Parties: ***Unknown***

Keywords

REFERENCE BY PARTIES TO "THE LAWS AND REGULATIONS OF THE INTERNATIONAL CHAMBER OF COMMERCE, PARIS, FRANCE" AS THE LAW GOVERNING THEIR CONTRACT – INEFFECTIVE BECAUSE TOO VAGUE AND IMPRECISE

REFERENCE BY PARTIES TO LEX MERCATORIA, UNIDROIT PRINCIPLES OR CISG (IN CASES WHERE CISG IS NOT APPLICABLE) AS THE LAW GOVERNING THE CONTRACT – NOT VERITABLE CHOICE OF LAW CLAUSE – MERELY AMOUNTS TO INCORPORATION OF SUCH NON-BINDING RULES INTO THE CONTRACT

REQUIREMENT CONTRACTS – COVERED BY CISG

SUPPLIER'S FAILURE TO DELIVER GOODS – AMOUNTS TO FUNDAMENTAL BREACH – BUYER ENTITLED TO TERMINATE CONTRACT (ART. 49(1)(B) CISG) - CONDITIONS

Abstract

Plaintiff, a Slovene rabbit breeder, entered into a contract with Defendant, an Italian company, for the supply on a regular basis of rabbits. The rabbits were raised by Plaintiff using special reproduction rabbits supplied by a third company. Subsequently Defendant asked Plaintiff to acquire the reproduction rabbits from a different company which however refused to supply the requested reproduction rabbits to the Plaintiff on the ground that the hygienic conditions on the Plaintiff's farm were inadequate. Faced with Plaintiff's failure to continue to supply rabbits, Defendant terminated the contract alleging breach of contract by Plaintiff. Plaintiff brought an action to have the termination declared unjustified and claimed damages.

The Court found that the contract was governed by CISG. Indeed, at the time the contract was concluded both Italy and Slovenia had ratified the Convention. As to the material scope of application, the Court held that the notion of sales contract underlying the Convention was broad enough to encompass not only contracts for a single delivery of goods or for delivery by instalments but also so-called requirement contracts involving the supply of goods on a regular basis in quantities as required by the buyer.

The contract contained a clause stating that "[t]his contract shall be governed by the laws and regulations of the International Chamber of Commerce of Paris, France", but the Court rejected the argument that such a provision could amount to a tacit exclusion of CISG. According to Italian conflict of law rules parties are free to choose the applicable law but in so doing they must choose a particular domestic law. A reference by the parties to non-State rules of supranational or transnational character such as the *lex mercatoria*, the UNIDROIT Principles or CISG in cases where the Convention as such is not applicable cannot be considered a veritable choice of law by the parties but amounts to an incorporation of such rules into the contract with the consequence that they will bind the parties only to the extent that they do not conflict with the mandatory rules of the applicable domestic law. In the case at hand even such incorporation into the contract must be excluded since the reference to "laws and regulations of the International Chamber of Commerce of Paris, France" was clearly too vague as to permit a precise identification of the kind of rules the parties had in mind.

As to the merits of the case, the Court held that the termination of the contract by Defendant was justified. Indeed the Plaintiff's failure to continue to supply rabbits amounted to a fundamental breach which entitled Defendant to terminate the contract in accordance with Articles 25 and 49(1)(b). It is true that according to Article 49(1)(b) the right to terminate presupposes that the non-performing party fails to deliver the goods within the additional period of time fixed by the aggrieved party or declares that it will not deliver within that period, and that Defendant has not fixed such an additional period of time. However, the Court held that in the case at hand there was no need to fix such an additional period of time since all parties involved had known from the outset that Plaintiff in the circumstances would have been in a position to deliver the rabbits only several months later.

Full Text

SVOLGIMENTO DEL PROCESSO

Con atto di citazione notificato il 21 marzo 2001, Ostroznik Savo, titolare dell'impresa denominata Vzerja Kuncev con sede in Celje (Repubblica Slovena), e Eurotrafic s.r.l. con sede in Feltre (BL) convenivano in giudizio La Faraona soc. coop. a r.l. con sede in Montagnana (PD) e la Banca di Credito Cooperativo di Roveredo di Guà (VR), sostenendo:

- che dal 1999 Eurotrafic s.r.l., depositaria in Italia della genetica francese Hyla per la cunicultura, forniva animali riproduttori alla ditta slovena;

- che il 7 luglio 1998 era stato stipulato un accordo tra i due attori, in base al quale Eurotrafic s.r.l. si era obbligata ad acquistare la produzione di conigli dell'allevamento sloveno, frutto di genetica Hyla;

- che Eurotrafic s.r.l. vendeva poi alla cooperativa La Faraona gli animali importati;

- che con successivo contratto 3 maggio 1999 si era pattuito che Ostroznik Savo vendesse direttamente i conigli alla cooperativa di Montagnana, la quale si obbligava a pagare a Eurotrafic s.r.l. una provvigione di £ 100 per ogni chilogrammo di carne viva acquistato dalla ditta slovena;

- che il 14 maggio 1999 la banca convenuta si costituiva fideiussore di La Faraona, garantendo a favore di Ostroznik Savo le obbligazioni della cooperativa fino all'ammontare di £ 35.000.000;

- che i rapporti si erano svolti regolarmente, fintanto che i responsabili della cooperativa si erano recati in Slovenia per consigliare all'attore di effettuare il "vuoto sanitario" e cambiare la genetica delle fattrici;

- che Ostroznik Savo, confidando nelle promesse dei responsabili della cooperativa, accettava di effettuare il "vuoto sanitario", svendendo gli animali presenti nell'allevamento, e di adottare la genetica della ditta Grimaud Italia;

- che senza motivo Grimaud Italia non forniva i conigli della genetica indicata, sicché Ostroznik Savo non era più in grado di consegnare animali alla cooperativa di Montagnana;

- che quest'ultima, con lettera 6 luglio 2000, risolveva unilateralmente il contratto, adducendo l'indisponibilità degli allevamenti di Ostroznik Savo a fornire conigli;

- che l'impossibilità a continuare le forniture dipendeva però dalla convenuta, la quale da un lato aveva richiesto il "vuoto sanitario" e dall'altro non si era adoperata affinché la ditta Grimaud consegnasse i propri riproduttori;

- che l'ingiustificata "rottura" del contratto aveva cagionato un rilevante danno a Ostroznik Savo, che aveva venduto a prezzo di carne da macello i riproduttori Hyla e si era trovato con un allevamento improduttivo;

- che Ostroznik Savo aveva tentato senza esito di escutere la garanzia bancaria;

- che La Faraona, contravvenendo a quanto pattuito al momento della cessione del contratto ed inducendo la ditta slovena a mutare genetica, aveva causato un danno anche a Eurotrafic s.r.l., consistente nella perdita della provvigione.

Ostroznik Savo e Eurotrafic s.r.l. chiedevano, pertanto, che la cooperativa La Faraona fosse dichiarata responsabile per inadempimento contrattuale e condannata al risarcimento dei danni a favore di entrambi gli attori; Ostroznik Savo chiedeva, inoltre, che la banca convenuta fosse condannata, in forza della prestata fideiussione, a pagargli la somma di £ 35.000.000.

Si costituiva La Faraona soc. coop a r.l., affermando:

- che con contratto del 7 luglio 1998 essa si era effettivamente impegnata a riconoscere a Eurotrafic s.r.l. una provvigione;

- che con successivo accordo del 3 maggio 1999, intervenuto tra tutte le parti, il contratto del 1998 veniva sostituito con un nuovo contratto, che prevedeva l'obbligo di La Faraona di acquistare tutta la produzione di conigli di Ostroznik Savo, precisando che gli animali dovevano essere esenti da malattie e malformazioni (dovendo poi essere allevati per l'ingrasso e la macellazione nelle strutture dei soci della cooperativa);

- che era pattuito che il contratto fosse regolato dalle leggi e regolamenti della Camera di Commercio internazionale di Parigi;

- che dall'inizio delle forniture La Faraona constatava che i conigli, oltre a non rispettare i quantitativi stabiliti, presentavano problemi sanitari e gravi "deficienze all'ingrasso", nel senso che, pur allevati secondo le specifiche tecniche, rimanevano sottopeso;

- che per risolvere i problemi Ostroznik Savo decideva liberamente di cambiare le fattrici, prendendo quelle della Grimaud Italia s.r.l., filiale italiana di nota società francese del settore;
- che quest'ultima società, conoscendo solo la convenuta, si rendeva disponibile alla fornitura, a condizione però che La Faraona trattenesse sulle somme da pagare a titolo corrispettivo alla ditta slovena una quota da rimettere direttamente a Grimaud, in modo che essa non dovesse richiedere pagamenti ad Ostroznik Savo;

- che Ostroznik Savo doveva effettuare, prima di ricevere le fattrici, il così detto "vuoto sanitario", purificando l'allevamento, al fine di evitare che le nuove fattrici venissero contaminate da preesistenti patologie;

- che, quando Grimaud avrebbe dovuto consegnare gli animali, l'allevamento non era ancora stato purificato (persisteva il vecchio letame e diffusa sporcizia), sicché Grimaud si rifiutava di consegnare le proprie fattrici;

- che conseguentemente Ostroznik Savo non era più in grado di fornire conigli alla cooperativa italiana, che perciò si decideva a risolvere il contratto con lettere del 6 luglio 2000;

- che, poiché l'attore non aveva rispettato nella fornitura le quantità e qualità promesse, il negozio di fideiussione non veniva perfezionato;

- che nulla era dovuto a Eurotrafic s.r.l., sia perché il contratto del 3 maggio 1999 non prevedeva alcuna provvigione, sia perché il rapporto negoziale è stato comunque risolto per inadempimento di Ostroznik Savo;

- che il predetto contratto conteneva all'articolo 7 una clausola compromissoria, la quale, attraverso il rinvio alle leggi e regolamenti della Camera di Commercio Internazionale di Parigi, affidava ogni controversia alla stessa Camera Arbitrale, con conseguente carenza di giurisdizione del giudice ordinario.

Per queste ragioni, La Faraona soc. coop a r.l. chiedeva, in via preliminare, che il giudice dichiarasse il difetto di giurisdizione, unica competente a risolvere la controversia essendo la Camera Arbitrale della Camera di Commercio Internazionale di Parigi, e nel merito che respingesse le domanda formulate dagli attori, pronunciando la risoluzione del contratto del 3 maggio 1999 per inadempimento di Ostroznik Savo e condannando quest'ultimo al risarcimento dei danni, con riserva di loro quantificazione in separato giudizio.

Si costituiva altresì la Banca di Credito Cooperativo di Roveredo di Guà, sostenendo che la fideiussione bancaria era stata anticipatamente estinta e che, comunque, venuto meno il contratto di fornitura, la garanzia era divenuta inefficace. Affermava infatti la convenuta che la fideiussione garantiva esclusivamente il pagamento delle fatture emesse in seguito a consegna di conigli svezzati, e non anche debiti di natura risarcitoria. In ogni caso, la banca chiedeva di essere manlevata dalla cooperativa La Faraona.

In via principale, la Banca di Credito Cooperativo di Roveredo di Guà domandava pertanto il rigetto della domanda proposta nei suoi confronti da Ostroznik Savo; in via riconvenzionale, domandava che La Faraona soc. coop a r.l. fosse dichiarata tenuta a manlevare la banca in caso di sua soccombenza.

Nel corso dell'istruttoria venivano assunte le deposizioni di De Carli Gianni, Hrastnik Uros, Carlo Orlando, Candeo Tonino e Fruscalzo Giovanni.

All'udienza del 22 settembre 2004, le parti precisavano le proprie conclusioni e la causa era trattenuta in decisione allo scadere dei termini concessi per il deposito delle comparse conclusionali e delle memorie di replica.

MOTIVAZIONE

Preliminarmente, occorre esaminare le eccezioni processuali sollevate dalla società cooperativa La Faraona.

L'art. 5 del contratto prevede testualmente che "in caso di disputa tra le parti contraenti sulla qualità del prodotto al momento della consegna, la decisione finale dovrà essere arbitrata dalla Camera di Commercio Ufficiale Italo-Slovena di Milano, Italia o qualsiasi altra Agenzia Ispettiva Ufficiale concordata reciprocamente". L'art. 7 dispone invece che il contratto "dovrà essere governato dalle leggi e dalle regolamentazioni della Camera di Commercio Internazionale di Parigi, Francia".

Il primo articolo non trova nella specie applicazione, poiché – se è vero che la cooperativa convenuta si lamenta in comparsa di costituzione della qualità dei conigli forniti da Ostroznik Savo – non è questa la ragione invocata per giustificare la risoluzione del contratto, bensì il fatto che l'attore avrebbe cessato, per causa a sé imputabile, di approvvigionare la convenuta. La controversia non verte pertanto sulla qualità di una o più partite di conigli, sì da richiedere, conformemente alla volontà dei contraenti, l'esame degli animali da parte di una qualificata commissione tecnica (indicata in contratto come "agenzia ispettiva"). Si è per tali ragioni al di fuori dell'ambito di operatività della clausola compromissoria voluta dai contraenti, espressamente limitata alla soluzione delle dispute concernenti la "qualità del prodotto al momento della consegna" (si aggiunga, peraltro, che la convenuta non ha fornito prova della presenza in Milano di una Camera di Commercio Ufficiale Italo-Slovena, e non essendo la sua esistenza un dato notorio può seriamente dubitarsi dell'efficacia della clausola).

Maggiore attenzione merita il secondo articolo, con cui sembrerebbe che le parti abbiano inteso sottoporre il loro rapporto alla "legge della Camera di Commercio Internazionale di Parigi", con ciò escludendo l'applicabilità sia del diritto nazionale italiano (ed anche sloveno), sia della Convenzione delle Nazioni Unite del 1980 sui contratti di vendita internazionale di beni mobili.

Si osserva, innanzitutto, che la presente controversia riguarda un rapporto d'indubbio carattere internazionale. Da ciò discende la necessità d'individuare il diritto sostanziale applicabile. Si potrebbe ritenere che l'individuazione debba essere compiuta sulla base delle norme di diritto internazionale privato, poiché esse rappresentano lo strumento più idoneo allo scopo (ed appositamente creato).

A questa soluzione "internazionalprivatistica" occorre preferirne una diversa, che favorisca, in quanto possibile, l'applicazione di norme di diritto sostanziale, quali quelle poste dalla Convenzione delle Nazioni Unite sui contratti di vendita internazionale di beni mobili del 1980, ratificata con legge 11 dicembre 1985, n. 765, ed entrata in vigore il 1° gennaio 1988 (v. Trib. Pavia, 29 dicembre 1999, in Corriere giuridico 2000, 932 s.; Trib. Vigevano, 12 luglio 2000, in Giurisprudenza italiana 2001, 280 ss.; Trib. Rimini, 26 novembre 2002, in Giurisprudenza italiana 2003, 896 ss.; Trib. Padova, 25 febbraio 2004, in Giurisprudenza italiana 2004, 1405 ss.; Trib. Padova, 31 marzo 2004, in Giurisprudenza di merito 2004, 1065 ss.).

La prevalenza della Convenzione delle Nazioni Unite (che è indubbiamente convenzione di diritto materiale uniforme, e non di diritto internazionale privato, come talvolta erroneamente affermato), sulle norme di diritto internazionale privato, è anzitutto dovuta al fatto che l'ambito di applicazione della Convenzione è speciale, poiché più limitato, rispetto a quello, più generale, delle norme di diritto internazionale privato. Essa, infatti, regola soltanto i contratti di vendita la cui internazionalità dipende dalla diversa ubicazione statale della sede d'affari delle parti contraenti, mentre - com'è noto – le norme di diritto internazionale privato riguardano ogni tipo di contratto "internazionale", senza limitazioni di sorta.

A giudizio del Tribunale, la specialità – e dunque la prevalenza – delle norme di diritto materiale uniforme si fonda, in secondo luogo, su altra considerazione che attiene al loro contenuto. Le norme di diritto materiale sono da considerarsi speciali perché risolvono "direttamente" le questioni sostanziale su cui verte la controversia, ossia evitando il doppio passaggio, consistente nell'individuazione del diritto applicabile prima e nell'applicazione poi dello stesso, che sempre si rende necessario quando si fa ricorso al diritto internazionale privato.

Ciò premesso, e passando all'esame dei presupposti di applicazione della Convenzione delle Nazioni Unite, si rileva che essa richiede la sussistenza di più condizioni.

Dal punto di vista materiale, occorre che il contratto sia un contratto di compravendita, di cui tuttavia la Convenzione non dà alcuna definizione. La mancanza di una definizione espressa non deve però indurre a ricorrere ad una definizione "nazionale", come ad esempio quella prevista dall'art. 1470 c.c. Il concetto di "compravendita" previsto dalla Convenzione deve piuttosto essere ricavato, come d'altronde la maggior parte dei concetti (tra i quali anche quello di "sede d'affari", di "residenza abituale", di "beni", ma non anche quello di "diritto internazionale privato", che corrisponde alla nozione propria del foro investito della controversia), in modo autonomo, ossia senza ricorrere a categorie peculiari di un determinato ordinamento. A tale proposito diventa rilevante il disposto degli artt. 30 e 53 della Convenzione (così anche Trib. Padova, 25 febbraio 2004, cit.; Trib. Rimini, cit.; Tribunal cantonal de Vaud, 11 marzo 1996, n. 01 93 1061, pubblicata in internet all'indirizzo *http://www.unilex.info/case.cfm?pid=1&do=case&id=302&step*), da cui si evince che è contratto di compravendita, alla luce della Convenzione, il contratto in forza del quale il venditore è obbligato a consegnare i beni, trasferirne la proprietà ed eventualmente rilasciare tutti i documenti relativi ad essi, mentre il compratore è obbligato a pagare il prezzo ed a prendere in consegna i beni.

Ci si deve chiedere a questo punto se il rapporto contrattuale oggetto della presente controversia, che nella prospettiva del diritto italiano verrebbe qualificato di somministrazione, rientri nell'ambito di applicazione ratione materiae della Convenzione. Alla domanda può darsi risposta affermativa (anche alla luce della giurisprudenza straniera di cui si deve tenere conto in virtù dell'art. 7, comma 1°, della Convenzione, la quale ha sempre ricompreso il contratto di somministrazione tra quelli rientranti nell'ambito di applicazione materiale della Convenzione: v., ad esempio, Cour d'appel de Colmar, 12 giugno 2001, pubblicata in internet all'indirizzo [...]; LG Ellwangen, 21 agosto 1995, pubblicata in internet al seguente indirizzo: CISG-online 279), giacché scopo della Convenzione è disciplinare tutti i contratti internazionali in cui vi è consegna di beni mobili e trasferimento della loro proprietà contro il pagamento di un prezzo, a prescindere dalla qualificazione giuridica che, secondo gli ordinamenti nazionali, tale operazione economica può assumere.

La risposta affermativa trova poi conferma nel dettato della Convenzione: l'art. 73 fa rientrare nel proprio ambito di applicazione tutti i "*contracts for the delivery of goods by installments*" ossia i "*contrats à livraisons successives*", espressioni che nel testo (non ufficiale) pubblicato nella Gazzetta Ufficiale sono state tradotte con la locuzione "contratto a consegne successive". Sulla base di ciò, la dottrina italiana ha creduto giustamente di dovere ricondurre alla normativa uniforme la vendita a consegne ripartite, essendo questa certamente "*contrats à livraisons successives*".

Non potendosi, tuttavia, dedurre dalla disciplina uniforme che la ripartizione delle diverse livraisons attenga esclusivamente alle modalità di esecuzione della prestazione di consegna, mentre l'effetto traslativo debba comunque verificarsi al momento della stipulazione (come nel caso, appunto, della vendita a consegne ripartite di beni determinati nella loro individualità), si deve giudicare con la migliore dottrina che la Convenzione si riferisce anche ai contratti di somministrazione, in cui l'effetto traslativo si verifica solo in occasione delle singole forniture.

La Convenzione richiede altresì che l'oggetto del contratto, tra cui quello di somministrazione, sia mobile e tangibile (per questo requisito, v. Cour d'appel de

Grenoble, 26 aprile 1995, pubblicata in internet al seguente indirizzo [...], nonché OLG Köln, 26 agosto 1994, in *Neue Juristische Wochenschrift Rechtsprechungs-Report*, 1995, 246).

Poiché il contratto oggetto della presenta controversia presenta i requisiti appena menzionati (in quanto anche gli animali sono beni mobili, ai sensi della Convenzione delle Nazioni Unite), sotto il profilo materiale la Convenzione risulta applicabile. Affinché la Convenzione possa applicarsi, occorre inoltre che il contratto sia internazionale, carattere che la stessa Convenzione, come la maggior parte delle convenzioni di diritto materiale uniforme, si preoccupa di definire. A tale proposito, è necessario che le parti contraenti abbiano, al momento della conclusione del contratto (per cui sarà irrilevante se questa circostanza muti successivamente alla conclusione del contratto), la loro sede d'affari – ossia il luogo dal quale viene svolta un'attività commerciale caratterizzata da certa durata e stabilità nonché da autonomia (per questa definizione vedi anche Trib. Rimini, cit.; Trib. Padova, 25 febbraio 2004, cit.; OLG Stuttgart, 28 febbraio 2000, in *Internationales Handelsrecht*, 2000, 66) – in Stati diversi. Con riferimento al contratto dedotto in giudizio, risulta evidente che questo requisito di internazionalità sussiste, avendo il fornitore la propria sede d'affari nella Repubblica Slovena, mentre il somministrato ha la propria sede d'affari in Italia. Inoltre, si osserva che tale internazionalità era ben conosciuta dalle parti al momento della conclusione del contratto, per cui essa non può considerarsi irrilevante ai sensi dell'art. 1, comma 2°, della Convenzione. Nel caso di specie, si evidenzia inoltre che la Convenzione è entrata in vigore sia nella Repubblica Slovena sia in Italia ben prima della conclusione del contratto. Essa deve pertanto considerarsi applicabile in virtù dell'art. 1, comma 1°, lett. a).

Si aggiunga che le parti non hanno fatto ricorso alla possibilità di escludere l'applicazione della Convenzione, ancorché detta facoltà fosse loro spettante ed esercitabile anche in forma tacita, come spesso affermato dalla giurisprudenza italiana (Trib. Vigevano, cit.; Trib. Rimini, cit.; Trib. Padova, 25 febbraio 2004, cit.) e straniera (si vedano, ad esempio, Oberster Gerichtshof, 22 ottobre 2001, pubblicata in internet all'indirizzo [...]; Cour de Cassation, 26 luglio 2001, all'indirizzo [...]; OLG München, 9 luglio 1997, in *International Legal Forum*, 1997, 159 s.). Infatti, la scelta operata dalle parti nell'art. 7 del loro contratto a favore delle "leggi e [delle] regolamentazioni della Camera di Commercio Internazionale di Parigi, Francia" non solo non costituisce un'esclusione espressa, ma neppure un'esclusione implicita della Convenzione (si è di fronte ad un'esclusione implicita, ad esempio, nei casi in cui le parti scelgano il diritto di uno Stato non contraente della Convenzione, o in cui scelgano il diritto di uno Stato contraente facendo però riferimento al suo diritto "interno", come nell'ipotesi in cui rinviassero al "diritto italiano non uniforme" oppure al "diritto italiano del codice civile").

Conviene sottolineare come il riferimento alle leggi e regolamenti della Camera di Commercio di Parigi non possa essere intesa come "scelta della legge" ai sensi del diritto internazionale privato, le cui norme – almeno quelle vigenti in Italia – non ammettono la possibilità di scegliere un insieme di regole non statali (ciò si evince chiaramente dal disposto dell'art. 2, comma 1°, della Convenzione concernente la legge applicabile ai contratti di compravendita a carattere internazionale di cose mobili del 1955 [ratificata con l. 4 febbraio 1958, n. 50 ed entrata in vigore il 1° settembre 1964], nonché dagli artt.

3 e 4 della Convenzione sulla legge applicabile alle obbligazioni contrattuali [ratificata con l. 11 dicembre 1985, n. 765, ed entrata in vigore il 1° gennaio 1988]). In altre parole, la scelta operata dalle parti con l'art. 7 del contratto non equivale alla scelta internazionalprivatistica di un diritto, ed è dunque inidonea a determinare la prevalenza della disciplina richiamata rispetto alle norme imperative del diritto altrimenti applicabile (ciò varrebbe, peraltro, anche se la scelta fosse caduta sulla c.d. *lex mercatoria,* sui Principi UNIDROIT dei contratti commerciali internazionali oppure sulla stessa Convenzione delle Nazioni Unite nei casi in cui essa non è applicabile). Per questa ragione la scelta operata dalle parti non può rappresentare un'implicita esclusione della Convenzione.

Quanto detto non esclude tuttavia che la scelta di un insieme di regole non statali possa avere una qualche efficacia. Potrebbe infatti sostenersi che tale scelta abbia l'effetto di una determinazione per relationem del contenuto contrattuale, cioè di una regolamentazione dall'interno del rapporto negoziale. In altri termini, scegliendo regole non statali, e richiamandole quali clausole contrattuali, le parti potrebbero derogare alle norme dispositive del diritto applicabile, e dunque anche alle disposizioni della Convenzione delle Nazioni Unite (questa, pur dovendo essere applicata *ex officio* dal giudice [vedi Cour d'Appel de Paris, 6 novembre 2001, pubblicata in internet al seguente indirizzo […]; Cour de Cassation, 26 giugno 2001, in Dalloz 2001, *Jurisprudence* 3607], ha pacificamente natura dispositiva: eccezion fatta per gli artt. 12, 28 e 89-101). Nel caso concreto, tuttavia, la scelta operata dalle parti non permette d'individuare le regole esatte del loro rapporto negoziale, in quanto il riferimento alle "leggi e regolamentazioni" delle Camera di Commercio di Parigi è estremamente vago ed impreciso.

Per completezza si aggiunga che la scelta delle parti non può neppure avere il significato di escludere qualsiasi diritto statale, che in astratto potrebbe essere idonea ad impedire l'applicazione della Convenzione delle Nazioni Unite, in quanto diritto recepito dagli ordinamenti degli Stati contraenti, poiché il diritto internazionale privato vigente in Italia, pur consentendo una scelta negativa del diritto, non ammette l'esclusione di ogni diritto statale.
In considerazione di quanto sopra affermato, si deve concludere per l'applicabilità della Convenzione delle Nazioni Unite.

Affrontando ora il merito della controversia, deve giudicarsi che le domande formulate dagli attori non siano fondate e non possano pertanto trovare accoglimento.

L'attività istruttoria ha infatti permesso di accertare che fu Ostroznik Savo a rendersi inadempiente, poiché, dopo avere accettato di sostituire i conigli di genetica Hyla con animali di genetica Grimaud, non predispose adeguatamente il proprio allevamento per ricevere i nuovi animali riproduttori, e non fu così in grado di proseguire le forniture alla cooperativa La Faraona.

Sebbene la richiesta di modificare la "genetica" dei conigli, previa disinfestazione dell'allevamento, provenisse dalla convenuta, la quale aveva sovente riscontrato varie malattie nei conigli ricevuti (patologie riscontrate anche dalla struttura sanitaria pubblica: v. la deposizione del dott. Orlando Carlo, veterinario dipendente dell'Azienda Sanitaria Locale n. 17; v., inoltre, la testimonianza di Candeo Tonino), Ostrosnik Savo vi aveva consentito, e a tal fine aveva personalmente contrattato con Grimaud Italia l'invio di circa 1300 conigli riproduttori (v. doc. n. 14 del fasc. dell'attore).

Il teste Fruscalzo Giovanni, dirigente di Grimaud Italia, ha dichiarato di essersi personalmente recato presso l'allevamento sloveno, onde verificare le condizioni del luogo. Grimaud aveva interesse ad accertare, prima di effettuare la consegna delle proprie fattrici, che non vi fossero problemi sanitari. Il testimone ha riferito che l'allevamento non era stato pulito e che erano presenti molte feci. In altri termini, sebbene non vi fossero più conigli, il "vuoto sanitario", ossia la sterilizzazione delle strutture destinate all'allevamento degli animali, non era stato compiuto. Conseguentemente, Grimaud si rifiutò di consegnare i propri conigli. Fruscalzo ha dichiarato che fu Grimaud Italia a decidere autonomamente di non fornire animali a Ostroznik Savo, non ritenendo che sussistessero le condizioni igieniche necessarie. La deposizione di Fruscalzo, il quale non ha un particolare interesse all'esito del presente processo, è sicuramente più attendibile di quella resa da Hrastnik Uros, dipendente dell'attore, il quale ha affermato che lo stabilimento era stato pulito e che "per la disinfestazione finale si attendeva la comunicazione della data di arrivo dei nuovi conigli". Poiché il dirigente Grimaud si era recato in Slovenia appositamente per verificare l'idoneità dell'allevamento ad ospitare i propri conigli, non si vede la ragione per la quale Ostroznik Savo dovesse indugiare prima di completare il "vuoto sanitario", tanto più che l'invio degli animali era stato contrattato ben due mesi prima. Si comprende, al contrario, che Grimaud Italia, constatato che il luogo non era stato adeguatamente ripulito e disinfettato, non si fidasse a spedire i propri animali riproduttori, sussistendo il concreto pericolo che i conigli procreati, destinati al mercato italiano, si ammalassero, con evidente danno (non solo di immagine) per il titolare del diritto di sfruttamento della "genetica" Grimaud.

Non fu quindi per volontà della cooperativa La Faraona se l'attore non ricevette i conigli riproduttori di genetica Grimaud.

Nessun elemento consente di presumere che la convenuta non intendesse più acquistare conigli da Ostroznik Savo (peraltro, se questa fosse stata la sua volontà, avrebbe potuto più semplicemente recedere dal rapporto, dando alla controparte il preavviso previsto in contratto).

Fu invece Ostroznik Savo a rendersi inadempiente, non effettuando il così detto vuoto sanitario, ossia non ripulendo e disinfettando adeguatamente i luoghi in cui i conigli erano destinati ad essere allevati. E' dunque colpa dello stesso attore se non gli pervennero fattrici di genetica Grimaud, e se di conseguenza non fu in grado di fornire ulteriori conigli alla cooperativa convenuta.

Non ricevendo più animali (e – ancor prima – venendo a conoscenza delle cattive condizioni igieniche dell'allevamento del fornitore), La Faraona ha legittimamente reagito all'inadempimento di controparte comunicando il 6 luglio 2000 la risoluzione del contratto. Questo prevedeva, infatti, la consegna settimanale di alcune migliaia di conigli. Constatando che il venditore non era più in grado di consegnare animali, la convenuta ha correttamente deciso di porre termine al contratto, giacché un'ulteriore attesa le sarebbe risultata pregiudizievole.

L'inadempimento di Ostroznik Sava deve perciò considerarsi, ai sensi dell'art. 25 della Convenzione, un "fundamental breach", ossia un inadempimento essenziale (a questo proposito, ritiene questo Tribunale che vi sia corrispondenza di significati tra l'inadempimento "fondamentale" dell'art. 25 e l'inadempimento di "non scarsa importanza" che, ai sensi dell'art. 1455 c.c., consente la risoluzione dei contratti corrispettivi, essendo entrambe le disposizioni espressione di un'esigenza di proporzionalità tra la rilevanza dell'inadempimento ed i rimedi concessi alla parte non inadempiente: la risoluzione del contratto, comportandone l'eliminazione e la rimozione degli effetti prodotti, è l'estremo rimedio, a cui si può ricorrere solo nei casi di grave inadempimento, quando ormai l'utilità connessa al contratto è, per la parte che subisce l'inadempimento, venuta meno).

Qualora la prestazione caratteristica (nella specie, la periodica consegna dei conigli) sia interrotta, e non si prospetti ragionevolmente la possibilità della ripresa della sua esecuzione, l'inadempimento non può che considerarsi fondamentale.

L'art. 49 della Convenzione, che specifica i casi in cui il compratore può ottenere la risoluzione del contratto, parrebbe distinguere tra inadempimento essenziale (richiamando il disposto dell'art. 25) e mancata consegna dei beni (a questo proposito deve rilevarsi l'erroneità di alcune traduzioni italiane non ufficiali della lettera b) del 1° comma dell'art. 49 – quale ad esempio quella che si trova in Nuove Leggi Civili Commentate 1989, p. 222 –, che ponendo un punto e virgola dopo l'espressione "in caso di mancata consegna" inducono il lettore a ravvisare in tale disposizione due differenti fattispecie: quella della mancata consegna; e quella in cui la mancata consegna segue alla scadenza di un termine fissato dal compratore).

In realtà, non può certo dubitarsi che la mancata consegna rappresenti sempre un inadempimento essenziale, giacché esclude a priori che il compratore abbia potuto trarre una qualche utilità dal contratto (*cfr.* Cour d'Appel de Grenoble, 21 ottobre 1999, CLOUT case n. 313; Oberlandesgericht Celle, Germania, 24 maggio 1995, CLOUT case n. 136). Lo stesso deve dirsi, in un rapporto di fornitura a tempo indeterminato, nel caso in cui il venditore interrompa le consegne, impedendo al compratore di trarre ulteriore utilità dal contratto.

Il problema è piuttosto stabilire, volta per volta, quanto tempo il compratore debba attendere dopo la scadenza del termine previsto per la consegna dei beni (o dopo l'interruzione della fornitura) per potere considerare l'inadempimento del venditore definitivo e quindi essenziale (e ciò nell'ipotesi in cui le parti non avessero espressamente pattuito in contratto che il rispetto del termine di consegna era da considerarsi essenziale e che la sua inosservanza, così come l'interruzione delle consegne, avrebbe consentito al compratore di dichiarare immediatamente la risoluzione della compravendita). Da un lato, un'attesa troppo breve prima di dichiarare risolto il contratto può favorire contestazioni circa la gravità del ritardo da parte del venditore, il quale potrebbe sostenere che, nel momento in cui ha ricevuto la comunicazione della risoluzione, era pronto ad effettuare la consegna dei beni. Dall'altro, un'attesa prolungata, se consente di ritenere definitivo l'inadempimento del venditore, può esporre il compratore ad un pregiudizio economico connesso alla situazione d'incertezza circa l'esecuzione del contratto (egli non può infatti contare sull'arrivo della merce, ma neppure escludere che la consegna verrà effettuata e quindi approvvigionarsi da altri fornitori). Si è quindi voluto con la disposizione della lettera b) del 1° comma dell'art. 49 offrire all'acquirente, che subisce l'inadempimento, la possibilità di sciogliersi dal contratto in un tempo ragionevole, evitando contestazioni in merito all'essenzialità dell'inadempimento. Scaduto il termine supplementare fissato dal compratore per la consegna dei beni, la vendita può essere senz'altro risolta (al venditore non rimarrebbe che una difesa: sostenere che il termine concessogli dalla controparte non era adeguato, ai sensi dell'art. 47, 1° comma).

Nella specie, non risulta che il compratore abbia fissato alla controparte un termine supplementare entro cui riprendere la fornitura dei conigli, a pena di risoluzione del contratto. Deve tuttavia osservarsi che, venuta a conoscenza delle cattive condizioni igieniche dell'allevamento, del fatto che non era stato effettuato "il vuoto sanitario" e che conseguentemente Grimaud Italia si era rifiutata di fornire le nuove fattrici, la cooperativa La Faraona poteva ragionevolmente escludere che Ostrosznik Sava fosse in grado di consegnare conigli nei mesi successivi. Lo stesso attore afferma difatti in atto di citazione che "il tempo fisiologico necessario a ricostituire un allevamento in grado di produrre animali svezzati da mettere in commercio" era "di almeno sei mesi". Ciò però presupponeva l'esecuzione del "vuoto sanitario", che comporta la pulizia e disinfestazione dell'intero allevamento. Il veterinario Orlando Carlo dell'Azienda Sanitaria Locale n. 17 ha precisato che le suddette operazioni, affinché siano correttamente eseguite, richiedono circa venti giorni, durante i quali non possono essere introdotti animali. Solo dopo una corretta esecuzione del "vuoto sanitario", l'attore avrebbe potuto riconvocare i tecnici di Grimaud Italia, per cercare di convincerli che l'allevamento era divenuto idoneo a ricevere le loro fattrici.

Si aggiunga che, quando il 6 luglio 2000 La Faraona comunicava per iscritto la propria volontà di risolvere il rapporto, era già maturato un ritardo di alcuni mesi. Gli accordi fra Ostroznik Savo e Grimaud Italia risalivano infatti all'inizio del maggio 2000 (v. lettera datata 11 maggio 2000 di Grimaud Italia: doc. n. 14 del fasc. dell'attore), sicché l'attore avrebbe dovuto prima dell'estate provvedere al "vuoto sanitario", onde predisporre l'allevamento per il ricevimento delle nuove fattrici. Ed invece nel luglio del 2000 – come ha dichiarato il teste Fruscalzo – il "vuoto sanitario" non era stato ancora effettuato, e l'allevamento si presentava in pessime condizioni igieniche.

A quel punto, non era ragionevole pretendere che La Faraona indugiasse ulteriormente, sopportando il pregiudizio dell'interruzione, ancora per lungo periodo, delle forniture di conigli, con la speranza – non suffragata da alcun elemento: Ostroznik Savo non aveva infatti manifestato né alla convenuta né a Grimaud la volontà di provvedere celermente all'idonea predisposizione della propria struttura, dopo che era stata constatata la mancata esecuzione del "vuoto sanitario" e la presenza di feci – che controparte potesse rimediare all'inadempimento. Ulteriori attese avrebbero potuto cagionare un serio pregiudizio economico alla cooperativa La Faraona, la quale necessitava di forniture settimanali di conigli.

Deve perciò concludersi che, nel luglio del 2000, l'inadempimento di Ostroznik Savo si presentava come "fondamentale", e pertanto legittimava la convenuta a dichiarare, ex art. 26 della Convenzione, l'immediata risoluzione del contratto.

Relativamente alla domanda risarcitoria formulata da Eurotrafic s.r.l., si rileva che l'unica obbligazione che La Faraona aveva assunto nei confronti di essa consisteva nel corrisponderle una provvigione di £ 100 "per ogni chilogrammo di carne viva" che fosse stata acquistata da Ostroznik Savo. La cooperativa non aveva promesso di proseguire i rapporti con l'impresa slovena, e neppure di richiedere esclusivamente conigli di genetica Hyla. Se dunque i rapporti tra La Faraona e Ostroznik Savo si fossero per qualunque ragione interrotti, Eurotrafic s.r.l. non avrebbe potuto avanzare alcuna pretesa, così come non avrebbe potuto impedire all'impresa slovena di modificare la genetica delle fattrici. La società attrice aveva esclusivamente diritto ad un compenso se (e fintanto) fosse proseguito il rapporto di somministrazione avente ad oggetto conigli vivi, geneticamente appartenenti al tipo Hyla (su cui pare che Eurotrafic s.r.l. avesse una privativa industriale nel territorio italiano), liberi somministrante e somministrato di mutare in ogni momento l'oggetto del contratto. Dunque, la domanda risarcitoria proposta da Eurotrafic s.r.l. è sprovvista di fondamento: legittimamente La Faraona ha richiesto ad Ostroznik Savo di modificare la genetica dei conigli riproduttori per migliorarne la qualità; in nessun modo la convenuta era vincolata, verso Eurotrafic s.r.l., a proseguire gli acquisti di conigli di genetica Hyla.

Il rigetto delle domande attoree esonera dall'esame della domanda di manleva formulata dalla Banca di Credito Cooperativo di Roveredo di Guà.

Dev'essere altresì rigettata la domanda riconvenzionale proposta dalla cooperativa La Faraona, giacché essa non ha provato di avere subito un pregiudizio di natura economica a causa dell'inadempimento di Ostroznik Savo. Cessato il rapporto con l'imprenditore sloveno, è presumibile che la convenuta abbia acquistato conigli da altri allevatori. Non sono stati indicati elementi – che ben potevano essere documentalmente forniti – dai quali possa evincersi un maggiore costo sostenuto da La Faraona per approvvigionarsi di conigli da terzi fornitori. In mancanza della prova della sussistenza di un danno di natura patrimoniale, la domanda risarcitoria non può essere accolta neppure limitatamente all'an della responsabilità (con liquidazione del quantum in separato giudizio).

Poiché Ostroznik Savo e Eurotrafic s.r.l. hanno dato origine al presente giudizio, in cui sono rimasti soccombenti, essi dovranno rifondere ai convenuti le spese di lite, così come liquidate in dispositivo.

P.Q.M.

Il Tribunale di Padova, sezione di Este, in composizione monocratica, definitivamente decidendo nella causa n. 40287 R.g. del 2001, promossa con atto di citazione notificato il 21 marzo 2001 da Ostroznik Savo, titolare dell'impresa denominata Vzerja Kuncev con sede in Celje (Repubblica Slovena), e da Eurotrafic s.r.l. con sede in Feltre (BL) (attori) nei confronti di La Faraona soc. coop. a r.l. con sede in Montagnana (PD) e della Banca di Credito Cooperativo di Roveredo di Guà (VR) (convenuti), ogni diversa e contraria istanza, domanda ed eccezione disattesa, così ha deciso:

1) rigetta l'eccezione pregiudiziale sollevata dalla convenuta La Faraona soc. coop. a r.l.;

2) rigetta tutte le domande proposte dagli attori;

3) rigetta la domanda riconvenzionale della convenuta La Faraona soc. coop. a r.l.;

4) dichiara solidalmente tenuti e condanna gli attori a rifondere a La Faraona soc. coop. a r.l. le spese di lite, che liquida nella complessiva somma di Euro 3.070,00, di cui Euro 1.300,00 per diritti ed Euro 1.400,00 per onorari, oltre IVA e CPA come per legge;

5) dichiara solidalmente tenuti e condanna gli attori a rifondere alla Banca di Credito Cooperativo di Roveredo di Guà (VR) le spese di lite, che liquida nella complessiva somma di Euro 2.850,00, di cui Euro 1.200,00 per diritti ed Euro 1.300,00 per onorari, oltre IVA e CPA come per legge.

Este, 11 gennaio 2005.
Il giudice
(dott. Alessandro Rizzieri)

Sources

Decision kindly provided by Professor Franco FERRARI.

Date: **March 29, 2005**
Adjudicating Court: **Arbitration Institute of the Stockholm Chamber of Commerce**
Number: **Unknown**
Parties: **Unknown**

Keywords

CONTRACT BETWEEN TWO COMPANIES FROM DIFFERENT STATES FOR THE SUPPLY OF GAS – BUYER'S FAILURE TO PAY THE PRICE DUE TO INSOLVENCY CAUSED BY INTERFERENCE BY ITS COUNTRY'S GOVERNMENT – GOVERNMENT LIABLE FOR DAMAGES VIS-À-VIS SELLER

INTEREST – TO BE CALCULATED ON THE BASIS OF INTERNATIONAL RULES – APPLICATION OF ART. 7.4.9 UNIDROIT PRINCIPLES CONSIDERED BY ARBITRAL TRIBUNAL "TO BE AN APPROPRIATE BASIS FOR DETERMINING THE INTEREST"

Abstract

Plaintiff, a trading company registered in Gibraltar entered into a contract with a State-owned Company X of an Central Asian Republic, for the supply of gas condensate over the course of a certain period of time on a monthly basis. While Plaintiff regularly fullfiled its obligations under the contract, Company X, after paying the first invoices, stopped making payments. When some months later the Government of the Central Asian Republic set up a new State-owned Company Y to replace Company X for the domestic supply of gas and transferred to Company Y the assets but not the debts of Company X, Plaintiff brought an action against the Central Asian Republic for the payment of the outstanding invoices and damages. According to Plaintiff Defendant, by depriving Company X of its assets and thereby causing that company's insolvency, had violated its obligation under the 1994 Energy Charter Treaty to ensure foreign investors fair and equitable treatment.

The Arbitral Tribunal decided in favour of Plaintiff and awarded damages to compensate the loss Plaintiff suffered by not being able to receive payment from Company X of its outstanding invoices. The Arbitral Tribunal also awarded interest which it held should be calculated on the basis of international rather than national rules: in this respect the Arbitral Tribunal referred to Article 7.4.9 of the UNIDROIT Principles which, with no further explanation, it considered "to be an appropriate basis for determining the interest".

Full Test

Full text available at *http://www.investmentclaims.com/decisions/Petrobart-kyrgyz-rep-Award.pdf.*

Date: ***April 28, 2005*** *Country:* ***People's Republic of China*** *Adjudicating Court:* ***Guangdong Intermediate People's Court*** *Number:* ***Unknown*** *Parties:* ***Hengxing Company v. Guangdong Petrochemical Subsidiary Company***

Keywords

LEASE CONTRACT BETWEEN TWO CHINESE COMPANIES – TERMINATED ON ACCOUNT OF HARDSHIP – APPLICATION OF THE RELEVANT PROVISIONS OF UNIDROIT PRINCIPLES

Abstract

The Court, in terminating a lease contract between Hengxing Company and Guangdong Petrochemical Subsidiary Company on account of hardship, based its decision on the relevant provisions contained in the UNIDROIT Principles of International Commercial Contract. An appeal by Defendant objecting that "according to their Introduction the UNIDROIT Principles are not binding and therefore cannot be applied compulsorily, is presently pending before the Guangdong High People's Court.

Full Text

[Not yet available]

Sources

Notice of the decision kindly provided by Ms. JING XI.

Date: ***August 2, 2005***
Country: ***U.S.A.***
Adjudicating Court: ***Overseas Private Investment Corp.; Administrative Determination***
Number: ***Unknown***
Parties: ***Ponderosa Assets, L.P.***

Keywords

LICENSING AGREEMENT BETWEEN A U.S. INVESTOR AND THE GOVERNMENT OF ARGENTINA – ADMINISTRATIVE DETERMINATION BY U.S. GOVERNMENTAL INSURANCE AGENCY ON EXPROPRIATION CLAIM

QUESTION AS TO WHETHER OR NOT A VALID CONTRACT HAD BEEN CONCLUDED BETWEEN U.S. INVESTOR AND THE GOVERNMENT OF ARGENTINA – REFERENCE TO THE TWO CRITERIA SET OUT IN ART. 2.1.1 UNIDROIT PRINCIPLES

Abstract

A U.S. investor acquired a 35% interest in a private Argentine gas company. The investor also secured a policy for political risk insurance from the Overseas Private Investment Corp (OPIC), an agency of the U.S. government designed to help U.S. businesses invest overseas. The company was subject to regulation by the government of Argentina. In the licensing agreement issued to the company by Argentina, the company was allowed to raise revenue by charging tariffs that were subject to change every six months based on the U.S. Producer Price Index, and which were to be calculated in U.S. Dollars but paid in Argentine Pesos.

In 2000, in response to a fiscal crisis, Argentina passed a law prohibiting the use of indexes from other countries in adjustment clauses governed by public law, and providing that in contracts governed by public law the exchange rate would be 1 U.S. Dollar = 1 Argentine Peso. As a result of the law, the company's tariffs were frozen at the January 2000 rate and had to be paid in the amount of Argentine Pesos numerically equivalent (as opposed to being equivalent in value) to the amount calculated using U.S. Dollars.

Investor claimed that its property had been expropriated by the government of Argentina in violation of international law and without adequate compensation. The matter between Argentina and investor was pending before the International Centre for Settlement of Investment Disputes (ICSID) when OPIC issued its Memoranda of Determinations in response to investor's claim that its policy should be disbursed because of the alleged illegal expropriation.

In making its determination as to whether or not the actions of Argentina constituted a repudiation of the contract between the company and Argentina amounting to an illegal expropriation of investor's property as defined by the insurance contract, OPIC first looked to whether or not a contract had actually been formed between those two parties. In doing so, OPIC quoted Article 2.1.1 of the UNIDROIT Principles, stating that a contract can be formed "by the acceptance of an offer." OPIC found that Argentina's licensing agreement constituted an offer that was duly accepted by the company, thus forming a contract. OPIC also quoted Article 2.1.1, according to which a contract can be formed by "conduct of the parties that is sufficient to show agreement." OPIC concluded that from 1992 until 2000 the conduct of each of the parties conformed to the terms of the agreement, thus indicating that it was their common intention to be bound by the terms of the licensing agreement.

Full Text

Available at: *http://www.investmentclaims.com/*

Sources

Notice kindly provided by Mr Bruno POULAIN.

Date: ***August 19, 2005***
Adjudicating Court: ***Ad hoc Arbitration, Brussels***
Number: ***Unknown***
Parties: ***EUREKO B.V. v. Republic of Poland***

Keywords

DISPUTE BETWEEN A STATE AND A FOREIGN INVESTOR – TO BE DECIDED ON THE BASIS OF THE BILATERAL TREATY FOR THE PROTECTION OF INVESTMENTS AND "THE UNIVERSALLY ACKNOWLEDGED RULES AND PRINCIPLES OF INTERNATIONAL LAW" – REFERENCE TO THE UNIDORIT PRINCIPLES

Abstract

In the privatisation process of a wholly State-owned Polish insurance company, a Dutch company acquired 30% of the shares and at the same time entered into an agreement with the State Treasury as the owner of the Polish company according to which the State Treasury was committed to sell subsequently another lot of shares so as to permit the Dutch company to become the majority shareholder. Immediately thereafter the two parties began to dispute a number of matters related to the deal but eventually made a settlement agreement whereby they re-affirmed the original schedule of privatisation and waived any previous claims between them. After the State Treasury's continuing not to sell the additional lot of shares to the Dutch company, the latter commenced arbitration against the Republic of Poland invoking the violation by the Republic of Poland of the Dutch/Polish Treaty for the protection of investments (hereinafter the "Treaty").

According to the Treaty the Arbitral Tribunal shall decide "on the basis of respect for the law, including particularly this Agreement and other relevant agreements existing between the two Contracting Parties and the universally acknowledged rules and principles of international law".

One of the objections raised by Defendant was that Claimant was barred from raising in the present proceedings claims which had been waived by the settlement agreement between Claimant and the State Treasury. On its part Claimant argued that, since the State Treasury had not performed the other terms of the settlement, it was justified in raising again even the pre-agreement claims in conformity with the so-called exception of non-performance (*exceptio non adimpleti contractus*). In deciding on this matter in favour of Defendant, the Arbitral Tribunal pointed out that the exception of non-performance essentially applies only to cases of simultaneous performance and in support of this argument referred to Article 7.1.3(1) of the UNIDROIT Principles providing that "where the parties are to perform simultaneously, either party may withhold performance until the other party tenders its performance". In the case at hand both parties had to, and actual did, perform simultaneously only their obligation mutually to waive and release all pending claims while the sale of the remaining shares by the State Treasury was clearly a distinct obligation to be performed at a later stage

Full Text

Full text available at: *http://www.investmentclaims.com/decisions/Eureko-Poland-LiabilityAward.pdf.*

Date: **December 4, 2005**
Country: **United Kingdom**
Adjudicating Court: **High Court of Justice (Queen's Bench Division)**
Number: **2004 Folio 272**
Parties: **Svenska Petroleum Exploration AB, Government of the Republic of Lithuania, AB Geonafta**

Keywords

JOINT VENTURE BETWEEN A SWEDISH COMPANY AND A LITHUANIAN COMPANY – SIGNED ALSO BY THE GOVERNMENT OF LITHUANIA – LITHUANIAN LAW APPLICABLE

INTERPRETATION OF THE AGREEMENT – LIBERAL INTERPRETATION IN ACCORDANCE WITH PARTIES' COMMON INTENTION – RELEVANCE OF PRELIMINARY NEGOTIATIONS – REFERENCE TO ARTS. 6.193 - 6.195 OF THE LITHUANIAN CIVIL CODE REPEATING ARTS. 4.1 - 4.6 OF THE UNIDROIT PRINCIPLES

Abstract

A Swedish petroleum company ("the plaintiff") and a previously state-owned Lithuanian petroleum company ("the defendant") entered into a joint venture agreement ("the agreement") for oil exploitation in Lithuania. The agreement contained an arbitration clause which indicated that the "founders," *i.e.* incorporating shareholders, would submit their disputes to arbitration under the ICC Rules of Arbitration. Moreover it stated that "This Agreement shall be governed by the laws of Lithuania supplemented, where required, by rules of international business activities generally accepted in the petroleum industry if they do not contradict the laws of the Republic of Lithuania." The Agreement also contained a separate provision stating that "The Government of the Republic of Lithuania hereby approves the above agreement and acknowledges itself to be legally and contractually bound as if the Government were a signatory to the Agreement."

After a dispute arose as to the rights to exploit certain oil fields, the plaintiff commenced arbitration against both the defendant and the Government of Lithuania, claiming, with respect to the latter, breach of its obligation to grant a license to exploit certain oil reserves. The Government of Lithuania argued that sovereign immunity shielded it from liability, and even if sovereign immunity did not protect it, the arbitration clause only applied to the plaintiff and to the defendant because Lithuania was not a "founder." In response, the plaintiff argued that in the agreement the Government of Lithuania had expressly waived sovereign immunity, and although the Government of Lithuania was not a founder, it was subject to the arbitration clause because it had signed the abovementioned separate clause in the agreement according to which it would be contractually bound as if it were a signatory to the agreement.

The Arbitral Tribunal found that because the Government of Lithuania had agreed it would be bound as if it were a signatory to the agreement, it was subject to the arbitration clause. As to the merits the Arbitral Tribunal held that the defendant and the Government of Lithuania were jointly and severally liable for payment of damages to the plaintiff.

The plaintiff then filed for enforcement and recognition of the award in England, which was granted. Against this decision, both the defendant and the Gvernment of Lithuania appealed.

On appeal, the Court considered both the issue of whether the Government of Lithuania had waived sovereign immunity and whether it had agreed to arbitration. In dealing with this latter issue, the Court looked to the relevant rules of contract interpretation contained in Articles 6.193 to 6.195 of the Lithuanian Civil Code, and also extensively quoted the commentary by an eminent Lithuanian scholar pointing out that those articles "repeat Articles 4.1 - 4.6 of the UNIDROIT Principles." The Court noted that contrary to English law, the above-mentioned rules of contract interpretation allow for a greater amount of factual material to assist in interpreting the meaning of a contract, particularly in allowing for evidence of pre-contractual negotiations, earlier drafts of the contract, and each parties subjective intent. Applying those rules, the Court looked to the parties' pre-contractual negotiations in the case at hand, including previous drafts of the agreement, to determine whether the parties had intended Lithuania to waive sovereign immunity and to be bound by the arbitration clause. The Court found that because previous drafts of the agreement contained terms waiving sovereign immunity for Lithuania and subjecting it to arbitration, the drafters had inappropriately used the term "founder" in stating which parties would be subject to arbitration. Furthermore, the Court found that at no point during negotiations did any of the contracting parties suggest that that the waiver of sovereign immunity only applied to the respondent. Accordingly, the Court found in favour of the claimant, finding that Lithuanian had waived its sovereign immunity and had agreed to settle disputes through arbitration.

Full Text

SVENSKA PETROLEUM EXPLORATION AB v. GOVERNMENT OF THE REPUBLIC OF LITHUANIA (NO 2) [2005] EWHC 2437 (Comm)

QUEEN'S BENCH DIVISION (COMMERCIAL COURT)

[2006] 1 Lloyd's Rep 181

HEARING-DATES: 4 November 2005

4 November 2005

Mrs Justice GLOSTER

The further facts are stated in the judgment of Mrs Justice Gloster.

INTRODUCTION

1. On 28 April 1993, the claimant, Svenska Petroleum Exploration AB ("Svenska"), the first defendant, the Government of the Republic of Lithuania ("Lithuania" or "the State"), and the second defendant, AB Geonafta ("Geonafta") (collectively "the defendants"), signed a Joint Venture Agreement (the "JVA") in relation to the planned exploitation of various oil fields in Lithuania.

2. Svenska, as its name suggests, is a Swedish company employed in the business of oil exploration and extraction. Geonafta, previously known as Gargzdai State Petroleum Geology Enterprise and sometimes referred to in the relevant documents as "EPG", was formerly a Lithuanian State enterprise. It was privatised on 16 June 2000 and has since then been privately owned.

3. In June 2000, a dispute arose between the parties as to who was entitled to exploit certain specific oil fields. Svenska brought a claim against both Geonafta and the State before an ICC arbitral panel sitting in Denmark ("the Tribunal"). The State took the preliminary objection that it was not a party to the arbitration agreement contained in article 9 of the JVA. On 16 and 17 October 2001 there was a two-day hearing before the three-member Tribunal in Copenhagen at which all parties were fully represented in relation to the issues of jurisdiction and arbitrability. In a 69-page interim award ("the Interim Award"), issued on 21 December 2001, the Tribunal, (having considered all the various arguments which have been deployed before me on this hearing) unanimously held that the State was a party to the arbitration agreement. The State made no challenge to that finding in the Danish courts, although it was common ground that it was open to it to have done so. It is relevant to quote the following passage from the Interim Award at page 68:

"It is undisputed that no provisions of any Lithuanian law prevented Government from signing an arbitration agreement at the time when the JVC was signed in 1993. The issue of arbitrability only arises due to subsequent Lithuanian laws, *i.e.* article 29 of the underground law from 1995 and article 11 in the Law of Commercial Arbitration from 1996.

The JVC is a commercial contract regarding the exploration and exploitation of oil fields within Lithuania. The dispute between Svenska and Government is a dispute which relates to an alleged breach of contract by Government. Such a dispute is clearly arbitrable. The claims of Svenska, *i.e.* the relief sought from this Tribunal are divided into three different claims, a request for a declaratory award sentence, a request for damages and a request for a specific performance award ordering Government to abrogate an existing licence and to issue a new licence. The alleged non-arbitrability can in the opinion of the Arbitral Tribunal at most be applicable to that part of Svenska's claim, which relates to the revocation and issuance of licences. It follows that Government is obliged to answer to the remainder of the claims in any event.

Under these circumstances, the Arbitral Tribunal has not found it appropriate - at this stage of the case - to make a final decision whether the claim for revocation and issuance of licences is arbitrable, or whether the relief sought would be an appropriate relief in this matter.

Accordingly, the parties are invited to elaborate further on this issue in the course of the dealing with the merits of the case."

4. Following a substantial hearing, in which the State fully participated, the Tribunal issued a final Award on 30 October 2003 ("the Final Award"). By that Award (which ran to 280 pages), the Tribunal held that the State and Geonafta were jointly and severally liable to pay the claimant the sum of US$12,579,000 by way of damages plus costs. That Award also determined the question of arbitrability, in relation to which the Tribunal (by a majority) held as follows:

"Arbitrability"

"In his dissenting opinion, Mr Gytis Kaminskas has addressed the issue of arbitrability, and has concluded that the dispute related to the Principal Claim is not arbitrable under Lithuanian law by virtue of article 29 of the Underground Law and Articles 2 and 11 of the Law on Commercial Arbitration of 1995.

We do not agree with Mr Kaminska's position, and we believe that this issue was already decided upon in our Interim Award, dated 21 December 2001, in which Award the unanimous finding of the Arbitral Tribunal was stated as follows. . . [Here the Tribunal set out the passage that I have already quoted above].

. . .

The claimant has after the Interim Award withdrawn its claim for a specific performance award ordering first respondent to abrogate an existing license and issue a new license. claimant's requested remedy is now limited to a claim for damages. This claim is in the view of the majority clearly arbitrable under Lithuanian law. The parties have not previously nor after the Interim Award argued that the claim for damages is not arbitrable or that the Arbitral Tribunal otherwise lacks jurisdiction with respect to this claim.

Article 29 of the Underground Law and article 11 of the Law on Commercial Arbitration governs the administrative legal relations, which disputes are decided by the Administrative court of Lithuania. These provisions are not applicable to disputes originating from a commercial contract, where relief sought is a claim for damages.

The claim for damages is a claim for breach of contract and does not depend on or relate to the validity of any administrative or Governmental act, including the grant or revocation of any rights in relation to the underground either to the claimant, the second respondent or the JV-Company."

5. The State made no challenge to that Final Award in the Danish courts. On the contrary, by resolution dated 11 February 2004 it resolved that:

"1.. . . It is not expedient to apply to a court for annulment of the award of the Arbitration Tribunal of the International Chamber of Commerce in the case considered in Copenhagen on 30 October 2003.

2.. . . to commission the state enterprise State Property Fund to notify [Svenska] or its representatives of the position of the [State] or its representatives of the position of the [State] on the award referred to in clause 1."

Neither Geonafta nor the State has honoured the Final Award.

6. On 2 April 2004, Svenska issued an arbitration claim form seeking permission to enforce the Final Award in England pursuant to section 101 of the Arbitration Act 1996. On 7 April 2004 Morison J gave Svenska permission to enforce the Final Award in England. Since the application had, in the usual way, been made without notice, the defendants were given a period of time in which to apply to set aside the order. Geonafta's challenge to the recognition and enforcement of the Final Award was dismissed by Cooke J on 24 August 2004. The State acknowledged service of the claim form on 31 August 2004, indicating in that acknowledgement that it intended to contest the court's jurisdiction. On the same day, the State issued an Application Notice pursuant to Part 11 of the CPR disputing the jurisdiction of the English court, and applied for an order that the claim form, the order of Morison J and the service of the enforcement proceedings on it be set aside on the grounds that, as an independent sovereign state, the State is immune from the jurisdiction of the English court, by virtue of section 1 of the State Immunity Act 1978 ("the Act"). This provides:

"A State is immune from the jurisdiction of the courts of the United Kingdom except as provided in the following provisions of this Part of this Act."

SUMMARY OF THE PARTIES' CONTENTIONS

7. Shortly stated, the State's argument is that none of the various exceptions contained in Part I of the Act apply. In particular, the State contends that it has not submitted to the jurisdiction of the English court (section 2); that the proceedings do not relate to a commercial agreement (section 3); and that the State has not agreed in writing to submit a dispute which has arisen to arbitration (section 9).

8. On the other hand, Svenska contends that:

(i) the State has expressly waived any entitlement to rely on State Immunity and has agreed to submit to the court's jurisdiction; accordingly it falls within the exception contained in section 2 of the Act;

(ii) it was party to a commercial transaction and the present proceedings relate to that transaction; accordingly it falls within the exception contained in section 3 of the Act;

(iii) it was a party to the arbitration agreement contained in article 9 of the JVA, alternatively is estopped from denying that fact by virtue of the Interim Award; accordingly it falls within the exception contained in section 9 of the Act.

FACTUAL BACKGROUND

9. It is necessary to set out the factual background to the JVA and the arbitration proceedings in some greater detail than the brief summary which I have already given.

10. In 1989, Swedish and Lithuanian parties commenced discussions concerning the exploitation of certain of Lithuania's oil reserves. Discussions were initially conducted between Svenska, on the one hand, and the Soviet Corporation of Geological Works ("LG") on the other. On 31 January 1991, Svenska and LG signed a Letter of Intent, outlining a framework for the development and exploration of Lithuanian oilfields. The parties to the letter of intent were defined as Svenska and LG only. In March of 1990 the Republic of Lithuania declared its independence. After independence, LG had to be liquidated. The liquidation of Soviet style companies was a common occurrence in all newly independent States following the collapse of the Soviet Union and the gradual replacement of Socialist law with legal systems more consistent with market economies. Geonafta succeeded to LG as the State Enterprise having a right to explore and develop oilfields in Lithuania. All rights and obligations under the Letter of Intent were transferred to Geonafta. This was confirmed by agreement between Svenska and Geonafta dated 13 June 1991. The parties to this agreement were Svenska and Geonafta only. Negotiations continued as I describe in greater detail below in relation to the concluding of an agreement for the development and exploration of the oilfields. Geonafta held the legal licence to exploit the oil reserves which were the subject matter of negotiations. The project would require State approval. In addition, petroleum exploration and exploitation were a priority in view of the trade embargo imposed by the Soviet Union in response to Lithuania's declaration of independence. Lithuania had been the very first of the Soviet States to restore its independence. Accordingly, the State Geological Survey ("SGS") participated in discussions and reported to the State on progress. Various drafts of the JVA were prepared by Svenska between 1991 and 1993. Some early versions of the arbitration agreements mentioned the State and it was proposed that the State should agree to an ICSID arbitration clause. As I shall describe below in greater detail, the final version of the JVA did not include such a provision.

11. It was eventually decided to create a joint venture company as the vehicle for cooperation between Svenska and Geonafta. This was reflected in the text of the draft JVA dated March 1992. This draft also introduces the concept of the "Founders" of the joint venture company. The term "Founder" has a legal meaning under Lithuanian law corresponding to that of an incorporating shareholder. All drafts of the JVA subsequent to March 1992 define Svenska and Geonafta as the "Founders". They also provide that Svenska and Geonafta are to be the incorporating shareholders of the joint venture company, each holding 50 per cent of the shares.

12. References to both the State and ICSID arbitration were removed from subsequent drafts of the arbitration clause which on its face refers only to arbitration between the two "Founders" of the JVA, Svenska and Geonafta, pursuant to ICC Rules.

13. By Government Resolution dated 27 March 1993, the State approved the terms of the JVA and the issuing of licences in relation to the Gencai oilfield. This resolution also specifically authorised Dr Gediminas Motuza, Head of SGS, to approve the JVA. On 28 April 1993, Svenska and Geonafta signed the JVA. The JVA provided for signature by each founder. The State also signed the last page of the JVA, but separately from the signatures of the Founders and under the following rubric in the English version:

"The Government of the Republic of Lithuania hereby approves the above agreement and acknowledges itself to be legally and contractually bound as if the Government were a signatory to the Agreement."

The Lithuanian text of the expression accompanying Lithuania's signature is slightly different. It states:

"The Government of the Republic of Lithuania approves this agreement and undertakes the obligations as a signatory thereto."

As the JVA was executed in both Lithuanian and English, article 37 of the JVA accords equal weight to both versions of the text. However I do not attach any significance to the slightly different wording for the purpose of the issues which I have to determine.

14. Pursuant to the terms of the JVA, a joint venture company was established by Svenska and Geonafta, called UAB Genciu Nafta ("the JV Company"). In the preamble to the JVA, Svenska and Geonafta were defined as "Founders". Svenska and Geonafta, as "Founders", each held 50 per cent of the share capital of the JV Company. The State was not defined as a "Founder" under the JVA and did not hold any shares in the JV Company.

15. Article 41 of the JVA provided that the parties would develop either or both of the Kretinga and Nausodis oilfields by a separate agreement. Disputes arose principally in respect of the development and exploration of the Kretinga and Nausodis oilfields. Article 41 of the JVA provided:

"Fields within the Agreement Area

As soon as practical after the Effective Date, Svenska shall carry out a technical economic feasibility study in respect of the Kretinga and Nausodis fields within the Agreement Area and the Parties shall, where the study, in the opinion of the Parties proves this to be economically feasible, develop either or both fields by a separate agreement."

16. Svenska and Geonafta failed to agree terms for the development of the Kretinga and Nausodis oilfields as envisaged at article 41 of the JVA. Geonafta, which held the licence to develop these oilfields prior to the JVA, continued to develop them independently of

Svenska. Svenska claimed that the JVA entitled Svenska to exclusive rights to develop the Kretinga and Nausodis oilfields. As a result, Svenska filed a Request for Arbitration with the ICC Secretariat on 12 June 2000. On 19 and 29 August 2000, the State wrote to Svenska and the ICC Secretariat stating an objection to jurisdiction on the alleged grounds that the State had not consented to arbitrate differences with Svenska. A three-member tribunal was appointed comprising Messrs Mogens Skipper-Pedersen, Edward Greeno and Gytis Kaminskas. Terms of Reference were agreed with the arbitral tribunal on 8 August 2001. These were signed with an express reservation in respect of jurisdiction on the State's part, in the following terms:

"[The State] declares that its signature of these Terms of Reference does not constitute an acceptance of the jurisdiction of the ICC Court of Arbitration and/or the Arbitral Tribunal."

17. On 16 and 17 October 2001, a hearing took place in Copenhagen on the issue of the arbitrators' jurisdiction over the State. As I have already stated, the Tribunal issued the Interim Award on jurisdiction on 21 December 2001 in which it held that it had jurisdiction over the State. The Tribunal held that the State was a party to the JVA. It relied, in part, on the words of the JVA which express the State's consent to be contractually bound by the JVA. At page 63 of the Interim Award the Arbitrators held:

"The Arbitral Tribunal holds that by signing the [JVA] and by acknowledging itself to be legally and contractually bound "as if the Government were a signatory to the agreement," Government became a party to the Joint Venture Agreement with Svenska and [Geonafta]. . . By this signature, the agreement became effective in accordance with article 11.1 of the [JVA]. This interpretation is supported by Government Resolution No 205 of 27 March 1993, in which the Government authorises the Minster of Energy and Mr Motuza to approve the founding agreement of the Genciu Nafta enterprise "on behalf of the Government." The Arbitral Tribunal cannot accept Government's allegation that this signature is merely an approval by Government in its administrative capacity. As pointed out by Svenska, the [JVA] vests a number of rights and obligations on the part of Government, and it needs a strong support, which is not available in this case, to consider that Government's signature is of no significance to such rights and obligations . . ."

In the absence of any indication in the wording of the JVA or any other indication of intentions in relation to the arbitration agreement, the Tribunal also relied on a presumption of Lithuania's intent. At pages 63 and 65 the arbitrators said:

"The Arbitral Tribunal also holds that by signing the [JVA], Government is bound by the arbitration clause in article 9. Although Government signed the [JVA] in a different capacity than a "Founder", we have found that Government is as a party to the [JVA] signed "as if it was a "signatory" and therefore became bound by the provisions of the [JVA], as if Government had been a "Founder". Government is therefore also bound by the arbitration provision in article 9 unless there is support for an allegation that Government intended a different dispute resolution mechanism. [. . .] Such support does not exist". . . .

"The [JVA] was an agreement between three parties, each having its rights and obligations. . . In such a contract there is an implicit assumption that the parties have agreed to the same dispute resolution mechanism."

Does the State fall within the exception contained in section 2 of the Act?

23. The first issue for my determination is whether the State falls within the exception contained in section 2 of the Act. Section 2 provides (so far as is material) as follows:

"(1) A State is not immune as respects proceedings in respect of which it has submitted to the jurisdiction of the courts of the United Kingdom.

(2) A State may submit after the dispute giving rise to the proceedings has arisen or by a prior written agreement; but a provision in any agreement that is governed by the law of the United Kingdom is not to be regarded as a submission.

(3) A State is deemed to have submitted

(a) if it has instituted the proceedings; or

(b) subject to subsections (4) and (5) below, if it has intervened or taken any step in the proceedings.

(4) Subsection (3)(b) above does not apply to intervention or any step taken for the purpose only of

(a) claiming immunity; or

(b) asserting an interest in property in circumstances such that the State would have been entitled to immunity if the proceedings had been brought against it."

24. One of the terms of the JVA was article 35, which provided as follows:

"GOVERNING LAW AND SOVEREIGN IMMUNITY

35.1 Government and EPG hereby irrevocably waives [sic] all rights to sovereign immunity.

35.2 This Agreement shall be governed by the laws of Lithuania supplemented, where required, by rules of international business activities generally accepted in the petroleum industry if they do not contradict the laws of the Republic of Lithuania."

25. However, the State contends that, on its true construction (as allegedly demonstrated by evidence as to the purpose of article 35, given by a Professor Katuoka and corroborated by a Mr Zukovskis), article 35 amounted to a waiver of Sovereign Immunity in respect of Geonafta only (Geonafta being at the time of entry into the JVA a state

enterprise), and that all that the State was doing under the terms of the clause was to give its consent to Geonafta's own waiver.

26. The JVA contains no express submission to the jurisdiction of the English court. Article 9 of the JVA does contain an arbitration agreement referring disputes between the two "Founders" (which is the collective definition set out in the preamble to the JVA of Geonafta and Svenska) to inter alia ICC arbitration and is in the following terms:

"9.1 Disputes between the Founders concerning the performance or interpretation of this Agreement are settled through negotiations between the Founders.

9.2 In the event that disputes cannot be settled within 90 days of the receipt of the written notice by either Founder about the existence of such disagreement, the disputable matter shall be submitted upon agreement of the Founders for consideration to:

(a) the court of the Republic of Lithuania; or

(b) independent arbitration in Denmark, Copenhagen, to be conducted in accordance with International Chamber of Commerce Rules of Arbitration in the English language. In case the Founders do not reach agreement on the institution where the dispute is to be settled, the disputable matter shall be submitted for consideration to an independent arbitration provided in sub-para (b) of this paragraph."

27. The State contends - and it is a critical plank of its case - that, because it is not a "Founder", it is not a party to the agreement to arbitrate. This is an issue to which I will have to turn later in this judgment in the context of the submissions on section 9 of the Act. It submits, that even if, contrary to its primary contention, the State itself agreed to waive its own, as opposed to Geonafta's, sovereign immunity under article 35, that waiver under article 35 did not per se amount to a submission to the English court's jurisdiction for the purposes of section 2; accordingly, article 35 cannot assist Svenska unless the State is also found to have agreed that it would be a party to arbitration proceedings under article 9 of the JVA.

28. Therefore the questions which, as I see it, I have to decide under this head are as follows:

(i) on the true construction of article 35, did the State waive its own sovereign immunity thereunder, or did article 35 amount to a waiver of Sovereign Immunity in respect of Geonafta only;

(ii) if the former, did the waiver of the State's immunity in clause 35.1 amount to a submission to the jurisdiction of the English court, irrespective of whether the State was a party to the arbitration agreement contained in article 9 of the JVA.

If the answer to sub-issue (ii) is that the waiver of the State's immunity contained in clause 35.1 amounts to a submission to the jurisdiction of the English court only if the State was in fact a party to the arbitration agreement under article 9 of the JVA, because only in that event would the court have jurisdiction to enforce the Award, then there is no separate or free-standing issue under section 2 of the Act, since in reality the issue falls to be decided under section 9.

29. Subject to the points referred to below, it was common ground that the JVA had to be construed in accordance with its governing law, namely Lithuanian law, and that the relevant principles of construction were contained in articles 6.193-5 of the Lithuanian Civil Code as elaborated in a commentary by a Professor Mikelenas ("the Commentary"). However, the parties were not in agreement as to the relevance and importance of the principal text of the contract or whether article 6.193 represents a complete statement. In addition, the State relied on "international law and practice", which Mr Shackleton identified as "the interpretations of similar situations by other arbitral tribunals and by the courts of the United States, France and Switzerland where these issues have arisen". It was also common ground that, although the expert as to foreign law has to provide the English court with the relevant foreign principles and rules of construction, in relation to a contract it was for the English court, in the light of those principles and rules to determine the meaning of the document; see DICEY and MORRIS, The Conflict of Laws (2000) (13th edn) at paras 19-019 and 32-188-9; the Fourth Supplement thereto (2004) at page 26 and authorities there cited; and Rouyer Guillet & Cie v. Rouyer Guillet & Co Ltd [1949] 1 All ER 244 (CA). Accordingly, both parties correctly accepted that the views, given by their respective experts as to the true interpretation of the contract, were not admissible evidence. Likewise, the subjective views of Mr Zukovskis as to the interpretation of article 35 were not legitimate aids to my determination.

30. Articles 6.193-5 of the Lithuanian Civil Code and the relevant commentary (excluding footnotes) are as follows:

"Article 6.193: Rules on Interpretation of Contracts

1. A contract must be interpreted in accordance with good faith. In interpreting a contract, it is necessary primarily to determine the parties' good intentions and not rely only on a literal interpretation of the text of the contract. In the event the real intentions of the parties cannot be established, the contract must be interpreted in accordance with the meaning that reasonable persons analogous to the parties would have attributed to it in the same circumstances.

2. All terms and conditions of the contract must be interpreted taking into account their interrelation, the essence of the contract as well as its purpose and the circumstances of its conclusion. When interpreting a contract, it is necessary to have due regard to usual terms and conditions, although they are not provided for in the contract.

3. In the event of doubt concerning terms which may have several meanings, the meaning, which is most suitable according to the nature, essence and subject-matter of the contract, shall be attributed to these terms.

4. In the event of doubt concerning contractual conditions, these shall be interpreted against the contracting party that proposed such conditions, and in favour of the party that accepted them. In all cases, the conditions of a contract must be interpreted in favour of consumers or a party who concludes a contract by way of adherence.

5. When interpreting the contract, pre- contractual negotiations, an established course of conduct between the parties, post-contractual conduct and existing usages shall be taken into consideration as well.

Article 6.194: Language Discrepancies

Where a contract is drawn up in two or more languages and all texts of the contract have equal legal force, in the case of discrepancy between the versions, preference shall be given to the text which was drawn up first.

Article 6.195: Filling in Gaps of a Contract

Where parties leave certain matters unagreed, which are necessary for the performance of the contract, the court, at the request of a party, may fill in such gaps in the contract by establishing appropriate conditions, taking into account non-mandatory legal norms, the intentions of the parties, the purpose and essence of the contract, standards of good faith, reasonableness and justice.

. . .

THE COMMENTARY:

1. The article commented on repeats articles 4.1-4.6 of the UNIDROIT Principles. The contract has to be interpreted when a dispute arises between the parties concerning its validity, type, nature, amendment, termination, true meaning of one or another condition, *etc.*

In accordance with article 45 of the Law on Approval, Entry into Force, and Implementation of the Civil Code of the Republic of Lithuania, articles 6.193-6.195 of the Civil Code are applied to the interpretation of contracts irrespective of the time of their conclusion. This rule is set out because the rules on the interpretation of contracts provided in the article commented on are not new - they were known and recognised by both legal doctrine and judicial practice before the entry into force of the Civil Code.

Paragraph 1 of the article establishes two significant principles of interpretation of contracts. First, contracts must be interpreted in good faith. This principle requires that consideration be given to the intentions of both parties, analysis of the contract as a whole, and not certain part[s] of it, and in case of doubt as to the validity of a contract, to give priority to an interpretation that confirms the validity of the contract, *etc.* In addition to good faith, the principles of justice and reasonableness must be applied when interpreting contracts. For instance, both good faith and justice require that a contract be interpreted in favour of a party which is economically weaker, *e.g.* for the benefit of the consumer or an employee or a party which concluded the contract by way of adherence. Second, the article commented on embodies the principle of subjective interpretation of contracts which requires the determination of the true intentions of the parties and not only the written text of the contract. This principle means that in case of any discrepancy between the textual meaning of provisions of the contract and the true intentions of the parties, priority must be given to the parties' true intentions which they had in mind when concluding the contract. However, this principle should not be overestimated. In case the parties' true intentions vary, attention should be focused on the textual analysis of the contract, since it might be helpful in determining which party's intentions correspond to the textual meaning of the contract. Therefore, the article commented on also establishes that when the parties' true intentions cannot be determined, the contract must be interpreted in the way a reasonable person, being a party under identical circumstances, *e.g.* having the same profession, experience or qualification, would understand its text.

2. Paragraph 2 of the article being commented on sets out several other principles of contractual interpretation. First, this article establishes the principle of systemic interpretation of the contract which requires any contractual condition to be interpreted with regard to the entire context of the contract. Furthermore, no part of the contract, annex or any other constituent part should be left without consideration or evaluation (eg it is necessary to have regard to the preamble of the contract, its annexes, subsequent amendments, etc). In this case, the presumption that each word or phrase has a certain meaning and significance is valid, as usually parties do not use them without a reason. Therefore, it is necessary to determine the meaning of each word or phrase, and not on the contrary, to state that one or another word or phrase is meaningless or insignificant. Also, it is necessary to bear in mind that terms and conditions of a contract are of two types: explicitly expressed and implicit (article 6.196 of the Civil Code). Therefore, when inter- preting a contract, due regard must be paid not only to explicitly expressed terms and conditions, but also to implicit terms and conditions, for instance, those which are usually found in contracts of a similar nature. When interpreting contracts, it is necessary to take into account traditions of the trade, mutual relations between the parties, the circumstances of the conclusion of the contract, *etc.*

Another principle of contractual interpretation is the determination of its objectives. The purposes of a contract may help to reveal the parties' true intentions, the meaning of one or another condition, *etc.* The purposes of the contract may help to determine the type, nature of the contract and the extent of mutual rights and duties of the parties.

3. Paragraph 3 of the article commented on sets out the rule of interpretation when polysemic words and definitions are encountered. Frequently, the same words may have several meanings. Sometimes parties indicate in the contract interpretations of definitions used in the contract. Definitions must be interpreted in the way they were defined in the contract by the parties. Words or definitions the meaning of which is not set out in the contract must be assigned the meaning which is most acceptable in terms of the type, nature, essence, subject-matter, parties of the contract and other important circumstances.

4. Paragraph 4 of the article being commented on embodies the so-called contra preferentem rule. This means that terms and conditions that are unclear and ambiguous in the contract are to be interpreted against the benefit of the party which proposed or drafted them. For instance, unclear and ambiguous terms and conditions of a contract are to be interpreted against the benefit of the party which drafted them and in favour of the party who concluded the contract by way of adherence. As most consumer contracts are contracts of adherence, the article being commented on sets a general rule that in case of doubt, it is necessary to interpret contracts for the benefits of users and the party which has concluded the contract by way of adherence, *i.e.* the party who is economically weaker.

5. Paragraph 5 of the article being commented on sets out the general rule that not only the text of the contract, but also the actual circumstances surrounding the conclusion and fulfilment of the contract as well as other action of the parties are important for the interpretation of the contract. Therefore, when interpreting a contract, it is necessary to take into account the parties' pre-contractual negotiations, signed documents of negotiations, verbal and written statements by the parties, exchanges of correspondence, established relations between the parties, traditions of the trade and other customs, actual acts of the parties when concluding, fulfilling or making any amendments, etc to the contract. Actual acts of the parties must also be interpreted in order to determine the true intentions of the parties (para 1 of the article being commented on). Frequently, after lengthy negotiations parties include in the contract a special condition indicating that this is to be the sole agreement and the whole previous correspondence of the parties or the signed documents become invalid (the reservation of integration or consolidation). However, such a contractual condition does not have any impact on the interpretation of the contract - the whole pre-contractual documentation between the parties may be used for the interpretation of the contract and for the determination of the common intentions of the parties."

31. In my judgment, and applying the rules and principles set out in article 6, as amplified by the Commentary, on the true interpretation of article 35 of the JVA, the State clearly waived its own sovereign immunity thereunder, and it is impossible sensibly to construe article 35 as amounting to a waiver of Sovereign Immunity in respect of Geonafta only. Every draft of the JVA, except the first draft, and the final version of the JVA, contained a clause by which both Geonafta and the State waived state immunity and submitted to arbitration under the auspices of ICSID (International Centre for the Settlement of Investment Disputes). At no point did either party ever suggest that the waiver of immunity was restricted to Geonafta and that was all to which the State was agreeing. Accordingly on this issue I construe the JVA against the State's contentions.

THE APPLICABLE PRINCIPLES OF LITHUANIAN LAW

80. I heard lengthy expert evidence, both written and oral, relating to Lithuanian law. However there was, in the main, agreement between the parties on the essential requirements under Lithuanian law for a valid arbitration agreement. The principal features may be summarised as follows:

(i) At the time that the JVA was concluded there was no requirement that an arbitration agreement had to be in any particular form; see Professor Katuoka's Report, §§62-64.

(ii) At the time that the JVA was concluded there was no legal impediment to the State's agreeing to arbitrate disputes that might arise under that contract; see the First Report of Dr Foigt, page 7; and Professor Katuoka's Report, §64.

(iii) The principle of the separability of arbitration agreements is well-recognized under Lithuanian law; *i.e.* arbitration agreements/ clauses are separable from the contracts in which they might be contained; see Professor Katuoka's Report, §§83-89 and Second Report of Dr Foigt, §§27-28.

(iv) A valid arbitration agreement required the parties to express their common will to submit disputes between themselves to arbitration in writing; see Professor Katuoka's Report §§71-73.

(v) Although the JVA was concluded in 1993, when construing it and, in particular, article 9, the Civil Code 2000 (which entered into force on 1 July 2001) must be applied; article 45 of the Law on Approval, Coming into Force and Enforcement of the Civil Code of the Republic of Lithuania, dated 18 July 2000; see Professor Katuoka's Report, §§76-77 pp 16-17 and Second Report of Dr Foigt, §16.

81. Article 6.193 of the Civil Code, "Rules of the Interpretation of Contracts", and the Commentary thereon, (which I have already set out in full above) make it clear that the process of interpretation of a contract under Lithuanian law is significantly different from the approach that is applied under English law. In particular, under Lithuanian law it is legitimate to have regard to a far wider range of factual material, than would be permissible under English law.

82. I accept Mr Bools' submissions that the following important principles of Lithuanian law relating to the interpretation of contracts can be derived from the expert evidence and the materials which they produced:

(i) The overriding principle is that a contract should be interpreted in good faith.

(ii) Thereafter, the court's search is for "the real intentions of the parties without being limited by the literal meaning of the words". In other words, unlike under English law, the primary objective is to ascertain what the parties subjectively actually intended, regardless of the words they used. In the present case, therefore, the enquiry becomes one into whether Lithuania and Svenska intended that disputes between them would be resolved by arbitration, regardless of the literal meaning of the words they used.

(iii) In seeking to ascertain the parties' actual intention, regard must be had to "the preliminary negotiations between the parties, practices which the parties have established between themselves, the conduct of the parties subsequent to the conclusion of the contract, and the existing usages". Consequently, and again contrary to the position in English law, the court must look at the negotiations which led to the conclusion of the contract, take into account earlier drafts of the contract and consider each party's subjective intention.

(iv) If, despite these sources, what the parties really intended cannot be ascertained then the court will apply an objective interpretation and give the contract "the meaning that could be attributed in the same circumstances by reasonable persons in the corresponding position as the parties".

83. The issue before the court in reality is whether the pre-contractual dealings between the parties demonstrate that they intended disputes between Lithuania and Svenska to be submitted to ICC arbitration. I should say that both experts gave their opinions as to whether or not, applying Lithuanian law to the facts, the State was a party to the arbitration agreement in article 9 of the JVA. Professor Katuoka concluded that it was

not; Dr Foigt concluded that it was. However, as I have already said above, both parties agreed that, although the expert as to foreign law has to provide the English court with the relevant foreign principles and rules of construction, it was for the English court, in the light of those principles and rules, and any relevant factual material, to determine the meaning of the JVA. Accordingly it is not necessary for me to analyse, accept or reject the respective opinions of the experts as to the true construction of the JVA.

CONCLUSION

139. In my judgment, the evidence of the parties' pre-contractual negotiations demonstrates the common intention of the State, Geonafta and Svenska that their disputes (including those involving the State) should be settled by arbitration and that the dispute resolution provisions of article 9 of the Final JVA should apply to disputes between the State and Svenska, notwithstanding the inappropriate use of the words "Founders" and other words in that clause. In reaching this conclusion I have given due weight to the wording in clause 9. However, despite the fact that it does not prima facie reflect the actual intentions of the parties as I have held them to be, the relevant principles of article 6.193 of the Lithuanian Civil code require the court to search for the parties' real common intention notwithstanding the literal meaning of the words used. Accordingly, it follows that, in my judgment, the State was indeed a party to the arbitration agreement in article 9 of the JVA and therefore it is not entitled to State immunity in the present proceedings by virtue of section 9 of the Act.

Date: ***December 20, 2005***
Country: ***Switzerland***
Adjudicating Court: ***Bundesgericht***
Number: ***Unknown***
Parties: ***Unknown***

Keywords

QUESTION AS TO WHETHER PARTIES CAN CHOOSE A-NATIONAL PRINCIPLES AND RULES AS THE LAW GOVERNING THE CONTRACT – OPEN QUESTION WITH RESPECT TO SETS OF GENERAL PRINCIPLES AND RULES PREPARED BY INDEPENDENT ACADEMICS AND COMPARABLE TO DOMESTIC LEGAL SYSTEMS AS TO INTRINSIC EQUILIBRIUM, COMPREHENSIVENESS AND GENERAL RECOGNITION SUCH AS THE UNIDROIT PRINCIPLES – QUESTION TO BE ANSWERED IN THE NEGATIVE WITH RESPECT TO SECTORIAL RULES PREPARED BY PRIVATE ASSOCIATIONS SUCH AS THE VARIOUS INTERNATIONAL SPORT ASSOCIATIONS

PARTIES' CHOICE OF THE FIFA RULES AS THE LAW GOVERNING THE CONTRACT – AMOUNTS TO CONTRACTUAL INCORPORATION OF THE FIFA RULES WHICH WILL BIND PARTIES ONLY TO THE EXTENT THAT THEY DO NOT CONFLICT WITH MANDATORY PROVISIONS OF THE APPLICABLE DOMESTIC LAW

Abstract

The facts are the same as those in the decision of the Handelsgericht St. Gallen of 12 November 2004 reported in UNILEX.

Concerning the question as to whether in disputes before domestic courts parties are entitled to choose a-national or supranational rules as the law governing their contract, the Supreme Court, as the Court of first instance, recalled that opinions were divided and that, at least with respect to sets of general principles and rules prepared by independent academics and comparable to domestic legal systems as to intrinsic equilibrium, comprehensiveness and general recognition such as the UNIDROIT Principles, the affirmative view prevailed.

However the Supreme Court overruled the decision of the Court of first instance according to which the FIFA Rules could be chosen by the parties as the law governing the contract. Indeed, like other sectorial sets of rules prepared by international sport associations such as the Rules of the International Ski Federation, also the FIFA Rules have been prepared by a private organisation and therefore cannot be considered rules of law applicable instead of a particular domestic law. Consequently, in the case at hand the parties' choice of the FIFA Rules as the law governing their contract amounts to a contractual incorporation of these Rules which would bind the parties only to the extent that they are not contrary to the mandatory provisions of the applicable domestic law.

As to the merits, the Court stated that the limitation periods provided by Swiss law are mandatory and would therefore prevail over the conflicting provisions of the FIFA Rules, with the result that the claim brought by Plaintiff was not too late.

Full Text

132 III 285

[...]

Die X. AG mit Sitz in St. Gallen (Klägerin), vertreten durch einen FIFA-Agenten, schloss am 16. August 1999 mit der Y. mit Sitz in A. (Beklagte), einer griechischen Aktiengesellschaft, einen Vertrag über den Transfer eines von der Klägerin vertretenen Spielers. Gemäss dieser Vereinbarung sollte die Klägerin zunächst USD 15'000.-, zahlbar bis 30.September 1999, erhalten, sodann weitere USD 15'000.-, zahlbar bis 30.Dezember 1999, sofern der Arbeitsvertrag zwischen der Beklagten und dem Spieler bis zum 30. Juni 2000 verlängert würde, und schliesslich USD 30'000.-, zahlbar bis 30. Dezember 2000, und nochmals USD 30'000.-, zahlbar bis 30. Dezember 2001, sofern das Arbeitsverhältnis um weitere zwei Jahre verlängert würde. Am 5. Februar 2003 reichte die Klägerin beim Handelsgericht des Kantons St. Gallen Klage ein und verlangte von der Beklagten "US$ 15'000.- nebst 5 %Zins seit 30.09.99", "US$ 15'000.- nebst 5 % Zins seit 30.12.99" und "US$30'000.- nebst 5 % Zins seit 30.12.00". Die Beklagte beteiligte sich nicht am Verfahren und reichte keine Klageantwort ein. Das Handelsgericht wies die Klage ab. Gegen dieses Urteil führt die Klägerin Berufung beim Bundesgericht. Sie beantragt, das angefochtene Urteil aufzuheben und hält an den bereits vor Handelsgericht gestellten Anträgen fest. Die Beklagte hat keine Berufungsantwort eingereicht.

AUS DEN ERWÄGUNGEN:

Erwägung 1

1. In Art. 3 des Vertrages vom 16. August 1999, auf welchen die Klägerin ihre Forderung stützt, haben die Parteien bestimmt, ihre Vereinbarung solle den FIFA-Regeln und dem Schweizer Recht unterstehen ("This agreement is governed by FIFA rules and Swiss law").
Die Vorinstanz hat diese Vertragsklausel als kumulative Rechtswahl in dem Sinne interpretiert, dass die FIFA-Regeln dem nationalen schweizerischen Recht als *lex specialis* vorgehen sollten. Sie hat das Reglement angewendet,das die FIFA speziell für Spielervermittlungen am 10. Dezember 2000 erlassen hat und das ein Verfahren für Streitigkeiten vorsieht. Danach sind unter anderem Rechtsvorkehren spätestens zwei Jahre nach den zugrunde liegenden Vorfällen den zuständigen Organen einzureichen. Die Vorinstanz hat diese Bestimmung als Verwirkungsfrist interpretiert und die Klage mit der Begründung abgewiesen, im Zeitpunkt der Klageeinreichung sei die zweijährige

Verwirkungsfrist bereits abgelaufen gewesen. Die Klägerin rügt, die Vorinstanz habe Art. 116 Abs. 1 IPRG verletzt, denn das FIFA-Reglement könne nicht Gegenstand einer Rechtswahl sein.

1.1 Nach Art. 116 Abs. 1 IPRG untersteht der Vertrag dem gewählten Recht. Die Rechtswahl als kollisionsrechtliche Verweisung hat zur Folge, dass sowohl die dispositiven als auch die zwingenden Normen der gewählten Rechtsordnung zur Anwendung gelangen und die Bestimmungen des ohne Rechtswahl (im Rahmen einer "objektiven" Anknüpfung nach Art. 117 IPRG) anwendbaren Vertragsstatuts ersetzen (KELLER/KREN KOSTKIEWICZ, Zürcher Kommentar, N. 7 zu Art. 116 IPRG; AMSTUTZ/VOGT/WANG, Basler Kommentar, N. 11 zu Art. 116 IPRG mit Hinweisen). Dagegen lässt die materiellrechtliche Verweisung die gewählten Normen zum Vertragsinhalt werden. Sie ermöglicht den Parteien, ihre Rechtsbeziehung in den Schranken des anwendbaren Sachrechts frei zu gestalten (AMSTUTZ/VOGT/WANG, Basler Kommentar, N. 11 zu Art. 116 IPRG; KELLER/KREN KOSTKIEWICZ, Zürcher Kommentar, N. 8 und 83 ff.zu Art. 116 IPRG).

1.2 Ob die Parteien im Rahmen von Art. 116 Abs. 1 IPRG nur staatliche Rechtsordnungen wählen können oder ob auch die Wahl anationaler Normen zulässig ist, geht aus dem Wortlaut der Bestimmung nicht eindeutig hervor(BUCHER/BONOMI, Droit international privé, 2. Aufl., Basel/Genf/München 2004, S. 258 f.; VISCHER/ HUBER/ OSER, Internationales Vertragsrecht, 2.Aufl., Bern 2000, S. 69), worauf schon in der Vernehmlassung zumGesetzesentwurf hingewiesen wurde (vgl. Bundesgesetz über das internationale Privatrecht, Darstellung der Stellungnahmen auf Grund des Gesetzesentwurfs der Expertenkommission und des entsprechenden Begleitberichts, Bundesamt für Justiz 1980, S. 380 f.). Obwohl in der Botschaft im Vergleich zum Gesetzesentwurf der Expertenkommission eine minime redaktionelle Änderung vorgenommen wurde (vgl. BBl 1983 I 498, Art. 113; Eidg. Justizabteilung,Bundesgesetz über das internationale Privatrecht [IPR-Gesetz],Gesetzesentwurf der Expertenkommission und Begleitbericht, S. 29, Art. 117),erfolgte diesbezüglich keine Klarstellung. Die Expertenkommission selbstging davon aus, die Wahl nichtstaatlicher Rechte sei ausgeschlossen(VISCHER, in: Freiburger Kolloquium über den Entwurf zu einem Bundesgesetz über das internationale Privatrecht, Zürich 1979, S. 49).
In der Lehre ist die Frage umstritten (zum deutschen Recht vgl. REITHMANN/MARTINY, Internationales Vertragsrecht, 6. Aufl., Köln 2004, S. 79 ff.). Ein Teil der Lehre spricht sich generell gegen die Gültigkeit kollisionsrechtlicher Verweisungen auf anationales Recht aus (SCHWANDER, Einführung in das internationale Privatrecht, Zweiter Band:Besonderer Teil, St. Gallen/Lachen 1997, N. 489, S. 227 f.; Vincent BRULHART, Le choix de la loi applicable - questions choisies,Habilitationsschrift St. Gallen 2004, S. 254; KARRER, Basler Kommentar, N.60 zu Art. 187 IPRG, allerdings unter anderem mit Hinweis auf HEINI, IPRGKommentar, N. 7 zu Art. 187 IPRG, der die entsprechende Passage in der neuenAuflage des Kommentars nicht beibehalten hat, vgl. HEINI, Zürcher Kommentar, 2. Aufl., N. 7 zu Art. 187 IPRG; zweifelnd: KNOEPFLER/ SCHWEIZER/ OTHENIN-GIRARD, Droit international privé suisse, 3.Aufl., Bern 2005, S. 254, N. 499). Andere befürworten die Zulässigkeit generell (PATOCCHI, Das neue internationale Vertragsrecht der Schweiz, in:Internationales Privatrecht/Lugano-Abkommen, Zürich 1989, S. 36), in Bezug auf internationale Handelsbräuche (AMSTUTZ/VOGT/WANG, Basler Kommentar, N.21 zu Art. 116 IPRG; vgl. auch BUCHER/BONOMI, a.a.O., S. 258) oder zumindestin Bezug auf bestimmte wissenschaftliche Regelungswerke, die bezüglich

Ausgewogenheit, Anerkennung, und Regelungsdichte mit staatlichen Rechtsordnungen vergleichbar sind (VISCHER/ HUBER/OSER, a.a.O., S. 67 ff.; VISCHER, Die kollisionsrechtliche Bedeutung der Wahl einer nichtstaatlichen Ordnung für den staatlichen Richter am Beispiel der UNIDROIT Principles of International Commercial Contracts, in: SCHWENZER/HAGER [Hrsg.], Festschrift für Peter Schlechtriem zum 70. Geburtstag, Tübingen 2003, S. 445 ff.,insbesondere S. 451 f.; Bernard DUTOIT, Droit international privé suisse: commentaire de la loi fédérale du 18 décembre 1987, 4. Aufl., Basel 2005, N.12 zu Art. 116 IPRG, S. 384 f.; BUCHER/BONOMI, a.a.O., S. 258; AMSTUTZ/VOGT/WANG, Basler Kommentar, N. 21 zu Art. 116 IPRG; vgl. auch Kurt SIEHR, Die Parteiautonomie im internationalen Privatrecht, in:FORSTMOSER/GIGER/ HEINI/SCHLUEP [Hrsg.], Festschrift für Max Keller zum 65.Geburtstag, Zürich 1989, S. 501 f.).

1.3 Nach der Praxis des Bundesgerichts kommt Regelwerken privater Organisationen auch dann nicht die Qualität von Rechtsnormen zu, wenn sie sehr detailliert und ausführlich sind wie beispielsweise die SIA-Normen (BGE 126 III 388 E. 9d S. 391 mit Hinweisen) oder die Verhaltensregeln des internationalen Skiverbandes (BGE 122 IV 17 E. 2b/aa S. 20; 106 IV 350 E. 3aS. 352, je mit Hinweisen). Von privaten Verbänden aufgestellte Bestimmungen stehen vielmehr grundsätzlich zu den staatlichen Gesetzen in einem Subordinationsverhältnis und können nur Beachtung finden, soweit das staatliche Recht für eine autonome Regelung Raum lässt (Jérome JAQUIER, La qualification juridique des règles autonomes des organisations sportives, Diss. Neuenburg 2004, Rz. 212). Sie bilden kein "Recht" im Sinne von Art.116 Abs. 1 IPRG und können auch nicht als "lex sportiva transnationalis" anerkannt werden, wie dies von einer Lehrmeinung befürwortet wird (Jérome JAQUIER, a.a.O., Rz. 293 ff.). Die Regeln der (internationalen) Sportverbände können nur im Rahmen einer materiellrechtlichen Verweisung Anwendung finden und daher nur als Parteiabreden anerkannt werden, denen zwingende nationalrechtliche Bestimmungen vorgehen (KELLER/KREN KOSTKIEWICZ, Zürcher Kommentar, N. 84 zu Art. 116 IPRG).

1.4 Die Vorinstanz hat dem Verweis auf die FIFA-Regeln in Art. 3 des Vertrages vom 16. August 1999 bundesrechtswidrig die Bedeutung einer Rechtswahl zuerkannt. Dem Verweis auf das FIFA-Reglement kann nur die Bedeutung einer materiellrechtlichen Verweisung, d.h. einer (globalen) Übernahme in den Vertrag der Parteien zukommen. Dies widerspricht übrigens der Regelungsabsicht der FIFA nicht, weist doch die Präambel des FIFA-Reglements über die Spielervermittlungen vom 10. Dezember 2000 die Nationalverbände an, gestützt auf die Richtlinien verbandsinterne Reglemente zu erstellen (Ziffer 2) und bei deren Ausarbeitung die nationaleGesetzgebung und die internationalen Staatsverträge zu berücksichtigen(Ziffer 3). Die FIFA anerkennt damit die Subordination ihrer Verbandsregelung unter die massgebende nationalstaatliche Rechtsordnung mitsamt den internationalen Verträgen. Die Bestimmung in Ziffer 3 des Vertrages der Parteien ist als materiellrechtliche Verweisung zu verstehen,während die Rechtswahl sich allein auf die schweizerische Rechtsordnung bezieht, deren zwingende Normen somit Anwendung finden.

Erwägung 2

2. Nach herrschender Meinung verbietet Art. 129 OR eine vertragliche Verkürzung der Verjährungsfrist (VON TUHR/ESCHER, Allgemeiner Teil des schweizerischen Obligatio-

nenrechts, 3. Aufl., Zürich 1974, Bd. II, S. 217; SPIRO, Die Begrenzung privater Rechte durch Verjährungs-, Verwirkungs-, und Fatalfristen, Bern 1975, Bd. 1, S. 867 f.; DÄPPEN, Basler Kommentar, 3. Aufl., N. 5 zu Art. 129 OR; ENGEL, Traité des obligations en droit suisse: Dispositions générales du CO, 2. Aufl., Bern 1997, S. 809; PICHONNAZ, Commentaire romand, N. 5 zu Art. 129 CO; GAUCH/SCHLUEP/SCHMID/REY, Schweizerisches Obligationenrecht, Allgemeiner Teil, Bd. II, 8. Aufl., Rz. 3566 mit Verweis auf BGE 63 II 180). Dies schliesst zwar nicht aus, dass eine Forderung von einer Resolutivbedingung abhängig gemachtwerden kann. Allerdings ist eine Bedingung, wonach die Forderung binnen bestimmter Frist irgendwie gerichtlich einzuklagen sei, der Abkürzung der Verjährungsfrist gleichzustellen. Indem die Vorinstanz Art. 22 Abs. 3 des FIFA-Reglements im Ergebnis als Abkürzung der gesetzlichen Verjährungsfrist (Art. 127 OR) ausgelegt hat, hat sie die zwingende Norm von Art. 129 OR des schweizerischen Rechts missachtet, das die Parteien in Ziffer 3 des Vertrages gewählt haben. Der angefochtene Entscheid ist aus diesem Grund aufzuheben. Da die Vorinstanz keine Feststellungen zur materiellen Begründetheit der eingeklagten Forderung getroffen hat, ist die Sache zur Neubeurteilung gestützt auf Art. 64 Abs. 1 OG an die Vorinstanz zurückzuweisen.

Date: **2006**
Country: **People's Republic of China**
Adjudicating Court: **Xiamen Intermediate People's Court**
Number: **Unknown**
Parties: **Xiamen Xiang Yu Group Ltd. v. Mechel Trading AG**

Keywords

SALES CONTRACT BETWEEN A SWISS AND A CHINESE COMPANY – CHOICE OF LAWS CLAUSE REFERRING TO CISG AND, FOR ISSUES NOT COVERED BY CISG, TO THE UNIDROIT PRINCIPLES

Abstract

A Chinese company and a Swiss company entered into a contract for the trade of steel. The contract, concluded on 26 March 2004, contained the following provisions: "The application and interpretation of this contract shall be governed by the United Nations Convention on Contracts for the International sale of Goods. On Issues not covered by this Convention, the UNIDROIT Principles (1994) shall apply. In case both instruments cannot cover the issue under dispute, international customs and the law of Seller's place of business (Swiss law) shall apply", and "All disputes arising from or related to this contract shall be decided in accordance with the ICC Arbitration Rules [...] The place of arbitration is Beijing, China, and the language of arbitration is Chinese and English". In August 2004 the Swiss company commenced an arbitration proceedings, and in a partial award rendered in December 2004 the Arbitral Tribunal affirmed its competence. The Chinese company challenged the validity of the arbitration agreement before the Chinese Court which rejected the application and confirmed the validity of the arbitration agreement.

Full Text

[Not yet available]

Sources

Notice of the decision kindly provided by Ms. JING XI.

Date: ***January 10, 2006***
Country: ***Italy***
Adjudicating Court: ***Tribunale Padova - Sez. Este***
Number: ***Unknown***
Parties: ***Unknown***

Keywords

JURISDICTION – EUROPEAN COUNCIL REGULATION NO. 44/2001 ON JURISDICTION AND RECOGNITION AND ENFORCEMENT OF JUDGEMENTS IN CIVIL AND COMMERCIAL MATTERS – JURISDICTION OF COURT FOR PLACE OF PERFORMANCE

NEED FOR AN AUTONOMOUS INTERPRETATION OF REGULATION – RECOURSE TO CISG IN VIEW OF ITS LARGE CONSENSUS WORLDWIDE AND ITS IMPORTANCE AS MODEL FOR OTHER INSTRUMENTS ADOPTED AT EUROPEAN LEVEL

NOTION OF "CONTRACT OF SALE" UNDER THE REGULATION (ART. 1(1)(B)) – DEFINED ACCORDING TO CISG

NOTION OF "PLACE OF DELIVERY" UNDER THE REGULATION (ART. 5 (1)(B)) – RECOURSE TO ART. 31(A) CISG – SOLUTION CONFIRMED BY OTHER "AUTONOMOUS" INTERNATIONAL INSTRUMENTS SUCH AS UNIDROIT PRINCIPLES OF INTERNATIONAL COMMERCIAL CONTRACTS (SEE ART. 6.1.6(1)(B)) AND PRINCIPLES OF EUROPEAN CONTRACT LAW (SEE ART. 7:101(1)(B))

Abstract

An Italian manufacturer and an English distributor concluded a sales contract on approval of two merry-go-rounds made and to be installed by the former in Great Britain. As neither the price was paid nor the goods returned to the manufacturer within the time provided in the contract, the seller brought an action against the buyer before an Italian Court.

The Italian Court declined jurisdiction on the ground of European Council Regulation no. 44/2001 on Jurisdiction and the Recognition and Enforcement of Judgements in Civil and Commercial Matters, which had to be applied in lieu of the 1968 Brussels Convention since the claim had been brought after the Regulation's entry into force and the dispute concerned a "civil or commercial matter" as required by its Art. 1(1).

After recalling that the Regulation, contrary to the Brussels Convention, expressly provides that in the case of a sales contract the place of performance for the purposes of Article 5(1)(b)is the place in a Member State "where the goods were delivered or should have been delivered under the contract", the Court first of all pointed out that the notion of "sales contract", which has not been defined by the Regulation, has to be interpreted autonomously. For this purpose, in view of its large consensus worldwide and its importance as a model for other instruments adopted at European level such as Directive no. 99/44 on the sale and consumer goods and associated guarantees, the Court decided to make recourse to CISG, according to which a sales contract may be defined as a contract whereby the seller is obliged to deliver the goods, transfer of the property in the goods and possibly to deliver the documents relating to the goods while the buyer is obliged to pay the price and to take delivery of the goods (see Arts. 30, 53 CISG). In the case at hand the contract was definitely to be considered a sales contract. The fact that the seller was also obliged to install the merry-go-rounds at the place of delivery was irrelevant since this latter obligation was not preponderant (Art. 3(2) CISG). Also with respect to the notion of the place of delivery under Art. 5(1)(b) of the Regulation the Court stated that it had to be interpreted "autonomously" and that, unless otherwise agreed between the parties, in cases where the contract involves the carriage of the goods the place of delivery is to be considered the place where the seller hands the goods over to the first carrier for transmission to the buyer. In reaching this conclusion the Court referred first of all to Art. 31(a) CISG, but at the same time it pointed out that "this solution is confirmed by two other equally autonomous, though not binding, instruments such as the UNIDROIT Principles of International Commercial Contracts (Art. 6.1.6(1)) and the Principles of European Contract Law (Art. 7:101(1)(b))". In the case at hand, however, since the seller was contractually bound to install the merry-go-rounds upon delivery in Great Britain, it could not be considered to have fulfiled its obligation of delivery by having handed the goods over to the first carrier. Consequently, in the case at hand the place of delivery was not located in Italy but in Great Britain and the Italian courts had therefore no jurisdiction.

Full Text

SVOLGIMENTO DEL PROCESSO

Con atto di citazione notificato il 9 agosto 2004, Pessa Luciano, esercente l'impresa individuale denominata Pessa Studio con sede in Montagnana (PD), conveniva in giudizio W.H.S. Saddlers International di Pradelles Lin con sede in Otterbourne, Hampshire (Inghilterra), affermando:

- che in data 23 maggio 2003 aveva concluso con la convenuta un contratto con cui era ad essa concesso di promuovere in via esclusiva la vendita dei prodotti dell'attore;

- che il 14 giugno 2003 la convenuta accettava due forniture di giostre del valore di Euro 12.791,65 e 10.469,68, pattuendo che le macchine sarebbero rimaste in visione per sei mesi, trascorsi i quali sarebbe stato pagato il relativo prezzo oppure restituite al venditore;

- che le giostre venivano consegnate e montate in data 23 giugno 2003 in due diverse località dell'Inghilterra;

- che l'attore aveva inoltre sostenuto le spese di trasporto;

- che trascorso il termine pattuito il prezzo dei beni non è stato pagato e la merce non è stata restituita;

- che l'inadempimento della convenuta era totale;

- che sussisteva la giurisdizione italiana, poiché il contratto era stato concluso in Italia ed il pagamento doveva essere effettuato al domicilio dell'attore.

Pessa Luciano chiedeva pertanto che W.H.S. Saddlers International di Pradelles Lin fosse condannata al pagamento della complessiva somma di Euro 26.452,72, oltre interessi legali dalla scadenza delle fatture al saldo.

La convenuta non si costituiva e all'udienza del 18 maggio 2005 ne veniva dichiarata la contumacia.

Con ordinanza del 25 ottobre 2005, il giudice non ammetteva le prove indicate dall'attore e fissava udienza di precisazione delle conclusioni.

All'udienza del 16 novembre 2005, erano precisate le conclusioni e la causa era trattenuta in decisione allo scadere del termine concesso per il deposito della comparsa conclusionale.

MOTIVAZIONE

Si osserva preliminarmente che il contratto datato 23 maggio 2003 non è stato sottoscritto dalla convenuta. E' vero tuttavia che con lettera 5 febbraio 2004 W.H.S. Saddlers International chiedeva di "rinnovare il contratto di vendita dei prodotti di Pessa Studio& sino al 31.12.2009" (v. doc. n. 2 del fasc. dell'attore). Si può perciò ritenere che il contratto fosse stato effettivamente concluso, almeno in forma orale. Rimane però il dubbio circa il luogo in cui sarebbe avvenuta la perfezione del negozio, giacché l'indicazione "Montagnana-Montanaro" presente in calce al documento non può essere presa in considerazione, in ragione della mancanza di contestuale sottoscrizione del testo contrattuale. E' possibile che l'accordo sia stato raggiunto telefonicamente oppure che la convenuta, ricevuto il contratto sottoscritto dall'attore presso la propria sede legale, l'abbia accettato dandone comunicazione orale al proponente. Si spiegherebbe così il fatto che l'attore non è in possesso di esemplare firmato da W.H.S. Saddlers International.

A prescindere da ciò, si rileva che l'accordo attribuiva alla parte convenuta la facoltà di promuovere, in condizioni di esclusiva, la vendita dei prodotti di Pessa Studio in Gran Bretagna "rendendosi acquirente diretto o acquistandoli per conto del cliente finale"; l'attore si obbliga fra l'altro a "fornire il materiale venduto e, se richiesto, montarlo nel luogo, entro il tempo e alle condizioni di volta in volta pattuite". Si trattava quindi di un contratto normativo, che avrebbe dovuto disciplinare successive forniture da eseguirsi in Gran Bretagna, ove la merce sarebbe stata consegnata ed eventualmente installata da Pessa Luciano.

Le due forniture del giugno 2003 sono state per l'appunto eseguite in Inghilterra, come attestano i documenti di trasporto allegati dall'attore. Si tratta di due compravendite di giostre, contenenti una clausola di gradimento, che consentiva al compratore di restituire la merce entro sei mesi dal ricevimento: in mancanza di restituzione, il prezzo doveva essere pagato, a prescindere dal fatto che W.H.S. Saddlers International avesse o no rivenduto le giostre.

Anche le modalità di conclusione di queste compravendite internazionali risultano incerte. La venditrice ha trasmesso la sua proposta per iscritto alla convenuta, inviandola presso la sua sede legale. Non è però dato sapere come W.H.S. Saddlers International abbia accettato l'offerta, non essendo stata prodotta alcuna documentazione in proposito.

E' comunque verosimile che l'accettazione sia intervenuta, considerato che le giostre sono state consegnate ed installate in due località inglesi (Tamporlay e Durley). Allo scadere del termine semestrale, l'attore ha richiesto il pagamento, senza ottenere risposta.

Questione pregiudiziale è stabilire se sussista la giurisdizione del giudice italiano. Per affrontare il problema, occorre dapprima individuare le norme di diritto internazionale processuale applicabili. Nella specie esse sono le norme poste dal Regolamento CE n. 44/2001 del Consiglio del 22 dicembre 2000, concernente la competenza giurisdizionale e l'esecuzione delle decisioni in materia civile e commerciale (regolamento cosiddetto Bruxelles 1, di seguito: Regolamento), che a partire dalla data di entrata in vigore - ossia dal 1° marzo 2002 - ha sostituito (fatta eccezione per le ipotesi in cui il foro adito sia un foro danese o in cui il convenuto abbia la propria sede d'affari in Danimarca, ma non anche per l'ipotesi in cui l'attore abbia la propria sede d'affari in Danimarca) la Convenzione di Bruxelles del 1968, relativa alla competenza giurisdizionale e alla esecuzione di decisioni in materia civile e commerciale.

Affinché il Regolamento - obbligatorio in tutti i suoi elementi e direttamente applicabile in Italia come negli altri Stati membri della Comunità Europea (nel limite già ricordato) in base al trattato che istituisce quest'ultima - possa trovare applicazione, debbono coesistere più requisiti, come chiarito anche dalla giurisprudenza straniera (v., ad esempio, OLG Düsseldorf, 30 gennaio 2004, pubblicata alla pagina web [...]), alla quale occorre fare riferimento (senza che però ad essa possa attribuirsi valore di precedente), al fine di assicurare al Regolamento la piena efficacia, nonché un'applicazione uniforme in tutti gli Stati contraenti: esigenza già sottolineata dalla Corte di Giustizia delle Comunità Europee con riferimento alla Convenzione di Bruxelles richiamata in precedenza (per tutte, v. sentenza 1° ottobre 2002, causa 167/00, Verein für Konsumenteninformation, punto 35).

Da un punto di vista temporale, è sufficiente che l'azione sia proposta posteriormente all'entrata in vigore del Regolamento, come si evince facilmente dal suo art. 66, 1° comma: condizione di applicabilità (temporale) che nel caso di specie senz'altro sussiste.

Da un punto di vista materiale occorre che la controversia verta su una questione "civile e commerciale" (art. 1, 1° comma, del Regolamento). Quando questo accada non viene precisato dal Regolamento, come non era precisato neppure dalla Convenzione di Bruxelles. Ciò non deve però indurre ad "interpretare i termini di tale disposizione come un semplice rinvio al diritto interno dell'uno o dell'altro degli Stati in questione" (Corte di Giustizia, sentenza 14 novembre 2002, causa 271/00, Gemeente Steenbergen, punto 28); occorre piuttosto interpretare il concetto in modo "autonomo", come affermato dalla giurisprudenza della Corte di Giustizia in relazione alla Convenzione di Bruxelles (v. sentenza 15 maggio 2003, 266/01, Préservatrice foncière TIARD SA, punto 20; sentenza 14 novembre 2002, causa 271/00, Gemeente Steenbergen, punto 28; sentenza 21 aprile 1993, causa 172/91, Volker Sonntag, punto 18; sentenza 16 dicembre 1980, causa 814/79, Niederlande, punto 7; sentenza 22 febbraio 1979, C-133/78, Henri Gourdain, punto 3): giurisprudenza alla quale, sulla questione in esame, ci si può senz'altro richiamare, anche allo scopo di "garantire la continuità tra la Convenzione di Bruxelles e il presente Regolamento" (esigenza a cui fa riferimento il considerando 19).

Nel caso in esame, non può esservi dubbio che la disputa rientri tra la "materia civile e commerciale", avendo l'attore richiesto il pagamento di una somma di denaro che rappresenta il corrispettivo della fornitura di beni mobili da lui professionalmente prodotti. Pertanto, non trattandosi di una delle materie che l'art. 1, 2° comma, del Regolamento esclude dal suo ambito di applicazione, può dirsi che esso risulti applicabile anche dal punto di vista materiale.

Come prima di esso la Convenzione di Bruxelles, anche il Regolamento prevede come criterio fondamentale di competenza il domicilio del convenuto. Infatti, l'art. 2, 1° comma, del Regolamento (come già l'art. 2, 1° comma, della Convenzione di Bruxelles), afferma che "salve le disposizioni del presente Regolamento, le persone domiciliate nel territorio di un determinato Stato membro sono convenute, a prescindere dalla loro nazionalità, davanti ai giudici di tale Stato membro". Nella specie, non sarebbe il giudice italiano, bensì quello inglese, in quanto alla luce dell'art. 60 del Regolamento - che rinvia a tre criteri alternativi di collegamento (sede statutaria, amministrazione centrale e centro di attività principale), utilizzabili per la determinazione della sede delle persone giuridiche - non si potrebbe asserire che il tribunale adito sia il foro generale del convenuto inglese (per un caso analogo, v. Trib. Rovereto, 28 agosto 2004, pubblicata alla pagina web [...]).

Ne consegue che la competenza del Tribunale di Padova non potrebbe che fondarsi su uno dei criteri speciali di giurisdizione tassativamente previsti dal Regolamento: dato l'oggetto della controversia, il criterio che verrebbe in considerazione sarebbe quello previsto in "materia contrattuale" dall'art. 5, n. 1, del Regolamento.

La lite verte senz'altro in "materia contrattuale" (concetto anch'esso non meglio precisato dal Regolamento, che necessita di una definizione autonoma, "facendo riferimento al sistema e agli scopi [del Regolamento] al fine di garantirne l'applicazione uniforme in tutti gli Stati", non potendo essere "interpretato come un rinvio alla qualificazione fornita dal diritto nazionale al rapporto giuridico dedotto dinanzi al giudice nazionale": così Corte di Giustizia, sentenza 5 febbraio 2004, causa 265/02, Frahuil SA, punto 22). Infatti, conformemente alla giurisprudenza sviluppatasi sulla Convenzione di Bruxelles - che per la ragione di "continuità interpretativa" già ricordata può essere utilizzata per interpretare il Regolamento, quando si tratti di disposizioni che ricalcano le norme della Convenzione di Bruxelles (in questo senso, v. anche Trib. Rovereto, cit.) -, la nozione di "materia contrattuale" deve essere senz'altro intesa come ricomprendente le situazioni in cui esiste "un obbligo giuridico liberamente assunto da una parte nei confronti di un'altra" (Corte di Giustizia, sentenza 20 gennaio 2005, causa 27/02, Petra Engler, punto 51; sentenza 5 febbraio 2004, causa 265/02, Frahuil SA, punto 24; sentenza 17 giugno 1992, causa 26/91, Handte, punto 15): è il caso di specie, avendo W.H.S. Saddlers International liberamente assunto l'obbligazione di corrispondere il prezzo delle giostre ad essa consegnata, qualora non fossero state restituite al fornitore nel termine pattuito.

Si pone quindi la questione se sussista la giurisdizione del giudice italiano in virtù del criterio speciale previsto dall'art. 5, n. 1, del Regolamento.

In materia contrattuale, tanto il Regolamento quanto la Convenzione di Bruxelles consentono all'attore di citare il convenuto, domiciliato nel territorio di uno Stato membro, davanti al giudice di un altro Stato membro, se questo corrisponde con il "giudice del luogo in cui l'obbligazione dedotta in giudizio è stata o deve essere eseguita". A differenza però di quanto previsto dalla Convenzione di Bruxelles - che imponeva dapprima l'individuazione analitica dell'obbligazione specificamente dedotta a fondamento della domanda (v., in merito, la giurisprudenza della Corte di Giustizia iniziata con la sentenza 6 ottobre 1976, causa 14/76, De Bloos, punto 9 ss.), e quindi la determinazione per mezzo del diritto internazionale privato dell'ordinamento nazionale applicabile, sulla base del quale poi determinare il locus solutionis di quell'obbligazione (v. la giurisprudenza della Corte di Giustizia a partire dalla sentenza 6 ottobre 1976, causa 12/76, Tessili, punto 13 ss.), almeno quando non era applicabile una convenzione di diritto materiale uniforme a mezzo della quale determinare il luogo di esecuzione dell'obbligazione posta a base della concreta domanda (v. Corte di Giustizia, sentenza 29 giugno 1994, Custom Made Commercial, punto 26 ss.) - il Regolamento non richiede, quantomeno per le tipologie contrattuali maggiormente diffuse a livello internazionale (ossia il contratto di compravendita di beni e quello di prestazione di servizi), che venga innanzitutto "localizzata" l'obbligazione controversa. Difatti, il legislatore comunitario, limitatamente alle ipotesi rientranti nell'ambito dell'art. 5 n. 1 lett. b), ha individuato ex auctoritate quale sia (con riguardo alle due tipologie contrattuali ricordate) il luogo di esecuzione dell'obbligazione dedotta in giudizio, cercando così di superare le critiche che la soluzione prevista dalla Convenzione di Bruxelles aveva suscitato.

Pur facendo salvo un diverso accordo delle parti, con una sorta di fictio legis il legislatore comunitario ha individuato, per quanto riguarda il contratto di compravendita di beni, il luogo di esecuzione dell'obbligazione dedotta in giudizio nel "luogo, situato in uno Stato membro, in cui i beni sono stati o avrebbero dovuto essere consegnati in base al contratto". E' una finzione giuridica perché il criterio vale per qualsiasi obbligazione facente capo al venditore e al compratore, si tratti dunque dell'obbligazione di pagamento del prezzo o dell'obbligazione di consegna dei beni.

Nel caso in esame, è dunque irrilevante che l'obbligazione dedotta in giudizio sia quella di pagamento del prezzo: ciò che conta, affinché si possa affermare la giurisdizione, è da un lato che l'obbligazione abbia fonte in un contratto di compravendita di beni, e dall'altro che il luogo di consegna dei beni non sia situato all'estero.

Al pari di altri concetti già menzionati, anche quello di "compravendita di beni" non è definito dal Regolamento. Anche con riferimento a questo non si potrà ricorrere a definizioni nazionali, non potendosi altrimenti garantire l'applicazione uniforme del Regolamento nei vari Paesi in cui è in vigore. Occorre, quindi, perseguire ancora una volta un'interpretazione "autonoma". A questo proposito può essere utile, malgrado una pronuncia contraria (v. Trib. Rovereto, cit.), fare ricorso alla Convenzione delle Nazioni Unite sui contratti di vendita internazionale di beni mobili, in Italia ratificata con l. 11 dicembre 1985, n. 765, ed entrata in vigore il 1° gennaio 1988, e ciò pur non essendo la Convenzione uno strumento di diritto internazionale processuale, come invece il Regolamento, bensì una Convenzione di "solo" diritto materiale (per questa qualifica v., recentemente, McDowell Valley Vineyards, Inc. v. Sabaté USA Inc. *et al.*, U.S. District Court, Northern District of California, 2 novembre 2005, pubblicata alla pagina web [...]; ma anche Corte di Cassazione, Sez. un., 20 aprile 2004, no. 7503, pubblicata alla pagina web [...]; Tribunale di Padova, 25 febbraio 2004, in Giurisprudenza italiana, 2004, p. 1403 ss.; HG Zürich, 26 aprile 1995, pubblicata alla pagina web [...]; Trib. Comm. Buxelles, 5 ottobre 1994, pubblicata in traduzione inglese alla pagina web [...]). L'attenzione rivolta alla Convenzione delle Nazioni Unite è giustificata, da un lato, dal fatto che il concetto da interpretare ("compravendita di beni") è sicuramente proprio del diritto materiale e, dall'altro, in considerazione del ruolo preminente assunto a livello internazionale dalla Convenzione e del suo carattere "espansivo", costituendo un corpo di regole sì autonomo, ma per nulla chiuso in se stesso: non a caso lo stesso legislatore comunitario ha inteso utilizzare la Convenzione quale modello per la Direttiva 99/44/CE del Parlamento europeo e del Consiglio, 25 maggio 1999, concernente alcuni aspetti della vendita e delle garanzie dei beni di consumo.

In base agli artt. 30 e 53 della Convenzione delle Nazioni Unite, può essere definito contratto di compravendita "il negozio in forza del quale il venditore è obbligato a consegnare i beni, trasferirne la proprietà ed eventualmente rilasciare tutti i documenti ad essi relativi, mentre il compratore è obbligato a pagare il prezzo ed a prendere in consegna i beni" (*cfr.* Trib. Padova, 11 gennaio 2005, in Rivista di diritto internazionale privato e processuale, 2005, p. 791; Trib. Padova, 25 febbraio 2004, in Giurisprudenza italiana, 2004, p. 1404). La circostanza che nella specie il contratto non preveda solo un dare ma anche un facere (essendo il venditore obbligato a montare le giostre) non esclude la possibilità di qualificarlo come compravendita ai sensi della Convenzione delle Nazioni Unite, in quanto quest'ultima "non si applica [soltanto] ai contratti nei quali la parte preponderante delle obbligazioni della parte che consegna i beni consiste nella consegna di mano d'opera o di altri servizi" (art. 3, 2° comma, della Convenzione delle Nazioni Unite). Nel caso in esame non sussistono elementi che permettano di sostenere che l'attività di montaggio delle giostre fosse preponderante rispetto a quella di produzione. Il valore dei beni appare superiore al costo della loro installazione. Inoltre, nel contratto "quadro" del maggio 2003 il montaggio non era previsto come modalità indefettibile della prestazione di consegna. Se ne deduce il carattere meramente accessorio di tale attività rispetto alle obbligazioni tipiche che discendono dalla compravendita.

L'applicabilità dell'art. 5, n. 1, lett. b) del Regolamento richiede altresì che il contratto di compravendita abbia ad oggetto "beni": termine che non trova definizione nel Regolamento, e neppure nella Convenzione delle Nazioni Unite. Dottrina e giurisprudenza hanno, tuttavia, avuto occasione di precisare che possono considerarsi tali soltanto le cose mobili e tangibili (così, ad esempio Trib. Padova, 25 febbraio 2004, cit.; Trib. Rimini, 26 novembre 2002, in Giurisprudenza italiana, 2003, p. 903). E' superfluo dire che le giostre rientrano nella suddetta definizione, anche quando la loro installazione richieda lo stabile ancoraggio al terreno.

In base a quanto sopra detto, non può negarsi che i contratti conclusi da Pessa Luciano con W.H.S. Saddlers International sono di compravendita di beni.

Rimane da chiarire quale fosse il luogo di consegna dei beni. Malgrado l'intento del legislatore comunitario di semplificare il problema (rispetto a come si poneva sotto la vigenza della Convenzione di Bruxelles), non risulta possibile, anche a causa del limitato ambito di applicazione territoriale dell'art. 5 n. 1 lett. b), individuare un unico criterio, che soccorra l'interprete in ogni occasione.

La finzione giuridica, secondo cui il luogo di esecuzione della prestazione coinciderebbe sempre con quello in cui i beni devono essere consegnati, opera unicamente nel caso in cui il luogo di consegna sia "situato in uno Stato membro" (diverso dalla Danimarca). Diversamente, la competenza non potrà affatto valutarsi ricorrendo all'art. 5 n. 1 lett. b): ai sensi delle lett. c) e a) dello stesso articolo dovrà invece farsi ricorso a quel procedimento che a partire dalle ricordate sentenze De Bloos e Tessili della Corte di Giustizia si era imposto sotto la vigenza della Convenzione di Bruxelles (individuazione sia dell'obbligazione specificamente dedotta a fondamento della domanda, sia del diritto nazionale applicabile [in base al diritto internazionale privato], per mezzo del quale poi determinare il locus solutionis dell'obbligazione).

La verifica della competenza giurisdizionale viene complicata soprattutto dal fatto che il Regolamento non definisce il "luogo di consegna". E' pertanto necessario stabilire se il Regolamento, quando pone la regola della competenza contrattuale legata al luogo di consegna della merce, intenda introdurre un concetto autonomo di consegna, conforme al significato letterale della parola, ovvero indichi un concetto giuridico suscettibile di diversa interpretazione secondo le leggi nazionali ovvero secondo la Convenzione di diritto materiale uniforme di Vienna (v. per questa problematica anche la sentenza del Trib. Rovereto, cit.).

Ritiene il Tribunale che la soluzione varii a seconda che la consegna sia o no effettivamente avvenuta. In caso affermativo, sarà il luogo dell'effettiva consegna (nel senso di località in cui il compratore accetta la consegna dei beni, liberando il venditore dalla relativa obbligazione) a rappresentare il "luogo di consegna", ai sensi dell'art. 5, n. 1, lett. b): si tratta di regola del luogo previsto in contratto. Tuttavia, il luogo dell'effettiva consegna costituisce "luogo di consegna", ai sensi della citata norma, anche nel caso in cui l'accordo della parti prevedesse una località diversa, ma il compratore ha accettato di ricevere i beni altrove: in questa ipotesi, con l'accettazione dei beni nel diverso luogo, le parti raggiungono un nuovo accordo circa il "luogo di consegna".

Anche con riferimento al contratto di compravendita di beni da "piazza a piazza" rileva, per stabilire se il giudice abbia giurisdizione, il luogo dell'effettiva consegna. In questa ipotesi ci si deve però domandare se il luogo della consegna sia da considerarsi sempre quello della destinazione finale dei beni (ammesso che i beni giungano effettivamente a destinazione), come suggerito da parte della dottrina e della giurisprudenza (v. Trib.

Brescia, 28 dicembre 2004, in Int.l Lis, 2005, p. 132), oppure quello in cui i beni sono stati consegnati al primo trasportatore, come previsto ad esempio dal codice civile all'art. 1510, 2° comma. Nel caso in cui le parti abbiano previsto contrattualmente quale tra questi due luoghi debba essere preso in considerazione, rileverà ovviamente il luogo individuato contrattualmente. In mancanza di accordo delle parti, la soluzione non deve essere rinvenuta nel diritto nazionale applicabile: al quesito occorre piuttosto dare una risposta "autonoma", svincolata dal diritto nazionale. La risposta non può però evincersi dal Regolamento, che non offre suggerimenti in proposito. E' invece necessario ricorrere alla disciplina prevista dalla Convenzione delle Nazioni Unite, in quanto rappresenta un insieme di norme che - come già osservato - è stato utilizzato dallo stesso legislatore comunitario come modello normativo, attesa la larga condivisione a livello internazionale e la capacità di suggerire soluzioni interpretative autonome ed uniformi. In base alla Convenzione, in particolare al suo art. 31, "se il venditore non è obbligato a consegnare i beni in un altro luogo determinato", il venditore adempie il proprio obbligo di consegna "(a) se il contratto di vendita implica il trasporto dei beni, nel rimettere i beni al primo vettore per la trasmissione al compratore". Giova poi ricordare che questa soluzione trova conferma nelle disposizione di altri due strumenti altrettanto "autonomi" (a differenza, però, della Convenzione delle Nazioni non vincolanti), ossia i Principi UNIDROIT dei contratti commerciali internazionali (v. l'art. 6.1.6., 1° comma, lett. b)) ed i Principi europei dei contratti (art. 7:101, 1° comma, lett. b)).

Nel caso in cui, invece, la consegna dei beni non sia stata effettuata o la messa a disposizione dei beni sia avvenuta in luogo diverso da quello contrattualmente stabilito ed il compratore non abbia accettato i beni, occorre fare riferimento unicamente al luogo contrattualmente stabilito dalle parti (per mezzo, ad esempio, dell'inserimento di una clausola Incoterm).

In mancanza sia di una consegna effettiva, sia di un luogo di consegna contrattualmente stabilito, cioè quando "non è applicabile la lettera b)", si deve in virtù della lett. c) dell'art. 5, n. 1, del Regolamento ricorrere al metodo utilizzato sotto la vigenza della Convenzione di Bruxelles per l'individuazione del luogo "in cui l'obbligazione dedotta in giudizio è stata o deve essere eseguita": si dovranno, in altre parole, utilizzare i principi fissati sia dalla sentenza Tessili, che dalla sentenza De Bloos.

Tornando alla controversia tra Pessa Luciano e W.H.S. Saddlers International, si può affermare che il "luogo di consegna" rilevante ex art. 5 n. 1 lett. b) era situato in Inghilterra, e non in Italia. Infatti, la consegna è effettivamente avvenuta in Inghilterra, in conformità con quanto contrattualmente previsto. Ciò si evince altresì dalla circostanza che il venditore si era impegnato a procedere al montaggio delle giostre, facendo sì che la consegna dovesse ritenersi effettuata solo con il compimento di tale attività. In altre parole, il venditore non si liberava della propria obbligazione rimettendo i beni al trasportatore, bensì montando le giostre in Inghilterra nelle località indicate dal compratore, ove dovevano pervenire a cura dell'attore. Pertanto, il "luogo di consegna", nel caso di specie, non può dirsi ubicato in Italia.

Va quindi dichiarata l'incompetenza giurisdizionale del giudice italiano a conoscere la controversia, a favore della giurisdizione del giudice inglese.

Nulla per le spese, attesa la contumacia della convenuta.

P.Q.M.

Il Tribunale di Padova, sezione di Este, in composizione monocratica, definitivamente decidendo nella causa n. 40346 R.G. del 2004, promossa con atto di citazione notificato il 9 agosto 2004 da Pessa Luciano, esercente l'impresa individuale denominata Pessa Studio con sede in Montagnana (PD) (attore) nei confronti di W.H.S. Saddlers International di Pradelles Lin con sede in Otterbourne, Hampshire (Inghilterra) (convenuta), ogni diversa e contraria istanza, domanda ed eccezione disattesa, così ha deciso:

1) dichiara il difetto di giurisdizione del giudice italiano;

2) nulla per le spese.

Este, 10 gennaio 2006
Il giudice
(dott. Alessandro Rizzieri)

Date: ***February 17, 2006***
Country: ***United Kingdom***
Adjudicating Court: ***Court of Appeal (Civil Division)***
Number: ***2006 EWCA Civ 69***
Parties: ***Proforce Recruit Limited v. The Rugby Group Limited***

Keywords

CONTRACT INTERPRETATION ACCORDING TO ENGLISH LAW – WRITTEN CONTRACT CONTAINING A MERGER CLAUSE – ADMISSIBILITY OF EXTRINSIC EVIDENCE AND IN PARTICULAR OF PRE-CONTRACTUAL NEGOTIATIONS – REFERENCE TO UNIDROIT PRINCIPLES (ARTS. 4.1 - 4.3) AND CISG (ART. 8)

Abstract

Two English companies entered into a contract whereby one party, an employment agency ("the Agency"), undertook to supply labor personnel and cleaning equipment to the other party ("the Customer") for a fixed period of time. The written contract contained a clause stating that during the period of time fixed by the contract, the Agency would have "preferred supplier status" with respect to the Customer. The contract did not define the meaning of the expression "preferred supplier status", and contained a clause stating "This Agreement [...] constitutes the entire contract between the parties and supersedes all prior representations, agreements, negotiations or understandings whether oral or in writing".

A dispute arose when the Customer contracted with a third party for labor needs above and beyond those specified in the original contract without consulting the Agency. While according to the Customer the expression "preferred supplier status" simply meant that the Agency was to be the preferred supplier for the specific cleaning and other services set out in the agreement and did not imply any further commitments with respect to additional services the Customer might require, the Agency maintained that the expression granted it a right of first refusal as to any further needs of the Customer beyond those fixed in the original agreement.

The issue at stake was whether for the purpose of construing a written contract it was admissible to take account of extrinsic evidence, in particular the parties' pre-contract negotiations and their subjective declarations of intent.

The High Court applied the traditional rule of English law according to which pre-contractual negotiations are not admissible as evidence in interpreting a written contract and accepted the Customer's motion for summary judgment in its favour. The Court of Appeal overruled this decision and, holding that pre-contractual negotiations could be used in interpreting the preferred supplier clause, dismissed the Customer's motion for summary judgment and deferred the case to trial for further findings of fact concerning the meaning the parties intended to attach to the expression in question in the course of pre-contractual negotiations.

In his opinion Lord Justice Mummery stated that, since the expression "preferred supplier status" had no obvious natural and ordinary meaning, "its meaning could only be properly determined in the context of the agreement read as a whole and of all the surrounding circumstances", and with respect to the "entire agreement clause" contained in the contract, after pointing out that a distinction should be made between, on the one hand, "ascertaining the contents of a written contract [...] by reference to prior representations, agreements, negotiations and understandings and, on the other hand, ascertaining the meaning of a term contained in a written contract by reference to pre-contract materials", concluded that in the case at hand it was reasonably arguable that the parties intended to exclude the former but not to inhibit the latter.

On her part Lady Justice Arden, in supporting in substance these conclusions, went even further and openly stated that consideration should be given to the possibility of admitting in the future evidence of pre-contractual negotiations in interpretation questions on any wider basis than the law presently permits. In her view in this context "it may be appropriate to consider a number of international instruments applying to contracts", such as the UNIDROIT Principles which "give primacy to the common intention of the parties and on questions of interpretation requires regard to be had to all the circumstances, including the pre-contractial negotiations of the parties (Article 4.3)" and CISG which "provides that a parties' intention is in certain circumstances relevant, and in determining that intention regard is to be had to all relevant circumstances, including preliminary negotiations".

Full Text

[2006] EWCA Civ 69, (Transcript: Smith Bernal Wordwave)
ProForce Recruit Ltd v. Rugby Group Ltd

COURT OF APPEAL (CIVIL DIVISION)
[2006] EWCA Civ 69, (Transcript: Smith Bernal Wordwave)
HEARING-DATES: 17 FEBRUARY 2006

MUMMERY LJ:

THE APPEAL

[1] This is an appeal by ProForce Recruit Ltd (ProForce), for whom Mr Derek Sweeting QC appears. The appeal is from an order made by Field J on 2 March 2005. He struck out

and dismissed a breach of contract claim by ProForce against the Rugby Group Ltd (Rugby Cement), for whom Mr Romie Tager QC appears. ProForce also appeals against the order to pay the costs of the action, of the hearing before the Master below and of the appeal. The costs were summarily assessed at £35,500.

[2] Field J made the striking out order, the dismissal order and the costs order on allowing an appeal by Rugby Cement against the decision given by the Senior Master (Master Turner) on 12 November 2004. The Master had dismissed Rugby Cement's application for a striking out order under CPR 3.4 or dismissal of the action by way of summary judgment under CPR Pt 24. On reviewing the Master's dismissal of the applications Field J held that he was wrong to take account of extrinsic evidence for the purpose of construing a written agreement between ProForce and Rugby Cement. According to Field J the evidence adduced by Rugby Cement of pre-contract negotiations between the parties was not admissible in aid of the construction of a 'preferred supplier status' term in the agreement.

[3] ProForce contended that the evidence in question, which was contained in a witness statement dated 26 October 2004 (plus exhibits) by Mr Allen Bloor, the Chairman and Managing Director of ProForce, is admissible. It was submitted that Mr Bloor's evidence relates to the circumstances in which the written agreement was made. It is part of the applicable matrix of fact, in that it evidences the meaning that the individuals responsible for negotiating on behalf of the parties ascribed to the expression 'preferred supplier status' in the course of negotiations and/or the representation made as to its meaning by Rugby Cement in its original offer, which was accepted and acted upon by ProForce. There was, ProForce contended, a reasonable prospect of succeeding at trial on the issue whether the parties had negotiated on an agreed basis or understanding as to the received meaning of the expression used by them in the terms of their written agreement.

[4] On the basis of those submissions permission for a second appeal was granted by this court (Waller and Clarke LJJ) on 24 May 2005. The court's suggestion of mediation did not, unfortunately, achieve a settlement.

[5] The arguments before the Master and the Judge focused on ProForce's prospects of succeeding on the construction of the written agreement and on the admissibility of the extrinsic evidence adduced by it. The critical question is whether this action should be decided summarily or whether it should be allowed to proceed to trial on the disputed issues of construction and admissibility of evidence.

THE FACTS

[6] ProForce runs an employment and recruitment agency in Rugby. Rugby Cement manufactures and supplies cement for use by the construction industry. Since 1997 ProForce has supplied temporary workers to Rugby Cement for work at a site located in the Rugby area.

[7] The parties entered into a written service cleaning agreement on 31 July 2001 (the agreement). It was signed by Mr Allen Bloor on behalf of ProForce, and by Mr Derek Bell, the Works Manager at the Rugby site, on behalf of Rugby Cement. The agreement

was for a fixed term. It provided for a fixed payment and fixed rate for specific cleaning and operator services with machinery which ProForce had purchased for the job.

[8] The introduction to the agreement stated that ProForce had 'pleasure in submitting the following proposals for a service cleaning contract' between them.

[9] Under the heading 'Terms and Conditions' it was agreed that:

'In addition to the normal terms and conditions that exist between Rugby Cement and ProForce, it is also agreed that, subject to contract, the following conditions will apply'

[10] The conditions included an agreement by ProForce to buy cleaning equipment from Rugby Cement and an agreement by ProForce to supply personnel for agreed weekly hours and at agreed hourly rates. There were also agreed equipment charges.

[11] The following provisions were also included:

'This contract will be of a minimum two-year period and will be re-negotiable at the end of that period. During that period ProForce will hold preferred supplier status.

9.2. This Agreement together with any other document expressed to being operated herein constitutes the entire contract between the parties and supersedes all prior representations, agreements, negotiations or understandings whether oral or in writing.

9.3 These terms and conditions are to prevail over any terms and conditions sought to be included herein by the Client.'

[12] It is common ground that the agreement was subject to ProForce's Standard Terms and Conditions for the provision of contract labour. Agreed sums were duly paid. The personnel identified in the agreement were supplied and paid for throughout the stipulated two year period. ProForce supplied increasing numbers of non-cleaning personnel to the Rugby site and invoiced increasing amounts.

[13] In November 2001 Rugby Cement began to use other employment agencies to satisfy requirements over and above those provided for in the agreement, though not to do cleaning work.

[14] ProForce immediately and persistently complained that Rugby Cement was not observing the agreement. ProForce claimed that Rugby Cement was in breach of the term in the agreement that it would have 'preferred supplier status,' in that it failed after November 2001 to look to ProForce to provide its additional personnel requirements before looking elsewhere. Its claim is based principally on a construction of the agreement, in the light of the evidence of pre-agreement negotiations, that would give ProForce a legally enforceable right of first refusal to supply labour to Rugby Cement. It is also pleaded that a term to the like effect should be implied into the agreement in order to give it business efficacy.

JUDGMENT OF FIELD J

[15] Field J rejected Rugby Cement's submission that the agreement was not an enforceable contract because it contained the expression 'subject to contract' (para 16). He also rejected ProForce's implied term argument as 'hopeless' (para 17).

[16] He disagreed with the Master about the admissibility of extrinsic evidence. He accepted Rugby Cement's submission that ProForce was not entitled to adduce the extrinsic evidence in Mr Bloor's witness statement and exhibits. After his review (in paras 18 to 20) of the legal principles laid down in the leading authorities on the admissibility of extrinsic evidence to construe a written contract, on admissible evidence of the factual matrix and on the inadmissible pre-contract negotiations of the parties and their subjective declarations of intent (ICS Ltd v. West Bromwich BS [1998] 1 All ER 98, [1998] 1 WLR 896, [1998] 1 BCLC 493, in which Lord Hoffmann discussed the earlier decisions of the House of Lords in Prenn v. Simmonds [1971] 3 All ER 237, [1971] 1 WLR 1381 and Reardon Smith Line Ltd v. Yngvar Hansen-Tangen [1976] 3 All ER 570, [1976] 1 WLR 989, [1976] 2 Lloyd's Rep 621) the judge concluded:

'21. In my judgment, the statement alleged to have been made by Mr Bell that ProForce might be given a Preferential Agreement if ProForce were prepared to take the machinery, the discussions that continued in that vein and the alleged statement made by Ms Gough that 'Preferred Supplier Status' meant that ProForce would have the opportunity to supply all labour and additional plant at the site all constitute negotiations and form no part of the factual matrix to be used in construing the agreement.'

[17] On the construction of the 'preferred supplier status' provision he found against ProForce. He concluded:

'24. In my opinion, construed against the relevant background, the words 'ProForce will hold preferred supplier status' mean that if Rugby choose to operate a system of contracting only with preferred suppliers in respect of the Rugby site, ProForce are to be treated as being one of those preferred suppliers for all categories of personnel, not just cleaners. The words do not mean that Rugby are obliged during the term of the agreement to contract only with preferred suppliers and that throughout the term of the agreement Rugby must operate a preferred supplier system.

26. As it happened, Rugby did not adopt a preferred supplier system for the site during the contractual term. Instead they looked to a number of suppliers of labour who did not have the status of preferred supplier to satisfy their non-cleaning requirements. In my judgment, in acting in this way Rugby were not in breach of the agreement.'

SUBMISSIONS OF PROFORCE

[18] ProForce submitted that the case should be allowed to go to trial in order to establish the factual matrix of the agreement in the light of the extrinsic evidence on which it relies.

[19] As indicated earlier, ProForce contended that the 'preferred supplier status' term should be construed by reference to the meaning ascribed to the phrase by the parties through the individuals who conducted the negotiations and/or the representation made as

to its meaning by Rugby Cement. Those matters were part of the basis on which the parties concluded the agreement. The only relevant evidence on the point of contractual formation before the court was the statement from Mr Bloor. The evidence was that the 'preferred supplier status' term was shorthand for a status that was well understood by those individuals responsible for negotiating the agreement. It did not mean simply that ProForce was to be the preferred supplier for the specific cleaning and other services set out in the agreement. During the two year period Rugby Cement was obliged to offer ProForce the opportunity to supply contract labour and hire equipment at the Rugby site in preference to other suppliers and would not engage other suppliers of contract labour and hire equipment without first having offered ProForce a reasonable opportunity of meeting Rugby Cement's requirements in such respects. Alternatively, a term to that effect should be implied as a matter of commercial efficacy.

[20] The facts were that Rugby Cement had no other preferred supplier agreement; that after the inception of the agreement ProForce supplied increasing numbers of non-cleaning personnel; and that the departure of the individuals responsible for negotiating the contract on the part of Rugby Cement led to an immediate reversal in this position.

DISCUSSION AND MAIN CONCLUSIONS

[21] I am satisfied that Master Turner was right to dismiss Rugby Cement's applications to have the case determined summarily. It follows that Field J was wrong to allow Rugby Cement's appeal and to decide the action summarily by dismissing ProForce's claim. He ought to have allowed the disputed issue of the 'preferred supplier status' term and the associated point on the effect of cl 9.2 to proceed to trial.

[22] If there is to be a trial it is undesirable to express at this stage and at this level concluded views on the construction and admissibility issues. The whole purpose of having a trial is to enable the court of first instance to reach a conclusion on the construction issues after having established the relevant facts in the light of the admissible documentary and oral evidence.

[23] I would allow ProForce's appeal for the short reasons that follow.

[24] The expression 'preferred supplier status' is not defined by the parties anywhere in the agreement. Apart from the case of Dunblane Property Ltd v. MotorCare Holdings [2003] EWCA Civ 1033, in which the agreement in question contained an express definition of that expression, its meaning has not been judicially considered in any reported case cited to the court.

[25] The expression does not, in my view, have an obvious natural and ordinary meaning. Its meaning can only be properly determined in the context of the agreement read as a whole and of all the surrounding circumstances.

[26] A range of meanings has been pleaded by the parties. The crucial point is whether, as ProForce contended, the 'preferred supplier status' provision created a binding obligation that Rugby Cement should, during the term of the agreement, give ProForce a right of first refusal to supply Rugby with labour; or whether, as Rugby Cement

contended, it only conferred on ProForce the commercial advantage of being a supplier of labour approved by Rugby and with whom Rugby can choose to place business, though without any obligation to do so.

[27] For ProForce it was argued that by virtue of the provision it clearly had that status, whatever it meant, and that 'preferred' meant that it had some positive advantage relative to other suppliers. It was contended with considerable commercial force that, if the preferred supplier status term did not confer on it a right of first refusal for the supply of labour to Rugby, it added nothing to what ProForce was already entitled to under the agreement. If the expression was to have any effect, it must, it was argued, be construed as conferring on ProForce a benefit additional to the benefits enjoyed by it under the agreement.

[28] Apart from that consideration, the remainder of the agreement and ProForce's standard terms and conditions did not throw any light on the meaning of the expression. It would be necessary to explore the factual hinterland of the agreement in order to see whether illumination of the meaning of the expression could be found: for example, in evidence showing that the parties had agreed upon the meaning of the terms or had a mutual understanding of the term and were using it in the agreement as a shorthand expression of their agreement or understanding.

[29] The exploration of the surrounding circumstances is not, in my view, as completely ruled out as Field J held, either by the authorities on the admissibility of extrinsic evidence or by cl 9.2 of the agreement.

[30] As for the authorities Mr Sweeting cited a pertinent passage from the judgment of Kerr J in The Karen Oltmann [1976] 2 Lloyds Rep 708 at 712:

'Take Prenn v. Simmonds [1971] 1 WLR 1381 as an example. The issue in that case was whether the reference to profits in the contract meant the profits of the holding company only or the consolidated profits of the whole group. If in the course of the negotiations one party had made anything in the nature of a representation to the other to the effect that references to profits were to be taken in one of the senses and not in the other, and the other party had thereupon negotiated on this basis, then extrinsic evidence to establish this representation would in my view be clearly admissible. Similarly, if it had been contended that the parties had conducted their negotiations on an agreed basis that the word 'profits' was used in one sense only, although in the contract it was capable of having two senses, and the contract had been executed on that basis, then I do not think that the court would be precluded by authority from admitting extrinsic evidence to see whether or not this agreed basis could be established. Both these situations would be a long way from the attempts made in Prenn v. Simmonds and Arrale v. Costain [1976] Lloyds Rep 98, to adduce extrinsic evidence to try to persuade the court that one interpretation of the contract was in all the circumstances to be preferred to the other. I think that in such cases the principle can be stated as follows. If the contract contains words which , in their context, are fairly capable of bearing more than one meaning, and if it is alleged that the parties have in effect negotiated on an agreed basis that the words bore only one of the two possible meanings, then it is permissible for the court to examine the extrinsic evidence relied upon to see whether the parties have in fact used the words in question in one sense only, so that they have in effect given their own dictionary meaning to the words as the result of their common intention. Such cases would not support a claim for rectification of the contract, because the choice of words in the contract would not result from any mistake. The words used in the contract would ex hypothesi reflect the meaning which both parties intended.'

[31] Also, as stated in Chitty on Contracts para 12. 119, evidence of facts about which the parties were negotiating is admissible to explain what meaning was intended and evidence of what the parties said in negotiations is admissible to show that the parties negotiated on an agreed basis that the words used bore a particular meaning.

[32] There is substance in ProForce's criticism of Field J that he failed to address this point by simply stopping at the question whether the exchanges between the parties relied on were 'negotiations' and then ruling them out as inadmissible extrinsic evidence. He had then proceeded to construe the expression without the benefit of evidence as to the factual matrix, including evidence as to a shared understanding of the expression derived from representations made by Rugby Cement, which would have been available to the trial judge.

[33] As pointed out by Arden LJ in the course of argument, a valuable contribution to the continuing debate on the question what surrounding circumstances are relevant to the construction of written contracts was made by Lord Nicholls in his Chancery Bar Lecture, which was published in (2005) 121 LQR 577, (especially at 582 to 588), after the hearing before Field J.

[34] In the view of Lord Nicholls the statement of the rule that pre-contract negotiations are irrelevant is too rigid. He said that (see p 583):

'. . . there will be occasions where the pre-contract negotiations do shed light on the meaning the parties intended to convey by the words they used. There will be occasions, for instance, when the parties in their pre-contract exchanges made clear the meaning they intended by language they subsequently incorporated into their contract. When pre-contract negotiations assist in some such way, the notional reasonable person should be able to take that evidence into account in deciding how the contract is to be interpreted.'

[35] He continued:

'This would not be a departure from the objective approach. Rather, this would enable the notional reasonable person to be more fully informed of the background context. This would recognise that pre-contract negotiations are themselves part of the background of a contract and that, like other background material, they may be relevant when interpreting a contract. They differ from other background material in that, unlike other background material, they may afford direct evidence of the parties' actual intentions. That is not a reason for banning their use. That would be perverse. That would mean that in deciding the meaning intended to be conveyed by the language chosen by the parties the notional reasonable person would always be barred from having regard to what may be the best evidence of all. He must always conjecture, he must never know. The preferable approach is to recognise that pre-contract negotiations are relevant and admissible if they would have influenced the notional reasonable person in his understanding of the meaning the parties intended to convey by the words used.

Whether the notional reasonable person would have been so influenced in a particular case depends upon the facts of that case.'

[36] In my view, a trial is necessary in this case in order to hear all the pre-contract evidence from both sides in order to establish the facts of the case, including any evidence of pre-contract negotiations that is relevant and admissible for the purpose of ascertaining the meaning of the Preferred Supplier Status provision in the agreement.

[37] In his detailed skeleton argument and in his forceful oral submissions Mr Tager QC cited further authorities and advanced arguments for upholding the judgment of Field J and his decision that there was no point in having a trial: that the preferred supplier status term should be given its natural and ordinary meaning that during the two years of the agreement ProForce would have the status of a supplier with whom Rugby Cement would prefer to do business; that it meant no more than that ProForce would be included on any list of suppliers holding that status as a pre-condition to Rugby Cement offering future business opportunities to ProForce; that it did not confer on ProForce any legally binding right of first refusal in relation to supplies to Rugby Cement: that the oral conversations and discussions forming pre-contractual negotiations were irrelevant to the meaning of the agreement and were inadmissible by virtue of the parol evidence rule and formed no part of the factual matrix to be used in construing the agreement; and that cl 9.2 prevented ProForce from relying on the pre-contract materials in the evidence of Mr Bloor.

[38] For the reasons already given the right time and place for a final decision by the court on Mr Tager's arguments on both construction and admissibility is at trial, not on an application to strike out or for summary judgment.

Clause 9.2

[39] Although I have already referred in general terms to cl 9.2, I should make some more specific observations on it. The judge's construction of the clause came in for substantial criticism by ProForce. Field J said:

'22. Even if I were wrong about this [see paragraph 21 of his judgment cited in paragraph above], in my view these statements are 'prior representations, negotiations or understandings' within clause 9.2 of the standard terms and by virtue of that clause cannot be relied on by ProForce in seeking to establish their claim for breach of the agreement. Mr Sweeting argues that the effect of clause 9.2 was limited to barring reliance on pre-contract statements that are later said to be terms of the agreement. Whilst the clause may not exclude liability for misrepresentation (*cf.* Thomas Witter Ltd v. TBP Industries Ltd [1996] 2 All ER 573) in my opinion the effect of the words 'This agreement supersedes all prior representations, agreements, negotiations or understandings' is that the things superseded are to have no bearing on the meaning of the agreement.'

[40] Mr Sweeting submitted cl 9.2 was an 'entire agreement clause' aimed at excluding attempts to use extrinsic evidence in order to incorporate further terms or representations into the contract, which the parties had not themselves included and thereby change the contents of the agreement. It was not apt to govern the construction of the written terms

that the parties had included or to exclude evidence relevant to the ascertainment of their meaning. ProForce argued that it was not attempting to use what was agreed, understood or said before the making of the written contract in order to introduce a new term or a collateral contract, but to arrive at the proper meaning of the expression 'preferred supplier status,' which had no plain natural and ordinary meaning and which was not defined in the written agreement.

[41] In my judgment, ProForce has a real prospect of succeeding at trial in its construction of cl 9.2. There is a reasonably arguable distinction between, on the one hand, ascertaining the contents of a written contract or setting up a collateral or side contract by reference to prior representations, agreements, negotiations and understandings and, on the other hand, ascertaining the meaning of a term contained in a written contract by reference to pre-contract materials. It is reasonably arguable that in cl 9.2 the parties intended to exclude the former, but not to inhibit the latter.

RESULT

[42] I would accordingly allow the appeal and restore the order made by the Master. It is unnecessary to express any separate view on the costs order made by the judge and appealed by ProForce on other grounds. It was made on the basis that Rugby Cement succeeded in their appeal to him and that ProForce's action would be dismissed. That is no longer the case.

[43] In the light of our judgments the parties should attempt to reach an agreement on the terms of the order on allowing ProForce's appeal, including the question of costs before the Master, Field J and on this appeal. If the parties cannot reach agreement they should make written submissions to the court on the disputed aspects of the order to be made consequent on allowing the appeal.

JUDGMENTBY-2: ARDEN LJ:

JUDGMENT-2:

ARDEN LJ:

[44] I agree that this appeal should be allowed but on a narrower basis than that set out in the judgment of Mummery LJ. I gratefully adopt his statement of the facts and submissions.

[45] This appeal concerns the question whether the appellants ('ProForce') has a real prospect of success as regards its claim for damages for the failure by the Respondent ('Rugby') to give it the opportunity to tender for the supply of personnel before engaging contractors through other agencies. As this appeal arises at an interim stage in these proceedings, this court must proceed on the basis that the ProForce's allegations can be proved at trial.

[46] ProForce's case is that the obligation to give that preferential opportunity arises from a service cleaning contract made on 31 July 2001 between ProForce and Rugby. The critical provision in that agreement is as follows:

'This contract will be a minimum two-year period and will be re-negotiable at the end of that period. During that period ProForce will hold preferred supplier status.'

[47] The principal issue is as to the meaning of the words 'preferred supplier status'. A major plank in ProForce's case is that the meaning of those words for which it contends was in fact the meaning which the parties placed on those words when they were negotiating the agreement. That evidence is disputed. In addition, the effect of cl 9.2 has to be considered. Clause 9.2 provides:

'This Agreement together with any other document expressed to be incorporated herein constitutes the entire [Contract] between the parties and supersedes all prior representations, agreements, negotiations or understandings whether oral or in writing.'

[48] The evidence as to the meaning of the term 'preferred supplier status' is set out in the witness statement of Mr Allen Bloor at para 13 of his witness statement, Mr Bloor states:

'Discussions continued in that vein until about May [2001] when Emma Gough offered ProForce 'preferred supplier status' explaining that we would have the opportunity to supply all labour and additional plant at the Rugby site.'

[49] The judge held that Mr Bloor's evidence as to what Miss Gough said in the course of discussions leading to the agreement constituted negotiations and was therefore inadmissible on the interpretation of the agreement (judgment para 21). He further held that, if he was wrong about this, Mr Bloor's evidence was excluded by cl 9.2 of the agreement (judgment, para 22).

[50] Mr Derek Sweeting QC, for ProForce, submits that Miss Gough's representation was that preferred supplier status would give ProForce an advantage relative to other suppliers. Accordingly 'preferred supplier status' means the opportunity to supply personnel in preference to other suppliers and that ProForce would be given a reasonable opportunity to supply personnel before other suppliers were approached. Mr Sweeting submits that both parties approached the contract on the basis that this is what the phrase 'preferred supplier status' meant and that this meaning was not only shared by both parties to the agreement but also communicated between them in the course of the pre-contractual negotiations. Mr Sweeting further submits that the admission of the evidence of Mr Bloor would illuminate and not add to the agreement. He contends that his evidence is relevant to interpretation and he reserves the question whether statements of subjective intention are admissible. Mr Sweeting relies on the decision of Kerr J in the Partenreedesei Karen Oltmann v. Scarsdale Shipping Co Ltd ('the Karen Oltmann case') [1976] Lloyd's Law Reports 708 at 712 (set out in para 30 of the judgment of Mummery LJ):

[51] Mr Romie Tager QC for the Respondents submits that evidence of negotiations cannot be admitted on questions of interpretation of a written document. He submits that if the parties had a common assumption as to the meaning of 'preferred supplier status' and the agreement does not on its true construction reflect that meaning, the only remedy which ProForce could have would be to establish an estoppel by convention or to apply for rectification. Neither remedy is open to it in the present case. He submits that the passage on which Mr Sweeting relies from the Karen Oltmann case does not represent the current law. He further submits that cl 9.2 excludes evidence as to any representation or agreement.

[52] In Investors Compensation Scheme Ltd v. West Bromwich Building Society [1998] 1 WLR 898 at 912-3, Lord Hoffmann, with whom the remainder of the House agreed, set out the principles for the interpretation of written documents. In the course of doing so, he specifically dealt with the admissibility, for the purpose of interpreting an agreement, of what parties said in the course of negotiating that agreement:

'(1) Interpretation is the ascertainment of the meaning which the document would convey to a reasonable person having all the background knowledge which would reasonably have been available to the parties in the situation in which they were at the time of the contract.

(2) The background was famously referred to by Lord Wilberforce as the 'matrix of fact', but this phrase is, if anything, an understated description of what the background may include. Subject to the requirement that it should have been reasonably available to the parties and to the exception to be mentioned next, it includes absolutely anything which would have affected the way in which the language of the document would have been understood by a reasonable man.

(3) The law excludes from the admissible background the previous negotiations of the parties and their declarations of subjective intent. They are admissible only in an action for rectification. The law makes this distinction for reasons of practical policy and, in this respect only, legal interpretation differs from the way we would interpret utterances in ordinary life. The boundaries of this exception are in some respects unclear. But this is not the occasion on which to explore them.'

[53] It is clear, however, that the courts do, for different purposes, admit evidence as to communications between the parties prior to the making of a written contract. This occurs, for example, where the parties made their agreement partly in writing and partly orally. It occurs where there are proceedings for rectification. Likewise the court may hear evidence as to pre-contractual communications where it is said that one party made a representation to another on which that other acts. It has been held that where a party makes an oral representation as to the effect of a document for the purpose of its being acted upon, and it is acted upon, and there is no qualification in the representation suggesting that the document is not to govern the relationship of the parties, the representor cannot afterwards be heard to say that the representation is not true: see De Tchihatchef v. The 'Salerni' Coupling Ltd [1932] 1 Ch 330, [1931] All ER Rep 233. In that case the representation was made after the agreement had been executed, but in my judgment the position would have been the same if the representation had been made before the agreement was executed.

[54] The examples so far given are not examples of pre-contractual communications between the parties being admitted in evidence for the purpose of interpreting their agreement, but examples of this can be found. For example, the court can admit evidence as to pre-contratual communications made orally where the subsequent written agreement refers to those prior oral discussions (see The Pacific Colocotronis [1981] 2 Lloyd's Rep 40). Similarly, evidence as to pre-contractual communications may be admitted to identify property referred to in a contract or a term of art which is used in the contract. Indeed, there is no reason in principle why a contract should not expressly state that a particular term used in the contract should bear the meaning which the parties gave to it in the course of their negotiations. Evidence as to the parties' negotiations would in those circumstances unquestionably be admissible to show what that meaning was.

[55] In this case, the parties have used a very unusual combination of words ('preferred supplier status'). These words are undefined and they are not introduced or accompanied by any words of explanation. In those circumstances it is in my judgment reasonably arguable that on their true interpretation those words bear the meaning that the parties in common gave them in their communications leading up to the signing of the agreement. In admitting evidence as to those communications, the court would be hearing that evidence not with a view to taking the parties' subjective intent into account for the purposes of interpretation (a purpose precluded by the principles laid down by Lord Hoffmann in the ICS case) but for the purpose of identifying the meaning that the parties in effect incorporated into their agreement in circumstances where the court was satisfied that on their true interpretation the terms of the agreement were to have this effect.

[56] In my judgment, there is a sufficient prospect of success in distinguishing this situation from the usual situation in which, in the course of negotiations, the parties agree a matter which is to become binding on them (only) when a written agreement has been drawn up and signed. In that situation, evidence of the parties' negotiations would in principle not be admissible: see per Lord Hoffmann in the ICS case and per Lord Wilberforce in Prenn v. Simmonds [1971] 1 WLR 1382 at 1314 to 1315. This court cannot, however, at this stage determine the points which I have identified as reasonably arguable because they depend upon the true interpretation of the agreement, and the court cannot determine the true interpretation of the agreement without making findings of fact as to the circumstances surrounding its execution. That cannot be done on a summary application.

[57] Evidence as to negotiations between the parties to a contract leading up to the making of that contract may be admissible for the purposes of interpretation in wider circumstances than I have indicated above, but it is unnecessary for me to go further than those circumstances for the purpose of this appeal. Lord Hoffmann recognises in the ICS case that the boundaries of the rule excluding evidence of pre-contractual negotiations on questions of interpretation is unclear. Moreover, Lord Nicholls has argued in the passage cited by Mummery LJ in para 34 of his judgment and elsewhere, that the rule should be relaxed. The exclusion of pre-contractual negotiations is not on the face of it consistent with the general principle that a contract should be interpreted in the light of its context. Nor, on the face of it, is the application of a meaning which is not that which the parties themselves gave to a term consistent with the general approach of contract law, which is to respect party autonomy. The results may be anomalous. If the judge's ruling in this case expresses the general position in law, the result would be that the parties' meaning

would be adopted if they defined the term in their written contract but not if they only did so only in the course of pre-contractual negotiations. Moreover, in that latter event, the meaning given to the term by the court would prevail, and (if the court's meaning is one which is different from that on which both parties in fact proceeded) a party would be able to avoid its contractual obligations deriving from the parties' meaning. That may be the law but, if it is, it is not, on the face of it, an attractive result. There are considerations that may go the other way. Lord Hoffmann's holding is that the exclusionary rule is based on reasons of practical policy (see para (3) of the passage cited above from the ICS case). That policy would have to be carefully considered if evidence of pre-contractual negotiations is to be admitted in evidence in interpretation questions in the future on any wider basis than the law presently permits. In that sense there may be parallels to be drawn with the use of legislative history in the interpretation of statutes. In addition, careful consideration may have to be given to the aims to be achieved by contractual interpretation and the precise extent to which the law requires an objective interpretation, as set out in para (1) of the passage cited above from the ICS case. It may be appropriate to consider a number of international instruments applying to contracts. It is sufficient to take two examples. The UNIDROIT Principles of International Commercial Contracts give primacy to the common intention of the parties and on questions of interpretation requires regard to be had to all the circumstances, including the pre-contractual negotiations of the parties (art 4.3). The UN Convention on Contracts for the International Sale of Goods (1980) provides that a party's intention is in certain circumstances relevant, and in determining that intention regard is to be had to all relevant circumstances, including preliminary negotiations. Consideration may also have to be given to the question whether some matters outside the text of a contract should be given less weight where (for example) the contract is one to which different persons adhere at different points in time, such as a company's constitution, than in the case of 'one-off' contracts between two persons, as in this case.

[58] In the alternative, in this case, there is a sufficient prospect of success on the further ground that the evidence will show that Miss Gough made a binding representation as to the effect that the subsequent agreement would have in regard to ProForce's preferred supplier status: see the De Tichihatchef case cited above. Accordingly, for that reason also the interpretation of the agreement cannot be determined on a summary application.

[59] As to cl 9.2 of the agreement, I agree with Mummery LJ that ProForce's argument on cl 9.2 has a real prospect of success for the reason he gives in para 41 of his judgment. In addition, the evidence may in due course show that the parties in effect agreed that their agreement or common understanding as to the meaning of 'preferred supplier status' was to displace anything in the written agreement that would otherwise override that meaning. There is in my judgment, a sufficient prospect of success on that ground also.

[60] For the reasons given above, I would allow this appeal.

JUDGMENTBY-3: RICHARDS LJ:

JUDGMENT-3:

RICHARDS LJ:

[61] I, too, would allow this appeal. The reasons given by Arden LJ provide a sufficient basis for doing so. I also agree with Mummery LJ, however, that it is not appropriate at this stage to express any concluded view on the extent to which the pre-contract negotiations can properly be taken into account in this case for the purpose of ascertaining the meaning of the contract. That question is best resolved in the light of detailed findings of fact made at trial.

Appeal allowed.

SOLICITORS:

LM; Cemex (UK) Legal Department

www.ingramcontent.com/pod-product-compliance
Lightning Source LLC
LaVergne TN
LVHW052200200926
848481LV00001B/2